Encyclopedia of Buddhism

Copyright © 2008 by Edward A. Irons

Facts On File, Inc.
An imprint of Infobase Publishing
132 West 31st Street
New York NY 10001

Library of Congress Cataloging-in-Publication Data
Irons, Edward A.
    Encyclopedia of Buddhism / Edward A. Irons.
        p. cm. — (Encyclopedia of world religions)
    Includes bibliographical references and index.
    ISBN 978-0-8160-5459-6 (alk. paper)
    1. Buddhism—Encyclopedias. I. Title.
    BQ128.I76 2007
    294.303—dc22   2007004503

Facts On File books are available at special discounts when purchased in bulk quantities for businesses, associations, institutions, or sales promotions. Please call our Special Sales Department in New York at (212) 967-8800 or (800) 322-8755.

You can find Facts On File on the World Wide Web at http://www.factsonfile.com

Text design by Erika Arroyo
Cover design by Cathy Rincon
Maps by Dale Williams

Printed in the United States of America

VB FOF 10 9 8 7 6 5 4 3 2 1

This book is printed on acid-free paper and contains 30% post-consumer recycled content.

ENCYCLOPEDIA OF WORLD RELIGIONS

ENCYCLOPEDIA OF
Buddhism

Edward A. Irons

J. Gordon Melton, Series Editor

Facts On File
An imprint of Infobase Publishing

ENCYCLOPEDIA OF
Buddhism

CONTENTS

ABOUT THE EDITORS AND CONTRIBUTORS

Series Editor

J. Gordon Melton is the director of the Institute for the Study of American Religion in Santa Barbara, California. He holds an M.Div. from the Garrett Theological Seminary and a Ph.D. from Northwestern University. Melton is the author of *American Religions: An Illustrated History*, *The Encyclopedia of American Religions*, *Religious Leaders of America*, and several comprehensive works on Islamic culture, African-American religion, cults, and alternative religions. He has written or edited more than three dozen books and anthologies as well as numerous papers and articles for scholarly journals. He is the series editor for Religious Information Systems, which supplies data and information in religious studies and related fields. Melton is a member of the American Academy of Religion, the Society for the Scientific Study of Religion, the American Society of Church History, the Communal Studies Association, and the Society for the Study of Metaphysical Religion.

Volume Editor

Edward A. Irons is director of the Institute for Culture, Commerce and Religion, in Hong Kong. He holds a Ph.D. from the Graduate Theological Union, Berkeley, California.

Contributors

David Gray received a Ph.D. in the history of religions, with a focus on Buddhism, from Columbia University, New York. He is an assistant professor of religious studies at Santa Clara University, California.

Gail M. Harley teaches religious studies at the University of South Florida. She is the author of several books, including Facts On File's *Hindu and Sikh Faiths in America*, and is the editor of the *Encyclopedia of Women in American Religious Life*.

Huang Zuei-jane (indigenous name Inai Savon) is a Daoist priestess in the Quanzhen Dao lineage. A member of the aboriginal Pazeh ethnic group in Taiwan, she serves as a committee member with the Indigenous Peoples Commission, Taipei City Government. She is currently a doctoral candidate at Taiwan National Cheng-chi University, Taipei, focusing on Daoist philosophy, postmodern educational philosophy, and ethics.

Charles B. Jones received a Ph.D. from the University of Virginia. He is a specialist in East Asian Buddhism and author of *Buddhism in Taiwan: Religion and the State 1660–1990* (University of Hawaii Press, 1999) as well as coeditor of *Religion in Modern Taiwan: Tradition and Innovation in a Changing Society* (University

LIST OF ILLUSTRATIONS

of Hawaii Press, 2003). He is currently an associate professor at The Catholic University of America, Washington, D.C.

Bill Magee received a Ph.D. in Tibetan Buddhism from the University of Virginia. He has published books and articles on Tibetan language and philosophy. He lives in Charlottesville, Virginia, and Taiwan, where he teaches Tibetan Buddhism at the Chung-hwa Institute of Buddhist Studies.

Ronald Y. Nakasone, Ph.D., is affiliated with the Center for Art, Religion and Education at the Graduate Theological Union, Berkeley, California, and the Stanford University Center for Geriatric Education.

Elijah Siegler received a Ph.D. in religious studies from the University of California at Santa Barbara. He currently teaches at the College of Charleston, South Carolina. He is the author of the textbook *New Religious Movements* (Prentice Hall, 2006).

Angela Sumegi received a Ph.D. in religious studies from the University of Ottawa. She is currently an assistant professor at the College of the Humanities, Carleton University, Ottawa, Canada, specializing in Indo-Tibetan Buddhism and the interface between Buddhism and Shamanism.

John M. Thompson, Ph.D., is assistant professor of Religious Studies at Christopher Newport University, Virginia. He is author of *The World's Religions: Buddhism* (Greenwood Press, 2006) and *Understanding Prajna: Sengzhao's "Wild Words" and the Search for Wisdom* (Peter Lang, forthcoming).

Alex Wilding, M.A. (Oxon.), M.Phil. (Leics.), MITI has practiced and studied Buddhism under Kagyu and Nyingma teachers since 1974. He has worked as an engineer, in education, and now as a freelance translator from the German to English.

Robert B. Zeuschner received a Ph.D. in comparative philosophy, specializing in Buddhist philosophy and ethics from the University of Hawaii at Manoa. He is associate professor of philosophy at Pasadena City College, Pasadena, California, and the author of *Edgar Rice Burroughs: The Exhaustive Scholar's and Collector's Descriptive Bibliography* (McFarland, 1996) and *Classical Ethics East and West: Ethics from a Comparative Perspective* (McGraw-Hill, 2000).

LIST OF MAPS

LIST OF TABLES

PREFACE

The Encyclopedia of World Religions series has been designed to provide comprehensive coverage of six major global religious traditions—Buddhism, Hinduism, Islam, Judaism, Roman Catholicism, and Protestant Christianity. The volumes have been constructed in an A-to-Z format to provide a handy guide to the major terms, concepts, people, events, and organizations that have, in each case, transformed the religion from its usually modest beginnings to the global force that it has become.

Each of these religions began as the faith of a relatively small group of closely related ethnic peoples. Each has, in the modern world, become a global community, and, with one notable exception, each has transcended its beginning to become an international multiethnic community. Judaism, of course, largely defines itself by its common heritage and ancestry and has an alternative but equally fascinating story. Surviving long after most similar cultures from the ancient past have turned to dust, Judaism has, within the last century, regathered its scattered people into a homeland while simultaneously watching a new diaspora carry Jews into most of the contemporary world's countries.

Each of the major traditions has also, in the modern world, become amazingly diverse. Buddhism, for example, spread from its original home in India across southern Asia and then through Tibet and China to Korea and Japan. Each time it crossed a language barrier, something was lost, but something seemed equally to be gained, and an array of forms of Buddhism emerged. In Japan alone, Buddhism exists in hundreds of different sect groupings. Protestantism, the newest of the six traditions, began with at least four different and competing forms of the religious life and has since splintered into thousands of denominations.

At the beginning of the 19th century, the six religious traditions selected for coverage in this series were largely confined to a relatively small part of the world. Since that time, the world has changed dramatically, with each of the traditions moving from its geographical center to become a global tradition. While the traditional religions of many countries retain the allegiance of a majority of the population, they do so in the presence of the other traditions as growing minorities. Other countries—China being a prominent example—have no religious majority, only a number of minorities that must periodically interface with one another.

The religiously pluralistic world created by the global diffusion of the world's religions has made knowledge of religions, especially religions practiced by one's neighbors, a vital resource in the continuing task of building a good society, a world in which all may live freely and pursue visions of the highest values the cosmos provides.

In creating these encyclopedias, the attempt has been made to be comprehensive if not exhaustive. As space allows, in approximately 800 entries, each author has attempted to define and explain the basic terms used in talking about the religion, make note of definitive events, introduce the most prominent figures, and highlight the major organizations. The coverage is designed to result in both a handy reference tool for the religious scholar/specialist and an understandable work that can be used fruitfully by anyone—a student, an informed lay person, or a reader simply wanting to look up a particular person or idea.

Each volume includes several features. They begin with an essay that introduces the particular tradition and provides a quick overview of its historical development, the major events and trends that have pushed it toward its present state, and the megaproblems that have shaped it in the contemporary world.

A chronology lists the major events that have punctuated the religion's history from its origin to the present. The chronologies differ somewhat in emphasis, given that they treat two very ancient faiths that both originated in prehistoric time, several more recent faiths that emerged during the last few millennia, and the most recent, Protestantism, that has yet to celebrate its 500-year anniversary.

The main body of each encyclopedia is constituted of the approximately 800 entries, arranged alphabetically. These entries include some 200 biographical entries covering religious figures of note in the tradition, with a distinct bias to the 19th and 20th centuries and some emphasis on leaders from different parts of the world. Special attention has been given to highlighting female contributions to the tradition, a factor often overlooked, as religion in all traditions has until recently been largely a male-dominated affair.

Geographical entries cover the development of the movement in those countries and parts of the world where the tradition has come to dominate or form an important minority voice, where it has developed a particularly distinct style (often signaled by doctrinal differences), or where it has a unique cultural or social presence. While religious statistics are amazingly difficult to assemble and evaluate, some attempt has been made to estimate the effect of the tradition on the selected countries.

In some cases, particular events have had a determining effect on the development of the different religious traditions. Entries on events such as the St. Bartholomew's Day Massacre (for Protestantism) or the conversion of King Asoka (for Buddhism) place the spotlight on the factors precipitating the event and the consequences flowing from it.

The various traditions have taken form as communities of believers have organized structures to promote their particular way of belief and practice within the tradition. Each tradition has a different way of organizing and recognizing the distinct groups within it. Buddhism, for example, has organized around national subtraditions. The encyclopedias give coverage to the major groupings within each tradition.

Each tradition has developed a way of encountering and introducing individuals to spiritual reality as well as a vocabulary for it. It has also developed a set of concepts and a language to discuss the spiritual world and humanity's place within it. In each volume, the largest number of entries explore the concepts, the beliefs that flow from them, and the practices that they have engendered. The authors have attempted to explain these key religious concepts in a nontechnical language and to communicate their meaning and logic to a person otherwise unfamiliar with the religion as a whole.

Finally, each volume is thoroughly cross-indexed using small caps to guide the reader to related entries. A bibliography and comprehensive index round out each volume.

—J. Gordon Melton

BUDDHISM
AN INTRODUCTION

This book is meant to serve as a general introduction to and resource for Buddhism and other major religious traditions of East Asia. We do not mention Islam or Christianity, traditions covered in other volumes. And although we provide introductions to Daoism, Shinto, Confucianism, and other religious practices in East and Southeast Asia, the primary focus of the volume is clearly on Buddhism, in all its forms.

Yet, as the reader will soon discover, it is impossible to cover every area in such a broad subject. Inevitably, we have had to choose certain emphases. In the text, we focus on key individuals, regions, places, and schools; on basic terms that may be useful to readers; and on themes of relevance today. These themes include art, popular festivals, ecology, the role of women, engaged Buddhism, globalization, sexuality, martial arts, psychology, titles, and war. Such topical themes reveal our own inclinations as much as current issues in the field of Buddhist studies, and if any issue of importance is overlooked, we can only plead guilty and trust that other sources exist that will cover the topic.

Buddhism, like the other major religious traditions, seems an impossibly broad subject because it means such different things to different people, and as with many of the products of ancient cultures, it has undergone layers of changes over centuries. These changes can be described historically, in periods. However, for many people, Buddhism is not simply a historical object; it is a living system of beliefs and devotion. For others, it may be a philosophical or psychological system of great subtlety, one that can lead to major lifestyle changes. And for still others, it may simply be a cultural influence, one of the many cultural fragments—for example, the familiar image of the bronze Buddha figure at Kamakura—that inform but do not determine worldview. In different places, most notably in medieval China, Buddhism has been an important economic institution. Simply to catalog the artistic and literary expressions of Buddhist culture is a lifelong task.

With a subject of such variety, one may wonder whether there is actually any unified thing called Buddhism. Is it not possibly a convenient category that may hinder us from deeper understanding of what is going on? Such speculation would be in line with the postmodern impulse. However, mainstream understanding, including that of modern Buddhist practitioners, views Buddhism as a great religious tradition comparable to the other universalizing religions of Christianity and Islam, religions that have spread well beyond their places of origin and continue to thrive in a

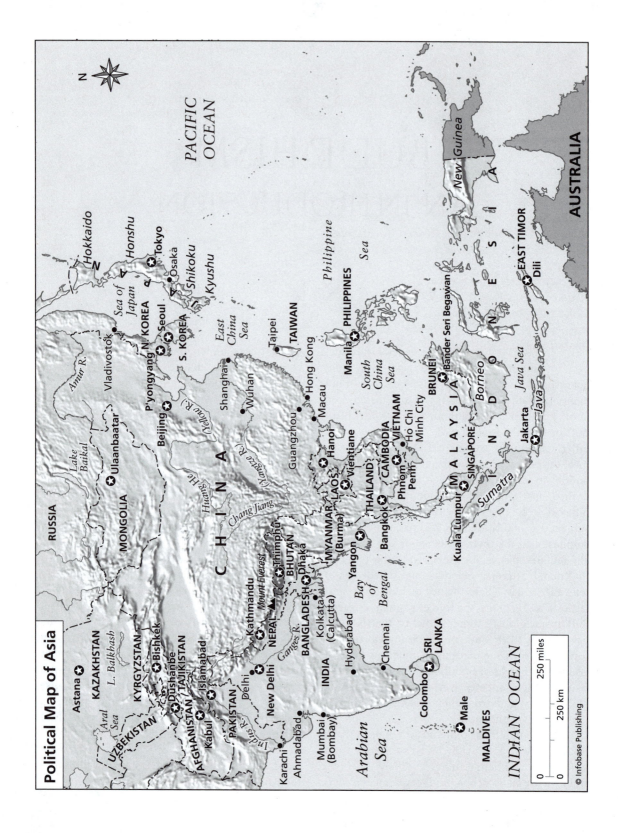

Political Map of Asia

N

PACIFIC
OCEAN

AUSTRALIA

New Guinea

Hokkaido

Honshu

Tokyo

Osaka

Shikoku

Kyushu

*Sea of
Japan*

Vladivostok

Amur R.

N. KOREA

P'yongyang

S. KOREA

Seoul

*East
China
Sea*

Shanghai

Wuhan

Taipei

TAIWAN

Hong Kong

Macau

Guangzhou

Philippine

Sea

PHILIPPINES

Manila

*South
China
Sea*

BRUNEI

Bander Seri Begawan

EAST TIMOR

Dili

I N D O N E S I A

Borneo

Java Sea

Yellow R.

Beijing

Ulaanbaatar

MONGOLIA

*Lake
Baikal*

RUSSIA

Huang He

Chang Jiang

C H I N A

Yangtze R. (Yangtze)

Hanoi

Vientiane

LAOS

VIETNAM

Ho Chi
Minh City

CAMBODIA

Phnom
Penh

THAILAND

Bangkok

M A L A Y S I A

Kuala Lumpur

SINGAPORE

Sumatra

Jakarta

Java

Astana

KAZAKHSTAN

L. Balkhash

*Aral
Sea*

UZBEKISTAN

Bishkek

KYRGYZSTAN

Dushanbe

TAJIKISTAN

Islamabad

Kabul

AFGHANISTAN

PAKISTAN

Indus R.

Karachi

Delhi

New Delhi

Ahmadabad

Mumbai
(Bombay)

*Arabian
Sea*

Kathmandu

NEPAL

Mount Everest

Thimphu

BHUTAN

BANGLADESH

Dhaka

Ganges R.

INDIA

Hyderabad

Kolkata
(Calcutta)

*Bay
of
Bengal*

Chennai

Colombo

SRI
LANKA

Male

MALDIVES

MYANMAR
(Burma)

Yangon

INDIAN OCEAN

0

250 miles

0

250 km

variety of cultures. As in other religions, believers refer to the founder to define the community.

The Buddha

The image of Buddhism's founder, who lived around 500 B.C.E., and all the ideas associated with that image continue to attract people. The Buddha left no writings of his own, but there is little reason to doubt his historicity—the number of stories and legends surrounding him points overwhelmingly to the presence of a powerful historical figure. There are, in addition, many written references to him; the famous edicts of Asoka were often carved in stone. These references are dated from well after his life, granted, but they nevertheless give strong material support to his influence.

The Term *Buddhism*

The term *Buddhism* did not exist in any language until the early 19th century, when scholars coined it in European languages to refer to the newly discovered complex of religious practices centered on the image or memory of the figure called Buddha, the Enlightened One. Early Buddhists, in fact, used such alternative terms as *dharma* or *dharma vinaya*, "law-rules," to refer to their belief system. In Sanskrit sources, these often became the Buddha Dharma, the "doctrines of the Buddha." In Sri Lanka, the teachings are still called *sasana*, the "teachings," while in China the traditional term is *fojiao* (Buddha doctrine or teachings), which is also now used as the translation for the European term *Buddhism*. The word *Boudhism* was introduced in the *Oxford English Dictionary* in 1801 and emerged as *Buddhism* in 1816.

Buddhist Spirituality

Students often look for a core teaching in Buddhism, and, indeed, different teachers and traditions do emphasize certain teachings over others. Some, for instance, emphasize the transient nature of reality, an aspect noted by the Buddha himself when he explained the nature of *dukkha,* or suffering. Others, however, emphasize Buddha nature, the underlying reality that gives us something to discover within. And others may emphasize the process of perceiving the unfolding of the world, through the concept of *pratityta samutpada,* codependent arising.

Focus solely on core teachings, however, obscures the essential spiritual nature of the Buddhist movement: personal spiritual development. Spiritual change and movement are assumed, longed for, and upheld as ideals. Regardless of tradition, all Buddhists who accept the Dharma, the Buddha's teachings, will in turn strive to make spiritual progress.

How does a follower of Buddhism approach spirituality, then? First, he or she seeks the clear perception of reality. The Buddha's teachings help clear away the cobwebs. However, individuals must also strive through their own efforts. Such efforts often include meditation techniques of some sort. *Meditation* is a term loosely referring to techniques of quiescence and observance. Monks and laypersons over the years have developed elaborate meditation exercises, from Theravadin *vipassana* to Tibetan visualizations and Chinese Tian Tai ritual. What will result from such techniques of discipline? First, the individual sees through the boundaries of the everyday self. The self is seen as a nonreality, a convenience that impedes clear perception. The meditator will experience non-self-based reality, achieving a "nondiscursive" awareness. The meditator will also cease to cling to the constructs of the mind, which are realized to be ephemeral and insubstantial.

Key Concepts

The Buddha left behind a set of core ideas, recorded in both the Theravada and Mahayana canons, which characterize Buddhist teachings in all regions. These ideas, along with the amazing resiliency of the sangha (monastic) organizational form, ensure Buddhism's essential identity, despite extreme diversity, over its vast geographic reach.

What are the key concepts? First is the idea that samsara, the cycle of earthly existence, can be removed through personal cultivation. Second, the idea that the world is ever-changing and impermanent. There is, then, nothing in the world of phenomena that possesses eternal existence; all phenomena are characterized by impermanence and lack of essential nature. Individuals become enmeshed in the cycle of existence through the chain of conditioned arising. Overcoming this cycle, one can experience nirvana, final release from the chain of suffering. The Buddha summarized these teachings in the formulations known as the Four Noble Truths, the Eightfold Path, and the 12-fold Chain of Causation.

The Buddha is often compared to a physician, who diagnoses the patient's ills, finds the source of the illness, prescribes countermeasures, and applies the cure. The Four Noble Truths nicely summarize a doctor's method: the diagnosis is that life is suffering (dukkha). The cause of that suffering is determined to be attachment. However, there is an antidote: release through nirvana. The prescription applied is called the Eightfold Path, or, in simplified form, the three elements of morality, concentration, and wisdom (sila, samadhi, prajna).

The 12-fold Chain of Causation is a model which illustrates the major teaching of codependent origination (pratitya samutpada). This teaching shows the sequence of events by which phenomena form and decay; they do not occur simply at random or as a result of the will of some individuals. This means there is an infinite web of relations among what we perceive in everyday reality to be separate events or things. The cycle begins with ignorance (stage 1) and runs through predispositions (2) to cause consciousness (3) of the present. With consciousness arise name and form (4), as well as the senses (5) capable of perceiving things. With the senses there are contact (6) and sensation (7). Sensation in turn leads to craving (8), then becoming (9), and, eventually, birth (10), old age (11), and death (12). The Buddhist practitioner, aware of this sequence, attempts to cut the link at any point that will break the cycle.

Another key teaching concerns the doctrine of non-self, or *anatman*. The everyday assumption of an everlasting soul is a delusion, the Buddha taught, a powerful and dangerous delusion, because it leads to attachment, egoism, cravings, and, ultimately, suffering. The Buddhist must observe his/her own nature and untangle the five *skandhas,* or aggregates (body, feelings, perceptions, dispositions, and consciousness), which we commonly misunderstand to be the individual soul. The Buddhist will not only perceive this, s/he will also see beyond this state to the underlying truth of nirvana, the cessation of all desires and karma.

These foundational concepts were augmented over the centuries with many additional ideas, such as emptiness (*sunyata*) and Buddha nature, which are described in individual articles.

Buddhism's Development

Buddhism, as a long-running tradition thriving in many cultures and epochs of history, is of course complex. The traditional description of what Buddhism entails is to point to the three jewels, the Buddha, the Dharma (teachings), and the sangha (community). This formulation, the *triranta,* gives wide scope to understand the phenomenon of Buddhism overall.

The first element, the Buddha, was Gautama Siddhartha, an enlightened being. His Dharma, the second element, was his vision, and all the understandings that relate to it. This vision, a kind of personal liberation, continues to motivate people as only a powerful utopia can. And his sangha, the third element, is the community of believers, who are traditionally grouped into separate groups of mendicants or settled recluses living separate from society. This style of living in tight-knit groups, primarily in monasteries, has had formidable staying power throughout history.

The Buddha's Age and Soon After

The time of the Buddha, c. sixth–fifth centuries B.C.E., was a time of social change and trade in India. Cities had developed and became places where wealth accumulated. Iron tools were widely used. A variety of social systems, including experiments with democracy as well as dictatorships, were tried. Slavery was a fact, as was the caste system, but the caste system was on the decline. The monetary system existed but was weak. Guilds were also weak.

The most important development was the merchant class, the members of which were readily attracted to the new system of thought. The Buddha's teachings offered an alternative to Brahmanism, the traditional belief system dominated by the Brahman, or priestly, caste.

The Buddha was born in the Sakya city of Kapilavastu. There is disagreement about where that site is today: one version is in southern Nepal, at Tilaurakot, Padaria. Another version, based on recent archaeological work, suggests Piprahwa in present-day India.

Although surrounded by luxury, the young prince Siddhartha was dissatisfied, and at the age of 29 he left home to seek answers to the questions of existence. After wandering for six years he achieved enlightenment at Buddhagaya, under a Bodhi tree. He at first did not wish to teach his conclusions, but, persuaded to do so by the brahman Sahamapati, he relented and decided to preach. The Buddha's first sermon was given at Benares, at Migadaya, where he explained the Four Noble Truths.

Indeed the Buddha was one leader among several heterodox (nonconformist) leaders, a group that included Nigantha Nataputta, founder of the Jain religion, which has continued to this day. Like many such leaders, the Buddha repudiated many of the religious assumptions of his time. He did not accept the Vedas as being infallible sources of truth. Nor did he put great importance in ritual. He did not accept the caste system, which rigidly categorized people, and he was especially critical of the Brahmanic classes. He advocated personal discipline but not extreme asceticism. His teachings were in this sense more an ethical code than a ritual practice. In all things the individual was urged to think matters through and make his or her own decisions. On the other hand, Buddhism retained many indigenous teachings from India, including the notion of samsara, the recurring cycle of the world, and karma, the notion that one builds up debts through deeds. He also accepted the widespread practice of the religious community remaining separate from society.

The Buddha was active for another 45 years, teaching in such urban centers as Rajagrha, Sravasti, and Vaisali. It was at Vaisali that the Buddha ate food offered by Cunda, a blacksmith, and passed away. In Buddhist writings this event is not called his death but his *parinirvana*, because an enlightened being has no possibility of a mortal death.

India was later unified under the Mauryan dynasty 317–180 B.C.E., and the rule of Asoka (c. 282–232 B.C.E.) was crucial in spreading Buddhist practice. Asoka established a centralized state and erected highways and canals. His edicts were often carved on rocks or pillars. Buddhist beliefs were also promoted by craftsmen and merchants, as well as members of the Sangha, the Buddhist order of monks. Also during the Mauryan period large structures such as the stupa at Sanci and stone *caitya* (shrines) were built to honor the Buddha. Asoka is thus closely associated with this first stage of Buddhism's development.

Mahayana

Mahayana is perhaps best seen as the second major stage in Buddhism's evolution; its literal meaning of "great vehicle" does imply superiority over the competing, lesser teachings, but we can use this term as simply a label without accepting such implications. Mahayana teachings, which took clear shape in the early Common Era, focused on the virtues of *metta* (loving kindness) and *karuna* (compassion), topics mentioned but not stressed in previous Buddhist teachings. In addition the Mahayana teachings focused on the role of bodhisattvas, compassionate beings (sometimes called Buddhist saints), who chose to remain in the world and not reach nirvana because they wished to help others. Mahayana also introduced eschatological elements, beliefs in the coming of savior figures, notably the Buddha Maitreya, the Buddha of the future.

Mahayana developed in Northwest India, in an area invaded by a sequence of powers, from the Greeks to the Parthians and the Kusanas. There was some additional development in South India, the region in which the philosopher Nagarjuna lived, and another area with close trading ties to the Mediterranean world. In the period between 100 and 400 C.E., there was widespread commerce among the regions of India, Kashmir, Parthia, Samarkand, and China. The Indian states of Gandhara and Mathura became important sources of Buddhist art. In this period also, Chinese monks began to travel to northern India, starting with Fa Xian in 399, who reached Ceylon (Sri Lanka) in 410. Later one Tang dynasty (618–907) Chinese source listed 61 Chinese monks who visited India. There were direct links between China and South India (as well as Arabia) by sea as well, as attested by the *Itinerary Book,* by Jia Dan (eighth century C.E.)

Buddhism Spreads: Southeast Asia

Following its initial development in India Buddhism spread throughout most of Asia, first going south, to Lanka (modern Sri Lanka) with Emperor Asoka's son, Mahinda, and daughter, Sanghamitta, around 250 B.C.E. The ruling king, Devanampiya, quickly converted, and subsequent rulers generally supported Buddhist establishment. Mahayana and Tantra were present in Sri Lankan Buddhism as well, but eventually the Theravada school became dominant. Since Indian independence from Great Britain in 1948,

Buddhism has had a revival in Sri Lanka and is today a major social institution.

Theravada practice spread to neighboring countries of Burma (modern-day Myanmar), Siam (Thailand), and parts of what is today Indonesia. Tradition in Burma is that King Asoka himself visited, and by the fifth century C.E., Buddhism was widespread. Both Theravada and other (Sarvastivadin and Mahayana) schools were active, until in the 11th century King Anaratha dictated that all Burmese should be Theravadin. Later, the form practiced in Sri Lanka, which recognizes only the Mahavihara Monastery, was adopted in Burma. The Buddhist faith today coexists with indigenous beliefs in folk spirits, called *nats.*

In Cambodia, Buddhism was present from at least the third century C.E., in various forms, including Mahayana. By the 14th century, Theravada seems to have become dominant in the Khmer empire, and it has persisted ever since.

Buddhism entered Thailand in the north, via Burmese influence, and in the south, through seaborne trade with India and Sri Lanka. The first Thai kingdom of Sukhothai, founded in 1238, was officially Theravadin. In the 19th century, under King Mongkut, a former monk, the Thai Sangha was reformed, resulting in formation of the Dhammayut school.

Buddhism entered the Indonesian region very early; statues dating to the third century C.E. are found, and the Chinese visitor Yi Jing noted Buddhist activity in Sumatra and Java. Borobudur, a major stupa complex in central Java, was built in the eighth-century Sailendra dynasty, who probably supported Mahayana. Beginning in the 14th century C.E., however, Islam began its great spread throughout the Indonesian islands, and today Buddhism exists only among immigrant communities such as the Chinese.

Northern Developments: China

Buddhism spread into China initially overland, via the Silk Road and the many small states and cities in Central Asia. By the time Buddhism reached China it had become a religion not simply

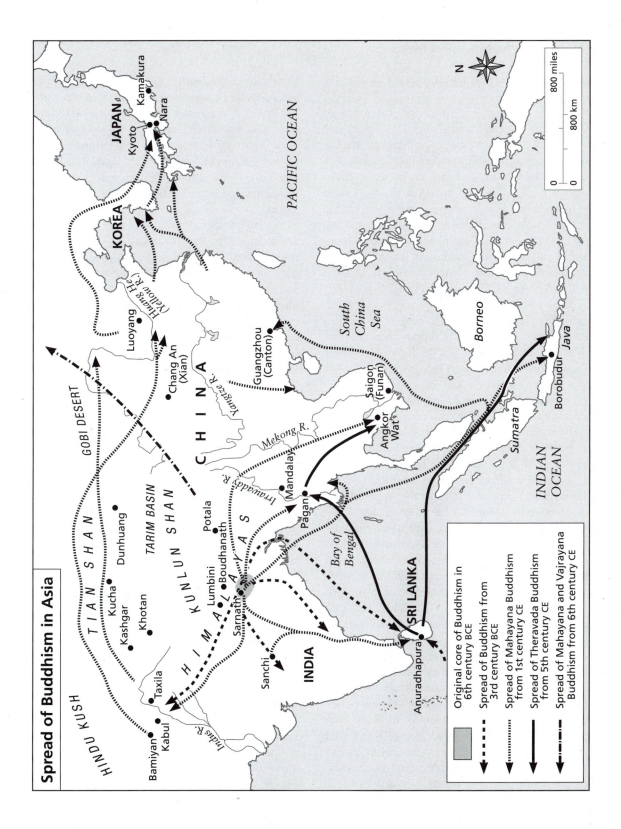

Spread of Buddhism in Asia

N

800 miles
800 km

PACIFIC OCEAN

JAPAN
Kamakura
Nara
Kyoto

KOREA

Huang He (Yellow R.)

Luoyang

Chang An
(Xian)

C H I N A

Yangtze R.

Guangzhou
(Canton)

*South
China
Sea*

Mekong R.

Saigon
(Funan)

Angkor
Wat

Mandalay

Pagan

Irrawaddy R.

Borneo

Borobudur
Java

Sumatra

INDIAN
OCEAN

*Bay of
Bengal*

SRI LANKA

Anuradhapura

HINDU KUSH

T I A N   S H A N

GOBI DESERT

Dunhuang

Kucha

Kashgar
Khotan

TARIM BASIN

K U N L U N   S H A N

Potala

Lumbini
Boudhanath
Sarnath

H I M A L A Y A S

Sanchi

INDIA

Taxila

Kabul

Bamiyan

Indus R.

Legend

Original core of Buddhism in
6th century BCE

Spread of Buddhism from
3rd century BCE

Spread of Mahayana Buddhism
from 1st century CE

Spread of Theravada Buddhism
from 5th century CE

Spread of Mahayana and Vajrayana
Buddhism from 6th century CE

of ascetics who renounce the world, but of lay believers.

To the Chinese, Buddhism was not a monolithic entity. Instead it was a collection of practices: worship of figures and sculptors, monastic institutions, chanting, teachings and literary activities such as translation and poetry, personal devotion, a moral code, plus mystical practices such as meditation. Buddhism was attractive because it was novel—the ceremony of baptizing statues, for instance—and colorful, with many ceremonies and chants, music and shrines. In the initial stages devotional assimilation into Chinese culture was still unknown. Intellectual assimilation is clearly marked out, however; such concepts as karma, emptiness, and *dhyana* were subject to endless discussion. The literate Chinese thinkers first interpreted these concepts in light of existing Daoist doctrines, only later recognizing Buddhism as a new system of thought.

Initial influence on Chinese society was limited to those who had contact with foreign travelers. By the Western Jin empire in 268–289 the aristocratic classes began to understand doctrinal elements of Mahayana. Buddhism then became a topic of interest in the aristocratic discussions (called *qing tan*) held as the upper classes migrated to the Yangtze (Chang) River area. These lay circles began to interact with literate monks, and a type of philosophical Buddhism resulted. Northern Chinese, in contrast, tended to be more interested in magical aspects of Buddhist masters.

By 400, with the advent of Kumarajiva (350–413) and Hui Yuan (334–417), Buddhism took deep root in Chinese society, as a wide-ranging religion. Buddhist piety developed on many levels of Chinese society. Communities appeared throughout China, symbolized by the erection of high pagodas, caves carved in rock, and monasteries dotting the countryside and the capital cities.

Monks also began to travel to India to study Buddhism. Several dynasties in the fifth and sixth centuries gave active support to Buddhism, including the building of monasteries and establishing of translation bureaus. Gifted translators such as Kumarajiva, Paramartha, and Xuan Zang helped spread Buddhist ideas deeply into Chinese culture.

The Sui and Tang dynasties (603–618 and 618–907) saw Buddhism reach its peak of influence as a social institution. Indigenous schools of thought, including Hua Yan, Tian Tai, Chan, and Pure Land, sprang up and were immensely influential for Buddhism's spread into Japan and Korea.

In later imperial dynasties such as the Song, Ming, and Qing, Buddhism lost its separate institutional vitality. Buddhism in a way merged with the other great schools of Chinese thought, Confucianism and Daoism. At the same time Buddhist ideas continued to circulate and became a fixed component of Chinese culture. The monastic system declined, however, and, despite its economic activity in Chinese society, became decadent. Reform occurred in the 20th century with Tai Hsu and, following the communist victory in 1949, complete reorganization under the control of the Communist Party. In practice, all the elements of Buddhist monastic and cultural life are under supervision of the state today; the Chinese Buddhist Association is the government unit that administers this institution. The Cultural Revolution of 1966–76 dealt a heavy blow to the Buddhist heritage, since many monasteries and works of art were destroyed or permanently defaced. In recent years monks have been allowed to repopulate the sangha once again.

Korea

Buddhism spread into Korea in the fourth century, a time when it was highly active in China. Buddhism was at a peak in the Three Kingdoms and Unified Silla periods (558–935), when it was officially supported. Such Buddhist schools as the Hua Yan, Chan, and Tantric Buddhism all thrived in Korea. In the Yi dynasty (1391–1910), however, Confucianism was made the state ideology, and Buddhism not only lost its privileged state but was at times actively suppressed. Since the end of Japanese occupation in World War II, Won Buddhism, an indigenous blend of various Buddhist teachings, has strengthened, and today in South Korea Buddhism is on an equal footing with the very strong faith of Christianity. North Korea, an iconoclastic communist state, initially suppressed and now tightly controls what remains of its Buddhist establishment.

Japan

Buddhism entered Japan from Korea as early as 522. It was actively promoted by Prince Shotoku (573–621) and became the official religion. During succeeding centuries there was active interaction between Japanese Buddhist leaders and visiting Korean and Chinese monks. Such figures as Kukai and Saicho founded important schools of Japanese Buddhism upon their return from China, most significantly the Shingon and Tendai schools. All these schools were involved in Japanese politics to some extent.

During the later Kamakura period (1185–1333), other schools moved to the fore, including Zen, Pure Land, and Nichiren, which remain the dominant forms of Japanese Buddhism today. During the Tokugawa period (1604–1868) Buddhism was both supported and highly controlled by the state. Then in 1868, Shinto became the dominant state religion, and Buddhism was forced to adjust to life as the underdog. Since Japan's defeat in World War II, however, Buddhism, especially through newly formed schools such as Rissho Kosei-kai and Soka Gakkai, has been reinvigorated.

Tibet

Tibetan culture has traditionally borrowed heavily from its two giant neighbors, India and China, while developing its own unique culture as well. When Buddhism was finally introduced into Tibet in the seventh century C.E., it was already on the decline in India and undergoing fiery evolution in China. The Mahayana and Vajrayana forms that finally took root in Tibet continued to develop, with great works of scholasticism and mysticism being written well into the 14th and 15th centuries. The culture became ingrained with Buddhist institutions, especially the monastery, and up to 20 percent of the total population at some points were monks and nuns. Tibetan Buddhism spread in addition into neighboring Nepal, Bhutan, and Mongolia.

According to tradition Buddhism arrived when King Songtsen Gampo married two wives, one from Nepal and one from China, and spread its doctrines. The great monastery of Jokhang, in Lhasa, dates from his reign. Later the king Trhisong Detsen called for the renowned master from Nepal Santaraksita. He in turn called for assistance from Padmasambhava, to whom legends ascribe the feat of subduing all the local demons who did not want Buddhism to enter Tibet.

A later event of significance was the debate in 792 C.E. between Hua Shang, a Chinese Chan monk in favor of sudden enlightenment, and Kamalasila, an Indian master who advocated the gradual path to enlightenment. The victory went to Kamalasila, an outcome that reflects the trend in Tibetan writings.

The Gelug school of Tibetan Buddhism gained political power in the 15th century, resulting in the rule by the Gelug leader, the Dalai Lama. The successive Dalai Lamas are considered to be incarnations of the bodhisattva Avalokitesvara and were chosen after searches for the correct successor and test questions. The Panchen Lama, whose main monastery was at Tashilhunpo, was a competing line of authority; the Panchen Lamas were all considered to be incarnations of the Buddha Amitabha.

Today Tibetan Buddhism is a vibrant part of Buddhist practice and in the late 20th century drew many adherents in the West as well as Asia, including China. The dispersal of the Tibetan religious leadership in 1959, with the flight of the Dalai Lama to India, although a crisis for the religious institutions, turned into a significant boost to this process of dissemination.

Buddhism Today

Today there are an estimated 500–700 million Buddhists, including those who profess to be Buddhists but also practice other faiths. Several trends characterize modern Buddhism's situation. One side effect of European colonization efforts in the 18th and 19th centuries was that subject populations, often in traditional Buddhist lands, became aware of other traditions in other places, all paying allegiance to the Buddha. Japanese Buddhists began to study and interact with those in Thailand and Sri Lanka. Chinese Buddhists discovered Tibetan Vajrayana. This process continues today as the different traditions coexist as varieties of Buddhism.

In addition Buddhism has sunk roots in most countries of the West, with creative results from the mixing of the concerns in these places with Buddhist perspectives. Western Buddhists have, for instance, shown keen interest in feminism and the role of sexuality.

Another important trend has been the worldwide spread of certain groups and traditions, in conjunction with the forces of globalization. This includes Tibetan Buddhism in general but also such individual well-organized newly formed institutions as Sokka Gakkai from Japan and the Compassion Relief Society from Taiwan.

As an Indian religion Buddhism was a minor sect among many, which grew somehow into a transnational institution. This worldwide movement has all the signs of and receives the recognition due to a major religion. It continues to attract talented and dedicated followers, some living in the monastic institution established by the Buddha, others living in society as lay followers. However, it remains firmly based on the simple ethical code and perceptions taught by the founder, more than 2,000 years ago.

Romanization Systems for Foreign Terms

Any work covering religions of Asia must refer to proper nouns and names from a variety of languages. In general, this text follows standard texts or transliteration forms for the various languages encountered. (These are Monier-Williams's *A Sanskrit-English Dictionary* for Sanskrit, pinyin for Chinese, *The Pali Text Society's Pali-English Dictionary* for Pali, simplified Wylie for Tibetan, McCune-Reischauer [Hangul] for Korean, and modified Hepburn for Japanese.) However, because this work is intended for a general readership, we do not use diacritics of any sort on Asian-language terms.

Terms not commonly accepted in English are italicized throughout. However, certain terms that through widespread usage have become accepted as English terms ("karma," for example) are not italicized.

The titles of nonreligious texts are italicized. Religious texts—recognized as sacred texts by followers within the tradition—are set in roman type. We generally adopt the most widely known version of a title, if there are several versions. For instance, we use "Lotus Sutra" instead of "Saddharmapundarika-sutra."

For technical terms we generally prefer to use the Sanskrit or other language version instead of the English translation, unless the English version is perfectly clear and nearly identical to the original term. Thus we refer to *desire* instead of *chanda,* but *pratitya-samutpada* instead of *codependent arising.* The first concept is clear to English speakers, but *codependent arising* is at best an approximate rendering of a complex Sanskrit concept. In cases where it could go either way, we generally choose the Sanskrit term, to encourage familiarity.

Some terms are known by both Sanskrit and Pali versions, and, depending on the background of the writer, a reader may encounter both versions. We tend by common practice to follow the Sanskrit versions, except where there is clearly a Theravada or Pali context and it makes no sense to introduce a spelling inappropriate to the tradition.

For Chinese terms, the pinyin system of romanization has become increasingly accepted. In this text, there are exceptions to its use. We retain the traditional, non-pinyin spelling for some individuals whose names have come down to readers in English in a widely recognized way. Two obvious examples are Confucius and Mencius, whose names would, strictly speaking, be transliterated as Kongzi and Mengzi, using the pinyin system. In addition, we retain the spelling used by the individual if that person is alive or only recently deceased, thus Sheng Yen instead of Sheng Yan. Also, the names of a few 19th-century Chinese masters are better known through spellings based on the Wade-Giles transliteration system, which we thus retain, for example, Cheng Yen (pinyin: Zheng Yan). For other well-known figures, such as Xuan Zang, older spellings are given in parentheses, as well as Sanskrit, Korean, and Japanese versions, if the terms are likely to be encountered frequently in those languages. However, in most areas, we resolutely follow the pinyin version—for instance, using the term *Daoism* instead of the increasingly outdated *Taoism*.

Pronunciation of Foreign Terms

Sanskrit and Pali terms can be sounded as in English without much difficulty. Chinese terms generally sound close if sounded according to the best guess in English. (Of course, the native speaker will miss the tones—pitch levels that are necessary for intelligibility.) There are, however, a handful of sounds that may prove tricky for English speakers:

xi	sound as "see"; hence xia = "see-ah"
long	the "lo" here is sounded like "loo" in loop
zhang	the "zh" sound like "j" in just
q	q is often paired with a vowel and always sounds like English "ch"; hence, qi = "chee," quan = "choo-an," and qu approximates "choo"
cu	"c" sounds like English "ts" in its; hence, cu = "tsoo"
sui	sounds like "sway"

Tibetan terms are found in many variants. We adopt the simplest, most widely used version of a term, even if it does not conform exactly to the strict romanization rule. This method often means leaving off unvoiced consonants.

CHRONOLOGY

Note: Dates for early, legendary events use traditional dating.

3000 B.C.E.

♦ The mythical emperor Fu Xi (r. 2952–2836 B.C.E.) creates writing, teaches cooking, fishing, and, most significantly, the ordering of the eight trigrams later recorded in the *Yijing* (*Book of Changes*). Fu Xi, married to his sister, Nyu Gua, was responsible for the general ordering of society and such civilizing institutions as marriage.

563

♦ Siddhartha Gautama (563–483), the future Buddha, is born in Kapilavastu, in present-day Nepal, and lives for 80 years. According to legend his mother, Maya, dreamed of a white elephant and became pregnant with the bodhisattva Buddha. The child was born from her right side. She died soon after, but the Buddha returns to heaven to teach her in the Dharma, thereby allowing her to attain enlightenment.

501

♦ Laozi and Confucius, China's great philosopher-teachers, are active and meet in China. According to tradition Confucius (551–470 B.C.E.) taught a band of disciples for many years until he died in his 70th year. Laozi, the central figure in early Daoist thought, is a much vaguer figure than Confucius. Laozi may be a compilation of several legends, including those concerning one called Lao Dan. The story was more or less fixed by 100 B.C.E. According to Daoist and Confucian tradition Confucius sought a meeting with Laozi to ask his opinion concerning mourning rites.

500–350

♦ The *Daodejing,* the most widely translated Chinese classic, is compiled and attributed to Laozi, the pseudolegendary founder of Daoism.

486

♦ The First Council of Buddhism is held at Rajagraha soon after the Buddha's *parinirvana* (death), to recite and check the complete Vinaya (rules of conduct for monks) and Sutras (the words of the Buddha). The council is presided over by Kasyapa.

450–050

♦ The early schools of Buddhism take shape in India. These sometimes developed as a result of doctrinal differences, sometimes of geographical differences. Some accounts cite the number of these schools at 18, although the actual number is difficult to pinpoint. The major schools include the Sthaviravadins, the Mahasanghikas, the Sarvastivadins, and the Sammatiyas. Although all of the schools are said to have recorded their own versions of the Tripitaka, only that of the Theravadins, an offshoot of the Sthaviravadins, survives in whole today, in the Pali language.

386

♦ The Second Council of Buddhism is held at Vesali (Vaisali), India. The first schism forms between two rival groups within the sangha, the Mahasanghikas and the Sthaviravadins.

371–289

♦ The great Confucian teacher Mencius is active during the Warring States period (c. 475–221 B.C.E.) of Chinese history. He emphasizes the teachings of righteousness and humanity, and the inherent equality of all people.

300–200

♦ The Daoist philosopher Zhuang Zhou teaches naturalness (*ziran*) and techniques of settling the mind, as found in the compiled classic *Zhuangzi*.

272–231

♦ Emperor Asoka reigns over the Maurya empire in northern India. He orders that edicts promoting the Buddha's Dharma be carved in stone on pillars and rocks showing his devotion to Buddhism. Thirty-three such carved edicts survive. The Mauryan empire declines soon after his death.

c. 250

♦ The Third Council of Buddhism is held at Pataliputra and in Pali accounts is presided over by Emperor Asoka. In this council disagree-

ments are debated by the Sarvastivadins and the Vibhajyavadins.

247

♦ Mahinda, son of Emperor Asoka, introduces Buddhism to Sri Lanka.

150

♦ The Questions of King Milinda, a sutra in the Pali language, appears in northern India and Pakistan. Milinda (or Menander) was an ethnic Greek ruler in northern India. This work expresses the idea that there can be only one Buddha in existence at one time.

100–0

♦ The Mahayana text Lotus Sutra is written, most likely in northern India. It is translated into Chinese at least six times, between 255 and 601. It was highly esteemed by the Tian Tai founder Zhi Yi (538–597) and the Japanese innovator Nichiren (1222–82).

55

♦ The *Analects,* the collected sayings of Confucius (551–479 B.C.E.), appear in the final form that we know today. According to tradition the text was collected after the master's death, but scholars believe it grew in several layers.

c. 25 B.C.E.

♦ Completion of the first writing of the Pali canon in written form in Sri Lanka.

0–100 C.E.

♦ The Tripitaka, the Buddhist canon, is recorded in final form in the language called Pali. This was a dialect of Middle Indo-Aryan used at the time of recording and differed from the Magadhi language spoken by the Buddha. Some of the early schools that formed by this period also used Sanskrit to record their canons, notably the Sarvastivadins.

0–100

♦ The Fourth Council of Buddhism, whose historicity is doubtful, is held at Kaniska during the reign of Kaniska I. The council is overseen by Vasumitra.

0–200

♦ Mahayana (Great Vehicle) teachings begin to appear in northern India and eventually spread to Central Asia, Tibet, parts of Southeast Asia, China, and other areas of East Asia. This major branch or Buddhist practice puts emphasis on the figure of the bodhisattva, an individual who decides to remain in the world of samsara (birth and death) out of great compassion for those still trapped within it. Mahayana schools develop complex, competing elaborations on the Buddhist tradition.

65

♦ The first written reference to a Buddhist vegetarian feast and community in China.

100–200

♦ Asvaghosa publishes the first biography of the Buddha, the *Buddhacarita* (Deeds of the Buddha). This work becomes the first authoritative account of the Buddha's life.

♦ Nagarjuna, one of Buddhism's greatest philosophers, is active in southern India. In the *Madhyamakasatra* (*Treatise on the Middle Way*) and other works Nagarjuna propounds the idea of *sunyata* (emptiness), which contends that all phenomena in the universe lack essential existence. They are, instead, empty. The idea opposed another powerful concept then gaining ground, Buddha nature (*tathagatagarbha*).

142

♦ The legendary founder of Daoism, Laozi, appears in a vision to the Sichuan hermit Zhang Daoling. Laozi confers the mandate of heaven (Tian Ming) on Zhang, who founds the Wudoumi (five pecks of rice) sect. Zhang's movement becomes a well-organized political institution, which briefly sets up its own state. Zhang is today recognized as the founder of religious Daoism.

185

♦ The popular Mahayana text Vimalakirti-nirdesa Sutra, which relates the teachings of a lay bodhisattva in dialog with the bodhisattva Manjusri, is first translated into Chinese. This version has been lost, and the current version is the translation by Kumarajiva (c. 406).

284

♦ Ge Hong (284–363) is born to a family of mystics and scholars. He writes the *Baopuzi* (*He who embraces simplicity*), a classic of early Daoist alchemy, and retires to Mt. Luofu in southern China to cultivate the techniques of immortality.

c. 360

♦ Yang Xi (330–386?) begins to receive the Shang Qing revelations from the spirit of Lady Wei Huacun (251–334), a Daoist adept who had been a practitioner of Celestial Master Daoism. The revelations eventually total 31 volumes of materials and become the foundation for a new school, Shang Qing Daoism, which developed on Maoshan (Mt. Mao) under the leadership of Tao Hongjing (456–536). The school put great emphasis on visualizations and decreased emphasis on alchemical practices. Shang Qing Daoism was later absorbed into the Orthodox Unity (Zhenyi) school.

300–400

♦ The brother philosophers Asanga and Vasubandhu are active in northern India, in the region of Kashmir. They establish the principles of the Yogacara school. Vasubandhu in addition writes the massive Abhidharma-kosa, a summation of early Buddhist philosophy that is regarded as a monument by later generations.

400–500

♦ The Pali scholar Buddhaghosa is active in India and Sri Lanka. He eventually writes the *Vasudimagga*, a classic summary of meditation techniques.

401

♦ The great translator Kumarajiva (344–413) arrives in the Chinese capital of Chang'an, under imperial escort. The emperor supports the establishment of the first translation bureau. Kumarajiva goes on to oversee the nuanced translation of many major texts, including the Lotus Sutra.

402

♦ The Chinese monk Hui Yuan (344–416) establishes a cult of worship of Amitabha and his Pure Land on Mount Lu.

420

♦ The encyclopedic Mahayana text the Avatamsaka (Flower Garland) Sutra is first translated into Chinese by Buddhabhadra. It is translated two more times, by Siksananda in 699 and Prajna in 798, and into Tibetan by Jinamitra in the 700s.

446

♦ Emperor Wu (r. 424–451) of the Northern Wei dynasty orders the destruction of all Buddhist temples and images, and the execution of many monks, in the first persecution of Buddhism in Chinese history.

500–700

♦ The major Chinese schools of Buddhism form under the influence of the Sui dynasty (589–617) and Tang dynasty (618–907). These schools include Tian Tai, Hua Yan, Pure Land, and Chan, all of which constitute the major strands of Chinese Buddhist thought and practice, which remain influential today.

526

♦ The first Chan (Zen) patriarch, Bodhidharma, arrives in the southern Chinese port city of Canton (Guanzhou) and proceeds north to meet Emperor Wu (502–549) of the Liang dynasty (502–557). The emperor does not receive the iconoclastic monk warmly. Bodhidharma eventually moves on to the Shao Lin Temple in northern China and meditates in a cave there for nine years. He dies at the age of 160, after passing the secret teachings to his disciple, Hui Ke. The tradition later called Chan Buddhism developed into a major movement highly critical of other schools of the time. The emphasis of this school was clearly on direct enlightenment. It later spread widely into Japan, Korea, and Vietnam.

527

♦ Rulers of the Korean kingdom of Silla adopt Buddhism. The new faith received official support and spread throughout the Korean peninsula once Silla unified the other two states, Paekche and Koguryo, in the so-called Unified Silla state (?668–935).

562–645

♦ The Chinese monk Dao Cho, second patriarch of Pure Land Buddhism, introduces the term *mofa* (*mappo* in Japanese) to indicate the end of the Dharma. This is Mahayana Buddhism's expression of an apocalyptic future in which the Buddha's teachings are falsified, reviled, and ultimately lost. The larger framework sees an initial period in which the true Dharma (*shobo*) prevails, followed by the era of the false Dharma, and finally by the period of the end of Dharma, when the Buddha's teachings are not passed on and each individual must practice spiritual cultivation independently.

597

♦ The Tian Tai school founder Zhi Yi settles at Xiuchan Monastery on Mount Tiantai in eastern China. He publishes a disciplinary code for the monks there, the *Li Zhifa* (Establishing monastic regulations), in 597. His follower Guan Ding later records Zhi Yi's teachings in the *Mohe Zhiguan* (Great calming and contemplation). In this work Zhi Yi spells out the equal importance given to practice and study in the monk's life of contemplation.

600–700

♦ The monk Pomnang (seventh century) introduces Son, the Korean form of Chan, into Korea.

604

♦ A Confucian constitution is adopted in Japan by Prince Shotoku (574–622). The prince had been named crown prince of the Japanese state in 593 and promoted Buddhism widely. The second clause of the constitution urges the ruler to value the three treasures of Buddhism.

617–686

♦ The great Korean syncretic thinker Wonhyo writes more than 80 works on Buddhism. Active during the Three Kingdoms Period (335–668) and, later, in the Unified Silla dynasty (668–935), Wonhyo systematized the thinking of many Buddhist schools then active in Korea.

His commentary on the *Awakening of Faith* in particular is a classic still popular today.

629

♦ The Chinese monk Xuan Zang (596–664) sets out on his pilgrimage to India, a 16-year odyssey that has since been memorialized in countless stories in Chinese literature. The ostensible reason for the journey was to collect new texts, but Xuan Zang took home such a complete understanding of Indian Buddhism that he was immediately acknowledged as a great master. Although the Chinese emperor did not originally support the project, upon his return Xuan Zang's scriptures were all housed in the newly donated pagoda Dayanci in the capital, Chang'an. Other famous Chinese travelers to India include Fa Xian (fourth–fifth centuries) and Yi Jing (635–713).

662

♦ Hui Neng (638–713), later the sixth patriarch of Chan Buddhism, hears a sutra recitation and decides to follow the path of the Buddha. He moves to the monastery in which the Chan master Hong Ren (602–675) resides. Hong Ren recognizes Hui Neng as his rightful successor and before his death passes him the two symbols of Chan authority—Bodhidharma's robes and alms bowl.

690

♦ Empress Wu (Wu Zetian) (625–705), China's only female emperor, founds the brief Zhou dynasty (690–705) and is formally declared emperor, after ruling China indirectly during the Tang dynasty reigns of her husband, Gao Zong (d. 683), and son (resigned 690). She provides major support for Buddhism, especially the Chan and Hua Yan schools.

691

♦ Empress Wu issues a decree giving Buddhism precedence over Daoism.

710–784

♦ Nara is designated Japan's capital, during a relatively brief period that corresponded to the introduction of Buddhism into Japan. Six schools were established in Nara, the Ritsu, Kegon, Hosso, Kusha, Jujitsu, and Sanron, although these were primarily centers of sutra study rather than full-blown practicing schools of Buddhism.

712/720

♦ The *Kojiki* and *Nihonshoki*, Japan's first national histories, appear. They contain original myths relating to the creation of Japan, as well as early political events. They later become symbols of "pure" Japanese culture in 20th-century nationalist polemics.

753

♦ After trying five times over 10 years, the Chinese Vinaya (rules of discipline) master Ganjin (Jin Jianzhen in Chinese) finally arrives in Japan. He and his companions then perform the first ordination ritual in Japan at Todai-ji in the capital of Nara. The Japanese sangha, the community of monks, can be said to date from Ganjin's arrival.

775

♦ Samye, the first monastery in Tibet, is built following the intervention of the legendary Indian saint Padmasambhava. After being invited to Tibet by King Trison Detsen (c. 740–798), Padmasambhava does battle with local demons before prevailing in order to set the stage for Buddhism's entry into Tibet.

788

♦ After returning from his study tour to China, the Japanese monk Saicho (767–822) establishes Enryaku-ji, the temple complex on Mount Hiei near Kyoto, as the headquarters of the Tendai school. The temple became involved in political struggles and even had its own army of "warriors," the *sohei*. Most major figures in Japanese Buddhism in the subsequent Heian (794–1185) and Kamakura (1192–1338) periods all studied first on Mount Hiei. The original temple was finally destroyed by the warlord Nobunaga in 1571 but was rebuilt and continues to serve as the Tendai main temple.

800–900

♦ The great stupa at Borobudur, in central Java, is built by the Sailendra and Sanjaya dynasties. The known stupa is a vast mandala built of five base layers. Seventy-two smaller stupas, each housing a seated Buddha figure, are scattered throughout the three upper platforms.

804

♦ The Japanese monk Kukai (774–835) sails for China, where he studies with various monks in temples throughout the empire, finally settling in the Tang dynasty (618–907) capital of Chang'an, at the Ching Long temple. Through his master there, Hui Guo, Kukai obtained instructions in esoteric Buddhism (*mikkyo*), which Kukai eventually established in Japan as the Shingon school. To this day Shingon remains an important if small sect of Japanese Buddhism. Its head temple is at Kongobu-ji on Mount Koya.

838

♦ The Tendai Japanese monk and disciple of Saicho Ennin (794–864) travels to China. He remains until 847 and keeps a detailed diary of his experience in China. His description of the Hui Chang Persecution is particularly valuable as an objective record of that key event in Chinese history. He later returns to Japan and incorporates Pure Land elements into Tendai practice.

845

♦ Hui Chang persecution takes place under the reign of Emperor Wu Zong (r. 841–846) in

Tang dynasty (618–907) China. Although this persecution lasted only four years, it was the culmination of a tendency toward official control of Buddhism in China and marks the point at which Buddhism became subservient to official interests. Many scholars see 845 as the beginning of Buddhism's decline in China.

868

♦ The Diamond Sutra is printed in Chinese, as confirmed by a copy of the sutra from this date. This woodblock print has since been confirmed to be the oldest extant book in print, in the world. This text was probably first composed between 100 and 300 C.E. and is part of the family of texts known as the *prajnaparamita* (perfection of wisdom). The Diamond Sutra opens with the Buddha speaking before a vast crowd including 1,250 monks in the Jeta Grove. The bodhisattva Subhuti approaches with a question, and the Buddha explains the practice of a bodhisattva, a key concept in Mahayana Buddhism.

900–1300

♦ The Five Dynasties (907–960)/Song-era (960–1279) monks Bu Dai and Ji Gong, famous for their eccentric behavior while alive, become popular folk heroes and are quickly deified in popular Chinese religion. Bu Dai is depicted as a fat, laughing monk. His image merges with descriptions of Maitreya, the Buddha of the future, who is henceforth depicted as the laughing Buddha. Ji Gong, in contrast, is a thin, half-drunk beggarlike figure later known as "Crazy Ji." Both figures remain staples in the religious imagination of China and East Asia.

c. 960

♦ The Korean monk Chegwan (d. 971) formulates the concept of five periods and eight teachings in his short work *Tiantai Sijiaoyi* (*Outline of the Tian Tai fourfold teachings*).

960–1279

♦ In the Song dynasty Chinese Buddhism shifted gears and took on an increasingly popular bent, with, however, less intellectual vigor than shown previously. As an intellectual movement Buddhism had to deal with a reinvigorated Confucian spirit, Neo-Confucianism. Unlike in previous periods, few new Buddhist schools appeared, and such major individuals as the Tian Tai monk Zhi Li (960–1028) tended to focus on rhetorical debates within the existing lineages.

983

♦ The first Chinese Buddhist canon is printed in Sichuan, China.

1000–1100

♦ The Nyingma, or "Red Hat," school, the oldest school of Tibetan Buddhism, is designated as a separate tradition of teachings following the second introduction of Buddhism into Tibet in the 11th century. Nyingma teachings focus on Dzogchen, or the great perfection, as the key doctrine in Buddhist teachings.

1000–1200

♦ Neo-Confucianism is established as the major ideology in China and, later, other East Asian cultures. The intellectual movement began with the philosopher Zhou Dunyi (1017–73 C.E.) of the Song (960–1279) and extended to the Ming (1368–1644) thinker Wang Yangming (1472–1529).

1085

♦ The Tibetan meditation master Milarepa (1040–1123) begins nine years of solitary meditation, after which he attained full enlightenment. His collected songs, the *Hundred Thousand Songs of Milarepa*, is a testimony to his teaching techniques and popularity.

1107

◆ The university monastic complex at Nalanda, India, originally established in the fifth century C.E., is destroyed by the Turkish-Afghan invader Mahmud Shabbudin Ghori. It had been a key structure for the maintenance of Buddhism, whose loss underlined the final decline from which Indian Buddhism never truly recovered.

1133–1212

◆ The Japanese monk Honen propounds the idea that recitation of the Buddha Amitabha's name (*nembutsu*) is the most appropriate form of worship for the current age of degeneration. Through such recitation the believer would be ensured of rebirth in Amitabha's western paradise. Honen's ideas were fought against, and he was defrocked. After this he collected his followers and eventually established the Jodo Shu school of Japanese Buddhism.

1158–1210

◆ Chinul, a Chan monk in Korea, promotes Hua Yan (Avatamsaka) and Chan practice in Korea; the latter came to be known as Son. He advocated a path of cultivation in which sudden enlightenment was followed by gradual awakening, as seen in his work *Susim kyol* (Secrets on cultivating the mind).

1192

◆ The Kamakura era (1192–1338) begins with the shogun (military ruler) assuming real power throughout Japan as opposed to the emperor, based in Kyoto. The shoguns favor Buddhism, especially Zen, and Pure Land and Nichiren schools also flourish.

1198

◆ The founder of the Japanese Rinzai Zen school, Eisai (1141–1215), publishes *Kozen Gogokuron* (Promote Zen to protect the kingdom's rulers),

his most influential work. Eisai had first visited China in 1169 and returned with Tian Tai texts. He later returned a second time to study Zen (Chan) teachings. His *Kozen Gogokuron* gave imperial approval to his efforts to establish a Zen school in Japan. Eisai is also remembered as introducing tea from China.

1207

◆ Shinran (1173–1262), the successor to Honen, is sent into exile at the same time as Honen. He went on to teach about *nembutsu* practice and raise his own family. Shinran further developed the Pure Land concepts that joined to establish the Jodo Shinshu sect of Japanese Buddhism. Shinran placed special emphasis in his teachings on *shinjin*, faith.

1225

◆ The Japanese monk Dogen (1200–53) attains enlightenment while studying with the Caodong Chan master Ru Jing (1163–1268) in China. He returns to found the Soto Zen school in Japan. His masterpiece, *Shobogenzo,* spells out his philosophical ideas on the nature of phenomena.

1229

◆ The koan collection *Wuman Guan* (Gateless gate) appears. It contains 48 classic koans, "cases" meant to help cultivating monks gain an immediate apprehension of a vital truth. The work and another collection of 100 cases, the *Blue Cliff Records,* constitute the most famous koan collections. Koans have been an important aspect of practice in the Linji/Rinzai traditions of Chan/Zen.

1260s

◆ The great cast bronze figure of the Amitabha Buddha in Kamakura, Japan, the Daibutsu, is completed, replacing a wooden one completed in 1243.

1273

♦ Nichiren (1222–82) publishes the *Kanjin honzon sho,* a text that explains how to perform contemplation in the age of *mappo,* or the end of Dharma. Nichiren established a very powerful, iconoclastic school, Nichiren Shu, which put primary emphasis on the Lotus Sutra as the most complete expression of the Buddha's wisdom. The *Kanjin honzon sho* took the ideas of the Tian Tai founder Zhi Yi (538–597) in the direction of making the contemplation techniques propounded by Zhi Yi available to all.

1300–1400

♦ Buston (1290–1364), a Tibetan monk-scholar from the Kagyu school, edits the Tibetan Buddhist canon. He helps to organize the entire corpus into two portions, the Tanjur (words of the Buddha) and the Tenjur (commentarial literature). He also writes a chronology of Buddhism in India and Tibet.

1357–1419

♦ Tsong Khapa founds the Gelug (Virtuous Ones) school of Tibetan Buddhism, after intensive study with Sakya, Kagyu, and Kadampa masters.

1360

♦ Theravada Buddhism is recognized as the official state doctrine in the Siamese Kingdom of Ayutthaya.

1578

♦ The Mongol ruler Altan Khan assigns the title *Dalai Lama* ("teacher of the great ocean of wisdom") to the Tibetan teacher Sonam Gyatso (1543–88), subsequently known as the third Dalai Lama. The individual occupying this position later became the political leader of Tibet, as well as spiritual leader of the Gelug school.

1603

♦ The Tokugawa shogunate takes power in Japan. While privileging Zen Buddhism, the government strongly regulates Buddhism during the next 264 years and establishes a nationwide registration system.

1770s

♦ The 99-meter-high stupa and temple complex at Shwedagon is built in Rangoon, Burma (Myanmar).

1860

♦ Angkor Wat temple complex is rediscovered by the French explorer Henri Mouhot. The original complex near the Khmer city of Angkor Thom was built by the Khmer rulers Jayavarman VII (1181–1220) and Suryavarman II (r. 1131–50). Angkor Wat was originally dedicated to Vishnu but later became a Buddhist temple.

1868

♦ The restoration of the Meiji emperor (1852–1912) to power marks the end of the Tokugawa era (1603–1868) and social structure in Japan. The new modernizing and outward-focused government rethinks the status of Buddhism and Shinto.

1869

♦ Yasukuni Jinja, a Shinto shrine in Tokyo, is built under imperial edict to commemorate the dead of the Boshin Civil War (1867–68). Over time the souls of others who died in later battles were also added. Most recently, in 1978 the souls of 14 leaders (and war criminals) from World War II were included in the shrine. Since 1979 several prime ministers have visited the shrine, causing diplomatic complaints and demonstrations in other Asian countries, whose people generally see the visits as a sign of Japan's lack of remorse for its actions during the war.

1871

◆ The entire Pali Tripitaka is carved on 729 marble slabs, as instructed by the Burmese king Mondon. This collection is still visible at the Kuthodaw temple in Mandalay, Myanmar.

1881

◆ The Pali Text Society is founded by Thomas W. Rhys Davids. The society, based in London, continues to publish the Pali canon of Buddhism as well as dictionaries and a journal.

1885

◆ The Buddhist flag is first unfurled on Wesak, the celebration of the Buddha's birth date, in Sri Lanka (then Ceylon). Originally intended for use only during Wesak, it later became associated with the struggle against colonialism. In 1950 it was adopted officially by the World Federation of Buddhists.

1891

◆ Angarika Dharmapala (1864–1933) founds the Maha Bodhi society to organize support for the preservation of Bodhgaya, the site of the Buddha's enlightenment. Today Bodhgaya is a major pilgrimage center and a United Nations World Heritage Site.

1893

◆ The Indian Buddhist Angarika Dharmapala (1864–1933) and the Japanese Zen leader Soyen Shaku (1859–1919) speak at the World's Parliament of Religions held in Chicago. After the parliament, Charles T. Strauss, a German-American businessman, becomes the first American who formally accepts the precepts and becomes a lay Buddhist.

1895

◆ The Japanese Buddhist scholar D. T. Suzuki (1870–1966) achieves enlightenment after training under Soyen Shaku (1859–1919). Suzuki later writes more than 100 books and is instrumental in explaining Buddhism to the modern West.

1899

◆ The Buddhist Churches of America (BCA) is founded in San Francisco when Sonoda Shuye and Nishijima Kakuryo arrive in the city as representatives of the Honpa Hongwanji sect of Jodo Shinshu.

1899

◆ The first Young Men's Buddhist Associations are founded in Colombo, Sri Lanka, by D. D. Jayatilaka.

1900

◆ More than 40,000 Buddhist and Daoist texts are discovered in a single cave storage room in Dun Huang, a city located on the edge of China's great western desert. The Hungarian-British explorer Aurel Stein (1862–1943) purchased the whole lot and transported it to British India. It is now held in the British Museum.

1918–1992

◆ Ajahn Chah, a major proponent of the Thai Forest Meditation Tradition, establishes Wat Pah Nanachat in northern Thailand. This in turn becomes a major center training Westerners in the Thai Forest Tradition.

1920

◆ The Chinese Buddhist reformer T'ai Hsu (1890–1947) visits Hong Kong and sparks a popular Buddhist revival there.

1924–1935

◆ The Chinese Tripitaka is published in Japan in what is today known as the Taisho edition (full name is Taisho Shinshu Daizokyo). Today the Taisho remains the authoritative edition of the Chinese Tripitaka, and each work is referenced by its *T* number. The Taisho contains 2,184 separate works in 55 volumes.

1933

♦ Zhang Tianran assumes leadership of a small Eternal Mother–worshipping sect based in Shandong, eastern China. In the 14 years before his death he builds a nationwide religious organization known popularly as Yiguandao (today often called Tian Dao). Although suppressed in mainland China, Tian Dao groups continued to flourish in Taiwan and other areas in Asia throughout the 20th century.

1937

♦ The lay Nichiren organization now known as Soka Gakkai International is founded by Makiguchi Tsunesaburo (1871–1944) in Tokyo. In the decades since World War II, it has become one of the most powerful Buddhist institutions in the modern world.

1952

♦ World Fellowship of Buddhism is established, with headquarters in Bangkok, Thailand, as the umbrella organization for all Buddhist groups.

1954–1956

♦ Buddhist Council at Rangoon sponsored by the Burmese government to review and collate the contents of the Pali canon.

1956

♦ The Indian independence leader Babasaheb Bhimrao Ramji Ambedkar (1891–1956) formally converts to Buddhism and encourages around 400,000 Dalits (members of the untouchable class) to convert in the same year as well.

1959

♦ The 14th Dalai Lama flees Tibet after Chinese occupation. This results in the migration of a significant number of Tibetans into exile and, concurrently, the spread of Tibetan Buddhism to most parts of the world.

1963

♦ The immolation of the Buddhist monk Thich Quang Duc on June 11 calls the world's attention to the growing conflict in Vietnam and helps ignite a global movement for peace.

1965

♦ Change of the immigration law in the United States launches the movement of people from Asian countries to North America with a resultant rapid expansion of Buddhism there.

1966

♦ The Buddhist compassion relief Tzu Chi Association ("Tzu Chi") is founded in Hualian, Taiwan, as a charitable institution by the nun Cheng Yen (1966–   ). It eventually became one of the most influential organizations in modern Buddhism.

1967–1976

♦ The Chinese Great Proletarian Cultural Revolution dominates events in China and results in the wholesale destruction of many Buddhist temples and works of art.

1970

♦ Chogyam Trungpa (1940–87), the first Tibetan *tulku* educated in the West, arrives in America and settles in Colorado. He founds the Vajradhatu Foundation in 1973 and Naropa University in 1974 and is instrumental in popularizing Tibetan Buddhism in the West.

1982

♦ The Vietnamese-born monk Thich Nhat Hanh (1926–) founds Plum Village as a meditation center in France.

1987

♦ American Buddhist Congress is organized in Los Angeles to provide a united voice for the Buddhist groups in the United States.

1989

♦ The 14th Dalai Lama, Tenzin Gyatso, receives the Nobel Peace Prize. He is born in 1935 in Tibet, chosen at two years old as the reincarnation of the Dalai Lama, and receives a traditional, rigorous education in Buddhism. In 1959, at the age of 24, he leaves India on foot with a large number of followers and henceforth lives in exile, based in the North Indian city of Dharmsala, where he establishes the Tibetan Government-in-Exile.

1994

♦ The *Journal of Buddhist Ethics*, the first electronic publication devoted to Buddhism, begins.

1994

♦ The entire Pali canon is made available online.

1998

♦ World Buddhist University is established by the World Fellowship of Buddhists.

2002

♦ The Mahabodhi Temple at Bodhgaya, the site of the Buddha's enlightenment, is named a United Nations World Heritage Site.

2006

♦ Plans are finalized to establish a modern university at the ancient Buddhist monastery complex at Nalanda in Bihar, India. Several Asian nations express official support for the project.

2007

♦ Buddhist monks take a leading role in organizing civil unrest in Myanmar. Sporadic demonstrations occur in such northern cities as Sittwe and Pakokku, initially to protest the doubling of diesel and the quintupling of natural gas prices announced by the ruling junta on August 15. Up to 100,000 demonstrators take to the streets of the capital on September 24, with civilians forming human barricades around the marching monks and nuns. These demonstrations are eventually quelled by police and army units, resulting in mass arrests and deaths of at least 15 people. Monasteries around Yangon are raided and surrounded by armed police.

ENTRIES A TO Z

A

Abhidharma/Abhidhamma

The Abhidharma is one of the three subsections or "baskets" of the TRIPITAKA, the traditional collection of the Buddhist sacred scriptures. The Abhidharma is sometimes also written as *Abhidharmapitaka,* meaning "the basket of the Abhidharma."

Abhidharma means, literally, "concerning the DHARMA. The term *Dharma* here refers to the teachings of the Buddha, which are mainly recorded in the *Sutrapitaka,* the SUTRAS, or "sayings," of the Buddha. The Abhidharma literature is a collection of commentaries on the sutras. It contains literature that we generally classify as philosophy, along with other works of a more religious or historical nature.

The earliest version of the Abhidharma was produced in the Pali language. Various schools of Buddhism quickly developed their own versions of the Abhidharma and argued strongly for the superiority of their own interpretations. However, only three Abhidharma literatures still exist today: the Pali Abhidhamma (using the Pali spelling for this term), the Sarvastivadin Abhidharma, and the Sariputra Abhidharma of the Dharmaguptaka school.

THE PALI ABHIDAMMA

Tradition states that the Pali Abhidamma developed when the Buddha visited his mother in Tusita, one of the Buddhist heavens, and taught her (along with MARA, the Buddhist devil, and all the remaining *devas,* or gods, in heaven) about the Dharma. He did this at night, and in the daytime he would repeat the same teachings to his major disciple, SARIPUTRA. Sariputra recited the comments to his disciple, who in turn passed them down until they were recited at the Third Council of Buddhism, held at Pataliputra in 251 B.C.E. At that time all seven books were recited accurately by Revata, who was the presiding monk of the council.

The Pali Abhidamma, still used throughout the Theravada world, consists of these seven major works of Buddhist philosophy (arranged in order of historical age):

1. Dhammasangani: This work gives a scheme to categorize all *dhammas* (DHARMAS), here meaning "phenomena." The types of *dhammas* are arranged in headings in a list called the Matika. In the Dhammasangani's Matika there are 122 headings in four categories: *cittuppada* (*dhammas* of consciousness), *rupa* (those of corporeality), *nikkhepa* (the way *dhammas* are distributed), and *atthakatha* (an additional summary section).

2. Vibhanga ("distinctions"): Called "the Book of Analysis," the Vibhanga complements the Dhammasangani by fully discussing all *dhammas*, in the same order as the Dhammasangani. There are 18 chapters in three groups: those dealing with mental phenomena, those dealing with the holy life, and supplemental categories.

3. Dhatukatha: This text concentrates on analyzing the *dhatus*, the physical elements, from 14 separate perspectives.

4. Puggalapannatti ("the designation of individuals"): This work discusses classifications of people, in 10 chapters.

5. Kathavatthu ("subjects of discussion"): This work deals with wrong views. It was compiled as a result of schismatic disagreements among the early 18 schools of Buddhism. Written as a debate between two people, it involves 1,000 statements about the Matika, each analyzed in depth. The Kathavatthu was said to have been recited at the Third Council of Buddhism.

6. Yamaka ("book of pairs"): This work discusses the relationship between *dhammas,* elements of existence, and *puggalas* (in Sanskrit, *pudgalas,* "individuals" or "selves"). The format it follows is to ask two questions concerning an unclear subject, the answers to which reveal important distinctions.

7. Patthana ("system of relations"): Also called the "Great Book," the Patthana presents the entire system of conditioned reality. This work deals with PRATITYA-SAMUTPADA and the interrelations among elements of reality. There are four divisions, each one discussing the 24 *paccayas* (in Sanskrit, *pratyayas,* or "conditions").

THE SARVASTIVADIN ABHIDHARMA

Although the Sarvastivadin version of the Abhidharma-pitaka also has seven texts, these do not generally coincide with those of the Pali Abhidhamma. And they are not generally taken as a "fixed" canon of seven texts. Instead there was an Abhidharma tradition of six smaller texts or "legs" that culminated in the development of a seventh, the massive Jnanaprasthana, which in turn led to the writing of the Mahavibhasa, another, later compilation of Sarvastivadin thought. The first seven texts of the Sarvastivadin Abhidharma are as follows:

1. Sangitiparyay ("section for recitation"): This work lists doctrinal concepts.

2. Dharmaskandha ("aggregate of Dharmas"): This work focuses on Sarvastivadin doctrines, especially concerning the stages of the ARHAT's progress.

3. Prajnapti ("book of manifestation"): This work explains cosmology and psychology.

4. Vinanakaya: This work discusses the nonexistence of the self.

5. Dhatukaya: This work is another psychological discussion.

6. Prakaranapada ("treatise"): This work discusses all the elements of reality.

7. Jnanaprasthana ("course of knowledge"): This work defines psychological terms.

The Sarvastivada Abhidharma has not survived in its Sanskrit original version—in other words, it does not exist today in Sanskrit. However, it had long before been translated into Chinese, and that version exists. While one part of the Sarvastivada Abhidharma, the Prajnapti, is not complete in Chinese, it is found in a Tibetan version. So today we are able to say we have complete access to the Sarvastivadin Abhidharma literature.

Chinese travelers collected works from many of the early Indian schools, such as Sthaviravada, Mahasnghika, Sammatiya, Dharmaguptaka, and Sarvastivadin, but only those from the Sarvastivadin Abhidharma were translated into Chinese. Thus the Abhidharma in the Chinese Tripitaka is, strictly speaking, that of the Sarvastivadins.

SARIPUTRA ABHIDHARMA

The Sariputra version summarizes the first two Abhidharmas without introducing much new material. It survives only in Chinese translation.

Further reading: Nina van Gorkom, *Abhidhamma in Daily Life* (London: Triple Gem Press, 1997); Herbert V. Guenther, *Philosophy and Psychology in the Abhidharma* (Berkeley, Calif.: Shambhala, 1976); Kogen Mizuno, *Basic Buddhist Concepts.* Translated by Charles S. Terry and Richard L. Gage (Tokyo: Kosei, 1987).

Abhidharma-kosa (Abhidharmakosa-basyam)

The Abhidharma-kosa, one of the greatest works of Buddhism, is a fundamental text studied to this day by most BHIKSU (Buddhist monks). It is, literally, a commentary (*basyam*) on the *kosha* ("storehouse") of the ABHIDHARMA. The Abhidharma is one of the three parts of the traditional TRIPITAKA, the writings accepted as scripture by Buddhists. The Abhidharma-kosa, as the work is usually referred to, is divided into chapters, each dealing with a major conceptual category, such as the *dhatus* (elements) or the *indriyas* (sense organs). It presents definitions of all fundamental concepts in Buddhist thought: *abhidharma* itself ("discernment of the dharmas"), dharma, *klesas, skandhas, rupas,* and more.

The Abhidharma-kosa was extremely influential, both in India and later in such areas as CENTRAL ASIA and CHINA. It generated a vast commentarial literature itself. The Abhidharma-kosa was written by the fourth-century Indian scholar VASUBANDHU (c. 316–396). At the time, he was a monk in Kashmir. He did not strictly adhere to the SARVASTIVADIN school, but he presented the Abhidharma-kosa as a careful exposition of the VAIBHASIKA philosophers, a branch of Sarvastivadin thought.

CONTENTS OF THE ABHIDHARMA-KOSA

There are two sections to Vasubandhu's work. The first is a *karika*, or verse section, known as the Kosha proper. The second is the commentary (*basyam*) to the verses, also written by Vasubandhu.

The *karika* section existed independently and has been translated into Chinese as an independent work. The *basyam* section was translated into Chinese but was until recently lost in Sanskrit. A Sanskrit version was rediscovered in 1935 in the form of a palm-leaf text in a monastery in Tibet. This manuscript dated from the 12th–13th centuries. Part of the text was missing. However, it did include 600 of the main *karikas*.

TRANSLATIONS OF THE ABHIDHARMA-KOSA

The Abhidharma-kosa was translated into Chinese by PARAMARTHA (563–567) and again by XUAN ZANG (651–654). It became the foundation of the Zhushe or Kosa School of early Chinese Buddhism developed by Xuan Zang's disciples. The importance of the Abhidharma-kosa was made known to modern scholarship after its translation into French by Louis de La Vallée Poussin, between 1923 and 1931.

Further reading: Herbert V. Guenther, *Philosophy and Psychology in the Abhidharma* (Berkeley, Calif.: Shambhala, 1976).

Abhidharma school

This Chinese school flourished in the initial period of contact with Buddhism, especially during the Northern and Southern Dynasties period (420–589 C.E.). It emphasized study and practice based on the works of the ABHIDHARMA, the commentary portion of the Buddhist canon. Specifically, the school taught that all DHARMAS are real and that they are produced by a combination of six primary and four subsidiary causes. Followers of the Abhidharma school studied such works from the early 18 schools of Buddhism as Dharmaratna's *The Heart of the Abhidharma.* The school later declined and was absorbed into the Zhushe (in Japanese, Kosa) school in the seventh century.

The importance of the Abhidharma school reflects the emphasis placed on study of Abhidharma literature in the early phase of Chinese Buddhism. Once Chinese Buddhists attempted their own interpretations of the Buddhist corpus of learning, such new Mahayana schools as CHAN and TIAN TAI absorbed the energies of Chinese thinkers.

Further reading: Kenneth K. S. Ch'en, *Buddhism in China* (Princeton, N.J.: Princeton University Press, 1964).

achan See TITLES AND TERMS OF ADDRESS, BUDDHIST.

Achan Mun See MUN, AJAAN.

Afghanistan, Buddhism in

Buddhism reached what today is Afghanistan in the third century B.C.E. having spread from the area ruled by King ASOKA. Over the next several centuries it spread among the population and during the second century C.E. assumed a more central role with the ascendancy of KANISKA to the throne.

Kaniska's empire reached from the Caspian Sea across Afghanistan and south across the Indus River into northern India. A convert to Buddhism, Kaniska became its great patron. He is remembered for holding a great council of Mahayana Buddhist leaders to seek reconciliation among various schools. He also helped nurture the new artistic synthesis that had arisen, the Gandhara school of art, which mixed elements of Greek realism and Indian mysticism.

With Kaniska's support, Buddhist art and culture permeated his kingdom and many images of the Buddha carved in stone were produced. The Gandhara approach represented a significant step, as previously Buddha had not been pictured in human form; rather he had been represented by some artifact of his earlier presence—an empty seat, a footprint, or a riderless horse. Gandhara artists began to show him with a serene face and a body posed to suggest peace and compassion.

Kaniska saw to the building of many Buddhist structures, especially STUPAS and monasteries. The Bamiyan Valley, some 150 miles north of Kabul, one of the region's trade and cultural centers (a stop along the Silk Road), became the site of a number of monasteries, though many monks chose to live in the more reclusive caves that honeycombed the valley walls. It would be here that some of the most important sculptures, gigantic statues of Buddha (the largest almost 175 feet in height), were carved out of the rock on the sides of the Bamiyan gorge. Carving of the two largest statues began during Kaniska's reign and was completed over the next century.

Afghanistan became both a conduit for Buddhism to pass from India to China and Tibet and a center of Buddhist dissemination in its own right. Buddhism remained the dominant religion in Afghanistan until the mid-seventh century, when Islamic forces overran the area. Kabul fell in 664. Over the next centuries, accounts of travelers in the areas suggest that the Buddhist artifacts remained largely untouched. However, disaster occurred in Bamiyan in the 13th century with the invasion of Genghis Khan. During the siege of Bamiyan, his grandson was killed and after the city was taken, every resident was killed.

Buddhism did survive, initially, although there is little mention of it from the 14th century. It appears to have died out gradually. By the time Afghanistan had contact with European colonial states there were no Buddhists, but a considerable amount of Buddhist art was scattered around the country. This remaining Buddhist presence in the country became a matter of heightened concern in March 2001, when the then-ruling Taliban regime decided to destroy the large statues of the Buddha located in the Bamiyan Valley. They were blown up, in spite of widespread pleas from the international community (including other Islamic countries) to prevent their destruction. In the years since the fall of the Taliban, efforts have been launched to rebuild the statues. Before their destruction, one of the statues was the largest statue of Buddha in the world.

Further reading: Simone Gaulier, Robert Jera-Bezard, and Monique Maillard, *Buddhism in Afghanistan and Central Asia* (Leiden: Brill, 1976); Cary Gladstone, *Afghanistan: History, Issues, Bibliography* (Huntington, N.Y.: Novinka Books, 2001); Monique Maillard and Robert Bézard, "Buddhism in Afghanistan and Central Asia," *Iconography of Religions* 13 (1976).

Africa, Buddhism in

Buddhism has had a relatively negligible presence in Africa's long history. Only since the 1970s has it become significant in the complex African religious scene.

Buddhism first appeared in 1686, when three Thai monks were shipwrecked along the coast of South Africa, but that is all we hear of it until early in the 20th century when some 450 Ceylonese Buddhists migrated to Zanzibar in search of employment. Around 1915 they formed a Sinhalese Buddhist Association and requested land from the British authorities to build a temple. In 1919 they obtained a sapling from the Bodhi tree in Sri Lanka. Their first worship hall was completed in 1927.

In 1962, the Buddhist Association received the first Buddhist monk to arrive in Africa since the 17th century. He worked in Zanzibar until 1964, when at the time of the revolution and the creation of the present state of Tanzania, all of the Buddhists (who now included people from a variety of Asian countries) moved to the African mainland and reestablished the Buddhist Association in Dar es Salaam. Dar es Salaam is now the home of the oldest Buddhist temple in Africa and serves a community of some 40,000 Buddhists, the second largest in Africa.

Meanwhile, early in the 20th century, some Hindus who had settled in Natal, South Africa, in the 19th century converted to Buddhism. Other Asian Buddhists arrived in South Africa by taking advantage of the liberal travel laws within the British Commonwealth. Among the first to form a community were Burmese in Natal, who erected the country's first Buddhist temple. Their efforts have more recently been bolstered by Jeffrey Oliver, an Australian who spent eight years in Burma practicing meditation and immigrated to South Africa to found a Burmese monastery.

The real growth of Buddhism, however, as in the Western world, began in the 1970s, a decade that saw the arrival of a variety of Buddhist teachers to spread their faith and the movement of religiously alienated South Africans to Asia in search of a new spiritual path. By the 1980s a spectrum of Buddhist groups had emerged in urban centers around the country that attracted South Africans of Dutch and British backgrounds. Buddhist traditions included those from Thailand, Japan, China (including Tibet and Taiwan), and Korea. Among the 14,000 Taiwanese who arrived in South Africa in the last half of the 20th century, many are affiliated with the Fo Guang Shan Order. In 1992, these Taiwanese Buddhists began an ambitious project of erecting a Buddhist temple complex, complete with a seminary for training Buddhist leaders, at Bronkhorstspruit, just outside Johannesburg. The South African temple now serves a diverse population of interested seekers. As the 21st century begins, South Africa is home to some 80,000 Buddhists.

Apart from Tanzania and South Africa, very few Buddhists can be found across the continent.

As early as the 1960s, President Daisaku Ikeda of SOKA GAKKAI INTERNATIONAL (SGI) had included Africa in his plans for the expansion of the organization, but it was not until the 1980s that real recruitment efforts began, with its greatest response in Ghana and South Africa. It now has centers in Uganda, Mozambique, and a number of other countries. SGI is the only Buddhist group making an effort to build an African membership outside South Africa. The only other organization with multiple centers in Africa is the Association Zen Internationale, based in Paris, which has several affiliate centers in some of the former French colonies (Burkina Faso, Cameroon, Ivory Coast, Mali).

Most northern African countries, where Islam is the primary religion, do not allow or encourage the development of other religions, especially any that would seek to build membership from among the Muslim population. There are a few Buddhist centers, but they exclusively serve expatriate residents.

Further reading: BuddhaNet. "Africa." Available online. URL: http://www.buddhanet.net/wbd/region.php?region_id=4. Accessed on September 6, 2007.

aggregates *See* SKANDHA.

Agon Shu

Agon Shu is a new form of Japanese Buddhism. Agon Shu teaches a doctrine called Jobutsu-ho, the teachings and practices needed to attain enlightenment and full salvation (NIRVANA). The route to salvation includes the practice of the meditation methods founded in Esoteric Buddhism (VAJRAYANA), bolstered by additional practices such as kundalini yoga, a form of yoga that emphasizes the spine.

Agon Shu has established its headquarters at its main temple located outside Kyoto. In 1986, the president of Sri Lanka donated a true relic of the Buddha for enshrinement at the temple. The temple grounds is the site of the main annual festival of Agon Shu, the Hoshi Matsuri, or fire ceremony, during which members throw prayer into the fire in the belief that the fire becomes the agent in realizing the answer to their prayer requests. A lesser form of the fire ceremony is held in the local Agon Shu centers each month.

Agon Shu was founded in 1978 by Seiyu Kiriyama (1921–   ), who serves as president of the organization. Followers call him Kancho, or director, acknowledging his role as the leader of a new Buddhist school. Kiriyama had been a member of several different groups, and he drew on THERAVADA, MAHAYANA, and TANTRIC Buddhism, as well as some aspects of SHINTO, in creating Agon Shu.

Agon Shu grew quickly in Japan and by the end of the century had established itself within Japanese communities in Taiwan, Brazil, and the United States.

Ahkon Norbu Lhamo, Jetsunma
(1949–   ) *first Western female tulku*
Jesunma Ahkon Norbu Lhamo, the first woman to be recognized by Tibetan Buddhist leaders as a TULKU, or reincarnated lama, was born Alice Zeoli in Brooklyn, New York. She had an awakening in her 19th year through a series of dreams in which she was instructed in a mode of meditation. The dreams would continue for more than a decade, during which she married and began to raise a family. After she moved to Washington, D.C., a following began to form around her and she emerged as the teacher at the Center for Discovery and New Life.

In 1985, she met H. H. Penor Rinpoche, the head of the NYINGMA school of Tibetan Buddhism. Though she was unaware of Tibetan Buddhism, when Renor Rinpoche queried her as to what she was teaching at the center, he identified it as MAHAYANA BUDDHISM. Subsequently, she was visited by other lamas, as Penor Rinpoche had concluded that she was a *tulku* (a reincarnated aspect of a BODHISATTVA). In 1988, Penor Rinpoche formally enthroned her as *tulku*. Her new name, Ahkon Norbu, tied her to a 17th-century female mystic and nun at the Palyul Monastery in Tibet. The contemporary Ahkon Norbu was designated the Western lineage holder of the Palyul lineage. In 1994, she was also recognized as an incarnation of the White Tara, one representation of GUAN YIN.

Ahkon Norbu Lhamo is now the head of the Kunzang Odsal Palyul Changchub Choling, in Poolesville, Maryland.

See also CHINA-TIBET, BUDDHISM IN.

Further reading: Vicki Mackenzie, *Reborn in the West: The Reincarnation Masters* (London: Bloomsbury, 1995); Andrew Rawlinson, *The Book of Enlightened Masters* (LaSalle, Ill.: Open Court, 1997).

Aitken, Robert Baker (1917–) *founder, Diamond Sangha*

Robert Aitken founded the Diamond Sangha, an organization of Zen Buddhist centers that encourages interreligious dialogue and activism on issues of social justice. The Diamond Sangha functions as one segment of the larger Sanbo Kyodan (Fellowship of the Three Treasures), a loose association of teachers in the lineage of Harada Dai'un Sogaku Roshi (1871–1961), the teacher of YASUTANI Hakuun Ryoko Roshi. The Sanbo Kyodan teaches RINZAI ZEN, the tradition that uses KOANS.

Aitken was born in Philadelphia, Pennsylvania, but grew up in Hawaii. He attended the University of Hawaii, but his study was interrupted by World War II. He joined the United States Army and was stationed on Guam at the end of 1942 when the Japanese invaded. Taken prisoner, he first learned about Buddhism from one of the guards at his detention camp, who lent him a book by the British Zen practitioner R. H. Blyth, a student of DAISETSU TEITARO SUZUKI. Aitken eventually met Blyth, who was interned in the same camp and after the war studied with him as preparation for

his journey to Japan to study with Nakagawa Soen Roshi (1907–84).

In 1959, with Nakagawa Roshi's permission, he began a Zen meditation group in his home in Hawaii, while periodically returning to Japan to sit with Yasutani Hakuun Ryoko Roshi (1885–1973) and his dharma heir, Yamada Koun Roshi (1907–89). Aitken received dharma transmission from Yamada Roshi in 1974 and was recognized as a Shoshike (Correctly Qualified Teacher) in the Shjobo Kyodan lineage of Yasutani Roshi in 1985.

Meanwhile, in 1969, Aitken founded the Diamond Sangha, a center in Honolulu where Japanese Zen teachers could meet American seekers. By this time, Aitken had developed some ideas that were quite distinctive within the larger Zen community. He had become a pacifist and peace advocate (during the Vietnam War), advocated changes relative to women's concerns, and opposed traditional authoritarian structure in Zen facilities. He became a cofounder of the Buddhist peace movement and nurtured female practitioners at his Zendo. In 1979, the Diamond Sangha gave birth to *Kahawai; A Journal of Women and Zen*. In 1991, Aitken appointed his first female assistant teacher, Subhana Barzaghi, who was named a *roshi* in 1996.

From the original center, other centers were opened in Hawaii, across the United States, and then in other countries—Australia, New Zealand, Switzerland, Germany, and Argentina. Among the many teachers he has trained, some have gone on to become Zen masters in their own right. They now lead Diamond Sangha centers, or, in a few cases, have founded their own independent centers.

As of 2005, Aitkin lived in retirement in Honolulu. He has become well known from his many books.

Further reading: Robert Aitken, *Zen Training. A Personal Account* (Honolulu: Old Island Books, 1960); ———, *Taking the Path of Zen* (San Francisco: North Point Press,

1982); ———, *The Mind of Clover: Essays in Zen Buddhist Ethics* (San Francisco: North Point Press, 1984); ———, *Zen Master Raven: Sayings and Doings of a Wise Bird* (Boston: Charles E. Tuttle, 2002).

ajahn   See TITLES AND TERMS OF ADDRESS, BUDDHIST.

Ajanta

Ajanta is a cave complex in western India, northeast of present-day Mumbai (Bombay), whose walls are richly decorated with Buddhist paintings and sculptures. Some of the caves date from the earliest phase of Buddhist history. The site has 36 separate building foundations, including VIHARAS and STUPAS. The caves are carved into a 250-foot-high wall of rock. Many of the caves' walls still show events from the Buddha's lives.

The monasteries at Ajanta were built in two stages. The first stage was from 100 B.C.E. to 100 C.E. Ajanta was at that time the intersection of trade routes linking the south and the north. But most of the ruins at Ajanta date from the second stage, around 460–480 C.E. Most of the benefactors who sponsored the buildings were from the court of the Vakataka king Harisena. Ajanta probably served the king as a military point, as well as a trade center. Once Harisena fell from power the complex was abandoned. By the time the Chinese traveler XUAN ZANG (596–664) visited India the caves had already become tourist attractions.

The Ajanta caves are a World Heritage Site. The advisory board, which recommended that Ajanta be included in World Heritage Sites in 1983, cited the caves' outstanding value as artistic creations. The decorations inside the caves, including painted or sculpted figures, reflect values of suppleness and balance. The caves have exerted a major influence on later artistic development.

Further reading: Benoy K. Behl, *The Ajanta Caves: Artistic Wonder of Ancient Buddhist India* (New York: Abrams, 1998); Richard S. Cohen, "Ajanta, India," in William M. Johnston, ed., *Encyclopedia of Monasticism* (Chicago and London: Fitzroy Dearborn, 2000), 18–21; Walter M. Sprink, "The Caves at Ajanta," *Archaeology* 45 (November/December 1992): 52–60; Volkmar Wentzel, "India's Sculptured Temple Caves." *National Geographic Magazine,* May 1953, pp. 665–678; UNESCO World Heritage. "Ajanta Caves." Available online. URL: http://whc.unesco.org/en/list/242. Accessed on December 3, 2005.

alaya-vijnana

The YOGACARA school of Mahayana developed a theory of a central consciousness of the universe that acts as the ground of reality. This central consciousness is the *alaya-vijnana,* or "storehouse consciousness." According to the Yogacara school, consciousness is real, but the objects of consciousness—the things we think we see and touch—are not real; they are illusion. This illusion is created through eight layers of consciousness. The eighth layer is the *alaya-vijnana,* called the "storehouse consciousness" because it acts as a storage place for karmic energy and serves as the basis for producing the other seven layers of consciousness. All actions create karmic energy. This energy—metaphorically called *bija,* or karmic seeds—is stored in the *alaya-vijnana.* As each individual's karmic seeds ripen, they produce other consciousnesses, such as thought, sight, and touch—in other words, action. The action combines with ignorance to create the effect of an individual person acting in a real world. The rising of this sense of individual essence creates a karmic impression that results in further individuation and action. The cycle is cut when the cultivator, through meditation and hard practice, realizes there is no world of objects separate from the mind.

Further reading: G. M. Nagao, *Madhyamika and Yogacara.* Translated by L. S. Kawamura (Albany: State University of New York Press, 1991); John Powers, *The*

Yogacara School of Buddhism: A Bibliography (Metuchen, N.J.: American Theological Library Association/Scarecrow Press, 1991).

alchemical suicide

Alchemy is the term most scholars use to refer to Daoist practices aimed at attaining "immortality." Some of the most intriguing and counterintuitive of these practices involved a practitioner's intentionally killing the body (usually by ingesting a poisonous compound) to attain "immortal" life. Daoists often speak of such alchemical deaths as *shijie* (liberation from the corpse). Most scholars agree that the idea developed in Daoist tradition as a way of explaining the physical death required as part of the transformation into an "immortal."

The theoretical basis for the practice of "alchemical suicide" is rooted in ancient Chinese beliefs concerning QI ("matter-energy," the basic "stuff" of existence), the "soul(s)," and the afterlife. In traditional Chinese thought, all of reality is made up of different sorts of *qi*. In terms of human existence, this *qi* forms not only the body (more or less "impure" *qi*) but also a person's two "souls"—the *hun* (spirit soul) and the *po* (earth soul). These two are formed from purer, primordial *qi* (especially in the case of the *hun*) and seem to join in the womb; they provide the life and consciousness we enjoy on Earth. At some point after physical death, the two "souls" separate, with the *hun* returning to its heavenly place of origin and the *po* remaining on Earth in the vicinity of the corpse. Both "souls" continue to exist for several generations before merging back into their source elements. Before such final dissolution, both are honored through ancestral rites.

In traditional Daoism, these theories suggested that a person was still "present" immediately after death and that some *qi* might still be active. Such conditions might be the ideal state for those who were properly trained to cultivate and refine their *qi* and so go on to attain immortality. This would not be an immortal existence in the earthly body (after all, the body is composed of *qi* in its most impure form) but rather in a body composed of pure and rarified *qi,* which would be immune to decay and dissolution. As such, the earthly body (corpse) would no longer be required for continued existence.

The actual practices involved in *shijie* were highly ritualized. They would typically include prior preparation through alchemy and other practices. Moreover, over the years the general understanding became that *shijie* was an acceptable response to an official summons from the celestial realms. One so summoned would quickly ingest the elixir that had been prepared beforehand. The more potent (i.e., poisonous) it was, the more quickly the adept could effect the transformation and so ascend to the immortal state. It is also important to stress that from a Daoist perspective, this procedure is not "unnatural" since it involves purifying one's primordial *qi* and hence returning to the natural state; it is ordinary life with its decay and bodily death ("proof" of a failure to maintain one's original harmonious endowment) that is "unnatural."

A typical feature of attaining immortality through *shijie* is the practice of leaving behind some sort of token of one's physical existence that would be discovered when the adept's coffin was opened. The most obvious token, of course, would be the corpse itself, but it might also include some symbolic object such as a sword, staff, sandals, or another piece of clothing belonging to the immortal. If the corpse is left, however, accounts typically state that it does not decay as an ordinary body would. Rather, it remains fresh—even "sweet"—and may be surrounded by clouds of pink vapors and strains of heavenly music. In some cases as well, it seems that the adept announced his intention to ascend and then entered into a deep meditative trance, "dying" while the body remained in meditative posture. This latter course seems to betray Buddhist influence, recalling as it does tales of the historical

Buddha as well as similar stories of the deaths of legendary Buddhist masters.

The SHANGQING (Highest Purity) school of Daoism, which arose on Mount Mao (Maoshan, another name by which the school is known) in the early Middle Ages and drew upon the teachings of the famed alchemist GE HONG, had some intriguing views of *shijie*. In part, these teachings seem to be based on Buddhist notions of rebirth. According to Shangqing teachings, *shijie* is a result of the "purification by the Supreme Yin." It is said that the gods watch over the body for 100 years. At the end of this period (during which the body may have even rotted away), the body rises up into the "Supreme Yin." According to the *Xiang'er* commentary to the DAODEJING, the "Supreme Yin" is a sort of "palace" or womb in which the body is prepared for a new birth. In essence, this means that even if the purification process is incomplete, one undergoes a more or less "partial death" and will be reborn in an intermediary place in which complete purification takes place. This would seem to be roughly equivalent to the idea of purgatory that gained so much credence in medieval Christianity. Other Shangqing traditions maintain that an adept can be reborn in one of the paradises located in the extreme southern regions (known variously as "Palace of Red Fire" or "Court of Liquid Fire"). There the adept undergoes an intense process of purification by fire and is reborn as a full-fledged immortal.

Chinese literature, both popular and elite, is filled with numerous accounts of Daoist adepts undergoing *shijie*. Among the most famous was none other than Ge Hong himself, the "Master Who Embraces Simplicity." One of the more whimsical tales of *shijie* concerns Wei Boyang, a figure often regarded as the "father of alchemy," who is alleged to have lived during the latter Han (25–220 C.E.). Wei was a hermit who lived with a few disciples in his laboratory deep in the mountains. There he experimented with concocting various elixirs. One day he refined a particularly potent batch and, for a test, fed one of the pills to his dog. Immediately the dog fell over dead and Wei's students were crestfallen. Apparently grieved but still confident, Wei said that the effect might be different on humans. When none of the students volunteered, Wei swallowed a pill and also fell down dead. Two of his students left, convinced their master had been a fool and they had wasted their time. Wei's last student, however, trusted his master and so also took a pill. He, too, fell over dead. Presently, however, Wei got up and began to feel light and weightless. His dog also recovered and ran to his master, as did the faithful disciple. Laughing, Wei clapped the latter on the back. Then all three ascended into the sky, much to the consternation of the other disciples, who saw them flying through the heavens. According to tradition, nothing was left of Wei's potion. He did, however, leave behind a treatise entitled the *Cantongqi* (Token of the triplex unity), which is often regarded as the ancestor of all Daoist alchemical texts.

Further reading: Livia Kohn, *Daoism and Chinese Culture* (Cambridge, Mass.: Three Pines Press, 2001), 56–57; ———, ed., *The Taoist Experience* (Albany: State University of New York Press, 1993), 305–313; Isabelle Robinet, *Taoism: Growth of a Religion.* Translated by Phyllis Brooks (Stanford, Calif.: Stanford University Press, 1997), 137–138, 220; Eva Wong, *The Shambhala Guide to Taoism* (Boston: Shambhala, 1997), 66–76; ———, *Tales of the Taoist Immortals* (Boston: Shambhala, 2001), 147–168.

alchemy   *See* DAOIST ALCHEMY.

All Ceylon Buddhist Congress

The All Ceylon Buddhist Congress (ACBC) was founded December 1919 in Colombo, Sri Lanka, and registered as a charitable organization. It was originally intended to act as a coordinating body for the various YOUNG MEN'S BUDDHIST ASSOCIATIONS. But the ACBC soon attracted such intellectuals such as Professor Gunapala Malasekere (1899–1973), who developed the organization into a position of community leadership. Malasekere was president of the ACBC between 1940 and 1958 and between 1970 and 1973. Today it is the largest lay Buddhist organization in Sri Lanka and works as a counterpart to the Buddhist SANGHA. Women were until 1924 denied membership.

The congress has 10 separate councils to handle such functional areas as religion and culture and education. Each council is presided over by officeholders and other volunteers. There is also an advisory board of 60 monks appointed from three monastic traditions.

The ACBC was involved in the formation of the World Buddhist Fellowship in 1950. It also sponsors a major TRIPITAKA translation project. The congress has since the 1940s become active in providing schools, vocational training, and hostels. One current project is the rehabilitation of ancient irrigation tanks in Sri Lanka, a project highly relevant today given recent drought conditions on the island.

Further reading: All Ceylon Buddhist Congress. Available online. URL: www.acbc.lk/index.html. Accessed on October 2, 2005; George Bond, *The Buddhist Revival in Sri Lanka: Religious Tradition, Reinterpretation and Response* (Columbia: University of South Carolina Press, 1988); H. L. Seneviratne, *The Work of Kings: The New Buddhism in Sri Lanka* (Chicago: University of Chicago Press, 1999).

alms bowl (Sanskrit *patta,* Japanese *jihatsu*)

The round bowl is one of the basic accessories of an ordained monk, along with the staff, an umbrella (*glot*), and three robes. The bowl is used to collect food donated by the laity each day. In Southeast Asian countries such as Thailand and Myanmar monks go forth each day, usually at dawn, to ask for food. The food is put into the bowl by the lay Buddhist, who prepares and offers it. The monk must accept all food offered, without asking or choosing. The monks then return to the monastery and eat the food in silence around 11 A.M. In general no more food is taken that day after noon.

The alms bowl is a powerful symbol of Buddhist monastic life and principles. It represents the monk's lifestyle and adherence to the VINAYA, the code of conduct. On an economic level it represents the Sangha's dependence on society at large for its continuance.

In Southeast Asia today most alms bowls are made of lacquer, a traditional light material easily cleaned, although metals have also been used. Alms bowls are generally round, around 15 cm in diameter, with walls that curve inward to the mouth. The bowl is often carried over the monk's shoulder in a fabric sling. It is also often carried under the monk's robes.

Further reading: Buddhamind. "Alms bowl." Available online. URL: www.buddhamind.info/leftside/arty/bowl.htm. Accessed on September 6, 2007; John S. Strong, *Relics of the Buddha* (Princeton, N.J.: Princeton University Press, 2004); Tahnissaro Bhikkhu, "An Economy of Gifts." Beliefnet.com. Available online. URL: www.beliefnet.com/story/47/story_4747_1.html, accessed January 18, 2006.

Altan Khan (Altyn Khan) (1507–1582)
Mongol ruler
Altan Khan reunited the Mongolian empire and spread VAJRAYANA BUDDHISM in Mongolia and Tibet.

He was the grandson of Dayan Khan, who had begun the effort to reunify the Mongolian peoples. Altan Khan reestablished ties between Mongolia and Tibet. At this time Tibet was largely ruled by the leaders of the SAKYA Buddhist sect. Altan Khan invited Sonam Gyatso (1543–88), the abbot of Tashilhumpo Monastery and leader of the GELUG sect, to Mongolia to spread Buddhism. This encounter would both establish Gelug Tibetan

Buddhism as the religion of Mongolia and lead to the rise of the Gelug sect as the dominant form of Buddhism in Tibet.

Gyatso made two trips to Mongolia, one in 1569 and then again in 1578. During his second visit Altan Khan formally converted to Buddhism. Sonam Gyatso then suggested that Altan Khan was both a reincarnation of Kubla Khan and the embodiment of the BODHISATTVA of wisdom, MAN-JUSRI. By this action he proclaimed the union of secular and religious power in the person of the khan.

The khan responded to Gyatso's action by naming the abbot DALAI LAMA, that is, "teacher of the ocean of wisdom." Gyatso, the third abbot of Tashilhumpo, also applied the title to his two predecessors. Thus Sonam Gyatso became known as the third Dalai Lama.

Further reading: Erik Hildinger, *Warriors of the Steppe: A Military History of Central Asia, 500 B.C. to 1700 A.D.* (New York: Sarpedon, 1997); David Morgan, *The Mongols* (Oxford: Blackwell, 1990).

Amaterasu Omi-Kami

Amaterasu Omi-Kami, one of the major SHINTO deities, is revered throughout Japan as the sun goddess. Amaterasu is the focus of a variety of Japanese myths, especially stories that concern the seasons and the rising of the sun each day. Equally important are the stories connecting her with the Japanese emperor. She is believed to be the mother of the imperial family; the first emperor was her son, whom she established on his throne. The status of Amaterasu reached its zenith in the early 20th century as the successive emperors made heightened claims to political power and directed the building of an expansive Japanese empire.

According to the ancient Shinto scriptures, Amaterasu appeared in the midst of the creation process after the death of Izanami, the female figure in the couple who initiated the creative process. In his grief, her mate, IZANAGI, engaged in a mourning and purification process. In the process of cleaning his left eye, he produced Amaterasu. Continuing with the process he additionally produced TSUKIYOMI NO MIKOTO, SUSANO-O NO MIKOTO, and a host of lesser deities (*KAMI*).

As the sun goddess, Amaterasu was assigned the sky as the realm over which she exercised her hegemony. With the death of Izanagi and the retirement of Izanami, Amaterasu emerged as the chief active deity in the Japanese traditional religion, and the ruler of the other deities. Shrines great and small emerged around the country. She is represented with a mirror and symbolized in the rising sun that appears on the Japanese flag.

Typical of the shrines devoted to Amaterasu is the Kumano Hongu Shrine at Hongu, a popular pilgrimage site in central Japan. The shrine itself is simple and even somewhat austere, but placed in a beautiful setting. The most well known shrine, of course, is the ISE SHRINE, located at the foot of Mount Kamiji in central Honshu (Japan's main island). The Inner Ise Shrine is closely related to the imperial family, and the emperor is the only one allowed to pass through its gates. The mirror at the Inner Shrine is considered one of Japan's great imperial treasures.

Further reading: Linda Kay Davidson and David M. Gitlitz, *Pilgrimage from the Ganges to Graceland: An Encyclopedia* (Santa Barbara, Calif.: ABC-Clio, 2002); Patricia Monaghan, *The New Book of Goddesses and Heroines* (St. Paul, Minn.: Llewellyn, 1997); Sokyo Ono, *Shinto: The Kami Way* (Rutland, Vt.: Charles E. Tuttle, 1991).

Ambedkar, Babasaheb Bhimrao Ramji

(1891–1956) *Indian independence invocate who led a mass conversion of Dalits, or Untouchables, to Buddhism*

A complex political figure, B. R. Ambedkar played a key role in the political struggle for equal rights for India's lowest class, the Dalits.

Under Ambedkar's guidance more than 5 million Dalits converted to Buddhism in the early 1950s. He was himself born a Dalit, but unusual for his position in society, was able to receive a good education that led to doctorates from both Columbia University and the London School of Economics. He also qualified for the bar in the United Kingdom.

Beginning with his return to India in 1927, he began a campaign for the uplift of his people, which he came to see as being coincidental with the rejection of Hinduism and the caste system. He went on to found several political parties and was instrumental in drafting India's constitution in 1947. After independence he became India's first law minister.

Meanwhile, his understanding of the Dalits evolved. Traditionally considered outside the caste system, they were consigned to work in the lowest of jobs and typically lived in slum areas. To escape from the rigid mindset associated with the caste system, he concluded it was best for Dalits not just to reject Hinduism but to convert en masse to a faith perceived as outside the rigid system, but at the same time perceived by all as innately Indian. That faith was Buddhism. In his 1948 book, *The Untouchables,* he advanced the theory that the Dalits were descended from the few Buddhists who remained in India when the Buddhist community was otherwise destroyed by the advance of Islam and revival of Hinduism in the Middle Ages.

Under Ambedkar's guidance more than 5 million Dalits converted to Buddhism. In 1955 he founded the Buddhist Society of India and himself formally converted, just months before his death. His role in the society was subsequently assumed by his son, Yeshwant Ambedkar (1913–77). It quickly grew into a national organization spearheading the post–World War II revival of Buddhism in India.

Further reading: Sangharakshita, *Ambedkar and Buddhism* (Glasgow: Windhorse, 1986); Eleanor Zelliot,

From Untouchable to Dalit: Essays on the Ambedkar Movement (New Delhi: Manohar, 1992).

America   *See* UNITED STATES.

American Buddhist Congress

The American Buddhist Congress is an ecumenical organization of the major Buddhist groups in the United States. The congress seeks to provide the Buddhist community with a united voice on matters of common interest, to foster fellowship among different Buddhist groups and traditions, and to facilitate cooperative action on matters related to the common good. It has also developed efforts to educate the largely Christian American public about Buddhism.

It was founded in 1987 at a gathering of representatives from different Buddhist organization held at Kwan Um Sa Korean Buddhist Temple in Los Angeles, California. The congress is a product of the radical expansion of the Buddhist community in America that followed the change in immigration laws in 1965 favoring Asian lands, and the additional immigration of refugees from Vietnam as the war came to a close. It includes all segments of the Buddhist community, though the older and more established Japanese community was reluctant to participate.

Among the leaders who made the congress a reality was the Venerable Dr. Havanpola Ratanasara (1920–2000), a Sri Lankan; Dr. Karl Springer, an American leader in a Tibetan Buddhist tradition; and the Venerable Karuna Dharma, an American teacher in the Vietnamese tradition.

The congress operates through a representative general council with administrative duties assigned to an executive council. The congress is headquartered in suburban Los Angeles.

Further reading: American Buddhist Congress. Available online. URL: http://www.americanbuddhistcongress. org/. Accessed on October 10, 2005.

Amida *See* AMITABHA.

Amitabha (Amida, Amitayus, "Infinite Light")

Amitabha is one of the most popular deity figures of Mahayana Buddhism. As Buddhism developed, various figures such as Amitabha were added to worship and became focal points for artistic expression and popular belief. Some of those figures were seen as Buddhas in addition to the historical Buddha, since the title *Buddha* indicated an enlightened individual in general, not solely the historical Buddha. Amitabha is the Buddha who rules over the Western Paradise of SUKHAVATI. Like a BODHISATTVA, Amitabha is said to have origi-

Seated Amitabha figure in wood and lacquer, from the Tokyo National Museum

nally been a human. He is most often associated with the figure Dharmakara, an Indian king who gave up his throne and became a monk. Dharmakara decided to become a Buddha and establish a realm where all souls may reside until they are ready to enter nirvana. This realm, Sukhavati, is best understood as a state of consciousness, although in many people's minds it is a kind of heavenly paradise. A practitioner need only recite Amitabha's name at the moment of death and Amitabha will appear and escort that person to his Western Paradise. Amitabha is in some traditions referred to as head of one of the five Buddha families, the Lotus Family.

Belief in Amitabha and Sukhavati was a relatively late development in Buddhism; the first mention was in the Sutra of the Buddha Amitabha, a text that entered China in the fifth century C.E. This text exists now only in the Chinese version—the Sanskrit original has been lost.

Amitabha's Western Paradise was a powerful force of popular belief and in large measure accounts for the spread of the PURE LAND and JODO schools in China and Japan. Entry into the Western Paradise allows the practitioner a shortcut on the road to NIRVANA. Instead of the path of constant discipline and rebirths into SAMSARA, a person need only have faith in Amitabha in order to achieve a sort of salvation. Entry into Sukhavati, although distinct from the final extinction of nirvana, would assure a person of ultimate entry into nirvana.

Amitabha's status as a Buddha is reflected in his depiction in art. Amitabha is often painted as one of a trio of figures. In the first trio Amitabha is seated in the center on a lotus blossom, with AVALOKITESVARA (GUAN YIN) on his left and the bodhisattva Mahasthamaprapta (he who has obtained great power) on his right. In another common triad Amitabha is drawn with BHAISAJYA-GURU, the Medicine Buddha. In addition, Avalokistesvara is often said to have been born from an emanation from Amitabha's brow. Because of this Avalokitesvara is often painted or carved into Amitabha's brow.

Further reading: Luis Gomez, "Shinran's Faith and the Sacred Name of Amida," *Monumenta Nipponica* 38, no. 1 (Spring 1983): 73–84; Tripitaka Master Hua, *A General Explanation of the Buddha Speaks of Amitabha Sutra* (San Francisco: Sino-American Buddhist Association, 1974).

Amitabha Buddhist Societies

Amitabha centers offer courses that lead to an understanding of Pure Land Buddhism and its practice. The basic course teaches a set of moral principles and the practice of reciting the Amida Buddha's name. Subsequent courses emphasize harmony and self-discipline. A final course centers upon the "Universal Worthy Bodhisattva's Ten Great Vows."

The idea of the founding of an association of independent Buddhist societies dedicated to calling upon the name of the bodhisattva AMITABHA was initially proposed by Xia Lian-Ju, an eminent Buddhist teacher in Taiwan. He was for a number of years the teacher of a monk later to be known as Master CHIN KUNG (1927–). In the 1970s, Chin Kung began an aggressive effort of propagating PURE LAND Buddhism through his lectures and classes. In 1977, he expanded his efforts beyond Taiwan and began traveling the world, primarily to those countries with a significant Chinese community. Picking up the idea of his teacher, he began founding Amitabha Buddhist Societies wherever he found response to his teachings.

The Pure Land Buddhist teachings offered at the centers are those found in the Infinite Life Sutra, the Amitabha Sutra, the Visualization Sutra, the "Chapter of Universal Worthy Bodhisattva's Conduct and Vows," the "Chapter on the Perfect and Complete Realization of Great Strength Bodhisattva," and VASUBANDHU Bodhisattva's Report. Members are expected to live according to the Five Guidelines of the Three Conditions (which include respect for elders, taking refuge in the Buddha, not killing, and encouraging people on the path to enlightenment), the Six Principles of Harmony (for living with others), the Three

Learnings (self-discipline, deep concentration, and wisdom), Six PARAMITAS (giving, self-discipline, patience, diligence, deep concentration, and wisdom), and the Ten Great Vows (which involve respecting all people, praising the virtues and kind practices of others, giving, repenting and reforming all the faults, rejoicing in the virtuous deeds of others, promoting the broad spread of the teachings, seeking the guidance of the societies' teachers, holding the Buddha's teachings in one's heart, seeking accord with the wishes of the people around us, and dedicating the peace gained from practicing to all living beings).

Amitabha Buddhist Societies may be found across Taiwan, the United States, Canada, Australia, the United Kingdom, Spain, Malaysia, Hong Kong, and Singapore.

Amoghavajra (Pu-k'ung, Pu Kong)

(705–774) *Vajrayana Buddhist teacher in China*
Amoghavajra was an Indian Buddhist monk who translated key texts into Chinese and is considered the sixth patriarch of CHINESE ESOTERIC BUDDHISM. Amoghavajra first traveled to Xi'an, the capital of China, in the eighth century C.E. with two prominent VAJRAYANA teachers, Subhakarasimha and Vajrabodhi (671–741), at the request of Emperor Xuan Zong (Hsuan Tsung) (r. 712–56). Vajrabodhi and Subhakarasimha learned both Confucianism and Daoism and created the unique form of Chinese Vajrayana by their synthesis of Indian and Chinese insights. Amoghavajra learned the art of translation from his two older companions.

In 741, following Vajrabodhi's death, Emperor Xuan Zong expelled all foreign monks working in China. Amoghavajra used the opportunity to travel in India and Sri Lanka gathering additional texts before returning to China in 746 with some 500 volumes. Among his notable accomplishments in the next years was the completion of a task begun by his older colleagues, the translation of the key text of Vajrayana Buddhism, the *Tattvasamgraha.*

In 756 the emperor Su Zong (r. 756–62) ascended the throne. In 759 Amoghavajra formally received Su Zong as an adherent of Buddhism. Amoghavajra had already become well known as a miracle worker, especially noted for rainmaking and stilling of storms. He was put to the test in 765 when Tibetan forces threatened an invasion. He performed an elaborate ritual, and afterward the invasion stopped, ostensibly because the leader of the opposing forces suddenly dropped dead. Amoghavajra had called upon the bodhisattva MANJUSRI as China's protector and now focused his attention on completing a temple on Mount Wutai dedicated to him.

Amoghavajra died in 774, a greatly honored personage. Among his most prominent successors were Hui Guo and Hui Lin. Hui Guo would later accompany the Japanese monk KUKAI to Japan, where they would establish SHINGON, the Japanese form of Vajrayana Buddhism.

Further reading: Kenneth K. S. Ch'en, *Buddhism* (Woodbury, N.Y.: Barron's Educational Series, 1968); Arthur F. Wright, *Buddhism in Chinese History* (Stanford, Calif.: Stanford University Press, 1959); Zhou Yiliang, "Tantrism in China," *Harvard Journal of Asiatic Studies* 8 (March 1945): 241–332.

amulets

Amulets are objects of worship and protection worn in many Buddhist cultures. A typical amulet is a triangular, flat Buddha image around 15 mm high that can be hung around a believer's neck on a chain or placed in other locations where it will protect the individual from evil. Amulets are distinct from talismans, which are objects designed to accomplish a goal desired by the object's possessor, though in practice amulets and talismans are more difficult to distinguish.

In the premodern world, amulets were often associated with spirit entities seen as freely populating the world. They were regarded as the home to spirits, and often as a protection from the actions of evil or mischievous spirits (demons). Amulets could thus protect someone from illness, injury, impotence, or various mental disorders deemed to be caused by demonic possession or obsession. Today, amulets are generally seen to be objects that contain or focus cosmic magical power, rather than being the abode of spirits or demons.

They are found everywhere in such Buddhist countries of Southeast Asia as Thailand and Kampuchea. Amulets in Thailand are often highly prized art pieces and so can be traded and sold.

Further reading: Sheila Paine, *Amulets: Sacred Charms of Power and Protection* (Rochester, Vt.: Inner Traditions, 2004); William T. Pavitt and Kate Pavitt, *The Book of Talismans, Amulets, and Zodiacal Gems* (Detroit: Tower Books, 1914); Stanley J. Tambiah, *The Buddhist Saints of the Forest and the Cult of Amulets* (Cambridge: Cambridge University Press, 1984).

anagarika   See TITLES AND TERMS OF ADDRESS, BUDDHIST.

Analects

The *Analects* is the collected sayings of the Chinese philosopher CONFUCIUS (551–479 B.C.E.). It is difficult to overstate the importance of this book in Chinese history. It stood at the core of traditional education for 2,000 years. Most scholars simply memorized the entire text, and their writings and conversations were liberally laced with quotes from Confucius as well as references to various characters, his disciples, and rulers from different states.

The ideas that permeate the *Analects* are the enduring themes of CONFUCIANISM: DAO, REN (humanity, benevolence), LI (ritual, propriety), and *xiao* (FILIAL PIETY). Confucius takes pains to explain the essence of these subjects. For instance, in explaining filial conduct, Confucius said "While [parents] are alive, serve them according to [the requirements of] proper ritual. After they are dead, perform burial rites as well as sacrificial rites [of remembrance] according to proper ritual" (*Analects* 2.5).

In addition to these enduring themes, Confucius left a hierarchy of ideal types that have served as moral standards for later generations. There is, first, the *shi,* a scholar-apprentice on the path (Dao) toward full realization. The realized *shi* will become a *junzi,* a "gentleman." The *junzi* is one whose actions are in harmony with proper ritual and Dao. His actions can be studied, but he himself requires no more instruction. An even higher category is the *shengren,* "a sage." The *shengren* is rare—Confucius did not consider himself to be one—and the *junzi* can only admire them from a distance.

The *Analects* consists of 499 short vignettes and quotes from the sage, who lived during the tumultuous later part of China's Zhou dynasty (1122–256 B.C.E.). According to tradition, after the master's death his disciples began to write down what they recalled of his words. Within 100 years there were 15 short books. Five more were added within another 100 years, and eventually 20 books were collected to form the *Analects,* the *Lun Yu,* or "Sayings of the Master."

More recent scholarship has revised the traditional account of the *Analects*' background. Books 4–8 are now seen to be the oldest sections and were most likely compiled by Confucius's disciples. Books 9–11 were probably prepared by the third generation of followers, and the remaining books were all written later. Book 20 is the newest book, probably added 225 years after Confucius's death. Archaeological finds, including text fragments found at Dingzhou, confirm the *Analects* existed in its current form at least from 55 B.C.E.

Further reading: Roger T. Ames and Henry Rosemont Jr., trans., *The Analects of Confucius: A Philosophical Translation* (New York: Ballantine Books, 1998); China the Beautiful. "Writings of Confucius—Kongzi [Kung Tze]." Available online. URL: www.chinapage. org/confucius/confucius.html. Accessed on September 7, 2007; Chinese Culture course, compiled by Paul Halsall. "Chinese Cultural Studies: Confucius Kongfuzi (c. 500 C.E.): The Analects, Excerpts." Available online. URL: http://acc6.its.brooklyn.cuny.edu/~phalsall/texts/analects.html. Accessed on January 25, 2006.

Ananda *the Buddha's principal assistant during most of his 45-year teaching career*

Ananda, one of the foremost DISCIPLES OF THE BUDDHA, was also the Buddha's cousin. In the first of the COUNCILS OF BUDDHISM after the Buddha's PARINIRVANA (death), Ananda recited all the Buddha's teachings by heart, a performance that was the first rendering of the Buddhist SUTRAS. He is said to have worked to achieve enlightenment before he was called on to recite, and he did so the night before the recital. During the recital he forgot some sections and was as a result asked to confess his faults before the assembly.

Ananda joined the Sangha along with three others near the time the Buddha visited the palace of his father, SUDDHODANA, in Kapilavatthu. Ananda figures prominently in several parts of the Buddhist canon. It was he who urged the Buddha to grant the requests of Mahaprajapati, the Buddha's aunt and stepmother, to allow women to join the Sangha.

Ananda acted as the Buddha's personal attendant for 25 years. However, he was not appointed personal attendant to the Buddha until after the Buddha had wandered for several years. Before that time various monks took turns to act as attendant. But the Buddha sensed he required a permanent helper and asked for volunteers. Ananda finally agreed to help, but under eight conditions. These conditions ranged from the authority to refuse certain things, such as an invitation, to not handling alms received by the Buddha.

Further reading: Edward J. Thomas, *The Life of Buddha as Legend and History* (New Delhi: Munshiram Manoharlal, 1992); C. B. Varma, *The Illustrated Jataka and*

Other Stories of the Buddha (New Delhi: Indira Gandhi National Centre for the Arts, n.d.). Available online. URL: http://www.ignca.gov.in/jatak.htm. Accessed on September 7, 2007.

anatman (non-self)

Anatman, or "non-self," is one of the four characteristic doctrines of Buddhism, what are called the "Seals of the Law." "All dharmas are devoid of self" is an expression found throughout Buddhist literature. "Self" in the abstract sense indicates atman, a self that is not subject to change. Buddhism consistently rejects that there can be a permanent self. All phenomena in the world are subject to change.

In the Buddha's teachings there is no true self. There is a conventional self, which we take on as a member of society. However, the sense of permanence that most people associate with the self has no foundation. According to Buddhism, nothing stable can be found in material reality, in the mind, in the experiences of life. What we inevitably find upon seeking a foundation for self is an unsatisfying sense of impermanence.

This concept is one of the greatest challenges for people beginning the study of Buddhism. It is particularly challenging for people from Western cultural backgrounds, given the Western emphasis on the individual as a core unit of society. Individualism validates a sense of the importance of self. When the Buddha denies this, many people react as though a cherished assumption were under threat. It need not be this way, however. The ego as constructed and maintained by each individual in this life is normal for the level of everyday reality. The point made by the Buddha is that there is no ultimate reality to this construct. Reality is not centered on the ego, or its substitute, the soul.

Further reading: Damien Keown, *Buddhism: A Very Short Introduction* (New York: Oxford University Press, 1996); Kogen Mizuno, *Essentials of Buddhism: Basic Terminology and Concepts of Buddhist Philosophy and Practice.* Translated by Gaynor Sekimori (1972. Reprint, Tokyo: Kosei, 1996); Walpola Rahula, *What the Buddha Taught* (New York: Grove Press, 1974).

ane/ani *See* TITLES AND TERMS OF ADDRESS, BUDDHIST.

Angkor Wat

Angkor Wat is a temple complex, spreading over 500 acres, in Cambodia. The ruins at Angkor Wat have been designated a World Heritage Site.

During the Funan period of Southeast Asian history (third–sixth centuries C.E.) both Hindu and Buddhist traditions entered the Khmer region. The court tended to practice Hinduism, while the populace followed Buddhism. By the classical period, ninth–11th centuries, a new, syncretic religion that combined elements of both had taken shape. Angkor Wat is an expression of this blend of Hindu and Buddhist ideas.

The founder of the line of Angkor monarchs was Jayavarman II (c. 802–850), who promoted the cult of the Devaraja king. In this concept the king was not only a CAKRAVARTIN, a World-Renouncing Monarch, but also acted as the highest priestly figure. Under the later ruler JAYAVARMAN VII (1181–1219) this concept was merged into the cult of the Buddharaja, a Buddhist-oriented king.

Angkor Wat was built during this period of the flowering of Khmer culture outside the capital of Yasodarapura by Suryavarman II (1113–45). In the complex, multiple rings of galleries surround the central temple; each ring represents a different level of spiritual cultivation. The first gallery is open, made of columns. The second gallery is closed. The third level of gallery is a portico. The inner temple, enclosed by walls, symbolizes Mt. SUMERU, which in Buddhist and Hindu cosmology sits at the center of the universe. The three rings can be interpreted to represent the levels of achievement strived for in VAJRAYANA Buddhism.

Although the buildings of Angkor Wat were originally constructed to promote a purely Hindu cult, not to commemorate Buddhism, the complex was almost certainly used for Buddhist worship as well as Hindu ceremonies. Carvings from Hindu mythology can still be seen, including dancers (*apsaras*) performing for the king, Suryavarman II.

A large range of Hindu and Mahayana deities were worshipped at Angkor. These included Garuda, the mythical bird from Hindu mythology, and Hevajra, a Vajrayana Buddhist deity. Laksmi, a Hindu deity, was also worshipped in a form very similar to that of the Buddhist Padmapani. The Buddhas MAITREYA and Prajnaparamita were also worshipped. Finally, Lokesvara, a form of AVALOKITESVARA, was associated with the figure of Jayavarman VII, the builder of the neighboring complex at Angkor Thom. After this king's death most worship at Angkor Wat became Theravada.

Angkor Wat and neighboring sites are also related to the Javanese site BOROBUDUR, because both sites used the terrace pyramid with a central temple representing Mt. Sumeru. In Angkor Wat's case the three elements of the universe are the ocean, represented by the surrounding moat; Mt. Sumeru, the central temple; and the surrounding mountain ranges, the walls around the temple.

The Khmers abandoned the Angkor site in 1432, for reasons not yet clear. Knowledge of its existence was gradually lost. It was "rediscovered" by French explorers in 1850. Restoration began in 1860. Henri Mouhot wrote the first detailed description of the Angkor Wat complex.

Further reading: Laura Porceddu, "Angkor Wat, Cambodia," in William M. Johnston, ed., *Encyclopedia of Monasticism* (Chicago and London: Fitzroy Dearborn, 2000), 26–28; Donald K. Swearer, *Buddhism and Society in Southeast Asia* (Chambersburg, Pa.: Anima Books, 1981).

anitya

Anitya is impermanence. In Buddhist theory all phenomena in existence are characterized by three things, known as the *trilaksana,* or "three marks," of conditioned phenomena. Impermanence is the first. From it follow suffering (DUKKHA) and nonessentiality (ANATMAN).

Anitya is thus the foundation of experience and life itself. Since all DHARMAS or elements of existence are characterized by SUNYATA, emptiness of permanent traits, we experience and know all phenomena as transitory. These impermanent phenomena include the idea of the soul or self. Realizing the impermanence of all experience is the first step on the Buddha's path of cultivation (MARGA), which ultimately ends in the release of NIRVANA.

Further reading: Kogen Mizuno, *Essentials of Buddhism: Basic Terminology and Concepts of Buddhist Philosophy and Practice.* Translated by Gaynor Sekimori (1972. Reprint, Tokyo: Kosei Publishing, 1996).

Annen (ninth century) *Esoteric Tendai Buddhist teacher*

Annen, who helped integrate esoteric (TANTRIC) teachings into the TENDAI tradition, began his study of Buddhism with ENNIN (794–864), who initiated the process of developing Esoteric Buddhism. Annen later studied with Henjo (816–890). In 884 he was appointed master of dharma transmission at Gangyo-ji monastery. He later constructed a new temple, Godai-in, on Mt. HIEI, where he would spend his last years.

Annen turned his attention to the reworking of the Tendai ordered system for classifying the Buddhist sutras and their teachings. In that system, the Lotus Sutra was seen as containing the highest teaching of Buddhism. In Annen's reworking of the classification system, the teachings of Esoteric Buddhism were placed above the Lotus Sutra. Annen's changes in the Tendai perspective freed the Esoteric teachings introduced by his first teacher to grow and develop within the Tendai context.

Further reading: Kazuo Kasahara, ed., *A History of Japanese Religion*. Translated by Paul McCarthy and Gaynor Sekimori (Tokyo: Kosei, 2001).

An Shigao (An Shih-kao) (second century C.E.) *pioneer Buddhist in China*

An Shigao was a Buddhist priest from the Central Asian state of Parthia who traveled to Luoyang, China's capital, around the year 148 C.E. He had been born as a crown prince but renounced his royal status for the life of a Buddhist monk. In China, An Shigao was responsible for the dissemination of texts related to meditation and breath, as well as many Dharma practices. He did not speak or write Chinese but worked orally with a bilingual interpreter. The interpreter would translate for a group of Chinese scholars, who then produced the written Chinese text. Using this process—which would be followed by Indian Buddhists in China until the seventh century—An Shigao produced 34 Chinese translations of Buddhist texts from Sanskrit originals.

According to one story, An Shigao presented the Chinese emperor with some Buddhist RELICS that he had found along the way. These relics had supposedly been buried by a group of monks who had been sent to China from India some four centuries earlier by King ASOKA. After presenting the relics, An Shigao additionally requested that the emperor disperse them to different parts of China to assist the spread of Buddhism. The emperor built a large STUPA at the site where the relics were found to house the Buddha's finger, and some 18 other stupas in different locations in his kingdom.

The stupa housing the finger, the Finger SARIRA, is located in Xian, which later became the capital of China. During the Tang dynasty (618–906) it served as the emperors' temple, but over the centuries the finger itself was lost. It was uncovered during archaeological excavation in 1987 in a secret chamber at the Famun Temple in Xian. It was subsequently deemed the most precious treasure possessed by Chinese Buddhists. Over the several decades since its discovery, the finger has been allowed to travel for viewing by devotees in Thailand (1994), Taiwan (2002), Hong Kong (2004), and the Republic of Korea (2005).

Further reading: CriEnglish.com. "Buddha Finger Sarira to Be Enshrined in ROK." Available online. URL: http://en.chinabroadcast.cn/2242/2005-11-11/177@281428.htm. Accessed on November 28, 2005; Richard H. Robinson and Willard L. Johnson, *The Buddhist Religion: A Historical Introduction* (Belmont, Calif.: Wadsworth, 1997); Arthur F. Wright, *Buddhism in Chinese History* (Stanford, Calif.: Stanford University Press, 1959).

anusaya (tendencies)

In Buddhist teaching, the *anusaya*—literally "outflow"—is a list of seven tendencies, or practices, to which humans lean. They are sensual desire (*kama*), recalcitrance (*dristi*), skepticism (*vichikitsa*), arrogance (*mana*), craving for existence (BHAVA), and ignorance (AVIDYA). Much of Buddhist practice is intended to eliminate these tendencies.

Further reading: Damien Keown, ed., *A Dictionary of Buddhism* (Oxford: Oxford University Press, 2003).

arannavasi (Sanskrit, aranyavasi)

Arannavasi, the Pali term for the forest dwelling tradition in early Buddhist practice, has become popular in modern THERAVADA Buddhism as well.

Forest dwelling monks are an important impulse in Buddhist monastic thought. Forest monks were seen as embodying the Buddha's recommendation that practitioners live apart from society. As a result, although all monks continue to live as part of a Buddhist community, the SANGHA, those living in forest environments have often been perceived as being different from those monks living near urban centers. In contrast to those in urban-based monasteries, monks in forest hermitages are thought to lead lives of simplicity in which they can devote more time to cultivation. Although *arannavasi* is today associated with Theravada Buddhism, all Buddhist cultures have seen some monks devoted more to meditative practices than to literary learning. *Arannavasi* monks may also have been instrumental in the early development of MAHAYANA.

In the premodern period forest dwelling monks in Thailand were known for their magical powers but did not strictly adhere to the VINAYA regulations specified for monks. However, Achan Sao and his student, AJAAN MUN (1870–1949), reinterpreted this tradition in the light of DHAMMAYUT ideas of following the ascetic practices of the Vinaya. They also added an emphasis on meditative practices as found in the master BUDDHAGHOSA's great work, Visuddhimagga. They moved away from an emphasis on magic. This reorientation has made the forest dwelling tradition extremely popular in Thailand.

In the modern period well-known practitioners of the Thai forest tradition include BUDDHADASA (1906–93) and his follower Phra Payom Kalayano (1949–   ). In contemporary practice the THAI FOREST MEDITATION TRADITION continues to attract followers throughout Theravada Buddhism.

Further reading: Damien Keown, ed., *Oxford Dictionary of Buddhism* (Oxford, New York: Oxford University Press, 2003); Donald K. Swearer, *The Buddhist World of Southeast Asia* (Albany: State University of New York Press, 1995); Kamala Tiyavanich, *Forest Recollections: Wandering Monks in Twentieth-Century Thailand* (Honolulu: University of Hawaii Press, 1977).

arhat (luohan)

An *arhat* is a fully enlightened person. In the Buddha's words, the *arhat* is one for whom "finished is birth, lived is pure life, what should be done is done, nothing more is left to be done." In other words, the *arhat* has realized ultimate truth and attained nirvana. He (or she) is free from all impu-

rities and no longer has a sense of self (atman) as a separate, concrete, substantial reality. While the figure of the lonely cultivator finally achieving *arhatship* was denigrated in Mahayana writings, the *arhat* has remained a powerful symbol of cultivation in all Buddhist cultures. The *arhat* is especially common as a figure of artistic portrayal and in temples.

Literally meaning "one worthy of respect," the term *arhat* was translated into Chinese in two ways. The first version was "one who has nothing more to learn" or "destroyer of bandits," the bandits meaning the illusions of thought and desire. The second translation was "no rebirth," since an *arhat* will not in theory be reborn into the cycle of SAMSARA.

A common sight in Chinese Buddhist temples are the 18 *luohan*, arhats depicted in various situations of intense focus and meditation. Each of the 18 *luohans* has an individual personality, yet each represents the path of cultivation so central to Buddhism. There was a tradition of 16 *arhats*—generally forest dwelling—found in such Indian texts as the Nandimitravadana, dating from the seventh century C.E. In China a further two figures were added to the Indian list.

Further reading: Kogen Mizuno, *Basic Buddhist Concepts.* Translated by Charles S. Terry and Richard L. Gage (1987. Reprint, Tokyo: Kosei, 2003); ———, *Essentials of Buddhism: Basic Terminology and Concepts of Buddhist Philosophy and Practice.* Translated by Gaynor Sekimori (1972. Reprint, Tokyo: Kosei Publishing, 1996); Reginald A. Ray, *Buddhist Saints in India: A Study in Buddhist Values and Orientations* (New York and Oxford: Oxford University Press, 1994).

Arnold, Edwin, Sir (1832–1904) *British poet, schoolteacher, and writer on Buddhism*

Edwin Arnold's epic poem on the life of Buddha, *The Light of Asia* (1879), became an early avenue of access for Westerners interested in Buddhism. Though Arnold never professed to be a Buddhist, his poem was a sympathetic treatment of Buddha's life and teachings that won praise from both Eastern and Western readers. Later in his life Arnold was active in the efforts to have BODHGAYA, the site of the Buddha's enlightenment, returned to Buddhist ownership, in which cause he joined forces with Anagarika DHARMAPALA and the MAHA BODHI SOCIETY.

Arnold was born at Gravesend, Kent, and educated at Kings College, London, and University College, Oxford. After his graduation in 1854, he became the master of a school in Birmingham. His first book of poems was published in 1852 while he was still a student.

In 1857 Arnold accepted an invitation to become the principal of Deccan College in Poona, India. Once in India, he learned Sanskrit and gave much time to the observation of Indian culture and religion. In 1861 he became a foreign correspondent for the *Daily Telegraph,* a London newspaper. He would stay with the newspaper when he returned to England in the mid-1860s and eventually become its editor.

In the early 1870s, he began to put together the idea of a work on the life of Buddha in the form of a book-length poem. He seemed to have worked on it in snatches for a number of years. It was originally published in 1879. Prior to his death in 1904, he was knighted by Queen Victoria.

Further reading: Sir Edwin Arnold, *The Light of Asia; or, The Great Renunciation (Mahâbhinishkramana): Being the Life and Teaching of Gautama, Prince of India and Founder of Buddhism (As Told in Verse by an Indian Buddhist)* (London: Trübner & Co., 1879); Rick Fields, *How the Swans Came to the Lake: A Narrative History of Buddhism in America* (Boston: Shambhala, 1992); Donald S. Lopez, Jr., *Modern Buddhism: Readings for the Unenlightened* (London: Penguin Books, 2002); Brooks Wright, *Interpreter of Buddhism to the West: Sir Edwin Arnold* (New York: Bookman Associates, 1957).

Aro gTer

Aro gTer (Mother Essence) is a relatively small and unrecognized lineage within NYINGMA Tibetan Buddhism. It is described as a nonliturgical, nonmonastic tradition that emphasizes the practice of DZOGCHEN. Aro gTer emphasizes the integration of Buddhist practice with everyday life, and everyday life as practice. It also teaches an equality of the sexes.

Aro gTer originated with a number of females who had experienced enlightenment. This lineage culminated in the career of Khyungchen Aro Lingma (1886–1923). The visionary Aro Lingma had received transmission from another enlightened female, Yeshe Tsogyel. She passed the lineage to her son, Aro Yeshe (1913–51), and through him it passed to the current lineage holders, Ngak'chang Cho-ying Cyamtso Ogyen Togden Rinpoche (1952–) and Khandro Dechen Tsedrup Yeshe. Khandro Dechen is a recognized master of the Dzogchen Long-de system, whose practices she teaches.

Ngak'chang Rinpoche is a German by birth. Raised in England, he developed an interest in Nyingma Buddhism and in 1971 traveled to the Himalayan Mountains to find a teacher. During his stay, he completed a four-year solitary retreat. Having encountered the followers of the Aro gTer, he was eventually recognized as the incarnation of Aro Yeshe, who had died the year before the new Rinpoche's birth. He now holds the lineage along with his wife, Khandro Dechen.

Since returning to the West to teach in 1979, Ngak'chang Rinpoche has opened Aro gTer centers in North America and across northern Europe. In England, the group is known as Sang-Kgak-Cho-Dzong.

See also TITLES AND TERMS OF ADDRESS, BUDDHIST.

Further reading: Ngakpa Chogyam, *Wearing the Body of Visions* (Ramsey, N.J.: Aro Books, 1995); ——— and Khandro Dechen, *Roaring Silence: Discovering the Mind of Dzogchen* (Boston: Shambhala, 2002); ——— and Khandro Dechen, *Spectrum of Ecstasy: The Five Wisdom Emotions according to Vajrayana Buddhism* (Boston: Shambhala, 2002).

art, aesthetics, and architecture

Art and design are major aspects of Buddhist practice. As Buddhist ideas spread into new regions they have invariably ignited creative surges and expressions in all aspects of culture. There is thus no single form or school of Buddhist art. Instead each culture has created its own unique mix—all centered on the teachings, images, and stories found in early Buddhism, along with later elaborations. Early artists, sculptors, architects, and artisans gave visual expression to the Buddha's spiritual vision by infusing new meaning in existing cosmological models, modes of expression, and material culture; subsequently others created fresh images that reflected the evolving visions and practical needs of the faith. Buddhists adapted and consigned innovative meanings to Hindu and Hellenistic ideas and motifs. Artists continue to recreate Buddhist symbols and narratives in accordance with local canons of taste in every region where Buddhism spread. Buddhist ideals are also apparent in the inexpensive utilitarian wares made and used by the common people.

Much Buddhist art and architecture falls into six broad areas: the STUPAS, monasteries and temples, the mountain temple, the Buddha image, paintings, and folk art.

THE STUPA

When Sakyamuni Buddha passed away in 483 B.C.E. his lay devotees divided and erected stupas over his cremated remains to honor his memory and his PARINIRVANA (more commonly, NIRVANA), a spiritual ideal that provided an alternative to endless cycles of life and death. Fusing the earthly and transcendent, this ancient sepulchral monument became the signature icon of Buddhism.

The stupa has evolved from a simple funerary mound to symbolize the *parinirvana* (death), to mark a sacred site associated with the Buddha, his earthly possessions, or other holy persons. Some scholars have suggested that the stupa is an expression of the Mount Meru cosmology.

The oldest example of the stupa is the Great Stupa at Sanchi, India (third century B.C.E.). Other important examples include the Great Stupa at Amaravati in present-day Andhra Pradesh; the cylindrical stupas at Karle and Ajanta, eastern India; the great stupa at Anuradhapura, Sri Lanka; and the bell-shaped stupas at Ananda Stupa in Pagan, Myanmar, and Phra Si Ratana Chedi in Bangkok, Thailand. By the Gupta period (c. 319–550 C.E.), sculptors placed the image of the Buddha on the elongated cylindrical base. Architects also experimented with square bases, cornices, articulated by pilasters, niches, and arcades, developments that prefigure the East Asian pagoda.

MONASTERIES AND TEMPLES

The VIHARA (monastery) and *caitya* (communal worship space) are the archetype Indian spiritual sanctuaries. *Viharas* and *caityas* were hewn out of living rock or constructed from brick and other materials. More than 1,000 were cut along the ancient trade routes in the Western Ghat range between 120 B.C.E. and 400 C.E. They were built near prosperous towns and on sites associated with the Buddha and other worthies. While some, like NALANDA in Bihar and Sirkap in Gandhara, grew into vast establishments, the *vihara* evolved from a simple cave or hut that housed, especially during the rainy season, a single cleric. As the number of clerics grew, living quarters were built around a common center where the community could gather for rites and for study. The ruins at Nalanda show that each cell contained a stone bed and pillow with a niche for a lamp. In contrast, *caityas* were designed with an apse or recess and two side aisles designed to accommodate circumambulation. Devotees proceeded between two rows of columns that formed a corridor that circled the stupa placed in the far end of the apse. The second century C.E. *caitya* at Karle, near Lonavla in Maharashtra, India, is of monumental proportions (125 feet in length, 46 feet in width and height).

Viharas and *caityas* continued to be hewn in the Tian mountains that linked Central Asia and northern China. The earliest Chinese cave-temples are in Gansu Province. Archaeologists have discovered new sites near the great cave-temples at Dunhuang. The Northern Wei dynasty (386–532) established cave temples at various sites in northwest China. While cave-temples continued to be hewn and maintained, urban temples and monasteries were laid out on a south-north axis based on Daoist geomancy. In the early layout, the devotee would immediately arrive at the pagoda after entering through a south facing gateway. The *kondo* (Japanese pronunciation), or Buddha hall; *kodo,* or lecture hall; and other structures were placed behind the pagoda. But the pagoda, essentially a foreign element, did not fit into the Chinese architectural layout. Between the sixth and eighth centuries, it was placed to the left of the central axis. At times a second pagoda was added, and in other cases the pagoda was eventually abandoned. The seventh-century Horyu-ji in Nara, Japan, is an example of this shift, which begins in the Six Dynasties period of Chinese history (220–589 C.E.) temple layout. The pagoda stands on the west and the *kondo* to the east. To the north and facing the central entry is a large *kodo,* or lecture hall, that houses the Buddha and subsidiary images. The *kondo* at Toshodai-ji, also in Nara, marks another shift. The VAIROCANA Buddha occupying the central seat in the *kondo* is intended to be viewed from the front and was not designed for circumambulation. In later developments, the altar is pushed to the back, opening up a space for congregate worship that is common in PURE LAND temples, where the AMITABHA Buddha occupies the central position. Over time, in East Asia the *kondo* replaces the *stupa* in importance.

THE MOUNTAIN-TEMPLE

In Buddhist architecture some structures function as representations of the cosmos, the *loka-dhatu,* or universe that comes into existence, is sustained and disintegrates through the collective karmic energy of all living beings. At the center of that cosmos sits MT. SUMERU. According to the *ABIDHARMA-KOSA* by VASUBANDHU (c. 420–500) Mt. Sumeru and the surrounding seven concentric square mountain ranges, each separated by vast oceans, are located in the middle of a great ocean. The five peaks region at the summit of Mt. Sumeru is the heavenly abode of the god Indra, the four great kings, and 33 lesser deities. Four heavenly palaces are located above the summit. MAITREYA, the future Buddha, resides in the Tusita Heavens. Mount Sumeru served as a model for temple design and layout and the *CAKRAVARTIN,* or ideal ruler, that guided earthly polity in Southeast Asia. Important cosmological temples include the Bayon, built by JAYAVARMAN VII (r. 1181–1219), the symbolic center of Angkor Thom, the capital city of the Khmer empire; the later ANGKOR WAT (early 12th century), the most ambitious architectural monument to recreate Mount Sumeru cosmology; and BOROBUDUR in Indonesia.

In East Asia Mt. Sumeru is preserved in the dais on which the Buddha rests. The dais, or bottom half of the rectangle platform, is in the form of a step pyramid; the upper half is an inverted step pyramid; the Buddha is portrayed as the lord of the physical and spiritual worlds. Often a lotus throne is placed on the dais, compounding the glory of the Buddha. Buddhism adopted the lotus to symbolize spiritual unfolding and the axis of the universe.

THE BUDDHA IMAGE

The third century B.C.E. bas-reliefs sculptured at Sanchi and Bharhut, India, are the earliest extant narratives that illustrate important events in Sakyamuni Buddha's life and *JATAKAS TALES,* stories of the Buddha's former lives that exemplify his wisdom and compassion. In these and other early visual representations, artisans depicted major personalities, but never the human Buddha. His presence was suggested by images of the *bo*-tree (BODHI TREE, *Ficus religiosa*) under which he realized ENLIGHTENMENT, or the cushion on which he rested at the moment of the enlightenment, or the stupa representing his PARINIRVANA, or his footprint(s) signifying his presence, or the *dharmacakra*, or Dharma Wheel, representing the first sermon. At times the Buddha is presented as part of a trident, a symbol of the TRIRATNA, or Triple Jewels—BUDDHA (the teacher), DHARMA (the Teaching), SANGHA (community)—that constitute the core of the faith.

Sculptors may have hesitated to portray the human Buddha because transcendence, purity, and spirituality are more effectively conveyed by symbols. Their reluctance may have been due to the belief that Sakyamuni had achieved *parinirvana* and thus ceased to exist; because he was not of this world, it was not possible to depict the Buddha and his spiritual accomplishments. The state of nonexistence presented the artist with a dilemma concerning how to present the formless and transcendental Buddha through form.

The shift from the aniconic (symbolic) to the iconic representation of the Buddha coincided with the rise of MAHAYANA and the spread of lay devotionalism (*bhakti*) at the beginning of the first and second centuries C.E. The heroic and sacrificial character of the BODHISATTVA, who vows to save all beings by sharing the merits he/she has accumulated over eons of discipline, is an outgrowth of the idealization of the historical Buddha. Other scholars have suggested that the bodhisattva ideal and the accompanying vision of *Suhkavati*, or PURE LAND, were of Mediterranean and Central Asian origin and filtered into Mahayana thought. At any rate Mahayana ideals departed from the understanding that the historical Buddha was an exceptional individual and teacher. This new vision together with the spread of the faith among the population required more readily accessible images to replace the highly abstract notions of enlightenment and *parinirvana* represented by the stupa and other symbols. The development of the Buddha image was one response.

The first Buddha image appeared more or less simultaneously in Mathura and Gandhara regions in the first century C.E. under the Kushan (c. 50–288) political hegemony; a flurry of images appeared during the reign of KANISKA (c. 78–101 C.E.). Their respective depictions of the Buddha emerged from different traditions. Artisans from Mathura in north central India near the modern-day city of Agra continued the sculptural forms of the *yaksa* and *yaksi*—male and female, respectively, fertility spirits. The blocklike compactness and smooth close-fitting robe, almost entirely devoid of folds, are replicated in the earliest standing Buddha image. The first Mathuran image makers, it seemed, never intended to sculpt an anatomically correct human Buddha. Their images were a composite of 32 major and 80 minor *laksana*, or marks. These literary descriptions were based on natural images and features associated with manly beauty and heroic ideals. Thus the Buddha, a noble being and a *cakravartin* (ideal ruler), has a smooth and perfectly proportioned body, an oval-shaped head, eyebrows in the shape of the curve of an Indian bow, eyes that recall a lotus bud, ears that evoke the shape of mangos, thighs that are like those of a gazelle, and limbs smooth like a banyan tree. The triple folds of the neck are derived from a conch shell, a symbol used to call the faithful to listen to the teachings. The broad chest and narrow hips recall the lion, the patriarch of the jungle; the arms that reach to the knees and webbed fingers symbolize the Buddha's great compassion. The long arms enable the Buddha to embrace all beings; his webbed fingers prevent those whom the Buddha has scooped from the sea of SAMSARA from dribbling back. The distended ear lobes, a feature of nobles, who wore heavy ear ornaments, recall his aristocratic birth. The colored gold body emits a wondrous scent.

Siddhartha's locks curled to the right after he cut his hair, a symbol of abandoning the secular life, and became a spiritual mendicant. He has 80 of these right-turning tufts of hair that never grew

Burmese Buddha figure, painted wood and lacquer, Mandalay, northern Myanmar (Burma)

again. His curls and lotus-petal lips prompted the early British explorers mistakenly to report Buddha images to have an "African cast." The palms of his hands and the soles of his feet bear the *dharmacakra*, "dharma wheel," or Buddhist SWASTIKA. The *urna*, the white lock curled to the right, emits the light of wisdom; the *urna* is depicted as a third eye in Tantric Buddhism. The Buddha image is often embraced by halo and aureole (circles of light) that symbolize the Buddha's immeasurable brilliance of truth and wisdom. The Buddha's extraordinary wisdom is represented by the *usnisa*, a "bump" or extra cranial protrusion. These various features are not afterthoughts, but integral parts of the Buddha's representation. Since the *laksana* (marks) were too numerous to include in any single image, the Mathuran artisans selectively chose the principal features to use for each Buddha image.

In contrast the Gandharan Buddha image was inspired by Hellenistic realism, tempered by Persian, Scythian, and Parthian models. Sculptors crafted Buddhist images with anatomical accuracy, spatial depth, and foreshortening. The straight sharply chiseled Apollonian noses, brows, and mustaches capture a "frozen moment." Their more

realistic tradition transformed the *usnisa* into a top-knot or turban; the Buddha's curls were altered into wavy hair. Another obvious Mediterranean feature is the diaphanous (thin), togalike robe. The emaciated Buddha, an image rarely seen in Mathura, is another evidence of Hellenistic realism.

From the close of the second century both the Mathuran and Gandharan styles experienced mutual cross-fertilization. The skillful incorporation of the *laksanas* suggests that the Gandharan image makers became more comfortable in incorporating native Indian notions of beauty. The bulky Mathura Buddha gradually gives way to the slender elegance of the Gandharan image. The result of this synthesis ennobled, refined, and purified the Buddha image that appeared in the Gupta period (c. 320–467 C.E.). The soft and supple body visible beneath the thin robe swells with life-giving breath. The round face sculpted with a feeling of perfect tranquility engaged in profound meditation conveys in the human form a sense of the transcendent. The Gupta style became the model for Southeast Asian images.

Transcendence in bodily form is also seen in the walking Buddha in the round created during Thai culture's Sukhotai period (c. 1240–1438). The Sukhotai-style image in the *maravijaya* (Victory over MARA) seated posture where the Buddha extends his right hand to touch the earth—a gesture known as *bhumisparsa-mudra*—signifying the defeat of Mara, lord of darkness, and the walking image with the *abhaya-mudra* (gesture of fearlessness and reassurance) are Thailand's best-known styles. Thai sculptors seamlessly blended literary description with aesthetic sensitivity to create a figure that emanates great spiritual power. The asexual images exhibit no anatomical or skeletal features; the head is shaped like an egg; the torso is lionlike with broad shoulders, the arms smooth and tapering; the thick thighs resemble the stalks of a banana tree. The downcast eyes and high flame *usnisa* finial (top decoration) convey a spiritual radiance. This distinctive Thai style emerged after the Thai overthrew their Khmer (Cambodian) overlords. Khmer images were square-faced and topped by a conelike *usnisa* or a wide crown. The figure of Muchilinda, the *naga*-king (water serpent), protectively hovering over the Buddha is especially popular in Southeast Asia.

While Theravada artists and sculptors of Southeast Asia have portrayed the historical Buddha and events related to his life, the ideas and goals of Mahayana introduced an important shift in visual and plastic representation. Mahayana artists in Central and East Asia have struggled to render the celestial Buddhas and bodhisattvas and transcendental Buddha Lands. Mahayanists understood nirvana to be the "other world" of Sukhavati, not the state of non-being of *parinirvana*. The Larger Sukhavativyuha Sutra and other Pure Land sutras describe in exquisite detail this "other world" that is reigned over by the AMITABHA Buddha. MAITREYA, or the future Buddha, was the most popular image during the Kushan period; this representation of the Buddha seems to have been influenced by Persian and Mediterranean messianic ideas. VAIROCANA, the universal Buddha; BHAISAJYA-GURU, the Medicine Buddha; and the bodhisattva AVALOKITESVARA are other popular

Head of large marble Buddha, Mandalay, Myanmar

images. These celestial beings and their realms inspired the creation of monumental images and spectacular symbolism. Thus we see the appearance of colossal Buddha images at Bamiyan in Afghanistan. The 175-foot-tall Vairocana Buddha, the universal monarch, was hewn into the cliff between the fourth and fifth centuries. After 15 centuries Taliban artillery destroyed this image and a smaller 120-foot-tall accompanying Buddha in 2001. The 53-foot-tall Vairocana Buddha at TODAI-JI in Nara, cast in 752 C.E., is another such example. The great size of these figures reflects the importance Mahayana placed on celestial realms that promise riches and rewards to those who would be reborn in such a paradise. Mahayana artists portrayed these Buddha lands with rich colors and vibrant imagination.

In another change, many of the early Buddha images were accompanied by pairs of bodhisattva images and other worthies. Unlike the simply dressed Buddha images, bodhisattvas were adorned with elaborate dress and ornamentation that reflected the tastes of princes. Bodhisattvas can often be identified by the objects and symbols that accompany them. Maitreya, the future Buddha, is displayed with a stupa on its crown; Vajrapani holds a thunderbolt; Avalokitesvara

Massive "sleeping Buddha" (with eyes open, indicating relaxation, not *parinirvana*) at Shwethalyaung Temple in Bago (Pegu), Myanmar

Feet of a sleeping Buddha figure at Shwethalyaung Temple, Bago (Pegu), Myanmar, with the *dharmacakra*, the Buddhist wheel in each sole

or GUANYIN (or Kannon in Japanese), "he or she who hears the pleas of the world," is especially popular in China; this bodhisattva has a seated Amida Buddha in his crown and holds a lotus. The bodhisattva MANJUSRI, the personification of wisdom, rides a lion; Samantabadhra sits on a six-tusked elephant.

The first Buddha images to enter China were probably transported in small portable shrines that were molded and carved in Central Asia. These images, a fusion of Gupta and later Gandharan styles, had a great impact on the early Northern Wei (386–535) style that formed the foundation of Chinese Buddhist art. The distinctive slender and frontal figure with its cascading robes of the Wei-style images appears during the Japanese Asuka period (552–646) in the Shaka Triad and Yumedo Kannon at Horyu-ji in Nara. A characteristic Chinese style appears in the Tang (618–907) period. The Tang style is rounder and bolder. A prime example of the classical Tang style is at the Yakushi Triad at Yakushi temple in Nara, Japan. The 751 C.E. Sokkuram Buddha in Korea is another fine example.

PAINTINGS

Visions of the various Buddhist paradises were executed with great delicacy and imagery on the walls and ceiling of the *viharas* and *caityas*. Mahayana inspired not only lofty images of the Pure Land, but also images of the horrors of HELL. Dating to the first century B.C.E. these paintings constitute, as do the bas-reliefs at Bharhut and Sanchi, a testament to the Indian artist's skill in narrative presentation, composition, and use of color. The majority of AJANTA's murals date from the fifth and sixth centuries; the tradition continues in the cave paintings of Central Asia and East Asia. The best example of Tang dynasty painting survived on the walls of the *kondo* at the Horyu-ji in Kyoto until it went up in flames in 1950. East Asian artists used the soft brush to create a diverse corpus of Buddhist paintings. Monochrome ink paintings of the Song dynasty (960–1178 C.E.) inspired great ZEN paintings in China and Japan. Most Thai paintings date from the 18th century. The delicate linear drawings, vibrant colors, and textile patterns give Thai paintings a distinctive look.

FOLK ART

Parallel to the development of "high" art, Buddhist culture and feeling are also found in folk art. The Japanese aesthetician Yanagi Soetsu (1889–1960) found profound beauty in the humblest and most commonplace utilitarian artifacts produced by unknown craftsmen. Yanagi's *mingei*, or folkcraft philosophy, relocates Buddhist art, not to Buddhist subject matter, but to the source of and manner of creativity. The artless spontaneity in the manner in which Korean Yi dynasty (1392–1912 C.E.) ceramic wares and their brushwork were created reveals the Pure Land of Beauty; it is a beauty of the nondual or Buddha mind. The task of the artisan is to give form to this formless mind. Yanagi derived the notion of the "Pure Land of Beauty" from the Larger Sukhavatīvyuha Sutra. The Zen philosopher Hisamatsu Shin'ichi (1889–1977) also proposed that the task of the Zen artist is to give form to the Zen experience. Spontaneity required in writing calligraphy is especially suited for mirroring such experiences. For Yanagi and Hisamatsu Buddhist art should express the Buddha mind and experience of the enlightenment; it is not about conveying Buddhist themes.

Further reading: A. L. Basham, *The Wonder That Was India: A Survey of the Culture of the Indian Sub-Continent before the Coming of the Muslims* (New York: Grove Press, 1989); Ananda K. Coomaraswamy, *History of Indian and Indonesian Art* (New York: Dover, 1965); Robert E. Fisher, *Buddhist Art and Architecture* (New York: Thames & Hudson, 1993); Anagarika Govinda, *Psycho-Cosmic Symbolism of the Buddhist Stupa* (Berkeley, Calif: Dharma, 1976); Partha Mitter, *Indian Art* (Oxford: Oxford University Press, 2001); Akira Sadakata, *Buddhist Cosmology, Philosophy and Origins* (Tokyo: Kosei, 1997); E. Dale Saunders, *Mudra, a Study of Symbolic Gestures in Japanese Buddhist Sculpture* (Princeton, N.J.: Princeton University Press, 1960); Dietrich Seckel, *The Art of Buddhism* (New York: Crown, 1963); Soetsu Yanagi, *The Unknown Craftsman Japanese Insight into Beauty* (Tokyo: Kodansha International, 1978).

Aryadeva (second century C.E.) *student of Nagarjuna and Chan patriarch*

Aryadeva, also called Kanadeva (god of a single eye), was a follower of NAGARJUNA, the great early Mahayana philosopher. He is considered the 15th patriarch in the CHAN (ZEN) lineage. He was killed after a debate against brahmanist teachers—that is, teachers representing rival Hindu beliefs. Aryadeva wrote several key texts in the MADHYAMIKA tradition, including *Aksarasataka* (One hundred verse treatise). This work, along with two others by Nagarjuna, in turn became the core works of the later San Lun (Japanese SANRON) school.

Further reading: Edward Conze, "Mahayana Buddhism," in *The Concise Encyclopedia of Living Faiths.*

Edited by R. C. Zaehner (New York: Hawthorn Books, 1959).

Asahara, Shoko   *See* AUM SHINRIKYO.

Asanga (fourth century C.E.) *one of the great founders of Yogacara thought and a key Mahayana writer*

Asanga converted from an early school of Buddhism to MAHAYANA and eventually succeeded in persuading his younger brother, VASUBHANDU, to convert as well. One version relates how he visited Tusita heaven and was taught the Mahayana doctrine on nonessence by MAITREYA, the Buddha of the future. In another version he received his understanding of Mahayana from his earthly teacher, who was named Maitreya. The two brothers founded the YOGACARA school of MAHAYANA Buddhism, which gave preeminence in its teachings to the nature of mind. Asanga wrote the *Yogacarabhumi Sastra*, the *Mahayana-samgraha*, and the *Abhidharma-samuccaya*.

Further reading: Kogen Mizuno, *Essentials of Buddhism: Basic Terminology and Concepts of Buddhist Philosophy and Practice*, trans. Gaynor Sekimori (1972. Reprint, Tokyo: Kosei, 1996).

Asita *prophet who forecast the Buddha's greatness*

Asita was a wise man of Kapilavastu, the capital of Sakya, the state in which the historical BUDDHA was born. After the son's birth his father, SHUDDHODANA, requested that Asita study the newborn's physical features. Asita recognized the 30 marks of a great person and forecast that Siddhartha would become either a great leader or, if he renounced the world, a Buddha.

Further reading: Edward J. Thomas, *The Life of Buddha as Legend and History* (New Delhi: Munshiram Manoharlal, 1992).

Asoka (Ashoka) (c. 304–232 B.C.E.)
greatest Buddhist monarch and proponent of early Buddhism

Asoka unified much of what is modern India but was shocked in 262 B.C.E. at the suffering he had caused in conquering the rebellious state of Kalinga (roughly corresponding to the modern state of Orissa). The horror of the war was so great that whereas earlier he had had a nominal commitment to Buddhism, it now became active in his life. He vowed to apply Buddhist principles to his rule. This vow included performing numerous good works such as building hospitals for people and animals, digging wells, and setting up travel facilities. Asoka played a crucial part in spreading Buddhism throughout India and abroad. He prob-

Three lions, the symbol of Emperor Asoka, atop a pedestal at the Kyauktawgyi Paya temple, Mandalay, northern Myanmar (Burma), which re-creates the Emperor Asoka's pedestals and stone edicts erected throughout India

ably built the first major Buddhist monuments. In Buddhist lore he is said to have overseen the third Buddhist Council at Pataliputra. He ordered the erection of inscribed pillars to commemorate the establishment of the Buddha's DHARMA, or rule, in his lands. He introduced Buddhism to Sri Lanka through his son, MAHINDA, and additionally sent his daughter, SANGHAMITTA, there with a cutting from the BODHI TREE to plant.

Though he is now one of the best known of Buddhist figures, many of the details of King Asoka's life are unknown and much that is known, such as his date of birth, is disputed by scholars. He was born about 304 B.C.E. He was the grandson of Chandragupta, founder of the Mauryan dynasty, and followed his father, Bindusara, to the throne. As king of MAGADHA he also held the title *Devanampiya Piyadasi* (Beloved-of-the-gods, he who looks on with affection.)

Asoka died in 232 B.C.E., in the 38th year of his reign. Asoka has since come to represent an ideal of close interaction between temporal ruler and Buddhist principles. He is the *CAKRAVARTIN*, the ideal ruler, who causes the wheel of the law—the Buddha's DHARMA—to turn.

Although he was a fabled king, little was known of Asoka from the time Buddhism was stamped out in India until the survey of Indian literature made by European scholars in the 19th century. In several books they found repeated references to a ruthless prince who rose to power over the bodies of his own brothers but who had a sudden conversion to Buddhism, after which he ruled justly and assisted the spread of Buddhism. Later in the century they began to associate the king Asoka in the literature with the King Piyadasi mentioned in the texts of edicts that had been carved into many stone monuments. Finally in 1915, a stone monument with the name *Asoka* was discovered. Incidentally, Asoka's edicts comprise the earliest decipherable corpus of written documents from India. They survived because they are written on rocks and stone pillars.

Further reading: Ven. S. Dhammika, *The Edicts of King Asoka: An English Rendering* (Kandy, Sri Lanka: Buddhist Publication Society, 1993); John S. Strong, *The Legend of King Asoka: A Study and Translation of the Asokavadana* (Princeton, N.J.: Princeton University Press, 1983); Romila Thapar, *Asoka and the Decline of the Mauryas* (Delhi and New York: Oxford University Press, 1997); Mortimer Wheeler, *Early India and Pakistan to Asoka* (New York: Praeger, 1959).

Association of Nuns and Laywomen of Cambodia

This association was established as a nongovernmental institution in 1995 to give voice to a group relatively marginalized in Cambodian Buddhism—unordained nuns, called *donchee* in the Khmer (Cambodian) language. One goal of the association is to improve the status of nuns in Cambodian society. As in Thailand, Cambodian nuns who may have taken the 10-fold precepts for nuns are nevertheless not allowed to become novices (*samaneri*) or fully ordained *bhiksuni* (female monks). In fact women were not ordained anywhere in Southeast Asia for over 1,000 years, following the collapse of the lineages of nuns in Sri Lanka and Burma. Much of the male SANGHA in Thailand and Cambodia today continues to resist allowing female ordination.

The founding group consisted of 107 women. Membership is open to Buddhist women only. There are today over 10,000 members, 65 percent of whom are nuns. The two Supreme Patriarchs of Cambodian Buddhism are patrons, and the queen, Queen Norodom Monineath Sihanouk, is sponsor. The Association of Nuns and Laywomen of Cambodia (ANLWC) is now found in all provinces throughout the country. It sponsors leadership and social work training for women. This program highlights one of the newest roles of nuns in Cambodian life, serving as social workers and family counselors. The ANLWC receives support from the Heinrich Boll Foundation in Germany.

Association Zen Internationale

The Association Zen Internationale, founded in Paris in 1970, has become the largest Zen Buddhist group in Europe. It was founded by Taisen Deshimaru Roshi (1914–82). The association's mission is to propagate Soto Zen as presented by Master Deshimaru.

Deshimaru Roshi grew up in an old samurai family. His mother was a follower of Shin Buddhism, and as a youth he was attracted to Christianity. He eventually found his way to Zen, traditionally associated with the samurai.

Deshimaru chose Kodo SAWAKI ROSHI (d. 1965), a SOTO ZEN master, as his teacher. He began studying with Kodo Sawaki in the 1930s and remained with him except when serving in the army during World War II. A married man with a family, Deshimaru did not become ordained as a monk until the time of his being commissioned to take Zen to the West just shortly before Sawaki's death in 1965.

Leaving his family in the care of his eldest son, Deshimaru moved to France in 1967. He entered without any resources or knowledge of French. From a primitive sitting space to do ZAZEN, he gathered a few followers and built an initial DOJO. He founded an association in 1970 and through the 12 remaining years of his life attracted students from across Europe. He eventually received dharma transmission from Master Yamada Reirin, head of Eihei Temple in Japan and was named *kaikyosokan* (head of Japanese Soto Zen for a particular country or continent) for all Europe.

In the late 1970s the association acquired an estate, La Gendronnière, where Deshimaru oversaw the construction of a temple in 1979 and then a new large dojo that could hold up to 400 practitioners. From there he trained and sent his students out to found centers across Europe. After his death, the association continued under the guidance of senior students.

As of 2005, the association oversaw some 200 DOJOS and practice centers, most in Europe. In

1983, a senior student, Robert Livingston Roshi, founded the first center in North America, in New Orleans, Louisiana. Association-related centers are now located in 36 countries.

Further reading: Taisen Deshimaru, *Questions to a Zen Master* (New York: E. P. Dutton, 1985); ———, *The Ring of the Way: Testament of a Zen Master* (New York: E. P. Dutton, 1987); ———, *Sit: Zen Teachings of Master Taisen Deshimaru.* Edited by Philippe Coupey (Prescott, Ariz.: Hohm Press, 1996); ———, *The Voice of the Valley: Zen Teachings* (Indianapolis, Ind.: Bobbs-Merrill, 1979).

asubha

Asubha, or ugliness, is a concept used in a standard Buddhist meditation practice in which the cultivator focuses on 10 "disgusting objects," including the body and its decay. To do this the meditator is advised to spend time observing decaying corpses in a burial ground. This list of 10 objects is part of the larger list of 40 subjects given in the VISUD-HIMAGGA, the standard text on Buddhist meditation written by BUDDHAGHOSA, c. 400 C.E.

Why do Buddhist texts encourage mediation on ugliness? The underlying idea is to reinforce the idea of decay and impermanence. All phenomena decay and change, a key idea in Buddhist practice and teachings.

asvabhava   *See* SVABHAVA.

Asvaghosa (second century C.E.) *Mahayana writer and poet*

Asvaghosa propagated Buddhism through his art in the second century C.E. Asvaghosa at first worked against Buddhism but later became a fervent champion. His *Budhacharita,* the story of the Buddha's life, is a key work of Indian literature. Asvaghosa in general put definite emphasis on the forest-dwelling aspect of the Buddha's life, as opposed to depicting the Buddha as an urban individual, as is the general tendency in the VINAYA, the part of the Buddhist canon that details rules for the monkhood. Asvaghosa is most remembered for his *Awakening of Faith in the Mahayana* (*Mahayana-sraddhotpada-sastra*). Some scholars contend this work, while attributed to Asvaghosa, was produced by later Chinese writers. Regardless, we may consider Asvaghosa to be the first major scholar of Mahayana.

Further reading: Asvaghosa, *Awakening of Faith.* Translated by D. T. Suzuki (Chicago: Open Court, 1900); Yoshito S. Hakeda, trans., *Awakening of Faith Attributed to Asvaghosa* (New York: Columbia University Press, 1967); Noble Ross Reat, *Buddhism: A History* (Berkeley, Calif.: Asian Humanities Press, 1994).

Atisa (11th century) *Indian Buddhist teacher instrumental in introduction of Buddhism to Tibet*

Atisa was the key person in the second transmission of Buddhism to Tibet. During the ninth century, the Tibetan king, Langdarma, had persecuted Buddhism and instigated a period of decline. Then in the next century several of the rulers in western Tibet sent Tibetans to India to recover the tradition. Of 21 who were sent, two returned in 978—Rinchen Zangpo and Lekpe Sherab—and they began the process of revival with new translations of Buddhist texts. The older texts being used by the NYINGMA practitioners were examined and anything not confirmed to have originated in India deleted. Thus, the attempt was made to exclude from the teachings any pre-Buddhist teachings from Tibetan religions.

Then in the 11th century, Lkhalama Yeshe-o, the king of western Tibet, invited the Indian teacher Atisa, a scholar from Vikramashila University in Bengal, to his land. While details of his life are few, he was the author of the *Bodhipathapradipa* (Lamp for the path of enlightenment), his summary of Tantric Buddhist teachings, which presents its material in such a way that the believer may

appropriate Buddhist teachings and enlightenment along a graded path of attainment. He
would spend his life in the revival of a reformed
Buddhism.

Atisa took with him a disciple, Dromtonpa,
who established Rva-sgreng monastery in 1056,
generally considered the date of the founding of
the KADAMPA school of Tibetan Buddhism. That
tradition would eventually be absorbed into the
Gelug school headed by the DALAI LAMA.

Further reading: Atisa, *Lamp for the Path to Enlighten-
ment: Commentary by Geshe Sonam Rinchen* (Ithaca,
N.Y.: Snow Lion, 1997); Graham Coleman, ed., *A
Handbook of Tibetan Culture: A Guide to Tibetan Centres
and Resources throughout the World* (Boston: Shambhala,
1994); Anil Kumar Sarkar, *The Mysteries of Vajrayana
Buddhism: From Atisa to Dalai Lama* (Colombia, Mo.:
South Asia Books, 1993).

atman   *See* ANATMAN.

Aum Shinrikyo/Aleph

Because of the homicidal actions perpetrated by
its leadership, Aum Shinrikyo, one of the late-
20th-century new religions of Japan, has attained
a pariah status in Buddhist circles generally. The
aura of evil that surrounds it has made analysis
difficult—no group, and rightfully so, wants to be
connected with it.

Aum Shinrikyo was founded by Shoko Asahara, born Chizuo Matsumoto in 1955. After failing the entrance examination to Tokyo University,
Asahara began studying Chinese medicine. He also
joined AGON SHU, a new Buddhist religion based
on the Agama sutras and efforts to remove one's
inherited karma through ritual activity. In 1984,
Asahara began holding yoga classes, through
which he gained his first followers. Through the
mid-1980s he visited India and attained enlightenment while absorbing some elements of Tibetan
Buddhism.

Upon his return to Japan, his following evolved
into the Aum Shinrikyo, the "teaching of the
supreme truth." *Aum* is a basic mantra recited in
India, the creative word by which the world came
into being. After overcoming some complaints
from the families of members, the group was registered with the government in 1989.

Aum Shinrikyo spread through Japan and
established a rural headquarters complex near
Mt. FUJI. It also continued to generate public controversy. Parents who disapproved of the group,
and especially the way in which some members
severed standard communications with their families after joining, persisted in attacking the group.
The families hired a lawyer, Sakamoto Tsutsumi,
to pursue their concerns. Sakamoto began aggressively and effectively to attack the group. Then
in November 1989, Sakamoto, his wife, and his
infant son suddenly disappeared. Foul play was
alleged, but there was no evidence.

Meanwhile, Asahara had been absorbing elements of Western apocalyptic thinking, primarily
from his reading of the Christian New Testament,
with an emphasis on the Book of Revelation, and
the prophetic writings of Nostradamus. He also
urged the group to follow the example of the SOKA
GAKKAI and become involved in running candidates for public office. With considerably less
following and no political skills, the Aum Shinrikyo candidates lost in an embarrassing defeat.

During the early 1990s, two different Aum
realities developed. Outwardly, and to most members, Aum presented a program that invited individuals to seek enlightenment through an eclectic
program of spiritual exercises derived from Agon
Shu, Tibetan Buddhism, modern technology in
altered consciousness, and the fertile imagination
of Asahara. In this endeavor a number of books
were published including the group's primary
text, *AUM Supreme Initiation* (1988).

At the same time, an increasingly apocalyptic
view of current events and the near future developed. As the tension with the public increased,
the vision of the future increasingly pictured Aum

Shinrikyo as an active force in bringing about those events. The apocalypticism increasingly took center stage in the core leadership group, though it is hard to know how much the ideology seeped to the larger membership. However, one important change within the group was the 1994 reorganization of the leadership structure to mirror the organization of the Japanese government, presumably to facilitate Aum's assuming power after the coming catastrophic events.

At the same time that Aum's ideology was transforming, within the top leadership strategies were discussed on blocking various official attacks on the group. As would later become known, some leaders had planned the death of Sakamoto Tsutsumi and his family, in 1989. In 1993, the group began to manufacture nerve gas, initially produced before the year was out. The gas was initially used in 1994 in Matsumoto, Japan, in an attempt to prevent some legal proceeding against Aum by injuring the judges. The relative success of the event prepared the way for the March 20, 1995, event in which the nerve gas was released at the Kasumigaseki Station in central Tokyo, which also happened to be near a number of government offices and the headquarters of the National Police Agency. Twelve people died and hundreds more were injured more or less severely.

This incident, more than any other, served to focus attention on Aum, which immediately rose to the top of the suspect list. Raids on Aum centers, including the main center near Mt. FUJI, followed and arrests were made. The volatile nature of the nerve gas agent used made analysis and hence evidence gathering difficult. However, in September, a major break occurred when a member involved in the disposal of the bodies of the Sakamoto family confessed and led police to the bodies.

Asahara, who had been in hiding in a secret room at the headquarters, was finally arrested along with most of the leadership and several hundred people deemed to have been involved in planning and executing the several incidents or in assisting and/or protecting the leaders in the weeks after the March gassing incident.

Over the next several years, the Japanese authorities worked slowly and methodically to build a case against Asahara and his major lieutenants. The case made through the trials and testimonies of those involved on the periphery of the crimes eventually led to the trial and conviction of the major perpetrators, including Asahara. Upon conviction, the leaders were sentenced either to death or to lengthy prison terms.

Meanwhile, attempts were made to disband the organization, which, in a greatly weakened state, had been held together by those few leaders not indicted in the gassing incident. As the great majority of the members were not involved in any illegal or violent activities, Aum was allowed to remain in existence. The continuing leadership made several public apologies for the actions of their colleagues and promised to show their regret by paying a large sum to the victims and their families. The group also changed its name to *Aleph,* under which it continues. The small group, of several thousand members, continues to be heavily monitored by the police.

Further reading: Robert J. Kisala and Mark R. Mullins, *Religion and Social Crisis in Japan: Understanding Japanese Society through the Aum Affair* (New York: Palgrave, 2001); Robert J. Lifton, *Destroying the World to Save It: Aum Shinrikyo, Apocalyptic Violence and the New Global Terrorism* (New York: Metropolitan Books/Henry Holt, 1999); Ian Reader, *Religious Violence in Contemporary Japan: The Case of Aum Shinrikyo* (Honolulu: University of Hawaii Press, 2000).

Australia, Buddhism in

Buddhism is an increasingly important religious presence in Australia. Buddhists first arrived in 1848 when some transient Chinese workers immigrated to work on the Victorian gold fields.

However, a permanent Buddhist community did not emerge until 1876, when Sri Lankans settled on Thursday Island, off the northern tip of Queensland, to work the sugarcane plantations. By the end of the decade they would be joined by a number of Japanese, who scattered across the northern coast to work in the gathering of pearls. Japanese immigration was stopped by the Immigration Restriction Act of 1901, part of a broad policy to maintain dominance of people of European descent. Through the next generations, Buddhism remained the faith of several shrinking ethnic communities. The community on Thursday Island eventually died out, and the temple site was replaced in later years by a post office. All that survives of the original community are two BODHI TREES, descendents of the tree under which Gautama BUDDHA found enlightenment.

The first Western Buddhist group, the Little Circle of the Dharma, emerged in Melbourne in 1925, but it was a community only until after World War II. Then in 1951, Sister Dhammadinna, an American-born Buddhist nun visiting Australia, prepared to spread the Theravada teaching she had acquired in Sri Lanka over the previous three decades. Her visit resulted in the formation of the Buddhist Society of New South Wales under the leadership of Leo Berkley, a Dutch-born businessman and resident of Sydney. Today the society is the oldest existing Buddhist group in Australia. It nurtured the growth of similar groups in other cities, which were united in the Buddhist Federation of Australia in 1958.

In 1971, Somaloka, a monk from Sri Lanka, traveled to Sydney at the request of the Buddhist Society of New South Wales. He opened a monastery and retreat center in the Blue Mountains west of the city. This effort signaled a new era of growth for Australian Buddhism. That growth was built upon by both the immigration of people from different nearby countries that are predominantly Buddhist as well as the conversion of native

Australians to the faith. Growth among the latter segment was spurred by the early visits of the DALAI LAMA in 1982, 1992, and 1996. By the time of his third visit, the Buddhist community claimed almost 200,000 residents, of whom some 30,000 were native Australians and the rest largely first-generation immigrants. Taiwanese members of FOGUANGSHAN have opened a temple complex at Wollongong, Nan Tien, which rivals its headquarters complex in Taiwan.

The rapid growth of Buddhism created a situation in the mid-1980s in which many diverse Buddhist centers carried on their programs oblivious to other nearby groups. This situation led officials from the WORLD FELLOWSHIP OF BUDDHISTS to go to Australia to promote the fellowship's goals of cooperation and coordination. In 1984, for example, Teh Thean Choo, an executive with the fellowship, traveled to Sydney and became the catalyst for the formation of the Sydney Regional Buddhist Council, which evolved into the Buddhist Council of New South Wales. Similar regional structures now draw the Western and Eastern ethnic Buddhists together on a regular basis.

The single largest segment of Australian Buddhism is found in the Vietnamese community. The Unified Vietnamese Buddhist Congregation of Australia-New Zealand, founded in 1980, now claims some 100,000 lay practitioners, about one-fourth of the entire Australian Buddhist community. It is the only association of centers with temples in each of Australia's states. Significant other ethnic Buddhist communities are found among the Burmese, Laotians, Thai, Cambodians, Sri Lankans, Koreans, Tibetans, and Chinese (including Chinese from Taiwan, Malaysia, and Singapore).

Further reading: Darren Nelson, "Why Is Buddhism the Fastest Growing Religion in Australia?" Available online at BuddhaSasana: A Buddhist Page by Binh Anson. URL: http://www.budsas.org/ebud/ebdha226. htm. Posted June 1, 1998. Accessed on September

14, 2005; Michelle Spuler, *Developments in Australian Buddhism: Facets of the Diamond* (London: Routledge Curzon, 2003).

Avalokitesvara

Avalokitesvara (He who gazes) is the Sanskrit name for GUAN YIN (*Kuan Yin,* Japanese *Kannon,* Tibetan *spyan-ras-gzigs*). Avalokitesvara was a major Mahayana bodhisattva figure in such sacred Buddhist texts as the LOTUS SUTRA. In India and Tibet, Avalokitesvara is pictured as a male. In China and other East Asian cultures Avalokitesvara has assumed female form, as Guan Yin. Avalokitesvara also became important as a Tantric deity, especially in Tibet. The bodhisattva is often shown with many heads (11) and multiple arms (four, six, or, often, 1,000).

What explains the importance of Avalokitesvara in most Buddhist cultures? This figure is most closely associated with *karuna,* "compassion," a key value in Mahayana Buddhism, as well as Tantric forms of Buddhist practice. The urge to personify this key value helps us understand the popularity of images of Avalokitesvara, and especially Guan Yin/Kannon.

Further reading: John Clifford Holt, *Buddha in the Crown: Avalokitesvara in the Buddhist Traditions of Sri Lanka* (New York: Oxford University Press, 1991); Chun-fang Yu, *Kuan-yin: The Chinese Transformation of Avalokitesvara* (New York: Columbia University Press, 2001).

avidya (ignorance)

Avidya, or ignorance, is the inability to distinguish between the transitory and eternal aspects of experience. The term has a specific sense in Buddhist philosophy. It means being unaware of the FOUR NOBLE TRUTHS, the three precious jewels (the BUDDHA, the DHARMA, and the SANGHA), and the truth of KARMA—in other words, the truths of Buddha's teachings.

Further reading: Kogen Mizuno, *Essentials of Buddhism: Basic Terminology and Concepts of Buddhist Philosophy and Practice.* Translated by Gaynor Sekimori (1972. Reprint, Tokyo: Kosei, 1996).

B

Baimasi

Said by tradition to be the first Buddhist temple in China, the Baimasi or "White Horse Temple" was ordered constructed by Emperor Ming (28–75 C.E.) of the later Han dynasty in the year 67 C.E. at Luoyang, his capital. It was called White Horse because the two Indian monks, KASYAPA MATANGA and Zhu Falan, who founded the temple, had arrived with a white horse that carried an image of the Buddha and a copy of the Sutra of Forty-two Sections.

The White Horse Temple has been regarded as the originating point of Chinese Buddhism but has not always been maintained as a place of honor. Damage at different times has meant it had to be rebuilt on several occasions, most recently during the Ming dynasty (1368–1644).

Further reading: Samuel Beal, *Buddhism in China* (North Stratford, N.H.: Ayer, 1977); Kenneth K. S. Ch'en, *Buddhism in China: A Historical Survey* (Princeton, N.J.: Princeton University Press, 1964); Hsuan Hua, trans., *Sutra in Forty-Two Sections Spoken by the Buddha* (Talmage, Calif.: Buddhist Text Translation Society, 1994).

Baiyun Guan

The most important Daoist temple in Beijing, Baiyun is also the seat of QUANZHEN Daoism. This means that in addition to being a functioning monastery, it holds the lineage records for any people who become Quanzhen priests.

Baiyun was founded in the 1200s, during the Yuan dynasty (1279–1368). It suffered greatly in the fighting at the end of the Ming dynasty (1368–1644). The temple's fortunes improved when WANG CHANGYUE was asked to take over as abbot around 1650. In the later part of the Qing dynasty (1644–1911) the dowager empress was said to visit the temple by barge and made significant donations to its enlargement.

Today Baiyun is more significant as a community temple than as a monastery. Thus it is busiest during the major holidays such as Chinese New Year. In addition to a hall housing the founders of Quanzhen Daoism (LU DONGBIN, WANG CHONGYANG, and QIU CHUJI), it has another hall with the three pure ones, the major Daoist deities, and a building housing large images of the 60 signs of the Chinese zodiac. Today the temple houses a handful of monastics as well as offices of the Chinese Daoism Association.

Further reading: *The White Cloud Daoist Temple (Baiyan Guan)* (Beijing: Chinese Daoist Association, 1994).

Ba Khin, Sayagi U (1899–1971) *Burmese vipassana meditation master*

U Ba Khin, founder of the INTERNATIONAL MEDITATION CENTRE, was born in Rangoon, Burma (now Yangon, Myanmar). As a young man he obtained a job as a civil servant in the British colonial government. He first encountered meditation in 1937 and responded so forcefully to the experience that he immediately sought out Saya Thetgyi, a VIPASSANA teacher who had a center at Pyawbwegyi, outside Rangoon.

He studied with Saya Thetgyi. Then in 1941 he met Webu Sayadaw, a monk proficient in meditation, who urged U Ba Khin to begin teaching. He did not do this, however, until some 10 years later. Meanwhile he worked at his government job even after Burma gained its independence. Only in the 1960s, four years before his death, did he retire and become a full-time meditation teacher.

Along the way, in 1950, he founded the Vipassana Association, to facilitate his coworkers' learning to meditate, and two years later he opened International Meditation Centre, where he received students from across the country and many foreign lands. He accepted an increasing number of Western students as he was one of the very few *vipassana* teachers who at the time spoke English.

Among his most prominent students was S. N. GOENKA, an Indian who grew up in Burma and after studying with U Ba Khin established the VIPASSANA INTERNATIONAL ACADEMY in India and developed an international following.

Since his death, U Ba Khin's work at the International Meditation Centre has been carried on by Mother Sayamagyi.

Further reading: *The Clock of Vipassana Has Struck: A Tribute to the Life and Legacy of Sayagyi U Ba Khin* (Igatpuri, India: Vipassana Research, 1999); U Ba Khin, *The Essentials of Buddha Dhamma in Meditative Practice* (Kandy, Sri Lanka: Buddhist Publication Society, 1981); Vipassana Research Institute. "Sayagyi U Ba Khin (1899–1971)." Available online. URL: http://www.vri.dhamma.org/general/subk.html. Accessed on June 5, 2005.

Bamiyan   *See* AFGHANISTAN, BUDDHISM IN.

Bangladesh, Buddhism in

There were approximately 625,000 Buddhists living in Bangladesh in 1991, mostly in the south near the MYANMAR border. This area, centered around the city of Chittagong, has traditionally been strongly influenced by the culture of the Arakan (Rakhaing) region of Myanmar. The region was accessible by land from India as far back as the Buddha's era. Arakan was a border region that fell alternately under the sway of Bengal or Burman power, depending on their relative strength.

From the 13th century, with the Muslim suppression of Buddhism in INDIA, Buddhism began a long period of assimilation and decline in Bangladesh. As in India, Buddhism was increasingly assimilated into Hindu, not Muslim, practice. Such Hindu deities as Ganesh and Siva were placed alongside images of BODHISATTVAS and the Buddha. Animals were sacrificed at such community events as Kalibari, a Hindu festival. And a class of Buddhist monks, called Rauli, began to marry and take on similar priestly roles, including setting up families, like those of the Brahman priestly class in Hindu society. Monks in general lost contact with the PRATIMOKSA, the rules of monastic conduct, and Buddhist scriptures in general.

As occurs often in the history of THERAVADA Buddhism, monks from neighboring regions went to the rescue of the community in Bangladesh. A monk from Burma, Saramitra Mahastabir, was invited to Bangladesh in 1856 by a leading monk from the Chittagong region, Radha Charan Mahasthabir. Saramitra returned in 1864 with a contingent of monks, determined to reform the

SANGHA in Bangladesh. He established a headquarters in Pahartali-Mahamuni, north of Chittagong. Ordinations, including the reordination of existing monks, were held at nearby Hancharghona. Today followers of this reform movement within the Bangladeshi sangha are known as the Sangharaj Nikaya or school.

Although most existing monks agreed to follow the reformist agenda, some refused and established a countermovement, known today as the Mahasthabir Nikaya. This group, still active in the Kamalapur monastery in Dhaka, today's capital, argued that the existing sangha was directly descended from original Buddhist practice and did not require reform.

Bunnachar Dharmadari became the second head of the Sangharaj movement in 1877. Dharmadari was a Bengali who had been ordained in Burma and spent 18 years studying abroad. He emphasized the spread of Buddhist learning by establishing Pali *tols* (schools). As a result of such efforts, Pali courses are today offered in public schools and at universities in Dhaka and Chittagong.

Today the Sangharaj and the Mahasthabir continue to be the two main divisions in the Bangladesh sangha, with the Sangharaj the larger of the two. Eventually the Mahasthabir instituted reforms that aligned practice more closely with that of the Sangharaj. Both are Theravada and follow the same VINAYA code. For lay followers, the differences between the two are minor and generally not important. However, monks of the two groups refuse to cooperate with each other in many contexts. Overall, however, monastic practice and learning in Bangladesh are in line with those in other South and Southeast Asian countries.

baojuan

Baojuan, "precious volumes," is a generic term for a type of moral literature produced mainly in the Ming and Qing periods of Chinese history (1368–1644 and 1644–1911, respectively).

Baojuan probably developed as a written form of lectures on Buddhist themes popular during China's medieval period (c. 280–1368). They are invariably composed of alternating sections of prose and short poetry, with the poetry forming the core of the message. They are usually dedicated to particular deities, and indeed an image of a deity often appears at the beginning of the text. Many dedication lists are added to show donors who supported the book's printing. The first *baojuan* texts were discussions of Buddhist teachings or stories. They began to appear around 1500 and were composed by monks. A second type soon appeared, closely associated with the teachings of Chinese sectarian religions. The first of these was written by Luo Qing (1442–1527), founder of one such group, the Wu Wei. And a third type focused on relating the story of the Mother Creator, a major deity popular in the Ming.

A fourth type includes longer stories meant to make a moral point. This type of *baojuan* was prevalent in the 19th century. By that time *baojuan* had become simply a literary category and did not necessarily reflect the thoughts of particular religious groups. These moral injunction–style *baojuan* were sold alongside texts created through FUJI (secret writing) revelation. Both types of literature preached essentially similar content: the need to lead moral lives and act in accord with proper ritual behavior. Nevertheless, many *baojuan* texts, influenced by sectarian religious ideologies, also urged readers to disregard distinctions of wealth and gender, since as spiritual individuals all were equal in the eyes of heaven (TIAN).

Further reading: David K. Jordan and Daniel L. Overmyer, *The Flying Phoenix: Aspects of Chinese Sectarianism in Taiwan* (Princeton, N.J.: Princeton University Press, 1986); Daniel L. Overmyer, "Values in Chinese Sectarian Literature: Ming and Ch'ing *bao-chuan*," in David Johnson, Andrew J. Nathan, and Evelyn S. Rawski, eds., *Popular Culture in Late Imperial China: Diversity and Integration* (Berkeley: University of California Press, 1985).

Baopuzi Neipian

The *Baopuzi Neipian,* "Inner Chapters of the Master Who Embraces Spontaneous Nature," is a major work of DAOIST inner ALCHEMY. First written in 317 C.E. and revised in 330, it is attributed to the southern Chinese master GE HONG (288–343 C.E.). The *Baopuzi* explains meditation as practiced in fourth-century China. The *Baopuzi* is in fact part of the tradition of the *Huangting jing* (Scripture of the Yellow Court), a third-century C.E. work that describes the human body and alchemical processes that give birth to the inner person. The *Baopuzi* gives additional detail about the body's alchemical composition. There are three *dantian,* or "Elixir Fields" (also called CINNABAR Fields), the head, the chest, and the abdomen. These are controlled by the One (*yi*), a divine force inside every person.

Ge Hong, who was as much a Confucian as a Daoist, intended to show how a Confucian sage could follow the Confucian DAO through the pursuit of immortality. The *pu* in the title means "simplicity," or, perhaps more generally, "wholeness." The text has 20 "inner" chapters detailing alchemical formulas and procedures, including lists of 282 types of talismans. The second, "outer" section consists of 50 chapters that discuss more general issues.

Works such as the *Baopuzi* and other texts of SHANGQING DAOISM were important elements in the "inner alchemy" (*neidan*) tradition of Chinese Daoism.

Further reading: Julian F. Pas, *Historical Dictionary of Taoism* (Lanham, Md.: Scarecrow Press, 1998); Fabrizion Pregadio and Lowell Skar, "Inner Alchemy (Neidan)," in Livia Kohn, ed., *Daoism Handbook* (Leiden: Brill, 2000), 464–497.

bardo (antarbhava)

The *bardo* is an intermediate state after an individual's death and before his/her rebirth into another life. The term is Tibetan and is known today primarily as a concept of Tibetan Buddhism. However, the concept was first used in Indian MAHAYANA writing. VASUBANDHU (c. fourth century C.E.), in his great work the Abhidharmakosabasyam, explained the *antarbhava* as a nonmaterial state in which individuals are immaterial and have the "divine eye," supernatural powers of observation, similarly to divine beings called *gandharvas.*

In India TANTRA techniques were later developed to explore the dying process. In Tibet the work *The Six Yogas of Naropa* gives meditation techniques to prepare for the advent of this state. A later work, the Book of the Dead (*bardo thodol,* literally "Liberation through Hearing in the Intermediate State"), attributed to PADMASAMBHAVA (eighth century C.E.), was a guide to navigating the process of transition from living to *bardo* to another lifetime. The Book of the Dead differentiates six different *bardo* states: the *bardos* of birth, dream, meditation, the moment of death, supreme reality, and becoming. People who have not prepared for the transition through meditation can still be helped by readings of the Book of the Dead (in the presence of their corpse) within the transitional period that immediately follows their death. This text is read aloud to the dying and for those recently deceased to remind them that the experiences are mental. NAROPA taught a set of six yogas designed to assist the practitioner to focus on the clear light and thus attain NIRVANA or liberation.

The idea of the *bardo* state was introduced to Westerners largely through an early English translation of the *Bardo thodol* by W. Y. Evans-Wentz. In an obvious reference to the popular Egyptian guide to the afterlife, it was called the TIBETAN BOOK OF THE DEAD (1927). Several new translations and commentaries on the *Bardo thodol* have more recently been released.

The *Bardo thodol* is one of the TERMA texts, that is, texts supposedly written at an earlier date and then left to be discovered and their contents revealed at a later time. Thus, it is ascribed to

Padmasambhava and said to have been transcribed from his oral teachings. Since its rediscovery by one Karma Lingpa in the 14th century, it has become part of the revered literature of the NYINGMA and KAGYU schools of Tibetan Buddhism.

It is to be noted that the term *bardo* is also occasionally used to describe other intermediate states such as those one passes through in moving from waking to sleep, though the primary reference is to the postdeath state.

Further reading: Bryan J. Cuevas, *The Hidden History of the Tibetan Book of the Dead* (London: Oxford University Press, 2003); W. Y. Evans-Wentz, *The Tibetan Book of the Great Liberation; Or the Method of Realizing Nirvana Through Knowing the Mind* (Oxford: Oxford University Press, 1927); Glenn H. Mullin, *Tsongkhapa's Six Yogas of Naropa* (Ithaca, N. Y.: Snow Lion, 1996); Padmasambhava, *Bardo Thödol: The Tibetan Book of the Dead.* Translated by Robert A. Thurman (New York: Bantam, 1993); ———, *The Tibetan Book of the Dead: The Great Liberation through Hearing in the Bardo.* Translated by Francesca Fremantle and Chogyam Trungpa (Boston, Mass.: Shambhala, 2003); Sogyal Rinpoche, *Tibetan Book of Living and Dying* (New York: HarperCollins, 1992).

Beat Zen

Beat Zen was a term coined by the American Buddhist philosopher ALAN WILSON WATTS to describe the form of Buddhism that was popularized in America in the 1950s by several "Beat" writers and poets. The term *Beat* had originated with the 1950s writer Jack Kerouac, who described his generation of alienated youth who were searching for a "beatific" vision, that is, a form of spiritual transcendence.

Watts saw the Beat generation as using Zen Buddhism as a means of dropping out of participation in the post–World War II American society. The revolt does not seek change in society, merely withdrawal from it by seeking reality in subjectivity. Watts criticized the Beats for using Zen to escape from the world (and the dominant Christianity) in which they found themselves, but failing actually to come to terms with Buddhism, its practice and teachings.

Watts called it "Beat Zen" because it was being advocated by some of the leading spokespersons of the Beat subcultures—Jack Kerouac in his *Dharma Bums* and the poets Allen Ginsberg and GARY SNYDER—and found its audience among the people (artists, musicians, and hangers-on) who frequent the beatnik nightspots. Watts then contrasted Beat Zen with "square Zen," which made Zen a process with guidelines for practice and standards for achievement. They analyze the traditional masters and rather than follow their path to the elusive reality of enlightenment, attempt to copy them, having already decided upon the nature of *satori*.

To Watts, both Beat Zen and square Zen miss the point. Allen Ginsberg later became a faculty member of the Jack Kerouac School of Disembodied Poetics at VAJRADHATU's Naropa Institute in Boulder, Colorado.

Further reading: Allen Ginsberg, *Howl and Other Poems* (San Francisco: City Lights Books, 1958); Jack Kerouac, *Dharma Bums* (New York: Viking, 1958); Gary Snyder, *Gary Snyder Reader: Prose, Poetry, and Translations, 1952–1998* (Washington, D.C.: Counterpoint, 1999); Anne Waldman and Marilyn Webb, *Talking Poetics from Naropa Institute: Annals of the Jack Kerouac School of Disembodied Poetics.* 2 vols. (Boulder, Colo.: Shambhala, 1978); Alan Watts, *Beat Zen, Square Zen, and Zen* (San Francisco: City Lights Books, 1959).

Bennett, Allan (Ananda Maitreya) (1872–1923) *early Western Buddhist convert*

Allan Bennett, an early British Buddhist, was born in London and raised a Roman Catholic by his mother, a widow. He was still a child when his mother died, however, and he was adopted by S. L. McGregor Mathers (1854–1918), one of the founders of the Hermetic Order of the Golden

Dawn, a ritual magic group. Bennett attended Hollesly College and after finishing his studies obtained a job as a chemist. By this time, Mathers had initiated him into the Golden Dawn. He had obtained the rather high grade Adeptus Minor by the time he turned 23. As an accomplished magician, he had contact with and became a teacher of Aleister Crowley (1875–1947). He also worked behind the scenes on the book *Liber 7777,* published by Crowley, a volume detailing correspondences used in magical operations.

Bennett seems to have been introduced to Buddhism through reading Sir EDWIN ARNOLD's *The Light of Asia.* At the time he encountered it, he was suffering from asthma, a condition that both made it difficult for him to hold a job and led to his dependence on a spectrum of drugs.

In 1900, Bennett sailed for Ceylon (Sri Lanka), where he studied Pali and yoga, then later with a Hindu teacher, Sri Parananda. While he was in Ceylon, Crowley caught up with him, and he introduced Crowley to the *asanas* (postures) that make up most of hatha yoga teachings.

A short time later Bennett moved on to Burma (MYANMAR), where he pursued his Buddhist studies in earnest and in 1902 became the first British person ordained as a *bhiksu* (monk in the THERAVADA tradition). Upon joining the sangha (community of Buddhists), he assumed the religious name Ananda Maitreya. Again Crowley caught up with Bennett while he was in Burma and cited Bennett as the catalyst for an intense experience he had while in Southeast Asia in 1905.

In 1903, Bennett founded the International Buddhist Society (Buddhasasana Samagama) in Rangoon (Yangon). Four years later he led the first Buddhist mission to England. In preparation for the arrival of Bennett and his Burmese colleagues, several leading British Buddhists formed the Buddhist Society of Great Britain and Ireland (later superseded by the presently existing BUDDHIST SOCIETY), under the presidency of T. W. Rhys Davids (1843–1922). During his time in England, Bennett participated in the founding of the *Bud-*

dhist Review, the first Buddhist journal published in the United Kingdom. In 1908 he returned to Burma. He remained there until 1914, when on the eve of World War I he resigned his monk's life and returned to England. It appears he was planning to move to California, where he hoped the dry climate would assist his health, but was trapped in England for the duration of the war. During this time, he continued efforts to spread Buddhism.

Among the people he met was Paul Brunton (1898–1981), a British journalist and theosophist who would later write several popular books on Eastern religion. Bennett introduced Brunton to Buddhist meditation, and Brunton assisted Bennett with the revival of the *Buddhist Review,* the publication of which had been suspended during the war. Also assisting him with the *Buddhist Review* was the playwright Clifford Bax (1886–1962).

In 1923, Bennett tried again to go on to California. He booked passage on a ship from Liverpool, but when he arrived at the dock, the ship's captain, seeing how ill Bennett was, refused him passage. Bennett died a few days later.

Benzaiten

Benzaiten is the Japanese version of the Indian *deva* (goddess) Sarasvati, the goddess of fortune. Sarasvati probably began as a goddess of the ancient river Sarasvati and later became associated with a range of themes concerning flow and movement: music, poetry, dance, art, and eloquence. Perhaps because of the association with fecundity and flow, Sarasvati also became known as the protector of children. She is mentioned in the Suvarnaprabhasa-sutra (Sutra of Golden Radiance) as a protector deity and the sister of King YAMA, the ruler in hell. She also appears in the LOTUS SUTRA.

As with many imported deities, their imported images merged with indigenous deities after they arrived in Japan. In Sarasvati's case the Indian

Stone image of the popular Japanese deity Ebisu, god of good fortune and protector of children, in a shrine at the Zuisen-ji Zen temple in Kamakura, Japan.

Thereafter Benzaiten is often depicted wrapped around by a white serpent that has the head of an old man—the popular god Hakuja (Ugajin). The white snake is, of course, the dragon. When the two deities are depicted together the composite is known as Uga Benzaiten. Because of the association between Benzaiten and Hakuja, white snakes are considered to be lucky in Japan. Benzaiten is in general closely associated with snakes and water.

In the Kamakura period Japanese artists began to draw nude images of certain gods, including Benzaiten and Jizo. Benzaiten is one of the seven Japanese gods of good fortune; the others are Ebisu, Daikokuten, Bishamon, Hotei, Fukurokuju, and Jurojin. Benzaiten is the sole female figure in the group. Benzaiten shrines are found throughout Japan; her main shrine is on Enoshima in Sagami Bay, south of Tokyo. Because of Benzaiten's clear association with prosperity, today her shrines often focus on money. In the Benzaiten shrine in KAMAKURA the worshipper can clean bills with sacred water and offer these to Benzaiten with the wish that she will bless all efforts to earn money. In this case the traditional deity supports the modern economic system.

deva, who began to appear in Japan around the sixth–eighth century C.E., merged with the indigenous Shinto goddess of rice, Inari. Benzaiten is usually pictured carrying a *biwa*, a Japanese stringed lute. Another form of depiction shows her with eight arms holding such objects as a musical instrument, a bow and arrow, a wheel, a sword, a key, or a jewel.

In one account (the *Enoshima Engi* written in 1047 C.E.) the goddess is said to have gone to the aid of local inhabitants of Koshigoe threatened by a five-headed serpent, in 552 C.E. The dragon was consuming the local children. After Benzaiten, described as the third daughter of the serpent king, Munetsuchi, descends from heaven, she marries the serpent and he ends his evil ways.

Further reading: F. Hadland Davis, *Myths and Legends of Japan* (London: George G. Harrap & Company, 1913); Robert A. Juhl, "The Goddess, the Dragon, and the Island: A Study of the *Enoshima Engi* (*History of Enoshima Temple*): Part 1." Available online. URL: http://www2.gol.com/users/bartraj/goddessindex-1.html. Accessed on February 13, 2006; Mark Schumacher, "Benzaiten, Benten." Shinto and Buddhist Corner. Onmark Productions.com and Above Average Productions. Available online. URL: http://www.onmark-productions.com/html/benzaiten.shtml. Accessed on September 7, 2007.

bhagavat *See* TITLES AND TERMS OF ADDRESS, BUDDHIST.

Bhaisajya-guru Buddha (Medicine-master Buddha, Yaoshifo, Yakushi Nyorai)

This Buddha is a symbol of the healing aspect of the enlightened being. Like AMITABHA he resides in a Pure Land. Baisajya Buddha's image is often found together with that of the historical Buddha and Amitabha in a triad, in which he sits to the left of Sakyamuni BUDDHA. He often holds a fruit, symbol of healing in his right hand. The Bhaisajya Buddha Sutra, which exists today only in Tibetan and Chinese versions, relates how Bhaisajya, then a famous teacher (guru), makes 12 vows, including guiding all beings to the Mahayana path and healing all illnesses. This figure is therefore of interest because he is worshipped as a Buddha but remembered equally for his bodhisattvalike vows which he strives to accomplish before becoming a Buddha.

Further reading: Raoul Birnbaum, *The Healing Buddha* (Boston: Shambhala, 1989).

bhava

Literally "being" or "becoming," in Buddhist theory *bhava* is the 10th link in the chain of reactions that explain the process of codependent arising (PRATITYA-SAMUTPADA). In this specialized sense of becoming, *bhava* refers to becoming while identifying with individuality. In other words, one is aware only of being as an individual entity, acting without connection to the web of other beings and DHARMAS (events) in the universe.

In addition *bhava* can refer to any one of the states of being in the three worlds (TRILOKA) of SAMSARA: *kamabhava* (being in the desire realm), *rupabhava* (being in the realm of desireless form), and *arupabhava* (being in the formless realm). Humans experiencing everyday, commonsense reality exist in the realm of desire.

Further reading: Damien Keown, ed., *bhava*, in *A Dictionary of Buddhism* (Oxford: Oxford University Press, 2003), 31; Edward J. Thomas, *The Life of Buddha as Legend and History* (New Delhi: Munshiram Manoharlal, 1992).

bhavana

Bhavana is a Sanskrit term for "dwelling," and, by extension, it evolved to refer to meditation. The meditator dwells in the state of meditative repose. The contemporary Theravada scholar WALPOLA RAHULA contends that this key term is widely misunderstood. According to him, *bhavana* should indicate a mental culture in which the individual is on a complete path of purifying the self of mental illusions, all disturbances, and impurities. It should not simply be seen as a series of exercises or practices separate from other parts of life. Similarly, the Indian scholar Sikimar Dutt emphasizes the revolutionary impact of the Buddha's message on the ancient Khmer peoples of Cambodia, who were used to living in a world where kings were gods and society was caste-based. According to Dutt, Theravada's emphasis on *bhavana,* which he translates as "becoming," was a call for each person to develop self-knowledge and begin the path of self-cultivation.

Two generations of monks in a temple in Wenzhou, on China's eastern seaboard

In general discussion today *bhavana* refers to Buddhist meditation practices. These are generally categorized into two types: SAMATHA (tranquility, calm) and VIPASSANA (insight).

Further reading: Sukumar Dutt, *Buddhism in East Asia: An Outline of Buddhism in the History and Culture of the Peoples of East Asia* (Bombay, India: Bhatkal Books, 1966); Walpola Rahula, *What the Buddha Taught* (New York: Grove Weidenfeld, 1974).

bhiksu/bhikkhu

A *bhiksu* (in Pali, spelled *bhikkhu*) is one who begs for food, and in Buddhism the term therefore refers to a Buddhist monk. It is used throughout Buddhist literature for a follower of the Buddha who has taken the precepts, vows taken in an initiation ceremony. They are then considered members of the SANGHA, or monastic community. The vows, as spelled out in the PRATIMOKSA, or rules of monastic conduct, are fixed at 217. In the beginning ORDINATION was informal, but as the sangha grew ordination became formalized and strict. All members of the sangha simply had to

Monks dressed in vermilion robes line up at the Magandha temple, outside Mandalay, northern Myanmar (Burma), to receive rice for their midday meal.

repeat the TRISARANA (Three Jewels) formula three times, and promise to follow the 10 vows. Monks later started as *pravrajya* (going forth), progressed to novice (*sramanera*), and once they were at least 20 were given full ordination in the *upasampada* ceremony. They traditionally possess only robes, an alms bowl, a razor, a needle, a staff, and a toothpick. *Bhiksus* were traditionally expected to beg for food and not maintain a fixed place of residence. Settled existence later became more common, in MONASTERIES. Although Buddhist monks were not expected to work or marry, in some locations (China, Japan) they were allowed to work, and in some (Tibet, Japan) to marry.

Further reading: Reginald A. Ray, *Buddhist Saints in India: A Study in Buddhist Values and Orientations* (Oxford: Oxford University Press, 1994).

bhiksuni/bhikkhuni

A *bhiksuni* is a female mendicant, a nun. In legend and the Buddhist canon the first *bhiksuni* was MAHAPRAJAPATI, the Buddha's aunt and stepmother. The regulations for a *bhiksuni* are stricter than for a BHIKSU (male monk). *Bhiksunis* must undergo a two-year probation if they had been previously married for more than 12 years or are less than 20 years old. The version of the PRATIMOKSA (rules of conduct) that applies to nuns has 100 more rules than the monks'. (The number of precepts for nuns varies slightly in the different Vinaya versions, totaling between 166 and 210.) And there are eight special rules, the GURUDHARMAS, that confirm the nun's secondary status in relation to monks. From the start, then, women were placed in a subsidiary position to men.

The details for *bhiksunis'* ORDINATION and precepts are found in the *bhiksunivibhanga*, part of the Dharmaguptaka Vinaya. The exact process of becoming a *bhiksuni* can be summarized as follows: There are three overall stages. First is going forth, *pravrajya*, followed by the two-year probationary period, in which the novice becomes

Mahayana Buddhist nun

a *siksamana,* and, finally, full ordination (*upasampada*). Going forth involves a ceremony of cutting the hair in which the assembly of nuns (*bhiksunisangha*) is asked to cut the candidate's hair, after which the candidate is also asked questions. The candidate then informs the assembly three times that she is taking refuge in the Buddha, the Dharma, and the Sangha (the Three Jewels) and thus becomes a *sramanera* (novice). She is then given the 10 precepts that will govern all *bhiksuni,* the *dasa siksapadani.* These include, in addition to the five precepts (*pancasila*) common to all Buddhists, proscriptions against wearing flowers, perfume, or jewels; singing, dancing, or making song; using a high or large bed; eating at the improper time (after noon); and keeping gold, silver, or other valuables.

At the age of 18 the *sramaneri* (novice) is allowed to ask the assembly of nuns to be allowed to study the precepts and become a *siksamana,* a probationary nun. This is the intermediate stage between novice and full monk/nun status, a stage that is not required for males. After making the request to the assembly the candidate is led away and a spokesperson asks the assembly on her account whether they will accept the candidate. The accepted *siksamana* must follow the six (sometimes 18) rules. Probably the oldest version of these rules is found in the Pali VINAYA, which lists prohibitions on sexual intercourse, stealing, taking human life, and lying, plus eating after noon and drinking alcohol. Since all of these prohibitions were already mentioned in the *dasa siksapadani* (above), the difference between a *sramaneri* (female) or a *sramanera* (male) novice and a *siksamana* (nun probationate) is, apparently, a formal distinction only and probably simply implies a slightly higher rank. Regardless of status, both *sramaneri* and *siksamana* are expected to follow the rules for *bhiksuni* in general, with a few formal exceptions.

In the final stage of ordination a spokesperson (*upadhayayini*) is also required to speak on the candidate's behalf before the assembly of nuns, the *bhiksunisangha.* In this case the candidate is also present. If the *bhiksunisangha* consents, the candidate, holding her robes and alms bowl, asks the *bhiksunisangha* three times for ordination. There is a public interrogation, and, if it is passed, the ordination ceremony. Two unique instructions are then given. First, the eight *parajayika* (from "disconnect" or "exclude") precepts are explained. These are prohibitions about sexual intercourse, stealing, taking human life, lying about one's (spiritual) achievements, having physical contact involving any area between the armpit and the knee, being with a man alone and doing any of the eight "wrong" things, hiding serious offenses of another *bhiksuni,* and following a *bhiksu* who has been suspended. The second instruction gives the four supports (*nisraya*): the *bhiksuni* should dress in rags, rely only on donated food, not live at the root of a tree, or use medicine made from "putrid" components.

Interestingly, Mahaprajapti, the Buddha's aunt, and her 500 followers completed ordination by accepting only the eight rules (*gurudharmas*). The Buddha confirmed these have the same validity as the longer ordination procedure.

Today nuns are ordained only in Chinese lineages; ordination was broken in the two other older traditions, both from Theravada, making them extinct. Therefore, Theravada nuns today often travel to China or Taiwan to complete ordination in the Chinese lineage.

Further reading: Tessa Bartholemeusz, *Women under the Bo Tree: Buddhist Nuns in Sri Lanka* (Cambridge: Cambridge University Press, 1994); Ann Heirmann, *Rules for Nuns According to the Dharmaguptakavinaya: The Discipline in Four Parts* (Delhi: Motilal Banarsidass, 2002); Friedgard Lottermoser, "Buddhist Nuns in Burma." BuddhaSasas: A Buddhist Page by Binh Anson. Available online. URL: http://www.budsas.org/ebud/ebidx.htm. Accessed on January 14, 2005; Liz Wilson, *Charming Cadavers: Horrific Figurations of the Feminine in Indian Buddhist Hagiographic Literature* (Chicago: University of Chicago Press, 1996).

bhumi

The Sanskrit term *bhumi* literally means "earth, locality, situation, rank, stage." In Mahayana Buddhist teachings there are FIFTY-TWO STAGES, or *bhumis*, in a BODHISATTVA's development toward Buddhahood. After completing the preparatory stages, the cultivator embarks on a voyage of cultivation of the first 10 *bhumis*, or the *dasabhumi*. There are several lists of these 10 stages. The most widely known are the 10 stages common to most Buddhist groups, including those of Mahayana as well as earlier schools. These 10 stages are spelled out in the Mahaprajnaparamita Sastra (Treatise

on the Ferrying Across by Means of the Great Wisdom), a work attributed to NAGARJUNA (but perhaps composed by KUMARAJIVA). They are the stages of dry wisdom (no Buddha truth introduced), embryo, the eight patient endurances, freedom from wrong views, freedom from the first six of the nine delusions in practice, freedom from the remaining three delusions, complete discrimination with regard to wrong views (the ARHAT stage), the *pratyekabuddha* stage, the bodhisattva stage, and Buddhahood.

The Mahayana also offers an additional version of 10 stages; the boddhisattva's 10 stages as given in the Dasabhumika Sutra, the Sutra on the Ten Stages. The 10 are the conditions of being *pramudita* (joyful), "joy at having overcome the former difficulties and now entering on the path to Buddhahood"; *vimala* (immaculate), the stage of perfected moral discipline; *prabhakari* (radiance), involving the cultivation of patience leading to further enlightenment; *arcismati* (blazing), characterized by vigor and flowing wisdom; *sudurjaya* (hard to conquer), where meditation is used to master final difficulties; *abhimukhi* (face to face), achieving wisdom above conceptions of impurity and purity; *durangama* (going far beyond), with skill in means, proceeding beyond ideas of self; *acala* (immovable), attaining calm and unperturbedness; *sadhumati* (good thought), fine wisdom, knowing how to save others, and having the 10 powers; and, finally, *dharmamegha*, achieving the powers of the law cloud, absolute knowledge. The 10 Mahayana stages became associated with the respective 10 PARAMITAS, or perfections.

Further reading: Charles S. Prebish, *Historical Dictionary of Buddhism* (Metuchen, N.J.: Scarecrow Press, 1993).

Bhutan (Druk-Yul), Buddhism in

Druk-Yul (land of the thunder dragon) is a small country sandwiched in between India and China known to most of the world as Bhutan. Most of the people are ethnically Tibetan. As the area emerged out of the prehistorical era, it was a land dominated by the BON RELIGION, an indigenous shamanistic religion that also held sway throughout Tibet. As Buddhism began to infiltrate into the area, Bon incorporated various elements of Buddhist practice, but in the end it lost its primary place to TANTRIC (VAJRAYANA) Buddhism in the form of DRUKPA Kagyu Tibetan Buddhism.

Drukpa, one of a number of subschools of the KAGYU Tibetan tradition, originated with Lingje Repe in the 12th century. Drukpa Kagyu quickly became the majority religion in Bhutan, but Bon retained a substantial following until the 17th century, when the country was united by Lama Ngawang Namgyal, who as the *shabdrung* held both spiritual and secular leadership roles. For over three centuries, the country was led by a lamist theocracy—political leadership by Buddhist clergy. In 1907, the structure led by the *shabdrung* was replaced with a secular monarchy led by Ugen Wangchurch. He established a national nine-member council, two of whom are appointed by the religious leadership. In addition many Buddhist monks are active in the national consultative assembly.

Bhutan maintains its Buddhist establishment, which serves approximately 75 percent of its 1.5 million citizens. However, approximately one-fourth of the residents of Bhutan are of the Butia people, who are traditionally Hindu. The majority of them continue to practice Hinduism with the government's cooperation. The Buddhist-dominated government has instituted laws to prevent other religions from entering and establishing themselves in Bhutan.

Further reading: John Berthold, *Bhutan: Land of the Thunder Dragon* (Somerville, Mass.: Wisdom, 2005).

bi gu

Bi gu, the Daoist idea of not eating any of the five grains (wheat, barley, rice, millet, beans), is an old concept dating at least to the Han period (207 B.C.E.–220 C.E.). The individual who avoided all grains, as well as alcohol and meats, avoided the influence of degeneration associated with the forces of the earth. He or she thus was able to lengthen the life span and become closer to immortality, a key goal of early DAOISM. There have been several cases of seekers after immortality who died as a result of the limited intake of grains and meats. This form of extreme dietary abstinence later mixed with Buddhist ideas about abstaining from meat in order to not take life, as the obligation not to take life is one of the five SILA precepts common to all Buddhists. The two perspectives form the foundation for current ideas of vegetarianism and dietary morality in Chinese thinking.

Another reading of the term *bi gu,* however, is that avoiding grains simply meant avoiding food in general. Daoist practitioners, according to this interpretation of *bi gu,* were focused on achieving immortality, and fasting was seen as a shortcut.

Further reading: Stephen Eskildsen, *Asceticism in Early Taoist Religion* (Albany: State University of New York Press, 1998), 43–44; Livia Kohn, *Daoism and Chinese Culture* (Cambridge, Mass.: Three Pines Press, 2001); ———, ed., *The Taoist Experience* (Albany: State University of New York Press, 1993); Isabelle Robinet, *Taoism: Growth of a Religion.* Translated by Phyllis Brooks (Stanford, Calif.: Stanford University Press, 1997).

bija

Bija, literally "energy" or "seed," refers to the seed energy present in every manifestation of reality. In particular, in TANTRA teachings *bija* refers to a particular MANTRA (sound of power) given by a guru to a follower, which entails the essence of a Tantric deity.

In terms of Buddhist doctrine the teachings of the *bija* make up part of the Mahayana teachings on the ALAYA-VIJNANA, the storehouse consciousness.

In this context the *bija* is a phenomenon deriving from a habit stored in the storehouse consciousness. So on a practical level all individuals have *bijas*, which in turn explain habitual actions and reactions. *Bijas* in this sense are powerful forces that impel action, the engines of karma.

Further reading: Kogen Mizuno, *Essentials of Buddhism: Basic Terminology and Concepts of Buddhist Philosophy and Practice.* Translated by Gaynor Sekimori (1972. Reprint, Tokyo: Kosei, 1996).

Blavatsky, Helena Petrovna (1831–1891)
cofounder of the Theosophical Society

Madam Blavatsky was one of the leading voices of Western esoteric thinking, a synthesis of many traditions including occultism, alchemy, and Rosicrucianism. She was born into a Russian family of the minor gentry in Ekaterinoslav, Russia. During her early life she moved around the world and finally landed in New York in 1873. Along the way she had been attracted to spiritualism. It was in connection with the activities of the Eddy Brothers, popular materialization mediums, that she met HENRY STEEL OLCOTT.

Together with a lawyer, Henry Q. Judge, the pair founded the THEOSOPHICAL SOCIETY, an organization dedicated to investigating occult realities, but plainly set to distance themselves from spiritualism. The society was also dedicated to exploring all religions and the truths to be found therein. In 1878, Olcott and Blavatsky sailed for India, leaving Judge in charge of affairs in the United States.

In India, Olcott became an enthusiastic Buddhist and led Blavatsky to join him in formally converting to the faith in 1880, even though Blavatsky's own approach was much closer to Hinduism. Through the 1880s, Blavatsky allowed Olcott to take the lead in promoting Buddhism in Sri Lanka, while she continued her occult explorations through the Esoteric Section. Olcott saw the society much more as a place to explore a wide range of spiritual alternatives, while Blavatsky saw her particular form of Western Esotericism as the heart of the society's work.

Blavatsky was also largely removed from Olcott's efforts on behalf of Buddhism in 1884 when she was accused of significant fraud by the Society for Psychical Research. Richard Hodgson, a young psychic researcher, had investigated a number of unusual occurrences reported to have occurred around Blavatsky at the society's Madras headquarters and concluded that they had been produced by trickery (similar to that being discovered to underlie many spiritualist phenomena). The Hodgson Report would cast a pall over Blavatsky for the rest of her life. She died in 1891.

In spite of the charges against her, many people were drawn to Blavatsky and her writings. She appointed a very capable young woman, Annie Besant, to take over the Esoteric Section. Besant would also eventually succeed Olcott as president and lead the society in its most expansive era in the decade following World War I. In recent decades there have been attempts by Theosophical scholars to rehabilitate the image of Blavatsky.

Further reading: Helena P. Blavatsky, *H. P. Blavatsky: Collected Writings.* Compiled by Boris de Zirkoff. 15 vols. (Wheaton, Ill.: Theosophical Publishing House, 1950–1995); Michael Gomes, *Dawning of the Theosophical Movement* (Wheaton, Ill.: Theosophical Publishing House, 1987); Marion Meade, *Madame Blavatsky: The Woman behind the Myth* (New York: G. P. Putman's Sons, 1980); Gertrude Marvin Williams, *Priestess of the Occult: Madame Blavatsky* (New York: Alfred A. Knopf, 1946).

Bodhgaya

Bodhgaya is the place in India where Sakyamuni became enlightened. It was originally called Buddhagaya. Emperor ASOKA built a monastery there, which was later visited by such Chinese travelers as FA XIAN and XUAN ZANG. By the 1800s,

Bodhgaya was under Hindu ownership. In the 1890s, ANGARIKA DHARMAPALA (1864–1933), a Sri Lankan Buddhist, founded the MAHABODHI SOCIETY for the purpose of raising money to buy back the Bodhgaya and return it to Buddhist control. That campaign had a partial victory in 1949, when a temple management committee took control of the site. It is still the case that a majority of the committee and its chairperson must be Hindus, but Buddhists participate. In 2002, the temple at Bodhgaya was named a World Heritage Site by the United Nations Educational, Scientific, and Cultural Organization (UNESCO).

See also BODHI TREE.

Further reading: Abdul Quddoos Ansari, *Archaeological Remains of Bodhgaya* (Delhi: Ramanand Vidya Bhavan, 1990); Norbert C. Brockman, *Encyclopedia of Sacred Places* (Santa Barbara, Calif.: ABC-Clio, 1997).

bodhi

Bodhi, or enlightenment, is a concept found throughout Buddhism and used in different ways by different schools. All understand *bodhi* as wisdom or understanding achieved through progress on the Buddhist path of CULTIVATION. Early Buddhist schools, such as THERAVADA, understand *bodhi* to mean awakening, the realization of the FOUR NOBLE TRUTHS. This process is split into three stages: the enlightenment of a disciple (SRAVAKA), that of an individual cultivator (a PRATYEKABUDDHA), and the enlightenment of a Buddha.

In Mahayana *bodhi* refers to understanding of the unity of SAMSARA (the world of rebirth) and NIRVANA (extinction), in other words, the realization of SUNYATA (emptiness). Early Mahayana delineated four types of enlightenment: setting the mind toward enlightenment, continuation of practice, no backsliding, and becoming a BODHISATTVA.

Further reading: Kogen Mizuno, *Essentials of Buddhism: Basic Terminology and Concepts of Buddhist Philosophy and Practice.* Translated by Gaynor Sekimori (1972. Reprint, Tokyo: Kosei, 1996).

Bodhi, Bhikkhu (Jeffrey Block)
(1944–) *American-born Buddhist monk*

Jeffrey Block was born into a Jewish family in Brooklyn, New York. He attended Brooklyn College (B.A., 1966), and later completed his Ph.D. in philosophy at Claremont Graduate School in 1972. He eventually took full vows of monkhood in Sri Lanka in 1973 with the monk Balangoda Ananda Maitreya. He was a confidant of the well-known teacher NYANAPONIKA, the president of the BUDDHIST PUBLICATION SOCIETY. Bhikkhu Bodhi returned for a period to the United States in 1977 but by 1984 was back in Sri Lanka, where he became the editor for English-language publications for the Buddhist Publication Society based in Kandy. In 1988 he succeeded Nyanaponika as the society's president. Over the years, he translated numerous works from the PALI canon of Buddhism into English.

Further reading: Venerable Kantasilo, "An Interview with Bhikkhu Bodhi," conducted June 20, 2001. BuddhaSasana: A Buddhist Page by Binh Anson. Available online. URL: http://www.Budsas.org/ebud/ebdha211. htm. Accessed on May 16, 2005.

bodhicitta

Bodhicitta (enlightened mind) is a philosophical concept in Mahayana Buddhism. The enlightened mind is one that holds a vision of the true nature of reality, or in Buddhist terms, SUNYATA, "emptiness." In Tibetan Buddhism one aim is to arouse the *bodhicitta*, which is interpreted as absolute commitment to the enlightenment of all beings.

Further reading: Gampopa, *The Jewel Ornament of Liberation: The Wish-Fulfilling Gem of the Noble Teachings.* Translated by Khenpo Konchog Gyaltsen Rinpoche and edited by Ani K. Trinlay Chödron (Ithaca, N.Y.: Snow Lion, 1998); Khunu Rinpoche, *Vast as the Heavens, Deep as the Sea: Verse in Praise of Bodhicitta* (Somerville, Mass.: Wisdom, 2003); Santideva, *The Bodhicarya-vatara.* Translated by Kate Crosby and Andrew Skilton (Oxford: Oxford University Press, 1995).

Bodhi Citta Buddhist Centre   *See* KHANTIPALO, PHRA.

Bodhidharma (Da Mo, Daruma Daishi)
(c. 470–c. 534) *first Zen patriarch and source of multiple legends*
We know little more than the basic facts about the man revered as the first patriarch of CHAN BUDDHISM, Bodhidharma (Da Mo in Chinese or Daruma Daishi in Japanese), about whom numerous legends have grown. He is said to have been the third son of an Indian king in southern India. He would spend much of his life as a wandering monk, mainly in northern China. He seems to have spent time (515–526) at the Yong Ming monastery in Luoyang, soon to become the Chinese capital, at some point prior to 534.

Bodhidharma's life is filled in with numerous stories of questionable historic value. Upon his arrival in China, for example, the emperor Wu Di, a Buddhist himself, met with Bodhidharma at Nanjing, but the latter was unable to convince the emperor of the value of the many temples he was having built. During his wanderings he found his way to the Song Mountain range, where the Shaolin Temple was located. Here he observed the poor physical condition of the Shaolin monks. To help them, he created a program of physical techniques that strengthened their bodies and allowed them to withstand the rigors of their isolated existence and the demands of a concentrated meditation program. In this version, these techniques evolved into what is today called Kung Fu (*gongfu*), the mother of all MARTIAL ARTS.

At some point, Bodhidharma practiced meditation long enough to attain ENLIGHTENMENT and to be able to pass along the "seal of enlightenment" (*INKASHOMEI*) to others who had a similar realization of the truth. This possibly occurred at Shaolin or later, when he was at Luoyang, the capital. One story has him meditating for nine years, so long that his legs atrophied from disuse. This legend is the source of the so-called *daruma* dolls in Japan—dolls that always move back to an erect sitting position when tipped over.

Bodhidharma is said to have passed his lineage to HUI KE (c. 487–c. 593), another vaguely known master who is cited as the second Chan patriarch. Much contemporary scholarship considers the later Zen master SHEN HUI (684–758 C.E.) the person who created the basic legend of Bodhidharma as the first patriarch of a Chinese lineage.

Further reading: Jeffrey Broughton, *The Bodhidharma Anthology* (Berkeley: University of California Press, 1999); Heinrich Dumoulin, *Zen Buddhism: A History.* Vol. 1; *India and China* (New York: Macmillan, 1988); *The Zen Teachings of Bodhidharma.* Translated by Red Pine (New York: North Point Press, 1987).

Bodhi Manda Zen Center   *See* SASAKI ROSHI, KYOZAN JOSHU.

Bodhiraksa (1934–   ) *founder of the Santi Asoka, a large contemporary Thai Buddhist movement*
Bodhiraksa, originally a Thai television entertainer and songwriter, was ordained as a monk in 1970 and founded the SANTI ASOKA temple and Buddhist movement five years later. He subsequently assumed an ever-increasing role of moral critic and guide in Thai society. In 1989 the leader and many of his monks and nuns were elected to the government and accused of "pretending" to be Buddhists. Educational activities have been limited since then. The group had 92 monks and 23 nuns in 1995.

Further reading: Donald K. Swearer, *The Buddhist World of Southeast Asia* (Albany: State University of New York Press, 1995).

Bodhiruci (c. 508) *early translator of Buddhist texts into Chinese*

Bodhiruci, a native of northern India who translated a number of Sanskrit texts into Chinese, settled at the old Chinese capital of Luoyang in 508. He would remain there the rest of his life, during which he would translate some 39 texts including the Lankavatara Sutra, The Treatise on the LOTUS SUTRA, and the DIAMOND SUTRA.

He had a major role in the development of PURE LAND BUDDHISM as the translator of the *Treatise on the Pure Land,* a copy of which he presented to TAN-LUAN, the major exponent of Pure Land doctrine in China in the sixth century. At the same time, Bodhiruci became the founder of the Di Lun school of Chinese Buddhism through his translation of the *Treatise on the Ten Stages Sutra,* a volume on BODHISATTVAS and the stages leading to enlightenment. He is also credited with initiating belief in the bodhisattva MANJUSRI, who became popular during the Tang dynasty.

A second translator of the same name (sometimes spelled Bodhiruchi) (652–710 C.E.) was active during the Tang dynasty (618–907 C.E.). This Bodhirucci translated the Maharatnakuta Sutra.

Further reading: Kogen Mizuno, *Buddhist Sutras: Origin, Development, Transmission* (Tokyo: Kosei, 1995).

bodhisattva (bodhisatta)

A bodhisattva is an advanced individual who chooses not to attain NIRVANA and instead remain in the world of SAMSARA in order to help others attain enlightenment. The bodhisattva ideal is a key element in Mahayana thought. The early Mahayanists desired to distinguish themselves from other Buddhist groups who placed emphasis on ARHATS, or fully enlightened persons. In Mahayana thought the *arhat,* although accomplished in self-cultivation, was lacking in compassion (KARUNA). The bodhisattva, in contrast, while able to attain final release through nirvana, chooses to delay this until all sentient beings are free of sufferings. The concept was a powerful image in many cultures. In China the self-sacrificing bodhisattva was in many ways diametrically opposite to many of the Confucian ideals of the cultivated scholar or the Daoist recluse. Here was an individual willing to sacrifice all selfish impulses for the sake of others. The most well-known bodhisattvas are found in Mahayana traditions, such figures as MAITREYA, MANJUSRI, AVALOKITESVARA (GUAN YIN), and KSITIGHARBA (JIZO).

The term *bodhisattva* appears in early, pre-Mahayana scriptures as well as in the Mahayana. In Pali the term is spelled *bodhisatta* and refers to a being "destined for enlightenment." This most often meant the Buddha himself, since technically he remained a bodhisattva until his final attainment of nirvana. Another bodhisattva figure still found in Theravada Buddhism is Maitreya, the bodhisattva who remains in Tusita heaven and is destined to become the Buddha of the future. A bodhisattva's conception is one cause of earthquakes, according to the Buddha's explanation to Ananda near the end of his life.

The doctrine of the bodhisattva is clearly key to understanding Mahayana. Although the term existed in early literature, as we have seen, it referred to one whose vow to become a Buddha is focused on his own cultivation path. In the Mahayana the scope of bodhisattva identity was expanded, in two directions. First, it became a term applicable to any person who has the determination to embark on the bodhisattva path. Today *bodhisattva* is often used in some Chinese Buddhist groups to refer to all believers in general. The second innovation in the concept of bodhisattva was to make it apply to the development of Bodhi in all sentient beings, and not simply to one's own enlightenment.

Further reading: Geshe Kelsang Gyatso, *The Bodhisattva Vow: A Practical Guide to Helping Others* (Conishead Priory, Cumbria, U.K.: Tharpa, 1995); A. G. S. Kariyawasam, *The Bodhisattva Concept.* Bodhi Leaves Publication No. 157 (Kandy, Sri Lanka: Buddhist Publication Society, 2002). Available online at BuddhaSasana: A Buddhist Page by Binh Anson. URL: http://www.budsas.org/ebud/ebdha238.htm. Accessed on September 7, 2007; Reginald A. Ray, *Buddhist Saints in India: A Study in Buddhist Values and Orientations* (Oxford: Oxford University Press, 1994); Edward J. Thomas, *The Life of Buddha as Legend and History* (New Delhi: Munshiram Manoharlal, 1992), 1, 29, 147, 223–224.

Bodhi tree

The Bodhi tree, a large fig (pipal) tree located in BODHGAYA, India, is honored by Buddhists as the originating location of their faith. As the story goes, Gautama BUDDHA, the Buddhism founder, had been engaged in various austerities in his search for enlightenment. After several years of such exercises, he realized their futility and changed his focus. He sat under a tree vowing not to rise until he attained his goal. Here he engaged in various mental disciplines, often pictured as battles with the lord of illusion (MARA), and subdued his mind. He followed his enlightenment with seven days of sitting meditation, seven days of walking meditation, and then seven more days under the tree. In 623 B.C.E., Gautama emerged from this period as the Buddha, the Enlightened One, ready to deliver his teachings to his close disciples.

Over the next centuries, the most famous incident concerning the tree relates to the conversion of King ASOKA (third century B.C.E.) to Buddhism. He subsequently found his way to Bodhgaya to meditate by the tree. As the story goes, his angry wife had the tree cut down. Asoka responded by having the tree stump covered with dirt, over which he poured milk. The tree miraculously revived. He later had a stone wall built around the tree's trunk to protect it.

SANGHAMITTA, Asoka's daughter and a Buddhist nun, took a cutting from a shoot of the tree to Sri Lanka, where the king, Devanampiyatissa, planted it at the Mahavihara monastery in the old capital of Anuradhapura. This tree, it is said, derives from the original tree and is now the oldest continually documented tree in the world.

A century after Asoka, the original Bodhi tree was destroyed by King Puspyamitra (second century B.C.E.), though an offshoot of the tree was planted in its place. Then in 600 C.E., King Sesanka, a zealous Hindu, destroyed the tree again. A new tree was planted in 620 by King Purnavarma. Little was heard of the tree for many centuries after Buddhism's destruction in India in the 12th century. In the 19th century, the British archaeologist Alexander Cunningham visited Bodhgaya on several occasions and documented the destruction of the tree as it was then constituted. Already weakened by rot, in 1876 the last remnant of the tree was destroyed in a storm. Several people had collected the seeds and in 1881, Cunningham planted a new Bodhi tree, which stands today. That tree is the fourth in lineage from the original tree. With the support of the British colonial authorities, Cunningham also began a restoration of Bodhgaya.

Today, a number of Buddhist temples around the world have Bodhi trees growing in or adjacent to them, all of which are believed to be offspring of the one from Sri Lanka.

Further reading: Anagarika Dharmapala, *The Arya Dharma of Sakya Muni, Gautama Buddha; or, The Ethics of Self Discipline* (1917. Reprint, Calcutta: Maha Bodhi Book Agency, 1989); H. S. S. Nissanka, *Maha Bodhi Tree in Anuradhapura, Sri Lanka: The Oldest Historical Tree in the World* (New Delhi: Vikas Publishing House, 1996).

Bon Festival (Obon)

The Bon Festival is a Japanese Buddhist commemoration of the dead that usually occurs over several days in July (traditional Japanese lunar calendar) or August (modern Common Era calendar). During this period, believers welcome the souls of the deceased into their homes and life, and offerings of food to the dead are made at family home altars.

The Bon Festival appears to have been introduced to Japan from China in the seventh century. One story told of its origin concerns the story of a young man who had a vision in which his mother's soul was trapped in the Realm of Hungry Ghosts. He asked Buddha how he could assist his mother and was told to perform some charitable act in his mother's memory. As he performed the act, he saw his mother's soul being released, and he realized her unselfishness in his own upbringing. In his joy at what had occurred, he broke into dance. That young man was the Buddha's major disciple MAUDGALYAYANA, and the same festival in China was of course the Ghost Festival, ULLAMBANA, still popular throughout East Asia.

Two major communal activities occur during the Bon Festival—the bon *odori* (dancing) and the floating of paper lanterns on the water to show the souls their way back to their year-round home. Many people travel back to their ancestral home for the period of the festival.

Today, the Bon Festival in Japan has become rather secularized and is celebrated largely as a time for a family reunion. Interestingly, in the West, Japanese Buddhists have used the festival as a time to introduce themselves to the larger non-Buddhist community. Temples will often offer a weekend of public events that include food, music and drumming, games, crafts, martial arts demonstrations, and tours of the temple.

Further reading: Dianne M. MacMillan, *Japanese Children's Day and the Obon Festival* (Berkeley Heights, N.J.: Enslow, 1997); Ruth Suyenaga, *Obon* (*Multicultural Celebrations*) (Cleveland, Ohio: Modern Curriculum Press, 1993).

Bon religion

Bon refers to the indigenous Tibetan religious tradition; the Bon tradition refers to itself as the Yungdrung Bon. For the tradition, the term *yung-drung* means "eternal," and the term *bon* designates "truth," "teaching," or "reality," a range of meaning similar to those of the term DHARMA (*cho* in Tibetan) in Buddhist literature. A believer in the Bon teachings is referred to as a Bon-po. Bon teachings, while in many ways close to those of the NYINGMA school of Buddhism, nonetheless constitute an independent system. The Bon tradition is particularly famed for its tradition of DZOG-CHEN, "Great Perfection," teachings. The literature of Bon has received very little academic study, so at this point it is not possible to generalize about its contents.

During the 10th century, the Bon tradition arose as an institutionalized, non-Buddhist religious movement. Not coincidentally, Buddhists also at this time begin referring to the Bon as a rival religious tradition. In literature from the 10th century onward, the term *bon* was deployed in an expanded sense. These Buddhist texts portray the Bon community in a hostile light, as opponents of Buddhism who went out of their way to obstruct the religion in Tibet. While these records likely reflect actual antagonism between advocates of the respective traditions, the Buddhist accounts, written centuries after the fact, are clearly overblown and had negative consequences in the religious history of Tibet.

The result was the active suppression of the Bon religious tradition, which was developing around the same time that these records were being composed, from the 10th century onward. The Bon religion, while claiming descent from an ancient tradition that far predates the imperial period, was in fact a "new" tradition developing in interdependence with the Buddhist traditions that were developing alongside it. Heavily influenced by Buddhism, particularly the NYINGMA tradition of Buddhism, the Bon religion developed an institutional structure identical to that of its Buddhist rivals, with monasteries inhabited by monks whose lifestyle was very similar to that of their Buddhist counterparts. While they had their own deities and a unique textual corpus, they also borrowed heavily from Buddhist iconography and textual models. The similarities are so great Bon has sometimes been described not as a distinct religion but as a Buddhist heresy, heretical because its advocates do not acknowledge the founder of Buddhism, SAKYAMUNI Buddha, as their founder. These similarities have also led some advocates of Bon in the West to refer to Bon as a form of Buddhism, although this claim may have been made for marketing purposes.

Despite, or perhaps because of, these similarities, most Tibetans would not accept that Bon is a form of Buddhism. Many Tibetan Buddhists, in part because of the attacks on Bon in their own religious literature, do not view Bon as Buddhist. Many premodern Buddhists have viewed Bon as a force hostile to Buddhism, and this belief has led to numerous Buddhist persecutions of Bon in Tibet. These persecutions have been so successful that the Bon tradition virtually disappeared in central Tibet. The tradition largely survived on the margins of the Tibetan world, in the Himalayan border regions as well as in far eastern Tibet, on the borders of China, in what are now Yunnan, Sichuan, Gansu, and Qinghai provinces. While most Tibetan Buddhists are no longer hostile toward Bon, the idea of difference remains; it is shared by most members of the Bon tradition, who have a strong sense of a distinct history and religious identity.

According to the Bon histories, the Bon tradition was founded by a figure named Tonpa Shenrab, a person of the distant past, who lived 18,000 years ago. He was the ruler of a land to the west of Tibet known as Tazik and was a fully enlightened being. Through his efforts, the Bon religion was disseminated to Zhangzhung, a region that now includes the western portion of Tibet as well as the Ladakh, Kinnaur, and Spiti areas of northwestern India. Bon was the dominant religion in Zhangzhung prior to its conquest by the Tibetan kings, a process that led to its decline as a "false religion" as Buddhism waxed in Tibet with the support of the kings.

Further reading: Samten G. Karmay, *Treasury of Good Sayings: A Tibetan History of Bon* (Delhi: Motilal Banarsidass, 2001); Samten G. Karmay and Yasuhiko Nagano, eds., *New Horizons in Bon Studies* (New Delhi: M. Saujanya, 2004); Anne C. Klein, *Unbounded Wholeness: Dzogchen, Bon, and the Logic of the Nonconceptual* (New York: Oxford University Press, 2006); Per Kvaerne, *The Bon Religion of Tibet: The Iconography of a Living Tradition* (Boston: Shambhala, 2001); David L. Snellgrove, trans., *The Nine Ways of Bon* (Boulder, Colo.: Prajna Press, 1980).

Book of Changes (Yijing, Zhou Yi, I Ching)

This text is an ancient Chinese collection of divination. It is one of the five Chinese classics of the Confucian tradition. It dates at least to early Zhou times in Chinese history (1111–249 B.C.E.). However, it almost certainly reflects divinatory methods used by people in preceding periods as well.

Another title of the *Book of Changes* is *Zhou Yi*, or *Changes of the Zhou.* Unlike the people of the preceding Shang dynasty (1751–1112 B.C.E.), who practiced divination by examining heat cracks on bones, the Zhou people of the Zhou dynasty had a "new" divination method. They used sticks to produce divinatory outcomes. Sticks were put into a container and a number of them were removed. An odd number was unlucky, an even number lucky. Later, the results were marked down as a whole line —— for lucky, and a broken line --- --- for unlucky. These results were then tabulated into possible combinations, leading to the eight trigrams, the *ba gua,* showing all possible combinations if the sticks are drawn three times.

These divinatory patterns later took on philosophical interpretations: 1 came to mean heaven, 8 earth, 3 water, and so on. 1 also came to mean father, 8 mother, 2–4 sons, 5–7 daughters. In all they became a shorthand for discussing various patterns of energy and juxtapositions of relationships. This layer of philosophic interpretation was not written in the *Book of Changes,* however; it represents a later development.

qian	zhen	kan	gen	dui	li	xun	kun

Chart showing the eight trigrams, according to the *Book of Changes (Yijing)*

The eight trigrams can be linked into 64 pairs of trigrams, called hexagrams, offering a wide spectrum of divinatory explanations.

The *Book of Changes* is still widely consulted today. Every combination of six binary (on/off) outcomes is covered in the *Book of Changes*. Therefore, individuals can toss coins six times or use some other method to obtain a hexagram. The important step after that is, of course, to interpret the result. The *Book of Changes* offers suitably cryptic guidance, often requiring meditation to be understood fully.

Further reading: Julian F. Pas, *Historical Dictionary of Taoism* (Lanham, Md.: Scarecrow Press, 1998).

Boowa Nanasampanno, Phra Ajahn Maha (1913–　) *Thai monk and Buddhist teacher*

Phra Ajahn Maha Boowa was born in Udornthani in northeast Thailand. He became a monk as a young man and concentrated on the study of Pali but did not find an answer to his spiritual quest until he met AJAAN MUN (1870–1949), the founder of the THAI FOREST MEDITATION TRADITION. He studied with Mun for seven years, during which he was told to forget his Pali studies and focus on meditation practice.

Boowa stayed with Mun until his teacher's death in 1949; by then he was beginning to gather his own students. Soon afterward he founded Wat (temple) Pa Bahn Tahd near the village where he was born. He is still the abbot of Wat Pa Bahn Tahd and has on several occasions left Thailand for visits to England. He speaks English and has attracted a number of non-Thai students who appreciate the strict manner in which he regulates the monks' lives.

Further reading: Joe Cummins, *The Meditation Temples of Thailand: A Guide* (Bangkok: Wayfarer Books, 1990).

Borobudur

Borobudur is the largest Buddhist site in insular Southeast Asia. Its scale is comparable only to that of the ANGKOR WAT complexes in Cambodia and the temples clustered at Pagan in Burma (Myanmar). Borobudur is a vast structure—it is perhaps too limiting to call it a STUPA—rising from the plains of east Java, Indonesia. On the basis of archaeological evidence and comparison with surrounding sites, it can be dated to the period 870–920 C.E., during the Sailendra dynasty (r. c. eighth–ninth centuries C.E.). It is a totally Buddhist design, in contrast to Hindu monuments built in areas nearby. Yet it is also uniquely Javanese, a blend of Buddhist influence with local creative urges.

The name *Borobudur* is probably a shortened version of *Bhumisambhara*, "merit and knowledge obtained in stages." The stages are replicated when one ascends the various levels. The structure contains 504 Buddhas enclosed in niches and in 72 bell-shaped stand-alone "cages" on the terraces. There are in addition five "directional Buddhas," identified as the Pancha Buddha Dhyani (Five Celestial Buddhas). The Buddha VAIROCANA sits in the center, Aksobhya to the east, Ratnasambhava to the south, AMITABHA to the west, and Amoghasiddhi to the north. There are also three Buddhas in the center, whose identifications are contested; they are probably related to Samantrabhadra-Vajradhara. The structure is in the shape of a stupa on the outside but inside follows a *prasada* archaeological form, a stepped pyramid like that found in other structures such as the Lohapasada at Anuradhapura in SRI LANKA.

Borobudur was first "discovered" by Western culture in 1814, when Sir Thomas Stamford Raffles, then the colonial governor, found out about it and sent an engineer there to investigate. Several famous names in European letters have studied the structure, including Wilhelm von Humboldt, who discussed it in his linguistic study *Uber die Kawi-Sprache,* published in 1936, as well as the scholar Paul Mus, who wrote on Borobudur in 1935.

The monument resembles a miniature Mt. SUMERU. The bottom has five levels, in square shape. The largest base is 479 feet on a side. All the walls are decorated with scenes in bas-relief, showing scenes from the well-known Mahayana text the Gandavyuha Sutra, as well as the *JATAKA TALES* and the Buddha's life. Farther up the structure, on the five terraces, are three round layers, atop which sits a single large stupa. These three elements—the square base layers, the middle round layers, and the top stupa—symbolize the universe with its constituent elements of earth, the land of deities, and the heights of purity, symbolizing *SUNYATA*. This symbolic geography makes the entire structure a giant MANDALA through which the pilgrim crosses.

Although Indonesia is today a majority Muslim state, Borobudur continues to be a major tourist and, increasingly, Buddhist pilgrimage site.

Further reading: Luis O. Gomez and Hiram W. Woodward, Jr., eds., *Barabudur: History and Significance of a Buddhist Monument* (Berkeley, Calif.: Asian Humanities Press, 1981); Donald K. Swearer, *Buddhism and Society in Southeast Asia* (Chambersburg, Pa.: Anima, 1993).

Boudhanath (Boudnath)

The Great Stupa (in Tibetan, Jarung Kashor) at Boudhanath is the largest stupa in Nepal and the greatest center of Tibetan worship outside Tibet. Located five kilometers from Katmandu, the stupa is noteworthy because of its square base. It is 36 meters high and the base measures 100 meters on each side. It is a United Nations Educational, Scientific, and Cultural Organization (UNESCO) World Heritage Site. In addition it continues to be a popular site of worship. Thousands of people can be seen circumambulating (walking around) the stupa all day.

A treasure text concerning the Great Stupa and the Tibetan sage PADMASAMBHAVA was found and rediscovered in the 16th century. The connection between Padmasambhava and the stupa is strong. He prophesied the stupa would deteriorate as a result of the laxity of moral practice and would require a devout hero to rebuild it.

The stupa was built in the fifth century C.E. in the reign of Manadeva. Since the 19th century the stupa has been managed jointly by Bazra (Vajra) and Chini (Chinese) lamas. This arrangement probably reflects competition for power between Tibetan monks and local landowners. When Tibetan refugees flooded into Nepal after the Chinese annexation of Tibet in 1959, many settled in the vicinity of Boudhanath. And since the discovery of Nepal as a travel destination on the "hippie trail" of the 1960s, the area has also become a vibrant center for travelers.

See also SHRINES.

Further reading: "Boudhanath" Khandro (1998–2006). Available online. URL: http://www.khandro.net/stupa_Boudhnath_KD.htm. Accessed on January 25, 2006.

Bu Dai (c. 906 C.E.) *monk whose laughing image became associated with the Buddha Maitreya*

Bu Dai was a historical figure, a monk from eastern China during the Liao dynasty (907–1125 C.E.). During his lifetime he was known as a wondering monk who appeared to do nothing. He is typically depicted as a fat, laughing monk carrying a simple cloth sack; the words *bu dai* (fabric bag) are often written on the bag. He represents the spirit of

CHAN (ZEN) paradox. Many stories surrounded this figure, and they continued to evolve after his death. His image as MAITREYA, the laughing Buddha, is widespread throughout China today and is found in many homes. Indeed the laughing Buddha is probably the single most common form in Buddhist iconography.

Further reading: Bernard Faure, *The Rhetoric of Immediacy: A Cultural Critique of Chan/Zen Buddhism* (Princeton, N.J.: Princeton University Press, 1991).

Buddha (Siddhartha Gautama) (563–483 B.C.E.) *the historical Buddha*

The Buddha was born Siddhartha to a royal family in a tiny kingdom of the Sakyas in what is now northern India, at the base of the Himalayas. In this period there were a multitude of tiny states competing for resources, including population. Trade flourished, and religious practices and doctrines vied for attention.

Even this basic account of the Sakya state is controversial. We know of the Sakyas only through Buddhist sources, and much elaboration has been added over time, including accounts of the descent of the Sakya kings. Sakya princes were exiled from a previous state—in one account identified as the Kingdom of Ayodhya—by an angry king and proceeded to found the state of Sakya. Despite the official account, it is possible the leader of this Sakya state was little more than a regional lord, the head of a tribe.

The Sakya state was centered at the city of Kapilavastu. Various ruins along the Nepal-Indian border have been found but none positively identified as Kapilavastu. In addition, Kapilavastu was not mentioned as a great city, even in the Buddhist canon. As among many similar groups in this period of Indian history the land of the Sakyas was most likely absorbed by the powerful empire of the Magadhas, which flourished during and after the Buddha's period.

FAMILY AND ANCESTRY

The rulers of the Sakya state were from the *ksatriya* (warrior) class of the Gotama clan. The original ancestor was a *rishi* (seer) named Gotama, a member of the *brahman* (priestly) class. (There is no adequate explanation as to why descendents of a *brahman* class would claim the status of *ksatriya*, a lower class. It may indicate that the Vedic system of strict membership in classes was not fully operational in the region of the Sakya tribe.)

Scholars have debated his actual birth dates, with some saying 566, others 563, and some 623. Some Theravadin traditions date him 100 years earlier, and some recent work has put his dates at 484–404 B.C.E. Throughout the 20th century most scholars used the 566–486 dating. This question of his dating is complicated because all records were oral, and legendary material was affixed to narratives about his life from an early period. Regardless of his actual birth date, all traditions agree that Siddhartha Gautama lived for 80 years and that such an individual did actually exist and taught in India.

His father was Suddhodana, king of the Sakyas, and his mother was MAYA. She bore him in the forest at LUMBINI but died in childbirth. Siddhartha was raised by her sister, MAHAPRAJAPATI, whom his father had married. He had no siblings we know of, but he had many cousins, including ANANDA, a major disciple, and DEVADATTA, who betrayed him.

Siddhartha also married, a beautiful woman named YASODARA. She bore him a son, but he interpreted the emotions engendered by the arrival of a son as a further impediment to his ability to practice spiritual discipline, and he left his family when he was 29.

LEGENDARY ASPECTS

Over the centuries a large body of legendary narrative has accrued around the topic of the Buddha's early years and his career as a teacher. Nearly all of what we know is found in the Pali canon,

Stone frieze showing the Buddha's mother, Maya, giving birth to the baby Prince Siddhartha, who emerges from her right side; scene taken from the life of the Buddha, second to third century C.E.; originally from Gandhara, Central Asia, now in the Freer Gallery, Smithsonian Museum, Washington, D.C.

in such texts as the Mahaparinibbana-sutta and the *JATAKA TALES*. Asvaghosa's *Buddhacarita* (Acts of the Buddha), composed in the second century C.E., is an important early biography. As with all legends, there is most likely a core of historical truth around which later generations attached other details and embellishments.

His father, King Suddhodana, took pains to spare his only son from contact with the unpleasant details of life. He was motivated also by the prophecy given by a wandering ascetic, who foretold that the young Siddhartha would become either a great king or a great spiritual leader. His father wanted him to rule as his successor. So while the young prince was given a high-quality education, with tutors for language and martial arts, he was not allowed to leave the royal compound. And his father decreed that all the prince's desires were to be met. He lived a life of refinement and luxury.

Yet Siddhartha yearned to know about the world outside the walls. He finally succeeded in persuading his charioteer, Channa, to take him for trips through the streets. Here he was shocked to see misery and pain. In particular

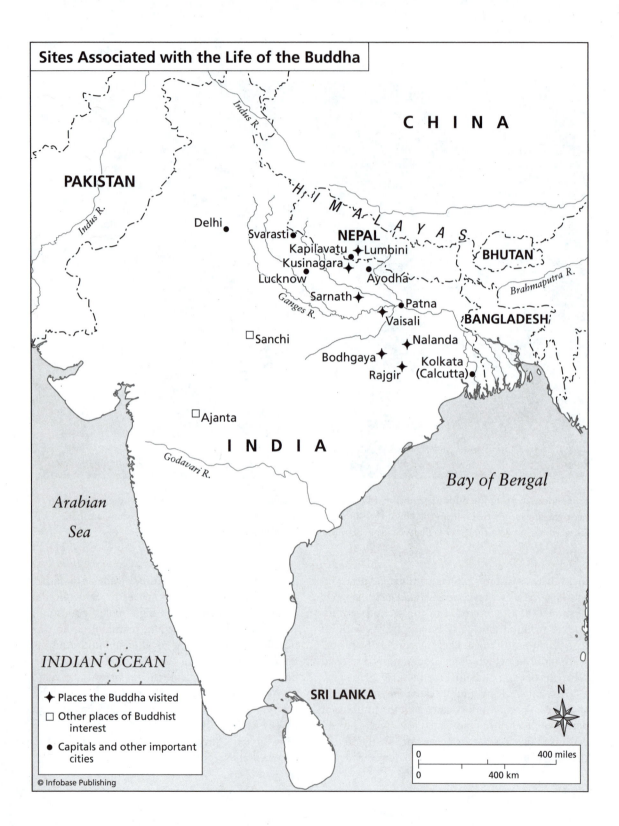

Sites Associated with the Life of the Buddha

CHINA

PAKISTAN

Delhi

Svarasti

NEPAL

Kapilavatu • Lumbini

Kusinagara

Lucknow

Ayodha

BHUTAN

Brahmaputra R.

Indus R.

Indus R.

HIMALAYAS

Sarnath

Patna

Ganges R.

Vaisali

BANGLADESH

Sanchi

Nalanda

Bodhgaya

Rajgir

Kolkata
(Calcutta)

Ajanta

INDIA

Godavari R.

Arabian
Sea

Bay of Bengal

INDIAN OCEAN

SRI LANKA

N

✦ Places the Buddha visited

☐ Other places of Buddhist
   interest

● Capitals and other important
   cities

0   400 miles
0   400 km

© Infobase Publishing

he saw feeble old people, sick people, and some who had died. These images did not match the narrow picture of the world he had constructed through his education. They troubled him so much that he resolved to leave home and seek truth by himself.

On the very night of his son's birth Prince Siddhartha rose and silently bade farewell to his wife, Yasodara, and baby son, RAHULA. He then rode with his horse and charioteer a distance, ordered them to return, and began wondering by himself.

ASCETIC WANDERING

He soon met five wandering ascetics. Such ascetics were typically people who gave up all attachments, physical and social, and in this way attempted to gain spiritual insights and wisdom. The ascetic impulse was a widespread tradition in the Indian subcontinent, as it was throughout the ancient world. Siddhartha decided to join the five ascetics on their quest for spiritual understanding.

During this time Siddhartha underwent ascetic practices such as fasting, extreme physical deprivation in order to overcome the influence of the physical body. But Siddhartha finally concluded this form of practice was simply another extreme that would not lead to true wisdom. He then chose to leave his small group and ponder the way of achieving truth by himself.

Siddhartha settled in a forest grove and began to meditate on his life experiences. After 40 days he achieved what is invariably described as ENLIGHTENMENT, a complete and pervasive shift in understanding of the nature of reality. Siddhartha, the former prince and wondering ascetic, had become the Buddha, the enlightened one.

RELIGIOUS LEADERSHIP

The Buddha's subsequent story involved his 45-year career as a teacher. He collected a band of followers who traveled together with him throughout northern Indian regions. The Buddha

The Buddha preaching his first sermon to the five wandering ascetics, a common theme reproduced in Theravada temples and folklore; from Mt. Popa, central Myanmar (Burma)

saw himself as a teacher, not as the founder of a religious organization or a deity. He stressed each person's obligation to use reason and judgment when evaluating life choices.

After 45 years he sensed his health was deteriorating. Later generations of followers state that he simply passed into NIRVANA, or the state of nonattachment, which knows no time or change. Being enlightened, the Buddha was no longer subject to the cycle of recurring births and death.

The figure of the Buddha is today an object of veneration for most Buddhists. And despite his clear teachings to the contrary, the Buddha has become a deity. Beyond this, however, the Buddha's life itself stands as a powerful model of the correct path. This individual avoided the extremes of careless hedonism and cruel asceticism to find a balanced view of the world and his place in it. He concluded that humans must develop wisdom and compassion in equal measure. And he taught others the results of his quest.

Further reading: E. H. Johnston, trans., *The Buddhacarita, or, Acts of the Buddha.* 3d ed. (Delhi: Motilal

Image of Gautama Buddha, from a temple near Kunming, southwestern China *(Institute for the Study of American Religion, Santa Barbara, California)*

Banarsidass, 1984); Trevor Ling, *The Buddha* (Harmondsworth, U.K.: Penguin, 1973); H. Saddhatissa, *The Life of the Buddha* (London: Unwin, 1976); Edward J. Thomas, *The Life of Buddha as Legend and History* (New Delhi: Munshiram Manoharlal, 1992).

Buddhabhadra (359–429) *translator of Buddhist texts into Chinese*

Born in Kapilavastu, northern India, Buddhabhadra traveled to China in 408 C.E. Settling at Chang'an, the capital city, he assisted KUMARAJIVA (c. 400) in translating scriptures but was later rejected by Kumarajiva's other disciples and left. Heading south—in some versions with 40 followers—he thereafter settled for a while at Mount Lu, where he worked with HUI YUAN (334–416) and taught meditation, and then at Nanjing, where he resumed his translation work. He translated 13 works, including the Dharmatara-dhyana-sutra (Yogacharabhumi-sutra), the Avatamsaka (Flower Garden) Sutra, and, with FA XIAN, the Vinaya and the Mahaparinirvirna Sutra.

Further reading: Kogen Mizuno, *Buddhist Sutras: Origin, Development, Transmission* (Tokyo: Kosei, 1995).

Buddhadasa (1906–1993) *Thai reformer monk*

Buddhadasa, who led a reformist movement opposing the corruption of mainstream Buddhist practice in Thailand, was born in Pum Riang, Chaiya District, Thailand, and as a young man became a BHIKSU. He settled in Bangkok to study. However, he found life in the city corrupting. In 1932 he moved to southern Thailand and founded Suan Mokkhabalarama (Grove of the Power of Liberation) near his hometown.

Suan Mokkhabalarama was one of the few places in all of southern Thailand to offer intensive instruction in and practice of VIPASSANA meditation. Buddhadasa began to attract likeminded Thai monks and, after World War II, many Westerners. His center became a fortress defending traditional Thai Buddhist practice from the "modernization" trends so evident among urban Buddhists. He championed what he termed "pristine Buddhism," which he saw as the original truth discovered by Buddha before the development of commentaries, rituals, clerical structures, and all of the paraphernalia that constitutes modern Buddhism. His view was developed out of his own study of the Pali canon.

He had received little formal education; the success of Buddhadasa's self-education was evident in the respect later shown to him in his mature years. He authored a number of books and is credited as a major force in the 20th-century revival of Buddhism in Thailand. He is seen as a link between traditionalism and modern engaged Buddhism with its emphasis on Buddhist outreach into a spectrum of social concerns from environmentalism to politics. He called upon religious people to unite against the creeping inroads of materialism.

Toward the end of his life he founded the International Dhamma Hermitage, which gave focus to his work with Western disciples and inter-Buddhist and interfaith work.

Buddhadasa died of a stroke in 1993.

Further reading: Buddhadasa, *The Handbook for Mankind.* Translated by Ariyananda Bhikkhu (Roderick S. Bucknell) (Bangkok: Mahachula Buddhist University Press, n.d.); ———, *Me and Mine: Essays.* Edited by Donald K. Swearer (New Delhi: Sri Satguru Publications, 1991); Peter A. Jackson, *Buddhadasa: Theravada Buddhism and Modernist Reform in Thailand* (Chiang Mai, Thailand: Silkworm Books, 2003); Donald S. Lopez, Jr., *Modern Buddhism: Readings for the Unenlightened* (London: Penguin, 2002).

Buddhaghosa (fifth century C.E.) *Buddhist philosopher*

Originally from the Indian subcontinent near BODHGAYA, Buddhaghosa moved to the Mahavihara monastery in Sri Lanka. There he wrote commentaries on the TRIPITAKA, the Buddhist scriptures. In some versions he moved to Sri Lanka in order to translate the great Sinhalese commentaries on the Pali canon from Singhalese into Pali. These are today collectively known as the Atthakathas, "talks about the contents." His first work, *Visuddhimagga* (Way of purity), is an overarching summary of Theravada doctrines. The book, a classic of meditation practice, has spawned a steady flow of commentaries over the centuries. He also wrote the *Atthasalini* and *Sammohavinodani* as commentaries on parts of the Abhidhamma (Sanskrit, ABHIDHARMA) section of the Tripitaka, and several more on the sutta (sutra) portion of the Tripitaka.

Buddha nature (*fo xing, buddhagotra*)

The concept of Buddha nature expresses the assumption that all beings, human or otherwise, possess a pure or original nature, which is the same as that possessed by Buddhas or otherworldly beings. Because of this, all beings have the *potential* to achieve Buddhahood. HINAYANA or THERAVADA teachings do not recognize this original nature of purity. Instead, in Theravada teachings the individual strives to understand the conditions associated with human life—for instance, the influence of the senses and materiality—and achieve a state in which those conditions are overcome. The idea of Buddha nature became important as Mahayana thought developed in northern India. Mahayana thought introduced the idea that one need only become aware of one's pure nature or TATHATA.

Transferred to Chinese Mahayanists, various theorists of the YOGACARA and MADHYAMKIA schools offered different interpretations while agreeing upon the universal presence of the Buddha nature or pure consciousness. Chingying Huiyuan (523–592) considered Buddha nature to be true consciousness, the fruit of Buddhahood (the DHARMAKAYA), and that which is recognized or comprehended by Buddha's consciousness. Buddha nature is thus present in all objects, sentient and nonsentient.

Zhi Zang, a later thinker (549–623) associated with the founding of the MADHYAMIKA school, takes Buddha nature as synonymous with *tathata*, DHARMADHATU (all that exists), *ekayana* (unity), and wisdom. In line with Madhyamika teachings of the Middle Way, Buddha nature is caused by the Middle Way between truth and nontruth.

In the TIAN TAI master ZHI YI's system of five periods, the teachings on Buddha nature are revealed by the Buddha in the third period, when he taught basic Mahayana doctrine. The greatest summation of Buddha nature thought is found in the Buddhagotra-sastra (Treatise on Buddha nature), attributed to VASUBHANDU (fourth–fifth centuries C.E.).

Further reading: Gampopa, *The Jewel Ornament of Liberation: The Wish-Fulfilling Gem of the Noble Teachings.*

Translated by Khenpo Konchog Gyaltsen Rinpoche and edited by Ani K. Trinlay Chödron (Ithaca, N.Y.: Snow Lion, 1998).

Buddharakkhita, Bhikkhu (1922–)
Theravada monk and founder of numerous centers

Buddharakkhita was born in Manipur, India, and studied engineering. He was ordained in 1949 and studied in Sri Lanka and Burma, under MAHASI SAYADAW. He founded the MAHABODHI SOCIETY in Bangalore, India, and numerous other centers, including the Institute of Buddhology and Pali Studies in Mysore, the Artificial Limb Centre in Bangalore, and the International Meditation Centre in Bangalore.

Further reading: buddhist studies: profiles of buddhist figures. "Profiles of Theravada Buddhists." Available online. URL: http://www.buddhanet.net/e-learning/history/theravada.htm. Accessed on May 24, 2005.

Buddha Sasana Nuggaha

This Burmese organization was founded in November 1947 for the purpose of promoting knowledge of Buddhist scriptures and the Dharma or truth of Buddhism. Sir U Thwin was the first president. He donated a five-acre property for the meditation center. U Thwin proposed that MAHASI SAYADAW be in charge of the meditation center. Mahasi moved to the center, called the Sasana Yeiktha, in 1949. Since Sayadaw's death in 1982 the organization has continued to flourish and has sent many missions to the West. It continues as one of the most active Theravada revivalist organizations.

Further reading: The Venerable Mahasi Sayadaw's Discourses & Treatises on Buddhism. "The Buddha Sasana Nuggaha Organization." Available online. URL: http://www.mahasi.org.mm/bsno.html. Accessed on January 14, 2005.

Buddha's Light International Association   *See* FOGUANGSHAN.

buddhas of the past

In traditional texts, six buddhas are said to have preceded SAKYAMUNI's appearance in the world: Vipasyin, Sikhin, Visvabhu, Krakucchanda, Kanakamuni, and Kasyapa. Stories of their lives and careers—and of the seventh, Sakyamuni—are found in the Maha-apadana-suttanta (Sutra of the Story of the Great Ones), part of the Digha-nikaya in the Pali canon.

Later Abhidharma texts added even more predecessors to the Buddha. The Buddhavamsa (Lineage of the Buddhas), in the Khuddaka-nikaya, lists 25 buddhas of the past. The Mahavastu (The Great Account), a work of the MAHASANGHIKA school, lists 4 billion buddhas, each having one of a list of 17 names, and another list of 128 separate buddhas. The Mula-Sarvastivadin school listed buddhas of the past as worshipped by Sakyamuni while he was a BODHISATTVA—that is, still in preparation for becoming the Buddha. In the first period (the *asamkhyeya kalpa*) he worshipped 75,000 separate buddhas. In the second he worshipped 76,000, and in the third he worshipped 77,000. In the final 100 *kalpas* (ages of the universe) before his appearance he worshipped only the six who immediately preceded him.

Further reading: Kogen Mizuno, *Essentials of Buddhism: Basic Terminology and Concepts of Buddhist Philosophy and Practice.* Translated by Gaynor Sekimori (1972. Reprint, Tokyo: Kosei, 1996), 56–57.

buddhavacana

Buddhavacana refers to "the word of the Buddha" and "that which is well spoken." This concept indicates the establishment of a clear oral tradition, and later a written tradition, revolving around the Buddha's teachings and the SANGHA, soon after the PARINIRVANA of the Buddha, in India. The teachings that were meaningful and important for doctrine became known as the *buddhavacana*. There were four acceptable sources of authority, the *caturmahapadesa*, "four great appeals to authority," for claims concerning the Buddha's teachings: words spoken directly by the Buddha; interpretations from the community of elders, the sangha; interpretations from groups of monks who specialized in certain types of doctrinal learning; and interpretations of a single specialist monk. In order to be considered as doctrinally valid statements, any opinion from one of the four sources had to pass three additional tests of validity: does the statement appear in the SUTRAS (1) or the VINAYA (2), and (3) does the statement conform to reality (*dharmata*)? These procedures were probably a means of allowing words not spoken by the Buddha to be deemed as doctrinally valid. *Buddhavacana*, then, is Buddhist truth, broadly defined. *Buddhavacana* became an important label of approval for commentary and statements from various sources. A statement labeled *buddhavacana* was equal to a statement made by the Buddha. Naturally *buddhavacana* included the Sutras, which in all versions and schools were defined as the words of the Buddha. But with the concept of *buddhavacana* nonsutra works could also be considered authoritative. This was convenient for new teachings attempting to gain acceptance. One early example was VASUBHANDHU's commentary (*bhasya*) on the Madhyantavibhaga of MAITREYA, an early Mahayana work. In Vasubhandu's commentary the words of Maitreya are considered *buddhavacana* because they were from Maitreya, an individual of near-Buddha qualities.

Further reading: Paul J. Griffiths, *On Being Buddha: The Classical Doctrine of Buddhahood* (Albany: State University of New York Press, 1994), 33–36, 46–53.

Buddhist Association of the Republic of China (Taiwan)

After the Chinese Revolution, the leadership of the defeated Chinese Nationalist regime and many of their supporters retired to the island of Taiwan. In what was seen as a continuing situation of war with the new People's Republic of China, martial law was declared and a rather authoritarian rule ensued. Religion was somewhat suppressed and, where allowed to exist, heavily regulated. The government encouraged the founding of the Buddhist Association of the Republic of China (BAORC), which was subsequently given the authority to supervise all Buddhist activities in Taiwan.

Among the many tasks adopted by the association was the reestablishment of the trappings of Chinese Buddhism (primarily in its Pure Land form) in Taiwan. That a number of qualified Buddhist clergy immigrated in the massive migration of Chinese to the island in the early 1950s allowed a Buddhist order to be recreated, and in 1953, the first ceremonies for the ordination of Buddhist priests were held.

The BAORC had a virtual monopoly on Taiwanese Buddhism through the 1980s, as until 1987, it was illegal for any other Buddhist institution to be established outside BAORC's authority. However, in the 1960s, at first under BAORC's umbrella and, since 1987, increasingly independently of it, a spectrum of new organizations have appeared and now claim the allegiance of the majority of the the Taiwanese Buddhist community, the most prominent of them FOGUANGSHAN, the BUDDHIST COMPASSION RELIEF TZU CHI ASSOCIATION, DHARMA DRUM MOUNTAIN, the AMITABHA BUDDHIST SOCIETIES, and the TRUE BUDDHA SCHOOL. In addition, the CHAN (ZEN) tradition in Taiwan has been developed by Master Weichueh (Wei Jue), who founded Chung Tai Chan Monastery and Chung Tai Buddhist Institute.

The BAORC remains the largest Buddhist organization in Taiwan, operating as both the nationally established religion and an ecumenical group drawing support from a number of very different Buddhist associations. The BAORC is headquartered in Taipei.

In 2001, the BAORC sponsored the International Conference on Religious Cooperation, a gathering of leaders from some 17 religious traditions from 29 countries. The Ching Hsin, president of the BAROC, chaired the gathering.

Further reading: Charles Brewer Jones, *Buddhism in Taiwan: Religion and the State, 1660–1990* (Honolulu: University of Hawaii Press, 1999).

Buddhist Churches of America

The Buddhist Churches of America (BCA) is an incorporated religious organization affiliated with the JODO SHINSHU Hongwanji. The HONPA HONGWANJI was a sect founded on the teachings of SHINRAN (1173–1262), a Japanese cleric active during the KAMAKURA period (1185–1333). The BCA is headquartered in San Francisco, California.

The Buddhist Churches of America celebrated its centennial in 1999. During the preceding century the teachings of Shinran and his American institutional incarnation had to respond and adapt to the American experience. This adventure began with the arrival of the Reverend Sonoda Shuye and the Reverend Nishijima Kakuryo in San Francisco on September 1, 1899; this date marks the official beginnings of the BCA. Their arrival was prompted by a plea in 1896 to the Honpa Hongwanji sect headquarters in Kyoto to dispatch priests to minister to the growing Japanese immigrant community.

U.S. government census figures noted that the number of Japanese immigrants had grown 10-fold from 2,039 in 1890 to 24,327 in 1900. Since most of the early immigrants were Jodo Shinshu devotees, they naturally appealed to the Honpa Hongwanji for a spiritual presence in new homes. In addition to serving constituents, the Hongwanji viewed its foray into the United States as an opportunity to propagate Shinran's teaching to the English-speaking community.

Uchida Koyu, who arrived in 1905 with his wife, Seto, laid the institutional foundation of the Buddhist Mission of North America, the forerunner of the BCA. During their 18 years, the Reverend and Mrs. Uchida witnessed the establishment of 13 temples and a number of fellowships in the western states of California, Oregon, and Washington. Temples were also built in Salt Lake City and Denver. Recognizing the growing number of temples and administrative complexity, Uchida was officially appointed *socho,* bishop, in 1918.

The sixth *socho,* Masuyama Kenju, arrived in 1930 and quickly surmised that the Buddhist mission would require ministers who could communicate fluently in English. Shortly thereafter he established the Buddhist Society of America to appeal to English speakers, as well as second-generation Japanese Americans. He enlisted the assistance of European-Americans and encouraged the American-born and -educated Tsunoda Noboru and Kumata Masaru, the first Japanese Americans to do so, to undertake ministerial training in Kyoto. The bishop created the Young Buddhist Association, moved to sponsor Boy Scouts groups, encouraged Dharma School expansions, and promoted English publications.

In 1935 Bishop Masuyama visited Thailand, where he received a portion of the corporeal relics of SAKYAMUNI Buddha from King Ananda Mahidol, Rama VIII. These remains of the Buddha were unearthed in the late 19th century in northern India and are now enshrined at the Buddhist Church of San Francisco. Bishop Masuyama left to his successor 48 temples and fellowships that extended from Vancouver, Canada, to the north and New York City to the east.

The outbreak of World War II and the subsequent internment of the Japanese community along the Pacific coast marked an important milestone in the American Pure Land experience. President Roosevelt's 1942 Executive Order 1099, the Civilian Exclusion Orders, legalized the removal of persons of Japanese ancestry from their homes, farms, and businesses. U.S. authorities closed all of the Buddhist temples and arrested most of their clerics and lay leaders, who were sent to various internment camps throughout the United States. Bishop Ryotai Mat-

sukage was sent to the Topaz Relocation Center in Utah and with him went the headquarters of the Buddhist Mission. Government officials allowed Buddhist groups to carry on their religious activities in the camps. In 1944 a general meeting of ministers and lay leaders from the various camps and from other noninterned communities gathered at Topaz to adopt the articles of incorporation that officially changed the name from *Buddhist Mission of North America* to *Buddhist Churches of America.*

Ironically, the internment provided new opportunities. The United States allowed the Japanese to relocate from the strategic Pacific coast states into the interior. Many found their way to such cities as Chicago; Detroit; St. Louis; New York; Philadelphia; and Seabrook, New Jersey, where they established Buddhist fellowships, many of which eventually evolved into full-fledged temples. The arrest and internment of the largely Japanese-speaking leadership thrust the younger American-born English-speaking clerics into leadership positions. After the war, great efforts were made to change temple-related activities from Japanese to English and to nurture a new generation of leaders and devotees. English is now the primary language used in religious services, and meetings are conducted and transcribed in English. In 1954 the BCA established the Buddhist Study Center in Berkeley, California, to provide instruction in English for ministerial aspirants. The center was renamed the Institute of Buddhist Studies (IBS) in 1966.

Between 1959, when Shinsho Hanayama ascended to the bishop's office, and 1980, when Kenryu Tsuji vacated the bishop's post, the BCA transformed itself into a modern American institution. In addition to initiating a number of innovative educational materials and programs, the BCA created a scholarship fund to assist ministerial aspirants, a ministerial Disability Income and Accidental Death Benefits Program, a financial foundation, and other institutional reforms.

In 1969 Kenryu Tsuji became the first Japanese American to assume the post of bishop. Under his watch the Hongwanji accredited the ministerial program at the Institute of Buddhist Studies in Berkeley, California. Ministerial training was now possible in English. Ordination, however, is still done in Kyoto.

As it did for other mainline U.S. religious denominations from the mid-1970s the BCA's vitality began a slow decline, due in part to declining membership, financial difficulties, an aging clergy, and uninspiring leadership. In an attempt to reverse this decline the BCA initiated the Campaign for Buddhism in America in 1982 with the goal of raising $15 million. The campaign was only able to raise approximately $10 million. Once again in 2003 the BCA embarked on a capital campaign to raise $31 million for Buddhist education and ministerial benefits and to secure a permanent facility for its seminary, the IBS in Berkeley.

Since its mid-1970 peak the BCA has had to trim back its administrative staff. The departments of Buddhist Education and Sunday (Dharma) school that produced many innovative programs and publications have been eliminated. The IBS sold its Berkeley facility in 1997 and moved to Mountain View, California. Its substantial collection of Buddhist books are in storage. Unable to sustain the BCA Archives that was begun with a grant from the National Historical Publications and Records Commission, the BCA transferred its archives to the Japanese National Museum in Los Angeles, California, in 1998.

From its headquarters in San Francisco, the BCA oversees 61 temples and five fellowships with approximately 17,000 dues-paying members throughout the contiguous United States, and an annual budget of approximately $1 million.

Administratively, the BCA consists of eight geographical districts, six of which are concentrated on the Pacific coast. This far-flung scattering of temples is governed by a board of directors composed of the bishop, the board president, the Ministerial Association chairperson, district-elected board members, board-members-at-large, and representatives from BCA-affiliated organi-

zations, including the Federation of Buddhist Women's Associations, the Western Adult Buddhist League, Federation of Dharma School Teacher's League, California Young Adult Buddhist League, and Western Young Buddhist League.

The Buddhist Mission of North America (BMNA) and the BCA have been instrumental in a number of historical events. In 1915 the BMNA hosted the World Buddhist Conference in San Francisco. This first international conference of Buddhists in the United States was held in conjunction with the International Exposition. In 1935 Bishop Masuyama traveled to Thailand to receive a portion of the holy relics of Sakyamuni Buddha. Through the efforts of Young Buddhist Associations in Hawaii and the continental United States, BCA lobbied the U.S. Department of Defense to recognize Buddhist as a legitimate religious designation. The Department of Defense now allows the Buddhist (Dharma) Wheel on grave markers.

The American Shin Buddhists within the state of Hawaii have a separate jurisdiction and administration. The Honpa Hongwanji Mission of Hawaii traces its beginnings to 1899. As do those in Hawaii, Shin Buddhists in Canada have a separate organization, headquartered in Richmond, British Columbia. Pure Land Buddhists arrived there in 1905.

Further reading: James C. Dobbins, *Jodo Shinshu, Shin Buddhism in Medieval Japan* (Bloomington and Indianapolis: Indiana University Press, 1989); Kimi Hisatsune, *Introduction to the 100-Year Legacy: Buddhist Churches of America, a Legacy of the First 100 Years* (San Francisco: Buddhist Churches of America, 1998); Ronald Y. Nakasone, *Ethics of Enlightenment: Essays and Sermons in Search of a Buddhist Ethic* (Fremont, Calif.: Dharma Cloud, 1990); Donald R. Tuck, *Buddhist Churches of America, Jodo Shinshu* (Lewiston, N.Y.: Edwin Mellon Press, 1987); Ueda Yoshifumi and Dennis Hirota, *Shinran: An Introduction to His Thought* (Kyoto: Hongwanji International Center, 1989).

Buddhist Compassion Relief Tzu Chi Association (Tzu Chi)

The Buddhist Compassion Relief Tzu Chi Association is the largest religious organization in the Republic of China (Taiwan). It was founded in 1966 by Dharma Master CHENG YEN (1937–) as a charitable organization whose primary goals were to assist the poor and educate the wealthy. It originated in Hualien, one of Taiwan's poorer counties. Those affiliated with the association were motivated to perform charitable work through both the Buddhist concept of compassion for all sentient beings and the belief that such activity earns the doer spiritual merit.

Cheng Yen, a native Taiwanese woman, was jolted onto a spiritual search by the unexpected death of her father in 1960. Her search led her to Buddhism, and in 1961 she decided to become a Buddhist nun. Two years later she placed herself under the spiritual care of the Venerable Master YIN SHUN (1906–2005), whose thought closely aligned with that of Chinese master TAI HSU (1890–1947), who emphasized the importance of lay people and their charitable works. Cheng Yen was formally ordained into the religious life. She established herself in a hut behind Pu Ming Temple, in Hualien, where the first women who wished to share her nun's life assembled. In the evenings Cheng Yen offered them teachings on the sutras.

The catalyst for founding the Buddhist Compassion Relief Tzu Chi Association occurred in 1966. One day while visiting the hospital, Cheng Yen was moved by a pool of blood from a woman too poor to afford treatment for a miscarriage. A short time afterward, she engaged in a dialogue with some Roman Catholic nuns, who pointed out that while Buddhism promoted love for its followers, it had failed to engage in those actions that would embody such teachings, such as building hospitals, schools, and temples in areas dominated by the poor. Cheng Yen accepted the truth of the observation. Thus, in 1966, with the assistance of the few nuns who had joined her, she founded the association.

At the time of its founding, all of Buddhism in Taiwan was under the control of the BUDDHIST ASSOCIATION OF THE REPUBLIC OF CHINA, an organization with close ties to the government, which discouraged the establishment of new competing Buddhist organizations. Thus the Tzu Chi Association was established as a charitable association rather than a temple-forming organization that would compete head to head with other Buddhist temples.

Beginning as a very small group, the association found an immediate appeal among the Taiwanese public, who were overwhelmingly Buddhist by tradition, and by the beginning of the 21st century there were more than 4 million members. At the same time, while it continues to be structured as a charitable organization, it has become a new Buddhist association with Cheng Yen as its primary teacher. Various centers of the association function as centers for the distribution of charitable services and temples where people worship.

Cheng Yen, though a somewhat humble and modest woman, has emerged as a beloved charismatic religious leader. Her followers compare her to Mother Theresa and with her teachings she inspires people to acts of mercy and self-sacrifice. Her life has drawn admiration from both Buddhists and non-Buddhists throughout Taiwan.

The Tzu Chi Association is somewhat unique in Buddhist circles because of the status and role it assigns to WOMEN. It was begun by a small group of Buddhists nuns who were not allowed to ordain men, and almost without conscious intent, women began to assume the leadership posts throughout the association.

Already in the 1970s, the organization began to spread beyond Taiwan as members migrated to other countries, especially the United States. Members in Los Angeles would help create a new thrust in the organization when they organized assistance of victims of a cyclone that struck Bangladesh in 1991. By the beginning of the 21st century, the association had spread to almost every land of the Chinese diaspora, and it is increasingly well known for its charitable activities.

Further reading: Yu-ing Ching, *Master of Love and Mercy: Cheng Yen* (Nevada City, Calif.: Blue Dolphin, 1995); Charles Brewer Jones, *Buddhism in Taiwan: Religion and the State, 1660–1990* (Honolulu: University of Hawaii Press, 1999).

Buddhist Fast Days (*uposadha*)

In ancient India, two days per month were set aside as days of reflection. On those days lay practitioners as well as monks were to review their conduct, their actions as well as speech, and vow to improve. Such an act of reflection was *uposadha*, faults broadly conceived. In ancient India such meetings were held every 14 or 15 days and gave all believers an opportunity to confess their faults.

The practice was continued under Buddhism. The *uposathagara* ceremony served several purposes. Besides allowing the individual to reflect on his or her own behavior, it reinforced the unity of the community; it was in fact a group ceremony that reinforced the relationship between individual and community. The main element of the ritual was the recitation of the PRATIMOKSA, the monastic rules, by a chosen monk. The *uposathagara* was in fact a statutory act required in the Pratimoksa—the entire body of ordained monks were required to be present. As the Buddha mentioned in the VINAYA, attendance at *uposathagara* was a sign of respect for the community.

In later times the *uposadha* signified fasting on six days of the month: the first, eighth, 14th, 15th, 23rd, and 30th. On these occasions the households would adhere to the eight fasting precepts of the monk, instead of to the five main precepts lay practitioners agree to follow. The eight precepts taken by the lay believer on *uposadha* days are as follows: one must abstain from killing; refrain from taking anything from another without permission; distance oneself from action not sacred or upright; refrain from damaging talk; abstain from all alcohol; not sleep in a bed higher than one foot six inches; refrain from decorating the body with perfume or jewelry, or dancing and singing; and abstain from eating at inappropriate times, in other words, after noon.

In China, the practice of refraining from taking meals after noon became known as holding a "fast." The food consumed by the sangha during the day, including the midday meal, later was referred to in Chinese by the preexisting term *zhai*, a religious ceremonial meal. *Zhai* eventually became a term for vegetarian food in general.

In fact, the original, core meaning of *zhai* in its Buddhist context is "cleansing." One cleanses one's actions, speech, and intentions through rituals of contrition and confession. The contemporary association between the term *zhai* and vegetarianism, began later.

In Chinese Buddhist practice today, *zhai* days are meant as days of reflection and purification. In addition the practitioner, whether residing at home as a lay follower or in the sangha, is expected to perform acts of positive moral value. These are enumerated specifically as releasing cows (or any other beings) *uposadha*.

The Agama Sutra, one of the earliest of all Buddhist sutras, lists three fundamental ways of observing *uposadha*. The first is by releasing animals without actually registering the significance of the act: one performs the action but in the heart retains the association with the eating of the animal. The second is the non-Buddhist form of *uposadha* in which the intent is stated to help sentient beings, but the action does not correspond to the intention. The third form of *uposadha* is the proper Buddhist approach: one gives up all association with the offered object and models one's action on the *arhats* (individuals advanced in cultivation practice) of the past. All action is taken for the sake of all sentient beings.

Further reading: Buddhanet. "Buddhist Ceremonies: Festivals and Special Days." Available online. URL: www.buddhanet.net/festival.htm. Accessed on October 9, 2005; George E. Shibata, *The Buddhist Holidays* (San Francisco: Buddhist Churches of America, 1974);

John Snelling, *Buddhist Festivals* (Vero Beach, Fla.: Rourke Publishing Group, 1987); ReligioNet at the Religious Studies Program, University of Wyoming. "Time and Worship." Available online. URL: http://uwacadweb.uwyo.edu/religionet/er/buddhism/BTIME. HTM. Accessed on October 7, 2005.

Buddhist flag

Buddhism in Sri Lanka underwent a revival in the 1870s as Buddhist leaders responded to what they saw as the colonial government's attempts to undermine the faith by support for Christian missionaries. An early victory in the revival was the government's declaration of Vesak Poya Day (WESAK) as a public holiday, beginning in 1885. In response, the Buddhist leadership selected a Colombo Committee to help plan the first celebration, to be held in May 1885. This committee, headed by the Venerable Hikkaduwe Sri Sumangala Thera, began to assemble a Buddhist flag to be used initially on the Full Moon Day of Wesak. HENRY STEEL OLCOTT, the president of the THEOSOPHICAL SOCIETY, who had publicly identified with Buddhism, became involved in the process, making the suggestion that the flag be the same size as the Ceylonese national flag.

The flag, as initially revealed to the public in April 1885, is composed of colored stripes, each color representing a quality of Buddhahood and referencing the aura emanating from the Buddha in his enlightened state. The colors used are blue (compassion), yellow (the Middle Way), red (benefits of the practice of the Buddha's teachings), white (purity), and orange (wisdom). The combination of the colors symbolizes the universality of the Buddha's teachings. The flag was seen as having a variety of virtues but, most important, became a symbol of unity to Buddhists struggling under colonial rule by non-Buddhists. It became a symbol calling Buddhists to maintain strong structures in the face of competition. It has also been seen as continuing the tradition of using flags by Tibetan Buddhists.

The flag took on new significance in 1950 when at the suggestion of the first president of the WORLD FELLOWSHIP OF BUDDHISTS, the organization adopted the flag as an official symbol for Buddhists globally. Since that time, the flag has permeated the Buddhist world. It had particular significance in Vietnam in the 1960s, when it became a symbol of the struggle of the Buddhist community against the presidency of Ngo Dinh Diem, whose government was attempting to make Roman Catholicism the state religion. The issue came to a head on May 8, 1963, when government forces entered a Buddhist gathering in Hue and tore down the Buddhist flags that had been hoisted against government regulations. In response, on June 11, 1963, a Buddhist monk, THICH QUANG DUC, immolated himself on a street in Saigon (now Ho Chi Minh City). This action (followed by several similar actions) highlighted the lack of support for the American-backed Diem regime.

It is to be noted that there is also a Thai Buddhist flag, a red wheel on a yellow background, which is closely associated with the Thai royal family, who are notable Buddhists.

Further reading: Newsfinder: A Literary Favour to World Culture. "The Buddhist Flag." Available online. URL: http://www.newsfinder.org/site/more/the_buddhist_flag/. Accessed on September 9, 2007; Buddhist Information of North America. "Self Immolation." Available online. URL: http://www.buddhistinformation.com/self_immolation.htm. Accessed on November 7, 2005; Upali S. Jayasekera, "Who Designed the Buddhist Flag?" *Lanka Daily News*, May 11, 2002. Available online. URL: http://www.quangduc.com/English/WorldBuddhism/35buddhistflag.html. Accessed on November 9, 2005.

Buddhist Publication Society

Buddhist Publication Society (BPS), one of the major Buddhist publishers of English-language texts, was founded in Sri Lanka in 1958 by two Sri

Lankans, A. S. Karunaratna and Richard Abeyasekera, and the German-born Buddhist monk NYANAPONIKA THERA (1901–94). Based in Theravada Buddhism, the BPS holds to the Pali canon as the most authentic account of the historical Buddha and what he taught. While by no means limited to English-language publications, its two long-standing English periodicals, the *Wheel* and *Bodhi Leaves,* have had a significant impact in making Westerners aware of Buddhism. Each issue of the *Wheel* is a substantial booklet on major topics within Buddhist studies (philosophy, psychology, meditation, social teachings, etc.). *Bodhi Leaves* differs only in being smaller. Both are published triannually. More recently, the BPS has begun publishing full-length texts.

The BPS is headquartered in Kandy, Sri Lanka, and its aggressive publication program reflects a reaction to the history of displacement, which the Sri Lankan Buddhist community experienced during the years of British rule, a reaction begun by ANGARIKA DHARMAPALA in the 1890s. The BPS also operates a large bookstore in Colombo, Sri Lanka's capital.

Nyanaponika Thera served as the editor of the society for more than a quarter of a century (1958–1984) and as president for three decades (1958–1988). He was succeeded by an American, BHIKKHU BODHI (formerly Jeffrey Block), a Pali scholar ordained in Sri Lanka who was an editor at the society from 1984 to 1988 and its president from 1988 to 2000.

Further reading: Bhikkhu Bodhi, *A Comprehensive Manual of Abhidhamma* (Kandy, Sri Lanka: Buddhist Publication Society, 2000).

Buddhist Society (United Kingdom)

The Buddhist Society is the oldest continuously existing Buddhist organization in the United Kingdom. It dates to 1907 and the founding of the Buddhist Society of Great Britain by THOMAS WILLIAM RHYS DAVIDS (1843–1922), E. T. Mills, and J. E. Ellam. The society had a two-pronged program—the dissemination of Buddhist beliefs in the country and the study of Pali, the language in which the oldest Buddhist texts were written. The original work of the society was delayed somewhat by the arrival in England of a Buddhist mission led by ALLAN BENNETT (1872–1923), who had been ordained as a *BHIKSU* (monk) in Burma and founded the International Buddhist Society (IBS) with the goal of evangelizing the West. After the completion of the first phase of the IBS work, the British society picked up its work.

In 1908, the society launched *The Buddhist Review,* the second English-language Buddhist periodical in the West (it was preceded by an American periodical, *The Buddhist Ray,* which had been launched in the 1880s). The society carried on through the years of World War I and experienced postwar revival somewhat countered by the death of three of its leading figures at the beginning of the 1920s. The vacuum created by their loss was filled by Francis Payne, who was already making an impact as a popular advocate of Buddhism. His speaking inspired the founding of what became the Buddhist Centre of the Theosophical Society.

Heading the Buddhist Centre was CHRISTMAS HUMPHREYS, a convert to Buddhism who had found the Theosophists to be people who welcomed his interests and provided a context for his future studies. In June 1924 the Buddhist Centre and the Buddhist Society of Great Britain merged to form the Buddhist Lodge. The lodge remained associated with the Theosophical Society until the end of 1926, when it became independent and has carried on as the Buddhist Lodge, London. Much of its work for the next decade would be in conjunction with the British section of the MAHA BODHI SOCIETY, which grew from the several visits of ANGARIKA DHARMAPALA (1864–1933) to England. The lodge did issue two important publications, a book, *What Is Buddhism?,* and a periodical, *Buddhism in England.* Through the 1930s the lodge nurtured various authors who were writing pioneering books on Buddhism, including ALAN WILSON WATTS (1915–1973), who began his journey to Buddhism at the lodge's headquarters in London.

The lodge's activity was thoroughly disrupted by World War II, but it emerged like a phoenix after the war with a new headquarters and a new name, the Buddhist Society. *Buddhism in Britain* was superseded by *The Middle Way*. Along with the Maha Bodhi Society, it was almost the only place one could find a group of Buddhists, and it opened its doors to believers from the whole perspective of Buddhist thought and practice.

In the years since World War II, the Buddhist scene in England has changed radically. Immigrants from former Buddhists colonies as well as refugees from China and Tibet flooded into the country and created a spectrum of Buddhist ethnic communities. At the same time, British citizens traveled to Asia and found Buddhist teachers. Upon their return, they founded a host of new Buddhist groups. The Buddhist Society now found itself as the oldest Buddhist center in the midst of a rapidly expanding Buddhist community. Through the last half of the 20th century, the society's role began to change. It emerged as a resource center for Buddhists with a large library and easily accessible bookstore. It also became a meeting place for Buddhists who followed the many variant paths available within the Buddhist tradition. One symbol of this changing role has been the Society's periodic publication of the *Buddhist Directory*, a listing of the Buddhist centers in the United Kingdom and Ireland.

The society remains but a single community in London but is recognized as the center of the British Buddhist community.

Further reading: *Buddhist Directory* (London: Buddhist Society, triannual).

Buddhist Society for Compassionate Wisdom

Founded in 1975 as the Zen Lotus Society, the Buddhist Society for Compassionate Wisdom is both a pioneer Buddhist organization in Canada and a pioneering Korean Buddhist organization for North America. The society is the lengthened shadow of the influential Buddhist master Samu Sunim, born Sam-Woo Kim in Korea in 1941. His parents died when he was a child and he grew up an orphan. He entered a SON Buddhist monastery at the age of 17. He completed three years as a novice, was ordained, and then studied under Master Slobong, a highly trained meditation teacher.

Samu Sunin's meditation training was interrupted by his induction into the army, but as he had become a pacifist, he deserted and took refuge in a monastery. In 1966 he fled to Japan and a year later to the United States. He finally settled in Canada in 1968. He became a Canadian citizen in 1972 and took up residence amid the Korean community in Toronto. Delayed somewhat by health problems, he finally founded the Zen Lotus Society in 1975. Affiliated temples were soon opened in Ann Arbor, Michigan (1981), and Mexico City (1983). During its early years, the focus of the society was on the recruitment of monks and their monastic training. The adoption of the present name in 1990 signaled a change of emphasis toward the development of a lay community and a new vision of the society's role in the planting of Buddhism in the West, a movement as important for Buddhism as was the spread of Mahayana Buddhism to China, Korea, and Japan in the first millennium C.E. This latter awareness has undergirded pan-Buddhist and interreligious activities promoted by the society.

To carry out its program, the Buddhist Society for Compassionate Wisdom operates the Maitreya Buddhist Seminary, which offers a three-year curriculum to produce Buddhist teachers, and a shorter Dharma Guardian program aimed at lay leaders, especially urban professionals. The society publishes the quarterly journal *Spring Wind: Buddhist Cultural Forum*. In 1992, a fourth center, in Chicago, Illinois, was opened.

Further reading: Geri Larkin, *First You Shave Your Head* (Berkeley, Calif.: Celestial Arts, 2001); Samu Sunim,

"Turning the Wheel of Dharma in the West: Korean Son Buddhism in North America," in Ho-Youn Kwon, Kwang Chung Kim, and Stephan Warner, eds., *Korean-Americans and Their Religions: Pilgrims and Missionaries from a Different Shore* (University Park: Pennsylvania State University Press, 2001): 227–258.

Bukkyo Dendo Kyokai (BDK)

The Bukkyo Dendo Kyokai (BDK), or Society for the Promotion of Buddhism, one of the most important independent organizations propagating Buddhism internationally, was founded in 1965 by the Reverend Dr. Yehan Numata, a businessman who is also a Shin Buddhist priest. Numata heads Mitutoyo Manufacturing Company, founded in 1934, and the founding of BDK was occasioned by his company's 30th anniversary and its success in the global market.

While building his company, Numata had nurtured a dream to make Buddhist teachings more widely available. He gathered a group of people from a spectrum of Japanese Buddhist groups to engage in a nonsectarian mission to transmit Buddhism around the world. The first project of the society was the publication of a new edition of *The Teachings of the Buddha,* initially published in 1925. It is a basic text on Mahayana Buddhism that had been compiled by a group of Japanese scholars and distributed throughout Japan in the closing years of the Meiji regime. An English edition was released in 1934. Numata had republished the English edition in 1962. The new BDK assembled a group of scholars to prepare a new English-Japanese edition. In the years since, it has been translated into 35 additional languages.

The BDK found in the program of the Gideons, an American group that specializes in placing Bibles in hotel rooms, a means of distributing *The Teaching of Buddha.* Over the last 40 years some 6 million copies have been placed in hotel/motel rooms in more than 50 countries. In the process DBK affiliates have been founded around the world.

BDK has developed an educational emphasis with the founding of a number of Numata Chairs in Buddhism at universities. It also launched the Tripitaka Translation Series, a publication program to issue copies of the Buddhist scriptures. In addition, Numata has established several Shin temples called Ekoji (Temple of the Gift of Light). Several are located in Japan and one each has been opened in the Washington, D.C., metropolitan area; in Dusseldorf, Germany; and in Mexico City. BDK is headquartered in Tokyo.

Further reading: *Buddhist Denominations and Schools in Japan* (Tokyo: Bukkyo Dendo Kyokai [Society for the Promotion of Buddhism], 1984); *The Teaching of the Buddha* (Tokyo: Bukkyo Dendo Kyokai [Society for the Promotion of Buddhism], 2001).

Burma   *See* MYANMAR.

Buton Rinchen Drup (Buston) (1290–1364) *scholar of Tibetan Buddhism*

Buton lived during a time of rapid transformation of Tibetan society. At the time of his birth, Tibet was administered by the SAKYA school under Mongol rule, although during his lifetime Mongol power would collapse, and with it the political power of the Sakyas. In their place there arose an indigenous Tibetan administration under Changchub Gyaltsen, which also led to a rise in power of the Phagmo Dru and DRIGUNG KAGYU schools. Buton was also born several centuries into the second dissemination of Buddhism into Tibet. Buton himself would play a very important role in the development of this process.

Buton was born into a learned and devout family and engaged in religious reading and practice from a young age. He studied with masters associated with the Sakya and Kagyu schools. As a monk, he excelled at scholarship. Over the course of his life he wrote a large number of commentaries on SUTRAS and TANTRAS. He was learned in SANSKRIT and was one of the last Tibetan translators of Indian Buddhist works. He was particularly known for his advocacy of the Kalacakra Tantra as well as the Yoga Tantras. His was a major figure in the systematization of Buddhism in Tibet. His greatest contribution was the compilation of the Tibetan canon, which he organized into two divisions, the Kanjur, or translations of works attributed to the Buddhas, and the Tenjur, translations of works of scholarship by Indian masters. This was an extremely important achievement and marked a major turning point in the development of Tibetan Buddhism. It was also controversial, for Buton excluded from the canon a number of works that were important for the NYINGMA school, because of lack of evidence that they were bona fide translations from Indian languages.

Buton was patronized by the princes of Zhva-lu (Shalu) in the Tsang region of Tibet and with their support built several temples and stupas there. He also gathered numerous disciples, who collectively constituted a distinct school known as the Zhva-lu-pa, which was also known as the Bu-lugs, the "system of Buton." While his school no longer exists as an independent institution, his influence lives on via the powerful impact he made on the study and practice of Tibetan Buddhism.

Further reading: Thubten Jigme Norbu and Colin M. Turnbull, *Tibet: Its History, Religion and People* (Harmondsworth: Penguin, 1983).

buxu

The *buxu* (pacing the void) dance and song sequence is found in many Daoist rituals today.

The earliest instance of this practice of pacing the void dates to a text from the fourth century C.E. In that example heavenly maidens sing a poem that mentions the practice of pacing the void. The void in this case is the cosmos, and "pacing the void" may refer to the practice of ritually marking off the constellations; it may also refer to a form of whistling. All these practices occurred to stabilize the ritual specialist's energy when in contact with the divine. The *buxu* ritual became fixed under the influence of *pradaskina*, the Buddhist ritual of circumambulation. The early LINGBAO Daoist texts contain such *buxu* hymns as the following:

> The Immortal Lads, with solemn expressions, perform the pure hymn while the Jade Maidens advance slowly and turn, with gracefully glowing dance movements.
> *(From Dongyuan lingbao yujing shan buxu jing, cited in Schipper, p. 113)*

This hymn is now used in Daoist *jiao* (audience) ceremonies. Its performance was often accompanied by meditation, along with such instructions as these: "Grind the teeth three times, swallow three times, and then concentrate on the vision of the sun and the moon, in front of one's face." (Schipper, p. 115).

Music, performed today alongside the ritual and mediations, serves to integrate the inner, visualized and outer, visible aspects of the ritual.

Further reading: Kristofer Schipper, *The Taoist Body.* Translated by Karen C. Duval (Berkeley: University of California Press, 1993); Pen-Yeh Tsao and Daniel P. L. Law, eds., *Studies of Taoist Rituals and Music of Today* (Hong Kong: Society for Ethnomusicological Research in Hong Kong, 1989).

C

cakravartin

A *cakravartin* is a wise monarch, one who "turns the wheel" of the world. The concept of the *cakravartin* is found in Indian sources well before the time of the historical BUDDHA. The myth of the *cakravartin* is first seen in the Buddhist canon in the Digha Nikaya, in a section entitled Cakkavatti Sihanada Sutta. The subject of this story is Dalhanemi. He rules over a golden age in which all live lives lasting 80,000 years. Dalhanemi rules through the DHARMA, the Buddhist law. Simply through his presence he maintains the prosperity and peace of his age. The spinning wheel itself is one of the seven jewels of his reign. The wheel appears in the air at the beginning of Dalhanemi's reign and remains suspended over his palace. Eventually the wheel begins to fall and finally sinks into the ground. At this point Dalhanemi retires and passes the crown to his son. Each king in turn must prove himself worthy of the wheel. Eventually one successor is not able to do so. No wheel appears, prosperity suffers, and an age of decline sets in. The king thus is responsible for the degradation of the world.

Later sources gave more detail about the types of *cakravartin*. VASUBANDHU, the great Indian philosopher, gives four categories: those with golden wheels, who were qualified to rule all four continents; those with silver wheels, who could rule three; those with copper wheels, who could rule two continents; and iron-wheeled *cakravartin*, who could rule only over the continent of Jambudvipa, the land in which we humans reside.

The Buddhist tradition gave the concept of the *cakravartin* great emphasis. This is because there was a historical figure who approximated this ideal of an enlightened Buddhist monarch. The great Mauryan king ASOKA was an iron-wheeled *cakravartin* (*ayascakravartin*). Asoka was the embodiment of the *dharmaraja,* the ruler who, as all *cakravartins,* ruled according to the DHARMA.

The idea of a *cakravartin* can be said to provide the foundation for Buddhist thinking on governance, and the relationship of the ruler to the subjects as well as the Buddhist community and the Dharma. Asoka ruled after the Buddha's departure, his PARINIRVANA. Asoka in a sense substituted for the Buddha, acting as the linchpin that orders the world. Asoka also actively supported the Dharma through building 84,000 stupas and many sites of pilgrimage. Asoka created, it has been noted, a MANDALA of the elements of the world that could then be understood by all.

Later rulers in all Buddhist cultures used the image of the enlightened Asoka as an ideal to strive for in their efforts at enlightened rulership.

Further reading: John S. Strong, *The Legend of King Asoka: A Study and Translation of the Asokavadana* (Princeton, N.J.: Princeton University Press, 1983).

Cambodia (Kampuchea), Buddhism in

Since the extreme violence and disruption of civil war in the 1970s, Buddhism is again a major institution in contemporary Cambodia, a reflection of its traditional status. As were neighboring countries of Southeast Asia, Cambodia was influenced by Indian culture from an early date. Mahayana Buddhism as well as Brahmanism were both well established by the fifth century C.E. There are records of a mission sent by the ruler of Fu Nan, an early state in Southeast Asia, to the Chinese emperor in 503. Among the gifts sent were Buddha images.

The Khmer civilization that developed in Cambodia centered on Angkor. A cult practice that associated the Khmer rulers with major Indian deities developed. Some were associated with the Buddha himself. The rulers in turn built monuments to themselves. The area around ANGKOR WAT is dotted with impressive, massive monuments.

These complexes were difficult to maintain, however, and Angkor was abandoned in 1431. From that time Theravada Buddhism became the dominant belief system. Theravada was actually introduced to Khmer civilization late, by means of monks from Burma. The first inscription relating to Theravada dates from 1230. The first Theravadin leader was King Jayavarman Paramesvara (r. 1327?–   ), who changed the language of ritual from Sanskrit to Pali.

Cambodia was a French colony between 1893 and 1975. After a fierce civil war, in 1975 Pol Pot and his forces established a communist regime, which lasted a mere four years but revolutionized society. The Pol Pot regime was antireligion; monks and nuns were forced into lay life, and monasteries were closed. This policy caused a radical shock from which Cambodian Buddhism is only now recovering.

After the Vietnamese invasion in 1979 Buddhism institutions began a gradual revival. With the newly elected government in 1993 Buddhism took central stage in Cambodian life. Prince Norodom Sihanouk, the new titular head of state, supports Buddhist rituals. Politicians today seek the blessings of monks at public gatherings.

Individual monks are now moving to the fore to take leadership of Cambodian Buddhism. For instance, a Cambodian monk living in exile in America, Mahaghosananda, has been involved in social Buddhism since the new regime began.

See also ASSOCIATION OF NUNS AND LAYWOMEN OF CAMBODIA.

Further reading: Chantou Boua, "Genocide of a Religious Group: Pol Pot and Cambodia's Buddhist Monks," in P. Timothy Bushnell et al., *State Organized Terror: The Case of Violent Internal Repression* (Boulder, Colo.: Westview Press, 1991), 227–240; Ian Charles Harris, *Cambodian Buddhism: History and Practice* (Honolulu: University of Hawaii Press, 2004); Khmer Buddhist Research Center, *Buddhism and the Future of Cambodia* (Phnom Penh, Cambodia: Rithisen News, 1986); John Powers, *A Concise Encyclopedia of Buddhism* (Oxford: One World, 2000); Donald K. Swearer, *Buddhism and Society in Southeast Asia* (Chambersburg, Pa.: 1981); ———, *The Buddhist World of Southeast Asia* (Albany: State University of New York Press, 1995); Yang Sam, *Khmer Buddhism and Politics from 1954 to 1984* (Newington, Conn.: Khmer Studies Institute, 1987).

Canada, Buddhism in

At present, there are several hundred Buddhist centers in Canada, which represent the entire spectrum of Buddhist schools in Asia. As the 21st century began, they served an estimated 250,000 adherents. A large but still partial listing of Canadian Buddhist centers may be accessed at http://buddhismcanada.com/.

Buddhism was introduced to the United States by Chinese who responded to news of the California gold rush of 1849–50. Once in California, they flocked to the foothills of the Sierra Nevada, where they attempted to search for gold and where they built the first joss (god) houses. In spite of the often unwelcoming atmosphere, the Chinese remained in California until 1858, when rumors of a new gold strike along the Fraser River in British Columbia led many to move north. Thus Buddhism entered Canada.

While many hoped to make their fortune and return home, the reality was that almost none became wealthy and year after year the migration from China continued. A subsequent gold discovery in the Cariboo region led to the founding of the first Chinese town, Barkerville, which became the home to some 4,000 by 1863. Most of the Chinese were Cantonese-speaking people from Hong Kong and Guangdong.

The migration to Canada was spurred by both hostility to their presence in the United States and the need for cheap labor. Many arrived to work on the transcontinental railway built across Canada in the mid-1880s. After the completion of the railroad, however, the Canadian government began to enact legislation to slow the immigration of further Chinese by periodically increasing the head tax that had to be paid by each immigrant. In the meantime, Japanese, many of them Buddhist, began to immigrate and found some success in the fishing business in Vancouver. Further Japanese immigration was limited by an agreement worked out between the Canadian and Japanese governments in 1909. Early in the 20th century, Japanese Buddhists were organized as part of the Buddhist Churches of America; the first "church" was formed in 1904.

During World War II, many Japanese were rounded up and placed in internment camps. This action totally disrupted the Buddhist churches but also provided the catalyst for the separation of the Canadian congregations as the Buddhist Churches of Canada soon after the war.

The small Chinese and Japanese Buddhist community in Canada grew very slowly until the 1960s, when changes in the immigration law again allowed Asians to migrate to Canada, and Asian immigration began to flow again, especially from Taiwan. Many of the new and old immigrants found a home in Richmond, a suburb of Vancouver, which has become the only city in Canada with a Chinese Canadian majority. A large temple built and maintained by the International Buddhist Society serves as an informal center of the Chinese Buddhist community. The Buddhist Churches of Canada also have their national headquarters in Richmond.

While Vancouver is the primary entrance point for immigrants into Canada, many have fanned out to cities across Canada, as far east as Toronto and Montreal. The several international Buddhist movements from Taiwan—the Amitabha Buddhist Societies, the Buddhist Compassion Relief Tzu Chi Association, Dharma Drum Mountain, Foguangshan, True Buddha school—all have multiples centers in various part of Canada.

As Asian immigration proceeded into the 1970s and 1980s, the rapid growth of Buddhism in Canada developed along three lines. First, as communities of immigrants formed, they attempted to recreate the religious lives of their former homes. Thus, as was true of their neighbor to the south, Canada saw the founding of a spectrum of not only new Chinese and Japanese Buddhist centers, but also Thai, Vietnamese, Laotian, Korean, and Sri Lankan centers. Canada and the United States have become important centers for the regrowth of the leadership of the Cambodian Buddhist community, which was almost completely eradicated by the Khmer Rouge regime.

Second, beginning in the 1950s, numerous Buddhist temple associations were formed in the United States founded both by Asian teachers and by Americans who had received a dharma transmission. The earliest of these were Japanese and a disproportionate number were from one of the Zen traditions. However, they were quickly followed by the whole spectrum of Tibetan schools, a selection of Theravada meditation (VIPASSANA) traditions, and several Korean Buddhist schools. The more successful of these not only spread across the United States, but took advantage of the relatively open border between the countries to establish centers in Canada.

American groups with significant presence in Canada would include Vrajadhatu International, a Tibetan group founded by the late Rinpoche Chogyam Trungpa (1939–87), which in 1985 actually moved its headquarters from the United States to Halifax, Nova Scotia. The Order of Buddhist Contemplatives, a Soto Zen group based in California, has two affiliated centers in Canada. The Insight Meditation Society, based in Barre, Massachusetts, which introduced *vipassana* meditation to North America, has now spread across the continent. The most successful Korean Buddhist group, the Kuan Um School of Zen, also has two centers in Canada.

Third, several Asian teachers moved to Canada and founded groups that have expanded to multiple locations both in the country and internationally. Among the first was Samu Sunim (Sam-Woo Kim) (1941–), who settled in Canada in 1968 and in 1975 founded the Zen Lotus Society, now the Buddhist Society for Compassionate Wisdom. The society first spread to Michigan and Illinois but has more recently developed an extensive program centered on the Toronto headquarters temple. In contrast is Sei'un An Roselyn E. Stone, a Canadian who went to Japan to study Zen in 1977. In 1985, she was authorized as a Zen Master in the SANBO KYODAN Zen Lineage, founded by YASUTANI HAKUUN ROSHI (1885–1973) and passed through Harada Daiun Sogaku Roshi (1940–). Stone now heads the independent Mountain Moon Sangha in Toronto

and its affiliated center in Australia. The ubiquitous SOKA GAKKAI INTERNATIONAL has seven Canadian centers.

Further reading: Frank Korom, ed., *Constructing Tibetan Culture: Contemporary Perspectives* (St. Hyacinthe, Quebec, Canada: World Heritage Press, 1997); Janet McLellan, *Many Petals of the Lotus: Asian Buddhist Communities in Toronto* (Toronto: University of Toronto Press, 1999); Daniel Metraux, *The Lotus and the Maple Leaf: The Soka Gakkai Buddhist Movement in Canada* (Lewiston, N.Y.: University Press of America, 1996); Duncan Ryuken Williams and Christopher S. Queen, eds., *American Buddhism: Methods and Findings in Recent Scholarship* (Richmond, U.K.: Curzon Press, 1999).

cancellation of evil Daoist ritual (*xiaozai jiangfu*)

The cancellation of evil ritual is a type of exorcism practiced today as part of popular Chinese religion. This ritual is performed by Daoist priests of several sects in a public temple or at a private altar. An article of clothing from a person represents the evil or negative influences that "stick" to a person. These influences may be the result of mistakes or transgressions a person has made in the past, or they may be due to birth dates that are not auspicious in a certain time. Whatever the reason, the individual, who is not necessarily present, is able to avoid calamity if this ritual is performed on his or her behalf.

Through ritual action, usually chanting and reading from a Daoist text, the priest transfers the negativity to a paper model, then burns the paper model, and so destroy the influences. A similar ritual can be performed by individual mediums who fall into trance possession states. In such cases the Daoist text may not be used.

Further reading: Pen-Yeh Tsao and Daniel P. L. Law, eds., *Studies of Taoist Rituals and Music of Today* (Hong Kong: Society for Ethnomusicological Research in Hong Kong, 1989), 28–35.

Caodaism

Caodaism is a Vietnamese religion that attempts to merge the principles of Buddhism, Daoism, and Confucianism. Dao Cao Dai (the Great Way), which originated from a merging of themes from Daoism and early 20th-century French spiritism, emerged in the 20th century as the largest indigenous religious movement in Vietnam. In the early 1920s a group of young Vietnamese who had become enthused over the possibilities of spirit contact through the use of mediums approached Ngo Van Chieu (1878–1932), a government official who had been involved with mediumistic phenomena in a Daoist setting. He assisted the group to organize but soon despaired of the direction in which their thought was developing and left. In his place Le Van Trung (d. 1934) and Pham Cong Tac (1890–1959) emerged as future popes. Cao Dai was formally established in a ceremony in 1926.

The new religious group made the séance, in which a medium sits with a number of believers and attempts to contact and relay messages from the spirit world, its central activity, and Dao Cao Dai grew rapidly. Through mediumship, the leaders have received a number of what are considered sacred texts. The mediums have suggested the texts for worship and prayer time. Also, the center shifted from Saigon (now Ho Chi Minh City) to Tay Ninh, where a large community assembled and a cathedral was built.

The Supreme Being is symbolized with a Great Eye (Thien Nhan). It is the center for meditative activity as members focus on the eye and hope to create conditions for internal changes. A variety of figures from different religions are assigned a lesser status in the divine hierarchy but are seen as objects to whom prayers may be addressed—BUDDHA, Confucius, Lao Tzu, Jesus, and the novelist Victor Hugo.

Caodaism was significantly affected by the Vietnam War. After the war it had to deal with a new government hostile to all religion, but especially wary of new religions. While the center in Tay Ninh remains the official international headquarters, most believers are now scattered in countries abroad. Most activity now occurs in the lands of the Vietnamese diaspora. A headquarters for believers outside Vietnam has been established at Redlands, California.

Further reading: Sergei Blagov, *Caodaism: Vietnamese Traditionalism and Its Leap into Modernity* (Huntington, N.Y.: Nova Science, 2001); Cao Dai Giao Hai Ngoai, *An Outline of Caodaism* (Redlands, Calif.: Chan Tam, 1994).

Caodong (Ts'ao Tung) school

Caodong was a major historical branch of CHAN Buddhism. The school's name is simply a combination of the surnames of the founder, Dongshan Lingjie (807–869 C.E.), and his successor, Caoqi Benzhi (840–901). As with all extant schools of Chan (Zen), Caodong ultimately descended from the so-called Southern school founded by HUI NENG (638–713), the sixth Chan patriarch. Dongshan Lingjie was a sixth-generation successor to Hui Neng. His lineage eventually resulted, another eight generations later, in the master DOGEN Zenji (1200–1253). This Japanese monk introduced the Caodong school to Japan, where it is known as SOTO.

It is also sometimes assumed that Caodong was influenced by SHEN XIU's Northern school and its YOGACARA BUDDHISM school leanings, and that is a possibility. The Cadong school is often seen as emphasizing quiet sitting and meditation, as opposed to the more active "sudden" techniques of such rivals as the LINJI CHAN, which included the use of KOANS. However, in fact all the "Five Schools and Seven Sects" of Chan used koans as instruction aids. Although the Soto line has thrived in Japan, Caodong did not last as a separate tradition in China much longer than the Dogen's time. Chan itself merged into the larger tradition of Chinese monastic practice, including PURE LAND and other schools, and did not retain its separate identity as a school.

See also CHAN BUDDHISM; SOTO ZEN.

Further reading: Andy Ferguson, *Zen's Chinese Heritage: The Masters and Their Teachings* (Somerville, Mass.: Wisdom, 2000); John Snelling, *The Buddhist Handbook: A Complete Guide to Buddhist Schools, Teaching, Practice, and History* (Rochester, Vt.: Inner Traditions, 1991).

Carus, Paul (1852–1919) *German-American scholar and early writer on Buddhism*

Though not a Buddhist, the publisher/editor Paul Carus emerged as a major spokesperson for Buddhism in the West in the early 20th century. He was born in Germany, where his father was the first superintendent of the Lutheran Church of Prussia. Carus received a Ph.D. from Tübingen and began a teaching career. He was eventually forced out of his position as a result of his liberal theological views.

In 1884, Carus moved to the United States. He became the editor of *Open Court,* an eclectic journal, and eventually married the owner's daughter. He attended the World Parliament of Religions held in 1893 in Chicago, where he met Anagarika DHARMAPALA and the Zen master Soyen SHAKU. He agreed to head the American chapter of the MAHA BODHI SOCIETY and later arranged Dharmapala's 1896 lecture tour in North America. He also worked with Shaku to host DAISETSU TEITARO SUZUKI, who lived with Carus from 1897 to 1909 and worked on translating a number of Buddhist works.

In 1894 he published his own book, *The Gospel of Buddha According to Old Records.* This work was one of the first interpretations of Buddhism in a Western language and continues to be used today. It has also been translated into a variety of languages.

Through the several decades after the Parliament of Religions, Carus wrote almost 50 books and published a spectrum of titles on Buddhism and other non-Christian religions. Carus also wrote some poems that were turned into hymns for use in the songbook of the BUDDHIST CHURCHES OF AMERICA.

Today the Hegeler Carus Mansion in LaSalle, Illinois, where the press was headquartered, houses a collection of Carus's work and a library. The building, designed by the well-known architect W. W. Boyington, is listed in the National Register of Historic Places. Here Suzuki worked with Carus for 12 years, before returning to his native Japan.

A major award, the Paul Carus Award for Outstanding Contributions to the Interreligious Movement, was announced in 2004, at the Parliament for World Religions meeting in Barcelona.

Further reading: Paul Carus, *The Gospel of Buddha* (Chicago: Open Court, 1915); ———, comp., *The Teachings of Buddha* (New York: St. Martin's Press, 1998); Rick Fields, *How the Swans Came to the Lake: A Narrative History of Buddhism in America* (Boston: Shambhala, 1992); William Peiris, *The Western Contribution to Buddhism* (Delhi: Motilal Banarsidass, 1973).

Caves of the Thousand Buddhas

The Caves of the Thousand Buddhas are located in Dunhuang, a town in northwest China along the ancient Silk Road. Buddhist monks began to settle here in the 360s, after a lone monk experienced a vision of 1,000 golden Buddhas. Over the next centuries, the monks turned the nearly 500 caves into a massive Buddhist shrine. Buddhas, BODHISATTVAS, and various divine figures were carved on the walls throughout the cave system.

Along the main route from Central Asia to China, monks wishing to contribute to the effort of transmitting Buddhism to China often stopped at Dunhuang to learn Chinese. Others traveled to the caves to seek certain benefits. For example, women would go to a famous statue of Guan Yin when trying to become pregnant.

Over the centuries, the caves came to house a large library of Buddhist texts. In more modern times they were largely forgotten as the Silk Road lost much of its importance as a trade route. Then in 1907, the explorer AUREL STEIN set out for Dunhuang to see whether the description of the place by the eighth-century traveler XUAN ZANG could be verified. There he found the large library of ancient texts that had apparently been sealed up in a room in Cave 17. By bribing the abbot of the surviving community of monks, he was able to acquire most of it and take it back to Europe. Among the major items Stein found was the world's oldest printed document, a copy of the DIAMOND SUTRA, dating to the ninth century.

Today, the caves have become a major tourist spot, and, while the site has been pillaged a number of times, a surprising amount of statues, carvings, and illustrations that decorated the caves have survived. A small community of monks continues to maintain the site.

Further reading: Norbert C. Brockman, *Encyclopedia of Sacred Places* (Santa Barbara, Calif.: ABC-Clio, 1997); Linda Kay Davidson and David M. Gitlitz, *Pilgrimage from the Ganges to Graceland: An Encyclopedia* (Santa Barbara, Calif.: ABC-Clio, 2002); Roderick Whitfield et al., *Caves of the Thousand Buddhas: Chinese Art from the Silk Route* (New York: George Braziller, 1990).

Central Asia (The Silk Road)

Over the many centuries of Buddhism's history Central Asia has played a crucial role in its growth and development. Central Asia includes those land-locked states north of the Indian subcontinent, north also of the Tibetan plateau, south of the Siberian landmass, and west of developed East Asia—those places today known as China, Korea, and Japan. For centuries Central Asia was crisscrossed by traders and armies carrying products, customs, and ideas. Their trails are today known as the Silk Road. Buddhism as well as other religions such as Manichaeism and Islam traveled over the well-worn trade routes. For Buddhism, the key period was approximately 100 B.C.E. to 1000 C.E., when many pilgrims and traders moved the Indian concepts and images of Buddhism into and out of the area. Central Asia

was a boiling cauldron as well as repository for Buddhist ideas.

Contact between India and Central Asia began very early. Emperor ASOKA sent missionaries to Bactria in Central Asia during the third century B.C.E. Inscriptions in stone left by Emperor Asoka's empire have been found in Gandhara, in present-day Afghanistan.

The best reflection of Central Asia's role is seen in the vast libraries recovered from Dunhuang, the cave complex at the eastern edge of Central Asia. The 20,000 texts and art pieces recovered there are written in many languages, including Sanskrit, Brahmi, Kharosthi, Tibetan, Turki, Tokharian, Manichean, Syriac, Sogdian, Uighur, and Chinese. Most of the works were written on palm leaves or birch bark, with carvings on wood or bamboo, leather, or, later, paper. In addition to this textual evidence are archaeological sites. There are stupas, temples, and caves still in existence, all decorated with Buddhism figures and frescoes. Luckily for scholars of Buddhism, many sites are well preserved as a result of the generally dry desert terrain. And especially for those areas near China there are many historical accounts of Buddhism's development in Chinese.

THE SILK ROAD

The sources clearly describe two major trade routes that constituted the Silk Road. These developed in the early years of the Common Era and passed north or south of the great Takla-makan desert, which includes the Tarim Basin. Going west from China, the northern passage transited through Hami, Turfa, Karasahr, Kucha, Aksu, Tumshuk, and Kashgar and finally ended at Samarkand. The southern road went through Miran, Cherchen, Keriya, Khotan, and Yarkand before ending at Herat and, finally, Kabul in present-day Afghanistan. The Silk Road passed through many such city-states, which were often established by groups from Kashmir and northern India, who often claimed connections with Indian royal families.

The MONASTERIES that grew up along these trade routes were often connected to the various schools of Buddhism that had developed in northern India and Kashmir. Many of the monasteries on the southern route followed MAHAYANA BUDDHISM, while those on the northern route (Kashgar, Kucha, and Turfan) were connected to HINAYANA or Theravadin teachings.

Of all the states on the Silk Route in this period probably Kucha and Khotan were the most important for Buddhism's history. Many manuscripts are in Kuchan Sanskrit, a form of Sanskrit. And the important scholar Kumarajiva (344–413 C.E.), who was taken to China in 401 C.E. to translate Buddhist texts, was from Kucha.

The northern and southern roads met in China at Yunmen Guan, to the west of Dunhuang. Yunmen is noted for its thousand grottoes or caves with Buddhist-inspired carvings carved between the fifth and eighth centuries C.E. Political developments in India also influenced the spread of Buddhism into Central Asia. The Mauryan prince Kunala is said to have migrated and settled in Khotan after leaving Taxila in northern Afghanistan. Chinese accounts note other Indian "colonies" established throughout the area. These oasis cultures played a key role in the Chinese importation of Buddhism.

INTERACTION WITH CHINA

There were most likely two major waves of importation of Buddhism from Central Asia into China. The first recorded instance was a mission headed by the Central Asian monks KASYAPA-MATANGA and Zhu Fa Lan to China, in 65 C.E. Around the same time the emperor Ming had a dream of a Buddha-like figure who instructed him to invite two Buddhist monks. A monastery, BAIMASI (the White Horse Monastery), was indeed constructed for these two missionaries in the Han capital of Luoyang, where they spent the remainder of their days.

As Buddhism became established in successive states throughout the area, more missionaries had contact with China. Tokharestan, a state north of modern Afghanistan, adopted Buddhism, as did the nearby Parthians. The Parthian prince Lokottama visited China with numerous Buddhist texts. He remained in China at Baimasi in 144. The Kushan monk AN SHIGAO visited the Han Chinese capital of Luoyang in 148 and began a translation center there. And Lokaksema, a Scythian, worked there from 147 to 189.

DHARMARAKSA, from Tokhara, settled in Dunhuang between 284 and 313; there he translated 90 Buddhism works. She Lun, also from Tokhara, arrived in 373, followed by Dharmanandi.

Chinese pilgrims also began to travel to the Central Asian places, and beyond, leaving detailed records. The great northern city of Kashgar was visited by numerous pilgrims. The monks there followed the SARVASTIVADIN school. The great Chinese translator XUAN ZANG (596–664 C.E.) records that the southern kingdom of Khotan had 100 monasteries and 5,000 monks, all following Mahayana. Chinese records from the Jin dynasty (265–316 C.E.) note that Kucha held 1,000 stupas and temples, including nunneries.

MATERIAL CULTURE OF THE SILK ROAD

Other religions flourishing in the Tarim Basin area included Hinduism, Zoroastrianism, Christianity, and Manichaeism, all of which influenced Buddhism's development. However, Buddhism appears to have been the most influential religion during this period, as is reflected in the material culture.

The material culture of the Silk Road was rich and confused. Most inhabitants were nomadic and pastoral. Buddhism, once introduced, became the common thread linking these various small states. Rulers often adopted Indian names and titles, for instance. Slavery was practiced, even in monasteries, and a mild form of caste consciousness appears to have been widespread, limiting intermarriage between different classes. Indian music and dress were also adopted throughout Central Asia.

Economically the societies in Central Asia were agricultural with trade as a sideline. Monks were prosperous and often could marry and own property.

Artistic production, centered on depictions of the Buddha and his lives, flourished. Multiple influences, including Greek, Roman, Persian, and Sassanian, all impacted Central Asian art. The closeness to the trade routes stimulated artistic production, since artists could make a living by selling to the traders. Overall Indian and Persian influences were dominant in the south, and Chinese, Tibetan, and Uighur styles were strong in the north. The earliest artistic influence on Central Asia was from Gandhara, in northeast India, which was a center of Greek-influenced art. The paintings in the caves at Dunhuang show a range of styles, including Indian and Tibetan. These date from the fifth to the eighth century C.E. Khotan as well as India also had strong influence on the development of art in Tibet.

Some scholars believe Central Asian beliefs influenced core Mahayana practices. For instance, the bodhisattva MANJUSRI, worshipped at Mt. Wutai in western China, is said to have been imported from Takharia. And the bodhisattva KSHITIGARBHA, while originally from India, did not flourish there and only became a major deity figure in Central Asia. AMITABHA, the Buddha of the Western Paradise, is said to have been borrowed from the Zoroastrian deity Ahuramazda.

In addition Tibetan culture had an intimate relationship with those around the Tarim Basin, since Tibetans occupied the area for a period.

LATER DEVELOPMENTS IN CENTRAL ASIA

While the first 500 years of the Common Era saw much Buddhist activity, this came to an end with a series of Arab invasions from the early 600s. In 642 a Sassanian ruler was defeated by Arab armies, and from that point on Buddhist civilization in Central Asia was dismantled, to be discovered by 19th-century archaeology.

Further reading: Simone Gaulier, Robert Jera-Bezard, and Monique Maillard, *Buddhism in Afghanistan and Central Asia* (Leiden: Brill, 1976); Damien Keown, ed., *Oxford Dictionary of Buddhism* (Oxford: Oxford University Press, 2003); John Powers, *A Concise Encyclopedia of Buddhism* (Oxford: One World, 2000); B. N. Puri, *Buddhism in Central Asia* (Delhi: Motilal Banarsidass, 1987).

Ceylon   *See* SRI LANKA.

Chah, Ajahn (1918–1981) *Thai Forest Meditation Tradition master*

The Venerable Ajahn Chah, one of the most well-known THAI FOREST MEDITATION TRADITION masters, was born in rural northeast Thailand. He worked on his parents' farm until the age of 20, then decided to enter the monastic life and was ordained as a BHIKSU. His first years as a monk were spent during World War II, which, along with the death of his father, set him upon an individual search to overcome suffering. While on a pilgrimage in 1946, he learned of the Venerable AJAAN MUN Bhuridatto (1870–1949) and sought him out. Ajaan Mun set him on the simple path of mindfulness meditation characteristic of the Thai Forest tradition. Ajahn Chah spent the next seven years as a wandering mendicant.

In 1954 he accepted an invitation to return to the town near his parents' farm. He settled in a forest near Ubon Rajathani, and as disciples gathered, he built Wat Pah Pong, which became the mother of other monasteries of a similar kind. In 1967 the first Westerner, a recently ordained monk named Sumedho, arrived. He adopted the strict and austere life at Wat Pah Pong. As the Venerable Ajahn SUMEDHO, he would found another monastery, Wat Pah Nanachat, in northeast Thailand, as a center administered by English-speaking monks for English-speaking seekers.

In 1977, Ajahn Chah, accompanied by Ajahn Sumedho and the Venerable Khemadhammo, visited England. Sumedho and Khemadhammo remained behind to establish the Forest Tradition in England and the West. He made a second visit to England in 1979. However, at the time his health was taking a downward turn. He returned to Thailand and died of diabetes two years later.

Further reading: Ajahn Chah, *Everything Arises, Everything Falls Away: Teachings on Impermanence and the End of Suffering.* Translated by Paul Breiter (Boston: Shambhala, 2005); ———, *Food for the Heart: The Collected Teachings of Ajahn Chah* (Somerville, Mass.: Wisdom, 2004); Jack Kornfield and Paul Breiter, *A Still Forest Pool: The Insight Meditation of Achaan Chah* (Wheaton, Ill.: Quest Books/Theosophical Publishing House, 1985).

Chajang (seventh century C.E.) *Korean Buddhist monk*

Chajang, a Korean Buddhist monk, emerged out of obscurity in the 630s when he became one of the first Korean monks to go to China to study. Born in a royal family, he rejected a promising career at court to become a monk. Early in his life he developed a desire to make the pilgrimage to Wutai Shan, a mountain in Shanxi said to be the home of the bodhisattva MANJUSRI, the embodiment of perfect wisdom. While at Wutai, Chajang chanted before a statue of Manjusri and was given a poem in a dream. Unable to interpret the poem, he consulted a local monk, who gave him several relics of the Buddha and told him to return to his home. After a further week of devotional practice, he had a vision in which he was told that the monk was in fact Manjusri and that upon his return home he must build a temple to the bodhisattva.

In 643, Chajang arrived at the mountain Odae-san in southern Korea, where after some waiting he had another encounter with Manjusri. He subsequently built Woljong-sa (Calm Moon Temple), later a major center for disseminating Buddhism throughout the peninsula. Three years later he

settled on Yongjuk-san Mountain and from there oversaw the building of Tongdo-sa Temple. Here he enshrined the relics of the Buddha acquired in China. (Woljong-sa was destroyed during the Korean War but rebuilt in 1969. Tongdo-sa had been destroyed during the Japanese invasion in 1592 and reconstructed in 1601.)

Chajang was aided in his Buddhist mission by Queen Sondok (r. 632–646), the daughter of King Chinp'yong (r. 570–632), who followed her father's program of utilizing Buddhist language to promote her own governmental program, as well as defend her position as a female ruler.

Further reading: *Focus on Korea.* 3 vols. (Seoul: Seoul International Publishing House, 1988); James Huntley Grayson, *Korea: A Religious History* (Oxford: Oxford University Press, 1989); Duk-Whang Kim, *A History of Religions in Korea* (Seoul: Daeji Monoonwha-sa, 1988).

Chan Buddhism

The emphasis on meditation as the essential tool for the practice of Buddhism and the realization of enlightenment is usually traced to India and the image of the BUDDHA sitting under the BODHI TREE. In India, the emerging movement encountered both Hinduism and Daoism, especially the concept of *dhyana*, the Indian word commonly translated as "meditation." *Dhyana* was a practice in Hinduism and Jainism (an Indian movement that grew up alongside Buddhism). Meditation was well established in Buddhism during the Indian era, as may be seen in such writings as the PRAJNAPARAMITA sutras, which date to the first century B.C.E.

It is in China, however, that the meditative practices that existed as one element in Buddhist practice became the basis of a separate school of Buddhism, which became known as Chan (a Chinese word derived from the Sanskrit *dhyana*). Most researchers now see the emergence of Chan as based on an isolation of meditative practice and the merger of Buddhist and Daoist

Lacquer image of Bodhidharma, the founder of Chan Buddhism, from the Hualin temple, Guangzhou, southern China

mystical concepts, though in Chan practice, meditation had always been more important than any metaphysical/theological speculation. Among the people important to the process of isolating and emphasizing meditation as a practice was DAO SHENG (c. 360–434), who advocated the idea of sudden enlightenment following the pattern set by the Buddha. He also manifested the Chan distrust of scriptures and their study.

The credit for actually founding Chan is usually assigned to BODHIDHARMA (c. 470–c. 534), the first patriarch in a lineage of enlightened masters who were able to recognize when others were enlightened and to pass to them a "seal of enlightenment." Bodhidharma is seen as initiating a tradition that understood the inadequacy of words to convey enlightenment and hence passed

truth directly to people, who intuitively apprehended it.

We know few details of Bodhidharma's life. He appears to have been born in southern India, moved to China relatively late in life, and died there around 534 C.E. Around him many semimythical stories accumulated. He ended his life as the abbot of the Shaolin (Young Forest) Temple/Monastery (located near Luoyang, west of the old capital of Xian), and he passed the leadership of the monastery to his successors, the next five of whom would be remembered as the patriarchs of the movement. Bodhidharma passed the INKASHO-MEI, or seal of enlightenment, directly to the second patriarch, HUI KE (c. 484–c. 590).

The person recognized as the fourth Chan patriarch, DAO XIN (580–651), settled in one place and built a community of monks who wished to practice meditation. The needs of the new community, not the object of charity from the nearby population, led to Dao Xin's introduction of a daily schedule that included time for the monks to engage in agricultural work to meet the community's food needs. Work subsequently was integrated into the monastic life and became another means of practice along with meditation. The development of communities centered on Zen practice also facilitated the participation of lay people in meditation activities in ways not previously available.

The fifth patriarch, Hong Ren (601–674), was the last to preside over a relatively united movement. He passed his lineage to two students, SHEN XIU (606–706) and HUI NENG (638–713). The former, actually the more dynamic of the two, established himself at Luoyang in northern China. Here he developed a variation on the Zen tradition by an emphasis on gradual enlightenment. He built a large following due to his charisma, but his approach to Zen did not long survive him.

Hui Neng has become known as the leader of the so-called Southern school of Chan that maintained the emphasis on instant enlightenment. He saw experience as the way to enlightenment, which occurred in a sudden, direct, and personal apprehension of the self. Word and scriptures were not essential and might actually be distractions. As the northern school of Shen Xiu died out, future Chan lineages would all be traced to Hui Neng, now considered the sixth patriarch. His status is manifest in the collection of his discourses in an authoritative volume, the PLATFORM SUTRA of the Sixth Patriarch.

And beginning with Hui Neng, Chan flourished in China, at least for the next century. During this time, the use of the KOAN (a practice usually attributed to Mazu [707–786]) would be introduced. The koan is a story or question or image that defies a rational response and hence pushes the student toward intuitive jumps. De Shan (780–865) is credited with introducing the stick with which the master would strike students to take them to the present and, it was hoped, shock them into sudden enlightenment. Bo Zhang (749–814) compiled and codified the rules that would regulate monastic life, the monasteries where people could engage in the daily routine of "work, live, meditate, sleep," advocated by Dao Xin. To Bo Zhang is attributed the saying "One day without work means one day without food."

The development of Hui Neng's students encountered a disastrous moment during the reign of the emperor Wuzong (r. 840–846). Rising to the throne during a time of economic crisis, the emperor eventually gazed upon the Buddhist monasteries as a solution to his cash flow problem. He confiscated many of the monasteries and scattered the monks, forcing them back into a secular lay existence. Wuzong's persecution (which extended to other religions as well) was an almost fatal wound to the Zen community. It took a generation to revive and never fully overcame the effects. During the late ninth century, the revived community would divide into five major sects, called the Five Houses. Of these, two would become dominant, the LINJI (later transferred to Japan as RINZAI ZEN) and the CAODONG (in Japan as SOTO ZEN) schools.

Linji Chan, which took its name from its main center located at Linji, was founded by Yi Xuan (also known as Gigen) (d. 867). He is most known for his emphasis on the koan, which he saw as the best tool for provoking sudden enlightenment. Later generations would collect the hundreds of koans into books. Over time, Linji Chan would divide into a number of different schools, each characterized by a unique lineage of leaders, though each could be traced to Yi Xuan.

Caodong Chan took its name from its two founders, Cao Shan (840–901) and Dong Shan (807–869), who in turn had adopted their religious names from the mountains on which they resided. Caodong emphasizes ZAZEN, sitting in meditation, a practice that if pursued over time leads to enlightenment. Caodong thus reintroduced a form of the gradual enlightenment advocated by Shen Xiu.

Stone image of Muso Kokushi (1327-1351), Rinzai Zen priest, founder of Zuisen-ji and builder of many Japanese gardens, in the garden of the Zuisen-ji, Kamakura, Japan

Chan would be introduced into Japan (where it would be called Zen) in the seventh century, and the island nation would receive regular new injections. The most important transmission of Chan would occur in the 12th and 13th centuries when Linji Chan would be introduced by EISAI (1141–1215) and Caodong by DOGEN (1200–53).

During China's Song dynasty (960–1279), Chan Buddhism was able to recover somewhat, and with Pure Land Buddhism would become one of two major schools of Chinese Buddhism. In many places, practitioners of the two schools shared a single monastic facility, a practice that led to the blurring of the lines between Pure Land and Chan life.

Among the interesting developments within the Chan community, the monks at Shaolin responded to the unrest in China during the time of Wuzong and his predecessors by inviting practitioners of the MARTIAL ARTS to the monastery. The monks compiled the knowledge from different teachers and over time developed the major center for the teaching and practice of kung fu, which was integrated into the Zen culture.

Chan survived through the centuries in China in spite of the ups and downs of various dynasties that favored other forms of Buddhism, including VAJRAYANA. It would face its greatest test in the 20th century after the Chinese revolution and antireligious policies adopted by the People's Republic of China, which led to the closing (and even destruction) of many Chan MONASTERIES and the transformation of many of the leading Chan monastic centers into tourist attractions.

The Chinese revolution also led to the diffusion of Chan Buddhism, first to Taiwan and then to other communities of the Chinese diaspora in Southeast Asia and the West. Prominent among the diaspora Chan communities are the DHARMA DRUM MOUNTAIN ASSOCIATION and FOGUANGSHAN, both based in Taiwan.

Further reading: Chang Chung-yuan, *Original Teachings of Ch'an Buddhism* (New York: Grove Press, 1982); Ken-

neth K. S. Ch'en, *Buddhism in China: A Historical Survey* (Princeton, N.J.: Princeton University Press, 1964); Andy Ferguson, *Zen's Chinese Heritage: The Masters and Their Teachings* (Somerville, Mass.: Wisdom, 2000); John R. McRae, *The Northern School and the Formation of Early Ch'an Buddhism* (Honolulu: University of Hawaii Press, 1986); Arthur F. Wright, *Buddhism in Chinese History* (Stanford, Calif.: Stanford University Press, 1959).

Channa *Prince Shakyamuni's groom*

Channa was the charioteer and companion to Siddhartha, the young Sakya prince who would go on to become the Buddha. Siddhartha had been restrained from leaving the palace by his father, who wished to spare his son from contact with the unpleasant realities of the world. However, Siddhartha eventually persuaded Channa to take him outside. Channa guided the prince through the city four times, when he was able to see old age, sickness, and death—symbols of human suffering—for the first time. Channa fielded Siddhartha's questions about the nature of human reality, including his own mortality. On the night of his final departure from his early family it was Channa who saddled the horse and accepted the symbols of Siddhartha's old life—his hair, his robe, and his jewelry.

Further reading: Edward J. Thomas, *The Life of Buddha as Legend and History* (New Delhi: Munshiram Manoharlal, 1992).

Chegwan (d. 971) *Korean monk and scholar during the Tang dynasty in China*

Chegwan was a Korean monk who spent several years studying in China. He was a key figure in the transmission of the teachings of the TIAN TAI school of Chinese Buddhism. The Tian Tai school rose in the early Tang (618–906) period as a result of the teachings of the founder, ZHI YI (538–597), and his key disciple, Guan Ding. Chegwan's key work was the *Tiantai Sijiaoyi* (*Outline of the Tian Tai Fourfold Teachings*), a text that has served as a foundational introduction to Tian Tai doctrine for generations of monks. Chegwan's writings were particularly important for presenting the concept of the Five Periods and Eight Teachings (*wushi bajiao*), a categorization system that has traditionally been seen as the core of Tian Tai teachings.

Further reading: The Korean Buddhist Research Institute, *The History and Culture of Buddhism in Korea.* (Seoul: Dongguk University Press, 1993).

Cheng Hao (Cheng Mingdao, Ch'eng Hao) (1032–1085)
Neo-Confucian philosopher
Elder brother of CHENG YI (1033–1107), nephew of ZHANG ZAI (1020–77), former student of ZHOU DUNYI (1017–73), and friend of Shao Yung (1011–77)—who together are often referred to as the "five masters of 11th century Chinese philosophy"—Cheng Hao was a key figure in the development of Neo-Confucian thought. The son of an official, Cheng Hao drifted away from Confucian studies during his teens, flirting with Daoism and Buddhism for a number of years, until returning to the study of the classics in his mid-20s. He obtained a *jinshi* (presented scholar) degree in 1057 and went on to have a distinguished career during which he served in various administrative posts and deeply impressed several Song dynasty (960–1279) emperors. Beloved by his disciples, Cheng Hao was said to be so understanding and amiable that for 20 years he never became angry.

Cheng Hao's teachings are often associated with his brother's (the two together are referred to as the "two Chengs"). Both thinkers hold that all things comprise QI (matter-energy) and LI (principle), the latter often termed *tianli* (the principle of heaven). In the case of human beings, *li* is structured as human nature (*xing*). Following MENCIUS, the Chengs understand human nature as originally good. Human nature finds its fulfillment in the virtue of REN (goodness, humaneness). One cultivates human fulfillment through a combination of investigation of things and spiritual introspection, primarily through the twin methods of study (*nian*) and *jing zuo* (quiet sitting). There do seem to be important differences between the Chengs, however, mainly concerning cultivation. Cheng Hao seems to lay more stress on the "learning of the mind" and "quiet sitting" than Cheng Yi. It has been suggested that Cheng Hao was more influenced by Zhou Dunyi as well as the teachings and practices of CHAN (ZEN) BUDDHISM than his brother, but this is a controversial claim. Some scholars have gone so far as to say that Cheng Hao's line of thought was the catalyst for the Ming dynasty (1368–1644) Neo-Confucian scholar WANG YANGMING's critical response to Zhu Xi's orthodox Confucian teachings.

Further reading: W. Theodore de Bary and Irene Bloom, eds., *Sources of Chinese Tradition.* Vol 1, *From Earliest Times to 1600.* 2nd ed. (New York: Columbia University Press, 1999), 689–697.

Cheng Yen (pinyin: Zheng Yan) (1937–)
founder of the Tzu Chi Association
Cheng Yen is a native Taiwanese nun whose devotion and frugality have inspired millions of followers. Born in southeast Taiwan, Yen was ordained as a nun in 1960 and subsequently established a nunnery in Hualian, her hometown. Today there are branches of the BUDDHIST COMPASSION RELIEF TZU CHI ASSOCIATION throughout the world. As the new century begins, it has become the largest Chinese lay Buddhist group and the largest civil society organization in Taiwan.

Further reading: Yu-ing Ching, *Master of Love and Mercy: Cheng Yen* (Nevada City, Calif.: Blue Dolphin, 1995).

Cheng Yi (Cheng Yichuan, Ch'eng I) 1033–1107) *Neo-Confucian philosopher*
The younger of the two Cheng brothers, Cheng Yi, had an even more decisive influence on

Neo-Confucian thought than his elder sibling, CHENG HAO. An outstanding student, he earned his *jinshi* degree, the highest accomplishment possible in the system of Chinese imperial degrees, in 1059 at the age of 27. He repeatedly declined various high positions, preferring to lecture on Confucian principles to the emperor and his court. Strict in his own behavior, he openly criticized those in power and so earned many enemies. For a time his teachings were even prohibited. Unlike his brother, Cheng Yi was grave and stern in his demeanor, sometimes even shouting at people. Yet it is also said that he was so in control of himself that he remained undisturbed when a boat in which he was riding was about to sink.

Cheng Yi's teachings are closely allied to his brother's in his focus on the basic metaphysical duality of QI (matter-energy) and LI (principle), the perfection of human nature (*xing*) through REN (goodness, humaneness), and its development through investigation of things and spiritual introspection. However, Cheng Yi lays more stress on extending knowledge, making it the cornerstone of his system. For Cheng Yi, one extends knowledge by investigating things, that is, through inductive and deductive study (*nian*) and handling of human affairs. All things, no matter how small, contain principle and so must be investigated. Such stress gives his philosophy a decidedly rationalistic flavor.

Cheng Yi's famous statement "Principle is one but its manifestations are many" is one of the most renowned sayings in Chinese philosophy. Fully in keeping with the traditional Chinese stress on cosmic harmony, it remains an elegant summary of Neo-Confucian metaphysics. It seems likely that Cheng Yi borrowed the basic idea from the HUA YAN school of Buddhism with its teaching of "All in one, one in all." Later, the Song (960–1279) thinker ZHU XI eagerly took to his teachings, once the official ban on them was lifted, and it is clear that much of Zhu's own work is based on Cheng Yi's views.

Further reading: W. Theodore de Bary and Irene Bloom, eds., *Sources of Chinese Tradition.* Vol. 1, *From Earliest Times to 1600.* 2nd ed. (New York: Columbia University Press, 1999): 689–697.

chi   See QI.

Chieu, Ngo Van (Ngo Mingh Chieu)
(1878–1932) *founder of Cao Dai religion in Vietnam*
Chieu was born into a genteel but impoverished Vietnamese family. From seven he lived with his aunt, whose Chinese husband encouraged Chieu to study Chinese spiritual beliefs. He attended French school and entered the civil service in 1899. He retired in 1931. During this time he became a member of the Dao Mindh Su (Dao Phat Duong) sect of Chinese Daoism. He also absorbed ideas from the French psychical researcher Camille Flammarion (1842–1925). He was in constant communication with spirits through séances. In 1919 during a séance Chieu met the spirit Cao Dai, and from 1920 this spirit dominated Chieu's activities. Cao Dai ordered him to use a Celestial Eye as a symbol and attract followers. The first altar was established in 1924 in the home of Vuong Quan Ky, a fellow clerk in the colonial administration.

As the fledgling group grew, Chieu became unsettled. He felt the group moved toward application and registration and inauguration too quickly. He also was probably unhappy with the large number of spiritual adepts, many from higher social levels, who had joined. After Cao Dai's official inauguration in 1926 he set up his own followers in Can Tho. He retired there after leaving the civil service and died in 1932.

His followers proclaimed his Esoteric School, Noi Giao Tam Truyen, as an institution without organization or priesthood. His second school, the Salvationish, or Ngoai Giao Cong Truyen, was a religious school set up for growth.

See also CAODAISM.

Further reading: Sergei Blagov, *Caodaism: Vietnamese Traditionalism and Its Leap into Modernity* (New York: Nova Science, 2001).

Chih-i   *See* ZHI YI.

China, Buddhism in

From the perspective of Chinese culture, Buddhism is that rarest of things: a cultural import. China has generated so much of its own great development that major cultural infusions are unusual. In fact, Buddhism has been a presence over so much of China's long history that most Chinese forget it was in fact a well-developed system of thought and religious practice well before it arrived in China around 100–300 C.E. It has since experienced varying fates yet today is so thoroughly part of Chinese culture that it is impossible to imagine one without the other. As with so many cultural borrowings, Buddhism in East Asia has become thoroughly sinicized, made "Chinese."

THE EARLY IMPACT OF BUDDHISM

Traditional accounts of Buddhism in China start with the dream of Emperor Ming (r. 58–75 C.E.). This emperor of the Han dynasty (206 B.C.E.–220 C.E.) dreamed of a "golden man." Assuming this might be the Buddha, a figure known to his advisers only vaguely, the emperor dispatched two emissaries to India. They returned with Buddhist monks, and the emperor built the BAIMASI (White Horse Temple) in the capital Luoyang for them. This story of Emperor Ming's dream is not based on factual evidence. Nevertheless, the first verifiable, written record of Buddhism in China does in fact date from his period. This was an edict issued in 65 C.E. stating that Buddhist rituals had been performed in the eastern province of Jiangsu, at a vegetarian feast presided over by Prince Ying, Ming's half brother. This and other factors show that Buddhism had been introduced even earlier than this edict or Emperor Ming's dream.

Other literary evidence points to the existence of Buddhist communities during the Han dynasty. These communities existed in the capital, Luoyang, in the east, as mentioned, and in southern China. *Mozi Lihuolun* (Mozu on the settling of doubts) is a work written in defense of Buddhism. It was collected probably in the early 200s C.E. but contains information from an earlier period. The preface mentions communities of Buddhists in southern China, at Tonkin, now part of Vietnam but then part of the Chinese empire. Most of the foreign monks at the southern center arrived by sea, not overland via the Silk Road. We can imagine that they may have traveled north from Southeast Asian cultures such as Champa (current-day southern Vietnam) or Sumatra, in addition to parts of India.

What the early stories show is China's first attempt to understand this imported system of thought. Buddhism was in some ways similar to existing systems in China, since China had familiarity with early philosophers such as CONFUCIUS and ZHUANGZI. However, the core Buddhist ideas—ENLIGHTENMENT, NIRVANA, SAMSARA, KARMA, *KARUNA* (compassion)—were probably very strange to Chinese. In addition there was a complex system of stories and divine figures, already fully developed. And to top it all off, Buddhism had an exotic and complex literary aspect. There were already written records of the Buddha's speeches, the SUTRAS, as well as written interpretations of philosophy, the ABHIDHARMA, and complex monastic regulations, the VINAYA. In other words, the TRIPITAKA of Buddhism had taken shape in India and now presented Chinese thinkers with a puzzle. Since China by the Han dynasty was itself a literary culture, it was only natural for emphasis to be put on the interpretation of these literary works, in an effort to make sense of Buddhism.

THE TRANSLATION TASK

Although traders and other travelers undoubtedly played a key role in Buddhism's entry into China, most of the recorded figures in early Buddhism in China were foreign monks and their converts. And according to our records these figures seem to have spent most of their time working with the books of Buddhism. Some went to great lengths to travel to obtain these new texts, to India and Central Asia. Others spent their entire lives translating them into Chinese. And others no doubt worked to smooth the way with local authorities, to enable this great translation project to proceed. And a great project it was indeed. Looked at over the period of Buddhism's gradual entry into China, from around 50 to 1000 C.E., the translation of Buddhist texts from the various Indic and Central Asian languages into literary Chinese was a massive intellectual effort. Seen in terms of cultural capital, meaning the things that a society decides are of vital importance and focus, Buddhism was a deep concern of Chinese people and their rulers.

By the end of the Tang dynasty (618–907 C.E.) this translation effort was essentially complete. Only a handful of translations were made in the later Song dynasty (960–1279 C.E.). The Chinese Tripitaka, in its final form, is today contained in 85 volumes, each of around 1,000 pages. The first translation efforts were by individual foreign monks, sometimes working alone, sometimes working with Chinese collaborators. DHARMA-RAKSA (c. 265–313 C.E.), for instance, worked with a father-son Chinese pair who wrote down his explanations in Chinese. There was little control over the actual translation, since neither side understood fully the other's language. In addition, since most of the foreign monks recited the original from memory, there were occasional lapses.

A later stage in translation was the formation of translation bureaus. The first was headed by AN SHIGAO, a Parthian prince who arrived in Luoyang in 148 C.E. DAO AN (312–385 C.E.), a Chinese monk, began to establish translation bureaus in order to translate the vast SARVASTIVADIN works. The translation bureau form of collaboration became the primary style of work when the great translation master KUMARAJIVA arrived at Chang

An, a major capital, in 401. Overall there were translation bureaus established in various cities and MONASTERIES under KUMARAJIVA, Gunabhadra, BODHIRUCI, Dharmakshema, Narendrayasas, and AMOGHAVAJRA. The ruler of the kingdom usually arranged and paid for all expenses of such bureaus, thereby giving their work extra significance.

Naturally this form of translation turned out to be more accurate than the first form of collaboration. It was also, in practice, extremely fast. The translation bureaus generally followed a detailed separation of labor. The chief translator, usually also a famous monk, would explain the text in Chinese. He would fill in missing sections. His team of Chinese translators would then find the right expression in literary Chinese. Finally the master would check the final product against the original, for accuracy, and ask for revisions.

A third stage in the translation of Buddhist works into Chinese began in the Sui and Tang dynasties (581–618 and 618–907 C.E.). In this period the great translators were Chinese monks who had become extremely familiar with the languages of the original texts, usually Sanskrit. The most famous of these translators were XUAN ZANG and YI JING (635–713). Their translations are today seen as the most accurate and literary of all.

As the number of texts translated became large, Chinese monks began to catalog them. The first catalog was produced by Dao An in 374 C.E. Another, and the oldest one we still have a copy of, was done by Seng Yu in 518 C.E. Today we have 18 catalogs from different times in Chinese history, all containing lists of the books of Buddhism. These listed the original and the Chinese translation and translator. In some cases more than one translation existed, especially for the major sutras.

Today the definitive version of the Chinese Tripitaka is the Taisho. *Taisho* refers to the reign name of the Japanese emperor during the period of printing, 1922–33. (The latest version, the *Taisho Daizokyo*, is in 85 volumes with 3,063 separate pieces of writing.) This collection includes works from so-called HINAYANA (or non-Mahayana) as well as Tibetan and Korean sources.

THE RECEPTION OF BUDDHISM AMONG THE CHINESE PEOPLE

But translating was only part of the process of absorption of Buddhist culture into China. Those early monks and traders who introduced knowledge of Buddhism had to deal with perceptions among the local peoples. In general, Buddhism was of intense interest only to the gentry, the upper classes, and did not become widely popular until much later in its history in China, with the Tang (618–907 C.E.). But the upper, educated classes in the many dynasties between the Han through the Tang all showed strong interest in this foreign religion.

Buddhism presented a handful of core concepts in the initial stages. In the Han many Buddhist ideas emphasized constant rebirth of the soul in the cycle of karma. Chinese used the concept of *shen-ling* to describe the soul that, though indestructible, is sent through successive rebirths without any other linking connections. The indestructible soul matched Daoist ideas of a spirit force that survived after death of the body.

Buddhism also emphasized cultivation through suppression or control of the passions, a new concept for Chinese culture. The conclusion from this teaching was that one who cultivates should withdraw from society and concentrate on inner cultivation. Because Chinese did not take to the strenuous and often extreme rules of conduct, the PRATIMOKSA, they tended to emphasize concentration or meditation on the breath. Such breath procedures were already present in Daoism.

Buddhism also put emphasis on charity and compassion. Charity included the donation of worldly possessions to the SANGHA, the Buddhist community of monks. Compassion led naturally to proscriptions against killing.

Many of these ideas were first interpreted in light of existing Chinese concepts, especially similar ideas from Daoism. Some ideas were superficially similar, both Daoism and Buddhism emphasized meditation and breath control, for instance. The Daoist search for immortality was reinterpreted in Buddhist terms as the cultivation toward liberation. The Buddhist ARHAT was simply translated into a version of the Daoist cultivated gentleman. Because of such similarities, early Daoists and Buddhists presented Buddhism as simply one aspect of DAOISM.

In addition early translations of Buddhist texts had no words at hand to express the technical concepts of Buddhism. As a result they often used Daoist terms. And many early translations focused on meditation and breath control instead of core Buddhist concepts such as the Four Truths.

In order to preserve the primacy of Laozi as founder and main deity of Daoism, a theory of *hua hu,* or "cultivating barbarians," was developed by the Daoists. LAOZI (LAO TZU) was said to have traveled to the far West and taught Daoism. In this view, the Buddha was in fact simply one incarnation of LAOZI. These ideas were collected in the *Huahu Jing,* the Sutra on the Conversion of the Barbarians, written by Wang Fu during the Western Jin dynasty (265–316 C.E.).

The major roadblock to acceptance of Buddhist ideas was, inevitably, the emphasis on becoming a monk, the idea of leaving the family and ties of home behind. Chinese society and Confucian teachings in particular emphasized filial piety and perpetuation of the family. To become a monk, to lead a life of poverty and nonworldly concerns, went against such family-centered assumptions. Thus when promising young members of wealthy gentry families began to enlist as monks, there were concern and strongly worded attacks on the foreign system of beliefs. The early Daoist work Taiping Jing (Sutra on Great Peace) stated that severe calamity would accompany failure to leave descendants. This would be the actual fate of a male who gave up marriage and entered the monkhood, of course. Such strong reactions are not perhaps so difficult for us to understand; compare, for instance, the reaction of many middle-class families to sons' or daughters' joining "cults" in the 1960s and 1970s in Europe and America.

BUDDHIST CULTURE IN CHINA, THE PERIOD OF POLITICAL DISUNITY

Between the end of the Han in 220 C.E. and the beginning of the Sui dynasty in 589 China was in a state of political confusion. Foreign groups repeatedly invaded and occupied the north, setting up dynasty after dynasty. The first to succeed were the Xong Nu, or, as they are more commonly labeled, the Huns. The capitals of Luoyang and Chang An fell to them in 311 and 316. With the foreign occupations many of the literary and ruling classes migrated south. These refugees included monks. Many at first settled in Jian Kang, present-day Nanjing, but they eventually scattered to other urban centers throughout China's south.

This vast migration in fact assisted in the spread of Buddhism, as the refined culture of the Han capitals was spread throughout other areas. As a result, Buddhism did not develop in parallel in the north and the south, and we cannot speak of a unified status of Buddhism in China until the empire was finally reunified by the Sui dynasty in 589.

The south developed a unique form of "gentry Buddhism," Buddhism for the upper classes. This brand of Buddhist practice put equal emphasis on philosophy and Daoist ideas and core Buddhism. And because the dynasties in the south were politically weak, the Buddhist establishment was able to act relatively independently. The religion was actively promoted by the Jin dynasty rulers Jian Wen (r. 371–373) and Xiao Wu (373–396). Records show there were 1,786 temples and 24,000 monks in the Eastern Jin area.

The popularity of Buddhism in the south led to political intrigue and complications. While the sangha had generally seen itself as independent in India, such a position was strongly criticized in China. Chinese thought had always given highest authority to the emperor, who was traditionally called the "Son of Heaven." But, it was argued, if the monks and monasteries were truly independent, monks should not need even to recognize or bow to the emperor. Monks requested exemption from the rule that all subjects must bow before the emperor because, it was reasoned, the emperor was in the end a householder, and a monk should not look up to a householder. Debates on this issue arose on several occasions. The famous monk HUI YUAN convinced the emperor Huan Xuan in 403 not to force monks to bow before him.

In the north the newly arrived foreign rulers generally wanted to establish their legitimacy within the framework of Chinese culture. These more dynamic political entities were able to control the Buddhist establishment easily, and for the first time Buddhism began to look like a state religion for many of these dynasties. The monks able to survive in such environments were skilled at political maneuvering and creation of magical displays, a very different kind of personality from that prevalent in the south.

The peak of Buddhism's strength in the north was under the Later Qin (384–417 C.E.) emperor Yao Xing (366–416). Yao continued to support Buddhism and, especially, the massive translation of the Sarvastivadin canon that had been started by the preceding dynasty. Yao Xing took Kumarajiva to the capital of Chang An in 401, a significant event in Chinese Buddhism because he systematized the translation process.

This period of political disunity was also a period of heightened activity on the SILK ROAD trade routes. The famous translator Dharmaraksa resided at the CAVES OF THE THOUSAND BUDDHAS at Dunhuang, and the first dated cave temple was dug there in 366 by the monk Luo Cun. Monks often fled to Dunhuang to escape political turmoil in northern China in this period.

At the same time Chinese monks began to travel abroad on pilgrimages. The first trip was started by FA XIAN in 399. Fa Xian was the first Chinese monk to visit India, study there, and return. He arrived in India via the southern route of the Silk Road, through the desert, and he returned after visiting Sri Lanka and Java, in 414 C.E. Overall this period was one of preparation for Buddhism's vast progress in the 600s. During this period key concepts were clarified and major Buddhist texts were translated.

INTERACTION WITH DAOIST THOUGHT

At this point two trends of Buddhism were popular in China, DHYANA, or concentration, and PRAJNA, or wisdom. The *dhyana* trend followed Hinayana writings while the *prajna* trend emphasized Mahayana texts. Gradually the *prajna* sutras became more popular, thus cementing Mahayana as the major brand of Chinese Buddhism.

It was the Prajna school that interacted most with Daoism of the period, creating a Buddhist-Daoist hybrid thought. This dialog began with realization that certain key concepts, such as Buddhist SUNYATA (emptiness) and Daoist WU WEI (nonaction), were similar. The literary thinkers then began to develop theories based on equivalencies. Both Buddhists and Daoists looked for and assumed similarities between the two religious currents, not differences. The best example illustrating this hybrid way of thinking was the monk Zhi Dun (314–366 C.E.), who was born in a ruling class family and lived in the new capital of the south, Jian Kang. Zhi Dun developed a new interpretation of the ancient Chinese concept of LI (principle). According to Zhi, *li* was a transcendental principle that could be contrasted with *shi*, or materiality.

The Buddhists developed a method of interpreting Buddhist ideas by using existing concepts from Chinese philosophy. This method, called GEYI, or "matching meaning," may have been useful in teaching Buddhist ideas, but as a translation technique it did not convey the full flavor of the independent system of thought that was Buddhism. Once Kumarajiva's translation bureau was established in the early 400s, this "matching meanings" technique died out.

INFLUENTIAL EARLY MONKS

Kumarajiva's translation activities resulted in the development of a new school, the MADHYAMAKA, or Middle Path, school. It was also called the San Lun, or three treatises, since it was based on three major works by the Indian philosopher NAGARJUNA (c. 100 C.E.). The most brilliant student of Kumarajiva's was SENG ZHAO (374–414 C.E.). Seng Zhao used the Daoist-Buddhist ideas of *ti* and *yong* (substance and phenomenon) to argue that these two essences are not separate. They are, in fact, the same. He sought to use Nargarjuna's ideas of synthesizing extremes to find a middle way in reconciling opposing concepts.

Other important monks in this period include DAO AN (312–385 C.E.) and HUI YUAN (344–416 C.E.). Dao An was important for collecting many disciples, whom he repeatedly scattered to many points in southern China, and for compiling the first catalog of the Chinese sutras, in 374 C.E. Dao An lived the final 15 years of his life in the northern capital of Chang An, where he urged the ruler to invite the eminent translator Kumarajiva to China.

One of Dao An's best-known disciples was Hui Yuan, who settled in Mt. Lu (Lu Shan) in present-day Jiangxi Province. The local governor built a monastery there for Hui Yuan, the Donglin Si (Eastern Grotto Temple), c. 386. Hui Yuan carried on a stimulating correspondence with Kumarajiva, which covered in particular questions of the nature of the DHARMAKAYA, the body of the dharma. Hui Yuan's community on Lu Shan was the first to begin the worship of AMITABHA and vow to be reborn in Amitabha's Western Paradise.

A final eminent monk of this period was DAO SHENG (c. 360–434). He had visited Hui Yuan on Lu Shan and had worked with Kumarajiva's translation bureau. He finally settled in Lu Shan. Dao Sheng was most interested in the NIRVANA SUTRA, a text from the Pali canon that was translated three times into Chinese. Dao Sheng taught and wrote on many key concepts taken from the Nirvana Sutra. Such concepts as sudden enlightenment, the idea that all beings have Buddha nature, and the idea of the true self in turn strongly influenced later Chinese Buddhism. Dao Sheng's teachings led to the development of a Nirvana school, which eventually was absorbed into the TIAN TAI school in the 600s.

BUDDHISM TRANSFORMS INTO A CULTURAL PRESENCE: THE PERSECUTIONS

In southern China the long-lasting Jin dynasty was finally overthrown in 420 C.E., and a succession of shorter-lived dynasties took over. In the north the non-Chinese tribes such as the Toba Wei (386–534), a Turkish tribe, continued to rule. There Buddhism continued to have a political function. Its political prominence was great, and it attracted as a result significant criticism. At this time northern China experienced the first of four major periods of persecution. Emperor Wu (Dai Wudi) (423–452), the third Toba Wei ruler, issued three increasingly harsh edicts related to Buddhism. In the first, in 438 C.E., the emperor ordered that no men below 50 were allowed to become monks. His final edict of 446 stated that all temples, STUPAS, and murals connected to Buddhism should be destroyed by the army, and Buddhism should be eradicated. Political intrigue, including the desires of Daoist and Confucian adversaries, were behind much of the strict treatment. Buddhism was easily restored to its previous position of prominence when Emperor Wu died in 452. However, this repression was to set a precedent for more severe repressions of Buddhism.

These periods of repression are traditionally seen as turning points in Buddhism's fortunes. In 574–577 Emperor Hou Zhu (r. 565–577, also called Gao Wei), of the Northern Qi dynasty (550–577), banned Buddhism. The actions taken were fairly standard for other persecutions as well. Monks were defrocked and forced to return to the lay life, to dress in everyday clothing, and to marry. Many monasteries and temples were destroyed, lands were confiscated, and wealth was appropriated. Daoism or Confucianism was declared to be a superior doctrine. Not long after the emperor died, Buddhism made a recovery and was reinstated in the imperial favor.

The most serious persecution occurred later, under Emperor Wuzong (r. 841–847) of the Tang (618–907 C.E.). In what is called today the HUI CHANG PERSECUTION, the emperor ordered the destruction of all Buddhist temples and monasteries, and the defrocking of all monks and nuns. Since the Tang ruled all of China, this persecution was the most widespread of all. It was over in 846, however, and many establishments were restored.

What such persecutions tell us is that Buddhism had found a place in Chinese economic and ideological life, as well as in the political arena. Buddhism was more often than not a unifying ideology. The Sui dynasty (589–618), which unified China, north and south, was strongly Buddhist. Emperor Wen (r. 589–605) actually explained his actions in terms of carrying out the Buddhist Dharma, or mission. He was most likely mimicking the actions of the Indian emperor ASOKA, who proclaimed the truths of Buddhism throughout his empire. And many individual emperors and empresses of subsequent dynasties followed Buddhism.

Overall it is clear that by the end of the period of disunity, 220–589 C.E., Buddhism had grown from a minority, imported religion into a force affecting all areas of Chinese life. The political disunity probably helped Buddhism's spread. And the use of spells and charms, especially in the north, made Buddhism more popular among the common people. The monasteries also served as an escape from military service for many young men. And Buddhism's message of salvation through cultivation attracted many caught in hopelessness. Buddhism taught that meritorious deeds would accumulate and reduce negative karma. In addition all creatures possessed BUDDHA NATURE, so regardless of social standing all could achieve release from suffering.

Although Buddhism was never again to be a state religion, its influence within Chinese culture was now ingrained. No longer could it be seen as a foreign system. It was instead an aspect of social life to be regulated and recognized, not ignored or suppressed. Buddhism had arrived.

THE BUDDHIST MONASTIC SYSTEM

One sign of this presence was the empire's effort to control Buddhist rules. In both the Tang and the later Five Dynasties (907–960) new rules were put into place to fix entry into the sangha. A person who desired to become a monk was required to lecture on the sutras, practice concentration (Buddhist meditation), memorize a text, compose an essay, and comment on a passage. A person who passed the examination would then be given an ordination certificate and was considered a SRAMANA, or novice. Some would then proceed to become full BHIKSUs, although most monks remained at the SRAMANERA level. Ordination was also possible through imperial declaration and through the purchase of certificates, which began in 1067. Such sales were especially popular during the Song (960–1279) dynasty.

Within temples several standard functions appeared. The most senior were the abbot, the rector, and the superintendent. Below them were various department heads, including controller, steward, and accountant.

Monks and the monasteries in which they lived were actually important economic centers. They always had substantial lands under cultivation. Some were involved in trade and even moneylending. Any property owned by a monk would pass to the sangha upon his death, so, as did the Catholic Church in Europe, the Buddhist sangha in China inevitably became a wealthy entity. In the Tang period, Buddhist temples also handled many aspects of economic production, including rolling mills (used to make flour), hostels, and pawnshops.

Temples were categorized as being contemplation temples (mainly those practicing Chan Buddhism), doctrinal temples, and *vinaya*, or regulation-focused, temples.

The government had an official bureaucracy set up to manage Buddhism and its assets. The earliest bureau was set up by the Northern Wei dynasty in 396 C.E. By the later part of the Tang dynasty a nonmonk was put in charge of Buddhist affairs. The office of the commissioner of religion is mentioned as early as 774 C.E.

POPULAR BUDDHISM

By the Song dynasty (960–1279) and beyond. Buddhism had become a popular religion. This means simply that it was an accepted part of everyday life for people of the lower stratum of society as well as for the upper classes. We saw that Buddhism initially appealed to the learned classes, and that monks were often from the ranks of the ruling classes. Temples and Buddhist towers dotted the landscape in all regions of China.

Buddhism's presence at the popular level is reflected in several areas. First were the popular festivals. Second were the many gods and deities worshipped by people, in Buddhist temples or outside. Finally, there is evidence of songs and stories with Buddhist themes.

Buddhist Festivals in China

The major festivals were observed already in the Tang dynasty by the Japanese monk ENNIN. These include the Lantern Festival, the Buddha's Birthday, and ULLAMBANA.

During the Lantern Festival, held on the 14th, 15th, and 16th of the first (lunar) month, the people would light lanterns and parade throughout the city or town streets. Temples competed with each other to build the most extravagant light structures, a practice still maintained in TIBET.

Popular Gods of Buddhism

By the Song dynasty (960–1279 C.E.) the full range of Buddhist deities had more or less solidified and become ingrained at all levels of society. And these deities did not always correspond to those popular during Buddhism's initial entry into China. MANJUSRI, the bodhisattva of wisdom, for instance, was not so popular by the Song period and had been overshadowed by the popularity of AMITABHA and GUAN YIN. Another popular figure was MAITREYA, the Buddha of the future, usually depicted as a fat, laughing Buddha. These deities were all imported from India and Central Asia, but over the centuries in China they became associated with other local figures and traditions. Guan Yin, originally AVALOKITESVARA, the bodhisattva of compassion, a male figure, in China became associated with feminine images of childbearing and devotion and to this day has remained a female figure, often pictured with children and dressed in white.

A Chinese original deity figure who has remained popular in both Buddhist and non-Buddhist circles

Worshipper before an image of Guan Yin, the Chinese Buddhist bodhisattva of compassion, at Jing An Temple, downtown Shanghai, China

since Song times is JI GONG. Ji Gong was originally a reclusive monk living in Hangzhou, one of the Song capitals. He was often seen drunk, disorderly, or acting crazy. Because of this he was called "Crazy Ji" and, after his death, worshipped as an enlightened being who, seeing the unreality of the everyday world, chose to ignore the false realities of that conventional world.

The indigenous deity figures were increasingly mixed with the imported Buddhist deities and worshipped side by side in temples. This form of religiosity—indiscriminate mixing at the popular level—is common in Chinese religious practice. At the popular level all religious traditions continue to learn from and borrow from one another to this day.

Buddhist Stories and Folklore

Buddhist storytelling lies at the heart of literature during the Tang period (618–907 C.E.). In this period, the recitation of stories, done at temples, often on feast days, was the only way popular audiences could learn about Buddhist ideas. This oral art developed into a form of literature called *bian wen*, "texts of marvelous events." The core event is usually taken from a Buddhist sutra, then embellished with additional events and characters. The two most popular *bian wen* were stories taken from the VIMALAKIRTI SUTRA and those revolving around Maudgalyayana's journey to save his mother.

By the later imperial periods, the Ming (1368–1644) and Qing (1644–1911), Buddhism was thoroughly mixed and reflected in popular culture, in both drama and, increasingly, fiction. The character of Maitreya, the laughing Buddha, often appeared in plays. Maudgalyayana's filial piety was a constant theme in plays performed on feast days, usually on stages set up in front of temples. And *Xiyouji* (*Journey to the West*), an adventure novel based loosely on the Tang monk *Xuan Zong*'s famous trip to India, was a frequent subject of dramas. The impact of Buddhist ideas is also seen clearly in printed literature, especially the popular novel, which expanded rapidly in the Ming. Today

Buddhist themes continue to be mixed with such popular forms as martial arts literature.

Religious Societies

Popular religiosity also led to the spread of folk-level religious groups not part of the officially recognized Buddhist sangha, or community of monks. These religious *hui* (societies) have been a constant part of Buddhism. But with the increasing popularity of Buddhism at the lower levels of society they became more significant.

Religious societies were often established to promote Buddhist ideas actively, much as missionary societies were established in 19th-century Europe and America. Some were of the nature of cults, meant to focus on the veneration of one certain deity, such as Amitabha. Others even took on political tasks, a feature of Chinese society back at least to Han times (226 B.C.E.–220 C.E.). However the majority existed simply to promote Buddhist ideas and practices. Members were encouraged to donate to new temples or support Buddhist art. Many of the cave temples at Yun Gang and LONG MEN, created during the Northern Wei dynasty (386–534 C.E.), were financed by groups of lay (nonmonk) Buddhists. Other groups joined together to recite sutras or organize feasts. They were often guided by monks and associated closely with temples. And they all engaged in some form of welfare activity.

By the Song period (960–1290 C.E.) popular Buddhist practice at times appeared to be more widespread than sangha/temple-based Buddhism. And that is certainly the case today, to some extent. However, such activities cannot exist without interaction with the living sangha, the groups of monks fully devoted to the Buddha's message.

THE SCHOOLS OF CHINESE BUDDHISM

We have seen already that two early schools, the Dhyana and the Prajna, were influential in early Buddhism in China. These two trends later interacted with the massive translation efforts undertaken in the early period of China's interaction with Buddhism and led to the development

Buddha image at Le Shan, Sichuan, western China, reproducing the original statue at the Yun Gang Caves, in northern Shaanxi, originally carved fifth to sixth centuries C.E.

of several clearly distinguishable schools. Scholars normally speak of eight SCHOOLS OF CHINESE BUDDHISM; the Tantric school is also sometimes added as a ninth. These eight are the Three Stages (San Jie) school, the Lu or Disciplinary (VINAYA) school, the Kosa (ABHIDHARMA-KOSA) school, the TIAN TAI school, the HUA YAN (Avatamsaka) school, the Fa Xiang (Characteristics of Dharma) school, PURE LAND, and CHAN (in Japanese, Zen). By far the most influential of these, in terms of both historical and contemporary Buddhism, are Tian Tai, Hua Yan, Pure Land, and Chan. These four schools are covered in depth in individual articles. The other schools are of relatively historical interest only. (Tantric exists today in China, but mainly in forms imported from Tibetan Buddhism.)

After the Hui Chang persecution of Buddhism in 845 C.E., most Buddhist schools lost influence and faded away. Only Pure Land and Chan remained as the two pillars of Chinese Buddhism. The others, especially Tian Tai and Hua Yan, while influential and admired, do not survive as separate organizations within the larger Chinese sangha.

The Le Shan Buddha, built into the mountainside and carved out of rock, near the congruence of the Minjiang Dadu and Qingyi Rivers, Sichuan, western China, dating from 1312 and said to be the largest stone-carved Buddha image

BUDDHISM IN CONTEMPORARY CHINA

Given the many persecutions of Buddhism in Chinese history, it is sobering to learn that by far the most damaging occurred during the modern era, that period after the fall of the last imperial dynasty, the Qing, in 1911, for it was under the influence of modern concepts that Buddhism experienced sustained criticism.

The republican government that took shape in the precommunist years, roughly 1927–49, was based on the ideas of the Chinese Renaissance, a movement in favor of modernity and science, and critical of traditional beliefs. Proponents of these ideas looked to the West, and, to some extent, modernized Japan, as role models for China. They saw Buddhism, Daoism, and the entire edifice of traditional structures that supported the imperial system, from examinations based on the Confucian classics to traditional dress, as backward and as obstacles to development.

As a result the new republican regime was highly critical of Buddhism's "preferential" position in the traditional scheme of things. In particular the government focused on the economic aspect of monasteries. Monasteries in the later part of the Qing dynasty continued to be independent entities that owned land and farmed. A simple solution to this "parasitic" relationship was to take over temple lands and convert them to other uses. A movement began to seize Buddhist monasteries and convert the buildings to public schools. While the movement did not go to the extreme of total expropriation, it was a widespread shock to the traditional relation between Buddhism and society.

Buddhism continued to flourish as a popular religion, of course. And there were exemplary monks and leaders during this brief period of republican rule. Foremost was TAI XU (T'ai Hsu, 1889–1947), a monk who spoke up to protect temple properties. Tai Xu was well traveled and educated. He started the WU CHANG BUDDHIST INSTITUTE in central China in 1922 to train a new generation of leaders. And he vigorously promoted the revival of the idealist school of Buddhist philosophy, based on the Fa Xiang teachings popular from the Tang dynasty.

Unfortunately no leaders of Tai Xu's caliber were allowed to rise up in the early communist years. And more shocks were ahead. With the advent of the People's Republic of China in 1949, Buddhism (as well as other religions) was singled out for additional measures. From 1950 Buddhism was deemed to be a feudal superstition, and abbots were treated as landlords; they did in fact traditionally often lease out land to tenants. Common monks were equated with the proletariat or peasants, while higher levels of monks were equated with the corrupt social classes, businessmen and landlords. In 1951 a land reform movement confiscated all land held by Buddhist temples, as well as ancestral halls in most villages. This move finally cut the economic legs out from the traditional support structure for Buddhism. Thereafter the remaining temples became completely dependent on government support. A CHINESE BUDDHIST ASSOCIATION established in

1953, for the first time in history, gave central organization to Buddhist groups and temples in China. It also allowed complete control by the central government.

The association today publishes newsletters, communicates with international Buddhist groups, and carries out some research. It has always followed central government policy on important issues, such as the status of Buddhism and the worship of the Dalai Lama in Tibet. As we have seen, central control over Buddhist institutions is not new in Chinese history and is not in itself a cause for worry. The greater issue in the post-1949 religious scene has been the depletion of trained clergy. Monks were forced into lay life or not allowed to teach widely, and new monks were either not recruited or given very little instruction.

At around the same time the CULTURAL REVO-LUTION period in China, 1967–76, severely damaged many Buddhist temples, images, and works of art. Cave frescoes were defaced. Buddha images were decapitated. Although this period of sporadic anarchy was brought under control, and rebuilding has also been constant since, to this day one runs into people who point out the extensive damage that occurred to Buddhism's legacy so recently. The Cultural Revolution is not widely discussed today in China, as the nation focuses on economic growth, yet for Buddhism it was without a doubt a great tragedy.

Since 1979, when China adopted an outward-looking approach to growth and economic integration, religious sites have been restored and the sangha has started to grow again. Local Buddhist activities have been widely allowed, and state control has relaxed. New temples, often built with overseas contributions, sprout up constantly, especially in Fujian and Henan provinces. Training for new monks is improving. It is thus not necessary to allow the tragedy of the Cultural Revolution to color our reading of Buddhism in the future. There is certainly the potential for strong grassroots forms of Buddhism to flourish once again in China.

OVERALL IMPACT OF BUDDHISM ON CHINA

Chinese Buddhism today exists as one single, broad stream, a tradition from which all Chinese culture learns. At the level of ideas certain philosophical concepts such as karma and merit making have passed into every corner of awareness. The language is also full of Buddhist-inspired phrases, just as the literature is filled with Buddhist stories and deities. Chinese regularly use such words as *gongde* (merit), *pusa* (bodhisattva), and *kuhai* (bitter sea), all of which are originally Buddhist. Chinese art and architecture would be unrecognizable without its Buddhist color. The pagoda, an elaboration of the Buddhist stupa, is a typical East Asian building form. Landscape painting is as much Buddhist as it is Daoist, and poetry owes a great debt to the massive influence of vivid Buddhist ideas. In terms of cultural attainment Buddhism has inspired Chinese people to an amazing level of creativity.

Buddhism has also deeply influenced all other traditional strands of Chinese thought. Daoism was hardly recognizable as a religion when Buddhism first arrived. It was so thoroughly affected by this exotic new import that it in effect modeled itself after Buddhism, organizing a corpus of canonic texts, in three parts; issuing ordination certificates for monastics; and appropriating Buddhist folklore into its own stories. As for Confucianism, its major renaissance, the *lixue* (or Neo-Confucian) movement of the Song (960–1279 C.E.) and Ming (1368–1644) dynasties, was heavily influenced by Buddhist ideas. Traditional Confucian concepts were in effect redefined in terms of Buddhist abstract concepts.

Buddhism influenced the traditional Chinese practices of medicine, astronomy, and linguistics. Buddhism in fact pervaded all aspects of traditional Chinese culture and continues to influence contemporary culture, despite the vast changes of the modern period.

While Buddhism's influence on China has been immense, we cannot simply say that China is a Buddhist country. It is in fact its own amalgamation, a creative mix unique to humanity. It is not a predominantly Buddhist culture, for Confucianism and Daoism, as well as utilitarianism and, now, industrialization, have shaped its fate in equally significant ways.

Further reading: Kenneth K. S. Ch'en, *Buddhism in China: A Historical Survey* (Princeton, N.J.: Princeton University Press, 1964); Frank Dobbins, *An Illustrated Comparative Study of Chinese and Japanese Buddhism* (Albuquerque, N. Mex.: American Classical College Press, 1988); Jacques Gernet and Franciscus Verellen, *Buddhism in Chinese Society: An Economic History from the Fifth to the Tenth Centuries* (New York: Columbia University Press, 1998); Nan Huai-Chin, *The Story of Chinese Zen* (New York: Charles E. Tuttle, 1995); W. Pachow, *Chinese Buddhism* (Washington, D.C.: University Press of America, 1980); Zenryv Tsukamoto, *A History of Early Chinese Buddhism: From Its Introduction to the Death of Hui-Yuan.* Translated by Leon Hurvitz (New York: Kodansha America, 1985); Arthur F. Wright, *Buddhism in Chinese History* (Stanford, Calif.: Stanford University Press, 1959); Erik Zurcher, *The Buddhist Conquest of China: The Spread and Adaptation of Buddhism in Early Medieval China* (Atlantic Highlands, N.J.: Humanities International Press, 1973).

China-Hong Kong, Buddhism in

Although Hong Kong's history as a large city began only in the 1840s, when Britain gained possession and built it into a strategic colony, Buddhism had a presence in the area long before the British arrived. Buddhist monasteries and nunneries coexisted with local temples dedicated to local gods, as well as Daoist institutions. Until the modern era, however, these institutions had limited interaction with the local people; they tended to be isolated buildings with monastics leading their own lifestyles. Despite the government's open preference for Christianity during most of Hong Kong's modern history, Buddhism today remains a major presence in Hong Kong society. The number of active Buddhist believers has been estimated at between 500,000 and 1 million (of a total of nearly 7 million), although many other inhabitants engage in Buddhist rituals on an occasional basis. In particular, most non-Christian funerals today are invariably Buddhist. It is a good bet that Buddhism will continue as a major part of Hong Kong's social fabric and cultural sensibilities.

The earliest proof of Buddhism in Hong Kong is found in three temples. The oldest are the Beiju Si and Lingdu Si in the New Territory towns of Tuen Mun and Yuen Long, respectively. They were said to have been renamed by a monk, Bei Du, in 428 C.E. Hence they were in existence before that time. Their locations in the New Territories, near the coastal forts guarding the approaches to the Pearl River, reflect the importance of the sea trade throughout most of China's imperial history. Interestingly, both of these early temples probably housed communities of unmarried, vegetarian women during parts of their histories. And the Bei Du temple was at one point (1829) converted into a Daoist monastery; it later reverted to a Buddhist institution in 1926. It has been called Qing Shan temple ever since.

Another well-known temple, the Ling Yun, was also a Buddhist nunnery for a period. Built originally between 1426 and 1435, it was in turn a private villa before reverting to a nunnery in 1911.

In the premodern period the landscape in Hong Kong was fluid and informal. Temples often switched between Buddhist and Daoist affiliations, and temples often converted to nunneries, as mentioned. Temples were found in both urban and rural settings. Those in the rural New Territories were basically retreats for religious hermits. Those in urban settings were used for ritual services. There was no strong sense of belonging to a single "Buddhist" religious community. Instead, different institutions lived independently.

In 1957, there were 83 Buddhist institutions in the whole of Hong Kong; a large part, 89 percent, were hermitages based in the New Territories island of Lantau. And the majority of those, some 70 percent, were not MONASTERIES but were female-led nunneries, called *zhai tang*, or "vegetarian halls." These halls served as places of solace for women who refused to marry (known as *zhushunu*), as well as lower-class, migrant, or otherwise unattached women who would otherwise have led a precarious life.

The early monasteries were not large public institutions, as were often found in other parts of China. Instead, they were smaller temples informally run by clergy and lay supporters together. Ownership and management responsibilities for these temples were passed from generation to generation in a kind of inheritance system.

THE BRITISH AND BUDDHISM

In 1841 the first governor of Hong Kong, Captain Charles Eliot (1801–75), proclaimed that "the natives of the island of Hong Kong and all natives of China thereto resorting, shall be governed according to the laws and customs of China, every description of torture excepted." The government went on to pursue a policy of benign neglect of the spiritual aspects of Chinese society. The Chinese population was generally left to fend for itself, and this included the establishment and management of Buddhist institutions. If any care was taken with regard to religious issues, it was to focus only on Christianity.

There was a minimal government structure to deal with Chinese society. The secretary for Chinese affairs was responsible for advising on issues of Chinese culture. In 1919 this official was put in charge of religious institutions as well. In fact the government's interest extended only to registration and landownership, and not to involvement with religious content or forms.

In 1928, a law that dealt with Chinese temples, the Chinese Temples Ordinance, was introduced. In order to prevent misuse of temple funds, all local temples (with the exception of five established ones) were put under a Chinese Temple Committee. The committee was in fact mainly composed of leading Chinese community leaders concerned with the proliferation of exploitive religious practices. Today the committee is concerned largely with registration of temples.

BUDDHIST REVIVAL

When a vigorous revival movement took hold on mainland China, Hong Kong was soon affected. In the 1930s new institutions such as the Tung Lin Kok Yuen introduced a new type of Buddhism to the local population, one characterized by active participation in society. The revival started with the visit of important clergy, such as TAI XU in 1920. It was also evident in the establishment of new institutions and the restoration of others. As in China, the Buddhist reform movement focused less on intellectual issues and more on institutional reform, often in the face of scorching criticism from such Chinese intellectuals as HU SHI.

Tai Xu visited Hong Kong seven times, beginning in 1910 and ending in 1936. However, he formally invoked the Buddhist revival only when he visited in 1920. Tai Xu's followers soon arrived to lecture and educate the local population in Buddhism. And unlike in the traditional model, in which lectures were held in monasteries, from the 1920s lectures were increasingly presented in public forums such as playgrounds, parks, and cinemas.

Many of the new Buddhist institutions were built in the rural areas, especially Lantau Island, Shatin, Tsuen Wan, and Taipo, in some cases along the rail lines. By 1927 three temples, the Qingshan in Tuen Mun, Lingyun in Yuen Long, and Po Lin Monastery on Lantau, were regularly performing ORDINATION ceremonies for new clergy.

The role of public lay supporters was redefined at this time. Public ordination ceremonies were held to admit lay followers as lay disciples (*guiyi dizi*) of the Buddha, a significant innovation for Hong Kong Buddhism. Tai Xu held such a ceremony during his visit in 1928 in which he admitted 3,000 as disciples.

This social atmosphere culminated in the establishment of the Hong Kong Buddhism Study Association. Its roots lay in the Buddhist Society, a private group formed in 1916. The group's purpose and title were revised in 1931 to the Buddhist Study Association. Another important institution, the Tung Lin Kok Yuen (Eastern Lotus Enlightenment Garden), was established in 1935 by Lady Clara Ho Tung (1875–1938) with the goal of becoming the center of Buddhist community in Hong Kong. The society and the Yuen coexisted well and led directly to the formation of the Hong Kong Buddhist Association in 1945.

THE HONG KONG BUDDHIST ASSOCIATION

The association was formed only after the end of the Anti-Japanese War in 1945. It first took over a former Japanese Buddhist temple, Dongbenyuan, in the urban district of Wanchai. The Japanese monks residing in the temple, seeing defeat as imminent, decided to donate their temple as long as it remained a Buddhist institution. They transferred ownership, on August 16, 1945, to two lay Buddhists who were also active as leaders of the Tung Lin Kok Yuen, Chen Jingtao and Lin Lingzhen. In 1967 the association moved to larger premises on Lockhart Road, where it continues today. The association's Web site claims a membership of 10,000 people, including clerics.

The association's leader, the Venerable Kok Kwong, is the de facto leader of Hong Kong's Buddhists, although other groups are not bound to follow his leadership. In fact, his major role is as a visible presence at formal ceremonies. He is also a delegate to the National People's Congress, a national-level role. In his rare public statements he has tended to support Beijing's policies strongly.

Further reading: David Faure, *The Structure of Chinese Rural Society: Lineage and Village in the Eastern New Territories, Hong Kong* (Hong Kong: Oxford University Press, 1986); Jean Gittins, *Eastern Windows-Western Skies* (Hong Kong: South China Morning Post, 1969); The Hong Kong Buddhist Association. Available online. URL: http://www.hkbuddhist.org/index.html. Accessed on January 6, 2006; Rubie Watson, "Girls' Houses and Working Women Expressive Culture in the Pearl River Delta, 1900–41," in Maria Jaschok et al., eds., *Women and Chinese Patriarchy* (Hong Kong: Hong Kong University Press, 1994), 25–44; Steve Tsang, *A Modern History of Hong Kong* (Hong Kong: Hong Kong University Press, 2004).

China-Taiwan, Buddhism in

Chinese Buddhism in Taiwan has thrived in the modern period. Taiwan is today a center of Buddhist development.

Scholars can document the existence of Buddhism in Taiwan only from the migration of Chinese fleeing to the island after the fall of the Ming dynasty (1368–1644). Many of the "monks" of this period were Ming loyalists who fled to the island in clerical disguise, and legitimate clerics were few in number and largely ignorant of Buddhist teachings. Those whose names appear in the records were noted for non-Buddhist accomplishments such as rainmaking, painting, poetry, and playing go. Most functioned as temple caretakers and funeral specialists and did not engage in teaching, meditation, or other Buddhist practices.

As the island became more settled, many more temples were founded, particularly around the capital city, Tainan. Despite this apparently vigorous activity, it is doubtful that very many of the monks and nuns who inhabited these temples had received more than the novices' ordination, since there was no ordaining monastery in Taiwan, and only scant records exist of those who journeyed to the mainland to receive the full ordination.

In 1895, the Chinese government ceded Taiwan to Japan, and when Japanese troops arrived, they were accompanied by Buddhist chaplains. These were eager to establish mission stations in order to propagate Japanese Buddhism to the native population, but funding from their head temples was insufficient, and only a very small percentage of the Chinese population ever enrolled in Japanese Buddhist lineages.

In fact, one of the most notable features of the Japanese period is the effort of the local Buddhists to keep their Chinese identity and traditions. This period saw the institution of the first facilities for transmitting the full monastic precepts in Taiwan. Four temples established "ordination platforms," and the leaders of these temples, all of whom had received ordination at the Yongquan Temple in Fuzhou, transmitted their tonsure-lineages to Taiwan. Ordinees from these temples went forth and founded other temples, giving rise to the "four great ancestral lineages" that defined and organized Buddhism during the Japanese period.

Even as Chinese Buddhism attempted to maintain its own distinctive identity, it still had to accommodate the government in some fashion, and so clergy and laity joined to form Buddhist organizations that functioned as governmental liaisons. The largest of these, founded in 1922, was the South Seas Buddhist Association, which operated until 1945.

The end of the Pacific war in 1945 saw the return of Taiwan to China, and in 1949, the mainland fell to the Communists and the Nationalists fled to Taiwan. All of these events kept the political and economic situation in turmoil, and Buddhist clerics experienced difficulty keeping their monasteries viable. A few monks of national eminence arrived, such as the Zhangjia Living Buddha (1891–1957), Bai Sheng (1904–89), Yin Shun (1906–). They were the leaders of the newly revived BUDDHIST ASSOCIATION OF THE REPUBLIC OF CHINA (BAROC) and went to Taiwan for reasons that paralleled the Nationalists': to use Taiwan as a base of operations until they could return home to rebuild Buddhism.

The BAROC mediated between Buddhism and the government in several ways: the government expected it to register all clergy and temples, organize and administer clerical ordinations, certify clergy for exit visas, and help in the framing of laws dealing with religion. In other areas, the BAROC confronted the government when it threatened religious interests. Two notable controversies concerned the failure of the government to return confiscated Japanese era temples to religious use, and the government's obstruction of efforts to establish a Buddhist university.

Because the laws on civic organizations allowed only one organization to fill any single niche in society, the BAROC enjoyed hegemony until the late 1980s. Then, in 1989, the government no longer dealt with Buddhist monks and nuns separately, but registered them under their lay names as ordinary citizens. Thus, the BAROC was no longer needed to certify their status. That same year, a new law on civic organizations took effect, abolishing the "one niche, one organization" rule and opening the way for competition. In the ensuing period, other Buddhist organizations took root. Some grew out of preexisting groups, most notably FOGUANGSHAN and the BUDDHIST COMPASSION RELIEF TZU CHI ASSOCIATION. Others were newly founded, such as DHARMA DRUM MOUNTAIN and Zhongtai Shan.

Further reading: Charles B. Jones, *Buddhism in Taiwan: Religion and the State 1660–1990* (Honolulu: University of Hawaii Press, 1999).

China-Taiwan, Daoism in

Daoism, as a major Chinese religion, is present in Taiwan at both official and unofficial levels. Officially there are an organization of Daoism and a handful of strictly Daoist temples. Yet the number of worshippers in this official Daoist religious practice is dwarfed by those who follow Buddhism and other Chinese religions. Unofficially, however, Daoism is an intrinsic part of popular religious practice in Taiwan. Indeed, popular religion in Taiwan, as well as China, is often termed "popular Daoism."

With the political and economic changes in contemporary Taiwanese society, the practice of

Chenghuang (City God) temple, built in 1748, Hsinchu (Xinzhu), central Taiwan *(Institute for the Study of Religion, Santa Barbara, California)*

maintaining *shentan*, or "spirit altars"—another term for Daoist temples—has become more streamlined than in traditional Chinese Daoism. As a result, Daoism in contemporary Taiwan is mixed with belief in the BUDDHA and additional folk beliefs common to southern China. These changes have the following background.

Inhabitants of the border regions of southern China migrated to Taiwan island during the Chinese Middle Ages—that is, between the Tang dynasty (618–907 C.E.) and the Ming-Qing period (1368–1911 C.E.). By the late Qing Taiwan was nominally ruled by the mainland Chinese imperial regime, but with little actual control or presence. During the subsequent Japanese occupation (1895–1945 C.E.) a colonial policy of "forbidding Daoism and promoting Buddhism" predominated. After the defeat of Japan in World War II the regime then ruling China, the Kuomintang (KMT), also assumed power in Taiwan. The KMT authorities intentionally ignored Daoism for the sake of their own political purposes. The regime feared

the accumulation of popular power anywhere in Taiwan. Because of such concerns the various Republic of China (ROC) Daoism associations offered no training in Daoism to their members, not even training in basic Daoist doctrine. The government feared that once the members became well educated, the ruling KMT authorities would ultimately lose control over the Taiwanese people. Therefore, the association headquarters functioned only to collect annual fees from the *shentans*, or temples, throughout the countryside. The consequence of this situation has been the entanglement of orthodox Daoist belief with Buddhist beliefs.

Excluding the small number of Christians in Taiwan today, most of the population can be considered as followers of popular religions. This term is widely used in academic and religious discussions today. However, few people have a correspondingly clear or distinct idea about the meaning of Daoism. In a broad sense most Taiwanese may be regarded as trustees of Daoism, whose number of adherents is several times that of Christianity in Taiwan. In spite of this, we must recognize that some forms of orthodox Daoist schools still exist at the local level in Taiwan, from north to south. These are the Zhengyi Pai (school), Chuanzhen Dao, Lingbau DAOISM, and Lushan Pai. Among them Zhengyi Pai and Lingbau Pai may be regarded as identical lineages, judging from the titles of deities who at the beginning of any Daoist ritual are asked by the Daoist priest (*daoshi* or *fashi*) to descend from heaven to the altar to listen to the needs of the trustees. Compared with the other three schools, Chuanzhen Dao is said to be the newest branch for most Taiwan people because it has only recently spread from Hong Kong and mainland China to Taiwan, over the past two decades.

According to historical records, during the earliest Spring and Autumn period (722–481 B.C.E.) of Chinese history the ancient Chinese worshipped many deities, including heaven, the earth deity, ghosts, and ancestral spirits, in various forms. At the same time they expressed a unique understanding, a belief in the cosmos and the living world, through a symbolic system. During the Eastern Han dynasty, in 384 C.E., ZHANG DAOLING, considered the founder of Daoism, collected folk magic practices and put them into the context of this ancient Chinese religious culture. He combined these elements into an integrated whole that thereafter was called "Daoism." The clearest expression of Daoism gradually turned toward those aspects related to the search for eternal life through many empirically oriented methods and procedures.

There should be no doubt that Daoism itself, like other religions, has its characteristic pattern of logic. With the exception of Lushan Pai, which is concerned solely with traditional forms of Daoist magic to satisfy the daily needs of trustees, the contents and expression of the other branches of Daoism can be classified into the following five aspects: canonical texts, teachings, divine spells and documents, divination, and inner meditation inside the human body.

Despite their various forms of expression, the different schools are all based on an identical system of cosmology, theology, ontology, and life values. This common ground is the conceptual system of YIN/YANG and *wuxing* (the five elements). The former is a set of contrasting concepts about positive and negative attributes of material in the universe, and the latter is the fivefold classification of earthly materials: wood, fire, soil, metal, and water. Both are original and fundamental beliefs of the Chinese, who thought everything in the world (plants, animals, human, nonliving things included) could be fully classified, recognized, and conceptualized within the scheme of yin-yang/*wuxing* without exception and must be understood from this point of view. As a result the most ideal situations are "the harmonious union of yin and yang" and "the genetic relation of *wuxing*."

Compared with the other religions of the world, from ancient times to the present, these principles can still be seen as the most cardinal and unique core beliefs of Daoism, although Daoist culture has progressively changed and developed over the past 5,000 years. All beings are regarded as the by-products of the functioning of Dao. Because of this we can realize why the ultimate and transcendental is nothing but the unification of humans and heaven (*tianren heyi*), an ideal value constantly searched for by all Chinese.

Further reading: William G. Goddard, *Formosa: A Study in Chinese History* (London: Macmillan, 1966); Margery Wolf, *Women and the Family in Rural Taiwan* (Stanford, Calif.: Stanford University Press, 1972).

China-Tibet, development of Buddhism in

The name *Tibet* is likely derived from the Mongolian word *Thubet* and is related to the Chinese *Tufan* and the Arabic *Tubbat*. Tibetans call their homeland *Bod* (pronounced with a "P" sound) and refer to it poetically as "the abode of snow." Tibet occupies the highest geographic region on Earth—"the roof of the world"—where people live at altitudes of 16,000 feet above sea level. Mostly it consists of a high plateau surrounded on three sides by massive mountain ranges; much of the area is uninhabitable except by the hardiest of Tibetan nomads and yak herders. However, it is not entirely a wilderness of snow and barren wasteland; there are numerous valleys and plains, pastures, fields, and woodlands, which create a great diversity of local growing conditions and wildlife habitat. The staple food, called *tsampa*, is made from roasted barley grains, ground into flour, and moistened with Tibetan butter tea.

The origins of the Tibetan people are unclear, especially since different peoples have migrated into the region during its history. One traditional origin story describes them as descendants of the Lord of Compassion AVALOKITESVARA, who in the form of a monkey took as his wife a mountain ogress. From their divine forefather, it is said, the Tibetans inherited gentleness, compassion, and a tendency not to talk more than necessary, and from their foremother, stubbornness, avarice, and love of meat.

There are varying accounts of the first king and the origins of the ancient Tibetan empire. One tells of a strange figure with long blue eyebrows and webbed fingers, an outcast from his native India who wandered north and appeared in the Yarlung valley. He encountered some farmers who asked him where he was from; not understanding their language, he pointed at the sky. Since the people of that time were said to worship the sky, they regarded him as a holy being descended from the sky and so acclaimed him as their ruler, hoisting him onto a chair on their necks to carry him to the village. So he was called the "Neck-Enthroned King," Nyatri Tsenpo. It was believed that the first seven kings after him had no tombs as upon death they ascended to their heavenly home by means of a rope of light that stretched from the crown of their head to the sky. In the life of the eighth king, however, this rope was accidentally cut and after that the kings of Tibet were buried in tombs.

Tibet enters into known history in the seventh century under the dominance of the Yarlung dynasty and the rule of King Songtsen Gampo (605?–649). At this time Tibet was surrounded by the Buddhist cultures of northwest India, Nepal, Central Asia, and China. Ironically, the people among whom Buddhism was to take such hold first appear in historical records as a fierce invading force known as "the Red-faces," a reference to the fact that their soldiers painted their faces with red ocher. The Tibetan empire was ruled from the seventh to the ninth centuries by three kings, who are traditionally known as the Dharma-kings or religious kings: Songsten Gampo (c. 618–650), Trisong Detsen (c. 740–798), and Relbachen (815–836).

Songsten Gampo is credited with sending scholars to India to develop a Tibetan script and grammar based on SANSKRIT, and with making Tibet open to the practice of Buddhism. He secured political alliances with both China and Nepal by marrying princesses from those Buddhist countries. His Chinese wife is said to have had an image of Sakyamuni BUDDHA, which was installed in the JOKHANG temple. The statue, known as Jowo Rinpoche, continues to be revered as the most sacred image in Tibet and the Jokhang, the most sacred temple.

From these beginnings, Buddhism took hold of the Tibetan spirit and was thoroughly established in the Tibetan court during the reign of King Trisong Detsen (c. 740–798), although not without the opposition of those who still held to earlier indigenous forms of religion. Under Trisong Detsen, the great Indian Buddhist scholar SANTARAKSITA and the great Tantric yogi PADMASAMBHAVA were invited to Tibet. Santaraksita's first visit coincided with climatic upheavals such as storms and floods, which were interpreted by Trisong Detsen's antagonists as the displeasure of the local spirits. In order to overcome this obstacle, he suggested that the king invite Padmasambhava, who was known for his magical arts. Through Tantric rituals and magic formulas, the opposing spirits of Tibet were subdued and bound to the service of the Buddha Dharma by Padmasambhava, known in Tibet as Guru Rinpoche.

Once the way was clear, Santaraksita returned and along with Padmasambhava oversaw the eventual construction of the first monastery of Tibet, Samye. Thus began the Tibetan monastic system and an extensive program of translation of Buddhist texts. During the establishment of Buddhism in Tibet, Buddhist teachers from both India and China were attracted to the region, where they promoted rival schools of thought. The Chinese approach to ENLIGHTENMENT proposed that it was a state achieved instantaneously when physical and mental processes fell away. Alternatively, the Indian teachers proposed that enlightenment was the result of a gradual process of mental purification, and the step-by-step accumulation of merit and wisdom. A famous debate called for by King Trisong Detsen between "sudden" and "gradual" enlightenment was held in 792 at Samye between the Chinese CHAN monk Hua Shang and Santaraksita's student, Kamalasila. Kamalasila was declared the winner and the Indian gradual method of training was accepted as the standard of Buddhism for Tibet.

By the time of the third religious king, Relbachen (r. 815–836), Buddhism was strongly supported by the ruling and educated classes of Tibetan society and was on its way to becoming the religion of the people. Relbachen is portrayed as a somewhat fanatic follower of Buddhism. Monks in his reign were known as "Priests of the King's Head," a reference to the practice of tying a string to his braided hair, to which was attached a cloth that the monks sat on during state ceremonies, signifying the king's subservience to the SANGHA. Opposition to the excesses of Relbachen's rule increased until he was assassinated and succeeded by his elder brother, Lang Darma, a bitter opponent of Buddhism. Lang Darma's reign ushers in a period of Buddhist persecution and marks the end of what is called the "first dissemination" of Buddhism in Tibet. His assassination in 842 ended the Yarlung dynasty and Tibet entered upon a period of political chaos.

The renaissance of Buddhism in Tibet, known as the "second dissemination," began in about 978 with the arrival of some Indian scholars. In 1042 the famous Indian scholar ATISA founded the first school of Buddhism in Tibet, the KADAMPA order. The main schools founded after this time, the GELUG, the KARGYU, and the SAKYA, are referred to as "new schools" to distinguish them from the NYINGMA, the "old school," which traces its origins to Padmasambhava and relies on texts and translations from the period of the first dissemination.

By the 12th century, Tibetan military power had long since waned in the region and the Mongolians with Genghis Khan at their head were the new power in Central Asia. The Mongolians moved to take control of Tibet, but the khan was converted to Buddhism and a "patron-priest" relationship developed between the Sakya chief priest and the ruling khan in which the Sakya lama became the spiritual adviser of the khan and the khan provided the military support for the priest's interests. In subsequent centuries, the dominance of the Sakya school in the Tibetan monastic system declined and was replaced by the Gelug, founded in 1409 by TSONG KHAPA. The Gelug system, anchored by the largest monasteries in Tibet—Gaden, Drepung, and Sera—became a spiritual powerhouse led by the institution of the DALAI LAMA, the supreme spiritual and political ruler of Tibet.

The institution of the Dalai Lamas started in 1578 when Sonam Gyatso, the head of the Gelug order, visited the ALTAN KHAN, the most prominent of the Mongol chieftains at that time. In return for his religious instruction, the khan bestowed the title of *Dalai*, "Ocean" (of Wisdom), on his teacher. From that time on, the successors of Sonam Gyatso as well as his two predecessors bore the title *Dalai Lama*. In the history of the Dalai Lamas, Ngawang Losang Gyatso, known as the "Great Fifth" (1617–82), is credited with being the first to rule over a united Tibet since the end of the Yarlung dynasty in the ninth century.

Currently DALAI LAMA XIV, Tenzin Gyatso, the 14th in this line, presides over the most dramatic upheaval in modern Tibetan history, the advance of Chinese armies into Tibet that began in 1950. In 1959 the Dalai Lama escaped to India, where he was given asylum and allowed to set up a Tibetan government in exile in Dharamsala. He was followed into exile by thousands of Tibetans who made the dangerous trek on foot across the mountains into India. The Chinese CULTURAL REVOLUTION of the 1960s was particularly hard on Tibet, where there were large-scale destruction of monasteries and suffering of thousands of monastics and lay people. Despite some continued human rights abuses reported by agencies such as Amnesty International, the 14th Dalai Lama has maintained his efforts to seek a political compromise with the Chinese government. In the meantime, economic development in recent years has dramatically transformed Tibetan life.

Further reading: John Powers, *Tibetan Buddhism* (Ithaca, N.Y.: Snow Lion, 1995); Geoffrey Samuel, *Civilized Shamans: Buddhism in Tibetan Societies* (Washington, D.C.: Smithsonian, 1993); Orville Schell, *Virtual Tibet: Searching for Shangri-La from the Himalayas to Hollywood* (New York: Henry Holt, 2000); Tsepon W. D. Shakabpa, *Tibet: A Political History* (1967. Reprint, New York: Potala, 1984); Tsering Shakya, *The Dragon in the Land of Snows: A History of Modern Tibet since 1947* (New York: Columbia University Press, 1999); David L. Snellgrove and Hugh E. Richardson, *A Cultural History of Tibet* (1968. Reprint, Boulder, Colo.: Prajna Press, 1980); R. A. Stein, *Tibetan Civilization.* Translated by J. E. Stapelton Driver (1962. Reprint, Palo Alto, Calif.: Stanford University Press, 1995).

Chinese Buddhist Association

In China today, Buddhism enjoys greater support from the government than either Daoism or Christianity. At the popular level, Daoism is far less popular than Buddhism, the largest religious community in China. Unlike Christianity, still suspect as a foreign-based faith, Buddhism is viewed as a more indigenous Chinese religion. There are an estimated 100 million Buddhists in China.

The Chinese Buddhist Association serves as a liaison between the government and the Buddhist community and has the responsibility of implementing government regulations related to religion in China. It is led nationally by a standing committee and its officers. The current chairman is the Venerable Master Yi Cheng. Leadership at the national level is supplemented with provincial leadership located in a prominent temple in each province.

During the early 20th century, Buddhists in China, who lacked strong national organization, attempted to create a China-wide association to represent Buddhist interests to the new secular government. An initial Chinese Buddhist Associa-

tion began to hold conferences in 1929 and met annually until World War II began in China with the Japanese attack on the country in 1937.

In 1945, as the war came to an end, the Venerable TAI XU (T'ai Hsu) (1890–1947) became head of a Committee for the Reorganization of Chinese Buddhism, which led two years later to the formation of a new Chinese Buddhist Association. It soon became moribund as the Chinese Revolution occurred. In 1953, yet a third attempt to form a Chinese Buddhist Association occurred in Beijing. A lay Buddhist, Zhao Puchu (1907–2000), was selected as general secretary. The organization functioned for 12 years, until the beginning of the CULTURAL REVOLUTION, when all religious activity was banned in the People's Republic of China.

In 1978, the Chinese Buddhist Association was revived with most of its former leadership, including Zhao Puchu, assuming their previous roles. Working with the leadership of the Communist Party of China, Zhao announced a program for the restoration of Buddhist activity throughout the country. After that announcement, Buddhist temples and monasteries were reopened and many damaged during the Cultural Revolution were refurbished—especially those located in major urban areas or known for their artistic or historical importance. During the 1980s, the study of Buddhism revived, Buddhist books and scriptures were published, structures created for the education of monks and nuns, and the association began to develop international relationships with Buddhists, especially in neighboring countries. The association affiliated with the WORLD FELLOWSHIP OF BUDDHISTS.

Further reading: Donald E. MacInnis, *Religion in China Today* (New York: Orbis Books, 1989); Holmes Welch, *The Buddhist Revival in China* (Cambridge: Harvard University Press, 1968).

Chinese Buddhist schools *See* SCHOOLS OF CHINESE BUDDHISM.

Chinese Esoteric Buddhism

TANTRIC BUDDHISM, or VAJRAYANA (or "Esoteric") Buddhism, entered China around 720 C.E. and for several centuries was a major school, before gradually losing influence. Vajrayana focuses more on practice than on teachings, which are fundamentally Mahayana-based. Vajrayana emphasizes the relationship between the teacher (guru) and disciple. Rituals are complex. Although it sprang from MAHAYANA BUDDHISM, Vajrayana claims to allow the practitioner to achieve nirvana quickly, in the current life.

Vajrayana migrated from its originating points in India through Afghanistan and Tajikistan to China and Mongolia. It reached Xian, the Chinese capital, at the height of the Tang dynasty (618–907 C.E.). Subhakarasimha (637–735) and two other Vajrayana priests, VAJRABODHI (671–741) and AMOGHAVAJRA (705–774), made the long trek to Xian at the request of the emperor Xuan Zong (r. 712–756). The trio are most remembered for their work of translating many Buddhist and Tantric works into Chinese. In the process, they mastered Confucian and Daoist teachings. The integration of Chinese and Indian thought created the unique Chinese form of Esoteric Buddhism, called in Chinese *hanmi*.

Subhakarasimha and Vajrabodhi initially established Vajrayana at the Great Propagating Goodness Temple (Daxingshan Si), and their young student Amoghavajra built on their accomplishments. Only 15 when he made the original trip to China, he returned in 732 to India, gathered more texts, and finally traveled back to Xian in 746. He became the instrument for receiving the emperor Xuan Zong into the Buddhist religion. The next emperor, Su Zong (r. 756–762), gave Amoghavajra the task of translating a library of texts, a program that absorbed most of his energy for the next two decades. When he died in 774, he had seen Vajrayana become a popular movement and himself a greatly honored Buddhist leader. Unfortunately, under the emperor Tang Wuzong (841–847), who banned Vajrayana teachings, much of Amoghavajra's work was undone. It would be several centuries before it would again rise to its former level of success. In the meantime, Hui Guo (746–805), Amoghavajra's disciple, went to Japan with KUKAI (774–835) to become the sources of the Japanese Vajrayana school, later known as SHINGON.

Integral to the story of Chinese Esoteric Buddhism was the introduction of Vajrayana into Tibet in the eighth century. PADMASAMBHAVA is generally considered to be the founder of the unique form of Vajrayana that would dominate Tibet. His work would result in the development of the old school of Tibetan Buddhism, the NYINGMA. Then in the 11th century, a new lineage of Vajrayana teachings would emerge with a set of five masters, beginning with TILOPA (988–1069). He would be followed by NAROPA (1016–1100) and MARPA (1012–97), the person who actually took the teachings to Tibet. Marpa's student MILAREPA (1052–1133) and his student GAMPOPA (1079–1153) established the teachings, now known as the KAGYU tradition.

A third Tibetan tradition originated within Tibet. Its founder, Khon Konchok Gyalpo (1034–1102), built the Gray Earth (Sakya) monastery in central Tibet, from which the tradition would take its name. The SAKYA tradition was firmly established in the 12th and 13th centuries.

After the death of Genghis Kahn in 1227, his son, Ogedei, and his progeny were awarded China and the other lands of East Asia. In the 1240s the decision was made to incorporate Tibet into the realm and Ogedei's son, Prince Godan, assumed the task. The conquest occurred with minimal opposition and afterward Godan invited the Sakya leader, the fourth Gongma Sakya Pandita (1182–1251), to his court in Mongolia. The relationship that grew from that visit began a second revival of the Vajrayana in China. Golan's conversion to Buddhism bore real fruit after his brother, Kublai Khan, became emperor of China. Kublai Khan invited the fifth Gongma, Drogon Chogyal Phagpa, to Mongolia. In gratitude for Phagpa's inventing a new script for written Mongolian,

Kublai Khan made Vajrayana Buddhism the state religion of his empire and awarded Phagpa political leadership over three Tibetan provinces. The Sakya leaders would also be the primary secular authority in Tibet for the next century.

With Vajrayana Buddhism now the religion of choice in China and Mongolia, the next development would occur in Tibet, where a new teacher, TSONGKHAPA (1357–1419), would take the lead in reforming Tibetan Buddhism. Ganden Monastery was the disseminating point for the new teachings, the GELUG tradition. One of his students, Gendun Drub (1391–1474), would found the Tashilhumpo monastery near Shigatse, west of Lhasa, the center that eventually solidified the position of the Gelug tradition in Tibet. Gendun Drub was succeeded at Tashilhumpo by Gendun Gyatso (1475–1542) and Sonam Gyatso (1543–88), the latter destined to change the historical trajectory of two countries.

In the centuries since the Sakya had been placed in power, the kingdom of Kublai Khan began slowly to disintegrate. Then with the fall of his dynasty, the Yuan, in 1368, Vajrayana Buddhism would fade and largely be replaced with PURE LAND BUDDHISM and CHAN BUDDHISM. It would fall to a later leader, ALTAN KHAN (1507–83), both to reunify the Mongol people in a semblance of Kublai Khan's old kingdom and to revive Esoteric (Vajrayana) Buddhism. Once in power, Altan Khan turned to Tibet for religious teachings that could unify his kingdom. Having heard of Sonam Gyatso, the khan invited the abbot to Mongolia. Sonam Gyatso proved a capable teacher for the khan's people, and before his return to Tibet a notable exchange occurred. Sonam Gyatso proclaimed his patron the reincarnation of Kublai Khan and the embodiment of the bodhisattva Vajrapari, thus uniting his political and religious credentials. In return, the khan, in his religious office, named Sonam Gyatso, DALAI LAMA, teacher of the ocean of wisdom. He would subsequently be seen as an incarnation of AVALOKITESVARA (or GUAN YIN), the bodhisattva of compassion. The title *Dalai Lama* was then retroactively applied to Sonam Gyatso's two predecessors.

The future Dalai Lamas would maintain their relationship with the khan of the Mongols, and Lozang Gyatso (1617–82), the Fifth Dalai, with the assistance of Mongol troops, secured authority as the political leader of all Tibet. In the process of establishing the Gelug in power, he suppressed those schools he perceived as possible competitors (such as the Sakya) and assisted others (such as the Nyingma). Esoteric Buddhism of the Gelug school was now established in Tibet and Mongolia and would remain dominant until the 20th century.

In China, Pure Land Buddhism would become the dominant form of Buddhism, though outposts of Esoteric Buddhism were scattered across the land. Then in the 18th century the spread of the Chinese empire during the Manchu (Qing) dynasty (1644–1911) would provide a context for a new revival of Esoteric Buddhism. Under the rule of the Manchu emperor Qianlong (1711–99), China incorporated Mongolia and Tibet into its territory. Qianlong even sent an army into Tibet to confirm the Dalai Lama's political authority.

A primary symbol of the new respect given Vajrayana Buddhism at this time was Qianlong's creation of the temple YONGHE GONG (the Palace of Harmony and Peace) as a new Buddhist center in Beijing. Originally built as a palace in the previous century, the huge complex was turned into a lamasery and a guesthouse for official visitors from Mongolia and Tibet. Qianlong subsequently erected a number of Vajrayana temples throughout his empire, especially in areas dominated by different ethnic minorities. The erection of these temples encouraged the migration of Mongolian and Tibetan priests.

In the 20th century, northwest (or Outer) Mongolia declared its independence from China (1911) and later emerged as the modern nation of Mongolia. The more southern and eastern parts of the land, Inner Mongolia, remained a Chinese province. Two years later, the Dalai Lama proclaimed Tibetan independence and then quickly moved to sign a treaty of mutual recognition with Mongolia. Vajrayana thus had three main centers in the greater Chinese region—Inner Mongolia, Outer Mongolia and Tibet—supplemented by many temples scattered across China.

Within China, Vajrayana practice would continue through World War II and the Chinese Revolution. However, in the 1950s and 1960s it would undergo significant suppression by the antireligion policies of the People's Republic of China, which also moved to incorporate Tibet back into its territory. The suppression of Tibetan and Mongolian Buddhism would have two unplanned consequences. First, a number of Chinese citizens, especially Tibetans, would leave and disperse throughout the world. Their migrations have led to a geographic spread and remarkable growth of Tibetan Buddhism. At the same time, relocation policies within China have seen Tibetans scattered across the country, further diffusing their religion as the repressive policies most in force in the 1970s have been greatly relaxed.

As the new century begins, many Tibetan and Mongolian temples have been restored and monasteries again opened. It is difficult to tell how many adherents remain. Among Han Chinese in the last generation, Vajrayana Buddhism has experienced a revival as demonstrated by new emergent groups such as the Taiwanese-based TRUE BUDDHA SCHOOL and the World Buddhist-Hanmi Association based in Manchuria, the People's Republic of China.

Further reading: Kenneth K. S. Ch'en, *Buddhism in China: A Historical Survey* (Princeton, N.J.: Princeton University Press, 1964); Donald S. Lopez Jr., *Buddhism in Practice* (Princeton, N.J.: Princeton University Press, 1995); Chogay Trichen, *The History of the Sakya Tradition* (Bristol, U.K.: Ganesha Press, 1983).

Ching Hai Meditation Association, Master

The Master Ching Hai Meditation Association is a Taiwanese group founded by Ching Hai Wu Shang Shih, "Supreme Master" or "Suma," Ching Hai. Though it is often described as a Buddhist group, the core teachings of Ching Hai derived from the Sant Mat tradition of the Punjab, India.

Ching Hai was born Hue Dang Trinh into an ethnic Chinese Roman Catholic family in 1950 in Vietnam. Her grandmother was a Buddhist. At the age of 18, she moved to England and was educated at several locations in Western Europe, where she met her husband, a Buddhist.

After several years of marriage, she began a spiritual quest. Crucial to her progress was the mention of what was termed the Quan Yin method in a Buddhist scripture, the Surangama Sutra. She began asking Buddhist teachers about the method, but no one understood of what it consisted. In her quest, she was led to northern India, where she met Thakur Singh, a teacher of *surat shabd yoga*. This form of yoga utilizes a variety of mantras as a means of attuning the self to the creative sound current and follow it back to the soul's point of origin. In the *surat shabd yoga* systems, the guru (teacher) is an important figure who guides his/her students on the inner path to ever higher levels. Ching Hai concluded that *surat shabd yoga* was identical to the Quan Yin method.

As she began to master the technique, she moved to Taiwan. There in 1983 she was ordained as a Buddhist nun. After several years in New York, she returned to Taiwan in 1986. There she encountered a group of devotees of AVALOKITESVARA (another name of Quan Yin or GUAN YIN), who requested knowledge of the Quan Yin method. She subsequently founded the Master Ching Hai Meditation Association.

Life for the new association member begins with initiation by Ching Hai or one of her representatives, and an introduction to some basic practices of *surat shabd yoga*. Members are also asked to follow the five basic moral precepts common to Buddhism: they are thus enjoined against killing of living beings, taking of what is not given (or stealing), sexual misconduct, false speech, and the use of intoxicating substances. In addition, members are expected to adopt a vegetarian diet.

During its first decade, the movement spread worldwide, with followers on every continent, though membership was concentrated around the Pacific Rim. The association has also nurtured a chain of vegetarian restaurants. Ching Hai's book *The Key to Enlightenment,* which has appeared under several slightly different titles in English, is the basic text for the movement.

Further reading: Rafer Guzmán, "Immaterial Girl." *Metro* (San Jose, Calif.), (28 March–3 April, 1996).

Chin Kung (Jin Kong) (1927–   ) *Taiwanese Buddhist leader*

Master Chin Kung Shi, the founder and leader of one of Taiwan's five prominent Buddhist groups, the AMITABHA BUDDHIST SOCIETIES, was born Hsu Yae-Hong in 1927 in Anhui province, China. In 1949 he migrated to Taiwan, where he studied for many years with several outstanding Buddhist teachers. In 1959, he became a monk at Linji Temple of Yuanshan, Taipei, where he received his religious name, Chin Kung. After his ordination in the Pure Land tradition, he began lecturing and teaching widely across Taiwan and was active in the BUDDHIST ASSOCIATION OF THE REPUBLIC OF CHINA. As he lectured, he also proposed and helped found a number of independent Buddhist centers focused upon the veneration of AMITABHA Buddha and the recitation of the NEMBUTSU. Thus over time an association of Pure Land centers tied together by the propagation activities of Chin Kung came into being. Along the way, he also led in the founding of the Hwa Dzan Dharma Giving Association, the Hwa Dzan Buddhist Library, the Corporate Body of the Buddha Educational Foundation, and the Hwa Dzan Pureland Learning Center, each of which has carried on a special program related to the overall propagation goal.

Master Chin Kung pioneered Buddhist broadcasting in Taiwan utilizing both radio and television and more recently the Internet. He has become more widely known for the publishing activity of the Buddha Educational Foundation, which annually prints and distributes tens of thousands of free copies of books, including both transcripts of his talks and volumes of Buddhist scripture.

Master Chin Kung first traveled abroad to teach in 1977. Subsequent international tours have led to the founding of Amitabha Buddhist Societies in Hong Kong, Singapore, Malaysia, North America, Australia, Spain, and England. These operate primarily within the Chinese diaspora. In 1985, he moved to the United States, and after more than a decade there he moved to Singapore (his home in 2005). His most recent project has been the founding of the Buddhist Educational College in Singapore for the training of Buddhist leaders.

Further reading: Master Chin Kung, *Buddhism: The Wisdom of Compassion and Awakening* (Taipei, Taiwan: The Corporate Body of the Buddha Educational Foundation, n.d.); ———, *Changing Destiny, Liao-Fan's Four Lessons: A Commentary* (Taipei, Taiwan: The Corporate Body of the Buddha Educational Foundation, n.d.); ———, *To Understand Buddhism* (Taipei, Taiwan: The Corporate Body of the Buddha Educational Foundation, 1998).

Chinp-yo (mid-eighth century) *prominent Korean monk*

Chinp-yo, a monk of the Dharma Characteristics or Dharma Aspects school (known in China as the Faxiang school and in Japan as the HOSSO SCHOOL), is one of the people responsible for the emphasis on Maitreya so noticeable in Korean Buddhism. He emerges out of obscurity in the 760s when he returned to Korea from China, just as the Korean peninsula was being unified by the Kingdom of SILLA. According to the stories told about him, he had a vision of the bodhisattva MAI-

TREYA, from whom he received a book of divination. He decided to build a temple to Maitreya and by supernatural means was directed to the Kumsan forest on Mt. Miak-san near Chonju. There he built Kumsan-sa (or Gold Mountain Temple). In fact, a small temple was already located at the site, dating from the beginning of the seventh century.

Central to the temple complex erected under Chinp-yo's direction was a large Maitreya Buddha Hall, in the center of which was a 39-foot statue of Maitreya. (The temple complex went through a variety of ups and downs through the years as political leadership changed and in the 16th century was largely destroyed during an invasion from Japan. The buildings one sees today on visiting Kum-san were erected in 1635.)

Further reading: Lewis R. Lancaster and C. S. Yu, ed., *Assimilation of Buddhism in Korea: Religious Maturity and Innovation in the Silla Dynasty* (Berkeley, Calif.: Asian Humanities Press, 1991). ———, *Introduction of Buddhism to Korea: New Cultural Patterns* (Berkeley, Calif.: Asian Humanities Press, 1989).

Chinul (1158–1210) *Korean Buddhist reformer*

The Korean Son Buddhist teacher Chinul was born to a well-to-do family near Kaegyong (Kaesong), then the capital of the country. Suffering from chronic illness as a child, Chinul was offered as a Buddhist monk by his father if he were healed. He was healed and at the age of seven was ordained. His training was unusual, however, as he was not placed in the care of a particular recognized teacher. Over the years as he matured he made his own way through the many Buddhist writings available to him. He developed an eclectic and ecumenical approach to the various schools of Son (Zen) meditative practices.

Chinul grew up in the small monastery in his hometown. When at the age of 42 he first traveled to the capital to take his examinations, he was negatively affected by what he saw as an inappropriate worldliness. He decided to form a retreat society to emphasize concentration and the acquisition of wisdom. Over the next nine years he traveled the land, studying at various monastic centers and allowing his thought to mature. These years were punctuated by three important experiences of the realization of the truth concerning the reality and experience of One Mind. His new comprehensive perspective, combining theory with the practice of meditation, would be summarized in his posthumously published work *The Complete and Sudden Attainment of Buddhahood.*

In 1190, Chinul formed his retreat society on Kong Mountain. Contemporaneously he wrote his first book, *Encouragement to Practice: The Compact of the Concentration and Wisdom Community.* The work attacked what he saw as a degenerate Buddhist community, especially the practices of PURE LAND BUDDHISM. He argued that each person is already an enlightened Buddha and what is needed is the recovery of one's pristine enlightened state. Within a few years, Chinul's teachings and personality had attracted attention and thousands flocked to King Mountain.

Within a few years, the facilities on Kong Mountain proved inadequate to deal with the crowds and a new center for his society was sought. Toward the end of the decade, a new temple was built at Songgwang Mountain in southern Korea. On his way to the new temple, Chinul stopped for a time at Chiri Mountain to make a retreat in preparation for his assuming leadership of the new community. During this retreat, Chinul and his companions experienced a variety of supernatural events. They interpreted these occurrences as confirmation that their leader had attained a final higher state of enlightenment.

At the new center, Chinul soon became the dominant voice in SON BUDDHISM. His first book issued from his new home, *Admonitions to Beginning Students,* emphasized the moral basis of the monastic life and is still given to all young Buddhist monks in Korea. It was followed by another classic text, *Secrets on Cultivating the Mind* (c. 1205), an outline of Son practice. Later in the decade, he would author his two major works, *Abridgment of the Commentary of the Flower Garland Sutra* (1207) and *Excerpts from the Dharma Collection and Separate Circulation Record with Personal Notes* (1209). The latter is a comprehensive survey of Buddhist thought and practice that soon became a standard work for students of Son meditation throughout Korea. He advocated an approach to Son based on sudden enlightenment to one's Buddhahood, to be followed by a life of CULTIVATION of Buddhism and a mature arrival at a mature realization. This approach would dominate Son practice in Korean Buddhism in later centuries.

As death approached in April 1210, Chinul engaged in a set of question and answer sessions with his close disciples. He died on April 22 and was buried in a STUPA at the monastic center. The Korean king named him *National Preceptor Pril Pojo* (or Buddha Sun Shining Universally).

Further reading: Robert E. Buswell, Jr., ed., *The Korean Approach to Zen: The Collected Works of Chinul* (Honolulu: University of Hawaii Press, 1983); Ian P. McGreal, ed., *Great Thinkers of the Eastern World* (New York: HarperCollins, 1995).

Chodron, Pema (Deirdre Blomfield-Brown) (1936–) *Tibetan Buddhist nun*

Pema Chodron, a leading spokesperson for the KARMA KAGYU Tibetan Buddhist tradition, was born Deirdre Blomfield-Brown in New York City. After her graduation from the University of California Berkeley, she began a career as an elementary school teacher. She married and bore two children. In the early 1970s, on a visit to France, she met Lama Chime Rinpoche. After several years of study, she took her first vows as a novice nun in 1974. She was soon afterward ordained by the Sixteenth Karmapa. She received the full BHIKSUNI ordination in the Chinese lineage in 1981 in Hong Kong.

Meanwhile, in 1972 she had encountered CHOGYAM TRUNGPA Rinpoche (1939–87). She became

his student and studied with him for the next 15 years. As VAJRADHATU INTERNATIONAL, Trungpa's organization, developed, Ane Pema became the director of Karma Dzong, its main center in Boulder, Colorado. In 1984, she moved to Cape Breton, Nova Scotia, as the new director of Gampo Abbey, the first Tibetan monastery established in North America for Westerners.

Her first two books, *The Wisdom of No Escape* (1991) and *Start Where You Are* (1994), found a popular response and she emerged as one of the leading female Buddhist teachers in the West and an advocate of spreading Tibetan monasticism.

Further reading: Pema Chödrön, *No Time to Lose: A Timely Guide to the Way of the Bodhisattva* (Boston: Shambhala, 2005); ———, *The Places That Scare You* (Boston: Shambhala, 2001); ———, *Start Where You Are* (Boston: Shambhala, 1994); ———, *When Things Fall Apart: Heart Advice for Difficult Times* (Boston: Shambhala, 1996); ———, *The Wisdom of No Escape* (Boston: Shambhala, 1991).

Chogyam Trungpa (1939–1987) *Tibetan Buddhist lama and teacher*

Chogyam Trungpa Rinpoche was an influential and controversial Tibetan Buddhist lama who played an important role in the dissemination of Buddhism to the West. He was born in eastern Tibet and was identified at the age of 13 months as the 13th incarnation of the Trungpa tulku, an important KARMA KAGYU teaching lineage. He was educated in the traditional fashion and installed as the head of Surmang monastery. In 1959, he fled Tibet and went into exile in India. The DALAI LAMA appointed him to a teaching position at the Young Lamas Home School in Dalhousie, India. While in India he married a Tibetan woman, Kunchok Palden, who in 1962 gave birth to their son, Osel Rangdrol Mukpo, now known as Sakyong Mipham Rinpoche.

In 1963 Chogyam Trungpa traveled to England to study at Oxford University, leaving his family behind in India. Four years later he moved to Scotland, where he founded the Samye Ling meditation center. Shortly thereafter, he was in a severe car accident, which left him partially paralyzed. He also entered into a romantic relationship with a young English woman, Diana Pybus, whom he married in 1970. In 1969, the first of his many books, *Meditation in Action,* appeared.

Chogyam Trungpa moved to the United States in 1970 and here he blossomed as a popular spiritual teacher. He settled in Barnet, Vermont, where he founded a meditation center called Tail of the Tiger. He attracted many students and wrote a series of books on Buddhism, the most popular of which was his work *Shambhala: The Sacred Path of the Warrior,* a work that attempted to present key teachings of Buddhism in a form more understandable to his American audience. He established several other meditation centers in North America, as well as the Naropa Institute (now Naropa University) in Boulder, Colorado, and founded the Vajradhatu International Buddhist Church. In the meantime he attracted a number of well-known students, such as the poet Allen Ginsberg.

Chogyam Trungpa was a controversial teacher who tended to make a strong impact not only upon his students, but also upon many of the other people with whom he interacted. He tended to be a polarizing figure and manifested what his defenders call the "crazy wisdom" style of spiritual teaching. He was an alcoholic, and critics have accused him of engaging in abusive behavior. It is reported that he frequently engaged in sexual activity with many of his students. Despite these allegations of abuse, he made a major impact upon the reception of Vajrayana (Tantric) Buddhism in North America.

He passed away in 1987 and was succeeded by his chosen successor, an American student named Osel Tenzin. Most recently, the various elements of the movement he created have been reorganized under the umbrella organization SHAMBHALA INTERNATIONAL.

Further reading: Stephen T. Butterfield, *The Double Mirror: A Skeptical Journey into Buddhist Tantra* (Berkeley, Calif.: North Atlantic Books, 1994); Charles S. Prebish, *Luminous Passage: The Practice and Study of Buddhism in America* (Berkeley: University of California Press, 1999); Chogyam Trungpa, *Meditation in Action* (Boston: Shambhala, 1991); ———, *Shambhala: The Sacred Path of the Warrior* (Boulder, Colo.: Shambhala, 1984).

Chogye Order

Korean Buddhism, though divided into a number of sects, is largely dominated by a single organization, the Chogye Order. The order was formally organized in 1935 when the two main branches of Korean Buddhism were merged, but its history really goes back to the 12th century and the revival of Son (Zen) Buddhism on the peninsula.

Though introduced earlier, SON BUDDHISM did not really take hold in Korea until CHINUL (1158–1210). While a young practitioner he became upset with contemporary practice and started a reform movement in Korean Buddhism. He eventually (1197) with his followers built a large temple and monastic complex, Songgwang-sa, on Songgwang Mountain, which he renamed Chogye Mountain after the home of HUI NENG (638–713 C.E.), the Chinese meditation master and sixth Chan patriarch. Two centuries later, the master TAEGO (1301–82) would succeed in uniting the various Son groups and, as did Chinul, work for the unification of the various strains of Buddhist thought.

In the years after Taego, the Yi dynasty adopted CONFUCIANISM as its dominant form of thought and pushed Buddhism from its favored position at the king's court. Out of favor, the monks were forced to abandon the population centers and retreat to the mountains, where they established new monastic centers. At times active suppression led to the destruction of temples, the confiscation of their possessions, and the secularization of the monks. In the 15th century, King Sejong (r. 1419–50) forced the consolidation of the different

Buddhist groups into two sects, the Son, with its emphasis on meditation, and the Kyo, with an emphasis on the study of the scriptural writings.

Buddhism experienced a revival at the end of the 19th century, an expansion that continued after the Japanese occupation of the country. The Japanese had a policy of manipulating Buddhist leaders in conquered countries to facilitate social control of the population. However, the leadership withdrew its support when they realized that the Japanese planned to incorporate the Son movement into the Japanese Soto Zen organization. The Japanese did, however, effect one important change in the Korean sangha: they moved against celibacy among the monks and most monks chose to marry.

Common opposition to the Japanese led the two Korean sects to reconcile their different approaches to Buddhism, and in 1935, the Son and Kyo merged, and the Chogye Mountain center gave the name to the united movement. A temple in Seoul, the only major temple within the old city walls, later named Chogye-sa, became the headquarters of the Chogye Order in 1936.

A united Korean sangha lasted two decades. When the dust settled from the Korean War, throughout the southern half of the peninsula, it was discovered that in the rural areas, a number of unmarried monks had honored their celibacy vows and were now free to voice their dissent from the earlier changes. By this time, however, the majority of monks were married. The celibate monks fought to regain control and in 1954 won the government to their cause. The unmarried monks took control of the order and the married monks and priests were forced out. The married group formed a new organization, the Taego Order, but had to start over as all the property of the Chogye stayed with the unmarried group. In 1985, an order of nuns was created as a Chogye Order affiliate.

In South Korea, the Chogye faces stiff competition from Christianity, as Korea has been the site of Christianity's most successful proselytizing effort, with more than 40 percent of the country adherents. Buddhism now claims less than 20 percent of the population. At the same time, Chogye teachers have migrated to other countries both to establish the movement within the Korean diaspora and to spread the teachings within the larger host populations. Of the latter, the most successful has been the KWAN UM ZEN SCHOOL started by Seung Sahn Sunim, with centers in more than 25 countries around the world.

Further reading: Robert E. Buswell, Jr., *The Zen Monastic Experience: Buddhist Practice in Contemporary Korea* (Princeton, N.J.: Princeton University Press, 1992); Sonsa Kusan, *The Way of Korean Zen* (New York: Weatherhill, 1985).

Christian-Buddhist relations

Christian-Buddhist relationships are a focus of modern scholarship, a reflection of the increasing prominence of Buddhism in contemporary Western culture as well as the impact of Western missionary activity on traditionally Buddhist cultures. Historically, Christian-Buddhist relations can be divided into two distinct phases. The first began with the ancient contacts between India and the Mediterranean Basin, which may date to the time of King ASOKA (eight century B.C.E.). After the establishment of Christianity there are passing references to Buddhism in the writings of several Christian church fathers, including Clement of Alexandria (c. 150–c. 215) and Origen (c. 185–c. 254), who resided in Egypt. Some have suggested that Buddhism influenced Christianity in its development of monasticism and in the cult of relics.

Beginning with Marco Polo, Westerners began to visit Buddhist lands, most notably China. The Jesuit Order (founded in 1534), inspired in part by news of the Asian world opened by the Portuguese, targeted India, China, and Japan for missionary activity. The missionary endeavor, which flourished in China for several generations, was remarkable for its grasp of Buddhist teachings and attempts to accommodate the local culture, though ultimately the techniques championed by Matteo Ricci (1552–1610) were rejected by the Catholic Church and the material on Buddhism sent back to Rome by his Jesuit colleagues was deposited unread at the Vatican. At worst, Westerners turned on Buddhists in lands they attempted to colonize, with resultant atrocities. However, through the 17th and 18th centuries, contacts between Buddhists and Christians were minimal, though remnants of the early Catholic efforts survived in places such as Macau, the Portuguese colony in China.

A new situation began late in the 18th century with the development of the world Protestant missionary movement. Blocked from entering India, such missionary churches as the Methodists began work in Sri Lanka, and the American Baptists settled in Burma (Myanmar). Through the 19th century, missionaries entered China, Japan, and Korea. By the end of the 19th century, China was the single country with the most missionaries. The emergence of the Protestant movement also encouraged a revival of missionary activity by Catholics throughout Asia.

From the beginning of the 19th century to the present, the attempts by Protestants to convert Buddhists has dominated Buddhist-Christian encounters. This effort was mirrored by Buddhist outreach efforts in the West throughout the 20th century. Buddhist evangelical activities have assumed a much lower profile than Christian efforts but have led to a remarkable growth of Buddhism in Europe and North America.

A different way for Christian, and Buddhists to relate to each other began at the end of the 19th century and had its initial significant manifestation in the World's Parliament of Religions held in Chicago in 1893. While the parliament masked a liberal Protestant evangelical thrust, the gatherings allowed Buddhist and Christian representatives to offer their views on a variety of religious and social issues and manifested the possibilities

of dialogue as a means of highlighting similarities and differences of beliefs; establishing working relationships between two religious communities, neither of which was ready to dissolve in the presence of the other; and providing a framework for mutual cooperation on shared goals. The parliament was succeeded later in the century by additional efforts at interreligious dialogue focused in such organizations as the World Congress of Faiths and the World Conference on Religion and Peace.

A new era in building positive Buddhist-Christian relations can be dated from 1961, when Christians from Burma, Ceylon (Sri Lanka), and Thailand gathered in Rangoon for an international consultation, "Buddhist Christian Encounter." The conference recommended that Christians begin to show a deeper concern for Buddhism.

In 1964, in the midst of Vatican II, the Roman Catholic Church established the Pontifical Council for Inter-religious Dialogue. One of its major departments is designed to build new levels of understanding of and respect for Buddhism. The council supported Pope John Paul II's (1920–2005) periodic meetings with Buddhist and other religious leaders voicing his concern for interreligious dialogue in which the followers of the various religions can discover shared elements of spirituality, while acknowledging their differences. Then as the 20th century came to a close, he offered an apology for the attitudes of mistrust and hostility occasionally assumed by Catholics toward followers of other religions, as part of a broad acknowledgment of the failings of Christians in their pursuit of their missions.

Among the first people to respond to the Vatican call for an exploration of spirituality in other religions was the Jesuit priest William Johnston, who moved to Japan in 1951 and began to practice ZEN meditation. As early as 1965 he visited the Christian mystic Thomas Merton (1915–68) and introduced him to Zen. With his two books, *The Still Point: Reflections on Zen and*

Christian Mysticism (1971) and the best-selling *Christian Zen* (1971), Johnston launched a movement of Christians, especially Catholics in religious orders, to appropriate Zen meditation as a means of Christian renewal. The CHRISTIAN ZEN movement became one of the most noticeable segments of a growing Christian-Buddhist dialogue effort that has flourished since the 1970s in both the East and the West.

It is to be noted that the widespread practice of Zen meditation paralleled a similar appropriation of Transcendental Meditation, a Hindu practice promulgated in the West by followers of Mahesh Maharishi Yogi. In 1989, Pope John Paul II called attention to the spiritual dangers to which Christians who followed either practice were opening themselves. His statement did much to quiet the enthusiasm for Christian Zen.

The pope's 1989 statement did little to squelch the large growing realm of Christian-Buddhist dialogue, which has done much to foster new levels of respect between the two large religious communities and contribute to a lessening of what are considered illegitimate conversion techniques (such as the use of coercive tactics), which dominated much 19th-century Christian work in predominantly Buddhist lands. Much of that dialogue has been built on the expansive arena of Buddhist religious studies. Most Western universities now have one or more faculty members who specialize in Buddhism, and most colleges offer classes on Buddhist history and beliefs.

As the 21st century begins, Christianity has established viable worshipping communities in almost every country of the world. At the same time, Buddhism has become a global religion. The presence of Buddhist and Christian communities in strength in so many major urban centers has created an environment in which Buddhist-Christian dialogue at all levels has become vital for the well-being of both communities.

Further reading: Educational Resources Committee of the Society for Buddhist Studies, *Resources for Buddhist-Christian Encounter: An Annotated Bibliography* (Wofford Heights, Calif.: Multifaith Resources, 1993); Aelred Graham, *Conversations: Christian and Buddhist, Encounters in Japan* (New York: Harcourt Brace, 1968); Rita Gross and Terry C. Muck, eds., *Christians Talk about Buddhist Meditation, Buddhists Talk about Christian Prayer* (New York: Continuum International Publishing Group, 2003); William Johnston, *Christian Zen* (New York: Harper, 1971); ———, *The Still Point: Reflections on Zen and Christian Mysticism* (New York: Fordham University Press, 1971); Joseph J. Spae, *Buddhist-Christian Empathy* (Chicago: Chicago Institute of Theology and Culture, 1980); Scott W. Sunquist, ed., *A Dictionary of Asian Christianity* (Grand Rapids, Mich.: William B. Eerdmans, 2001); D. T. Suzuki, *Mysticism: Christian and Buddhist* (New York: Harper, 1971).

Christian Zen

Christian Zen is an approach to Christianity through the practice of Zen. During the second Vatican Council (1962–65), the bishops gave considerable consideration to reorienting the church relative to other large religious traditions, including Buddhism. It established the Pontifical Council for Inter-religious Dialogue, which included a department mandated to build new levels of understanding of Buddhism. The impetus launched by the council prepared the way for numerous dialogical efforts from the international to the local level. One early suggestion concerned the potential for followers of the various religions to share elements of spiritual practice, while acknowledging differences in theology and belief.

Even as Vatican II proceeded, the Jesuit priest William Johnston, who had moved to Japan in 1951, had begun to practice ZEN meditation. By the time the council ended, he was active in promoting Zen as a useful practice for Christians and as early as 1965 shared his views with the Christian mystic Thomas Merton (1915–68), whom he introduced to Zen. Merton was on a trip to Asia in 1968 when he died in a tragic accident. Johnston went on to become the leading voice in the English-speaking world in promoting Zen as a Christian practice through his two books, *The Still Point: Reflections on Zen and Christian Mysticism* (1971) and the best-selling *Christian Zen* (1971).

Through the 1980s, an increasing number of Roman Catholics began to study Zen; leadership was assumed by a number of people, both male and female, in religious orders. Paralleling Johnston in their study in Japan were two Roman Catholic priests, Hugo Makibi Enomiya-Lassalle (1898–1991) and Willigis Jäger (1925–   ). Enomiya-Lassalle, like Johnston a Jesuit, began studying Zen with Harada Roshi, the founder of the SANBO KYODAN lineage as early as 1956 and two years later published his enthusiastic response to what he had discovered, *Zen: A Way to Enlightenment.* He continued his study under Harada's successor, Yamada Roshi, and steered many of his colleagues to the Sanbo Kyodan. He was certified as a teacher of Zen in the late 1960s and spent the rest of his life leading Zen events in Europe, especially in German-speaking countries.

The Benedictine priest Willigis Jäger followed a similar course and, after his certification as a Zen teacher, returned to Austria and settled at Münsterschwarzach Abbey in the Würzburg diocese, which became the center from which he spread his version of Christian Zen. Other leaders in the growing movement who studied with the Sanbo Kyodan included Niklaus Brantschen, Pia Gyger, Ruben Habito, Thomas Hand, Patrick Hawk, Robert Kennedy, Elaine MacInnes, Kathleen Reiley, and Ana Maria Schlütters.

In the late 1980s, the Vatican, especially the office of Cardinal Joseph Ratzinger (now Pope Benedict XVI), took under consideration what it saw as the spread of both the Transcendental Meditation taught by Maharishi Mehesh Yogi and Zen meditation within the church. In 1989, Pope John Paul II (1920–2005) called attention to the spiritual dangers to which Christians opened themselves by engaging in such practices. This statement did much to quiet (but by no means end) the enthusiasm for Christian Zen.

A more definitive step against Christian Zen occurred in 2002 when Ratzinger moved against Willigis Jäger, at the time the most prominent Christian Zen teacher in Europe. He ordered Jäger to cease all public activities, with special reference to his teachings and writing, at the same time accusing him of abandoning the idea of a personal God and downplaying the importance of doctrine.

After a generation of enthusiastic practice, Christian Zen survives but at a much diminished level from the heights of the 1980s. Meanwhile, it has done much to popularize Buddhism in the West.

Further reading: Tom Chetwynd, *Zen and the Kingdom of Heaven: Reflections on the Tradition of Meditation in Christianity and Zen Buddhism* (Somerville, Mass.: Wisdom, 2001); H. M. Enomiya-Lassalle, *Zen Meditation for Christians* (LaSalle, Ill.: Open Court, 1974); John Dykstra Eusden, *Zen and Christian: The Journey Between* (New York: Crossroad, 1981); William Johnston, *Christian Zen* (New York: Harper, 1971); ———, *The Still Point: Reflections on Zen and Christian Mysticism* (New York: Fordham University Press, 1971); Robert E. Kennedy, *Zen Spirit, Christian Spirit: The Place of Zen in Christian Life* (New York: Continuum International Publishing Group, 1995).

Chuang-tzu   *See* ZHUANGZI.

Chung Hwa Institute of Buddhist Studies

The Chung Hwa Institute, a major Buddhist studies institute in Taiwan, traces its roots to 1965 and the establishment of the Institute of Buddhist Studies within the Academica Sinica, the leading scholarly organization in Taiwan. The Institute of Buddhist Studies was founded by Chang Chi-yun (1900–85). Its first director was Chow Pang-tao.

The Institute of Buddhist Studies evolved into the Chung Hwa Institute in 1978, at which time

SHENG YEN, a Buddhist Zen master and head of DHARMA DRUM MOUNTAIN ASSOCIATION, became the new director. Darma Drum has subsequently become the institute's major sponsor. The institute publishes the *Chung Hwa Buddhist Journal* and the *Hwakang Buddhist Journal*. The institute has targeted graduate level university students in its attempt to woo people into Buddhist studies. Each year more than 50 students attend classes developed by the institute. The overall goal has been the production of scholars of international stature.

Further reading: The Chung Hwa Institute of Buddhist Studies. Available onlne. URL: http://www.chibs.edu.tw/e-index.htm. Accessed on June 20, 2007.

cinnabar

One of the most mysterious yet important substances in Daoist alchemy is cinnabar. Known in Chinese by the generic term *dan* (lit. "pill" or "elixir"), cinnabar is a mineral compound that (along with gold, mica, and other substances) was used extensively in concocting potions that Daoist masters ingested in their quest for immortality. Since cinnabar is reddish in color, it was associated with yang, or male, energies and thought to "revitalize" the blood. Indeed, ancient Chinese regarded cinnabar as the most powerful natural form of *yang* energies, concentrated sunlight, the very power of life. It is typically found along riverbanks or in rocky, mountainous areas. According to Daoist lore, to find a deposit of cinnabar one should look for a special mushroom that takes the shape of deer antlers. This mushroom (*Ganoderma lucidum*) grows in damp, secluded places over which cinnabar can be found. Its fantastic shape is said to be evidence that the fungus itself is the product of natural alchemical processes and some accounts say it even glows at night.

Cinnabar was highly prized as a means of attaining powers of longevity and often paired with gold (whose yellow color was associated with yin, or female, energies) in the preparation of various potions and elixirs. The close relationship between both substances was, thus, crucial for alchemists to understand. According to traditional wisdom, gold naturally transmutes into cinnabar over time, much as *yin* and *yang* give way to each other as part of the natural processes of Dao. Evidence for this intimate connection was also supplied by the fact that deposits of cinnabar are typically found beneath veins of gold.

Chemically, cinnabar is a mercury sulfide that, when heated, separates into its constituent parts, only to reconstitute itself when cooled. As is well known, mercury is toxic and when taken internally often results in "mercury poisoning," a condition marked by delusions and brain damage. In large doses it is fatal. Daoists of ancient and medieval times were well aware of this fact; accounts of their efforts (as well as archaeological discoveries of bodies) indicate that some suffered slow poisoning involving the failure of the liver and spleen, dementia, hallucinations, or even the collapse of the nervous system. Others died quick, agonizing deaths. Still, alchemists continued to work with tinctures of cinnabar as a primary means of attaining immortality through the late Tang dynasty (618–907).

Despite the obvious dangers, the logic behind such practices is quite simple: cinnabar, gold, and other such minerals do not decay. In fact, in the case of gold, they do not even tarnish. Following traditional Chinese reasoning, Daoist masters concluded that preparations of such substances could help prevent bodily decay. There is also evidence that in minute amounts, concoctions of such minerals are actually beneficial and formed an important part of Chinese medical (or perhaps more appropriately, "wellness") practice. Moreover, such chemical preparations have been proved to have preservative powers.

The preparation of cinnabar was carefully guarded by practitioners of "external alchemy" (*waidan*). Almost all of these masters also engaged in strict regimens of meditation, calisthenics (e.g., QIGONG), and even sexual yoga to prepare the body for the ingestion of cinnabar concoctions. Instructions for the preparation of cinnabar outlined in such texts as the *Xuzhen lijian miaotu* (Subtle illustrations of experiences in cultivating the real) specify proper techniques in the use of laboratory equipment (furnaces, bellows, cauldrons, etc.) in order to refine and purify cinnabar potions. Although highly artificial, such practices were modeled on natural processes involving minerals and stones that absorbed *yin* and *yang* energies (from exposure to sunshine, moonlight, etc.) over a long period. The most potent forms of cinnabar were said to have undergone nine cycles of refining under carefully controlled conditions that mimicked the "natural furnace and cauldron" (the earth and sky).

In the *Baopuzi,* GE HONG states that cinnabar is far superior to herbal potions, going on to detail the preparations and effects of the nine cycles of cinnabar, each of which promises extraordinary powers. Ge Hong writes, "Acquire any one of these nine elixirs and you will be an immortal! There is no need to prepare all nine. Which one you prepare depends entirely on your preference. After taking any one of them, if you wish to ascend to heaven in broad daylight, you can do so. If you wish to remain on this earth for some time, you can come and go freely wherever you wish, no matter what the barriers. Nothing and nobody will harm you." In some of his writings Ge Hong even laments that he lacks the money to purchase the quantities of cinnabar needed to concoct elixirs—an indication that cinnabar, despite its potentially dangerous powers, had a high market value in early medieval China.

In so-called internal alchemy (*neidan*), the language of cinnabar and its preparations is highly symbolic. Generally, though, it represents the combining of yin and yang energies—a process that takes place in the lower "cinnabar field" (*dantian,* the lowest of three energy centers in the body, located in the region of the navel) through breathing techniques. Ultimately such practices are thought to result in the spiritual immortality of the practitioner.

Further reading: Julia Ching, *Chinese Religions* (Maryknoll, N.Y.: Orbis Books, 1993), 104–111; Livia Kohn, *Daoism and Chinese Culture* (Cambridge, Mass.: Three Pines Press, 2001), 83–86; ———, ed., *The Taoist Experience* (Albany: State University of New York Press, 1993), 305–313; Isabelle Robinet, *Taoism: Growth of a Religion.* Translated by Phyllis Brooks (Stanford, Calif.: Stanford University Press, 1997), 97, 103ff.; Kristofer Schipper, *The Taoist Body.* Translated by Karen C. Duval (Berkeley: University of California Press, 1993), 174–178; Eva Wong, *The Shambhala Guide to Taoism* (Boston: Shambhala, 1997), 66–76.

codepend arising   *See* PRATITYA SAMUTPADA.

compassion   *See* KARUNA.

Confucian Classics

The traditional Chinese scholar was expected to master the four books and five classics. The Four Books are the four basic texts of CONFUCIANISM—the ANALECTS, the *Book of Mencius,* the *Great Learning,* and the *Doctrine of the Mean.* These four were the basis for the imperial examination system between 1313 and 1905. The Five Classics were works of even greater antiquity—the *Book of Odes* (*Shi Jing*), the *Book of History* (*Shu Jing*), the *Book of Rites* (*Li Ji*), the *Spring and Autumn Annals* (*Chun Qiu*), and the BOOK OF CHANGES (*Yijing*). The *Books of History* and *Rites,* and the *Spring and Autumn Annals* were traditionally attributed to CONFUCIUS. A sixth classic, the *Book of Music,* has been lost.

Further reading: John H. Berthrong and Evelyn Nagai Berthrong, *Confucianism: A Short Introduction* (Oxford: Oneworld, 2000); Jennifer Oldstone-Moore,

Confucianism: Origins, Beliefs, Practices, Holy Texts, Sacred Places (Oxford: Oxford University Press, 2002).

Confucianism

Confucianism is an indigenous Chinese philosophy and moral code that, among other tenets, puts great emphasis on maintenance of proper social relations. Today Confucianism is a religion with a mere handful of temples, a faith with virtually no distinct followers, and a philosophy associated with a bygone era, that of imperial China. How, then, can we say it continues as a living tradition that lies at the heart of the East Asian worldview?

Traditionally grouped together with Buddhism and DAOISM as one of the three "Chinese" religions, Confucianism pales when compared to the other two as a complex religious system. Certainly it sparks little religious fervor in its adherents. But looking at Confucianism on its own terms will help us understand its continuing importance.

Confucianism is certainly a major strand of Chinese history, associated with the teachings of CONFUCIUS (551–479 B.C.E.), who lived during the Spring and Autumn period (722–481 B.C.E.), and his followers. The period was one of disintegrating political entities, constant warfare, and competing schools of thought. Confucius was simply one of the teachers often hired by the rulers of the states in northern China. Confucius emphasized certain points in his teachings. First, he held up rulers of the past, especially the founders of the Zhou dynasty, King Wen, King Wu, and the duke of Zhou, as exemplary models of righteousness. These leaders were successful because they had modeled themselves on the sage kings of the past, so contemporary leaders should do the same and follow the lead of the Zhou kings. Confucius tried to reform society through teaching ancient wisdom.

What was at the heart of Confucius's teachings? He emphasized, first, the importance of REN, or humaneness. This kind of virtue was not limited to the ruling classes; instead, any person of commitment could strive to attain the virtue of humanity. In addition, Confucius taught the importance of empathy and reciprocity. The goal was for the individual to attain the status of a true gentleman (*junzi*), an idealized individual who embodied learning and virtue.

Confucius's teachings might have died with him, for his followers constituted a mere handful. But the disciples succeeded in writing down many of his teachings, and these in turn were picked up by a group known as the *ru*, or ritual specialists. Henceforth Confucianists were known as *rujia*, the school of *ru*.

The second great spur to growth was provided by MENCIUS (Mengzi), the second great sage in the Confucian tradition, who is believed to have lived in the fourth century B.C.E. Like Confucius he was a thinker who gave advice to rulers. He was also a seasoned street fighter in the contest of ideas that characterized his times. He argued with such schools as the legalists, proponents of raw power, and the Daoists, who advocated nonaction. Mencius emphasized that each person contained the seeds of goodness, which could be nurtured. Once a ruler found such energy within, he would be able to rule by example.

The third great sage of Confucianism was XUNZI, who lived in the fourth–third centuries B.C.E., a time just prior to the eventual unification of China under the Qin emperor. Xunzi disagreed with Mencius concerning human nature, which he considered to be fundamentally evil; however, through cultivation one could become good. In order to achieve this transformation Xunzi emphasized education and especially knowledge of Confucian ritual.

HAN DYNASTY CONFUCIANISM

The Qin dynasty (221–206 B.C.E.) had banned Confucius's writings. By the Han period (206 B.C.E.–220 C.E.) the followers of Confucius were determined to make Confucian thought the official state dogma. They accomplished this by subtly grafting other theories onto a core set of Confucian social ethics. They did not, in other words, seek to discredit other schools completely. They simply appropriated elements from the different sources. The Han scholars also excelled in collecting texts from the past and in writing histories. By the end of the Han period the stage was set for the complete domination of the Confucian way as state policy.

The system of thought that took shape in the Han put emphasis on the individual's moral CULTIVATION. Of course, there was a larger cosmos with many unknowns. However, the Confucian "persuasion" is to start with things close at hand, then move outward. In other words, such issues as the extent and mystery of the cosmos were not of primary concern. What did matter was the society one found around oneself, in particular the family and relationships there derived. In addition a fixed canon of texts, mainly written by the three great masters but also supplemented with minor texts, was finalized. This Confucian Way emphasized moral cultivation. The first step in developing oneself as a person was to have concern, to care—in modern language, to take things seriously. The Confucian is nothing if not dedicated and conscientious, the polar opposite

Confucius Temple at Nanjing, eastern China

of the caricature of the Daoist social dropout. The Confucian focus was on cultivating the mind, actually thought of as the heart-mind, and one's responsibilities as a member of a community.

NEO-CONFUCIANISM

The end of the Han era opened Chinese society to a new force, Buddhism. This foreign import generally held sway in Chinese intellectual history for the 700-odd years between the end of the Han and the Song dynasty (960–1279 C.E.). Although political theory remained focused on Confucian values, the truly new and fresh developments were in Buddhism. By the end of the Song, however, Confucianism responded with its own revival, what we call NEO-CONFUCIANISM (in Chinese, *lixue*). The primary figure in this period was Zhu Xi, a philosophical genius able to synthesize various strands of traditional and new thought. He and his followers picked up the grander cosmic vision that seemed to characterize Buddhist thought and grafted it onto the Confucian core message of moral cultivation. They were supplemented by the work of WANG YANGMING in the Ming (1368–1644 C.E.). The final edifice of Confucianism was erected in the Qing period (1644–1911 C.E.), before the advent of the modern period.

With the republican revolution of 1911, and subsequent political and social turmoil, many thoughtful Chinese recognized the need to discard outdated ways of thought and modernize. They quickly concluded that everything associated with the imperial system and its centralized, autocratic power structure and palace intrigue had to change. This also meant the replacement of the grounding political philosophy that had guided the Chinese state over the previous 2,000 years, Confucianism. It was easy, from the vantage point of the 1920s, to conclude that Confucianism was finished. However, it was not. Indeed there were value restoration movements in play from the minute the old regime died in 1911. These included religious movements as well as

social movements. Confucian scholars argued that there was a core of value in the Confucian heritage. These so-called New Confucians have continued to meet and study and today form the main impulse behind a revaluation of Confucianism. The best known figure in this group is Tu Weiming, a scholar and proponent of third wave Confucianism. The assumption is that just as Confucianism benefited from and responded to the challenge of Buddhism, so will it regroup after the impact of Westernization and the industrial age.

CONFUCIAN SELF-CULTIVATION

For Confucians, the individual is always a social being. From the awareness of one's place within the group—family, nation, whatever—arises an overriding concern for the world. But the definition of the human condition is essentially as a social condition, because family ties, reverence for authority, and social stability are linked through the individual's actions.

Here we can see the dual nature of Confucian thinking: while emphasizing internal cultivation, it also stresses social ties. The individual component of experience is thus often seen to be overshadowed by the push for social stability. Hence Confucianists are accused of being overly rigid and conservative.

The individual is bound by vertical, social ties that connect him or her to TIAN (heaven) and the cosmos. But horizontal, social ties also constrict and connect. The human condition is social, and there is no need to focus excessively on the impact of forces beyond society, forces that at any rate are beyond comprehension. Ethical cultivation is true cultivation.

Traditionally, the gentleman (the referent was always male) cultivated his self by means of education and meditation. Here education meant constant study and refinement of literary skills, always highly prized. There was in addition a uniquely Confucian type of meditation. Confucian meditation had several forms. First there was a type of "honoring," which focused on human nature as perceived. Later a type of "quiet sitting" was developed from the Song period on. The practitioner sat quietly in a chair, with eyes looking down, and began to still the mind. One should realize a state of calm before engaging with the world. Once the scholar is able to attain quiet, a balance with active engagement can be maintained. Wang Yangming later refined this technique to add focus on the individual will, the ability to concentrate. But the goal of all cultivation, ultimately, was to enable oneself to become more fully human, to apprehend the true nature of *ren,* humaneness.

This survey illuminates the elitist attraction of Confucianism. It was not bashful about focusing on the leadership stratum. At the same time its emphasis on human relations feels particularly modern. There are in fact many today who feel our period could do with a healthy dose of Confucian values. This practical and morally principled persuasion and its adherents continue to attract us to this day.

Further reading: John H. Berthrong and Evelyn Nagai Berthrong, *Confucianism: A Short Introduction* (Oxford: Oneworld, 2000); Ch'u Chai and Winberg Chai, *Confucianism* (Woodbury, N.Y.: Barron's Educational Series, 1973); James Huntley Grayson, *Korea: A Religious History* (Oxford: Clarendon Press, 1989); Ian P. McGreal, ed., *Great Thinkers of the Eastern World* (New York: HarperCollins, 1995); Jennifer Oldstone-Moore, *Confucianism: Origins, Beliefs, Practices, Holy Texts, Sacred Places* (Oxford: Oxford University Press, 2002).

Confucius (Kongzi, Kongfuzi, K'ung Fu-tzu) (551–479 B.C.E.) *founder of Confucianism*

One of the world's greatest philosophers, Confucius may have been the most influential person in China's long history.

He was a wandering teacher who worked on assignment for various rulers and gentry families during China's early history. During his wander-

ings he lectured his hosts and soon attracted a small band of followers. These included the beloved YAN HUI as well as others. Because of his desire to surround himself with scholar-gentlemen, he can be said to have started the Chinese literati tradition. He was originally from Lu, roughly equivalent to modern Shandong province in eastern China. His family was noble but fairly impoverished. From his youth he decided to devote his time to teaching. However, he also acted as an administrator in the state of Lu. At 51 he became a magistrate and, subsequently, a minister of justice. He resigned and, at the age of 56, began to travel. At 68 he returned to Lu. He died at 73, having taught, according to some sources, 3,000 pupils.

Many works are attributed to Confucius, but not all are accepted by modern scholars as his own work. The one we can most reliably conclude contains his thoughts is the ANALECTS, a collection of short vignettes and exchanges between the "master"—Confucius—and his pupils and others. Other works attributed to Confucius include the *Chun Qiu (Spring and Autumn Annals)* and the *Zuo Zhuan,* a commentary on the *Chun Qiu.*

Further reading: John H. Berthrong and Evelyn Nagai Berthrong, *Confucianism: A Short Introduction* (Oxford: Oneworld, 2000); Ian P. McGreal, ed., *Great Thinkers of the Eastern World* (New York: HarperCollins, 1995).

Conze, Edward (1904–1979) *early British Mahayan Buddhist scholar*

Edward Conze, the author and translator of numerous Buddhist books, was born in London and as a youth moved to Germany, where he attended high school and college. He studied at Tübingen, Heidelberg, Kiel, and Cologne. He received his Ph.D. from the latter school in 1928. He pursued further postdoctoral studies in Germany and England and gradually moved to his life work, the translation of the many works of Indian (Sanskrit) and Tibetan Buddhist literature.

The culmination of his years of study and work began to appear in the 1950s; his first books were a basic text, *Buddhism: Its Essence and Development* (1951), and *Buddhist Texts through the Ages* (1954), a coedited volume. These would be followed over the next 20 years with a prodigious output of translations and papers and books on Buddhism. Much time was spent on translating the PRAJNAPARAMITA sutras.

In 1963, Conze became the Distinguished Visiting Professor of Indian Studies at the University of Wisconsin. This appointment was the first of a number of short-term posts as visiting professor at different schools in the United States, England, and Germany. His last years were spent at the University of Lancaster and the University of California Santa Barbara.

Further reading: Edward Conze, *Buddhism: Its Essence and Development* (New York: Harper & Row, 1959); ———, *Further Buddhist Studies: Selected Essays* (Oxford: B. Cassirer, 1975); ———, *A Short History of Buddhism* (London: Allen and Unwin, 1980); Lewis Lancaster, *Prajnaparamita and Related Systems: Studies in Honor of Edward Conze* (Seoul, Korea: The Group in Buddhist Studies and Berkeley: The Center for South & Southeast Asian Studies, University of California, 1977).

councils of Buddhism

There were four major councils held in ancient times. In the modern period, a major fifth council was held in MYANMAR (then called Burma) in 1871, and a sixth in 1954–56.

In Buddhist literature the first three councils are the most often mentioned. There are in fact two competing traditions regarding the fourth— one from Sri Lanka and one from Kashmir. Just as the early Christian councils guided the new faith in certain directions, the early Buddhist councils reflected many critical issues.

Several of these councils were presided over or sponsored by a secular authority, usually the king or emperor, or, today, a modern secular government. In fact the councils were often *called by* the ruler, often because of concerns about the direction of development in the SANGHA. We can make various readings concerning the true reasons a secular power would want to be involved in such councils, but at the very least it confirms the close connection throughout Buddhism's history between sangha and state.

Another theme in many councils is concern for accuracy and the imperative to retain traditional knowledge. In a period when civilization moved from oral recitation to written records there was understandable anxiety to record all material that existed in oral forms. In fact, Buddhism's long history reflects the impact of this major transition in the form of knowledge management. Not surprisingly, as we today face another transition to digital knowledge, there are new concerns about the *fragility* of transferring the teachings into digital formats.

Finally we should note that the major councils were primarily held in South and Southeast Asian cultures. The major councils were not held in East Asia. They may thus represent a cultural expression and method of dealing with overriding concerns in the south. Practitioners in the north faced different conditions: often fragmented into competing schools, hampered by mountains and oceans, and not always supported by the state, Buddhist leaders in China, Korea, Japan, and Tibet found other ways to deal with concerns for accuracy, knowledge retention, and institutional reform.

RAJAGRHA

The First Buddhist Council, at Rajagrha, took place in 486 B.C.E., a mere three months after the Buddha's death, his PARINIRVANA. In that meeting, his disciple ANANDA is said to have recited the Buddha's sermons, which later became the SUTRAS. Upali, another of the major disciples, recited the monastic rules, which became the VINAYA. And Purna began the collection of commentaries, the ABHIDHARMA, although the early recitals were probably limited to *matrkas,* lists of key concepts. To this day, these three areas together form the body of the Buddhist canon, the TRIPITAKA.

While some scholars doubt that the first council ever truly took place, in Buddhist literature and legend it remains an important event. The meeting is said to have been held in a splendid hall built by the local king, Ajatasatru. The council was presided over by MAHAKASYAPA, the Buddha's successor. One account indicates that Mahakasyapa decided to convene the council with 500 selected monks in order to counter the effects of one blasphemous monk (a Subhadra or, in some accounts, Balanda). Mahakasyapa may also have felt it important to clarify the DHARMA (teachings) so that the Buddha's impact would not fade with the passing of his person. With this council the outlines of the Buddha's teachings, the BUDDHAVACANA, was now formalized.

THE VAISALI COUNCIL
This Second Buddhist Council was held after around 100 years, in 386 B.C.E. (some traditions say 326 B.C.E.). Some monks from Vaisali, in the east, were criticized for following the 10 tenets, which did not match the PRATIMOKSA, the rules for monks. The 10 tenets related to carrying or keeping salt, to eating after noon, to going to a village intending to eat but not practicing the ceremony of dealing with leftover food, and to various other practices that to us may perhaps seem minor. But the 10th tenet, that a monk could accept gold or silver from the hands of lay people, was seen as a serious issue.

The situation was debated by the full body present, with monks from the west disapproving. Finally a committee of eight was appointed to decide, and they ruled to reprimand the monks who followed the 10 tenets. In response the monks from the east simply held their own congress. They later became known as the MAHASANGHIKA, the "large majority." The remaining members were known as the STHAVIRAVADINS, the "elders." Thus while the council of Vaisali resulted in the broad separation into the Mahasanghika

and the Sthaviravatins camps, this outcome probably also reflected tensions between east and west as well as doctrinal issues.

PATALIPUTRA COUNCIL
The Pali canon states that the Third Buddhist Council was held during the time of King Dharmasoka, 236 years after the Buddha's *parinirvana,* in 250 B.C.E. Pataliputra was the capital city of the time. This council expelled monks who had been attracted to the SANGHA by the comfortable lifestyle in monasteries. It also aired out doctrinal disagreements. The Vibhajyavadins argued that elements (DHARMAS) were impermanent by nature, while the SARVASTIVADINS argued that elements were incorruptible. Although Emperor ASOKA was said to have presided over this council, many scholars doubt the likelihood of this.

THE COUNCIL OF KING KANISKA
One famous council—in some traditions called the Fourth Buddhist Council—was called by King KANISKA (r. c. 79–101 C.E.). Kaniska was ruler of the Kusanas in Central Asia, a region that included modern Kashmir. He decided to call the council in Kashmir because of confusion he felt about Buddhist teachings. Monks and scholars gathered at Gandhara for seven days. From this group the king selected 499 ARHATS to attend, and he later added one Vasumitra, who although not an *arhat* was urged forward by divine influence and agreed to preside over the council. The actual council was held somewhere in Kashmir—some accounts say Kundalavana; some say the Kuvana monastery at Jalandhara. Once gathered, the participants focused on preparing commentaries on the TRIPITAKA. The resulting commentaries were written on copper plates and stored in stone boxes. It is most likely, although not known definitely, that the commentaries were written in Sanskrit, perhaps used for this function for the first time.

The historical truth of this synod is in doubt; it was not mentioned by Southern school records or by the Tibetan historian BUSTON. It may be a reconstruction that reflects the rise of Mahayana at this time.

ADDITIONAL COUNCILS

Several other synods were held in Ceylon (Sri Lanka), Thailand, and Burma (Myanmar). The first in Ceylon occurred when King Devanamapi-yatissa erected a monastery and attended the council with thousands of participants. This was the council in Thuparama monastery, with 1,000 monks led by Thera (elder) Aritto and featuring Thera Mahinda, the great missionary. The meeting was held 238 years after the death of the Buddha, therefore around the time of the third council at Pataliputra, mentioned earlier.

A second synod was held in Ceylon during the rule of King Vatthagamini Abhaya, 57 years later, in the Aloka Lena cave near present-day Matale. The council was convened because of the fear that the contents of the Tripitaka could not be reliably retained in memory and had to be written. Five hundred monks recited the Buddha's words and wrote the contents on palm leaves. Today it is called the Council of Tambapanni, and in many Theravada accounts is called the Fourth Buddhist Council.

Another council in Ceylon was held in 1865 at Ratnapura under the Venerable. Hiddaduve Siri Suamhala. It lasted five months.

In Thailand the *Sangitivamsa* (History of the recitals), written in 1789, records councils held in Sri Lanka and one at Chiangmai, northern Thailand, the so-called eighth council. It was held under the King Sridharmacakravarti Tilakarajad-hipati. This eighth council is recognized in the Thai tradition only.

Unlike many of the smaller councils in Sri Lanka and Thailand, two in Myanmar are recognized as major councils. The Fifth Buddhist Council was held in 1871 in Mandalay, the old imperial capital in the north of Myanmar. It was sponsored by the reigning king, Mindon. The Dharma was recited jointly by 2,400 monks in

an effort to find alterations and distortions. As a result of this council the entire Pali Tripitaka was inscribed on stone slabs; this massive library can still be viewed today at Kuthodaw Pagoda.

And the Sixth Buddhist Council was held in Rangoon in May 1954, to celebrate the 2,500th anniversary of Buddhism; 2,423 monks from Burma and 144 from other countries attended. During the council, which lasted for two years, leading Theravada monks edited and restored an "original" version of the Pali Tripitaka. This meeting was sponsored by the Burmese government.

Additional recent international meetings include a World Buddhist Summit held at Lumbini, Nepal, in 1998 and, in 2000 and 2002, the Second and Third World Buddhist Propagation Conferences held in Thailand and Cambodia, respectively. A World Buddhist Summit was held at the Mahapasana Cave in Yangon (Rangoon) in December 2004. Finally, a first major effort in modern China, the World Buddhist Forum, was held in the Chinese cities of Hangzhou and Zhoushan in April 2006.

Further reading: Francis Brassard, "Councils, Buddhist," in William M. Johnston, ed., *Encyclopedia of Monasticism* (London: Fitzroy Dearborn, 2000), 331–332; Rewata Dhamma, "Buddhist Councils." Available online. URL: http://www.nibbana.com. Accessed on September 10, 2007; Pandit Moti Lal, *Being as Becoming: Studies in Early Buddhism* (Boston: Intercultural, 1993); Amarnath Thakur, *Buddha and Buddhist Synods in India and Abroad* (Delhi: Abhinav, 1996).

cultivation

Broadly conceived, *cultivation* means following a program that will result in spiritual attainment. The term is used in Christian contexts for following the path of Christ. In Buddhism it refers to the path of Buddhism, following the DHARMA taught by the BUDDHA. In the Daoist context it means consciously working to achieve unity with the DAO. And in Confucianism it refers to the efforts to lead the life of a true gentleman, the Confucian ideal who embodies Confucian concepts of humanity. Other Chinese religious traditions such as TIAN DAO (Yiguandao) constantly speak of cultivating the way (*xiu dao*) as the goal of religious participation. One may thus speak of cultivating a path in any tradition; the main assumption is that as a patient gardener one exerts effort to follow a fixed program.

In Buddhism there are various interpretations, with each school and period perhaps providing a different perspective on the Buddhist path. The Buddha's original emphasis was on the EIGHTFOLD PATH, a scheme that remains at the core of Buddhist practice. However, even in the earliest stages certain individuals were said to have attained special states upon hearing the Buddha teach the FOUR NOBLE TRUTHS. These individuals are separated into the three groups of Voice Hearers, who include many of his 10 major disciples. There quickly developed a scheme of progress on the path of Buddhism. The individual would pass through three stages, the three paths. In the path of insight the individual perceives the Four Noble Truths and discards all illusions in thought. In the stage of practice the individual cuts off all desire. And in the final stage, that of the ARHAT, all illusions of all sorts are discarded and the individual is fully enlightened.

A slightly more elaborate scheme breaks out four stages of ENLIGHTENMENT: the stream-winner, the once-returner, the nonreturner, and the ARHAT. The stream-winner is one who has entered the stream leading to NIRVANA and has conquered illusion of thought. The once-returner is one who has passed through six of the illusions of desire. Having attained this level the person will be reborn once in the realm of the gods and one more final time as a human. Therefore, the individual will return to the world of SAMSARA only once more. The non-returner is just that person who has been reborn after seeing through the six illusions of desire and so will not need to return. Having eliminated the final three illusions of desire, the individual achieves the status of *arhat*. The *arhat*, by definition, has passed beyond all illusions of thought and desire and is henceforth free from being reborn in the world of samsara.

This schema sums up the situation for early Buddhist thought. The Mahayana writers accepted this but built on it, adding many stages on the BODHISATTVA path. There are in BODHISATTVA practice 52 stages. These are spelled out in the Jeweled Necklace Sutra, a work probably first produced in China in the fourth century C.E. The text describes 10 stages in each of the areas of faith, security, practice, devotion, and development, followed by the 51st stage of near-perfect enlightenment and the final stage of perfect enlightenment. This scheme had a wide-ranging influence on Mahayana thought, for instance, on the teachings of the TIAN TAI school, which developed in China from the seventh century C.E.

A common saying in Buddhism is that there are 84,000 different *famen,* or Dharma gates. This means the Buddha's Dharma is approached from many angles and methods. There are thus multiple methods of cultivation, and each individual must find the most appropriate after investigation and consideration.

Further reading: Samuel Bercholz and Sherab Chodzin Kohn, *Entering the Stream: An Introduction to the Buddha and His Teachings* (Boston: Shambhala, 1993); Rick Fields, with Peggy Taylor, Rex Weyler, and Rick Ingrasci, *Chop Wood, Carry Water: A Guide to Finding Spiritual Fulfillment in Everyday Life* (Los Angeles: Jeremy P. Tarcher, 1984).

Cultural Revolution (China)

The Cultural Revolution is a period of Chinese history still only partially understood, mainly because it is too near to our own period. It began in 1967 and lasted through 1976, basically ending with the death of Mao Zedong (1893–1976) and the loss of power experienced by his key lieutenants. It began as a political movement and power struggle within the ruling elite but ended by affecting every corner of Chinese society and culture. It is fair to say there is not a Chinese alive today whose family has not been directly affected by the Cultural Revolution in some way. As such it is not always an easy topic to discuss. While the official line on this period is that it was one of excess and mistakes, many who actually lived through that period prefer not to dwell on the suffering it caused.

The effects of the Great Proletarian Revolution on Buddhism were widespread and devastating. Signs of its approach were evident as far back as 1964, when fewer and fewer accounts of Buddhism appeared in news reports. Holmes Welch, one of the first commentators on Buddhism in this period, speaks of the virtual "disappearance" of the religions. Buddhism was, in fact, as close to extinction in China during this period as it has ever been.

The Cultural Revolution buildup started in 1964 with a concerted campaign against the Four Olds—Ideas, Customs, Habits, and Culture. By September 1966, every monastery and temple had closed in the cities. This was the first time monasteries had been ordered closed since the HUI CHANG PERSECUTION of 845 C.E. Some were covered with political slogans, some were stripped bare, and most were converted to other uses such as offices. The headquarters of the CHINESE BUDDHIST ASSOCIATION were closed and the monks expelled. Monks and nuns were ordered to revert to lay life and marry. Red Guards forced people to destroy sacred images. Many leaders were subjected to criticism, abuse, and torture or prison. The Religious Affairs Bureau itself ceased to function.

The Cultural Revolution affected not only Buddhism, but all religions. QIGONG research, for instance, which in the 1950s and 1960s had built up an aura of scientific validity, was attacked. Qigong clinics were often vandalized, and as a result qigong masters sometimes redefined their practices to emphasize bodily movement. And the Red Guards often took aim at archaeological sites of some value; an early site of a "parish" arranged around an earthen altar, established by the first Daoist Celestial Master patriarch ZHAO DAOLING, was destroyed near Mt. Longhu, for instance.

With regard to religious issues, the policies of the Cultural Revolution were formally repudiated at the 11th general assembly of the Central Committee of the Chinese Communist Party, held in December 1978. The Cultural Revolution was then officially recognized as a "mistake."

Further reading: Thomas H. Hanh, "Daoist Sacred Sites," in Livia Kohn, ed., *Daoism Handbook* (Leiden: Brill, 2000), 683–708; Yan Jiaqi and Gao Gao, *Turbulent Decade: A History of the Cultural Revolution* (Honolulu: University of Hawaii Press, 1996); Kam-yee Law, ed., *The Chinese Cultural Revolution Reconsidered: Beyond Purge and Holocaust* (New York: Palgrave Macmillan, 2003); Holmes Welch, *Buddhism under Mao* (Cambridge: Harvard University Press, 1972).

D

Daibutsu

Daibutsu is the popular name of the Great Buddha located at KAMAKURA, Japan. It is a large bronze statue of AMITABHA (Amida) Buddha, the primary object of worship in PURE LAND BUDDHISM, standing some 27.4 feet high. The statue is located in an open courtyard west of the city of Kamakura, its location chosen to symbolize the belief that the paradise to which Amitabha welcomes believers is in the West.

The idea for building the Daibutsu originated in 1195 when Minamoto Yoritomo (1147–99), the shogun who ruled from Kamakura, attended a ceremony in NARA at which the statue of Buddha at TODAI-JI, which had been reconstructed, was rededicated. He decided that Kamakura needed such a Buddha but was unable to act upon the idea during the four years of life remaining to him.

After his death, some Pure Land followers close to Yoritomo followed through with the idea, a project delayed by some years of political unrest and the final consolidation of power in the hands of the family of his widow, Hojo Masako. The Hojo family favored the RINZAI ZEN Buddhists and did not financially support the building of the Daibutsu, though they did not oppose it.

A Pure Land priest named Joko began raising money for the project in 1238, and the original statue, carved in wood, was completed in 1243, along with a hall to house it. In 1247, one of the many storms that afflicted Kamakura in the mid-13th century destroyed the statue and its hall. Devotees again raised money and this time replaced the wooden statue with a bronze one; its casting began in 1252. It was finished in the mid-1260s. The hall in which it then rested was again attacked in a storm in 1335 and destroyed. By this time, the Kamakura shogunate had been defeated and national leadership moved to Kyoto. A new hall was built, but it was destroyed by an earthquake in 1495. Afterward, the hall was not rebuilt and the statue has since been located outdoors.

Over the years, at times, the statue was totally neglected as Kamakura's role in the national life receded into obscurity. Then, early in the 18th century a JODO-SHU priest named Zojoji (1637–1718) launched an effort to restore the statue. He raised enough money to restore the statue, but not enough to construct a new hall.

In the 20th century, especially since the end of World War II, the Daibutsu has become one of Japan's most visited tourist and pilgrimage sites. It currently rests in the open within a courtyard.

The Great Buddha, or Daibutsu, bronze statue at Kamakura, Japan

Immediately to the east of the courtyard is the Kotoku-in temple, which is not accessible to the casual visitor. The statue on view today is the same statue cast in the 13th century. Since its restoration in the 18th century, it has undergone repairs twice, in 1923 and 1960.

The statue shows Amida Buddha sitting in a meditative position. The hands rest on his lap, palms up and the tips of the thumbs touching each other, positioned in what is termed the Samadhi MUDRA.

Further reading: Hisashi Mori, *Sculpture of the Kamakura Period* (Tokyo: Heibonsha and New York: John Weatherhill, 1974); Iso Mutsu, *Kamakura: Fact and Legend* (Rutland, Vt.: Charles E. Tuttle, 1918).

daisho *See* TITLES AND TERMS OF ADDRESS, BUDDHIST.

dakini

Dakinis are female semidivine beings who seem to have emerged out of the folklore of India and assumed prominent positions in Tantric Hinduism, whence they passed into Tibetan Buddhist lore. In Hindu lore, *dakinis* are generally negative beings—demonic in both appearance and behavior.

Dakinis assumed a much more positive position in VAJRAYANA (Tantric) Buddhism, seen as personifications of various levels of the spiritual universe. In Tibet they are known as *khadromas* and are assumed to exist on the highest spiritual levels. They are often pictured as nude, to symbolize the clarity of truth as it is unveiled.

While usually seen as a purely spiritual supernatural being, a *dakini* could also be a human female who had attained a high level of spiritual awareness and accomplishment, or even the incarnation of a deity. PADMASAMBHAVA (eighth century) indicated that no fewer than five of his female disciples were *dakinis*. It appears that these disciples, possibly consorts in sexual rituals, are the source of the other use of the term, to refer to the female partner in those Tantric yogas involving sexual intercourse. The most prominent of the five was YESHE TSOGYAL, who wrote not only the biography of Padmasambhava but her own autobiography. NAROPA's student NIGUMA (11th century) was also thought of as a *dakini*.

Further reading: Erik Pema Kunsang, *Dakini Teachings: Padmasambhava's Oral Instructions to Lady Tsogyal* (Boston: Shambhala, 1990); Thinley Norbu, *Magic Dance: The Display of the Self-Nature of the Five Wisdom Dakinis*. 2d ed. (Boston: Shambhala, 1985); Judith Simmer-Brown, *Dakini's Warm Breath: The Feminine Principle in Tibetan Buddhism* (Boston: Shambhala, 2001); Yeshe Tsogyal, *The Lotus-Born: The Life Story* of *Padmasambhava*. Translated by Erik Pema Kunsang (Boston: Shambhala, 1993).

Dalai Lama

Dalai Lama, or "teacher of the ocean of wisdom," is the title of the leader of the GELUG school of Tibetan Buddhism and, from the 17th century C.E., political leader of Tibet. The title was first given to Sonam Gyatso by a Mongolian prince, ALTAN KHAN, in 1578, as an honor. Sonam Gyatso subsequently applied the title to his predecessors, Gendun Drub (1391–1474) and Gendun Gyatso (1475–1542), and became known himself as the third Dalai Lama. There have since been 11 Dalai Lamas. The current one, DALAI LAMA XIV, Tenzin Gyatso, is at the time of this writing living in exile in DHARMASALA, India, where he fled in 1959.

The Dalai Lama is considered by those in the Tibetan tradition to be an incarnation of the BODHISATTVA AVALOKITESVARA. In addition each is a *TULKU*, or rebirth, of the preceding Dalai Lama.

See also CHINA-TIBET; DALAI LAMA I; DALAI LAMA II; DALAI LAMA III; DALAI LAMA V; DALAI LAMA VII; DALAI MAMA XIII; DALAI LAMA XIV.

Further reading: Ardy Verhaegen, *The Dalai Lamas: The Institution and Its History* (New Delhi: D. K. Printworld, 2002); Ya Hanzhang, *The Biographies of the Dalai Lamas* (Beijing: Foreign Languages Press, 1991).

Dalai Lama I, Gendun Drub (Pema Dorje) (1391–1474) *first in line of Dalai Lamas*

As a child of seven, Pema Dorje, possibly a relative of TSONG KHAPA (1357–1419), the founder of the GELUG school of Tibetan Buddhism, was sent to study with the famous teacher. The Gelug school was a 15th-century reform movement in Tibetan Buddhism that drew heavily on the KADAMPA reform instituted by ATISA in the 11th century. Tsong Khapa emphasized themes of universal compassion and the doctrine of emptiness. He

also moved to reform the system of discipline of the monasteries and insisted on the avoidance of illicit sex and alcohol.

After years as a disciple, Pema Dorje, now known by his religious name, Gendun Drub, became the abbot of Gaden monastery, founded by Tsong Khapa, and then founded the Tashil-humpo monastery, west of Lhasa. This latter monastery soon became the largest in Tibet and the center of the Gelug school. Gendun Drub emerged out of the shadow of his teacher as a scholar of note and the author of a number of books, possibly the most famous of which was a commentary on the ABHIDHARMA-KOSA. He also wrote two well-known poems, one in praise of the Buddha and one in praise of Tsong Khapa. For a period, Gendun Drub established his residence at the Ganden Phodang, the Palace of Joy, at Drepung monastery.

The title *Dalai Lama*, roughly translated "ocean of wisdom," was not applied to the lineage of reincarnated lamas that began with Gendun Drub until the next century. It is the case that Gendun Drub emphasized the idea of looking for his reincarnation, which led to the establishment of the lineage through his successor, Gendun Gyatso (1475–1542), several years after his death.

Further reading: Martin Brauen, *Dalai Lamas: A Visual History* (Chicago: Serindia, 2005); Glen H. Mullin, trans. and ed., *Selected Works of the Dalai Lama*. Vol. 1, *Bridging the Sutras and Tantras* (Ithaca, N.Y.: Snow Lion, 1985); Ya Hanzhang, *The Biographies of the Dalai Lamas* (Beijing: Foreign Language Press, 1991).

Dalai Lama II, Gendun Gyatso (1475–1542) *second Dalai Lama*

As a young boy, Gendun Gyatso was recognized as the reincarnation of the leader of the GELUG school of Tibetan Buddhism, Gendun Drub (1391–1474). According to the story, even as a child, he identified himself as Pema Dorje, the birth name of the Gendun Drub. He then indicated a desire to move to Tashil-humpo monastery, the community founded by Gendun Drub, to reside among the monks. The leadership at the monastery confirmed his identity as the return of their recently deceased leader.

He grew up at the monastery and matured into a notable scholar and accomplished poet. He later authored a history of Buddhism, a volume of the different forms of Buddhism in India, and his autobiography. However, in his younger adult years, after assuming his post as head of the order, he concentrated on traveling and spreading the Gelug movement around the country. In 1509, he founded the picturesque Chhokhorgyal Monastery, adjacent to LAKE LHAMO LATSO, southeast of Lhasa. He then successively became the abbot of three additional monastic centers: Tashil-hunpo (1512), Drepung (1517), and Sera (1526). From these four monastic centers the Gelug school permeated Tibet and set the order in a position to reap the opportunity that would arise with Gendun Gyatso's successor. Drepung soon surpassed Tashil-humpo as the largest Gelug center and became closely identified with the future Dalai Lamas.

Gendun Gyatso died at the Ganden Phodang, the Palace of Joy, his residence at Drepung monastery. He was not, during his lifetime, known as the Dalai Lama. That title was applied to him posthumously by his successor several decades later.

Further reading: Martin Brauen, *Dalai Lamas: A Visual History* (Chicago: Serindia, 2005); Glen H. Mullin, trans. and ed., *Selected Works of the Dalai Lama*. Vol. 2, *The Tantric Yogas of Sister Niguma* (Ithaca, N.Y.: Snow Lion, 1985); Ya Hanzhang, *The Biographies of the Dalai Lamas* (Beijing: Foreign Language Press, 1991).

Dalai Lama III, Sonam Gyatso (1543–1588) *first recognized Dalai Lama*

Sonam Gyatso was born in Khangsar, a community not far from Lhasa. As a child he was identified as the reincarnation and successor of Gendun Gyatso (1475–1542), the head of the GELUG school of Buddhism and abbot of Drepung monastery. The leadership at Drepung recognized and verified his identity. The child would then grow up at Drepung and Chhokhorgyal monasteries. He became well known in Tibet and beyond as an outstanding scholar. In his many travels around the country, Sonam Gyatso took time to found the Champaling Monastery (in eastern Tibet), Kumbum Champaling (a monastery in northern Tibet), and Sandal Khang, the Sandalwood Temple, also in northern Tibet.

Life would change for both Sonam Gyatso and Tibet in 1578 when he visited eastern Mongolia at the invitation of ALTAN KHAN (1507–82), the Mongolian ruler who was in the process of building a great empire. Altan Khan saw Buddhism as a tool that would unify the Mongol tribes. It was, of course, the Vajrayana (Tantric) Buddhism in its Gelug Tibetan form that he taught. Sonam Gyatso proved successful in his assigned task, and as he made plans to return to Tibet, he proclaimed Altan Khan the reincarnation of Kubla Khan and the embodiment of the bodhisattva of wisdom. These twin titles united the khan's political and religious status. The khan then reciprocated by naming Sonam Gyatso the Dalai Lama, teacher of the ocean of wisdom. As the Dalai Lama he would also be seen as an incarnation of AVALOKITESVARA (or GUAN YIN), the bodhisattva of compassion.

The Mongols subsequently built their first Buddhist monastery in 1586. In 1588, Sonam Gyatso visited Mongolia again, but he died on his way back to Tibet. His body was cremated and his ashes taken back to Drepung monastery, where he had resided.

Sonam Gyatso, as the incarnation of a lineage of high lamas, considered it only right that the title that had been given to him be applied to his predecessors, Gendun Drub (1391–1474) and Gendun Gyatso (1475–1542), who thus became known as the first and second Dalai Lamas, respectively.

Further reading: Martin Brauen, *Dalai Lamas: A Visual History* (Chicago: Serindia, 2005); Glen H. Mullin, trans. and ed., *Selected Works of the Dalai Lama*. Vol. 3. *Essence of Refined Gold* (Ithaca, N.Y.: Snow Lion, 1985); Ya Hanzhang, *The Biographies of the Dalai Lamas* (Beijing: Foreign Language Press, 1991).

Dalai Lama V, Lobsang Gyatso (1617–1682) *first politically powerful Dalai Lama*

Lobsang Gyatso, the Fifth Dalai Lama, spent the early years of his life in some obscurity. He was identified as the new incarnate lama at the age of two. A year later he was publicly identified but not enthroned until he was eight (1625). This delay seems to be related to the political climate. The GELUG and the KAGYU schools were vying for control of different parts of the country. In the late 1630s, the Dalai Lama made common cause with the Mongol leader Gushri Khan (d. 1655). Gushri Khan marched into Tibet and made Lobsang Gyatso (the Dalai Lama) both the secular and the spiritual leader of the country and in addition, the head of all Buddhist groups in Asia.

With real political authority, the Dalai Lama proclaimed a new operating principle, Chhosi Shungdel, the integration of religion and politics. He began to define that principle through a claim that the lineage of the Dalai Lamas was the continuation of the lineage of the kings of ancient Tibet all the way back to Songsten Gampo (c. 618–650), the first king. Members of this lineage were to be seen as incarnations of the founder of the Tibetan race, who in turn was the product of the union of Chenrezig, the Buddha of Compassion, and Dolma, a feminine deity of wisdom.

King Songsten Gampo had founded Lhasa, and Lobsang Gyatso now made the city the seat of his government. Here he established two schools, the Tsedung and Shodung, to train the people who would assist him in running the country. He oversaw the construction of the POTALA Palace built atop the site where Buddhism was introduced to Tibet and in 1649 moved there from the traditional residence of the Dalai Lamas at the Palace of Joy in Depung Monastery.

It was for his public life that Lobsang Gyatso became one of the two Dalai Lamas called "the Great." Apart from his political activities, the Fifth Dalai Lama wrote a number of books, including the biographies of his immediate predecessors. He also composed a new code for the monastic orders.

Toward the end of his long life, the Dalai Lama quietly withdrew into a private world and left the country in the hands of a regent. He died in 1682, but it would be 1697 before a public announcement of his death was made. It appears that the regent wished to maintain the new order that the Fifth Dalai Lama had established. The delay seems to have had disastrous results as the Sixth Dalai Lama, Tsangyang Gyatso (1683–1706), though officially discovered as a child, was not publicly acknowledged until his teen years. He turned out to be unsuitable for the task, and the Mongols invaded the country and deposed him. He disappeared (probably murdered) and died at the age of 23.

See also CHINA-TIBET.

Further reading: Martin Brauen, *Dalai Lamas: A Visual History* (Chicago: Serindia, 2005); Lobsang Gyatso, *The Four Noble Truths*. Translated by Sherab Gyatso (Ithaca, N.Y.: Snow Lion, 1994); ———, *The Harmony of Emptiness and Dependent Arising* (Dharamsala: Library of Tibetan Works and Archives, 1992); ———, *Nyung Nä: The Means of Achievement of the Eleven-Faced Great Compassionate One, Avalokiteshvara of the (Bhikshuni) Lakshmi Tradition*. Translated by Lama Thubten Zopa Rinpoche and George Churinoff (Boston: Wisdom, 1995); Ya Hanzhang, *The Biographies of the Dalai Lamas* (Beijing: Foreign Language Press, 1991).

Dalai Lama VII, Kelzang Gyatso (1708–1757) *seventh Dalai Lama*

The death of the Sixth Dalai Lama, under mysterious circumstances, and the discovery of a new child believed to be the real incarnation of the Fifth Dalai Lama drew the Chinese into the affairs of Tibet in opposition to the Mongols, the traditional supporters of the Dalai Lama. Ousting the Mongols in 1720, it was the Chinese (of the Manchurian Qing dynasty) who backed the installation of Kelzang Gyatso as the Seventh Dalai Lama. They, in turn, left behind an official called the *amvan,* who actually held the political reins of the government. For the next century, the Dalai Lama's political power remained quite limited.

Having little taste for politics, Kelzang Gyatso was a scholar and poet and took some interest in the religious life of his people. He founded the Tel-ing Monastery, located near his birthplace, Gethar. He died relatively young, during his 49th year.

See also CHINA-TIBET.

Further reading: Martin Brauen, *Dalai Lamas: A Visual History* (Chicago: Serindia, 2005); Ya Hanzhang, *The Biographies of the Dalai Lamas* (Beijing: Foreign Language Press, 1991).

Dalai Lama XIII, Thupten Gyatso (1876– 1933) *reformist Dalai Lama*

The 13th Dalai Lama rose to power after more than a century during which the authorities in Tibet adopted a more and more isolationist approach both to individual foreigners and to foreign countries. Much of this change was related to the decline of the Qing dynasty and a resultant weakening of the role of China in Tibetan affairs, and some to the growing power of the British in India. It fell to the new Dalai Lama to hold the country together.

A regent ruled the country while Thupten Gyatso was a minor. However, in 1904, at the beginning of his 19th year, the British invaded Tibet, using as an excuse the rising power of Russia. To handle the crisis, the regent ceded his power to Gyatso, who began to exercise his authority as the 13th Dalai Lama.

Soon after the British invasion, Thupten Gyatso fled to Mongolia. While in exile, he received a message from the emperor in Beijing requesting him to visit. When he returned to Tibet, he found the Chinese in control of his country and ready to depose him. He then left for India, where he tried to persuade the British to stop the Chinese. They refused to act and it was not until a popular revolution in 1911–12 toppled the Chinese forces in Tibet that the Dalai Lama was able to return. He declared Tibet independent of China.

His rule reestablished, the Dalai Lama moved to reverse Tibet's isolationist policies, though he faced stiff opposition from the conservative majority. He was able to improve communications with a postal, telephone, and telegraph system. He extended the use of electrical power and began modernizing roads for the future use of automobiles. He also issued the first paper money. Among the few things he did approved by the conservatives was the reintroduction of monastic discipline.

Thupten Gyatso died on December 17, 1933. He was the second Dalai Lama to be honored with the title "Great." He made a prediction that Tibet could very well return to Chinese control.

See also CHINA-TIBET.

Further reading: Charles Bell, *Portrait of a Dalai Lama: The Life and Times of the Great Thirteenth* (Somerville, Mass.: Wisdom, 1987); Martin Brauen, *Dalai Lamas: A Visual History* (Chicago: Serindia, 2005); Ya Hanzhang, *The Biographies of the Dalai Lamas* (Beijing: Foreign Language Press, 1991).

Dalai Lama XIV, Tenzin Gyatso (1935–) *14th Dalai Lama*

The current Dalai Lama was born in Takster, a village in northeast Tibet. At the age of two he was recognized as the reincarnation of the 13th Dalai Lama and taken to Lhasa for his education. His formal enthronement took place in Lhasa in 1940. He completed the Geshe Lharampa degree, roughly equivalent to a doctorate, in 1959. Prior to that he completed his examinations at the three main universities, Drepung, Sera, and Ganden, with a final examination at Jhokang Monastery during the Tibetan New Year, as is the custom.

The Dalai Lama held meetings with both Chinese and Indian leaders beginning in 1950. He attempted to broker an end to border tensions between China and India, which eventually culminated in the Sino-Indian border war of 1962. The relations between China and Tibet worsened after a popular uprising in 1959, which was quickly put down. At that time the Dalai Lama concluded that it was best for him and his government to leave Tibet. He took 80,000 followers with him. Today there are 120,000 Tibetans living in exile in India. The TIBETAN GOVERNMENT-IN-EXILE, which he leads, is centered in DHARMASALA.

Since arriving in India the Dalai Lama has concentrated on the well-being of Tibetans in exile as well as preserving Tibetan culture. Numerous MONASTERIES—more than 200—have been established worldwide. The Dalai Lama acts as spokesperson for his organizations as well as his religious order, the GELUG Buddhists. As leader of a government-in-exile he oversaw the promulgation of a (proposed) new constitution for Tibet, in 1963, as well as a five-point peace plan for Tibet, in 1987. These efforts have met no response from the Chinese government, which does not recognize the Dalai Lama's political authority.

The Dalai Lama has been more successful in contacts with other political and religious leaders. He has visited more than 40 countries and met with both Pope Paul VI (r. 1963–78) and Pope John Paul II (r. 1978–2005), the latter on numerous occasions. His position on other religious traditions seems to fit the mood in many Western multicultural societies. Contact with other religions is to be encouraged, in his opinion, because "each religion has certain unique ideas or techniques, and learning about them can only enrich one's own faith." Through constant media exposure the Dalai Lama has become a world-renowned figure. His status as an international celebrity reached a peak when he was awarded the Nobel Peace Prize in 1989. "The prize," he said

at the time, "reaffirms our conviction that with truth, courage and determination as our weapons, Tibet will be liberated. Our struggle must remain nonviolent and free of hatred."

Today the Dalai Lama exists as both a spiritual and a political leader. As a *spiritual leader* he is widely admired; indeed he represents the achievements of a cultured civilization that has given special attention to spiritual attainment. He has made it his job to focus the world on spiritual themes and values. He has emerged in the popular consciousness as a spokesperson for Buddhism in general, a position at times reinforced by the language used in his many books, lectures, and public pronouncements, though in fact he speaks out of his own segment of the Buddhist community. As a *political figure,* he has had limited effectiveness. He chose exile rather than cooperation with the Chinese authorities and in the intervening years has been forced to deal with China from a position of confrontation. While he has had some success in mobilizing support for his cause on the international level, his efforts have not been able to prevent the dramatic changes that continue in Tibet; nor has he been allowed any input in guiding those changes.

The Dalai Lama's years of leadership of Tibet were the subject of a book, *Seven Years in Tibet,* written by the explorer Heinrich Harrer, who spent World War II in Tibet. His book was made into a movie in 1997.

See also CHINA-TIBET.

Further reading: The Dalai Lama of Tibet, Tenzin Gyatso, *The Dalai Lama at Harvard: Lecture on the Buddhist Path to Peace* (Ithaca, N.Y.: Snow Lion, 1988); ———, *Freedom in Exile: The Autobiography of the Dalai Lama* (New York: Harper Collins, 1990); ———, *Ocean of Wisdom: Guidelines for Living* (San Francisco: Harper & Row, 1990); The Government of Tibet in Exile. "The Dalai Lama's biography." Available online. URL: http://www.tibet.com/DL/biography.html. Accessed on January 25, 2006; Nobelprize.org. "The 14th Dalai Lama-Biography." Edited by Tore Frängsmyr, [Nobel

Foundation], Stockholm, 1990. Available online. URL: http://nobelprize.org/nobel_prizes/peace/laureates/1989/lama-bio.html. Accessed on September 11, 2007.

Dam Luu (1932–1999) *Vietnamese nun*

Dam Luu lived in a monastery from the age of two and was ordained as a BHIKSUNI when she was 19. In 1980 she emigrated to the United States. She founded Duc Vien Temple, which is now located in San Jose, California. In 1983 she established the first Vietnamese nunnery in America. She has championed the chanting of sutras and prayers in vernacular language.

Further reading: Karma Lekshe Tsomo, ed., *Innovative Buddhist Women: Swimming against the Stream* (Richmond, U.K.: Curzon, 2000).

dana

Dana, "giving," is a concept found in both Theravada and Mahayana contexts. In Theravada *dana* relates to merit building, while in Mahayana it generally refers to donations.

Buddhist monastics were always supported by lay contributions. Such contributions were interpreted as acts that would generate a store of merit for each individual. In return the lay people would receive the Dharma from monastics, in the form of blessings or teachings. Both types of transactions are *dana.*

In Mahayana theory *dana* is one of the six PARAMITAS, or perfections, which the cultivator on the BODHISATTVA path will practice. The bodhisattva gives completely, to the extent that the ego is overcome and all action is selfless. In practice Mahayana communities today also encourage extensive almsgiving to the sangha.

There are two categories of *dana,* acts of pure charity and those that seek personal benefit. There are further distinctions, including divisions into three (goods, doctrine, and courage).

Tharmanay Kyaw, a contemporary Burmese teacher, notes the distinction between material giving and *cetana,* or the volition that leads to the act of giving. In response to a question from Anathapindikata, a lay follower, the BUDDHA himself stated: "Householder, whether one gives coarse alms or the finest alms, if one gives casually, without thought, not with one's own hand, with no thought to the future, then, wheresoever that almsgiving bears fruit, his mind will not turn to the enjoyment of excellent food, of fine clothes and rich carriages, the enjoyment of the five senses; and his sons and daughters, slaves, and workers will not respect and honor his words. Such, householder, is the result of a deed done casually."

Further reading: Bhikkhu Bodhi, ed., *Dana: The Practice of Giving.* Wheel No. 367/369 (Kandy, Sri Lanka: Buddhist Publication Society, 1990); Ellison Banks Findly, *Dana: Giving and Getting in Pali Buddhism* (Delhi: Motilala Banarsidass, 2003); Tharmanay Kyaw, "The Buddha's Teachings for Peace on Earth." Buddhist Information of North America. Available online. URL: http://www.buddhistinformation.com/great_gifts_and_giving_well.htm. Accessed on January 15, 2006; Phra Ajaan Plien Panyapatipo, *How To Get Good Results from Doing Merit.* Translated by Benja Jeensnga and Wanchai Jeensnga (Chiangmai, Thailand: Wat Aranyawiwake (Baan Pong), 1991); Charles S. Prebish, *Historical Dictionary of Buddhism* (Metuchen, N.J., Scarecrow Press, 1993).

Dao (Tao)

Dao is the central concept in Daoism. Indeed, as a term it is found in all religious discourse, including Buddhism, CONFUCIANISM, folk religions, and Christianity, throughout all the cultures of East Asia.

Dao is a linguistic term in Chinese and other languages. Its many meanings include "way" of proceeding, "way" of doing, and, in philosophical discourse, "way" of action and thought—in other words, an ideology. The Buddhists used this term to translate the Sanskrit *marga,* in particular the path of Dharma, that is, Buddhism itself. *Dao* can also be used as a verb, meaning "to speak."

In Daoist philosophy *Dao* has several senses. Most important, it signifies an absolute, ultimate reality that lies beyond the visible. This is the Dao of the first line of the *DAODEJING:* "The Way which can be spoken of is not the true way." Here Dao is a primordial substance that makes up the universe, including all life.

But the Dao is also something of a great mystery. The Chinese created a special term to describe that sense of mystery, *xuan,* perhaps best rendered by the Latin *mysterium.* This mystery presumably results from the limitations of the human condition. Because we cannot possibly comprehend all facets of the unlimited Dao, much remains hidden. By extension this implies we can only connect with the Dao through quieting our everyday mind, stilling our desires. Approaching the Dao was always a goal of Daoist cultivation.

Dao is more than a static lump of material, however. It is in constant change. The Daoist conception of the universe was extremely dynamic, with Dao constantly reinventing itself. In philosophical DAOISM the Dao predated all matter; the myriad things—in the Chinese expression, the 10,000 things—issued from the Dao as an expression of itself.

Dao is thus a dynamic that creates change while it ensures existence. Practically speaking, he who has access to a direct understanding of this Dao is one who has true power. "He who holds fast to the Way is complete in Virtue," according to the *Daodejing.*

In the Heavenly Masters school, that first definable school of religious Daoism that arose in the second century C.E., Dao also represented the central deity, who was none other than LAOZI, the purported founder of Daoism. Laozi was the incarnation of the Dao in flesh, a concept not unlike Christ's nature in Christianity. However, unlike Christianity, Daoism added a string of additional god figures to the altar, in practice reducing the relative significance of Laozi. Of course the additional deities were also products of the ultimate Dao. Thus in religious Daoism the Dao represented a creator force behind the universe.

The Dao then became an element in the religious theology of Daoism.

Further reading: Alan K. L. Chan, "The Daodejing and Its Tradition," in Livia Kohn, ed., *Daoism Handbook* (Leiden: Brill, 2000), 1–29; Julian F. Pas, *Historical Dictionary of Taoism* (Lanham, Md.: Scarecrow Press, 1998); Kristofer Schipper, *The Taoist Body* (Berkeley: University of California Press, 1993).

Dao An (Tao An) (312–385) *early Chinese Buddhist priest and translator*

Dao An was a leading monk in Chang An, the capital of the Former Qin dynasty, just before the time the master translator KUMARAJIVA arrived and began his epic translation work in 401 C.E. Before that time Dao An had completed a catalog of the SUTRAS that had been translated into Chinese. This list, which has now been lost, enabled later Chinese scholars to organize the TRIPITAKA, the Buddhist canon. Dao An had already decided to stop using the facilitating technique of GEYI, "matching terms," which clouded many early translations of Buddhist works. Thus Dao An's work in a sense laid the foundation for Kumarajiva's translations.

Dao An and his followers were so dedicated in spreading the word of Buddhism that he sent followers to all corners of China. His disciples included HUI YUAN (334–416 C.E.), who later went on to found an important center of practice on Mt. Lu.

Further reading: Kogen Mizuno, *Buddhist Sutras: Origin, Development, Transmission* (1980. Reprint, Tokyo: Kosei, 1995), 49–54.

Daodejing (Tao Te Ching)

The *Daodejing,* the *Classic of the Way of Power,* is perhaps the best-known book of Chinese DAOISM and is a classic of world literature and spirituality. It is the most widely translated work from Chinese, translated into English alone more than 30 times. It is organized into two books that total 81 chapters. The work was originally simply called the *Laozi,* the book of Laozi. But by the second century C.E. it was also called the *Daodejing.* The first half is in fact the *Dao Jing,* the second the *De Jing.* These titles do not indicate significant themes of the two parts; they reflect simply the first words in each half. At 5,000+ Chinese ideographs the *Daodejing* is a relatively short work.

The *Daodejing* is traditionally attributed to Laozi, who lived roughly around the time of Confucius, in the fourth–fifth centuries B.C.E. The work is clearly an anthology, a collection assembled from various sources and by different individuals. What unites the passages is that they relate to the school of Daoism (*dao jia*), one of the competing philosophic schools of the period. In this school the idea of Dao is central. Dao is inexpressible. It is the source of all things and events. It prexisted the universe. It transcends distinctions and is the key to all possibilities.

This foundational work in Chinese spirituality is well worth reading and rereading. It is difficult to top this opening:

The Dao that can be told of is not the eternal Dao;
The name that can be named is not the eternal name.
The Nameless is the origin of Heaven and Earth;
The Named is the mother of all things.
Therefore let there always be non-being so we may see
their subtlety,
And let there always be being so we may see their
outcome.
The two are the same,
But after they are produced, they have different names.
They both may be called deep and profound.
Deeper and more profound,
The door of all subtleties!

(Wing-Tsit Chan, *A Source Book in Chinese Philosophy* [Princeton, N.J.: Princeton University Press, 1963] 139)

Further reading: D. C. Lau, trans., *Chinese Classics: Tao Te Ching* (Hong Kong: The Chinese University Press, 1963, 1982); Lao Tsu, *Tao Te Ching.* Translated by Gia-Fu feng and Jane English (New York: Vintage Books, 1972).

Daoism (Taoism)

Daoism as a formal, organized religion is not as widespread or popular as other Chinese religions, for instance, Buddhism or Christianity. However, as a system of concepts, a way of interpreting the world, Daoism exerts a strong pull on many people. And in Chinese culture, as well as many other Asian cultures, Daoism continues to live in a range of popular level practices, from medicine to martial arts to ritual feasts in villages.

Daoist teachings focus on humanity's relationship with nature. Unlike in many religious systems, there is no all-powerful deity figure who created the universe. All phenomena, instead, enter into existence through a process of constant multiplication and decay. Tuning into this process is a major goal of the Daoist practitioner. Daoist teachings also include political considerations, such as the correct role of the ruler in regard to the subjects, as well as issues of correct diet and regulation of the body.

Daoism is the most uniquely Chinese religion, and yet it remains a subject of great misunderstanding. Some see it as identical with the early texts *Daodejing* and *Laozi.* Others see it as an imitation of Buddhism.

There are four periods in Daoist history: proto-Daoism, classical Daoism, premodern Daoism, and contemporary Daoism.

PROTO-DAOISM

In proto-Daoism there was no formal religious organization. The earliest "Daoists" were most likely shamans who helped people in this world understand "secret" or hidden phenomena. Still, many core Daoist ideas and beliefs formed at this time. Several classic books on philosophy and mysticism were written in this period, including the *Laozi, Zhuangzi,* and *Neiye.*

LAOZI

Sima Qian, an early Chinese historian, stated that LAOZI was an "archivist" who lived in the Zhou dynasty (1027–221 B.C.E.) and was one of Confucius's teachers. Laozi retired and journeyed west but was stopped at the Hangu Pass by Yin Xi, the gatekeeper. Yin Xi asked him to write a text containing his philosophy. The result was the DAODE-JING, the Scripture of the Way and Its Power.

The Daodejing, or Laozi, is a terse statement of important philosophical positions. It explains the creation of the universe and the forces at work in it.

The Daoist myth states that Laozi continued on to India and appeared there as SAKYAMUNI, the Buddha. He then traveled farther west and became Mani, the founder of Manichaeanism, a dualistic Christian sect.

ZHUANGZI

ZHUANGZI was a Daoist leader who lived a few hundred years after Laozi. The classic that is known by the philosopher's name has never been used much by Daoists. Instead it is important because it explains the concept of the sage, the enlightened being who can live without being fettered by social and cultural conventions. This perfected person was called a zhenren, a "true person." In this image, Daoism becomes a personal spiritual quest.

NEIYE

A third proto-Daoism text is the Neiye, "inward training," which is a smaller section of a larger work, the Guanzi. The Neiye is the first of a long line of Daoist writings to focus on such techniques for longevity as breath meditation. In the inward training the practitioner focuses on internal energy, and especially the QI or "vital energy." The refined form of qi is jing, or "essence." The person who can cultivate jing can improve the circulation of qi in the body. Through cultivation of such qi the person becomes attuned to the energy of the cosmos, the universal Qi.

CLASSICAL DAOISM

Classical Daoism began in 142 C.E., when ZHANG DAOLING started the Way of Orthodox Unity, the first organized Daoist religion. In this period two other important Daoist groups started as well: SHANGQING DAOISM (the Way of Highest Clarity) and LINGBAO DAOISM (the Way of Numinous Treasure). Classical Daoism took general shape in this period as an organized religious spirit. It developed fixed rituals and important texts. Classical Daoism thus corresponds roughly with medieval Chinese history—from the Han (221 B.C.E.–220 C.E.) through the Tang (618–906 C.E.) dynasties. Politically, Daoism reached the peak of its influence as the official religion of the Tang during the reign of the emperor Xuan Zong (713–756). During the Tang, Daoism also spread into neighboring countries, such as Korea, Japan, and Vietnam. Several important new Daoist religious movements developed in China during the classical period.

ZHENGYI DAO
(WAY OF ORTHODOX UNITY)

The end of the Han dynasty saw several revolutionary movements spring up. Zhengyi Dao (or, in another name, the Way of Celestial Masters—Tianshi Dao) was founded in 142 C.E. by Zhang Daoling, in Sichuan, in far western China. Zhengyi Dao was a theocracy—civil and religious administrations were the same. The group also used public ritual to expatiate or atone for sins. It taught that Laozi was a god. All offices in Zhengyi Dao were hereditary. So eventually Zhang Daoling's son and grandson took over. Zhang Lu, the grandson, finally surrendered power to the revolutionary leader Cao Cao in 215 C.E. At this point all Zhengyi followers dispersed to different regions of China.

SHANGQING
(WAY OF HIGHEST CLARITY) SCHOOL

This movement arose among the higher classes in southern China, in the 300s C.E. The pronouncements of a Daoist immortal, Lady Wei Yang, who had lived on Mt. Mao near Nanjing, in central China, were collected by Tao Hongjing (456–536 C.E.), who founded the Shangqing school.

Shangqing Daoism was not a communal movement. Instead it emphasized personal self-cultivation and the deities of the stars and the Big Dipper. These gods were seen to enter the person's body during meditation. They then helped the cultivator to transform into a celestial immortal. The goal, then, was immortality.

THE LINGBAO (WAY OF NUMINOUS TREASURE)

The Lingbao were probably originally spirits or shamans who guarded certain places. Later, LINGBAO referred to talismanic objects such

Large incense burner, Daoist temple in Guangdong, China; names of donors are listed on the side of the burner

as small books, chants, or diagrams that had spiritual powers of protection. The Lingbao school was centered around belief in five sacred diagrams, one associated with each of the five directions. These diagrams were in a collection of texts written by Ge Chaofu and made public in 401 C.E.

Numinous Treasure Daoism is clearly influenced by Buddhist ideas. The talismans and charts were said to help all sentient beings to attain salvation, which is a key goal of Buddhist practice. Lingbao liturgies and rituals showed a way to save people from a complex series of hells and purgatories where people suffered for karmic sins. All these were Buddhist ideas. Daoism also borrowed the idea of taking precepts or vows to abstain from meat and sex.

Lu Xiujing (406–477) was the seventh celestial master. He standardized the Lingbao texts and broke Daoist ritual into three types: ordinations (*jie*), fasts (*zhai*), and offerings (*jiao*). These three types were all practiced at the imperial courts whenever Daoism was in favor. Lu also developed popular rituals. Today *jiao* is the main kind of public ritual performed by Daoist priests.

PREMODERN DAOISM

The premodern period of Daoism began with the Song dynasty (960–1279). In this period the borders between Buddhism and Daoism became blurred. There was another kind of influence at work as well: local cults. All over China people worshipped local heroes and gods. Such worship practices became mixed into the Daoist hierarchy of gods.

In this period the most significant new movement was QUANZHEN DAO (the Way of Complete Perfection), which was started by WANG CHONGYANG (1112–70), a former official of the Liao dynasty (907–1125). Quanzhen is significant today as one of the two organized forms of Chinese Daoism still practiced. Quanzhen was based on Chinese alchemy ideas. However, over the years its focus has shifted more to community religion. It is also a blend of Confucian, Daoist, and Buddhist ideas. Quanzhen was most influential under the Yuan dynasty (1279–1368). Qiu Chanchun (1148–1227), a famous Quanzhen leader, visited the Mongol emperor Genghis Khan and debated Buddhists at his court. Quanzhen had influence at court, clearly. However, such political support could come and go: a later debate with Buddhists in 1281 was lost.

Daoism later made a comeback during the Ming dynasty (1368–1644). It was during the Ming, in 1445, that the Daoist Canon (DAOZANG), or collection of Daoist written works, was first compiled, under the Yongle emperor. This collection included around 1,500 different texts, including hymns, liturgies, recipes, and myths.

CONTEMPORARY DAOISM

The final period, the modern or contemporary, started with China's modernization in the late 19th century. Daoism, along with Buddhism and Confucianism, gradually lost influence among China's educated elite. By the time the last empire was overthrown, in 1911, the educated classes were clearly looking for alternatives to traditional religious systems of thought. Institutional Daoism, including its system of monasteries and rituals, experienced financial problems.

Today Daoism survives in three major ways. First, it remains a powerful system of ideas and mysticism. Such a cultural network influences Chinese culture in many areas, for instance, in martial arts training, art, and literature.

A second form of influence is institutional. Daoism as an institution takes two forms today. First is Zheng Yi, or "Orthodox One," Daoism. Zheng Yi Daoists are individual Daoist teachers who pass their ritual knowledge to disciples. This is not a communal religious practice, although Zheng Yi Daoists do officiate at local community temple celebrations. Quanzhen Daoism, in contrast, is communal and, in a limited way, monastic. There are networks of Quan Zhen temples now in Hong Kong and China that perform com-

Large stone stele, or memorial, placed on a turtle, symbol of the East, in the Qingyang gong, a Quanzhen Daoist temple in Chengdu, Sichuan, western China

munity functions such as holding funerals and celebrating major holiday.

A third form of Daoism active today is best understood as "popular Daoism." There are ritual specialists who, though not formally ordained or trained as Quan Zhen or Zheng Yi Daoists, are nevertheless called "Daoists" in many villages and towns. These specialists are called on to perform rituals at village feasts and important celebrations. They are respected, and paid, because of the ritual knowledge they possess. Such specialists may also tell fortunes and dabble in FENG SHUI. Other people offer Daoist knowledge in the marketplace, including divination using the BOOK OF CHANGES (Yi Jing) and Chinese medical advice based on Daoist principles.

Further reading: Livia Kohn, *Daoism and Chinese Culture* (Cambridge, Mass.: Three Pines Press, 2001); ———, ed., *Daoism Handbook* (Leiden: Brill, 2000); James Miller, *Daoism: A Short Introduction* (Oxford: Oneworld, 2003); Isabelle Robinet, *Taoism: Growth of a Religion.* Translated by Phyllis Brooks (Stanford, Calif.: Stanford University Press, 1997).

Daoist alchemy

Daoism includes a number of intriguing practices, many of which can be considered more or less mystical, and at times highly esoteric (secret). Some of the most misunderstood of these traditions have been focused on transcending death and attaining "immortality." It has become common among scholars to label such traditions *alchemy*, a term usually associated with occult practices in the West.

One type of Daoism closely associated with alchemy is "hermit Daoism." As might be surmised, hermit Daoism is particularly associated with mysterious "hermits" who lived in seclusion far off in the mountains. In their hidden dwellings, these hermit alchemists spent their days working with the cosmic forces in the body, practicing intense meditations, and concocting (and consuming) magical elixirs intended to promote longevity or even to enable the practitioner to transcend the mortal realm.

These practices and the ideas behind them are not necessarily as far-fetched as they may appear. Daoist alchemy is rooted in important philosophical texts (e.g., the BOOK OF CHANGES and DAODEJING), and probably dates to ancient—even prehistoric— shamanistic practices that formed the original basis of Chinese culture. In whatever form we find it, Daoist alchemy is premised on understanding and acceptance of life and death, sickness and health, and a conviction that these dualities can be transcended. Such views are fully in keeping with the ideals of "free and easy wandering" and radical freedom (even invulnerability) espoused in the Daoist sage MENCIUS's great work *Zhuangzi.*

ORIGINS AND BASIC FEATURES OF ALCHEMY

The Chinese term most often translated as "alchemy" is *jindan* ("gold-cinnabar"), undoubtedly because it names the two principal ingredients in most alchemical elixirs.

Daoist alchemy was encouraged by techniques of metallurgy. China was one of the first ancient civilizations to attain high levels of development in the casting and smelting of bronze. Some of the earliest masterpieces of Chinese art were the great bronze vessels of the Shang (1766–1027 B.C.E.) and Zhou (1122 B.C.E.–256 B.C.E.) dynasties, and the earliest dynastic histories speak of such vessels as among the most treasured royal objects. Such vessels (often tripods or cauldrons) were only used in official sacrificial ceremonies. By serving as containers for sacrifical offerings, the vessels themselves became sacred; they became bridges to heavenly realms. The effect was to engender a deep-seated cultural association between prized bronzes (cauldrons and the like) and the divine. It is but a short step to putting such sacred vessels to other uses such as preparing special mixtures for attaining a divine state of immortality.

Daoist alchemy essentially shares the same theoretical basis as most Chinese medicine. Since the Chinese have generally not maintained a strict separation of "mind" and "body" (both were thought to be composed of the same essential stuff), it was not difficult to conceive of survival after earthly life in some sort of transcendent bodily form. Daoists speak of the body as comprising three forces or life principles: QI (matter-energy, "breath"), *jing* ("essence," often equated with semen), and *shen* ("spirit," or more appropriately, "consciousness"). Each of these principles is also present in the larger cosmos. In such a cosmos it is relatively easy (at least theoretically) to transform from one level to another; such changes are essentially changes in form, not in substance.

"IMMORTALITY"?

The goal of Daoist alchemy has long been said to be "immortality," which referred to more than a simple "deathless state." Daoist "immortality" could be understood as physical, as a type of afterlife beyond the mortal body (as pure "spirit"), or perhaps a more mystical sense of merging with Dao. The latter would seem to be based on mystical experiences in which the practitioner realized she or he would never lose her/his true identity, even in physical demise. In some later forms of Daoism, the immortals ascend to the heavenly realms, where they take their places in an elaborate bureaucracy.

The most common Chinese term for "immortal" is *xian,* a word composed of the characters for "human being" (*ren*) and "mountain" (*shan*), making for a more or less literal translation of *xian* as "mountain man." In some respects this is actually a rather apt translation when we bear in mind the prominent role mountains have played in Daoist lore. Some scholars have tried to avoid the problematic associations with the term *immortal* by translating *xian* as "sylph," originally a Latin term that denotes a type of fairy (often female) supposed to inhabit the air. However, this rhetorical move conveniently avoids the whole matter of death and how it is to be overcome, the main Daoist concern in alchemical practice. The recent scholarly consensus is to stay with *immortality* for the sake of continuity with the understanding that Daoist "immortality" might best be conceived as a type of transcendence and transformation.

TYPES OF ALCHEMY

It has become customary for scholars to distinguish two forms of Daoist alchemy: "external alchemy" (*waidan*) and "internal alchemy" (*neidan*). "External alchemy" focuses on preparing various herbs, drugs, and elixirs that are consumed in order to prolong life or achieve immortality. There is some indication that these procedures were the outgrowth of the search for a way to turn baser substances into gold, the guiding idea in Western alchemy as well. By contrast, "internal alchemy" is a path of meditative cultivation that includes strict moral discipline, a regimented diet, and specialized exercises to nourish and purify *qi*.

"External" and "internal" alchemy were never truly separate in ancient and medieval China. In addition, various learned scholars (e.g., GE HONG, 283–343) were deeply involved in alchemical pursuits. Toward the end of the Tang dynasty (618–906), however, "internal" alchemy was predominant, in large part because of the numbers of adepts who died of poisoning after consuming CINNABAR elixirs. Nonetheless, it is helpful to consider both forms of Daoist alchemy separately with the understanding that aspirants engaged in practices from both.

"EXTERNAL ALCHEMY" (*WAIDAN*)

Although "external alchemy" is undoubtedly a very ancient practice, the first clear evidence of it is from the pre-Han and Han (206 B.C.E.–220 C.E.) eras with the rise of a certain class of proto-Daoists usually called "*fangshi*" (lit. "Masters of Techniques"). A very eclectic group, the *fangshi* were essentially magicians and thaumaturges ("wonder workers") who had great reputations among the Chinese populace and were often sought after by various rulers.

Among the most famous of the *fangshi* was Li Shaojun (d. 133 B.C.E.), a powerful sorcerer who allegedly persuaded Emperor Wudi (r. 140–87 B.C.E.) to permit alchemical experiments that included invoking the aid of the STOVE GOD in the transformation of cinnabar mixtures. The purified cinnabar concoction would be fashioned into special vessels and those eating from such dishes would be assured of immortality. Although his techniques differed from those of later alchemists, in the case of Li Shaojun, we clearly see evidence of someone engaged in alchemical practices aimed at transcending the bounds of mortal life. By the late Han and the ensuing "Period of Disunity" (220–589 C.E.), small groups of *wai dan* practitioners were widespread throughout China.

Followers of the Way of *wai dan* needed to prepare rather rigorously. Such training would typically include progress in various forms of meditation, calisthenics (e.g., QIGONG), and strict ethical striving. Serious Daoists have consistently maintained that pursuit of immortality required detachment from sensual desires and the purging of negative attitudes such as hatred, which were considered harmful to the aspirant. Only with a firm foundation made strong through such CULTIVATION could one actually begin procuring and mixing the ingredients necessary for the elixir that would confer immortality.

Actual consumption of an elixir might have any number of effects, depending on its potency and on the adept's constitution. In theory it could transform the alchemist's body into one of pure light and air, enabling him to soar into the heavens to join the other immortals. In practice, though, the effects were rather different. Texts indicate that the elixir was to be taken in small doses at regular intervals and accompanied by a special diet. Some alchemists, however, took large doses that invariably caused their deaths. In small doses elixirs seem to have had a sedative effect, aided the breathing, warmed the body, and even promoted hair growth. In addition, those who took the elixirs experienced heightened sexual energy, general sensory arousal, and possibly even hallucinations. Perhaps the most important side effect was the preservation of bodily tissues. The bodies of those who died of elixir consumption resisted normal decay, retaining a lifelike appearance that may have been taken as direct proof of immortality.

External alchemy continued to be practiced throughout the medieval period, yet during the latter sixth century there is evidence of growing skepticism in some alchemical circles. Thus, for instance, we read of instances when condemned prisoners facing execution were used as guinea pigs to test various elixirs. Nonetheless, the Way of *waidan* enjoyed something of a renaissance in the Tang dynasty (618–907 C.E.). During this remarkable period of cultural flowering many wealthy and powerful patrons employed professional alchemists who worked to perfect their techniques. Yet invariably there were many poisonings. In fact, during the Tang more emperors died of ingesting alchemical elixirs than in any other period. The increasing evidence of failure provoked a major rethinking of the entire art of alchemy and the eventual decline of *waidan* as a viable practice.

"INTERNAL ALCHEMY" (*NEIDAN*)

The Way of "internal alchemy" developed originally from meditation techniques used by practitioners of "external alchemy." We can see such ideas at the fore in the life and work of GE HONG. Ge Hong was a well-known scholar who actively sought ingredients for concocting elixirs but who also led a disciplined personal life. He was an accomplished practitioner of complex meditations, notably techniques of visualization known as *shouyi* ("Guarding the One"). In his masterpiece, the BAOPUZI, he writes:

Guard the One and visualize the True One; then the spirit World will be yours to peruse!
Lessen desires, restrain your appetite—the One will remain At rest!
Like a bare blade coming toward your neck—realize you Live through the One alone!
Knowing the One is easy—keeping it forever is hard.
Guard the One and never lose it—the limitations of man will Not be for you!
On land you will be free from beasts, in water from fierce Dragons.
No fear of evil spirits or phantoms,
No demon will approach, nor blade attain!

In this and other passages Ge Hong seems to promise freedom and superhuman powers merely from practicing the mysterious meditation techniques rather than ingesting actual elixirs. As time went on, alchemists increasingly began to turn to such practices as offering an alterative path to ultimate transformation.

It is really only in the late Tang and the period immediately following the dynasty's collapse that we find Daoist thinkers self-consciously distinguishing the Ways of "external" and "internal" alchemy. In part this was due to growing skepticism among alchemists that immortality (in at least the grossest, most literal sense) was even possible. Under the steady influence of Buddhism, some alchemical thinkers concluded that immortality properly construed was really liberation (nirvana) from the beginningless cycle of life and death (SAMSARA). Others took a more rationalist view and maintained that so-called immortality was really about cultivating health and longevity. In their entertaining such notions, we see that many Daoists in the later Middle Ages were actively reinterpreting their received traditions. Most also began to emphasize the various meditations and systems of bodily exercise that had traditionally been regarded as adjunct practices in the concocting of elixirs.

It is often difficult to decipher instructions for practices of *neidan*, since alchemy is generally an esoteric tradition passed on only to initiates who have been trained in its secret lore. As such, the language typically found in alchemical texts is cryptic and highly symbolic, resembling the "twilight language" of Hindu and Buddhist *tantras*. The guiding principle seems to be visualizing the body and its energies as the furnace and cauldron in which the elixir of immortality (the "Golden Elixir" or "Golden Flower") is purified. Essentially then, the same steps in "external alchemy" are still performed albeit *internally*.

Actual methods of *neidan* seem to vary tremendously but share a view of the body as being divided into three "cinnabar fields" (*dantian*) located in the abdomen, chest, and head. Practitioners would engage in special techniques of breathing, visualizing light (*qi* made visible) and then circulating it through the "cinnabar fields" in what was sometimes called a "microcosmic orbit." With practice, this might be extended to the limbs in a "macrocosmic orbit." Other practices involved nourishing the YIN-YANG energies of the body and uniting them to create a "spirit body" (often described as the "embryo") that would depart the body at death and live on beyond the gross material realm.

Neidan probably reached its height in the period from the late 10th to mid-14th centuries during the Northern and Southern Song (960–1279) as well as the Yuan (1279–1368) dynasties. One important "internal" alchemist was Zhen Xiyi, who allegedly studied under LU DONGBIN. The most important master of *neidan*, though, was Zhang Boduan (987–1082), a government official who received revelations from Lu Dongbin and retired to alchemical pursuits. He earned great fame for a collection of poems entitled the *Wuzhen pian* (Awakened to reality). Other practitioners founded rival lineages that used other techniques. Despite their differences, however, nearly all practitioners of *neidan* agreed that the proper Way required physical *and* psychological cultivation. Thus, we can say that Daoist alchemy became a means of training both mind and body or, as some scholars have recently put it, a "biospiritual" tradition.

DAOIST ALCHEMY TODAY

Daoist alchemy (particularly *neidan*) is still actively practiced. It has transformed over the years and can now be found most obviously in the various movements of *qigong*. *Qigong* is a generic term for various complex systems that include meditation, gymnastics, martial arts, and breath control. Although it has ancient origins, it only developed into an integrated system during the mid-20th century. It is in this form (along with the related art of TAIJIQUAN) that teachings and practices based on methods of "internal alchemy" have been most often made available to Western students. The stated aims of both arts are to promote physical and mental balance, health, and so on, although reports of developing supernatural powers (e.g., clairvoyance, telepathy) are not uncommon.

The renowned psychoanalyst C. G. Jung (1875–1961) was very interested in Western forms of alchemy, and in conjunction with his friend Richard Wilhelm (1873–1930), a renowned orientalist, published a new translation of an alchemical treatise entitled the *Taiyi jinhua zong-zhi* (Supreme unifying secret of the golden flower) with his own commentary. The resulting volume (translated into English as *The Secret of the Golden Flower*) has become a classic of Jungian psychology and has opened up the exploration of Daoist alchemy to many contemporary people.

See also QUANZHEN DAOISM; QIGONG.

Further reading: Chikashige Masumi, *Oriental Alchemy* (New York: Samuel Weiser, 1936, 1974); Julia Ching, *Chinese Religions* (Maryknoll, N.Y.: Orbis Books, 1993), 104–111; Livia Kohn, *Daoism and Chinese Culture* (Cambridge, Mass.: Three Pines Press, 2001), 83–86, 145–149, 193–202; ———, ed., *The Taoist Experience* (Albany: State University of New York Press, 1993); Isabelle Robinet, *Taoism: Growth of a Religion.* Translated by Phyllis Brooks (Stanford, Calif.: Stanford University Press, 1997); Richard Wilhelm and Carl G. Jung, *The Secret of the Golden Flower: A Chinese Book of Life* (London: K. Paul, Trench, Trubner, 1931); Eva Wong, *The Shambhala Guide to Taoism* (Boston: Shambhala, 1997), 66–79.

Daoist liturgies and rituals

Daoist liturgies are *keyi*. A *ke* originally meant a "rule." A *keyi* was a liturgical instruction, the actual texts that Daoist priests follow during rituals. Early Daoist collections of the ZHENGYI school, the Celestial Masters, founded by ZHANG DAOLING in 142 C.E., included five separate works that included rules. These liturgies became increasingly important in Daoist practice. There were liturgies associated with exorcism, meditation, alchemy, and priestly ordination, as well as such practical issues as marriage.

One important form of ritual throughout Daoist history has been the *zhai*, or "fast." The word originally meant the fast undertaken by the emperor and officials in preparation for sacrifices. It later meant a formal audience accompanying worship. The structure of such worshipping sessions continued to retain the flavor of imperial rites, however. Today the *zhai* is still performed and has taken on a colorful aspect, with dramatic performances and feasting for the entire community. *Zhai* community rituals typically last three, five, or seven days.

Further reading: Charles D. Benn, "Daoist Ordinations and Zhai Rituals in Medieval China," in Livia Kohn, ed., *Daoism Handbook* (Leiden: Brill, 2000), 307–339; Michael Saso, *Blue Dragon White Tiger: Taoist Rites of Passage* (Washington, D.C: The Taoist Center, 1990).

Dao Sheng (Tao-sheng) (c. 360–434) *early Chinese interpreter of Buddha nature*

Dao Sheng was an early Chinese master whose chief contribution was a commentary on the LOTUS SUTRA. He was born during the Eastern Jin dynasty (317–420 C.E.), a very active period in the importation of Buddhism into China. And he was born in the early Buddhist center of Peng Cheng, in eastern China (modern Jiangsu). His father was a local magistrate. Dao Sheng began to study with a Buddhist master, Zhu Fatai (319–387 C.E.) from the age of 11. Given his background, Dao Sheng's involvement in Buddhism is not surprising.

Zhu Fatai, who had been a student of the Kuchean missionary Fotudeng (d. 349), did not emphasize textual knowledge. Thus Dao Sheng had only limited knowledge of some PRAJNAPARAM-ITA (wisdom) texts. Nevertheless he became a well-known teacher and debater. When Zhu Fatai died in 387, Dao Sheng began to travel. He eventually settled in the major Buddhist center of Mt. Lu in 397 C.E. Here he had contact with Sanghadeva, a Kashmiri missionary and ABHIDHARMA expert. Although Dao Sheng stayed at Mt. Lu for seven years, there is no evidence that he became close to or was much influenced by the famous Hui Yuan (334–417), who had also moved to Mt. Lu.

In 405 or 406, Dao Sheng departed Mt. Lu and moved to Chang An to study with KUMARAJIVA, one of the greatest translators in Buddhist history. Kumarajiva had arrived in 401 and soon attracted more than 3,000 hopeful students. Dao Sheng was perceived as being highly knowledgeable and competent, but it is unclear to what extent he actually assisted in Kumarajiva's various translation projects. Nevertheless, Dao Sheng was present in the capital during the period of feverish translation of such important texts as the *Great Wisdom Treatise* (*Mahaprajnaparamita-sastra, Ta Zhi Du Lun*), the VIMALAKIRTI-NIRDESA SUTRA, the LOTUS SUTRA, and the *Astasahasrika-prajnaparamita*. He soon wrote commentaries on the last three.

In 408 Dao Sheng returned to Mt. Lu in the south and the following year settled in Jian Kang, at the Qingyuan Temple, where he continued to write. One conclusion he reached was that ICCHAN-TIKAs (condemned people), who were generally seen as being outcasts in the path to enlightenment, had BUDDHA NATURE just as everyone else had. For this controversial stand he was expelled from the Buddhist sangha in 428 or 429.

Dao Sheng retreated once more to Mt. Lu, where his risky belief was exonerated once the complete translation of the NIRVANA SUTRA (by Dharmaksema) was disseminated. In this translation it was clear that *icchantikas* were indeed seen to have Buddha nature. Vindicated, Dao Sheng died on Mt. Lu in 434, having first composed a commentary on the Lotus Sutra.

Dao Sheng's life was spent in three major centers of Buddhism, and on many subjects he occupies an intermediary position among the three. In his thinking he particularly emphasized the doctrine of sudden enlightenment and the doctrine of Buddha nature.

Further reading: Young-ho Kim, *Tao-sheng's Commentary on the Lotus Sutra: A Study and Translation* (Albany: State University of New York Press, 1990).

Dao Xin (Tao-hsin) (580–651) *fourth Chinese patriarch of Chan Buddhism*

Dao Xin lived in the early days of the Tang dynasty (618–906 C.E.), a period in which Buddhism vied with DAOISM for influence over the Chinese court. He is said to have been commanded to visit the emperor but refused, an action for which he was willing to risk death.

Dao Xin introduced a method of training using *ekavyudi-samadhi,* "the SAMADHI of specific mode." In this practice the cultivator practices *nienfo chan,* or "reciting the Buddha's name." This term does not refer to the PURE LAND repetition of the name of AMITABHA Buddha. Instead Dao Xin taught that it is up to the practitioner to decide which particular Buddha's name he recites. Dao Xin referred to the first chapter of the LANKAVATARA SUTRA as scriptural authority for this practice.

While previous masters normally lived alone in thatched huts, Dao Xin established a community of several hundred monks near Mt. Shuangfeng in Huangmei. Another innovation he introduced was to emphasize work as part of CHAN practice, making his community of monks economically self-sufficient.

Dao Xin is said to have slept sitting up for most of his life, a practice still common among Chinese monks. He is also said to have died seated, in meditation. His body is still preserved, one of many famous Buddhist mummies.

Further reading: Heinrich Dumoulin, *Zen Buddhism: A History.* Vol. 1, *India and China* (New York: Macmillan, 1988); Venerable Jing Hui, "Dao Xin's Gate," in "The Gates of Chan Buddhism." buddhanet.net, Buddha Dharma Education Association. Available online. URL: http://www.buddhanet.net/pdf_file/gates_of_chan.pdf. Accessed on March 19, 2005.

Daozang (Tao-tsang, Daoist Canon)

A general term for the texts used by Daoists, the *Daozang* contains 5,485 separate works. It was compiled in 1445 during the Ming dynasty

(1368–1644), during the reign of one emperor, Zhengtong, and issued again under Emperor Wanli. The *Daozang* is divided into three overall categories, or *dong* (grotto, cavern), and further divided into four *fu* and 12 *lei*, or types (explained later). The three *dong* are Dongzhen (The Cavern Truth, containing the SHANGQING revelation), Dong Xuan (The Cavern Mystery, containing the LINGBAO revelations), and Dong Shen (Cavern Spirit, containing the Sanguang revelations). Each of the three "caverns" is preceded by an introduction said to have been dictated by a major deity: Dongzhen by the Celestial Venerable of the Primordial Beginning (Yuanshi Tianzun), Dongxuan by the Supreme Lord of the Dao (Taishang Daojun), and Dongshen by the Supreme Master Lao (Taishang Laojun), or LAOZI.

All of the three *dong* are divided into 12 types or forms of writings, such as original documents, charms, and spiritual diagrams. The key point about the *dong* literature, and most of the *Daozang*, is that the material is revelatory, that is, revealed by a deity figure and written by a chosen follower.

There is a further category of texts, called collectively the *sifu*, or "Four Lacunae." These are texts that did not fit the original categorization by *dong*. They contain, nevertheless, great works of Daoist literature: the Taixuan, or Great Mystery; the Taiping, or Great Peace; the Taiqing, or Great Purity; and the Zhengyi, or Orthodox Oneness.

There were several attempts to collect the major texts of Daoism throughout Chinese history, beginning in the eighth century C.E. That effort collected between 3,744 and 7,300 volumes of material, which unfortunately was lost by the 10th century. In the Song dynasty (960–1279 C.E.) another effort resulted in 4,359 volumes of text, expanded later into 4,565. By the Yuan dynasty this collection was expanded to 5,481 volumes. Some of this was lost during the Yuan. With additions the current, Ming dynasty version was finalized. It was reissued in Shanghai in 1923–25.

The study of the *Daozang* has been part of Daoist practice for centuries. Chinese scholars are perennially drawn to the *Daozang*; however, serious modern scholarly research into the *Daozang*, by scholars from all cultures, is still in its infancy. Much of the *Daozang* remains untranslated, understudied, and, perhaps fittingly, a mystery.

See also FUJI.

Further reading: Judith M. Boltz, *A Survey of Taoist Literature: Tenth to Seventeenth Centuries* (Berkeley: University of California China Research Monograph 32, 1987); CHINAKNOWLEDGE—a universal guide for China studies. "Religious Daoism." Available online. URL: www.chinaknowledge.de/Literature/Religion/daozang.html. Accessed on January 18, 2006; Daoist Studies Website. Available online. URL: www.daoist-studies.org. Accessed on January 19, 2006. Laurence Thompson, "Taoism: Classic and Canon," in Frederick M. Denny and Rodney F. Taylor, ed., *The Holy Book in Comparative Perspective* (Columbus: University of South Carolina Press, 1985), 204–223.

darsana

Darsana is the Buddhist concept of seeing, or gaining knowledge by seeing. *Darsana* was a Hindu term meaning a school of philosophy, a teaching, and philosophy in general. In Buddhist ABHIDHARMA theory *darsana* was a stage attained by those on the path of enlightenment. This scheme was first elaborated on the basis of the Buddha's lecture to the five ascetics in the Deer Park at SARNATH. These five ascetics went through three stages of progress, the so-called three turns of the wheel. The first of the turns, when the cultivator gains theoretical awareness, is *darsana-marga*. (The second and third turns are *bhavana-marga*, the Way of Practice, and *asaiksa-phala*, the stage of knowing there is no more to learn—that is, an ARHAT.) *Darsana* is thus the first step in this scheme of Buddhist ENLIGHTENMENT.

These teachings also developed into an eight-stage path to the goal of becoming an *arhat*, beginning with the *dharsana-marga*. A person at this stage is a stream-winner, one who enters the stream of the sages. The Mahayana teachings also recognize *darsana-marga* as a stage on the BODHISATTVA path.

Further reading: Kogen Mizuno, *Buddhist Sutras: Origin, Development, and Transmission* (Tokyo: Kosei, 1995); ———, *Basic Buddhist Concepts*. Translated by Charles S. Terry and Richard L. Gage (1965. Reprint, Tokyo: Kosei, 1996); ———, *Essentials of Buddhism: Basic Terminology and Concepts of Buddhist Philosophy and Practice*. Translated by Gaynor Sekimori (1972. Reprint, Tokyo: Kosei, 1996) 153, 186, 191–196.

David-Néel, Alexandra (1868–1969)
transmitted Tibetan Buddhism to the West

Alexandra David-Néel, who wrote and lectured about her explorations of Tibetan Buddhism in the early 20th century, was born in Paris in 1868. Six years later, the family moved to Ixelles, near Brussels, where she grew up and developed her passion for travel.

In 1889, she left her family, who had continually blocked her efforts to move out and see the world. She settled in Paris, where she could attend meetings of the Theosophical Society and audit classes in Oriental languages at the several Paris universities. She joined secret societies and associated with anarchists.

In 1899 she authored her first writing for publication. However, no Parisian publisher would print it. Her significant other, Jean Haustont, saw to its private publication. Still not satisfied, she studied music and received favorable reviews for her starring roles in several operas.

Her life changed considerably in 1890. With a small inheritance from her godmother, she was able to spend a year in India, where she first heard Tibetan music, and she studied with a guru, Swami Bhaskarânanda. Her next trip was to North Africa. In Tunis she met her future husband, Philippe Néel. They were married in 1904.

He was wealthy enough to support her desire for further travel.

In 1911 she left on what would be a 14-year journey. She arrived in Sikkim in 1912. While there she met the young Aphur Yongden, whom she later adopted, and made several forays into Tibet, for which she was expelled from Sikkim in 1916. After World War I began, she moved on to Japan. There she met the philosopher Ekaï Kawagushi, who had disguised himself as a Chinese monk and spent 18 months in Lhasa. She next headed for Korea and then China. She made her way across the Gobi desert and spent three years studying at a Tibetan monastery. She and Aphur Yongden then abandoned all their possessions, adopted local dress, and headed for Lhasa. They arrived in 1924. After two months the pair were discovered, and David-Néel and her young companion had to leave quickly via Sikkim and India.

In 1928, she settled at Digne in Provence, France, and built a home for meditation and contemplation, Samten-Dzong. She now focused on writing books about her travels and what she had learned. She also went forth on lecture tours throughout Europe.

By 1937, the wanderlust had risen again and with money from her husband, who remained her close friend despite their separation in 1928, she and Yongden set off via Russia for China, now at war with Japan. This journey lasted 10 years and was marked by visions of the war and ended in India only in 1946. She subsequently returned to Digne to write and lecture. She died in 1969, having passed her 100th birthday. In 1973 her ashes and those of her adopted son were scattered in the Ganges.

While David-Néel left behind a number of books, she is most remembered for two of them, *My Journey to Lhassa* (1927) and *With Mystics and Magicians in Tibet* (1929, English edition, 1931), which recounted her appropriation of Tibetan Buddhism.

Further reading: Tiziana Baldizzone and Gianni Baldizzone, *Tibet on the Paths of the Gentlemen Brigands:*

Retracing the Steps of Alexandra David-Neel (London: Thames and Hudson, 1995); Jacques Brosse, *Alexandra David-Néel* (Paris: Retz, 1978); Alexandra David-Néel, *My Journey to Lhassa* (New York: Harper, 1927); ———, *With Mystics and Magicians in Tibet* (London: John Lane The Bodley Head, 1931).

Deer Park   See SARNATH.

defilements   See KLESA.

Dengyo   See SAICHO.

desire (*canda*)

Desire (*canda*) is a recurring topic in Buddhist discourse, although it is not the fundamental focus. In early Buddhist writings of the SARVASTIVADINS, *canda* was simply one of the 10 mental functions. Different people would have minds characterized by certain functions. Thus one person's nature may be heavily associated with desire, while another's would be heavily associated with feeling (*vedana*). In the Buddha's formulation of the 12-fold Chain of Origination, desire is a result of craving, which in turn is a result of ignorance. Thus ignorance is a root cause, while cravings and desires are expressions. But desires are only one type of craving—the others are craving for existence and craving for nonexistence. The particular subtypes of desires are those associated with the five senses: touch, smell, sight, taste, and hearing.

It is perhaps common to assume that Buddhism involves the control or overcoming of natural desires and urges. But it is a mistake to see the Buddhist as simply a world renouncer. Instead Buddhism teaches the need to understand the place of desire in nature, the importance of observing how desires arise and fade away, the thoughts associated with desires, and the effect of desire on our actions.

Further reading: Kogen Mizuno, *Essentials of Buddhism: Basic Terminology and Concepts of Buddhist Philosophy and Practice.* Translated by Gaynor Sekimori (1972. Reprint, Tokyo: Kosei, 1996).

Devadatta (c. 500 B.C.E.) *early follower of the Buddha who turned against him*

Devadatta was a disciple (and a cousin) of the Buddha who later denounced him. Devadatta had vied with Prince Gautama for the hand of YASODARA, Gautama's eventual wife. After becoming a disciple he grew jealous and fomented discord within the order. He is said to have arranged several attempts on the Buddha's life. He finally fell into hell. Nevertheless, the Buddha, in chapter 12 of the LOTUS SUTRA, is said to have predicted that Devadatta would eventually become a Buddha called Tian Wang (*Devaraja*, "heavenly king").

Despite his overwhelmingly negative associations, the treatment of Devadatta in the Buddhist literature is not consistent. In the Sarvastivadin VINAYA he is said to have acted as a saint for the first 12 years after his ordination as a monk. He meditates frequently and lives as an ascetic in the forest. Therefore, Devadatta is a complex character, an accomplished master as well as a diabolical person.

One interpretation of the presence of this personality within the Buddhist literature is that he represents a schism within the sangha, one that actually occurred *after* the major split between the MAHASANGHIKAS and Sthaviravadins (c. 350 B.C.E.). The two Chinese pilgrims FA XIAN and XUAN ZANG, who visited India between the fourth and seventh centuries C.E., report the presence of individuals who were actual followers of Devadatta. These followers did not worship SAKYAMUNI; nor did they drink milk products. Indeed his followers may have adhered to very strict dietary codes, something forbidden for Buddhist monks.

Further reading: Reginald A. Ray, *Buddhist Saints in India: A Study in Buddhist Values and Orientations*

(Oxford: Oxford University Press, 1994), 162–178; John Snelling, *The Buddhist Handbook: A Complete Guide to Buddhist Schools, Teaching, Practice, and History* (Rochester, Vt.: Inner Traditions, 1991).

Dhammakaya

The Dhammakaya (body of the Dharma) movement began in the early 1970s in Thailand. Dhammakaya is influential for several reasons, including its ability to attract educated urban dwellers as well as politically powerful followers. Dhammakaya controls most of the Buddhist associations in Thai universities. And overall its image is one of purity and noncorruption—in stark contrast to its frequent criticism of Thai society, including the sangha, for corruption and materialism. In contrast to traditional Buddhist monks, Dhammakaya followers wear white robes.

Two students at Kasetsart University in Bangkok, Chaiyaboon Sitthiphon (b. 1944) and Phadet Phongasawad (b. 1941), studied meditation with the monk Monkhon Thepmuni (LUANG PHO SOT) and the lay teacher Khun Yay (1909–) at Wat Paknam Phasi Charoen in Bangkok. Both Sitthiphon and Phadet were ordained as monks (in 1969 and 1973, respectively), after graduating. The Wat Dhammakaya movement was officially registered in 1978 and has been the fastest growing organized movement in Thai Buddhism since.

Dhammakaya grew quickly from 1970, when 80 acres was donated to the movement by a wealthy widow. Its rapid growth is due to the focus on urban residents, especially college-educated youth. Dhammakaya generally presents an image of being nonmaterialistic and free of corruption, qualities that resonate with urban Thai.

The movement is headquartered on 1,000 acres at Pathum Thani, north of Bangkok. Here ceremonies such as the Buddhist Rains Retreat are attended by up to 100,000 people.

Dhammakaya has been criticized for its wealth and influence. It is active in recruitment, creating a nearly evangelistic atmosphere. And some see it as simply a mouthpiece for the politically powerful elements in Thai society. Despite such criticisms Dhammakaya is in many ways the face of modern Thai Buddhism.

Further reading: Phra Maha Sermchai, *The Heart of Dhammakaya Meditation* (Pathum Thani: Dhammakaya Buddhist Meditation Foundation, 1997); Donald K. Swearer, *The Buddhist World of Southeast Asia* (Albany: State University of New York Press, 1995).

Dhammapada

The *Dhammapada,* literally "the sayings of the dhamma [dharma]," is perhaps the most popular book in the Pali canon of THERAVADA Buddhism. It consists of some 423 verses, all said to be the words of the Buddha. Many of these verses are also found in other parts of the Buddhist canon, and there are very similar works in other, non-Buddhist Indian texts such as the *Mahabharata.* The contents of the *Dhammapada* were collected over time. We therefore can say that they carry a large amount of local folk wisdom from ancient Indian times, as well as Buddhist thought.

A tradition of commenting on the *Dhammapada* quickly developed. The commentaries helped explain the texts, some of which may have become difficult to understand. They also took on the character of a narrative linking the various verses. When monks arrived in Sri Lanka around 300 B.C.E. to spread Buddhism, they also introduced an understanding of these commentaries. When this commentarial material was finally written down in Sinhalese, the local language in Sri Lanka, it became known as the Sinhala Commentary, or *Sihalatthakatha.*

By the fifth century C.E., a movement under the direction of the great scholar BUDDHAGHOSA began to translate Sinhalese materials back into Pali, the language of the Theravada canon. Although Buddhaghosa himself did not translate the *Dhammapada,* it too was translated into Pali around this time. The Singhalese version and commentary thus fell into disuse, though it was relatively older.

The tradition of commenting on the *Dhammapada* died out during Sri Lankan Buddhism's dark age of decline, from the 1500s through the 1700s. After Buddhism was revived in the late 18th century by the arrival of monks from Thailand, the commentaries started again. By the late 1800s, study of and publishing on the *Dhammapada* were growing in Sri Lanka.

Today the *Dhammapada* is used by practicing Buddhists in all countries as a concentrated selection of Buddhist wisdom, and by non-Buddhists as a clear introduction to Buddhist thought. Here is one example:

> Verse 25—On Awareness (Appamada-vaggo)
> The path to the Deathless is awareness;
> Unawareness, the path of death.
> They who are aware do not die;
> They who are unaware are as dead.
> [from Carter and Palihawadana, p. 25]

Further reading: Thomas Byron, *The Dhammapada: The Sayings of the Buddha* (New York: Vintage Books, 1976); John Ross Carter and Mahinda Palihawadana, trans., *The Dhammapada* (Oxford: Oxford University Press, 1987).

Dhammayuttika Nikaya

Dhammayuttika Nikaya (school) is the reform branch of Thai Buddhism, established in the mid-19th century by King Mongkut or Rama IV (r. 1851–68 C.E.). Mongkut had spent 25 years as a monk while his brother was on the throne of the Thai state. As a monk he focused on scholarly activity and reform, in addition to learning English and gaining knowledge of the West. (King Mongkut was in fact the king in the play *The King and I,* although the depiction bears little resemblance to the historical Rama IV.)

Once he assumed the throne Mongkut focused on reform of the Thai sangha. He tightened monastic examinations and called for a revision of the Thai Buddhist canon that was already under way. His reform efforts in general were known as *dhammayuttika,* or "adherence to the dharma," and this became the label of a new sect within Thai Buddhism, the Dhammayut. Today the Dhammayut is the second largest branch of Thai Buddhism.

Mongkut attempted to interpret the Thai canon in several ways. First, he made a distinction between early TRIPITAKA elements and later additions. Second, he attempted to reinterpret the mystical or magical elements in the light of Western notions of rationality. These efforts may have been a reaction to the criticisms of Western missionaries. Similar efforts were under way in Sri Lanka and Burma, both of which were also under the influence of Western colonial forces.

Further reading: Phra Rajavaramuni, *Thai Buddhism in the Buddhist World* (North Hollywood, Calif.: Wat Thai of Los Angeles, 1984); Noble Ross Reat, *Buddhism: A History* (Fremont, Calif.: Jain, 1994).

Dharma/dharmas (dhamma)

Dharma is a fundamental concept in Buddhism, and one easily misconstrued. There are two major senses. The first sense is the Buddha's teachings, or Law. Dharma in this sense is the second of the three treasures of Buddhism. The second sense is dharma as a constituent of nature. For convenience, the first sense is usually capitalized, as in "The Buddha's Dharma," and the second sense is written in lowercase and usually pluralized, as in "the conditioned dharmas of existence."

The Buddha's Teachings: Dharma as the Law refers to the teachings of the Buddha, as well as the canonical expression of those teachings in the Buddhist TRIPITAKA. Early Buddhism considered only the Buddha's teachings, the part of the Tripitaka called the SUTRAS, to be Dharma. Later the concept was expanded to include the other two "baskets" of the Tripitaka, VINAYA and ABHIDHARMA.

As doctrine, *Dharma* means the teachings of Buddha, and Buddhism in general. Dharma is a moral imperative for a Buddhist, for it is through observing the Buddha's teachings that one can reach enlightenment and nirvana. By following the Dharma one will see immediate results; one will experience it at once, without lag. Dharma in this sense is a means toward salvation. This then is the religious imperative behind Buddhism as a whole. Dharma is what makes Buddhism relevant, today as well as in the past.

The dharmas of existence: Early Buddhism used the idea of dharmas to mean elements of existence. The idea embraced all aspects of reality, including mind. Some schools also included unconditioned aspects of reality, such as those found in the state of NIRVANA, while other schools meant the term *dharmas* to apply to only the objects of consciousness. In Buddhism there were three types of dharmas: the five aggregates (SKANDHAS), the 12 sense fields, and the 18 elements of existence. Later schools expanded upon these categories to form complex lists of dharmas. The SARVASTIVADINS, for instance, counted 75 dharmas in five categories. And the YOGACARINS had their own list of 100 dharmas in five categories. Pali philosophy, not to be outdone, had a separate list of 170 dharmas in four categories. Regardless of the details, these schemes served as detailed road maps of reality for Buddhist practitioners. While these analytical structures remain in place today, such thinking was deemphasized in Mahayana practice with the development of the concept of SUNYATA, teaching on the emptiness of all dharmas.

Further reading: David J. Kalupahana, *Buddhist Philosophy: A Historical Analysis* (Honolulu: University Press of Hawaii, 1976); Kogen Mizuno, *Essentials of Buddhism: Basic Terminology and Concepts of Buddhist Philosophy and Practice.* Translated by Gaynor Sekimori (1972. Reprint, Tokyo: Kosei Publishing, 1996).

Dharma Drum Mountain Association

The Dharma Drum Mountain Association is one of the larger Buddhist groups in Taiwan. It exists to promote the teachings of Chinese Chan Buddhism, especially as taught by Master SHENG YEN (1931–). The organization was first formed as Dharma Drum Mountain in Taiwan in 1989. It was reorganized as an international organization in 1996 by the merger of the International Cultural and Educational Foundation of Dharma Drum Mountain with the Institute of Chung-Hwa Buddhist Culture in New York. More than 300,000 people now view themselves as adherents of the Dharma Drum Mountain Association.

These two organizations had emerged over the previous decades as the primary expressions of the work of the CHAN master Sheng Yen. Sheng Yen was born in China and moved to Taiwan in 1949 at the time of the Chinese Revolution.

In 1959 he was named a Dharma heir (successor) in both the LINJI and CAODONG CHAN traditions, completed his education at Rissho University in Japan (M.A., 1971; Ph.D., 1975), and received full transmission in the two Chan traditions, Caodong (1975) and Linji (1978).

Since his reception of the higher Chan credentials, Master Sheng Yen has moved to spread Chan meditation practice throughout Taiwan, around the Pacific Basin, and in Europe. In 1979 he became the abbot of Nung Ch'an Monastery in Taiwan, which became a seedbed for ordained monks and nuns who currently assist with the growing movement. In 1980, he founded the Ch'an Meditation Center and the Institute of Chung-Hwa Buddhist Culture in New York to help develop the work in North America. In 1985 he added a graduate school, the Chung-Hwa Institute of Buddhist Studies, in Taipei. His growing following in Taiwan was organized into the International Cultural and Educational Foundation of Dharma Drum Mountain in 1989.

Further reading: Sheng Yen, *Complete Enlightenment: Translation and Commentary on the Sutra of Complete Enlightenment*. Translated by Bhikkhu Guo-Gu (Elmhurst, N.Y.: Dharma Drum, 1997); ———, *Dharma Drum: The Life and Heart of Ch'an Practice* (Elmhurst, N.Y.: Dharma Drum, 1995); ———, *Two Talks on Buddhism* (Kaohsiung, Taiwan: Fo Kuang, 1987); Edmund Newton, "East Settling into West." *Los Angeles Times*, 10 January 1988.

Dharmaguptaka school

The Dharmaguptaka is one of the 18 SCHOOLS OF EARLY BUDDHISM that flourished in India. The Dharmaguptaka derived from the Mahisasaka school, which in one version (the Singhalese) was derived from the THERAVADA. An alternative tradition (the Sammatiya) is that both Dharmaguptaka and Mahisasaka derived from the Mulasarvastivadins, a section of the Sthaviravadins. And a third tradition, from the Kashmir region, derives the Dharmaguptaka from the Mahisasakis, who descended from the Sarvastivadins, who in turn were from the STHAVIRAVADA SCHOOL. Regardless of exact lineage, the Dharmaguptaka school was named after one Dharmagupta, a follower of the Buddha's disciple MAUDGALYAYANA. Dharmagupta is considered by many to be a legendary figure.

Although there were doctrinal differences between the Dharmaguptakas and their predecessors, the Mahisasaskans, the two groups most probably split simply because of geographic and temperamental differences. The Dharmaguptakas were active in the northwest region near modern-day Afghanistan and Iran, from the third century B.C.E. They used the Gandhari language. By the 300s C.E. they had become one of the major Buddhist schools. By the time of the Chinese pilgrim XUAN ZANG's visit to India in the early 600s the school had declined in influence.

However, the Dharmaguptaka school remained important because of its influence on China. Many of the first VINAYA texts translated into Chinese were from the Dharmaguptaka Vinaya, written in Gandhari. These were joined later by additional Vinaya translations into Chinese, including those of the Sarvastivadin, Mahasanghikan, and Mahisasaka schools. The Dharmaguptakan version had high prestige, however, because the first ordinations in China were performed with the Dharmaguptakan Vinaya. Eventually the Dharmaguptaka Vinaya became the only Vinaya used in Chinese ordination and study.

The Dharmagupta Vinaya also contains the *bhiksunivibhanga*, which gives rules for ordination of nuns. Therefore the term *Dharmagupta* also refers to the lineage of BHIKSUNIs, or nuns, introduced from Sri Lanka to China in the fifth century. Unlike the Theravada and Mulasarvastivada lineages for nuns, the Dharmagupta lineage has survived to this day.

Further reading: Ann Heirmann, *Rules for Nuns According to the Dharmaguptakavinaya: The Discipline in Four Parts* (Delhi: Motilal Banarsidass, 2002).

Dharma heir

A Dharma heir is a designated successor to a Buddhist master. It is a term used often in ZEN (CHAN) Buddhism, since it involves the notion of transmission. What can be transmitted between master and disciple is of great importance to the Zen ideological message. A successor is a designated leader for a lineage. Finding and designating a successor are essential to ensuring the continuity of a lineage tradition after the death of a master.

The first instance of a succession was from the Buddha to his designated successor, MAHAKASYAPA. In the Chan tradition perhaps the most famous example is the fifth patriarch Hong Ren's (601–674) designation of HUI NENG (638–713) as his Dharma heir and successor as patriarch. In passing over the brilliant Dharma heir SHEN XIU

(605?–706) in favor of the relatively uncultured Hui Neng, Hong Ren confirmed the principle that enlightenment is accessible to all.

Today a master may have many Dharma heirs; the term becomes a generic way to refer to major followers trained in and carrying on a master's work. The Taiwanese monk SHENG YEN, for example, has introduced four non-Chinese monks (John Crook, Simon Child, Max Kalin, and Zarko Andricevic) as Dharma heirs. In Zen the students will in principle also attain a level of wisdom and understanding equal to the master's, but strictly speaking this does not occur through receiving anything from the master. The master serves only as catalyst for the student's own enlightenment experience. There is no material or content transmitted. Once one receives the INKASHOMEI, a kind of designation from the master, one can become a Dharma successor.

See also TITLES AND TERMS OF ADDRESS, BUDDHIST.

Further reading: Master Sheng Yen et al., Chan Comes West (Elmhurst, N.Y.: Dharma Drum, 2002).

dharmakaya

The dharmakaya is the "dharma body" of the Buddha. The dharma body is the essence of the Buddha, which is eternal and bears no dualities. YOGACARA school authors mention the dharmakaya as the principle that allows one to move to the final stage of enlightenment. Therefore, the dharmakaya is the body of the Buddha, which represents his ultimate reality—his essence.

Further reading: Robert E. Buswell, Jr., The Formation of Ch'an Ideology in China and Korea: The Vajrasamadhi-Sutra, A Buddhist Apocryphon (Princeton, N.J.: Princeton University Press, 1989), 83–84; David J. Kalupahana, Buddhist Philosophy: A Historical Analysis (Honolulu: University Press of Hawaii, 1976), 149–152; Hajime Nakamura, Indian Buddhism: A Survey with Bibliographical Notes (Delhi: Motilal Banarsidass, 1996).

Dharmapala, Angarika (1864–1933) Buddhist reformer

Dharmapala, who founded the MAHA BODHI SOCIETY and became a major figure in the revival of Buddhism in SRI LANKA in the early 20th century, was born David Hewivitane at a time when England dominated Sri Lanka, then called Ceylon. When the island was subjected to government-supported attempts to convert the population to Christianity, Hewivitane was raised a Buddhist and survived his years at St. Benedict's Anglican School and St. Thomas' Collegiate School. He finally left school at the age of 19 after he was repulsed by what he saw as the extremely hypocritical behavior of the Christian leadership.

Shortly thereafter he joined the Theosophical Society, based in Madras, India, which had developed strong Buddhist leanings especially in the person of its president, HENRY STEEL OLCOTT. Dharmapala joined Olcott in the effort to found Buddhist schools and in 1888 accompanied Olcott on a visit to Buddhists in Japan.

In 1891, Dharmapala visited BODHGAYA, the site where Buddha gained his enlightenment. He found it rundown and in response founded the Maha Bodhi Society to raise funds to restore and maintain it. On all of his future travels, he made the founding of local Maha Bodhi Society chapters part of his work.

In 1893, Olcott assisted Dharmapala in his journey to Chicago, where he became one of the spokespersons for Buddhism at the World's Parliament of Religions. While there he met PAUL CARUS, an American publisher/editor, whom he persuaded to become the head of the society's American chapter. He would later preside at a ceremony at which C. T. Strauss became the first American to take refuge in the Buddha (formally convert). On a later trip to America in 1896–97, he organized the first WESAK festival in America.

In the years after World War I, Dharmapala would make trips to England, where he founded the British Maha Bodhi Society and helped stimulate the growth of the small Buddhist community.

In 1933, he was honored at SARNATH, India, where the Buddha preached his first sermon, and finally was ordained as a BHIKSU. This was the first such ordination on Indian soil in more than seven centuries. Dharmapala died later that year.

Further reading: Stephen Prothero, "Henry Steel Olcott and 'Protestant Buddhism,'" *Journal of the American Academy of Religion* 63, no. 2 (1995), 281–302.

Dharmaraksa (1) (239–316 or 233–310)
translator of Buddhist scriptures

Dharmaraksa was originally from the Dunhuang region of western China. A monk since childhood, he was descended from the nomadic Yue Zhi (Yueh-chih) tribe, a group identified early in Chinese records who were probably related to the Tocharians of the Tarim Basin. Dharmaraksa traveled extensively throughout Central Asia and is said to have learned 36 languages. He arrived in the Chinese capitals of Chang An and Luoyang during the Western Jin Dynasty (265–316 C.E.), a time of frantic activity and interest in Buddhism. There was in particular a tremendous thirst for translations of texts from this foreign religion. Until 308 Dharmaraksa devoted himself to translation work. He is said to have translated 159 separate scriptures. Dharmaraksa was the first to translate the Lotus of the True Law, the LOTUS SUTRA, into Chinese. He also translated the Vimalakirti and Flower Garland (Hua Yan) Sutras.

Further reading: Hajime Nakamura, *Indian Buddhism: A Survey with Bibliographical Notes* (Delhi: Motilal Banarsidass, 1996).

Dharmaraksa (2) (385–433 C.E.) *first translator of the Nirvana Sutra*

There are two significant figures named Dharmaraksa. The first (239–316 or 233–310) (DHARMARAKSA (1)) was from the Dunhuang region. The second Dharmaraksa was also a foreign monk who settled in China and translated key texts. However, unlike the first Dharmaraksa, he was originally a HINAYANA monk from India. He read the NIRVANA SUTRA and switched his allegiances to the Mahayana school. He settled in the northern China state of Liang Zhou in 412 C.E. He was taken on as an adviser to the ruler, Ju'chu Mengxun, and encouraged to translate Buddhist sutras. He eventually produced the first translation of the Nirvana Sutra, a massive task resulting in 40 volumes. He returned to India once to collect more texts. On a second return journey he was murdered by the very ruler of the Liang Zhou who sponsored him.

Further reading: Hajime Nakamura, *Indian Buddhism: A Survey with Bibliographical Notes* (Delhi: Motilal Banarsidass, 1996).

Dharmasala

Best known today as the site of the TIBETAN GOVERNMENT-IN-EXILE, Dharmasala sits in the middle of an area rich in Buddhist history, in the hill station region of northern India. XUAN ZANG, the famous Chinese traveler, visited the area in 635 and noted 50 monasteries and thousands of monks.

Dharmasala is sited in a valley at a relatively high altitude—1,250–1,800 meters. Most of the Tibetan inhabitants are concentrated in the McLeod Gunj area, which is the town at the highest elevation. The Dalai Lama's residence, the Tsuglag Khang, is also in McLeod Gunj. The Library of Tibetan Works and Archives was established there in 1971. Other important institutions include the Norbulingka Institute of Tibetan Culture, the Amnye Machen Institute, a Tibetan studies center, and Namgyal Monastery, named after the Namgyal Monastery in the Potala Palace, which now has 180 monks.

Further reading: Graham Coleman, ed., *A Handbook of Tibetan Culture: A Guide to Tibetan Centres and Resources* throughout the World (Boston: Shambhala, 1994); Nanci H. Rose, Living Tibet: The Dalai Lama in Dharmasala (Lanham, Md.: National Book Network, 2005); Jeremy Russell, Dharmasala: Tibetan Refuge (Torrance, Calif.: Heian International, 2002).

dhyana (jhana, chan)

Dhyana is the Sanskrit term meaning "trance," "absorptions," or "meditation." The Pali equivalent, jhana, refers to the four meditative states in THERAVADA tradition that lead to salvation. These four jhana are taught to all those who learn meditation in the Theravada tradition.

In Mahayana Buddhist teachings dhyana is the fifth PARAMITA or perfection. Dhyana meditation is intended to overcome ego. In China dhyana was transliterated as "chan" and so became associated with the CHAN (in Japanese, ZEN) school of Buddhism.

Chan meditation spells out eight stages of dhyana practice, four with form, and four formless. Typically, a meditator first focuses on any sense object. While meditating this way, achieving the first of the dhyanas involves detaching oneself from one's negative tendencies. To achieve the second dhyana one goes beyond thoughts and attains the level of faith. In stages three and four one fights the tendency to grope toward the unknown with elation. By the fourth dhyana the cultivator is detached from the emotions of the self.

In practicing the next four dhyanas, the formless group, the cultivator continues to overcome the remains or vestiges of the sense object.

Further reading: Edward Conze, Buddhism: Its Essence and Development (New Delhi: Munshiram Manoharial, 2001), 100–101; Kogen Mizuno, Essentials of Buddhism: Basic Terminology and Concepts of Buddhist Philosophy and Practice. Translated by Gaynor Sekimori (1972. Reprint, Tokyo: Kosei Publishing, 1996), 177–178; Santideva, The Bodhicaryavatara. Translated by Kate Crosby and Andrew Skilton (Oxford: Oxford University Press, 1995).

Diamond Sutra (Vajracchedika-prajnaparamita-sutra)

The Diamond Sutra is an early Mahayana text dating from 150–200 C.E. that has continued to be popular into modern times. The sutra means literally "The sutra of diamond-cutting ultimate wisdom." It is part of the vast PRAJNAPARAMITA (perfection of wisdom) literature.

The Diamond Sutra is a SUTRA and so is believed by most Buddhists to record the words of the Buddha, passed down to later generations by disciples who were present when the words were spoken. The sutra tells how the Buddha answered a disciple's question concerning the means to gain enlightenment. His answer focused on the understanding of emptiness (SUNYATA). Emptiness here refers not to a vacuum or meaninglessness, but to the conditioned nature of all phenomena, and the true absence of attachments among phenomena. All things are interrelated and connected, empty of isolated identity, and this is the nature of reality. Furthermore, emptiness itself is empty.

This train of thought remains difficult for many to accept, for it leads to difficult conclusions regarding the self. As chapter 3 states:

> A bodhisattva who creates the perception of a being cannot be called a "bodhisattva." And why not? Subhuti, no one can be called a bodhisattva who creates the perception of a self or who creates the perception of a being, a life, or a soul. (Red Pine, p. 71)

Fundamentally, there is no self. Realizing this is the key to liberation, in the Buddha's teachings. There is no atman (self); no sattva (being), no jiva (life), and no pudgala (soul). Enlightened beings continue to have perceptions but do not have views (DRISTI). Attachment to the idea of a self, to the ultimate existence of a self, is such a view.

Further reading: Red Pine, trans., The Diamond Sutra: The Perfection of Wisdom (Washington, D.C., and New York: Counterpoint, 2001); A. F. Price and Wong

Mou-lam, trans., *The Diamond Sutra and the Sutra of Hui-Neng* (Boston: Shambhala, 1974); Mu Soeng, *The Diamond Sutra: Transforming the Way We Perceive the World* (Somerville, Mass.: Wisdom, 2003); Thich Nhat Hanh, *The Diamond That Cuts through Illusion: Commentaries on the Prajnaparamita Diamond Sutra* (Berkeley, Calif.: Parallax Press, 2005).

Diamond Way Buddhism

The Diamond Way is a Western association of Tibetan Buddhist centers that offer Karma Kagyu teachings as providing verifiable nondogmatic teachings, an easy means of meditation, and ways to solidify the levels of awareness one attains. There are now more than 200 Diamond Way centers. They recognize the authority of the 17th Karmapa Thaye Dorje (1983–   ).

The centers are tied together by the leadership of Lama Ole Nydahl, who, with his wife; Hannah, traveled to Nepal in 1968. There they met Lopon Tchechu Rinpoche, who became their teacher and under whose guidance they became Buddhists. He also arranged for the pair's initial meeting with Rangjung Rigpe Dorje (1924–1981), the 16th Gyalwa Karmapa, the head of the KARMA KAGYU school of Tibetan Buddhism. The Karmapa had settled at Runtek Monastery, in Sikkim. The Nydahls became his first Western students and spent three years (1969–72) in study of the Kagyu teachings and intensive practice. During this time they received a variety of empowerments (rituals designed to awaken the potentials in the individual).

The Gyalwa Karmapa recognized Ole as a protector of the Karma Kagyu lineage and gave him the mission of spreading the Karma Kagyu teachings in Europe and the West. Nydahl also received a transmission of a practice called Phowa. Phowa teaches an individual the way, at the moment of death, to transfer one's consciousness to a state of high bliss.

Upon his return to Denmark in the early 1970s, Ole Nydahl began to teach and organize centers, while Hannah has spent most of her time translating Tibetan texts. His winsome down-to-earth persona drew many to Nydahl, and centers spread across Europe. The first North American center was opened in the 1980s. Nydahl has himself trained more than 30 students, who now work with the Diamond Way.

Further reading: Ole Nydahl, *Entering the Diamond Way: My Path among the Lamas* (Nevada City, Calif.: Blue Dolphin, 1985); ———, *Ngöndro: The Four Foundational Practices of Tibetan Buddhism* (Nevada City, Calif.: Blue Dolphin, 1990); ———, *Riding the Tiger: Twenty Years on the Road: The Risks and Joys of Bringing Tibetan Buddhism to the West* (Nevada City, Calif.: Blue Dolphin, 1992).

disciples of the Buddha

The BUDDHA taught for 60 years before departing from the world of form in his PARINIRVANA. In this period he attracted a large group of followers. In Buddhist legend and history a key number of these figures receive great focus. The 10 major disciples are normally listed as follows:

1. SARIPUTRA
2. MAUDGALYAYANA (in Pali, Moggallana)
3. ANANDA
4. MAHAKASYAPA (in Pali, Mahakassapa)
5. Aniruddha (in Pali, Anuruddha)
6. Katyayana (in Pali, Kacchayana or Kacchana)
7. Upali
8. Subhuti (in Pali, Subhadda)
9. Purna (in Pali, Punna)
10. RAHULA

Each of these figures became associated with special abilities or aspects of Buddhist practice.

Sariputra and Maudgalyayana were childhood friends from privileged, Brahman families. They had become ascetics before the Buddha himself. Their search for spiritual masters took them to several individuals, and at the time of the Buddha's enlightenment they were followers of one Sanjaya. Eventually they found the Buddha and joined him at Rajagaha, in a bamboo grove, taking several other students with them. Upon hearing the Buddha's first teachings the entire group is said to have achieved the state of *arahatship*. The Buddha then appointed Sariputra to be his chief disciple and Maudgalyana to be his deputy. Sariputra was famous for his wisdom, while Maudgalyayana was known for his transcendent powers.

Ananda, the Buddha's cousin, was known for his personal devotion to the Buddha. In addition to that he was an excellent listener and had a phenomenal memory. Therefore, he was central in the act of recording the Buddha's teachings after the Buddha's death. After Mahakasyapa, Ananda became the second of the Buddha's 24 successors.

Mahakasyapa (also written as KASYAPA) was originally a fire worshipper and wandering ascetic. He is said to have been impressed with a demonstration of magical powers by the Buddha and took 500 followers into the Buddha's sangha. He was foremost in ascetic practices, called *dhuta*. Although they were the same age, Mahakasyapa outlived the Buddha, and he presided over the first Buddhist Council. Upon his death he passed leadership of the Sangha to Ananda.

Another of the Buddha's cousins, Aniruddha, was famous for his "divine insight." One story in the Agama Sutras narrates how he vowed never to sleep because he had fallen asleep during one of the Buddha's lectures. His eyesight damaged to the state of blindness, Aniruddha gained a kind of extraordinary discernment of reality.

Katyayana was best known as a debater. He was originally a senior adviser to a ruler of Avanti in southwestern India. Sent by his ruler to investigate the Buddha, he converted on the spot and in turn converted the king.

Subhuti was the nephew of Sudatta, the patron who donated Jetavana Monastery to the Buddha. He was one of the four Voice Hearers who attained enlightenment upon first hearing the Buddha's teachings. He was renowned for having a special understanding of the doctrine of nonsubstantiality, a concept that is troubling to many students of Buddhism today, just as it was in the past.

Purna excelled at preaching the DHARMA of Buddhism and was able to convert hundreds through his sermons. There are conflicting accounts of his background. In one version he was an ascetic living on Snow Mountain who joined the Buddha and attained the state of ARHAT. In another version he was a merchant who was converted by fellow travelers who were lay Buddhists.

Originally a barber living the small state of Kapilavastu, Upali was an expert in VINAYA, the rules of discipline of the sangha. During the first Buddhist Council he recited the entire Vinaya from memory, just as Ananda recited the sutras.

When the Buddha returned home for the first time after leaving to follow his path of cultivation, his young son, Rahula, met his father for the first time. Rahula was converted and became one of the Buddha's 10 major disciples. He is known as a symbol of "inconspicuous practice." This refers to his devotion to the precepts, the rules governing a monk's life, and his constant study under fellow monks Sariputra and Maudgalyayana. He was earnest and did not find pride in his status as the son of the Buddha.

See also ANANDA; MAUDGALYAYANA; RAHULA; SARIPUTRA.

Further reading: Radhika Abeysekera, "Relatives and Disciples of the Buddha." Buddhist Information of North America. Available online. URL: www. buddhistinformation.com/relatives_and_disciples_ of_the_b.htm. May 13, 2000. Accessed on November 25, 2005; Nyanaponika and Hellmuth Heckler, *Great Disciples of the Buddha* (Kandy, Sri Lanka: Buddhist Publication Society, 1997); Serizawa Keisuke, *The Ten Disciples of Buddha* (Japan: Ohara Museum of Art, 1982); Hajime Nakamura, *Indian Buddhism: A Survey with Bibliographical Notes* (Delhi: Motilal Banarsidass, 1996).

Dogen (1200–1253) *founder of Japanese Soto Zen Buddhism*

Dogen, who introduced Chinese CAODONG CHAN BUDDHISM to Japan, was born into a well-to-do Japanese family and received a good education in Chinese literature. Orphaned by the age of seven, he was subsequently raised by an uncle who lived near TENDAI BUDDHISM's headquarters on Mt. HIEI. He affiliated with the Tendai and began a spiritual quest that eventually led him to the recently established RINZAI ZEN center established by EISAI (1141–1215) in Kyoto. In 1223, he left for China, where he could explore the Chan centers directly.

Dogen began his stay in China at Diang Tong monastery, where Eisai had studied. However, he did not thrive under its then leader, Wu Ji. He left for a period and upon his return learned that Wu Ji had died and that the monastery had not only changed abbots but had moved from the LINJI (Rinzai) camp to the CAODONG fold. He placed himself under Ru Jing (1163–1228), from whom he received his acknowledgment of ENLIGHTENMENT.

Dogen returned to Japan in 1227 and settled back at Kyoto, where he wrote an initial short treatise, *General Teaching for Zazen*. He then moved on to Fukakusa around 1230; while there he would author his most notable work, the *Treasury of Knowledge of the True Law* (SHOBOGENZO), the basic text of what would come to be known as SOTO ZEN. There he would also build the first Zen temple in Japan, Koshohorin-ji. He emphasized the model of the BUDDHA, sitting in meditation (ZAZEN) under the BODHI TREE.

In 1247, Dogen withdrew from the turmoil that his teachings had caused in the larger Japanese Buddhist world and moved to Echizen province, where in 1248 he founded EIHEI-JI, the monastic complex that would become the major training center and point of dissemination for Soto Zen. With occasional side trips, he would remain there for the rest of his life. In 1253 he went for a visit to Kyoto to receive some medical care, but before he could return to Eihei-ji, he passed away. He was succeeded by his major disciple, Ejo (1198–1280).

Further reading: Maseo Abe, *A Study of Dogen: His Philosophy and Religion* (Albany: State University of New York Press, 1992); Carl Bielefeldt, *Dogen's Manuals of Zen Meditation* (Berkeley: University of California Press, 1988); Thomas Cleary, trans., *Shobogenzo: Zen Essays by Dogen* (Honolulu: University of Hawaii Press, 1986); Steven Heine, *Dogen and the Koan Tradition* (Albany: State University of New York Press, 1994); Kazuaki Tanahashi, ed., *Moon in a Dewdrop: Writings of Zen Master Dogen* (San Francisco: North Point Press, 1985); Kazuaki Tanahashi and John Daido Loori, trans., *The True Dharma Eye: Zen Master Dogen's Three Hundred Koans* (Boston: Shambhala, 2005).

dojo (*daochang*)

Dojo is the Japanese term for a place of practice. In Buddhism this usually refers to a meditation room or, on a larger scale, an entire temple or monastery. The term is also used by martial arts disciplines such as judo to mean the place of practice or instruction.

Dojo is pronounced *daochang* in Chinese, and from this we see it is composed of the term DAO plus "chang," meaning place, hence "a place of the Way." The Chinese word *daochang* was also used to translate the Sanskrit term *bodhimandala*, or "truth-plot." A *daochang* is thus a sacred place, one used for teaching, worship, or ritual, which is therefore also the original sense of *dojo*.

A *daochang* may also refer to the entire field of the Dao. It also refers to a Buddha's or BODHISATTVA's field of influence. In this sense AMITABHA's field of influence, for instance, is the Western Paradise, and VAIROCANA Buddha's field of influence is the transcendent or the universe. A bodhisattva's field of Dao is, properly speaking, the world of sentient beings, since every bodhisattva makes the Mahayana vow not to move to NIRVANA until all suffering beings in SAMSARA are freed of suffering.

In some Chinese texts *daochang* is used to indicate the place where Buddha attained enlightenment, or BODHGAYA, or the BODHI (pipal) tree under which he attained enlightenment. In very early Buddhist art, the Buddha himself was not depicted, and the tree stood as a symbol of the Buddha, his promise of enlightenment, and his power—in a word, his *daochang*.

don chee   See TITLES AND TERMS OF ADDRESS, BUDDHIST.

Dong Zhongshu (Tung Chung-shu) (195–105 B.C.E.) *early systematizer of Chinese thought*

Dong Zhongshu is one of the great lights of CONFUCIANISM. Although not necessarily an original thinker, he was a first-rate systematizer and the chief architect of the basic metaphysical system of the Han dynasty (206 B.C.E.–220 C.E.). During his life he was the acknowledged "leader of the literati," and he served as chief minister for two Han emperors. His work is preserved in the masterful anthology *Chunqiu fanlu* (Luxuriant gems of the spring and autumn annals), a collection of materials compiled in the early Middle Ages.

Dong Zhongshu's system of Han Confucianism, based on the premise that the details of state must harmonize with heaven and earth, set the pattern for all later dynasties. It was a complex system governing all dimensions of political and religious life and became one of the hallmarks of Chinese civilization.

Dong's thought is Confucian in orientation but decidedly syncretistic as well. He draws on other schools of thought, especially DAOISM with its views of naturalness and self-cultivation. His imagery and language often resemble the DAODEJING. For Dong, the cosmos is a large organism in which human beings have a vital role. Because the cosmos is a large organism, it is a finely balanced, interactive system in which all parts are inter-related. Disturbance in one area leads to disruptions in others. The world needs constant, careful attention, which is the responsibility of humanity. Human beings are fully integrated into the cosmic order, so much so that the human body replicates in miniature all the structures of the cosmos. Moreover, the cosmic order is also replicated in the sociopolitical order. Harmony, the overriding concern in all Chinese traditions, is thus a cosmic, political, and moral ideal.

For Dong, the emperor (*tianzi*, Son of Heaven) has the key role in the world. He is a man among men, the cosmic pivot. The emperor must model himself on heaven and its workings just as his ministers must model themselves on earth. His duties and responsibilities are awesome, for he must order the state in line with the cosmos. Above all he must be virtuous, for it is through his moral charisma (*de*) that he leads and educates the people. The emperor's influence must sway the people to the good through imperial policy, promotion of the common good, and proper ritual performance.

Proper performance of the LI (rituals, rites) is central to the way the "Son of Heaven" leads his people. To do this, he needs the guidance of able Confucian ministers to ensure that his activities accord with the time and season. In actual practice, this required not just proper training in the various ritual procedures but also attention to the color of imperial clothes at each seasonal ritual, the direction in which the emperor traveled, the type of transportation used, and other details. It was also crucial to have the exact number of officials working with the emperor at all times.

Further reading: W. Theodore de Bary and Irene Bloom, eds., *Sources of Chinese Tradition.* Vol. 1, *From Earliest Times to 1600,* 2d ed. (New York: Columbia University Press, 1999), 292–310; Christian Jochim, *Chinese Religions: A Cultural Perspective* (Upper Saddle River, N.J.: Prentice Hall, 1987).

Dosho (629–700) *Japanese monk who built the first Hosso hall in Japan*

Dosho entered the priesthood after his initial studies at Gango-ji, an early Buddhist temple at Asuka (moved to Nara in 718). In 653 he went to China, where he became a student of the famous Chinese traveler and translator XUAN ZANG (602–664). Xuan Zang taught YOGACARA BUDDHISM teachings to the young student. He also introduced Dosho to CHAN.

Upon his return to Japan, Dosho passed along the Yogacara teachings as the Hosso, or Dharma Marks, school. He built the first HOSSO meditation hall in Japan, adjacent to Gango-ji, and there deposited a number of texts he transported from China. Dosho is considered the founder of the Hosso school, which took root in Nara in the eighth century and had some importance for several centuries. He did not successfully establish the Hosso lineage, however, since he did not receive his teachings from an enlightened master.

Dosho's body was cremated after his death, seemingly the first incident of cremation in Japan.

Further reading: Kazuo Kasahara, ed., *A History of Japanese Religion.* Translated by Paul McCarthy and Gaynor Sekimori (Tokyo: Kosei, 2001); K. Krishna Murthy, *Buddhism in Japan* (Delhi, India: Sundeep Prakashan, 1989).

Dozan (d. 1593) *outstanding Jodo-Shu priest*

The Nagoe subgroup of JODO-SHU taught that multiple invocations of AMITABHA were not needed; even a single sincere repetition of the *NEMBUTSU* was all that was necessary for salvation. There was no special benefit from multiple repetitions of the *nembutsu*—daily or for a lifetime. This group spread primarily through the northern half of Honshu, the largest of Japan's four main islands, and it failed to found a temple in Kyoto. Such was still the case when Dozan appeared on the scene in the 16th century. Dozan emerges out of obscurity as the student of Ryoga (1507–85), who resided in Shinano Province, with whom he continued to work into the mid-1560s. Dozan began his career as a Pure Land priest spreading the teachings in towns along the Shinano River.

In the 1570s he worked in Echizen Province and recruited a number of PURE LAND BUDDHISM temples formerly associated with another Jodo subgroup into the Nagoe camp, beginning with the Saifuku-ji temple in Matsubara. Saifuku-ji became the headquarters temple for the Nagoe and from it Dozan planned the group's entrance into Kyoto. It would be 1582, however, before he received imperial sanctions to begin work in the big city. He began work at Shojoke-in, a Pure Land temple, and gradually rose to become its head priest. He led it into the Nagoe group, and eventually it became the group's new headquarters temple.

While acquiring a foothold in Kyoto, Dozan was still not satisfied. He wanted to assume control of a temple with some direct connection to HONEN (possessing relics of Honen or an image carved centuries earlier while he was still alive) but was unable to secure the cooperation of the leadership at Shojoke-in.

Further reading: Kazuo Kasahara, ed., *A History of Japanese Religion.* Translated by Paul McCarthy and Gaynor Sekimori (Tokyo: Kosei, 2001); E. Dale Saunders, *Buddhism in Japan* (Philadelphia: University of Pennsylvania Press, 1964).

Drigung Kagyu

Drigung Kagyu is one of the eight lineages within the KAGYU school of Tibetan Buddhism, all deriving from GAMPOPA (1079–1153). The Drigung Kagyu was one of the first schools to establish the uniquely Tibetan institution of transmission of authority via reincarnation. The Drigung lineage of the Kagyu school was founded by Jikten Gönpo (1143–1212), a disciple of Phagmo Drupa (1118–70), who, in turn, was a disciple of Gampopa. According to his biographies, he was born into the O-tron branch of the Kyura clan. Jikten Gonpö's father died when the boy was young, and as a result his family fell on hard times. He turned to the practice of Buddhism at an early age and, as a layman, became an accomplished spiritual practitioner. He first studied with a master of the KADAMPA school and later became the disciple of Phagmo Drupa. He was ordained as a monk at Phag mo Dru monastery. He later set out on his own and established the Drigung monastery in 1179 C.E.

The Drigung lineage was named after the monastery. Jikten Gonpo was succeeded by his nephew, On Sherab Jungne. Both Jikten Gonpo and On Sherab Jungne were noted for their scholarship, and together they formulated the influential "single intention" teachings, which sought to harmonize the Kagyu Mahamudra teachings with the "Path-Fruit" teachings of the Sakya school.

The Drigung lineage never became widespread and was based at the monastery that gave it its name. Eventually, authority in this tradition was passed down from generation to generation by reincarnation, as was also the case in the Karma Kagyu school. During the CULTURAL REVOLUTION, the Drikung monastery was destroyed in Tibet. However, the lineage reestablished its institutional basis with the completion of the Jangchubling Drikung Kargyu Institute in 1989, at Dehra Dun in India.

Further reading: Ronald M. Davidson, *Tibetan Renaissance: Tantric Buddhism in the Rebirth of Tibetan Culture* (New York: Columbia University Press, 2005); David Snellgrove and Hugh Richardson, *A Cultural History of Tibet* (Boston: Shambhala, 1986).

dristi

Literally, "seeing, sight, view," *dristi* usually refers to false views. The Buddha emphasized that such views were dangerous because they led to unwholesome action and thus rebirth. Some sources list seven *dristi*: belief in an ego, repudiation of the law of karma, eternalism, nihilism, observing false SILAS (precepts), regarding karma resulting from bad deeds as good, and doubting the truths of Buddhism. The SARVASTIVADA (SARVASTIVADIN) SCHOOL originally developed a list of 62 separate *dristi*, which was later reduced to a standard list of five: the view that the aggregates (*skandhas*) are equal to the self; such extreme ideas as that the body and spirit are eternal, or that death ends all existence; perverse ideas that reject the function of cause and effect; stubborn views that one's ideas alone are correct; and, last, attachment to wrong positions, such as ascetic practices. This list of five was later adopted by YOGACARA BUDDHISM as well.

Further reading: Kogen Mizuno, *Essentials of Buddhism: Basic Terminology and Concepts of Buddhist Philosophy and Practice.* Translated by Gaynor Sekimori (1972. Reprint, Tokyo: Kosei, 1996), 186, 209–212; Francis Story, "Suffering," in *The Three Basic Facts of Existence.* Vol. 2 (Kandy, Sri Lanka: Buddhist Publication Society, 1983).

Drukpa Kunleg (1455–1570) *Tibetan Buddhist master*

Drukpa Kunleg, credited with converting Bhutan to Buddhism in the 16th century, was a practitioner of Drugpa, one of the subschools of KAGYU BUDDHISM. Rather than living in a monastery, however, he chose a wandering life modeled on those of the *mahasiddhas*, the name given to a set of independent Buddhist adepts who lived in the period from the sixth to the 12th century. They were distinguished by the individualistic search for liberation in a single lifetime, a quest that often led them into extremes and/or the use of sexuality as a tool for enlightenment. Tales of the *mahasiddhas* were especially valued within the Kagyu school.

Drukpa Kunleg was seen as a reincarnation of several of the *mahasiddhas* and some saw him as a "holy madman." He impressed the followers of the indigenous Bon religion throughout the Himalayas, where he chose to spend most of his life, and the poems and songs attributed him have become part of the folklore. Among his many accomplishments was, reputedly, the defeat of the local demons.

Further reading: Keith Dowman, *The Divine Madman: The Sublime Life and Songs of Drukpa Kunleg* (Clearlake, Calif.: Dawn Horse Press, 1983).

dukkha

Dukkha is a key concept in Buddhism. It is often translated into English as "suffering," but this translation is limited. The Pali/Sanskrit word means, among other things, "discomfort," "impermanence," and "imperfection." Life is not simply pain and suffering; life is filled with unsatisfying events and sensations, and overall impermanence. Thus even experiences that we would normally perceive as happy are part of *dukkha*.

Dukkha comes into being through craving (TANHA). These cravings may be for sensual pleasures or they may be for more fundamental aspects, such as the very desire to be (volition). The Buddha taught that *tanha* is the mechanism through which *dukkha* (suffering) comes forth. *Dukkha* is thus the fundamental ground of SAMSARA.

Further reading: Walpola Rahula, *What the Buddha Taught* (New York: Grove Press, 1974).

Dzogchen

The term *Dzogchen* is an abbreviation of the Tibetan term *dzog pa chen po,* which means "Great Perfection." It refers both to the natural and primordial state of the enlightened mind that all sentient beings possess, and to a set of teachings that are designed to aid one in the realization of this. According to both the Nyingma school of Tibetan Buddhism and the BON tradition of Tibet, it is the ultimate state, the realization of which is equivalent to enlightenment, and the Dzogchen teachings that bring this about are considered the highest "vehicle" or spiritual approach by both traditions. Dzogchen teachings aim to attain a state of nonperception. Dzogchen differs from ZEN BUDDHISM and *VIPASSANA* (insight) traditions of meditation—which also cultivate nonperception—in its incorporation of indigenous Tibetan techniques, for instance, visualizations.

According to the NYINGMA tradition, the teachings of Dzogchen were first taught in India by a master named Garab Dorje, who was from Oddiyana, the Swat valley in present day Pakistan. These teachings were taken to Tibet in the late eighth and early ninth centuries by the Indian saint PADMASAMBHAVA, who arrived in Tibet in the late eighth century at the invitation of the Tibetan king, Trisong Detsen (r. 755–797). He was aided in this transmission process by two Indian masters named Vimalamitra and Vairocana. These three figures were responsible for the transmission to Tibet of three distinct series, known as the Mind Series (*sem-dé*), Space Series (*long-dé*), and Secret Instruction Series (*men-ngak-dé*). In these one is first introduced to the primordial state of mind, then given exercises and instructions to deepen one's experience of this.

The Bon tradition holds that Dzogchen teachings originated with the founder of the Bon tradition, Tönpa Shenrab, who lived 18,000 years ago, ruling the kingdom of Tazik to the west of Tibet. He transmitted these teachings to the region of Zhang-zhung, which is the far western portion of the Tibetan cultural world, including the contemporary region of Ladakh. The Bon tradition also divides Dzogchen into three distinct systems, known as Dzogchen, A-tri, and the Zhang-zhung Aural Lineage (*zhang-zhung nyen-gyü*).

Despite the claims that Dzogchen has an ancient lineage originating in India or Tazik, there is no record of Dzogchen prior to the 10th century, when Tibetans began writing texts concerning it. It is certainly possible that Dzogchen is a unique

Tibetan teaching, and there is also interesting (but inconclusive) evidence suggesting that there may have been a connection between the Tibetan Dzogchen and Chinese Chan traditions. A pivotal figure in the history of Dzogchen was Longchenpa Rabjampa (1308–64, possibly 1369), who systematized the somewhat haphazard collections of Dzogchen teachings that were circulating in Tibet at this time.

While Dzogchen is primarily taught by Nyingma and Bon lamas, Dzogchen is also traditionally studied, practiced, and taught by a number of lamas in the Kagyu. It has also been practiced by several of the Dalai Lamas of Tibet, most notably by the Fifth Dalai Lama, Lobsang Gyatso, who was originally trained in the Nyingma tradition, as well as the current DALAI LAMA Tenzin Gyatsu (1935–   ), who has actively encouraged nonsectarianism among Tibetans and has specifically sought to ameliorate the hostility that has characterized relations between the GELUG and Nyingma schools for the past several centuries.

Further reading: The Dalai Lama, *Dzogchen: Heart Essence of the Great Perfection* (Ithaca, N.Y.: Snow Lion, 2004); Shardza Tashi Gyaltsen, *Heart Drops of Dharmakaya: Dzogchen Practice of the Bön Tradition* (Ithaca, N.Y.: Snow Lion, 2002); Matthew Kapstein and Gyurme Dorje, trans., *The Nyingma School of Tibetan Buddhism: Its Fundamentals and History* (Boston: Wisdom, 2002).

E

ecology and environmentalism in Buddhism

The numerous problems of human coexistence with nature are a widespread concern in all places today. Indeed characteristic of our times are widespread anxiety and disillusionment about the environment. These concerns can be summarized as human effect on the global climate and atmosphere; toxic wastes; land loss, including deforestation, loss of agricultural land and topsoil, erosion, desertification; the reduction in biodiversity, including the loss of sources for medicine and traditional habitats; overall loss of wilderness areas; reduction in the numbers of native peoples previously able to lead lifestyles separate from mainstream societies; a lifestyle of massive, unsustainable consumption; and genetic engineering, which, although not yet proved to be damaging, causes consternation concerning its future impact on life.

To varying degrees, modern religions have responded to the environmental concerns. Some have stuck to traditional views on nature. Others have incorporated environmental concerns, just as they have incorporated the points of view of feminism and multiculturalism. Ecotheologies have developed in four general directions:

1. A reinterpretation of traditions—rereading classical texts in the light of current crisis
2. An extension of traditional beliefs to include nature
3. A creative synthesis of views on nature from different traditions, for instance, incorporating Daoist concepts into Christian thinking
4. Creation of new concepts on religion's role in nature

Today some Buddhist leaders are actively involved with environmental issues while others do not appear concerned at all. Indeed it is difficult to speak of a single Buddhist perspective on contemporary ecological problems. The best we can do is illustrate possible directions that incorporate a Buddhist perspective.

BUDDHISM'S TRADITIONAL PERSPECTIVE ON THE ENVIRONMENT

Buddhism seen as a whole is a flexible set of viewpoints and practices that has generally excelled at adapting to local circumstances. Nevertheless there are ingrained perspectives and leanings seen from the first teachings of the Buddha. The earliest depictions of the Buddha and his followers in fact show them living in close harmony with nature.

Such trees as the *sal*, the BODHI (or *pipal, Ficus religiosa*), and the banyan figure prominently in Buddhist stories. There is an overall respect for nature and other beings. For instance the PRATIMOKSA (rules for monks) forbids monks to cut down a tree, dig the earth, or empty a container of water with living creatures onto the ground. Such teachings parallel and resonate with the modern perspective of ecology.

Respect for animals reinforces the idea of karma, in which humans may be reborn as animals. In the *JATAKA TALES*, which relate the past lives of the Buddha, an animal is the central character in half of the narratives. Given the recognition that animals are beings in the six paths of SAMSARA, the world of suffering, Buddhism argues consistently for fair treatment of animals and indeed all living beings. And any individual whose living involves the killing of animals will bear karmic consequences.

The early Buddhist emperor ASOKA also followed a strict conservation program. He planted trees throughout his realm and called for medicinal herbs and fruit trees to be available to all. In addition he planted shade trees by roadsides. He also forbade the needless burning of forests.

Philosophically, Buddhism's emphasis on the individual's analysis of craving and its cause has potential influence on today's culture of consumption. In this sense Buddhism offers a radical rethinking of modernity's materialist obsession, and the attendant attitudes toward exploiting the natural environment.

A second concept in Buddhist philosophy that resonates strongly with ecology is PRATITYA-SAMUTPADA, codependent arising, a concept that emphasizes the interconnected nature of all life.

Socially, monasticism, the central institution of Buddhism, can be viewed as a radical alternative to modernity's forms of social organization, which in turn influence attitudes toward the environment. The monastery is a relatively frugal community that fits easily into the local economy and environment.

Despite such ecological leanings, it is also true that Buddhist-oriented societies, today as in the past, are perfectly capable of allowing ecological degradation. The contemporary ecological movement is essentially a response to modernity and its impact on the environment. Modernity interacts with Buddhism in a variety of ways in different cultures. We may best look at individual cases to see how Buddhist culture and values apply to ecological thinking. Two well-known cases are Ladakh, a Buddhist culture in northwest India, and Thailand. Ladakh has struggled to deal with the severe degradation brought on by tourism and dependency on imports. As a result a strong self-sufficiency movement has taken root. For its part Thailand has responded to severe deforestation, drought, and sedimentation with a strong ecological movement. Activist leaders there, such as the monk BUDDHADASA, have built on Buddhist concepts to motivate social action.

Further reading: Christopher K. Chapple, "Animals and Environment in the Buddhist Birth Stories," in Mary E. Tucker and Duncan R. Williams, eds., *Buddhism and Ecology* (Cambridge: Harvard Center for the Study of World Religions, 1997); David L. Gosling, *Religion and Ecology in India and Southeast Asia* (London: Routledge, 2001); Roger S. Gottlieb, "Introduction: Religion in an Age of Environmental Crisis," in Roger S. Gottlieb, ed., *This Sacred Earth: Religion, Nature, Environment.* 2d ed. (London: Routledge, 2004), 3–20; Chatsumarn Kabilsingh, "Early Buddhist Views on Nature," in Roger S. Gottlieb, ed., *This Sacred Earth: Religion, Nature, Environment.* 2d ed. (London: Routledge, 2004), 130–133; Leslie E. Sponsel and Poranee Natadecha-Sponsel, "Illuminating Darkness: The Monk-Cave-Bat-Ecosystem Complex in Thailand," in Roger S. Gottlieb, ed., *This Sacred Earth: Religion, Nature, Environment.* 2d ed. (London: Routledge, 2004), 134–144.

18 schools of early Buddhism

Buddhism had a complex development in India before the development of MAHAYANA and its major thrust into Central and East Asia. Several schools developed from this early, pre-Mahayana period, of which only the THERAVADA has survived into the modern period. These schools are traditionally numbered at 18, although a strict count would total 25 or 26. The last of these early schools was founded in the fourth century C.E.; the cutoff time for the first 18 would be around 50 B.C.E. All of the schisms that divided these early schools concerned points of doctrine. One school, the DHARMAGUPTAKA, for instance, agreed with the doctrines of the STHAVIRAVADA SCHOOL except it placed extra emphasis on gifts and donations made to the Buddha as opposed to gifts made to the community (the sangha). The Dharmaguptaka also emphasized the honoring of PAGODAS (shrines). The Dharmaguptaka school broke away around the third century B.C.E. and later experienced much success in spreading into Central Asia.

At the same time there were geographic reasons for the division into different groups. There was from the beginning—in the time of the Buddha—a distinction between the Mathura area in the west of India and the Vaisali area to the east. The very first schism, between the Sthaviravadins and the MAHASANGHIKAS, found the Sthaviravadins less popular in the east. The Mahasanghikas remained firmly based in the capital of Pataliputra and other areas to the east. In the third major division of Buddhist schools, Mathura split off and became, with the areas north, the region of the SARVASTIVADA SCHOOL. This split was reflected in traditions concerning the Third Council of Buddhism.

It is interesting to note that schisms were more common during the period of greatest growth in India, when monks were moving great distances and setting up new communities in an almost pioneer effort. It is perhaps inevitable that periods of growth will lead to different points of view.

The major early schools include four groups that had the greatest impact on Buddhism's later development. The Sthaviravada and the MAHASANGHA formed after the first great schism, in

Vesali in 350 B.C.E. The Sthaviras (elders) were the conservative faction who followed closely the VINAYA, the monastic code, and who held to the Buddha's exact words and did not adapt easily to new interpretations. The Sthaviravada TRIPITAKA was written in Pali, the first of several SACRED LANGUAGES used by Buddhists, and is therefore one of the most authentic and oldest of all the Tripitakas from the different schools—that is, it contains few later additions.

The second school that resulted from the schism at Vesali was the Mahasangha, or "great assembly." The Mahasanghikas are associated with a democratic tendency within the sangha, as well as a liberal interpretation of doctrine. Significantly, the Mahasanghikas started to elucidate the image of the BODHISATTVA, an ideal type that would be definitively described by the Mahayana school.

A third major early school is the Sarvastivada, which means literally "those who hold the doctrine that all is." The Sarvastivadins were an outgrowth of the Sthaviravada. By the time of the fourth of the COUNCILS OF BUDDHISM held during the reign of KANISKA, around 100 C.E., the Sarvastivadins are mentioned as a widespread school. The school dominated that council and wrote commentaries, inscribed on copper plates, on the Tripitaka. This school is important because it occupied the key crossroads between India and CENTRAL ASIA, the area around Gandhara in what is today northern Pakistan and Afghanistan. Sarvastivadins are largely responsible for the transmission of much of the literary record of Buddhism to Central Asia and CHINA.

The Sarvastivadins had a particularly large commentarial literature. Today only a few sections of the Sarvastivadin canon exist in SANSKRIT, the original language. However, all of the Sarvastivadin Tripitaka was translated in China, and the canon can today be studied in its entirety.

The fourth important early school, and the only one that exists today, is the Theravada. By the time of the Council of Asoka, around 250 B.C.E., the earlier Sthaviravada school had split into three other groups, the Vatsiputriya-Sammatiyas, the Sarvastivadins, and the Vibhajyavadins. The Vibhajyavadins later split into two others, the Mahisasakas and the Theravadins. Theravada eventually spread throughout Southeast Asia and today remains dominant in the region. The entire Theravada Tripitaka is still in existence, in the Pali language, along with a major noncanonical commentarial literature, including such great works as the *Visuddhimagga* by the great Theravadin monk BUDDHAGHOSA.

Further reading: Edward Conze, *Buddhism: Its Essence and Development* (New York: Philosophical Library, 1951); Charles S. Prebish, ed., *Buddhism: A Modern Perspective* (University Park: Pennsylvania State University Press, 1975), 42–45; A. K. Warder, *Indian Buddhism* (Delhi: Motilal Banarsidass, 1970).

Eightfold Path

MARGA, the correct path, is the fourth of the Buddha's FOUR NOBLE TRUTHS. Teachings on *marga* are traditionally broken down into eight interrelated sections: right understanding, right thought, right speech, right action, right livelihood, right effort, right mindfulness, and right concentration. These categories cover nearly all of the Buddha's teachings and can be seen as the core of his message. The Eightfold Path is not sequential. Individuals are expected to begin at any point and cultivate all sections simultaneously. Work in one section will assist progress in the others.

The Eightfold Path is called in Sanskrit *arya-astangika-marga*, the "noble way of eight parts." This title implies it is the way of the *arya*, or sage. It is, however, not other-worldly. It is expressly designed to be practiced in the world of everyday life.

The Eightfold Path is often summarized by a threefold formula of *SILA* (morality), *SAMADHI* (concentration), and *PRAJNA* (wisdom), what some writers call the "threefold practice," or the three "trainings." Right view and right thought are associated with wisdom; right speech, right action, and right livelihood with morality; right mindfulness and right concentration with *samadhi*; and right effort with all three areas of practice.

See also DRISTI; SMRTI.

Further reading: Thich Nhat Hanh, *Heart of the Buddha's Teaching: Transforming Suffering into Peace, Joy, and Liberation: The Four Noble Truths, the Noble Eightfold Path, and Other Basic Buddhist Teachings* (Berkeley, Calif.: Parallax Press, 1998); Kogen Mizuno, *Essentials of Buddhism: Basic Terminology and Concepts of Buddhist Philosophy and Practice*. Translated by Gaynor Sekimori (1972. Reprint, Tokyo: Kosei, 1996); Piyadassi Thera, *The Buddha's Ancient Path* (1964. Reprint, Kandy, Sri Lanka: Buddhist Publication Society, 1996); ———, *The Teaching of the Buddha* (Tokyo: Bukkyo Dendo Kyokai, 2001).

eight immortals (ba xian)

The eight immortals are popular figures in Chinese legend and literature. These eight figures are found throughout Chinese-speaking cultural regions, as well as in Japan. Some were historical figures, while others were deities of unknown origin. It is not known why the eight became grouped together from the end of the Tang dynasty (618–906 C.E.). In subsequent periods stories about the eight continued to be told at all levels of society. By the Yuan dynasty (1279–1368) the stories had become more or less fixed and thereafter were transmitted without major revision. Thus the figures included in the list of eight are first of all folk heroes. The following list summarizes the eight:

1. LU DONGBIN is the most popular of the eight because of his association with longevity, healing, and powerful spells. He is a powerful deity. He carries a sword, the *zhanyaoguai* (devil slayer), which he uses to combat evil spirits whenever he is invoked.

He also carries a fly whisk, symbolizing his ability to fly.

2. Li Tieguai is associated with medicine. His iron crutch is a traditional symbol for a pharmacy. His second symbol is a gourd. He is imagined as a beggar, one with a feisty temper who is willing to fight for the rights of the downtrodden.

3. Zhang Guolao (Zhang Guo) is seen riding a donkey, often backward, and playing a bamboo mouth organ. He helps to bring offspring, so his image is often hung over newlyweds' beds.

4. Cao Goujiu was a powerful court official, a dangerous man to cross. His symbol is either a pair of wooden sounding blocks or an imperial tablet used for official pronouncements. He is dressed as an official.

5. Han Xiangzi is the patron of musicians. He is seen holding a jade flute. He symbolizes also the love of nature and solitude.

6. Zhungli Quan (Han Zhongli) was a court official in the Han dynasty (207 B.C.E.–220 C.E.). He is said to have invented the pill of immortality. He is seen in full beard, sometimes dressed as a general. He carries a feathered fan, by which he can control the oceans, or a peach, symbolizing immortality.

7. Lan Caihe, along with Li Jieguai, is another trickster figure in the group. Lan's gender changes; usually depicted as male, he is at times depicted as female. He is seen as somewhat crazy. He carries a basket of flowers.

8. He Xiangu is revered as a powerful religious ascetic; she was made immortal because of her meditational attainments. She holds a lotus flower, symbol of wisdom.

With the exception of Lu Dongbin, Li Guaili, and Zhang Guolao, these figures are not worshipped alone; they are most often seen together in a group.

There is some question as to how this group of eight merged in popular consciousness. Possibly the best explanation is the manner in which they seem to reflect the functions of the eight trigrams (*ba gua*). The eight trigrams, ancient divinatory tools found in the BOOK OF CHANGES, symbolize fundamental forces in nature. And each of the eight immortals is closely associated with one of the eight *gua*. Thus He Xiangu, the lone complete woman in the group, is associated with the trigram *kun*, composed of three broken lines. Her polar opposite, Li Jieguai, is known for his hot temper and so is associated with the strong *yang* trigram of three unbroken lines, *qian*. Each trigram is also correlated with a particular direction, a constellation, and many other elements. If we see the interaction of the eight fundamental trigrams as the underlying processes of nature, then the dramatic interaction of the eight immortals, as found in numerous plays and stories, is simply the in-the-flesh depiction of these forces at work. The eight immortals, then, embody basic notion of religious DAOISM.

See also BOOK OF CHANGES.

Further reading: Kwok Man Ho and Joanne O'Brien, trans. and ed., *The Eight Immortals of Taoism* (New York: Penguin, 1990); W. Percevel Yetts, "The Eight Immortals," 1916. Internet Sacred Text Archive. Available online. URL: http://www.sacred-texts.com/journals/jras/1916-21.htm. Accessed on December 5, 2005.

Eihei-ji

Eihei-ji is the lead temple of the SOTO ZEN community in Japan. It was founded in 1243 by DOGEN (1200–53), who had earlier introduced Soto practice from China. As part of his activity to spread Zen, in 1243 Dogen published his book, *SHOBOGENZO*. In it he argued that Zen was a better form of Buddhism in terms of its essential national duty. Buddhism was seen as an essential national asset shielding the nation from a variety of evils including wars and natural disasters. The book created a firestorm in the larger Buddhist community with even the supporters of RINZAI ZEN joining the attack.

Dogen concluded that withdrawal from the conflict was his best course, and at the end of the summer in 1243 he moved to Echizen Province (contemporary Fukui Province) and an estate owned by a staunch lay disciple, Hatano Yoshishige. He opened a temple and lived a secluded existence. This temple was renamed *Eihei-ji,* "Temple of Eternal Peace," in 1246, the new name referring to the period when Buddhism was initially transmitted to China from India. Dogen emphasized the monastic ideal. After Dogen's death, his primary disciple, Koun Ejo (1198–1280), became the abbot. He was succeeded by Tetsu Gikai, then Gien (d. 1314), and Giun (1253–1333).

Eihei-ji grew into a large monastic complex over the years, its remote location serving it well. In the 20th century, it began to welcome Western Zen practitioners, and from its facilities Soto Zen has spread to the West. Every 50 years a memorial service for Dogen is held, most recently in 2002.

Further reading: Steven Heine, *Dogen and the Koan Tradition* (Albany: State University of New York Press, 1994); Yuho Yokoi, *Zen Master Dogen: An Introduction with Selected Writings* (Tokyo: Weatherhill, 1976).

Eisai (Yosai) (1141–1215) *Japanese Rinzai Zen master who was first transmitter of Zen to Japan*

Eisai was a Buddhist priest who visited China in 1168 and 1187 C.E. During his second visit, he received the "seal" (*INKASHOMEI*) of ZEN transmission from Xuan Huaichang. Eisai then established the Shofuku-ji in Kyushu, the first RINZAI temple in Japan. He was later, in 1204, appointed abbot of the Kennin-ji monastery in Kyoto. It was here that Eisai was the first master of DOGEN, who went on to transmit SOTO Zen to Japan. Finally, he established the Jufuku-ji in Kamakura.

As most monks of his time did, Eisai studied TENDAI and SHINGON at Mt. HIEI. However, after his discovery of RINZAI in China he became a critic of Tendai. Tendai monks in Japan were as a result quite antagonistic to Eisai; his school was banned for a while. However, he gained the support of the Kamakura era shogun Minamoto Yoriie, support that allowed him to teach in the centers of Kyoto and Kamakura.

Ironically Eisai's own lineage, the Oryo lineage of Rinzai, died out a few generations after his death. His importance lay in his transmission of Rinzai teachings and, in his own writings, his new synthesis of SHINGON, TENDAI, and ZEN elements. He is considered the first monk to have established Zen teachings in Japan.

Further reading: Kazuo Kasahara, ed., *A History of Japanese Religion.* Translated by Paul McCarthy and Gaynor Sekimori (Tokyo: Kosei Publishing, 2001), 227–229.

ekayano magga (Sanskrit: *ekayana marga*)

Literally "one path," the term *ekayano magga* (Pali: *ekaayam*) was used by the Buddha when describing the Four Foundations of Mindfulness in the Mahaasatipatthaana Sutta, a Pali work. In this sutra, the Buddha explains that there is only one way or path to achieve purification, only one method to overcome the pains and discomforts of life, only one way to achieve nirvana. The one path consists of practicing the Four Foundations of Mindfulness: dwelling in contemplation of the body, dwelling in contemplation of the feelings, dwelling in contemplation of the consciousness, and dwelling in contemplation of the dharmas. Essentially, only mindfulness can allow one to achieve nirvana.

The concept of "one way" indicates that the Buddha's method is certain; there are no forks or deviations in the path. In addition, it is a method to be employed by each as an individual, as a "one," and not as a group. It can also be interpreted to mean the "Path of the One," referring to the Buddha himself as the One, a totally unique being.

Further reading: Ven. Sayadaw U Liilaananda, "The Four Foundations of Mindfulness (a Summary), A Talk Given at the Buddha Saasana Yeikthaa, Severn Bridge, Ontario, Canada." BuddhaSasana Homepage. Available online. URL: www.budsas.org/ebud/ebmed906.htm. Accessed on January 5, 2007.

emptiness   *See* SUNYATA.

Enchin (Chisho) (814–891) *founder of the Jimon sect of Tendai Buddhism*

Enchin (Chisho), founder of the Jimon sect of TENDAI BUDDHISM, was the nephew of KUKAI, the founder of Japanese SHINGON BUDDHISM, but instead of following his uncle's teachings, Enchin affiliated with TENDAI Buddhism. He traveled to China for six years (852–858) and upon his return to Japan opened a study center at the Miidera temple on Mt. HIEI, where Tendai was headquartered.

Miidera was soon directly affiliated with ENRYAKU-JI, the lead Tendai temple, over which Enchin became abbot in 868, shortly after the death of ENNIN (794–864). Enchin would remain at Enryaku-ji for the rest of his life.

In 866, Enchin also became head of Onjo-ji, the traditional temple of the powerful Otomo family, in Otsu City. For several decades after Enchin's death, monks in the lineage of Enchin and/or Ennin would head Enrayaku-ji. In 933, however, a dispute over the leadership succession led to a schism and the faction who traced their lineage to Enchin left Enrayaku-ji and established themselves at the Onjo-jo Temple, which became the headquarters of the Jimon sect of Tendai Buddhism.

Further reading: Bibhuti Baruah, *Buddhist Sects and Sectarianism* (Delhi: Sarup, 2000); H. Byron Earhart, *Japanese Religion: Unity and Diversity.* 3d ed. (Belmont, Calif.: Wadsworth, 1982); Paul Groner, *Ryōgen and Mount Hiei: Japanese Tendai in the Tenth Century.* Kuroda Institute Studies in East Asian Buddhism Series, 15 (Honolulu: University of Hawaii Press, 2002); Kazuo Kasahara, ed., *A History of Japanese Religion.* Translated by Paul McCarthy and Gaynor Sekimori (Tokyo: Kosei, 2001); E. Dale Saunders, *Buddhism in Japan* (Philadelphia: University of Pennsylvania Press, 1964).

engaged Buddhism

The idea of "engaged Buddhism" first emerged within the Zen Buddhist community in Vietnam during the ongoing conflict that began with the defeat of French colonial powers and continued as the Vietnam War in the 1960s. The Vietnamese monk THICH NHAT HANH gave voice to a dilemma faced by his community. As the war began to affect their neighbors, they asked themselves how they should react. Their first reaction was to maintain their monastic organization emphasizing their inner cultivation and not react to the transitory events around them. However, the suffering of people called them to move out from the monasteries and begin to assist those suffering physically and psychologically from the bombs. They decided to go forth into the world out of the insight (mindfulness) they had obtained from their meditative practices.

As Thich Nhat Hanh put it in his book *Peace Is Every Step,* "Mindfulness must be engaged. Once there is seeing, there must be acting." Hanh's new approach, while not altogether unique, has become a vital element in the emergent Buddhist community in the West. Hanh and his compatriots moved from simply assisting individuals who were hurrying to protest the war that caused their suffering to an analysis of the conditions of peace to the development of a way for Buddhists to be in the world and relate to the many socially upsetting phenomena they would have to encounter.

Through the mid-1960s, Hanh and his colleagues established a study center in Saigon, the

An Quang Pagoda, and began to organize people to provide services for the population victimized by the war. In the process of opposing the war he began to adopt the nonviolence activism articulated by Mahatma Gandhi and the Reverend Martin Luther King, Jr. (the U.S. civil rights movement was then at its height).

There are two main centers from which the engaged Buddhist approach is disseminated. Hanh now lives at Plum Village, a monastic community in Loubes-Bernac, France. Here the Unified Buddhist Church is headquartered as well as the Order of Interbeing, the international association founded in 1968 for people committed to engaged Buddhism. Plum Village itself exists as a place where people involved in the work of social transformation can receive rest and spiritual nourishment while improving their skills for introducing mindfulness into everyday life. It welcomes thousands of visitors annually.

Community of Mindful Living (CML) was formed in 1983 to promote and support the practice of mindfulness for individuals, families, and societies inspired by Thich Nhat Hanh. It is now an official arm of the Unified Buddhist Church and part of a collection of church agencies operating in and around Berkeley, California, including the church publishing arm, Parallax Press, and Deer Park Monastery.

Engaged Buddhist SANGHAS are now found around the world. The concept has been so successful that it is now applied to most instances in which Buddhist groups become involved in social causes. It no longer refers solely to Thich Nhat Hanh's groups or his teachings.

Further reading: Thich Nhat Hanh, *Be Free Where You Are* (Berkeley, Calif.: Parallax Press, 2002); ———, *Creating True Peace: Ending Violence in Yourself, Your Family, Your Community, and the World* (New York: Free Press, 2003); ———, *The Heart of the Buddha's Teaching Transforming Suffering into Peace, Joy, and Liberation* (New York: Broadway Books, 1999); ———, *Peace Is Every Step: The Path of Mindfulness in Everyday Life* (New York: Bantam Books, 1991); Robert H. King, *Thomas Merton and Thich Nhat Hanh: Engaged Spirituality in an Age of Globalization* (New York: Continuum, 2001); Christopher S. Queen, ed., *Engaged Buddhism in the West* (Somerville, Mass.: Wisdom, 2000).

***engi* (co-dependent arising)** See PRATITYA-SAMUTPADA.

enlightenment (*bodhi, satori*)

Enlightenment is the common English translation for the Sanskrit term *bodhi*. However, the English word *enlightenment* enjoyed a long history before Buddhism was introduced to the West and carried certain connotations, such as introducing light and clarity to one's vision of the world. With the discovery of the Buddhist tradition by scholars in the West in the late 19th century, the term was applied to what was seen to be the goal of Buddhist practice. However, the Sanskrit root *budh* actually means "awaken." Rather than a brighter, better-lit view of a familiar reality, BODHI is an awakening, an awareness of the true nature of reality as if seeing it for the first time.

One PALI commentary (the *Vibhangatthakatha*) describes this by saying that the enlightened person will "emerge from the sleep of the stream of defilements." This emergence is characterized by complete understanding of the FOUR NOBLE TRUTHS or a direct realization of NIRVANA. In general the Pali scriptures and commentaries see *bodhi* as a kind of knowledge, part of wisdom. Awakening experience, the activation of knowledge of reality, brings about a change in the quality of the DHARMAS (components of reality) that, when arising, constitute the individual. The entity that experiences this knowledge is defined simply as a collection of *skandhas* or aggregates; the individual does not in any ultimate sense exist as a separate entity. The awakened person becomes a noble person, a *bhodin*, or awakened one.

Stone image of the Buddha informing the universe of his enlightenment by touching the earth (*bhumisparsa mudra*); from a carved relief depicting the life of the Buddha, second to third century C.E.; originally from Gandhara, Central Asia, now in the Freer Gallery of Art, Smithsonian Museum, Washington, D.C.

The first enlightened one to share with others the experience of *bodhi* was the Buddha—the "awakened one." The Buddha was a man who through self-effort attained a certain understanding and perception of reality. While sitting under the BODHI TREE, he saw through everyday perceptions to the underlying nature of the universe. In MAHAYANA terms that nature is SUNYATA, emptiness. He also saw that this emptiness was not separate from the world of perceptions. It is a profound vision of unity, without dualities.

After the Buddha's death Buddhist practitioners developed techniques of religious cultivation to help a practitioner attain enlightenment. In classic Buddhist theory these consist of 37 practices—called *bodhipaksikiadharma*—categorized into seven groups. The 37 practices entail more than simple techniques of meditation, and it is important to note that Buddhist practice extends to issues of moral reflection as well as consciousness.

The first group includes the four fields of mindfulness: contemplating the body (and its impure nature), contemplating feeling to register suffering, contemplating mind to see impermanence, and contemplating phenomena to be able to notice that phenomena do not contain self.

The second group, the four right efforts (*catvari samyakprahanani*), are to eradicate evil already present, to prevent evil not yet arisen, to help good to arise, and to improve the good already present. Kogen Mizuno, a contemporary writer, cautions that evil here means simply that which leads away from an ideal, while good is its opposite.

The third group is the set of four psychic powers, which all relate to DHYANA, or a state of meditation: the will to obtain *Dhyana*, the effort to obtain *Dhyana*, the mind to attain *Dhyana*, and the research into wisdom to attain *Dhyana*.

The fourth group is the five roots of freedom that lead to good conduct: faith, endeavor, mindfulness, concentration, and wisdom.

In the fifth group are five "excellent" powers (*panca balani*), which correspond to the five roots listed in the fourth group. They are simply the roots as practiced by an experienced cultivator, at an advanced level.

In the sixth group are seven factors of enlightenment, on which the cultivator should focus just prior to reaching enlightenment. These help the cultivator obtain liberation and supernatural knowledge. They are mindfulness; investigation of the DHARMA, the Buddha's doctrines; endeavor;

joy; tranquility; concentration; and equanimity—seeing all mental phenomena with dispassion.

The final, seventh group of the 37 consists of the EIGHTFOLD PATH as originally taught by the Buddha—right view, right thought, right speech, right action, right livelihood, right effort, right mindfulness, and right mindfulness.

As a result of the complexity and variety of practices that developed later, the 37 practices were often summarized by reference to the three overall Buddhist practices of *sila, samadhi,* and *prajna,* a formula that continues to be a succinct description of Buddhist cultivation.

The 37 practices are described in detail by two great ABHIDHARMA masters, BUDDHAGHOSA, who wrote from the THERAVADA perspective (in his Visuddhimagga), and Vasubandhu, who wrote from the SARVASTIVADA perspective (in his ABHIDHARMA-KOSA). For Buddhaghosa all 37 practices occur in a single moment, the *eka-citta,* which corresponds to the moment when the four knowledges come to the cultivator. (The four knowledges are those of the path of stream-attainment, once returned, non-returned, and the ARHAT.) For Vasubandhu the 37 practices constitute the entire path of Buddhist development.

Chan and Zen developed further emphasis on meditation. Although the Chinese word *chan* was originally a translation for the Sanskrit *dhyana,* in practice the Chinese term (and its Japanese equivalent, *zen*) represented more than the traditional three practices of *sila, samadhi,* and *prajna.* Zen practice includes these, plus the six perfections, the PARAMITAS, as well as a focus on gaining an intuitive understanding of the true nature of the practitioner's mind. A further way to refer to enlightenment in Zen practice is *satori,* which indicates enlightenment, broadly speaking.

See also CULTIVATION.

Further reading: R. M. L. Gethin, *The Buddhist Path to Awakening: A Study of the Bodhi-Pakkhiya Dhamma* (Leiden: E. J. Brill, 1992); Kogen Mizuno, *Essentials of Buddhism: Basic Terminology and Concepts of Buddhist Philosophy and Practice.* Translated by Gaynor Sekimori (1972. Reprint, Tokyo: Kosei, 1996); Isabelle Robinet, *Taoism: Growth of a Religion.* Translated by Phyllis Brooks (Stanford, Calif.: Stanford University Press, 1997), 101–102.

Ennin (Jijaku) (794–864) *Japanese Tendai leader*

Ennin, the third chief-priest of ENRYAKU-JI, is famous in Japan as the student and successor of SAICHO, who established TENDAI as a major strain of Buddhist orthodoxy. He was born in Shimotsuke Province. Already a serious student of Buddhism, he traveled to Mt. HIEI to study Tendai Buddhism with Saicho at Enryaku-ji in 808. He subsequently spent a number of years in China studying both TIAN TAI (of which Tendai is the Japanese version) and esoteric, VAJRAYANA, BUDDHISM. He believed the esoteric practices he had mastered to be of equal merit to the LOTUS SUTRA, the text so valued in the Tendai teachings.

Upon his return to Japan in 847, he began to introduce esoteric practices into Tendai. The positive response he received was manifested in his being chosen the new abbot of Enryaku-ji in 854. Through much of his life, he engaged in a struggle with another Tendai leader, ENCHIN, the head of another Tendai temple on Mt. Hiei. Only after Ennin's death was Enchin able to move into a position of power at the monastery.

Ennin is equally famous for a journal he kept relating his nine-year travels through China. He witnessed in particular the HUI CHANG PERSECUTION of Buddhism throughout China in 845 C.E. His eyewitness account is an invaluable record of this key event in Chinese Buddhism.

Further reading: Edwin Reischauer, trans. *Ennin's Diary* (New York: Ronald Press, 1955); ———, *Ennin's Travels in T'ang China* (New York: Ronald Press, 1955); E. Dale Saunders, *Buddhism in Japan* (Philadelphia: University of Pennsylvania Press, 1964).

Enryaku-ji

Enryaku-ji is the head temple of the TENDAI school on Mt. HIEI, northeast of Kyoto, Japan. It was founded by SAICHO in 788 C.E., as part of his process of establishing the new Tendai teachings he had imported from China.

The site for the temple was carefully chosen, as the northeast was considered the direction from which evil inevitably arose. Hence, by placing his center on Mt. Hiei, Saicho was asserting its role as the protector of the nation in general and the capital in particular. Thus, after the capital was moved from Nara to Kyoto in 794, Enraku-ji was formally assigned the title "protector of the nation."

In 806, Saicho officially established the Tendai school, an event marked by his requesting the right to ordain his students using the Mahayana ritual and precepts, as opposed to the HINAYANA precepts used at TOADAI-JI in NARA, where all Japanese Buddhist priests were ordained at the time. Permission to erect a Mahayana ordination platform was approved just days after Saicho's death and put into effect by his successors. Enryaku-ji went on to become the major Mahayana ORDINATION center in Japan for centuries, and the training ground for such future leaders as HONEN, DOGEN, and NICHIREN.

Further reading: Paul Groner, *Ryôgen and Mount Hiei: Japanese Tendai in the Tenth Century*. Kuroda Institute Studies in East Asian Buddhism Series, 15 (Honolulu: University of Hawaii Press, 2002); ———, *Saicho: The Establishment of the Japanese Tendai School* (Honolulu: University of Hawaii Press, 2000); Kazuo Kasahara, ed., *A History of Japanese Religion*. Translated by Paul McCarthy and Gaynor Sekimori (Tokyo: Kosei, 2001); E. Dale Saunders, *Buddhism in Japan* (Philadelphia: University of Pennsylvania Press, 1964).

Esala Perahera (Buddha's Tooth Day)

The Festival of the Tooth takes place in Kandy, in central SRI LANKA, and commemorates the sacred Buddha RELIC, a tooth of the Buddha, housed there. There is an elaborate procession on the full moon in the eighth lunar month. As the focus of devotion for all Buddhists in Sri Lanka, the Tooth Relic has deep symbolic meaning in Sri Lanka. It is a symbol of the nation itself, of sovereignty and self-determination.

Esala Perahera is a *poya* (fast) day that commemorates the day the Buddha taught his first sermon. It is also the day of his conception by his mother, Queen MAYA, as well as of his teaching of the ABBHIDHARMA (Abhidhamma) to her in heaven.

ethics, traditional Buddhist

Buddhism has not developed a single, separate ethical system as a philosophical category. Rather, ethical considerations spring forth from existing Buddhist concerns. We may call these core concerns, since they are ideas with which Buddhist thinkers have wrestled for centuries. Buddhist ethics is in fact a secondary ordering, a "second-order reflection," of other systems. Of more vital importance to Buddhist writers is the person's moral standing, and as with all religious systems ethics are derived from moral considerations.

Because morality is anchored in culture and historical context, the various Buddhist interpretations of moral behavior must be understood within their cultural contexts. Ethics are meaningful only as they are practiced, and they are practiced in various cultural settings by different peoples.

THE DEVELOPMENT OF BUDDHIST ETHICAL CONCEPTS

Buddhism started in the fourth century B.C.E. with the teachings of SIDDHARTHA GAUTAMA (c. 490–410). Siddhartha was born as a prince into the SAKYA tribe in northern India. Despite living in the midst of great luxury he was able to observe his surroundings carefully. He noticed the universality of birth, aging, old age, and death. After leaving home to devote himself to spiritual goals, he announced, at age 35, that he had seen through this condition and attained nirvana.

Buddhism developed in response to the highly ritualized Vedic religious practices then dominant in India. Vedic religion was controlled by brahmans, hereditary priests. There were also many competing teachings, including skeptics and individual ascetic teachers. Buddhism was at that time simply one competing system of many. Because of this, there were some ideas that Buddhism shared with the other groups, and others that were unique. The Buddha rejected such practices as animal sacrifice, complex ritual, and the caste system. On the other hand, he adopted these key conventional ideas:

DHARMA: This indicates a universal law that governs the universe. It also indicates the teachings of the Buddha, which reflect the operation of the universe. One who lives according to the Dharma will live a righteous path, in accordance with the Buddha's teachings. This natural law of Dharma was not created by the Buddha; he simply discovered and described its operations. To follow the Dharma is a moral choice.

KARMA: This is the idea that all actions have consequences in the moral realm. There is a dimension of action that is moral, not simply material. And all people are part of this system. Since moral action is needed in order to achieve NIRVANA, someone following the Buddha's Dharma must recognize the moral significance of all actions.

Rebirth: Rebirth means the return in another body, another identity. That identity may be better or worse, depending on moral behavior in the previous existence. This idea of a string of existences, all linked by karma, was prevalent in India and became a part of Buddhist thought.

In addition to these existing concepts the Buddha naturally developed his own. These include the following novel ideas:

The Four Noble Truths: The FOUR NOBLE TRUTHS state the Buddha's fundamental understanding of reality. Suffering (DUK-KHA) is part of life. Suffering is caused by desire (TANHA). There is a way to end this suffering, and that way is nirvana. In order to achieve nirvana the person should follow the EIGHTFOLD PATH.

The Middle Way: The Buddha taught that people should not go to excess. Since he had tried extreme asceticism as well as extreme hedonism, he felt a "middle way" was the only method to cultivate the moral life. This led to the formulation of the Noble Eightfold Path:

Right view
Right resolve
Right speech
Right action
Right livelihood
Right effort
Right mindfulness
Right meditation

These eight are traditionally grouped into three parts: morality (SILA), concentration (SAMADHI), and wisdom (PRAJNA). View and resolve lead to wisdom. Speech, action, and livelihood concern morality. And effort, mindfulness, and meditation relate to the development of *samadhi,* or meditative calm. This list describes the ideal Buddhist: one who is aware of wisdom, attempts to follow a moral life, and uses meditation to gain spiritual progress.

The Precepts: In addition to the threefold description of morality (*sila*) given in the Noble Eightfold Path, there are detailed descriptions of moral codes found throughout the Buddhist literature. The most basic, the Five Precepts (PANCA SILA), are the five elements of right action: no killing, no stealing, no sexual immorality, no lying, and no taking of intoxicants. These five are the basic precepts that all lay people in Buddhism follow. Monks, nuns, and others preparing for the SANGHA have additional lists found in the PRATIMOKSA.

Virtues: The precepts listed actions that followers were not allowed to do. In contrast, virtues are lists of positive traits. There are countless lists of virtues and vices in Buddhist literature. But in the earliest period the virtues can be narrowed down to the following:

Alobha (unselfishness): The person acts without selfish desire.

Adosa (Benevolence): The person wishes goodwill to all living beings.

Amoha (Understanding): The moral person understands human nature as described in the Four Noble Truths.

The Four Sublime States (*Brahma-viahara*): There were in addition some states associated with meditative practice. These four subtle conditions required constant application and cultivation as a Buddhist: love (*metta*), compassion (KARUNA), gladness for others (*mudita*), and equanimity (*upekkha*). The literature gives directions about how each person can develop these four qualities through conscious application, for instance, by spreading positive feelings of *karuna* (compassion) to everyone in one's surroundings.

A Middle Ground: Finally, traditional Buddhist ethics stress the absolute importance of leading a moral life. Buddhism revolves around gaining wisdom and translating that wisdom into action. Buddhist thinkers argued from the very beginning against dogmatic positions and favored the individual's using his or her innate powers of reasoning. They rejected eternalism (*sassatavaada*) as well as nihilism (*sabba atthii ti*), hedonism as well as self-mortification. Such extremes, they taught, led away from the development of wisdom and self-knowledge. Buddhism from the very beginning emphasized finding the middle ground between extreme views.

Further reading: David J. Kalupahana, *Ethics in Early Buddhism* (Honolulu: University of Hawaii Press, 1995); Damien Keown, *Buddhist Ethics: A Very Short Introduction* (Oxford: Oxford University Press, 2005); Hammalawa Saddhatissa, *Buddhist Ethics* (Somerville, Mass.: Wisdom, 1997); William Schweiker, ed. *The Blackwell Companion to Religious Ethics*, (Malden, Mass.: Blackwell, 2005); Jamgon Kongtrul Lodro Taye, *Buddhist Ethics* (Ithaca, N.Y.: Snow Lion, 2003).

Europe, Buddhism in

In 1966, when Kosho Yamamoto made his trip through Europe surveying the spread of Buddhism in the West, he found a fledgling community that was still in its first generation; the oldest Buddhist association was the Buddhist group at Leipzig, Germany, founded by Kurt Seidenstüxker (1876–1936). That picture is radically different from the image presented a mere 30 years later in 1996 by Peter Lorie and Julia Foakes in *The Buddhist Directory,* which surveys a thriving Buddhist community across Europe with all of the major elements—Theravada, Tibetan, Zen, Pure Land, Nichiren, and new Western forms of faith well represented.

BACKGROUND

The movement of Buddhism into Europe began with the first scholars (both professional and amateur) who became aware that Buddhism existed. This awareness followed close on the heels of the efforts of Great Britain to establish its hegemony in Southeast Asia and push northward into the Himalayas and even Tibet. Notable in the transmission of information about Buddhism would be, for example, Brian H. Hodgson (1800–94), who lived in Nepal and began publishing essays in *Asiatic Researches* as early as 1828. These would later be collected in a book, *Essays on the Lan-*

guages, Literature and Religion of Nepal and Tibet (1874). By the end of the century, travelogues and memoirs of Westerners who moved through Buddhist lands helped excite individuals about the exotic worlds and unfamiliar religious practices to be found in Asian lands.

Essential to the spread of Buddhism would be the availability of Buddhist sacred literature in Western languages. A few translations began to appear in the middle of the 19th century—as early as 1860 Albert Weber published a translation of the DHAMMAPADA into German and Vincent Fausboll first issued a copy of the JATAKA TALES in 1877. However, the real dissemination awaited the work of MAX MULLER's Sacred Books of the East project and the massive translation of Theravada literature by the PALI TEXT SOCIETY, founded in 1881.

Because the publication of Buddhist texts originated with Sanskrit and Pali scholars, it is not surprising that the first hints of the conversion of Europeans to Buddhism was to Theravada Buddhism as found in Sri Lanka, Burma (Myanmar), and Thailand. The first people who publicly identified themselves with Buddhism in England and Germany were followed by the first ordinations of Europeans into the sangha—C. H. ALLAN BENNETT (1872–1923) in 1901 and Anton W. F. Gueth (1878–1957) in 1904.

Meanwhile, in the British colony of Ceylon (Sri Lanka), the cofounder of the Theosophical Society, the American HENRY STEEL OLCOTT (1832–1907), had publicly identified with Buddhism and become an early supporter of ANGARIKA DHARMAPALA and the MAHABODHI SOCIETY he founded to return the place of the Buddha's enlightenment to Buddhist ownership. While Dharmapala's earliest focus was on the United States and the 1894 World Parliament of Religions, his more persistent efforts would emphasize Europe in general and England in particular. In the meantime, while the Theosophical Society was more closely aligned to Hinduism, it persistently created avenues for the dissemination of Buddhism in the West.

In England, the emergence of Buddhism would build around the Buddhist Society of Great Britain and Ireland, founded in 1907 by THOMAS WILLIAM RHYS DAVIDS, who had earlier founded the Pali Text Society. That society would welcome the first Buddhist mission to Europe, in which Allan Bennett, now known as Ananda Metreyya, led a group of several Burmese monks to England in 1907. They stayed for eight months. In 1908, the first European Buddhist periodical, The Buddhist Review (the precursor of The Middle Way), made its appearance.

The original Buddhist Society was joined by the Buddhist Lodge of the Theosophical Society, founded by the great pioneering force in British Buddhism CHRISTMAS HUMPHREYS (1901–83) at the beginning of the 1920s. Those two organizations merged in 1924 and became the current BUDDHIST SOCIETY. Dharmapala arrived in 1924 to found the British branch of the Mahabodhi Society and a short time later the London Buddhist Vihara. Though Humphreys would favor Zen Buddhism, and later invite DAISETSU TEITARO SUZUKI to England to teach, Theravada would dominate Buddhism in Britain well into the post–World War II period. Assisting this dominance would be the many German writings of Anton W. F. Gueth, better known by his religious name MAHATHERA NYANATILOKA, who spent much of his career in Sri Lanka.

The same early dominance of Theravada Buddhism was manifest in Germany, both in the Leipzig group and in the other prominent early pioneers of Buddhism such as Paul Dahlke (1865–1928) and GEORGE GRIMM (1868–1945). That dominance would not be broken until 1952 with the founding of the Arya Maitreya Mandala, a Tibetan Buddhist group headed by LAMA ANAGARIKA GOVINDA, the religious name of E. L. Hoffmann (1898–1985), who beginning from Germany opened centers across Europe. Also in the 1950s an initial European branch of the Jodo Shinshu opened in Berlin under the leadership of Harry Pieper.

In the 1960s, Buddhism began its growth, a growth that paralleled the rise of a host of alternatives to the Christianity that had previously dominated the scene. A place for Buddhism had been prepared to some extent by the skeptical critique of Christianity, which caused some to search for a non-Western religious alternative. Also, as in North America, youthful Europeans, who had encountered Buddhism as a result of their service in World War II, pursued Buddhist studies in the East after the war. Finally, after the war the number of immigrants from countries dominated by Buddhism increased dramatically. In most cases, such immigration occurred unnoticed, as there were no barriers to immigration like those that prevented Asians from entering the United States.

POSTWAR GROWTH

After World War II, the rapid growth of Buddhism can be seen in three areas. First, Buddhist teachers moved to Europe and began new centers. Most notable among the new teachers were the two Japanese Zen exponents, Taisen Deshimaru Roshi (1914–82) and Testu Nagaya Kuchi Roshi (1895–1993), and THICH NHAT HANH from Vietnam. Deshimaru Roshi settled in Paris in 1967 and founded the ASSOCIATION ZEN INTERNATIONALE, now the largest Zen organization in Europe with *zendos* in most European countries (and more than 90 places for meditation in France alone). Two years before Deshimaru's arrival, Nagaya Kiichi, a lay Buddhist practitioner, settled in Berlin and began the propagation of Zen. His work soon spread through the German-speaking countries of Europe. Unable to return to Vietnam, in the 1970s Thich Nhat Hanh settled in France, where he built a large community called Plum Village and built an international following for his socially active spirituality, called ENGAGED BUDDHISM.

Tibetan Buddhism, as popular in Europe as in America, was introduced to Europe in the person of Chogyam Trungpa, who moved to England in 1963 as a university student and stayed to found the Samye Ling meditation center, the first Tibetan Buddhist practice center in the West, in Scotland in 1967. Several years later, he moved to the United States and built a large organization in North America, but Samye Ling has continued as a pioneering Tibetan center. It was supplemented in the 1970s by the FOUNDATION FOR THE PRESERVATION OF THE MAHAYANA TRADITION, founded by two Gelug teachers, Lama Thubten Yeshe (1936–84) and Lama Thubten Zopa Rinpoche. The foundation spread the form of Buddhism most associated with the Dalai Lama from its European headquarters in Pisa, Italy. No more important Tibetan teacher has moved to Europe than Geshe Kelsang Gyatso, the Gelug leader who in the 1990s had a falling out with the Dalai Lama, but who in the meantime had built the largest Buddhist organization in England and has subsequently established centers of the NEW KADAMPA TRADITION across Europe and around the world.

Along with Asian teachers moving to the West, Westerners traveled to the East to sit under leading Buddhist instructors. Notable among these Westerners was the Dane Ole Nydahl, who in 1969 met the head of the KARMA KAGYU sect of Tibetan Buddhism and was later confirmed as a teacher. Since the 1970s he has built the largest Tibetan Buddhist organization, the DIAMOND WAY, with centers across Europe and now reaching other continents.

Theravada Buddhism in Europe was reinforced by the movement of AJAHN SUMEDHO (also known as Robert Jackman) to England in the mid-1970s. In 1978 he founded the Chithurst Forest Monastery, destined to be the source of a number of centers in the THAI FOREST MEDITATION TRADITION across Great Britain and then Switzerland, Germany, and Italy.

In addition to the Europeans who became teachers of Buddhism are the Americans who became teachers, developed work in North America, and subsequently expanded their organizations to Europe. Prominent examples would include Jiyu Kennett Roshi, founder of the Order of Buddhist Contemplative (a Soto Zen group), and Philip Kapleau, founder of the Zen Center of Rochester, who has sanctioned teachers in Germany and Sweden. Supplementing the American teachers have been Asian teachers who settled in America and from there built international associations of Buddhist centers; Seung Sahn, founder of the Kwan Um School of Zen, is a prominent example.

A third element of the burgeoning European Buddhist scene are the immigrant communities that became visible in the 1960s. Taking the lead were people from former British colonies (Sri Lanka, Burma/Myanmar, Malaysia, Hong Kong) who took advantage of liberal travel regulation through the British Commonwealth to move to England. People from the former Indochina (Vietnam) would move to France, and people from across Asia would begin to filter into different countries, many of them refugees who left their homes as political powers changed (most notably the Tibetans).

By the 1980s, first-generation immigrant Buddhists outnumbered European-born practitioners, and their organizations became a source from which the further spread of Buddhism among Europeans could proceed, in spite of their tendency to form somewhat separated ethnic religious conclaves. By the beginning of the 21st century, temples serving predominantly Chinese, Japanese, Korean, and southern Asian communities could be found scattered across Europe.

In light of the growth of European Buddhism, in 1975 a European Buddhist Union (EBU) was founded to include primarily those organizations serving European-born Buddhists, but reaching out to the ethnic communities. The formation of the EBU and similar national cooperative organizations highlights the gap between various segments of the Buddhist community (only a minority of Buddhist groups participate), especially the credentials of non-Asian Buddhist leadership. No more divisive issue emerged than that surrounding the SOKA GAKKAI. This expansive lay organization, which originated in the Japanese Nichiren Shoshu tradition, has become the largest Buddhist group in Europe and in various countries. In Italy, for example, it forms over half of the total Buddhist community. In spite of its impeccable Buddhist credentials, it has been a most controversial group. Many Buddhists refuse to engage in dialog or cooperative activities with Soka Gakkai.

The next question to be faced by the European Buddhist community, which will in all likelihood remain a distinct religious minority, is how the various elements will grow and change. European Buddhists have placed the different Asian traditions into relatively close proximity. Their minority status (with both Christian and irreligious communities continually challenging them) gives them motivation to develop a united front and to develop as a new Buddhist community at home in its European setting. At the same time, the different groups have a distinct investment in the diverse Asian traditions with which they practice. It is yet to be seen how Buddhism will respond to the new situation.

Further reading: Martin Bauman, "Creating a European Path to Nirvana: Historical and Contemporary Developments in Europe," *Journal of Contemporary Religion* 10, no. 1 (1995): 55–70; *Buddhist Directory* (London: Buddhist Society, triannual); Graham Coleman, ed., *A Handbook of Tibetan Culture: A Guide to Tibetan Centres and Resources throughout the World* (Boston: Shambhala, 1994); Christmas Humphreys, *Sixty Years of Buddhism in England, 1907–1967* (London: Buddhist Society, 1968); Peter Lorie and Julie Foakes, *The Buddhist Directory* (London: Boxtree, 1996); Paul Weller, *Religions in the U.K.: A Multi-Faith Directory* (London: Russell Press, 1993); Kosho Yamamoto, *Buddhism in Europe* (Ube City, Japan: Karinbunko, 1967).

Evans-Wentz, Walter Yeeling (1878–1965)
early Western Buddhist and translator of the Tibetan Book of the Dead

W. Y. Evans-Wentz, who studied Buddhism in the early years of the 20th century, prepared the first English translation of the Bardo Thodol under the title *The Tibetan Book of the Dead*. Evans-Wentz was born and raised in a Unitarian family in Trenton, New Jersey. He dropped out of high school to become a journalist. He worked at various jobs before landing in Palo Alto, California, in 1901. After taking some remedial courses, he was admitted to Stanford University in 1902. After graduation, Evans-Wentz pursued a master's degree with a focus on the Celtic influence on English literature. He also met William James, the visiting professor of philosophy. With his master's degree in hand (1907), he went to Europe and continued to study Celtic at the University of Rennes, where he received his doctorate in 1909. His studies led directly to his first book, *The Fairy-Faith in Celtic Countries* (1911).

By the time his first book appeared, Evans-Wentz had developed a primary interest in comparative religion, to which he now turned his attention. He traveled in the Mediterranean basin for several years and then wound up in India in 1917. He would spend the next five years in India, Sikkim (now a state in India), and Ceylon (Sri Lanka). His most important time was in the Himalayas, where he studied Tibetan Buddhism. He spent two years as a novice monk in Sikkim (1920–22).

In Sikkim he studied with Lama Kazi Dawa-Samdup (d. 1922), who was at the time translating Tibetan Buddhist texts into English. Evans-Wentz took his translations, edited them for English-speaking readers, and published them in four books: *Tibet's Great Yogi, Milarepa* (1928); *The Tibetan Book of the Dead* (1929); *Tibetan Yoga and Secret Doctrines* (1935); and *The Tibetan Book of the Great Liberation* (1954). For this work, in 1931, Oxford University awarded him an honorary doctorate.

His last book, *The Sacred Mountains of the Western World*, remained unpublished at the time of his death in 1965. He left an inheritance to Stanford University, which is used to support an annual lectureship.

Further reading: W. Y. Evans-Wentz, *The Tibetan Book of the Dead* (Oxford: Oxford University Press, 1929); ———, *The Tibetan Book of the Great Liberation* (Oxford: Oxford University Press, 1954); ———, *Tibetan Yoga and Secret Doctrines* (Oxford: Oxford University Press, 1935); ———, *Tibet's Great Yogi, Milarepa* (Oxford: Oxford University Press, 1928); Thomas V. Peterson and William A. Clebsch, "Walter Yeeling Evans-Wentz, Biographical Note." Stanford University, Special Collections and University Archives. Available online. URL: http://www-sul.stanford.edu/depts/spc/xml/m0278.xml#target4. Accessed on October 5, 2005.

F

fa chang (fa ch'ang, rituals of method)

Fa chang is an exorcism ritual series performed to expel evil from a sick person. It is performed by "redhead" Daoists in northern Taiwan, ritual specialists who perform the sequence theatrically. The sequence involves some 16 separate ritual actions that take place over several hours. The specialist performs in front of an altar surrounded by nine deities, including the Queen Mother of the West as well as the Three Ladies, the original deities who are said to have learned the *fa chang* ritual from the deity Xu Zhenren on Mt. Lu. All objects involved in the ritual are divinized, meaning they are imbued with divine power. Once an object is transformed into something divine, and the deities have been invoked, the priest performs some action that inverts or changes the situation and transfers the evil from the subject. The action may also involve a request that is sent to heaven.

Further reading: John Keupers, "A Description of the Fa-ch'ang Ritual as Practiced by the Lu Shan Taoists of Northern Taiwan," in Michael Saso and David Chappell, eds., *Buddhist and Taoist Studies* I (Honolulu: University Press of Hawaii, 1979), 82–92; Pen-Yeh Tsao and Daniel P. L. Law, eds., *Studies of Taoist Rituals and Music of Today* (Hong Kong: Society for Ethnomusicological Research in Hong Kong, 1989).

faith, practice, and study

In the Japanese Buddhist leader NICHIREN's theory, faith, practice, and study are the three fundamentals. *Faith* refers to the belief in the GOHONZON of the Three Great Secret Laws. *Practice* refers to understanding the Buddha's teachings, and *Study* means to teach on and help others chant the *daimoku* mantra and practice it oneself. Nichiren considered faith to be fundamental and believed that it gave rise to practice and study.

Falun Gong (Falun Dafa)

Falun Gong is a new Chinese religion that draws on a variety of older themes. Most notably it gives a central role to the practice of QIGONG, a set of practices that are believed to yield health and well-being. *Qigong* practice is based upon the idea of QI (*chi* or *ki*), the universal energy believed to undergird the cosmos, the same belief that underlies acupuncture. In Chinese theory, the body has a set of channels through which the *qi* flows. When that flow is obstructed, various negative conditions result. When it flows freely, the individual is healthy, vigorous, and mentally alert. According to Falun Gong teachings, the most critical part of the human anatomy is the Falun, a center of energy located in the region of the lower abdomen. It is a microcosm of the universe and contains all of its secrets.

On April 25, 1999, the movement emerged out of obscurity when some 10,000 of its members, without prior warning, appeared on Tiananmen Square in Beijing, China, to protest some articles that had appeared in several periodicals attacking it. Before the Chinese parliament, the protesters quietly practiced their spiritual exercises and then disappeared into the city. The Communist Party leadership felt threatened and the security forces were embarrassed.

After a period in which information was gathered on this group that had had the demonstration, the government acted. On July 22, 1999, Falun Gong was outlawed. It was declared a destructive cult and the government accused it of a laundry list of negative traits. Most significantly it had threatened the government and was harming the nation's social fabric. In the months ahead, the government moved to discredit it in the eyes of the public with a massive propaganda campaign. Members of the group who did not immediately withdraw were in many cases arrested.

The attempts to suppress the group within China led followers in other countries to launch public protests based upon religious freedom considerations. In the wake of the attacks upon the movement inside China, protests have been held outside Chinese embassies and consulate offices around the world daily to the present. Meanwhile, Falun Gong has been totally suppressed within China and no longer exists in any public or communal form, although there are underground members.

The controversy surrounding Falun Gong has somewhat obscured its existence as a religious community. It was founded by Master Li Hongzhi. Master Li claims to have been born in Changchun, Jilin, China, on May 13, 1951; according to the group's literature, that would give him the same birthday as Gautama BUDDHA. His claim is contested by the Chinese government, whose records indicate a birthday of July 7, 1952. Be that as it

may, he founded Falun Gong in 1992 and has authored its two main textbooks, *Zhuan Falun* (*Revolving the Law Wheel*) and *China Falun Gong.*

In China, *qigong* practices were traditionally passed orally from teachers to students. Knowledge of the *qigong* methods was otherwise found in closely guarded secret texts. After the Chinese Revolution, many of these texts were destroyed or confiscated and placed in government archives. Then, after the CULTURAL REVOLUTION, the practice of *qigong* resurfaced and was even promoted by the government as part of a new emphasis on traditional culture. A national *qigong* federation emerged with chapters across the country. The foundation of Falun Gong coincides with Master Li's withdrawal from the national *qigong* federation.

Master Li offers an expansive form of *qigong* that includes not only the performance of specific exercises (five basic exercises) but also the "cultivation of the *xinsheng*," a way of life that emphasizes truthfulness, benevolence, and forbearance. Practice leads to enlightenment. Li had, on the one hand, suggested that he alone knew the exact format of exercises people should practice, but he also made all of this information public in his book *China Falun Gong.*

Master Li has also taught that individuals must pass through tribulations in this life, and that dealing with tribulations is a means of ridding oneself of past karmic debts. He pictures a universe of many spiritual entities, including evil ones that interfere with life on earth.

In 1998, the year before Falun Gong was outlawed in China, Master Li moved to the United States. By this time the movement had already become international, spreading quietly through the Chinese diaspora. The controversy has attracted many people to it and with the translation of the basic texts into different languages it has been able to move out beyond the Chinese communities. The movement has a massive presence on the Internet, including the complete texts of Master Li's two books.

Further reading: "Falan Dafa." Falun Dafa. Available online. URL: http://www.falundafa.org/. Accessed on December 14, 2005; Li Hongzhi, *Zhuan Falun (Revolving the Law Wheel)* (Hong Kong: Falun Fo Fa, 1994); ———, *China Falun Gong* (Hong Kong: Falun Fo Fa, 1998); John Wong and William T. Liu, *The Mystery of China's Falun Gong: Its Rise and Its Sociological Implications* (Singapore: World Scientific and Singapore University Press, 1999).

Fa Xian (Fa-hsien) (377–422) *first Chinese pilgrim to visit Indian Buddhist sites*

Fa Xian was a Chinese monk who traveled to India, Sri Lanka, and Sumatra, studying with masters and collecting Buddhist scriptures. He left a record of his experiences in *Travels to Buddhistic Kingdoms* (*Foguo Ji*), one of the earliest and most detailed records of early Indian cultures.

Fa Xian lived during the turbulent period following the fall of the Han dynasty (221 B.C.E.–220 C.E.). It was precisely at this time of uncertainty that Buddhism began to make a strong impact on Chinese culture. There was a great hunger for more knowledge of the new teachings reaching China overland from Central Asia.

Fa Xian left China in 399 C.E. via Dunhuang, the Central Asian state of Khotan, and the Himalayas to India. Along the way he collected many important Buddhist scriptures, such as the NIRVANA SUTRA. He studied with masters active in India. He visited many major sites in India, Sri Lanka, and Sumatra (then a largely Buddhist culture). He finally returned to China by sea, in 414 C.E.

In China he continued to work on the material he had collected. He translated the Mahaparinirvana Sutra, with BUDDHABHADRA.

Further reading: Faxian, *The Travels of Fa-hsien (399–414 A.D.), or Record of the Buddhistic Kingdoms*. Translated by Herbert Allen Giles (Cambridge: Cambridge University Press, 1923); Kanai Lal Hazra, *Buddhism in India as Described by the Chinese Pilgrims*, A.D. 399–689 (New Delhi: Munshiram Manoharlal, 1983).

Fa Xiang (Fa-hsiang) school   *See* HOSSO SCHOOL.

Fa Zang (Fa-tsang) (643–712) *systematizer of Hua Yan Buddhist doctrine*

Fa Zang was the third patriarch of the HUA YAN school of Chinese Buddhism. Although he was born in the Tang dynasty capital of Chang An (now Xian), his parents were from Sogdia, or Samarkand, one of the Central Asian ministates. When he was 16 he was said to have burned off one finger to show his devotion to the BUDDHA. After the death of his first master, Zhi Yan, in 668, Fa Zang was ordained and joined the newly constructed Taiyuan Temple built by the Empress WU CHAO in Chang An. He early on was an assistant to XUAN ZANG, the great translator. He left Xuan Zang after disagreements and began to develop his own line of thinking based on the perspective of the monks Du Shun (557–640) and Zhi Yan (602–68).

Fa Zang's most famous work is probably the *Jin shizi zhang* (Essay on the gold lion). In this work he uses the allegory of a golden lion to represent the nature of substance. Substance is the true dharma nature, pure and complete in its own nature. Fa Zang argued that the outward appearance of the lion image is characterized by SUNYATA, voidness, yet the lion is nevertheless real. He then proceeded to explain the 10 "gates" or stages by which one may achieve NIRVANA, using the image of the golden lion to illustrate the nature of each gate. For instance, the fact that the lion may be revised, melted down, modified, while the gold itself remains intact, illustrates the principle of nongeneration.

Fa Zang is also well known as the systematizer of Hua Yan doctrine. As did the TIAN TAI founder ZHI YI, and the later Hua Yan master MI ZONG, Fa Zang worked with classification systems, called PANJIAO. Fa Zang used his writings to argue that Hua Yan was the highest form of Buddhist teaching.

Fa Zang was also known for clarifying a vision of PRATITYA-SAMUTPADA, codependent arising. In Fa

Zang's formulation, matter and truth were identical. All phenomena, he taught, interacted and interpenetrated infinitely.

Further reading: Yves Raguin, "Ways of Contemplation East and West: Xuan Zang, Fa Zang, Jing Jing." *Renlai Monthly.* Available online. URL: www.riccibase.com/docfile/rel-cw94.htm. Accessed on January 6, 2006.

feng shui

Literally "wind and water," feng shui is traditional Chinese geomancy, divination through study of the land and interaction between geophysical and human energies. It is widely practiced by professional feng shui experts in nearly all places with Chinese populations, as well as related East Asian cultures such as Korea and Japan. In recent years the principles of feng shui have also been picked up by other cultures; today awareness of this practice in Europe and America is being spread along with understanding of Chinese culture and religions.

There were antecedents for feng shui practice dating to the Han (221 B.C.E.–220 C.E.) and Tang (618–960 C.E.) periods. Classic texts dating from those periods include the *Zang Shu (Burial Book)*, *Zai Jing (Classic of Dwellings)*, and *Guanshi Dili Zhinan (Geographic Guide of the Guan Clan)*. However, as a systematic practice feng shui dates from the Song dynasty (960–1278). In the Song two distinct schools of feng shui appeared, the Jiangxi school and the Fujian (or magical) school. In general the Fujian school emphasizes the use of the geomancy compass, the *luopan,* while the Jiangxi school emphasizes observation of the environment and symptoms of "dragon" and "tiger" energies.

Feng shui incorporates a wide spectrum of popular religious thought, including Chinese astrology, YIJING divination, and a healthy dose of common sense. For instance, feng shui incorporates such religious concepts as QI (energy) and *taiji,* the "great absolute." Feng shui theory is also a repository of religious linguistic terms. While the details of feng shui theory cannot be adequately covered here, they are a fascinating and barely understood window on the Chinese imagination. The popularity of feng shui ideas in today's society is perhaps a reflection of people's desire to mix well into a complex industrial environment and not lose touch with the energy flows of nature.

Further reading: Ernest J. Eitel, *Feng-Shui: The Science of Sacred Landscape in Old China* (1873. Reprint, London: Sybergetic Press, 1984); Du-Gyu Kim, "Intuition in Korean Fengshui." Chinese University of Hong Kong. Available online. URL: http://www.cuhk.edu.hk/rih/phs/PEACE/papers/DuGyuKIM.pdf. Accessed on January 25, 2006; Evelyn Lip, *Chinese Geomancy* (Singapore: Times Books International, 1979); Sara Rossbach, *Feng Shui: The Chinese Art of Placement* (New York: E. P. Dutton, 1983); Eva Wong, *Feng-Shui: The Ancient Wisdom of Harmonious Living for Modern Times* (Boston: Shambhala, 1996).

Fenollosa, Ernest Francisco (1853–1908)
American artist and early convert to Buddhism

Ernest Francisco Fenellosa, one of the first Americans to convert to Buddhism, was born and raised in Salem, Massachusetts. He later graduated from Harvard (1874) and did postgraduate studies at the Boston Museum of Fine Arts. Having received an invitation to teach at the Imperial University in Tokyo, in 1878 he moved to Japan. His students would include many of the next generation of Buddhism's leadership.

Once in Japan, he studied Buddhist art and architecture, many aspects of which were being neglected because of the anti-Buddhist atmosphere of the Meiji regime. He worked with several prominent artists to revive the Nihonga (Japanese) style of painting and in 1886 helped found the Tokyo Fine Arts Academy and the Imperial Museum (for which he served as the director for a brief period).

Along the way Fenollosa converted to Buddhism and assumed the name *Tei-Shin.* He also on occasion referred to himself as Kano Yeitan Masanobu, suggesting that he had been admitted into the ancient Japanese art academy of the Kano. Fenollosa's main accomplishments welded his interest in Buddhism and art. For example, he inventoried Japan's national treasures (which included many Buddhist items), for which the emperor of Japan honored him. In 1886, Fenollosa sold his art collection to a colleague who deposited it at the Boston Museum of Fine Arts. Four years later, Fenellosa returned to the United States as the museum's curator of Oriental art. His outstanding career at the museum was brought to an abrupt end in 1895 by a public scandal accompanying his divorce.

He returned to Japan to teach for three years and then spent the rest of his life writing and lecturing on Buddhism and Japanese art. After his death in 1908, his widow and his colleague Ezra Pound compiled his notes into some of his most notable books, including the two-volume *Epochs of Chinese and Japanese Art.* Though widely read when published, the book was full of errors that unfortunately detracted from Fenellosa's importance in stimulating Western interest in Asian art.

See also MEIJI RESTORATION.

Further reading: Van Wyck Brooks, *Fenollosa and His Circle with Other Essays in Biography* (New York: E. P. Dutton, 1962); Lawrence W. Chisolm, *Fenollosa: The Far East and American Culture* (New Haven, Conn.: Yale University Press, 1963); Ernest F. Fenollosa, *The Chinese Written Character as a Medium for Poetry* (London: Stanley Nott, 1936); ———, *East and West: The Discovery of America and Other Poems* (New York: Thomas Y. Crowell & Co., 1893); ———, *An Outline of the History of Ukiyo-ye* (Tokyo: Kobayashi Bunshichi, 1901).

Festival of All-Souls   *See* ULLAMBANA.

festivals, Buddhist

Festivals are a major aspect of Buddhist religious practice. The commemoration of the Buddha and

his major disciples through rituals and festivals probably began as soon as the Buddha's PARIN-IRVANA, or death, around 417 B.C.E. Although the Buddha had specifically warned against practices that deified his person, the urges to remember, to honor, and to worship this unique figure could not be stopped. Today the festivals of Buddhism, those days of commemoration and celebration that punctuate the calendars, have merged into the cultural landscape in all Buddhist cultures.

Festivals of Buddhism are present in all the cultures deeply influenced by Buddhism—a belt of countries stretching from Japan to Indonesia to Nepal, and most countries in between. These festivals can be categorized into five main types. First, some days commemorate Buddhas and bodhisattvas, of which the most obvious is WESAK, or the Buddha's birthday, a national holiday in at least 10 Asian countries.

Second, similar days are set aside to commemorate well-known cultivators and patriarchs of the Buddhist tradition. Such days as Zen's BODHIDHARMA Day and NICHIREN BUDDHISM's June Assembly reflect the unique history of Buddhist traditions in each country.

Third, a set of more localized celebrations reflect preexisting local practices before the entry of Buddhism, as well as Buddhist-inspired events. These festivals are usually confined to a country, province, or even single city or shrine; for instance, the Aoi Festiva, a Shinto event held every May 15 at Kamigamo Shrine in Kyoto, is said to be the oldest festival in the world. In these festivals we can see the presence of other traditions that have been integrated with Buddhist practice.

Fourth, another set of festivals are held for particular purposes, for instance, festivals that involve opening new temples or Buddha images, festivals of purification, and festivals of initiation. Such festive events mix religious ceremony and purpose with local customs and needs (and are not discussed here, unless they coincide with other festival days).

Fifth, a final category are festive events tied to the sangha, the community of monks and nuns. As a unique form of social organization that has endured for more than 2,000 years, the sangha naturally has many special occasions that relate to life within it.

The major festivals common to most Buddhist traditions begin with the single most popular festival: the Buddha's birthday. Note that in discussing Buddhist festivals all dates are lunar calendar dates, unless specifically noted as solar calendar dates.

WESAK AND OTHER DAYS COMMEMORATING SAKYAMUNI BUDDHA'S LIFE

BUDDHA's birthday is perhaps the most widely celebrated festival in Buddhist cultures. It is generally called Wesak (Vesak), or Visakah Puja, "ritual of Viskah," reflecting the month of the Buddha's birth according to the Indian calendar. It is celebrated on the full moon in (lunar) May in many countries. In the Chinese calendar it is celebrated on the eighth day of the fourth lunar month. The event commemorated was the Buddha's birth to *Maya*, his biological mother, in the park at LUM-BINI, under a tree. The infant is said to have immediately stood up, raised his right hand, and sworn to give solace to all suffering beings.

Additional holidays reflect key events in the Buddha's life. The first is his moment of enlightenment. Although this event is normally assumed to have happened while the Buddha meditated under the banyan tree, there are varying traditions. In Thailand he is said to have achieved enlightenment when he watched ploughing work by his father's side—when he was seven. This event is commemorated with the Ploughing Festival in the first part of the fifth month. In this celebration two white oxen pull a gold plough. They are followed by four girls dressed in white who throw rice seeds. This Thai festival, called Raek Na, is clearly also related to the beginning of the planting season, just prior to the rains.

The Chinese celebrate various events in the Buddha's life beginning with the Buddha's enlightenment on the eighth day of the 12th month. The Buddha's renunciation day, recalling the day he renounced his status and privileges as a prince and lord and gave up family as well as power, is celebrated in Chinese cultures on the eighth day of the second month. On the 15th of the second month, the Chinese acknowledge the Buddha's *parinirvana,* his final extinction and departure after 80 years of life.

While Mahayana and Vajrayana (Tantric) cultures celebrate the four key dates in the Buddha's career as separate days, Theravada countries generally believe that all four days occurred on the same day and so celebrate only Buddha Day (Visakha Puja).

See also FESTIVALS, CHINA; FESTIVALS, JAPAN; FESTIVALS, MONGOLIA; FESTIVALS, SANGHA-SPECIFIC; FESTIVALS, THERAVADA CULTURES; FESTIVALS, TIBET.

Further reading: "Buddhist Ceremonies: Festivals and Special Days." Buddhanet. Available online. URL: www.buddhanet.net/festival.htm. Accessed on October 9, 2005; George E Shibata, *The Buddhist Holidays* (San Francisco: Buddhist Churches of America, 1974); John Snelling, *Buddhist Festivals* (Vero Beach, Fla.: Rourke Publishing Group, 1987); "Time and Worship." ReligioNet at the Religious Studies Program, University of Wyoming. Available online. URL: http://uwacadweb.uwyo.edu/religionet/er/buddhism/BTIME.HTM. Accessed October 10, 2005.

festivals, China

Beyond those festivals common to Buddhism internationally, a variety of Buddhist festivals are unique to or had their greatest development in China and in the modern period have been exported to Chinese communities around the world. Many of the Buddhist-related festivals are directly related to one of the BODHISATTVAS so prominent in PURE LAND and other schools of Chinese Buddhism. For example, the Buddha

MAITREYA has symbolic importance in Chinese culture as he represents hope and renewal for the future. Maitreya Buddha's birthday is celebrated on the first day of the first (lunar) year. The major bodhisattva-related festivals are discussed here.

MAHASTHAMAPRAPTA'S (BODHISATTVA OF GREAT POWER)'S BIRTHDAY

Mahasthamaprapta (in Japanese, Seishi Bosatsu) is one of the bodhisattvas associated with AMITABHA's Western Paradise. She is most often depicted as the assistant to Amitabha, along with AVALOKITESVARA. The three are known as the Three Saints of the Western Paradise. Mahasthamaprapta's halo of wisdom permeates all creation. She is often seen in feminine form, with a jeweled water vase in her crown. Mahasthamaprapta's birthday is celebrated on the 13th of the seventh month in the Chinese calendar.

SAMANTABHADRA'S (UNIVERSAL WORTHY'S) BIRTHDAY

SAMANTABHADRA is normally depicted riding on a white elephant. Along with MANJUSRI and Sakyamuni Buddha, Samantabhadra makes up the three lead characters in the massive Flower Garland Sutra, one of the great works of MAHAYANA literature. Samantabhadra is particularly associated with DHARMA practice—that is, the efforts and focus needed to follow one's religious obligations. Simply stated, he symbolizes the spirit of Mahayana. He is said to reside on Mt. EMEI in Sichuan province, one of the four sacred mountains of Chinese Buddhism. In the Chinese tradition Samantabhadra's birthday is celebrated on the 21st day of the second month, two days after Guan Yin's.

GUAN YIN'S (THE GODDESS OF MERCY'S) BIRTHDAY

There are in fact three key days associated with GUAN YIN: her birthday on the 19th of the second month, her enlightenment day on the 19th of the sixth month, and her renunciation day—when she become a nun—on the 19th of the ninth month.

These three days are celebrated most seriously on Mt. PUTUO, the island off China's east coast with which Guan Yin is most often associated. On these days there is a huge influx of pilgrims, in the tens of thousands, as befits the days celebrating the best known figure in Buddhism. Celebrations at the three main temples on Mt. Putuo take place over three days. These celebrations date back at least to the Sui dynasty (581–617 C.E.); they are recorded in a stone stele (carved memorial) found on Mt. Wutai, in the Hu Guang Temple, that dates from that period. The stele records that Guan Yin transformed herself into a monk and subdued an evil dragon on Mt. Putuo. A temple was built to commemorate this event, and on the 19th day of the sixth month a series of wonderful apparitions appeared in the sky.

MANJUSRI'S BIRTHDAY

Manjusri, the symbol of great wisdom, is usually depicted riding on a lion, holding in his hand a sword symbolizing the sharpness of his discrimination. As mentioned previously, Manjusri along with Samantabhadra and Sakyamuni make up the "Three Saints of the Flower Garland."

Manjusri is said to manifest himself on Mt. Wutai, in China's Shanxi Province. The many Buddhist temples on Mt. Wutai hold two major celebrations. The first, the Assembly of the Sixth Month, is a time of pilgrimage visits. The second, in the fourth month, involves four days of rituals in 10 of the largest temples. This ritual cycle coincides with Manjusri's birthday on the fourth day of the fourth lunar month.

In Japan the celebrations in honor of Manjusri can be traced to the ninth century C.E. His veneration is still practiced in the Manjusri Assembly in Japan. Since Manjusri is said to transform himself in the guise of beggars, food and drink are prepared on this day to feed all beggars, and the names of Manjusri and the Medicine Buddha are recited 100 times each, each day. This traditional ritual is performed today in only two temples.

ULLAMBANA (RELEASE FROM SUFFERING) FESTIVAL

ULLAMBANA is the SANSKRIT name for the occasion on the 15th day of the seventh month when the human and ghostly realms are connected. The original story of Ullambana's origin is given in the Ullambana Sutra. In that sutra the Buddha, out of compassion for the suffering of those condemned to suffering in hell, explains the path of salvation to his disciple MAUDGALYAYANA (in Chinese, Mu Lian). The method of salvation is to make food offerings on the 15th of the seventh month to seven generations of one's ancestors. The festival symbolized a time of making offerings to all the dead. Since Maudgalyayana became a bodhisattva, the Ullambana festival, as the others under discussion, is closely affiliated with a bodhisattva.

KSHITIGARBHA'S BIRTHDAY

The bodhisattva KSHITIGARBHA (in Japanese, JIZO) is normally depicted as a monk, with a monk's shaved head, holding a staff and a precious stone. He is popularly associated with saving the souls of those suffering in hell; in fact he can appear at any place in the six realms of existence, to any being (including nonhumans) who calls on him. His place of "residence"—where he is most often sited—is Mt. Jiu Hua in China's Anhui Province, one of the four sacred mountains of Chinese Buddhism. His main temple there is Hua Cheng Temple, which was founded in 401 C.E.

Kshitigarbha's birthday is celebrated throughout East Asia on the first day of the eighth lunar month (some celebrate on the last day of the seventh month).

AMITABHA'S BIRTHDAY

Amitabha Buddha, the Buddha of the Western Paradise, is celebrated on the 17th day of the 11th month. Along with Guan Yin, Amitabha is the best known Buddhist figure in Mahayana, including Tibetan Buddhism. Amitabha's vow is to establish the Western Paradise, the most sublime environment for cultivation, in order to assist all beings in the quest to realize perfect enlightenment.

See also CHINA; CHINA-TAIWAN; FESTIVALS, BUDDHIST.

Further reading: "Chinese Buddhist Festivals." Buddhanet. Available online. URL: www.buddhanet.net/ Carol Stepanchuk and Charles Wong, *Mooncakes and Hungry Ghosts: Festivals of China* (South San Francisco, Calif.: China Books & Periodicals, 1992); "Ullambana." Surf India. Available online. URL: www.surfindia.com/festivals/ullambana.html. Accessed on October 9, 2005.

festivals, Japan

Buddhist-inspired festivals can be found everywhere in Japan; there are at least 100 major events in the Buddhist calendar. Most of these relate to local temples or specific schools and are not national in scope. Nevertheless, the variety of Buddhist events reflects the importance of Buddhism in Japan's history, especially the medieval period, in which Buddhist ideas dominated cultural expression. We summarize the major Buddhist festivals in the following, as well as some more specialized or local festivals of note.

NEW YEAR'S AND SETSUBUN

The most important holiday in modern Japan is January first, a chance to clean house and dress up. There is little religious significance. However, the advent of the traditional, lunar-based year is still celebrated in the Setsubun (the Bean Throwing Ceremony), celebrated today on February 3 (solar). Setsubun celebrates the establishment of spring, as well as the exorcism of wandering spirits. There was an ancient belief that ghosts wandered the streets at night in the new season. The Spring Assembly is an exorcism performed before their arrival. The ceremony was originally performed on New Year's Eve by the imperial court. In the performance some actors took on the role of blue and red ghosts, who were chased by the others. Beans were also thrown around the ground to ward off devils. The festival gradually spread into the general populace. People today throw roasted soybeans in and around their homes, intoning, "In with good luck, out with devil." This is a ceremony to drive out demons. In shrines and temples well-known celebrities perform the same actions.

Another feature of Setsubun in many households is to put food out for the Mother Deity, HARITI. The traditional legend is that Hariti was a demon who ate the children of humans, until finally her own child was hidden by the Buddha. From that point she became a disciple of the Buddha.

Spring Assembly festivals are held at many SHINGON temples in Japan, such as Hoko-ji and Eifuku-ji in Nara.

HIGAN (PARAMITA, EQUINOCTIAL WEEK)

There are two Higan festivals, each lasting seven days, to mark the spring and fall equinoxes. Today the spring festival (Shunbun no Hi) is celebrated during the seven days surrounding the 20th of March (solar). The fall festival (Shubun no Hi) falls around the 23rd of September. These two days have been made into official holidays in the secular calendar, the first to commemorate the environment, the second to respect ancestors.

OBON

The festival of all souls, BON or Obon, corresponds to the ULLAMBANA festival popular in China. In this period people make bonfires to lead spirits to visit their homes. Many people visit their hometowns during Bon. This is because in Japan the Ullambana festival has become associated almost exclusively with veneration of ancestors. It normally takes place from the 13th to the 16th of the seventh lunar month. Processions are mounted at the beginning to greet the ancestors and, at the end of the celebration, to send them off on their return journeys. The Daimonji Yaki (Okuribi; Great Bonfire Event) held at Kyoto during this period (discussed later) is a variation on the practice of lighting bonfires; in the

Daimonji Yaki giant written characters are lit on the mountainsides.

On the day before the festival most areas in Japan perform Flower Dances along with fireworks. Shoro Nagashi (Floating of Lighted Lanterns) is held at the end of the Obon festival period. On the 15th of August (lunar) the floating lanterns guide spirits back to their proper place, the realm of the dead. Small candles are set on small boats and sent onto rivers or the sea.

KAMBUTSUE (BUDDHA'S BIRTHDAY ASSEMBLY)

The Buddha's birthday is celebrated on the eighth day of the fourth lunar month. The celebration in Japan dates from 606 C.E. Flowers are arranged in a dragon line that symbolizes LUMBINI, the site of the Buddha's enlightenment. A Buddha figure is placed in the center and, during worship, sprinkled with sweetened tea water.

JUNE ASSEMBLY

This festival held on June fourth generally commemorates Saicho, the founder of the Japanese Tendai school. However, another June Assembly is held to commemorate NICHIREN, founder of Nichiren Buddhism.

SENNICHIKEI (THOUSAND DAYS TEMPLE VISIT)

This celebration originally meant visiting the temple (or shrine) on 1,000 consecutive days. Later it was shortened to one day, which, however, had the same efficacy. The festival is held on different days for different temples; on those days the number of visitors is massive.

BUDDHA'S NAMES ASSEMBLY

This three-day ritual was imported from China and began in the imperial household in 774 C.E. In the ritual all past, present, and future names of the Buddha are recited as an act of confession to remove the collected karmic burdens accumulated over the previous year. The ritual soon spread to outside temples and was performed on the 15th to the 17th day of the 12th lunar month. It was later moved to the 19th through the 21st, and, finally, shortened to one day. It is today performed in only a handful of Buddhist temples.

THOUSAND LANTERNS ASSEMBLY

Several Buddhist scriptures such as the Bodhisattva Sutra mention the benefit of lighting lanterns to worship and commemorate confession. The lights symbolize the brightness of enlightenment. The ritual has roots in India and was popular in China as well as Japan. In Japan the first recorded procession occurred in 651 C.E. In Japan the celebration has become a major part of most temples' calendars, as will be apparent in the regional listing that follows. The four processions at Todai-ji are particularly well known.

JIZO'S BIRTHDAY

The bodhisattva Jizo (in Chinese, KSHITIGARBHA) is popularly associated with saving the souls of those suffering in hell; in fact, he can appear at any place in the six realms of existence, to any being (including nonhumans) who calls on him. Jizo's birthday is celebrated throughout East Asia on the first day of the eighth lunar month (some celebrate on the last day of the seventh month). The practice of celebrating Jizo's birthday was imported from China to Japan. In Japan the 24th of *every* lunar month is Jizo's day, and the 24th of the seventh month is the assembly in his honor. Today the largest celebration is held on the 23rd and 24th of the eighth month in Kyoto and greater Kansai.

To this day lectures are held on the 24th of each month, particularly in the Kansai region of western Japan. These lectures predominantly focus on prayers for the welfare of children, in line with Jizo's role as protector of children.

REGIONAL FESTIVALS

A sampling of the many regional festivals in Japan would include the following:

Wakakusayama Yama Yaku Turf burning

Opposing monks burn the ground on hills above Wakakusayama. This ritual began as a dispute between two neighboring temples.

Hadaka Matsuri

In late February at the Saidaiji Temple, Okayama, young men dressed only in *fundoshi* (loincloths) rush into the temple and plunge themselves into the nearby Yoshii River. At midnight they compete to find a pair of *shingi* (sacred wands) thrown into the night darkness.

Omizutori (Sacred Water-Drawing)

At TODAI-JI Temple, Nara, to mark the arrival of spring, participants are bathed in the sparks from torches. This is said to give protection against evil. Priests then offer water from a sacred well to Kannon, the goddess of mercy. This ceremony is part of the Todai-ji monks' training program, the Shunie.

Awashima-jinja Nagashi-bina (Doll-floating Ceremony)

Held at Awashima jinja (shrine) in Wakayama in early March, the ceremony sends Hina dolls, made from clay and paper, to sea in small boats. The traditional explanation is that ailments or impurities are transferred to the figures, and with offerings the problems are resolved. The act also protects from calamities. Not particularly Buddhist, this ceremony is a fascinating parallel to the Thai ceremony of casting small boats to sea (see FESTIVALS, THERAVADA CULTURES).

The Awashima-jinja Nagashi-bina is a type of Tenjin Matsuri. Such celebrations involve sending a fleet of decorated boats to sea. The goal is to prevent plague and disease. The Gion and other festivals with elaborate float processions (discussed later) also spring from this tradition.

Takayama Matsuri

This spring festival in Takayama, Gifu Prefecture, involves a procession of 12 large wagon floats with intricate decorations. Many include puppets. Along with the Gion Festival from Kyoto and the Chichibu Night Festival from Saitama—all processions of floats—this festival is of interest because of similarities with the Tibetan Butter Lamp Festival. It is held April 14–15.

Dojou-ji Temple Kane Kuyo (Requiem Service)

This honors a legend in which a princess becomes a snake and burns a priest using a *kane* (bell). It takes place on April 27 at Dojo-ji in Wakayama.

Takigi Noh (Open-air Noh Drama)

Held May 11–12 at Kofukuji in Nara, this drama is performed on a stage near a shrine. This practice harks back to the close relationship that previously existed between religion and drama, with stages often set up in temple grounds. Another Noh-related festival is held at the Heian Jingu in Kyoto on June 1.

Gion Matsuri

Held at the Yasaka Jinja in Kyoto, this festival lasts for one month in June. Twenty-nine floats are built on frames, seven large and 22 small. These are decorated with lanterns and traditional motifs.

Nachi no Himatsuri

Held at Kumanonachi taisha in Wakayama, the Nachi no Himatsuri is a ceremony involving a staged confrontation between two groups in front of the shrine: 12 priests carrying torches and 12 carrying portable shrines.

Asakusa Kannon Yonman rokusen nichi (Hozuku Ichi) (46,000 Days)

At the Senso-ji Temple, in Tokyo, each visitor's prayer is said to equal 46,000 normal visits to the same temple. The Hozuki (ground cherry) fair is held nearby.

Daimon-ji Yaki (Okuribi; Great Bonfire Event)

Held in Kyoto on August 16, this is a variation of the Nagashi, rituals of cleansing. A fire is lit over five mountains, each fire spelling out one large kanji (Chinese written character). A similar fire ceremony is held at the beginning of Obon.

Shunie (Second Month Assembly)

This ceremony held at Nara's Todai-ji Temple involves reciting one's faults and sins in front of the 11-faced Kannon (GUAN YIN) figure. The formal name is the *Second Month Eleven-Faced Confessional Assembly*. The ceremony is old, with the first recorded performance in 809 C.E. It is held today in March.

See also FESTIVALS, BUDDHIST; FESTIVALS, JAPAN.

Further reading: H. Byron Earhart, *Japanese Religion: Unity and Diversity*. 3d ed. (Belmont, Calif.: Wadsworth, 1982); George E Shibata, *The Buddhist Holidays* (San Francisco: Buddhist Churches of America, 1974)

festivals, Mongolia

Many Mongolian festivals such as the Naadam and Sagaalgan (the White Moon Festival, New Year) are not specifically Buddhist. However, festivals played a key role in the spread of Buddhism from Tibet into Mongolia in the 16th and 17th centuries. Many of the Buddhist festivals involved ritual dances, called TSAM, that exorcised evil.

The Transformation of Maidar (MAITREYA) Festival honoring Maitreya is described in a separate entry.

See also FESTIVALS, BUDDHIST; MONGOLIA.

Further reading: "Face Music—Projects—Tsam Dance Mongolia." Face Music. Available online. URL: http://www.face-music.ch/tsam/tsamhistory_en.html. Accessed on July 10, 2006; "Festivals:" Asia Society. Available online. URL: http://www.asiasociety.org/arts/mongolia/festivals.html. Accessed on July 10, 2006; Walther Heissig, *The Religions of Mongolia*. Translated by G. Samuel (Berkeley: University of California Press, 1980); L. W. Moses and S. A. Halkovic, Jr., *Introduction to Mongolian History and Culture* (Bloomington: Research Institute for Inner Asian Studies, Indiana University, 1985).

festivals, sangha-specific

Certain festival days are not widely celebrated in the culture in general but are important milestones within the Buddhist monastic community (the SANGHA). This discussion uses the Chinese monastic example but can be said to pertain to Buddhist monastic practice in general.

VASSA

VASSA, the rains retreat, marks the beginning of the annual period when the monks settle down in one place.

PAVARANA DAY

The 15th of the seventh month marks the traditional end to the rainy season retreats. Monks normally recite sutras on the evening of the 14th. On the 15th they enter the hall and prepare cakes.

On the final day the monks also hold a special ritual of confession and contrition, Parvana. They review their faults and publicly call on others to review those faults of which they are unaware. This confessional practice takes place on the final evening of Vassa. The practice also served as the origin of the Ullambana festival.

JIANGHU ASSEMBLY

From the 10th month to the 15th day of the first lunar month the sangha holds another retreat period, which mirrors the summer retreats and is called in Chinese jie dong, "breaking the winter." The celebration summons all the monks in the various "rivers and lakes"—in other words, near and far—to assemble together and cultivate and is thus called the "Assembly of Rivers and Lakes." From the Qing dynasty (1644–1911) to today another habit has developed within the Chinese sangha of not holding the summer retreat and staging only a winter retreat. Instead of holding Vassa during the summer months the sangha during winter focus on lectures and study of the vinaya (rules and regulations for monks). This practice has become codified in the Chinese sangha, leading to the saying "Meditate in the winter; lecture in the summer."

BUDDHIST FAST (ZHAI) DAYS

In ancient India two days per month were set aside as days of reflection. On those days lay practitioners as well as monks were to review their conduct, their actions as well as speech, and vow to improve. Such an act of reflection was uposadha, "faults broadly conceived." In ancient India such meetings were held every 14 or 15 days and gave all believers an opportunity to confess their faults.

The practice was continued under Buddhism. The Uposathagara ceremony served several purposes. Besides allowing the individual to reflect on his or her own behavior, it reinforced the unity of the community; it was in fact a group ceremony that reinforced the relationship between individual and community. The main element of the ritual was the recitation of the PRATIMOKSA, the monastic rules, by a chosen monk. The uposathagara was in fact a statutory act required in the Pratimoksa—the entire body of ordained monks were required to be present because, as the Buddha mentioned, attendance at such statutory acts as Uposathagara was a sign of respect for the community. The Uposathagara also later became associated with the practice of fasting on six days of the month.

Further reading: "Buddhist Ceremonies: Festivals and Special Days." Buddhanet. Available online. URL: www.buddhanet.net/festival.htm. Accessed on October 9, 2005; George E Shibata, The Buddhist Holidays (San Francisco: Buddhist Churches of America, 1974); John Snelling, Buddhist Festivals (Vero Beach, Fla.: Rourke Publishing Group, 1987); "Time and Worship." ReligioNet at the Religious Studies Program, University of Wyoming. Available online. URL: http://uwacadweb.uwyo.edu/religionet/er/buddhism/BTIME.HTM. Accessed October 9, 2005.

festivals, Theravada cultures
SRI LANKA

ESALA PERAHERA (Buddha's Tooth Day)
The Festival of the Tooth takes place in Kandy to commemorate the sacred Buddha RELIC housed there.

Vesak Poya Day

WESAK or Vesak, the Buddha's Birthday, is celebrated in Sri Lanka on the full moon of the fifth month. *Poya* is a term derived from the Pali and Sanskrit word *uposatha/uposadha,* which implies a "fast day." In Sri Lanka, just as in Chinese traditions, several days are seen as "*poya* days," during which the practitioner is expected to fast and follow the eight precepts.

Vesak Poya Day is the foremost *poya* day in Sri Lanka, for not only does it commemorate the birth of the Buddha, it also commemorates his enlightenment, his PARINIRVANA (death), and his visit to Sri Lanka. The tradition states that eight years after his enlightenment the Buddha visited Sri Lanka. Kelaniya continues to be a place of pilgrimage today because the Buddha is said to have visited it.

THAILAND
Buddhist New Year

In Southeast Asian countries the New Year holidays fall on the first three days of the full moon in April. This no doubt reflects the intense heat of the period, prior to the onset of the monsoon rains. It also coincides with the popular festival of Songkran, in which people playfully splash water on each other and participate in boat races.

Elephant Festival

On the third Saturday in November is the Elephant Festival in Thailand. This commemorates the Buddha's use of an elephant as a metaphor in the study of Buddhism. Just as a wild elephant can be tamed by pairing it to a tame one, taught the Buddha, so a person new to the Dharma should study with an experienced one.

Magha Puja Day ("Sangha Day")

This day falls on the full moon in the third lunar month. It commemorates the visit of the Buddha to Rajagaha in India for an assembly of 1,250 *arhats* who all felt drawn to meet there without prior arrangements. This assembly is also called the "Fourfold Assembly" because the participants were all *arhats,* they were all ordained by the Buddha, they assembled without consultation, and the meeting occurred on the full moon of the traditional month of Magha.

Today Magha Puja is an opportunity to show respect to the sangha in general, as an important institution in Thai society.

Asalha Puja Day (Dhamma Day)

This day, on the full moon of the eighth lunar month, celebrates the Buddha's first teaching. After his enlightenment he taught the truth of the Dhamma (Dharma) to the five ascetics in the Deer Park at SARNATH.

Kathina (Robe Offering) Ceremony

This ceremony is held within one month after the Vassa, or rains, Retreat. During this ceremony robes and other offerings are given to monks. Since the monks were not allowed to travel during the Vassa period, Kathina is an opportunity for lay supporters to check on the welfare of monks and offer them things before they travel. Again, this practice reflects the high status accorded the sangha in Thai and Theravada cultures, as well as the dependence of the sangha on the laity.

Today in the formal Kathina ceremony a lay representative offers fabric robes to two chosen *bhiksus* (monks) who represent the sangha. The two *bhiksus* then pass the offering to the sangha. The sangha together say, "Sadhu," [it is well], confirming agreement. The ceremony is finalized later that day when the robes are completed and presented to the honored *bhiksus.*

Loy Krathong
(Festival of Releasing Dharma Boats)

In the full moon of the 12th lunar month the water level is highest in Thailand's waterways. People make bowls of leaves, add candles or incense sticks, and release the bowls onto the water. The boats are said to carry bad luck away. The festival in fact commemorates a holy footprint left by the Buddha by the banks of the Namada River in India.

MYANMAR (BURMA)
Abhidhamma Day

The Burmese celebrate the day when the Buddha visited his mother in Tusita Heaven. The purpose of the trip was to teach her the Abhidhamma, those philosophical teachings that explain the sutras of Buddhism. This celebration is held on the 15th day of the seventh month in the Burmese calendar, which falls in October in the solar calendar.

See also FESTIVALS, BUDDHIST; MYANMAR, BUDDHISM IN; SRI LANKA, BUDDHISM IN; CAMBODIA, BUDDHISM IN; THAILAND, BUDDHISM IN.

Further reading: A. G. S. Kariyawasam, "Buddhist Ceremonies and Rituals of Sri Lanka." The Wheel. Available online. URL: www.accesstoinsight.org/lib/authors/kariyawasam/wheel402.html#ch3. Accessed on September 13, 2007; Mohan Wijayaratna, Buddhist Monastic Life: According to the texts of the Theravada Tradition, trans. Claude Grangier and Steven Collins (Cambridge: Cambridge University Press, 1990).

festivals, Tibet

Above and beyond those festivals common to Buddhists around the world, at least 30 major festivals mostly associated with Tibetan or TANTRIC BUDDHISM remain popular in Tibet.

The calendar of festivals associated with Buddhism begins with the New Year and the Grand Summons Ceremony LOSAR, which is described in a separate entry.

GAHDEN-NAMGYE (ILLUMINATION) FESTIVAL

Small lantern festival is held on the 25th day of the 10th month. It commemorates the day in which TSONG KHAPA, the founder of the GELUG school, died. Lamps are placed on roofs of monasteries and homes. On the ground Buddhist practitioners take ritual walks and place tree branches into incense burners in front of the Jokhang Monastery.

BELHA RABZHOL (AUSPICIOUS HEAVENLY MAID) FESTIVAL (FAIRY MAIDEN FESTIVAL)

This festival, held on the 15th day of the 10th month, commemorates the Auspicious Heavenly Maid, the protector of the Jokhang Monastery. A portrait of the Maid is carried to the main hall on the evening of the 14th and placed opposite the statue of Sakyamuni Buddha. On the 15th, monks from Moru Monastery carry her portrait along Barkor Street in Lhasa. Along the way onlookers present offerings, in particular the hada scarves. The festival is particularly popular with women.

SAGA DAWA FESTIVAL

The Saga Dawa commemorates Sakyamuni's birth, Buddhahood, and parinirvana. It occurs on the 15th day of the fourth lunar month. It is also known as the Festival for Releasing Living Things. Many Tibetans refrain from eating meat for the entire month to prepare for this festival. On the holiday people wear formal dress and often hold picnics.

THE LINGKA WOODS FESTIVAL (WORLD'S INCENSE BURNING DAY)

The Lingka Woods Festival, held on the 15th of the fifth month, commemorates PADMASAMBHAVA. Padmasambhava overcame evil in this month. Today it is an opportunity for Tibetans to dress up and enjoy displays, folk arts, and the arrival of spring. The festival, which normally lasts a month, is a major social gathering of the year for many nomadic Tibetans.

THE SHOTON (SOUR MILK DRINKING) FESTIVAL

This uniquely Tibetan festival was originally an occasion to celebrate the end of the monk's three-month period of confinement during the Vassa. Local people prepared yogurt and a feast for the monks on the first day of the seventh month. But starting in the mid-17th century a new element was introduced in the celebration—opera. The festival also became known as the Tibetan Opera Festival and was held outside the monasteries. In the early 18th century the Dalai Lama's new summer residence, Norbu Lingka, became the site of the Shoton Festival. The festival continues today.

Today different opera troupes continue to compete for honors.

See also CHINA-TIBET, BUDDHISM IN; FESTIVALS, BUDDHIST.

Further reading: Charles Allen, *A Mountain in Tibet* (London: Futura, 1985); Geshe Kelsang Gyatso, *Heart Jewel: The Essential Practices of Kadampa Buddhism.* 2d ed. (London: Tharpa, 1997); "Kagyu Monlam Chenmo." Kagyu Monlam Chenmo. Available online. URL: http://www.kagyumonlam.org/. Accessed on July 10, 2006; Richard J. Kohn, *Lord of the Dance: The Mani Rimdu Festival in Tibet and Nepal* (Albany: State University of New York Press, 2001).

52 stages

In general Mahayana theory, the BODHISATTVA advances through 52 distinct stages in his development toward enlightenment. In the Sutra of the Bodhisattva's Prior Jewel-like Acts these are grouped into sections, as follows: 1–10 the Ten Stages of Faith; 11–20 the Ten Stages of Security (the 10 abodes); 21–30 the Ten Stages of Practice; 31–40 the Ten Stages of Devotion (transference of merit); 41–50 the Ten Stages of Developing Buddha Wisdom (*dasabhumi*), 51 the stage of Near Enlightenment; 52 the Stage of Supreme Enlightenment (*myogaku*). These teachings on the 52 stages are laid out in a variety of sutras developed in China, including the Jeweled Necklace Sutra, the Benevolent Kings Sutra, and the Brahma Net Sutra.

Different schools had variations of this general scheme of 52 stages. The Fa Xiang (Vijnanavada) school outlined 41 stages. However, the TIAN TAI and HUA YAN schools both agreed on the scheme of 52 stages, and this model has since dominated Mahayana practice.

Lists of 10 stages can be found in the Mahavastu, a pre-Mahayana work, and the Avatamsaka Sutra. However, these longer, 52- (or sometimes 41-) stage schemes of bodhisattva development are unique to Chinese Mahayana, since they are not found in Indian or Tibetan sources.

See also BHUMI; CULTIVATION.

Further reading: *The Buddha Speaks: The Brahma Net Sutra* (Talmage, Calif.: Dharma Realm Buddhist Association, 2003); C. M. Chen, "How to Become a Bodhisattva." Buddhist Information of North America. Available online. URL: http://www.buddhistinformation.com/howtobecome.htm. Accessed on January 19, 2006; Kogen Mizuno, *Essentials of Buddhism: Basic Terminology and Concepts of Buddhist Philosophy and Practice,* trans. Gaynor Sekimori (1972. Reprint, Tokyo: Kosei, 1996), 193–202.

filial piety (*xiao, xiaoshun, hsiao, hsiao-shun*)

Filial piety entails respecting, caring for, and honoring parents and ancestors. Filial piety is a deeply rooted value throughout eastern Asian cultures, especially those influenced by the teachings of the Chinese philosopher CONFUCIUS. Confucius was clear in favoring ordered relations between family members. "Filial piety and brotherly respect," he is recorded to have said, "are the root of humanity [*ren*]" (*Analects* 1:2). The requirements to respect parents extended into the afterlife: "When parents are alive, serve them according to the rules of propriety. When they die, bury them according to the rules of propriety and sacrifice to them according to the rules of propriety" (*Analects* 2:4).

The idea of filial piety took deep root in Chinese culture after Confucius's time. The primary expression of the value of filial piety is found in the *Classic of Filial Piety (Xiaojing)*, a work dating from the Zhou dynasty (1027–221 B.C.E.), which was often memorized by students in later periods. There are texts focusing on filial piety in all the major religious traditions of China. For instance, in Buddhism the Sutra about the Deep Kindness of Parents and the Difficulty of Repaying It (*Fumu enbao nan jing*) and the Sutra on the Profound Kindness of Parents (*Fumu en zhong jing*) focused on filial piety. These Buddhist works did not concentrate solely on filial piety, however. In contrast, strong emphasis has generally been given to this theme in popular literature from all traditions. In Buddhism the most obvious formats in which filial piety is discussed are popular lectures (*sujiang*) and the precious scroll (BAOJUAN) literary form, which developed with mass printing in the 1600s.

Nevertheless, Buddhism was often attacked for breaking up families by forcing monks and nuns into celibacy. However, as Buddhism grew to be part of Chinese life it took on Chinese cultural values, including such aspects as filial piety and obedience.

A paradigmatic expression of filial piety was *gegu*, "cutting the thigh." *Gegu* involved cutting and boiling a piece of one's leg, then feeding the broth to a sick parent to nurse him or her to health. Although it was normally condemned officially, the practice was symbolic of absolute devotion and reverence. Such prototypical stories were found in Buddhist popular literature as well as other traditions in Chinese history. In the story of GUAN YIN the goddess is said to have offered her arm and an eye to save her father from disease, although he had behaved terribly toward her.

Perhaps the most filial of all Buddhist acts is to perform funeral rites for the deceased parent. Traditionally Buddhist services are held on the seventh day after death, until the final ceremony on the 49th day. The background of these observances is to guide the soul of the dead individual through a series of obstacles, such as gates guarded by obstinate officials in hell. Once all the obstacles are overcome the soul finally reaches AMITABHA's Western Paradise.

As Chinese culture spread to neighboring countries so did the notion of reverence for parents. These values are alive today, although experiencing modification along with rapid industrialization. A recent survey covering China, Korea, Japan, and Taiwan confirmed the importance of such traditional Confucian values as filial piety.

Further reading: Lewis Hodus, "Buddhism and the Family," from *Buddhism and Buddhists in China,* book published on Authorama: Public Domain Books. Available online. URL: www.authorama.com/buddhism-and-buddhists-in-china-6.html. Accessed on January 7, 2006; Susan Mann, trans., "The Story of Wang Wenlan's Wife, nee Yun," in Victory H. Mair, Nancy S. Steinhardt, and Paul R. Goldin, eds., *Hawaii Reader in Traditional Chinese Culture* (Honolulu: University of Hawaii Press, 2005); Yan Bing Zhang, Mei-Chen Lin, Akihiko Nonaka, and Khisu Beom, "Harmony, Hierarchy and Conservatism: A Cross-Cultural comparison of Confucian Values in China, Korea, Japan and Taiwan," *Communication Research Reports* 22, no. 2 (June 2005), 107–115.

five elements

Early Indian thought taught there were five fundamental types of materials in the universe: space, air, fire, water, and earth. Space (*akasa*) was seen as the material that tied the other four together, a type of glue. Buddhism incorporated the Indian concept of five elements, called the *Mahabhutas* in Sanskrit and translated into Chinese as the "five greats." These gross elements, space, air, fire, water, and earth, corresponded to the five *tanmatras,* or subtle types of matter: sound, touch, form, taste, and smell.

Over time Buddhist thinkers developed additional elaborate associations of the five elements with Buddhas, bodhisattvas, symbols and, functions. For instance, water is associated with the Buddha Askobhya, with the bodhisattvas MAITREYA and KSHITIGARBHA, with wisdom, diamonds, and the five-prong VAJRA thunderbolt symbol.

In China this scheme coexisted with but was kept separate from the native Chinese theory of the materials or processes (WU XING): wood, fire, earth, metal, and water.

Further reading: Kelley L. Ross, "The Indian and Buddhist Elements, and the Gunas." The Proceedings of the Triesian School, Fourth Series. Available online. URL: www.friesian.com/elements.htm. Accessed on December 2, 2005.

five hindrances

In Buddhism the hindrances are the five factors that will delay and deflect the cultivator from achieving progress. They are sensual desire, ill will, sloth and torpor, restlessness and worry, and doubt. Such roadblocks are overcome through constant effort and gathering with fellow cultivators, for instance, in the SANGHA. One must overcome the five hindrances in order to develop DHYANA (in Pali, *jhana*), the state of "absorption."

Further reading: Nyanaponika Thera, comp. and trans., *The Five Mental Hindrances and Their Conquest: Selected Texts from the Pali Canon and the Commentaries* (Kandy, Sri Lanka: Buddhist Publication Society, 2003). Available online. URL: http://www.accesstoinsight.org/lib/authors/nyanaponika/wheel026.html. Accessed on January 19, 2006.

Five Patriarchs and Seven True Daoists

The QUANZHEN Daoist tradition recognizes five founders and seven lineage founders. Their images are found in Quanzhen temples, where they are worshipped as deities. The first four of the founders are legendary figures found in other Chinese religions as well:

Wang Xuanpu (also called Donghua Dijun) and Zhongli Quan (also called Zhengyang, Yunfang) (both said to date from the Han dynasty, 206 B.C.E.–220 C.E.)
Lu Dongbin (Tang dynasty, 618–907 C.E.)
Liu Haichan (also called Liu Cao); (Liao dynasty, 907–1125)
Wang Chongyang (1112–70); (Song dynasty 960–1129)

The first three figures are almost certainly mythical characters. Wang Xuanpu is said to have been an emanation of LAOZI. Zhongli Quan, the teacher of Lu Dongbin, is in turn said to have been a government official in the late Han period (206 B.C.E.–220 C.E.). Lu Dongbin has been the most popular Daoist figure since the Song dynasty (960–1279). He is also one of the EIGHT IMMORTALS. Liu Haichan was a master of inner alchemy during the Northern Song period. Only the last, the founder Wang Chongyang, is probably historical.

But addition of these legendary figures to the genealogy of founders helped to date Quanzhen's genesis back to the Han period and, ultimately, to transmission from Laozi, the founder of Daoism.

Traditional Quanzhen accounts also describe the seven key disciples, or the Seven True Daoists (*qi zhenren*) of the North, who succeeded the Quanzhen founder Wang Chongyang. In contrast to the first four patriarchs, these seven lineage founders are historical figures. Note each individual had two or three names. The third names were later used to identify their lineages within the Quanzhen tradition. Qiu Chuji's followers, for instance, were known as the "Longmen school."

Qiu Chuji (Changchun, 1143–1227), also called Longmen (Dragon Gate)
Liu Chuxuan (Changsheng, 1147–1203), also called Suishan (Mount Sui)
Tan Chuduan (Changzhen, 1123–85), also called Nanwu (Southern Void)
Ma Yu (Danyang, 1123–84), also called Yuxian (Meeting the Immortals)
Hao Datong (Guangning, 1140–1212), also called Huashan (Mt. Hua)
Wang Chuyi (Yuyang, 1142–1217), also called Yushan (Mount Yu)
Sun Bu'er (1119–83), also called Qingjing (Clarity and Stillness)

The formula of the Five Patriarchs and Seven True Daoist immortals first appeared in 1326 but can possibly be traced back to 1269 because the formal titles used refer to titles given by the emperor in that year.

Further reading: Estephen Eskildsen, *The Teachings and Practices of the Early Quanzhen Taoist Masters* (Albany: State University of New York Press, 2004); Bartholomew P. M. Tsui, *Taoist Tradition and Change: The Story of the Complete Perfection Sect in Hong Kong* (Hong Kong: Christian Study Centre on Chinese Religion and Culture, 1991); Eva Wong, *Taoism: A Complete Introduction to the History, Philosophy, and Practice of an*

Ancient Chinese Spiritual Tradition (Boston: Shambhala, 1997).

Foguangshan

Foguangshan (Buddha's Light Mountain) is one of several new Buddhist groups founded in Taiwan in the 1970s. While primarily a Chan Buddhist organization, Foguanshan freely mixes elements of PURE LAND BUDDHISM in its life and work. Its headquarters complex near the southern Taiwanese city of Kao-hsiung boasts an eight-story-high statue of AMITABHA Buddha as well as a Pure Land Cave. However, it has become even better known for its espousal of the perspective of the Venerable TAI HSU (1890–1947), teachings generally termed humanistic Buddhism, which call for a reorientation of Buddhist life away from otherworldly concerns (such as rebirth into the Pure Land after death) and toward a remaking of the world into a pure land in which people can live.

After the transfer of the government of the Republic of China to Taiwan in the 1950s, the BUDDHIST ASSOCIATION OF THE REPUBLIC OF CHINA (BAORC) was founded to supervise Buddhist activities in Taiwan, and for several decades religious freedom was severely restricted. However, with the lessening of tensions with the People's Republic of China, there was a loosening of restrictions signaled by the end of martial law in 1987.

Among the groups established initially under the authority of the BAORC was Foguangshan, founded in 1967 by Master Xingyun (also known as Hsing Yun) (1927–   ). As a youth of 12, he entered a LINJI CHAN Buddhist monastery in Nanjing, China, and took his initial vows of renunciation. He was fully ordained in 1941 and is today the 48th patriarch of the Linji school. In 1949, he left China for Taiwan as the Nationalist Army made its retreat from the Communist forces that subsequently founded the People's Republic of China.

Master Xingyun has rejected radical social action as a means of achieving change; rather, he calls upon members to act at their own self-cultivation and then to assist others in improving their condition in the world. Foguangshan has founded a number of social service organizations to embody its approach to change.

To facilitate its members' self-cultivation, Foguangshan has developed an extensive publishing program. To further its social goals, Xingyun has nurtured the assistance of both government and corporate leaders to back his social programs.

As Taiwanese have moved to other countries, especially the United States, Foguangshan has followed them and established an extensive international network. Its temple complex in Southern California is the largest outside China. It has also established large temple complexes in Australia and South Africa. In the West, Foguangshan is better known through its lay organization, the Buddha's Light International Association. The International Buddhist Progress Society is the group's educational and outreach organization. Internationally, the group claims more than a million affiliates.

Further reading: Hsing Yun, *Buddhism Pure and Simple* (New York: Weatherhill, 2001); ———, *Where Is Your Buddha Nature? Stories to Instruct and Inspire* (New York: Weatherhill, 2000); Charles Brewer Jones, *Buddhism in Taiwan: Religion and State, 1660–1990* (Honolulu: University of Hawaii Press, 1999).

Foster, Mary Elizabeth (1844–1930)
Buddhist philanthropist in Hawaii

A Hawaiian native and member of the royal family, Mary Foster was a founder of the Hawaiian branch of the Theosophical Society as well as a staunch supporter of the Hawaiian queen. She met Angarika Dharmapala, the founder of the MAHABODHI SOCIETY, in 1893 and became his most devoted follower. She was a major benefactor for the Mahabodhi Society, which supported schools and hospitals in South Asia. Mary and her husband, Captain Thomas Fields, purchased the Hillebrand garden property in central Honolulu and bequeathed what is now known as the Foster Botanical Gardens to the city.

Further reading: Rick Fields, *How the Swans Came to the Lake: A Narrative History of Buddhism in America* (Boston: Shambhala, 1992); Louise M. Hunter, *Buddhism in Hawaii: Its Impact on a Yankee Community* (Honolulu: University of Hawaii Press, 1971).

Foundation for the Preservation of the Mahayana Tradition

The Foundation for the Preservation of the Mahayana Tradition (FPMT) is an international association of GELUG Tibetan Buddhist centers that emerged in stages through the 1960s and 1970s. The founders, Lamas Thubten Yeshe (1935–84) and Thubten Zopa Rinpoche (1946–), had left Tibet in 1959. They met when the younger Zopa Rinpoche arrived in Buxaduar, India, to become the student of Thubten Yeshe. Shortly thereafter, a Russian woman, Zina Richevsky, also became Thubten Yeshe's student. She was ordained as a nun in 1967. Two years later, the three established Kopan monastery near Kathmandu, Nepal. Kopan became a magnet for Westerners wishing to learn Tibetan Buddhism, and in 1973 the International Mahayana Institute was opened to accommodate them.

The work in Kathmandu began at a time when the survival of Tibetan Buddhism was in question. News of the destruction of monasteries and libraries in Tibet threatened the still largely disorganized refugee community in India and Nepal. The preservation of the beliefs and practices of Tibetan Buddhism in its various manifestations became a high priority for the community leadership. It led, among other things, to the adoption of an aggressive outreach program by lamas who heretofore had been very reluctant to share teachings with non-Tibetans.

In 1972, Lamas Yeshe and Zopa opened the first center in India, the Tushita Retreat Center in Dharmasala (where the Dalai Lama had settled). In 1974 they made their first trip to the West. As a result, they gained many students in Europe and North America, the majority of whom could not make the trek to the Himalayan centers. Gradually, they refocused their work to the West and moved the international headquarters of the FPMT to Pisa, Italy. In the United States, two pieces of land given to the foundation became the Vajrapani Institute at Boulder Creek, Colorado, and the Milarepa Center in rural Vermont. In the 1990s, the FPMT headquarters was relocated to California, and the relics of Lama Thubten Yeshe, who died in 1984, placed in a STUPA at the Vajrapani Institute.

The foundation attracted much attention in 1985 when a Spanish child, later known as Tenzin Osel Rinpoche, was identified as the lama's reincarnation. This event was hailed by Western Buddhists as a sign that the tradition had truly passed into the West and would continue as a global movement.

One of the largest organizations within the Tibetan Buddhist community, the FPMT sponsors Wisdom Publications, now based in suburban Boston, Massachusetts, which has become a major publisher of Tibetan Buddhist books in English.

Further reading: Vicki Mackenzie, *The Boy Lama* (Boston: Wisdom, 1996); Jamyang Wangmo, *The Lawudo Lama: Stories of Reincarnation from the Mt. Everest Region* (Kathmandu: Vajra, 2005); Thubten Yeshe, *The Tantric Path of Purification: The Yoga Method of Heruka Vajrasattva* (Boston, Mass.: Wisdom, 1995); ——— and Thubten Zopa Rinpoche, *Wisdom-Energy: Two Tibetan Lamas on a Lecture Tour in the West* (Honolulu: Conch Press, 1976); Thubten Zopa Rinpoche, *The Door to Satisfaction: The Heart Advice of a Tibetan Buddhist Master* (Boston, Mass.: Wisdom, 1994).

Four Noble Truths

The Four Noble Truths are a teaching tool. The Buddha's first sermon was presented to his five wandering ascetic friends at the Deer Park in Varanasi, near modern Sarnath. Here he first presented the idea of the Four Noble Truths (*catvari aryasatyani*). The Four Noble Truths present the Buddha's fundamental understanding of reality. Suffering (DUKKHA) is part of life. Suffering is caused by desire (TANHA). There is a way (MARGA) to the cessation of suffering (NIRODHA).

These ideas are found throughout Buddhist literature. It is said the Buddha first decided to teach the Four Noble Truths because he felt the Twelve-fold Chain of Dependent Origination, his detailed explanation of PRATITYA-SAMUTPADA (codependent arising), would be too difficult for people to grasp. The Four Noble Truths are a way of helping people understand this concept.

Further reading: Thich Nhat Hanh, *Heart of the Buddha's Teaching: Transforming Suffering into Peace, Joy, and Liberation: The Four Noble Truths, the Noble Eightfold Path, and Other Basic Buddhist Teachings* (Berkeley, Calif.: Parallax Press, 1998); Thera Piyadassi, *The Buddha's Ancient Path* (1964. Reprint, Taipei: Corporate Body of the Buddha Educational Foundation, n.d.); *The Teaching of the Buddha* (Tokyo: Bukko Dendo Kyokai, 2001); Geshe Tashi Tsering, *The Four Noble Truths*. Vol. 1, The Foundation of Buddhist Thought (Somerville, Mass.: Wisdom, 2005).

Friends of the Western Buddhist Order

The Friends of the Western Buddhist Order (FWBO) is an international fellowship of Buddhists founded self-consciously as a new Western approach to Buddhism that would draw on the many different Asian traditions. It shares characteristics of both a monastic order and a lay fellowship.

FWBO was founded in 1967 by the Venerable Maha Sthavira Sangharakshita (1925–). Born Dennis Lingwood, he was attracted to Buddhism through theosophy. As a young man he went to India and after several years wandering around the country, found a Theravada Buddhist teacher and was ordained as a BHIKSU in 1950. He subsequently founded the Vihara of the Three Ways in Kalimpang, India, and participated in the efforts generally associated with BABASAHEB BHIMRAO RAMJI AMBEDKAR to reach the Dalits for Buddhism. He expanded his study of Buddhism and was eventually also ordained in the MAHAYANA and Tibetan Vajrayana (Tantra) traditions. He also learned several languages—Pali, Sanskrit, Tibetan—important for Buddhist studies.

By the 1960s, Sangharakshita began to think about a new approach to Buddhism that would be relevant to the modern West. As a starting point, FWBO emphasized the central principles affirmed by Buddhists of all traditions. He also eschewed the idea that one tradition was better than the others. In each he found everything necessary to lead people to the enlightenment the BUDDHA intended. This ecumenical approach is reflected in the new order he founded.

Those who join FWBO are not ordained as either monks or nuns or laity; they are ordained as simply Buddhists. In the ordination process, no distinction is made between men and women—those of the same gender decide upon the appropriateness of any individual ordination. Ordination involves commitment to taking refuge in the Three Jewels (Buddha, Dharma, and Sangha) rather than to a particular lifestyle. Members are expected to follow the 10 precepts expected of any lay Buddhists, but there are no initial vows involving poverty or chastity. They may take vows of poverty or chastity, but that is purely an individual decision. After ordination members may live in community or alone.

Organizationally, the FWBO is a network of autonomous local chapters. Most of these chapters evolved into single-sex communities. Among the unique characteristics of the FWBO has been the open acceptance of homosexuality among the members. Order members have concluded that precept rules against abusing sexuality do not relate to the formal structure of sexual relations so much as to the nature of the relationship itself. Thus sexual relations are permitted both within and apart from marriage and of both a hetero- and a homosexual nature.

It is the goal of the chapters to be centers in which individuality can flourish, rather than places where sameness with a group ideal dominates. There are a set of materials, including the many books written by Sangharakshita, that the order draws upon, but otherwise it presents a very diverse face to the world. The order has spread worldwide, with about a thousand members who have taken vows but many more who participate in order activities. In the 1990s, the order spread throughout India and Indian members now make up approximately half of the formal membership. Other members are scattered primarily in countries with a large English-speaking population.

Further reading: Dhaemachari Subhuti (Alex Kenedy), *Buddhism for Today: A Portrait of a New Buddhist Movement* (Glasgow: Windhorse, 1988); Richard P. Hayes. "Androgyny among Friends." Available online. URL: http://www.unm.edu/~rhayes/afterpat.pdf. Accessed on December 15, 2005; Sangharakshita, *A Survey of Buddhism* (Boulder, Colo.: Shambhala, and London: Windhorse, 1980); ———, *The Three Jewels: An Introduction to Buddhism* (London: Rider, 1967).

fuji (*fu-chi*, spirit writing)

The practice known today as *fuji* was widespread in China at least from the Song dynasty (960–1279 C.E.) and it is part of the usual operations of sectarian religious groups to this day. It bears many similarities to the spirit writing or automatic writing seen in Europe from Roman times. The European version used a planchette (in French, literally a "little plank"), a heart-shaped piece of wood with wheels or rollers and a pencil attached. With hands on the wood, the medium could chan-

nel the pencil's movements in accordance with the spirit's intentions—at least this is the intent.

In China the related practice involved possession by a spirit and writing with a stylus, a penlike instrument, usually in sand. *Fuji* was used to write a large volume of different literary works. A god dictated his own autobiography to a spirit medium in 1181 C.E. (*A God's Own Tale*). The tradition continues today among a wide variety of Chinese religious groups, including Xiantiandao, the Taiwan Compassion Society, and TIAN DAO (YIGUAN DAO). The vast amount of *fuji* literature produced by such groups makes *fuji* a major genre of religious expression in Chinese religiosity.

There are indications the tradition of spirit contact was not originally a communication using words and was instead a form of nonverbal communication used by common people to communicate with deities. In particular there are records of people creating images of Zigu, goddess of the latrine, on her death anniversary, and inviting the goddess to descend into the image. The participants would than ask the image yes or no questions; if the image danced, it indicated a "yes" answer.

By the 1100s *fuji* had become an exclusively written communication between deities and the living. As a literary form it was most often used by the upper, literary class, often to divine such topics of concern as success or failure at official examinations. The revelations often contained moral injunctions. Before long these often became book-length expositions. In this case they performed the same function as BAOJUAN (precious scriptures)—moral instruction. The major difference between the two forms, of course, is that in *fuji* a human was involved in a type of possession by a god.

The earliest known Chinese text written under the influence of possession are certain parts of the *Taiping Jing* (*Classic of Great Peace*), dating from the first century B.C.E. *Fuji* was thereafter a very common way of creating Daoist texts.

Today a typical *fuji* session performed in a Tian Dao meeting involves at least four participants: three pubescent girls, dressed in white robes, and one senior leader, who may be a man or woman. The three girls gather around a table on which sits a rectangular box filled with a thin layer of sand. One of the girls is "possessed," or in contact with the deity. She stands at the head of the box and writes characters in the sand, normally upside down and reversed, while holding a ring with a stick attached. A second girl stands to the side of the box, reads each line as it is formed, and with a squeegee clears off the writing after every line is completed. And the third girl sits at the table writing down the communication with pen and paper. There is often a video camera placed over the sand box, allowing other watchers to see the lines of text being formed in the sand. The writing and recording are extremely fast—the girl writing on paper is barely able to keep up with the recitation.

Each page is handed to the session leader, who reads the message to the god. She or he will often speak to the gathered group about the messages received. They sometimes are targeted at individuals in the congregation, with words of encouragement or castigation. And they sometimes contain general moral lessons. The entire performance is highly dramatic, with the congregation curious about the god's message, as well as impressed with the solemn actions of the team of intermediaries with the gods.

There have been admissions by Tian Dao leaders that the contents of the messages were prepared in advance and given to the performers. Some Tian Dao groups have given up the process entirely. However, for the majority of believers there appears to be no question of the accuracy of this traditional way to communicate with the gods.

Further reading: "Ancient Ouija Boards: Fact or Fiction?" Museum of talking boards. Available online. URL: www.museumoftalkingboards.com/ancient.html.

Accessed on January 6, 2005; David K. Jordan and Daniel L. Overmyer, *The Flying Phoenix: Aspects of Chinese Sectarianism in Taiwan* (Princeton, N.J.: Princeton University Press, 1986); Terry F. Kleeman, trans., *A God's Own Tale* (Albany: State University of New York Press, 1994).

Fuji, Mt. (Fuji san)

One of the most well-known sites in the world, Japan's Mt. Fuji has, as have many of the world's spectacular peaks, attracted a range of religious sentiments and aspirations. Its textbook conical appearance and snow-capped top rising more than two miles (12,387 feet) above sea level have drawn religious seekers and secular pilgrims for centuries.

Buddhists see the mountain as the home of Dainichi Nyotai, an enlightened being (a Buddha) who embodies spiritual wisdom. A temple to him, constructed on the mountain's summit, was active by the 12th century. Some Buddhists have also described the mountain and its surrounding territory as constituting a large MANDALA. Eight smaller peaks that surround Fuji are likened to the petals of a lotus (a sacred flower in both Hinduism and Buddhism) that surround the Buddha's home.

Several Japanese Buddhist sect groups claim a special relation to Mt. Fuji. In 1289, NIKKO, one of the successor disciples to NICHIREN, left his master's temple at Minobu and moved to the foot of Fuji and on the southwest flank of the mountain erected Taiseki-ji, a temple that became the headquarters of the NICHIREN SHOSHU. SHUGENDO, the Buddhist group oriented toward mountain life and its austerities, found their way to Fuji in the 14th century and for several centuries controlled access to the summit.

Fuji has been especially significant to Shintoists. The earlier signs of worship directed at the mountain occurred in the ninth century, when a variety of ways of appeasing and relating to the various deities (KAMI) associated with the mountain led to the creation of a variety of Shinto shrines around the mountain. Also, quite early, religious activity developed around the many caves created by the mountain's formation. Female shamans often took up residence in a cave. During the Edo period, legends developed about two mythical women, Konohana Sakuyahime and Kaguyahime, both known for their beauty. The presence of the female shamans seems to be related to stories of Kaguyahime's entering one of the Fuji caves.

The development of a new religion focused on Fuji but outside the official channels of any Buddhist or Shinto organization is attributed to Kakugyo (1541–1646). He entered one of the larger caves, called Hitoana, which had already collected legends as a supernatural location, and while there had a revelation. He later became the center of a new religion with practice built on various magical operations and a set of moral teachings known as Fuji Ko. Fuji Ko spread rapidly after its then-leader, Jikigyo Miroku (1671–1733), starved himself to death on the mountain's summit in an act aimed at ending a famine that had struck in 1731. Fuji Ko, along with a splinter group called Fujido, was suppressed in the l850s and has largely died out.

Today, images of Fuji are so ubiquitous in Japan that it is difficult at times to separate religious worship and secular appropriation of the mountain. A number of Shinto shrines have constructed replicas of the mountain that provide a local means of building reverence before the actual mountain is approached. Most pilgrims who attempt to climb Mt. Fuji do so in July or August. There are four main routes up the mountain. Along each route SHUGENDO followers, still present though no longer in control, have established rest stops. Religious pilgrims generally carry a staff and as they progress on their way to the top, the name of each rest station is burned into the staff. Some spend the night on the mountain so as to be at the top at sunrise.

Further reading: Edwin Birnbaum, *Sacred Mountains of the World* (San Francisco: Sierra Club, 1990); Linda Kay Davidson and David M. Gitlitz, *Pilgrimage from the Ganges to Graceland: An Encyclopedia* (Santa Barbara, Calif.: ABC-Clio, 2002); *Mt. Fuji* (Tokyo: Japan Times, 1970).

Fuke Zen

Fuke Zen was a practice active in Japan during the Edo period (1603–1867) when the shogun ruled the country from Edo (Tokyo). A hallmark of Fuke practitioners was playing the bamboo flute, or *shakuhachi,* as a form of meditation. Eventually, the group developed a reputation for abusing people and committing crimes. The government moved against it on several occasions and largely suppressed it in the 1870s. A few remnants have survived as small religious associations.

The practices associated with Fuke Zen first entered to Japan from China. Its founder was Pu Hua (P'u-hua) (ninth century), known in Japan as Fuke. A wandering, eccentric RINZAI ZEN priest, Pu Hua was known for carrying a large bell that he would ring just prior to his recitation of verses from Buddhist sutras. In the 13th century, a Rinzai priest, Muhon Kakushin (1207–98), traveled to China and a priest who followed Pu Hua returned with him. As the movement developed a following, the priests of the group were known for not shaving their heads, for carrying straw mats, and for playing the *shakuhachi.* From their mat (*komo*) people called them the *komuso,* which means "priests of nothing." Three types of religious functionaries eventually developed within the movement: the long-haired priests who wandered the countryside living off what they could beg by playing their flutes, wandering ascetics who also played the flute, and resident priests who did shave their head.

The problems with Fuke developed when over a period of time they became the home to a variety of people who had unsavory backgrounds—especially former members of the samurai class who had violated the rules of their caste. They also drew to them a number of people who were outlaws or outcasts. This pattern eventually led to the government suppression of the sect.

The Fuke flute players developed a repertoire of music used as an aid to meditation that came to be known as *honkyoku*. Contemporary musicians who use the flute in Japan have rediscovered both *honkyoku* and the Zen teachers who produced the music.

Further reading: Heinrich Dumoulin, *A History of Zen Buddhism* (New York: Pantheon Books, 1963); Kazuo Kasahara, ed., *A History of Japanese Religion*. Translated by Paul McCarthy and Gaynor Sekimori (Tokyo: Kosei, 2001).

Fukko Shinto (Restoration Shinto)

Literally, *fukko* is "resurgence," a return to tradition. The Fukko Shinto movement began with the writings of Motoori Morinaga (1730–1801), who initiated scholarly research into Shinto literature. Morinaga was intimately involved in the Kokugaku (national learning) movement during the Tokugawa (Edo) era (1600–1867).

One of Norinaga's students, Hirata Atsutane (1776–1843), took these ideas in the direction of theology and nationalism and started Fukko Shinto. Atsutane taught that Japan was the religious center of the world, and that Shinto was the original religion of humankind. These teachings were accepted by late Tokugawa thinkers and influenced imperialist interpretations of Shinto in the 1900s.

Further reading: Kazuo Kasahara, ed., *A History of Japanese Religion*. Translated by Paul McCarthy and Gaynor Sekimori (Tokyo: Kosei, 2001).

Fu Xi (Fu Hsi) *mythological Chinese emperor credited with introduction of the eight trigrams*

Fu Xi was the first of three mythical emperors traditionally credited with introducing innovations to humanity. He is said to have ruled around 3000 B.C.E. Fu Xi invented music, painting, the feeding of silkworms (used to produce silk), the oracle bones used in divination, and the most common Chinese surnames. But his most important invention was without doubt the introduction of the eight trigrams, or *ba gua*. These are the eight possible combinations of short and long lines, which in turn form the building blocks of the 64 hexagrams in the BOOK OF CHANGES.

Further reading: Eva Wong, *Taoism: A Complete Introduction to the History, Philosophy, and Practice of an Ancient Chinese Spiritual Tradition* (Boston: Shambhala, 1997), 119, 162.

G

Gampopa (1079–1153) *teacher in the Kagyu Tibetan school*

Gampopa Sonam Rinchen, the primary student of the Tibetan teacher MILAREPA, founded the monastic tradition within the KAGYU school. He was born Dharma Drak at Nyal, central Tibet. He was known as Gampopa ("man of Gampo") because he spent years living in the Gampo region. At his father's direction, Dharma Drak was trained as a physician. Only after the death of his wife and children in an epidemic did he begin serious study of Buddhism. In his mid-20s he began study with a NYINGMA teacher but soon found his way to the KADAMPA reformist movement. He was 26 when he received his monastic initiation from Geshe Loden Sherap. He had studied the Kadampa teachings for several years when he heard of the Kagyu teacher Milarepa (1012–97) and set out in search of him.

Milarepa gave Gampopa several tests to gauge his seriousness. Then, recognizing Gampopa's talent, Milarepa began to transmit all the Kagyu teachings to him. Gampopo eventually emerged as Milarepa's primary student and lineage holder. However, Gampopa did not simply pass on Milarepa's teachings; he also developed them further.

Gampopo founded the Dhaklha Gampo Monastery, the fountainhead of the monastic order within the Kagyu tradition. He also worked to integrate into the Kagyu school the basics of the Kadampa reform, which was known for the orderly way it introduces the student to basic Buddhist insights. Gampopa's approach was embodied in his most famous text, *The Jewel Ornament of Liberation,* and in his other writings.

Gampopa had four main students from whom the four primary Kagyu schools emerged, including Baram Dharma Wangchuk (Baram Kagyu), Pagtru Dorje Gyalpo (Pagtru Kagyu), and Sahang Tsalpa Tsondru Trag (Tsalpa Kagyu). His fourth student, Dusum Khyenpa, became the founder and first Karmapa, or figurehead, of the KARMA KAGYU lineage, the most famous Kagyu school in the West. In addition, Pagtru Dorje Gyalpo had eight students from whom eight lesser Kagyu lineages emerged, including the Drakpa Kagyu school, which has become the dominant form of Buddhism in BHUTAN.

Further reading: Graham Coleman, ed., *A Handbook of Tibetan Culture: A Guide to Tibetan Centres and Resources throughout the World* (Boston: Shambhala, 1994); Gampopa, *The Jewel Ornament of Liberation: The Wish-Fulfilling Gem of the Noble Teachings.* Translated by Khenpo Konchog Gyaltsen Rinpoche and edited by Ani K. Trinlay Chödron (Ithaca, N.Y.: Snow Lion, 1998).

Ganjin (Jin Jianzhen) (688–763) *founder of Ritsu school of Japanese Buddhism*

Ganjin was a Chinese TIAN TAI master from Yang-zhou in central China. He moved to Japan after two visiting Japanese priests asked him to go there to induct Japanese Buddhists as monks. Doing so was critical for Buddhism in Japan because an official ordination platform (or sanctuary) had yet to be established there.

By the time Ganjin arrived in Japan in 753 he had lost his eyesight. Nevertheless, he quickly established an ordination platform at TODAI-JI temple, where he inducted the retired emperor Shomu and several hundred others as monks. The RITSU, or precepts, school in Japan was established in that same year, under his direction. Ganjin was later made general administrator of all priests in Japan. He established the Toshodai-ji temple in NARA in 759.

Further reading: "Ganjin," in *Soka Gakkai Dictionary of Buddhism* (Tokyo: Soka Gakkai, 2002), 245.

Gautama Buddha *See* BUDDHA.

Gedatsu (Gedatsu-kai)

Gedatsu is an eclectic Buddhist group founded by Shoken Okano (1881–1948) (later given the honorific title Gedatsu Kongo). Gedatsu offers a threefold method for finding enlightenment: developing wisdom, purifying emotions, and improving willpower. Wisdom is developed through meditation. Emotions are purified by service to one's ancestors and various spiritual entities (such as the BODHISATTVAS). The emotions may be purified by what is termed the Way of Holy Goho, a disciplined technique for training the mind offered through Gedatsu.

Gedatsu Kongpo saw the universe as held together by a universal law, the power of nature. This law provides enlightenment to any who seek the truth. The path to truth begins with a realiza-tion that the source of human problems is the focus on self-satisfaction through wealth, fame, food, sex, and rest. The focus on self-satisfaction can be replaced by a focus on attaining enlightenment—a state of calm and peace.

Worship in Gedatsu is centered on the act of *kuyo,* which is defined as humbly offering respect and gratitude to all those to whom one is indebted. Thus one acknowledges one's ancestors, the bodhisattvas (especially Fudo-myo-o, a bodhi-sattva important to Shingon Buddhists, and Kan-non, or GUAN YIN), and the spirit of the supreme creator, Tengenchigi.

Okano was born in Saitama, Japan, and spent much of his adult life as a successful business-man and a member of a SHINGON group. He had repeated experiences of communication with the spirit world that provided the foundation of Gedatsu. Okano received many of his communi-cations at Saitama-ken, Japan, at a location that has become the spiritual center for the movement, the Goreichi Spiritual Sanctuary. A shrine at the Goreichi is dedicated to Gedatsu Kongo as a token of gratitude to him.

In the years after World War II, Gedatsu began to spread to the Americas. There are now several churches in California and one in Hawaii, as well as centers in Brazil.

Further reading: H. Byron Earhart, *Gedatsu-Kai and Religion in Contemporary Japan* (Bloomington: Indiana University Press, 1989); Archbishop Eizan Kishida, *The Character and Doctrine of Gedatsu Kongo.* Translated by Louis K. Ito (San Francisco: Gedatsu Church of America, 1969); *Manual for Implementation of Gedatsu Practice* (San Francisco: Gedatsu Church of America, 1965).

Ge Hong (Ke Hung) (284–363 or 283–343 C.E.) *Daoist mystic and alchemist*

Ge Hong was an official in China's Eastern Jin dynasty (317–420). Frequent changes of political regime often left him out of power or persecuted, and he eventually retired to Mt. LUOFU (Luofu Shan) in Guangdong Province to focus on inner cultivation. He is most famous as the author of the BAOPUZI NEIPIAN (One who embraces simplicity), an important text in the DAOIST ALCHEMY tradition.

Ge is most closely associated with the southern branch of DAOISM, which developed from efforts to attain immortality through alchemy and magic. However, Ge Hong was not the typical Daoist hermit; he was as much a Confucian scholar as a Daoist alchemist. In order to attain immortality, Ge recommended that all cultivators practice QI retention through such practices as breathing exercises, sexual techniques, and diet. He also advocated the ingestion of rare substances produced through alchemy. In accommodating the needs of both CONFUCIANISM and Daoist alchemy, Ge Hong became one of the earliest syncretic thinkers.

He was also an iconoclast, criticizing equally the excesses of superstition and of Confucianism. In regard to alchemy he showed a practical, experimental bent. He insisted on experiments with various elements and stated his preference for those derived from minerals over those from herbs, because of their longer-lasting effects. He was openly critical of belief in shamanistic ritual and gods as opposed to practical approaches to healing. He also criticized the typical Confucian scholar's ignorance of metaphysics and the workings of nature.

Ge Hong made major contributions to the field of pharmacology. He also studied individual diseases. He had an advanced understanding of tuberculosis, for instance. And he records the first historical method to treat smallpox. He personally collected many folk prescriptions and formulas.

Because he retired to Mt. Luofu and eventually died there, Ge Hong became a cult figure in the Luofu Shan region. His image is worshipped there to this day, along with that of his wife, Bao. One legend has it that Ge was able to concoct two and a half doses of an alchemical substance that would grant immortality. He and his wife took

one dose each, and he handed the remainder to his disciple, Huang Ba Hu. Since Huang did not attain full immortality, he has remained a presence on the mountain to this day. He is depicted as a half-wild man, existing in a state of primitive oneness with nature.

As the scholar Nathan Sivin notes, Ge was not affiliated with any organized Daoist tradition. This made it possible for his charisma to be associated with place and easily appropriated by others, as happened when QUANZHEN Daoists later settled on Mt. Luofu.

Further reading: Robert Ford Campany, To Live as Long as Heaven and Earth: A Translation and Study of Ge Hong's Traditions of Divine Transcendents (Berkeley: University of California Press, 2002); Lai Chi-Tim, "Ko Hung's Discourse of Hsien-Immortality: A Daoist Configuration of an Alternate Ideal Self-Identity," Numen 45 (1998): 183–220; David C. Yu, trans., History of Chinese Daoism. Vol. 1 (Lanham, Md.: University Press of America, 2000).

Gelug (Yellow Hat school)

The Gelug school is a major school of TIBETAN BUDDHISM. The term literally means "virtuous ones." The school began in the 14th century through the efforts of TSONG KHAPA (1357–1419), the great teacher from Amdo in central Tibet. Since Tsong Khapa had studied with so many teachers—according to tradition, more than 100—the Gelug school teachings include elements of many other traditions. The school stresses ethics and careful scholarship. Gelug teachings are collected into Lamrim lectures. The Dalai Lama is always from the Gelug school.

By the 14th century the four major Tibetan Buddhism schools of NYINGMA, KAGYU, SAKYA, and Gelug had formed. The Gelug-pa wore yellow hats, which served to distinguish them from the Nyingma-pa (old school), who wore red hats.

The Gelug school rose to political prominence in Tibet through the support of the powerful

Mongol ALTAN KHAN in 1578. In 1642 Lobsang Gyatso, the Fifth Dalai Lama, was made the ruler of Tibet. Although all Dalai Lamas are of the Gelug school, they are not, strictly speaking, the heads of the school. The head of the Gelug-pa is called the Gaden Tripa. TSONG KHAPA died at the age of 60 and passed his position as head of the monastery of Ganden, which he had founded in 1409, to a successor. Today that position or "throne" is held by the 99th successor, Yeshi Dhondup. The major Gelug-pa monasteries are now Ganden, Sera, Drepung, and Tashi Lhunpo. Since the Dalai Lama's retreat from Tibet in 1959, Gelug-pa Tantric colleges have also been established in India, and leadership of the school is now based in a set of institutions at DHARMASALA.

See also CHINA-TIBET; TITLES AND TERMS OF ADDRESS, BUDDHIST.

Further reading: "The Gelug Tradition," Government of Tibet in Exile. Available online. URL: http://www.tibet.com/Buddhism/gelug.html. Accessed on July 5, 2005; Geshe Kelsang Gyatso, *Buddhism in the Tibetan Tradition: A Guide* (London: Tharpa, 1984); Tenzin Gyatso, H. H. the Fourteenth Dalai Lama, *The Buddhism of Tibet and the Key to the Middle Way.* Translated by Jeffrey Hopkins (Ithaca, N.Y.: Snow Lion, 1987); ——— and Alexander Berzin, *The Gelug/Kagyü Tradition of Mahamudra* (Ithaca, N.Y.: Snow Lion, 1997); Vijay Kumar Singh, *Sects in Tibetan Buddhism* (New Delhi: D. K. Printworld, 2006); "A View on Buddhism: Buddhism in Tibet," Kalachadranet. Available online. URL: http://buddhism.kalachakranet.org/tibet.html. Accessed on July 5, 2006.

Genshin (Eshin) (942–1017) *one of the founders of Jodo Buddhism in Japan*

Genshin, a Japanese TENDAI priest who influenced the development of Japanese PURE LAND BUDDHISM (JODO-SHU), was born at Taima, Yamota province. He went to Mt. HIEI to study with the great Tendai monk Ryogen (912–85) and was eventually ordained there. He later served in the imperial court and composed a major work on logic.

Around his 40th year, Genshin retired to Mt. Hiei to devote himself to Pure Land practice built around the recitation of the NEMBUTSU (in the Tendai style). His practice led to his most famous work, the poem *Ojo yoshu* (Compendium on the essence of rebirth), which reviewed all Pure Land literature up to his day. He recommended various means of meditation upon AMITABHA Buddha, different methods suited to different people. This widely read work helped promote devotion to Amitabha Buddha and prepare the way for HONEN (1133–1212) and the emergence of Pure Land Buddhism as a separate Buddhist sect in Japan.

Genshin also painted (or perhaps simply directed) what one scholar calls the greatest Japanese religious painting: *The Descent of Amida from Heaven.* This vast canvas in three sections is based on Genshin's vision of heaven and hell.

Further reading: Allen A. Andrews, *The Teachings Essential for Rebirth: A Study of Genshin's Ojoyoshu* (Tokyo: Sophia University Press, 1973); University of Wisconsin-Eau Claire, Philosophy and Religious Studies. "The Descent of Amida." Available online. URL: www.uwec.edu/philrel/shimbutsudo/descent_of_amida.html. Accessed on June 15, 2005; *The Descent of Amitabha and the Heavenly Multitude* (Mt. Koya, Japan: Museum Catalogue of the Museum Reihokan, 1997); Joseph M. Kitagawa, *Religion in Japanese History* (New York: Columbia University Press, 1966); Ishida Mizumaro, *Genshin* (Tokyo: Iwanami Shoten, 1970).

Ge Xuan and the Ge family tradition

Ge Xuan was the granduncle of the DAOIST ALCHEMY master GE HONG. In later Daoist writings Gu Xuan is mentioned as an immortal.

The Ge family were aristocratic landowners in southern China from the Three Kingdoms Period (220–280 C.E.). The family members were known as seekers after immortality. They are associated with the development of alchemical techniques; Ge Hong in this case is perhaps the most prominent in a long line of inner cultivation experimenters. The family is associated with such charts as the *Wuyue zhenxing tu* (True shape of the five peaks).

Another well-known member of the Ge family was Ge Chaofu (456–536 C.E.), of the second generation after Ge Hong. Ge Chaofu studied Ge Hong's writings and was instrumental in the development of the LINGBAO tradition in Daoism.

Further reading: Yamada Toshiaki, "The Lingbao School," in Livia Kohn, ed., *Daoism Handbook* (Leiden: Brill, 2000), 225–255.

geyi (ke-yi, matching concepts)

Geyi is a Chinese term whose literal meaning is "parallel concepts." It describes a method used in post–Han dynasty China (after 220 C.E.) to understand and interpret Buddhism, then a new and often incomprehensible system of ideas. Since educated Chinese were familiar with Daoist philosophical concepts, they tried to match unfamiliar concepts with familiar ones. For example, the Sanskrit concept TATHATA (suchness, ultimate reality) was matched with the Daoist concept *benwu* (original being).

Daoists at this time, especially in southern China, engaged in detailed investigation of such Buddhist concepts as the nature of being and nonbeing. These investigations resulted in the seven early schools of Chinese Buddhism that arose during the Six Dynasties period (222–589 C.E.). Neo-Daoism and such tools as *geyi* were instrumental in the establishment of these schools' identities.

Early Chinese translators eventually concluded that the material described by Buddhist texts and experience went beyond anything they knew. They discarded *geyi* and existing Daoist concepts in favor of a completely new vocabulary, the Chinese vocabulary of Buddhism.

Further reading: Wing-Tsit Chan, *A Source Book in Chinese Philosophy* (Princeton, N.J.: Princeton University Press, 1963), 336–337.

Ghosananda, Maha (1929–) *supreme patriarch of Buddhism in Cambodia*

Maha Ghosananda is the leader of an international effort to rebuild Cambodian Buddhism after the devastation of the Pol Pot regime. Born in Takeo Province in south central Cambodia, Ghosananda became a monk in 1943 at the age of 14. He later studied at the Buddhist University in Phnom Penh and at Nalanda University in India, where he received his doctorate in 1969. Because Cambodia was involved in a civil war when he completed his formal education, he took up residence at a meditation center in Thailand managed by Achan Dhammadaro.

Between 1975 and 1978, one of the modern world's greatest tragedies took place in Cambodia. Approximately 1.7 million people (21 percent of the country's population) were killed during the reign of the Khmer Rouge, including most of the thousands of Buddhist monks in Cambodia; only about 80 survived.

Ghosananda survived because he was in Thailand. Beginning in 1978, he became active in establishing Buddhist temples in the refugee camps along the Thai-Cambodian border.

After the collapse of the Pol Pot regime, Ghosananda became the head of an international effort to rebuild Buddhism in Cambodia. Through much of the 1980s he lived in Rhode Island and directed the revival of Buddhism in the Cambodian resettlement communities in North America, Europe, and Australia. He also worked to recruit and educate a new generation of Buddhist monks and launched an array of programs to garner support to rebuild Cambodia and work for peace in general. In 1988 he was elected the Supreme Patriarch of Buddhism in Cambodia.

In 1992 Ghosananda led delegations to the United Nations–sponsored peace negotiations that preceded the Cambodian elections. He also guided Pope John Paul II around the Cambodian killing fields during the pope's visit to Cambodia. He has been nominated for the Nobel Peace Prize four times and is popularly known as "The Gandhi of Cambodia."

Further reading: R. Scott Appleby, *Ambivalence of the Sacred: Religion, Violence, and Reconciliation* (Lanham, Md.: Rowman & Littlefield, 1999); Somdet Phra Maha Ghosananda, *Step by Step: Meditation on Wisdom and Compassion* (Berkeley, Calif.; Parallax Press, 1992); Buddhanet. "Masters and Their Organizations." Available online. URL: http://www.buddhanet.net.master/maha-gosanada.htm. Accessed on June 20, 2005.

globalization and Buddhism

Globalization refers to the widespread convergence of communications and interaction, an intensified increase in contact between previously separate peoples. Although not a new phenomenon in history, technological change and economic interdependence are currently unprecedented in scale and a source of social disruption.

Buddhist groups have responded to this convergence in a range of ways. First, many focus on counteracting what is seen as a growing monoculture, the loss of indigenous cultures and the growing formation of a single economy and monolithic cultural forms. Many Buddhists see the "invisible hand" of the Western economic model in the rise of global cities and mass consumption trends. Buddhist groups point to the Buddhist sangha as a democratic social form that runs counter to such tendencies. Unlike authoritarian forms of social life, the sangha develops values of social interdependence.

A second Buddhist response to globalization is an emphasis on Buddhist-inspired individual values. To counter the widespread belief in the value of advanced technology, Buddhist social critics such as Sulak Sivaraksa argue for nonat-

tachment to such notions as technology, the belief in progress, and the idea that the individual is in ultimate control. Sivaraksa recommends a renewed emphasis on small scale over large scale. The ideas of the economist E. F. Schumacher in his 1973 work *Small Is Beautiful: Economics As If People Mattered* seem to match such Buddhist thinking on community. Schumacher's emphasis on small-scale economic activity fits well with the Buddhist emphasis on generosity, compassion, nonattachment, and community.

In particular, economic globalization has resulted in a renewed awareness of the value of right livelihood, a component of the EIGHTFOLD PATH taught by the Buddha. Right livelihood traditionally means shunning certain occupations, such as hunting. It also means ethical behavior in business. The serious Buddhist has an obligation to define and follow a clear code of business ethics.

A fourth broad trend is an awareness of individuals as "global citizens." In this sense the sangha is a model for all of society. Each member should treasure and balance society in addition to seeking economic growth for the sake of growth. The sangha model results in an emphasis on general welfare through focus on each individual's compassion toward others.

Such a general concern for all members of society has led certain Buddhist groups to focus on world peace. SOKA GAKKAI INTERNATIONAL, itself a thoroughly globalized Buddhist movement, cautions that the benefits of globalization should not divert attention from such horrors as war. Soka Gakkai in 1993 founded the Boston Research Centers for the 21st Century to foster peace.

Not all Buddhist groups focus on peace movements. In fact many traditional teachings focus on self-cultivation and do not comment on geopolitical issues. However, leading contemporary spokespersons for modern Buddhism, such figures as the DALAI LAMA and THICH NHAT HANH, consistently support the ideal of peace.

A fifth response of Buddhism to globalization has been ecumenical. Globalization has reconfigured the way Buddhists see themselves, resulting in a pan-Buddhist movement in which Buddhists of many types meet and discuss issues felt to be common to all Buddhists. The World Fellowship of Buddhists, founded in Sri Lanka in 1950, reflects a revised sense of what it means to be a Buddhist in the modern world. An international Buddhist university focused on countering some of the effects of globalization was established in Bangkok in 2000. The new school, called the WORLD BUDDHIST UNIVERSITY, was sponsored by the WORLD FELLOWSHIP OF BUDDHISTS.

Further reading: Nolan Pliny Jacobson, *Buddhism and the Contemporary World: Change and Self-Correction* (Carbondale: Southern Illinois University Press, 1983); ———, *The Heart of Buddhist Philosophy* (Carbondale: Southern Illinois University Press, 1988); Peter Kakol, "A Socially Engaged Process Buddhism," *Journal of Buddhist Ethics* 7 (2000); Helena Norberg-Hodge, "Buddhism in the Global Economy: Economic Globalization Endangers Democracy, Community, Cultural Diversity and Spirituality." Resurgence. Available online. URL: http://www.resurgence.org/resurgence/articles/norberg_hodge_buddi.htm. Accessed on August 2, 2005; Ira Rifkin, *Spiritual Perspectives on Globalization: Making Sense of Economics and Cultural Upheaval* (Woodstock, Vt.: Skylight Paths, 2003); Robert Thurman, *Inner Revolution: Life, Liberty, and the Pursuit of Real Happiness* (New York: Riverhead Books, 1998); Lance Woodruff, "Buddhists Open Worldwide 'University without Walls' in Thailand." *Worldwide Faith News*, (11 December 2000). Available online. URL: http://www.wfn.org/2000/12/msg00077.html. Accessed on August 6, 2005.

Goddard, Dwight (1861–1939)
early proponent of Buddhism in North America
Dwight Goddard, a former Christian missionary in Fujian, southern China, founded the Fellowship Following Buddha, an early Buddhist monastery in the United States.

Goddard was born in Worcester, Massachusetts. After working for 10 years as a mechanical engineer, he entered Hartford Theological Seminary with the goal of becoming a Baptist missionary. He left for China in 1894.

Goddard worked for 20 years as a missionary but slowly began to believe that he should be looking toward a syncretism of Christianity and Buddhism. In 1924, he proposed the formation of a Christian/Buddhist Fellowship. In 1927 he published a brief work, *Was Jesus Influenced by Buddhism?* In the meantime, having concluded that it was closest to the teachings of the BUDDHA, he had begun to study ZEN BUDDHISM at Shokoku-ji, a RINZAI ZEN temple in Kyoto, Japan.

By the early 1930s he had created a vision of an American Buddhist organization, the Fellowship Following Buddha. He hoped to have two centers, one in Vermont and one in California, and in 1934 he settled in Union Village, Vermont, as a first step. He also founded a magazine, *Zen*. Though a few people adhered to the fellowship, it never developed as Goddard had hoped.

In 1938 Goddard published the volume that proved his major contribution to the emergent Buddhist community, *A Buddhist Bible*, an anthology of key Buddhist writings. He died in 1939.

Further reading: Rick Fields, *How the Swans Came to the Lake: A Narrative History of Buddhism in America* (Boston: Shambhala, 1992); Dwight Goddard, *Buddha Truth and Brotherhood: An Epitome of Many Buddhist Scriptures Translated from the Japanese* (Santa Barbara, Calif.: author, 1934); ———, *The Buddha's Golden Path* (London: Luzac, 1930); ———, ed., *A Buddhist Bible*. Rev. ed. (Thetford, Vt.: author, 1938 and London: George Harrap, 1956); ———, *Followers of Buddha: An American Brotherhood* (Santa Barbara, Calif.: author, 1934).

Goenka, Satya Narayan (1924–)
Burmese vipassana teacher
The THERAVADA Buddhist leader Satya Narayan Goenka established the VIPASSANA INTERNATIONAL ACADEMY in 1976. Goenka is an unusual Buddhist leader in that he is not a monk and has a business

background. Goenka was born and raised in Burma (Myanmar). While still a young man he met the Burmese meditation master U BA KHIN (1899–1971). He initially studied meditation in order to cure his migraine headaches. However, after 14 years with Ba Khin, he had become an accomplished practitioner. Goenka later moved to India and in 1969 began teaching vipassana. He has increasingly devoted his time to teaching and establishing Vipassana training centers, in the United States, Japan, Europe, and other areas.

Further reading: S. N. Goenka, *The Discourse Summaries* (Seattle: Pariyatti, 2000); ———, *The Gracious Flow of Dharma* (Igatpuri: Vipassana Research Institute, 1994); William Hart, *Vipassana Meditation: As Taught by S. N. Goenka* (San Francisco: HarperSanFrancisco, 1987).

Gohonzon

Gohonzon, the Great Object of Devotion, was created by the Japanese prophet NICHIREN (1222–82) as an expression of his devotion to the LOTUS SUTRA as the preeminent written text of Buddhism. The Gohonzon is a large MANDALA originally inscribed by Nichiren, before which believers repeat the mantra *namu myoho renge-kyo,* that is, "devotion to the marvelous Dharma of the Lotus Flower teachings." Nichiren believed that in this time of MAPPO, in which the Buddha's teachings are degraded, the correct object of devotion for people is the title (*diamoku*) of the Lotus Sutra, and that title, *namu myoho renge-kyo,* is the essence of the sutra.

The text of the Gohonzon is centered on the words *namu myoho renge-kyo,* which are written vertically in the middle of the mandala. On the four sides are written the names of the four main points of the compass. To the right and left are the names of Sakyamuni BUDDHA and another Buddha named Taho (Prabhutaratna, or Many treasures), who is mentioned in the 21st chapter of the Lotus Sutra. Flanking the two Buddhas are four leading BODHISATTVAS, whose names in English mean "Superior Practices," "Boundless Practices," "Pure Practices," and "Firmly Established Practices." The rest of the Gohonzon carries the names of many other bodhisattvas and lesser spiritual beings representing the various cosmic realms. Toward the bottom are the names of Tien Tai and Dengyo, honored teachers who transmitted the true lineage of Buddhism. Nichiren also left a declaration, "This is the great mandala never before known in the entire land of Jambudvipa [Indian subcontinent] in the more than 2,230 years since the Buddha's passing."

Copies of the Gohonzon dominate Nichiren temples, and individual members often have a smaller version on an altar in their homes. The Gohonzon is used by all Nichiren-shu sects including the NICHIREN SHOSHU and its former lay affiliate group the SOKA GAKKAI INTERNATIONAL, and by various new groups such as RISSHO KOSEI-KAI and REIYUKAI.

Soka Gakkai International, the largest Nichiren Buddhist organization in the world, had operated as the lay arm of Nichiren Shoshu since its founding. Members had looked to priests of Nichiren Shoshu to issue their own authorized reproduction of the Gohonzon. In 1993, after the break between the Soka Gakkai and Nichiren Shoshu, Soka Gakkai International began to issue reproductions of its own.

Further reading: Gosho Translation Committee, eds. *The Writings of Nichiren Daishonin* (Tokyo: Soka Gakkai, 1999); Nikkyo Niwano, *Honzon: The Object of Worship of Rissho Kosei-Kai* (Tokyo: Hinode Printing Company, 1969); E. Dale Saunders, *Buddhism in Japan* (Philadelphia: University of Pennsylvania Press, 1964).

Goma Fire Rite

This purification ritual dating from Vedic times (c. 1500 B.C.E.) in India was introduced to Japan by the early Buddhist masters SAICHO and KUKAI. To this foundation were added elements of the mystical practices of *yamabushi* (mountain ascetics) in medieval Japan.

In theory, the Goma Fire Rite can be performed anywhere. The first step is to transform a place into a sacred spot with an altar and a pile of wood. In some interpretations 108 pieces of wood are burned, symbolizing the 108 human sins. The fire burns off the human passions, the KLESAS (defilements).

The Goma Fire Rite is performed in six stages: a fire offering to Agni, the Vedic god of fire; a fire offering to Buddha-Locana, one form of the Buddha; a fire offering to the Usnisa Buddha in the Golden Moon (Ichiji Kinrin), envisioned as the 11-headed Kannon (GUAN YIN) with 42 arms; a fire offering to Acala Buddha (who eliminates that which is against Buddhist teachings) and VAIRO-CANA (the supreme Buddha in the universe), both of whom symbolize the supplicant's good and bad deeds; a fire offering to the Buddha, Lotus, and Vajra (diamond) worlds; and a fire offering to the spirits of Vedic, Daoist, and SHINTO deities. Finally, after the flames are extinguished, the monks involved meditate. During each stage the monks throw three sets of various offerings into the flames. Each offering and action has symbolic meaning, and each stage is envisioned as part of a MANTRA or MANDALA (a patterned cosmic chart with a Buddha at the center).

Today both SHINGON and TENDAI schools of Japanese Buddhism perform the ritual. The two versions share the same MUDRA hand symbols, the same Sanskrit mantras (magical chants), and the same mandalas. However they support different philosophical interpretations, with the Tendai version tending toward a MADHYAMIKA (rationalist) interpretation and the Shingon a YOGACARA (idealistic) interpretation.

A large Goma Fire Rite is performed annually in Kyoto by AGON SHU Buddhists.

Further reading: Richard Karl Payne, *The Tantric Ritual of Japan: Feeding the Gods—the Shingon Fire Ritual* (Delhi: Aditya Prakashan, 1991); Michael Saso, *Homa Rites and Mandala Meditation in Tendai Buddhism* (Delhi: Pradeep Kumar Goel, 1991).

gong an *See* KOAN.

Govinda, Lama Anagarika (1898–1985)
early Western Buddhist

Anagarika Govinda is the religious name of Ernest Lothar Hoffmann, an early 20th-century Western adherent of and writer about Buddhism. He was born in Waldheim, Germany. He served in World War I and subsequently attended the University of Freiburg. In 1918 he moved to Sri Lanka. The following year he was ordained as a Buddhist monk and received the title Anagarika in Burma (Myanmar). Over the next years he continued his studies in Buddhism and Pali. Then, in 1931, he encountered Tibetan Buddhism for the first time.

As a result of his discovery of Tibetan Buddhism, Hoffman traveled to Darjeeling, where he met Tomo Geshe Rinpoche, who became his primary teacher. He would remain in the Himalayan region through the World War II era (during which he was interned). When his guru died, he founded Arya Maitreya Mandala as an organization to spread Tibetan Buddhism in the West. In 1947 he became a citizen of India. He eventually settled at the Kasar Devi Ashram in northern India.

In 1952 he ordained Hans Ulrich Rieker and sent him to Germany to found the first Western chapter of the Arya Maitreya Mandala. It opened in 1953. The organization spread through Europe and soon developed an Eastern European headquarters in Budapest, Hungary.

During the postwar years, he began to write, and several of his books became classic presentations of Tibetan Buddhism, especially *Foundations of Tibetan Mysticism* (1959) and *Way of the White Clouds* (1966). In the 1960s and 1970s he traveled widely in the West to lecture on Buddhism, and a U.S. chapter of the Arya Maitreya Mandala appeared.

In 1980, he traveled to the United States for medical treatment. His health did not allow his return to India, and he settled in Mill Valley, California, where he lived out the rest of his life.

Further reading: Lama Anagarika Govinda, *Foundations of Tibetan Mysticism* (London: Rider, 1959); ———, *The Inner Structure of the I-Ching: The Book of Transformations* (Tokyo: Wheelwright Press and John Weatherhill, 1981); ———, *Way of the White Clouds: A Buddhist Pilgrim in Tibet* (London: Hutchinson, 1966); Kosho Yamamoto, *Buddhism in Europe* (Ube City, Japan: Karinbunko, 1967).

Grimm, George (1868–1945) *pioneer of Buddhism in Germany*

George Grimm was one of the leading Buddhist figures in Germany in the first half of the 20th century. Grimm grew up in Germany at a time when Western intellectuals were first becoming aware of Buddhism and basic texts were becoming available in European languages. He started on a career in theology but, after completing his studies, switched to law. He became a judge in Bavaria and had a distinguished life of public service.

He seems to have been introduced to Buddhism through reading the works of the philosopher Schopenhauer (1788–1860). He then developed long-term relationships with the Indologist K. E. Neumann (1865–1915), who made many of the original translations from the Pali canon into German, and the philosopher Paul Deussen (1845–1919), who introduced Germans to Indian philosophy.

Grimm began his own study of Sanskrit and Pali in 1908. The first result of his study was his most famous book, *Die Lehre des Buddha* (translated into English in 1926 as *The Doctrines of the Buddha*).

By 1920 he had retired. He spent the rest of his life in quiet seclusion, his primary activity being the writing of additional books. He did, however, in cooperation with the Indologist Karl Seiden-stucker (1876–1936) found the Altbuddhistische Gemeinde (Old Buddhist Community) in 1921. This group survived until closed by Nazi authorities in 1933.

Further reading: George Grimm, *Buddhist Wisdom: The Mystery of the Self.* Translated by Carroll Aikins. (Delhi: Motilal Barnasidass, Delhi, 1982); ———, *The Doctrine of the Buddha: The Religion of Reason and Meditation* (Delhi: Motilal Barnasidass, 1982); ———, *Perennial Questions* (Delhi: Motilal Barnasidass, 1979).

Guan Gong (Guang Ti, Kwan Kong)

Guan Gong, or "Duke Guan," the god of war, is one of the most popular gods in popular Chinese religion. Guan Gong is depicted in a general's clothing, usually carrying a halberd, with a furious scowl on his face. The scowling face is often painted red.

Guan Gong is an example of a deity based on a historical figure, Guan Yu (162–219 C.E.). Guan Yu is a well-known figure from the *Sanguo yanyi* (Romance of the three kingdoms), a 15th-century novel written by Luo Guanzhong and edited in the 17th century by Mao Lun and Mao Zhonggang. The novel was in turn based on the *Sanguo zhi* (Records of the three kingdoms), a work by Chen Shou describing political events in the immediate post-Han period (220–280 C.E.).

Guan Yu was a confidant of Liu Bei, ruler of Shu. Both Guan Yu and Zhang Fei (167–221 C.E.) had sworn loyalty to Liu Bei (161–223 C.E.), and both are today symbols of absolute loyalty. Chen Shou, author of the *Sanguo zhi*, classed Guan Yu as one of the powerful five tiger generals; his courage was widely known. At the same time, he also criticized Guan Yu for being overly stubborn and proud.

Guan Yu was not worshipped as a god until the seventh century, when his image took on both Daoist and Buddhist qualities. As a Daoist deity he was known as the protector of officials.

Temple to the popular Chinese deity Guan Gong, Taipei, Taiwan *(Institute for the Study of American Religion, Santa Barbara, California)*

As a Buddhist figure Guan Gong was treated as a bodhisattva and protector of Buddhist temples. In the popular imagination he was also known as the "Ruler Who Banishes Demons." He was portrayed in painting and sculpture in two major poses: either in military garb, holding his halberd, often standing next to his horse, or sitting in official clothes, holding a Confucian classic, the *Spring and Autumn Annals (Qunqiu)*.

Guan Gong's popularity increased with time. He was given numerous titles by successive emperors, culminating in his promotion to "Military Emperor" during the 19th century. He was officially worshipped twice a year by state officials,

and numerous temples dedicated to him were built throughout the empire. After the fall of the Chinese Qing dynasty in 1911 he became solely a figure in popular religion. Along with JI GONG he was a popular subject of *FUJI*, revealed texts. He is known as the god of war. Also, perhaps curiously, he has become associated with success in one's studies and is today often worshipped by families of students.

Further reading: Prasenjit Duara, *Culture, Power, and the State: Rural North China, 1900–1942* (Stanford, Calif.: Stanford University Press, 1988); Jonathan Wu, "Guan Yu (Yunchang)," Kongming's Archives. Available online. URL: http://www.kongming.net/novel/kma/guanyu.php. Accessed on January 25, 2006.

Guan Yin (Kuan Yin, J. Kannon; Chenresi in Tibetan, Kuan-em in Korean)

The goddess of compassion in Mahayana Buddhism, and arguably the most widely worshipped Buddhist deity figure, strictly speaking, Guan Yin is a BODHISATTVA, an enlightened being who, moved by KARUNA (compassion) for the suffering of living beings, has taken a vow not to proceed to NIRVANA until others are enlightened.

Guan Yin sculptures and paintings often show the goddess with a vase (filled with the holy dew of compassion), a prayer book, a willow branch used to sprinkle holy nectar, a dove, and a rosary.

Guan Yin, or Guan Shi Yin, literally "he who hears the calls of the world," was originally an Indian figure known as AVALOKITESVARA. This deity figures prominently in the Lotus Sutra, where in chapter 25 he is depicted as one who will respond to any person calling out his name:

> If any, carried away by a flood, call upon his name, they will immediately reach the shallows. . . . Or if anyone cries who is in deadly peril by the sword, the sword will be snapped asunder. If wicked demons attack, the one who cries will become invisible to them. . . . If a woman desires a son, worships and pays homage, she will bear a son, virtuous and wise; or if a daughter, then of good demeanor and looks.

This passage reflects that Avalokitesvara was ever-ready to help those in need. In performing acts of assistance the deity would frequently transform his image. The passage also shows that Avalokitesvara was originally a male figure. Over the centuries, and certainly by the 700s, the bodhisattva's figure was depicted as female. This transformation probably resulted from a merging of worship traditions with existing practices of veneration of feminine deities. Feminine deities were prominent in early Chinese religions, a period best described as shamanistic. With the dominance of the Confucian worldview, the goddess aspects were gradually suppressed in Chinese culture. Alternative images such as the Queen Mother of the West (Xiwang Mu) reemerged during the Han period (226 B.C.E.–220 C.E.). Buddhism may have appropriated such feministic leanings in order to maintain popularity within the culture at large.

Guan Yin was in one version created as an emanation of light from the Buddha AMITABHA, the Buddha of the Western Lands. Guan Yin is depicted as a small figure on Amitabha's forehead

Large painted Guan Yin figure at the True Buddhist School main temple in Taiwan *(Institute for the Study of American Religion, Santa Barbara, California)*

or headpiece. Guan Yin was also later associated with the legend of Miao Shan, a princess said to have lived around 700 B.C.E.

Guan Yin worship spread quickly throughout China in the Tang and Song dynasties, and it later entered Korea and Japan. In each area the broad stream of Guan Yin worship absorbed local legends and stories. In China a widely accepted account states that Guan Yin resides on Mt. PUTUO (Putuo Shan), a small mountain island near Ningbo on China's eastern coast. This island later became identified with Potalaka, the magical island mentioned in the *Hua Yan Jing* (Flower Ornament Sutra). As Guan Yin's place of residence, Putuo Shan is one of the four sacred mountains of Chinese Buddhism.

Further reading: John Blofeld, *Bodhisattva of Compassion: The Mystical Tradition of Kuan Yin* (Boulder, Colo.: Shambhala, 1978); Sandy Boucher, *Discovering Kwan Yin, Buddhist Goddess of Compassion* (Boston: Beacon Press, 1999); Glen Dudbridge, *The Legend of Miao-shan* (London: Ithaca Press, 1978); Martin Palmer and Jay Ramsay with Man-Ho Kwok, *Kuan Yin: Myths and Revelations of the Chinese Goddess of Compassion* (London: Thorsons, 1995); Chun-fang Yu, *Kuan-yin: The Chinese Transformation of Avalokitesvara* (New York: Columbia University Press, 2001).

gurudharma

The *gurudharma* are the eight special rules imposed on women by the BUDDHA, which have served to ensure the subordinate status of women within the sangha (monastic community) and have greatly influenced the role of women throughout Buddhism. The sangha was established by the Buddha very early in the movement. The opening of the sangha to females was in part due to the entreaties of the Buddha's foster mother, MAHAPRAJAPATI GOTAMI, who over the course of five years persuaded the Buddha to allow their entry. The rules reflect the dominant gender relationships of the time and the opinion prevalent in male-dominated societies

that women are the major cause of men's violating sexual mores.

The eight rules are summarized as follows:

1. A BHIKSUNI (nun) must always give precedence to a BHIKSU (monk), regardless of their relative seniority; she must always offer him a place to sit.
2. *Bhiksunis* may not observe the annual retreat (*vassa*) in a district where there are no *bhiksus*.
3. *Bhiksus* will be asked to establish the dates for *bhiksuni* Uposatha (full moon and new moon) ceremonies of renewal.
4. Every two weeks the *bhiksuni* sangha must send a representative to ask the sangha of *bhiksus* for "instructions." Such "instructions" generally entail a reiteration of the *gurudharma's* eight rules.
5. Certain judicial processes in the case of *bhiksunis* must be undertaken by both sanghas; those for *bhiksus* need only take place before the *bhiksu* sangha.
6. The Upasampada (full ordination) ceremony for *bhiksunis* should take place before the *bhiksu* sangha as well the *bhiksuni* sangha.
7. A *bhiksuni* should never abuse or revile a *bhiksu*.
8. *Bhiskus* can officially admonish *bhiksunis*, but not vice versa.

These rules, which clearly placed the community of nuns in a subordinate position to the community of monks, were later incorporated in the *bhiksuni* VINAYA *pitaka*. However, the order of *bhiksunis* was allowed to become moribund. The modern revival of that order, combined with the general critique of traditional gender subordination of females, has led to widespread discussion of the *guarudhamma*, with several female Buddhist spokespersons questioning its relevance to the modern age.

Further reading: Swarna de Silva, "The Place of Women in Buddhism." Enabling Support Foundation.

Available online. URL: http://www.enabling.org/ia/vipassana/Archive/D/DeSilva/WomenInBuddhism/womenInBuddhi smSwarnaDeSilva.html. Accessed on January 15, 2006; Ven. Professor Dhammavihari, "Women and the Religious Order of the Buddha." Buddhism Today. Available online. URL: http://www.buddhismtoday.com/english/sociology/021-religiousorder.htm. Accessed on January 14, 2005; I. B. Horner, *Women under Primitive Buddhism* (New York: E. P. Dutton, 1930); Mohan Wijayaratna, *Buddhist Monastic Life: According to the Texts of the Theravaada Tradition.* Translated by Claude Grangier and Steven Collins (Cambridge: Cambridge University Press, 1990); Ann Heirmann, *"The Discipline in Four Parts": Rules for Nuns according to the Dharmaguptaka-vinaya* (Delhi: Motilal Banarsidass, 2002).

Gyoki (Gyogi) (668–749 C.E.) *prominent Hosso monk in Japan*

Gyoki was a monk at the Yakushi-ji temple in NARA, where he studied the teachings of the HOSSO school. He propagated Buddhist doctrines widely and assisted the emperor Shomu's efforts to build a huge VAIROCANA Buddha figure. Because of these efforts he was made chief administrator of all priests in 745 C.E.

For more than a thousand years, the Japanese Buddhist priest Gyoki has been well known for his seventh-century charitable religious activities. His biographies and hagiographies tell that not long after the "official introduction" of Buddhism into Japan, Gyoki roamed the countryside propagating the teachings together with farming techniques to oppressed people hungry for both. His activities, in defiance of secular law, were carried out in a time when the government maintained strict control of Buddhists by confining them to temple grounds for academic study. With supporters outside the capital swelling to thousands, an imperial edict was issued against his actions, and Gyoki was arrested. This attempt to quell the growth of Gyoki's hero status backfired, however, and popular support for him increased. As a result the government reversed its stance toward Gyoki, and he was awarded the rank of high priest (*daisojo*). Meanwhile, among the masses he became known as the BODHISATTVA Gyoki (Gyoki Bosatsu). Subsequently, he became the first person in Japan to be awarded the title Bodhisattva by the government as an official rank.

In 744 Gyoki built a temple at Nannou, called the Temple of Bodhisattva of Mt. Garyu. It burned in 1336, a victim of war. When rebuilt in 1700, it was renamed Gyoki's Temple. The gate was constructed in 1820 and the main temple rebuilt separately in 1832.

Further reading: Jonathan Morris Augustine, *Buddhist Hagiography in Early Japan; Images of Compassion in the Gyoki Tradition* (London: Routledge/Curzon, 2005); Ronald S. Green, "Gyoki, Bodhisattva of Japan (668–749): A Biography of the Life and Legacy of the Bodhisattva Gyoki." Ronny Green. Available online. URL: http://www.ronnygreen.us/gyoki.htm. Accessed on January 14, 2006.

H

Hachiman (Yawata)

As Buddhism began to grow in Japan, it met opposition from the older Shinto faith. Among its many strategies to accommodate itself to its new home was the incorporation of Shinto deities into the Buddhist worldview. One popular example of such integration is the god Hachiman, a deity who had hegemony over, among other realms, agriculture and blacksmithing. Hachiman was originally identified as the continuing spirit of the early Japanese emperor Ojin (fifth century?). He also has an alternative name, Yawata, "god of eight banderoles [ornamental banners]" He is frequently symbolized by the dove.

Hachiman seems to have entered the Buddhist world in the eighth century at the time the large bronze statue of VAIROCANA Buddha was being forged for the TODAI-JI Shrine in Nara. During the casting of the statue, Hachiman was invoked as the god of blacksmiths. He was subsequently worked into the Buddhist pantheon as a BODHISATTVA. The process culminated in 781, when the Heian emperor gave him the title *Daibosatsu,* or Great Bodhisattva. He would later become closely associated with the Minamoto clan, which rose to power in 1185. Minamoto no Yoritomo, the first shogun at KAMAKURA, believed that Hachiman was a manifestation of AMITABHA Buddha and built a shrine to him in the new capital city.

NICHIREN (1222–82), who settled in Kamakura as a young priest, saw Hachiman as a manifestation not of Amitabha Buddha but of the Eternal Sakyamuni BUDDHA. He also considered Hachiman in terms of his traditional role of generating agricultural fertility. As such, Hachiman is one of the deities mentioned on the GOHONZON, the great object of worship for Nichiren Buddhism.

Today, the main Hachiman shrine is the Usa Shrine in Oita, though it is closely followed in importance by the Iwashimizu Hachiman Shrine on Mt. Otoko southwest of Kyoto, which dates to 859, and the Tsurugaoka Hachiman Shrine in Kamakura, both attached to the Minamoto clan. An ancient Hachiman figure is housed in the Hachimangu Shrine, built near the Todai-ji Temple in Kyoto. Through the years, Hachiman became a favorite deity of the warrior class (hence one of his titles as the "Shinto god of war"). Worship of Hachiman then filtered down to the peasants. He subsequently became one of the most honored of KAMIs by Shintoists as well as one of the most acknowledged bodhisattvas by Japanese Buddhists. Tens of thousands of small shrines dedicated to him now exist across the country. The Hachiman shrines are a vivid example of the japanization of Buddhism through syncretism with Shintoism.

Further reading: Christine Guth Kanda, *Shinzo: Hachiman Imagery and Its Development* (Cambridge, Mass.: Harvard University Press, 1985); Donald A. Mackenzie, *China and Japan Myths and Legends* (London: Bracken Books, 1986); Ryuei Michael McCormick, "Kami: The Shinto Deities." LotusSutra.net. Available online. URL: http://nichirenscoffeehouse.net/ShuteiMandala/kami.html. Accessed on October 9, 2005; Virtual Museum of Japanese Arts. "Hachiman." Available online. URL: http://web-japan.org/museum/shinto/shinto01/shinto01.html. Accessed on October 9, 2005; Onmark-Productions.com. "Hachiman." Available online. URL: http://www.onmarkproductions.com/html/tsurugaoka-hachiman.shtml. Accessed on October 9, 2005.

Hanmi school   *See* CHINESE ESOTERIC BUDDHISM.

Han Yu (768–812) *archconservative writer in Tang dynasty China*

Although the Tang dynasty (618–906) is known mainly for its cosmopolitan atmosphere, heavily Buddhist-flavored CONFUCIANISM (*rujia*) remained an abiding presence. Perhaps the greatest proponent of Confucian thought in the Tang was Han Yu. Distinctly conservative in his social and cultural views, Han Yu saw his mission as restoring China to its earlier Confucian social and political order. His most famous work, *Yuandao* (Essentials of the moral way), argues against Daoist and Buddhist teachings on economic, social, and moral grounds.

Han Yu was a great essayist who reaffirmed the CONFUCIAN CLASSICS (*jing*) as central to the Chinese heritage and patterned his own style of writing on them. He had a profound dislike for Buddhism (except for its focus on ethics). His famous "Memorial on the Bone of Buddha," occasioned by Emperor Xianzong's (r. 806–820) support of a large-scale public ceremony venerating a Buddhist relic, is a classic example of a Confucian reproach to a ruler who strays from the true Way. Instead, Han Yu advocated a return to the "Way of the sages," all the way back to MENCIUS. According to his reckoning, the orthodox transmission of the Way (*daotong*) had been cut off since the Han and needed to be recovered. For Han Yu, this Confucian tradition was the true source of Chinese civilization. Over time, however, Buddhism and Daoism gradually led Chinese culture astray. As part of his program of cultural recovery, Han Yu recommended forcing Buddhist and Daoist clergy back to lay life, confiscating their temples, and burning their books.

Although Han Yu and his fellow Confucians had no direct hand in it, the sentiments he expressed eventually led to the suppression of Buddhism and other "foreign *daos*" under the Emperor Wuzong (r. 841–846). His staunch advocacy of Confucianism and his prose style were major factors in the Confucian resurgence in the Song dynasty (960–1279).

Further reading: W. Theodore de Bary and Irene Bloom, eds., *Sources of Chinese Tradition.* Vol. 1, *From Earliest Times to 1600.* 2d ed. (New York: Columbia University Press, 1999), 568–585.

Hariti (*guizimu, jiuzimu,* Kariteimo)

Hariti was a minor Hindu folk deity famous for eating human children. She was eventually converted by the Buddha and afterward became a protector of children. She is first recorded in the Hariti Sutra, a short work translated into Chinese in the third century C.E. This sutra describes how the Buddha arranged for her 1,000 children to be kidnapped and held in a monastery. He only released them after Hariti recognized her evil deeds. After this incident she became especially associated with helping childless couples.

Hariti was particularly popular in the northern India/Central Asian area of Gandhara. She is depicted in sculpture of that area as relatively plump, half-naked, and surrounded by children. She is later often depicted in paintings and sculpture, always surrounded by children or nursing a baby. In China she took on another name, *jiuzimu,* "mother of nine children." This image of succoring children eventually merged with that of Xiwangmu, the Mother of the West. In Japan she is known as Kariteimo and is venerated as a protector of many family activities. Because she appears in the LOTUS SUTRA, she is very popular among NICHIREN Buddhists.

Hariti is also often depicted in violent encounter with the Buddha. Scrolls depicting this event are often called "raising the alms bowl" because one text, the *Samyuktaratna-pitaka,* states that the Buddha hid her favorite child under his alms bowl. These paintings depict a grand battle between demons and the Buddha.

Further reading: Buno Kato, Yoshiro Tamura, and Kojiro Miyasaka, trans., *The Threefold Lotus Sutra* (New York: Weatherhill, 1975); Geoffrey Samuel and Santi Rozario, eds., *Daughters of Hariti: Childbirth and Female Healers in South and Southeast Asia* (London: Routledge, 2003).

Healing Tao

The Healing Tao, founded by Mantak Chia (1944–), is among the best known of the popular Daoist groups in the West. It is an organization that promotes, through books and seminars, a system of breathing, visualization, meditation, and postures that streamlines the Daoist practice of inner alchemy (*neidan*). In Chinese Daoism, inner alchemy's ultimate goal was the attainment of immortality through the transformation of energy within the body, but many adherents follow the Healing Tao teachings for increased health, vitality, and spiritual contentment. These exercises have all been described in Chia's books, but the program emphasizes personal instruction. The full Mantak Chia program consists of 15 courses, the first nine introductory, the next three intermediate, and the final three advanced courses concerned with spiritual immortality.

Mantak Chia is an ethnic Chinese born in Thailand. Chia is said to have begun self-cultivation at the very young age of six with Buddhist meditation training, MARTIAL ARTS, Tai Chi, and Kundalini yoga. He also has some training and interest in Western medicine. Of his many teachers, his most influential was a Daoist hermit living in a mountain cabin in the Hong Kong New Territories. This teacher, called One Cloud, gave him transmission and a mandate to teach and heal using inner alchemy.

In 1979, Chia moved to New York and opened the Healing Tao Center, attracting Euro-American students, who helped him organize a national seminar circuit. Around the same time as Kundalini and Tantra were becoming popularized in the West, Chia's books about "Daoist sexual practice" circulated and his Healing Tao grew to one of the largest Western Daoist groups, today comprising over 1,000 certified instructors in many countries, who can be found by location or qualification at a central Web site.

In 1994, Chia moved back to Thailand to establish Tao Garden, an international Healing Tao Center in Chiang Mai, where Europeans and Americans train to be Healing Tao instructors. Tao Garden also functions as an alternative therapy spa. Chia's former student Michael Winn now leads Healing Tao USA and leads an annual retreat at Tao Mountain in the Catskill Mountains in New York State. Winn also leads three-week guided tours of sacred sites of China.

Further reading: Mantak Chia, *Awaken Healing Energy through the Tao* (New York: Aurora Press, 1983); ———, *Taoist Ways to Transform Stress into Vitality: The Inner Smile/Six Healing Sounds* (New York: Aurora Press, 1985); ———, with Michael Winn. *Taoist Secrets of Love: Cultivating Male Sexual Energy* (New York: Aurora Press, 1984).

Hearn, Lafcadio (1850-1904) *influential translator of Japanese culture and Buddhism*

Lafcadio Hearn was the first great sympathetic interpreter of Japan to the English-speaking world. Hearn was born on the Greek island of Lefkas but raised in Ireland by a great-aunt after his parents' divorce when he was still a small child. When he was 19 he moved to Cincinnati, Ohio, where he eventually found work as a newspaper reporter. He moved on to New Orleans in 1877 and emerged as an accomplished writer.

In 1889 he moved to Japan, where he found a job teaching school in Matsue. He fell in love with the country, became a Japanese citizen (1895), and assumed a Japanese name, Yakumo Koizumi. At Matsue, he also found a wife, the daughter of a samurai.

He completed his first book on Japan in 1894, *Glimpses of Unfamiliar Japan,* a collection of short works about his adopted country. He would thereafter write almost a book a year exploring different aspects of life in Japan; the first one on Buddhism appeared in 1897 as *Gleanings in Buddha-Fields: Studies of Hand and Soul in the Far East.* Hearn was much admired for his mastery of the English language and his ability to use the language to invite readers into the sometimes exotic environment surrounding his subject.

In 1894, he also secured a job writing for the English-language Kobe newspaper, the *Chronicle.* The work on the *Chronicle* helped him secure a position teaching English literature at the Imperial University in Tokyo, where he taught for seven years. He died in 1904.

Further reading: Carl Dawson, *Lafcadio Hearn and the Vision of Japan* (Baltimore, Md.: Johns Hopkins University Press, 1992); Lafcadio Hearn, *Gleanings in Buddha-Fields: Studies of Hand and Soul in the Far East* (Boston: Houghton, Mifflin, 1897); ———, *Glimpses of Unfamiliar Japan* (Boston: Houghton Mifflin, 1894); ———, *Karma* (New York: Boni and Liveright, 1918); Shoko Watanabe, "Hearn's View of Japanese Buddhism," *Today's Japan* 4, no. 1 (January 1959).

Heart Sutra

The Heart Sutra is an early Mahayana text from the Greater Perfection of Wisdom (PRAJNAPARAMITA) family of texts that remains one of the most popular texts in East Asian Buddhism today. The Heart Sutra (Prajna-paramita-hrdya-sutra) is the shortest of the group. It can be interpreted as a brief compilation of *Prajnaparamita* (wisdom) thought, with a focus on the SUNYATA (emptiness) of all phenomena.

The Heart Sutra was originally translated into Chinese by KUMARAJIVA in the fourth century and later by Xuan Zang (602–664) in 649. Because of its relative brevity it is often found carved on fans and used as a subject for calligraphy. In Japan it became a favorite text for ZEN and SHINGON practitioners. A Sanskrit version handwritten on palm leaves, now kept in the National Museum, Tokyo, dates from 609 C.E.

Further reading: Geshe Kelsang Gyatso, *Heart of Wisdom: The Essential Wisdom Teachings of Buddha* (Cumbria, U.K.: Tharpa, 1996); Hsuan Hua, *The Heart of Prajna Paramita Sutra: With "Verses without a Stand" and Prose Commentary* (Talmage, Calif.: Dharma Realm Buddhist University, 2002); Donald Lopez, *Elaborations on Emptiness: Uses of the Heart Sutra,* (Princeton, N.J.: Princeton University Press, 1996).

hell

As nearly all religions have, Buddhism has a well-developed concept of hell. The Sanskrit term used to refer to hell is *naraka* or *niraya,* literally "devoid of happiness." Ideas of hell were developed over many centuries within Indian culture and thus show broad similarities to those from other Indian traditions such as Jainism and Hinduism. The oldest Buddhist texts such as *Verses on the Law* and the Group of Discourses (Sutta Nipata, third century B.C.E.) describe hell as simply the place where those who do evil are sent. The *Kokaliya-sutta* chapter in the Group of Discourses, an early Indian Buddhist text, describes a monk who visits hell and witnesses such punishments as trees with blades and balls of heated iron.

The Buddhist concept of hell was eventually further refined and systematized. It is found in its complete form in the ABHIDHARMA-KOSA, that great summary of early Buddhism. The *Abhidharma-kosa* describes many hells, starting with the eight hot hells. These are separated from the world of everyday reality, which is traditionally called Jambudvipa, by a layer of white clay. The eight hells are arranged from top to bottom in this order: Samjiva (reviving), Kalasutra (black string), Samghata (dashing together), Raurava (weeping), Maharaurava (great weeping), Tapana (heating), Pratapana (greatly heating), and Avici (no release).

Naturally, individuals receive different punishments in the various hells. In Samjiva they are killed with blades, revived by a wind, and killed again in a self-perpetuating cycle. In the lowest hell, Avici, individuals receive no respite at all: the torture is constant. In Kalasutra (black string) people lie on boards and are marked with black lines before being cut along the lines. In Samghata (dashing together) the inhabitants endure various forms of smashing and cutting. Raurava (weeping) and Maharaurava (great weeping) accurately describe the extent of the people's agony, while Tapana (heating) and Pratapana (greatly heating) indicate the extent of thermal discomfort.

Each hell has four doors, one in each direction, and each door leads to four subhells, called *utsadas*. Each of the four types of *utsada* contains a special horror. For instance, in the Kukula (heated by burning chaff) subhell, people are forced to walk over hot ashes. There are thus 16 subhells associated with each major hell, for a total of 128 subhells.

The list of hells is not yet complete without the cold hells. There are eight cold hells, arranged below the surface of the world parallel to the hot hells. Each of these produces a unique effect on the skin: In Arbuda (abscess) the skin erupts in frostbite. In Nirarbuda the skin cracks open. The names of the Atata, Hahava, and Huhuva hells refer to the quality of the sound of the cries of the sufferers. The final three, Utpala, Padma, and Mahapadma, refer to colors of three lotus types—blue, red, and deep red—indicating perhaps a strong association of those colors with fear and discomfort, perhaps as they relate to the skin.

Adding the 128 subhells to the eight hot hells and the eight cold hells, one arrives at 144 hells in the traditional Buddhist conception of the universe. There are in addition "minor" hells that are created for certain classes of people or even single people. This realm of suffering, developed in India but spread with Buddhism throughout Asia, was described with some care.

LATER MAHAYANA CONCEPTS OF HELL
The traditional images of hell expressed in the *Abhidharma-kosa* are still widespread in all Buddhist cultures, including the Mahayana areas of East Asia. However, there were significant additions. Most important, a king of hell, YAMA, was added. Originally a god living above Mt. SUMERU, Yama is a very ancient Indian deity, one of the twin progenitors of the human race. As the first man, Yama lived in a heavenly realm after dying.

Gradually Yama's heavenly realm was shifted to a subterranean place and became less than a paradise. This shift may have reflected the difference between funerary practices of cremation (associated with the Aryan culture of the Indian Rg Veda, an ancient religious text) and burial. Regardless, by the time Yama's realm was associated with the underworld it was a place of discomfort. In particular, hell was a place for hungry spirits, PRETA, including those who did not leave behind any descendents. In the Abhidharma-kosa, Yama was the deity who decided which individuals are thrown into hell. After the period of the Abhidharma-kosa, Yama was seen to reside in the lower hells himself, one of a staff of 10 warders. Yama was, in effect, the judge who oversaw who was sent to hell and how long they stayed. Thus the role of Yama in Mahayana ideas of hell reflects the idea of judgment of the deeds of the living.

The concept of the 10 kings, each presiding over a different stage of purgatory, probably developed in China. One early source to reflect this structure was *The Scripture on the Ten Kings,* a text collected before 908 C.E., during the Tang dynasty (618–906 C.E.) in China. In this text, Yama and nine other "kings" preside over their own jurisdictions and act as judges for the dead. Yama is here simply the fifth of the 10 kings, called in Chinese *Yanlo Wang.* The text describes how the Buddha explains that King Yama will eventually become fully enlightened as the bodhisattva SAMANTABHADRA. Below ground, King Yama and the other kings performed good deeds for the benefit of the suffering individuals; they acted out of compassion.

Individuals move through each department in a fixed cycle of days, spending seven days in each of the first seven departments, 100 days in the eighth, one year in the ninth, and three years in the realm of the 10th king. After this period the individual is assigned a new place within the SIX REALMS OF EXISTENCE. Thus the 10 kings ruled over a transitional space in the individual's journey from one existence to another. This medieval Chinese conception of purgatory was clearly correlated with ritual approaches to death.

In Mahayana Buddhism the 10 kings were also supplemented with the image of the bodhisattva KSHITIGARBHA. This figure became associated with hell and those suffering there. His bodhisattva vow in fact promised not to proceed to NIRVANA until all beings in hell had attained enlightenment. Kshitigarbha finally became the dominant deity figure in hell. Paintings often show the 10 kings arranged in a circle with the larger image of Kshitigarbha in the background.

Individual cultures took the idea of hell and purgatory in new directions. In Japan, for instance, the idea of a "riverbank of suffering" (Sai no kawara) developed. This probably had a real-world referent in a burial ground at the intersection of two rivers in Kyoto, a place referred to in sources from the ninth century C.E. The Sai no Kawara then became a kind of boundary point between the living and the dead. In Japanese Buddhist thought the Sai no Kawara was particularly a place of torture of children. They were forced to build stone mounds without ceasing, only to have them knocked down by the guards of hell. The cries of the children are said to disturb the parents who still reside in the world of the living. The parents then turn to the bodhisattva Kshitigarbha (in Japanese, JIZO), who visits the children and holds their hands. Kshitigarbha thus represents the face of compassion, an exalted being who softens the brutal impact of judgment.

Further reading: Akira Sakakata, *Buddhist Cosmology: Philosophy and Origins* (Tokyo: Kosei, 1999); Stephen F. Teiser, *The Scripture on the Ten Kings and the Making of Purgatory in Medieval Chinese Buddhism* (Honolulu: University of Hawaii Press, 1994).

Hesse, Hermann (1877–1962) *German novelist*

The works of Hermann Hesse, the Nobel Prize–winning author, enjoyed a new birth of life in the 1960s as a new generation of alienated youth discovered his writings. One novel in particular stood out, *Siddhartha*—originally published in 1922 and originally translated into English in 1951. This novel transcended his other writings as it became part of the emergence of Western Buddhism in the last half of the 20th century.

Hesse was born in Germany. He began to write in his teen years. His early novels were expressive of the young adult rejection of his upbringing, which he considered repressive in the extreme. After World War I, he gave up much of his youthful idealism, including his pacifism, and he also went through extensive Jungian psychoanalysis, a treatment that encouraged his own inner explorations.

Hesse visited India in 1911, the catalyst for his interest in Eastern religions. That interest culminated in the novel *Siddhartha* (1922). In the novel, the main character makes a pilgrimage of self-discovery. He is religious, but dissatisfied. He spends time with Hindu ascetics but is not helped. So, with a friend named Govinda, he goes in search of a teacher of whom they have heard. The teacher is Gautama BUDDHA, and once introduced, he is allowed to articulate the basic precepts of his enlightenment. Hesse emphasizes the Buddha's humanity. He is a man who has found a way. While Govinda decides to stay with the Buddha, Siddhartha chooses to become his own pupil and to learn the truth of himself. He thus takes a very Buddhist approach to the search for reality by individual internal self-reflection.

Hesse continued to write novels into the war years but for the last two decades of his life concentrated on essays, poems, and letters. He won the Nobel Prize in 1946 and died in 1962.

Further reading: Mark Boulby, *Hermann Hesse: His Mind and Art* (Ithaca, N.Y.: Cornell University Press, 1967); Ralph Freedman, *Hermann Hesse: Pilgrim of Crisis, A Biography* (New York: Pantheon Books, 1978); Hermann Hesse, *Siddhartha* (New York: New Directions, 1951).

Hiei, Mt. (Heizan)

This mountain of 848 meters overlooks Japan's Kyoto basin. (In current parlance, Mt. Hiei also loosely refers to the chain of mountains from Kyoto in the south to Otsu in the north.) In 788 C.E., SAICHO built a small Buddhist temple there. This was the beginning of the TENDAI presence in Japan. Until it was destroyed by Oda Nobunaga in 1571, the Tendai complex on Mt. Hiei, also known as ENRYAKU-JI, would dominate much of Japanese Buddhism.

Saicho almost certainly had no inkling that Hiei would become an influential political site. This occurred only when the capital was moved to Kyoto from Nara in 720. In fact Saicho desired to establish an ordination platform (*kaidan*) that would be separate from the Buddhist schools then dominant in Nara. The monastery's subsequent closeness to the court almost certainly played a role in many monks' gaining positions with the government. Among the most famous monks from Hiei are HONEN, NICHIREN, and KUKAI.

The Enryaku-ji complex at Mt. Hiei continues today as the main temple for Japanese TENDAI. Buildings there date from 1642, after the complex was rebuilt. At the center is the *honzon*, or "object of reverence," carried by SAICHO. This is housed in the Konponchudo, or Central Prayer Hall.

Further reading: Paul Groner, *Ryogen and Mount Hiei: Japanese Tendai in the Tenth Century* (Honolulu: University of Hawaii Press, 2002); ———, *Saicho: The Establishment of the Japanese Tendai School* (Honolulu: University of Hawaii Press, 2000); Richard Hines, "Mount Hiei and the Tendai School." Japanese Buddhism. Available online. URL: www.wsu.edu:8080/~dee/ANCJAPAN/HIEI.HTM. Entry updated June 6, 1999. Accessed on September 22, 2005.

Higashi Hongwanji

The Higashi (east) Hongwanji, part of the JODO SHINSHU movement, was one of the larger Japanese Buddhist groups during the early years of the TOKUGAWA SHOGUNATE. It had no real doctrinal differences with its sister group, the HONPA HONGWANJI; the split between the two groups was based rather on a single event.

The Jodo Shinshu movement was a Japanese PURE LAND BUDDHISM group that traces its origin to SHINRAN (1173–1262). Through the 1570s, the head of the Shin Buddhists, Kennyo (1542–92), who served as chief abbot of the movement's head temple, had conducted a war against Oda Nobunaga (1534–82), a warlord who wanted the temple for his own use. In 1580, the Japanese emperor interceded in the situation and ordered Kennyo to give up his temple. Kennyo, an officer of the court, obeyed and subsequently moved to Saginomori, near Wakayama.

The move to Saginomori caused a split in Kennyo's family. His older son, Kyonyo (1558–1614), who would normally inherit Kennyo's lineage, strongly opposed the action. Thus Kennyo passed his lineage to his second son, Junnyo (1577–1630). Kyonyo had enough support that he was able to organize his following separately from that of his father and brother, forming the Higashi Hongwanji. Both brothers saw themselves as continuing the lineage from Shinran and both designated themselves the 12th Shinshu abbot of their respective *hongwan-ji,* or head temple.

Kyonyo received some unexpected support from Ieyasu (1543–1616), the first Tokugawa shogun. Ieyasu saw two weaker Shinshu groups as easier to manage than one larger one. Thus in 1602, he gave land to Kyonyo in Kyoto, where a new temple was built. In the mid-17th century, Higashi Hongwanji established Takakura Gakuryo, a school that grew up to become the present Otani University.

Unlike the Honpa Hongwanji, until the early 20th century, the Higashi Hongwonji showed little interest in expanding overseas. Work began in Hawaii in 1899, and its movement to the U.S. mainland was occasioned by a split in the Honpa Hongwanji temple in Los Angeles in 1921. Later temples were opened in Berkeley, California, and Chicago. DAISETSU TEITARO SUZUKI, famous in the West as a Zen teacher, was a longtime professor at Otani University. The Higashi Hongwanji expanded to Brazil in the 1950s.

Further reading: Haya Akegarasu, *The Fundamental Spirit of Buddhism.* Translated by Gyomay M. Kubose (Chicago: Buddhist Temple of Chicago, 1977); *Jodo Shinshu* (Tokyo: Otani University, 1961).

Hinayana

Hinayana, literally "lesser vehicle," is a Sanskrit term of derogation used in Mahayana literature to describe other Buddhist groups, which were considered to be lesser forms of understanding.

For their part, the so-called Hinayanists, whom we can generally equate with the early 18 schools, ignored the Mahayana and their distinctions. To this day the Theravadins of Sri Lanka and other countries do not recognize the term *Hinayana* except as a label given them by other Buddhists. As such it is a word with very limited practical application today. It is found usually in print and should be approached with caution. The term *Theravada* is sufficient and preferred as a way to refer to contemporary practitioners of schools descended from the original 18 SCHOOLS OF EARLY BUDDHISM.

The early Mahayana writers considered their version "great" because of its all-encompassing doctrines of sympathy, its refined notion of SUNYATA (emptiness), and the goal of attaining Buddhahood. The Hinayanaists, they said, were content with individual cultivation and the lesser ideal of the ARHAT.

Early Mahayana writers in fact used the term rarely, preferring the alternative description "the disciples and *pratyekabuddhas.*" A *pratyekabuddha* is defined in the early literature as one who is enlightened through self-effort but dies without spreading the word of enlightenment. The disciples were, of course, the *arhats,* the body of original followers of the Buddha.

The Mahayanists were at first a minority within the body of Buddhism. The scholar of Buddhism EDWARD CONZE believed the Mahayanaists became the majority around 800 C.E., just before Buddhism's precipitous decline in India. In shifting focus to other areas such as Central and East Asia, the Mahayana apologists became fiercer in their arguments against the Hinayana. They struggled with ways to handle their sectarian competitive nature while being good, compassionate Buddhists, and so often gave contradictory accounts.

Further reading: Edward Conze, *Buddhism: Its Essence and Development* (New York: Philosophical Library, 1951); Nalinaksha Dutt, *Buddhist Sects in India* (Delhi:

Motalal Barnarsidass, 1978); Eytienne Lamotte, *History of India Buddhism: From the Origins to the Saka Era* (Louvain-La-Neuve: Institut Orientaliste, 1988).

homosexuality, Buddhist attitudes toward

The emergence of the gay community in the West in the last generation has raised the question of homosexuality in a new way for rapidly growing Western Buddhism as well as Buddhism worldwide. The gay issue was primarily set in Christian terminology, given the dominance of Christianity in the West, and called for an alteration of moral categories to make room for homosexual activity. One new observation that demanded reconsideration of homosexuality was the distinction between homosexual orientation, the desire for sex with people of one's own gender rather than the opposite gender, and homosexual activity, the acting on one's sexual desire.

Quite apart from any significant reconsideration of homosexuality within Buddhism by SANGHA leaders, community administrators, or scholars, gay Buddhist groups have emerged and leaders who have made their homosexual orientation known have taken their place in the pluralistic community with relatively little negative criticism. A reconsideration of homosexuality within the community has begun; in it the 1998 anthology *Queer Dharma: Voices of Gay Buddhism* is a landmark statement.

The discussion of homosexuality in the Buddhist community began not so much as pertaining to an ethical issue as to one concerning practice. The original Buddhist community was the sangha, a community of monks and nuns for whom the effort to gain enlightenment was foremost. Engaging in sex was seen as a distraction to practice. Thus the issue was not heterosexuality versus homosexuality, but celibacy versus engagement in any form of sexual activity.

When the VINAYA, the rules governing the sangha, was committed to writing, sexual conduct was dealt with broadly. Engaging in sexual intercourse is grounds for expulsion. Sexual intercourse includes genital, anal, and oral sexual acts. The rules for nuns go beyond those for monks and prohibit touching another's body or meeting alone with another person—male or female.

While the discussion of homosexuality in history continues, the present consensus, articulated by José Ignacio Cabezón in his essay "Homosexuality and Buddhism," is that overall Buddhism has been neutral on homosexuality, in contrast to the Jewish-Christian-Muslim tradition, which is decidedly antihomosexual. Throughout its history, Buddhism offers no definitive stance on homosexuality and at different times and places Buddhist spokespersons have both strongly condemned it and offered it high praise. It is the case that, as with Christian monastic communities, the act of becoming a Buddhist monk (or nun) allowed people who lacked heterosexual desires to escape the requirement to enter into marriage relationships. In particular, it allowed men who did not desire the company of women to spend their time with male companions and to develop deep friendships quite apart from any overt sexual expressions.

The primary support for homosexuality is from Japan and Tibet. KUKAI, the founder of SHINGON Buddhism, is cited in some sources as the one who introduced homosexuality from China to Japan, meaning that he introduced forms of homosexual activity into Buddhist monasticism. Certainly, in the medieval period, a positive attitude developed in Japan and produced a set of literature built around the theme of relationships between an older and a younger monk.

In Tibet, monasteries developed communities of what were termed "working monks," young men who desired to participate in the sangha but did not feel called to the rigors of full monastic life. They lived on the fringe of the sangha and performed the practical maintenance tasks to allow the monks to carry on with their religious activities undistracted by the practical necessities of the monasteries' upkeep. While they were not exclusively homosexual, homosexuality was certainly an aspect of their life.

The flexibility of Buddhism toward homosexuality has provided space for a new generation of gay and lesbian Buddhists to emerge, both as members of older Buddhist groups and as architects of new predominantly gay and/or lesbian communities. The raising of the question of gender-exclusive relationships, other than asexual monastic life, has also provided the environment in which new forms of the religious life such as that which has arisen within the FRIENDS OF THE WESTERN BUDDHIST ORDER can emerge.

See also SEXUALITY, BUDDHIST APPROACHES TO.

Further reading: José Innacio Cabezón, *Buddhism, Sexuality and Gender* (Albany: State University Press of New York, 1992); ———, "Homosexuality and Buddhism," in Winston Leyland, ed., *Queer Dharma: Voices of Gay Buddhism* (San Francisco: Gay Sunshine Press, 1989); Tsuneo Watanabe and Junichi Iwazta, *The Love of the Samurai: A Thousand Years of Japanese Homosexuality* (London: GMP, 1989).

Honen (1133–1212) *founder of Jodo (Pure Land) Buddhism in Japan*

Honen, the founder of PURE LAND BUDDHISM in Japan, was born into a prominent family in Mimasaka Province. His parents early encouraged him to enter the Buddhist priesthood and as a youth he studied at the famous TENDAI center at Mt. HIEI. After his ordination he began a period of retreat when he concentrated on prayer and the study of Buddhist scriptures. He absorbed a belief in AMITABHA (Amida) during this period from the reading of a work by Genshin that introduced him to the idea that Amitabha had vowed to save all sentient beings and that faith in his vow would lead one to the Pure Land, the western paradise.

In 1175 he began publicly to advocate his faith in Amitabha. In 1198 he published his *Collection of Passages*, an anthology of selected works on Amidism along with Honen's own opinions. This work created a strong reaction from the Tendai leadership. A scandal that broke out within the Pure Land community related to the indiscretion of two Pure Land followers became the occasion for his enemies to act, and the Emperor Toba II (r. 1184–98), though Honen's friend, was forced to exile him, in 1206. A number of his more prominent students, including SHINRAN (1173–1262), were also forced into exile.

His formal exile lasted less than a year, but he was not allowed to return to Kyoto, the capital of Japan, until 1211. He was by that time near the end of his life and passed away the following year. His work would be carried on by six primary students. Of these, Shokobo (1162–1238) would lead the most conservative faction, which would later mature into the JODO-SHU sect. Shinran would lead one of the more popular factions, which would later be the JODO SHINSHU; it would still later divide into the HONPA HONGWANJI and the HIGASHI HONGWANJI.

Further reading: Allen Andrews, "Myth and History in the Life and Biographies of Honen." *Pure Land: Journal of Pure Land Buddhism* n.s. 2 (1985): 21–29; Atone Joji and Hayashi Yoko, *An Anthology of the Teachings of Honen Shonin* (Los Angeles: Bukkyo University-Los Angeles Extension, 1998); Soho Machida, *Renegade Monk: Honen and Japanese Pure Land Buddhism.* Translated and edited by Ioannis Mentzas (Berkeley: University of California Press, 1999); Taitstsu Unno, *River of Fire, River of Water: An Introduction to the Pure Land Tradition of Shin Buddhism* (New York: Doubleday, 1998).

hongaku (benjue)

Hongaku, "innate enlightenment," was a TENDAI Buddhism concept that exerted strong influence over all schools during the KAMAKURA period (1192–1333) of Japanese Buddhism. The concept *hongaku,* or *benjue* in Chinese, was first used in the influential Chinese text *The Awakening of Faith in the Mahayana* (*Dacheng qixin lun*), in which it refers to the potential for enlightenment. It was contrasted with *shijue* (Japanese *shikaku*), the process of actualizing enlightenment. KUKAI (774–851), founder of the Japanese SHINGON School, incorporated the term into his esoteric—secret and transmitted—teachings. Tendai thinkers later associated *hongaku* with the LOTUS SUTRA. Tendai taught that Buddhahood was inherent in all sentient beings, not an external goal to which one needed to work. Tendai held that the world as it exists is a realm of enlightenment, pure TATHAGATA. Essentially the distinction, cause of much debate in Kamakura era Buddhism, contrasts achieving enlightenment through effort, what we normally think of as cultivation practice, as opposed to achieving the realization of one's inherent BODHI, or enlightened state.

The JODO SHU founder HONEN was familiar with *hongaku* thought and concluded it was dangerous in that it led people to conclude strict practice was not critical. His final emphasis on NEMBUTSU teachings underlies his belief that humans are far from the state of the Buddha's awareness.

Further reading: Jacqueline Stone, "Medieval Tendai Hongaku Thought and the New Kamakura Buddhism: A Reconsideration," *Journal of Japanese Religious Studies* 22 nos. 1–2 (1995): 17–48; Jodo Shu Research Institute. "Exclusivity (*senju*) and Innate Enlightenment (*hongaku shiso*) in Kamakura Buddhism." Available online. URL: www.jsri.jp/English/Honen/TEACHINGS/kamakurab.html. Accessed on January 19, 2006.

Honpa Hongwanji

The largest branch of PURE LAND BUDDHISM in Japan traces its origin to SHINRAN (1173–1262), founder of a variation on the JODO-SHU doctrine of HONEN. After Shinran's death, his daughter (who had become a Buddhist nun) established a shrine at Kyoto in her father's honor. Emperor Kameyama (r. 1249–74) gave this shrine the name Kuon Jitsujo Amida Hongwan-ji and it became the first head temple (HONGWANJI) of the

JODO SHINSHU (or the True Pure Land school). The special emphases of Shinshu Buddhism can be found in a book, the *Tannisho,* a collection of the sayings of Shinran compiled several decades after his death by his disciple Yui-en, who also wrote the prologue and epilogue. Several sections of the book highlight points of controversy with which Shinran contended.

Leadership of the movement passed through a series of abbots of the *hongwanji,* the first several direct descendants of Shinran. The movement experienced a significant revival under RENNYO (1415–99); however, his success led some rivals to attack the head temple and destroy it. In 1482, Rennyo returned to Kyoto and built a new *hongwanji* at Yamashina. He also built a second temple at Ishiyama in 1496.

All was calm for a generation, but in 1532 the Yamashina temple was burned down by soldiers. The then-abbot, Shonyo (1516–54), moved to the Ishiyama temple at Osaka, which became the third Shinshu head temple.

Shonyo's successor, Kennyo (1542–92), ran into trouble with Oda Nobunaga (1534–82), a warlord who wanted the Ishiyama temple as his own headquarters. Kennyo refused to abandon the temple and war ensued (1570–80). In 1580, the emperor interceded to stop the fighting and commanded Kennyo to surrender. Obeying the emperor, Kennyo moved to Saginomori near Wakayama. Then in 1582, Toyotomi Hideyoshi (1536–98) replaced Nobunaga as the true power in Japan. Friendly to the Shinshu, he gave them 700 acres of land at Nishi Rokujo, Kyoto, where a new *hongwanji* was established. A school established adjacent to this temple would become Ryukoku University.

At the time that Kennyo surrendered Ishiyama (1580), his two sons developed opposing views of his action: his elder son, Kyonyo (1558–1614), opposed his father's action, which the younger son, Junnyo (1577–1630), supported. Kennyo passed leadership of the Nishi Hongwanji to Junnyo. The followers of Kyonyo organized separately and went on to become a second substantial Shinshu organization, the HIGASHI HONGWANJI.

Junnyo's lineage continued in control of the Nishi (west) Hongwanji in Kyoto and its members would become the largest Pure Land organization and one of the largest Buddhist communities in Japan.

In the late 19th century, the Honpa Hongwanji would begin its expansion outside Japan following the Japanese diaspora. It would initially establish temples in Hawaii, and as the century ended, launch a mission in San Francisco. Through the 20th century it would expand into South America and Europe. The San Francisco Mission would mature as the BUDDHIST CHURCHES OF AMERICA from which the Buddhist Churches of Canada would emerge. The Hawaiian work continues as the Honpa Hongwanji Mission of Hawaii.

Further reading: Masao Kodani and Russell Hamada, *Traditions of Jodoshinshu Hongwanji-Ha* (Los Angeles: Senshin Buddhist Temple, 1962); Tosui Imadate, trans., *The Tannisho* (Kyoto: Eastern Buddhist Society, 1928); *Jodo Shinshu, a Guide* (Kyoto: Hongwanji International Center, 2002).

Horyu-ji (Ikaguradera)

The Horyu-ji is a temple built by the regent Prince SHOTOKU during the reign of Empress Suiko (592–628 C.E.) in Japan. The actual year of its founding is debated, but it was most likely around 607 C.E. The temple served as head temple of the SANRON school and later promoted teachings of the HOSSO school, two early schools of Buddhism in Japan.

The presently existing Horyu-ji complex, the central pieces of the ancient temple, includes the oldest presently existing wooden buildings in the world. Though the original temples built by Shotoku were burned in 670, they were rebuilt in the first decade of the eighth century, prior to the removal of the imperial court to Kyoto in 710. The buildings are most unusual as they have escaped the many destructive forces that occurred around them—including war, fires, and earthquakes.

Horyu-ji contains statues of the Medicine Master (BHAISAJYA-GURU BUDDHA) and Sakyamuni, the historical BUDDHA.

Further reading: Nishi Kazuo and Hozumi Kazuo, *What Is Japanese Architecture?* (Tokyo: Shokokusha, 1983); Seiichi Mizuno, *Asuka Buddhist Art: Horyuji* (New York: Weatherhill, 1974).

Hosso school (Faxiang, Fa-hsiang, Dharma Marks school)

The Hosso school is the Japanese form of the Faxiang school of MAHAYANA Buddhism started by the Chinese translator XUAN ZANG. It was based on the YOGACARA BUDDHISM teachings of VASUBHANDU and his brother, ASANGA (c. fourth century C.E.). Hosso teachings were absorbed by the Japanese monk DOSHO, who spent nearly 10 years in China as Xuan Zang's student. Dosho returned to Japan and founded the Guango-ji monastery. He in turn taught GYOGI, who founded the Southern Monastery lineage. A second lineage of Hosso was founded by Gembo, who visited China for 10 years from 716 C.E. He returned to Japan and taught Genju, who started the Northern Monastery lineage.

Despite all this activity in the end Hosso never took root in Japan, at least not to the extent it did in China. Japan, after the initial importation of Buddhist schools during the Kyoto period, has tended to favor development of CHAN BUDDHISM and PURE LAND BUDDHISM (JODO SHINSHU).

See also NARA SCHOOLS.

Further reading: Ichiro Hori et al., eds., *Japanese Religion: A Survey by the Agency for Cultural Affairs* (Tokyo: Kodansha International, 1972); Yusen Kashiwahara and Koyu Sonoda, *Shapers of Japanese Buddhism* (Tokyo: Kosei, 1994); K. Krishna Murthy, *Buddhism in Japan* (Delhi: Sundeep Prakashan, 1989).

Hsing Yun (pinyin: Xing Yun) (1927–) *Zen master and founder of Foguangshan*

Hsing Yun, founder of the FOGUANGSHAN International Buddhist Order, was born in Zhejiang Province in eastern China. He joined the Buddhist SANGHA in 1941 and lived at a monastery near Nanjing. He is the 48th patriarch of the LINJI (RINZAI ZEN) school of CHAN (ZEN) BUDDHISM. In 1949 he moved to Taiwan and settled in the southern city of Kaohsiung (Gaoxiong). He established the Foguangshan International Buddhist Order at Mt. Foguang. The foundation has since grown to be the largest Buddhist organization in Taiwan, with branches in many countries and two universities. The Hsi Lai Monastery in Los Angeles is affiliated with the Fo Guang Foundation.

Hsing Yun's lectures focus on such traditional themes in Chinese Buddhism as *prajna*, the wisdom that perceives the true nature of things, as well as such popular texts as the HEART SUTRA. His publications include *Humanistic Buddhism A Blueprint for Life.*

Further reading: Ju Chang, ed., *Cloud and Water: A 50 Year Anniversary Photobiography of Master Hsing Yun* (Taiwan: Fo Guangshan Foundation for Culture and Education, 2003); Fu Chi-Ying, *Handing Down the Light: The Biography of Venerable Master Hsing Yun.* Translated by Amy Lui-Ma (Hacienda Heights, Calif.: Buddha's Light, 2004); Hsing Yun, *The Lion's Roar: Actualizing Buddhism in Daily Life and Building the Pure Land in Our Midst* (New York: Peter Lang, 1991); ———, *Only A Great Rain: A Guide to Chinese Buddhist Meditation* (Somerville, Mass.: Wisdom, 1999); ———, *Sutra of the Medicine Buddha with an Introduction, Comments and Prayers* (Hacienda Heights, Calif.: Buddha's Light, 2002).

Hsuan Hua (pinyin: Xuan Hua) (c. 1908–1995) *modern Chan master and founder of the Dharma Realm Buddhist Association*

Hsuan Hua is a major figure in the survival and transmission of a relatively strict monastic version of Chinese MAHAYANA BUDDHISM. The Dharma Realm Buddhist Association, which he founded, sponsors the Buddhist Text Translation Society, which has taken the lead in translating Buddhist texts in English and other Western languages.

Hsuan Hua was born in Shandong Province, northeastern China, and became a monk at an early age. During the 1940s he spent time in monasteries in China, and in 1947 the Venerable Abbot Hsu Yun passed the Wang Yin lineage to him.

In 1949, reacting to the Chinese Revolution, he moved to Hong Kong. He lived alone in hills above Shatin and spent time assisting other refugee monks. He built two temples in the Hong Kong countryside. In 1959 he founded the Sino-American Buddhist Association, later renamed the Dharma Realm Buddhist Association. In 1960 he moved to Taiwan; in 1962 he moved to San Francisco, where he took charge of the San Francisco Buddhist Lecture Hall founded by some of his students. As Americans were attracted to his teaching, he began training them to assume the role of Buddhist monks. The first group was received as novices in 1973 in Taiwan.

In 1972 he founded the Gold Mountain Monastery in San Francisco. While the whole spectrum of Chinese Buddhist perspectives (in which the divisions between schools is not as rigid as in other cultures) were taught, Chan Buddhism was at the heart of his instructions. In 1976, he established the Wan Fo Cheng (City of Ten Thousand Buddhas) in Talmage, California, now the site of a monastery, a convent, and the Dharma Realm University.

Through the 1980s, Hsuan Hua traveled the world spreading the work of the Dharma Realm Buddhist Association. He also invited religious leaders to a series of interfaith conferences he held at the City of Ten Thousand Buddhas. He attracted a loyal following of well-educated Chinese and American individuals who were attracted to his strict approach to cultivation practice. He died in 1995.

Further reading: Dharma Realm Buddhist Association Staff, Buddhist Text Translation Society Staff (ed.), Heng Yin (ed.), Buddhist Text Translation Society Staff (trans.), *In Memory of the Venerable Master Hsuan Hua.* 3 vols. (Talmage, Calif.: Buddhist Text Translation Society, 1995, 1996); Hsuan Hua (Master), *Biographical Sketch of the Elder Venerable Hsuan, Noble Hua* (Burlingame, Calif.: Dharma Realm Buddhist Association, 1995); ———, *Buddha Root Farm* (San Francisco: Buddhist Text Translation Society, 1976); ———, *A General Explanation of the Buddha Speaks of Amitabha Sutra* (San Francisco: Buddhist Text Translation Society, 1974); ———, *Great Compassion Dharma Transmission Verses of the Forty-Two Hands and Eyes* (Talmage, Calif.: Buddhist Text Translation Society, 1983); ———, *Listen to Yourself; Think Everything Over.* 2 vols. (Talmage, Calif.: Buddhist Text Translation Society, 1978, 1983); ———, *Propagating the Dharma: The City of Ten Thousand Buddhas* (Talmage, Calif.: Buddhist Text Translation Society, 1996)

Hsuan-tsang   *See* Xuan Zang.

Hsu Yun (pinyin: Xu Yun) (1839–1959) *Buddhist monk associated with early modern renaissance in Chinese Buddhism*

Hsu Yun, who is known for his efforts to revive a declining Buddhism in China, was born in the middle to late Qing dynasty (1644–1911) and died after the dawn of the communist regime. He lived for 120 years, 101 of them as a monk. From Guangzhou, in southern China, he originally focused on stringent practice, including periods of silence and isolation with extremely limited food intake. His final years were spent living in the cowshed at the Zhen Ru Monastery.

In order to stem the decline of Buddhism in China, Hsu Yun traveled widely and gave Dharma talks in public. He also urged the rebuilding of important Buddhist sites, including the Nan Hua temple in Guangdong Province, home of Hui Neng, the sixth patriarch of Chan Buddhism, as well as the Yunmen Monastery.

Further reading: Hsu Yun Buddhist Association. "Master Hsu Yun's Biography." Available online. URL: http://www.hsuyun.net/hsuyunbio.html. Accessed on January 26, 2006; Zen Buddhist Order of Hsu Yun. Available online. URL: http://www.hsuyun.org/Dharma/zbohy/HsuYun/hsuyun-home.html. Accessed on January 25, 2006.

Huanglu Jing   *See* Three Register Rituals.

Hua Yan (Avatamsaka) school

Hua Yan is the Chinese translation of *Avatamsa*, the Sanskrit term for "garland." The Hua Yan school is that branch of Chinese Buddhist thought centered on the Flower Garland (Avatamsaka) Sutra. The school is also focused on worship of the bodhisattva Manjusri. It was sometimes called the Dharma nature school because of its focus on Dharma nature (*dharmata, faxing*). It was founded by Dixin Dushun (557–640), who was succeeded by four major patriarchs: Yunhua Zhiyan, Xianshou Fa Zang (643–712), Qingliang Chengguan (737–820), and Guifeng Zong Mi (780–841). In 740, Shen Xiang (Shinso) introduced Hua Yan teachings to Japan, where the school was known as Kegon. Although the school continued as a presence in Japanese Buddhism, in China the Hua Yan did not survive long past the death of Zong Mi, who represents the culmination of this strand of Chinese Buddhism. As an intellectual current, however, Hua Yan teachings continue as an integral part of Chinese Mahayana.

The Avatamsaka Sutra is a massive work of Mahayana Buddhism. It was translated three times into Chinese, first by Buddhabhadra (c. 406 C.E.), in 60 volumes; second by Siksananda (c. 700) in 80 volumes; and finally by Prajna (c. 800) in 40 volumes. The depth of this work created numerous treatises, called collectively in Chinese the *Hua Yan Bu*.

Hua Yan starts with a complete understanding of the absolute interdependence of all phenomena. This unity of the universe, the *dharmadhatu* (dharma realm, *fajie*), is the source of multiplicity; all phenomena ultimately unite into and spring from this single unifying principle. The concept of *dharmadhatu* was in fact held by most East Asian Mahayana schools of the time, such as TIAN TAI and, in Japan, SHINGON. The *dharmadhatu* is static and dynamic, as an ocean can be still in parts and produce waves in others. The static state of phenomena is that of the TATHATA (suchness), which is also equal to SUNYATA (emptiness). The dynamic state equates with all phenomena. In experience the two realms interact, a situation described by the Buddha's teaching of codependent arising (PRATITYA-SAMUTPADA).

The Hua Yan used two terms taken from Chinese philosophy to describe the static and dynamic nature of all dharmas (phenomena): *li* (principle) and *shi* (phenomena, things). The interaction of the two principles was famously illustrated by Fa Zang's description of the golden lion, in which the gold is the principle (*li*) and the lion is the lion (*shi*). The aspects of "gold-nature" and "lion-nature" exist together in the reality of the golden lion.

As did other schools of Chinese Buddhism in the Tang dynasty (618–907 C.E.), Hua Yan developed an elaborate PANJIAO (classification of doctrine) system. In the Hua Yan system there were five types of Buddhist teachings, each associated with particular branches or schools: Hinayana, as reflected in earliest writings, the Agamas; elementary Mahayana (FA XIANG and San Lun schools); fully formed Mahayana (the TIAN TAI school); sudden teachings of CHAN (ZEN); and rounded teachings of MAHAYANA, as found in Hua Yan itself. Unsurprisingly, Hua Yan writers considered their own teachings to be the most sublime teachings of Buddhism.

Further reading: Thomas Cleary, *Entry Into the Inconceivable* (Honolulu: University of Hawaii Press, 1995).

Hui Chang persecution

Between 845 and 847 the Chinese state vigorously and openly suppressed Buddhist and Daoist institutions, the temples and monasteries. The events of persecution had been prepared for by a regulation issued by the government after the An Lu-shan Rebellion (755–764). To raise quick money, authorities allowed anyone to be ordained as a monk or nun who applied and paid a flat fee, regardless of preparation for or motivation to live the religious life. While the regulation raised the necessary cash for the treasury, it was never taken off the books and over decades allowed many to enter the religious life to avoid paying taxes. The monasteries became filled with tax dodgers.

A succession of emperors avoided dealing with the problem prior to Emperor Wu Zong (r. 840–846) of the Tang dynasty (618–908), a dedicated Daoist. He found a variety of reasons to move against the Buddhist community including his frustration at the bickering between the different sects and the urging of Taoist and Confucian scholars, some of whom saw a chance to wipe Buddhism out of China.

Wu Zong began issuing edicts in 842 that ordered all monks and nuns to return to lay life (and hence the tax rolls), along with the destruction of monasteries and shrines and the confiscation of the property upon which they had rested. The destruction of the Buddhist community was thorough except in areas where Buddhist government officials refused to carry out the edicts' directives. Much of what we know of the effects of the persecution is from ENNIN, the Japanese monk visiting China at the time, who left behind an account of what he saw.

Wu Zong died in 846, seemingly of the effects of an immortality medicine he was taking at the direction of his Daoist advisers. He was but 32, and

Buddhists were quick to blame his actions against their community for his early demise. Xuan Zong (r. 846–859) moved immediately to reverse the effects of Wu Zong's actions as much as he could.

Further reading: Stanley Weinstein, *Buddhism under the T'ang* (New York: Cambridge University Press, 1987); E. Zurcher, *The Buddhist Conquest of China: The Spread and Adaptation of Buddhism in Early Medieval China* (Atlantic Highlands, N.J.: Humanities Press International, 1973).

Hui Ke (Hui-k'o) (c. 487–c. 593) *successor to Bodhidharma and the second Chan (Zen) patriarch*

As for his predecessor, little is known of the life of Hui Ke, the second patriarch of CHAN BUDDHISM, and what is known is thoroughly mixed with legendary tales. Possibly the most famous story concerns his initial encounter with BODHIDHARMA, the first Chan patriarch. In a vision Hui Ke was encouraged to seek out Bodhidharma, then residing at the Shaolin temple in Henan, in central China. To show the sincerity of his request to become a student he waited for many days, eventually even in the snow. Finally, as the story goes, to convince Bodhidharma of his desire to become his disciple, he cut off his arm, which he showed to his future master.

Hui Ke witnessed much political turmoil, including the Northern Zhou emperor Wu's suppression of Buddhism and DAOISM in 574. After Bodhidharma's death, Hui Ke spent the remainder of his long life wandering among temples and mountain residences in central China, in particular the capital of Luoyang, and An Yang.

Further reading: Kenneth K. S. Ch'en, *Buddhism in China: A Historical Survey* (Princeton, N.J.: Princeton University Press, 1964); Heinrich Dumoulin, *Zen Buddhism: A History: India and China* (New York: Macmillan, 1988); John R. McRae, *Seeing through Zen: Encounter, Transformation, and Genealogy in Chinese Chan Buddhism* (Berkeley: University of California Press, 2004).

Hui Neng (Caoqi Huineng) (638–713) *sixth patriarch of Chinese Chan Buddhism*

One of the most important Chinese Chan Buddhist teachers is Hui Neng, the sixth Chan patriarch of the Southern line of CHAN. He is the key link connecting India, previous intellectual Chan, and later irrational Chan. All of the later Chan Buddhist and ZEN teachers and sects trace their lineage and origins to Hui Neng and two of his students. However, most of what we think we know about Hui Neng is legend, originating from two problematic sources: a text entitled the PLATFORM SUTRA OF THE SIXTH PATRIARCH and the potentially biased sermons of a student of Hui Neng named SHEN HUI, and his followers.

The basic biography of Hui Neng originates in the introduction to the Platform Sutra, which tells us that Hui Neng was born in the Tang dynasty (618–906) in southern China in 638 C.E. and describes numerous miracles that accompany his birth and early years. Then at age 24, he heard a SUTRA and was awakened to the Buddha's pathway. He went to the northern temple of Hong Ren (602–675), called the fifth patriarch, where Hui Neng defeated the chief priest, SHEN XIU (605?–706), in a poetry contest.

Shen Xiu's verse: *The body is like the Bodhi tree, the mind is like a clear mirror. At all times we must strive to polish it, And do not let any dust land on it.*

Hui Neng's verse: *Originally there is no tree of Awakening, Nor is there a stand for the clear mirror. From the very beginning, not one thing; Where could the dust land?*

According to the legend created by Shen Hui, Hong Ren acknowledged Hui Neng's deep understanding, named him the successor and sixth patriarch, and gave Hui Neng two important symbols of authority: the robe of BODHIDHARMA and the begging bowl of Bodhidharma. Hui Neng then returned to the south of China and remained in obscurity for 16 years, until he was finally ordained as a monk in 676. He established the Baolin (treasure forest) temple in the mountains, taught students, and gave talks about the Buddha teachings. He received honors from the court and trained 10 great disciples, including the monk Heze Shenhui. Eight months before his death, he predicted his passing; then, accompanied by many miracles, he died in 713.

As Philip Yampolsky persuasively argues, most of the preceding account is legend and it is very unlikely that the Platform Sutra quotes the actual words of Hui Neng. The student of Hui Neng, Heze Shenhui, never once quotes from the Platform Sutra or mentions its existence, and even the epitaph for Hui Neng written by Wang Wei makes no mention of the Platform Sutra. Shen Hui's own writings are so similar to the Platform Sutra that it has been suggested that sermons and talks by Shen Hui were incorporated to create the document we now know as the Platform Sutra. A hypothesis is that the Platform Sutra attributed to Hui Neng was a compilation of Shen Hui's ideas mixed with a shorter text belonging to the Ox-head school of Chan, and perhaps some other sources.

In addition, in genuinely early sources the name *Hui Neng* appears as merely one of 10 disciples of Hong Ren, the fifth Chan patriarch, and not a particularly important disciple. The poetry contest appears impossible, since reliable biographical data show that the head monk, Shen Xiu, left the monastery of Hong Ren before Hui Neng arrived.

The teachings attributed to Hui Neng in the Platform Sutra place emphasis upon sudden awakening (*dun wu*), no-mind (*wu xin*, being free from conceptualization), the *prajna* wisdom of the Prajnaparamita Sutras (especially the Diamond Sutra), the claim that all things are empty of essence (*sunyata*) including one's true Buddha nature (from the Nirvana Sutra), and the identity of wisdom and focused concentration. Echoing

Heze Shenhui, it says that people of lesser talent pursue a gradual path, and people of greater spiritual talent take the sudden path, but the truth itself is neither sudden nor gradual.

As a result of the political maneuvering of Heze Shenhui, disciple of Hui Neng, Hui Neng was declared the official sixth patriarch of Chan Buddhism. In the early ninth century, there were already numerous "houses" of Chan. The Chinese place great stress on genealogy, and we see this in the new Chan, called the "patriarchal chan." The patriarchs start with Bodhidharma as the first patriarch in China and reach the apogee with Hui Neng, the sixth patriarch. Since through Hui Neng each Chan school could connect itself to the Buddha, the method for legitimization was to connect one's own "house" with Hui Neng's disciples. There were two disciples of Hui Neng about whom very little was and is known. These two names provided the necessary link. One was Nanyue Huaijing (677–744) and the other Chingyuan Xingsi (660–740). Each of the surviving branches of Chan Buddhism tracks its own genealogy and legitimacy through these two names, perhaps by making their own prior generation of teachers in turn students of one of these two teachers.

Further reading: Thomas Cleary, *The Sutra of Hui Neng: Grand Master of Zen with Hui Neng's Commentary on the Diamond Sutra* (Boston: Shambhala, 1998); Heinrich Dumoulin, *Zen Buddhism: A History: India and China* (New York: Macmillan, 1988); Philip B. Yampolsky, *The Platform Sutra of the Sixth Patriarch* (New York: Columbia University Press, 1967).

Hui Si (Nanyue Huisi) (515–577) *teacher of Zhi Yi, the founder of Tian Tai Buddhism*

Hui Si was a meditation specialist from northern China who settled in the south at Nanyue, near present-day Heng Shan, Hunan, southern China, one of China's most sacred mountains. Here he built Fu Yan Temple (Temple of Blessings through Persevering in Cultivation) and Can Jin Hall (The Hall of Buddhist Scriptures Library). They still exist on Mount Heng to the present. While there, he transmitted his meditation techniques to ZHI YI (Chih-i), founder of the TIAN TAI school of Buddhism.

Further reading: David W. Chappel, ed., *T'ien-t'ai Buddhism* (Tokyo: Daiichi-Shobo, 1983); Kenneth K. S. Ch'en, *Buddhism in China: A Historical Survey*. Vol. 1, *Studies in History of Religion* (Princeton, N.J.: Princeton University Press, 1964).

Hui Yuan (1) (334–416) *founder of Pure Land Buddhism in China*

Hui Yuan was born in northern China, and became a Buddhist priest and later a disciple of DAO AN (312–385), who had established a center for translating Buddhist texts with the patronage of the Chinese emperor at Chang An. After his teacher's death, he traveled into southern China and in 402 founded a community on Mt. Lu called the Bailianshe, or White Lotus Society. The emphasis of this group was to cultivate in order to gain entry into the Western Paradise of AMITHABA. Hui Yuan was thus the founder of PURE LAND BUDDHISM in China. The Dong Lin Monastery on Mt. Lu became the initial major center for the dissemination of Pure Land Buddhism across China.

In later periods other groups, some Buddhist, some political, borrowed the name *White Lotus*. There does not appear to be any direct link between these later groups and Hui Yuan's community.

Further reading: Mark L. Blum, *The Origins and Development of Pure Land Buddhism: A Study and Translation of Gyonen's Jodo Homon Genrusho* (Oxford University Press, 2002); Kenneth K. Tanaka, *The Dawn of Chinese Pure Land Buddhist Doctrine: Ching-ying Hui-yuan's Commentary on the Visualization Sutra* (Albany: State University of New York Press, 1990); B. J. Ter Haar, *The White Lotus Teachings in Chinese Religious History* (Kinderhook, N.Y.: E. J. Brill, 1992); Zenryv Tsukamoto, *A*

History of Early Chinese Buddhism: From Its Introduction to the Death of Hui-Yuan. Translated by Leon Hurvitz (New York: Kodansha America, 1985).

Hui Yuan (2) (523–592) *monk who restored Buddhist traditions during the Sui dynasty*

Hui Yuan (not to be confused with the other Chinese monk of the same name, who founded PURE LAND BUDDHISM) was born in northern China, where he became a priest of the Di Lun school. He emerged out of obscurity when he attempted to persuade the emperor Wu (502–549) to stop any planned actions against the Buddhist community. Failing initially, he worked to restore Buddhism after Wu died and later found favor with Emperor Wen (541–604) of the Sui dynasty (589–618).

Hui Yuan was a scholar of note. He authored commentaries on a number of sutras and a widely read text, a *Treatise on the Meaning of the Mahayana*. In his last years he lived at Jingyingsu Temple.

Further reading: Kenneth K. S. Ch'en, *Buddhism in China: A Historical Survey* (Princeton, N.J.: Princeton University Press, 1964).

Humphreys, Christmas (1901–1983) *English judge and writer who established the Buddhist Society*

A key figure in the development of Buddhism in Britain, Christmas Humphreys was born in London. He studied law at Cambridge, eventually becoming a barrister and a circuit judge (1968–75). In the meantime, at age 17, Humphreys had discovered Buddhism and soon afterward joined the Theosophical Society, one of the few organizations that would nurture his interest. His continued pursuits led to the formation of the Buddhist Lodge as an association within the society with Humphreys its president. Two years later, the lodge disaffiliated from the Society and emerged as the Buddhist Lodge, London. Though the lodge broke with the society, Humphreys did not and remained active in the organization for the rest of his life.

Over the next years, Humphreys worked closely with ANGARIKA DHARMAPALA, who had founded a chapter of the MAHABODHI SOCIETY in London in the mid-1920s. Humphreys continued to lead the fledgling group through the years of World War II. In 1943, the organization changed its name to the BUDDHIST SOCIETY.

As the war closed, Humphreys began to work on a document that would delineate the basic teachings of Buddhism and be representative of both Theravada and Mahayana Buddhism while honoring each's unique perspective. The result was a brief statement, "Twelve Principles of Buddhism," the publication of which set the tone for Humphreys's world tour soon after the war. The document was welcomed by Buddhist leaders and has been used in subsequent efforts to draw Buddhists together across national and school lines.

While serving as the leader of an organization serving Buddhists of all persuasions, Humphreys was himself drawn to Zen, a fact that became evident in his 1949 book, *Zen Buddhism*. Three years later he welcomed DAISETSU TEITARO SUZUKI to the society to give classes and instruct the Zen subgroup that had emerged.

During his last years, he was honored both nationally and internationally for his decades of work in building Buddhism in England. He also wrote a host of books, including an autobiography, *Both Sides of the Circle* (1978).

Further reading: Christmas Humphreys, *A Popular Dictionary of Buddhism* (London: Arco, 1962); ———, *Sixty Years of Buddhism in England, 1907–1967: A History and a Survey* (London: Buddhist Society, 1968); ———, *Studies in the Middle Way: Being Thoughts on Buddhism Applied* (London: Routledge, 1996); ———, *A Western Approach to Zen* (Wheaton, Ill.: Theosophical Publishing House, 1972).

Hunt, Ernest (1878–1967) *pioneer American Buddhist leader*

Ernest Hunt, a European American Buddhist priest in Hawaii in the middle of the 20th century, worked to reconcile the Japanese community with the larger English-speaking population that dominated the islands. Hunt, an Englishman by birth, had converted to Buddhism just as he completed his studies for the priesthood in the Church of England. Then in 1915, he and his wife moved to Hawaii. In the 1920s, the pair opened Buddhist Sunday school classes for English-speaking children, and in 1924, Hunt was ordained by Bishop Yemyo Imamura, the head of the Hawaiian branch of the HONPA HONGWANJI Buddhists. At that time he assumed the religious name *Shinkaku*. Two years later Imamura named him the head of the Honpa Hongwanji's English Department.

By 1928, some 60 students had formally been initiated into Buddhism through Hunt's efforts. Hunt also promoted a nonsectarian approach to Buddhism, whose Japanese community was divided among a half-dozen competing Japanese groups. His ideal was pursued through the Hawaiian branch of the International Buddhist Institute, which he and Imamura founded. Hunt served as the organization's first vice president.

The direction of Hunt's work suddenly changed in 1932 when Bishop Imamura died. Three years later, Bishop Giyko Kuchiba became the new leader. The opposite of Imamura in both temperament and belief, he was a dedicated Japanese nationalist and a rigid advocate of SHIN BUDDHISM. He soon fired Hunt and disbanded the English Department. Fortunately, Hunt, who had made many friends, soon found shelter in the SOTO ZEN temple. He would eventually be ordained as a Soto priest and later receive recognition for his accomplishments in Zen. Until shortly before his death, he remained the Buddhist ambassador to the English-speaking community and frequently met with and gave talks to the islands' many tourists.

Further reading: Louise H. Hunter, *Buddhism in Hawaii* (Honolulu: University of Hawaii Press, 1971).

Hu Shi (Hu Shih) (1891–1962) *Chinese modernizer*

Hu Shi is a key figure in early modern Chinese history. A leader of the New Culture movement in China, he also served as ambassador to the United States (1938–42) and chancellor of Peking University (1946–48). He was an early proponent of the use of the vernacular language (in today's term, *putong hua*) in Chinese writing, as opposed to the traditional use of literary Chinese. In a series of path-breaking articles he also traced the development of ZEN (CHAN) BUDDHISM in China. Although he was eventually bypassed as China's history turned toward war and revolution, his influence as a literary figure was immense.

Born in Shanghai, Hu received his early education in China. Sent to the United States in 1910, he studied at Cornell University and Columbia University and was strongly influenced by the pragmatic philosophy of John Dewey (1859–1952). Hu returned to China in 1917.

Hu was highly critical of both CONFUCIANISM and Buddhism. These traditional systems were unsuited to the modern era, he felt. He was highly skeptical in general. However, this attitude was not simply slavish copying of overseas fashions. His skeptical outlook was based on the writings of the great Song dynasty historian Sima Guang (1019–86 C.E.). As a writer Hu Shi was active in interpreting and investigating China's religious traditions. He was generally opposed to the extreme expressions of superstitions and such expressions of devotion as self-sacrifice and worshipping of Buddha's RELICS. He valued, in contrast, China's humanist tradition.

Further reading: Jerome B. Grieder, *Hu Shih and the Chinese Renaissance: Liberalism in the Chinese Revolution, 1917–1937* (Cambridge: Harvard University Press, 1970); Hu Shi, "Ch'an (Zen) Buddhism in China: Its History and Method," *Philosophy East and West* 3, no. 1 (January 1953): 3–24; Ma Keke "One of PKU's Historic Figures: Hu Shi," *PKU News.* Available online. URL: http://ennews.pku.edu.cn/news.php?s=72166732. Accessed on January 7, 2005.

Hwaom Buddhism

Hwaom Buddhism is the Korean form of the Chinese HUA YAN, or Flower Garland, school of MAHAYANA Buddhism. In Korea, Hwaom Buddhism became one of the five doctrinal schools that stood in contrast (because of their emphasis on study of the sutras and doctrinal teachings) to SON BUDDHISM, the Korean form of the meditational approach (generally called Zen).

The Flower Garland school takes its name from the Avatamsaka (Flower Garland) Sutra, which had been translated into Chinese as early as the fifth century. The Avatamsaka Sutra is a philosophical treatise on the nature of phenomena. It was and is mainly studied by monastic adherents as a means of understanding ultimate reality. Hua Yan developed in China complementing the TIAN TAI school (which favored the LOTUS SUTRA) under five patriarchs—Du Shun (557–640), Chih-yen or Zhi Yan (600–668), Fa-tsang or FA ZANG (643–712), Cheng Guan, and Zong Mi. The Tian Tai had developed a classification of Buddhist schools and SUTRAS, ranking them from the lowest to the highest, with the Lotus Sutra at the top. The Hua Yan adopted a similar system but placed the Avatamsaka Sutra on top.

UISANG (625–702) traveled to China and studied with Zhi Yan and upon his return to Korea introduced Hua Yan teachings there. He also founded Pusok Temple, which became the group's headquarters. He stayed in touch with the Chinese leadership and later corresponded with Fa Zang.

In Korea, Hwaom Buddhism would be caught up in the periodic Korean endeavor to synthesize and harmonize all the different approaches to Buddhism. WONHYO (617–686), Uisang's colleague and a leader in the harmonization process, suggested all phenomena are merely products of the mind, and as one awakens to that fact, doctrinal disputes are resolved.

In 740, Sinjo, a Korean Hwaom priest from the Korean kingdom of Silla and student of Fa Zang, introduced the Flower Garland school to Japan. Here it would be called KEGON and would become institutionalized at TODAI-JI, the main temple in Nara.

Further reading: Sae Hyang Chung, "The Silla Priests Uisang and Wonhyo," *Korean Culture* 3, no. 4 (December 1982): 36–43; Peter H. Lee, "Fa-tsang and Ŭisang," *Journal of the American Oriental Society* 82 (1962): 56–62.

I

icchantika

An *icchantikia* is, literally, a "nonbeliever." One Chinese definition is "one who has severed his good roots" and so allows himself to be full of desires. There are three kinds of *icchantikas*: the wicked, those BODHISATTVAS who choose to become *icchantikas,* and those without a nature (or *bodhi* mind) to attain final NIRVANA.

The "*icchantika* of great mercy" is another term for a bodhisattva, who vows not to proceed to Buddhahood until all sentient beings are saved.

Further reading: Nirvana Sutra. "Mahayana Mahaparinirvana Sutra." Available online. URL: http://www. nirvanasutra.org.uk/. Accessed on January 19, 2006; William Edward Soothill and Lewis Hodous, comps., *A Dictionary of Chinese Buddhist Terms: With Sanskrit and English Equivalents and a Sanskrit-Pali Index* (London: Kegan Paul, Tranch Trubner, 1937).

ichinen

The Japanese term *ichinen* is, literally, "one mind." It refers to the ultimate reality that is present in every moment. In TIAN TAI SCHOOL thought, the experience of Buddhahood is inherent in all life experiences, or the 10 worlds, 10 factors, and three realms of existence. NICHIREN later taught that this same buddhahood was manifest in the Gohonzon MANDALA. Another related Tian Tai term is *ichinen sanzen,* indicating that the 3,000 (*sanzen*) worlds are present in a single instant.

Further reading: Nyanatiloda, *Buddhist Dictionary Manual of Buddhist Terms and Doctrines* (San Francisco: Chinese Materials Center, 1997).

Ikeda, Daisaku (1928–) *president of Soka Gakkai International*

Ikeda is the photogenic, globe-trotting spokesperson for SOKA GAKKAI INTERNATIONAL, one of the largest Buddhist organizations in Japan and a growing power in Japanese religion since the 1950s. Ikeda grew up in Tokyo and completed his elementary school education as World War II was heating up. He worked in an iron manufacturing plant during the war. Two years after the war, a devastated Ikeda met JOSEI TODA (1900–58). Toda dealt with his despair over Japan's loss of the war and drew him to faith in Nichiren Buddhism. Ikeda began to work with Toda in rebuilding

Soka Gakkai, the Nichiren lay organization that the government had suppressed during the war. He also continued his schooling and eventually graduated from the Taisei Institute.

In 1952, Ikeda began to work on building the Komeito, a political party that embodied Soka Gakkai policies. In 1958, Toda died; Ikeda was first named executive director and then in 1960 became Soka Gakkai's third president.

Toda had initiated a strong program of proselytization that had led to Soka Gakkai's spectacular growth. Ikeda continued Toda's policies and both Soka Gakkai and the Komei (Clean Government) Party grew tremendously. Soka Gakkai became known for its aggressive recruitment practices, and the Komei Party moved from local involvement to successes in national elections. As the organization grew, Ikeda began to found a variety of educational institutions that embodied the educational ideal of Soka Gakkai's founder, TSUNESABURO MAKIGUCHI. In 1964 he announced the plans for the global center of Nichiren Buddhism, the Sho Hondo, completed in 1970.

In 1974, Ikeda suddenly resigned as president of Soka Gakkai. The next year he became the president of Soka Gakkai International and assumed duties related to the spread and development of the movement worldwide. He retired in 1979 and was named honorary president.

Through the 1980s to the present, Ikeda has kept up an active schedule of traveling the world, encouraging believers, and building new institutions incarnating various Soka Gakkai ideals. Ikeda has initiated a variety of efforts in higher education, both with the founding of Soka Gakkai universities and with sponsoring of scholarly research facilities at secular universities, such as the Toda Institute for Global Peace and Policy Research and the Boston Research Center for the 21st Century. He has been particularly interested in world peace and to that end strongly supports the United Nations. He has received the United Nations Peace Award.

Amid all of his travels and administrative duties, he has authored or collaborated in more than 170 works.

Further reading: Daisaku Ikeda, *Daily Guidance* (Los Angeles: World Tribune Press, 1983); ———, *A Lasting Peace.* 2 vols. (New York: Weatherhill, 1987); ———, *My Recollections* (Los Angeles: World Tribune Press, 1980); David Machachek and Bryan Wilson, eds., *Global Citizens: The Soka Gakkai Buddhist Movement in the World* (Oxford: Oxford University Press, 2000); Richard Hughes Seager, *Encountering the Dharma: Daisaku Ikeda, Soka Gakkai, and the Globalization of Buddhist Humanism* (Berkeley: University of California Press, 2006).

Ikkyu (1394–1481) *beloved "madman" monk of Japanese Zen legend*

Ikkyu was an eccentric Japanese poet, painter, calligrapher, and monk in the RINZAI ZEN tradition. He was unsparing in his criticism of Zen in his day. In his opinion contemporary practice was degraded from that of the masters of the past.

Ikkyu was the son of the Japanese emperor Go-komatsu (r. 1382–1412) but was unable to benefit from his relationship as his mother was a member of a family who were rivals for the imperial throne. He is said to have gained enlightenment when he heard a crow's call. As he matured, he became particularly critical of Yoso Soi (1376–1458), head of Daitaku-ji, the RINZAI ZEN temple at Kyoto. Ikkyu chose to live away from Kyoto at the nearby monastery on Mount Jou. As a protest at the degraded state of Zen BUDDHISM he did not declare a DHARMA HEIR (successor) before his death, and he tore up his own confirmation certificate. Ironically, Ikkyu was later named abbot of Daitoku-ji and so given an institutional platform for his brand of Rinzai. Ikkyu is also well known for his sponsorship of the tea ceremony.

Ikkyu can be compared to the Chinese monk BU DAI, who lived approximately 300 years before Ikkyu. Like Ikkyu, Bu Dai was considered slightly crazy and acted inexplicably because he was enlightened. Both figures are extremely popular in their respective cultures. The large number of stories about each of these legendary monks reflects popular attempts to understand Buddhist goals.

Further reading: Stephen Berg, *Crow with No Mouth: Ikkyu: Fifteenth Century Zen Master* (Port Townsend, Wash.: Copper Canyon Press, 2000); Ikkyu, *Ikkyu and the Crazy Cloud Anthology: A Zen Poet of Medieval Japan.* Translated by Sonja Arntzen (Tokyo: University of Tokyo Press, 1987); Kazuo Kasahara, ed., *A History of Japanese Religion.* Translated by Paul McCarthy and Gaynor Sekimori (Tokyo: Kosei, 2001); John Stevens, *Three Zen Masters: Ikkyu, Hakuin, Ryokan* (Tokyo: Kodansha International, 1993).

Imamura, Yemyo (1867–1932) *Hawaiian Buddhist leader*

Bishop Yemyo Imamura, who led the Shin Buddhist community in Hawaii for more than 30 years, was born in Japan. He became a schoolteacher but later in life studied for the priesthood and finally arrived in Hawaii in 1899 as a priest for the HONPA HONGWANJI Buddhists. His first task was overseeing the building of their first temple in Honolulu. He then took upon himself the task of organizing the scattered Buddhist believers, many of whom resided on the islands' plantations. He founded the Young Men's Buddhist Association and then led in the construction of many temples. In 1900 he became the *katouku*, or bishop, of the Hawaiian mission.

An amiable and personable man, Imamura won the cooperation of the plantation owners, most of whom generally favored Christianity. His position was sealed when he intervened in a riot in 1904 and was able to contribute substantively to its ending. In 1906, his Japanese superiors designated the work in Hawaii a detached branch, which allowed Imamura to apply for corporate status for the mission. In 1908 he received a license to perform marriages, the first issued to an American Buddhist. For his leadership, as the work grew, Imamura was given the title bishop.

Imamura came to believe that Buddhism had a place in America and that his members could integrate into American life. He worked to support democracy and separated himself from any meaningful support for Japanese nationalist ambitions. His designs led him into contact with ERNEST HUNT, a British citizen who had moved to Hawaii after his conversion to Buddhism. The two worked to create an English Department for the Honpa Hongwanji and Imamura assigned Hunt leadership of it. He also blessed Hunt's advocacy of a nonsectarian approach to Buddhism and took the lead in founding the Hawaiian branch of the International Buddhist Institute, an organization to spread nonsectarian Buddhism in the West.

Imamura died in 1932. Hunt carried on the English Department until 1935, when a new bishop, Giyko Kuchiba, assumed leadership of the Honpa Hongwanji mission. He opposed most of Imamura's policies and developed a program exclusively focused on the Japanese community and aimed at keeping tied to Japan as closely as possible. He fired Hunt and closed the English Department. Only after World War II was the vision of Imamura once more appreciated and the mission returned to the course he had set. Later, Bishop Imamura's son, Kanmo Imamura, would serve seven years (1967–74) as leader of the Hawaiian work.

Further reading: Louise H. Hunter, *Buddhism in Hawaii* (Honolulu: University of Hawaii Press, 1971); Yemyo Imamura, *Democracy According to the Buddhist Viewpoint* (Honolulu: Honpa Hongwanji Mission, 1918); ———, *A Short History of the Hongwanji Buddhist Mission of Hawaii* (Honolulu: The Mission, 1927); George Y. Yamamoto, *The Origin of Buddhism in Hawaii* (Honolulu: YMB of Honolulu, 1955).

India, Buddhism in

Buddhism began in India as a movement against the order of the day. That order was Brahmanism, the system of ideologies and beliefs that people in the BUDDHA's day took for granted. The Buddha was born as a prince to an aristocratic family in the SAKYA tribe, sometime around 500 B.C.E. This was a period of change in many parts of the world, including the Indic world. India's civilization was a churning pot of various languages and cultures. There were, however, two basic streams: the Indic and the Vedic. The Indic was associated with the Indus Valley civilization in today's Pakistan—such sites as Mohenjo-daro and Harappa. Dravidian languages were spoken. The people worshipped goddess images and had a matrilineal society. This Indic civilization flourished between 2500 and 2000 B.C.E. Around 2000 B.C.E. another civilization, that of the Aryans, the Vedic, entered the scene. These people spoke Indo-European languages. They moved east into the Gangetic plains, the busy region around the Ganges River. Unlike the Indic peoples, the Vedis were pastoral nomads. Their economy was centered on cattle. The lifestyle was based on warfare and acquisition. The Vedic magical worldview was based on the *rta*, or universal principle/law.

THE BUDDHA

At the time of the BUDDHA these two historical forces, the Indic and the Vedic, produced different social forms. First was the tribal, class-structured *gana-sanghasa*, characteristic of Indic influence, and second was the monarchical, city-based kingdoms, reflecting Vedic culture. Eventually the kingdoms consolidated power and absorbed the *gana-sanghasas*. These city-states were in turn finally absorbed into the vaster MAGADHA kingdom, after the Buddha's death.

The Buddha, Sakyamuni, was born into a *gana-sanghasa*, or tribal group. He borrowed this same concept for his SANGHA, or monkhood, from these tribal forms of organization. In addition there were current two types of religious traditions, the *sramana* (ascetic) and the Brahmanic. The *sramanas* were essentially people who separated themselves from society. These individuals simply "dropped out" and led unconventional lives. There were many groups, such as the Ajivikas and the Jains. Many were extreme ascetics who lived in the forest. All the groups generally accepted the idea of karma and rebirth.

The Brahmans, in contrast to the *sramanas*, developed from Vedic culture, in which they were priests and, perhaps, shamans. However, not all Brahmans were actual descendants of the Aryan tribes who invaded India from around 2000 B.C.E. Instead they are best seen as ritual specialists who possessed high knowledge and moral status. The Brahmans transformed and reinterpreted the ancient Vedic traditions. They did this through such works as the Upanisads, sacred texts that which were first compiled around 700 B.C.E. The Upanisads emphasized such doctrines as a universal, eternal self, the ATMAN, which is reborn continually.

Although early Buddhism was a shamanic organization that opposed much Brahmanic thinking, in many ways the Buddha's teachings synthesized both traditions. In early Buddhism SRAMANA and *Brahman* essentially mean ARHAT, one who has cultivated. The Buddha developed a teaching, his DHARMA, which steered a middle path between the extreme ascetic practices of many *sramana* groups and the householder-based options of Brahmanism. He psychologized much of the teachings of KARMA, saying the intent of action was more important than the ritual action itself. In regard to meat eating, he said it was not the act of eating meat itself that counted; it was whether the person acting intended harm and pain that counted. Killing is not to be condoned, but eating meat by itself is not proscribed. The Buddha's teachings invariably focused on the individual's state of mind.

The Buddha's Dharma was, in addition, meant for all, both householders and ascetics. Ascetics could join the sangha, his band of roving "drop-outs." And householders, including kings and soldiers, could adhere to his teachings in daily life. The sangha had a set of strict rules, called the VINAYA. The householder followed the EIGHTFOLD PATH, which would give rules for living, SILA, and result in ultimate understanding, insight.

A DEVELOPING RELIGIOUS SYSTEM

In the centuries after the Buddha's death, what is called his PARINIRVANA, his followers, spread his Dharma message throughout the many societies in Asia. The missionaries connected with all levels of society and in doing so generally used the local vernacular language. The elite classes preserved the Buddha's teachings in the written records of the SUTRAS, eventually written in such educated languages as Pali, Sanskrit, literary Chinese, and Tibetan. The teachings also traveled through the popular levels of society, often as stories or songs (GATHAS). The JATAKA TALES of the Buddha's early incarnations, his earlier lives, were taken from local languages and eventually recorded in Pali.

The monastic system grew in India, with the distinction between householders and monks or BHIKSUS, growing increasingly clear. Eventually householders were encouraged to give gifts or donations to the MONASTERIES in order to build up positive KARMA. The monasteries became wealthy and the lifestyles of the monks were often leisurely.

Doctrinally three forms of Buddhism took root in India. First was THERAVADA, or the Way of the Elders. Second was MAHAYANA BUDDHISM, a spiritual movement within Buddhism that focused on the impetus to give to others, on compassion. The third was VAJRAYANA, or TANTRIC BUDDHISM, a philosophical movement that focused on the union of absolute opposites. Tantricism developed around 700–1000 C.E. Mahayana began to form in the first century B.C.E. and gradually developed a sense of its own separate identity over the next 600 or so years.

Buddhism was an important religion—but never the single religion—throughout India from around the third century B.C.E. to the third century C.E. The first major boost to its fortunes occurred when ASOKA (r. 276–236 B.C.E.), third emperor of the Mauryan dynasty (322–185 B.C.E.), converted. Under Asoka's patronage Buddhism spread throughout southern India. The numerous stone pillars that he left in all corners of his empire illustrate his devotion to the Buddhist ethical code of tolerance, harmony, generosity, and nonviolence. After the Mauryans, Buddhism continued to gather support and patronage. Large monasteries would typically be supported by the regime in power and by wealthy patrons near cities.

BUDDHIST DECLINE

However, by the time of the ruler Harsavardhana in the 600s of the Common Era, Buddhism was beginning its general decline. When the Chinese traveler XUAN ZANG visited in 633 he noticed many abandoned temples. Xuan Zang visited Sravasti, Kapilavastu, Kusinara, Benares, Vaisali, Pataliputra, Bodhgaya, and Nalanda. At BODH-GAYA, where the Buddha gained enlightenment, Xuan Zang saw the statue of AVALOKITESVARA, the BODHISATTVA of compassion. It had sunk halfway into the ground. An ancient prophecy had claimed that when the statue disappeared, then Buddhism would also disappear. To Xuan Zang this image seemed to foretell Buddhism's impending fate in the land of its birth.

Buddhism's decline was due less to military invasion and more to its absorption into Hinduism. The process of absorption had begun even before Xuan Zang's visit. Mahayana Buddhists often adopted Hindu deities into the Mahayana pantheon in order to win over local Hindu worshippers. But this type of accommodation with Hinduism had an unexpected result: the local people increasingly saw Buddhism as simply another branch of Hinduism. The Buddha became, in local eyes, another of the many incarnations of Lord Vishnu. By the eighth century C.E. it was difficult for the common people to see the distinction between Hinduism and Buddhism. The Muslim invasions simply brought the process to its final conclusion.

With the Turkish invasions of India that began around 1000 C.E., Buddhism went into final and near-complete decline. The remaining monasteries and universities, clustered in the north, were easy targets for the invading armies; the Turkic sultan Mahmud Shabuddin Ghori (Muhammad Ghori) (1162–1206) attacked the university-monastery at NALANDA in 1197 and the university complex at Vikramasily in 1203. Unlike Hinduism at the time, the Buddhist tradition had been centered in these great monastery complexes in northern India. Therefore, the Buddhist, sangha-based system did not survive among the general population after the monasteries were destroyed.

The obliteration of Buddhism in India had a vast impact on the other Buddhist countries. Innovative thought and texts no longer emerged from India to be interpreted and argued over in other lands. Such centers as Sri Lanka and China were now cut off from a long and noble source of religious inspiration.

THE BUDDHIST HERITAGE RECLAIMED

Indian history continued down its unique, spectacular path after the demise of Buddhism. Still, Buddhism remained a factor in the Indian self-awareness. For many it was perhaps nothing more than one of the many cultural memories that stalk the landscape in India. But for others it was a jewel to be rediscovered and appreciated. This process of discovery was spurred on by the British unification of the Indian subcontinent during colonial rule (c. 1776–1947). Buddhism was recognized and studied in the West as a complex, admirable religion. When India attained independence as a secular, multiethnic entity it naturally claimed Buddhism as its heritage, one of which contemporary Indians can be proud.

Buddhism's status in contemporary India was also influenced by political events in the young Indian nation. A key influence was BABASAHEB BHIMRAO RAMJI AMBEDKAR, a member of the Maharashtran Dalit (untouchable) class and leader in the struggle for independence. After much soul searching Ambedkar lost hope in the possibility of reform of Hinduism. He made a sudden and dramatic conversion to Buddhism in 1956. His influence convinced many of his political followers to follow suit, and today there are more than 4 million Indian Buddhists. In addition, Tibetan Buddhism has had an impact on modern Indian history due to the influx of Tibetans after the Chinese annexation of Tibet from 1959. Buddhism, against all odds, has made something of a comeback in the contemporary period. It remains a tiny religion in today's India, yet its staying power cannot be denied. It is an intrinsic part of the current landscape and India's historical imagery.

Further reading: D. C. Ahir, *Buddhism in Modern India* (Delhi: Sri Satguru, 1991); Kenneth K. S. Ch'en, *Buddhism in China: A Historical Survey* (Princeton, N.J.: Princeton University Press, 1964); Edward Conze, *Buddhist Thought in India* (1962. Reprint, New Delhi: India Munshiram Manoharlal, 2002); Akira Hirakawa, *A History of Indian Buddhism: From Sakyamuni to Early Mahayana.* Translated and edited by Paul Groner. Asian Studies at Hawaii, No. 36. (Honolulu: University of Hawaii Press, 1990); Trevor Ling, *Buddhist Revival in India: Aspects of the Sociology of Buddhism* (New York: St. Martin's Press, 1980).

Ingen (Yin Yuan) (1592–1673) *founder of Obaku Zen*

The monk Ingen (in Chinese, Yin Yuan), who founded the OBAKU ZEN school in Japan, was born in China. As a young man, he moved to Wan Fu CHAN temple on Huang Po Mountain to study with the Chan master Jian Yuan. He eventually became abbot of the temple.

In 1644 there was a significant political change in China with the fall of the Ming dynasty. Many people fled to Japan and settled in Nagasaki. Some of the Nagasaki Chinese, including a colleague, Itsunen, invited Yin Yuan to their new home. He traveled there in 1654 and settled in at the Sufuku-ji temple.

Over the next few years he gained some reputation, and in 1661 he met and gained permission from the Tokugawa shogun to construct a temple in the Uji district near Kyoto. The shogun gave land for the temple, which was built out of the memory of the temple in China that Ingen headed as abbot. He named the new temple *Mampuku-ji* (the Japanese equivalent of *Wan Fu Temple*).

Ingen taught a form of Zen quite reminiscent of RINZAI ZEN practice but to it added an emphasis on the veneration of AMITABHA through the repetition of the NEMBUTSU. It was this latter practice that distinguished the Obaku Zen approach. Ingen also introduced a new vegetarian cuisine from China, *fusa ryori*, which had been popular in Chinese temples.

Ingen was succeeded by Mu An as abbot at Mampuku-ji.

Further reading: Helen J. Baroni, *Obaku Zen: The Emergence of the Third Sect of Zen in Tokugawa Japan* (Honolulu: University of Hawaii Press, 2000); Kazuo Kasahara, ed., *A History of Japanese Religion.* Translated by Paul McCarthy and Gaynor Sekimori (Tokyo: Kosei, 2001).

inka See INKASHOMEI.

inkashomei

The Japanese term *inkashomei* (legitimate seal of clearly furnished proof), often abbreviated as *inka,* is a key concept in ZEN BUDDHISM practice. The *inkashomei,* or "seal," is the confirmation that more than teachings or philosophy had been passed from master to student; in CHAN and ZEN theory the master passes enlightenment itself. The seal is a confirmation from the master that the student has received and grasped the teachings of enlightenment. In practices centered on the use of KOANS, receiving the *inka* signifies the student has studied and passed each koan test. Once a student receives the *inka* from the master he or she is then allowed to take on students and to be called a *roshi,* an enlightened master. As an example, the modern Zen master Hakuun Tasutani-roshi (1885–1973) received the *inkashomei* from his master, Harada-roshi, when he was 58.

See also ISHIN DENSHIN.

Further reading: Victor Sogen Hori, *Zen Sand: The Book of Capping Phrases for Koan Practice* (Honolulu: University of Hawaii Press, 2003); Roshi Philip Kapleau, *The Three Pillars of Zen: Teaching, Practice, and Enlightenment* (1965. Reprint, Garden City, N.Y.: Anchor, 1980), 367.

International Buddhist Progress Society *See* FOGUANGSHAN.

International Meditation Centre

The International Meditation Centre (IMC) was originally founded in 1952 by U BA KHIN, a Burmese master of VIPASSANA meditation, specifically to teach THERAVADA Buddhist doctrine and meditation. After U Ba Khin's death, his closest disciple, Mother Sayamagyi, assumed leadership of the IMC. Over the years a global network of centers affiliated directly with the IMC in Rangoon have emerged. They may be found in Australia, Singapore, Japan, the United States, Canada, Italy, the United Kingdom, Belgium, Denmark, Germany, and Switzerland.

In 1999, the Vipassana International Academy in India opened the Sayagyi U Ba Khin Village, one of the three projects to mark the birth centenary of Sayagyi U Ba Khin.

Further reading: *The Clock of Vipassana Has Struck: A Tribute to the Life and Legacy of Sayagyi U Ba Khin*

(Igatpuri, India: Vipassana Research, 1999); U Ba Khin, *The Essentials of Buddha Dhamma in Meditative Practice* (Kandy, Sri Lanka: Buddhist Publication Society, 1981).

Ippen (1239–1289) *inspired founder of Ji-shu sect*

Ippen, the founder of the Pure Land JI-SHU sect of Japanese Buddhism, was born into a formerly wealthy family on Shikoku Island. His family had, however, lost its position as a result of choosing the losing side in the Kokyo Disturbance (1221). His mother died when he was 10 and he entered a Buddhist order. He studied at various temples, but in 1271, at a Jodo temple, he had a remarkable religious awakening.

At the Senko-ji temple in Shinano Province, he saw a painting, which pictured the path to the PURE LAND, the paradise that is the object of the religious life in JODO SHINSHU. As a result of his contemplation of the picture, he became convinced of the basic Pure Land belief that entrance into the heavenly realm is the destiny of all who repeat the NEMBUTSU, a MANTRA calling upon the grace of AMITABHA. He believed that to recite the *nembutsu* was to become one with Amitabha.

On the basis of a message he had received from an oracle at the Kumano Shrine, a SHINTO shrine at Hongu, Japan, in 1274, he began traveling around Japan giving people a *nembutsu* medallion and practicing a *nembutsu* dance. The dancing was seen as an ecstatic expression of his realization that all were going to be saved by the *nembutsu*. He concentrated his travels in the rural areas, and many adopted his dance. It is said that he distributed more than 2 million *nembutsu* talismans. Members of Ji-shu consider the date of the oracle as their founding date.

He died in 1289 believing that no new sect needed to be founded as a result of his work. However, Shinko-ji temple was erected at the spot where he died in Settsu Province. One of his followers, SHINKYO (1237–1319), eventually emerged to continue his work and found the Ji sect that advocated his teachings.

Further reading: Dennis Hirota, *No Abode: The Record of Ippen* (Honolulu: University of Hawaii Press, 1997).

Ise Shinto (Watarai Shinto)

During the Kamakura period (1192–1333), when Japan was ruled by the shoguns based in KAMAKURA, Buddhism was privileged at the expense of traditional SHINTO. One prominent family who favored more traditional beliefs, the Watarai family, who supplied the priests at the Outer ISE SHRINE, took the lead in developing a new revitalization of Shintoism. Ise Shinto stresses purity and honesty as ideals, with the goal of religious practice to perfect purity and honesty. The Ise Shinto priests attempted to reverse the Buddhist dominance by, among other things, seeing the Buddhas and BODHISATTVAS as manifestations of Shinto KAMI, or deities.

The major text of the movement is the *Shinto gobusho* (Five books), which dates from the Muromachi period (1334–1592).

Further reading: Kazuo Kasahara, ed., *A History of Japanese Religion*. Translated by Paul McCarthy and Gaynor Sekimori (Tokyo: Kosei, 2001), 299–302.

Ise Shrine (Jingu Shrine)

There are two major Shinto shrines in Ise, on Japan's eastern coast in Mie Prefecture. The Inner Shrine (Naiku) contains AMATERASU OMI-KAMI, said to be the grandmother of Ninigi, who unified Japan. Six kilometers distant, the Outer Shrine (Geku) houses the Ise deity, Toyouke. Toyouke is also the SHINTO goddess of agriculture. Ise was unusual because even in early periods Buddhist rituals as well as terminology were prohibited. Ise is today still the imperial household shrine.

The Ise Shrine is ancient, certainly dating more than 1,000 years. But no old structures remain. This is because in the rite of *shikinen sengu* the wooden buildings are burned and rebuilt every 20 years. This custom was first carried out in 690 C.E. It is only during the ceremony that the general public is allowed to be close to the shrine—once every 20 years.

Further reading: Brian Bocking, "Changing Images of Shinto: Sanja Takusen or the Three Oracles," in John Breen and Mark Teeuwen, eds., *Shinto in History: Ways of the Kami* (Richmond, U.K.: Curzon, 2000), 167–185; Teiji Itoh, *The Roots of Japanese Architecture: A Photographic Quest by Yukio Futagawa* (New York: Harper & Row, 1963); Kenzo Tange and Noboru Kawazoe, *Ise: Prototype of Japanese Architecture* (Cambridge: M.I.T. Press, 1965); Yasutada Watanabe, *Shinto Art: Ise and Izumo Shrines* (New York: Weatherhill, 1974).

ishin denshin

In ZEN practice, the Buddhadharma, the essential truth of the Buddha's message, is transmitted from master to disciple. This transmission forms a strong link and perpetuates the lineage for each tradition or school. The Japanese term *ishin denshin* literally means "transfer from heart-mind [*ishin*] to heart [*shin*]." The emphasis is clearly on nonverbal and nontextual transmission of truth. A common phrase often heard in Zen practice is *ishin-denshin, furyu-monji*—"Communicate truth without written words." This form of insight is, then, beyond book learning. Today this term is often translated as "thought transference," "being on the same wavelength," or, at times, "telepathy." *Ishin denshin* is widely used in popular conversations and business for unspoken understandings between people.

The original term can be traced to the PLATFORM SUTRA of HUI NENG, recognized generally as the sixth CHAN patriarch.

Further reading: Japanese 1-2-3.com. "ishin denshin." Available online. URL: http://www.japanese123.com/businessjapanese2.htm. Accessed on December 5, 2005.

Ito Jinsai (1627–1705)
Japanese Confucian scholar

Ito Jinsa was a member of the Japanese school of Ancient Learning, which promoted a version of Confucianism free of the influence of Buddhism. The Ancient Learning movement was less a revival than a criticism of the overly formal approach to Confucianism.

Ito was a writer and educator. In his writings he emphasized the early brand of CONFUCIUS and MENCIUS thought and criticized NEO-CONFUCIANISM, the revision of Confucianism that was popularized in Song dynasty (960–1279) China. Ito established the Kogaku school of Tokugawa CONFUCIANISM as well as the Kogido academy in Kyoto. One particular innovation was the concept of *sakumon,* or "problems." *Sakumon* originally meant the questions given to students on the Chinese imperial examination. Ito used the term for a part of his group learning when students took turns explaining and posing questions on particular texts. *Sakumon* was a continuing technique at the Kogido academy. *Sakumon* was also used in group learning by the *shingaku* (learning of the mind) movement in early Tokugawa (1600–1868) Japan.

Further reading: Masaharu Anesaki, *History of Japanese Religion with Special Reference to the Social and Moral Life of the Nation* (Rutland, Vt.: Charles E. Tuttle, 1963); Janine Anderson Sawada, *Confucian Values and Popular Zen: Sekimon Shingaku in Eighteenth-Century Japan* (Honolulu: University of Hawaii Press, 1993).

Itsuku-shima

Itsuku-shima, a prominent Shinto shrine, is located on the sacred Miya Island, located in the middle of the bay at Hiroshima, Japan. Three ocean goddesses—Ichikishima, Tagori, and Tagitsu, the daughters of SUSANO-O NO MIKOTO—are thought to live at the center of the shrine. They are believed to be the protectors of mariners and their ships.

The shrine dates at least to the sixth century, though, as have most of Japan's older sacred structures, it has been rebuilt several times. The present shrine dates to the 12th century, though the main building was last reconstructed in 1875.

Visitors today are welcomed to the shrine and the island by a TORII (gate) that sits in the water offshore. Many of the buildings at Itsuku-shima Shrine are built over the water and rest on stilts to protect them from the high tides. It seems that the Heike clan who owned the island did not allow common pilgrims to the shrine to set foot on the island itself. There are more than a dozen additional temples and shrines on the island.

In 1996, the shrine was placed on the United Nations Educational, Scientific, and Cultural Organization (UNESCO) World Cultural Heritage List. It is now administered by the Daishoin Temple, located on the mountainside behind the shrine. Incense burns inside the temple and is said to have been kept burning continuously for more than 12 centuries. From this fire, a flame was taken to light the Eternal Flame at Peace Park in Hiroshima.

Further reading: Linda Kay Davidson and David M. Gitlitz, *Pilgrimage from the Ganges to Graceland: An Encyclopedia* (Santa Barbara, Calif.: ABC-Clio, 2002).

Iwashimizu Shrine

A major Shinto shrine, Iwashimizu is dedicated to the Buddhist-Shinto bodhisattva HACHIMAN. Established in 859 by the Buddhist monk GYOKI, it sits on a mountain southwest of Kyoto. The deity Hachiman was associated with the legendary Japanese emperor Onin. During the Kamakura era (1192–1333), the Iwashimizu Shrine was sponsored by the ruling Minamoto clan, a powerful family in medieval Japanese history.

Further reading: Brian Bocking, "Changing Images of Shinto: Sanja Takusen or the Three Oracles," in John Breen and Mark Teeuwen, eds., *Shinto in History: Ways of the Kami* (Richmond, U.K.: Curzon, 2000), 167–185.

Izanagi/Izanami

Along with AMATERASU OMI-KAMI, Izanagi no Mikoto and Izanami no Mikoto are the main deities (KAMI) in the ancient SHINTO creation story. They are venerated in relation to their sexual mating, which led to the creation of Japan. They entered the story when the primordial deities sent Izanagi and Izanami to earth with orders to make something useful. The gods created an initial place, Orogoro, from which the two deities could work.

From their copulation came forth 14 islands and 35 *kami* (deities). In birthing the fire god, Kagu-Tsuchi, Izanami was burned so badly she died. In his grief, Izanagi beheaded their child. From his blood flowed numerous lesser *kami*. Izanagi then searched for his mate in the underworld. Unable to take her back, and after facing a set of terrors, Izanagi returned. He underwent a set of purification rituals that led to the emergence of Amaterasu, the sun goddess; TSUKIYOMI NO MIKOTO, the moon god who rules the night; and SUSANO-O NO MIKOTO, who ruled the sea (with different accounts assigning the three slightly different realms). Susano-o's three daughters, Ichikishima, Tagori, and Tagitsu, are thought of as the protectors of seamen and their ships. They are the focus of worship at the famous Shinto shrine ITSUKU-SHIMA.

After completing his purification work, Izanagi had finished his assigned task and retired from the scene (with different accounts offering different final resting places). Amaterasu Omi-Kami, Tsukiyomi no Mikoto, and Susano-o would then emerge as the main deities recognized in Shinto worship.

Further reading: Joseph M. Kitagawa, *On Understanding Japanese Religion* (Princeton, N.J.: Princeton University Press, 1987): Joseph W. T. Mason, *The Meaning of Shinto: The Primæval Foundation of Creative Spirit in Modern Japan* (Port Washington, N.Y.: Kennikat Press, 1967); Sokyo Ono, *Shinto: The Kami Way* (Rutland, Vt.: Bridgeway Press, 1962); Ian Reader, *Religion in Contemporary Japan* (Honolulu: University of Hawaii Press, 1991).

Izumo Taisha

Izumo Taisha, one of the oldest, largest, and most honored Shinto shrines in all Japan (second in honor only to the ISE SHRINE), is in the town of Izumo on the northern coast of western Honshu (the main island of Japan). It is dedicated to Okuninushi no Kami. The total shrine complex covers some 27 hectares. For many centuries it has been under the care of the Senke family.

The shrine was active in the prehistoric era and over the centuries has accumulated several stories concerning its origin. One story identifies Izumo as the location where the brother of AMATERASU OMI-KAMI, one of the main Shinto goddesses, slew a dragon. He later married a local princess and from her was born Okuninushi no Kami. Okuninushi no Kami is a patron of farming, medicine, and silk but, more important, oversees the linking of couples. Hence Izumo has become the favorite pilgrimage point for people seeking a mate or for parents seeking the best mate for their son or daughter.

The first written mention of the shrine is in *Nihonshiki,* the early chronicles of Japan, which dates to the eighth century. The *Nihonshiki* describes the main hall as having been some 50 meters, which would have made it the larg-est wooden structure in Japan. It was, however, rebuilt at a later date and is now only half the original height. The present shrine was constructed in 1774. Several of the associated buildings in the shrine complex date to the 1660s, including the Kagura-Den, a hall for sacred dance and today a popular site for weddings. Other important buildings were rebuilt in 1874.

There are three major festivals at Izumo Taisha, including the New Year and the rice planting festival in May. Then in late October/early November each year it is believed by many that all of the many Shinto deities (KAMI, some 8 million in number) gather at Izumo Taisha for their annual meeting. At Izumo, this period is the month of the gods (*kami-arizuki*) and in the rest of Japan the month of no gods (*kannazuki*).

Further reading: Linda Kay Davidson and David M. Gitlitz, *Pilgrimage from the Ganges to Graceland: An Encyclopedia* (Santa Barbara, Calif.: ABC-Clio, 2003); Ian Reader, *Religion in Contemporary Japan* (Honolulu: University of Honolulu Press, 1990); Yasutada Watanabe, *Shinto Art: Ise and Izumo Shrines.* Translated by Robert Rickets (New York: Weatherhill, 1974).

J

Japan, Buddhism in

Buddhism did not reach Japan until a millennium after the seminal events in the life of the Buddha, but Japan has subsequently emerged as one of the most important Buddhist countries in the world. While Buddhism may have entered the country earlier, its formal introduction occurred in the 550s as the rulers of the Korean kingdom of PAEKCHE presented the Japanese emperor with an image of Sakyamuni BUDDHA, scrolls recounting his life, and vessels to be used to keep the image clean. The Buddhist movement went on to develop several major sects and schools, including Zen, Nichiren, Jodo, and Shingon, all of which remain active. There are an estimated 50 million Buddhists in Japan today.

Not all of the emperor's supporting leadership welcomed the Korean gift, but the Soga family accepted the image and over local religious opposition enshrined it in what would later become the first Buddhist temple in Japan. Later in the century, the Sogas would create a shrine to MAITREYA, the future Buddha. However, the real development of broad support for the new faith would await the tenure of regent Prince SHOTOKU (r. 592–628). A scholar proficient in Chinese, he reoriented attention from Korean to Chinese Buddhism and sent scholars and other representatives to the mainland to acquire the faith in more depth. He subsequently funded the erection of a number of temples around his realm and saw to the sculpting of many images of the Buddha.

Continuing Chinese influence manifested in 710 with the creation of the city of NARA as the new capital of Japan on a Chinese pattern. One Nara temple, TODAI-JI, would become the center of Japanese Buddhism, and at Todai-ji a large bronze statue, 53 feet high, of the Buddha and a hall to house it were erected. Todai-ji would become the site of ordinations of Japanese Buddhist priests. The other temples in Nara as well as the temples now scattered throughout the country all looked to Todai-ji for leadership.

During its first century in the country, Buddhism was a religion of the elite and functioned in close relationship with the government. The emperor granted the land for the erection of each temple; saw to the appointment of priests, monks, and nuns; and gave land that supplied income for the temple's maintenance. Initially, four schools that had entered Japan from China in the seventh century—the KUSHA, JOJITSU, SANRON, and HOSSO—established themselves at Nara. Each specialized in the study of specific Buddhist sutras and related texts and represented four theological variants on Buddhist theology. Shortly after the founding of Nara, two additional schools—the RITSU and KEGON—would also open temples. The Ritsu would specialize in the study of the rules governing the priests and monks.

In 794, the capital of Japan was moved to Kyoto, then called Heian, a second city created on a Chinese model. Its creation would also set the stage for the introduction of two new schools of Chinese Buddhism. In 807 SAICHO (767–822), one of two monks who had recently spent time in China, introduced TENDAI BUDDHISM. While having one center inside the city, it would establish its headquarters just outside Heian at Mt. HIEI. Tendai would prove to be an eclectic sect. It would emphasize the teachings of the LOTUS SUTRA and a variety of practices, including veneration of AMITABHA through the chanting of the NEMBUTSU mantra and meditation. It also placed an emphasis on the discipline to be followed by monks at a time in which the standards at Nara had begun to slip.

KUKAI (774–835), who went to China at the same time as Saicho, was most impressed with CHINESE ESOTERIC BUDDHISM and upon his return founded the SHINGON movement. While beginning his work in Heian, Kukai wished to take the monks under his care outside the chaos of urban life and eventually was able to establish his new Buddhist group at the more remote Mt. KOYA, where he would later retire. Shingon would eventually operate from its two centers, To-ji inside Heian, and Mt. Koya.

The move to Heian led to a deemphasis in the role of the Nara schools, only three of which would survive; only one, the Kegon, would develop into a separate sect that would play any significant role in the future of Japanese Buddhism. Todai-ji, by keeping a stranglehold on ordinations, would continue to hold a strong position in the larger Buddhist community until other ordination sites were designated over the centuries.

THE KAMAKURA ERA

The year 1183 saw the rise of the shogun, a military ruler who turned the Japanese emperor into

a figurehead, and his establishment of his throne at KAMAKURA. The shift of power away from Heian also saw a significant change in culture as the love of things Chinese gave way to a new emphasis on Japanese culture. At the same time, as power flowed to Kamakura so did the older Buddhist groups, most of which established new centers as close to the shogun as possible. The move to Kamakura was symbolic of the popularization of Buddhism, which had heretofore remained largely a movement among the elite—courtiers, the powerful families, the intelligentsia, and the military leadership. The popularization of Buddhism set the context in the 13th century for new forms of Buddhism, attuned to the shifting situation.

Among the early Kamakura era Buddhisms to arise, PURE LAND BUDDHISM was built around the chanting of the *nembutsu* as a means of expressing faith in AMITABHA (Amida). While use of the *nembutsu* had been part of Tendai practice, a former Tendai priest named Honen (1133–1212) would claim that the recitation of the *nembutsu* as an expression of one's faith in Amitabha would be all that was necessary to attain entrance into the Pure Land paradise, believed to be located in the west.

Honen emerged at the close of the Heian period, and much of his later years would be spent fending off the attacks of the priests of the older Buddhist groups. It would be left to his disciples to found the several Pure Land sects. Shokobo (1162–1238) carried on Honen's teachings with the least modification and became the founder of the Chinzei school, known today as the Jodo-shu sect. Most prominent of Honen's students, however, was SHINRAN (1173–1262). He differed from Honen in his disavowal of the monastic ideal and favoring of the marriage of priests. Also Shinran focused exclusively on Amitabha, while Honen merely favored Amitabha among the other Buddhist deities and BODHISATTVAS. The JODO SHINSHU sect that Shinran founded would later become the most popular form of Buddhism in Japan. Jodo Shinshu currently exists in two main factions, the HONPA HONGWANJI and the HIGASHI HONGWANGI.

The rise of the Kamakura shogun also provided an opportunity for the transmission of Chinese CHAN BUDDHISM to Japan. While some ZEN BUDDHISM had existed in Japan as early as the seventh century, it did not make headway until EISAI (1141–1215) traveled to China and discovered LINJI CHAN BUDDHISM on Mt. TIAN TAI. Upon his return he built the first Zen temple of what would become known in Japan as RINZAI ZEN. He was able to fend off his former colleagues among the Tendai Buddhists as he found favor with the shogun, Minamoto Yoriie (1182–1204), and invited his founding of a monastery, Jufuki-ji, in Kamakura.

Eisai also opened a monastery in Kyoto and found among his students DOGEN (1200–53), who also moved from his Tendai training and in 1223 traveled to China to see Chan practice there. In China he encountered CAODONG Chan Buddhism and received his seal of enlightenment (INKASHO-MEI). Upon his return to Japan in 1227, he settled at Eisai's Kyoto center and began the work that led to the founding of Soto Zen in the country. His career climaxed with the opening of EIHEI-JI monastery, in Echizen Province, the fountainhead center of the movement. Dogen's Soto practice was distinguished from Eisai's Rinzai Zen by its disavowal of the use of the KOAN.

The third addition to the Buddhist community during the 13th century was not imported from China but grew from the distinctive approach to the faith by another former Tendai Buddhist, NICHIREN (1222–82). Convinced that Tendai Buddhism had left its roots through the centuries since its founding, he sought to reform it by a renewed emphasis on the LOTUS SUTRA. However, instead of merely valuing the Lotus Sutra as the best among others, he grew to believe that it was the only sutra of note and made calling upon the "wonderful law of the Lotus" the cornerstone of practice. Nichiren's proposal for a single simple practice, "calling upon the Lotus," in Japanese,

namu myoho renge-kyo, was also based upon his strong belief that Buddhism had entered the age of MAPPO, when it would fall away from its essential teachings, and people needed a clear path to enlightenment.

Nichiren's career (and the formative years of his movement) was determined not so much by his own approach to Buddhism as by his harsh condemnation of all other forms. His uncompromising stance led to his being exiled from Kamakura in 1261 and even being sentenced to death a decade later. His execution was not carried out and he eventually settled at Minobu, on the western slope of Mount Juji. After his death, his main disciples divided over upkeep of his tomb, and two primary groups emerged, the Nichiren-shu and the NICHIREN SHOSHU.

With the rise of Nichiren Buddhism the basic outlines of the Japanese Buddhist community were set. Through the years of the Tokugawa shogunate (1600–1868), the older groups such as Kegon, Shingon, and Tendai would survive and grow slightly. Zen would spread with the support of the ruling warrior class (the samurai), though eventually the Pure Land groups would enjoy the largest popular support. Each of the groups would also split into several factions, analogous to Christian denominations. Rinzai Zen, for example, experienced no fewer than a dozen schisms.

MEIJI RESTORATION

Buddhism retained a privileged position relative to the government through the mid-19th century in Japan. It had also suffered from its subversion by the government, which saw Buddhism as an obedient arm of the state. Buddhism began to identify itself with the shogunate and was ill equipped to deal with the transformative events that were to overtake the country. In 1854, the United States forced the opening of the increasingly isolationist state into which the shogunate had led Japan. Then in 1867, the shogunate collapsed, and the emperor again took control of the country.

With the restoration of the imperial office as the real leader of the country, Buddhism was immediately faced with disestablishment, announced officially in 1869. Now in a privileged position, Shinto leadership turned on Buddhism with a vengeance. Buddhist images were defaced, and temples confiscated. Meanwhile, Christianity had been reintroduced into Japan. Thus, as Buddhism felt the attacks from Shintoism, proclaimed the national religion in 1870, it suffered new competition from a highly evangelical Western faith.

Pure Land Buddhists were the quickest to react to their new situation, and leadership emerged that sought reform and modernization emerged through the latter decades of the 19th century. They were supplied some opening when a new law on religious freedom was issued in 1887 but were hindered by the ever increasing need to assume a strong nationalist stance.

POSTWAR RELIGIOUS FREEDOM
The eight decades of the new order came crashing down in 1945 with Japan's loss of World War II and the devastating destruction of Hiroshima and Nagasaki by atomic bombs. After the war, an American-style freedom of religion law was adopted and a new era for Buddhism began, to which different groups have responded with more or less success.

The most important new reality of the post–World War era has been the rise of the so-called new religions. While the new religions cover the spectrum of religious practice worldwide, overwhelmingly the new groups represent new forms of Buddhism and Shintoism. New Buddhist groups include REIYUKAI, RISSHO KOSEI-KAI, SHINNYO-EN, KOFUKU NO KAGAKU, and AGON SHU. Most notorious of the new groups was AUM SHINRIKYO, whose leadership perpetrated the notorious gassing of the Tokyo subway system in 1995 that led to multiple deaths.

The most successful of the Buddhist new religions was SOKA GAKKAI, which through the 1970s and 1980s became the most controversial religious body in the country because of its aggressive proselytization activities and its development of a new political party, the Komeito. Controversy peaked in the 1990s with the break between Soka Gakkai, which had served as the lay organization of the Nichiren Shoshu, and its parent organization. The organization was subsequently targeted by legislators who reacted to the Aum Shinrikyo incident, proposing new laws specifically aimed at limiting Soka Gakkai's growing influence. Then suddenly, after the election of 1999, the Komeito Party was needed by the ruling party in the government to constitute a new ruling coalition. Overnight the organization, now known as SOKA GAKKAI INTERNATIONAL, completely changed its position in the country.

THE TWENTY-FIRST CENTURY
Buddhism is currently the dominant religion of Japan, with slightly over half of the population identifying themselves as adherents. That is a somewhat deceptive figure, as Buddhism mixes with Shintoism in the lives of many Japanese. Observers have noted the manner in which Shintoism and its rituals carry people in their formative years and Buddhism in their more mature years. Japanese Buddhists do not see the contradiction in participation in the activities of other faiths that is typical of, for example, Christians or Muslims.

Japanese Buddhism also, beginning in the late 19th century, initiated a move outside the country. The first temples were founded in Hawaii, and then in North and South America. In the 20th century, Japanese immigration into Europe led to the development of Buddhist communities in Germany, Italy, and the United Kingdom. Immigration increased after World War II, and the whole spectrum of Japanese Buddhism, including the new religions, is now present in the West. Soka Gakkai has also repeated its success and is now the largest Buddhist group in many Western countries.

Further reading: Peter B. Clarke, *Bibliography of Japanese New Religious Movements* (Richmond, U.K.: Japan

Library, 1999); H. Byron Earhart, *Japanese Religion: Unity and Diversity.* 3d ed. (Belmont, Calif.: Wadsworth, 1982); Kazuo Kasahara, ed., *A History of Japanese Religion.* Translated by Paul McCarthy and Gaynor Sekimori (Tokyo: Kosei, 2001); E. Dale Saunders, *Buddhism in Japan* (Philadelphia: University of Pennsylvania Press, 1964); Koyu Sonoda and Yusen Kashiwahara, eds., *Shapers of Japanese Buddhism* (Rutland, Vt.: Charles E. Tuttle, 1994).

Japan, Daoism in

The precise time of the arrival of DAOISM in Japan is not clear. There are records of an effort to seek immortality in the NIHONSHOKI (*Chronicle of Japan,* 720 C.E.) which are similar to Daoism's central theme of the search for immortality. Concrete evidence of Daoism in Japan, however, is found in the use of such practices as talismans and YIN-YANG divination. In addition Daoist influences can be found in early Japanese literature.

KUKAI (774–835), the founder of the SHINGON school of Japanese Vajrayana Buddhism, was well aware of the differences among Buddhism and Daoism and CONFUCIANISM. An esoteric Buddhist text, the *Gorin kuji hishaku* (Secret formula of the five chakras and nine worlds), from the 12th century describes MANTRAS and MUDRAS within a mystical body composed of the five organs, a common conception in Daoism as well as Chinese medicine. In addition such Daoist gods as the Great One (Taiyi) and Leigong (lord of thunder) were worshipped from an early period in Japan.

Daoism also exerted strong influence on SHUGENDO, an ascetic practice founded in the sixth century that integrates mountain shamanic worship with Buddhist and Shinto elements.

The belief in the THREE WORMS (*sanshi*) led in Japan to the development of the Koshin cult. The *koshin* (in Chinese, *gengshen*) referred to the day the three worms ascend to heaven to report on the person's sins. If people take ritual precautions prior to that day the three worms can be prevented from ascending. And if this happens seven times the worms will all die together. This form of vigil was practiced in Tang China and was known in ninth-century Japan. In Japan the event became an excuse for a banquet. And by the Tokugawa period (1600–1964 C.E.) it had become an occasion for lectures.

One final point: Daoism has a close though often unrecognized connection with ZEN BUDDHISM, for instance, the Zen emphasis on harmony with nature. Overall, Daoism, with Shinto and popular Buddhism, is present in Japanese culture in many ways. There are today a few overtly Daoist congregations and temples, usually associated with overseas Chinese or Japanese who have lived in Chinese society. But more important, Daoism's influence is found beneath the surface in many areas of Japanese life, for instance, in considerations taken regarding the location of buildings, in folk medicine, and in Japanese shamanistic rituals.

See also UNITED STATES, DAOISM IN.

Further reading: Masuo Shin'ichiro, "Daoism in Japan," in Livia Kohn, ed., *Daoism Handbook* (Leiden: Brill, 2000), 821–842.

Japan Buddhist Federation

An association of established Buddhist groups in Japan, numbering 103 denominations and many regional associations, the Japan Buddhist federation claims to include more than 90 percent of all Buddhist institutions in Japan. In 1900 a loosely organized group called "Buddhist Interfaith" formed to oppose the government's efforts to control religion. This group later became the Buddhist Confederation of Japan and, in 1957, the Japan Buddhist Federation. The federation is active in such projects as the restoration of the LUMBINI Sacred Garden, the Buddha's birthplace, and education efforts to fight discrimination against the Buraku minority in Japan. In 2001 the federation also voiced criticism of Prime Minister Koizumi's controversial visit to the YASUKUNI

SHINTO Shrine. The visit was heavily criticized in Asia because Yasukuni houses the remains of 14 major war criminals from World War II. The federation criticized the act as counter to the principle of separation of state and religion.

The federation publishes a periodical, *Zenbutsu,* thrice annually.

Further reading: Japan Buddhist Federation. Available online. URL: http://www.jbfne.jp/index_e.html. Accessed on January 19, 2006.

Jataka Tales

The *Jatakas* are a series of hundreds of legendary stories about the past lives of Shakyamuni BUDDHA prior to his life in the fifth century B.C.E. in India. These were collected in the first few hundred years following the Buddha's PARINIRVANA (death). They helped to popularize Buddhism in Indian culture in those periods.

Each of the 547 stories includes an associated moral point. For instance, "Buried Treasure" relates the story of a servant who refuses to disclose the location of a deceased father's inheritance. It illustrates the point that "a little power soon goes to the head of one not used to it."

These stories are now included in both the Theravada and Mahayana SUTRA and VINAYA collections. They may have been the basis for parts of *Aesop's Fables, Sinbad the Sailor,* and *The Arabian Nights.*

Further reading: Ethel Beswick, *Jataka Tales: Birth Stories of the Buddha* (London: Murray, 1956); V. Fausböll and Dines Anderson, *The Jataka Together with Its Commentary: Being Tales of the Anterior Births of Gotama Buddha.* 7 vols. (Oxford: Pali Text Society, 1992); H. T. Francis and E. J. Thomas, *Jataka Tales: Selected and edited with introduction and notes* (Cambridge: Cambridge University Press, 1916); Noor Inayat, *Twenty Jataka Tales* (Philadelphia: McKay, 1939); John Garrett Jones, *Tales and Teachings of the Buddha: The Jataka Stories in Relation to the Pali Canon* (London: George Allen & Unwin, 1979).

Jayavarman VII (1125?–1215?; r. 1181–1220) *great Angkor king*

Jayavarman VII was the Cambodian chief who rose out of relative obscurity to become the ruler of medieval Angkor (Cambodia). In 1177, forces from Cham (Vietnam) captured much of Cambodia and Jayavarman led the opposition that eventually recaptured the country. In the years following his ascending the throne formally in 1181, he extended his kingdom into what today is Thailand. At this time, a form of Hinduism centered on the worship of the god Shiva was dominant in the area. However, Jayavarman was a Buddhist and imposed his faith on the people.

The major expression of the new rulership and its religion was the city of Angkor Thom. A walled city, eight miles in circumference, it was surrounded by a crocodile-filled moat. Each of city's entranceways was crowned with a statue of the bodhisattva AVALOKITESVARA (GUAN YIN). The towers located along the city's walls were decorated with huge smiling faces of Jayavarman as the Buddha.

The primary religious building within Angkor Thom was the Bayon Temple, a Buddhist temple that retained elements of the preceding Hinduism. The temple was originally a Shiva temple and only converted to a Buddhist worship center as it was being constructed, a process stretched out over several decades. The top of the temple followed the theme of the city gates with some 50 towers, each with a representation of Avalokitesvara with four faces to greet individual worshippers from whatever direction they approached the temple. In addition to Angkor Thom, Jayavarman built other impressive temples such as Preah Khan and Ta Phrom.

Much of the power Jayavarman and his successors wielded was due to their identification with Buddhist deities and bodhisattvas such as Avalokitesvara. However, over the next centuries, the Jayavarman rulers' Mahayana Buddhism was slowly replaced with Theravada Buddhism, which had never adopted the belief in multiple deities and hence undercut the royal family's authority.

Then in the 15th century, a Thai army looted Angkor, and the city was abandoned and lost to the memory of the locals. It was rediscovered in the 19th century by Western explorers. Jayavarman was succeeded by his son, Indravarman II (r. 1220–43), who lost much of the territory previously conquered by his father, and the decline of the Khmer kingdom began.

Further reading: Joan Lebold Cohen, *Angkor: The Monuments of the God Kings* (New York: Harry N. Abrams, 1975); Michael Freeman and Roger Warner, *Angkor: The Hidden Glories* (Boston: Houghton Mifflin, 1990).

Jeung San Do

Jeung San Do (the Dao of Jeung San) is a Korean spiritual movement. Jeung San Do members chant as a meditation practice. There are eight separate MANTRAS used. The primary mantra is the Tae-eul Mantra, which offers healing and protection. In addition there is a series of 16 *taiji*-like physical exercises known as Tae-eul-ju Exercise. It is based on a healing meditation technique taught by Jeung San Sangjenim.

Jeung San Sangjenim (also called Gang Il-sun Sah-ok, or Sang Je Nim; 1871–1909) was born in a village in the south of Korea. He was a healer and local sage. In Jeng San Do teachings he is the embodiment of the key deity of the universe, an amalgamation of the Confucian Shang Di, the Daoist Jade emperor MAITREYA, and God. Although his first spiritual awakening occurred when he was seven, the key event in his early years was the Donghak (Eastern Learning) Uprising, a farmers' revolt that ultimately resulted in the Japanese occupation of Korea. After observing this key event in Korean history, Jeung San Sangjenim resolved to dedicate his life to reducing suffering. After several years of traveling he attained final enlightenment in 1901.

Sangjenim called his work the renewal of heaven and earth. He established an organization called the Creative Government, which included several types of spirits. Together he and the spirits worked on shifting the course of events. Sangjenim was thus more than a prophet, because he took steps to fix the balance of forces in the universe. This spiritual work is called Cheonjigongsa, "the work of renewing heaven and earth."

Before his death Jeung San Sangjenim pronounced that men and women were equal. It was thus no surprise that a woman, Lady Ko Pam-lye (1880–1935), known as Taemonim, "Great Mother," took over the movement in 1909. Today the movement's leader is Ahn Oon-sahn, whose title is *Tai-sa-bu-nim*, "great-teacher-father." His son, Ahn Gyung-jun, called *Sa-bu-nim*, "teacher-father," is also active.

Jeung San Do has grown since the Korean War period and has spread internationally. It is often classed as a new age religion.

Further reading: *JeungSanDo DoJeon* (Seoul, Korea: Daewon, 1995); Jeung San Do. Available online. URL: www.jeungsando.org/main/index.asp. Accessed on October 2, 2005.

Jien (1155–1225) *Japanese Tendai head priest*

Jien, the chief priest of Japanese TENDAI BUDDHISM at the beginning of the 13th century, was born as the son of the emperor regent Fujiwara Tadamichi (1097–1164) and as a youth began his training as a Tendai monk/priest. He rose steadily during the last decades of the 12th century and in 1203 was appointed the general administrator of priests of the Tendai sect. He on occasion also served as the chief priest at ENRYAKU-JI, the Tendai head temple.

Jien is remembered for his response to the growing belief among Japanese Buddhists that Buddhism was entering the MAPPO period, when belief in the Buddhist teachings would disintegrate. This belief was one manifestation of the anxiety over the rise of the shogunate at Kamakura. As opposed to trends emphasizing meditation and the sudden insight into one's nature it provides, and the magical approach provided by SHINGON Buddhism, Jien emphasized the need to study the great texts and master Buddhist teachings. To that end he sponsored and himself gave a number of lectures to assist Buddhists in general, and the monks under his direction in particular, to master the Dharma. His emphasis formed the thread in his major written work, *A Personal View*, in which he commented on the works of the Chinese T'IAN TAI scholar ZHI YI (538–597).

In seeming contradiction to his doctrinaire religious stance, Jien was also a poet of note and left behind a major collection, *The Gathering of Jewels*. After his death he was honored by the emperor's court.

Further reading: Delmer M. Brown and Ishida Ichirō, trans., *The Future and the Past: A Translation and Study of the Gukanshō, an Interpretative History of Japan Written in 1219* (Berkeley: University of California Press, 1979); Kazuo Kasahara, ed., *A History of Japanese Religion*. Translated by Paul McCarthy and Gaynor Sekimori (Tokyo: Kosei, 2001).

Ji Gong (Dao Ji; Crazy Ji; Beixian, Chi Kung)
(d. 1209 C.E.) *deified monk famous as Daoist trickster figure*

Ji Gong, "Duke Ji," an extremely popular figure in Chinese religions, was originally a Buddhist monk during the Song dynasty (960–1279 C.E.). He was known for being eccentric and for not fitting in well in monastic life. Born in Tian Tai, in eastern China, he lived most of his life in monasteries around the capital of the Southern Song dynasty, Hangzhou. His final position was as abbot of the Jingci Monastery. He was known as a poet and is said to have written verse on the walls of his residences. He lived for decades as a vagabond and wore rags. He had a sharp wit and cared little for those who had power, including powerful monks. His failure to adhere to monastic rules is reflected in his practice of drinking.

Upon his cremation his *sarira* remains (RELICS from those of noble character, usually objects resembling small pebbles or bone fragments) sparkled and reportedly caused a furor among the local people. He was, the people realized, a saintly figure.

Ji Gong's figure is not unique in Chinese religious history. Many Daoists were renowned for their disregard for secular rules and their bouts of drunkenness. "Holy fools" was a tradition in Buddhist literature as well, especially among the Chan masters. There were also influences from outside China, for instance, the Indian Tantric idea that great saints (Mahasiddhas) could cultivate while immersed in everyday reality, even in base occupations like prostitution and garbage collecting.

In Ji Gong's period there was most probably a large increase in traveling "miracle workers," mainly due to the dramatic increase in issuing of ordination certificates (*dudie*) to raise funds. These miracle workers were popular among the public as healers. They were venerated during their lives and cults often grew around them after they died. Ji Gong was one of those figures around whom a cult formed. (Another is the Song dynasty figure BU DAI.) The popularity of such figures may reflect resentments against the organized monastic institutions.

Over time all these influences, as well as the historical figure, merged into the figure of Ji Gong. By the Ming and Qing period of Chinese history (1368–1911 C.E.), Ji Gong had become a stalwart figure in drama. He had originally survived as a major figure in oral storytelling traditions of the Hangzhou region. When drama flourished in the Ming dynasty, it was natural for dramatists to fall back on this rich tradition. He was also used in novels; the earliest was *The Recorded Sayings of the Recluse from Qiantang Lake, the Chan Master Crazy Ji* (*Qiantang hu yin Jidian Chanshi yulu*), dating to 1569. In the many works that followed Ji Gong is depicted as an enlightened monk, a magician, a poet, and a miracle worker. The stories in these texts, including fictional accounts, were accepted as official history by the Qing (1644–1911 C.E.), and their accounts of Ji Gong's life are found in many official Qing temple records. Additional works featuring Ji Gong include *Drunken Puti* (*Zui puti*) (written in the late 1600s) and *The Storyteller's Jigong*, a 240-chapter novel published in the 1890s and written by Guo Guangrui. In *The Storyteller's Jigong*, Ji takes on many additional powers, such as MARTIAL ARTS.

Just as he became a literary figure throughout China, so the cult of Ji Gong the god has spread through much of the Chinese-speaking world. He is a major figure in spirit possession and spirit writing cults (*FUGI*), including *yiguandao* groups. He was also a figure venerated by rebels behind the Boxer Rebellion. One intriguing aspect of Ji Gong's popularity is that it was apparently enhanced by his literary popularity. *The Storyteller's Jigong* in particular stimulated worship of Ji Gong in the 20th century. Prior to modern times, then, he was a relatively obscure cult figure popular mainly in the Hangzhou region, where he had lived. Today Ji Gong is a major deity who actively communicates with worshippers.

Further reading: Meir Shahar, *Crazy Ji: Chinese Religion and Popular Literature* (Cambridge: Harvard University Press, 1998).

Jingtu Zong (Ching-t'u Tsung) *See* PURE LAND BUDDHISM.

jinja (kami tsu yashiro, mori)

A *jinja* is a Shinto shrine. Historically they were known as *kami tsu yashiro* or *mori*, terms that mean "*kami* grove." These terms go back at least to the eighth century. A *yashiro* was a sacred place to worship a KAMI, or deity. Typically the most sacred place was roped off, and no one was allowed entry into that zone.

The oldest form of shrine was a wooded hill (*moriyama*). Rituals were performed in the open at the foot of mountains, also known as *kami* mountains. Several shrines such as Omiwa near NARA have preserved this form and so have no worship hall.

An additional form of shrine is the village shrine, where the mountain *kami* would be encouraged to stay when visiting. Buildings were later added in the groves near villages.

Kamiyado or *otabisho* are temporary or "field" shrines placed outside the village. They are seen as temporary resting spots for the *kami*, especially during festivals.

Typical festival rituals would see the *kami* being taken on roads from the mountain shrine to the village shrine (*jinja*) to the field shrine (*kamiya* or *kamiyado*).

Further reading: Sonoda Minoru, "Shinto and the Natural Environment," in John Breen and Mark Teeuwen, eds., *Shinto in History: Ways of the Kami* (Richmond, U.K.: Curzon, 2000), 32–46.

jiriki (own-power)/tariki (other-power)

Jiriki, or "own power," is a term developed in JODO SHINSHU, or PURE LAND BUDDHISM, thought in Japan. It indicates attaining enlightenment through one's own efforts, or "own-power," as opposed to the practice of *tariki*, attaining enlightenment through the "other-power" of some other figure, such as a benevolent bodhisattva. *Jiriki* is associated with ZEN BUDDHISM practices of self-cultivation, while *tariki* is associated with Jodo practices of chanting and depending on the benevolent figure of AMITABHA. In fact, in early Pure Land thought in China progress was accomplished through a combination of *jiriki* and *tariki*.

After the Japanese Pure Land thinker HONEN, the object of Jodo practice focused entirely on *tariki*. In contrast to *tariki, jiriki* can be considered the "difficult path," one of extensive meditation, purifications, and discipline. In Buddhist debate during the Kamakura period (1192–1333), *jiriki* was a term of abuse, indicating a deluded approach that assumed that traditional practice was sufficient to become a BODHISATTVA. It was also used to criticize Pure Land followers who did not follow the orthodox approach as taught by Honen. The term was used once by Honen but frequently by such other religious leaders of the period as SHINRAN, Gyonen, and NICHIREN.

Further reading: Mark L. Blum, *The Origins and Development of Pure Land Buddhism: A Study and Translation of Gyonen's Jodo Homom Genrusho* (Oxford: Oxford University Press, 2002); Kogen Mizuno, *Essentials of Buddhism: Basic Terminology and Concepts of Buddhist Philosophy and Practice.* Translated by Gaynor Sekimori (1972. Reprint, Tokyo: Kosei, 1996), 24.

Ji-shu

Ji-shu, a subsect of Japanese Pure Land Buddhism, was inspired by the life and work of IPPEN (1239–89). In 1271, he had a deep religious experience that convinced him of the truth of the PURE LAND approach to Buddhism and three years later was sent out on a mission to spread word of the value of practicing the NEMBUTSU, a mantralike prayer in veneration of AMITABHA. Ippen pushed Pure Land belief almost to a form of universalism in his conclusion that Amitabha would save all who said the *nembutsu*.

Ippen spent the last years of his life traveling around Japan to spread the word. Shortly before Ippen died, he proclaimed the end of his mission. SHINKYO (1237–1319), his successor as head of his following, initially accepted what Ippen said at face value. However, he was soon convinced that many people had yet to hear the message of the *nembutsu*. Thus, Shinkyo began to travel around

the country preaching and dancing as his master had. He also began to form temples and ordain priests. His organization of the movement brought the Ji sect into existence.

Contemporary followers of Ji-shu follow Ippen's practice. They focus worship on the repetition of the *nembutsu* and continue to practice the dance. They also offer people cards promoting the saying of the *nembutsu*.

Ji-shu is headquartered at Fujisawa city, Kanagawa Province. It has in recent years celebrated two important dates. In 1886, the emperor gave Ippen the honorary name *Ensho Daishi* (great teacher). In 1975 Ippen was memorialized on the occasion of the 700th anniversary of his beginning his mission. There are more than 400 Ji-shu temples in Japan.

Further reading: *Buddhist Denominations and Schools in Japan* (Tokyo: Bukkto Dendo Kyokai, 1984); Kazuo Kasahara, ed., *A History of Japanese Religion.* Translated by Paul McCarthy and Gaynor Sekimori (Tokyo: Kosei, 2001).

Jizo   *See* KSHITIGARBHA.

jnana

Jnana is knowledge or "gnosis," but in Buddhism it indicates knowledge of a certain kind. In contrast to *prajna*, wisdom in general, *jnana* indicates knowledge of enlightenment itself, transcendental knowledge. Such knowledge is therefore more complete and "final" than knowledge in the usual sense. Mundane or everyday-world knowledge is characterized by wisdom of dealing with the defilements.

In Buddhism *jnana* is often associated with stages of cultivation. *Jnana paramita* is the perfected knowledge available to a bodhisattva who has attained the 10th stage of practice, according to the Flower Garland Sutra (Avatamsaka-sutra, Huayan Jing).

Further reading: Kogen Mizuno, *Essentials of Buddhism: Basic Terminology and Concepts of Buddhist Philosophy and Practice.* Translated by Gaynor Sekimori (1972. Reprint, Tokyo: Kosei, 1996); Santideva, *The Bodhicaryavatara.* Translated by Kate Crosby and Andrew Skilton (Oxford: Oxford University Press, 1995).

Jodo   *See* JODO-SHU; PURE LAND BUDDHISM.

Jodo Shinshu (Shin, Pure Land)

Jodo Shinshu, a branch of PURE LAND BUDDHISM, is one of the most widely practiced forms of Buddhism in Japan. Adherents believe that the teachings of SHINRAN contained in *Kyagyo shinshu* and his other writings crystallize the spiritual vision articulated in the Larger Sukhavati-vyaha-sutra, or the Larger Pure Land Sutra; the Amitiyurdhyana-sutra, or the Meditation Sutra; and the Smaller Sukhavativyaha-sutra, or the Smaller Pure Land Sutra. These three texts make up the core canon of all Pure Land Buddhism. Pure Land belief centers on the role of AMITABHA Buddha, who resides in his Western Paradise and welcomes all who repeat his name devoutly. It is thus a practice based on faith in the salvation of Amitabha.

Pure Land Buddhism emerged in China in the early fifth century and was transmitted to Japan in the ninth century, when devotion to Amitabha, generally called Amida in Japan, became an element in TENDAI Buddhism. However, it was in the 12th century that HONEN (1133–1212) established a separate Pure Land organization, which focused exclusively on devotion to Amida through the reccitation of the NEMBUTSU, a short mantralike prayer that acknowledges the believer's taking refuge in Amida Buddha.

Honen initially encountered devotion to Amida at Mt. HIEI, the headquarters of Tendai Buddhism. He left Mt. Hiei and in 1175 began to preach his more exclusive approach. He gained a substantial following but ran afoul of the government as a result of the debate over the extent of the power of the *nembutsu* to cancel out a life of extreme immorality. Could merely reciting the *nembutsu* take away the consequences of murder or other horrendous acts? Some followers said yes, and as a result, the government saw the new movement as subversive of the social order and prohibited it. Honen was exiled. Only after some years passed was he allowed to return and the movement to be propagated again. The year before his death, Honen settled in Kyoto at Chion-in Temple, which remains the headquarters of the group.

After Honen's death, a range of ideas were debated within the Jodo-Shu community. The most important development, however, occurred when one of Honen's students, SHINRAN, left the order of monks and married. He developed a lay-oriented from of Pure Land Buddhism that eventually eclipsed its parent organization.

Inspired with the insights from these three sutras, Shinran stressed the centrality of *shinjin,* true or sincere faith. He also assumed that the devotee possesses nothing true or absolute. Spiritual release occurs when the devotee perceives his or her inadequacies and surrenders to the absolute Other Power (see JIRIKI/TARIKI) of Amitabha, or Amida Buddha. Amida Buddha's compassionate efficacy is the sole power that confers salvation. Even *shinjin,* the prime condition for birth in the Pure Land, is a gift, and the sincere utterance of the NEMBUTSU is an invocation of gratitude and joy for Amida's compassion. For Shinran, birth in the Pure Land is the most conducive waystation for the ultimate realization of enlightenment (BODHI) or NIRVANA. Subsequently Kakunyo (1270–1351), Shinran's grandson, and his 10th-generation successor, RENNYO (1415–99), clarified and articulated his ideas into cogent vernacular. For example, in an attempt to communicate the notion of Other Power, Rennyo coined the expression *tasuke tamae to tanomu,* "relying on [Amida's power] to please save me." Rennyo's efforts won many devotees and transformed the Hongwanji school of Jodo Shinshu from a peripheral movement into a powerful Buddhist school, a position it still holds.

Further reading: Alfred Bloom, *Shinran's Gospel of Pure Grace* (Tucson: University of Arizona Press, 1965); *Buddhist Denominations and Schools in Japan* (Tokyo: Bukkto Dendo Kyokai, 1984); James C. Dobbins, *Jodo Shinshu: Shin Buddhism in Medieval Japan* (Bloomington: Indiana University Press, 1989); Daigan Matsunaga and Alicia Matsunaga, *Foundation of Japanese Buddhism,* Vol. 2. (Los Angeles: Buddhist Books International, 1976); E. Dale Saunders, *Buddhism in Japan* (Philadelphia: University of Pennsylvania Press, 1964).

Jodo-Shu

Jodo-Shu is the original organization of PURE LAND BUDDHISM in Japan. Pure Land Buddhism is focused on devotion to AMITABHA (or Amida) Buddha, which is believed to lead to rebirth into the heavenly realm overseen by Amitabha (the Pure Land). The Pure Land perspective originated in three SUTRAS—the Amida Sutra, the Buddha Infinite Life Sutra, and the Meditation on the Buddha Infinite Life Sutra.

In 1175, HONEN (1133–1212) established a Pure Land organization, Jodo-Shu, that was separate from the Tendai school of Japanese Buddhism practiced on Mt. Hiei. Honen eventually ran into government opposition. He was exiled and only allowed to preach freely a year before his death. He made Chion-in Temple the headquarters of the group. Although the form of Pure Land championed by his follower SHINRAN later came to eclipse the original organization established by Honen, Jodo-Shu Buddhism is still headquartered at Chion-in Temple in Kyoto. Temples are found across Japan and in the 20th century, Jodo-Shu joined the Japanese diaspora and now has temples in North and South America. Shinran's movement, known as JODO SHINSHU, currently exists through two large groups, the HONPA HONGWANJI and the HIGASHI HONGWANJI.

Further reading: Bukkyo Dendo Kyokai, *Buddhist Denominations and Schools in Japan* (Tokyo: Bukkyo Dendo Kyokai, 1984); Kodo Matsunami, *Introducing Buddhism* (Honolulu: HawaiiJodo Mission, 1965); K. Krishna Murthy, *Buddhism in Japan* (Delhi: Sundeep Prakashan, 1989); E. Dale Saunders, *Buddhism in Japan* (Philadelphia: University of Pennsylvania Press, 1964).

Jojitsu

The Jojitsu (Establishment of Truth) school was one of the six schools originally founded at NARA. It traced its origin to a fourth-century Indian Buddhist, Harivarman, who authored the Satyasiddhi Sastra (*Treatise on the Establishment of Truth*). This text was translated into Chinese by KUMARAJIVA in the fifth century. It emphasizes two propositions, that phenomena are transitory and that both the self and the world lack essential substantiality. It then offers a set of practices that will allow one to experience the truth and become free of illusions.

Some of Kumarajiva's students established a school of thought based upon the view of nonsubstantiality championed in Harivarman's *Treatise,* which spread in popularity through the seventh century. The view on substance it propounded was opposed by the San Lun school (known in Japanese as the SANRON, or Three Treatises, school), which saw it as too extreme. The San Lun school gradually replaced the Jojitsu movement in China but not before it spread to Korea and then Japan.

The teachings of the Jojitsu school were studied by the Japanese regent Prince SHOTOKU (573–621), who received them from Korea (and was almost simultaneously also introduced to the opposing Sanron teachings). Thus in Japan the Jojitsu and Sanron approaches to the study of phenomena were generally tied together, even at NARA, where separate schools for each were established. Over time the Sanron school absorbed the Jojitsu, but eventually both lost support and died out.

Further reading: K. Krishna Murthy, *Buddhism in Japan* (Delhi: Sundeep Prakashan, 1989); E. Dale Saunders,

Buddhism in Japan (Philadelphia: University of Pennsylvania Press, 1964).

Jokhang

Jokhang is the central religious site for Tibetans. Jokhang is a United Nations Educational, Scientific, and Cultural Organization (UNESCO) World Heritage list site (added in 2000, along with the Potala Palaces). It is located in the center of Lhasa, Tibet.

Jokhang was built during the reign of King Songtsem Gampo (617–650), who according to tradition had married two princesses, one from Nepal and another from Tang dynasty China. Each arrived in Lhasa with an image of the Buddha, and Songtsem Gampo built the vast temple complex to house these images.

Jokhang is divided into eight temples. These are housed in a structure of four stories, constructed around a central square. One statue of Sakyamuni Buddha found in the temple pictures him at the age of eight and is said to be the same image carried to Tibet by Princess Wen, the Chinese bride of Songtsem Gampo.

The story of the temple is connected with the entry of Buddhism in Tibet and the founding of the city of Lhasa. The site of the temple was originally a vast lake. After the lake was filled in, the site was called Ra Sa (Sheep-earth) Vphrul Snang—or Lhasa, for short.

Further reading: "Lhasa—Jokhang Temple." Travel China Guide.com. Available online. URL: www.travelchinaguide.com/attraction/tibet/lhasa/jokhang.htm. Accessed on October 25, 2006.

K

Kadampa

The Kadampa tradition in Tibetan Buddhism is a medieval (11th-century C.E.) school of philosophy that was later absorbed into the GELUG school. Kadampa is generally traced to the 11th-century reformer Atisa and his student Dromtonpa, who in 1056 established Rva-sgreng monastery in western Tibet. Beginning in the 1070s, the kings of western Tibet had attempted to revive Buddhism, which had reached a low point from its original transmission, and at the same time reform it by removing accretions it might have picked up from the pre-Buddhist local religion.

Atisa, the author of the *Bodhipathapradipa* (Lamp for the Path of Enlightenment), had emphasized a practical approach to Buddhism. He offered a gradual process by which the teachings could be learned and progress toward the BODHISATTVA ideal realized. The reform movement would soon spread to all parts of Tibet and compete with the NYINGMA tradition for the allegiance of Tibetan Buddhists. The evolving teachings of Atisa's successors would later be assembled as the Lojong (Thought Transformation) writings.

The Kadampa school would later divide into three lineages, the Lamrimpa, the Shungpawa, and the Mengagpa. In more recent centuries, the Kadampa school would be absorbed into the Gelug school, though it would be remembered through the continued respect for the Lojong writings. In the late 20th century, some Gelug Buddhists led by Geshe Kelsang Gyatso, who objected to some of the decisions made by the DALAI LAMA, would organize separately as the NEW KADAMPA TRADITION, now based in England.

Further reading: Atisa, *Lamp for the Path to Enlightenment* (Ithaca, N.Y.: Snow Lion, 1997); Graham Coleman, ed., *A Handbook of Tibetan Culture: A Guide to Tibetan Centres and Resources throughout the World* (Boston: Shambhala, 1994); Anil Kumar Sarkar, *The Mysteries of Vajrayana Buddhism: From Atisa to Dalai Lama* (Colombia, Mo.: South Asia Books, 1993).

Kagyu

Kagyu means literally "lineage of oral transmission." This Tibetan school emphasizes the MAHAMUDRA and the teachings of NAROPA. The Kagyu schools form one of the main groupings in the various strands of Buddhism developed in Tibet, along with the GELUG, NYINGMA, and SAKYA traditions. Many of the central Kagyu practices were introduced to Tibet by MARPA the Translator (1012–1197 C.E.). The Kagyu tradition was said to have four main branches and eight smaller ones, and several of these are active today. The largest is the Karma Kagyu. The Drikung Kagyu and the DRUKPA KAGYU also have considerable followings, both in Asia and in the Western world.

The differences between these schools of Tibetan Buddhism have as much to do with the details of ritual forms of meditation practice as they do with doctrine. All of them start by indicating that ordinary life is often very painful and at best unsatisfactory and does not last. All of them stress the possibility and the need to free ourselves from the cycle of birth and death, and all teach that developing compassion for every suffering being is vitally important.

Intensive practice is heavily emphasized, and a Kagyu "lama," or teacher, must include at least one close, guided retreat of over three years in his or her training. This might include the advanced practices known as the Six Teachings of Naropa—yogas that deal with the inner heat as practiced by Milarepa, illusory body, the dream state, the clear light of sleep, the state between one life and the next (Tibetan, BARDO), and transfer of consciousness at the time of death.

Another practice emphasized by the Kagyu schools is the teaching of MAHAMUDRA (Tibetan: chagchen). This system of meditation and practice makes less use of elaborate visualizations and focuses instead on recognizing the true nature of the mind, which is said to be naturally clear, luminous, empty of anything that can be grasped, and yet blissful. The advanced practitioner should remain in this state, so that all appearances, good or bad, are naturally liberated.

Further reading: Garma C. C. Chang, trans., *The Hundred Thousand Songs of Milarepa.* (Boston: Shambhala, 1999); Khenpo Karthar Rinpoche, *The Instructions of Gampopa: A Precious Garland of the Supreme Path* (Ithaca, N.Y.: Snow Lion, 1996); Lobsang P. Lhalungpa, trans., *The Life of Milarepa* (Boston: Shambhala, 1985); Jampa Thaye, *The Garland of Gold: The Early Kagyu Masters in India and Tibet* (Bristol, U.K.: Ganesha Press, 1990); The Third Jamgön Kongtrül, *Cloudless Sky: The Mahamudra Path of the Tibetan Buddhist Kagyü School.*

Translated by Tina Drasczyk, Alex Drasczyk, and Richard Gravel (Boston: Shambhala, 2001); Chögyam Trungpa, *The Life of Marpa the Translator* (Boston: Shambhala, 1986).

kaigen (kaiyan)

The *kaigen* (eye opening) ceremony is performed commonly in China, Korea, and Japan to commemorate the establishment of a new Buddha image. In NICHIREN SHOSHU practice each GOHONZON, or object of worship (usually a calligraphic scroll), should be properly consecrated in a *kaigen* ceremony in order to have potency. Otherwise the object remains artwork on the wall. Similarly, a Buddha image must be offered and consecrated in an unveiling ceremony for it to be perceived as effective by worshippers.

Further reading: Senchu Murano, "Dai Mandala Kaigen Shiki: Great Mandala Eye Opening Ceremony." Article excerpted from Manual of Nichiren Buddhism (1995), translations of portions of Nichiren Shu Hoyo Shiki. Nichiren Coffeehouse. Available online. URL: http://nichirenscoffeehouse.net/Gohonzon/EyeOpeningCeremony.html. Accessed on May 19, 2006.

Kailas, Mt./Lake Manasarovar

The spectacular Mt. Kailas in western Tibet and the equally beautiful Lake Manasarovar that lies at its base are sacred to both the Buddhists and followers of the BON religion in Tibet, as well as to Hindus in India. The waters that flow from the glaciers on Mt. Kailas feed the lake (the highest freshwater lake of any size in the world) and four rivers—the Indus, Brahmaputra, Sutlej, and most significantly, Ganges.

Tibetan Buddhists identify Mt. Kailas with Mt. SUMERU, the mythological center of the universe and symbolic of the single-pointedness of mind sought by Buddhist practitioners. The mountain embodies the principle of fatherhood. Furthermore, to bathe in Lake Manasarovar is to assist one's entrance into paradise, and to drink the water can lead to healing. Pilgrims walk around the lake occasionally stopping to bathe in its waters and quench their thirst. The lake embodies the mother principle. The completed trek around the lake (which takes three days or more) leads to instant Buddhahood.

Among the important mythological events to occur at the mountain and lake was that encountered by the Buddhist pioneer MILAREPA and a representative of the traditional Tibetan Bon religion. They held a competition demonstrating their spiritual powers. At one crucial point, the Bon leader flew to the top of the mountain on his drum. Unfortunately, when he arrived, Milarepa was waiting for him. As pilgrims make their circumambulation of the mountain, they will pass by a set of what are believed to be Milarepa's footprints and a shrine that houses a silver-covered conch shell that belonged to him.

Over the centuries, the Buddhists built some 13 monasteries near the mountain and lake and along the path taken by pilgrims to them. During the Cultural Revolution (1966–76), the sites fell victim to damage by Red Guards. Many of the artworks were taken and buildings destroyed. Pilgrimages began again in 1981, and subsequently most of the monasteries have been rebuilt, though resident to only a token number of monks. They now serve the pilgrims and mark the progress of their trek around the mountain. Among the best descriptions of the region are those from the accounts of modern pilgrims.

Many Hindus consider the mountain the axis of the world, and its sacredness interacts with the sacred quality of the rivers that have it as their source. Among the many stories told of the mountain is its being the site of the god Shiva's meeting one of his consorts, Meenakshi. Meenakshi was a king's daughter born with three breasts. It was said that she would lose one of them when she met her future husband. When she met Shiva, the third breast disappeared. Their wedding took place at Madurai, Tamil Nada, now the site of a temple built in 1560 in Meenakshi's honor. Each evening, the temple is closed and the main statue of Shiva is taken from its daytime spot to a room designated as Meenakshi's bedroom as music is played. It is returned at six the next morning. Three festivals annually mark the lovers' life together.

Jains believe that Rishaba, the first of their *tirthankaras* (teachers), received enlightenment at Mt. Kailas.

Further reading: Russell Johnson and Kerry Moran, *The Sacred Mountain of Tibet: On Pilgrimage to Kailas* (Rochester, Vt.: Park Street Press, 1989.); Swami Pranavananda, *Kailas-Manasarovar* (Calcutta: S. P. League, 1949); Robert A. F. Thurman, *Circling the Sacred Mountain: A Spiritual Adventure through the Himalayas* (New York: Bantam, 1999).

kaimyo

The *kaimyo* is a Buddhist name given to the deceased in Japan. It may be given to a Buddhist who has taken an oath to follow the five fundamental precepts—not to kill, lie, steal, commit adultery, or take intoxicants. In modern Japan it more often refers to a posthumous name given to a deceased individual. The *kaimyo* is usually written on a black hanging ornament.

The ceremony and fee to receive a *kaimyo* can be expensive today, often costing 1 million yen. (U.S.$8,600) and sometimes up to U.S.$80,000. Performing and assigning *kaimyo* have become an important revenue source for Buddhist temples in Japan. These costs have in turn generated widespread criticisms.

Further reading: Yoshiharu Tomatsu, "Transforming Ritual Transforming Japanese Funeral Buddhism." Jodo Shu Research Institute. Available online. URL: http://www.jsri.jp/English/Jodoshu/conferences/ritual-tomatsu.html. Accessed on January 19, 2006.

Kalu Rinpoche (1905–1989) *prominent contemporary Kagyu teacher in the West*

Kagu Rinpoche, who founded many KAGYU centers in the West in the 1970s and 1980s, was born in eastern Tibet, the son of a notable Kagyu TULKU, and at the age of 13 began formal studies toward assuming a leadership position in the tradition. His early years combined study with a series of notable Kagyu teachers (including the leading exponents of the eclectic RIME MOVEMENT) and a three-year retreat (begun in his 16th year) and a 12-year solitary retreat (begun in his 25th year). He then became the director of three-year retreats at Palpung monastery, the most prominent center of the KARMA KAGYU school.

During these years, the KARMAPA, or figurehead of the Karma Kagyu school, revealed him to be the reincarnation of Jamgon Kontrul Lodro Taye (1813–99), one of his father's teachers. At this point, Kalu Rinpoche became an inheritor of the little-known Shangpa Kagyu lineage, whose teachings, as revived by Jamgon Kontrul Lodro Taye, were passed to him. These teachings are traced back to two 11th century *yoginis,* NIGUMA and Sukhasiddhi.

In 1955, at the direction of the *karmapa* (the head of the Karma Kagyu school of Tibetan Buddhism), Kalu Rinpoche left Tibet to prepare the way should the Chinese assume control over Tibet and the Kagyu leadership need to move into India and Bhutan. He initially established two centers in Bhutan. In 1965 he opened a monastery, Samdrub Dhargye Ling, at Darjeeling, India, and established an accompanying three-year retreat center, over which he assumed direct authority. This became the center from which others would be established in India.

In 1971, Kalu Rinpoche began to travel throughout the West. Those centers in Europe and North America under his leadership were united under the collective title *Kagyu Dharma.* Besides his work of founding centers, he authored a number of books that have been translated into English.

Three years after his death in 1989, a young boy, now known as Yangsi Kalu Rinpoche (1990–), was recognized as his reincarnation. Kalu Rinpoche passed the Shangpa lineage to Bokar Tulku Rinpoche (1939–), who had studied the Six Yogas of Niguma under his guidance.

Further reading: Nicole Riggs, trans., *Like an Illusion: Lives of the Shangpa Kagyu Masters* (Fremont, Calif.: Dharma Cloud Press, 2000); Kalu Rinpoche, *The Dharma That Illuminates All Beings like the Light of the Sun and the Moon* (Albany: State University of New York Press, 1986); ———, *Excellent Buddhism: An Exemplary Life* (San Francisco, Calif.: ClearPoint Press, 1995); ———, *Profound Buddhism: From Hinayana to Vajrayana* (San Francisco, Calif.: ClearPoint Press, 1995); ———, *Secret Buddhism: Vajrayana Practices* (San Francisco, Calif.: ClearPoint Press, 2002).

Kamakura

The village of Kamakura contains some of Japan's greatest Buddhist treasures. Kamakura was a small fishing village on the southern coast of Honshu, Japan's main island. In 1185, the Minamoto family took control of Japan, and in 1192 its leader, Minamoto Yoritomo, was named shogun (military ruler). He established his regime in Kamakura, effectively making it the capital of the country, though the emperor still ruled ceremonially from Kyoto. Yoritomo died in 1199 and a struggle for control eventuated in the rise of his widow's family, the Hojo. They attained complete hegemony over the country and a succession of Hojo men would serve as regents until 1333. During this period, the political leadership of Japan remained at Kamakura, with the emperor reduced to a figurehead.

The Kamakura leadership showed great favor to Buddhism in general and ZEN in particular, and given the traditional alignment of Buddhism with the Japanese government, older groups moved to establish new centers in Kamakura and new groups emerged to court the shogun's and regent's favor. The new leaders, founders of new forms of Buddhism, would set the tone for the development of the Japanese Buddhist community, especially in the 13th century. The rise of the new leadership in Kamakura moved the military leaders, the samurai, forward. Their favoring of Zen did much to promote the new meditational practices across the country.

Zuisen-ji, Kamakura, Japan, showing the classical roof lines characteristic of the great Kamakura Zen temples

Interestingly, the main symbol emerging the Kamakura era was the DIABUTSU, the giant statue of AMITABHA (Amida) Buddha. Originally conceived as a rival to the giant VAIROCANA Buddha at TODAI-JI, the main Buddhist temple in Nara, it was the idea of Minamoto Yoritomo, who died before it could be constructed. Since the Hojo leaders favored Zen, Yoritomo's friends (who favored PURE LAND BUDDHISM) had to raise the money to build the statue.

At the time the Daibutsu was being constructed, the Hojo regent was putting his financial support into the construction of Kencho-ji, the emerging city's first major Zen temple. The two rival projects focused the religious ferment besetting the city. HONEN (1133–1212), the first of five notable religious leaders to descend on the city, initiated PURE LAND BUDDHISM in the country. His disciple SHINRAN (1173–1263) initiated what would become the most popular variation on the Pure Land approach, known as JODO SHINSHU, or the True Pure Land, school. The most prominent Pure Land temple in Kamakura is the Hase Temple, whose central attraction is the 27-foot statue of Kannon (GUAN YIN) along with statues of Amida, JIZO, and BENZAITEN.

RINZAI ZEN was introduced to Japan and Kamakura by EISAI (1141–1215), who was responsible for the building of the Kennin-ji in Kyoto, and then received the support of Hojo Masako, Minamoto Yoritomo's widow, to build Jufuku-ji, the first Zen center in Kamakura. Later in the century, Jufuku-ji would be somewhat overshadowed by Kencho-ji, built with the support of Hojo Tokiyori (1227–63), the regent. With the support of the regents, three more large Zen temples would be built—ENGAKU-JI, Jochi-ji, and Zuisen-ji. Eisai would be followed by DOGEN (1200–53), who introduced SOTO ZEN to Japan. Though based far away from Kamakura, Dogen appeared in the city in 1247 to spend time instructing Hojo Tokiyori and receive his favor for the development of Soto.

Possibly the most controversial of the new Buddhist leaders to settle in Kamakura was NICHIREN (1222–82), the prophet of the LOTUS SUTRA. He first entered Kamakura in 1237 and eventually settled there in 1253. He turned his attention to the storms affecting the city, especially the very destructive one of 1257. He would attribute the disasters that afflicted the city to the attention given false forms of Buddhism, especially Pure Land teachings. In response, Pure Land supporters drove him from the city, beginning years of tension between him and the regency and the people of the city. In the 1270s he would be exiled but was pardoned in 1274 and returned to Kamakura to advise the regent on an expected Chinese/Mongolian invasion. When the regent did not accept his advice to adhere to Nichiren's teachings exclusively, Nichiren quit the city. Today, the relatively modest Ankokuron-ji, which Nichiren founded, is the primary remnant of his stay in the city.

The Hojo regency declined in power during the first decades of the 14th century and was eventually overthrown in 1333. Power reverted to Kyoto and Kamakura would never return to its former glory. Just before its demise, the regent designated the five Kamakura Zen temples as Gozan, of the highest rank. This initiated a system of ranking of Zen temples across the country that has continued in modified form to the present.

The many temples in Kamakura suffered through the years as the country's leadership settled first in Kyoto and then in Tokyo. The Zen centers fared best, with the continued support of Zen by the Tokugawa Shogunate (1603–1868). The Buddhist sites were somewhat neglected during the years of the Meiji government (1868–1912), when Shinto replaced Buddhism as the country's official faith. In the years since World War II, the city has revived as a major tourist center and pilgrimage site for Buddhists. In recent decades, Western Zen aspirants have targeted Kamakura, especially Engaku-ji, as sites to receive Zen training.

It should also be noted that among its more than 70 temples, Kamakura is the home to the famous HACHIMAN temple, dedicated to the Shinto deity Hachiman, believed to be the protective deity of the Minamoto clan, to which Minamoto Yoritomo, who initiated the Kamakura era of glory, belonged.

Further reading: Kazuo Kasahara, ed., *A History of Japanese Religion.* Translated by Paul McCarthy and Gaynor Sekimori (Tokyo: Kosei, 2001); Hisashi Mori, *Sculpture of the Kamakura Period* (Tokyo: Heibonsha, and New York: John Weatherhill, 1974); Iso Mutsu, *Kamakura: Fact and Legend* (Rutland, Vt.: Charles E. Tuttle, 1918); George B. Sansom, *A History of Japan to 1334* (Stanford, Calif.: Stanford University Press, 1958).

kami

The Japanese term *kami* is difficult to render into English, as there is no exact English equivalent. It is often translated as "god," especially when talking about the major deities in Shinto mythology. All of the prominent deities such as AMATERASU OMI-KAMI and SUSANO-O NO MIKOTO, the objects of worship at shrines throughout Japan, are *kami.* However, the number of deities (to whom both good and bad qualities may be ascribed) is quite

large. And the term is not limited to these deities but emerges as a designation for all beings that are deemed to possess extraordinary and surpassing qualities, abilities, or virtues and are thus seen to be awe inspiring and worthy of reverence. The related term *yao-yorozu no kami* (literally, "ever-increasing myriad deities") refers to the fact hat the number of *kami* is believed to be continuously increasing.

Humans are believed to be close to the *kami* in their daily existence and might even become *kami.* The emperor is revered as a *kami,* by fact of his descending from the original Japanese deities. An individual may be designated as a *kami* if he or she lives an extraordinary life or does some particularly meritorious deed.

Kami are seen to reside at shrines dedicated to their veneration. A smaller shrine erected in one's home is termed a *kamidana.* The *kamidana* frequently contains one or more AMULETS acquired at one of the major shrines, such as the ISE SHRINE. Acknowledgment of the *kami* is made with offerings of food that are placed on the shrine.

Worship of the *kami* is performed in a ceremony (*kamimukae*) conducted by a Shinto priest during which the deity is summoned. The ceremony is followed by a similar one (*kamiokuri*) in which the *kami* is sent from the place of worship.

Further reading: H. Byron Earhart, *Japanese Religion: Unity and Diversity.* 3d ed. (Belmont, Calif.: Wadsworth, 1982); Hope Huntly, *Kami-No-Michi: The Way of the Gods in Japan* (London: Rebman, 1910); Sokyo Ono, *Shinto, the Kami Way* (Tokyo: Charles E. Tuttle, 1995).

Kaniska (Kanisska) (second century C.E.)
Buddhist ruler of Afghanistan

Little is known of this Buddhist ruler, though Kaniska is honored among Mahayana Buddhists in the manner in which Theravadists honor King ASOKA. What is known is that in the first century C.E. an Indo-Scythian people moved into what is now Afghanistan from the north and took control of it and the surrounding land in northern India and westward toward the Caspian Sea. Their leaders formed the Kushan dynasty. Kaniska I was one of their rulers in the second century, though he may have been but one of several rulers to bear that name. Estimates for his ascendancy to the throne vary between 78 and 230 C.E., but most scholars now focus on the period between 110 and 139 C.E.

Buddhism had already entered the land ruled by the Kushan kings, but during Kaniska's reign it flourished as never before. He nurtured the arts, and numerous Buddhist buildings (temples and monasteries) and STUPAS were built. These were most notable at his two capitals and the Bamiyan Valley some 150 miles north of Kabul. The Bamiyan Valley would become both a Buddhist cultural center and a prosperous trading community because of its location along the SILK ROAD. Here, Kaniska would initiate a project to build two large statues of the Buddha (completed during the reign of his successors). The largest of these (175 feet tall) would for many years (until the statues' destruction in 2001) be the largest statue of the Buddha in the world. Kaniska was the student of Sangharaksa, a contemporary of ASVAGHOSA, and exponent of the Sarvastivadin school. During his reign, several Buddhist schools competed for the allegiance of the faithful, and the king called the so-called fourth Buddhist council to resolve the issues, primarily variant opinions on a set of abstract metaphysical questions. These issues were decided in favor of the Sarvastivadin. The *Mahavibhasa,* a book on the council's deliberations, documented the substance of the discussions. This council is sometimes used to date the beginning of MAHAYANA BUDDHISM.

The reign of Kaniska seems to represent the height of both the Kushan empire and Buddhism in the region, though both survived until the Muslim invasion in the seventh century.

See also COUNCILS OF BUDDHISM.

Further reading: Simone Gaulier, Robert Jera-Bezard, and Monique Maillard, *Buddhism in Afghanistan and* *Central Asia* (Leiden: Brill, 1976); C. S. Upasak, *History of Buddhism in Afghanistan* (Sarnath, Varanasi, India: Central Institute of Higher Tibetan Studies, 1990).

Kantaka

Kantaka was the horse of Prince Siddhartha, who became the Buddha. When Prince Siddhartha left his youthful life, he also relinquished his horse Kantaka. According to the Buddhist canon Kantaka had been born at the same time as the Buddha, along with 499 other horses. Kantaka was the color of a polished conch shell and possessed speed and strength. On the night of Siddhartha's departure from the palace the horse's footsteps and neighing were muffled by four guardian deities, so their departure did not awaken anyone.

After traveling all night for a distance of 30 leagues and passing through three kingdoms the Buddha, his horse Kantaka, and his groom Channa stopped on the banks of the river Anoma. Kantaka jumped over the river. At that point the Buddha left them. After leaving his master's sight Kantaka could not bear the pain of parting and fell down dead. He was then reborn in Tusita heaven as Kantaka, a god.

In Buddhist imagery the horse is often a symbol of the senses. Hence Prince Siddhartha's giving up of his horse may be a symbol of his turn away from sensuality.

Further reading: Edward J. Thomas, *The Life of Buddha as Legend and History* (Delhi: Munshiram Manoharial, 1992).

karma

Karma is "deed" or "action," and the accumulated results of action. Karma is a widespread concept used to explain events. In classical Indian writings one's karma is the result of actions in the past—rich or poor, healthy or diseased, born well or born low, all people were said to be in their current situation as a result of the seeds planted by previous actions. Naturally these actions included those taken in previous lives.

The QUESTIONS OF KING MILINDA, an early Buddhist text, contains extensive discussion of karma. The sage Nagasena explains to the king that not all suffering and evil can be attributed to the function of karma. Suffering results from the fact of being in SAMSARA, not from karma alone. Karma is here seen as "retributive justice," which must be repaid. An enlightened being, a Buddha, will have worked off all his karmic load.

The Buddha stated that karma causes results in this life, the next lifetime, and all successive births. Humans are reborn into samsara because of the thirst (TANHA) for existence. Inanimate things appear mechanically and disintegrate eventually, in a mechanical process. And, generally, karma is increased through intentional action by people. Finally, there is karma on a cosmic level, which affects large units of people, whole nations, planets, and whatever lies beyond.

In Buddhist doctrine karma relates to volitions (*cetana*), both wholesome and unwholesome, that shape individual destinies and cause rebirth. The volitions in turn are manifested in bodily actions, speech, and mind. Unwholesome karma (*akusala*) are caused by the three bad roots (*mula*) of greed, hatred, and delusion. Wholesome karma (*kusala*) are caused by unselfishness; hatelessness, or *metta*; and undeludeness, or knowledge. Karmic results (*vipaka*) are countered through counteractive karma that becomes weak and fails to effect a result.

Karma functions in four ways: first, as regenerative karma, which functions at rebirth and throughout life; second, as supportive karma, which assists already manifested karma; third, as counteractive karma, which suppresses karmic results; and, fourth, as destructive karma, which destroys a weaker karma.

Further reading: David J. Kalupahana, *Buddhist Philosophy: A Historical Analysis* (Honolulu: University of Hawaii Press, 1976); Nyanatiloka, *Buddhist Dictionary*

Manual of Buddhist Terms and Doctrines (San Francisco: Chinese Materials Center, 1997).

Karma Kagyu

Karma Kagyu is one of the eight lineages within the KAGYU school of Tibetan Buddhism. The Karma lineage of the Kagyu school was founded by Dusum Khyenpa (1110–93), who is identified as the first KARMAPA, or figurehead of the Karma Kagyu school. He was born into a family of commoners in Khams in eastern Tibet and at age 18 began to travel in search of enlightenment. He befriended Phagmo Drupa (1118–70), and together they studied with Gyamarpa. He then studied with the Kadampa master Pa-tsap Lotsawa both exoteric (everyday) and esoteric (hidden and mystic) teachings of Kadampa. At age 30 he reached Daklha Gampo and began studying with Gampopa, who subjected him to a rigorous course of study in the fundamentals of Buddhism, followed by rigorous meditation practice. He founded Tsurpu monastery in central Tibet in 1185, as well as several monasteries in Kham.

Prior to his passing, Dusum Khyenpa is reported to have made a prediction regarding his rebirth. Unlike most of the others of this time, the Karma Kagyu became one of the first Tibetan schools to transmit authority from generation to generation by reincarnation, as opposed to transmission within a family, from father to son or uncle to nephew, as was the case in the Sakya and most of the other Kagyu lineages. He thus gave rise to the institution of the *karmapa*, the figurehead of the Karma Kagyu school. Because of the prestige of this lineage, the Karma Kagyu has become the best-known Kagyu lineage. The Sixteenth Karmapa, Rangjung Rikpe Dorje (1924–81), was an active teacher in exile, particularly in the United States. In recent years the school has been divided by a controversy over his succession, resulting in the enthronement of two candidates for the position of the Seventeenth Karmapa, Orgyen Trinley Dorje (1985–   ), who is the most widely accepted candidate, and Trinley Thaye

Dorje (1983–   ), who is the candidate advanced by Shamar Rinpoche.

Further reading: Ronald M. Davidson, *Tibetan Renaissance: Tantric Buddhism in the Rebirth of Tibetan Culture* (New York: Columbia University Press, 2005); David Snellgrove and Hugh Richardson, *A Cultural History of Tibet* (Boston: Shambhala, 1986); Lea Terhune, *Karmapa of Tibet: The Politics of Reincarnation* (Boston: Wisdom, 2004).

karmapa

The *karmapa* is the head of the Karma Kagyu school. The first *karmapa* was Dusum Khyenpa (1110–93). All subsequent *karmapas* have been recognized as reincarnations of the first. He was recognized as the *tulku,* or incarnation, in 1987.

Further reading: Karmapa.org. "H. H. 17th. Karmapa Trinlay Thaye Dorje." Available online. URL: www.karmapa.org. Accessed June 12, 2006.

karuna

Karuna, or compassion, is the essential quality of a BODHISATTVA. *Karuna* is also one of the four Brahma VIHARAS, or "sublime states." *Karuna* indicates the qualities of the heart—love and respect for all living beings. *Mahakaruna* (great compassion) is the last of the 18 virtues of a Buddha. It became a high-priority ideal with the rise of MAHAYANA ideology from the first century C.E. With PRAJNA, "wisdom," the individual cultivated the widest possible perspective on the suffering of others. Although not a separate section of the EIGHTFOLD PATH, nor one of the *paramitas,* or perfections, so strongly emphasized in Mahayana practice, the concept of *karuna* is present throughout both these schemes and is an essential quality in Buddhist cultivation.

Further reading: Kogen Mizuno, *Essentials of Buddhism: Basic Terminology and Concepts of Buddhist Philosophy and Practice.* Translated by Gaynor Sekimori (1972. Reprint, Tokyo: Kosei, 1996).

Kasuga Taisha

This SHINTO shrine located near Nara was for much of its history combined with the nearby Buddhist KOFUKU-JI temple. The deity in the area, Kasuga Daimyojin (Great Deity of Kasuga), was the ancestral deity of the powerful Fujiwara clan. The shrine was officially established in 768. By the end of the Heian period (794–1185) Kasuga Taisha was merged with Kofuku-ji to reflect the official policy of fusion of Shinto and Buddhism. The two centers of worship were not separated until the MEIJI period (1868–1912). Because of its association with the powerful Fujiwaras and its closeness to the original home of the gods, Kasuga Taisha is one of the most important Shinto shrines.

Further reading: Brian Bocking, "Changing Images of Shinto: Sanja Takusen or the Three Oracles," in John Breen and Mark Teeuwen, eds., *Shinto in History: Ways of the Kami* (Richmond, U.K.: Curzon, 2000), 167–185.

Kasyapa (first century C.E.) *monk said to have transmitted Buddhism to China*

Kasyapa was a Buddhist monk who is said to have been the first to transmit Buddhist teachings to China. According to the story, around 67 C.E., the Chinese emperor Ming had a dream of the Buddha. He subsequently sent two envoys to India to locate some Buddhist scriptures. As the envoys made their way to India, in what is now Afghanistan, they encountered two monks, Kasyapa-matanga and Zhu Fa Lan (also known as Gobharana or Dharmaratna). The monks were on their way to China. The envoys reversed their steps and led Kasyapa and his companion back to the emperor's court at Luoyang, Henan Province. (Some modern scholars have cast severe doubt on this story.)

Kasyapa introduced Buddhist sutras and, while in the environment of the court, edited a selection of the Buddha's sayings that has survived to the present as a popular introduction to Buddhism, The Sutra in Forty-two Sections Spoken by the Buddha. The text was edited in the style of the ANALECTS of CONFUCIUS.

Kasyapa-matanga and Zhu Fa Lan also presented the emperor with a picture of Sakyamuni Buddha seated on a white horse. The emperor saw to the building of the first Buddhist temple in China and named it the BAIMASI (or White Horse) Temple after the horse.

Two other individuals known as Kasyapa—MAHAKASYAPA and KASYAPA OF URUVELA—were contemporaries of the historical Buddha.

Further reading: Kenneth Ch'en, *Buddhism in China: A Historical Survey* (Princeton, N.J.: Princeton University Press, 1964); Kasyapa-matanga and Gobharana, trans., "The Sutra in Forty-Two Sections Spoken by the Buddha." Buddhanews.biz. Available online. URL: http://www.buddhanews.biz/sutra.asp. Accessed on October 12, 2005.

Kasyapa of Uruvela *early follower of the Buddha*

Kasyapa, a fire-worshipping ascetic, became an early follower of the Buddha. Uruvela Kasyapa and his two brothers took 500 of their matted-haired followers into the SANGHA. This Kasyapa was a well-known ascetic in his day, and it took an example of the Buddha's use of magical powers to persuade him to join. In the account the Buddha battled two smoke-breathing *nagas* (serpents), read the thoughts of Uruvela Kasyapa, and performed many other miracles—a total of 3,500—before Kasyapa and his followers agreed to follow him. After all the followers of the three brothers had been ordained, the Buddha taught them the fire sermon on Mt. Gaya. (This person shares the name with KASYAPA THE GREAT and KASYAPA of the first century C.E.)

Further reading: Edward J. Thomas, *The Life of Buddha as Legend and History* (Delhi: Munshiram Manoharlal, 1992).

Kasyapa the Great (Mahakasyapa) *foremost among the Buddha's followers*

Kasyapa is an important figure in early Buddhism. Two additional Kasyapa figures—KASYAPA of the first century C.E. and KASYAPA OF URUVELA—pale in significance to this Kasyapa, who was the Buddha's official successor. Through his saintliness, his possession of great merit, and his quick enlightenment, he was seen as worthy of being the Buddha's successor. Kasyapa is a paradigmatic Buddhist saint; in other words, stories were created around his image and using his spirit to guide subsequent schools. Mahakasyapa was a widely popular saint in northern and southern India in the pre-Islamic period of Buddhist influence. He is most famous as a forest renunciant and meditator.

Mahakasyapa was born into a wealthy family but abandoned the wealthy lifestyle and wandered for a year before he met the Buddha. Both immediately recognized each other as master and disciple. The Buddha then began a detailed instruction in the techniques of meditation, including mindfulness. After eight days of practice, Kasyapa attained enlightenment as an ARHAT on the ninth day. The Buddha continued to give Kasyapa preeminence among his followers; in one example they exchanged robes, a mark of high honor.

Kasyapa was enlightened and so possessed such magical abilities as flight. He was also known as a strict disciplinarian.

Upon the Buddha's PARINIRVANA (death), the community of monks could not light the funeral pyre until Kasyapa arrived. He immediately assumed leadership of the sangha. He realized they had a mission to recall and pass on the teachings of the Buddha, and so he proposed and convened the first Buddhist council.

In one Chinese version of the *Asokarajavadana* (the story of King Asoka) after the completion of the council Kasyapa transmits his lineage to Ananda. He then travels to Mt. Kukkutapada, where he dies while in meditation. Thereafter his presence is associated with that mountain, and King Asoka visits the mountain to address him.

Further reading: Reginald A. Ray, *Buddhist Saints in India: A Study in Buddhist Values and Orientations* (Oxford: Oxford University Press, 1994).

kathina (robe offering) ceremony

This ceremony is held in THAILAND and other countries where a majority practices THERAVADA Buddhism, within one month after the VASSA RAINS RETREAT. During this ceremony robes and other offerings are given to monks. Since the monks were traditionally not allowed to travel during the Vassa period, *kathina* is an opportunity for lay supporters to check on the welfare of monks and make offerings to them before they resume their wanderings. This practice reflects the high status accorded the SANGHA in Thai and Theravada cultures, as well as the dependence of the sangha on the laity.

Today in the formal *kathina* ceremony a lay representative offers fabric robes to two chosen BHIKSUS (monks) who represent the sangha. The two *bhiksus* then pass the offering to the full sangha. The sangha together chants *sadhu*, ("It is well"), confirming agreement. The ceremony is finalized later that day when the robes are completed and presented to the honored *bhiksus*.

Kaundinya (Ajnata Kaundindya; in Pali, Kondanna) *first Buddhist monk*

Kaundinya was one of the five ascetics who first wandered with the Buddha prior to his enlightenment. He achieved enlightenment in a flash of insight when listening to the Buddha expound the FOUR TRUTHS. He was thereafter held up as a symbol of the possibility of "sudden" enlightenment.

Kaundinya was the prototypical loyal follower of the Buddha, his right-hand person. In many religions it is this person who receives the leader's mantle and shepherds the fragile new group into its postleader stage. But in the Buddhist tradition this did not happen. Instead the mantle of leadership went to KASYAPA, the most eminent of the Buddha's followers, and Kaundinya, the loyalist, was left out. In some collections of the lives of the greatest 33 ARHATS, Mahakasyapa is listed first, and Kuandinya last.

Kaundinya played a part in the Buddha's birth as well as later, as a companion. On the fifth day after the prince Siddhartha was born, his father, King SUDDODHANA, summoned 108 Brahmans (wise men) to the palace to prophesy the young prince's future. Kaundinya was the youngest of the group of eight whose comments are recorded. Alone of the eight Kaundinya prophesied that the child would without doubt become a Buddha and fully comprehend the nature of reality. It was Kaundinya who also informed the king that his son would renounce the world after seeing the four signs: an aged person, a sick person, a dead person, and an ascetic.

Further reading: Edward Conze, *Buddhism: Its Essence and Development* (New York: Philosophical Library, 1951); Reginald A. Ray, *Buddhist Saints in India: A Study in Buddhist Values and Orientations* (Oxford: Oxford University Press, 1994); Edward J. Thomas, *The Life of Buddha as Legend and History* (Delhi: Munshiram Manoharial, 1992); A. K. Warder, *Indian Buddhism* (Delhi: Motilal Banarsidass, 1970).

Kegon

Kegon is the Japanese pronunciation of the Chinese term HUA YAN, or "Flower Ornament," a reference to the Avatamsaka Sutra. The Hua Yan school, which flourished in the medieval period of Chinese Buddhism, around the Tang dynasty (618–907), was introduced to Japan by the Chinese monk Shen Xiang around 740, during the Nara period (710–784) of Japanese history. It was vigorously promoted through the lectures of Ryoben (689–773), a disciple of the Korean Hua Yan monk Shinjo (d. 742). Emperor Shomu promoted this Buddhist school because its teachings of the central role of the VAIROCANA Buddha meshed with his own desire to strengthen central political authority. He authorized a temple to be built at Nara, TODAI-JI. Inside this temple he added, in 749, a vast statue of the Buddha Vairocana. The Kegon school was of interest to the social elite and not the common people, however, and after the Nara period it lost influence. In the HEIAN period it was almost completely overshadowed by the TENDAI school.

Further reading: Yoshiro Tamura, *Japanese Buddhism: A Cultural History*. Translated by Jeffrey Hunter (Tokyo: Kosei, 2000).

Keizan Jokin (1268–1325) *innovative Soto Zen leader*

Keizan Jokin was a second-generation SOTO ZEN leader who championed a lay-oriented form of the faith. He emerged as a young man as a student of Tettu Gikai, the third abbot of EIHEI-JI, the main Soto center. However, he left Eihei-ji to study with several RINZAI ZEN teachers who were still operating in a TENDAI context. While still dedicated to the Soto emphasis on ZAZEN, sitting meditation, he did begin to see the possibilities of reconciling Zen with some of the practices of other schools.

He eventually moved to Noto Province, a peninsula on the northern shore of Japan's main island, Honshu. Here he had great success at building the Soto movement. However, in winning the people, he departed from the practice at Eihei-ji in that he absorbed elements of the popular faith of the region, especially devotion to Kannon (GUAN YIN). He also emphasized the role of the lay people as opposed to the monks. From Soto-Ji, the temple Keizan founded, the movement spread from Noto to different parts of the country.

Under his leadership, his faction soon became the largest segment of the Soto movement, and Soto-ji rivaled Eihei-ji in importance as a leadership training center.

Keizan left behind two important disciples, Gasan Joseki (1275–1365), who succeeded him as abbot of Soto-ji, and Meiho Sotetsu (1277–1350), who became the abbot of Daijo-ji, another important Soto temple. The success of Keizan's faction over the next two centuries would allow it to take over Eihei-ji and eventually reunify the Soto movement, which had split into several factions after the founder Dogen's death.

Further reading: Kazuo Kasahara, ed., *A History of Japanese Religion*. Translated by Paul McCarthy and Gaynor Sekimori (Tokyo: Kosei, 2001); Keizan Jokin, *The Record of Transmitting the Light*. Translated by Francis Cook (Los Angeles: Center Press, 1991); ———, *Transmission of Light: Zen in the Art of Enlightenment, by Zen Master Keizan*. Translated by Thomas Cleary (San Francisco: North Point Press, 1990).

Kenchen Thrangu (1933–) *Karma Kagyu leader traditionally in charge of Thrangu monastery*

The Thrangu monastery was established around 1500 in Chinghai, now a province of China. The head of the monastery is known as the Thrangu Rinpoche. The first Thrangu Rinpoche was Sherap Gyaltsen, who was appointed by Chodrak Gyatso, the Seventh Karmapa.

The current Thrangu Rinpoche, Kenchen Thrangu, was born in 1933 in Kham, Tibet. He was recognized as the Ninth Kenchen Thrangu when he was four. He received full ordination when he was 23. In 1959, when he was 27, he left Chinghai, via Nepal, with approximately 70 followers.

In Rumtek, Sikkim, he was made abbot of Rumtek Monastery and the Nalanda Institute for Higher Buddhist Studies. He is currently abbot of Gampo Abbey in Nova Scotia, Canada. He has established monasteries, nunneries, and research centers throughout the world.

Further reading: "Biography of Thrangu Rinpoche" Venerable Thrangu Rinpoche. Available online. URL: www.himalayahchildren.org/rinpoche/. Accessed on August 25, 2005; "The Venerable Kenchen Thrangu Rinpoche" Gampo Abbey. Available online. URL: www.gampoabbey.org/home/abbot.htm. Accessed on August 25, 2005.

Khantipalo, Phra (Lawrence Mills)

(1932–   ) British-born Theravada teacher and founder of Bodhi Citta Buddhist Centre in Australia
Khantipalo was born near London and took his preliminary vows in London. He later lived in India, Thailand, Australia, and Sri Lanka. He established Wat Buddharangsee in Sydney and, in 1978 with Ayya Khema, the Wat Buddha Dhamma forest retreat at Wisemans Ferry, north of Sydney. He also founded the Bodhi Citta Buddhist Centre in Cairns, Australia.

Khantipalo eventually left the life of a monk and married. He continues to live in Cairns and is active in the Bodhi Citta Buddhist Centre.

Further reading: Buddhist Studies: Profiles of Buddhist Figures. "Profiles of Theravada Buddhists." Available online. URL: www.buddhanet.net/e-learning/history/theravada.htm. Accessed on June 9, 2005.

Khyentse Rinpoche

The term *Khyentse Rinpoche* refers to a lineage of reincarnating masters in the Nyingma school of Buddhism, all of whom originate in the figure of Jamyang Khyentse Wangpo (1820–92). He was a renowned master in the nonsectarian RIME MOVEMENT that flourished in eastern Tibet during the 19th century. He studied with teachers from all of the major Tibetan Buddhist traditions and was distinguished discoverer of hidden teachings.

His successor was Jamyang Khyentse Chökyi Lodrö (1894–1959). He was a prominent lama in eastern Tibet who instructed many other lamas, particularly in the Nyingma and Kagyu schools,

most notably Dilgo Khyentse Rinpoche. He has been succeeded by Dzongsar Jamyang Khyentse Rinpoche (1961–   ), an important Nyingma lama who trained under Dilgo Khyentse Rinpoche and currently oversees Dzongsar Monastery in eastern Tibet as well as branch monasteries established in India and Bhutan. He has also established Buddhist Centers in North America, Australia, and East Asia. He is thus an influential contemporary Nyingma teacher.

There is also a branch lineage deriving from Jamyang Khyentse Wangpo. The great Nyingma master Dilgo Khyentse Rinpoche (1910–91) was recognized by the illustrious Mipham Rinpoche (1846–1912) as an incarnation of Jamyang Khyentse Wangpo. He undertook a religious life at age 11, studying initially at Shechen monastery in eastern Tibet and later with Jamyang Khyentse Chökyi Lodrö. He was not a celibate monk, but a married lama. He was married to Khandro Lama, with whom he had two daughters. After the Chinese invasion of eastern Tibet, he and his family fled first to central Tibet and then to Bhutan, where he was well received as a teacher. He founded Shechen Tennyi Dargye Ling Monastery in Boudhnath, Kathmandu, in 1980; the current abbot of this monastery is his grandson, Shechen Rabjam Rinpoche (1966–   ). He became one of the best known Nyingma lamas, with numerous distinguished students, such as Trulshik Rinpoche (1923–   ).

He passed away in Bhutan in 1991, and his cremation and other observances, held in Bhutan and Nepal in 1991 and 1992, were attended by thousands of students and prominent lamas from around the world. His successor is Khyentse Yangsi Rinpoche, who was born in Nepal in 1993 and discovered as Dilgo Khyentse's successor by Trulshik Rinpoche.

Further reading: Matthieu Ricard, *The Spirit of Tibet: The Life and World of Khyentse Rinpoche, Spiritual Teacher* (New York: Aperture Foundation, 2000); E. Gene Smith, *Among Tibetan Texts* (Boston: Wisdom, 2001).

Kito Buddhism

Kito is a Japanese term referring to the popular practice of asking Buddhist deities and bodhisattvas to intercede in personal matters. Seeking such intercession usually involves the performance of particular magical-ritual acts. Such practices have always been and continue to be a part of popular religious practice in Japan (and China) in Buddhism as well as other religions. During the Tokugawa Shogunate, Buddhism was both elevated as the state religion and reorganized as a department of the government. Kito Buddhism was discouraged as an attempt was made to regularize religious practice. As priests assumed a number of functions administering temples and responding to government regulations, the personal religion of those who attended the temples suffered.

The formalized life of the temples led many individuals to turn toward a variety of unofficial priests and religious functionaries who offered cures from disease, glimpses of the future, and the alleviation of immediate painful situations. This more informal life was carried on outside the temple structures throughout the Tokugawa (1603–1868) and Meiji (1868–1912) periods, in spite of periodic attempts by the government to suppress it and has experienced a comeback in the years since World War II in the atmosphere of religious freedom.

Further reading: Ichiro Hori, *Folk Religion in Japan: Continuity and Change.* Edited by Joseph M. Kitagawa and Alan L. Miller (Chicago: University of Chicago Press, 1994); Kazuo Kasahara, ed., *A History of Japanese Religion.* Translated by Paul McCarthy and Gaynor Sekimori (Tokyo: Kosei, 2001).

Kiyozawa Manshi (1863–1903) *Japanese Buddhist reformer*

Kiyozawa Manshi, a JODO SHINSHU priest in the HIGASHI HONGWANJI, emerged at the end of the 19th century as a major voice for the reform of Buddhism and its realistic encounter with Western thought. A graduate in philosophy of the Tokyo Imperial University, he had studied Western philosophy and studied with Western teachers. In his younger years, he became an educator, holding various positions with the Higashi Hongwanji that led to his becoming president of Shinshu University (now Otani University), and taught history of philosophy.

At the time of his emergence, Japanese Buddhism had suffered a double blow, both being displaced from its formerly favored position by the Meiji government and having to deal with the growth of Protestant Christianity, which had been introduced in the 1850s. He rejected both identification with the heightened nationalism of the government and the harsh polemic against Christianity. Rather, he called upon Buddhism to reform internally with a new emphasis on religious experience and upon his own organization to rededicate itself to the teachings of its founder, SHINRAN (1173–1262). From his position at the university, he called upon the Jodo Shinshu to respond to Western intellectual currents without becoming subordinate to them. He motivated his students to develop contemporary interpretations of Shinran.

Kiyozawa's career took off in the mid-1890s and he obtained a wide audience for his calls for reform but in 1903 died at 40 years old. His approach would have far-reaching results, however, as its influenced several generations of Japanese Buddhist scholars and religious leaders. His thought provided the foundation for the spread of Japanese Buddhism in the West through the 20th century.

Further reading: Alfred Bloom, "Kiyozawa Manshi and the Renewal of Buddhism." Shin Dharma Net. Available online. URL: http://www.shindharmanet.com/writings/renewal.htm. Accessed on December 5, 2005; Mark Blum, "Kiyozawa Manshi and the Meaning of Buddhist Ethics." *Eastern Buddhist* 21, no. 1 (Spring 1988): 61–81; Frederick Franck, ed., *The Buddha Eye:*

An Anthology of the Kyoto School (New York: Crossroad, 1982); Kiyozawa Manshi, *December Fan: The Buddhist Essays of Manshi Kiyozawa.* Translated by Nobuo Haneda (Kyoto: Higashi Honganji, 1984).

klesa

In Buddhist thought the *klesas* refer to defilements or passions. The *klesas* are those properties of mind that create dullness and lead to unwholesome actions. These are eliminated in the path to *arhathood,* which by definition means the elimination of *klesas.* The *Bodhicaryavatara,* an eighth-century work by Santideva (685–763), lists three types of *klesa*: craving (*rgag*), hatred (*dvesa*), and delusion (*moha*). The *Visuddhimagga,* a standard work on Buddhist practice dating from the fifth century C.E., lists 10 *klesas*: desire, hate, delusion, pride, false views, doubt, rigidity, excitability, shamelessness, and lack of conscience.

Further reading: Kogen Mizuno, *Essentials of Buddhism: Basic Terminology and Concepts of Buddhist Philosophy and Practice.* Translated by Gaynor Sekimori (1972. Reprint, Tokyo: Kosei, 1996); Santideva, *The Bodhicaryavatara.* Translated by Kate Crosby and Andrew Skilton (Oxford: Oxford University Press, 1995).

koan (gong'an)

The koan is a Buddhist literary form. Literally a "public case" or file, the koan is an important tool in Zen/Chan training. Koans are usually short literary puzzles based on incidents from Buddhist history. These incidents generally involve "crazy Chan" practices popular in the Tang dynasty (618–960) in China—such actions as a master's hitting students, yelling into their ears, or speaking in riddles. The "solution" to the koan riddle is never based on rational thinking, however. The student is encouraged to develop "out of the box" insight in order to solve the paradoxes inherent in the puzzle. The idea is to stimulate the student into "sudden" enlightenment through focus on the paradoxes.

The koan was not originally a separate literary form. Instead the short scenes were embedded in longer commentary works, the *yu lu* (discourse records) of masters, in particular the "transmission of the lamp" style histories. The first of these longer works, *Jingde chuandeng lu*, was written in 1004 C.E. Koans were also found in biographies of famous Buddhist masters. It was only later that koans were extracted from such larger works and established as a separate literary form, koan collections.

Koans were not, however, simply extracts or summaries. A koan as a "case" reflects roots not in Buddhist practice but in legal practice in Tang dynasty China (618–907 C.E.). In medieval China the *gong'an* referred to the table (*an*) of the judge (*gong*), or, by extension, a written brief placed on the judge's table. As a case it was meant to illustrate a point, whether it be of civil law or Dharma.

In the Buddhist context the conversations of famous masters were deemed particularly worthy of recording and study. The key sections of conversations were commented on and used as meditative devices to increase the understanding of the disciple. Some koans have only one commentary. Some have commentaries on the original commentary. Still others have three or more levels of commentary.

The purpose of the koan was to aid in understanding of Buddhist principles. Not only did they record famous examples about legendary figures, they also expressed deep insights from the Buddhist perspective. In later practice in Japanese Zen monasteries, masters used koans to assist monks in gaining enlightenment, often in conjunction with physical punishment or nonconventional behavior. If a practitioner attains a complete understanding of the koan's case, including the paradox usually contained inside, he or she may suddenly attain complete understanding, or *SATORI*. This enlightenment is reflected in the practitioner's ability to explain the koan.

The koans are found in such collections as the Gateless Barrier (Chinese *Wumen Guan*,

Japanese *Mumonkan*) and the Blue Cliff Collection (Chinese *Biyan Lu,* Japanese *Hekiganroku*); the first contains 48 "cases," and the latter 63. These koans, originally compiled in China during the Song dynasty (960–1268), are used most commonly in the RINZAI tradition in Japanese Zen. The use of koans is sometimes criticized as being simply wordplay, and there are collections of answers intended to help students pass koan tests. For Chinese Buddhists, of course, the koan literature simply makes up part of the vast body of Buddhist literature.

Further reading: T. Griffith Foulk, "The Form and Function of Koan Literature: A Historical Overview," in Steve Heine and Dale S. Wright, eds., *The Koan: Texts and Contexts in Zen Buddhism* (Oxford: Oxford University Press, 2000), 15–45; Steven Heine and Dale S. Wright, "Introduction," in Steve Heine and Dale S. Wright, eds., *The Koan: Texts and Contexts in Zen Buddhism* (Oxford: Oxford University Press, 2000), 3–14; Isshu Miura and Ruth Fuller Sasaki, *Zen Dust: The History of the Koan and Koan Study in (Linji) Zen* (New York: Harcourt, Brace & World, 1966).

Kobo Daishi   *See* KUKAI.

Kodo Kyodan

Kodo Kyodan is an offshoot of REIYUKAI, the lay Buddhist organization founded in Japan in 1920. Kyodan emphasizes study of the LOTUS SUTRA. Much of the group's activity focuses on searching for the Lotus Sutra's core meaning. In addition emphasis is placed on the idea of filial piety. An assumption is that honoring of ancestors will yield positive results.

Reiyukai put emphasis on self-reliance and personal responsibility. Okano Shodo (1900–78) was a TENDAI monk and an officer in Reiyukai. He and his wife, Kimiko, had joined Reiyukai in 1934. They began to feel the organization emphasized recruitment of new members too much by, for instance, setting quotas. In 1936 they set up a branch organization called Kodokai in Yokohama, east of Tokyo. The Kodokai became independent in 1939, under the name Kodo *Kyodan,* or, literally, the "Filial Piety Teaching Hall." Okano's son, Okano Shokan, became leader in 1975, just before his father's death.

Kodo Kyodan's main festival is the Hana Matsuri, which celebrates the birth of the Buddha Sakyamuni. Members also celebrate the Obon festival for ancestors. Kodo Kyodan today reports having over 300,000 members.

Kofuku-ji

Kofuku-ji means "temple of renewed prosperity." There are a number of Kofuku temples in Japan. One in the Teramachi District of Nagasaki, central Japan, is the head temple of the OBAKU sect of Japanese Zen. It was constructed in 1620.

The Kofuku-ji in Nara is far older. It was originally built in Kyoto in 669 by the powerful Fujiwara clan to help a leader recover from illness. The temple was later moved to Nara in 710 when Nara became the capital. There were originally 175 buildings, of which only a few remain. It is today the head temple of the HOSSO sect of Japanese Buddhism. The Nara Kofukuki is a United Nations Educational, Scientific, and Cultural Organization (UNESCO) World Heritage Site.

Further reading: "Kofuku-ji." Destinations///Japan Travel Guide, Yamasa Institute Multimedia Studio. The Yamasa Institute. Available online. URL: www. yamasa.org/japan/english/destinations/nara/kofukuji. html. Accessed on May 5, 2006; Yoshiro Tamura, *Japanese Buddhism: A Cultural History.* Translated by Jeffrey Hunter (Tokyo: Kosei, 2000).

Kofuku no Kagaku

Kofuku no Kagaku is, literally, the Institute for Research in Human Happiness. Kofuku is a very recent religion started in 1986 in Tokyo, Japan, by Okawa Tyuho (1956–   ). Basic teachings of Kofuku no Kagaku include the four Principles of

Happiness: love, knowledge, development, and self-reflection. However, the group increasingly mentions such Buddhist concepts as the three treasures as well. At one point, in 1991, the group said there were 5 million members. Today Kofuku is probably declining in membership.

The founder of Kofuku no Kagaku, Okawa Tyuho, is a graduate in law of the University of Tokyo. He says he is able to communicate with Buddhist figures such as SAKYAMUNI. Although the group was not particularly Buddhist when it began, it has increasingly taken on the flavor of a Buddhist-inspired religious movement.

Membership in Kofuku no Kagaku requires that each person read 10 books written by Okawa. Members are also encouraged to attend lectures, to develop wisdom and practice "love that gives," and to meditate daily.

The role of Okawa remains central. He is said to be the incarnation of El Cantare, a "grand spirit" of the "terrestrial" spirit group, and within the movement he is addressed as "El Cantare." Such figures as Sakyamuni and Hermes developed as incarnations of El Cantare in the past.

As the group grew in its first 15 years Okawa attracted criticism. He was said to suffer from mental imbalances. At the same time Kofuku no Kagaku announced major expansion plans. In 1990 the group announced the goal of promoting Kofuku no Kagaku throughout Japan. This was followed in 1994 by a missionary program to establish centers throughout the world, starting with London and New York. There ensued an increasingly negative media campaign.

Okawa is said to have written more than 100 books. The best known is the 1990 *Laws of the Sun*, a description of Koguku no Kagaku's cosmology. Consistently, Okawa is depicted as the one who reveals God's truth to humanity. Okawa also favors themes of apocalypse and subsequent utopia. In his vision of utopia all beings can freely declare their happiness, living in full love and compassion.

The largest Kofuku no Kagaku centers are at Utsunomiya, north of Tokyo. These include the Shoshin-kan (House of the Right Mind) and the Mirari-kan (House of the Future).

Further reading: Trevor Astley, "The Transformation of a Recent Japanese New Religion: Okawa Ryuhu and Kofuku no Kagaku," *Japanese Journal of Religious Studies* 22, nos. 3–4 (1995): 343–380; Peter B. Clarke, *A Bibliography of Japanese New Religious Movements* (Richmond, U.K.: Japan Library, 1999); Masaki Fukui, "Kofuku no Kagaku: The Institute for Research in Human Happiness (IRH)," in Peter B. Clarke, ed., *A Bibliography of Japanese New Religions* (Eastbourne, U.K.: Japan Library, 1999): 149–167; Ryuhu Okawa, *The Laws of Eternity* (Tokyo: IHR Press, 1991); ———, *The Laws of Gold*. Tokyo: IHR Press, 1991); ———, *The Laws of the Sun: The Revelations of Buddha That Enlightens the New Age* (Tokyo: IRH Press, 1990).

Koguryo (Gogoryo)

Koguryo, one of KOREA's ancient three kingdoms, included not only all of what is now North Korea but much of Manchuria and some of Inner Mongolia. It was formed in 57 B.C.E. and would continue into the seventh century C.E.

Buddhism was introduced into Koguryo from China by the monk SUNDO (or Shun Daop) around 372 C.E.; there it found the approval of the new king, SOSURIM (r. 371–384). He made Buddhism the state religion, and it would flourish over the next centuries.

Koguryo would reach its zenith under King Kwang-gae-to (r. 391–412 C.E.). Only 18 when he ascended the throne, he would rule for 22 years during which he would push the boundaries of his kingdom south toward Beijing and into northern Manchuria. At the same time Koguryo grew to dominate the several kingdoms that existed on the southern half of the Korean Peninsula.

Koguryo's long existence was largely attributed to China's internal chaos with a number of petty rulers fighting for control. Once China was unified in the seventh century, a large army of the Sui emperor Yang-ti entered Koguryo (610 C.E.) but was soundly defeated by Korean forces. The inability to take Koguryo was a significant reason for the replacement of the Sui dynasty by the Tang in 618. Finally, in 668, China made common cause with the kingdom of SILLA, south of Koguryo, and together they were able to defeat Koguryo, which ceased to exist in the 670s. Its territory was annexed to China. The fall of Koguryo also led the way for the rise of Silla, which soon controlled the whole peninsula.

Further reading: James Huntley Grayson, *Early Buddhism and Christianity in Korea: A Study in the Emplantation of Religion* (Leiden: Brill, 1985); Lewis R. Lancaster and C. S. Yu, eds., *Introduction of Buddhism to Korea: New Cultural Patterns* (Berkeley, Calif.: Asian Humanities Press, 1989); Ki-baek Yi, *A New History of Korea* (Cambridge, Mass.: Published for the Harvard-Yenching Institute by Harvard University Press, 1984).

Kojiki and Nihonshoki (Nihongi)

These two works, dating from 712 and 720, respectively, are Japan's first national histories. They contain the earliest Japanese religious materials we have. They also record the Japanese myth of creation, in which the first deities, Izanaki and Izanami, are ordered to mate to "consolidate the land." They give birth in turn to many islands, collectively called the "land of the Eight Great Islands."

The *Kojiki* (Chronicle of ancient events) dates from a period in which Japan had no fixed written script. It describes a time dating as far back as 660 B.C.E. The scribe Yasumaro attempted to use Chinese characters to represent existing Japanese words, as dictated to him by well-known storytellers, called *kataribe*. There were no rules to the use of Chinese to transcribe Japanese at that time. Therefore, the contents of the *Kojiki* remained a

mystery until a group of researchers known as Native Scholars studied and were finally able to explain the way Yasumaro worked.

As does the *Kojiki*, the *Nihonshoki* (also called the *Nihongi*) relates mythological events. However, its focus is on contemporary events of the period, especially the reigns of emperors such as Tenji, Tenmu, and Jito. As with Chinese historical works, the *Nihonshoki* brings out the moral qualities of good and bad rulers. It also records diplomatic contacts with China and Korea. Unlike the *Kojiki*, the *Nihonshoki* was written in classical Chinese.

While the *Nihonshoki* and the *Kojiki* are invaluable as historical documents, they began to have new uses in modern Japanese history. With the rise of nationalism in the early 1900s these two works were held up as symbols of the early, pre-Chinese period of Japanese history, a time seen as "purely" Japanese, unpolluted by foreign influence.

Further reading: Mori Mizui, "Ancient and Classical Japan: The Dawn of Shinto," in Inoue Nobutaka, ed., Mark Teeuwen and John Breen, trans., *Shinto—a Short History* (London: Routledge Curzon, 1998), 12–64; Edwin O. Reischauer, *Japan: The Story of a Nation.* Rev. ed. (Rutland, Vt., and Tokyo: Charles E. Tuttle, 1974), 29–31.

Kokuchu-Kai

Kokuchu-Kai, or "Pillar of the Nation Society," is an offshoot of NICHIREN SHOSHU Buddhism. It is of interest as a Buddhist form of ultranationalist religion.

Tanaka Chigaku (1861–1939) founded Kokuchu-Kai in 1914. Prior to this time he had been lecturing on the Buddhist saint NICHIREN and had attracted a following. He published a magazine, *Myoushuu,* on Nichiren from 1897, which helped attract followers. He had earlier established the Kokuchu-Kai Shinbon (national Pillar News) in 1912.

Tanaka had been a novice in Myokakuji, a Nichiren Buddhist temple in Tokyo. Disillusioned with traditional practices, he left the priesthood in 1879 to start his own movement, the Renge-kai (Lotus Society), in Yokohama, to the east of Tokyo. The group shifted to Tokyo in 1884 and was renamed Rissho Ankoku-kai. Finally, he established the Kokuchu-Kai in Miho village, Shizuoka Prefecture, to the west of Tokyo. The title *Kokuchu* refers to a quote from Nichiren, in which he states, "I am the pillar of the state [Kokuchu]."

Tanaka was an innovator of Buddhist practice and ritual. He felt that monks and nuns should be seen as lay Buddhists and that celibacy and dietary rules were holdovers from older practice that was out of date. He thus advocated that monks and nuns marry and eat meat. He also believed Buddhism should be part of each person's daily life. He was the first to design a Buddhist marriage ceremony, in 1887, and he created a ceremony to confer the LOTUS SUTRA on newborns. In terms of practice, then, he was an innovator.

But Tanaka was also active on the national stage. The newly established Meiji government in this period was aggressively promoting state Shinto and consciously neglecting Buddhism. Some Buddhist groups not only accepted their new standing in society but incorporated the ideas of emperor worship into their own doctrine. One group, the Gyodo Kai (Association for the Practice of Imperial-Way Buddhism), in 1938 began to promote the idea of unity of Buddhism and the imperial Japanese state. This overall movement was known as Kodo Bukkyo (Imperial Way Buddhism).

Given this context, Tanaka's nationalist ideas found fertile ground. He believed that Buddhism should be reformed in the image of Nichiren. His strong promotion of Nichiren's ideas, including protection of the state, was called *Nichirenshugi*—"Nichirenism." But Tanaka's ideas extended beyond the realm of Buddhist institutions and took in all of society. Most important, he emphasized *shakubuku,* forceful proselytization, as a means to reform the entire Japanese nation. In Shumon no Ishin ("Reformation of the Sect," 1901) he called for the unification of all Japanese Buddhist groups into a state religion. Eventually, he excused Japan's imperialist adventures abroad as a form of *shakubuku.*

Since Tanaka Chigaku's death in 1939 Kokuchu-Kai has been run by his descendants, first his son, Tanaka Houkoku, then Tanaka Koho in 1949, and, most recently, Tanaka Kikyu in 1996. The group today has a relatively small membership of around 20,000 and is involved mainly in publications and symposia. There are 84 branches, including one in Brazil.

Despite its small size, Kokuchu-Kai is important as an example of ultranationalist Buddhism in the modern period. In addition it has had significant influence on several well-known people, including the writer Miyazawa Kenji and the military officer Ishiwara Kanji. Finally, Kokuchu-Kai's reforms and emphasis on *shakubuku* had a strong influence on such other Buddhist groups as Seiyu-kai and RISSHO KOSEI-KAI.

Further reading: Edwin B. Lee, "Nichiren and Nationalism: The Religious Patriotism of Tanaka Chigaku," *Monumenta Nipponica* 30 (Spring 1975): 19–35; Ryuei Michael McCormick, "Nichiren Buddhism in the 20th Century." NichirensCoffeehouse. Available online at Lotus Sutra.net (Nichiren's Coffeehouse). URL: http://nichirenscoffeehouse.net/Ryuei/nichirenbudd_20th.html. Accessed on October 2, 2005; GeoCities. "Tanaka Chigaku and Emperor Worship." Available online. URL: http://www.geocities.com/chris_holte/Buddhism/IssuesInBuddhism/tanaka.html. Accessed on August 25, 2005.

Konkokyo

Konkokyo, "Religion of Golden Light," was founded in 1859, immediately before the formal inauguration of modernization during the Meiji period (1868–1911). In Japanese religious studies it is classed as a "new religion," despite being now nearly 150 years old. There are today approximately 400,000 members, and the church is active in America, Canada, Brazil, Paraguay, and South Korea.

The founder was Konko Daijin (1814–83), a farmer from Konko-cho, Okayama, in Japan's west. Konko lost three children and two oxen. He attributed his misfortune to the god Konjin. He later began to communicate directly with Konjin and discovered that the god was good-natured and desired to produce happiness. Konko then renamed the god Tenchi Kani No Kami, and the deity began to speak through Konko's voice. Konko would pass questions to Tenchi Kani no Kami. These question-and-answer sessions eventually evolved into meditation sessions, called *toritsugi,* between humans and Tenchi Kane No Kami. The god in 1859 instructed Konko to cease farming and dedicate all his time to *toritsugi.*

Konko Daijin eventually applied for a SHINTO priest certificate. But the newly installed Meiji government did not recognize these certificates. Konko continued without official permission until he died in 1883. In 1885 his followers succeeded in obtaining government recognition as a Shinto organization, although in fact there were no Shinto rituals or deities involved in Konkokyo practice. In 1900 Konkokyo was officially recognized as a religion separate from Shinto.

Konkokyo followed the expansion of Japan's military occupation in Asia until the end of World War II. Those churches established in the areas occupied by Japan did not last. The religion was reorganized in 1954 in an effort to separate itself from the wartime legacy.

The key Konkokyo text is *Tenchi Kakitsuke,* "Divine reminder." This text explains the reciprocal relationship between humanity and this deity, also called Principle Parent. If people ignore the concept of reciprocity, suffering results. The Principle Parent is the source of all humanity. *Toritsugi* meditation connects individuals with the Principle Parent and all other *kami.* The leader of Konkokyo is chosen from Konko Daijin's descendants.

Further reading: Peter B. Clarke, *A Bibliography of Japanese New Religious Movements* (Richmond, U.K.: Japan Library, 1999); Helen Hardacre, "Creating State Shinto: The Great Promulgation Campaign and the New Religions," *Japanese Journal of Religious Studies* 12, no. 4 (1986): 29–64; Konkokyo English. "Welcome to Konkokyo." Available online. URL: www.konko-kyo.or.jp/eng/. Accessed on August 26, 2005; H. Neil McFarland, *The Rush Hour of the Gods: A Study of New Religious Movements in Japan* (New York: Macmillan, 1967); Susumu Shimazono, "The Living Kami Idea in the New Religions of Japan," *Japanese Journal of Religious Studies* 6, no. 3 (1979): 389–412.

Korea, Buddhism in

Spread from China in the fourth century of the Common Era, PURE LAND BUDDHISM made its first appearance in northern Korea in what was then the kingdom of Goguryeo (or KOGURYO) around 372 C.E. Introduced from China by the monk Sundo (or Shun Daop), the new faith was found useful by King Sosurim (r. 371–384), who worked to give it an initial home. Buddhism subsequently moved south to the kingdoms of PAEKCHE and SILLA. A united Korea was created in 668 C.E. as the Silla kingdom expanded. Buddhism flourished and Son BUDDHISM (ZEN BUDDHISM or CHAN BUDDHISM) joined its Pure Land rival. Some nine different schools of Buddhism developed around nine prominent teachers. Buddhism competed for its place in Korean society with Confucian thought and a strongly entrenched shamanistic indigenous religion. The Buddhist tradition in Korea would be characterized by the periodic emergence of outstanding teachers who attempted to reconcile the differences among the several Buddhist schools and call for a unified Buddhist movement.

Korean Buddhists would take the lead in transmitting Buddhism to Japan. At some point in the middle of the sixth century Korean monks initially took Buddhist texts and images to the island kingdom; then after the request of Japanese authorities, a contingent of Korean Buddhists settled at Nara to initiate the spread of Buddhist teachings, practices, and culture. The presence of Koreans in Japan would continue for several centuries before being replaced by Chinese influence.

As the Korean Peninsula was united in the seventh century, two of the land's most important scholar-preachers emerged in the persons of WONHYO (617–686) and his colleague UISANG (625–702). The story is told that on their way to China to study with a famous monk, they were caught in a rainstorm and took refuge in an underground shelter for the night. The next morning they discovered their shelter to be an old tomb. Before the rain ceased, Wonhyo had an intense spiritual experience that included his seeing the ghosts of the deceased. The result was an enlightenment of sorts, summarized in his conclusion that a person who has the right state of consciousness experiences no difference between a temple sanctuary and a tomb. Soon afterward, Wonhyo abandoned his monk's status and as a layman spent his life spreading Buddhism among the masses. His efforts included the penning of some 80 books focused on the underlying unity of Buddhist thought.

Uisang finally made his way to China, where he stayed for 20 years. Upon his return, he found favor in the imperial court and was able to continue the spread of Buddhism throughout the Unified Silla kingdom. Other monks who studied in China and later contributed significantly to Buddhism's spread in Korea would include Gyeomik (sixth century) and CHAJANG. To some extent, Wonhyo is also responsible for Korean Buddhism's unique emphasis on MAITREYA, the future Buddha (Enlightened One). According to Wonhyo, Gautama Buddha predicted the arrival of another enlightened figure who would assist humanity in the establishment of an ideal society characterized by righteousness and peace.

Zen (or Son) Buddhism would experience a revival in the 12th century under the leadership of CHINUL (1158–1210). Working at a time during which the Son leadership had become corrupted, he articulated a fresh perspective based on his understanding of the unity of Buddhist thought amid the outward divisions and a sudden-enlightenment approach to theory and practice. He called believers to understand their actual accomplished identity with the Buddha. This fact underlies a belief that Buddhists can experience a sudden enlightenment that then should be followed by a life of cultivating the insights that follow such enlightenment. Chinul's contemporaries received his message uniting the thought of the several Zen schools, though an actual union of the several Zen schools would not be accomplished until the 14th century. For his accomplishment in merging of the several Zen schools, the later Master T'aego (1301–82) is remembered as one of the several "national teachers" of Korean Buddhism.

In the century after Master T'aego, the Yi dynasty (1392–1910) rose to power. It was generally hostile to Buddhism and attempted to suppress it in favor of its rivals. As a result, the embattled Buddhist camps found reasons to unite, in part as a means of sheer survival. Two major Pure Land sects emerged, the Sonjong (1424) and Kyojong. In 1592, Japan invaded Korea and Buddhists suffered alongside the entire country. However, as they remained out of favor, they received no postwar government support to rebuild. Though Buddhism never gained official support, a relaxing of government opposition in the 19th century allowed a period of revival and recovery. This revival was accomplished in part by assistance from Japan. In the late 19th century, a number of Japanese priests moved to Korea to assist the local leadership.

The 20th century became a time of significant ups and downs for the Buddhist community. It began with the government's relaxing its control over the Buddhist temples. Then in 1910, Japan seized control of the peninsula. As an occupying force, it reassumed governmental oversight. Reaction to the brutal occupation government led to alienation between Korean and Japanese Buddhists, and to further uniting of the Koreans, symbolized by the 1936 merger of the Sonjong and Konjong sects into the presently existing Chogje sect, the dominant force in Korean Buddhism.

The Korean Peninsula suffered greatly in the years of World War II, but even more so in the aftermath when the United States and Russia assumed control over the southern and northern halves of the country, respectively. The inability of the two countries to work out an agreement over an independent country led directly to the Korean War (1950–53) and the establishment of two separate countries, the Republic of (South) Korea and the People's Republic of (North) Korea. In the north, Buddhism was suppressed along with all religions and has largely disappeared. Less than 2 percent of the population identify themselves as Buddhist, and few temples remain open. In the south, Buddhism has revived significantly but faces continued competition for varieties of tradition Korean folk religions and has fallen significantly behind Christianity, which now has the allegiance of some 40 percent of the public.

Some 80 percent of Korean Buddhists are affiliated with the Chogje sect with its headquarters at the Chogyesa Temple complex in Seoul. This 600-year-old temple has served as the Chogye's life center since its formation in 1936 and the Japanese used it as the administrative center for the entire Buddhist community. While Chogje Buddhism remains the dominant force in Korean Buddhist life, a spectrum of new Buddhist sects have also emerged. For example, WON BUDDHISM was created in the years of World War I with a distinct focus on the Diamond Sutra. It is a modern secularized version of Buddhism whose temples are devoid of image and whose programmatic thrust is very this-worldly.

Through the 20th century, Buddhists' migrations to other countries have occasioned the spread of Korean Buddhism, especially to Japan and North America. Post-1965 migrations to the United States (contemporaneous with the migration of a variety of South Asian Buddhists) have been followed by the building of numerous Buddhist temples, and the emergence of a number of organizations, some of which are new to the Buddhist world and have no Korean affiliate. Korean Buddhists have helped remold the American religious landscape. A Korean temple in Los Angeles became the site of the first meeting of what became the AMERICAN BUDDHIST CONGRESS.

Further reading: *Focus on Korea.* 3 vols. (Seoul: Seoul International Publishing House, 1988); James Huntley Grayson, *Korea: A Religious History* (Oxford: Oxford University Press, 1989); Duk-Whang Kim, *A History of Religions in Korea* (Seoul: Daeji Monoonwha-sa, 1988); Lewis R. Lancaster and C. S. Yu, eds., *Assimilation of Buddhism in Korea: Religious Maturity and Innovation in the Silla Dynasty* (Berkeley, Calif.: Asian Humanities Press, 1991); Lewis R. Lancaster and C. S. Yu, eds., *Introduction of Buddhism to Korea: New Cultural Patterns* (Berkeley, Calif.: Asian Humanities Press, 1989).

Korean Buddhist Federation

The Korean Buddhist Federation is the official organization for Buddhists in the Democratic People's Republic of Korea (DPRK), commonly called North Korea. The DPRK was established in 1945, at the end of the Second World War. Soviet and American forces that occupied the northern and southern halves of the country were unable to agree on the future of Korea and two countries resulted. The 1950 Korean War initiated by the DPRK was an attempt to reunite the country that failed. By the end of the war more than 400 Buddhist temples had been destroyed. Today only around 60 temples remain though among them are several prominent older centers, Pohyon Temple at Mt. Myohyang, Kwangpop Temple near Pyongyang, and Pyohun Temple at Mt. Kumgang.

The Korean Buddhist Association was formed in 1945 and almost immediately became moribund as the new government articulated a policy supportive of atheism and began a systematic suppression of all religion, including Buddhism. Buddhism survived as an underground movement.

Some liberalization of the antireligious policy was noticed in the 1970s, and the Korean Buddhist Federation was reorganized in at least a rudimentary fashion. It is led by a central committee with subordinate provincial, city, and county committees. The central committee is currently led by its chairman, Pak Thae Hwa. It was able to affiliate with the Asian Buddhist Committee for Peace in 1976, the World Federation of Buddhists in 1986, and the Asia Buddhist Conference in 1990. It also cooperates with the Korea Buddhist Federation in Japan.

In 1992, a new constitution for the DPRK was adopted that includes provisions for the freedom of religious belief and the right to erect buildings for religious use. In practice, only religion that supports the active interests of the state is permitted any public activity. Officially, the government emphasizes that it views religion as a purely private affair for individuals. Thus the government strives not to interfere with it nor to maltreat or approve religious beliefs.

At present, the public celebration of some Buddhist holidays, such as Buddha's birthday (VESAK), is allowed. The federation has been especially active in events calling for Korean unification, including some that involved colleagues from South Korea. An eight-year course of study, which around 50 men may enter each year, begins with a five-year course in Buddhism through the Philosophy Department of Kim Il Sung University (initiated in 1989) and completed at a three-year Buddhist school in Pyongyang managed by the federation.

It is difficult to estimate the number of Buddhists in the DPRK as the 21st century begins, but some learned observers have suggested that they number around 10,000.

Further reading: Choson Sinbo. "Buddhism in DPRK." Available online. URL: http://www1.korea-np.co.jp/pk/. Accessed on November 28, 2005.

Korean shamanism

Although most Koreans associate it with superstition, shamanism is widely practiced in modern South Korea. Indeed it may be more widespread in Korea than in other East Asian societies, although shamanistic elements are found in spiritual and medical practices in many countries. Shamanism generally entails practices in which an individual communicates with both spirit and human realms and often uses soul flight to leave the body and travel to other realms. Although separate from practitioners of indigenous medicine (*hanbang*), shamanism in Korea is a form of healing. It is a mistake to see the shaman as simply another medical alternative, however. The shaman operates in the "field of misfortunes," helping the supplicants deal with their bad luck. Ritual deals with illness caused specifically by misfortune, called in Korean *byonghwan*, "illness-misfortune."

MUDANG AND OTHER TYPES OF SHAMANS

Scholars generally refer to shamanism as *musok*, "shamanistic folklore." But ordinary Koreans simply refer to shamanism as *misin*, "superstition." The practitioners are called *mudang*. This title is in fact derogatory, and many practitioners do not like to be called *mudang*. Other words for shamans vary with different regions. However, the *mudang* type is the most common, making up around 50 percent of all contemporary practitioners. The shamans themselves prefer such titles as *mansin* (10,000 gods) or *boasla* (bodhisattva or, in current usage, a female Buddhist). In fact many shamans go under the guise of being Buddhists.

Most researchers divide Korean shamans into two main types, the *mudang*, who practice ecstasy, and the *tangol*, who do not. *Mudang* are masters of trance and depend on entry into states of ecstasy.

This means the *mudang* approximates a classical definition of the *shaman,* that given by Mircea Eliade: "the shaman specializes in the trance state, during which his soul is believed to leave his body and ascend to the sky or descend to the underworld" (Eliade 1987: 202).

The *tangol* shamans work together with another specialist, called *myeongdu,* who uses divination not trance. The *myeongdu* work with a *tangol* to find the relevant spirit and hold a ceremony, called a *kut.* The *tangol* holds the *kut* without entering a trance, thus not quite corresponding to the image of the shaman given by Eliade.

None of the Korean shamans engage in soul flight, another classic practice of shamans. Because of these deviations from the "classic" model of the shaman, it is possible simply to view these Korean practitioners as followers of a single religious tradition, called by one writer (Suk-Jay Yim) *mu-ism.* Practically speaking, then, Korean shamanism can be seen as the fourth, or "folk," tradition of Korean religions, after Buddhism, Christianity, and Confucianism.

SHAMANIC RITUAL, THE *KUT*

The most accurate way to describe Korean shamanic practice is through reference to ritual. The *kut* ritual is practiced by all shamans, regardless of their other characteristics, whether the trance is entered into by the shaman, the supplicant, or not at all; whether the shaman assumes his or her duties after illness or through hereditary tradition; whether a spirit stick is used or not.

In the *kut* the spirit is given a voice and then openly engages in dialog with people. The spirits express strong emotions through laughter or anger. The shaman performs the key function of invoking the spirit so that he or she can then speak. Unlike in ancestor-worship rituals such as the *chesa,* in which the spirits of the deceased are silent, in the *kut* they actively participate and express their emotions. And unlike in current Christian exorcism rites, the spirit is invoked not to be expelled, but to be engaged in nego-

tiation. Korean shamans show a sympathetic understanding of the spirit world and the plight of the deceased. The relationship between the supplicant, a living being, and the deceased, a spirit, is one of misfortune, and the *kut* functions to heal the pain through mutual understanding. This dialog is the defining characteristic of Korean shamanism.

There are two type of *kut* ritual, the sitting (*anjeun kut*) and the standing (*seon kut*). A spirit stick (*sinjangdai*) is used only in the sitting version. The spirit stick is a divining stick made of wood. While the supplicant holds the stick, the shaman asks questions. Answers are given through the stick: nodding means yes, shaking sideways means no, and so on. In general nearly anyone who holds the stick is possessed by the spirit—it is the participant's job to become possessed—while the shaman simply manages the *kut* ritual.

Unlike in many ritual performances, in the *kut* there is often no audience; only the shaman, the supplicant, and the deity are present. However, close relatives may also attend. As part of the ritual performance, the shaman may preside over a wedding or even a murder of the spirit, to complete some unfinished or painful issue. Many of these actions are performed to ward off misfortune, not simply to fix an existing condition.

Shamanism in Korea is a contested category. People would generally prefer not to recognize it, yet they continue to consult the *mudang* when a situation warrants it. Shamanism is looked down on because it is seen as superstition and, it would appear, invalid. Historically, shamanism has run against all dominant ideologies, including Confucianism and, today, Christianity and modernism. Spirits' speaking, the key ingredient of Korean shamanism, is an idea that runs counter to everyday, commonsense reality. Nevertheless shamans appear to perform an important, subterranean function in Korean society, one not likely to disappear soon.

Further reading: M. Eliade, *Shamanism: Archaic Techniques of Ecstasy.* Translated by W. Trask (London: Routledge & Kegan Paul, 1964); Chongho Kim, *Korean Shamanism: The Cultural Paradox* (Aldershot, U.K.: Ashgate, 2003); T. G. Kim, "The Realities of Korean Shamanism," in M. Hoppal and O. von Sadovsky, eds., *Shamanism: Past and Present.* Part 2 (Budapest: Ethnographic Institute, 1989), 271–282; ——— and K. Howard, "Without Ecstasy, Is There Shamanism in South-West Korea?" in M. Hoppal and K. Howard, eds., *Shamans and Cultures* (Budapest: Korrekt, 1993), 3–14.

Kornfield, Jack (1945–   ) *American lay practitioner and teacher of vipassana meditation*

After his graduation from Dartmouth College in 1967, the future Buddhist teacher Jack Kornfield joined the Peace Corps. He was assigned to northeast Thailand, where his stay provided the occasion of his meeting with AJAHN CHAH (1918–81), then at the height of his fame as a leading force in the THAI FOREST MEDITATION TRADITION. Kornfield took the opportunity to study THERAVADA BUDDHISM and practice meditation intensively. After his time in the Peace Corps, he became a monk.

He returned to the United States in 1972 and joined Sharon Salzberg and Joseph Goldstein in the founding of the Insight Meditation Society, based in Barre, Massachusetts. This organization began to offer the intensive practice of insight meditation to the American public. Kornfield later founded Spirit Rock Center, in California, north of San Francisco, as a West Coast center for insight meditation practice.

Since the mid-1970s, Kornfield has traveled extensively offering classes and workshops in VIPASSANA meditation and has authored a number of books. He also obtained a doctorate in clinical psychology.

Further reading: Joseph Goldstein and Jack Kornfield, *Seeking the Heart of Wisdom* (Boston: Shambhala, 1987); Jack Kornfield, *A Path with Heart: A Guide through the Perils and Problems of Spiritual Life* (New York: Bantam Books, 1993); Jack Kornfield and Christina Feldman, *Soul Food: Stories to Nourish the Spirit and the Heart* (San Francisco: HarperSanFransisco, 1996); Jack Kornfield and Paul Breiter, *A Still Forest Pool: The Insight Meditation of Achaan Chah* (Wheaton, Ill.: Quest Books, 1985).

Kosai-ji

This Buddhist temple at Kukuchi, near Amagasaki City, Japan (near Osaka), is well known as the burial place of Chikamatsu Monsaemon (1653–1724), the best-known Edo era (1603–1868) playwright. The temple is now a national heritage site.

Further reading: "Chikamatsu Monzaemon and Amagasaki." Amagasaki, the City of Chikamatsu. Available online. URL: http://www.city.amagasaki.hyogo.jp/web/contents/info/city/city03/chikamatsu/english/C1_p1.html. Accessed on May 19, 2006.

Koya, Mt.

Mt. Koya, the center of SHINGON Buddhism in Japan, is located in Wakayama prefecture (near Osaka). In 816, KUKAI, the founder of Shingon, resided in Kyoto. Wishing to escape the general chaos and corruption of city life, he requested a grant of land for a rural retreat where Shingon monks could concentrate on meditation and the development of their ritual and meditation skills. The emperor Saga (809–823) granted the mountain and Kukai moved immediately to construct a temple and other necessary building for a monastic community. Unfortunately, because of his duties in Kyoto, he was unable to move there until 832. He would remain on Mt. Koya for the rest of his life and eventually be buried there.

In the years after Kukai's death, a rivalry developed between the Shingon center in Kyoto (To-ji) and Mt. Koya. To-ji, given to Kukai in 823, remained the primary place for training students, but their final examination and ordination took place on the mountain. As the number of ordained priests was rigidly regulated, the right to examine and ordain carried much power. The ongoing tension between the two centers led the emperor to step in on several occasions. In 853 he ordered the candidates for ordination to be examined at To-ji and ordained at Mt. Koya. Nine years later, Mt. Koya was given full jurisdiction over ordinations. Finally, in 902, the number of ordinations was increased and split between the two centers.

Through the 10th century, Kukai became an increasing object of veneration. The cult of Kukai was further stimulated by the emperor's giving him the posthumous honorary title *Kobo daishi* (great teacher). Many of the Shingon believed that Kukai had not died but had entered a deep trance state awaiting the appearance of MAITREYA, the future Buddha. Through time, Kobo Daishi was viewed by some as an incarnation of Maitreya and Mt. Koya was part of Maitreya's heavenly realm.

A large stupa was erected over his tomb, and in 1107, the emperor Horikawa (r. 1086–1107) was buried in front of the STUPA. Mt. Koya subsequently became a pilgrimage site and a popular place to be buried.

Of some interest, Kukai believed that women could not attain Buddhahood (a popular opinion in the Buddhist community at the time), and thus women were not allowed to go to Mt. Koya, visit its temple, or participate in any of its activities. However, in 1160, Bifukumon'in, a consort of the emperor, requested that her body be buried on Mt. Koya. Her request was granted. She was the only woman to violate the standing rule prior to 1872, when it was abandoned.

Today, To-ji is considered the headquarters temple of Shingon Buddhism and Mt. Koya the center for monastic practice and pilgrimage.

Further reading: Shinryu Izutsu and Shoryu Omori, *Sacred Treasures of Mt. Koya: The Art of Japanese Shingon Buddhism* (Honolulu: Koyasan Reihokan Museum. 2002); Kazuo Kasahara, ed., *A History of Japanese Religion.* Translated by Paul McCarthy and Gaynor Seki-

mori (Tokyo: Kosei, 2001); E. Dale Saunders, *Buddhism in Japan* (Philadelphia: University of Pennsylvania Press, 1964).

Kshitigarbha (Jin Dizang, Ti-tsang, Jizo)

Kshitigarbha (Earth Repository), a popular bodhisattva in Mahayana Buddhism, is believed by devotees to have been entrusted with the task of saving souls in the era between Sakyamuni BUDDHA, the past Buddha, and MAITREYA, the future Buddha. Kshitigarbha appears to have originated from a female earth deity in Hindu mythology. He initially attained some popularity as a Buddhist figure in China during the Tang dynasty (618–906) as Mahayana Buddhism rose to prominence. Known as Jin Dizang, he first appeared in the fifth century when the Sutra of the Ten Chakras was translated. From China Kshitigarbha found his way to Korea and was introduced in the eighth century in Japan, where he became known as Jizo. In Japan Jizo was always second to VAIROCANA

Small stone images of Jizo (Kshitigarbha), the bodhisattva concerned with those in the afterlife. In Japan these are often dressed as babies or given toys as acts of remembrance by couples or women who have performed *mizuko Kuyo,* the ceremony of remembrance for aborted fetuses.

Bronze image of the bodhisattva Kshitigarbha in Qinglong temple, Xi'an, China

Buddha. However, he gained a new following during the 13th century and has grown in popularity ever since.

Kshitigarbha is valued for his reputed power to grant long life and to give mothers easy childbirth. He is generally pictured as a monk carrying a pilgrim's staff and a bright jewel representing the Dharma truth, whose light banishes fear. As the equally popular GUAN YIN, he is often associated with Amida Buddha (AMITABHA) and is seen assisting people trapped in hell to find their way to Amida's Western Paradise.

As Jizo, he has become an integral part of the modern cult of children in Japan, where numerous attributes found nowhere in the older sutras are ascribed to him. He is now, for example, seen as the guardian of unborn, aborted, miscarried,

and stillborn babies. He is often portrayed as a cute figure quite accepting of children, and Jizo festivals in Japan have become family affairs with special activities just for kids.

Further reading: Jan Chozen Bays, *Jizo Bodhisattva: Guardian of Children, Travelers, and Other Voyagers* (Boston: Shambhala, 2003); ———, *Jizo Bodhisattva: Modern Healing and Traditional Buddhist Practice* (Rutland, Vt.: Charles E. Tuttle, 2002); Samuel Beal, *A Catena of Buddhist Scriptures from the Chinese* (London: Trubner & Co., 1871).

Kuan Yin   *See* GUAN YIN.

Kukai (Kobo Daishi) (774–835) *Japanese Buddhist leader and founder of Shingon*
Kukai founded the influential branch of Japanese esoteric (hidden and mystical) Buddhism, SHINGON. Born to a provincial gentry family, Kukai studied Confucian classics until he suddenly left his studies to focus on Buddhist cultivation at age 14. He followed a strict ascetic lifestyle.

He was finally ordained as a priest when he was 30. He visited Tang dynasty China, where he learned further esoteric techniques and was allowed to initiate others. He was later appointed abbot of To-ji, a temple and monastery complex in Kyoto, which then became the center of Kukai's new sect, the Shingon. He spent his final years building a new center on Mt. KOYA.

Cultic worship of Kukai as Kobo Daishi, an incarnation of the bodhisattva MAITREYA, continues today.

Further reading: Ryuichi Abe, *The Weaving of Mantra: Kukai and the Construction of Esoteric Buddhist Discourse* (New York: Columbia University Press, 1999); Yoshito S. Hakeda, trans., *Kukai: Major Works* (New York: Columbia University Press, 1972); Richard K. Payne, "*Ajikan*: Ritual and Meditation in the Shingon Tradition," in Richard K. Payne, ed., *Re-Visioning "Kamak-*

ura" Buddhism (Honolulu: University of Hawaii Press, 1998), 219–248; Jacqueline I. Stone, *Original Enlightenment and the Transformation of Medieval Japanese Buddhism* (Honolulu: University of Hawaii Press, 1999); Yoshiro Tamura, *Japanese Buddhism: A Cultural History.* Translated by Jeffrey Hunter (Tokyo: Kosei, 2000).

Kumarajiva (344–413) *translator of Buddhist works into Chinese*

Kumarajiva was born into a royal family in Kucha, Central Asia. His mother, a devout Buddhist, became a nun when Kumarajiva was but seven years old, and under her guidance the boy began to learn Buddhist sutras, many of which he memorized. He traveled with his mother to study with the noted monks Bandhudatta (who lived in what is today Kashmir) in India and Buddhayashas in Kucha. Raised in a Theravada Buddhist atmosphere, he later adhered to Mahayana Buddhism. He was ordained around 364.

Kumarajiva attained a high profile for his knowledge of the Buddhist scriptures. His fame was great enough that the king of a short-lived Chinese dynasty, the Former Qin, ordered his general Lu Kuang to attack Kucha in order to take Kumarajiva to his capital. On the way there the Former Qin was overthrown. Lu Kuang subsequently settled at Liang-chou, where he maintained his custody over Kumarajiva. He finally arrived in Chang An, the capital of the new dynasty of the Later Qin, in 401.

Kumarajiva was treated as a major asset and spent the remainder of his life translating texts. The 35 texts he and his teams translated included the NIRVANA SUTRA and the Avatamsaka (Flower Garland) Sutra, the latter leading directly to the formation of the HUA YAN SCHOOL. The development of Buddhism in China, including the emergence of its major sects, was largely based on the appropriation of the Kumarajiva's translations.

Further reading: Jacques Gernet, *Buddhism in Chinese Society: An Economic History from the Fifth to the Tenth Centuries.* Translated by Franciscus Verellen (New York: Columbia University Press, 1995); Burton Watson, *The Flower of Chinese Buddhism* (New York: Weatherhill, 1986); Arthur F. Wright, *Buddhism in Chinese History* (Palo Alto, Calif.: Stanford University Press, 1959).

Kuon-ji

Kuon-ji is the head temple of the NICHIREN SHOSHU sect, on Mount Minobu, in Yamanashi Prefecture, Japan. In 1274, NICHIREN's relationship with the shogun in Kamakura came to a head. The shogun offered to build him a temple, but Nichiren turned it down because the shogun was continuing to support the other Buddhist sect groups. Thus in the middle of 1274 he left Kamakura and went to Mount Minobu. There he spent the next years teachings, writing, and training his closest disciples.

Kuon-ji was actually founded by Nichiren in 1281. It was built by Hakiri Sanenaga, a follower who was steward of the area around the temple. Sanenaga gave the building to Nichiren After Nichiren's death, Sanenaga had a disagreement with NIKKO, one of Nichiren's primary disciples, who left (1289) to found the Nichiren Shoshu. Another disciple, Niko, assumed control of Kuon-ji.

Further reading: Bruno Petzold, *Buddhist Prophet Nichiren: A Lotus in the Sun* (Tokyo: Hokke Janaru, 1978).

Kusha

The Kusha (Dharma analysis) school was one of the six schools of Buddhist thought established in the eighth century at NARA, Japan. *Kusha* here is short for the ABHIDHARMA-KOSA, the school based on the work of that name by the great Indian philosopher VASUBANDHU. At that time Vasubandhu was a committed Sarvastivadan, and the Kusha can be seen as a summation of SARVASTIVADA (SARVASTIVADIN) SCHOOL and indeed all HINAYANA doctrine. The 564 translation of the Abhidharma-kosa into Chinese gave birth to a school of Chinese Buddhism, which was introduced to Japan in the eighth century.

Vasubandu suggested that while the self lacked substantiality, matter really existed. It was composed of very fine particles that are continually rearranged to produce the ever-changing state of things we see in the world. He also considered the past and the future as having a real existence.

At Nara (as previously in China), the view of the Kusha school was opposed to the perspective being offered by the JOJITSU school (which denied the substantial existence of matter) and the SAN-RON school, which saw both the Kusha and Jojitsu schools as erroneous. The debate among the three schools and the study of the texts upon which they were based became lively pursuits in the eighth and ninth centuries in Japan but gradually lost the attention of Buddhist leaders and all three schools eventually disappeared.

Further reading: K. Krishna Murthy, *Buddhism in Japan* (Delhi: Sundeep Prakashan, 1989); E. Dale Saunders, *Buddhism in Japan* (Philadelphia: University of Pennsylvania Press, 1964); Yoshiro Tamura, *Japanese Buddhism: A Cultural History.* Translated by Jeffrey Hunter (Tokyo: Kosei, 2000).

Kushi, Michio   *See* MACROBIOTICS.

Kusinagara (Kusinara)

Kusinagara, a town in eastern Uttar Pradesh, India, was the capital of the Malla state during the lifetime of the historical Buddha. Kusinagara was later absorbed in the expanding Magadha state. Gautama Buddha, after a long and successful life in laying the foundations of Buddhism, spent his last days at Kusinagara. Here the Buddha delivered the MAHAPARINIRVANA SUTRA on the subject of diligence and admitted the last followers to be received as Buddhists by him personally. After the Buddha's death, his body was cremated and the remains divided among eight Buddhist kings from different parts of India. Some of his ashes were enshrined at Kusinagara.

Kusinagara grew in importance during the reign of the Buddhist king ASOKA in the third century B.C.E. He initiated a period during which most of the religious structures in the community were constructed. Kusinagara remained an active Buddhist center for many centuries, but then the Buddhist community was destroyed during the years of Muslim rule beginning in the ninth century. For almost a thousand years Kusinagara was lost in the jungles. It was rediscovered in 1878 by British explorers. Extensive excavations have uncovered the remains of a large monastic community that survived into the 11th century.

Today, the Chankhandi Stupa marks the spot where many believe that Buddha was cremated. In the midst of the ruins is a large pillar originally erected by King Asoka. None of the Buddha's relics originally placed in the stupa are known to exist. Close by is the Mahaparinirvana Temple in the midst of which was found a large statue of a reclining Buddha. Burmese Buddhists restored the temple in 1927 and 1956.

In a joint effort, Indian, Japanese, and Sri Lankan Buddhists have built a modern Buddhist pilgrimage center. In 1994, to commemorate the 50th anniversary of the enthronement of King Bhumibhol of Thailand, and to contribute to the effort to reestablish Buddhism in India, Thai Buddhists constructed Wat Thai Kusinara Chalermraj in Kushinagara.

Further reading: Trilok Chandra Majupuria, *Holy Places of Buddhism in Nepal and India: A Guide to Sacred Places in Buddha's Lands* (Columbia, Mo.: South Asia Books, 1987); Tarthang Tulku, ed., *Holy Places of the Buddha.* Vol. 9, *Crystal Mirror* (Berkeley, Calif.: Dharma, 1994).

Kuya (Koya) (903–972)   *earliest Japanese Buddhist monk to popularize the use of nembutsu*

After becoming tonsured as a novice priest around the age of 20, Kuya became a wanderer, and the first of a new class of wandering monks, the *hijiri*, "NEMBUTSU wanderers." He was respected among the common people for his willingness to live among them and forgo creature comforts.

In 948 he settled at Mt. HIEI (the headquarters of the TENDAI sect) and was ordained as a priest. This event seemed to have been a watershed in his life. He began to accept support from the imperial court and in 963 founded Saiko-ji temple in Kyoto. He lived there quietly for the rest of his life. Though a precursor to the distinctive PURE LAND BUDDHISM later promoted by Honen (1133–1212) and the JODO-SHU in the 13th century, he is a prime representative of the AMITABHA devotion cult that had become an integral part of Tendai Buddhism.

Further reading: W. Theodore de Bary, ed., *Sources of Japanese Tradition* (New York: Columbia University Press, 1958); August Karl Reischauer, *Studies in Japanese Buddhism* (New York, Macmillan, 1917); Yoshiro Tamura, *Japanese Buddhism: A Cultural History.* Translated by Jeffrey Hunter (Tokyo: Kosei, 2000).

Kwan Um school

The Kwan Um school of Zen is a Western expression of Korean SON BUDDHISM founded by Seung Sahn Sunim (1927–2002), generally called Dae Soen Sa Nim by his students. Seung Sahn was ordained as a novice monk at Magok-sa temple in Korea in 1948. Two years of study and examinations by several masters led to his receiving his INKASHOMEI (seal) of enlightenment.

Seung Sahn served in the South Korean Army during the Korean War, after which he became the abbot of a Buddhist temple and served on the board of directors of the Chogye Order. In the 1960s he founded temples among Korean expatriates in Japan and Hong Kong. In 1971 Seung Sahn moved to the United States and opened a Zen center in Providence, Rhode Island, the first of many. In 1983, he formally organized the Kwan Um school of Zen as an umbrella organization for the many centers related to him. Several years later he founded the first Korean style Zen monastery, the Diamond Hill Zen Monastery, in Rhode Island. It became the training ground for his more advanced students, a number of whom were given their *inka* by Seung Sahn.

Through the 1990s, the school spread internationally. A European headquarters in Paris oversees temples across the continent including in Russia and the countries of Eastern Europe. A center in Seoul oversees temples in Korea, Malaysia, Hong Kong, and Singapore. There is also work in Australia, Brazil, and South Africa.

Seung Sahn became one of the most well-known teachers in the Western Buddhist community. He authored several books in which he expounded the mixture of SOTO and RINZAI ZEN traditions he taught.

Further reading: Seung Sahn, *Bone of Space: Poems by Zen Master Seung Sahn* (San Francisco: Four Season's Foundation 1976); ———, *Dropping Ashes on the Buddha: The Teaching of Zen Master Seung Sahn.* Translated by Stephen Mitchell (New York: Grove Press, 1976); ———, *Only Don't Know: Selected Teaching Letters of Zen Master Seung Sahn* (San Francisco: Four Season's Foundation, 1982); ———, *Zen: The Perfect Companion* (New York: Black Dog & Leventhal, 2003).

L

Laity, Annabel (Chan Duc, "True Virtue")

(b. unknown) *follower of Thich Nhat Hanh and major contemporary translator*

Annabel Laity is a key lieutenant in THICH NHAT HANH'S Buddhist organization. She became a follower in 1986 and a Dharma teacher in 1990. She was director of the Maple Forest Monastery, USA, from 1997 and abbess of the Green Mountain Dharma Centre from 1998. She was born in England and studied Sanskrit in India. She has translated many of Thich Nhat Hanh's books, such as *Breathe! You Are Alive* (1998) and *Thundering Silence: Sutra on Knowing the Better Way to Catch a Snake* (1993).

Further reading: Thich Nhât Hanh, *Teaching on Love.* Translated by Mobi Warren and Annabel Laity (Berkeley, Calif.: Parallax Press, 1997).

Lama
See TITLES AND TERMS OF ADDRESS, BUDDHIST.

Laos, Buddhism in

Buddhism appears to have been introduced into Laos as early as the 10th century. Today, after a turbulent period during the 20th century, it remains the religion of most Laotians.

During the reign of King Fa Ngum (1316–73), founder of the Lao kingdom of Lan Xang in the mid-14th century, Buddhism played a dominant role in Laotian society. Over successive centuries the Lao Buddhist SANGHA (community of monks) promoted morality and an attitude of respect for the ruler. In return, the successive Lao kings generously supported the sangha. By the time Westerners first explored Laos in the 17th century, they were able to see a relatively wealthy monastic establishment that was consuming a significant portion of the kingdom's income.

In 1707, the Lan Xang kingdom fell apart and several rival kingdoms emerged. That action also split the community of monks, each group of which adhered to the ruler in the territory in which they resided. As Thailand (Siam) established control over the various parts of Laos in the 19th century, the sangha had largely lost its former privileged position. Laotian Buddhism's low point was reached in the years after the Thais sacked Viang Chan (now Vientiane, the Laotian capital) in 1828. The sangha was further split as different reform movements emerged. The DHAMMAYUTTIKA NIKAYA reform movement founded by the future Thai king Rama IV (1804–68) was also influential in Laos. Just as in Thailand, there was a dominant MAHANIKAYA as well as a reformist DHAMMAYUTTIKA NIKAYA.

The arrival of the French in the 1890s to establish a protectorate did little to change Buddhism's or the sangha's position, beyond opening the country to Christian missionaries. An independent Kingdom of Laos was founded in 1953 after the French pullout, and the new government restored Buddhism's privileged position. However, the new government was almost immediately drawn into conflict with the Communist Pathet Lao movement. To keep the Buddhist community loyal, the government imposed a new administrative structure on it that at every level paralleled the government's hierarchy. The sangha was led by the *sangharaja,* a monk selected by the senior abbots and approved by the government. The Pathet Laos encouraged different factions among the sangha to oppose the government.

In 1975, the Pathet Lao took control of the country. Most of those monks formerly loyal to the government left Laos. They were part of an exodus that saw approximately 10 percent of the population become refugees. They founded a number of Laotian ethnic temples and monasteries in their new countries of residence—France, Australia, Canada, and the United States.

Within Laos, the new government completely reorganized the Buddhist community. They abolished all the sectarian groupings and founded the Lao United Buddhists Association (LUBA), a substructure within the government-supported Lao Front for National Construction. The office of *sangharaja* was abandoned and leadership given to the new president of the LUBA. After a sharp decline in support, Buddhism has recovered and continues as the religion of the majority of Laotians.

Further reading: Grant Evans, *The Politics of Ritual and Remembrance: Laos since 1975* (Chiang Mai, Thailand: Silkworm Press, 1998); *Life after Liberation: The Church in the Lao People's Democratic Republic* (Nakhon Sawan, Thailand: Lao Christian Service, 1987); B. L. Smith, *Religion and the Legitimization of Power in Thailand, Laos, and Burma* (Chambersburg, Pa.: Anima, 1978); Martin Stuart-Fox, *Historical Dictionary of Laos* (Metuchen, N.J.: Scarecrow Press, 2000); ———, *The Lao Kingdom of Lan Xang: Rise and Decline* (Bangkok: White Lotus Press, 1998).

Lao Tzu   *See* LAOZI.

Laozi (Lao-tzu) (c. 500 B.C.E.)   *Chinese philosopher of the Dao*

Laozi is the most enigmatic of China's great philosophers. He is traditionally said to be the author of the DAODEJING. He was said to have lived during Confucius's time and to have debated with him. Depending on which school wrote the account, Laozi sometimes bested CONFUCIUS, and at other times served to illustrate Confucius's point.

The first biographical reference is in the *Shiji* (Records of the historian), a massive work from the early Han dynasty (221 B.C.E.–220 C.E.). According to this source Laozi (surnamed Li) was born in Chu, a state in what today is central China, and he kept the archives at the Zhou ruler's court. He resigned and went west, where he met one Yin Xi, "Guardian of the Pass," at the Xiangu mountain pass. Yin Xi requested that Laozi write down his wisdom before he would allow him to pass. At this request Laozi wrote the *Daodejing*. After this there are no more reports on his whereabouts. Nevertheless, his recorded age was at least 160 years, according to the *Shiji.*

Laozi's association with Daoist concepts meant that he soon became a figure of religious veneration. He is now worshipped as one of the highest deities in the Daoist pantheon, under the title *Taishang Laojun,* or simply *Laojun.*

Laozi was also used as a tool in debates between Buddhists and Daoists. Daoists often insisted that Laozi continued west to India, where he taught disciples, including Sakyamuni Buddha. Thus all Buddhist teachings originated with Laozi, a claim unsupported by evidence but sure to cause controversy.

Further reading: Max Kaltenmark, *Lao Tzu and Taoism.* Translated by Roger Greaves (Stanford, Calif.: Stanford University Press, 1969 [1965]).

Lhamo Latso, Lake (Oracle Lake, Vision Lake)

Lake Lhamo Latso is one of the holy natural sites in Tibet. The lake is located some hundred miles southeast of Lhasa. Above the lake on the hillside is a throne where the DALAI LAMA and others over the years have traveled to sit, meditate, and receive a vision and/or information on a particular question. It is often the place where Tibetan leaders go for information to assist them in identifying a new incarnation of a deceased lama.

The power possessed by the lake is derived from an ancient Tibetan belief that every country has a *la,* or "life-spirit." The lake is the home of the *la* of Tibet. The lake has also become associated with the *la* of each Dalai Lama.

The lake's most famous use in the 20th century occurred in 1933 after the death of the 13th Dalai Lama. The regent, who assumes power after the death of the Dalai Lama until the next one is identified and comes of age, made a pilgrimage to Lhamo Latso, where he was able to discern the information that led him and his colleagues to Tenzin Gyatso, the young boy then living in central Tibet who became the 14th Dalai Lama. More recently, in 1995, four monks from Tashil-humpo monastery, the monastery founded by TSONG KHAPA, who originated the GELUG school of Buddhism to which the Dalai Lama belongs, made the trek to Lhamo Latso, to gather information on the next PANCHEN LAMA (second only to Dalai Lama) in the Gelug community.

Further reading: Keith Dowman, *The Power Places of Central Tibet: The Pilgrim's Guide* (London: Rout-

ledge and Kegan Paul, 1987); Martin A. Mills, *Identity, Ritual and State in Tibetan Buddhism: The Foundations of Authority in Gelukpa Monasticism* (London: Routledge, 2003).

li (1) (principle, pattern, form)

Li is the ultimate structure(s) of both reality and human nature—it is essential to learn as one strives to become a sage. Western scholars of Chinese thought often speak of NEO-CONFUCIANISM when referring to the Confucian renaissance during the Song dynasty (960–1279). The term *Neo-Confucianism* is somewhat misleading; Chinese traditionally speak of later Confucianism as *lixue* (the learning of principle) in reference to the centrality of metaphysics in this later reinterpretation of Confucian teachings. It is this notion of *li,* which might best be conceived as the abstract "essence" of something that makes it what it is, that became the linchpin for Neo-Confucian views of reality, the place of human beings, and harmonious relationships between them exemplified by the sage.

Li originally referred to the veins within a piece of jade, its elemental and essential structure revealed through careful inspection and observation. We already see the word used in a more or less metaphysical sense in the BOOK OF CHANGES, where it is spoken of in conjunction with instructions on the use of the *Yi* as a way of understanding the cosmos and developing one's moral nature. The pre-Han thinker Hanfeizi (d. 233 B.C.E.), known for his association with "legalism," also speaks of *li* as both the cosmic pattern/order established by Dao and the ordering (patterning) process itself. Neo-Daoist thinkers such as Wang Bi (226–249) also speak of *li* in this latter sense, stressing it as the unity behind the diversity of existence. However, it is in the doctrinal schools of Chinese Buddhism (HUA YAN and TIAN TAI) that we first see a fully sketched out metaphysics involving the harmonious interpenetration of *li,* the abstract principle of reality, and the concrete, individual "things" (events, phenomena) that compose existence. It is almost certain that this Buddhist metaphysical scheme of *li*, as the "absolute" manifesting in actual events, was borrowed and reinterpreted by the great Song Neo-Confucians.

Although ZHOU DUNYI (1017–73) speaks of *li* in sections of his work, it really is the Cheng brothers, particularly CHENG YI (1033–1107), who elaborate upon it in detail. And it is through their influence that Zhu Xi (1130–1200), the great Neo-Confucian systematizer, formulates his own ideas. According to Zhu's interpretation (which became the standard one among Neo-Confucian thinkers), all things are to be understood as combinations of *li* (principle) and QI ("matter-energy"). *Li* is the principle that gives an individual thing its structure, whereas *qi* is the basic "stuff" that *li* informs. Neither *li* nor *qi* are "things" in the ordinary sense. Rather, all things are the result of *li*'s becoming instantiated within *qi*; one never finds *li* apart from *qi* nor *qi* apart from *li*, although the latter is, in some sense, logically and ontologically prior to the former. A reasonable analogy to Zhu's scheme is Aristotle's distinction between "form" and "matter." Just as with the ancient Greeks, so we can view the Neo-Confucian metaphysical scheme of *li-qi* as a way of accounting for the relationship of the "One and the Many." Zhu compares this relationship of *li-qi* to seeds of grain: each seed has a certain particularity yet also shares generic elements of structure, growth, use, and so forth. As a Confucian, though, Zhu insists (unlike the Buddhists) that *li* is absolutely real in substance and functional expression, not "illusory" or "empty."

As the absolute principle, *li* has various dimensions. Cosmically, *li* is the *Taiji*, the "Great Ultimate" (lit. "great ridgepole") from which all individual things derive. Again, using analogies from Western philosophy, we might conceive the *Taiji* as the "*Li* of *li*" similar to Plato's description of the Good as the "Form of forms" or Aristotle's concept of God. *Li* in this cosmic sense is an impersonal principle, but Zhu equates it with references in earlier Chinese texts to Shangdi, the "Lord on High."

However, it is the presence of *li* in human beings that is of most concern to Zhu and his fellow Confucians. The *li* of human beings is their intellectual and moral nature (intellect and morality are rarely separated in the traditional Chinese view). It is in essence identical with the "Mind of Heaven" (*li* in its most abstract sense) and can "penetrate" all things in order to understand their principles. Cheng Yi even went so far as to claim, "When one finally understands principle, even millions of things can be understood." Interestingly, it is *li* in the sense of this innate, original "moral mind" that receives the most emphasis in the later challenge to Zhu Xi's philosophy, the "School of Mind" associated with Wang Yangming (Wang Shouren, 1472–1529). Wang speaks of *li* in this existential sense as a person's "original substance" (*benti*), "heavenly principle" (*tianli*), or even more commonly, "True Self." The obvious influence of Chan Buddhism in this understanding of *li* reflects the mystical and phenomenological bent of Wang's philosophy, which has sometimes been misunderstood as a kind of metaphysical idealism.

Despite its variety of interpretations, there can be no doubt that *li* as "principle" or "absolute" is the key concept in Neo-Confucian metaphysics. As both an ontological and a mystical absolute, the Neo-Confucian *li* invites intriguing comparisons to the "godhead" spoken of medieval Christian mystics.

Further reading: Wing-tsit Chan, trans., *Reflections on Things at Hand: The Neo-Confucian Anthology, Compiled by Chu Hsi and Lu Tsu-ch'ien* (New York: Columbia University Press, 1967), xxvi–xxiv, 16–18, 26, 28; Julia Ching, *Chinese Religions* (Maryknoll, N.Y.: Orbis Books, 1993), 158–164; W. Theodore De Bary, and Irene Bloom, eds., *Sources of Chinese Tradition*. Vol. 1, *From Earliest Times to 1600*. 2d ed. (New York: Columbia University Press, 1999), 379, 689–692, 697–701.

li (2) (rites, rituals)

As opposed to the term *li* that refers to the absolute principle in reality, this second term *li* concerns ritual action. The emphasis on *li* (ritual) is one of the most enigmatic but crucial features of CONFUCIANISM. As with many Chinese terms, it is difficult to find an adequate translation for *li* because it has such a broad range of meanings. The term has been variously rendered as "rites," "ceremony," "propriety," "decorum," even "etiquette," although it seems to have originally referred to sacrificial rituals. Some scholars have even suggested translating *li* as "civility." While none of these translations are adequate, together they do convey a sense of the complexity and importance of this term in ancient China. The *li* are the complex body of manners guiding social behavior as well as court rituals, ancestor rites, worship of gods, and so on. In a sense, the *li* comprise a blueprint for social interaction. Proper adherence to the *li* is one of the hallmarks of a cultivated person, someone who knows the "social graces." The *li* epitomize the aesthetic and social dimensions of Chinese (and all of East Asian) culture. They also underscore the basic Chinese notion of harmony between the cosmic and human realms. So important are the *li* for Confucians that they were sometimes known as the "school of *li*."

In the Confucian view, the *li* have their roots in antiquity, in the ancient customs of the great societies of the past, particularly the early Zhou, when a just society following Dao had been established. CONFUCIUS himself appears to be the first thinker to recognize the importance of *li* in founding a good social order, and he often speaks of the *li* in the *Analects*. For Confucius, it seems that the *li* are the channels and forms of proper behavior for a *junzi*, a "noble person." As an ethical person, a *junzi* expresses himself through them. Ideally they are ingrained so that a properly cultivated person can follow them effortlessly (*wuwei*) and thus put others at ease. Above all the *li* are the means by which a ruler should govern his people rather than through law and punishments.

MENCIUS also maintains the centrality of the *li*, regarding respect for them as one of the four innate "buds" of virtue within all human beings.

However, of all the early Confucians it is Xunzi who provides the fullest discussion of *li*. For XUNZI, *li* are necessary for making a person truly human. Human beings are born "evil" (selfish, lustful) according to Xunzi but become good through education. The key component to such education are the *li,* which shape and restrain one's natural impulses so that one can take one's place in society. In his discussion of the ways *li* functions, Xunzi evinces a keen psychological and sociological understanding of the role of socialization in forming human character. Quite simply, one becomes fully human by learning the ways human beings should behave in various circumstances. The examples of such proper behavior are found in the *li.*

There can be little doubt that Confucian stress on *li* and their importance for individual moral/spiritual development and social order was a major reason for Confucianism's being adopted as the state ideology during the Han dynasty. The *li* were a means of maintaining the hallowed traditions of the past and giving the new rulers an air of legitimacy in the eyes of the populace. They also provided the emperor with a concrete example of orderly social interaction, thus serving as a model for the functioning of the well-run empire. One of the great Confucian classics compiled during the Han was the famous *Liji* (Record of rites), a collection of ancient materials stressing the role of the *li* in human society. During the Song dynasty (960–1279), the Neo-Confucian thinker Zhu Xi (1130–1200) selected two chapters from this work, assigning them independent status in the Confucian canon—the *Daxue* (Great learning) and the *Zhongyong* (The mean). Both are classic expressions of Confucian spirituality in which the *li* serve as the basis for self-cultivation.

Further reading: W. Theodore De Bary and Irene Bloom, eds., *Sources of Chinese Tradition.* Vol. 1, *From Earliest Times to 1600.* 2d ed. (New York: Columbia University Press, 1999), 43, 46–48, 55–56, 137–138, 174–177, 329–330; Herbert Fingarette, *Confucius—the*

Secular as Sacred (New York: Harper & Row, 1972); David L. Hall and Roger T. Ames, *Thinking through Confucius* (Albany: State University of New York Press, 1987), 83–110; Frederick W. Mote, *Intellectual Foundations of China*. 2d ed. (New York: McGraw-Hill, 1989), 27–28, 42, 46–50, 57, 106.

liangzhi (innate knowledge)

Liangzhi ("innate knowledge") is the path to knowledge advocated by the Confucian thinker WANG YANGMING (1472–1529). Knowledge has never been a purely intellectual matter in Confucianism. Rather, the tradition has long advocated the necessity of extending one's learning into daily life. Simply put, the focus from the time of Confucius has always been ethical in the broadest sense; the Confucian Dao is the Way of acting in concert with others to ensure a harmonious society. All training, therefore, should contribute to this end—a process outlined in the classic work, the *Da xue* (Great Learning). However, from the time of the rise of Neo-Confucianism, Confucian thinkers have differed on the details of this training. For Zhu Xi, one needs to cultivate oneself by "investigating things." Wang Yangming, by contrast, repudiates this intellectual approach, opting for a more intuitive and active path centered on what he called *liangzhi*.

For Wang, *liangzhi* is not something acquired but is a basic part of any human being. As he says, "It is my nature, endowed by Heaven, the original substance of my mind, naturally intelligent, shining, clear, and understanding." Wang even equates this with Mencius's reference to humanity's shared sense of right and wrong. In Wang's view, this innate *moral knowing* does not require learning or deliberation but must be developed and extended outward. One does this by acting rightly. Thus, in the fullest sense one's "innate knowing" is demonstrated not just by the feeling of alarm one experiences at seeing a child about to fall into a well but in the action of saving her by, for instance, seizing her hand.

Perhaps the best way to understand Wang's position is that *liangzhi* is the inherent capacity for moral behavior that we must realize (i.e., "make real") through our personal actions. Ultimately one cannot separate action and knowledge. Wang's understanding of "innate knowledge" has some affinity with the position of Socrates, who famously maintained that "to know the good is to do the good." It also suggests similarities with Martin Heidegger's analysis in *Being and Time* in which he seeks to uncover our basic "understanding of being" revealed in everyday behavior.

Further reading: W. Theodore De Bary and Irene Bloom, eds., *Sources of Chinese Tradition*. Vol. 1, *From Earliest Times to 1600*. 2d ed. (New York: Columbia University Press, 1999), 844–850; Fung Yu-lan, *A History of Chinese Philosophy*. Vol. 2, *The Period of Classical Learning (from the Second Century B.C. to the Twentieth Century A.D.)*. Translated by Derk Bodde (Princeton, N.J.: Princeton University Press, 1953), 599–605.

Li Hongzhi   *See* FALUN GONG.

Lin-chi Chan   *See* LINJI CHAN.

Lingbao Daoism (Lingpao Taoism)

The Lingbao (numinous treasure) school is the branch of religious Daoism based on the Lingbao Scriptures. These 40 texts date from the third century C.E. and contain information on such issues as ritual, the gods of the Daoist pantheon, and funeral ceremonies. The name *Lingbao* was given to these texts by Lu Xiujing (406–477), who cataloged them. These texts continue to make up a major part of the *Daozang*, the Daoist Canon.

There are three divisions to the Lingbao texts. The first consists of two relatively old works from the later Han period (206 B.C.E.–220 C.E.). They were compiled sometime in the fourth century C.E., one (the Wupian zhenwen, Perfect text in five tablets) by Ge Chaofu, a descendant of the famous alchemist GE HONG (283–343). These two works include ritual spells that probably dated back to the magicians of the Han period, called *fangshi*.

The second group of Lingbao Scriptures were issued at the birth of creation and are communicated by the Daoist deity Yuanshi Tianzun, the Celestial Venerable of the Primordial Beginning. They include teachings on universal salvation and karma and reflect the strong influence of Buddhist ideas then entering China.

The second group, nine works, are associated with Ge Xuan, a *fangshi* who was great uncle of GE HONG. While these texts contain magical spells and emphasize worship of ZHANG DAOLING, the first Celestial Master, and LAOZI, they also show Buddhist influence. Lingbao did not become an organized system or "school" until Lu Xiujing synthesized all these disparate materials in the fifth century C.E. Eventually the texts became part of the SHANGQING category, or "Cavern," in the *Daozong*. However, Lingbao rituals continued to be recognized and are performed today.

Lingbao was an early term for a kind of spirit medium who contacted and indeed controlled dead spirits. Such shamans were found throughout southern China as far back as the *Shijing*, or Book of songs, c. 700 B.C.E. Lingbao were related to a ceremony in which the soul of a departed ancestor was called back, and a young child, for instance, a grandson of the departed, would "wear" the skull and act as the "guardian" of the. numinous spirit. Later the skull was dropped and a wooden tablet that similarly represented the spirit of the ancestor set in place. Later Lingbao ritual was fixed by Lu Xiujing. He decided on standard formats for ordinations, purifications, feasts (*zhai*), and offerings (*jiao*). Lingbao ritual centered on nine *zhai,* or purification rites. Each rite included physical purifications (bathing, fasting, avoiding sex), mental purification (confession and meditation), and prayers. The *zhai* was not a new ceremony in China. It was originally a purification and fast-ing rite associated with certain deities. After Lu Xiujing's revisions it also became associated with prayers and repentance.

Lingbao texts are important because they reflect the incorporation of the five phases (*wuxing*) cosmology into standard Daoist thinking. Overall, the Lingbao corpus, as formalized by Lu Xiujing, was a grand compilation that involved reference to the *Daodejing,* the Ge family, Shangqing, and Buddhism.

See also DAOZANG; GE HONG; GE XUAN AND THE GE FAMILY TRADITION.

Further reading: Stephen R. Bokenkamp, *Early Daoist Scriptures: With a Contribution by Peter Nickerson* (Berkeley: University of California Press, 1997); Yamada Toshiaki, "The Lingbao School," in Livia Kohn, ed., *Daoism Handbook* (Leiden: Brill, 2004).

Lingyin

Lingyin (Soul's retreat, or the place the gods go to find rest) temple is located near Hangzhou, eastern China, in the mountainous area near Hangzhou's West Lake. At its height more than 1,000 monks resided in its many dormitories. First constructed in the fourth century, it is still a working temple today that houses a large monastic community but is also daily filled with visitors to what has become a major Chinese tourist attraction.

Lingyin temple dates to the early fourth century C.E. and the arrival of a monk from India, Hui Li. He began what would become a large monastic complex around 326 C.E. CHAN BUDDHISM emerged in China in the fifth century and Lingyin became identified with Chan as one of its most prominent centers.

Among the notable features of the land upon which Lingyin rests is Feilai Feng, or "Peak that flew from afar." According to the story, Hui Li believed that the mountain had been transported to China from India because it looked so much like ones he had seen in his homeland. Over the centuries the mountain was decorated with numerous carvings of bodhisattvas and other enlightened beings, most carved between the 10th and 14th centuries. The most famous of the carvings is a large one of MAITREYA, the Future Buddha.

Lingyan has survived through the many ups and downs of Chinese history. Its buildings have been destroyed and rebuilt more than a dozen times. It was a favored spot during the Qing dynasty (1644–1911). Lingyin escaped much of the harm done to religious structures in the Hangzhou region during the Cultural Revolution in the 1960s.

The current structures date from the 19th century. The main buildings that survive to the present include the Great and Magnificent Hall (or Mahavira Hall), which houses large statues of BUDDHA and GUAN YIN, and the Front Hall, which has statues of Buddha's four warrior attendants. The statue of Sakyamuni Buddha is 18 feet high. It was constructed during the Tang dynasty (607–960) from 24 pieces of camphor wood. It is one of the larger wooden Buddhas in the world. The Hall of the Five Hundred Arhats, as its name implies, contains hundreds of life-size statues of enlightened personages. A more recent, post-Qing building is the Hall for BHAISAJYA-GURU BUDDHA, also known as the Medicine Buddha, for his healing powers.

Further reading: *The West Lake of Hangzhou* (Beijing: China Travel & Tourism Press, 1999).

Linji Chan (Lin-chi Chan)

Linji is a major branch of CHAN BUDDHISM and the forerunner of the Rinzai school of Japanese Zen. The Linji school is renowned for its "lightning" or "shock" techniques. In these practices the master suddenly shocks the student, for example, by striking him or her, often with a fly swatter. For instance, in one example, a monk asked the master Linji, "What is the basic idea of the Law preached by the Buddha?" The Master lifted up his swatter. The monk shouted, and the Master beat him" (recorded conversations of Master Zen Master I-hsuan, d. 867, from Chan, 1963, p. 445). Such extreme techniques contrasted with the CAODONG (SOTO ZEN) school, which emphasized "quiet illumination," silent meditation on innate Buddha nature. After a series of debates between Caodong and Linji masters in the early 1100s, the Linji school was known as "KOAN contemplation Chan" for its emphasis on the study of koans.

The Linji school was founded by Linji Yixuan (d. 867), a Chan master who lived in the Linji Monastery in Hebei, northern China. Linji was one of the seven schools that derived from the Southern school of Chan, traditionally said to descend from HUI NENG (638–713), the sixth Chan patriarch. The Linji school followed a single lineage for six generations after Linji Yixuan. However, in the seventh generation it split into two competing camps, those of Yangqi Fanghui (992–1049) and Huanglong Huinan (1001–69). Eventually the Yangqi school eclipsed the Huanglong.

By the end of the Song dynasty (960–1279) the Caodong and Linji schools had absorbed all the other branches of Chan. However, neither school had a major impact in the post-Song period, when a resurgent CONFUCIANISM gained the attention of the ruling classes. The Linji school was later introduced to Japan by EISAI (1141–1215), where it eventually became the Rinzai school of Japanese Zen.

Further reading: "Lin-chi school," in Damien Keown, ed., *Oxford Dictionary of Buddhism* (Oxford: Oxford University Press, 2003).

Lin Zhaoen (Lin Chao-en) (1517–1598) *Chinese syncretic religious leader*

Lin Zhaoen was an intellectual and religious leader who founded the "Three-in-One" movement that combined elements of Confucianism, Daoism, and Buddhism. Lin was one of the best-known proponents of religious and philosophical syncretism ("mixing") in Ming dynasty (1368–1644) China. The long-standing tendency in China to combine religions and philosophies had increased in the 16th century, with the general populace blending Confucian, Daoist, and Buddhist ideas and practices. This syncretism underlies the spread of "morality books" (*shanshu*) and novels such as *Xiyouji* (*Journey to the West*). Lin himself had pursued Daoism and Buddhism early in life but returned to Confucianism as time went on. In this he was no different from several of the Song Neo-Confucians (e.g., ZHOU DUNYI, CHENG YI). Lin, however, went further in that he sought to merge all three ways into a new sect. Perhaps not surprisingly, he developed an enthusiastic following.

Lin's focus was on cultivating the mind common to CONFUCIUS, LAOZI, and BUDDHA. He was aided in this pursuit by Daoist "inner alchemy" (*neidan*) as well as Chan seated meditation (*zuo chan*). Much of Lin's aim was to help his followers restore their spiritual and physical health, the two understood as intimately related to each other and to one's moral state. Lin urged his followers to take special vows to heaven (TIAN), forming an almost personal relationship with heaven itself. The strongly individualistic quality inherent in Lin's teachings appealed to many people.

The late Ming government saw such views as an affront since from time immemorial only the emperor (*tian zi*, the "Son of Heaven") could relate directly to heaven on the people's behalf. Edicts were issued banning Lin's teachings, while many books and temples associated with the "Three-in-One" sect were burned. Yet as is often the case in China, official condemnation merely drove a popular movement underground, where it continued to flourish.

The Three-in-One sect remains alive today along China's southern coast and in Taiwan. Recent sources indicate that there are seven temples in Taiwan where incense is regularly offered to Confucius, Laozi, Buddha, and Lin himself. Another new sect, officially recognized by the Taiwanese government and seemingly related to Lin's movement, venerates *five* great figures—Confucius, Laozi, and Buddha as well as Jesus Christ and the prophet Muhammad.

Further reading: Judith Berling, *The Syncretic Religion of Lin Chao-en* (New York: Columbia University Press, 1980); Julia Ching, *Chinese Religions* (Maryknoll, N.Y.: Orbis Books, 1993), 217–218.

Lion's Roar

The Buddha often compared himself to a lion. The lion here symbolizes qualities of courage and nobility. His teachings became known as the "Lion's Roar."

There are two Pali *suttas* (Sanskrit: sutras) that refer to the Buddha's "Lion's Roar." The first, the Shorter Discourse on the Lion's Roar, discusses separate spiritual paths available to people. The second, the Great Discourse on the Lion's Roar, discusses his own spiritual qualities.

Further reading: Hsing Yun, *The Lion's Roar: Actualizing Buddhism in Daily Life and Building the Pure Land in Our Midst* (New York: Peter Lang, 1991); Bhikkhu Nanamoli, *The Lion's Roar Two Discourse of the Buddha*. Translated by Bhikkhu Nanamoli and edited by Bhikkhu Bodhi (Kandy: Buddhist Publication Society, 1993). Available online. URL: www.skepticfiles.org/mys5/contents.htm. Accessed on January 15, 2006.

Lion's Roar of Queen Srimala Sutra

This MAHAYANA sutra was first translated into Chinese in 436 C.E. by Gudabhadra. A second translation was made into Chinese by BODHIRUCI in the early 700s. The Sanskrit text exists today only in fragments, and we depend on the Chinese and Tibetan translations. In the sutra Lady Srimala, the daughter of a king of Kosala, a Buddhist kingdom in northern India, discusses in depth the doctrine that Buddha nature is present in all living beings.

Further reading: Alex Waymen and Hideko Wayman, trans., *Lion's Roar of Queen Srimala: A Buddhist Scripture on the Tathagatagarbha Theory* (New York: Columbia University Press, 1974).

Longchenpa (Rabjam Klongchen) (1308–c. 1364) *Tibetan Buddhist Dzogchen master*

Longchenpa was a 14th-century Nyingma teacher best known for combining two sets of DZOGCHEN meditation teachings into a workable single system—the Longchen Nyingthig. His work has been integrated over the years into mainstream NYINGMA teachings.

Longchenpa was for a time the abbot at Samye, one of the most important Tibetan Buddhist monasteries, but spent a considerable amount of time wandering around the countryside. His wandering for a time took him to BHUTAN, where he fathered two children, a son and a daughter. His son, Trungpa Odzer (1356–c. 1409), later became the primary Nyingma lineage holder.

Longchenpa was also a prolific writer with more than 250 texts attributed to him. His main work, the *Three Treasures*, was a summary of Buddhist history in Tibet to his lifetime. His work is gradually being translated into English.

Further reading: Rabjam Longchen, *The Practice of Dzogchen*. Translated by Tulku Thondup and edited by Harold Talbott (Ithaca, N.Y.: Snow Lion, 2002); ———, *The Dzogchen: Innermost Essence Preliminary Practice*. Translated by Tulku Thondup, ed. Brian Beresford (Ithaca, N.Y.: Snow Lion, 2001); Longchenpa, *Kindly Bent to Ease Us*. Translated by Herbert V. Guenther. 3 vols. (Berkeley, Calif.: Dharma, 1975–1976).

Longmen Daoism   *See* QUANZHEN DAOISM.

Losar (Tibetan New Year)

In Tibet the calendar of major festivals associated with Buddhism or Buddhist figures begins with the New Year. The Grand Summons Ceremony is the largest on the Tibetan Buddhist calendar. It lasts from the third or fourth day of the New Year until the 25th and takes place in Lhasa. It was started by the great Buddhist innovator TSONG KHAPA in 1409. The purpose of the ceremony was to honor Sakyamuni, the historical Buddha, while praying for the stability and well-being of the nation. The intent was to gather monks from all schools and tradition together and by joint vows revive Buddhist practice. The preparations for the first festival took two years and involved a complete refurbishing of the JOKHANG temple. Tsong Khapa himself donated 500 *taels* of gold to add a golden crown to the temple's reclining Buddha.

The literal meaning of the name of the festival, *Losar,* is "wish" or "request." At the start of the festival the 20,000-some monks resident around Lhasa gather together for a 21-day assembly. On the 15th day of the first month, which is Sakyamuni's day of enlightenment, the streets surrounding the temple are filled with lanterns in the colorful Butter Lamp Festival (discussed later).

THE SUTRA DEBATES

The Grand Summons festival is managed by the GELUG school. From the time of the fifth Dalai Lama the festival has included a sutra debate competition that chooses the best speakers from three large temples in Lhasa. The top seven *gesu* (scholars) among them join in a procession through the streets led by the Gandan Chiba, the successor to Tsong Khapa.

Besides the debates, another main activity during the festival involves chanting. The body of lamas chant, often in the open, on six separate occasions each day. Onlookers surround the chanting monks on balconies around three sides of the temple. From there they throw money into the midst of the monks as offerings.

FOOD AND WATER PROVISIONS

Massive amounts of food are required by the monks gathered for the Losar festival. The vat cooking tea alone is one and a half times as high as an average person, and each lot of tea requires four or five mule loads of tea leaves. The food and herbs are stacked in Lubu Square starting six months before the festival. Once the ovens are fired up they emit an odor throughout the city.

The water requirements during the festival are managed by a select group of young girls recruited from local tribes surrounding Lhasa. These girls constantly ferry water containers between the Dingba Qumi wells and the food halls. They need to handle the water carefully—since the temperatures are so low at that time of year, if the water spilled on them it would freeze them immediately. To ensure they control the water they sing a unique song. The tune remains the same but the lyrics change each year. The lyrics make fun of the local government's corruption and invariably mention names of local worthies accused of inappropriate behavior. The lyrics are a constant focus of attention. The people mentioned are, naturally, often unhappy. When they ask the water bearers what they mean by building such accusations into their songs, the girls consistently reply that they do not know the meaning of the words and simply sing what they are taught by the White Lamu Protective Deity of Jokhang Temple. The songs are therefore known popularly as White Lamu Songs.

THE ARCHERY CONTEST AND SORCERER'S DANCE

Unique aspects of the Great Summons festival are the Archery Contest and Sorcerer's Dance held on the 24th day of the first month, near the end of the festivities. The Gandan Chiba leads the Recitation for Expelling Ghosts texts at Potala Palace. Tribesmen on horseback play the part of 500 Mongol warriors who in the past attacked Lhasa and burned the Potala.

THE MAITREYA PROCESSION

On the morning of the 25th, all participating monks perform a ceremony welcoming the advent of the future Buddha Qiangba Tongzhen (Maitreya). This includes a procession of the silver Maitreya Buddha image through the streets of Lhasa.

THE BUTTERED SCULPTURE FESTIVAL (JIANE SUBA)

This lantern festival is the highlight of the Grand Summons festival. It is held on the 15th of the first month. It begins when the Dalai Lama visits the White Lamu, the protective deity of the Jokhang Temple. He then leads monks in a sutra recitation.

The night of the 15th sees a multitude of floats assembled in the eight-sided street surrounding Jokhang Temple. This ceremony was traditionally handled by an official responsible for religious affairs. The main temples and gentry families of Lhasa were each given sections of the street in which to build their floats and competed to attract the attention of the Dalai Lama. The floats themselves were built using a foundation of wood frames and ox skin upon which sculptures, made from a mixture of barley oil and wheat flour, were molded and painted into elaborate configuration. The contraptions, some reaching heights of 22 meters, were taken out to line the Eight-Side Road around four or five in the afternoon—any earlier and they are in danger of melting in the afternoon sun.

The barley oil lanterns in fact represent an important form of traditional Tibetan art, called "butter art." Barley flour is easily mixed with various minerals and molded into relatively permanent shapes. The same art form is practiced at Qing Hai's Da Er Temple. Subject matter for oil sculpture art normally includes Buddhist deity figures, feminine gods, and Tibetan mandalas.

Once night falls the lanterns are lit, producing a wonderland effect on the streets. However, no commoners are allowed to view the sculptures until after the Dalai Lama has seen them. At the appropriate time he leaves the Jokhang Temple and, with his retinue, inspects each work. Once he has returned to the temple the ropes holding back the common people are lowered and they flood in from the adjourning side streets to gape at the artistry.

THE LUBU DOJIA (EXPELLING DEMONS) FESTIVAL

This festival is in fact in preparation for the New Year. On the 29th day of the final lunar month monasteries hold ceremonies to drive off demons in the coming year, and lay people clean their homes.

See also CHINA-TIBET; FESTIVALS, BUDDHIST.

Further reading: Charles Allen, *A Mountain in Tibet* (London: Futura, 1985); Geshe Kelsang Gyatso, *Heart Jewel: The Essential Practices of Kadampa Buddhism.* 2d ed. (London: Tharpa, 1997); "Kagyu Monlam Chenmo." Available online. URL: http://www.kagyumonlam.org. Accessed on July 10, 2006; Richard J. Kosh, *Lord of the Dance: The Mani Rimdu Festival in Tibet and Nepal.* (Albany: State University of New York Press, 2001).

Lotus Sutra (Saddarma-pundarikia-sutra, "Lotus of the Superb Religion")

The key idea in the Lotus Sutra is the existence of a single "vehicle," the EKAYANO (Sanskrit, *ekayana*), which is the message of the Buddha that will transport cultivators to the final goal of liberation. Although there are three separate groups of followers of the Buddha, those who are disciples, PRATYEKABUDDHAS (those who cultivate the path in solitude), and bodhisattvas, the Lotus emphasizes that the true vehicle of the Buddha is open to all people. In fact, all people are bodhisattvas. The Lotus thus offers the laity the possibility of enlightenment. Many devotees of this sutra believe strongly in the value of reciting and copying the sutra as an act of merit and devotion.

The Lotus Sutra is arguably the most influential Buddhist text in history. Various Sanskrit versions exist; it was translated at least 17 times into Chinese, although only three translations survive, including one by KUMARAJIVA. Studies date the origin of the oldest parts of this text to between 40 and 220 C.E. The TIAN TAI school of Chinese Buddhism considered the Lotus Sutra to be the most sublime and all-encompassing of the sutras. It is still widely read today and can be considered a classic of trans-Asian literature.

The text begins with the Buddha in SAMADHI and emitting a light from between his brows that illuminates the universe. The Buddha then goes on to prophesy that several of his disciples will achieve Buddhahood. He emphasizes that there is but one Path, not three. To illustrate this he relates the well-known parable of the burning house:

> A rich man had a very large house. The house had only one entrance, and the timber of which it was made had dried out thoroughly over the years. One day the house caught fire, and the rich man's many children, heedless of the fire, continued to play in the house. Their father called to them from outside that the house was afire and that they would perish in the flames if they did not come out. The children, not knowing the meaning of "fire" or "perish," continued to play as before. The man called out once more, "Come out, children, and I will give you ox-drawn carriages, goat-drawn carriages, and deer-drawn carriages!" Tempted by the desire for new playthings, the children left the burning house, only to find a single great ox-drawn carriage awaiting them.

Using this example, the Buddha explains that the father was not deceiving the children. Instead, he used skill in means (UPAYA) to save them. It is the same with the Buddha's teaching: such a scheme as the three paths to salvation may be used to save some people, but in essence there is only one Path.

Further reading: Leon Hurvitz, trans., *Scripture of the Lotus Blossom of the Fine Dharma (The Lotus Sutra)* (New York: Columbia University Press, 1976); Bunno Kato, Yoshiro Tamura, and Kojiro Miyasaka, *The Three-fold Lotus Sutra* (New York: Weatherhill, 1975); W. E. Soothill, *The Lotus of the Wonderful Law* (London: Curzon Press, 1987); George Tanabe and Willa Jane, *The Lotus Sutra in Japanese Culture* (Honolulu: University of Hawaii Press, 1989); Burton Watson, *Lotus Sutra* (New York: Columbia University Press, 1993).

Lotus-womb meditation (Taizo-kai)

This Japanese ritual, a representative ritual of TENDAI BUDDHISM's esoteric (hidden) teachings, is divided into eight segments and can take days to complete. The ritual involves dancing or acting out internal visions of a fire created by the Buddha Acala (also known as Fudo myo-o in Japanese), the Buddha who destroys delusion and protects Buddhism. Each celebrant must envision a Lotus-womb world at the center of which is a VAIROCANA Buddha, the cosmological Buddha, seated on an eight-petaled lotus. The meditator attempts to merge himself or herself with the figure of Vairocana.

Further reading: Michael Saso, *Homa Rites and Mandala Meditation in Tendai Buddhism* (Delhi: Pradeep Kumar Goel, 1991).

Lu Dongbin (Lu Tung-pin)

Few figures in Chinese history have proved to be as consistently endearing as the famous "EIGHT IMMORTALS" (*ba xian*). These mythical personalities are some of the true folk heroes of Chinese DAOISM, particularly among peasants. While all eight continue to be favorites among storytellers and those who retain allegiance to traditional Chinese folkways, the most popular by far is Lu Dongbin. Statues of Lu (depicting him as the refined Confucian gentleman he apparently was

in life) can often be found in small temples and shrines, and numerous grottoes located on China's sacred mountains are dedicated in his honor.

As do several other "immortals," Lu appears to have been a real historical figure who lived from the late Tang dynasty (618–908) into the early Song (960–1279). From a strictly historical perspective we can say little about him beyond this. However, there are various traditional stories about him that are clearly the stuff of myth and folklore. Legend has it that he was born Lu Yan in 798 into a family of civil servants in northern China. Later tradition relates that his birth was marked by mysterious perfumes filling his family home and the strains of celestial music wafting from the sky. A mystical white crane descended from the heavens to hover over his birthing bed before vanishing. One story has it that in his youth he traveled south to Lushan, a mountain famous for its magical associations with both Daoism and Buddhism, where he encountered a mysterious fire dragon (a secret Daoist master). The dragon presented Lu with a magical sword and instructed him in methods that bestowed on him the power of invisibility. This sword, named "Demon Slayer," is a major source of Lu's powers.

The most important tale of Lu concerns his journey to the capital to follow an official career in government. During a stop along this trip he met Zhongli Quan, a fabled immortal who was busily warming some wine. Under the influence of Zhongli (and the wine presumably), Lu fell into a deep sleep and had his famous "Yellow Millet Dream." In this dream, Lu attained his government post and, as a result, accumulated great wealth and prestige. He enjoyed this privileged mortal life for some 50 years until he was accused of a great crime. Found guilty, he was stripped of all property, his family was separated from him, and he himself was banished into the mountains. With this Lu suddenly awoke to find his meal of yellow millet had still not finished cooking; his entire official career had lasted for only a few moments.

Realizing that ordinary life is but a fleeting dream, Lu decided to abandon his worldly aspirations and become Zhongli's disciple, taking the Daoist name *Dongbin* ("Guest of the Cavern") as a sign of his new religious life. After passing numerous tests, Lu underwent training in the secrets of alchemy. His powers were said to be so great that he retained a youthful appearance even past age 100. He could change his shape and even travel 100 miles in a matter of seconds. Lu Dongbin eventually became a high-ranking immortal, but he turned down the offer to ascend to the celestial realm with his master, preferring to remain on earth to aid all those earnestly seeking Dao. Because of his compassion, Lu was regularly sought after for oracles, healing, and spiritual advice.

Lu is especially known for his healing powers (he is sometimes said to be the "doctor of the poor") and his ability to subdue evil spirits. His sword and his bushy flywhisk symbolize these powers. For Lu, the sword is not a weapon of aggression, but a means of cutting through ignorance and the passions. It also is the means by which he can control evil spirits. Lu's flywhisk, a traditional symbol of a cultured scholar-gentleman, symbolizes his ability to fly at will.

Daoist tradition holds that Lu made many important contributions to the sacred arts. For example, Lu is credited with stressing the importance of developing compassion in Daoist self-cultivation—a sign, perhaps, of Buddhist influence. He is also credited with transforming the ancient methods of "external alchemy" (*waidan*) to those of "internal alchemy" (*neidan*). To this day, Lu Dongbin is regarded as one of the mythic "founders" of the Quanzhen (complete perfection) school of Daoism, the major monastic order. His official biography is in the *Zengxian liexian zhuan* (Illustrated biographies of the immortals). Various treatises and poems attributed to Lu have been collected in the *Luzu quanshu* (complete works of Patriarch Lu). Because of his importance, Lu Dongbin continues to be honored in Daoist tem-

ples, which usually hold special feasts in his honor on the 14th day of the fourth lunar month.

Lu has particular honor in Daoist tradition because he is alleged to have passed on his teachings to students who went on to become major Daoist figures in their own right. One of his students was Zhen Xiyi, said to have been a major innovator of techniques of *qigong*. An even more famous student of Lu's was WANG CHEN CHONYANG, the official historical founder of QUAN-ZHEN DAOISM and central character in the popular Chinese novel *Seven Daoist Masters*. Because of his contributions to these lineages, Lu is sometimes regarded as the grand patriarch of "internal alchemy."

Further reading: Kwok Man Ho and Joanne O'Brien, trans. and ed., *The Eight Immortals of Taoism: Legends and Fables of Popular Taoism* (New York: Penguin, 1991), 23–25; Livia Kohn, *Daoism and Chinese Culture* (Cambridge, Mass.: Three Pines Press, 2001), 154–155, 165; ———, ed., *The Taoist Experience* (Albany: State University of New York Press, 1993), 126–132; Eva Wong, *Tales of the Taoist Immortals* (Boston: Shambhala, 2001), 11–15.

Lumbini

Though most of the biographical facts concerning GAUTAMA BUDDHA are matters of scholarly dispute, tradition locates his birth place as Lumbini, in present-day Nepal. It is now considered one of four major holy places of international Buddhism. Many accept the story that MAYA Devi, Buddha's mother, gave birth while traveling to her parents' home in Devadaha. She took a rest in Lumbini under a sal tree. The event is dated as early as 642 B.C.E., and as late as 566. The infant is also said to have spoken immediately after separating from his mother, saying, "This is my final rebirth." He then took seven steps to the four cardinal points of the compass, and a lotus flower sprang forth with each step.

It would be several centuries later (249 B.C.E.) when King ASOKA visited the area. He erected a stele commemorating the event, ordered the building of a wall around the village, and erected a stone pillar and four STUPAS to mark the spot. He also reduced the taxes that the village would have to pay in the future.

Lumbini remained a Buddhist center until the ninth century C.E. During the next millennium when first Muslims and then Hindus controlled the region, the Buddhist structures were destroyed and even the memory of the location lost. Then in 1895, Alois A. Feuhrer, a famous German archaeologist, discovered the Asoka stele. Further probing led to the uncovering of a temple, which included scenes of the Buddha's life. This temple was probably constructed over one of the stupas originally erected by Asoka. Through the 20th century, further excavations were carried out and many of the Buddhist sites rediscovered. Japanese Buddhists raised money to have the area restored and in recent decades it reemerged as a place for Buddhist pilgrims in spite of its remoteness and the difficulty of travel to it.

Today, Lumbini is home to a Tibetan Buddhist monastery, a Nepalese temple (which the Burmese former United Nations secretary general U Thant helped finance), the Maya Devi Temple, and the pillar with the Asoka stele. The garden, where the birth actually occurred, is now well kept and visitors may also go to the nearby Puskarmi pond in which the infant Buddha had his first bath.

Further reading: Trilok Chandra Majupuria, *Holy Places of Buddhism in Nepal and India: A Guide to Sacred Places in Buddha's Lands* (Columbia, Mo.: South Asia Books, 1987); Tarthang Tulku, ed., *Holy Places of the Buddha.* Vol. 9, *Crystal Mirror* (Berkeley, Calif.: Dharma, 1994).

Lung-shan Temple

Lung-shan Temple in Taiwan was originally constructed for the veneration of GUAN YIN, but over the years other bodhisattvas and many non-

Buddhist deities have taken their places in the temple. Currently more than 50 different bodhisattvas and deities are found at Lung-shan. Guan Yin remains popular, and the most significant date in the temple's annual calendar is Guan Yin's birthday every spring.

The temple is a product of Chinese immigration to Taiwan during the Qing dynasty. After considering various options related to Taiwan, the Manchurian authorities decided in 1684 to occupy the island, at least to the extent of preventing it from becoming a center for piracy or antigovernment revolts. In the process, it moved many people thought loyal to the previous dynasty off the island and replaced them with others, many of them from Fujian Province, immediately across the Taiwan Straits. In the early 18th century, Chinese settlers in Taiwan built five temples all modeled on the Lang-shan Temple in Anhai, Fujian. The temples were erected at Tainan, Fengshan, Lukang, Tamsui, and Wanhua, a district of the future city of Taipei. As Taipei grew in importance, the Lung-shan Temple became an important center of PURE LAND BUDDHISM on the island.

The settlers who built Taipei's Lung-shan Temple arrived in the area in the mid- to late 1720s. According to a legend, they hung some incense on a tree and lighted it. During the night, they saw the incense glowing bright and interpreted the sight as a sign of the presence of a deity. Thus was the site of the proposed temple decided. (A similar story is told of other temples on Taiwan.) The temple was built in the 1730s and finished in 1738. It was to be dedicated to GUAN YIN. An expert on geomancy was hired to determine the correct alignment of the temple according to FENG SHUI. Also, as the temple was to be home to Guan Yin, an area immediately in front of the temple was set aside for a reflecting pool, symbolizing the feminine deity desire and ability to look into the mirrorlike waters.

On several occasions the temple suffered severe damage and required restorations, the

last after the end of Japanese occupation and the settlement of the Nationalist Chinese on the island. In 1951 the Taipei Municipal Government designated Lung-shan a historic site. A restoration program began two years later and continued for two decades.

Further reading: Li Chien Lang, *The Lung-shan Temple at Wan Hun, Taipei* (Taipei: Hsing Shih Art Books, 1989); April C. J. Lin and Jerome F. Keating, *Island in the Stream: A Quick Case Study of Taiwan's Complex History* (Taipei, Taiwan: SMC, 2000).

Luofu, Mt.

A sacred mountain in Guangdong, southern China, Mt. Luofu was home to hermit practitioners as far back as the first century C.E. It was here that GE HONG, the famous author of *BAOPUZI NEIPIAN*, retired and died—or, in some accounts, flew into the realm of the immortals. The mountain was thereafter associated with worship of Ge and his disciples, such as Huangba Hu. In the 17th century Luofu was a center of QUANZHEN practice in southern China. Existing temples were converted to Quanzhen centers and in some cases rebuilt.

Congxu Daoist temple, Mt. Luofu, southern China

Today Luofu remains an important religious center. There are four functioning Daoist temples and one substantial Buddhist temple on the mountain. Huang Long Guan is the largest, best endowed temple today on Luofu Shan. It has been actively supported by the Hong Kong master Hao Baoyuan. Cong Xu Guan, however, is the oldest temple on Luofu Shan, and the site of the original Ge Hong cult. Su Liao Guan is related to Chen Botao, a 17th-generation Quanzhen master from Dongguan.

By the mid-Qing (1644–1911) period Luofu Shan's transition into a Quanzhen site was accomplished. It remained for a crop of talented Quanzhen leaders to build on this foundation and spread beyond Luofu Shan. As a result major Quanzhen temples were founded in Guangzhou, Huizhou, to the east, and Panyu, to the west. These in turn were the springboards for Quanzhen leaders to spread into Hong Kong in the early years of the 20th century.

Mt. Luofu is one of the 10 mountains known as *Dongtian* (Heaven grottoes) in Daoism.

Further reading: Gregor Benton, *Cave Paradises and Talismans: Voyages through China's Sacred Mountains* (Leeds, U.K.: University of Leeds, 1995); Mary Augusta Mullikin and Anna M. Hotchkis, *The Nine Sacred Mountains of China: An Illustrated Record of Pilgrimages Made in the Years 1935–1936* (Hong Kong: Vetch and Lee, 1973); Susan Naquin and Chun-fang Yu, eds., *Pilgrims and Sacred Sites in China* (Berkeley: University of California Press, 1992).

luohan   See ARHAT.

Lu Sheng-Yen (pinyin: Lu Shengyan)
(1945–   ) *founder of the True Buddha school*
Master Lu Sheng-Yen, the founder of the TRUE BUDDHA SCHOOL, one of a small number of relatively new Taiwanese Buddhist groups that have emerged as international movements, was born in 1945 in Jiayi (or Chiai) in south central Taiwan. He attended Chun-Jen Polytechnic College in the 1960s and after completing his work joined the army. Lu was raised as a Presbyterian (the oldest Christian movement in Taiwan); however, in 1969, while visiting a Taiwanese temple, the Palace of the Jade Emperor, he encountered a medium named Qiandai, who was a member of a new Taiwanese group called the Compassion Society, based on worship of Xi Wangmu, the Royal Mother of the West, under the name *Jinmu*. During her presentation, Qiandai told Lu that the gods of the temple wished him to acknowledge them. Thrown into a state of confusion, he found himself able to communicate with the spirit world. Communications continued daily for the next three years. He also met a Daoist master who taught him the range of popular divinatory arts. Lu opened a temple in his home and began to offer his services as a diviner and leader of popular rituals. He later identified himself as a Daoist but also began to study Buddhism. Two Buddhist figures, SAKYAMUNI Buddha and the bodhisattva KSHITIGARBHA, have the dominant positions in his temple.

Lu was introduced to Tantric Buddhism in 1976. He met Rangjung Rigpe Dorje (1924–81), the 16th Karmapa of the KARMA KAGYU school of Tibetan Buddhism, and five years later was formally initiated into Tibetan Buddhism by the KARMAPA. By this time, however, Lu had emerged as a prominent up-and-coming figure in Taiwanese religion. A good writer, he began to turn out several books annually. His following across Taiwan grew. Then suddenly in 1982, he withdrew from his public in Taiwan and moved to the United States. Coincidentally with his withdrawal, on July 10, 1982, a Tibetan Buddhist deity appeared and told Lu that he had been chosen to spread VAJRAYANA teachings. The deity also bestowed upon him a title: "Holy Red Crown Venerable Vajra Master."

The radical change of residence marked the culmination of Lu's pilgrimage from his Presbyterian youth to his present role as the founder and master teacher of the TRUE BUDDHA SCHOOL. It was only a year after his move that he reorganized his following as the True Buddha school and established its headquarters in a newly constructed temple in Redmond (suburban Seattle), Washington. He announced his plans to build an international movement in the Vajrayana (Tantric) Buddhist tradition.

Over the next few years he had a number of contacts with a variety of beings in the spiritual world—Gautama BUDDHA, AMITABHA Buddha, MAITREYA Buddha, and PADMASAMBHAVA. From these contacts he assumed the title of *TULKU*, the emanation of a deity. He is considered by his followers to be a Living Buddha. He finished the decade by launching a four-year (1989–93) world tour on which he visited local Chinese diaspora residents. In the midst of the tour, in 1992, he opened Rainbow Villa, in Washington's Cascade Mountains, as a facility for training senior leaders. In 1993 he named a number of teaching masters, and since the tour he has taken a backseat in favor of his senior teaching masters and those disciples who have formed the several hundred local centers.

Through his adult life, Lu wrote a large number of books, in Chinese. In the 1990s, his students made a significant effort to translate these into other languages. A selection of titles is currently available in Malay, Indonesian, English, French, Spanish, and Russian.

Further reading: Lu Sheng-Yen, *Dharma Talks by a Living Buddha* (San Bruno, Calif.: Amitabha Enterprise, 1995); ———, *The Inner World of the Lake* (San Bruno, Calif.: Amitabha Enterprise, 1992); ———, *A Complete and Detailed Exposition of the True Buddha Tantric Dharma* (San Bruno, Calif.: Purple Lotus Society, 1995); Tam Wai Lun, "Integration of the Magical and Cultivational Discourses: A Study of a New Religious Movement called the True Buddha School," *Monumenta Serica* 49 (2001): 141–169.

M

macrobiotics

Macrobiotics is a spiritual teaching that finds its major manifestation in a comprehensive vegetarian diet and the lifestyle it suggests. The teachings were initially developed in the late 19th century by Sagen Ishizuka (1850–1901), somewhat in reaction to the wave of Western ideas, and especially Western foods, which had been flowing into Japan since the 1840s. Ishizuka developed what he saw as a modern scientific defense of a traditional Japanese diet in a technical text published in 1897. He then issued a popularized version of his ideas, *A Method of Nourishing Life,* that became a best seller in Japan. Drawing on a variety of traditional Asian teachings, especially Taoist ideas of balancing yin and yang, he argued for a cereal-based and vegetarianism diet with a proper balance between sodium and potassium.

In 1908, Ishizuka founded the Food Cure Society. An active leader in the society, Yukikazu Sakurazawa, introduced Ishizuka's ideas to the West in 1929. Settling in Paris, he Westernized his name to George Ohsawa (d. 1965) and coined the term *macrobiotics* to describe the teachings. He returned to Japan for a period after World War II, but then in 1959 settled in America and published his book *Zen Macrobiotics,* drawing on the attention being given to Zen Buddhism in the Beat culture.

Macrobiotics might not have become so well known had not Ohsawa recruited two dedicated students, Herman Aihara and Michio Kushi. Kushi immigrated to America in 1949 and with his wife, Aveline, founded the Ohsawa Foundation and developed the macrobiotic community in New York. Aihara joined them in 1952. The movement developed slowly but steadily until 1965. That year a woman who had adopted an extreme form of the macrobiotic diet died. Authorities raided the Ohsawa Foundation. In the wake of the controversy, Aihara moved the foundation to California, and Kushi moved to Boston and made a new beginning. Kushi's work soon flourished as it was identified with the emerging New Age movement. Through the 1970s, macrobiotic centers appeared in urban centers across the United States. Aihara's work, under several names, also grew.

Their work spread as Kushi was able to develop what many saw as a bland cereal-based diet as an attractive tasty and varied vegetarian cuisine. Gatherings of macrobiotic enthusiasts frequently were built around cooking classes. Kushi's diet included fresh fruit, common vegetables, and even some fish. Walking a legal tightrope, he also suggested that the diet was not just adequate for a normal person, but good for the healing of a spectrum of illnesses.

Further reading: Herman Aihara, *Basic Macrobiotics* (Tokyo: Japan, 1985); Michio Kushi, *The Book of Macrobiotics* (Tokyo: Japan, 1977); ———, with Stephen Blauer, *The Macrobiotic Way* (Wayne, N.J.: Avery Publishing Group, 1985); George Ohsawa, *Zen Macrobiotics* (Los Angeles: Ohsawa Foundation, 1965).

Madhyamika

The Mahdhyamika school is one of the two major schools of Mahayana Buddhism. The Madhyamika school promotes the "middle way." It is based on the writings of the early Indian philosopher NAGARJUNA. In his major work, *Madhyamaka-karika,* Nagarjuna discusses the function of SUNYATA, or emptiness, and truth. *Emptiness* here means the egolessness of the self as well as the liberation of the individual into the absolute. Nagarjuna concluded that not only is the self essentially "empty" or lacking in ego, this emptiness is also equivalent to the absolute. Therefore, union with the absolute is a form of liberation or release. Because of the importance of this idea of emptiness, the Madhyamika school was also known as the Shunyatavada, or school of emptiness.

Nagarjuna also emphasized the idea of two truths. The first truth is that of everyday reality, or *samvritit-sayta.* This is the world of appearances in which we live. The second truth is that of the absolute, or *paramartha-satya.* In this there are no opposites or things of relative value; everything is of ultimate reality.

Nagarjuna used philosophical techniques to prove his assertions about the two truths. He developed a procedure of applying the eight negations to any statement to prove that it was relative and that any such statement does not describe ultimate reality. Later Indian philosophers, such as Buddhapalita, Bhavaviveka, and Chandrakirti, developed his philosophical ideas further in India.

The Madhyamika school was influential in China and led directly to the Sanlun (Japanese SANRON) school. The idea of two truths was also later developed into a theory of three truths by the TIAN TAI school. But Madhyamika ideas were most influential in Tibet. Nagarjuna's ideas of *sunyata* and two truths are found throughout the four major Tibetan schools.

Further reading: Christian Lindtner, *Nagarjuniana: Studies in the Writings and Philosophy of Nagarjuna* (Copenhagen: Akademisk Forlag, 1987); Gadjin M. Nagao, *Madhyamika and Yogacara* (New York: State University of New York Press, 1991); Peter Della Santina, *Madhyamaka Schools in India* (Delhi: Motilal Banarsidass, 1986).

Magadha

Magadha was a north Indian kingdom at the time of the Buddha, around the third century B.C.E., where Buddhism first developed. It was located in the area of the present Indian states of Bihar and Jharkhand. Around 325 B.C.E., Magadha fell to Chandragupta, the founder of the Maurya dynasty. Chandragupta was the grandfather of the Buddhist ruler ASOKA.

Magadha was the site of numerous Buddhist events. At BODHGAYA, Sakyamuni BUDDHA received ENLIGHTENMENT. Buddha reportedly expounded the LOTUS SUTRA at Eagle Peak, a mountain north of Rajagriha, the capital city in Buddha's day, which became the base from which Buddhism spread. By the time of Asoka, the capital had been moved to the city now known as Patna.

The first, second, and third COUNCILS OF BUDDHISM were all held in Magadha, using the local language, Magadhi (a dialect of Sanskrit). Magadha was also the site of Jainism's origin.

Further reading: H. G. Rawlinson, *India: A Short Cultural History* (New York: Frederick A. Praeger, 1952);

Romila Thapar, *Asoka and the Decline of the Mauryas* (Delhi: Oxford University Press, 1997); Edward J. Thomas, *The Life of Buddha as Legend and History* (Delhi: Munshiram Manoharlala, 1992).

Mahabodhi Society

The Mahabodhi Society was a group founded by the Sri Lankan monk DHARMAPALA in 1891 for the purpose of reviving BODHGAYA, the Buddhist sacred site. By the 19th century C.E. Bodhgaya had become a decaying Hindu temple site. Dharmapala organized an international conference on the state of Bodhgaya in 1891. In 1892 the society began to publish the periodical The *Mahabodhi Society and the United Buddhist World*. The society used legal procedures to promote its position during the British period in India. The case was finally settled after India's independence in 1949.

Today both Hindus and Buddhists manage Bodhgaya. The Mahabodhi Society manages schools and hospitals there. The society also continues to publish translations of Pali works.

Further reading: Banglapedia. "Mahabhodhi Society." Available online. URL: http://banglapedia.search.com. bd/HT/M_0044.htm. Accessed on May 15, 2006; Anagarika Dharmapala, *Return to Righteousness: A Collection of Speeches, Essays and Letters of the Anagarika Dharmapala.* Edited by Ananda Guruge (Colombo: Ministry of Educational and Cultural Affairs, 1965); *Mahâbodhi Society of India, Diamond Jubilee Souvenir 1891–1951.* Edited by Suniti Kumar Chatterji et al. (Calcutta: Mahabodhi Society of India, 1952); Stephen Prothero, "Henry Steel Olcott and 'Protestant Buddhism,'" *Journal of the American Academy of Religion* 63, no. 2 (1995): 281–302.

Maha Boowa, Ajahn   *See* BOOWA NANASAMPANNO, PHRA AJAHN MAHA.

Mahakasyapa   *See* KASYAPA THE GREAT.

Mahamaya   *See* MAYA.

mahamudra

Mahamudra, or "great seal," is a Tibetan Buddhist meditation tradition used especially in the KAGYU school. The main teachings of this tradition involve recognition that compassion and insight (KARUNA and PRAJNA) as well as SAMSARA and SUNYATA are united and inseparable. The tradition was taken to Tibet by MARPA, who received it from NAROPA.

There are two forms of the practice, an ordinary form based on reading of the sutras or Buddhist scriptures and a second "extraordinary" form based on the TANTRAS, the specialized treatises central to TANTRIC BUDDHISM.

Further reading: Karma Chagmé, *Naked Awareness: Practical Instructions on the Union of Mahamudra and Dzogchen.* Translated by B. Alan Wallace (Ithaca, N.Y.: Snow Lion, 2000); Keith Dowman, trans., *Masters of Mahamudra: Songs and Histories of the Eighty-Four Buddhist Siddhas* (Albany: State University of New York Press, 1985); Herbert V. Guenther, *Meditation Differently: Phenomenological-Psychological Aspects of Tibetan Buddhist (Mahamudra and Snying-Thig) Practices from Original Tibetan Sources* (Delhi: Motilal Banarsidass, 1992); Geshe Kelsang Gyatso, *Clear Light of Bliss: Mahamudra in Vajrayana Buddhism* (London: Tharpa, 1982); Tenzin Gyatso, H. H. the Fourteenth Dalai Lama, and Alexander Berzin, *The Gelug/Kagyü Tradition of Mahamudra* (Ithaca, N.Y.: Snow Lion, 1997); Takpo Tashi Namgyal, *Mahamudra: The Quintessence of Mind and Meditation.* Translated by Lobsang P. Lhalungpa (Boston: Shambhala, 1986).

Mahanikaya

The Mahanikaya is a division of Thai THERAVADA Buddhism. The Mahanikaya meant simply the greater SANGHA or community of monks until the future King Mongkut (r. 1851–61) established a competing group, DHAMMAYUTTIKA NIKAYA, in

1833. The label *Mahanikaya* was used from that period as a means to distinguish the two groups. *Mahanikaya* means simply the "Great Body." Mahanikaya has always indicated the majority of Thai Buddhist monks, while the Thammayuttika from its inception has always been in the minority.

Today both groups are recognized under the successive Sangha Acts of 1902, 1941, 1962, and 1992. Both are regulated by the Supreme Sangha Council and the Supreme Patriarch. There are currently very few substantial distinctions between the two groups.

Further reading: "Buddhism in Contemporary Thailand." Available online. URL: http://www.dhammathai. org/e/thailand/contemperary.php. Accessed on January 19, 2006.

mahaparinirvana

The Buddha's death is referred to as his *parinirvana,* "complete NIRVANA," or sometimes as the *mahaparivirvana,* "great complete nirvana." Nirvana is the state of extinction. A Buddha's or *arhat's* attainment of nirvana is also described as nirvana with no remainder (*anupadisesa*), meaning both body and awareness are extinguished. Buddhism teaches that the Buddha attained only partial enlightenment from his efforts under the BODHI TREE. He completed his transition into full nirvana, extinction, upon his death. This traditional account of the Buddha's passage into nirvana is from the Pali Tripitaka.

The Buddha passed away in Kusinara, where he lay after eating a meal of truffles and rice offered by Chunda, a metalsmith. The Buddha, knowing this would be his final meal, ordered that all uneaten truffles be buried and not served to any others, who were instead given sweet rice and cakes. Hence only the Buddha experienced severe dysentery. Later, in the Sala grove at Kusinara, ANANDA made a bed for the Buddha to lie on, and from it he addressed the gathered sangha. His final words were as follows: "Inherent in all compounded things is decay and dissolution. Strive well with full mindfulness."

At this point the Buddha moved into the first stage of *jhana,* a meditative state, then the second, the third, and the fourth. From this he passed by stages into nirvana. The successive stages were consciousness of the infinity of space, consciousness of the infinity of thought, consciousness of nothing, a state between consciousness and unconsciousness, and finally a state without consciousness of sensation or ideas.

The Buddha appeared dead to his followers. But still his consciousness continued to progress, this time in reverse: from a state without consciousness of sensations or ideas, to a state between consciousness and unconscious, to a state in which nothing is present, to a state of consciousness of the infinity of thought, to a state conscious of the infinity of space, then, continuing, to the fourth stage of *jhana,* then the third, second, and first. Then he passed from the first stage of *jhana* to the second, then the third, then the fourth. At this point he died. His passing was accompanied by an earthquake and mighty thunder.

Further reading: E. H. Brewster, *The Life of Gotama the Buddha: Compiled Exclusively from the Pali Canon* (1926. Reprint, London: Routledge, 2000); David J. Kalupahana, *Buddhist Philosophy: A Historical Analysis* (Honolulu: University of Hawaii Press, 1976).

Mahaparinirvana Sutra   *See* NIRVANA SUTRA.

Mahaprajapati Gotami   *the Buddha's aunt*

When his birth mother died, Sakyamuni's father married her sister, so she became Sakyamuni's stepmother as well as aunt. After her husband, Suddhodana's death and the ordination of her other son, Nanda, and grandson, RAHULA, Mahaprajapiti asked that the Buddha ordain her as well. He refused her pleas three times but finally agreed only after ANANDA, his assistant, made a special plea. Mahaprajapati has remained a symbol of both motherly devotion and devotion to the DHARMA. She was the first ordained BHIKSUNI.

Further reading: E. H. Brewster, *The Life of Gotama the Buddha: Compiled Exclusively from the Pali Canon* (1926. Reprint, London: Routledge, 2000); Edward J. Thomas, *The Life of Buddha as Legend and History* (Delhi: Munshiram Manoharlal, 1992).

Mahasangha   *See* MAHASANGHIKA.

Mahasanghika (great assembly school)

Mahasanghika is one of the two schools into which the Buddhist community split after the second council of Buddhism, held at VAISALI c. 300 B.C.E. The second group was the Sthaviravada, or, in the PALI language, the THERAVADA. The two split over doctrine, with the liberal Mahasanghika accepting a new interpretation and the conservative Sthaviravadas rejecting it. What was the doctrinal question? There are two versions of the doctrinal debate. One story states that a monk named Mahadeva held that a monk who had become an ARHAT continued to have certain human weaknesses, such traits as ignorance, doubt, and capacity to be misled. Mahasanghikas accepted this interpretation while Sthaviravadins did not. Another version is that disagreement arose over the monastic rules (the VINAYA) of a certain Vriji tribe.

Regardless of which version of the doctrinal dispute is correct, the Mahasanghika spread over many areas of India and continued to split into other schools over time. Some scholars consider the Mahasanghika to be the forerunner of the MAHAYANA school of Buddhism. However, it is possible that Mahayana ideas influenced Mahasanghika, instead of the other way around. This topic is one of the unanswered questions about early Indian Buddhism.

Further reading: Edward Conze, *Buddhism: Its Essence and Development* (Delhi: Munshiram Manoharlal, 2001); J. J. Nattier and Charles S. Prebish, "Mahasanghika Origins," *History of Religions* 16 (1976–1977): 237–272.

Mahasi Sayadaw (Shin Sobhana) (1904– 1982) *Burmese vipassana teacher and scholar*

The Venerable Mahasi was born to a prosperous family in upper Burma. He became a BHIKSU, a full-time Buddhist monk, at the age of 19. By 1941, when he passed the government's Dhammacariya (dhamma teacher) examination, he had become abbot of Taik-kyaung monastery in Taungwaing-gale. With the outbreak of the war against Japan in 1941 he moved to the Mahasi Monastery at Seikkhun. He was henceforth known as Mahasi Sayadaw, or the Mahasi monk. During this period he wrote the Manual of *Vipassana* Meditation, an explanation of *satipatthana* meditation.

From 1949 Mahasi was head of the Sasana Yeiktha (meditation center) in Rangoon. He began to train students in VIPASSANA meditation. Related centers spread throughout Burma (Myanmar) and into neighboring countries such as Thailand and Sri Lanka. A 1972 estimate put the number of people trained by Mahasi centers at 700,000 worldwide. Mahasi Sayadaw was awarded the *Aggamahapandita* (exalted wise one) title by the government. Mahasi Sayadaw actively participated in the Sixth Buddhist Council, which was held in Burma from May 17, 1954. He acted as *osana* (final editor), *pucchaka* (questioner), and critic of the final commentaries produced at the council.

Prior to his death in 1981, Mahasi Sayadaw made several trips to India, Japan, Europe, and Indonesia to promote *vipassana* meditation.

Mahasi Sayadaw was criticized for promoting a focus on the rise and fall of the abdomen during *vipassana* meditation. This was seen as an innovation introduced by Mahasi Sayadaw himself. The point was argued vigorously in the pages of *World Buddhism,* a newspaper published in Sri Lanka.

Mahasi Sayadaw authored more than 60 works in Burmese. He had a major impact of Buddhism in the 20th century through both his teaching and his writing.

Further reading: Anne Teich, ed., *Blooming in the Desert: Favorite Teachings of the Wildflower Monk: Taungpulu Tawya Kaba-Aye Sayadaw Phaya* (Berkeley, Calif.: North Atlantic Books, 1996); U Nyi Nyi, "Venerable Mahasi Sayadaw: A Biographical Sketch." Buddha.net. Available online. URL: http://www.buddhanet.net/mahabio. htm. Posted on October 18, 1978. Accessed on March 5, 2005.

Mahavamsa

An early history of SRI LANKA, the *Mahavamsa,* or "Great Story," contains important stories of the historical Buddha and the development of Lanka (current Sri Lanka), including the initial movement of the Dharma to Sri Lanka with the missionary MAHINDA. It is generally ascribed to Mahanama, who lived in the sixth century C.E. The *Mahavamsa* is written entirely as PALI language poetry (3,000 verses) and covers 37 chapters. The *Mahavamsa* is in turn based on an older work, the *Dipavamsa* (History of the island). The *Mahavamsa* ends with events from the reign of King Mahasena in the fifth century C.E.

Further reading: Douglas Bullis and Thera Mahanama-Sthivara, *The Mahavamsa: The Great Chronicle of Sri Lanka* (Fremont, Calif.: Asian Humanities Press, 1999); Wilhelm Geiger, *The Culavamsa: Being the More Recent Part of the Mahavamsa.* 2 vols. (Colombo: The Ceylon Government Information Department, 1953). ———, trans., "The Mahavamsa: The Great Chronicle of Sri Lanka." Vipassana Fellowship. Available online. URL: http://www.vipassana.com/resources/mahavamsa/index. php. Accessed on May 20, 2006.

Mahayana Buddhism

Mahayana in Sanskrit is, literally, the "Great Vehicle." As a school of thought it refers to the school of Buddhist practice and teaching that developed around 200 B.C.E., probably in northern India and Kashmir, and then spread east into CENTRAL ASIA, East Asia, and parts of Southeast Asia. Mahayana is generally seen as one of the two main schools of Buddhism—the other is THERAVADA, or, in terms of the Mahayana writers, HINAYANA, or the "Lesser Vehicle."

The way that Mahayana first developed is not clear. It probably started as a movement in opposition to the formal, scholastic approach to Buddhist practice. Mahayana stressed instead meditation and assistance of the spiritual development of others. Some theories suppose it was influenced by the Theravada emphasis on *saddha,* or faith. Another theory holds that it was an outgrowth of Hinduism. Just as the *Bhagavad-Gita* teaches the need to act, Mahayana emphasizes the importance of disengaged, non-selfish action. It is also possible that Iranian ideas, mainly the teachings of Zoroastrianism, influenced Mahayana. The Zoroastrian idea of a heaven of light ruled over by a deity of light is similar to the Mahayana concept of the Buddha AMITABHA and his Western Paradise.

The key teachings in Mahayana revolve around the idea of the BODHISATTVA. The bodhisattva is a saintlike individual who has advanced along the way of cultivation. Instead of deciding to move on to the final extinction of NIRVANA, the bodhisattva decides to remain in the world of SAMSARA, of constant rebirth, in order to help others achieve enlightenment. The bodhisattva is motivated by a strong sense of compassion (KARUNA), and compassion is the primary religious emotion stressed in Mahayana writings. In juxtaposition is wisdom (PRAJNA). The bodhisattva must develop *karuna* and *prajna* equally during the cultivation process.

Mahayana quickly developed its own subdivisions. The major statement of its philosophy is contained in the PRAJNAPARAMITA (perfection of wisdom) texts. The *prajnaparamita* sutras developed the concept of SUNYATA, or emptiness. The idea of the Buddha also shifted; the Buddha was increasingly seen as a spiritual, cosmic being. Later schools developed out of this tradition, including YOGACARA BUDDHISM, MADHYAMIKA, PURE LAND BUDDHISM, and VAJRAYANA BUDDHISM. Eventually all beings were seen as possessing Buddha nature, and so all beings had the potential to be enlightened.

Today the major division in Buddhism is between Theravada and Mahayana. Some people also differentiate two other forms of popular Buddhism, Vajrayana, the "Diamond Vehicle" (equivalent to Tantric Buddhism), and CHAN (ZEN). Strictly speaking these are subdivisions within the Mahayana family. Vajrayana was strongly influenced by Tantric ideas, which were added to a Mahayana foundation; Vajrayana is today prominent in Nepal and in Tibetan Buddhism. Chan developed in China from the influence of Daoist ideas on Mahayana. Chan is today prominent in all East Asian cultures, primarily China, Korea, Japan, and in Southeast Asia, Vietnam. All of these East Asian Buddhist areas teach Mahayana ideas, in particular Pure Land and Chan, as a matter of course.

Further reading: Kenneth K. S. Ch'en, *Buddhism in China: A Historical Survey* (Princeton, N.J.: Princeton University Press, 1964); William Montgomery McGovern, *An Introduction to Mahayana Buddhism, with Especial Reference to Chinese and Japanese Phases* (New York: E. P. Dutton, 1922); Michael Pye, *Skilful Means: A Concept in Mahayana Buddhism* (London: Duckworth, 1979); Beatrice Lane Suzuki, *Mahayana Buddhism.* Edited by D. T. Suzuki (New York: Macmillan, 1959).

Mahikari

Mahikari ("true light") is the popular name of Sekai Mahikari, one of the more successful of the Japanese New Religions. Mahikari has centers in more than 75 countries. There are an estimated 800,000 members worldwide, 500,000 of whom are in Japan. It was founded in 1959 by Okada Kotama (1901–74), formerly a member of the Church of World Messianity, a church that had emerged out of one of the older Japanese New Religions, Omoto. The Church of World Messianity was built around spiritual healing accomplished by *johrei,* God's healing light.

In 1959, Okada had a personal revelation concerning Mahikari, the Divine Light of Sushin, the Creator. Mahikari is a cleansing energy that can yield health, harmony, and prosperity by its ability to tune the soul to its divine purpose. Humans have been sent to Earth to realize God's Divine Plan. It is their job to learn to use the material resources available to them to create an evolved civilization grounded in spiritual wisdom.

Okada began to teach the ideas derived from his revelation to any who would listen. He evolved a format for three-day seminars in which people learn to use the Mahikari energy for healing. They receive a pendant, the Omitana, which is believed to focus the light. It is then dispensed through the palm of the hand of the Mahikari practitioners. A summary of the teachings is found in a book, the *Goseigen, The Holy Words,* originally published in English in 1982.

After the death of Okada, who had become known as Sukuinushisama (Savior), the movement split. He left the movement to his daughter, Keishu Okada, known as Oshienushisama. She set about the task assigned to her to build Suza, "God's Throne," or the world shrine dedicated to creator god, which was erected in Takayama City, Japan. However, some members dissented from Oshienushisama's leadership claims and believed that Sakae Sekiguchi (1909–94), a prominent member, should be the new leader. The dispute led to a court case. The court recommended a settlement that would recognize two independent Mahikari organizations. The two would share the *Goseigen (The Holy Words)* and the *Norigotoshu* (the group's prayer book). The court proposal was accepted by both groups. Sekai Mahikari remains the larger group. The group led by Sekiguchi is known as Sekai Mahikari Bunmei Kyodan. After Sekiguchi's death in 1994, he was succeeded by Katsutoshi Sekiguchi (1939–   ).

In the 1990s, Mahikari became the subject of bitter controversy when it was charged that its founder had taken part in one of the more horrendous atrocities of World War II, the so-called Rape of Nanking, in 1937. These charges, though still widely promulgated on the Internet, remain unsubstantiated.

Further reading: Peter B. Clarke, *A Bibliography of Japanese New Religious Movements* (Richmond, U.K.: Japan Library, 1999); Winston Davis, *Dojo* (Stanford, Calif.: Stanford University Press, 1980); *Goseigen, The Holy Worlds* (Tujunga, Calif.: Sekai Mahikari Bunmei Kyodan, 1982); Richard Fox Young, "Magic and Morality in Modern Japanese Exorcistic Technologies—a Study of Mahikari," *Japanese Journal of Religious Studies* 17, no. 1 (1990): 29–50.

Mahinda (third century B.C.E.) *introducer of Buddhism to Sri Lanka*

Mahinda was the son of the Indian king and Buddhist convert ASOKA and brother of SANGHAMITTA. As a young man, following the urging of his father, Mahinda became a Buddhist monk. Shortly thereafter, he traveled to Sri Lanka and introduced Buddhism to the island nation. He is said to have delivered his first discourse to the king at Mihintale, a few miles from the old capital at Anuradhapura. The year 247 B.C.E. is generally accepted as the date of King Devanampiyatissa's (c. 250–210 B.C.E.) conversion.

After Devanampiyatissa accepted Buddhism, Mahinda would spend the rest of his life establishing it throughout Sri Lanka and seeing to the building of temples across the island. His most important construction project was the monastic complex at Mihintale. While it was being built, he sent for and received some RELICS of the Buddha, now housed there in the Ruwanweliseya, the "Great Stupa," at Anuradhapura. His sister took a branch of the BODHI TREE, which was planted there.

When Mahinda died, his body was cremated and a *cetiya* (earthen mound) erected over it. A mythological account of Mahinda is found in the MAHAVAMSA, the chronicle of ancient Sri Lanka.

Further reading: Douglas Bullis and Thera Mahanama-Sthivara, *The Mahavamsa: The Great Chronicle of Sri Lanka* (Fremont, Calif.: Asian Humanities Press, 1999); Wilhelm Geiger, *The Culavamsa: Being the More Recent Part of the Mahavamsa*. 2 vols. (Colombo, Sri Lanka: The Ceylon Government Information Department, 1953); Donald K. Swearer, *The Buddhist World of Southeast Asia* (Albany: State University of New York Press, 1995).

Maidari festival

The Transformation of Maidar (MAITREYA) is a Mongolian festival that honors Maitreya, the Buddha of the Future. It was introduced in 1656 by Zanabazar from Tibet, where it was first held in 1049. In Mongolia it takes place in each monastery for a day, usually some time after the lunar New Year.

During the festival, a sculptural depiction of Maidar is transported on a horse-drawn cart, which is also filled with banners and scriptures. Although the cart is pulled by lamas, a horse-head sculpture is placed on the front to simulate being pulled by a horse. Maitreya is said to descend into the figure, and all those in the procession are reborn as disciples of Maitreya.

The festival from the beginning took on political connotations, as it symbolized the desire for a new age of Mongol preeminence, similar to the golden age under Genghis Khan. During the era of Soviet domination of Mongolia in the 1930s, the sacred chariot used in the ceremony in the capital city of Urga (Ulaan Baator) was destroyed. A new chariot has been built and donated by the

DALAI LAMA. Today the Maidari festival has been revived.

See also FESTIVALS, BUDDHIST; MONGOLIA.

Further reading: "Face Music—Projects—Tsam Dance Mongolia." Available online. URL: http://www.face-music.ch/tsam/tsamhistory_en.html. Accessed on July 10, 2006; "Festivals:" Available online. URL: http://www.asiasociety.org/arts/mongolia/festivals.html. Accessed on July 10, 2006; Walther Heissig, *The Religions of Mongolia.* Translated by G. Samuel (Berkeley: University of California Press, 1980); L. W. Moses and S. A. Halkovic, Jr., *Introduction to Mongolian History and Culture* (Bloomington: Research Institute for Inner Asian Studies, Indiana University, 1985).

Maitreya (Milefo, Miroku)

Maitreya is the Buddha of the future. Within Buddhist thought, Maitreya is the last of the five earthly Buddhas. Until he enters this world of phenomena, he resides in his own heavenly realm, the *tusita*. There, he currently preaches to other heavenly beings. When he returns, he will deliver three sermons to those who have formed a personal bond with him. Those who relate to him as

Contemporary image of the Buddha Maitreya, the Buddha of the future, carved into a rock at the Da Yan Pagoda, Da Qian Temple, Xi'an, western China

Rare double-image of two seated Buddhas, in plaster with gold foil on the faces, in the Dhammayangyi Pahto temple at Pagan, central Myanmar (Burma), from 12th century C.E. The image on the left is Maitreya Buddha, on the right, Gautama, the historical Buddha.

a bodhisattva attempt to create a relationship that will guarantee their being present for the three sermons. One way to attain their goal is to work in this life so they may be reborn in the *tusita* and thus be with Maitreya when he descends to earth.

Maitreya appears in both THERAVADA and MAHAYANA Buddhism, but his figure is more developed and worshipped in Mahayana cultures. He is usually depicted on a seat with his feet on the ground, showing his willingness to enter the world. Elevation of Maitreya can be traced to the Northern Wei dynasty in China (386–534). Worship of him appears to have been introduced to Japan in the seventh century. The Maitreya cult thrived for several centuries but was eventually displaced by attention to rebirth in the western paradise of AMITABHA as advocated by PURE LAND Buddhism. Veneration of Maitreya is most alive in Korea.

In China, Maitreya's image became mixed with that of BU DAI, a monk of the Song (960–1279) dynasty. Bu Dai is a fat figure always depicted laughing and carrying a bag. As a result in many drawings and sculptures of Maitreya in China and Japan he is fat, the "laughing Buddha."

Further reading: Inchang Kim, *The Future Buddha Maitreya* (New Delhi: D. K. Printworld, 1997); Alan Sponberg, *Maitreya, the Future Buddha* (West Nyack, N.Y.: Cambridge University Press, 1988).

Maitripa (11th century) *major transmitter of Buddhism to Tibet*

Though many details of his life are missing, Maitripa emerges in the 11th century as a major impetus in the introduction of Indian Vajrayana teaching to Tibet through his most famous student, MARPA (1012–96).

Maitripa studied at NALANDA University at the time NAROPA served as its head. He also studied at Vikramasila University but was forced to leave because of sexual aspects of the Vajrayana practices—the monks at Vikramasila had taken a vow of chastity. He then took Savari, one of the *mahasiddhas* (masters of the *mahamudra*), as his guru.

At one point, Marpa, one of the founders of the KAGYU tradition in Tibet, traveled to India. On his initial trip, he spent 12 years with Naropa and on a later trip spent some time with Maitripa. Maitripa is credited with passing to him the MAHAMUDRA teachings and the teachings on the Buddha nature contained in the *Uttara Tantra Sastra* written by the fourth-century Indian teacher ASANGA. Marpa helped make Asanga's work popular in Tibet.

Further reading: Trhangu Rinpoche and Geshe Lharampa, *The Uttara Tantra: A Treatise on Buddha Nature: A Translation of the Root Text and a Commentary on the Uttara Tantra Sastra of Maitreya and Asanga.* Translated by Ken Holmes and Katia Holmes (Delhi: Sri Satguru, 2001).

Makiguchi, Tsunesaburo (1871–1944)
founder of Soka Gakkai

Tsunesaburo Makiguchi, the founder of the Nichiren Buddhist lay organization Soka Gakkai (now SOKA GAKKAI INTERNATIONAL), was born in Niigata Prefecture, Japan. He attended college in Sapporo, a city on Japan's northern island. He taught at the normal school for several years but eventually moved to Tokyo and obtained a job in the public school system. An early book he wrote was published in 1903 as the *Geography of Life*. It contained the germ of his idea concerning the creation value (or *soka*). In the 1920s, Makiguchi converted to NICHIREN SHOSHU.

In 1937, he formed the Soka Kyoiku Gakkai (Society for the Education in the Creation of Value). The 60 original members elected him president. The original purpose of the Soka Kyoiku Gakkai was to reform education so that it aimed at assisting people to attain happiness, which would arise in lives that create the values of beauty, benefit, and goodness. This goal set the group at odds with the government, which was already in a state of war and required social groups to give priority to the war effort.

As the war heated up, in 1941, Makiguchi was forced out of his job as an elementary school principal. He had started a magazine, *Kachi Zsozo* (Creation of value), which was suppressed in 1942. He was arrested in 1943 and died in prison in 1944. Twenty other leaders of his group were also arrested, including its vice president, JOSEI TODA, who would succeed Makiguchi and revive the Soka Gakkai after World War II.

Further reading: Dayle M. Bethel, *Makiguchi, The Value Creator: Revolutionary Japanese Educator and Founder of Soka Gakkai* (New York: Weatherhill, 1973); Noah S. Brannen, *Soka Gakkai: Japan's Militant Buddhists* (Richmond, Va.: John Knox Press, 1968); David

Machachek and Bryan Wilson, eds., *Global Citizens: The Soka Gakkai Buddhist Movement in the World* (Oxford: Oxford University Press, 2000); Tsunesaburo Makiguchi, *Education for Creative Living: Ideas and Proposals of Tsunesaburo Makiguchi.* Edited by Dayle M. Bethel and translated by Alfred Birnbaum (Ames: Iowa State University Press, 1989).

Malaysia, Buddhism in

Malaysia is a Muslim country created after the British relinquished control and the several former British colonies merged in 1963. The country traces its history to the second millennium B.C.E., when Chinese moved into the area to join the native Malay population. Today the country is approximately 60 percent Malay and 26 percent Chinese and 6 percent Indian and indigenous. Almost all of the Malay are Muslim and conversion to any other faith is strongly discouraged. The Chinese are divided among various Christian and Buddhist groups, with the former slightly larger.

Buddhism was the majority religion among the Chinese Malays for many centuries. Forms of Mahayana (mixed with Daoism), which had spread in China, predominate, though a few Theravada Buddhists of Sri Lankan extraction are also present. The later formed the Sasana Abhiwurdhi Wardhana Society as a national body for Sri Lankan Buddhists in 1894. In the 19th century, Christianity began to make inroads into the predominantly Buddhist community and a strong Protestant Christian mission has been active to the present. In the face of the strong Christian proselytization, in the last half of the 20th century, Malay Buddhists formed several organizations to strengthen and increase the Buddhist community.

The Young Buddhist Association of Malaysia, founded in 1970, is the most active of several national Buddhist associations. It works with Buddhists of all traditions to nurture Buddhist practice among the younger generation and to further the cause of Buddhism in a variety of social and cultural settings. It has more than 250 affiliated units.

The majority of Malaysian Buddhists are part of the temple associations affiliated with the Malaysian Buddhist Association, which formed to represent Buddhists in the new country. It was originally headed by the Venerable Chuk Mor (1913–   ), a Chinese-born Buddhist priest who left China after the revolution and settled in Malaysia in 1953. He founded the major Buddhist intellectual center, Malaysian Buddhist Institute. After many years as chairman, he passed the leadership of the association to the Venerable Kim Beng (1913–99), a writer, artist, and Mahayana monk. Among Kim Beng's major accomplishments, he worked to have the Malaysian government declare WESAK as a public holiday and helped form the Malaysian Multi-religious Council. He was succeeded by the Venerable Chip Hong, also the chief abbot of a temple in Seremban.

Recent growth of the Malaysian Buddhist community has been largely attributed to the work of the Venerable Dr. K. Sri Dhammananda (1919–   ), a Sri Lankan immigrant to Malaysia, who has since his arrival in 1952 become the most well-known missionary for Buddhism throughout the country, especially in the English-speaking communities. In the 1990s he put together a set of videos under the collective title *Introducing Buddhism.*

Most recently, a variety of groups have entered Malaysia from Taiwan. FOGUANGSHAN, the BUDDHIST COMPASSION RELIEF TZU CHI ASSOCIATION, the AMITABHA BUDDHIST SOCIETIES, and the TRUE BUDDHA SCHOOL have been active in the Chinese-speaking community, the latter reporting that its growth in Malaysia now rivals that in Taiwan. SOKA GAKKAI, established in Malaysia in 1984, is the primary Japanese Buddhist group working in the country.

Further reading: "Buddhism in Malaysia." URL: http://www.geocities.com/~buddhistnews/. Accessed on August 15, 2005; Linda Y. C. Lim and L. A. Peter Gosling, eds., *The Chinese in Southeast Asia.* Vol. 2, *Identity, Culture and Politics* (Singapore: Maruzen Asia, 1983); Colin McDougall, *Buddhism in Malaysia* (Singapore: Donald Moore, 1956); Ven. Piyasilo, ed., *New Directions in Buddhism Today* (Petaling Jaya, Malaysia: Dharmafarer Enterprises, 1992); Cheu Hock Tong, ed., *Chinese Beliefs and Practices in Southeast Asia* (Selangor Daruk Ehsan, Malaysia: Pelunduk, 1993).

mandala

Mandala (Sanskrit, circle) is an object of devotion found in Tantric Hindu and Vajrayana Buddhist practice. In addition the mandala may serve as a model of the universe and the place of humans within. The Tibetan mandala often depicts a central mountain, Mt. SUMERU, surrounded by protecting layers. The path into the mantra thus becomes a symbol of the spiritual journey. The mandala may be painted on a wall, cloth, or paper. Occasionally it is rendered through sand painting or in other sculpted materials.

The mandala usually includes a variety of geometric shapes, using patterns that have evolved from the YANTRA (a symbol of the cosmos). The mandala is also often understood as a symbolic palace. The palace contains four gates oriented to the four corners of the Earth and is located within circles that form protective barriers, symbolic of qualities (purity, devotion, resolve, etc.) that one must attain prior to entering the palace.

Inside the palace, the mandala contains symbols of the deities and/or the faith—a diamond (clear mind), a *ghanta* (or bell, symbol of the female), the yantra (or thunderbolt, symbol of the male), a Dharma wheel (EIGHTFOLD PATH), and/or a lotus (teachings).

Precise methodology is followed in creating the mandala and its construction integrated with a ritual, notable for the chanting of MANTRAS, words of power. The ritual accomplishes the empowerment of the mandala, now seen as an object of cosmic energy. As one meditates with a mandala, she or he is given access to the energy it embod-

Large bronze combination mandala and incense burner, from Yonghe Gong in Beijing, China.

ies. In Tibetan Buddhism, whole temples may be constructed as giant mandalas.

In the 20th century, the use of the mandala moved into Western esoteric thought, a complex amalgamation of ideas based on alchemy, occultism, and other mystical teachings, largely as a consequence of its being introduced to the West by the THEOSOPHICAL SOCIETY. In addition the mandala has often attracted people initially as simply an object of aesthetic appreciation.

Further reading: José Arguelles and Miriam Arguelles, *Mandala* (Boston: Shambhala, 1995); Martin Brauen, *The Mandala: Sacred Circle in Tibetan Buddhism.* Translated by Martin Wilson (Boston: Shambhala, 1997); Geshe Kelsang Gyatso, *Essence of Vajrayana: The Highest Yoga*

Tantra Practice of Heruka Body Mandala (Delhi, Motilal Banarsidass, 2000); Chogyam Trungpa, *Orderly Chaos, the Mandala Principle* (Boston: Shambhala, 1991); Giuseppe Tucci, *The Theory and Practice of the Mandala: With Special Reference to the Modern Psychology of the Subconscious* (London: Rider, 1961).

Manjusri

Manjusri, a prominent bodhisattva in MAHAYANA BUDDHISM, is usually pictured as one of two bodhisattvas attending Sakyamuni BUDDHA (along with SAMANTABHADRA). He is seen as representing the perfection of wisdom and riding a lion, the voice of the dharma. He carries a sword to sever worshippers from illusion.

Manjusri appears in the Flower Garland Sutra (especially favored by the Japanese KEGON school) as having hegemony over the Eastern realm, the Mt. Clear and Cool, frequently identified as Mt. Wutai in China. In the LOTUS SUTRA, he preached to the dragon kings who resided at the bottom of the ocean. The daughter of one of the kings desired ENLIGHTENMENT and immediately became the subject of a debate over whether or not she could attain Buddhahood quickly. That she did attain enlightenment is seen today by many who revere the Lotus Sutra as a statement supportive of women. He also appears as a main character in the Manjusri-Parinirvana Sutra, the Vimalakirti-Nivdesa Sutra, and the Lankavatara Sutra.

Belief in Manjusri emerged in China during the fourth century and was passed to Japan (where he is known as Monju) at the end of the eighth century. It was believed by many that the Japanese monk GYOKI (668–749), a HOSSO school priest and an important figure at TODAI-JI at NARA as general administrator of Buddhist priests, was a reincarnation of Manjusri. From China (where he is known as Wen-shu), Manjusri became a popular figure in Tibetan Buddhism (known as Jamdpal) and began to play an important part in the story of the creation of Nepal. As the story goes, Vipaswi Buddha threw lotus seeds into a lake. One seed produced a 1,000-petaled lotus flower from which shone five beams of light. Looking over the lake, Manjusri pondered the possibility of draining it and thus allowing people access to the light. Using his sword, he cut through the mountains. The sword came to rest on Swayambhu hill. The place where the lake formerly existed is now called Kathmandu Valley. Swayambhunath Stupa, a prominent Buddhist shrine, is now at the top of the hill. In Tibet, wise rulers are often seen as incarnations of Manjusri.

Further reading: Raoul Birnbaum, *Studies on the Mysteries of Manjusri: A Group of East Asian Mandalas and Their Traditional Symbolism* (N.p.: Society for the Study of Chinese Religion, 1983); Keith Dowman, *A Buddhist Guide to the Power Places of the Kathmandu Valley.* Available online. URL: http://www.keithdowman.net/essays/guide.htm. Accessed on December 14, 2005; Alex Wayman, *Chanting the Names of Manjusri: The Manjusri-Nama-Samgiti, Sanskrit and Tibetan Texts* (Boston: Shambhala, 1985).

mantra

Nearly all Buddhist forms of meditation use mantras. They are seen as manifestations of Buddhas and are usually given/assigned by a teacher to a student for use in meditation. One common mantra recited is the phrase *nam-myoho-renge-kyo* (devotion to the essence and teachings of the Lotus Sutra), used by NICHIREN SHOSHU groups in Japan and overseas. Possibly, the most well known mantra is *Om mani padme hum,* a Sanskrit phrase meaning "Hail to the jewel in the lotus," used throughout Tibetan Buddhism. In most traditions, the use of the mantra is accompanied by the performance of visualizations or placement of the body into prescribed postures. Tibetan traditions also involve focusing on the written form of the mantra, as well as the sound itself.

Mantra was rendered into Japanese as *shingon,* or "true word," the name of the major school of Japanese Buddhism based on Tantric practices.

Further reading: Harvey P. Alper, *Mantra* (Albany: State University of New York Press, 1989); Harold G. Coward and David J. Goa, *Mantra: Hearing the Divine in India and America* (New York: Columbia University Press, 2004); Lama Anagarika Govinda, *Foundations of Tibetan Mysticism (According to the Esoteric Teachings of the Great Mantra Om Mani Padme Hum)* (London: Rider, 1959); Tsong-ka-pa, *The Yoga of Tibet: The Great Exposition of Secret Mantra*. Edited and translated by Jeffrey Hopkins. 3 vols. (London: George Allen & Unwin, 1977–1981).

Maoshan (Mt. Mao) school

The Maoshan school of Daoism is based on the teachings of three brothers, named Mao, who were active during China's Han dynasty (221 B.C.E.–220 C.E.). The group they founded was originally named the Dharmic Altar of Highest Clarity. The three brothers were said to have all attained immortality and today are called the Three Mao Nobles. Both the mountain in eastern China where they attained immortality and the movement that they founded have since been called MAOSHAN, "Mt. Mao."

In the sixth century another Daoist who lived on Mt. Mao, Tao Hongjing (456–536), built on the SHANGQING scriptures that had been developed there and founded the Shangqing school, the Way of Highest Clarity. The Maoshan school is thus often confused with the Shangqing school.

By the Tang dynasty (618–907 C.E.) Mt. Mao and the Shangqing school centered there had become the main current of Daoist practice in China. Shangqing was able to absorb many of the teachings of competing Daoist schools such as the Numinous Treasure (LING BAO) and Orthodox Oneness (ZHENG YI). The school was well organized and not overly involved in political controversies of the time. As a result it increased in power and influence throughout the Tang period. This allowed Daoist doctrine to enter a phase of solidification. While the Shangqing school was later absorbed into the Orthodox Unity school and is no longer a separate institution, Mt. Mao continues to be influential in Daoism today.

Nearly all of the many temples and monasteries on Maoshan were destroyed during the Taiping Rebellion of 1851–64. Today there are four major temples on the mountain, which is located in Jiangsu Province in eastern China. Maoshan is one of the 10 Dongtian (grotto heavens) of Daoist folklore.

Further reading: Isabelle Robinet, *Taoist Meditation: The Mao-shan Tradition of Great Purity*. Translated by Julian F. Pas and Norman J. Girardot (Albany: State University of New York Press, 1993); Yin Zhihua, "Mt. Mao." Translated by Chen Xia and edited by Eli Alberts. Taoist Culture and Information Centre. Available online. URL: http://www.eng.taoism.org.hk/general-daoism/grotto-heavens&blissful-realms/pg1< 0x2013>5-5–6b.asp. Accessed on May 19, 2006.

mappo (*mofa*)

Mappo is a Japanese term meaning "latter day Dharma." *Mappo* is the final period in which the DHARMA, the Buddha's teachings, will be in decline. The Chinese term was first used by Dao Cho (562–645), who taught that PURE LAND practice was most suited to the period of *mappo*. Many people associated the KAMAKURA (1192–1338) period in Japan with the period of *mappo* because of the decline of the older Buddhist groups and the rise of new groups such as NICHIREN, PURE LAND, and ZEN

The concept of *mappo* was part of an understanding of history that divided Buddhism into periods. In the first phase, seen to have lasted 500 years, Buddhism gained acceptance and spread from India across Asia. In the second phase, which lasted some 1,000 years, Buddhist practice was observed to have weakened. In the last phase, which many saw as beginning in 1052 C.E., and hence already begun by the time of the new teachers in Kamakura (the 13th century), Buddhist faith was believed to be in a deteriorating state and even no longer being practiced within the Buddhist community. The new forms of Buddhism sold themselves in part as the most valid way to find enlightenment in the *mappo* period. Nichiren believed that the first phase of Buddhist history lasted 1,000 years and hence the *mappo* period was beginning in the 1200s.

Further reading: Charles S. Prebish, "Mappo," in *The A to Z of Buddhism* (Lanham, Md.: Scarecrow Press, 2001), 181; Jackie Stone, "Seeking Enlightenment in the Last Age: *Mappo* Thought in Kamakura Buddhism," *Eastern Buddhist* 18, no. 1 (Spring 1985): 28–56; 18, no. 2 (Autumn 1985): 35–64.

Mara

Mara, along with DEVADATTA, the "Buddhist Judas," is often referred to as an enemy of the Buddha and his teachings. Mara is a deity who tempts humans to take the path of evil. Although Mara is a Buddhist god, not found in Hindu literature, she or he is roughly equivalent to Kama, the Hindu force of lust or passion who leads humans to destruction. Kama was an ancient god, first seen in the Rg Veda, the oldest Indian text, as the creative principle and not then associated with evil. Kama does not rise to importance until later, in the Puranas, another ancient collection of Indian texts, as the son of Dharma and, much later, another name for the god Agni. In Indian cosmology Mara is defined as being more powerful than Indra, the deity who sits atop the world's axis, Mt. Sumeru.

But the Buddhist Mara is more truly evil than Kama. There is no deity figure in Indian mythology closer to being the embodiment of evil, a Satan-like presence, than Mara.

Mara and Kama are also closely associated with YAMA, the god who supervises the souls of the dead.

In ASVAGHOSA's *Buddhacarita,* a life of the Buddha written in the first century C.E., Mara is often depicted as scheming to put obstacles in the Buddha's way. It is Mara who attempts to persuade the Buddha to give up his quest for enlightenment just at the point when he is about to achieve it. Mara promises all sorts of enticements to the meditating Buddha. Mara is, then, a symbol of evil. The Buddha is apparently in constant dialog with Mara, perhaps a reference to the presence of evil throughout reality. The Buddha even agrees to fix the exact time and date of his death with Mara, indicating that he does not fear death.

After the period of the Buddha's earthly presence Mara continues to dog his followers. In fact, it is Mara who will bring about the period of decay of the Dharma, MAPPO, that time when the genuine Dharma will decline. At this time Mara will cause confusion among followers of the Buddha; they will reject the true Dharma in favor of lesser truths.

Mara is a symbol of the enticements of evil, and many subsequent Buddhist saints must engage in battle with Mara. In one story the Mathuran (northern Indian) SARVASTIVADIN patriarch Upagupta actually succeeds in converting Mara to Buddhism. This occurs while Upagupta is preaching the DHARMA. Mara diverts the attention of Upagupta's listeners. Upagupta, seeing this, uses his magical powers to hang garlands of flowers on Mara's neck. These turn into carcasses of a snake, a dog, and a human, which Mara cannot discard. Mara finally succumbs to the power of the Buddha's Dharma and takes refuge in Buddhism.

Further reading: Reginald A. Ray, *Buddhist Saints in India: A Study in Buddhist Values and Orientations* (Oxford: Oxford University Press, 1994); Edward J. Thomas, *The Life of Buddha as Legend and History* (Delhi: Munshiram Manoharlala, 1992).

marga (*magga*)

In Buddhist thought *marga,* or "path," indicates the fourth of the FOUR NOBLE TRUTHS. The Buddha not only points the way to the solution to life's problems, Nirodha, he gives a detailed plan of development for all people. That plan is the Middle Path (*marga*), which avoids the extremes of abandonment to sensual pleasures and self-mortification, a solution discovered by the Buddha himself in his cultivation. This path is broken down into eight linked sections, the Noble EIGHT-FOLD PATH. With his teachings on *marga* the Buddha has delivered his solution to the problem he posed by the first three Noble Truths. Perceive the reality of life, he says, and strike out on the path of *marga*. It is a simple yet powerful message that continues to resonate today.

While the Sanskrit word *marga* is often seen as equivalent to the Chinese term DAO, the Chinese term is used in a broader context and can mean many more things. In Buddhism *marga* more properly refers to the Eightfold Path.

Further reading: Robert E. Buswell, *Paths to Liberation: The Marga and Its Transformations in Buddhist Thought* (Honolulu: University of Hawaii Press, 1992); Thera Piyadassi, *The Buddha's Ancient Path* (1964. Reprint, Taipei: Corporate Body of the Buddha Educational Foundation, n.d.); Thich Nhat Hanh, *Heart of the Buddha's Teaching: Transforming Suffering into Peace, Joy, and Liberation: The Four Noble Truths, the Noble Eightfold Path, and Other Basic Buddhist Teachings* (Berkeley, Calif.: Parallax Press, 1998).

Marpa (1021–1097) *introducer of Kagyu teachings to Tibet*

Marpa Chokyi Lodro, one of the founders of the KAGYU Tibetan Buddhist school, was born in Lhodrak Chukhyer, southern Tibet, into a well-to-do family. A precocious child, he began his study of Buddhism with Drokmi Shakya Yeshe. He studied Sanskrit, the mastery of which provided the occasion for his going to India by way of Nepal. While in Nepal he set out with Chitherpa and Paindapa, two of NAROPA's students, the latter of whom traveled on to India with Marpa.

Marpa spent 12 years under Naropa's guidance and then returned to Tibet. In later years, Marpa

would make two additional trips to India to work with Naropa (1016–1100) and other Indian teachers, especially Maitripa.

Upon his return to Tibet, Marpa put his Sanskrit skills to use and concentrated on rendering Indian Vajrayana texts into Tibetan. As he translated the text he was engaged in the practices and experiencing the states of consciousness about which the texts taught. Only in experiencing the realities to which the texts referred did he gain the understanding of the occult realms and hence the knowledge of the correct translation.

Though an accomplished student of Naropa's teachings, Marpa had a personality—aggressive, impatient, and energetic—that tended to drive students away. Among the many who started with him, four remained to gather to them the major aspects of what he taught, the most prominent among them MILAREPA (1012–97), who emerged as his spiritual heir and bearer of the lineage of Naropa. The three other students were Ngok Choku Dorje, Tsurton Wanggi Dorje, and Meyton Chenpo.

On his last trip to India, Marpa, now in advanced years, was given Naropa's last teachings, the so-called six doctrines. Naropa also appointed Marpa to continue his lineage. His four students effectively spread his teachings to a larger audience.

Further reading: Chögyam Trungpa, *The Life of Marpa the Translator* (Boston: Shambhala, 1986); Brook Webb, "The Life of Marpa," *Buddhism Today* 4 (1988): 17–24.

martial arts

The development of personal fighting systems has its origins in prehistory but seems not to have emerged as an organized system until the fifth century C.E. in China, where it had an intimate connection to Buddhism. The development of what became known as kung fu (*gong fu*) is generally credited to the fabled BODHIDHARMA (c. 470–c. 534), best known as the founder of

CHAN BUDDHISM. As the story goes, Bodhidharma settled in at Shaolin (small forest) Temple near Luoyang, China, where he would teach Chan meditation to the monks.

While at Shaolin, Bodhidharma developed a set of physical and breathing exercises, the former derived from observing various animals, for whom they are named: tiger, crane, horse, monkey, snake, and others. Each technique drew upon a particular quality of the animal and extended that quality into a particularly effective action in fighting. The breathing became a means of building stamina and accessing additional reserves of inner strength. The disciplined practice of kung fu, the name given Bodhidharma's techniques, was easily integrated into the Zen practice as a whole.

While the techniques taught at Shaolin were kept somewhat confidential, they did spread among Zen practitioners and beyond over the next centuries, and other teachers furthered the process of evolution. Then during the ninth century, China went through a period of social and political turmoil. The Buddhist community felt the effect especially during the reign of the emperor Wuzong (r. 840–846), who in 845 turned on the MONASTERIES, confiscating the property of many as a means of filling the coffers of a financially distressed nation. The monks at Shaolin countered this unrest by inviting practitioners of the martial arts from around the country to visit their monastery, where they absorbed his teachings and integrated them into kung fu as they knew it. Until its destruction in the 15th century, Shaolin monastery remained the center of the most advanced and comprehensive kung fu teachings.

In the middle of the 18th century, kung fu spread to the royal court in Okinawa. Here it encountered an older local style of hand-to-hand combat called *te* (hand). *Te* had evolved over centuries and was spurred by periods in which the average citizen was denied possession of weapons. *Te* thus developed as an effective fighting skill supplemented by the use of common farm implements as weapons. At the time kung fu was introduced to Okinawa, the island was under Japanese control, and the Japanese authorities had forbidden Okinawans the possession of any weapons. The mixing of kung fu and *te* led directly to a new and uniquely Okinawan form of the martial arts that became known as *Kara-te-do,* or the "empty hand Way."

Soo Bak, an ancient hand-to-hand system of fighting, developed in Korea. During his reign, Chin Heung, the 24th king of SILLA (one of the ancient Korean kingdoms), saw to the organization of an elite fighting group, the Hwa Rang. These highly trained warriors developed Soo Hak by adding several new hand techniques, but most uniquely, a set of kicks. This new discipline developed by the Hwa Rang became known as Tae Kyon. Tae Kyon spread as a practice into the Korean monasteries, and on several occasions, the monasteries fielded armies to fight in local wars.

Beginning in the 14th century, during the Yi dynasty, militarylike training outside the army was strictly discouraged. The practice of Tae Kyon was suppressed, and while it did not disappear, it was continued primarily by groups operating sub rosa. The level of secrecy in teaching tae kyon was heightened during the years of Japanese occupation (1909–45), when the practice of martial arts was forbidden. In part, it was kept alive by Koreans who lived outside their homeland. After World War II, many Koreans who had learned martial arts skills returned to Korea to revive Tae Kyon and create a new eclectic Korean martial art, which in 1955 was given the name *Taekwondo* (or *Tae Kwon Do*), "the way of striking with hand and foot."

Jujitsu is the uniquely Japanese style of the martial arts perfected by the samurai warriors, who had closely identified with ZEN BUDDHISM (the Japanese form of Chan). The primary period of development of its many schools occurred in the period from the eighth to the 16th century. The peculiar techniques of jujitsu derived from the fact that samurais wore body armor and preferred chokes and joint locks to kicks or hand punches.

Judo ("the gentle way") emerged from jujitsu in the 1880s, its development being attributed to Dr. Jigoro Kano at the Kodokan Judo Institute at the Eishoji Buddhist Temple in Tokyo. Kano, a pacifist, developed judo around the idea that one should use the energy of one's opponent to defeat his or her aggression.

Aikido was developed in the early part of the 19th century by Morihei Uyeshiba, who as a young man studied Zen Buddhism. Though later he converted to one of the Japanese new religions called Omoto, he also made himself familiar with a spectrum of martial arts, especially jujitsu. Combining his spiritual and martial quests, he proposed Aikido as a Way of Peace. The Aikido practitioner attempts to evade and then redirect any opponent's attack.

All of the martial arts became immensely popular in the last half of the 20th century, as reflected in martial arts movies. At the same time, they have become secularized, especially as they have moved into the West. Some martial arts teachers have become famous by developing new forms, none more so than the actor Bruce Lee, who in the 1960s created Jeet Kune Do as an eclectic martial art that absorbed insights and techniques from the various systems he encountered. At the same time, the martial arts have been able to retain some ties to their religious roots and those who train for any length of time will encounter the Buddhist (or in some cases the Daoist) roots of their discipline.

See also QIGONG; TAIJIQUAN.

Further reading: David Carradine, *Spirit of Shaolin* (Tokyo: Charles E. Tuttle, 1991); John Corcoran and Emil Farkas, *Martial Arts: Traditions, History, People* (New York: Gallery Books, 1983); Louis Frederic, *Dictionary of the Martial Arts*. Translated and edited by Paul Crompton (Rutland, Vt.: Charles E. Tuttle, 1991); Joe Hyams, *Zen in the Martial Arts* (New York, Bantam, 1982); Andy James, *The Spiritual Legacy of Shaolin Temple* (Somerville, Mass.: Wisdom, 2004). Michael Maliszewski, *Spiritual Dimensions of the Martial Arts* (Rutland, Vt.: Charles E. Tuttle, 1996).

Maudgalyayana (Moggallana, Mu Lian)
disciple of the Buddha known for his occult powers
Maudgalyayana was born into a Brahman family in MAGADHA. He and his close friend SARIPUTRA joined the Buddha's followers together. He was killed while begging some time before the Buddha's PARINIRVANA. Maudgalyayana, in his Chinese name of Mu Lian, became a key figure in China's cult of veneration of parents. He is the hero in many Chinese operas and stories depicting his descent into hell to save his suffering mother.

See also DISCIPLES OF THE BUDDHA.

Further reading: Greg Bailey and Ian Mabbett, *The Sociology of Early Buddhism* (Cambridge: Cambridge University Press, 2003); Edward J. Thomas, *The Life of Buddha as Legend and History* (Delhi: Munshiram Manoharlala, 1992).

maya
Maya is the Sanskrit term for "illusion." In Hindu theory, maya is the force of Brahman, the absolute, which maintains the universe. As cosmic illusion, maya covers the true nature of Brahman and so does not allow humans to realize the unity of the universe.

In Mahayana Buddhist thought, maya refers to the seeming reality of SAMSARA (the cycle of birth, death, and rebirth), which exists but lacks ultimate metaphysical reality and will eventually disappear.

Further reading: Agehananda Bharati, *The Tantric Tradition* (New York: Samuel Weiser, 1975); Richard H. Robinson and Willard L. Johnson, *The Buddhist Religion: A Historical Introduction* (Belmont, Calif.: Wadsworth, 1997).

Maya (Mahamaya) *the Buddha's mother*

Maya died seven days after the Buddha's birth, and her younger sister, MAHAPRAJAPATI, then raised the young prince. Maya and her seven sisters were all married into the Sakya clan of Sakyamuni's father, SUDDHODANA. One text states that there were only two sisters, Maya and Mahamaya, and it was Mahamaya who bore Sakyamuni.

Further reading: Edward J. Thomas, *The Life of Buddha as Legend and History* (Delhi: Munshiram Manoharlala, 1992).

Mazu (Tian Hou)

Mazu is one of the most popular deities in modern China. Often called the goddess of the sea, she is worshipped actively along China's rugged southeast coastal areas—in Fujian, Taiwan, Guangdong, and Hainan—as well as overseas in locations where immigrants from those areas now live.

Mazu's story is well documented in official edicts, the Daoist Canon (DAOZANG), and local folklore. The young woman Lin Mo Niang (960–987) was a well-known healer who was also able to perform miracles such as stopping storms and predicting weather. She was born on the island of Meizhou on the Fujian coast in 960 C.E. She began to study Buddhism early and died at the young age of 28.

Her birthday is still a major popular festival occasion up and down the Chinese coast. The processions at Beigang in central Taiwan and at her birthplace in Meizhou are particularly well known. She is venerated by sailors and fishermen, whom she helps return to shore safely.

Further reading: Kenneth Dean, *Taoist Ritual and Popular Cults of Southeast China* (Princeton, N.J.: Princeton University Press, 1993); Goddess Gift. In "Mazu, Chinese Goddess of the Sea." Available online. URL: www.goddessgift.com/goddess-myths/chinese/goddess-mazu.htm. Accessed on January 27, 2007.

Meiji Restoration

By the time that America forced the opening of Japan to Western trade in 1854, the country had been ruled for many centuries by a SHOGUN (military leader) and his allies in the warrior class (the samurai), and some 260 years by the Tokuwara family. The entry of the Americans in 1853–54, the revelation of Japan's inability to compete militarily with the modern West, and the forced opening of Japan to Western trade and intellectual influences revealed inherent weaknesses in the shogunate and led to its relatively speedy collapse at the end of 1867. During the centuries of rule by the shogun, the office of the Japanese emperor did not end. The emperor had merely become a figurehead, though in every generation he received support from those who longed for the return of imperial power. In 1868 the emperor Meiji (1851–1912), only 17 years old, assumed authority to rule the country.

The effect on Buddhism was immense and quick. Under the Tokuwara shogunate, Buddhism, especially ZEN BUDDHISM, had been privileged and Shinto subordinated to it. Buddhist images could be found throughout Shinto shrines and Buddhist priests were often in control. The government supported Buddhist institutions and Buddhism supported the government. In its assumptions of political powers, Buddhist leadership had been permeated with corruption and to some extent alienated the masses. Its primary advantages were a clergy that was better educated than its Shinto rivals and its traditional and important hegemony over funerals. The Meiji government revived Shinto as the new state religion, and among the government's first decrees were several that sought to clearly distinguish Shinto from Buddhism and attempted to remove Buddhist influence. Capping the immediate changes was a 1872 law specifically removing many of the regulations governing the behavior of Buddhist priests, monks, and nuns from the secular code of law. Thus behavior previously forbidden to Buddhist clerics, such as eating meat, marrying, cutting hair, or dress in public was no longer to be considered a matter of interest to the authorities.

Popular response to the government changes was manifested in physical attacks on Buddhist temples, which were looted, vandalized, and destroyed. At the same time, the first wave of what would become the new religions appeared—the sectarian Shinto movements such as KONKOKYO, TENRIKYO, Shinrikyo, Shinshikyo, and Kurozum-kikyo. Meanwhile, Christianity grew into a force to be reckoned with as the underground Christians reemerged and new missionaries from the Roman Catholic and many Protestant churches spread across the country.

Shinto was restored to its privileged position in steps. In 1869, the Office of Kami Worship (Jingikan) was given authority over all Shinto shrines and at the same time placed directly under the emperor apart from the secular government's administration. The emperor empowered a new office of propaganda to disseminate Shinto teachings. In 1871, the priesthood and the shrines were reorganized nationally, and the Ise Shrine named the head of all the nation's shrines. Through the 1870s, the role of religion in the country was continually revised as the government replaced the Office of Kami Worship with a new Ministry of Religion, subsequently superseded by the Bureau of Shrines and Temples (1877).

While official acts were implemented to change the power relationships among the religious communities in Japan, scholars and other leading proponents of Shintoism and Confucian public morality issued a wave of anti-Buddhist literature, addressing inimical Buddhist thoughts or practices. Attacks ran the gamut from calling names (referring to Buddhists as barbarians) to criticizing Buddhism's otherworldliness as undercutting public morality.

Among the most important efforts by Buddhists both to respond to critics concerning Buddhist morality and to hold on to their lay support was the Ten Precepts movement. The Shingon priest Shaku Unsho (1827–1909), for example, organized the Association for the Ten Precepts to spread the basic notions that should guide a Buddhist. She or he should not kill, steal, engage in immoral sexual activity, lie, use immoral language, slander, equivocate, covet, give way to anger, or hold false views.

Buddhist groups sought to find ways to dispose of any erroneous teachings that might have entered the community over the centuries. The pressures on the community to deal with all of the attacks would lead to what in hindsight is one of the more creative periods in Japanese Buddhist history. It is in the context of the changing roles assigned to religion that a new generation of Buddhist leaders such as SHIMAJI MOKURAI (1838–1911) emerged to call for internal Buddhist reform and the separation of religion and government, an idea suggested by their knowledge of American and French religious life. Other Buddhists sought to make common cause with the new government, emerged as vocal nationalists, and argued for recognition of all that Buddhism had done to build the Japanese nation. Various revitalization movements appeared both to spread Buddhist teachings and to encourage the ethical life.

At the same time, intellectuals pursued various efforts to engage Western currents of thought and to purify their own traditions. These concerns would give rise to a new tradition of critical thought, which bore fruit in a new appreciation of the history and development of Buddhism. A key element in that development was the acceptance of Mahayana as a later (not an original) form of Buddhism.

By the beginning of the 20th century, the changes in Buddhism initially prompted by its disestablishment in 1868 would give birth to a variety of movements that would push the community into the self-conscious world of modernity. A new generation that grew up in the wake of the Meiji Restoration would create a more positive set of programs for Buddhist life, spirituality, and intellectual activity, built on both the large public support for Buddhism in the population and the structural distance the community now had from the government. In this regard, Buddhism prepared itself for the radical change that would occur in 1945 with the defeat of Japan and the imposition of an American-style government and its even more radical separation of religion and the state.

Further reading: W. G. Beasley, *The Meiji Restoration* (Stanford, Calif.: Stanford University Press, 1972); James Edward Ketelaar, *Of Heretics and Martyrs in Meiji Japan: Buddhism and Its Persecution* (Princeton, N.J.: Princeton University Press, 1990); Peter F. Kornicki, ed., *Meiji Japan: Political, Economic and Social History, 1868–1912.* 4 vols. (New York: Routledge, 1998); Ian Reader, *Religion in Contemporary Japan* (Honolulu: University of Hawaii Press, 1991); George Wilson, *Patriots and Redeemers in Japan: Motives in the Meiji Restoration* (Chicago: University of Chicago Press, 1992).

Meiji Shrine

The Meiji Shrine, a major structure of Japanese Shintoism, was constructed to memorialize Emperor Meiji (1851–1912) and his wife, Empress Shoken (1850–1914). Emperor Meiji was the first ruler of Japan after the fall of the Tokugawa shogunate at the end of 1867. In previous centuries, while Japan was ruled by a shogun, the emperors and their court continued to exist, though they were little more than figureheads. However, in 1868 the emperor moved from the old imperial residence in Kyoto to Tokyo and power passed to him and a small group of nobles and former samurai who supported him.

Emperor Meiji died in 1912, when Japan was at the height of its revival. He not only was given credit for the national revival, but had become the object of a popular cult. Thus it was that in 1920, some 100,000 workers donated their time to create the shrine and the grounds in which it is set.

Once completed, it became the center of state Shinto and many people arrive on its steps daily for worship of the KAMI, often by presenting offerings of food or money. It is busiest on Sundays and Thursdays, days set aside for couples to present their babies (somewhat analogously with Christian christening ceremonies). The Meiji Memorial Hall in the Outer Garden is a popular site for weddings.

The shrine was destroyed toward the end of World War II in an air raid (1945) but rebuilt in 1958. Among its more impressive features are the huge TORII (gates), which were built from 1,700-year-old cypress trees imported from Taiwan.

Further reading: D. C. Holtom, *Modern Japan and Shinto Nationalism* (1947. Reprint, New York: Paragon Book Reprint, 1963); S. Ono, *Shinto: The Kami Way* (Rutland, Vt.: Bridgeway Press, 1962).

Mencius (Mengzi, Meng-tzu) (371–289 B.C.E.) *great Confucian thinker*

Mencius, the second great thinker in the Confucian tradition, was a profound philosopher in his own right. As Confucius had he served for a time as an official. He was a great teacher but retired a disappointed man.

Mencius's greatest contribution to Confucian teachings was the idea that humans are innately good. Confucius had implied that human nature was good. Mencius's teaching of innate goodness led to further philosophical developments, including Li Ao's teachings on the recovery of original nature, WANG YANGMING's teachings on innate knowledge, and Confucianism's overall emphasis on the goodness of human nature.

Another key concept in Mencius is righteousness (*yi*), which he joined with *ren* (humanity) to argue against competing teachings such as those of the Moists. While the *Analects* clearly focused on *ren* as the key concept, Mencius argued that *ren* resulted in a concern for others, a kind of compassion, which would naturally lead one to

Marble image of the philosopher Mencius, from Confucius Temple, Nanjing, eastern China

think of righteousness, justice. Mencius argued that righteousness was an inherent part of humanity, not simply something external picked up from the environment.

Politically, Mencius taught that all people are potentially sages, and thus they are equal. He thus advocated a form of democracy. He also taught that people have the right to revolt if necessary.

Mencius operated out of the Confucian tradition, but he was more than a systematizer or recorder. He added important innovations and distinctions to Confucius's original teachings. Most of Mencius's work is included in the *Book of Mencius* (*Mengzi*), one of the Four Books of the Confucian tradition.

See also CONFUCIANISM; MOZI.

Further reading: Cho-yun Hsu, "The Unfolding of Early Confucianism: The Evolution from Confucius to Hsuntzu," in Irene Eber, ed., *Confucianism: The Dynamics of Tradition* (New York: MacMillan, 1986).

Meru, Mt.   *See* SUMERU, MT.

Middle East, Buddhism in

Buddhism is almost nonexistent in the Middle East, where Islam is the dominant faith and in most countries has the backing of the government. The non-Islamic religious communities of any size in these countries were present prior to the establishment of Islam and have survived as ethnic religions through the centuries. Small Buddhist groups exist in Bahrain, Dubai, Oman, and Morocco but operate almost exclusively among expatriates with no outreach to the larger society. The one exception related to Buddhism occurs in Israel. The relative religious freedom allowed in Israel has allowed Buddhism to emerge; however, those groups that exist are all relatively recent, introduced to the country by immigrants from Europe and North America. Buddhism, which exploded in the West in the 1970s, has had a particular appeal among Westerners of Jewish heritage, and in some Western Buddhist group Jews make up 25 percent or more of the membership. Buddhism provided Jews who did not practice Judaism with an alternative religion, which, unlike Christianity, has no history of persecuting Jews.

Buddhism was introduced to Israel by ethnic Jews who practiced Buddhism rather than Judaism. Among the several Buddhist groups that have formed multiple centers, the Community of Mindful Living related to the Vietnamese peace activist Thich Nhat Hahn, the Diamond Way led by the Western Karma Kagyu lama Ole Nydyhl, Zen Buddhism in the tradition of the Kwan Um school (Korean), and *vipassana* meditation in the tradition of S. N. Goenka appear to have the greatest support. Although a beachhead has been established, the total Buddhist community consists of only a few thousand practitioners.

Further reading: BuddhaNet. Available online. URL: http://www.buddhanet.org/. Accessed on August 25, 2005.

Milarepa (1052–1135) *pioneer of Kagyu Tibetan Yoga*

Milarepa, one of the founders of the KAGYU Buddhist school in Tibet, was born in Upper Tsang, in northern Tibet, into a family of wealth and status. He was still a child when orphaned and received cruel treatment from his aunt and uncle, who raised him. He began his religious quest attempting to work black magic against his guardians. Having received some retribution, Milarepa was regretful of his actions and set his mind on a more positive course.

He initially sought out a lama in central Tibet, Rongton Lhaga. Rongton Lhaga sent him to MARPA (1012–97), a student of NAROPA's, who lived in southern Tibet. Marpa, sensing that Milarepa was to be an outstanding student, put him through several difficult tests at the very beginning of their relationship. Milarepa, being desirous of learning the teachings, performed as asked, and finally Marpa gave him the refuge vows and began teaching him. He noted that Naropa (1016–00) had also gone through a similar slow start with his teachers, who tested his perseverance and love of his teachers.

Marpa gave Milarapa the Chakrasamvara initiation, during which Milarepa saw the face of the deity Chakrasamvara and then the full MANDALA, with the deity and the surrounding retinue. Marpa then offered a prophecy, based upon a pot with four handles that Milarepa had given to Marpa early in their relationship. He likened the four handles to his four main students, who besides Milarepa were Ngok Choku Dorje, Tsurton Wanggi Dorje, and Meyton

Chenpo. He also predicted a fruitful future for Milarepa's work.

Milarepa studied with Marpa for some 12 years after his initiation and from him learned the full range of Tantric Buddhism as passed to Marpa from Naropa. Having reached a state of full enlightenment (termed *vajradhara*) he was given his religious name by which he would then be known.

Now in his mid-40s, he established himself at Drakar Taso, which became a center from which he traveled widely across Tibet. He authored a number of poems and songs that conveyed his teachings in an easily remembered form. Unlike his teacher, Milarepa attracted a number of disciples, the most prominent of them GAMPOPA (1079–1153), who would found the Kagyu monastic lineage. After more than a quarter of a century of teaching activity, Milarepa died in 1135.

Further reading: Garma C. C. Chang, trans., *The Hundred Thousand Songs of Milarepa* (Boston: Shambhala, 1999); W. Y. Evans-Wentz, ed., *Tibet's Great Yogi Milarepa: A Biography from the Tibetan* (London: Oxford University Press, 1951); Lama Kunga Rinpoche and Brian Cutill, trans., *Drinking the Mountain Stream: Songs of Tibet's Beloved Saint, Milarepa* (Somerville, Mass.: Wisdom, 2003); Lobsang Lhalungpa, trans., *The Life of Milarepa* (Boston: Shambhala, 1985).

mindfulness   *See* SMRTI.

Miroku   *See* MAITREYA.

Moggallana   *See* MAUDGALYAYANA.

Mohe Zhiguan

Mohe Zhiguan, or "Cessation and Contemplation," is the major work by ZHI YI, one of Chinese

Buddhism's most important thinkers. This work is important as a summation of the TIAN TAI school's philosophy, ritual, and such practices as healing. The title in Sanskrit would be *maha-samatha-vipasyana,* or "great stillness and insight," a title that gives some indication of the book's emphasis on meditation. But Zhi Yi's concept went beyond technique to total religious practice, including the need to develop morality, SILA, and wisdom, PRAJNA, as part of *zhiguan* practice.

Further reading: David Chappell, *T'ien-t'ai Buddhism: An Outline of the Fourfold Teachings* (Tokyo: Daiichi shobo, 1983); Neal Donner and Daniel B. Stevenson, *The Great Calming and Contemplation: A Study and Annotated Translation of the First Chapter of Chih-i's Mo-ho chih-kuan* (Honolulu: University of Hawaii Press, 1993); Paul L. Swanson, *Foundations of T'ien-t'aio Philosophy: The Flowering of the Two Truths Theory in Chinese Buddhism* (Berkeley, Calif.: Asian Humanities Press, 1989).

monastery, Buddhist

The Buddhist monastery evolved in India and other areas into a unique cultural, architectural, and institutional form that, despite regional variety, has retained remarkable cohesion. This survey discusses examples of Buddhist monasteries in India, Sri Lanka, Thailand, and China.

THE *VIHARA* AND *CAITYA*

The VIHARA (monastery) and *caitya* (communal worship space) are the archetype Indian Buddhist spiritual sanctuaries. *Viharas* and *caityas* were hewn out of rock in hills or caves or constructed from brick and other materials. More than 1,000 were cut along the ancient trade routes in the Western Ghat range between 120 B.C.E. and 400 C.E. They were built near prosperous towns and on sites associated with the Buddha and other worthies. While some, like NALANDA in Bihar and Sirkap in Gandhara, grew into vast establishments, the *vihara* evolved from a simple cave or hut that

housed, especially during the rainy season, a single cleric. As the number of clerics grew, living quarters were built around a common center where the community could gather for rites and for study. The ruins at Nalanda show that each cell contained a stone bed and pillow with a niche for a lamp. In contrast, *caityas* were designed with an apse or recess and two side aisles designed to accommodate circumambulation. Devotees proceeded between two rows of columns that formed a corridor that circled the STUPA placed in the far end of the apse.

Viharas and *caityas* continued to be hewn in the Tian mountains that linked Central Asia and northern China. The earliest Chinese cave-temples are in Gansu Province. Archaeologists have discovered new sites near the great cave-temples at Dunhuang. The Northern Wei dynasty (386–532) established cave temples at various sites in northwest China. While cave-temples continued to be hewn and maintained, urban temples and monasteries were laid out on a south-north axis based on Daoist geomancy.

INDIA

The earliest dwellings of Buddhist monks were either clusters of huts, known as *avasa,* or enclosed sites with permanent structures, known as *arama.* These two types were mentioned in the early Buddhist literature, in particular the Vinaya, the section of the Buddhist canon that lists disciplinary codes. The structures were all meant to be temporary and were used only during VASSA, the rain retreats, since by definition the life of a monk was a mendicant's life, involving ceaseless wandering. The site at Jivakarama, used during the Buddha's time, reveals the foundations of four long halls, which were probably used as dormitories. In India these two types of complexes were either built on open ground or carved in caves. These were usually built within a day's walking distance from a major town, usually a seat of political power.

Three hundred years or so after the Buddha's PARINIRVANA a new monastic layout developed in which a square, open space was surrounded by a quadrangle of monks' living cells. This became the typical pattern throughout India, both in caves and in the open. These quadrangles were usually close to a large stupa, a round monument meant to house a relic of the Buddha. Eventually these stupas were included in the dwellings of the monks, usually in the center of the courtyard or near the entranceway. Smaller shrines or stupas were also added in the courtyard. And under the influence of Mahayana Buddhist practices these often housed images of Buddhas. The stupa also began to be placed within the courtyard. The reason the stupa or shrine was integrated inside may be related to the influence of *bhakti* or devotional practices, especially the practice of circumambulating around the shrines or stupas as an act of devotion. The layout of the monastery at Paharpur, in present-day Bangladesh, dating from the late 700s C.E., is a spectacular example. The huge central temple, with a square cross base, sits at the center of the courtyard. The outside walls form a perfect square lined with 177 monks' cells. Various other buildings such as a kitchen are within the courtyard.

Gradually the following basic elements of Buddhist monasteries became fixed:

The Stupa: The stupa began as a type of funerary tumulus but soon evolved into a grand memorial site. In later periods Buddha images were placed in niches around the stupa's surfaces. Smaller stupas, *caityagrha,* could be placed within shrines.

The Shrine: These were usually oblong in shape and included a cult object. From the fifth century C.E. on, shrines were generally placed near the monastic dwellings.

The Hall: Early texts stated that the PRATI-MOKSA, or rules for monks, must be recited in a hall and that all monks without exception must attend. The open central space of the central quadrangle was ideal for this function. Later special buildings were erected for this function.

One important development in monastic design were the Mahaviras ("great" *viharas*) built for educational purposes. These were found throughout India, especially at the great learning centers of NALANDA, Vikramasila, Nagarjunakonda, Valbhi, and Odantapuri. Today we usually think of these as the early "universities." The actual learning probably took place in the monasteries' assembly halls.

Monks' Quarters: These were generally single cells, each one perhaps two by three meters in size, with a door and, sometimes, a window.

EARLY MONASTIC LIFE

The first Buddhists were groups of mendicants, wanderers (in Sanskrit, *parivrajakas*). There were in fact many such groups in India, and an observer at the time would have been hardpressed to find anything unique about this group, which followed the former prince of the Sakyas, Sakyamuni Buddha. As a group of wandering ascetics, the Buddhists took a break during the rainy season. They used the opportunity to work on community-building skills. They established rules that regulated their communal life, which they called *varsa.* This act, which resulted in the PRATIMOKSA (code of monastic law) and the more elaborate Vinaya literature, was one step that differentiated this group from others in India at the time, such as the Jains. Other institutions sprang from this first step.

The early groups living in their *avasa* or *aramas* dwelled in *viharas,* or monastic dwellings. The accommodation was simple: a board for a bed and a mat for sitting, the *sayanasana.*

Group activities included the recitation of the monastic codes twice a month; the distribution of robes, called KATHINA, in a special ceremony; a special Pravarana at the end of the *varsa* residence; and ordination ceremonies for individual monks, known as *pravrajya* for initial ordination and *upasampada* for full ordination.

Monks eventually ceased to wander and lived in their monasteries. From this point the single, unified sangha split into sanghas with unique characteristics.

SRI LANKA

Buddhism reached Sri Lanka probably at the same time it reached southern India. The visiting Chinese monk FA XIAN records that the Abhayagiri monastery near the capital, Anuradhapura, housed nearly 14,000 monks. These monastic establishments were arranged in concentric circles around a central stupa. The stupa was nearly always built by the king as an expression of faith, and the monasteries grew around it later.

The Jetavananihara at Anuradhapura, the ancient Sri Lankan capital, is a good example of the scale of such ancient complexes. In the fourth century C.E. the Jetavana stupa was 120 meters high, one of the highest structures in the world at that time. The central stupa was raised on a square platform. Each complex housing monks was called a "college" (*pancayatana*). These surrounded the stupa on three sides and used different architectural schemes. They were united only in that the monastery's main entrance faced the stupa.

Each monks' complex had a gate house (*valhalkada*) and a brick wall (*prakara*). The thick walls maintained privacy as well as security from wild animals. Bathing facilities were usually placed near the gates.

The living quarters had separate *prakara* walls and included five buildings: a central rectangular building (*pasada*) and four smaller ones at the corners, called *kuti*. The central building probably housed the senior monks and the *kuti*, the students.

The *pancayatana* style was the most common style in early Sri Lankan Buddhism and indicates that students probably were organized under the tutelage of a master. Over time other forms developed. In the *pabbata vihara* form four main ritual

buildings (the stupa, the BODHI TREE shrine, the image house, and the chapter house) were place on a rectangular terrace at the center of an open space. The monks' dwellings were smaller *kuti* scattered around the compound. And the entire complex was surrounded by a rectangular moat and walls.

Another form of monastery was the *padhanaghara parivena*. In this building style two stone platforms were connected by a stone bridge. Structures were built on the platforms. The complex was then circled by a *prakara* wall. There is also a *cankamana* meditation path within the *prakara* walls. These monasteries had no stupas or shrines and were probably used by forest ascetics.

Today every Sri Lankan village has a monastic complex, which will include a stupa; an image house; the Bodhi tree, and a chapter house; a *dharmasala,* used for teaching; a library; a residence (*pansala*); and a refectory. The chapter house (*uposathaghara*) is where religious ceremonies are conducted, in particular the recitation of the Patimokha, the monastic rules which are read twice a month. Roofs, a distinctive part of Sri

Monks' quarters, with robes hung out to dry, at the Maha Ganayon monastery, Amarapura, outside Mandalay, northern Myanmar (Burma)

Lankan monasteries, are either thatched or tiled. Roofs often protect the stupa.

THAILAND

Stupas existed in Thailand as far back as the Dvaravati period (sixth–13th centuries C.E.), but the earliest monasteries, called *wat* in Thailand, are from northeastern Thailand and date from the seventh to the ninth century. Monasteries were generally located near rivers or canals, or in the city centers.

Today there are more than 30,000 separate monasteries in Thailand, and more than 270,000 monks resident during the raining season, the time of peak residence. Around half of these monasteries were constructed in the 20th century. The monasteries belong to either Mahanikaya or DHAMMAYUTTIKA NIKAYA orders, 95 percent and 5 percent, respectively; there are also eight Chinese monasteries and 11 Vietnamese style monasteries, according to 1997 figures. Wats are further classified as royal (*phra aram luang*) or common (*aram rat*).

Historically Thai *wats* were arranged in rectangular courtyards that surrounded a central *chedi* (STUPA). The *wihan* (VIHARA) was linked to the chedi area along an east-west axis. The ordination hall (called a *ubosot, bosot, bot,* or *sim*) was also arranged along the east-west axis. In the Bangkok period, from 1782, there is a formal distinction between the *Buddhavasa,* the inner part of the monastery, surrounding the *chedi,* Buddha image, and other sacred buildings, and the *Sanghavasa,* an outer area added along one side of the Buddhavasa, with the monks' buildings.

Today in Thai monasteries the *ubosot* and *wihan* are often very similar, distinguished only by the presence of boundary stones (*sima*) marking the ordination hall (*ubosot*). Not all monasteries today have ordination halls, however. They do all have a *wihan,* a *chedi,* an image house (*mondop*), and a gallery (*rabiang*). In the Sanghavasa they have a *sala kanparian,* or preaching hall; a pavilion (*sala*); a library; the monks' quarters (*kuti*), the

abbot's residence, a bell tower, a drum tower, and a crematorium (*men*).

CHINA

Chinese monastic design does not look much like that in India or Sri Lanka. Most monasteries are modeled after imperial palaces. Chinese monasteries are usually called *si* or *yuan,* terms signifying bureaucratic offices. A smaller form of monastery, the *an,* is a hermitage and the term is commonly used to refer to convents. Although there was overlap in function and meaning, there is a significant difference between temples and monasteries. A temple was a collection of buildings housing deities with very little space for monastics, while a monastery had halls for living and communal practice. In practice a temple could easily be converted to a monastery if the monks enacted the liturgy there, and a monastery could cease functioning if the monks left or the abbot converted it to a hereditary temple.

Certain monasteries were called doctrinal, Vinaya, or meditative. This scheme dates from the 10th century C.E. and signified that some focused on TIAN TAI doctrinal studies, some on ordinations, and some on CHAN meditation. In modern times, however, there is no distinction, and monks can travel to any monastery. This is not the case in Japan, where school affiliation remains important.

Most Chinese monasteries have a central pavilion (*dian*), a library, bell and drum towers, an abbot's quarters, and shrines. In addition they have specifically Buddhist elements: the meditation hall, a 500 *arhat* hall, and the stupa, in China called a *ta* (or PAGODA) tower. As in traditional architecture in China in general, the buildings all face south.

The Chinese word for a monastery, *si,* originally meant an "office," most likely the government bureau charged with handling foreigners, for it was the foreigners from Central Asia who introduced the idea and form of the monastery to China. The Chinese Buddhists quickly learned the

official religion of his empire. During his reign it became the religion of the ruling class, with less success among the common people.

Sakya Buddhism remained strong during the years of the Yuan dynasty, which Kublai Khan founded, but after the dynasty's fall in 1368, it gave way to resurgent competitors—DAOISM, CONFUCIANISM, and PURE LAND Buddhism. Mongolia declined into a somewhat disunited feudal state. Then in 1552 Altan Khan (the leader of Khalha Mongols) reunited the Mongolian tribes into a single political entity (1552). As Kublai had, he looked to Tibet for assistance.

By this time the GELUG reform sect had arisen in Tibet and its leader, SONAM GYATSO, traveled to Mongolia to respond to the khan's call. As he was about to return to Tibet, Sonam Gyatso proclaimed his patron the reincarnation of Kublai Khan as well as the embodiment of the BODHISATTVA of wisdom, thus uniting his political and religious credentials. In return, the khan named Gendun Drub *Dalai Lama,* "teacher of the Ocean of Wisdom" in acknowledgment of his success in spreading the Gelug teachings and helping him unify the land. The title DALAI LAMA was then retroactively applied to Sonam Gyatso's two predecessors, while his successors, the future Dalai Lamas, maintained their relationship with the khan of the Mongols. LOBSANG GYATSO (1617–82), the fifth Dalai Lama, secured his new role as the political leader of Tibet with the assistance of the khan's troops.

After Sonam Gyatso's time in Mongolia, Tibetan Buddhism reemerged as the religion of the Mongolian ruling elite and over the next century was adopted by most Mongolians. Following the Tibetan model, church and state were merged, and organizationally the head of the Buddhist community became the priest to the Mongol ruler. In turn, the successive rulers supported the Buddhist monasteries, the centers of the monk-leaders, whose holdings and wealth steadily increased. By the end of the 19th century, it is estimated that the monasteries controlled over a third of Mongolia's

wealth. Meanwhile, leadership of the Buddhist community was vested in the khan's priest, who attained some autocratic powers as a lama, a living Buddha, and incarnation of a BODHISATTVA/deity.

Over time, the leadership of the Buddhist establishment grew corrupt. The last leader, who held kingly powers over the faithful, was known as the Bogdogagen. As Mongolia's spiritual leader, he gained a reputation for his sexual adventures and eventually contracted syphilis. He did severe harm to Buddhism's reputation. When he died in 1924, there was not a tremendous outcry when the Mongolian Communists (who took power in 1921) announced that a reincarnation for the Bogdogagen could not be found. The country's new ruler also adopted a generally antireligious stance and viewed the continuing Buddhist community as a threat.

Systematic suppression of the 2,500 temples and monasteries in Mongolia began in 1929. The government was responsible for the death of more than 20,000 monks and the destruction of more than 800 temples and monasteries in the 1930s alone. Suppression did not end until the 1960s. As part of a new policy that included a more favorable view of religion, the government supported the building of the Gandan Monastery at Urga (Ulan Bator) and the reappearance of the leadership of a Living Buddha (lama). The monastery has served as headquarters of the Asian Buddhist Conference for Peace.

Since the 1960s, Buddhism has experienced a revival. By the beginning of the 21st century, it claimed some 22 percent of the population and was on a growth trajectory. A Buddhist Association founded in the 1990s serves as an organizational vehicle for the community. The revival has been assisted by Bakula Rinpoche, a monk who also has been the Indian ambassador to Mongolia and founded a school to train priests, and the Foundation for the Preservation of Mahayana Buddhism, which entered the country at the end of the 20th century.

Mongolian Buddhism expanded to the West in 1955 when Geshe Ngawang Wangyal (d. 1983), a Mongolian lama, was allowed to migrate to the United States. He settled in Howell, New Jersey, and founded the Lamist Buddhist Monastery of America (now the Tibetan Buddhist Learning Center), to serve a small community of Kalmack Mongolians and a small but expanding group of non-Mongolians who gathered around Wangyal.

Further reading: Hok-lam Chan and W. Theodore de Bary, eds., *Yuan Thought: Chinese Thought and Religion under the Mongols* (New York: Columbia University Press, 1982); W. Heissig, *The Religions of Mongolia.* Translated by G. Samuel (Berkeley: University of California Press, 1980); L. W. Moses, *The Political Role of Mongol Buddhism* (Bloomington: Research Institute for Inner Asian Studies, Indiana University, 1977); L. W. Moses and S. A. Halkovic Jr., *Introduction to Mongolian History and Culture* (Bloomington: Research Institute for Inner Asian Studies, Indiana University, 1985); Geshe Wangyal, *The Door of Liberation* (New York: Maurice Girodias Associates, 1973).

Mo-tzu   *See* Mozi.

mountain shrines   *See* ART, AESTHETICS, AND ARCHITECTURE.

Mozi (Mo-tzu) (fl. 479–438 B.C.E.) *leader of early Chinese philosophy school teaching nonaggression*
As CONFUCIUS and MENCIUS were, Mozi was a roving intellectual during the later part of the Zhou dynasty (1111–249 B.C.E.). Mozi moved from state to state during this period, offering his services as adviser to rulers. His followers were in most areas strongly opposed to Confucianists and locked horns often. Not only did they hold opposing views, they also probably represented different sectors of society, with Moists representing the working class and Confucians striving to form an elite core of cultivated *junzi,* or gentlemen.

Mozi taught a well-known doctrine of universal love that surprises many with its parallel to Christian teaching. All people are to be treated with love, without distinction. According to Mozi, those who practice love toward others will naturally be loved in return. This view contrasts sharply with the Confucian ideal of a society ordered by regularized relations, in which love and reverence depend on the relationship. The two worldviews were essentially incompatible. Thus the two camps frequently debated each other, especially in the time of Mencius, in which the Moists were one of the leading schools of thought.

The Moists probably lived communally and practiced asceticism. However, they did not make a lasting impact on Chinese thought. By the second century B.C.E. they had died out, totally overshadowed by the Confucianists.

Further reading: Wing-tsit Chan, *A Source Book in Chinese Philosophy* (Princeton, N.J.: Princeton University Press, 1969).

mudita (sympathetic joy)
Mudita, or sympathetic joy, is one of the four VIHARAS, or "immeasurables." Sympathetic joy is meant to focus on others' joy and happiness instead of their misfortunes. In particular, the greatest joy is the awareness of the liberation of other people from suffering. In meditation the person should manifest *mudita,* then radiate it in all directions.

Further reading: Eileen Siriwardhana, "Mudita." Buddhist Information. Available online. URL: http://www.buddhistinformation.com/mudita.htm. Accessed on April 10, 2006.

mudra
Mudra (literally a "seal") refers to the symbolic hand gesture generally assumed by the statues

of Buddhist deities and bodhisattvas. The different *mudras,* consisting of hand gestures and finger positions, represent a nonverbal system of communication common to both Hinduism and Buddhism. *Mudras* are designed to evoke both meaning and power among those who understand their significance. Throughout Asia *mudras* also appear in rituals, dance, and the performance of spiritual exercises.

Of the many *mudras,* five have become central to the presentation of images of the BUDDHA and the BODHISATTVAS. The Dharmachakra *mudra,* for example, recalls the Buddha's first sermon at SARNATH. Both hands are pictured with the thumb and forefinger touching to form a circle (the Wheel of the Dharma), and the three remaining fingers extended, to which additional meaning is ascribed. The Bhumisparsa *mudra* recalls the Buddha's enlightenment with the right hand touching the earth and the left hand placed flat in the lap. The Varada *mudra,* emphasizing the Buddha's charity and compassion, shows the left hand, palm up and fingers extended. The Dhyana *mudra* is made with the left hand placed in the lap, a symbol of wisdom (a feminine virtue). Various symbolic objects may then be placed in the open palm. The Abhaya *mudra,* usually pictured with a standing figure, shows the right hand raised and the palm facing outward. The left hand is at the side of the body, often with the palm also facing outward.

Throughout the Buddhist world, one often finds statues of GUAN YIN/AVALOKITESVARA showing one of the five *mudras* or their variations. In one form, the thousand-armed Kwan Yin, each hand is arranged to show a different *mudra.*

Mudras may be very complicated; among the most intricate is the *yonilingum mudra,* one of a set of *mudras* symbolic of the human generative organs and used in Tantric practice.

In practicing ZAZEN, sitting meditation, the individual hands are placed in the form known as the cosmic *mudra* in which one hand rests on top of the other, with palms open and up. The joints of the two middle fingers rest on top of each other, and the tips of the thumbs touch lightly.

Further reading: Likes Chandra, *Mudras in Japan* (New Delhi: Vedam Books, 2001); Tyra De Kleen, *Mudras The Ritual Hand-Poses of the Buddha Priests and the Shiva Priests of Bali* (1924. Reprint, New Hyde Park, N.Y.: University Books, 1970); Gertrud Hirschi, *Mudras: Yoga in Your Hands* (Weirs Beach, Maine: Weiser Books, 2000); E. Dale Saunders, *Mudra: A Study of Symbolic Gestures in Japanese Buddhist Sculpture* (London: Routledge & Kegan Paul, 1960); Chogyam Thrungpa, *Mudras* (Berkeley, Calif.: Shambhala, 1972).

Müller, Max (1823–1900)
European scholar of Asian languages and religions

Müller was one of the first of the 19th-century Western scholars to investigate the then-little-known religion of Buddhism. He was puzzled by what he found—"How a religion which taught the annihilation of all existence, of all thought, of all individuality and personality, as the highest object of all endeavors, could have laid hold of the minds of millions of human beings . . . is a riddle." He concluded that the founder had been nihilistic, but later Buddhists moved toward theism and immortality and hopefulness. "Müller translated the Dhammapada, a text containing many of the Buddha's shorter sayings (1881).

Müller was born at Dessau, Germany, and studied at the University of Leipzig, where he was introduced to Sanskrit. He later studied comparative philology at the University of Berlin and had his first immersion in Eastern religions at the University of Paris. In 1846 he began to work with H. H. Wilson in England on a translation of the Rg Veda. The first of the six volumes of the Rg Veda was published in 1849 by Oxford University Press, and Muller subsequently settled at Oxford. In 1850 he became the deputy Taylorian Professor of Modern Languages. He began his illustrious career exploring Eastern religions and their texts. He remained at Oxford for the rest of his life.

Beginning in 1875, he devoted his time away from the classroom to editing the 51-volume *Sacred Books of the East,* a monumental project that largely opened Eastern literature to the West.

Further reading: F. Max Müller, "Buddhist Pilgrims," in *Chips from a German Workshop.* Vol. 1 (1869. Reprint, Chicago: Scholars Press, 1985); Jon R. Stone, *The Essential Max Müller: On Language, Mythology and Religion* (Basingstoke, U.K.: Palgrave MacMillan, 2003); Thomas A. Tweed, *The American Encounter with Buddhism, 1844–1912 Victorian Culture and the Limits of Dissent* (Bloomington: Indiana University Press, 1992).

Mun, Ajaan (Phra Mun Bhuridatta Thera)
(1870–1949) *Thai monk in the forest tradition*
Phra Ajaan Mun was ordained as a Buddhist monk in 1893, at the age of 23. He spent most of his life wandering in forests in northern Thailand, Burma, and Laos. He focused on meditation practice and helped establish the dominance of the forest tradition in Thai Buddhist practice. This dominance resulted from the high respect in which he was held as a teacher, and the large number of students then attracted to him.

He wrote few works, but a poem composed by him in the 1930s was found after his death. Most of his impact on Buddhism has been through others. His teachings influenced most contemporary Thai Buddhist leaders.

Further reading: Ajaan Mun, *A Heart Released (Muttodaya): The Teachings of Phra Ajaan Mun Bhuridatta Thera.* Translated by Thanissaro Bhikkhu, 1995. Access to Insight: Readings in Theravada Buddhism. Available online. URL: http://www.accesstoinsight.org/lib/thai/mun/released.html. Accessed on September 22, 2005; Buddhism Society at Brown University. "Ven. Phra Ajaan Mun." Available online. URL: http://www.brown.edu/Students/Buddhism_Society/profiledir/ajahnmun.html. Accessed on March 5, 2005; Venerable Acariya Mun Bhuridatta. *The Biography of the Venerable Acariya Mun.* Available online. URL: http://www.luangta.or.th/english/site/books.php. Accessed on September 22, 2005.

Myanmar/Burma, Buddhism in
Myanmar (previous known as Burma) is a predominantly Buddhist Southeast Asian country immediately east of the nation of India. Buddhism had become firmly established in Burma by the fifth and sixth centuries C.E. A significant development was the conversion of King Anawrahta to THERAVADA Buddhism in the 11th century. In 1044, King Anawrahta (r. 1044–77) unified the land and founded the first Myanmar dynasty. With the assistance of Shin Arahan, a monk from Thaton, he designated Theravada Buddhism as the established religion of his land. Among the religious losers of the time was the MAHAYANA TANTRIC Buddhism popular in the central part of Myanmar.

The Myanmar dynasty was disrupted by the invasion of the Mongols at the end of the 13th century, and when they withdrew, the Burmese divided into several competing kingdoms. In the 1540s, King Tabinshwehti (r. 1531–50) reunited

Images of *nats* (folk spirits) from Mahagiri shrine near Mt. Popa, central Myanmar (Burma)

Myanmar. His successor, Bayinnaung (r. 1551–81), was a great patron of Buddhism who built pagodas, supported the monasteries, and developed relations with the Buddhist kingdom of Sri Lanka. He turned Pegu, a southern city, into one of the richest cities in Southeast Asia.

The British moved into Myanmar in three stages, beginning in the 1820s. King Mindon (r. 1853–78), the last king before the British took over completely, led the country into a time of prosperity and advancement. In 1857 he built his new capital, Mandalay, which he turned into a center of Buddhist learning. In 1871 he called together the Fifth Buddhist Council, which worked on revising and purifying the Pali scriptures.

In 1886 the British annexed Burma, as it was then called. The Burmese were restless under British rule and in the 1930s, a monk, U Ottama, organized Buddhists and Marxists in a vain attempt to drive out the British. World War II provided conditions through which the Burmese were able finally to gain their independence. A secular government moved into power and the country has struggled to establish a democratic tradition.

The government headed by U Nu that accompanied independence in 1948 financially supported a new Buddhist University of Pali. However, the government changed in 1962, and the new government withdrew recognition of Buddhism as the state religion and ordered all religious groups to register. In 1966, the government nationalized all the religious schools. With the announcement of a military government in 1962 Myanmar entered a period of relative political suppression. Political power has been held by a junta composed of military professionals, called first the Revolutionary Council, from 1974 the State Law and Order Reconciliation Committee (SLORC), and from 1997 the State Peace and Development Council. There have been periodic outbursts of civil unrest throughout this period, including student demonstrations against the military takeover in 1962; rice shortage riots and riots associated

Burmese monk, photographed in Kunming, southwestern China (*Institute for the Study of American Religion, Santa Barbara, Califonia*)

with former UN secretary-general U Thant's state funeral in 1974; student demonstrations in 1988; and fuel price-related street demonstrations in 2007. All such expressions of dissent have been violently suppressed by the state. As in the British era, Buddhist monks have been active in the popular political opposition. At the same time, various governments have called additional councils to "purify" Buddhism, with the result that the SANGHA is under nominal government control.

Various Buddhist organizations in Myanmar (the name adopted by the country in 1990) represent the several factions of Theravada Buddhism. The largest number identify with the Thudharma, which grew out of a controversy concerning the

Massive (900-ton) marble seated Buddha at the Soon U Ponya Shina Paya (temple) in Saigaing, northern Myanmar (Burma)

N.Y.: Cornell University Press, 1973); Ray Niharranjan, *Theravada Buddhism in Burma* (Calcutta: University of Calcutta 1946); Emmanuel Sarkisyanz, *Buddhist Backgrounds of the Burmese Revolution* (The Hague: Martinus Nijhoff, 1965); Melford E. Spiro, *Buddhism and Society: A Great Tradition and Its Burmese Vicissitudes* (Berkeley: University of California Press, 1982).

clothing of monks. After decades of arguments, King Bodawpaya (1782–1819) finally stepped in and ruled that all BHIKSUS had to cover both shoulders on the daily rounds to collect alms. For the time being, this ruling unified the community, the Thudharma Sayadaws, under the council of senior *bhiksus*, also appointed by the king.

Various reform movements that emerged at the end of the 19th century, and periodically through the 20th, have led to emergence of additional factions in opposition to the Thudharma; the Shewgyin and Dwara sects are important minorities.

In the last generation, several Burmese meditation masters, most notably Masahi Sayadaw (1904–82), U BA KHIN (1899–1971), and SATYA NARAYAN GOENKA (1924–   ), have built large international followings. Their teachings are now being spread by the Insight Meditation Society, the International Meditation Centres, and the Vaipassana Meditation Centres.

Further reading: Roger Bischoff, *Buddhism in Myanmar: A Short History* (Kandy, Sri Lanka: Buddhist Publication Society, 1995); E. Michael Mendelson, *Sangha and State in Burma.* Edited by John P. Ferguson (Ithaca,

Myochikai Kyodan

Myochikai Kyodan is an offshoot of REIYUKAI, a Japanese new religion. Today there are more than 650,000 adherents in Japan. (The movement itself counts more than 1 million followers.) Myochikai was started by Miyamoto Mitsu (1900–84) in 1950. Miyamoto Mitsu is today known as *Kaishu,* "great spiritual master," within Myochikai. She and her husband, Miyamoto Kohei, known within the movement as *Daionshi,* or "great spiritual leader," had joined Reiyukai in 1934. Both the Daionshi and the Kaishu are venerated by followers today. Myochikai holds ceremonies honoring the Kaishu (Mitsu) and the Daionshi (Kohei) in the spring and fall, respectively.

When she announced the establishment of the movement in 1950, Mitsu focused on the goal of world peace. This emphasis is not unusual for postwar new religious movements in Japan. In addition Myochikai focuses on spreading Buddhist teachings, on prayer for individuals and ancestors, repentance, and, especially, the concept of *ninzen,* perseverance. As with all NICHIREN-inspired groups, the LOTUS SUTRA is the primary text emphasized by the group. Today Myochikai is led by the Reverend Takeyasu Miymoto. In 1990 he started the Arigatou Foundation, which he characterizes as a faith-based nongovernmental organization focusing on children in crisis. In 2000 Myochikai established the Global Network of Religions for Children to promote children's rights.

Further reading: Keishin Inaba, "Myochikai Kyodan," in Martin Baumann and Gordon Melton, eds., *Religions of the World: A Comprehensive Encyclopedia of Beliefs*

and Practices (Santa Barbara, Calif.: ABC-Clio, 2002); Takeyasu Miyamoto, "Message from Rev. Takeyasu Miyamoto." Global Network of Religions for Children (GNRC). Available online. URL: www.gnrc.ne.jp/AF-introTOC.pdf. Accessed on October 2, 2005.

Myoe (Koben) (1173–1232) *Japanese Kegon priest*

Myoe, who is credited with reviving KEGON BUD-DHISM in the face of challenges by PURE LAND BUD-DHISM, was raised an orphan and entered religious life as a child. He studied both Kegon and Shingon Buddhism prior to his ordination in 1188 at TODAI-JI in NARA (also the headquarters temple of the Kegon school).

He would be especially honored by Hojo Yasutoki (1183–1242), the third regent of the Kamakura shogunate. In 1206, he requested and received a grant of land from the then-retired Emperor Gotoba (r. 1184–98) and subsequently took possession of an estate in Kyoto, where he established a Kegon temple he called Kozan-ji. The gift showed the respect that both the imperial court and the regent then residing in KAMAKURA had for Myoe, who had emerged as a significant scholar of his generation.

As he settled in at the estate, Pure Land Buddhism was being established by Myoe's older contemporary, HONEN (1133–1212). In 1212–13, Myoe wrote two harsh condemnations of Honen's emphasis on the recitation of the NEMBUTSU (the prayer calling upon the BODHISATTVA AMITABHA for salva-

tion). In part, Myoe, a staunch devotee of Sakyamuni BUDDHA, did not like the diversion of devotion to Amitabha. He practiced the daily devotion of taking refuge in the Three Treasures—the Buddha, the Dharma, and the SANGHA—which he claimed were sufficient for salvation for lay believers.

Myoe also condemned Honen for neglecting the "aspiration to enlightenment," the belief that all beings have the potential for ENLIGHTENMENT and the need to realize that potential. According to Myoe, Honen saw this as too difficult for the average believer and compared those groups who taught it to a band of robbers. To Myoe, Honen was the chief destroyer of the dharma in his generation.

Along the way, Myoe had also studied SHINGON BUDDHISM and offered lay believers entrance into esoteric Buddhism by use of the "mantra of light," an esoteric practice that sought union with the five qualities of the Buddha through meditation upon the MANDALA that pictured the Diamond Realm of the bodhisattva VAIROCANA.

Myoe died in 1232 much honored by the older schools of Japanese Buddhism.

Further reading: Hayao Kawai, *The Buddhist Priest Myoe: A Life of Dreams.* Translated by Mark Unno (Venice, Calif.: Lapis Press, 1991); George J. Tanabe Jr., *Myoe the Dreamkeeper: Fantasy and Knowledge in Early Kamakura Buddhism* (Cambridge: Harvard University Press, 1992); Mark Unno, *Shingon Refractions: Myoe and the Mantra of Light* (Somerville, Ma.: Wisdom Publications, 2004).

N

Naeb Mahaniranonda, Ajahn (1897–1983)
female Thai meditation teacher

Ajahn Naeb (or Naep) Mahaniranonda, one of the leading meditation teachers in 20th-century Thailand, emerged to prominence in the decades after World War II as various students recognized her abilities. Born into a prominent Thai family, she had a vivid experience of her true self at the age of 34. The experience led her to search out a Burmese monk, Pathunta U Vilasa, of Wat Prog in Bangkok, where she began the practice of VIPASSANA meditation and then the study of the ABHIDHAMMA, one section of the Theravada Buddhist scripture. By the end of the 1930s, she had become a teacher of *vipassana* meditation and Buddhist philosophy. In 1963, a group of students led by Boon Charoenchai, the minister of industry in the Thai government at the time, founded the Boonkanjanaram Meditation Center near Pattaya, Chonburi Province, as a place for Ajahn Naeb to live and teach. She taught there until her retirement in 1979.

Ajahn Naeb is credited with reviving studies of the Abhidhamma in Thailand with a special emphasis on mindfulness and living in the present moment. The practice of meditation, she taught, clarified the often difficult to understand elements of Buddhist thought, such as the manner in which change is motivated by DUKKHA (suffering). Naeb also developed a dialogical style of teaching (centered on questions posed by students).

Since her retirement (and death four years later), Naeb's work has been carried on by her students both at Boonkanjanaram and at additional centers that have arisen around Thailand.

Further reading: Boonkanjanaram Meditation Center. "Boonkanjanaram Meditation Center." Available online. URL: http://meditationboonkan.org/Profile.htm. Accessed on November 14, 2005; Joe Cummins, *The Meditation Temples of Thailand: A Guide* (Bangkok: Wayfarer Books, 1990).

Nagarjuna *one of the greatest Buddhist philosophers*

Though Nagarjuna, the founder of the MADHYAMIKA (Middle Way) school, was one of the most important teachers and transmitters of Buddhism, details of his life are vague. He is thought to have lived in southern India in the third century C.E. His major works include the *Mula madhyamakakarika* (Memorial verses on the middle teaching). Nagarjuna took the concepts found in the PRA-

JNAPARAMITA (wisdom) texts and elaborated them into a major philosophical school. These concepts included especially the idea of SUNYATA, or emptiness. Philosophically he is known for a distinctive dialectical methodology of reducing arguments to absurdity and concluding with a middle position that would eliminate all dichotomies and extremes. His philosophy is known, therefore, as the Middle Way, or MADHYAMIKA.

Further reading: David Burton, *Emptiness Appraised: A Critical Study of Nagarjuna's Philosophy* (Richmond, U.K.: Curzon, 1999); David J. Kalupahana, *Nagarjuna: The Philosophy of the Middle Way: The Mulamadhyamakakarika of Nagarjuna* (Albany: State University of New York Press, 1986); Nagarjuna, *The Fundamental Wisdom of the Middle Way: Nagarjuna's Mulamadhyamakakarika* (New York: Oxford University Press, 1995); Joseph Walser, *Nagarjuna in Context: Mahayana Buddhism and Early Indian Culture* (Irvington, N.Y.: Columbia University Press, 2005).

Nalanda

Known as "the Buddhist University," Nalanda (the place that confers the lotus) was a vast Buddhist monastic complex. Located in northeastern India near present-day Bihar, Nalanda was visited by such Chinese travelers to India as XUAN ZANG and YI JING, who left colorful descriptions of the place. At its height Nalanda housed more than 10,000 monks studying the full range of Buddhist topics, including mathematics, medicine, and logic. However, as it grew in influence, its curriculum was increasingly influenced by Hinduism.

Traditional accounts say that Nalanda was founded by the Magadha dynasty in the fifth century C.E. However, no archaeological evidence has been uncovered to support this claim. It was almost certainly founded by rulers of the Gupta dynasty (320–c. 620 C.E.). It was also strongly supported by the Pala rulers (eighth–12th centuries C.E.). The complex was ultimately destroyed in the Muslim invasions of the 12th and 13th centuries, beginning with the attack of Mohammad Bakhtyar in 1193. In addition to being a center of learning, Nalanda was significant as a site of contact with Tibetan culture. A second Nalanda University was founded in Tibet, near Lhasa, by the monk-scholar Rongston Sengge (1347–1449). And a third Nalanda Monastery was founded in Toulouse, France, in 1981, by Lama Zopa Rinpoche and Lama Thubten Yeshe.

The site of the original Nalanda was first excavated in 1872 by Alexander Cunningham. Today, tourists may visit the vast ruins of Nalanda. In recent years a Nalanda Institute of Pali Studies, established adjacent to the ruins, has attempted to capture the past glory of the site.

Further reading: G. C. Chauley, *Art and Architecture of Nalanda* (New Delhi: Sundeep, 2002).

Nanamoli, Bhikkhu (Osbert Moore)
(1905–1960) *English Theravada monk and translator of Buddhist works*

Nanamoli, a prominent 20th-century British convert to Buddhism, was born Osbert Moore. He discovered Buddhism while serving in Italy during World War II. He was posted to Sri Lanka in 1949 while working for the British Broadcasting Company, was ordained in 1950 at the Island Hermitage near Dodanduwa, and subsequently spent 11 years in the Sangha Ven. While there he translated a number of Theravada texts into English, including the great PALI meditation manual *Visuddhimagga*. He later completed translations of the entire Majjhima Nikaya, a major section of the Pali canon. Nanamoli's popular *The Life of the Buddha* is based entirely on the Pali canon and provides a good depiction of the Buddha based on the earliest sources.

Further reading: Bhikkhu Nanamoli, trans., *Life of the Buddha as It Appears in the Pali Canon, the Oldest Authentic Record* (Kandy, Sri Lanka: Ceylon Buddhist Publication Society, 1972); ———, *The Path of*

Purification—Visuddhimagga: The Classic Manual of Buddhist Doctrine and Meditation (Kandy, Sri Lanka: Buddhist Publication Society, 1991); Bhikkhu Nanamoli and Bhikkhu Bodhi, trans., *The Middle Length Discourses of the Buddha* (Somerville, Mass.: Wisdom, 1995).

Nara

Nara, a small city in south central Honshu, Japan's main island, a short distance south of present-day Kyoto, was the capital of Japan for part of the 700s and the site of six schools of Buddhism. The site was designated Japan's new capital in 710 and a city modeled on the Chinese capital, Chang An (now Xian City in Shaanxi Province, China), was constructed. Though Nara was the Japanese capital for less than a century, the important period for the large-scale introduction of Buddhism, it would serve as the major center from which Buddhism permeated the country for several centuries.

Nara is known as the site of six schools of Buddhism, each temple/school specializing in the study and teachings of particular Buddhist texts. Young monks would attend one or more of these schools for their training. One school, the RITSU, was especially concerned with the VINAYA, the document outlining the rules by which monks lived. It is difficult to determine the exact order and dates when most of the schools (all from China) arrived, though the KEGON school, established in 751, was the last to organize.

The 730s were a difficult time in Japan. Relations with Korea, from which Buddhism had originally been introduced, deteriorated. At the same time a smallpox epidemic spread across the land. The emperor Shomu (r. 724–749) called upon Buddhists to assist the government in meeting the crisis. In steps he ordered each province of the country to built Buddhist temples and make copies of Buddhist scriptures. Then in 743 he decreed the casting of a giant statue of the BODHISATTVA VAIRO-CANA Buddha, which was completed in 749 and formally dedicated in 752. In the meantime, TODAI-JI,

the head temple of all the Buddhist temples across the country, had been built at Nara and the statue of Vairocana was erected in a building adjacent to Todai-ji. Todai-ji would become the headquarters temple of the Kegon sect. In 754, GANJIN, a Chinese priest of the Ritsu school, erected a platform (formal place of ordination) at Todai-ji, and here Japanese Buddhist monks could be officially ordained in the manner common in China.

It is suggested that a major reason for the removal of the capital from Nara was the growth of Buddhism, which exerted a powerful force on politics and the affairs of the country. However, once the government was established in Heian (Kyoto) in 794, all of the Buddhist groups opened branch temples close to the imperial court, and thus Nara continued to exert a degree of power for many years.

Though the wooden temples that housed the various schools of Buddhism in Nara have been damaged and even destroyed by war- and weather-related causes over the years, they have been rebuilt. Much of Todai-ji was destroyed by fire and the giant Buddha statue damaged during the Gempei war (12th century). It was the restoration and rededication of the Buddha statue in 1195 that triggered the building of the DAIBUTSU in KAMAK-URA in the next century. The main hall of Todai-ji that houses the statue was last destroyed in the late 16th century but was rebuilt and stands today as the largest wooden building in the world.

Today the Kegon, Ritsu, and Hosso schools maintain their national headquarters in Nara.

Further reading: Inoue Hakudo, *Nara / the Yamato Road: Villages of Spirit and Body* (Kyoto: Kyoto Shoin 1988); Asako Matsuoka, *Sacred Treasures of Nara* (Tokyo: Hokuseido Press, 1935); *Nara* (Tokyo: Japan Times, 1972); Minoru Ooka, *Temples of Nara and Their Art*. Translated by Dennis Lishka (New York: Weatherhill, 1973); Hikosaku Yanagishima, *Kyoto and Nara: Where the Japanese Heart Goes Alive Everywhere* (Kyoto, Japan: Ranshobo Co., 1960).

Nara, Six Buddhist schools of

The Six Buddhist schools of Nara were the six categories into which Buddhism was divided in the earliest period of its history in Japan, during the Nara period (710–784). The six schools actually refer to groups of scholar-monks who coalesced around their respective interests into the Kusha, JOJITSU, Sanron, Hosso, KEGON, and Ritsu scholastic traditions introduced from Tang China (618–905 C.E.). Unlike in China the six schools were not distinct sects associated with specific temples. Their primary sponsor was the Ritsuryo government, which wanted to understand and promote Buddhism. The government therefore charged these scholar-clerics, in addition to conducting rites and ceremonies for the protection of the nation, the imperial family, and aristocracy, with undertaking a comprehensive study of Buddhist culture. While these study groups had little actual impact on the spiritual life of the general population, their efforts provided the basis for the subsequent development of Japanese Buddhism. The clerical leadership became increasingly influential in the Nara court, forcing Emperor Kammu (r. 781–806 C.E.) to relocate his government to Nagaoka, a move that encouraged SAICHO (767–822 C.E.), KUKAI (774–835 C.E.), and others, to experiment with more broad-based Buddhist movements that would eventually permeate the entire nation.

The six schools inherited the Buddha's original anguish over human suffering, its causes, remedy, and extinction. Their respective attempts to clarify the meaning of the Buddha's insight on PRATITYA-SAMUTPADA, NIRVANA, ANATMAN, the Middle Way, and other notions, represent different understandings of and developments of Buddhist thought and practice.

KUSHA

The Kusha school is based on VASUBANDHU'S (c. 320–400 C.E.) text, usually assigned to the SARVASTIVADA tradition, which appeared in the middle of the third century in northwestern India.

Kusha is the abbreviated Japanese translation of ABHIDHARMA-KOSA (Abhidharma kosha-basyam), introduced to the Japanese through the Chinese translations by the Indian monk PARAMARTHA (499–569 C.E.) and by XUAN ZANG (600–664 C.E.). The Japanese scholar-monks Dasho (638–700 C.E.), Joe (644–714 C.E.), Chitatsu (dates unknown), and others who studied with Xuan Zang's direct disciples introduced the school to Japan. The Sarvastivada school of early Buddhism sought to demonstrate rationally the truth of Buddha's insight of ANATMAN and to establish a method to realize NIRVANA, or enlightenment. To do this, they set out to clarify the relationship between *anitya* and *anatman* with *pratitya-samutpada* through the analysis of DHARMAS, the elemental building blocks of phenomenal reality. The school identified six direct causes and four indirect causes and five varieties of results that explain the causal efficacy of conditioned dharmas and their effects. Dharmic events do not occur simply through a single cause but are the result of a multiplicity of causes and conditions. In the act of perceiving, conceiving, willing, thinking, and doing, an individual continually generates karmic energy that collectively constitutes an ever-evolving personal existence.

JOJITSU

The JOJITSU school is based on the ideas articulated in *Satyasiddhi śāstra* (Establishment of truth) by Harivarman (c. 250–350 C.E.). We know almost nothing of the intellectual lineage of Harivarman or whether there ever was a *Satyasiddhi* school in India; scholars speculate that he belonged to the Sautrantikavada, a tradition critical of the Sarvastivada. The appearance of KUMARAJIVA'S (344–413 C.E.) Chinese translation of the text, in 412, quickened considerable interest because of the presence of both pre-Mahayana and Mahayana ideas. The Korean monk Hyegwan is credited with transmitting Jojitsu teachings to Japan along with the SANRON school into which they were eventually incorporated.

Critical of the overly intellectual efforts of the Sarvastivada and other schools to prove the validity of *anatman,* Harivarman hoped to reinstill the spirit of the FOUR NOBLE TRUTHS as the path to enlightenment by emphasizing nirvana and its attainment. In the process he adapted and expanded the fivefold categories of dharmas developed by the Sarvastivada. Unlike the Sarvastivada, Harivarman asserted the nonsubstantiality of dharmas. He was able to avoid asserting or denying the substantiality of dharmas and the self by claiming that dharmas are provisionally true (*samvrti satya*) in their transitory aspect, but are ultimately true (*paramatha satya*) in their essential nonsubstantial aspect.

SANRON

The Sanron (Three treatise) school represents a number of Indian Madhyamika strands of thought that emerged from NAGARJUNA's (c. 100–200 C.E.) *Mulamadhyamaka karika* (Middle stanzas) and Pigala's commentary, *Sata sastra* (Treatise of one hundred verses) by Aryadeva (c. 100–200 C.E.), in addition to the *Dvadasadvara sastra* (Treatise of twelve categories) attributed to Nagarjuna. These texts advocated the refutation of all views that impede the attainment of enlightenment and the establishment of correct views through the Middle Path of the two levels of truth.

The Sanron school was introduced to Japan along with the Jojitsu school by Ekwan, a Korean monk, in 625 C.E. It never developed into an independent school, but the study of these texts continues even today.

HOSSO

The Hosso (also known as Vijnanavada, or YOGACARA) school derives its name from its special interest in the characteristics of dharmas associated with the various phases of cognition; *hosso (dharma laksana)* means "characteristics of dharma." The school is based on the writings of MAITREYA (c. 270–350 C.E.), ASANGA (c. 410–500 C.E.), and VASUBANDHU, the author of the Abhidharma-kosa, who posited the idea of mind or consciousness-

only and asserted that the phenomenal reality that we know is manifestation of mental functions. These thinkers do not deny the reality of the physical world; rather, they maintain that we know the world through the sensory and cognitive data that are manipulated by the mind. The most important text of this school is DHARMAPALA's (439–507 C.E.) *Vijnaptimatratasiddhi (Joyuishikiron;* Perfection of consciousness-only). Vasubandhu reflects on the characteristics of dharmas and explores the process of transformation from ignorance to enlightenment, which had been neglected by Madhyamika and other schools.

Unable to locate key documents the Chinese monk-traveler XUAN ZANG left China and made his way to NALANDA University to study with the Yogacara master Silabhadra (529–645 C.E.). On his return in 645 he translated the *Vijnaptimatratasiddhi* and established the Fa Xiang (Hosso) school. The Japanese priest Dosho (628–700), who studied with Xuan Zang, returned home with its teachings.

In contrast with the earlier Kusha's limited interest in the functions of mind, the Yogacara system distinguishes eight varieties of mind-consciousness. The first five associated with the sensory organs are the consciousnesses of sight, sound, smell, taste, and touch. The sixth is mind-consciousness, which coordinates the sensory information that is received from five organs of sense and cognitive data from the seventh. The seventh is *manas*-consciousness. The seventh consciousness receives data from the exterior world processed through mind-consciousness and compares them with information stored in the eighth, the *alaya*-consciousness, and reroutes the synthesized information to the sixth consciousness, enabling it to respond. These multiple levels of mind account for cognitive understanding of the physical world, imagination, dreams, and memory.

KEGON

The Kegon (in Chinese, HUA YAN) school is based on the three recessions of the Avatamsaka Sutra that first appeared in northeast India between the first and second centuries. Hua Yan emerged as an independent tradition in China through the efforts of Du Shun (558–640 C.E.), Ji Yan (602–667 C.E.), and FA ZANG (643–712 C.E.), who systemized the various strands of Buddhist thought under the Hua Yan aegis. Fa Zang's disciples Dao Xuan and Shen Xiang traveled to Japan to lecture on Kegon doctrine. Inspired by the universal vision of Hua Yan doctrine, Emperor Shomu (724–748 C.E.) ordered the construction of TODAI-JI to house an image of the Mahavairocana, the primary Buddha in the Avatamsaka Sutra. MYOE (1185–1333 C.E.) attempted but failed to establish a new Kegon school in the KAMAKURA period. Hotan's (1657–1738 C.E.) attempt to establish an institute for Kegon studies in the Tokugawa period also failed.

Kegon masters explored the vision that transformed Siddhartha Gautama into the Buddha, the Enlightened One, who on the morning of the enlightenment saw that all dharmas appearing before his mind's eye were mutually related and interdependent. From this vision, the masters reasoned that the realm of dharmas, or the *dharmadhatu*, is embraced within a single thought and proceeded to describe a psychocosmic "metaphysics" that they crystallized in the doctrine of *hokkai engi* (*fajie yuanqi*; *dharmadhatu pratityasamutpada*). *Hokkai* or *dharmadhatu* points to the subjective reality of the enlightenment; it is the absolute truth and the universal principle. *Pratitya-samutpada* refers to Buddha's original insight and his ideological standpoint. *Hokkai engi* includes four visions of reality that correspond to the four levels of spiritual maturity. First, *jihokkai*, or the world of phenomenal reality, is the commonsense understanding that all existents are independent and distinct. Second, *rihokkai*, or the realm of universal truth, is the realm that sustains the phenomenal world; it is the realm of SUNYATA, which can be only intuitively apprehended. Third, *rijimuge hokkai*, the realm of the nonobstruction of phenomena and truth, is a vision that can be

seen only by enlightened beings. Enlightened beings apprehend the truth present in every individual existence. Fourth, *jijimuge hokkai*, the realm of the interfusion of things, articulates the Kegon vision that all existents, while maintaining their individual identity, mutually interrelate and interfuse with each other to create a harmonious whole. Kegon thought exerted considerable influence on later Buddhist developments, in particular Zen.

RITSU

In contrast to the five scholastic schools, the Ritsu school focused on the practical matters of the faith and the maintenance of the institution. *Ritsu* is the Japanese translation of VINAYA, or "precepts," the moral discipline and monastic codes of Buddhism. Emperor Shomu (r. 724–749 C.E.) was especially interested in establishing an ordination procedure to ensure that future clerics had a proper understanding of the responsibilities of the office. He sent the priests Eiei and Fusho to China to determine how the proper *vinaya* could be introduced to Japan. On their arrival they discovered that unless a candidate pledged to observe the 250 *vinaya* rules at the time of ordination, he was not considered to be a monk. Concerned, they appealed to Dao Xuan (702–760 C.E.) to leave for Japan immediately and offer instruction to their Japanese cohorts. He arrived in 736. Ten years later, Jin Jianzhen (GANJIN, 687–763 C.E.) was invited to establish the sect formally in Japan. After five unsuccessful attempts Jianzhen finally reached Japan in 754. Two months later the first ordination platform was constructed at Todai-ji and 80 monks of other schools received their priestly ordination. Emperor Shomu and other laypersons received the lay precepts. The formal transmission of the *vinaya* from China to Japan represented the actual establishment of the Buddhist community. The Ritsu school acted as the interdenominational guardian of the initiation into the clergy. This gate-keeping privilege was the cause of great controversy when Dengyo

Daishi Saicho (767–822 C.E.), the founder of Japanese Tendai, wanted to establish an ordination platform on Mt. Hiei.

In China and subsequently in Japan a person was not considered to be a cleric until he or she had stepped on the *kaidan,* or ordination platform, and pledged to observe the *vinaya* codes. The Chinese *kaidan* evolved from the early Buddhist *sima,* a sacred site in which the ordination took place. The candidate alighted the ordination platform by ascending three steps, representing the emptiness of self, dharmas, and both self and dharmas. The formal ceremony required the presence of at least 10 clerics, who would determine the suitability of the candidate.

Unfortunately by the time Ganjin arrived, politically well-placed clerics persuaded the Ritsuryo government to institute guidelines for clerical conduct that did not meet the rigorous *vinaya* requirements. Ganjin's presence served simply to lend legitimacy. In 758 Ganjin resigned his post with the bureau of priests and was permitted to establish his own *kaidan* and center for Buddhist studies at Toshodai-ji in 759. Formal *vinaya* discipline never took hold in Japan, partly because of the rise of Mahayana *vinaya,* which was part of the Tendai school.

The original purpose of the Vinaya was a confession of faith and affirmation of community. However, during the Buddha's lifetime the community instituted 250 articles for monks and 348 for nuns that set forth the rules that govern ordination, retreats, study, the celibate life, judicial codes, voting, and decision making. The Ritsu school maintained that the commitment and faithful observance of the *vinaya* are essential steps to the purification of the mind and to enlightenment. The study of the Vinaya as canonical text has always been part of Buddhist curricula for all traditions.

Further reading: Sukumar Dutt, *Buddhist Monks and Monasteries of India* (London: George Allan and Unwin, 1962); Erich Frauwallner, *Studies in Abhidharma Literature and the Origins of Buddhist Philosophical Systems.* Translated by Sophie Francis Kidd (Albany: State University of New York Press, 1965); Daigan Matsunaga and Alicia Matsunaga, *Foundation of Japanese Buddhism.* Vol. 1, *The Aristocratic Age* (Los Angeles: Buddhist Books International, 1974); Junjiro Takakusu, *The Essentials of Buddhist Philosophy* (Honolulu: University of Hawaii, 1947).

Narada Maha Thera (1898–1983) *Sri Lankan monk and teacher*

Narada Maha Thera, a Sri Lankan THERAVADA monk, is most remembered for his disciplined and saintly life. He was born Sumanapala Perera at Kotahena, a suburb of Colombo. He attended a Christian secondary school prior to entering St. Benedict's College, located in his hometown. He turned down offers to become a Roman Catholic priest. As a high school student he had begun studying Sanskrit and was taking instruction in Buddhism at the local VIHARA under Vajiranana Maha Nayaka Thera. Sumanapala received his initial ORDINATION as a Buddhist monk at the age of 18, at which time he took the religious name *Narada.* Continuing his Buddhist studies, he received his second ordination two years later.

He later became an external student at Ceylon University College, where he studied ethics, logic, and philosophy. During this time he attended the weekly meetings of the Servants of the Buddha society.

Then in 1929 at the age of 31, he accepted an invitation from ANGARIKA DHARMAPALA to attend the opening of Mulagandhakuti Vihara at Saranath (India). Once there he was called upon to conduct the meeting because of his knowledge of English. The trip became the first of many journeys outside Sri Lanka, especially to countries in Southeast Asia (where Theravada was the dominant form of Buddhism). Here he was welcomed as a missionary by an often-faltering Buddhist community. On a 1934 visit to Indonesia, he took a sapling from the BODHI TREE at Anuradhapura and planted it at the famous BOROBUDUR temple. He was the first Theravada BHIKSU to travel to Indonesia for many centuries.

In 1954 he went to England to celebrate the opening of the London Buddhist Vihara in Kensington. He stayed on to become the resident monk for the *vihara*'s first year.

Upon his return to Sri Lanka, he spent the next decades in missionary visits around Southeast Asia. He was especially active in Vietnam, where he planted many saplings of the Bodhi tree. He spent the last years of his life in the United States.

Further reading: Olcott Gunasekera, "Venerable Narada Maha Thera: A Buddhist Missionary Par Excellence," BuddhaSasana: A Buddhist Page by Binh Anson. Available online. URL: http://www.budsas.org/ebud/ebdha296.htm. Accessed on November 1, 2005; Narada Maha Thera, *The Buddha and His Teachings* (Colombo, Sri Lanka: Messrs. Apothecaries', 1973); ———, *The Dhammapada* (Calcutta: Karunaratne & Sons, 1995); ———, *Manual of Abhidhamma* (Yangon, Myanmar: Buddha Sasana Council, 1970); ———, and Kassapa Thera, *The Mirror of the Dhamma* (Singapore: Nanyang Buddhist Culture Services, n.d.).

Naropa (956–1040) *influential Indian Tantric Buddhist yogi*

Naropa, a key figure in the development of Indian Tantric Buddhism, played an essential role in the dissemination of Tantric Buddhist traditions to Nepal and Tibet. Accounts of his background vary. He was most probably born in Kashmir, although several biographies place him in east India. His best-known Tibetan biography holds that he was born a prince and became a monk as a young man. As he excelled at debate, he was made the warden of the northern gate at the illustrious NALANDA monastic complex in northeastern India, where he was responsible for debating visiting scholars. Despite his high status, he eventually tired of the scholastic life and was drawn to Tantric practice.

Other accounts, however, claim that he was of humble social status, the mixed-caste son of a liquor dealer.

All accounts agree, however, that he eventually sought out the famous Tantric guru Tilopa. Before accepting him as a pupil, Tilopa subjected him to a series of grueling ordeals. Upon his completion of these, he was accepted as a disciple and instructed in Tantric practice. Naropa excelled in these studies and eventually settled at Pulahari, a retreat center located near Nalanda monastery. There he attracted numerous disciples from India, Nepal, and Tibet, most notably MARPA (1012–97), who played a key role in the dissemination of Tantric Buddhism to Tibet.

In addition to serving as a Tantric guru, Naropa is credited with several important works, most notably commentaries on the *Hevajra Tantra* and the *Sekoddesha,* an important work associated with the Kalacakra Tantra. He is also the reputed founder of an important system of advanced Tantric yogic techniques known among the Tibetans as the "Six Yogas of Naropa."

Further reading: Herbert V. Guenter, trans., *The Life and Teaching of Naropa* (Oxford: Clarendon Press, 1963); Glenn H. Mullin, trans., *Tsongkhapa's Six Yogas of Naropa* (Ithaca, N.Y.: Snow Lion, 1996); Lama Yeshe, *Becoming Vajrasattva: The Tantric Path of Purification* (Somerville, Mass.: Wisdom, 2004).

nature *See* ECOLOGY AND ENVIRONMENTALISM.

nembutsu (Chinese, *nian fo*)

Nembutsu is, literally, "reciting the Buddha." The recitation of the BUDDHA's name was an early practice in Buddhism and stems from the concept of the MANTRA, a sound of power. Later *nembutsu* was the practice of reciting the name of AMITABHA, the Buddha of the western lands. The PURE LAND tradition, first established in China by HUI YUAN (336–416 C.E.), taught the importance of rebirth in Amitabha's Pure Land. SHAN TAO in seventh-century China declared that recitation of the Buddha's name equaled meditation on the Buddha. The idea was further expanded by HONEN (1133–1212) in Japan, who declared that reciting the name of Amida (Amitabha) Buddha was the *sole* means of rebirth into the Pure Land.

Further reading: Daien Fugen, ed., *The Shoshin Ge: The Gatha of True Faith in the Nembutsu* (Kyoto: Ryukoku University Press, 1966); Hisao Inagaki, *The Way of Nembutsu-Faith, a Commentary on Shinran's Shoshinge, Hymn of True Faith and Nembutsu* (Kyoto: Nagata Bunshodo, 1996); Shinei Shigefuji, *Nembutsu: Nembutsu in Shinran and His Teachers: A Comparison* (Toronto: Toronto Buddhist Church, 1980).

Neo-Confucianism (*lixue*)

Neo-Confucianism is a label given to a development in Chinese intellectual history that incorporated some of the metaphysical aspects of Buddhism into Confucianism. The Song dynasty (960–1279) saw an amazing convergence of talent and creativity in most areas of Chinese culture. Philosophically the major tenor of the age was a reenvisioning of the orthodoxy that had guided Chinese regimes since the Han dynasty (206 B.C.E.–220 C.E.), Confucianism. The scholars of the day were familiar with Buddhist principles and the many newly translated Buddhist texts, works often of great subtlety. These Confucian thinkers incorporated and modeled the vast amount of metaphysical and speculative material in Buddhism and created a complete system that, unlike early Confucianism, had answers to metaphysical questions. Their results are nevertheless still recognizable as Confucianism. The fundamental bases are humanity (REN) and the cultivation of mind and morality. The Neo-Confucians also believed in the essential rationality of the universe: the human mind is capable of comprehending the universe, despite its complexity.

The founding philosopher in this school was ZHOU DUNYI (1017–73 C.E.). In his Taiji tushuo (An Explanation of the diagram of the great ultimate) and Tongshu (Penetration of the *Book of Changes*) he presented a metaphysical vision that paved the way for later Neo-Confucian thinkers. His philosophy was essentially based on an interpretation of the *Book of Changes* (*Yijing*). By doing this he grouped the key concepts of principle (*li*), nature, and destiny together. His work shows the obvious influence of Daoist ideas then current in intellectual circles.

With the exception of Zhou Dunyi, Neo-Confucianism is divided into two major schools, the school of principle (*lixue*) and the school of mind (*xinxue*). They were associated with different thinkers, but many of their differences came down to pedagogy, or what we would today perhaps term *methodology*. The *lixue* thinkers, particularly Cheng Yi (1033–1107) and Zhu Xi (1130–1200), believed in gradual learning, which would eventually illuminate *xing*, true nature. The term *li* in *lixue* is simply the principle associated with *xing*, the reflection of (human) nature. The individual should follow Confucius's recommendations in, for instance, the *Da xue* (Great Learning), and move from investigations of things to investigation of knowledge itself.

Proponents of *xinxue*, the school of mind, put emphasis on intention (*cheng yi*). One need not go outside to accumulate understanding; one need simply realize the principle (*li*) already inherent within. This process is LIANGZHI, innate knowledge. Major thinkers in the *xinxue* camp include Lu Xiangshan (1139–93) and Wang Yangming (1472–1529).

All Neo-Confucians put emphasis on realizing one's status as a sage (*shengren*). This was formerly a label reserved for the grand masters of the past, the enlightened figures from antiquity who passed down essential knowledge. Now every cultivator could achieve sagehood. Just as the Buddhist practitioner aims to achieve enlightenment, the

Confucian scholar's efforts to cultivate sagehood became a religious goal. And how is sagehood defined? Simply, as complete unity between the individual and heaven (TIAN).

Invigorated with this religious interpretation of cultivation, and the perspective afforded by metaphysics, Neo-Confucianism became the de facto official dogma for all major states in East Asia: China, Korea, Japan, and Vietnam.

Further reading: Rodney L. Taylor, *The Way of Heaven: An Introduction to the Confucian Religious Life* (Leiden: E. J. Brill, 1986).

Nepal, Buddhism in

The modern nation of Nepal was created in the 18th century by King Prithvi. It is a long, thin, largely mountainous country in the Himalayan mountains, home to Mt. Everest. It is the only officially Hindu nation in the world, and more than 75 percent of the people follow the state-sponsored faith. There is, however a strong Buddhist minority of approximately 2 million, or about 8 percent of the population.

A number of ethnic Tibetans reside in the higher mountains. They seem to have migrated to Nepal in the 16th and 17th centuries and follow a form of NYINGMA religion. Among the most interesting Buddhists are the Newar people, whose beliefs and practices appear to date to the third century B.C.E. The Nepal community remained in contact with like-minded VAJRAYANA BUDDHISM believers in India until the 10th century C.E., when Buddhism was suppressed in northeast India by the Muslim conquerors. Many Indians fled to Nepal at this time. Newar Buddhism thus maintains the pre-Tibetan forms of Vajrayana practice.

Further reading: David N. Gellner, *Monk, Householder, and Tantric Priest: Newar Religion and Its Hierarchy of Ritual* (Cambridge: Cambridge University Press, 1992): ———, "Nepal," in J. Gordon Melton and Martin

Six-armed white Avalokitesvara (Amoghapasa Lokesuam) bodhisattva figure, made by a Nepalese artist in carved wood and plaster, in *tribhanga* pose (with hip to the side); from the 14th-century Malla dynasty; now housed in the Freer Gallery of the Smithsonian Museum, Washington, D.C.

Baumann, eds., *Religions of the World: A Comprehensive Encyclopedia of Beliefs and Practices* (Santa Barbara, Calif.: ABC-Clio, 2002), 925–927; S. Ortner, *High Religion: A Cultural and Political History of Sherpa Buddhism* (Princeton, N.J.: Princeton University Press, 1989).

Newar Buddhism

The Newar inhabit the Kathmandu Valley and make up 5.5 percent of Nepal's population Today most of the 540,000 Newars are Hindu, and some are Buddhist. One form of Buddhism practiced by the Newari is VAJRAYANA BUDDHISM, or TANTRIC Buddhism. This form, usually called Newar Buddhism, is the oldest continuous form of Buddhism still practiced anywhere. It also has characteristics found only in Nepal.

Most obviously, there is no separate SANGHA operating in Newar Buddhism. Instead certain individuals become monks and function much as Hindu priests—that is, as individual masters, not living in a separate community of practitioners. These are members of the Vajracarya/Sakya caste. The priests help perform rite-of-passage rituals for local believers. They are married and live in temples usually constructed in the *baha* style.

Baha is derived from the Sanskrit term VIHARA, or monastery building. Most Newar *baha* complexes are buildings constructed around a courtyard. Today there is usually a Buddha image, called a *Kapa-dya,* in the center of the courtyard. This image is generally performing the earth-touching gesture with its hands. This image in most cases faces north; in no cases does it face south, which is the direction associated with Yamaraja, the lord of the underworld.

The area of the courtyard with the Kapa-dya is the public, or Mahayana, section. All other areas of the complex are secret, or Vajrayana, and therefore not open to casual entry. Today there are 363 Buddhist *viharas—bahas—*in the Kathmandu Valley.

Celibate monks at one time did exist in Nepal, living in temple complexes called *bahis,* which were distinct from the *bahas.* The practice of having celibate monks died out around 400 years ago.

The cultural role of the Vajracarya priests in Newar Buddhism leads to several unique aspects. Since there is no full-fledged sangha, there is no practice of PRATIMOKSA/PATIMOKKHA, the rules followed by Buddhist monks. Theravadin practitioners are often critical of this aspect. A second unique area is the performance of ritual. In particular, the Homa Yajna, a ritual using sacrificial fire, is very common in Newar Buddhism. This practice is familiar to Tantra but not found in Theravadin or Mahayana practice. Newars also practice other rituals that are not used in other cultures today.

Newar Buddhists worship a wide pantheon. But AVALOKITESVARA remains the most popular deity figure. There are 108 ways in which Avalokitesvara manifests himself and is depicted in Newar art. The BODHISATTVA Amoghapasa Lokesvara and the Buddha VAIROCANA are also common figures in Newar temples.

There is today a lack of educated monks in Newar Buddhism. There are few individuals with specialized knowledge of sutras and Buddhist history such as exist in THERAVADIN and Mahayana Buddhist cultures as in Japan or Thailand. Local practitioners as a result are not particularly respected in Nepal.

Newar Buddhism probably dates to the time of ASOKA (d. 232 or 238 B.C.E.). During the late 12th century, when the great Buddhist centers of learning in India were under attack, a surge of refugees moved into Nepal, introducing another form of Buddhism, Pala Vajrayana. By the mid-1400s, when Buddhism finally died out in India, Newar Buddhism adjusted its identity to see itself as a separate tradition. The Newar texts dating from that time are in fact the last Sanskrit Buddhist sutras ever produced anywhere. These texts mix elements of Mahayana and Vajrayana thought.

A modern Nepal state was formed under Gorkha leadership from 1768. This regime was antagonistic to Buddhism. As a result many Buddhists took Hindu names, and Newar Buddhism began a long decline.

In the 20th century Buddhism in Nepal took on new life. While traditional Newar Buddhism is still practiced by the Vajracarya priests, it is a secret transmission. In contrast, a form of Newar Theravada has developed in Nepal, from the 1930s. And, since 1959, Tibetan Buddhism has been influential as many refugees entered Nepal.

Finally, Nepal's status as a center for Western and Japanese "seekers" has added to the eclectic mix.

Two sites in Nepal are of particular importance in Newar Buddhism. The first is the STUPA (*caitya*) of Svayambhu. The second is the Lokesvara figure at Bungamati.

Further reading: David N. Gellner, *Monk, Householder, and Tantric Priest: Newar Buddhism and Its Hierarchy of Ritual* (London: Cambridge University Press, 1992); Todd T. Lewis, *Popular Buddhist Texts from Nepal: Narratives and Rituals of Newar Buddhism* (Albany: SUNY Press, 2000); John K. Locke, "Unique Features of Newar Buddhism." Nagarjuna Institute of Exact Methods. Available online. URL: www.hagarjunainstitute.com/articles/unique_features.htm. Accessed on October 1, 2005; Alexander von Rospatt, "On the Conception of Stupa in Vajrayana Buddhism: The Example of the Svayambhucaitya of Kathmandu." *Journal of the Nepal Research Centre* 11 (1999): 121–147; Min Bahadur Shakya, "A Study of Traditional Vajrayana Buddhism in Nepal." Lotus Research Centre. Available online. URL: www.lrcnepal.org/papers/nbcp-ppr-3.htm. Accessed on October 1, 2005.

New Kadampa Tradition

New Kadampa Tradition (NKT) is an international Tibetan Buddhist organization in the GELUG tradition founded in the 1970s by the Venerable Geshe Kelsang Gyatso (1931–   ). He was among many Tibetan leaders who fled Tibet at the time of the Chinese takeover. In 1977, he was invited to England, where he has remained the resident teacher at the Manjushri Mahayana Buddhist Centre to the present. It was from that post that he turned the NKT into the largest Buddhist group in the United Kingdom and founded affiliated centers across Europe and North America.

The NKT's name recalls the work of ATISA (982–1054) and his disciple Dromton (1088–1164), who led a revival and reformation of Buddhism in Tibet in the 11th century. The KADAMPA school they founded was eventually absorbed into the GELUG school in the 15th century. The NKT was shaped to present the authentic Tibetan teachings in a way that would communicate with a new generation of Western believers.

Soon after moving to England, Geshe Kelsang Gyatso became involved in a controversy with the DALAI LAMA, the head of the Gelug school and head of the Tibetan Government-in-Exile. On July 13, 1978, Dalai Lama made a speech in which he denigrated the veneration of Dorje Shugden. Dorje Shugden is acknowledged as one of the tradition's dharma protectors, that is, an emanation of a BODHISATTVA who acts to avert any obstacles that block practitioners from reaching their spiritual goals. The Dalai Lama continued to speak out against the veneration of Dorje Shugden through the 1980s and actions were taken against those in the Gelug school who continued the once-popular practice. The discussion of Dorje Shugden reached a new height in 1996, when the Dalai Lama declared the dharma protector to be an evil Chinese spirit who was blocking Tibetan independence.

At this point, many, of whom Geshe Kelsang Gyatso was the most prominent, felt that the Dalai Lama had departed from traditional faith and practice. He placed the NKT in opposition to the Dalai Lama and his leadership and became very visible when NKT members protested his 1996 visit to England. In subsequent public appearances, the Dalai Lama faced demonstrations organized by the NKT. Though the heat of the controversy has lessened, the issue continues to divide the Gelug community.

Further reading: Stephen Batchelor, "Letting Daylight into Magic: The Life and Times of Dorje Shugden," *Tricycle: The Buddhist Review* 7, no. 3 (Spring 1998): 60–66; David Kay, "The New Kadampa Tradition and the Continuity of Tibetan Buddhism in Transition," *Journal of Contemporary Religion* 12, no. 3 (October 1997): 277–293; Geshe Kelsang Gyatso, *Buddhism in the Tibetan Tradition: A Guide* (London: Tharpa, 1984); ———, *Clear Light of Bliss: Mahamudra in Vajrayana*

Buddhism (London: Tharpa, 1982); ———, *Heart Jewel: The Essential Practices of Kadampa Buddhism* (London: Tharpa, 1997).

Nichiren (1222–1282) *Japanese Buddhist teacher and founder of Nichiren school of Buddhism*

Nichiren, the founder of the Japanese Buddhist tradition named after him, emerged in the 13th century as an advocate of the superiority of the LOTUS SUTRA and the practice of calling upon the Buddha through the sutra by reciting the mantra *nam-myoho-renge-kyo*. Nichiren believed that *nam-myoho-renge-kyo* was the essence of the Lotus Sutra's teachings.

Nichiren was born Zennichi-maro in Tojo Village, Awa Province, Japan. He was 11 when he began to study TENDAI BUDDHISM at a nearby temple. After ordination as a monk in 1237, he moved to KAMAKURA. He became convinced of the central Tendai teaching that the Lotus Sutra contained the highest Buddhist teachings and hence was superior to all the other Buddhist sutras. He also gradually concluded that he was now entrusted with the mission of Bodhisattva Superior Practices, to whom the Lotus Sutra assigns the task of propagating the Dharma in the Latter Days. That task included not only touting the superiority of the Lotus Sutra but pointing out the errors of other Buddhist groups.

He launched his mission in 1253 at Seicho-ji by preaching a sermon on the Lotus Sutra and taking the name *Nichiren* (sun lotus). This sermon included an attack on the currently expanding practice of reciting the NEMBUTSU (calling upon AMITABHA Buddha) being advocated by the Pure Land Buddhists. Nichiren, ever direct and harsh in his criticism, was subject to an immediate reaction by local Pure Land believers and quickly left for Kamakura. Over the next several years he gained an initial following and attracted the first members of what would become an inner core of monk disciples.

In 1260 Nichiren offered a treatise, *On Establishing the Correct Teaching for the Peace of the Land,* to government authorities. He suggested the disasters were due to widespread slander of true Buddhism by the Pure Land Buddhist and others. When word of the content got out, an angry crowd attacked Nichiren's dwelling and drove him from the city. When he tried to return, the shogunate imposed formal exile. He remained in exile on the Izu Peninsula for three years.

By 1268 he was back in Kamakura and wrote a letter noting that he had eight years earlier predicted the current threatened invasion by the Mongols. When a drought hit in 1271, he publicly denounced the ability of Ryokan, a leading Shingon Buddhist in Kamakura, to have any role in ending the drought. In reaction, Nichiren was arrested and threatened with execution. In the end he was again exiled. Returning to Kamakura in 1274, he turned down an offer by the shogunate to set him up on an equal footing with the other Buddhist schools. In his opinion he represented superior teachings, not just another variant set of Buddhist teachings. He left Kamakura for Mt. Minobu.

At Mt. Minobu he concentrated on writing and on training the inner core of disciples. Among the most important events during these years was his inscription (1279) of the giant mandalalike Object of Worship, the GOHONZON. He dedicated it for the attainment of Buddhahood by all humanity.

After his death, the care of his tomb on Mt. Minobu occasioned a split among his disciples. One of the six, NIKKO, broke with his brethren and established himself separately at a temple near Mt. Fuji. The effort of the five disciples would be carried forward by the NICHIREN SHOSHU. That group would in turn nurture the formation of a 20th-century lay organization, now known as SOKA GAKKAI INTERNATIONAL, which has in recent decades taken Nichiren's faith into most of the world's countries.

Further reading: Anesaki Masaharu. *Nichiren, the Buddhist Prophet* (Boston: Harvard University Press, 1916); Daniel B. Montgomery, *Fire in the Lotus: The Dynamic*

Buddhism of Nichiren (London: Harper-Collins, 1991); Nichiren, *The Writing of Nichiren Daishonin* (Tokyo: Soka Gakkai, 2003); Bruno Petzold, *Buddhist Prophet Nichiren: A Lotus in the Sun* (Tokyo: Hokke Janaru, 1978); Laurel Rasplica Rodd, ed., *Nichiren: Selected Writings* (Honolulu: University of Hawaii Press, 1980); Philip B. Yampolsky, *Selected Writings of Nichiren* (New York: Columbia University Press, 1990).

Nichiren Shoshu

Nichiren Shoshu is a branch of the Nichiren school, founded by one of Nichiren's disciples, NIKKO (1246–1333). After the death of Nichiren (1222–82), the six disciples he named to take charge of his movement built a tomb for their departed master on Mt. Minobu and agreed to take turns guarding it. In 1285 one of the six, Nikko, called attention to its neglect and took up residence on Mt. Minobu until a dispute with Hakii Sanenaga, a leading lay follower who was also a powerful figure in the region, forced his departure. Nikko settled near Mt. Fuji, where he built a temple, Taiseki-ji, and found some lay support. Over the next years, he became alienated from the other five Nichiren leaders.

Nikko's following became known as the Fuji school of Nichiren and through the years became the most conservative of the many divisions into which Nichiren Buddhism fell. In 1876, after the MEIJI RESTORATION, eight major temples of the Nikko lineage, including Taiseki-ji, united and formalized the establishment of what was termed the Essential Teachings school of Nichiren Buddhism. In 1899, however, Taiseki-ji withdrew from the Essential Teachings school and assumed the name *Fuji branch of the Nichiren school*. In 1912, this group took the name *Nichiren Shoshu*.

Nichiren Shoshu was a relatively small Nichiren group when in 1930, two lay converts, TSUNESABURO MAKIGUCHI (1871–1944) and JOSEI TODA (1900–58), founded an education-oriented lay society called Soka Kyoiku Gakkai (Value-Creating Education Society). Makiguchi and Toda ran into conflict with the demands of the Japanese government as World War II began and eventually were arrested. Makiguchi died in prison, but Toda survived the war and began the rebuilding of Soka Gakkai, which became a large international organization through the last half of the 20th century. As Soka Gakkai grew, so did Nichiren Shoshu, which founded a number of temples in countries such as the United States where Soka Gakkai had great success. While most Soka Gakkai members had little to do with temple worship, the Nichiren Shoshu priests performed an essential role by supplying replicas of the GOHONZON, the Object of Worship, to them.

In the late 1980s, the leadership of Nichiren Shoshu and what had by this time become SOKA GAKKAI INTERNATIONAL (SGI), came into conflict. SGI had been a controversial organization, as tension emerged from its high-pressure recruitment tactics, while most of its members did not show any loyalty to the priestly leadership of Nichiren Shoshu. As the conflict continued, the charges made by each side against the other multiplied. The issues climaxed in 1991 when the head of

Signpost for Nichiren Shoshu Myosen-ji, Silver Spring, Maryland *(Institute for the Study of American Religion, Santa Barbara, California)*

the Nichiren Shoshu excommunicated the international president, DAISAKU IKEDA (1928–) and the SGI leadership. Subsequently, the two organizations went their separate ways.

As the dust settled from the break between SGI and Nichiren Shoshu, the latter found itself with some 700 temples in Japan and 21 temples and outreach centers outside the country, including six temples in the United States.

Further reading: Tasiji Kirimura, *Fundamentals of Buddhism* (Tokyo: Nichiren Shoshu Center, 1977); *The Liturgy of Nichiren Shoshu* (Etiwanda, Calif.: Nichiren Shoshu Temple, 1979).

Niguma (11th century) *female yoga master*

Niguma was a teacher who practiced and conveyed to her pupils a path that centered on "Relying on the Body of Another Person" as a means of enlightenment, an obvious reference to sexual tantrism. Niguma was a student and consort of the Indian Vajrayana Buddhist teacher Naropa (1016–1100). To her he imparted the teachings known as the six yogas. As she matured, she became a teacher in her own right and was viewed as an enlightened one, a *dakini*.

Niguma's teachings were carried to Tibet by Khyungpo Naljor (978–1079), the founder of the Shangpa subschool of the Kagyu Tibetan Buddhist school. According to the tradition, when he arrived at Niguma's residence (she lived in a burial ground), she appeared to him in the sky dancing and wearing decoration made of human bones, an apparition not unlike that offered by the goddess Kali to her disciples.

Originally circulating as a set of oral instructions, they were finally written down in the 16th century by the second DALAI LAMA, GENDUN GYATSO (1475–1542), who is said to have received the teachings directly from Niguma in a dream. As appropriated by the Dalai Lama, the teachings are clearly describing the use of sexual intercourse as a tool for progress in the spiritual life.

Further reading: Gendun Gyatso, *Selected Works of the Dalai Lama II: The Tantric Yogas of Sister Niguma*. Translated by Glenn Mullin (Ithaca, N.Y.: Snow Lion, 1985).

Nihonshoki   See KOJIKI AND NIHONSHOKI.

nikaya

Nikaya is, literally, "corpus." In terms of the Buddhist canon, the TRIPITAKA, "The Nikayas" refers to the early sutras. For the Pali canon that means the entire *sutta-pitaka*, which is divided into five Nikayas. For the Mahayana canon, *nikaya* is roughly equivalent to the *agamas*. Because of its close association with the Pali canon, the phrase *Nikaya Buddhism* is sometimes used as a term to refer to Theravada, or "early," Buddhism. *Nikaya* also means a "fraternity," "branch," or "sect" when used in Sri Lanka and Thailand to describe major divisions in the *sangha*.

Nikko (1246–1333) *founder of Nichiren Shoshu*

Nikko, one of NICHIREN'S primary disciples and the founder of what today is known as NICHIREN SHOSHU, was born in Kajikazawa in Kai Province, Japan. In his youth he entered a temple of the Tendai sect and took his training in Buddhism and Chinese literature. In 1258, he visited another Tendai temple at Iwamoto and there met Nichiren (1222–82), the great Japanese Buddhist prophet. He became Nichiren's close disciple and accompanied him on his several periods of exile. He also made the arrangements for Nichiren to move to Mt. Minobu where Nichiren would spend his last days.

Nichiren died in 1282. Shortly before his death, he designated six of his elder monks to direct the movement that had grown up around him: Nissho (1221–1323), Nichiro (1245–1320), Niko (1253–1314), Nitccho (1252–1317), Nichiji (1250–?), and Nikko (1246–1333). Each of these elders headed a center in a different part of Japan.

These six agreed upon the enshrining of Nichiren's cremated remains in Kuon-ji (the Temple of Eternity) on Mt. Minobu and subsequently provided for someone to guard the reliquary, maintain the temple grounds, and provide instruction in Nichiren's teachings to the younger disciples at the mountain site. The arrangements included the regular appearance at the temple of each of the six during different parts of the year.

The agreement soon fell apart as most of the six stopped traveling to Mt. Minobu and the shrine fell into disrepair. Since Nikko was closest to the mountain, he soon assumed custodial duties and was joined by Niko, who was in charge of the instructions to disciples. The two soon fell out, however, over the strictness with which Nichiren's teachings should be followed. The situation was aroused by some actions of a wealthy patron of the shrine. Among the issues that bothered Nikko was the willingness of Nichiren's followers to install statues of Gautama Buddha in the temples. As the quarrel heated up, Nikko left Kuon-ji. He later established Taiseki-ji, a temple located at the foot of Mt. Fuji in Suruga Province. From this temple, his following and the lineage of priests that grew from his work would be named the *Fuji school of the Nichiren sect,* and later the *Nichiren Shoshu.* In fact, each of the six elder disciples created a Nichiren lineage that only merged as a single organization in the 20th century.

Nikko founded a seminary at Omosu, not far from the Fuji Temple, in 1298. He moved to the seminary and there lived the rest of his life. He died in 1333.

In the years immediately prior to Nichiren's death, Nikko reportedly recorded a set of lectures given by Nichiren to his six primary disciples. In 1287 Nikko obtained Nichiren's seal of endorsement for his transcript. This manuscript would later be published in Japanese as The Record of Orally Transmitted Teachings. The Nichiren Shoshu consider this volume a part of Nichiren teaching material. Some controversy has arisen about the authenticity of this work, as no mention of it occurs independently in the 16th century.

Further reading: Alicia Matsunaga and Daigan Matsunaga, *Foundation of Japanese Buddhism* (Los Angeles: Buddhist Books International, 1976); Paul Wersant, trans. and ed., "Record of the Orally Transmitted Teachings of Nichiren Daishonin." Buddhist Information of North America. Available online. URL: http://www.buddhistinformation.com/record_of_the_orally_transmitted.htm. Accessed on September 15, 2005.

nirmanakaya

Nirmanakaya refers to the "transformation body" of the Buddha. In the Mahayana TRIKAYA concept, this is the body in which the Buddha appeared to others. It is not a true physical body, however, merely the appearance of one.

Further reading: David Snellgrove, *Indo-Tibetan Buddhism,* Vol. 1. Boston: Shambala, 1987.

nirodha

Nirodha, "the cessation of DUKKHA," is the third of the Buddha's FOUR NOBLE TRUTHS. It promises a way to freedom from *dukkha,* suffering. That route to freedom is nirvana. Attaining NIRVANA means the extinction of TANHA, or cravings. The Buddha states, "A person so endowed is endowed with the absolute wisdom, for the knowledge of the extinction of all *dukkha* is the absolute noble wisdom." Thus the solution to the never-ending chain of SAMSARA is to realize nirvana.

The Buddha describes a state of the fully realized person who has perceived nirvana, all complexes and cravings eliminated; the enlightened person achieves a full and lasting happiness in this lifetime. This is the promise of *nirodha.*

Further reading: Thera Piyadassi, *The Buddha's Ancient Path* (1964. Reprint, Taipei: Corporate Body of the Buddha Educational Foundation, n.d.); *The Teaching* *of the Buddha* (Tokyo: Bukko Dendo Kyokai, 2001); Geshe Tashi Tsering, *The Four Noble Truths*. Vol. 1, *The Foundation of Buddhist Thought* (Somerville, Mass.: Wisdom, 2005).

nirvana/*nibbana*

Nirvana literally means "extinction," as when a candle's flame is extinguished. In Buddhist thought, nirvana has a very specific meaning and is perhaps the most misunderstood Buddhist concept among people of other religious traditions. Nirvana is not an "absence" or lack. It is instead a state of being. Nirvana is strictly defined as a state without conditioned aspects. Nirvana is without arising, subsisting, changing, or passing away.

In Hindu thought nirvana is a state of liberation from individuality and the suffering of SAMSARA, the cycle of birth and death. But it also assumes the individuality is lost through merger with the divine, or Brahman. Buddhist thought carries a similar sense of the extinction of the individual consciousness and liberation from samsara. But the early Buddhist philosophers took the concept in a new direction by carefully describing the states a person passes through on the path of Buddhist cultivation. Buddhist nirvana assumes the individual overcomes desire, hate, and delusion, the three poisons, and is no longer subject to the dictates of KARMA. This formulation is found throughout the PALI scriptures.

MAHAYANA writers took the idea of nirvana in a new direction. Mahayana practitioners concluded that nirvana was equivalent to and existed concurrently with samsara; the two states are at bottom indistinguishable.

Nirvana is often depicted as "bliss" or the cessation of suffering, DUKKHA. These are all senses in accord with the basic sense of nirvana as being a state without the conditioning aspects—arising, subsisting, changing, or passing. Some Westerners, however, saw nirvana as a nihilistic goal, a complete annihilation of consciousness, a con-

notation that many people found troubling. Buddhists, to the contrary, insist that the idea of nirvana should not lead to despondency. Nirvana is a condition in which suffering is not present, its most appealing aspect. Nirvana, in conclusion, is the goal of Buddhist practice and the culmination of the long process of self-cultivation.

Further reading: K. N. Jayatilleke, *The Message of the Buddha* (New York: Free Press, 1974); Rune E. A. Johansson, *The Psychology of Nirvana* (Garden City, N.Y.: Doubleday, 1970); David J. Kalupahana, *Buddhist Philosophy: A Historical Analysis* (Honolulu: University Press of Hawaii, 1976); F. Theodore Stcherbatsky, *The Conception of Buddhist Nirvana* (New York: Samuel Weiser, 1978); Guy Richard Welbon, *The Buddhist Nirvana and Its Western Interpreters* (Chicago: University of Chicago Press, 1968).

Nirvana Sutra (Mahaparinirvana Sutra)

Translated accurately as the "Sutra of the Great Decease," the two works by this title are said to be the final sermon of the Buddha before his entry into nirvana. There are two versions of the Nirvana Sutra. The older, in Pali, is normally written "Maha-parinibbanasuttanta." The Mahayana version is the "Mahaparinirvanasutra." Today in English it is common to refer to the "Nirvana Sutra," but it is important to distinguish between the Pali and the Mahayana works, since the two are separate texts.

The Maha-parinibbanasuttanta is a Pali text that probably dates from the period of ASOKA, around 250 years after the Buddha's *parinirvana*. It relates the Buddha's final days. Beginning in Rajagaha, the Buddha moved to Patali, a village, where he lectured on the moral life, before proceeding to Koti. Then he settled in the village of Natika. Later, he took a large group of BHIKSUs to Vesali, then to Veluva, where he fell ill. At Vesali the Buddha decided to proceed to the final stage of *parinirvana* and die in three months. He assembled the sangha and informed them of his decision.

He then continued to teach, moving to Bhanda, Bhoga, and Pava. He finally prepared his deathbed while at Kusinara, in a grove of sal trees.

The Maha-parinibbanasuttanta is part of the Digha-nikaya, the Long Discourses, one of the four divisions of the Pali Sutta-pitaka, those listing the teachings of the Buddha. The Maha-parinibbanasuttanta contains six chapters. The text exists in four Chinese versions as well as in the Pali—in Chinese the *nikayas* of the Pali canon are called the Agama-sutras—and the two languages' versions agree without major differences.

The Mahayana Mahaparinirvana Sutra was a grand collection of sutras most probably produced in the Kashmir region between 200 and 400 C.E. It was translated into Chinese by Faxian, in a six-volume work. Fragments of Sanskrit versions have been found, but not the entire work in Sanskrit. Unlike the Pali Maha-parinibbanasuttanta, the Mahaprinirvana Sutra mentions the idea that the DHARMA (the Buddha's teachings) will be degraded. The Buddha is said to predict that MARA, the Buddhist equivalent of the devil, will gradually destroy the Dharma after 700 years. Since the Gupta dynasty in India (320–520 C.E.) did in fact favor Hinduism over Buddhism, it is not unlikely that the sutra was written during this period of decline and persecution in Indian Buddhism. This idea of decline struck a chord in China also, since the period prior to the reunification of China under the Sui and Tang dynasties (581–618 and 618–907 C.E., respectively) was characterized by great uncertainty and political change.

The Mahaparinirvana Sutra introduced other key elements of Mahayana thought as well. It taught that the Buddha's Cosmic Body, the Buddhakaya, is eternal. In addition, every person has Buddhahood, or *buddhadhatu*. The text is also quite partisan: it elevates Mahayana teachings and casts aspersions on the teachings of other schools. It even recommends that those who slander Mahayana should be punished severely, something rarely seen in Buddhist sutras.

The Mahaparinirvana Sutra was extremely influential in China. A "school," actually more a field of interest than a formally organized tradition, formed around its study. This work can also be said to have begun the Chinese practice of classifying teachings (*pan jiao*). This arose because of the Nirvana Sutra's claim to be the Buddha's final words. If this claim was accepted, then other sutras could be classified as belonging to other stages or periods of the Buddha's life. Eventually all schools of Chinese Buddhism developed competing versions of classificatory schemes.

Further reading: Kogen Mizuno, *Essentials of Buddhism: Basic Terminology and Concepts of Buddhist Philosophy and Practice.* Translated by Gaynor Sekimori (1972. Reprint, Tokyo: Kosei, 1996); Hajime Nakamura, *Indian Buddhism: A Survey with Bibliographical Notes* (1980. Reprint, Delhi: Motilal Banarsidass, 1996).

nonaction (*wuwei*)

Nonaction is a key virtue in the writings of LAOZI. The wise ruler or "sage," according to Laozi, must adhere to a policy of nonaction. Such a policy will prevent the negative effects of the rulers' own desires on reality, and the resultant disorder. The ruler will practice self-cultivation, which will in turn result in his taking no such coarse actions as taxation or war. The *Laozi* (*Daodejing*) emphasizes the contrast between nonaction and action characterized by desire. The first major commentator on the *Laozi*, WANG BI, emphasized this as one of the first principles governing the universe. Dao, in fact, is characterized by nonaction, as should be people's actions. This concept in fact sums up the political principles advocated by the early Daoist thinkers, and it illustrates the immense gap separating Daoism from Confucian ideas of governance.

Further reading: Alan K. L. Chan, "The Daodejing and Its Tradition, in Livia Kohn, ed., *Daoism Handbook* (Leiden, Boston, and Koln: Bill, 2000), 1–29.

non-self *See* ANATMAN.

Nu Gua (Nu Kua) *feminine creator of mankind and founder of marriage in Chinese mythology*
A mythical Chinese deity, Nu Gua (or Nu Wa) was born with the separation of heaven and earth. She then created individual humans from mud. She was the companion of FU XI, the mythical creator of the eight trigrams collected in the *Book of Changes*. Nu Gua's symbol is a compass. She also taught humanity how to tame wild animals and control water.

Further reading: Keith G. Stevens, *Chinese Mythological Gods* (London: Oxford University Press, 2001)

Nyanaponika Thera (1901–1994) *cofounder of the Buddhist Publication Society*
Nyanaponika Thera, a prominent contemporary Theravada Buddhist monk, was born Siegmund Feniger into a Jewish family in Hanauam-Main, Germany. He found his way to Buddhism through reading and in the early 1920s moved to Berlin, where he associated with the early circle of German Buddhists at the Buddhistische Haus headed by Paul Dahlke (1865–1928). He later formed and led a Buddhist study circle in Konigsberg, East Prussia.

In 1936, Feniger traveled to Sri Lanka, where he received his initial ordination as a Buddhist monk at the Island Hermitage at Dodanduwa, where he became the pupil of a fellow German, NYANATILOKA MAHATHERA. He became a fully ordained BHIKSU the next year.

As a German, he was interned during World War II by British authorities and unable to move back to Sri Lanka immediately after the war, and he moved about for several years. In 1951, he accompanied his teacher to Burma for the Sixth Buddhist Council and afterward became an active leader in the WORLD FEDERATION OF BUDDHISTS. In 1952 he was finally able to return to Sri Lanka and he settled at the Forest Hermitage in Kandy, Sri Lanka, where he would live for the next several decades. In 1958 he became the cofounder and first president of the Buddhist Publication Society. He remained as editor until 1984 and as president to 1988. He was succeeded in both offices by BHIKKHU BODHI.

During his long career he was the author of a number of books. He died in 1994 at the age of 93.

Further reading: Buddha Dharma Education Association and Dharmanet. "Profiles of Theravada Buddhists." Available online. URL: http://www.buddhanet.net/e-learning/history/theravada.htm. Accessed on February 12, 2005; Nyanaponika Thera, *The Heart of Buddhist Meditation: A Handbook of Mental Training Based on the Buddha's Way of Mindfulness* (London: Rider, 1962); ———, *The Power of Mindfulness* (San Francisco: Unity Press, 1972); ———, *The Vision of Dhamma: Buddhist Writings of Nyanaponika Thera* (Kandy, Sri Lanka: Buddhist Publication Society, 1994); ———, Helmuth Hecker, and Bhakkhu Bodhi, eds., *Great Disciples of the Buddha: Their Lives, Their Works, Their Legacy* (London: C. W. Daniel, 1997).

Nyanatiloka Mahathera (Walter Florus Gueth) (1878–1957) *German-born Theravada monk and Pali scholar*
Walter Gueth first made contact with Buddhism during a trip to India and Sri Lanka and in 1903 took his vows as a Buddhist monk in Burma. He then took the Buddhist name *Nyanatiloka*. He founded a monastery in Sri Lanka in 1911, at Ratgama Lake, Dodanduwa, which over the years hosted many Western Buddhist practitioners. At the outbreak of the First World War he was expelled from Sri Lanka and traveled to the United States, China, and Japan. In 1920 he taught at Komazawa University in Japan. He returned to Sri Lanka in 1926. As a German national he was interned during World War II, and he finally returned in 1946. Because of his many translations Nyanatiloka was an influential scholar as well as teacher.

Further reading: Nyanatiloka, *Buddhist Dictionary: A Manual of Buddhist Terms and Doctrines* (Colombo, Sri Lanka: Buddhist Publication Society, 1972); ———, *A Guide through the Abhidhamma Pitaka* (Kandy, Sri Lanka: Buddhist Publication Society, 1971).

Nyingma

One of the four branches of Tibetan Buddhism, Nyingma Buddhism teaches that DZOGCHEN, or "the great perfection," is the most important doctrine in Buddhism and the final, complete teaching of the Buddha. A Dzogchen practitioner holds pure awareness at all times. Nyingma is, literally, the "school of the ancients." It probably includes the oldest Buddhist teachings transmitted to Tibet from India in the eighth century C.E. by PADMASAMBHAVA and his followers, in the first wave of transmission of Buddhism to Tibet.

There are three lineages within the Nyingma. The *kama* (utterance), or historical, lineage is for teachings from SAMANTABHADRA that were passed from teacher to student in succession. The TERMA, or direct, lineage is for all texts hidden away by Padmasambhava that could later be recovered and taught. The *Bardo thodol*, or the Tibetan BOOK OF THE DEAD, is the most famous example of such teachings. And the third lineage, the visionary, involves direct communication with a past teacher who has already passed away.

The Nyingma school is popularly called the Red Hats because their monastics wear red hats in ceremonies. However, there has always been a tradition of Nyingma lay, or nonmonastic, practice in addition to the monastic tradition.

Nyingma monasteries were built from the 15th century in such locations as Mindroling, Dorje Drag, Palyul, Dzogchen, and Zhechen, in Kham Province of Tibet, and at Dodrupchen and Darthang in Amdo Province. Since 1949 additional Nyingma monasteries have been set up in India.

At this time the highest-ranking member of the Nyingma is Penor Rinpoche.

Further reading: Government of Tibet in Exile. "The Nyingmapa Tradition." Available online. URL: http://www.tibet.com/Buddhism/nyingma.html. Accessed on February 12, 2005; Dudjom Rinpoche and Jikdrel Yeshe Dorje, *The Nyingma School of Tibetan Buddhism: Its Fundamentals and History.* 2 vols. Translated by Gyurme Dorje (Boston, Mass.: Wisdom, 1991); Khetsun Sangpo Rinbochay, *Tantric Practice in Nying-ma.* Translated by Jeffrey Hopkins (Ithaca, N.Y.: Snow Lion, 1996); Tulku Thondup Rinpoche, *Hidden Teachings of Tibet: An Explanation of the Nyingma School of Buddhism.* Edited by Harold Talbott (London: Wisdom, 1986)

O

Obaku Zen

Along with RINZAI ZEN and SOTO ZEN, Obaku is one of the three recognized schools of Zen Buddhism. Though less well known in the West than the other Zen schools, Obaku Zen is an important element in the Japanese religious community. Obaku is unique in that it has maintained a strong Chinese character for most of its history; the first 13 abbots of Manpuku-ji, the head temple, were Chinese, and to this day many Obaku practices reflect Ming era Chinese Buddhist customs, including an emphasis on sutra chanting.

Obaku's origins can be traced back to 17th-century China. With the fall of the Ming dynasty in China in 1644, many people displaced by the shift in political power fled to Japan. In 1654, at the request of some Chinese residents of Nagasaki, Yin Yuan (1592–1673), a prominent Chan/Zen teacher, known in Japan as INGEN, moved to Japan. In China Ingen had been the abbot of Wan Fu temple on Mt. Huangbo (*Obaku* in Japanese). In 1661 he had an audience with the shogun, Tokugawa Ietsuna (1641–80), who gave him land and money to build a temple in the Uji District, near Kyoto; Ingen named the temple *Mampuki-ji.* Mampuki-ji continues to be the head temple of Obaku Zen today.

Mampuki-ji became the center for the development of Ingen's variation on Rinzai Zen, which included an emphasis on the veneration of AMITABHA and chanting of the *NEMBUTSU,* practices associated with the PURE LAND school. During the years of the Tokugawa shogunate, Zen was an especially privileged form of Buddhism in Japan. Within a century, more than 400 Obaku Zen centers had been established across the country.

Mampuki-ji also became the center of a new diffusion of Chinese art and culture in Japan. The temple was built using Ming style architectural forms, and its Chinese residents introduced Chinese painting, crafts, and cooking. The influence of the new group was multiplied as priests from the Soto and Rinzai schools flocked to Uji to study the new teachings. In the late 20th century, the Obaku school was headed for more than three decades by Okuda Roshi, a renowned calligrapher.

Most recently there has been some merging between Rinzai and Obaku Zen elements, with a Joint Council for Japanese Rinzai and Obaku Zen established.

Further reading: Stephen Addiss and Kwan S. Wong, *Obaku, Zen Painting and Calligraphy* (Lawrence, Kans.: Helen Foresman Spencer Museum of Art, 1978); Helen

J. Baroni, *Obaku Zen: The Emergence of the Third Sect of Zen in Tokugawa Japan* (Honolulu: University of Hawaii Press, 2000); Kazuo Kasahara, ed., *A History of Japanese Religion*. Translated by Paul McCarthy and Gaynor Sekimori (Tokyo: Kosei, 2001).

Okinawa, religions in

Okinawa is the largest island of the Ryukyus, a chain of islands that stretch from Japan to Taiwan. The Ryukyuan Kingdom (1422–1879), centered in Shuri on the island of Okinawa, skillfully plied the trade routes and its people created a distinctive spiritual and cultural sensibility from diverse influences.

Okinawa was home to an indigenous primal religion centered on belief in the *kami* spirits. Over the centuries, Daoism, Buddhism, and Shinto all spread to Okinawa, and today the island's religious life somewhat reflects its history; the Japanese influence that has dominated recent centuries is most pronounced. A spectrum of Japanese Buddhism can now be found on the island.

HISTORY

Okinawa emerges out of prehistory in the seventh century when China extended its influence to the island. China ruled Okinawa until overthrown by Okinawans in the 12th century. Five centuries of self-rule ended with the entry of the Japanese at the beginning of the 17th century. From 1609 through the 1870s, although an Okinawan king ruled, samurai from Satsuma in Japan exercised hegemony over Okinawa. This authority would be passed to the Meiji emperor. In 1879, the emperor dissolved the Okinawan royal government and formally incorporated Okinawa into Japan.

Okinawa became the site of one of the most deadly battles of World War II. The Americans won control some two months before the Japanese surrender. In 1951 the United States assumed complete administrative control of the Ryukyus, which were passed back to Japan in 1972. Okinawa now exists as a prefectural district of Japan, though there is still a strong American military presence.

INDIGENOUS RELIGION AND *KAMI*

The outlines of indigenous beliefs must be extrapolated from the *Omorosōshi,* an anthology of ancient shamanic and folk lyrics that reflect the aspirations of the Okinawans, their relations and feelings toward with nature and the KAMI, or gods. "Worship of the sunrise" (*Omorosōshi* XIII78823) reveals a reverence for nature and conveys a deep sense of gratitude. "Great Master of the East," it states, "Let us all be of one mind before you. And say, 'How revered! How august!'" The "Great Master of the East" refers to the Sun; both the "east" and the "Sun" refer to *niraee kananee* (Japanese, *nirai kanai*), the home of the *kami,* the ancestral spirits, who give happiness, riches, and knowledge on visits to their earthly descendants. The ancestral *kami* have the capacity to supervise, influence, and alter events. Individuals and families have an obligation to observe memorials and other rituals at appropriate intervals. Should the family neglect its responsibilities, the ancestral spirit(s) may seek retribution on progeny through some unusual or ominous event.

The *kami* are contacted at the *utaki* (Japanese, *otake*), or sacred grove, a prominent feature in Okinawan life, associated with the memory of the earliest ancestors. Today villagers identify their *utaki* with the burial site of their founder, who with the passage of time has become deified as a protector *kami.* Even today the village priestesses perform their sacrifices, offer prayers of gratitude, and solicit favors of good harvest at the *utaki.*

Such village rituals correspond with rituals performed by the *chifijin* (Japanese, *kikoe-ogimi*), the national priestesses, at Seefa Utaki, the spot where the earliest ancestors arrived before migrating to other parts of the island. Every village, except those that were established in more recent times, has a sacred grove. The founding family—*niiya* (Japanese, *neya*), or root house—

provides the village's political and administrative leadership through the root man, *nichu* (Japanese, *nebito*), and its spiritual authority through the root deity, *nigan* (Japanese, *negami*), a female, usually the sister of the *nichu*. The *nigan* oversaw the ritual observances.

Historically, this brother-sister dual sovereignty system served as the model for administering the Ryūkyūan kingdom. The king held sway over political matters and his sister counterpart served as the national priestess. Both worked closely together to ensure the welfare of the nation. The power of the *chifijin* waned with the growing influence of Confucianism and was systematically undermined after the Japanese annexation. The last chief priestess died in 1944.

Until the introduction of the Buddhist altar in the 18th century, the *fii nu kang* was the primary deity enshrined in the home. Three stones placed in an altar of sand represent the most distant ancestor and family continuity. The shrine is located on the lower left corner of the main room of the house; it is part of the ancestral shrine. More recently three small stones are placed in a ceramic censer filled with ashes beside the kitchen stove. The female occupants of the house make offerings to ancestors and *fii nu kang* on the first and the 15th days of each month. Scholars trace the *fii nu kang* to the Chinese STOVE GOD.

If the family fails in its observances to the *kami* and suffers misfortune, the individual or family may wish to consult a *yuta* (shaman, usually female), whose powers of clairvoyance and possession qualify her to discern the causes of misfortune and to suggest or direct remedial action.

While the *yuta* are believed to be selected by the gods, the *kaminchu* and *nuru* (Japanese, *noro*), the principal village ritual functionaries, are hereditary positions. The *kaminchu* is a priestess who handles ritual. Originally they also underwent possession, but today they focus solely on ritual performance. The *nuru*, "divine priestesses," continue to serve the function of contacting ancestors and giving spiritual advice. During the Ryukyuan Kingdom these shaman types were organized nationally and headed by the *chifjin*.

BUDDHISM IN OKINAWA

The Rinzai Zen Buddhists erected the most impressive Buddhist temple complex on Okinawa. Enkaku-ji was for many years the family temple of the Okinawan king. It is located on the grounds of Shurijo Castle (now a park). It was built in the 1490s by King Sho Shin in honor of his father. It suffered greatly in the battle to take Okinawa during World War II but has been restored.

THE MARTIAL ARTS IN OKINAWA

It appears that in the middle of the 18th century Shaolin Kung Fu, the form of the martial arts developed by Chan Buddhist monks in China, spread to the court in Okinawa. Over the next years, the Chinese style of fighting mixed with a local style of hand-to-hand combat called *te* (hand). The Okinawans were motivated to develop the martial arts as the Japanese authorities forbade the possession of any weapons and confiscated any they found. Through the next centuries, Okinawans trained secretly and developed *te* into a sophisticated form of martial art. As part of their training, they also improvised with the use of common farm implements as weapons. Thus emerged the unique Okinawan form of the martial arts known worldwide as *Kara-te-do*, or empty hand Way.

Further reading: John Corcoran, *The Martial Arts Companion: Culture, History and Enlightenment* (New York: Friedman Group, 1992); George H. Kerr, *Okinawa: The History of an Island People* (Rutland, Vt.: Charles E. Tuttle, 1964); William P. Lebra, *Okinawan Religion, Belief, Ritual, and Social Structure* (Honolulu: University of Hawaii, 1966); Ronald Y. Nakasone, ed., *Okinawan Diaspora* (Honolulu: University of Hawaii Press, 2001); James C. Robinson, *Okinawa, a People and Their Gods* (Rutland, Vt.: Charles E. Tuttle, 1969; Mitsugu Sakihara, *A Brief History of Early Okinawa Based on the Omoro Soshi* (Tokyo: Honpo Shoseki Press, 1987).

Olcott, Henry Steel (Colonel) (1832–
1907) *a founder of the Theosophical movement and
a key figure in the popularization of Buddhist ideas in
the West*

Henry Steel Olcott, cofounder and first president
of the Theosophical Society, was born in Orange,
New Jersey, and grew up on his father's farm. He
later became the agricultural editor of the *New
York Tribune.* He served in the Union Army (1861–
65), achieving the rank of colonel. He passed the
bar in New York in 1868.

In 1874, while associated with the *New York
Daily Graphic,* he was assigned to write a story on
the Eddy Brothers, spiritualist mediums then operating in Vermont. His trip to Vermont resulted in
his meeting Madame HELENA PETROVNA BLAVATSKY,
which led to their founding the Theosophical
Society the next year in New York. In 1878, when
Olcott received a commission to study American
and Indian trade relations, the pair sailed for
India.

The society cast its net wide, making room for
various religions, and Olcott became an enthusiastic
Buddhist, an enthusiasm he initially made public
in 1880. That year, both he and Blavatsky formally
converted to Buddhism, though Blavatsky's commitment remained largely with Western esotericism. Esotericism in the European tradition implies
a mystical path that includes such traditions as
alchemy, Rosicrucianism, cabala, and occultism.
Over the next decade, Olcott involved himself (and
the society) in the Buddhist political efforts in Sri
Lanka (then called Ceylon). The main thrust of
such campaigns was to reverse the effects of the
British colonial government's attempts to impose
Christianity on the local culture. In 1881, he published the *Buddhist Catechism,* which went on to
become a popular introduction to Buddhism for
many Westerners. He promoted Buddhism through
the theosophical periodicals. He also began to found
Buddhist schools and youth associations in Ceylon
to counter the Christian hold on public education.

In 1884 he became involved in the Buddhist
effort to have WESAK declared a national public
holiday in Ceylon, and when that effort proved
successful, he suggested the construction of a
Buddhist flag as a community symbol. That project was carried out by the Wesak celebration
committee, with Olcott's input. Olcott later wrote
a Buddhist Platform for the Buddhists of Ceylon,
Burma, and Japan that was published in 1891 as
part of the effort to support an International Buddhist League.

Olcott was influential in the West as well
as in Asia. He helped popularize such imported
concepts as *chakras* (subtle energy centers in the
body) and reincarnation. However, he is probably most remembered for his relationship with
ANGARIKA DHARMAPALA, founder of the MAHABODHI
SOCIETY, and his support of Dharmapala's travel
to the United States to speak before the World's
Parliament of Religions.

Olcott remained president of the Theosophical
Society until his death in 1907. He was succeeded
in office by Annie Besant. He is remembered in Sri
Lanka with an annual Olcott Day (February 17).

Further reading: Henry Steel Olcott, *A Buddhist Cat-
echism* (1881. Reprint, Wheaton, Ill.: Theosophical
Publishing House, 1970); ———, *Old Diary Leaves: The
History of the Theosophical Society.* 6 vols. (Adyar, India:
Theosophical Society Press, 1974–1975); Stephen R.
Prothero, *The White Buddhist: The Asian Odyssey of
Henry Steel Olcott* (Bloomington: Indiana University
Press, 1996); Thomas A. Tweed, *The American Encoun-
ter with Buddhism, 1844–1912: Victorian Culture and
the Limits of Dissent* (Bloomington: Indiana University
Press, 1992).

Order of Interbeing

The Order of Interbeing is a Buddhist organization founded by THICH NHAT HANH in 1966.
The order was originally established because of
the perception that the Buddha's teachings were
needed to counter the violence then enfolding
Vietnam. It continues to publish and report on
Buddhist practice, Thich Nhat Hanh's teachings,

and Vietnam. There are four categories of membership: monks, nuns, laymen, and laywomen. The order publishes a journal, *The Mindfulness Bell*, three times a year.

The Community of Mindful Living, a sister organization, was legally registered in Berkeley, California, in 1983 and became a nonprofit religious organization in 1990. In 1999 its status was changed to an arm of the Unified Buddhist Church, known as "Doing Business As" (DBA).

Further reading: Community of Mindful Living. "Order of Interbeing-Tiep Hien Order." Available online. URL: www. iamhome.org/oi.html. Accessed on May 5, 2005.

ordination (*upasampada*)

Ordination is the process by which a novice monk, a SRAMANERA/SRAMANERI, takes vows of becoming a monk, a BHIKSU. The precise ceremonies of ordination, called *upasampada,* are governed by the VINAYA, that portion of the Buddhist sacred canon, the TRIPITAKA, that deals with discipline. There are, however, some important differences between the Pali and the Chinese versions of the Vinaya.

THE FIRST *UPASAMPADA*

Kondanna, one of the five ascetic companions of the Buddha, heard the Buddha's first sermon, the "Sutra of Turning the Wheel of the Doctrine," and immediately understood the concept of PRATITYA-SAMUTPADA, codependent origination. The Buddha noticed this. Kondanna then asked to receive the ceremony of *pabbajja,* leaving the world, and *upasampada,* ordination. The Buddha said, "Come, monk, well proclaimed is the doctrine; lead a religious life for making a complete end of pain." This is generally regarded as the first ordination ceremony.

THE PALI *UPASAMPADA*

This ceremony is still held for each full ordination, when one becomes a BHIKSU. The details differ slightly in different Buddhist traditions. In the Pali version the *upasampada* is a series of questions and discussions posed to the novice to ensure he is suitable for the life of a monk, the *bhikkhu-bhava*. First, explanations are given regarding the four resources of a monk's life:

1. The requirement that the monk will go forth every morning to search for food.
2. The requirement that one wear robes for life, and the particular requirements of materials.
3. That one will seek out suitable lodging.
4. That one can seek out certain medicines (ammonia, ghee, butter, honey) for medicinal purposes.

A second discussion explains the four things to be done after ordination. These four are actually regulations, known as the *samana-sila,* the moral code of the recluse; they include:

1. There can be no sexual intercourse, including with animals, for life.
2. No monk can intentionally deprive another living thing of life.
3. A monk cannot claim a state or condition of superiority to others.

These four things *mirror* but do not coincide with the *parajika,* the first four items in the list of the monk's code of discipline, the *patimokkha* (in Sanskrit, PRATIMOKSA), which forbid sexual intercourse, theft, killing, and boasting of higher states. The difference between the *parajika* and the *samana-sila* is that the *parajika,* which disciplines monks, emphasizes expulsion and other penalties for nonadherence. The four parts of the *samana-sila,* in contrast, spell out a moral ideal.

Taken together, the *samana-sila* and the *bhikkhu-bhava* (way of the monk) formed parallel codes for the monks under the Buddha. The *samana-sila* was a general code followed by many ascetic wanderers, not only by Buddhists. The *parajika* and the other rules, later called the *patimokkha,* took form as the Buddha laid down rules over time. The *patimokkha* eventually totaled 227 separate rules, arranged into eight chapters. We can say that the purpose of these rules was to ensure that monks adhered to the ideals of the *samana-sila*.

THE CHINESE *UPASAMPADA*

In China the translators of the *vinaya-pitaka* interpreted the *upamasada* as a ceremony. The translation in Chinese is *shou jie,* meaning "to receive the precepts." In the Chinese version the new monk makes a vow to observe the four things to be done. This was a Chinese innovation, since no such vow is mentioned in the Pali Tripitaka. In addition, the Chinese translations of the *upasamada* blurred the distinction between the *samana-sila,* the moral ideal, and the *parajika,* the first four of the 227 regulations.

Further reading: Robert E. Buswell Jr., *The Zen Monastic Experience: Buddhist Practice in Contemporary Korea* (Princeton, N.J: Princeton University Press, 1992); Edward J. Thomas, *The Life of Buddha as Legend and History* (Delhi: Munshiram Manoharlal, 1992).

Ouchi Seiran Koji (1845–1918) *Soto Zen lay leader*

Ouchi Seiran Koji, who developed a lay movement for the SOTO ZEN sect in Japan early in the 20th century, became a Soto priest but later returned to lay status. In the mid-1870s, at a time when Buddhism was being suppressed by the government in favor of Shintoism, he began to call for rethinking of the role of the clergy and elevating of the role of the laity. He used the periodical *Mekyo Shinshi* as his medium and began his call for more lay involvement with discussions of the writings of Jiun (1718–1804), a Shingon priest of a previous generation who had proposed what were termed the "ten lay precepts."

He began to construct a perspective by which the average lay Buddhist could acquire the basic concepts for an active Buddhist existence. These concepts were published in 1888 as *Shushogi* (Meaning of practice and enlightenment for lay members of the Soto sect). In this work Seiran took passages from *SHOBOGENZO* by the Zen founder DOGEN and rearranged them into a simple digest of Soto Zen. In this book, he not only summarized the basics of Soto practice but also advocated four essential principles: repentance of shortcomings, reception of the precepts, vows to be of benefit to all beings, and gratitude to the Buddha for helping practitioners persevere in practice. His text was widely reprinted and placed in the hands of the movement's lay people.

Seiran is credited with jolting the thinking of Soto leaders about their awareness (or lack thereof) concerning the changes occurring all around them as Japan moved into the 20th century. No longer the darling child of the government, Soto Zen had to learn to reach out to the general public if it was to survive and maintain its membership. Seiran also stimulated other Buddhist groups to respond to their disestablished status and the introduction of religious freedom after World War II.

Further reading: Kazuo Kasahara, ed., *A History of Japanese Religion.* Translated by Paul McCarthy and Gaynor Sekimori (Tokyo: Kosei, 2001); Ouchi Seiran Koji, ed., *Shushogi.* Zen Temple Kosanryumonji. Available online. URL: http://www.kosanryumonji.org/65.0.html?&L=1. Accessed on October 11, 2005.

P

Padmasambhava (Guru Rinpoche)

(c. eighth century C.E.) *semilegendary Tantric yogi who introduced Buddhism to Tibet*

Padmasambhava, popularly known as Guru Rinpoche (precious teacher), is credited with introducing Buddhism into Tibet from India in the eighth century during the reign of the Tibetan king, Trisong Detsen. His name, which means "lotus-born," derives from the legend of his miraculous birth in Oddiyana, an area around the border of Afghanistan and Pakistan. There, it is said, Padmasambhava appeared in the form of an eight-year-old boy sitting in the center of a lotus flower in the middle of a sacred lake. He was adopted by the king of the land and raised as a prince in his court. Later, in order to follow a spiritual path, because the king would not agree to let him go, he arranged for his own exile by apparently causing the death of a minister's son. As he planned, the king banished him for the crime and Padmasambhava spent many years living in cremation grounds. These were terrifying places of death where yogis went to practice meditation and to overcome fear. During this time, he was initiated into esoteric (involving hidden teachings and initiations) Tantric practices by wisdom DAKINIS (female guides to enlightenment) and developed the miraculous spiritual powers for which he became renowned.

Padmasambhava's fame as a powerful yogi spread and he was invited to Tibet by King Trisong Detsen (c. 740–798 C.E.) to defeat the local demons and other obstructing forces so that Buddhism could be established in Tibet. Padmasambhava is associated with the founding of Samye in 775 C.E., the first Buddhist monastery in Tibet, and he is especially revered as a "second Buddha" by the oldest school of Tibetan Buddhism, the NYINGMA. This school recognizes eight major forms of Padmasambhava known as his eight manifestations; they range in appearance from a peaceful gentle monk to the wrathful and terrifying Dorje Drolod. In the Nyingma religious calendar, the 10th day of each lunar month is dedicated to the commemoration of the major events of Padmasambhava's life.

Padmasambhava's main consorts were the Indian princess Mandarava and the Tibetan noblewoman Yeshe Tsogyal. They are often portrayed in paintings standing to the left and right of him. As his biographer and chief disciple, Yeshe Tsogyal also helped to conceal his teachings as *terma* (treasure) to be discovered and revealed in the far future by spiritually advanced ones called *tertons* (treasure revealers). Padmasambhava traveled throughout the country and many of Tibet's mountains, lakes, and caves are considered to have been blessed as places of spiritual power by his presence. Eventually he left Tibet to continue his work of subduing demons and spreading the Buddha's teaching in wild and untamed lands. Padmasambhava is considered to be a fully enlightened Buddha who remains as an active presence in this world working for the benefit of all sentient beings.

Further reading: Lama Chonam and Sangye Khandro, trans., *The Lives and Liberation of Princess Mandarava: The Indian Consort of Padmasambhava* (Boston: Wisdom, 1998); W. Y. Evans-Wentz, ed., *The Tibetan Book of the Great Liberation: Or, the Method of Realizing Nirvana through Knowing the Mind* (Oxford: Oxford University Press, 1983); Erik Pema Kunsang, *Dakini Teachings: Padmasambhava's Oral Instructions to Lady Tsogyal* (Boston: Shambhala, 1990); Padmasambhava, *Natural Liberation: Padmasambhava's Teachings on the Six Bardos.* Translated by B. Alan Wallace (Somerville, Mass.: Wisdom, 1997); John Powers, *Introduction to Tibetan Buddhism* (Ithaca, N.Y.: Snow Lion, 1995); Yeshe Tsogyal, *The Lotus-Born.* Translated by Erik Hein Schmidt (Boston: Shambhala, 1993).

Paekche

Paekche (or Kudara) was one of three kingdoms that existed on the southern half of the Korean Peninsula in the fourth and fifth centuries C.E. It appears to have been formed in the third century, possibly by remnants of the former Puyo state that had existed in Manchuria (the most northeastern area of contemporary China). Paekche emerged in strength in the fourth century and added to its power by developing close ties with Japan, which on occasion supported it when it was at war with its neighbors SILLA and KOGURYO.

Buddhism was introduced to Paekche by an Indian monk named Maranant'a in 384, some 12 years after its arrival in Koguryo. King Ch'imnyu adopted Buddhism as the state religion that same year. An initial temple was constructed the next year in Hansong (Seoul).

Paekche continued to exist until 660, when the combined forces of the Chinese Tang dynasty and the neighboring kingdom of Silla defeated it. At that point, Paekche was incorporated into Silla.

Further reading: *Focus on Korea.* 3 vols. (Seoul: Seoul International Publishing House, 1988); James Huntley Grayson, *Early Buddhism and Christianity in Korea: A Study in the Emplantation of Religion* (Leiden: E. J. Brill, 1985); Lewis R. Lancaster and C. S. Yu, eds., *Introduction of Buddhism to Korea: New Cultural Patterns* (Berkeley, Calif.: Asian Humanities Press, 1989); Chong-wuk Lee, "The Formation and Growth of Paekche," *Korea Journal* 18, no. 10 (October 1978): 35–40.

pagoda

The pagoda is an East Asian architectural form that evolved from the Buddhist STUPA. The Indian stupa was a round structure that housed sacred relics of the Buddha or, sometimes, the remains of famous masters. As of the stupa, the pagoda's function is to hold Buddha RELICS, or *sharira*. The pagoda form is found throughout China, Korea, and Japan. While each culture has developed its own style, all are multistoried towers with four or eight corners. (Some may occasionally be round.) Each floor has prominent overhanging eaves. And on the top roof is a central post composed of several rings stacked vertically. This post is supported by a round pediment.

Contrary to Western practice, Buddhist relics were not normally viewed by worshippers. Instead the devout walked around, or circumambulated, the stupa and so paid homage to the relics housed within, their knowledge of their presence substituting for any actual sight of them. Since pagodas have stairs that wrap around the structure as it rises up several floors, walking up

Da Yan Ta (pagoda), at Da Qian temple, built in 652 C.E. to house the scriptures collected by the Chinese traveler Xuan Zang, in Xi'an, western China

and down the stairs in a pagoda are also forms of circumambulation.

In China a pagoda is usually sited in a place that will be a good influence, in line with Chinese principles of geomancy, FENG SHUI.

There are a number of very famous pagodas such as the Silver Pagoda in Phnom Phen, Cambodia, constructed in 1892 by King Norodom; the Shwedagon Pagoda in Yangon, Myanmar (Burma); the Sanzang pagoda, in Nanjing, China; and the Leifeng Pagoda, in Hangzhou, China. The Miruksa temple is one of the largest and oldest of the Korean pagodas.

See also ART, AESTHETICS, AND ARCHITECTURE; SHRINES; STUPAS.

Further reading: Su-yong Hwang, "The Pagoda as an Art Form and Object of Faith in the Three Kingdoms Period." *Korea Journal* 6, no. 4 (April 1966): 16–20; Elizabeth Moore, *Shwedagon: Golden Pagoda of Myanmar* (New York: Thames & Hudson, 1999); Sam Y. Park, *An Introduction to Korean Architecture* (Seoul: Jungwoo Sa, 1991).

Pali

Pali and its cousin Sanskrit are two of the earliest sacred languages of Buddhism. The label *Pali* refers today to a west Indian language from the area of Avanti. This language is descended from the speech of the Vedic Aryans—some scholars treat it as a vernacular form of classical Sanskrit—and it was one of the many languages in use at the time of the historical Buddha. However, it was not the language actually spoken by the Buddha—he spoke Magadhi or some similar dialect of north-central India (the region near modern Varanasi).

Pali means, literally, "line" or "text." In Buddhist usage the label *Pali* began as a way to refer to the text used to record the Buddha's spoken words and teachings, and to distinguish those works from commentaries. Therefore, in the beginning Pali did not actually exist as a separate language under that name. This language used to record the words of the Buddha was simply one of the dialects of Middle Indo-Aryan that was available for use as a standardized dialect so that the material could be recorded. Eventually the chosen dialect itself became known to later times as Pali.

Pali is generally written in the Devanagari alphabetic script. Today it is not considered to be a living language, although monks and scholars of Theravada Buddhism generally gain proficiency in reading Pali.

See also SACRED LANGUAGES OF BUDDHISM.

Further reading: Wilhelm Geiger, *Pali Literature and Language* (Calcutta: University of Calcutta, 1943);

Bimala Charan Law, *A History of Pali Literature*. Vols. 1 and 2 (Calcutta: University of Calcutta, 1933).

Pali Text Society

The Pali Text Society, founded in 1881, was designed to publish Pali texts in roman characters, translations in English, and associated study tools such as dictionaries, concordances, books for students of Pali, and a journal. Its history is intimately connected with the life of its founder, THOMAS WILLIAM RHYS DAVIDS, a lawyer and amateur Buddhist scholar. He went to Sri Lanka in 1864 as a civil servant. While there, he served as a magistrate and had to decide a case that hinged on a document written in Pali. As he had already learned Sanskrit and Sinhala, the incident led him to master Pali; that knowledge led to his discovery of the original Buddhist writings that wore written in that language, that is the Pali Canon.

After his return to England, in 1881 he was invited to give the annual Hibbert Lectures. During the course of these lectures he announced his intention to found the Pali Text Society to make accessible to Westerners the teachings of the Buddha. The society was formed that same year. He saw its work as requiring about 10 years. The society's journal appeared, generally annually, from 1882 to 1927, after which there was a gap; publishing resumed in 1981. The society has since completed publication of the Pali suttas (Sanskrit, SUTRAS) and commentaries, the ABHIDHARMA-KOSA.

The society has had a precarious existence, as a small translation and publishing concern, serving primarily libraries and scholars. It has been relatively successful in keeping most of its publications in print. It tries to produce at least two new books and a volume of its *Journal* each year. Since it has completed the work originally assigned to it, the society has expanded its scope and now cooperates with a variety of efforts to preserve and make available the literature of Theravada Buddhism.

Today the society is headquartered in Headington, Oxfordshire, England.

Further reading: Caroline A. F. Rhys Davids, *A Buddhist Manual of Psychological Ethics* (London: Pali Text Society and Routledge & Kegan Paul, 1974); T. W. Rhys Davids, *Dialogues of the Buddha*. 3 vols. (Reprint, for the Pali Text Society, London: Luzac, 1956, 1957).

panca sila (*pansil*, Chinese *wu jie*)

The *panca sila* are the five moral rules that are the fundamental vows taken by lay Buddhists, the *upasaka* (male devotees) and *upasika* (female devotees). They are included in the 10 SILA (morality) vows taken by nuns and monks as well, and they function as the core of individual morality for Buddhists. The five precepts are do not kill, do not steal, do not engage in inappropriate sexual activity, do not use unjust speech, and do not take intoxicants. These rules are moral conventions common to all humans. In contrast, the Vinaya rules are specific to Buddhist monastic practice and are therefore complex and comprehensive.

Further reading: Walphida Rahda. *What the Buddha Taught: Revised and Expanded Edition with Texts from Suttas and Phammapada* (New York: Grove, 1974).

Panchen Lama

The Panchen Lama is today the second most significant position in Tibetan Buddhism, after the DALAI LAMA. Traditionally the Panchen Lama was also the abbot of Tashi Lhunpo Monastery. The title, which means "great scholar," was actually not used until the fifth Dalai Lama conferred it on his own master in 1642. As the Dalai Lama is considered to be an incarnation of AVALOKITESVARA, the Panchen Lama is considered to be an incarnation of the Buddha AMITABHA. Traditionally the Dalai Lama and Panchen Lama act as tutor to each other in a constant cycle of mutual dependency.

The Panchen Lama traditionally played no political role. This changed in the 20th century, however. The ninth Panchen Lama had died in 1937, and the 10th Panchen Lama was not recognized until 1944. He quickly fell under communist control when the armies of the Chinese Communists, already locked in civil war with the Nationalist Chinese, invaded the Tibetan province of Amdo. The 10th Panchem Lama spent the remainder of his life under the control of the Chinese Communist government, which assumed full power in China in 1949. Although he was accused by some of being a "puppet," the relationship between the Panchen Lama and the Chinese authorities was in fact more complicated. He called for the return of the Dalai Lama on several occasions and never ceased to honor the legitimacy of the Dalai Lama. He spent 10 years under solitary confinement and was released in 1978.

Because the Dalai Lama had fled Tibet in 1959, the 10th Panchen Lama's death in 1989 triggered a political crisis. The new Panchen Lama is traditionally chosen or "recognized" as a TULKU (reincarnation) by the current Dalai Lama, after a suitable search of several years is made. In this case the Dalai Lama, while still in exile in India, was able to recognize and announce the discovery of the 11th Panchen Lama on May 14, 1995. The child, Gedhun Choekyi Nyima, then living in Tibet, was quickly taken into custody by the Chinese government, who said they were protecting him. The Chinese government has confirmed that he is still alive and in custody today.

At the same time the Chinese authorities announced another Panchen Lama had been found. This child, Gyaltsen Norbu, was proclaimed and ceremoniously confirmed on November 30, 1995. He has been schooled in a tightly controlled environment. In contrast to the strict rules concerning showing the Dalai Lama's image, images of the current (Chinese-chosen) Panchen Lama are spread throughout Tibet. Thus the Panchen Lama dispute is a major element of the current political-religious scene in Tibet.

The government-backed Panchen Lama resurfaced in Tibet in 1999 and has since, along with continuing his Buddhist studies, assumed leadership over a select number of rituals as a Buddhist lama. His most important duties are yet to occur. Those duties involved in the selection of the next Dalai Lama will move to the fore immediately after the present Dalai Lama passes away.

Further reading: *The Confirmation and Enthronement of the 11th Bainqen Erden* (Beijing: China Tibetology Publishing House, 1996); Vicki Mackenzie, *Reborn in the West: The Reincarnation Masters* (London: Bloomsbury, 1995); The Tibet Society. "The Current Panchen Lama." Available online. URL: http://www.tibet-society.org.uk/pcurrent.html. Accessed on March 7, 2005.

panjiao (p'an chiao) (doctrinal classifications)

Panjiao is a system first developed in the fifth and sixth centuries to classify Buddhism's major schools and sutras into one unified system. Since Buddhism was introduced to China in the first century C.E., Chinese thinkers had been exposed to many Buddhist texts from a variety of schools. Accurate translations were available of such key texts as the Lotus Sutra, the Nirvana Sutra, the Abhidharma-kosa, and the Avatamsaka Sutra. They had been able to digest and make sense of the claims and subtleties of various Buddhist schools.

The TIAN TAI school thinker ZHI YI (538–597) and his successors developed an influential and in many ways prototypical scheme, the *wushi bajiao* (five periods and eight teachings) system. The theory behind this system is that the Buddha taught over five periods in his life, the HUA YAN period, the Deer Park period, the "Expanded" period, the Wisdom period, and the Lotus and NIRVANA period. In each period he used one of four methods of converting listeners: sudden, gradual, secret, or variable. In addition there were four doctrines of conversion: the TRIPITAKA, shared, distinctive, and complete. The sudden method of conversion, in which a select group of listeners instantly recognized the truth of the Buddha's teachings, was used only in the Hua Yan period. Some of the listeners to that first sermon also became enlightened through the secret and variable method. During the Deer Park, Expanded, and Wisdom periods, only the gradual, secret, and variable methods were used. Key sutras were associated with each period. In the Hua Yan period it was the HUA YAN SUTRA, in the Deer Park it was the (so-called) HINAYANA Tripitaka, in the Wisdom period the *PRAJNAPARAMITA* family of texts, and in the Lotus and Nirvana Period it was the LOTUS SUTRA and the NIRVANA SUTRA.

Zhi Yi, Tian Tai's founding figure, probably did not develop this theory of the five periods and eight teachings. His recorded lectures instead emphasize three kinds of teachings, three forms of meditation, and five flavors. The system was most probably elaborated by ZHAN RAN, the sixth Tian Tai patriarch, and later preserved in his text.

Other *panjiao* systems include Ji Cang's San Lun school *panjiao,* Yuan Zang and Kui Ji's Fa Xiang school *panjiao,* Dao Xuan's Lu (VINAYA) school *panjiao,* and Fa Cang's HUA YAN school *panjiao.* The last and in some ways most comprehensive *panjiao* system was that of ZONG MI, the great Hua Yan systematizer.

Further reading: Neal Donner and Daniel B. Stevenson, *The Great Calming and Contemplation: A Study and Annotated Translation of the First Chapter of Chih-I's Mo-Ho Chih-Kuan* Honolulu: University of Hawaii Press, (1993); Kogen Mizuno, *Essentials of Buddhism: Basic Terminology and Concepts of Buddhist Philosophy and Practice.* Translated by Gaynor Sekimori (1972. Reprint, Tokyo: Kosei, 1996); Paul L. Swanson, *Foundations of T'ien-T'ai Philosophy: The Flowering of the Two Truths*

Theory in Chinese Buddhism (Fremont, Calif.: Asian Humanities Press, 1989).

Paramartha (499–569) *translator of Buddhist classic texts into Chinese and founder of the She-lun school*

While recognized as the founder of one of the early SCHOOLS OF CHINESE BUDDHISM, the She-lun (Summary of the Mahayana) school, Paramartha is most remembered for his translation work. He translated the ABHIDHARMA-KOSA, the Mahayan-samparigraha, and the DIAMOND SUTRA into Chinese. His version of the Abhidharma-kosa is written in clear language that is often more precise than the more popular translation of XUAN ZANG.

A native of Central Asia, Paramartha traveled to China in 546, during a time of political turmoil. He was welcomed by Emperor Wu and given leave to travel throughout his territory. He traveled throughout southern China and eventually settled in Guangzhou.

Further reading: Diana Y. Paul, *Philosophy of Mind in Sixth-century China: Paramartha's "Evolution of Consciousness"* (Stanford, Calif.: Stanford University Press, 1984).

paramita

A *paramita* is a "perfection." The term has been translated in Buddhist texts with two senses, first meaning "other shore," indicating the means for the individual to leave the shore of life and reach the shore of nirvana; the second, "supreme." A list of six perfections (*sat-paramita*) was an original formulation of the BODHISATTVA's form of practice. These included donation, morality, forbearance, effort, concentration, and wisdom.

Eventually two lists of 10 *paramitas* developed, one from the PALI tradition and another from the MAHAYANA. The Pali (THERAVADA) tradition lists the 10, called the *dasa-parami*, as donation (*dana-parami*), morality (*sila-parami*), release from the world of delusion, wisdom (*panna-parami*), effort (*viriya-parami*), forbearance, truth, determination, benevolence (*metta-parami*), and equanimity.

The Mahayana list contrasts in many areas. The *dasa paramita* are donation (*dana-paramita*), morality (*sila-paramita*), forbearance (*ksanti-paramita*), effort (*virya-paramita*), meditation (*dhyana-paramita*), wisdom (*prajna-paramita*), skillful means (*upaya-paramita*), vows (*pranidhana-paramita*), purpose (*bala-paramita*), and transcendental knowledge (*jnana-paramita*). These 10 Mahayana *paramitas* corresponded to the 10 BHUMIS, or stages, through which a bodhisattva progresses. They thus form the core of the bodhisattva's practice and in theory require many ages to complete.

Further reading: Kogen Mizuno, *Essentials of Buddhism: Basic Terminology and Concepts of Buddhist Philosophy and Practice.* Translated by Gaynor Sekimori (1972. Reprint, Tokyo: Kosei, 1996; [1972]); Santideva, *The Bodhicaryavatara.* Translated by Kate Crosby and Andrew Skilton (Oxford: Oxford University Press, 1995).

parinirvana

The final NIRVANA of the Buddha, or, in common speech, his death. While the Buddha had attained nirvana when he achieved enlightenment, the point at which he left his human body was his final nirvana.

Further reading: Edward J. Thomas, *The Life of Buddha as Legend and History* (New Delhi: Munshiram Manoharlal, 1992).

Perfection of Wisdom Sutra in One Letter

While many Buddhist SUTRAS, or sacred texts, are known for being long, repetitive, and filled with evocative language, some do not fit that description. "The Blessed Perfection of Wisdom, the Mother of All the Tathagatas, in One Letter," is probably the shortest and most concise of all Buddhist texts:

Homage to the Perfection of Wisdom!

Thus have I heard at one time. The Lord dwelt at Raajag.rha, on the Vulture Peak, together with a large congregation of monks, with 1,250 monks, and with many hundreds of thousands of niyutas of kotis of Bodhisattvas. At that time the Lord addressed the Venerable Aananda, and said

"Aananda, do receive, for the sake of the weal and happiness of all beings, this perfection of wisdom in one letter, i.e., A."

Thus spoke the Lord. The Venerable Aananda, the large congregation of monks, the assembly of the Bodhisattvas, and the whole world with its gods, men, asuras and gandharvas rejoiced at the teaching of the Lord.

Further reading: Edward Conze, *Perfect Wisdom: The Short Prajnaparamita Texts* (Totnes, U.K.: Buddhist Publishing Group, 2003).

Philangi Dasa (1849–1931) *influential early American convert to Buddhism*

Philangi Dasa, the editor/publisher of the first English language Western Buddhist periodical, *The Buddhist Ray*, was born Carl Herman Vetterling in Sweden. Around 1872 he migrated to the United States. A student of the new religious currents of the day, he left the Lutheran church of the Sweden in which he was raised and became a student of the writings of the Swedish visionary Emanuel Swedenborg (1688–1772) and a member of the Theosophical Society. He studied for the Swedenborgian ministry and was ordained in

Stone carving showing the Buddha peacefully entering nirvana, called his *parinirvana*; from a carved relief depicting the life of the Buddha, Kushan dynasty (second to third century C.E.); originally from a stupa in Gandhara, Central Asia, now in the Freer Gallery, Smithsonian Museum, Washington, D.C.

1877. He subsequently served in several Church of the New Jerusalem pulpits but left the church in 1881. He subsequently studied at the Hahneman College in Philadelphia and became a homeopathic physician.

Continuing as a theosophist, he attempted to merge theosophy, Swedenborgian thought, and a new interest in Buddhism, stimulated somewhat by the 1883 publication of *Esoteric Buddhism* (1883) by Alfred P. Sinnett (1840–1921). His resultant synthesis appeared in 1887 as *Swedenborg the Buddhist*. At the same time, he vowed to publish a Buddhist journal for a period of seven years. The first issue of *The Buddhist Ray* duly appeared in 1887 and was continued through 1894, as promised. The magazine was devoted to expounding the philosophy of Buddhism, which focused on karma, reincarnation, and mystic communion with the divine. A theme of recovering the lost wisdom of Tibet also filtered through the issues.

Philangi Dasa's ideas, tying together Swedenborgianism and Buddhism, made their way to Japan, where his articles were translated and reprinted. In the West, the approach had more currency among Theosophists than Swedenborgians, who saw their teacher as a Christian.

A number of details of Philangi Dasa's life remain obscure, such as when and why he adopted his religious name, or details of his life after the last issue of *The Buddhist Ray*. He continued to develop his thinking and in 1923 issued a study of Jacob Boehme (1575–1624), the German esoteric thinker.

Further reading: Rick Fields, *How the Swans Came to the Lake: A Narrative History of Buddhism in America* (Boston: Shambhala, 1992); Philangi Dasa [Carl Herman Vetterling], *Swedenborg the Buddhist, or the Higher Swedenborgianism: Its Secrets and Tibetan Origins* (1887. Reprint, Charleston, S.C.: Arcana Books, 2003); Thomas A. Tweed, *The American Encounter with Buddhism, 1844–1912* (Bloomington: Indiana University Press, 1992).

phra *See* TITLES AND TERMS OF ADDRESS, BUDDHIST.

phurba

The *phurba* is a ritual three-sided dagger, still used in Tibetan VAJRAYANA rituals today. The *phurba* is driven into the heart of a doll that represents a demon. This is interpreted as an act of compassion (KARUNA) since it liberates the demon from its entrapment in this existence. Thus, far from being a tool of violence, the *phurba* is an instrument of liberation and compassion. In the original Tantra rituals introduced into Tibet by PADMASAMBHAVA, the *phurba* was also a deity figure. The *phurba* deity also appeared in several TERMA (discovered) texts in the 19th century.

Further reading: Robert, Bees. *The Encyclopedia of Tibetan Symbols and Motifs* (Boston: Shambala, 1999).

Platform Sutra (Tanjing, T'an-ching)

The Platform Sutra is purportedly the teaching of the sixth patriarch of the Southern school of CHAN (ZEN), HUI NENG. It dates from the second half of the Tang dynasty (618 C.E.–906 C.E.). The text is centered on the notion of the "formless precepts," a form of initiation knowledge, and the ceremony during which they are transmitted to acolytes. The "platform" (*tan*) in the title refers to the ordination platform necessary when one takes the Buddhist vows and becomes a monk. There are several surviving versions, including one from the Dunhuang caves rediscovered in 1900.

A later version of the text, dating from the Ming dynasty (1368–1644), deemphasizes this ritual and instead focuses on Hui Neng's sermon on the PRAJNAPARAMITA, the Buddhist teachings on the perfection of wisdom. The text describes Hui Neng's teachings to his disciple Fa Hai. A large part of the book also contains Hui Neng's biography. This Ming version was clearly influenced by various Chan factions of the time, including the SHEN HUI (Southern school) group centered around Hui Neng's disciple Shen Hui, and the NIU TOU (Oxhead) school, which also taught the formless precepts.

Further reading: Hsuan Hua (Tripitaka Master), *The Sixth Patriarch's Dharma Jewel Platform Sutra with Commentary* (San Francisco: Buddhist Text Translation Society, 1977); Huineng, *The Platform Sutra of the Sixth Patriarch*. Translated by Philip B. Yampolsky, (New York: Columbia University Press, 1967).

Potala

The winter palace of the Dalai Lama in Lhasa, Tibet, the Potala is now a World Heritage Site. The name *Potala* is taken from *Potalaka*, a mythical island said to be located in the Indian Ocean that was the residence of AVALOKITESVARA, the BODHISATTVA of compassion.

The Potala was originally built by the fifth DALAI LAMA (1617–82) beginning in 1645. The site had previously been a palace of the earlier Tibetan king Songtsen Gampo. Until 1959, it was also the seat of government for the Tibetan government. Since China's annexation of Tibet in 1959 it has become a museum.

Further reading: Linda Kay Davidson and David M. Gitlitz, *Pilgrimage from the Ganges to Graceland: An Encyclopedia* (Santa Barbara, Calif.: ABC-Clio, 2002); Namgyal Phuntsok, *Splendor of Tibet: The Potala Palace, Jewel of the Himalayas* (Dumont, N.J.: Homa & Sekey Books, 2002).

prajna/panna

Prajna is a key concept in Buddhist thought that is only roughly equivalent to the English term *wisdom.* In the Buddha's noble Eightfold Path, *prajna* indicates the sections of right thought and right understanding. Right thought indicates self-less renunciation, love, and nonviolence, extended to all sentient beings. Right understanding means an awareness of the fundamentals of reality. A penetrating grasp of ultimate reality is possible once one's mind has been conditioned by meditation. By pairing right thought and right understanding, Buddhist thought reinforces the necessary application of compassion (*karuna*) to create true wisdom.

Further reading: *The Teaching of the Buddha* (Tokyo: Bukko Dendo Kyokai, 2001); Geshe Tashi Tsering, *The Four Noble Truths.* Vol. 1, *The Foundation of Buddhist Thought* (Somerville, Mass.: Wisdom, 2005).

prajnaparamita

Prajnaparamita, or "the perfection of wisdom," refers to a vast series of texts that contain expositions on Mahayana themes, especially such key Mahayana concepts as SUNYATA (emptiness). There are some 40 *prajnaparamita* texts of varying length. The most popular today continues to be the HEART SUTRA, which is widely memorized throughout East Asia. Other works of *prajna-*

paramita literature include such works as the *Perfection of Wisdom in 100,000 Lines,* the *Perfection of Wisdom in 25,000 Lines,* the *Perfection of Wisdom in 18,000 Lines,* and the DIAMOND SUTRA (Vajracchedika-prajnaparamita Sutra).

Further reading: Donald S. Lopez, *The Heart Sutra Explained* (Albany: State University Press of New York, 1988).

pranidhana

Pranidhana is the BODHISATTVA's vow not to proceed to enlightenment until all sentient beings are liberated from the SAMSARA cycle of rebirth. This is the first of the 10 BHUMIS, or stages, on the path of the bodhisattva. As such the *pranidhana* is intimately connected to the Mahayana concept of compassion for all beings. Lay people as well as monks and nuns take this vow.

Further reading: Hisao Inagaki, *Nagarjuna's Discourse on the Ten Stages (Dasabhumika-vibhasa): A Study and Translation from Chinese of Verses and Chapter 9* (Kyoto: Ryukoku gakkai, Ryukoku University, 1998); Charles S. Prebish, *Historical Dictionary of Buddhism* (Metuchen, N.J.: Scarecrow Press, 1993).

Pratimoksa/Patimokkha

The Pratimoksa is part of the VINAYA, the part of the Buddhist canon that deals with discipline for monks and nuns. The Pratimoksa is a collection of rules for daily affairs. The lists are so detailed that they give a very vivid picture of life in ancient India, when they were first collected around 500 B.C.E. And the ways they have been interpreted in various cultures give insight into the different cultures. The Pratimoksa has always been recited twice every month in every monastery or wherever there are several monks collected together, at the Posadha ceremony. Reciting the Pratimoksa Sutra, or Classic of monastic discipline, gives each monk a chance to recite his own sins and failings.

The word *Pratimoksa* originally had two senses. In Chinese and Tibetan translations it is usually taken to mean "deliverance" or "liberation." It has also been interpreted to mean "chief." In this last sense the Pratimoksa are simply the chief rules to be followed by all monks. Since the different schools of Buddhism had different versions of the *vinaya-pitaka,* they often disagreed on such details as the number of rules. Various texts in early Buddhist sources put the number of Pratimoksa rules at 200, 150, or 250. The highest number is found in the SARVASTIVADA (SARVASTI-VADIN) SCHOOL version of the Pratimoksa, which totals 263 rules. Today the number for monks has been finalized at 227. The corresponding number for nuns is longer, at 348.

Further reading: Charles S. Prebish, *Buddhist Monastic Discipline: The Sanskrit Pratimoksa Sutras of the Mahasanghikas and Mulasarvastivadins* (State College: Pennsylvania State University Press, 1975); Karma Lekshe Tsomo, *Sisters in Solitude: Two Traditions of Buddhist Monastic Ethics for Women: A Comparative Analysis of the Chinese Dharmagupta and the Tibetan Mulasarvastivada Bhiksuni Pratimoksa Sutras* (Albany: State University of New York Press, 1996).

pratitya-samutpada

Pratitya-samutpada, "codependent arising," is a key concept in Buddhism—some would contend the key concept. *Pratitya-samutpada* was developed over the centuries by many thinkers. According to this concept, all phenomena depend on preceding causes. Each can only arise if the one before it is present. A simple example of this is death, which cannot take place unless birth has first taken place.

A complete cycle of codependent arising includes 12 links, each of which affects the arising of the next one. In a typical chain, when ignorance arises, it leads to action; action leads to consciousness, which leads to a form and a name, which leads to the six senses (the five physical senses and the mind). The six senses lead to sense impressions, which lead to feelings, which lead to desire (TANHA). Desire leads to attachment. Attachment leads to becoming. Becoming leads to birth, which leads, finally, to death.

Some writers contend the various links in the chain arise simultaneously, not in sequence, each one's presence reinforcing the other's. The cycle of 12 links is often illustrated in the WHEEL OF LIFE (*bhavachakra*), in which various individuals and objects represent each link.

Further reading: *The Teaching of the Buddha* (Tokyo: Bukkyo Dendo Kyokai, 2001).

pratyekabuddha

A *pratyekabuddha* is a practitioner of the Buddha's teachings who is able to attain NIRVANA through his or her own efforts, without the assistance or direction of a teacher. The *pratyekabuddha* serves in Mahayana teachings as a symbol of a solitary practitioner, who, unlike the BODHISATTVA, is limited in his impact on others.

Further reading: Ria Kloppenburg, *The Paccekabuddha: A Buddhist Ascetic* (Leiden, Netherlands: Brill, 1974).

preta

Preta is the Buddhist term for "hungry ghosts." There are six forms of life in Buddhist teachings, and the hungry ghost is one of the lower forms. Beings born into such destinies are described as having huge bellies and tiny mouths. They can thus never satisfy their cravings. This fate is explained as the result of greed in an individual's earlier life. Later texts divided *pretas* into many categories, including lightly tormented, assistants to YAMA, the king of hell, some in constant pain, and some who wander among humans.

One contemporary interpretation of the concept of the *preta* is given by the American poet

GARY SNYDER: "The conditions of the Cold War have turned all modern societies—Communist included—into vicious distorters of man's true potential. They create populations of 'preta'— hungry ghosts, with giant appetites and throats no bigger than needles. The soil, the forests and all animal life are being consumed by these cancerous collectivities; the air and water of the planet is being fouled by them."

Further reading: Charles S. Prebish, *Historical Dictionary of Buddhism* (Metuchen, N.J.: Scarecrow Press, 1993); Richard H. Robinson and Willard L. Johnson, *The Buddhist Religion: A Historical Introduction* (Belmont, Calif.: Wadsworth, 1997); Carol Stepanchuk and Charles Wong, *Mooncakes and Hungry Ghosts: Festivals of China* (South San Francisco, Calif.: China Books & Periodicals, 1992); Laurence G. Thompson, *Chinese Religion* (Belmont, Calif.: Wadsworth, 1996).

psychology

Buddhism has similarities to psychology, the modern science that studies the mind, and psychiatry, the branch of medicine dealing with mental disorders. It can be argued that Buddhism is more akin to psychiatry than psychology, since Buddhism provides diagnosis and treatment for the fundamental disease to which all humans are subject: *dukkha* (suffering). However, the field of psychology is the more interesting to compare, since it entails the broader perspective on the study of mind. Despite the areas of overlap, Buddhism has also reached conclusions that run counter to psychology, in particular concerning training, the idea of the self, and the role of the emotions.

One branch of psychiatry with particular relevance here is psychoanalysis. This is the treatment originally championed by Sigmund Freud, which emphasizes free association, dream interpretations, and such mechanisms as transference and repression. The theory of personality that Freud spelled out, involving id, ego, and superego, has

wide currency throughout Western society today, although not every psychologist or psychiatrist adheres to this theory by any means.

The psychology of religion has had a prominent place in religious studies since the work of William James (1842–1910), whose *Varieties of Religious Experience* (1902) looked at the actual experiences of people while practicing religion. James was interested in the kinds of motivations and thought patterns that characterize the devout, as opposed to those without belief in sacred reality.

In studying the non-Western religions now widespread throughout the West, psychologists soon found that many of them had their own traditions of the study of the mind. Buddhism in particular makes awareness of mental processes a cornerstone of religious practice. Here was a tradition capable of observing itself, perhaps making the observing psychologist unnecessary. It was inevitable that the two viewpoints would meet, compare notes, and cross-fertilize. At the very least contemporary psychologists are curious to know what conclusions Buddhism may have reached over its long history concerning the nature of mind. After all, as a relatively young science, psychology should be aware of alternative results reached through different methodologies.

What psychologists discover in Buddhist practice is an independent, well-developed psychology. The results of Buddhist psychology correspond in many ways to the conclusions of contemporary psychology, something we would expect to some extent, since both Buddhism and psychology aspire to universal truths. At the same time the methods and assumptions of this alternative psychology often contrast with the academic discipline. The following gives a summary of some parallels and differences.

TRAINING

Traditional Buddhist training emphasizes meditative practice, in particular the focus on developing *sila* (discipline), *samadhi* (meditation), and *prajna* (insight). While *sila* can be seen as the preparatory grounds for meditation, *prajna* is the fruit toward which the cultivator reaches.

In contrast, the contemporary psychologist and therapist receives academic training and uses observation. However, there is a relative neglect of experiential training of the practitioner's own mind, something emphasized by Buddhism. The conclusions drawn by Buddhist thinkers through years of traditional techniques are impossible without direct experience.

TRANSFORMATION

Both Buddhism and psychological therapies aim to transform people. They provide practical tools that can be used by all to achieve this aim. In order to help people understand their conditions they each offer psychological analyses, and they in particular focus on the role of suffering. For Buddhists the suffering is the fundamental human condition. For psychoanalysis, and especially for Sigmund Freud, its founder, suffering resulted from neurotic symptoms that were simply defense reactions caused by the frustration of needs. Freud isolated such phenomena as repression, regression, isolation of the ego, denial, projection, compensation, reaction formation, rationalization, identification, and aggressiveness.

In Buddhism frustration of basic needs is a condition that is described in detail, especially in the early literature, the NIKAYAS. We can draw an analogy between Freudian "needs" and the Buddhist concept of TANHA, cravings. In Buddhist thought *tanha* is derived from sensations (*vedana*). *Tanha* leads eventually to a collection of forces (*upadana*) that ultimately results in suffering and rebirth into the next life. *Tanha* is not unlike Freud's idea of libido, seen broadly as a vital life force. *Tanha* often takes the form of immoral activities of desire, hatred, and illusion (*raga, dosa,* and *moha*), the "three poisons." But the experience of various *tanhas* or cravings is always first conditioned by the perceptions of qualities: for *raga* one first perceives the quality of beauty (*patighanimitta*); for *dosa* one perceives the disgusting quality (*patighanimitta*); and for *moha* one experiences "improper attention" (*ayonisomanasikara*).

Buddhism sees having a desire to obtain something and yet not being able to get it as the root of all suffering. In psychological terms this is equivalent to frustration. And a close reading of the *nikaya* literature will show examples of each of the Freudian frustrations described. Both Buddhism and psychology dealt with the same territory, it seems.

THE SELF

Psychoanalysis distinguishes between the ego, a collective name for the conscious processes, and the self-image, a partly realistic, partly idealized image. Buddhism here distinguishes between *citta,* "true mind," and *atta,* an idealized essence. The person's sense of self-identity is "conditioned" by influxes (*asava*), undesirable psychological states allowed to "flow" in toward the *atta*. These result in a sense of individuality (*sakkayaditthi*), a false apprehension of the self as a collection of sensations, ideas, consciousness, and others. The individual in essence identifies his own self with this bundle of phenomena. The ego in fact is one such identification; it is illusory.

EMOTIONS

Recent medical focus on emotions and their relationship to overall health finds several parallels in Buddhist thought. Such phenomena as heart attacks, accidents, and serious physical injuries have been linked in recent medical literature to anger, depression, and stress. Buddhist meditative practice in particular is now actively studied as a possible countermeasure to such problems.

EARLY YEARS AND KARMA

Psychoanalysis in particular focuses on early childhood development and the influence of traumatic events on the formation of the personality. Buddhism in contrast offers the mechanism of karmic dispositions to explain much adult behavior.

MENTAL HEALTH

NIRVANA, the goal of Buddhist practice, is described in detail in the *nikaya* literature. It is associated with the positive emotions of happiness, peace, security, calm, humility, and kindness. It stands in contrast to DUKKHA, suffering or unpleasantness. Nirvana is in fact a state without strong emotions in which there are no needs or desires. It is defined as freedom from those emotions and desires, those same impulses that surround the psychological concept of ego. Once such attachments are overcome, the person is motivated by purely positive energies such as compassion. Here the goals of practice, NIRVANA in one case and "mental health" in the other, turn out to be surprisingly similar. And just as Buddhist nirvana does not refer to utter annihilation, so too does the psychological goal of the healthy personality not assume a life completely devoid of neurosis and frustrations.

In psychology, mental health has been characterized by adaptation (physically, morally, and socially), adjustment (no internal frictions), and integration of values and purposes. Buddhism agrees but adds new emphasis: for adaptation, the Buddha put greater stress on morality; for adjustment, insight into one's own self will yield freedom from inner conflicts and emotional stability; and for harmony, the enlightened person will function effectively and will be fully aware. However, the ultimate purposes of the two disciplines do not match. Psychology aims to achieve complete adjustment of the individual in society, while Buddhism strives to develop internal freedom and judgment, release from the everyday world.

Regardless, Buddhism today offers an alternative psychological perspective that complements and has added much to the overall discipline of psychology.

Further reading: Daniel Goleman, ed., *Healing Emotions: Conversations with the Dalai Lama on Mindfulness, Emotions, and Health* (Boston: Shambhala, 2003); Rune E. A. Johansson, "Defense Mechanisms According to Psychoanalysis and the Pali Nikayas," in Nathan Katz, ed., *Buddhist and Western Psychology* (Boulder, Colo.: Prajna Press, 1983); ———, *The Psychology of Nirvana* (London: George Allen and Unwin, 1969); Barry Magid, *Ordinary Mind: Exploring the Common Ground of Zen and Psychoanalysis* (Somerville, Mass.: Wisdom, 2005); Jeremy D. Safran, *Psychoanalysis and Buddhism: An Unfolding Dialogue* (Somerville, Mass.: Wisdom, 2003).

Puggalavadins

Known as "The Personalists," this group of early Buddhists in India split from the orthodox STHAVIRAVADA SCHOOL over their insistence that the *pudgala* (person) does have an ultimate reality. This reality is not tied to our modern concept of the individual. Instead, it centers on a subtle self that can be seen only by an enlightened being. The Puggalavadins were active in the early stages of Buddhism in India. By around 100 C.E. they had ceased to exist as a separate philosophical school.

Further reading: Richard H. Robinson and Willard L. Johnson, *The Buddhist Religion: A Historical Introduction* (Belmont, Calif.: Wadsworth, 1997).

puja

A *puja* is a ritual offering food or other valuable things; it is the essential ritual of honor and obeisance in both Hindu and Buddhist practice. Typically a *puja* is an offering to a Buddhist deity such as GUAN YIN or Sakyamuni. In VAJRAYANA Buddhism of Tibet, Bhutan, and Mongolia, the *puja* offering includes recitations and visualizations. The *puja* is also a concept in Hindu worship, in which it includes symbolic offerings.

Further reading: Ngawang Paldan of Urga, *Shakyamuni Puja: Worshipping the Buddha with "The Vow of the Conduct of Bhadra."* Translated by M. Willson (London: Wisdom, 1988); Sangharakshita and Padmasri Adiccabandhu, *FWBO Puja Book: A Book of Buddhist Devotional Texts* (London: Windhors, 2004); Gregory

Sharkey, *Buddhist Daily Ritual: The Nitya Puja in Kathmandu Valley Shrines* (Bangkok: Orchid Press, 2001); Musashi Tachikawa, Shoun Hino, and Lalita Deodhar, *Puja and Samskara* (New Delhi: Motilal Banarsidass, 2001)

Pure Land Buddhism

Pure Land Buddhism is a general name for a variety of Buddhist groups—for instance, Jingtu Zong in China, Jodo Shinshu in Japan—that focus upon the worship of AMITABHA Buddha and express their faith in him through the recitation of the NEMBUTSU. Amitabha Buddha is believed to inhabit a paradisiacal land located in the west, often described as the Western Pure Land, to which those who recite the *nembutsu* are welcomed after death, a move toward their eventual goal, NIRVANA.

Emphasis on Amitabha (or Amida—from which the alternate name *Amidism* is taken), one of several important figures in Mahayana Buddhism, emerges around the third century C.E. in India, though some see in him a reflection of the Zoroastrian deity, Ahura Mazda, who also inhabited a western paradise. Worship of Amitabha was, according to some, initially advocated by Nagajuna (c. 150–c. 250) and passed to Vasubandhu (c. 320–400). The basic texts supporting Amitabha worship, the Larger and Smaller Sukhavati-vyuha, were translated into Chinese by Samghavarman and Kumarajiva (344–413), respectively. HUI YUAN (344–417) is generally credited with founding Pure Land Buddhism in China. Once introduced, it became one of the most popular forms of Buddhism in the country.

Amidism begins with the BODHISATTVA Dharmakara, who in the mythological past vowed to save all sentient beings before he gained his own Buddhahood. Dharmakara subsequently became the Buddha Amitabha. Amitabha now inhabits the western paradise, where he welcomes all who have faith in him. He thus emerges as a savior figure who saves the believer, and Amidism emerges as having a very different dynamic than most forms of Buddhism, which are built around one's own spiritual accomplishments, generally the mastery of meditation, yogic, and/or magical techniques.

Acknowledgment of and access to Amitabha could involve several different practices. In Tendai Buddhism, for example, one popular practice was the circumambulation of a statue of Amida. However, the most popular method was the simple calling upon his name through repeating the *nembutsu*.

Amidism was introduced into Japan during the Nara period; there it became one among many practices. It was also known in both TENDAI and SHINGON Buddhist circles. The elevation of Amidism began in the 11th century with such advocates as GENSHIN (942–1017), Yokan (1032–1111), and Ryonin (1071–1132), all of whom wrote treatises on Amida and his western paradise. However, it was HONEN (1133–1212) who saw faith in Amitabha and the use of the *nembutsu* as a separate and superior form of Buddhism and created the first separate Buddhist group built exclusively around the Pure Land idea, the JODO-SHU.

Honen left behind six prominent disciples. One of these, Shokobo (1148–1227), remained closest to Honen's thought. His most brilliant follower, SHINRAN (1173–1262), created a popular variation on Honen's work by jettisoning the monastic establishment and allowing priests to marry. Shinran founded the JODO SHINSHU sect. Other teachers founded additional variations. Today there are no fewer than a dozen Shinshu sects active in Japan. The primary division in the Jodo Shinshu community occurred at the end of the 16th century, resulting in the two largest groups, the HONPA HONGWANJI and HIGASHI HONWANJI, both headquartered in Kyoto.

Further reading: Alfred Bloom, *Shinran's Gospel of Pure Grace* (Tucson: The University of Arizona Press, 1965); *Buddhist Denominations and Schools in Japan* (Tokyo: Bukkto Dendo Kyokai, 1984); Dennis Hirota, ed., *Toward a Contemporary Understanding of Pure Land Bud-*

dhism: Creating a Shin Buddhist Theology in a Religiously Plural World (Albany: State University of New York Press, 2000); Gendo Nakai, *Shinran and His Religion of Pure Faith* (Kyoto: Shinshu Research Institute, 1937).

Putuo, Mt.

Mt. Putuo is actually an island off the coast of eastern China, near the city of Ningpo. It is renowned as the residence of GUAN YIN, the Chinese goddess of mercy. As such Mt. Putuo is in Chinese Buddhism one of the four SACRED MOUNTAINS OF CHINA, along with Mount Emei, Mount Jiutai, and Mount Wu tai. Putuo is often identified in popular thought with Potakala, the mythical island of perfection and legendary home of Guan Yin.

The name *Putuo* is actually a transliteration (phonetic rendering) of a Sanskrit original, *Potalaka*. Potalaka is the name of an island in the Indian Ocean on which the BODHISATTVA AVALOKITESVARA is said to live. Although Mount Putuo is the lowest of the four sacred mountains of Buddhism in elevation, it certainly receives the largest number of pilgrims every year. This is a reflection of Guan Yin's continued popularity in China. At one time, there were around 100 temples served by some 4,000 monks around Mount Putuo.

Today, visitors to Mt. Putuo may visit the Puji Temple, the largest and most famous temple on the island, originally constructed in 916 C.E., and Putuo Buddhist College, a training center for novice nuns. In 1980, the Unwilling-to-leave Quanyin Temple was rebuilt. The oldest temple on the island, it dates to 859 C.E. According to the story, a Japanese monk named Huier purchased a Guan Yin statue from Mt. Wu tai. Attempting to return it to Japan, he found his ship stalled and seemingly unable to sail beyond the island. Eventually he decided that the statue belonged on the island and it was installed in a temple on land donated by a local farmer.

Further reading: Mary A. Mullikin and Anna M. Hotchkis, *The Nine Sacred Mountains of China: an Illustrated Record of Pilgrimages Made in the Years 1935–1956* (Hong Kong: Vetch and Lee, 1973); Susan Nasquin and Chin-fang Yu, eds., *Pilgrims and Sacred Sites in China* (Berkeley: University of California Press, 1992).

Q

qi (chi)

Qi is the unseen energy that flows throughout all of creation, something akin to a life force that energizes matter. *Qi* (pronounced like the first syllable of *cheetah*) is a central concept in Chinese philosophy and, indeed, everyday discourse. In the *Daodejing qi* is seen as the force through which all elements and manifestations in the universe are bound together. *Qi* allows for the universe to attain a state of harmony and balance. In order to maintain dynamic stability there must be the alternation of yang, or male, *qi* and yin, or female, *qi*. In addition, a third *qi*, generated by harmony, allows for the presence of humans in the picture; we would not be possible without the dynamic interplay between heaven and earth. Seen through the lens of *qi* energies, then, the universe is more than simply the interplay of yin and yang. The union of the *qi* of heaven with that of earth and the two again with the *qi* of harmony creates absolute nurtured growth and communication.

One conclusion of this view, taken from the Han dynasty text *Taiping Jing*, is that humans are charged with the responsibility of preserving harmony in the universe. Humans are the unique conduits for the *qi* of harmony.

Qi manifests itself throughout the universe. In Chinese medicine *qi* is associated with the blood in the form of *xueqi*, "blood *qi*," and in FENG SHUI it is associated with water, the source of life energy. However, *qi* is separate from both: water channels *qi* but does not limit its convergence. According to the *Zangshu*, or *Book of Burial*, a feng shui classic dated to c. 300 C.E., *qi* is seen as the "mother" to water and wind, riding the forces of nature to collect them in specific points.

One of the oldest sources, the *Zuozhuan*, describing *qi* distinguishes six types: cold, heat, wind, rain, dark, and lightness. This use of *qi* is similar to the idea of humors in Greek and Arab medicine. (Yin and Yang are closely associated with cold and heat and have not become the universal forces they would later develop into during the Han dynasty.)

Further reading: Stephen L. Field, "In Search of Dragons: The Fold Ecology of Fengshui," in N. J. Girardot, James Miller, and Liu Xiaogan, eds., *Daoism and Ecology: Ways within a Cosmic Landscape* (Cambridge: Harvard University Press, 2001), 185–200; Chi-tim Lai, "The Daoist Concept of Central Harmony in the Scripture of Great Peace: Human Responsibility for the Maladies of Nature," in N. J. Girardot, James Miller, and Liu Xiaogan, eds., *Daoism and Ecology: Ways within a Cosmic Landscape* (Cambridge: Harvard University Press, 2001), 95–111.

qigong (ch'i-kung)

Qigong, literally "energy technique," is QI cultivation for health and spiritual advancement. The concept covers a range of related practices taught in China and abroad by Chinese popular masters. These individuals developed mass followings in mainland China during a brief period in the 1980s and early 1990s, after which the movement in general stalled and was officially discouraged. They taught daily exercise regimens involving breathing, body movement reminiscent of TAIJIQUAN, and, in some cases, meditation. *Qigong* is a very modern phenomenon that uses traditional concepts. It is first of all a repackaging of the popular concept of *qi,* or subtle energy, possessed by all phenomena, including people. *Qi* is an ancient term found in much writing related to Daoism and Confucianism. However, the modern *qigong* movement per se was separate from any traditional, recognized religious groups, including sectarian groups often discouraged by imperial Chinese regimes in the past. It is useful to see *qigong* not as a traditional religious practice, but as a response to the pressures of modernization as they played themselves out in China's social context of the 1980s and 1990s.

The CULTURAL REVOLUTION (1967–76) created a vacuum in Chinese society, a failure of "political utopianism." This gap was filled from the 1980s with increasing commodification and, in response, cynicism. *Qigong* provided an antidote to this cynicism. It called for a mild form of personal and social regeneration that gave hope to individuals at many levels of Chinese society. The individual need only practice *qigong* techniques of breathing and bodily movement, and health and social energies would all improve, the masters taught. The old (1949–76) socialist system based on *danwei* (work unit) control of each person was clearly

not going to work in the new era of liberalization. Yet these market-oriented reforms offered by the Deng Xiaoping era were fraught with uncertainty. In *qigong* was an alternative utopia separate from these disconcerting changes.

Many in Chinese society responded to the *qigong* vision, and *qigong* experienced rapid growth in the 1980s, to the point where Chinese media talked about "*qigong* fever." Groups could be seen practicing *qigong* exercises in parks in many Chinese cities. Rural practitioners also responded strongly to this practice. This mass movement was tolerated politically because it was seen as benign, something that could in fact be used by the leadership of the Chinese state. It was in addition something of which China could be proud, a traditional practice or "invention" that quickly gained scientific legitimacy. Such legitimacy was attributed very quickly once prominent scientists, including physicists, gave their support to *qigong* principles.

However, *qigong* eventually proved unable to manage all the utopian hopes that it created. It was not, it turned out, scientific enough. And throughout Chinese society of the 1980s and early 1990s practices based on individualism and commodity-driven capitalistic forms of expression gained ground. A pseudotraditional practice did not, many discovered, always fit the needs of a modernizing populace.

The movement after 1989 split into two directions. First was a commodified version easily managed through official definitions of orthodoxy: in other words, simple health exercises. The second direction was one based on serious moral criticism of society and, increasingly, millennial beliefs that great social change was coming to China. The standard bearer of the second movement was FALUN GONG, a group that had started in northeast China around the figure of Li Hongzhi, a former bureaucrat. Li innovated in terms of doctrine and organization and created a movement capable of organizing mass protests in the heart of Beijing. When these protests were public in 1995, the

Chinese state took official steps to disband and suppress this movement, then branded illegal.

Qigong became associated with Falun Gong in the minds of many. However, many qigong practitioners did not participate for religious reasons. Today qigong practitioners are still a common sight in parks throughout China, performing morning qigong exercises.

Further reading: Roger Jahnke, *The Healing Promise of Qi: Creating Extraordinary Wellness Through* Qigong *and Tai Chi* (Chicago: Contemporary Books, 2002); Richard E. Lee, *Scientific Investigations in Chinese* Qigong (San Clemente, Calif.: China Healthways Institute, 1999); Sat Chuen Hon, *Taoist* Qigong *for Health and Vitality: A Complete Program of Movement, Meditation, and Healing Sounds* (Boston: Shambhala, 2003).

Qiu Chuji (Ch'iu Ch'u-chi) (1148–1227)

founder of the Longmen lineage of Quanzhen Daoism

Qui Chuji was also called Longmen (Dragon Gate) in reference to the cave in which he lived for many years. Qiu had audiences and was honored by both the Jin ruler Shizong and the Mongol chief Genghis Khan. Qiu oversaw the building of many monasteries and the development of a more sedate lifestyle for QUANZHEN DAOISM adepts. He died at the Baiyun Temple in Beijing, which today remains the main temple for Quanzhen lineage.

Further reading: Bartholomew P. M. Tsui, *Taoist Tradition and Change: The Story of the Complete Perfection Sect in Hong Kong* (Hong Kong: Christian Study Centre on Chinese Religion and Culture, 1991).

Quanzhen Daoism

Quanzhen (pronounced "choo-en jen") Daoism is a major Daoist sect that was begun in China by WANG CHONGYANG (Wang Zhe, 1113–70), a member of the literati, during the Jin dynasty (1115–1234). This was a period of sudden political dislocation, with the passing of the Song and

the advent of a new dynasty ruled by foreigners. Wang had retired to a solitary life in the mountains, when he had several meetings with such immortals as LU DONGBIN. Impelled to start a tradition of teaching, he developed a highly syncretic mixture of practices and morality well suited to the times. Wang's Quanzhen, or Complete Perfection, sect put greater emphasis on self-cultivation and less emphasis on intricate visualization exercises, elaborate rituals, or talismanic magic. The particular goal was to refine the body's energies through the practices of inner alchemy (neidan). Wang called his meditative practice jing zuo, "quiet sitting," a term probably borrowed from CHAN BUDDHISM. He borrowed from Confucianism an emphasis on filial piety and ascetic practices. His teaching emphasized abstaining from sex, alcohol, and strong vegetables (wu xin). He and his disciples lived a rustic lifestyle. When he died in 1127 he had around 15 followers.

Later Quanzhen practitioners evolved a monastic lifestyle, in contrast to most other Daoist groups. Quanzhen monks were expected to own only seven articles: a meditation cushion, a robe, a bowl, a straw hat, a horsehair whisk, a scripture bag, and a staff. Images of Wang Yangqun typically depict him holding a whisk.

In the Yuan and Ming periods, two events affected Quanzhen. The first was a series of debates. Quanzhen was in direct competition with Buddhism and other Daoist schools during the Yuan and Ming periods. In a famous series of debates hosted by the emperor in 1281, Quanzhen adepts were consistently bested by Buddhists. The defeat meant Quanzhen did not receive imperial sponsorship or patronage.

The second was an amalgamation with Jindan Dao (Golden Elixir Way) practitioners in the latter half of the Yuan. This school, which predated Quanzhen, had developed in the south and shared some similarities with Quanzhen. While both schools recognized some of the same patriarchs, including Lu Dongbin and Liu Haichan, Jindan Dao had a separate list of five patriarchs, starting with Zhang Boduan, author of *Wuzhen pian* (Essays on realizing truth). The two groups shared some common terms and a focus on inner alchemy, but unlike followers of Quanzhen, Jin-dan followers were not celibate; nor did they follow strict dietary strictures such as vegetarianism or rules against eating grains.

While there is some disagreement, most sources say that Quanzhen and Longmen, its major school, suffered a long decline during the Ming. It was revitalized with the appearance of WANG CHANGYUE (d. 1680) in the final days of the Ming. According to legend Wang met the "transition" master (*chuanjie lushi,* a master who passes secret knowledge to an initiate) Jiao Zhensong and accepted him as a disciple but refused to transmit the true teachings. They separately wandered an additional 10 years. When they met again, in 1628, on Mt. Jiugong in Hubei, Jiao relented and agreed to transmit the liturgy to Wang.

In 1655, after the An Lushan rebellion and the triumph of the Manchu forces over the Ming, Wang settled in Beijing. The fighting had emptied Beijing's most important Daoist temple, the BAI-YUN GUAN, except for one caretaker, who invited Wang Changyue to live there. Wang then set about building an organization. Significantly, he established an ordination process for Quanzhen monks. An ordained monk would then be able to travel freely to any Quanzhen temple. The ordination process involved 100 days of lectures and ritual, including passing of the precepts to the initiate. Initiates were expected to study for at least three years. A ranking system, the ordination register (*dengzhenlu*), determined whether a monk could have a position in a monastery or would adopt the wandering lifestyle of the itinerant (*canfang*).

One strength of the Quanzhen monastic network was the maintenance of wandering monastics. And with the spread of literacy and prosperity of the Ming, it was natural to set out in new directions. Wang Changyue, having established himself in Beijing, began to hold ordination ceremonies. Two were held in Beijing, in 1658 and 1659. He then proceeded to Nanjing and held an ordination ceremony in 1663. Thereafter he urged his disciples to move south and hold ordinations on their own. Arriving on the scene at a time of traumatic dynastic transition, Wang's revitalized Quanzhen attracted many new adherents. He is the primary source of the Longmen Renaissance.

See also QIU CHUJI.

Further reading: Vincent Goossaert, "The Quanzhen Clergy, 1700–1950," in John Lagerwey, ed., *Religion and Chinese Society: The Transformation of a Field* (Hong Kong: École Française d'Extrême-Orient and Chinese University of Hong Kong, 2001); Bartholomew P. M. Tsui, *Taoist Tradition and Change: The Story of the Complete Perfection Sect in Hong Kong* (Hong Kong: Christian Study Centre on Chinese Religion and Culture, 1991).

Questions of King Milinda (Milindapanha)

The *Questions* is a Pali book that, while not part of the Theravada official canon, has nevertheless been influential. It recounts a dialog between a monk, Nagasena, and King Milinda. King Milinda (in Greek, Menandros) (r. c. 155–130 B.C.E.) ruled one of the Greek-controlled states in northern India established after Alexander the Great's incursion into the region in the third century B.C.E. The dialog involves a clear explanation of the basic teachings of Buddhism for the benefit of the king, who eventually converts to Buddhism. The book seems to have been designed as a tool to assist the conversion of Greeks to Buddhism.

Further reading: T. W. Rhys Davids, trans., *The Questions of King Milinda.* Vols. 25 and 36, *Sacred Books of the East* (1894. Reprint, New York: Dover, 1963).

R

Rahula *only son of the Buddha*

Rahula was born to Prince Siddhartha and his wife, YASODARA, when the prince was 29. Rahula later joined the Buddha's roving band and became a devout disciple. In later lore Rahula was grouped with the list of 16 (later 18) ARHATs, or enlightened ones, found in many Buddhist temples.

Rahula literally means "obstacle," a word used by Prince Gautama because he saw the birth of a son as an obstacle to his dream of leading an ascetic lifestyle. His father, Suddhodana, promptly named the child Rahula, since he did not want his son to pursue that life. In fact, Gautama decided to depart quickly in order not to develop strong emotional ties to his son, and he left the very night the child was born.

Years later when the Buddha was passing through his father's kingdom his wife, Yasodara, and son, Rahula, met him on the street. Yasodara said to Rahula, "Ask your father for your inheritance." The Buddha then made Rahula a novice (*sramanera*) and he spent the rest of his life in the sangha, or Buddhist community.

The Chinese traveler XUAN ZANG relates a story of meeting Rahula, something physically impossible in normal terms, since their lives were separated by more than 1,000 years. An old man with bushy eyebrows appears at the doorway of a good-natured brahman. The old man is offered milk. He drinks and afterward says its taste is worse than that of the water in which he had washed the Buddha's bowl in RAJGIR. The old man then admits that he is Rahula, who has delayed his entry into NIRVANA.

Further reading: P. V. Bapat, *2500 Years of Buddhism* (Delhi: Publications Division, Ministry of Information and Broadcasting, 1959); Reginald A. Ray, *Buddhist Saints in India: A Study in Buddhist Values and Orientations* (Oxford: Oxford University Press, 1994).

Rahula, Walpola (1907–1997) *Sri Lankan monk and Buddhist critic*

Walpola Rahula was born in the village of Walpola in southern Sri Lanka, the son of Hettigoda Gamage Don Carolis De Silva, a devout Buddhist, astrologer, and Ayurvedic physician. He grew up at a time when Buddhism was experiencing a significant revival in the face of the government-backed growth of Christianity in the 19th century. He emerged after World War II as a leader in the revivalist movement and an advocate of Buddhism's being named the state religion. In that cause he founded the Buddha Sasana Samithis in 1952.

Rahula also became a learned student of the THERAVADA Buddhist scriptures and was for many years an active correspondent with the PALI TEXT SOCIETY. He taught at Vidyopaya University and rose to be vice-chancellor. From his knowledge of Theravada, in 1959, he wrote what became a popular international best-selling book on Buddhism, *What the Buddha Taught*. In 1964, that book led Edmund Perry, chairman of the Department of History and Literature of Religion (one of the pioneer university religious studies departments) at Northwestern University in Illinois, to invite Rahula to teach at Northwestern, the first Buddhist monk to hold a professorship at a major Western university. While there, he became instrumental in the founding of the Washington (D.C.) Vihara, the first Theravada temple in the United States.

Upon his return to Sri Lanka after some years in the United States, he served as chancellor of Kelaniya University.

The author of many items on Buddhism, Rahula is still best remembered for *What the Buddha Taught*. It is a popular college text in introductory courses and has been translated into a number of languages, including French, German, Spanish, Italian, Serbo-Croatian, Sinhalese, Chinese, Burmese, Thai, Korean, Vietnamese, and Tamil.

Further reading: Somaratna Balasoonriya et al., eds., *Buddhist Studies in Honor of Walpola Rahula* (London: Gordon Fraser, 1980); Guònadasa Liyanagâe, *On the Path: Biography of the Venerable Aggamahapandita Professor Dr. Walpola Sri Rahula, Chancellor of Kelaniya University, Supreme Master of Buddhist Scriptures* (Dehiwala, Sri Lanka: Buddhist Cultural Centre, 1995); Walpola Rahula, *The Heritage of the Bhikkhu: The Buddhist Tradition of Service* (New York: Grove Press, 2003); ———, *The History of Buddhism in Ceylon: The Anuradhapura Period: 3rd Century B.C.–10th Century A.D.* (Colombo, Sri Lanka: M. D. Gunasena, 1956); ———, *What the Buddha Taught* (New York: Grove Press, 1959, 1974).

Rajgir (Rajagriha, Rajgiri, Rajghir, New Rajagriha)

Rajgir, the ancient capital city of the MAGADHA kingdom, was among the first places visited by GAUTAMA BUDDHA as he began to spread the teachings of his new religion. It is located some 20 miles from BODHGAYA, where the Buddha attained enlightenment. Meaning literally "Royal Palaces," Rajgir can be considered the first Buddhist city. The Magadha kings from Bimbisara to ASOKA resided in Rajgir. As with most early Buddhist centers, little remains of Rajgir's past as a Buddhist center today. The once-flourishing city is today just a small town. Only ruins remain of Venuvana Venuvana Vihar, the monastery constructed by King Bimbisara as a residence for Buddha. Japanese Buddhists recently constructed a contemporary STUPA on top of Gridhakuta Hill, known as the Shanti Stupa, or Peace Pagoda.

Among the converts of the Buddha's 12-year stay was King Bimbisara, who attended his talks on Gridhakuta Hill (Vulture Peak). Here the Buddha would deliver what are termed the Wisdom Sutras (some of his first words recorded in writing). Buddha also frequently spent periods of meditation at the Jivkamaravana monastery, then located in a beautiful orchard. The nearby Saptaparni caves were the site of the first Buddhist council called by his leading followers after the Buddha's death. Ajatsatni (Asvajit; Pali, Assaji), one of the Buddha's leading disciples, received some of his ashes and built a stupa to hold them as well as a monastery. That site is now a mound used as a graveyard.

Rajgir was also the site of the monk Devatta's treachery. DEVATTA, a cousin of the Buddha, arranged for King Ajatasatru, Bimbisara's son, to make the wild elephant, Nalagiri, drunk, so it would attack the Buddha. The elephant stopped in its tracks and knelt down when addressed by the Buddha.

The Chinese pilgrim FA XIAN visited Rajgir and left a detailed description in his *Record of Buddhistic Kingdoms (Foguo ji),* written around 400

C.E. He mentions there were three monasteries in the old city, but other sources indicate there were 16 built by King Bimbisara. Already in Fa Xian's day the old city of Rajgir was deserted.

Further reading: Trilok Chandra Majupuria, *Holy Places of Buddhism in Nepal and India: A Guide to Sacred Places in Buddha's Lands* (Columbia, Mo.: South Asia Books, 1987); Tarthang Tulku, ed., *Holy Places of the Buddha.* Vol. 9, *Crystal Mirror* (Berkeley, Calif.: Dharma, 1994).

Rampa, T. Lobsang (c. 1911–1981)
fraudulent Tibetan lama

T(uesday) Lobsang Rampa is the pseudonym of Cyril Henry Hoskins (c. 1911–81), who claimed that he had traveled to Tibet and been initiated as a lama. His story became the subject of a set of autobiographical books by him and his wife, Sanya, that became quite popular in the 1960s and 1970s.

Hoskins was born in Devon, England. The son of plumber, he worked as a young man in his father's shop. He grew up in England and eventually settled in Nottinghamshire, where he worked for a surgical instrument company and then became a clerk with a correspondence school. At some point in the late 1940s–early 1950s, he shaved his head and began referring to himself as "Dr. Kuan-suo." In 1956, he published his first book, *The Third Eye*. By this time he had moved to Ireland.

The Third Eye, the first of almost a dozen books, written under the name Lobsang Rampa, claimed that the author had travelled to Tibet, where he had undergone lengthy training and been initiated as a Tibetan lama. Among the most memorable claims in the book was that the author had undergone a surgical operation that opened his third eye, the psychic center believed by many occultists to be located between and just above the two eyes. At the time this book appeared, there was a tremendous interest in Tibet, viewed by many as a land of mystical accomplishment,

and there were few firsthand accounts to satisfy the hunger for information.

The Third Eye was followed by a sequel, *Doctor from Lhasa*, in 1959. Both books sold well to a public otherwise ignorant of Tibet and its ways. However, as they found their way into the hands of people knowledgeable about Tibet and Tibetan Buddhism, a number of obvious errors were readily identified. An initial negative review appeared in the parapsychological journal *Tomorrow*, in which a Tibetan scholar, Chen Chi Chang, branded the book entertaining fiction. Subsequently, a private detective, Clifford Burgess, tried to find Rampa and eventually tracked him to his home in Ireland. He revealed the fact that Rampa had never been anywhere near Tibet and that, of course, the claimed operation had never occurred.

In the face of the exposure of his hoax, Hoskins would later claim that his body had been taken over by the spirit of a Tibetan lama. Also, aware that the consumers of his books either had not read of or did not care about the exposure of his hoax, through the 1960s and into the early 1970s Hoskins continued to turn out additional Rampa titles, which have continued to be reprinted to the present. Thus the hoax is perpetuated even in the face of the presence of many Tibetan teachers in the West and the ready availability of authoritative books on Tibetan Buddhism.

Further reading: Chen Chi Chan, "Tibetan Phantasies," *Tomorrow* 6, no. 2 (Spring 1958): 13–15; T. Lobsang Rampa [pseudonym of Cyril Henry Hoskins], *Doctor from Lhasa* (1959. Reprint, New Brunswick, N.J.: Inner Light-Global Communications, 1991); ———, *The Rampa Story* (London: Souvenir Press, 1960); ———, *The Third Eye* (Garden City, N.Y.: Doubleday, 1956); Gordon Stein, *Encyclopedia of Hoaxes* (Detroit: Gale Research, 1993).

refuge, to take (*saranagamana*)

In the traditional formulation, common to all forms of Buddhism, the individual "takes refuge" in the three treasures—the Buddha, the Dharma, and the Sangha. Taking refuge in the three treasures is the foundation of Buddhism as a religious system. It is the critical first step to be taken by any individual. In the Pali formulation, the individual recites:

> I go to the Buddha for refuge.
> I go to the Dharma for refuge.
> I go to the Sangha for refuge.

These three objects are also known as the "three refuges" (*trisarana*).

Taking refuge is not, strictly speaking, a commandment or regulation. The action is more an aspiration to lead a life centered around these three elements. (The statement is a vocative statement that alters the status of the participant.) After performing this ceremony one becomes a devotee, an *upasaka* (feminine: *upasika*), and attempts to follow the five precepts (PANCA SILA). In Tibetan Buddhism a fourth object is added, the guru. The master embodies the spirit of the Buddha dharma to which the individual orients himself or herself. In other words, the first three refuges, the three treasures, are embodied in the moment in the person of the guru. Naropa stated that his mind was the Buddha, his speech the Dharma, and his body the community.

Further reading: Mohan Wijayaratna, *Buddhist Monastic Life: According to the Texts of the Theravada Tradition.* Translated by Claude Grangier and Steven Collins (Cambridge: Cambridge University Press, 1990).

Reiyukai

Reiyukai, one of several 20th-century groups inspired by the life and teachings of the Japanese prophet NICHIREN (1222–82), is a lay Buddhist organization that aims to help individuals achieve their potential through practicing self-reliance and taking control of their own destiny. Members of Reiyukai are asked to build their religious life around four practices: recitation from the LOTUS SUTRA, appreciation of one's ancestors, interaction with fellow members of Reiyukai, and sharing of Reiyukai teachings with others. As other Nichiren groups do, Reiyukai considers the Lotus Sutra the most important of all Buddhist writings. Early in the organization's history, the cofounders, Kubo and Kotani, selected the most insightful passages of the Lotus Sutra to create what is now termed the Blue Sutra. Members are asked to recite the Blue Sutra every day.

Reiyukai's origins can be traced to 1920 and the attempt of a young Buddhist layman, Kakutaro Kubo (1892–1944), to find a practical alternative to the rather formal Buddhism of post–World War I Japan. He combined a religious perspective derived from Nichiren's emphasis on the Lotus Sutra with themes of hope, self-reliance, and assuming of control of individual destiny. From a small beginning in 1920, with the assistance of his brother's wife, Kimi Kotani (d. 1971), an organization emerged. Kotani was named Reiyukai's first president in 1930, when Reiyukai was formally organized. Kubo died during World War II, and after the war, Kotani led Reiyukai in an expanding program of social betterment, with a special emphasis on its youth program.

International expansion began in 1972 with the opening of the first Reiyukai center in the United States. Work followed in Brazil and Mexico and eventually around the Pacific realm, especially in places with a local Japanese community. The first European center was opened in 1978. Highlighting its international development was the organization's sponsoring of the LUMBINI International Research Institute in Nepal.

The original headquarters of Reiyukai was completed in 1937 at Azabu-Iigura, Tokyo. In 1975, the current leader of the organization, Tsugunari Kubo (1936–   ), the founder's son, opened the Shakaden, the present headquarters–meeting hall complex, constructed on the site of the former one. The meeting hall is dominated by a six-meter-high statue of Buddha carved from a single log of camphor wood.

Further reading: Tsugunari Kubo, *The Development of Japanese Lay Buddhism* (Tokyo: Reiyukai, 1986); Helen, Hardacre, *Lay Buddhism in Contemporary Japan: Reiyukai Kyodan* (Princeton, N.J.: Princeton University Press, 1984); *Reiyukai: Awareness, Action, and Development* (Tokyo: Reiyukai, 1997).

release of the burning mouth ceremony (*fangyan kou*)

This ritual of Chinese Buddhism is meant to release the PRETA, or hungry ghosts, from hell. It is performed as part of the Ullambana, or Yupan, festival for departed spirits in July of the lunar calendar. Typically lasting five hours, the burning mouth ceremony requires the performing monks to use ritual implements such as the *dorje*, or bells, to break through the barriers of hell, open the mouths of the hungry ghosts, and pour blessed water down their parched throats. The *pretas* then take refuge in the Buddha and recite the BODHISATTVA vow. They are thereby reborn, either in human form or in the western paradise presided over by AMITABHA.

The burning mouth ritual is said to have originated in a dream Ananda experienced. He asked the Buddha to give him *dharanis* (strings of mantras) to use to alleviate the suffering of hungry ghosts.

relics of the Buddha

GAUTAMA BUDDHA, the founder of Buddhism, died around 480 B.C.E. at KUSINAGARA, a town in the northeast corner of Uttar Pradesh, India, near the border with Nepal. Various Buddhist scriptures tell of his death and the events immediately following it. According to the story, the Buddha's body was cremated. In the ashes were found a number of relics—teeth and bones. A number of Buddha's followers of royal status expressed their desire to have the relics, and a Brahmin priest named Drona emerged to divide them equally. His initial decision was to create eight sets, one for each ruler desirous of having them. However, Drona was discovered to have hidden some relics, which were later stolen. By this process, the relics were distributed to the eight cities in various parts of India, and those stolen to a ninth. Drona retained the vase that had previously held the relics. At each site to which the relics were dispersed, a STUPA was built to hold them. Drona also built a stupa to hold the vase. Then a century later, King ASOKA conquered all the lands where the relics had been sent, regathered the relics, and redistributed them to a variety of places throughout southern Asia from Sri Lanka to China.

Buddhism, as Christianity, does not need relics as an essential part of its practice. They do serve to humanize the often-austere faith and provide a local focus for a faith that originated in a distant land many centuries ago. They have been seen as a constant sign of the Enlightened One's constant presence. Also, as with the relics associated with Jesus (his cross, Veronica's veil, the shroud of Turin, etc.), there are usually significant gaps in the historical record tying those items presently claimed to be genuine relics of the Buddha to the events reputed to have immediately followed his death.

Some of the more important relics that may be seen at Buddhist shrines around the world would include the following:

Sri Lanka—At Anuradhapura a stupa, Thuparama Dagabawhich, houses what is said to be Buddha's alms bowl and his right collarbone. In Kandy, at the center of the island nation, one may visit the Buddha's tooth, now housed in a golden stupa, known as Malagawa Vihara (or Dalada Maligawa). In 1986, the president of Sri Lanka donated a true relic of the Buddha to the leader of the Japanese Buddhist group AGON SHU for enshrinement in their temple near Kyoto.

- Myanmar—Several strands of hair are to be found in the Buddha Relics Chamber at Myingyan (Bagan). A tooth recovered from a collapsed pagoda in Mrauk-U, Myanmar, has been sent to the Golden Pagoda Buddhist Temple in Singapore.
- China—China is home to two of the most famous relics of the Buddha. In the present capital, Beijing, Ling Guang Si Monastery is home to one of Buddha's teeth. The medieval capital, Xian, had been the home to Buddha's finger bone, housed in Fa Men Si Monastery, That relic had been lost, however, in the changes that had occurred in China, including the rise and fall of various forms of Buddhism and then the rise of a secular government in the 20th century. However, in the 1980s, during archaeological exploration in Xian, the subterranean crypt where the finger had been housed was rediscovered.
- Thailand—In 1994, the Kingdom of Thailand initiated a project at KUSINAGARA (KUS-INARA), where Buddha died, as part of a larger movement to reestablish Buddhism in the land of its origin. One part of the impressive monastic complex is the Maha Chetiya, a shrine designed by the Thai king Bhumibhol Adulyadej. Here Buddha's relics originally held in Thailand have been placed.

Further reading: J. F. Fleet, "The Tradition about the Corporeal Relics of Buddha," *Journal of the Royal Asiatic Society* (1907): 341–363. Available online at Lightwatcher: An Oasis for the Heart, Mind and Spirit. URL: http://www.lightwatcher.com/old_lightbytes/buddha_on_tour.html. Accessed April 2, 2006; T. W. Rhys Davids, "Asoka and the Buddha-Relics," *Journal of the Royal Asiatic Society* (1901): 397–410; John Strong, *Relics of the Buddha* (Princeton, N.J.: Princeton University Press, 2004).

ren (benevolence)

Ren is the highest virtue taught in CONFUCIANISM. It is translated by several terms in English—"love," "goodness," "benevolence," or "humanity"—none of which is exact. In human relations *ren* is expressed in loyalty between two people: a ruler is kind to his subjects, a husband is good to his wife, and the subject or wife is loyal in return.

Further reading: Roger T. Ames and Henry Rosemont, Jr., *The Analects of Confucius: A Philosophical Translation* (New York: Ballantine, 1998).

Rennyo (1415–1499) *proponent of Jodo Shinshu teachings in Japanese Buddhism*

Rennyo, the leading proponent of JODO SHIN-SHU Buddhism in the 15th century, was born at Hongan-ji, the head temple of the Jodo Shinshu movement temple. Rennyo was the son of Zonnyo (1396–1457), the seventh grand abbot. Rennyo would later succeed his father.

Rennyo grew to adulthood at a time when the Jodo Shinshu movement was split into several competing factions. In the meantime, Hongan-ji, the site of the grave of the movement's founder, SHINRAN, was neglected. Rennyo lived quietly until 1457, when he was chosen to assume the abbot's job.

He began to place himself in the center of the Jodo Shinshu disputes through a series of epistles. Each discussed one of Shinran's main teachings and attacked those who deviated from it. His success at winning new converts, especially in Kyoto and its immediate environs, and criticizing rival Jodo Shinshu groups attracted many followers but also led to repeated attacks, both rhetorical and military, on him and those temples associated with Hongan-ji. However, his following continued to grow across the country.

In 1471, Rennyo relocated to Yoshizaki in Hukurokudo, where he enjoyed great success in winning over the public. The spread of the Jodo Shinshu message led to a series of armed clashes between believers and both secular authorities and rival Buddhists. As a whole, the Jodo Shinshu forces won and in the process assumed a quite critical attitude toward other Buddhist groups and the deities they acknowledged. Shinshu Buddhists tend to relate exclusively to AMITABHA Buddha. While having great success in promoting the Shinshu faith, Rennyo had less success in restraining his followers from denouncing the other Buddhist BODHISATTVAS and Buddhas.

Rennyo spent the last years of his life in Kyoto, where he died in 1499.

Further reading: Minor Rogers and Ann Rogers, *Rennyo: The Second Founder of Shin Buddhism* (Berkeley, Calif.: Asian Humanities Press, 1991).

Rhys Davids, Caroline Augusta (née Foley) (1858–1942) *early Pali scholar in Britain*

Because she was the wife of THOMAS WILLIAM RHYS DAVIDS, the accomplishments of Caroline Rhys Davids have been somewhat obscured. However, before meeting her future husband, she was a graduate of University College in London, where she received her master's and doctoral degrees. She subsequently became a reader in Pali at the London School of Oriental and African Studies and later moved on to Manchester University. She was 36 when she married Rhys Davids (who was himself 52). Beginning in 1900, she produced more than 20 volumes of translations of Pali texts. Thus it was not mere sentimentality for her to succeed her husband as president of the PALI TEXT SOCIETY after his death in 1922. She led the society for the remaining two decades of her life. She also became deeply interested in theosophy and psychological interpretations of Buddhist terms.

Further reading: Caroline Rhys Davids, *Buddhist Manual of Psychological Ethics* (London: Pali Text Society, 1974); ———, *Sakya or Buddhist Origins* (London: South Asia Books, 1978); T. W. Rhys Davids, trans., and C. A. F. Rhys-Davids, trans., *Dialogues of the Buddha*. 3 vols. (London & Boston: Luzac, 1899–1921).

Rhys Davids, Thomas William (1843–1922) *pioneering British scholar of Pali and Buddhism*

T. W. Rhys Davids spent much of his life working on translations of the Pali canon and promoting awareness of THERAVADA Buddhism. Rhys Davids was born in Colchester, England, the son of a Congregational minister. He attended the university of Breslau, where he studied Sanskrit, and after receiving his Ph.D. he took a position with the Ceylon Civil Service in 1871. In Sri Lanka, he learned both Sinhalese and Tamil. He first became aware of Pali while serving as a magistrate in a court case and soon added it to his linguistic repertoire.

He returned to London after only two years in Sri Lanka and in 1873 became a barrister. He authored his first book, on Singalese coins, in 1877 but began to promote the study of Pali. In 1881, he delivered the Hibbert Lectures at Manchester College, Oxford, during which he announced the formation of the PALI TEXT SOCIETY. The following year he secured an appointment as the professor of Pali and Buddhist literature at University College, London.

Rhys Davids would spend the rest of his life working on translations of the Pali Canon. His work would be published by the society and appear in the Sacred Books of the East series edited by his colleague MAX MÜLLER. In the process, he met another Pali scholar, Caroline Foley, 15 years his junior, whom he married in 1894. Soon after their marriage, the pair went to America, where he lectured at Cornell University; the lectures were published as *Buddhism: Its History and Literature* (1896). They had three children, and she would later succeed him as president of the Pali Text Society.

In 1904, he became the professor of comparative religion at Victoria University in Manchester (his wife, CAROLINE AUGUSTA RHYS DAVIDS, was a professor at Manchester University). In 1910 he also became president of the India Society (later the Royal India Pakistan and Ceylon Society) based in London. The need to divide time between

London and Manchester led to his retirement in 1915. He settled in Surrey, where he lived the last years of his life, much of which was devoted to the compilation of a new *Pali-English Dictionary*.

Rhys Davids campaigned tirelessly to promote awareness of Theravada Buddhism. Some of Rhys Davids's ideas were at times controversial, however. For instance, he felt there was a racial affinity between the British nation and Buddhism. Nevertheless, such opinions are outweighed by his very real accomplishments.

Further reading: T. W. Rhys Davids, trans., *The Questions of King Milinda*. Vols. 25 and 36, *Sacred Books of the East* (1891, 1894. Reprint 1967); —— and C. A. F. Rhys-Davids (trans.), *Dialogues of the Buddha*. 3 vols. (London & Boston: Clarendon Press, 1899–1921); —— and William Stede, *The Pali Text Society's Pali-English Dictionary* (London: Pali Text Society, 1979); Ananda Wickremeratne, *The Genesis of an Orientalist: Thomas William Rhys Davids and Buddhism in Sri Lanka* (Delhi: Motilal Banarsidass, 1984).

Rime Movement (Tibet)

The Rime Movement was an effort by a set of leading Tibetan teachers in eastern Tibet to construct an eclectic approach to Buddhism that drew on all of the major Tibetan Buddhist schools. Jamyang Khyentse Wangpo (1820–92), Chogyur Dechen Lingpan (1829–70), Ju Mipham Gyatso (1846–1912), and Jamgon Kongtrul Lodro Thaye (1813–99) were among the major exponents of the Rime Movement. Jamgon Kongtrul Lodro Thaye was also notable for reviving the formerly prominent Shangpa Kagyu lineage, which had almost disappeared but which could be traced back to a famous 11th-century female *yogini*, NIGUMA. He would be the teacher of Karma Lekshe Drayang, the father of KALU RINPOCHE (1905–89). Kalu Rinpoche would be recognized as the reincarnation of Jamgon Kongtrul Lodro Thaye and the inheritor of the Shangpa lineage.

The Rime Movement was notable for its production of a set of new books—compendiums of materials from the various Tibetan schools arranged topically. The most important expression of the tradition was Jamgon Kongtrul's multivolume *Five Great Treasures*.

As Tibetan Buddhism had grown in the West, the Rime, or nonsectarian, approach to its study has been appealing to people who are not interested in the historical differences that have divided the schools and wish to draw broadly on the teachings presented by different teachers. A variety of different independent Rime centers have begun to emerge.

Further reading: Jamgön Kongtrul Lodrö Tayé, *The Great Path of Awakening: A Commentary on the Mahayana Teaching of the Seven Points of Mind Training*. Translated by Ken McLeod (Boston: Shambhala, 1987); ———, *Jamgön Kongtrul's Retreat Manual*. Translated by Ngawang Zangpo (Ithaca, N.Y.: Snow Lion, 1994); Ringu Tulku, "The Rimé Movement of Jamgon Kongtrul the Great." Buddhist Information of North America. Available online. URL: http://www.buddhistinformation.com/tibetan/rim%E9_movement_of_jamgon_kongtrul.htm. Accessed on October 15, 2005.

rinpoche   See TITLES AND TERMS OF ADDRESS, BUDDHIST.

Rinzai Zen

Rinzai Zen is one of the two main forms of ZEN BUDDHISM to emerge in Japan in the 13th century, along with SOTO ZEN. During the Kamakura shogunate (1185–1333) Rinzai was the dominant school of Buddhism in Japan, largely because of its practices emphasizing sudden enlightenment and KOAN. It later declined but enjoyed a revival in the 18th century and today is a major presence in Japan and internationally.

Rinzai was introduced to Japan by Japanese teachers who had traveled to China and subsequently attempted to duplicate what they had learned and experienced in their homeland. During the 10th–12th centuries in China, LINJI CHAN had divided into a number of schools each characterized by a unique lineage of enlightened leaders that could be traced to the early patriarchs of ZEN BUDDHISM practice in China and an emphasis on the use of koans, the questions and stories presented to the individual practitioner that attempt to confound the intellect and lead to intuitive jumps toward the realization of truth.

Zen had been practiced in Japan prior to the arrival of EISAI (1141–1213) in Japan from his years of study in China and his attempt to reform Tendai Zen along Zen lines beginning in 1200. However, Zen meditation was integrated as a relatively minor practice in other Buddhist groups. Eisai had gone to China to seek the origin of TENDAI Buddhism (known in China as the TIAN TAI SCHOOL) but upon his arrival at Mt. Tian Tai, discovered that the monastic community had become a Chan community. He would on his second trip to China in 1187 study for four years with the leadership of the Huang-Long Linji school and return to Japan in 1191 with authority to teach.

When Eisai found the Tendai leadership uninterested in his campaign to reform Tendai along Rinzai lines, he sought support among the shogunate's court in Kamakura. A main line of argument was presented in his book *On Promoting Zen to Protect the Nation,* which followed the attempt of Buddhist leaders for centuries to argue that Buddhism in general and their version of Buddhism in particular was the best religion to rely upon for its ability to protect Japan from various calamities.

With the shogunate's support, Eisai was able to found Jufuku-ji in Kamakura. Then two years later he opened Kennin-ji in Kyoto. From these two temples, he attempted to spread Zen within the Tendai establishment. Instead of reforming Tendai, however, he succeeded in founding Zen as a separate Buddhist sect in Japan.

During the early and mid-13th century, additional schools of Linji Chan would be introduced into Japan both by Japanese who traveled to China to study and by Chinese priests who traveled to Japan to teach. For example, in 1235 Enni Bennen (1202–80), who had studied with Eisai's students, traveled to China, where he studied with Wu-chun Shih-fan (1178–1249), of the Yangji Linji school. Upon his return in 1241, he founded a new temple, Tofuku-ji, in Kyoto. His temple flourished as he promoted Zen within a larger philosophy of its harmony with the main forms of Buddhism of the time—Tendai and SHINGON.

Enni's contemporary, Muhon Kakushin (1207–98), began his career as a Shingon priest. In China, he studied with Wumen Huikai (1183–1260). Upon his return in the 1260s, he founded Kokoku-ji, located in Kii Province south of Kyoto, which would become the head temple of the Saiho school.

Among the Chinese who taught in Japan was Lanji Daoling (Rankei Doryu) (1213–78), who settled in KAMAKURA, where he drew an increasingly larger following. After several years he had to abandon the small temple that he had originally inhabited and built the expansive Kencho-ji, which would later become the head temple of the Daikaku school of Rinzai. Another Chinese priest, Wuxue Zuyuan (Mugaku Sogen) (1226–86), was sent to Kamakura from China as a successor to Lan-chi. He headed Kencho-ji but then also became the first abbot of Engaku-ji, the large monastic complex immediately north of Kamakura. Mugaku Sogen was a dominant influence in the city for the seven years he resided there, just enough time to establish the Bukko school of Linji.

Those 13th-century Zen teachers in Kamakura set the tone for Buddhism in the city and had the effect of identifying Zen with the shogun, his court, and the samurai warriors in and around the city. For several centuries, Kamakura Zen would be the dominant force across the country, though never to the extent of subverting Tendai Buddhism or preventing the rise of PURE LAND BUDDHISM.

Without really changing the practice at different temples, in the 1330s, the various Zen groups were joined into what was termed the Gozan system. Five temples in Kyoto and Kamakura were designated as the major, or Gozan, temples—Kencho-ji, Engaku-ji, Kennin-ji, Jufuku-ji, and Tofuku-ji. The number and designation of these main temples varied over the next two centuries. A second ranking was subsequently added and then the great majority of temples fell into a third level. Apart from the officially recognized temples were a number of private Zen centers. This system facilitated secular control of the Zen community.

It was during this period that the tea ceremony was established as part of Zen practice. Eisai had emphasized tea drinking for health; in 1211 he had written the treatise *On Drinking Tea and Prolonging One's Life*. However, it would be at Daitoku-ji, the great temple founded in the 14th century by Shuho Myocho (1282–1337), an outstanding representative of the Daio Rinzai school, that the tea ceremony developed. A low-ranking priest during his life, he had a role in reviving Zen in his day that was only recognized after his death. One of Shuho's successors, Ikkyu Sojun (1394–1481), drew a host of artists and writers to Daitoku-ji, and among some of them, such as the tea master Murata Juko (1423–1502), the TEA CEREMONY began to take shape, later to be perfected by Takeno Joo and others (1502–55). The ceremony is designed to focus attention on the present moment, the only real moment, and calls for a total involvement in one's life in the present.

Rinzai Zen, with its identification with the shogunate, prospered into the middle of the 19th century. Then suddenly in 1868, with the fall of the shogunate and the restoration of the emperor, Buddhism was disestablished and found itself in a new world. It had to compete with an emerging Christian movement (not to mention a number of Japanese new religions); deal with the influx of Western knowledge, both philosophical and technological; and find its place in the new government system in which Shintoism predominated.

In 1945, after World War II, the Rinzai Zen groups joined the other Buddhist sects in coping with the new world under an American-style constitution that mandated religious freedom and a separation of religion and government. Between 14 and 20 different Rinzai groups have emerged, each with a head temple and a number of associated temples around the country. The largest such groups are headquartered at the old, large, and famous temple-monastic complexes—Kennin-ji, Kencho-ji, Tofuku-ji, and Engaku-ji.

In 1893, a Rinzai priest, SOYEN SHAKU (1859–1919), traveled to Chicago to speak to the World's Parliament of Religions, at which he gave two major lectures. In this act he became the first representative of Rinzai Zen in the West. He would later return to America to spend time in San Francisco, where Rinzai practice was first taught. From his pioneering experience, he would encourage his students, including DAISETSU TEITARO SUZUKI (1870–1966), Nyogen Senzaki (1876–1958), and Sokatsu Shaku, to go west.

The efforts of these pioneering priests would be supplemented in the years after World War II by the discovery of Rinzai by a number of Americans. For example, Philip Kapleau was a court reporter in Japan in 1946. Attracted to Zen, he met D. T. Suzuki after he returned to America and then returned to Japan to study under several teachers. When he later settled back in the United States, he founded the Rochester Zen Center, which subsequently grew into an international association of Zen centers.

Shigetsu Sasaki Roshi (1882–1945), out of the same tradition as Soyen Shaku, settled in New York in 1928 and created the First Zen Institute of America. He later would marry one of his students, RUTH FULLER EVERETT SASAKI (1893–1967). After his death, Ruth Fuller Sasaki moved to Japan and at Daitoku-ji organized the First Zen Institute of America in Japan, to help Americans who wished to study Zen. Among those she assisted was the poet GARY SNYDER. With Sasaki's center, the world of Rinzai Zen had come full circle.

Further reading: Thomas Cleary, *The Original Face: An Anthology of Rinzai Zen* (New York: Grove Press, 1978);

Heinrich Dumoulin, *Zen Buddhism: A History.* 2 vols. 2d ed. (New York: Macmillan, 1988); Kazuo Kasahara, ed., *A History of Japanese Religion.* Translated by Paul McCarthy and Gaynor Sekimori (Tokyo: Kosei, 2001); Martin Roth and John Stevens, *Zen Guide* (New York: Weatherhill, 1985); E. Dale Saunders, *Buddhism in Japan* (Philadelphia: University of Pennsylvania Press, 1964); Irmgard Schloegl, *The Zen Teaching of Rinzai* (Berkeley, Calif.: Shambhala, 1975); Toichi Yoshioka, *Zen* (Kawamata, Japan: Hoikusha, 2002).

Rissho Kosei-kai

Rissho Kosei-kai (the Society for the Establishment of Righteous and Friendly Relations) is one of several 20th-century groups inspired by the life and teachings of the Japanese prophet NICHIREN (1222–82). As do other Nichiren groups, Rissho Kosei-kai builds its belief and practice on the LOTUS SUTRA, which it considers the primary Buddhist sacred text. The practice of chanting the title of the Lotus Sutra, *namu myoho renge-kyo,* and veneration of one's ancestors are basic to group participation. Members also recite selections from the Lotus Sutra twice daily.

Members meet in what are called instruction halls. They participate in chanting and listening to a sermon, though there are no formal clergy, and then engage in small groups for investigation of deeper aspects of the religious life, the sharing of experiences, and counseling.

Rissho Kosei-kai was founded in 1938 by Nikkyo Niwano (1906–99) and Naganuma Myoko (1899–1957). Nagamuna, a woman who had suffered physical problems for many years, met Niwano in the 1930s, when he was a member of REIYUKAI, a recently founded new Nichiren group, and he suggested that Naganuma's way to health lay in joining the organization. She took his advice and was healed. However, a short time later, the two left Reiyukai and formed their own organization.

Rissho Kosei-kai spread rapidly through Japan in the decades after World War II. It reached the United States at the end of the 1950s, and has also opened centers in Korea, Hong Kong, Thailand, and Brazil. It claims more than 5 million members internationally.

During the years of Rissho Kosei-kai's growth, Niwano emerged on the world stage. He had received little formal education but educated himself. As the leader of the organization, he developed its institutions, including a large headquarters complex in Tokyo, and became an active participant in interfaith dialogue. He became a friend of Pope Paul VI (r. 1963–78), attended the sessions of the Second Vatican Council, and subsequently made a number of visits to the Vatican. He was succeeded as president of Rissho Kosei-kai by his son, Nichiko Niwano.

Further reading: Stewart Guthrie, *A Japanese New Religion: Rissho Kosei-Kai in a Mountain Hamlet* (Ann Arbor: University of Michigan Press, 1988); Nichiko Niwano, *My Father, My Teacher* (Tokyo: Kosei, 1982); Nikkyo Niwano, *Buddhism for Today: A Modern Interpretation of the Threefold Lotus Sutra* (Tokyo: Kosei, 1978); ———, *Lifetime Beginner* (Tokyo: Kosei, 1978); ———, *Travel to Infinity: An Autobiography of the President of an Organization of Buddhist Laymen in Japan* (Tokyo: Kosei, 1968).

Ritsu school

One of the original six Buddhist schools established at NARA, Japan, in the eighth century, the Ritsu (or *Risshu,* Japanese, precepts) school concentrated on introducing the VINAYA, the rules of discipline for monks, into Japan. The Vinaya, which was initially written in the first century B.C.E., was transmitted to China from the third century. Of the several variant texts of the Vinaya, one known as *The Fourfold Rules of Discipline* emerged as the primary text in China for what came to be known as the Precepts school.

In 742, two Japanese Buddhist priests, Yoei and Fusho, at the command of the emperor Shomu (r. 724–748), traveled to China, where they met a learned Chinese monk of the Precepts school, Chin Chien-chen (688–763). They requested that he relocate to Japan and transmit the knowledge of the Vinaya there. The monk, later known in Japan as GANJIN, was ordered by the Chinese emperor not to go, but after several unsuccessful attempts finally arrived in Japan in 753. The Japanese emperor established him and the large number of monks and nuns who accompanied him at TODAI-JI, the main temple at Nara. His arrival became the occasion of erecting the ordination platform at Todai-ji.

Over the next decade, Ganjin assumed a prominent role in Japanese Buddhism. In 754 he led the ceremony at which Shomu, now retired, formally received the Precepts. He then established the Ritsu school at Todai-ji and in 756 was named the general supervisor and administrator of Buddhist priests in Japan. Three years later with the support of Empress Koken, he established Toshodai-ji temple as the new headquarters for the Ritsu school. Ganjin was greatly honored in death, named the Great Teacher Kakai (one who crossed the sea). His school continued to be the place where Japanese monks and priests studied the Vinaya, the discipline by which they would be expected to conduct their life. Over the next centuries, as Japanese Buddhism grew and differentiated itself into various sectarian groups, each with its own rules and ordination platform, the Ritsu school transformed into a sect in its own right and as such has survived to the present.

The Ritsu school's teachings had declined by the 12th century but were given new life by the work of Eizon (1201–90). He was an adherent of SHINGON when he became aware of the neglect of the monastic precepts in his own day. He found his way to Kyoto and conducted a ceremony in which he formally received the Precepts. In 1261, as the request of government authorities, he moved to Kamakura to disseminate the teachings in the capital and its environs. He finally settled at Saidai-ji temple in Kyoto, which became the headquarters of a new Shingon Ritsu school.

The Toshodai-ji temple in Nara remains the headquarters of the original Ritsu group.

Further reading: *Buddhist Denominations and Schools in Japan* (Tokyo: Bukkto Dendo Kyokai, 1984); K. Krishna Murthy, *Buddhism in Japan* (Delhi: Sundeep Prakashan, 1989); E. Dale Saunders, *Buddhism in Japan* (Philadelphia: University of Pennsylvania Press, 1964).

Ryobu Shinto

Ryobu (literally, "dual-aspect") was a syncretic Shinto group that combined SHINGON, or esoteric (concerning secret knowledge), Buddhism with SHINTO. Ryobu flourished during the Heian (794–1185) and Kamakura (1192–1333) periods of Japanese history. In Ryobu thought the sun goddess, AMATERASU, is equated with the Buddha Mahavairocana (Great Sun Buddha). In addition the dual realms of Mahavairocana were the same as the two *kami* (deities) housed at the ISE SHRINE. The first, Amaterasu, was equated with the *taizo kai* (womb world). The second, Toyuki Ikami, the god of food, clothing, and shelter, was equated with the *kongo kai* (diamond world). Ryobu and its several branches finally died out after the 18th century. However, it did influence other sects of Shinto, such as SANNO ICHIJITSU SHINTO.

Further reading: Kazuo Kasahara, ed., *A History of Japanese Religion.* Translated by Paul McCarthy and Gaynor Sekimori (Tokyo: Dosei, 2001), 306–309.

Ryokan (1758–1831) *independent Soto Zen mendicant and poet*

Ryokan was the most outstanding of a number of SOTO ZEN monks who, separating themselves from the mainstream Soto establishment, chose to live a quiet life of meditation and teaching on their own. He had a modest background and decided not to follow his father's occupation and to enter a Buddhist monastery. He studied with Dainin Kokusen (1723–91) at Entsu-ji Temple for almost a decade.

He then left Entsu-ji and established himself on Mount Kugami, where he informally taught the local residents and lived through their generosity. He developed a reputation for kindness and compassion, and as his fame spread by word of mouth, he began to influence many. He is regarded by many as an exemplar of the Buddhist ideal. Some of Ryokan's fame arose from his poetry, which in the 20th century was republished and translated into English.

Further reading: Misao Kodama and Hikosaku Yanagishima, *The Zen Fool: Ryokan* (Rutland, Vt.: Charles E. Tuttle, 2000); *Ryokan, One Robe, One Bowl: The Zen Poetry of Ryokan*. Translated by John Stevens (Tokyo: Weatherhill, 1977); Burton Watson, trans., *Ryokan* (New York: Columbia University Press, 1992).

Ryonin (1072–1132) *Japanese Shn Buddhist priest and founder of Yuzu-Nembutsu movement*

Ryonin, an advocate of simultaneous chanting of the NEMBUTSU and the founder of the YUZU-NEMBUTSU sect, was an early student of TENDAI Buddhism and resided at various Tendai centers near Mt. HIEI. Here he was introduced to the practice of reciting the *nembutsu*, calling upon the grace of AMITABHA to carry him to the western paradise after death, which he would repeat while circumambulating a large statue of Amitabha It was common for the residents at the Tendai centers to recite the LOTUS SUTRA in the morning and the *nembutsu* in the afternoon. However, over time, he became disillusioned with the atmosphere at ENRYAKU-JI, the main Tendai temple at Mt. Hiei, and he moved to an affiliated temple near Kyoto.

At Kyoto, he began to develop the logic of the Tendai thought and practice in which he engaged. He started from an understanding of the interconnectedness of all things and the belief that in one thing all things are contained. From that base, he concluded that in reciting the *nembutsu*, one's chanting merges with that of all others who chant to produce great merit. Continuing his logic, he arrived at the idea of chanting the *nembutsu* in unison with a group. Such *yuzu*, or "mutually inclusive," chanting multiplies the effect and permeates all beings to their good.

Around 1123, Ryonin left Kyoto and began traveling across Japan teaching his new insight. Wherever he found a response he organized *yuzu-nembutsu* societies that grew into a separate Buddhist subsect. He also called upon people to sign a pledge to chant the *nembutsu* daily. He continued to work until his death in 1133, and the organization he founded remains to this day.

Further reading: *Buddhist Denominations and Schools in Japan* (Tokyo: Bukkyo Dendo Kyokai [Society for the Promotion of Buddhism], 1984); Kazuo Kasahara, ed., *A History of Japanese Religion*. Translated by Paul McCarthy and Gaynor Sekimori (Tokyo: Kosei, 2001).

S

sacred languages of Buddhism

A sacred language is generally a language used in liturgy or ceremony. It may be a living language but it is often dead, one no longer spoken in everyday life. In Buddhism there are four major sacred languages today: PALI, SANSKRIT, Tibetan, and Chinese. Although Tibetan and Chinese languages today have many forms, the forms used for Buddhist texts are no longer spoken. Therefore, none of the sacred languages of Buddhism is a living language today. The various Buddhist cultures generally use liturgies in these four languages, even though communication and commentary may be in their own native languages.

Further reading: Kogen Mizuno, *Buddhist Sutras: Origin, Development, Transmission* (Tokyo: Kosei, 1982); Edward J. Thomas, *The Life of Buddha as Legend and History* (Delhi: Munshiram Manoharlal, 1992).

sacred mountains of China

Mountains have been seen as places of potency from the earliest times. As a vast and mountainous territory, China has many potential sacred sites, and mountains of power and mystery dot the Chinese landscape. Immortals were said to reside on sacred mountains, living in unity with nature and cultivating the Way. Mountains are also typical subjects of art.

Over time standard lists of sacred mountains developed, five for Daoism and four for Buddhism. These and other sites are recognized as places of cultural meaning, often involving pilgrimage.

THE DAOIST MOUNTAINS

The five Daoist peaks are known in Chinese as the Five Peaks (*wu yue*). They correspond to the four cardinal points on the compass, with a fifth, Song Shan, in the center (*shan,* mountain). Heng Shan Bei (Heng Shan), at 2,017 meters, in Shanxi Province, represents the north. Heng Shan Nan (also called Heng Shan), representing the south, is actually an area of 72 peaks, the highest rising to 1,290 meters. Mt. Hua, to the west, in Shaanxi Province, is the most inaccessible of China's Daoist mountains—a narrow one-meter-wide path is the only way up the 1,997-meter peak. Mt. Song (Song Shan) has long been claimed by Daoists. In fact, Mt. Song is near Shaolin Temple, so the connection with Buddhism is also strong. Mt. Tai (Tai Shan), in the east, was the place Chinese emperors held sacrificial rites from the Qin dynasty (221–209 B.C.E.).

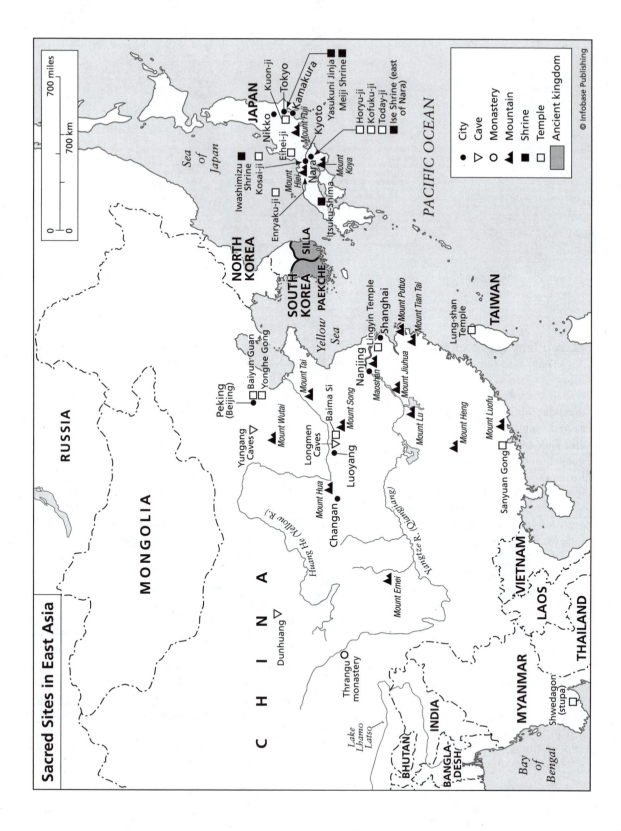

Sacred Sites in East Asia

RUSSIA

MONGOLIA

CHINA

NORTH KOREA

SOUTH KOREA

SILLA

PAEKCHE

JAPAN

TAIWAN

MYANMAR

VIETNAM

LAOS

THAILAND

BHUTAN

INDIA

BANGLA-DESH

Sea of Japan

PACIFIC OCEAN

Yellow Sea

Bay of Bengal

Huang He (Yellow R.)

Yangtze R. (Qiantang)

Lake Lhamo Latso

Tokyo
Kamakura
Kuon-ji
Yasukuni Jinja
Meiji Shrine
Nikko
Mount Fuji
Eihei-ji
Kyoto
Horyu-ji
Kofuku-ji
Today-ji
Ise Shrine (east of Nara)
Iwashimizu Shrine
Kosai-ji
Mount Hiei
Nara
Mount Koya
Enryaku-ji
Itsuku-Shima

Peking (Beijing)
Baiyun Guan
Yonghe Gong
Mount Tai
Yungang Caves
Mount Wutai
Longmen Caves
Baima Si
Mount Song
Luoyang
Changan
Mount Hua
Mount Emei
Dunhuang
Thrangu monastery
Nanjing
Lingyin Temple
Shanghai
Maoshan
Mount Putuo
Mount Tian Tai
Mount Jiuhua
Mount Lu
Mount Heng
Mount Luofu
Sanyuan Gong
Lung-shan Temple
Shwedagon (stupa)

Legend

- ● City
- ▽ Cave
- ○ Monastery
- ▲ Mountain
- ■ Shrine
- ▢ Temple
- ▨ Ancient kingdom

0   700 miles
0   700 km

© Infobase Publishing

Carved image of a protector deity, Virudhaka, one of the four Deva Kings (Caturmaharaja) usually found at the entrance to Buddhist temples in East Asia; from Wangnian Temple, Mt. Emei, Sichuan, western China

THE BUDDHIST MOUNTAINS

Mt. Emei, at 3,099 meters high, is the place where the BODHISATTVA SAMANTABHADRA is said to live. Mt. Jiu Hua, in central Anhui Province, contains more than 60 Buddhist temples. It is the residence of the bodhisattva KSHITIGARBHA. Mt. PUTUO, at a relatively low 284 meters, is nevertheless one of the greatest pilgrimage sites in China. Putuo is said to be the residence of the bodhisattva GUAN YIN.

Mt. Wu Tai, at 3,061 meters, lies in Shanxi in western China. Mt. Wutai is said to be the residence of the bodhisattva MANJUSRI, the bodhisattva of wisdom. There are as a result frequent sightings of Manjusri on Wu Tai, and more than 70 Buddhist shrines dot the mountain.

OTHER SACRED MOUNTAINS IN CHINA

Huang Shan in Anhui Province, central China, is famed for its cloud-girded peaks and majestic scenery. Mt. LUOFU in Guangdong, southern China, is a local center of Daoist practice. And Wu Dang Shan, in Hubei Province, not far from Mt. Hua, a World Heritage Site, is also associated with the development of TAIJIQUAN and MARTIAL ARTS.

Further reading: Linda Kay Davidson and David M. Gitlitz, *Pilgrimage from the Ganges to Graceland: An Encyclopedia* (Santa Barbara, Calif.: ABC-Clio, 2002); Martin Gray, "Sacred Mountains of China." Places of Peace and Power. Available online. URL: http://www.sacredsites.com/asia/china/sacred_mountains.html. Accessed on June 10, 2005; Mary Mullikan and Anna Hotchkis, *The Nine Sacred Mountains of China* (Hong Kong: Vetch and Lee, 1973); Susan Naquin and Chunfang Yu, *Pilgrims and Sacred Sites in China* (Berkeley: University of California Press, 1996); Bill Porter, *Road to Heaven: Encounters with Chinese Hermits* (San Francisco: Mercury House, 1993); Suzhou International Exchange Center. "Famous Mountains in China." Available online. URL: siecpage.3322.net/chmounts.htm. Accessed on May 15, 2005.

Saicho (767–822) *Japanese monk who established Tian Tai (Tendai) Buddhism in Japan*

Sent to China by the emperor to study and observe Chinese Buddhism, Saicho later introduced the teachings of the TIAN TAI SCHOOL to Japan, founding the TENDAI school. Saicho, the son of a Chinese family who had settled in Omi, Japan, entered the religious life as a child of 11. He was ordained as a novice priest at the age of 14 and fully ordained four years later in NARA at TODAI-JI, the lead temple of Japanese Buddhism at the time. Three months after his ORDINATION, Saicho left Nara and made his home on nearby Mt. HIEI, where he built a small hermitage. Here he made a set of vows about his own search for purification and enlightenment. He concentrated on the study of Buddhist sutras, such as LOTUS SUTRA and the Perfection of Wisdom Sutra, but found his direction from the Tian Tai writings of ZHI YI that had fallen into his hands. These writings extolled the virtues of the Lotus Sutra.

In 797, shortly after the imperial court was moved from Nara to Heian (Kyoto), he was called to serve as the court priest; that required frequent trips from Mt. Hiei but also extended his influence. Then in 804, the emperor sent him to

China to study and observe Chinese Buddhism. While in China he was exposed to the Esoteric (VAJRAYANA BUDDHISM) tradition, while also receiving transmission from the Tian Tai. He returned to Japan with copies of hundreds of the Tian Tai books.

Soon after resettling in Japan, Saicho was ready to build the Tian Tai sect (called Tendai in Japan). He petitioned for and received permission to ordain priests. And his small hermitage was developed into ENRYAKU-JI, the temple that would become the headquarters of the Tendai sect.

As the work on Mt. Hiei grew, Saicho engaged in an important debate with Tokuitsu of the HOSSO sect based at Nara over the nature of Buddhahood, specifically over whether all being had the innate potential for enlightenment. Saicho said they did. Shortly thereafter, in 818, he renounced his Todai-ji ordination (representing his break with the Nara leadership) and petitioned the emperor for the right to ordain priests separately. He also devised a new strict rule for prospective ordinands that included 12 years of strict practice on Mt. Hiei. In the training he offered to Tendai priests, he emphasized that their spiritual work was not solely for their salvation, but that they should think of themselves as similar to bodhisattvas. In helping others find enlightenment, they were coincidentally helping themselves.

Saicho nurtured close relations with the imperial court. He promoted the idea that MAHAYANA in general and Mt. Hiei in particular constituted the protector of the nation, an idea that he periodically revived in later years. He used the high esteem that the court held him in to petition for status as an independent sect for him and his students. He died in 822 without an answer. It arrived the following year, with a set of decrees, including the official naming of his temple Enryaku-ji.

Further reading: Paul Groner, *Saicho: The Establishment of the Japanese Tendai School* (Seoul: Po Chin Chai, 1984); Yūsen Kashiwahara and Kōyū Sonoda, *Shapers*

of Japanese Buddhism. Translated by Gaynor Sekimori (Tokyo: Kōsei, 1994); Umehara Takeshi, "Saicho," in Takeuchi Yoshinori, ed., in association with James W. Heisig, Paul L. Swanson, and Joseph S. O'Leary, *Buddhist Spirituality: Later China, Korea, Japan, and the Modern World* (New York: Crossroad, 1999), 164–173.

Sakya

The Sakya school of Tibetan Buddhism is today still one of the most vital and active, with monasteries in Asia and the West. It can be traced to the eighth century, when Khon Lui Wangpo Sunngwa became a student/disciple of PADMASAMBHAVA, the Indian saint who built Samye monastery and was largely responsible for the first significant transmission of Buddhism to Tibet. The NYINGMA school was the major result of his work and the Khon family staunchly supported it through the next centuries. Then in 1073, Khon Konckok Gyalpo built Sakya (Gray Earth) Monastery and began to build a great library of Buddhist texts.

The son of Khon Konckok Gyalpo, Sachen Kunga Nyingpo (1092–1158), is seen as the real founder of the Sakya school. He assembled the texts and oral tradition that distinguished the teachings emanating from the monastery from those currently taught by Nyingma teachers. These texts became the basic Sakya canon. Sachen Kunga Nyingpo is recognized as the first of five Gongma Nga (or exalted ones). He was succeeded by Lobpen Sonam Tsemo (1142–82), Jetsun Dakpa Gyaltsen (1147–1216), and Sakya Pandita (1182–1251).

Sakya Pandita, the fourth Gongma, excelled as a scholar, gaining an international reputation. His fame drew him to the attention of Genghis Khan's grandson, Prince Golan, in 1242. Golan subsequently invited Sakya Pandita to his court in MONGOLIA. That relationship had the effect of creating a revival of VAJRAYANA BUDDHISM teachings in Mongolia, which bore real fruit during the reign of Kublai Khan, who invited the fifth Gongma,

Drogön Chogyal Phagpa (1235–80), to Mongolia. While there, Phagpa invented a new script for written Mongolian. In return, Kublai Khan made Tibetan Buddhism Mongolia's state religion and presented Phagpa with political leadership over three Tibetan provinces. Phagpa emerged as the primary religious and secular authority in Tibet, and his successors ruled the land for the next century. Thus during the era of the five Gongmas Sakya Buddhism had moved from the teachings available at a single monastery to a dominant position in the land.

The most definitive teachings of the Sakya school are found in the Hevajra Tantras, writings generally traced to the Indian Mahasiddha Virupa that had been introduced to Tibet during the years of Drokmi the Translator (992–1072), the teacher of Khon Konckok Gyalpo. The Sakya tradition emphasizes the acquisition of truth through meditation and study (and the Sayka school has produced both enlightened masters and outstanding scholars). The basic insight they have proposed is termed the nondifferentiation of SAMSARA (the cycle of death and reincarnation) and NIRVANA (the state beyond suffering) to be found in a state of nonduality generally referred to as emptiness.

The Sakya political leadership of Tibet continued for a number of centuries but was eventually replaced by that of the DALAI LAMA in the 16th century. By that time, however, the Sakya school had spread throughout Tibet and the religious lineage continued. The current patriarch of the Sakya tradition is His Holiness Sakya Trizin (1945–   ). He became the 41st patriarch in 1959 and immediately after assuming power left Tibet in the face of the Chinese's assertion of hegemony over the country. He established his new headquarters at Rajpur, Uttar Pradesh, India. Nearby is Sakya College, where leaders are trained.

Beginning in 1974, Sakya Trizin began to travel globally and has inspired the founding of related centers through Southeast Asia and in the West. Among the prominent Western-affiliated institutions is the Sakya Institute for Buddhist Studies in Cambridge, Massachusetts, founded in 1990.

Further reading: Chogay Trichen Rinpoche, *The History of the Sakya Tradition*. Translated by Jennifer Stott (Bristol: Ganesha Press, 1983); Graham Coleman, ed., *A Handbook of Tibetan Culture: A Guide to Tibetan Centres and Resources throughout the World* (Boston: Shambhala, 1994); Ngorchen Konchog Lhundrub, *The Three Visions: Fundamental Teachings of the Sakya Lineage of Tibetan Buddhism*. Translated by Lobsang Dagpa and Jay Goldberg (Ithaca, N.Y.: Snow Lion, 2002); Sakya Pandita, *Ordinary Wisdom: Sakya Pandita's Treasury of Good Advice*. Translated by John T. Davenport (Boston: Wisdom, 2000).

Sakyadhita

Sakyadhita is the International Association of Buddhist Women, its name meaning "Daughters of the Buddha." The organization has 1,900 members and friends in 45 countries around the world. The objectives of Sakyadhita, as expressed at its founding meeting in 1987, are the following:

1. To promote world peace through the practice of the Buddha's teachings
2. To create a network of communications for Buddhist women throughout the world
3. To promote harmony and understanding among the various Buddhist traditions
4. To encourage and help educate women as teachers of Buddhadharma
5. To provide improved facilities for women to study and practice the teachings
6. To help establish the Bhiksuni Sangha (community of fully ordained nuns) where it does not currently exist

Since 1987, Sakyadhita has been working to benefit Buddhist women around the world. Every two years an international conference is held to draw laywomen and nuns from different countries and traditions together to share their experiences on issues of mutual interest and encourage projects to improve conditions for Buddhist women, especially in developing countries. At the Sakyadhita International Conference in February 1998, at BODHGAYA, India, 134 women took part in a full ORDINATION ceremony.

Working at the grassroots level, Sakyadhita provides a communication network among Buddhist women internationally. The organization promotes research and publications on Buddhist women's history and other topics of interest. It supports Buddhist women's initiatives to create education projects, retreat facilities, training centers, women's shelters, and local conferences and discussion groups. Members strive to create equal opportunities for women in all Buddhist traditions.

Further reading: Yuchen Li, "Ordination, Legitimacy, and Sisterhood:" "The International Full Ordination Ceremony in Bodhgaya," in Karma Lekshe Tsomo, ed., *Innovative Buddhist Women: Swimming against the Stream* (Richmond, U.K.: Curzon, 2000), 168–198; Sakyadhita. "Sakyadhita: The International Association of Buddhist Women." Available online. URL: www.sakyadhita.org. Accessed on April 13, 2006; Karma Lekshe Tsomo, ed., *Buddhist Women and Social Justice: Ideals, Challenges, and Achievements* (Albany: State University of New York Press, 2004); ———, ed., *Sakyadhita: Daughters of the Buddha* (Ithaca, N.Y.: Snow Lion, 1989).

Sakyamuni   *See* BUDDHA.

samadhi

Samadhi or, literally, "mental discipline," by itself indicates a state of bliss and focused concentration. In the Buddha's teachings *samadhi* is also the group of components of the noble EIGHTFOLD PATH, which includes right effort, right mindfulness, and right concentration. Right effort indicates an individual's determination to eliminate unwholesome states of mind from consciousness. Right mindfulness indicates the individual's awareness of the body, sensations, the mind, and all thoughts that arise in the mind. Development of right mindfulness requires meditation of some sort. Finally, right concentration is the sequence of mental development that leads the cultivator to increasingly higher states of perception. These states are the *Dhyanas* and can be likened to trance states. Attainment of the higher states of DHYANA results in a sense of perfect equanimity.

Further reading: Kogen Mizuno, *Essentials of Buddhism: Basic Terminology and Concepts of Buddhist Philosophy and Practice.* Translated by Gaynor Sekimori (1972. Reprint, Tokyo: Kosei, 1996); Sadhu Mouni, *Samadhi* (London: George Allen & Unwin, 1962); *The Pratyupanna Samadhi Sutra and the Surangama Samadhi Sutra* (Honolulu: University of Hawaii Press, 2006).

Samantabhadra (Chinese Pu Xian, or P'u-hsien, "Universal Worthy")

Samantabhadra, or "he who is all-pervadingly good," is a major BODHISATTVA figure in Mahayana and Tantric Buddhist texts (including the Avatamsaka Sutra), where he represents the unity of all creation. Samantabhadra protects the teachers of the DHARMA. He is often depicted as one of the trio of Shakyamuni BUDDHA and MANJUSRI. He invariably rides a white elephant with six tusks; the elephant is the power of wisdom, the tusks represent overcoming of the six senses. In China Samantabhadra is said to dwell on Mount Emei, in Sichuan, one of the four sacred Buddhist mountains in China.

In VAJRAYANA-influenced practice in Tibet, China, and Japan, Samantabhadra is depicted with blue skin and is usually seen in intimate embrace with his white-skinned consort.

Further reading: Thomas Cleary, trans., *The Flower Ornament Scripture: A Translation of the Avatamsaka Sutra.* 3 vols. (Boston: Shambhala, 1984–1987); Matthew T. Kapstein, *The Tibetan Assimilation of Buddhism: Conversion, Contestation, and Memory* (Oxford: Oxford University Press, 2000).

samapatti

In Buddhist philosophy, *samapatti,* or "the attainments," is a label for nine separate states. They are the four absorptions (DHYANAS) as well as the four types of formlessness, and, finally, the state of extinction (NIRODHA).

The attainments were mentioned in early Buddhist literature as well as Mahayana writings. In the Discourse on Effacement (Sallekha Sutta), a text from part of the Pali canon (Majjhima Nikaya), the Buddha notes that the achievement of the eight *Dhyanas* results in a state of "abiding in ease."

Further reading: Kogen Mizuno, *Essentials of Buddhism: Basic Terminology and Concepts of Buddhist Philosophy and Practice.* Translated by Gaynor Sekimori (1972. Reprint, Tokyo: Kosei, 1996); Charles S. Prebish, *The A to Z of Buddhism* (Lanham, Md.: Scarecrow Press, 2001).

samatha

In Buddhist philosophy, *samatha,* or "cessation," refers to the cessation of contact with the senses. In Sanskrit texts the term is associated with SAMADHI, "concentration," but emphasizes the stopping of the mind's mental activity in order to allow *samadhi* concentration. In Chinese Buddhism the term *zhi,* "cessation," was a key part of TIAN TAI, ZHI YI's theory of religious practice.

See also MOHE ZHIGUAN.

Further reading: Kogen Mizuno, *Essentials of Buddhism: Basic Terminology and Concepts of Buddhist Philosophy and Practice.* Translated by Gaynor Sekimori (Tokyo: Kosei, 1996); "Samatha," in Charles S. Prebish, ed., *The A to Z of Buddhism* (Lanham, Md.: Scarecrow Press, 2001), 221–222; Santideva, *The Bodhicarya-*

vatara. Translated by Kate Crosby and Andrew Skilton (Oxford: Oxford University Press, 1995).

sambhogakaya

The *sambhogakaya,* or "bliss body," is one of the Buddha's apparent forms. The *sambhogakaya* is the body of the Buddha visible to BODHISATTVAS residing in their heavenly realms. Thus the average person has little hope of seeing this aspect of the Buddha. The *sambhogakaya* is one element of the MAHAYANA TRIKAYA theory, in which the Buddha's body is said to manifest in three different forms.

Further reading: Kogen Mizuno, *Essentials of Buddhism: Basic Terminology and Concepts of Buddhist Philosophy and Practice.* Translated by Gaynor Sekimori (1972. Reprint, Tokyo: Kosei Publishing, 1996); "Sambhoga-kaya," in Charles S. Prebish, ed., *The A to Z of Buddhism* (Lanham, Md.: Scarecrow Press, 2001), 222.

Sammatiya school

Although they later declined in importance, the Sammatiyas were one of the more important of the 18 schools of early Buddhism. The Sammitiyas engaged in debate over the nature of the self, the concept of SKANDHAS (aggregates), and the concept of ANATMAN. The Sammitiyas held that a person is not simply the sum of the five aggregates (matter, feelings, mind, perception, and consciousness). This was the view of the rival Vaibhasika school. According to the Sammatiyas, the distinction between the five aggregates and the individual exists but is so subtle that it is inexpressible. Unlike in the concept of the five aggregates, the person does not cease to exist at death. However, unlike in the Hindu concept of the *atman,* or self, the person is not eternal.

The Chinese travelers XUAN ZANG (c. 600–664) and YI JING (634–713) taught that the Sammityas, along with the SARVASTIVADA, MAHASANGHIKA, and STHAVIRAVADA, made up the main four categories of ABHIDHARMA Buddhism.

Further reading: Daniel Cozort and Craig Preston, *Buddhist Philosophy: Losang Gonchok's Short Commentary to Jamyang Shayba's Root Text on Tenets* (Ithaca, N.Y.: Snow Lion, 2003); Kogen Mizuno, *Essentials of Buddhism: Basic Terminology of Buddhist Philosophy and Practice.* Translated by Gaynor Sekimori (1972. Reprint, Tokyo: Kosei, 1996).

samsara

In traditional Indian thought, samsara is the cycle of birth, decay, death, and rebirth to which all living beings are subject until they achieve release through ENLIGHTENMENT. *Samsara* literally refers to "journeying." The YOGACARA school of Buddhism states that samsara and NIRVANA are equal, since all experiences of the world are mental representations. Realization of the true base of reality will destroy such dichotomies as a simple distinction between samsara and nirvana. Most schools agree that there is no beginning to the chain of samsara. The Buddha taught that it is pointless to search for one.

Further reading: Hoyu Ishida, "Nietzsche and Samsara: Suffering and Joy in the Eternal Recurrence," *The Pure Land,* Journal of Pure Land Buddhism, New Series, 15 (December 1998): 122–145; Sangharakshita, *A Survey of Buddhism* (Boulder, Colo.: Shambhala and London: Windhorse, 1980); Matsui Takafumi, *Samsara: Earth, Universe, Man: Where Are We Going?* (Tokyo: Tokuma Shoten, 1990).

Samu Sunim   *See* BUDDHIST SOCIETY FOR COMPASSIONATE WISDOM.

Sanbo Kyodan

Sanbo Kyodan, the Three Treasures school of Zen, is a relatively small ZEN BUDDHISM community that has nevertheless exerted considerable influence in the development of Zen in the West. It is characterized by the teaching of a mixture of SOTO ZEN and RINZAI ZEN and lessening of the distinctions between monastic and lay practitioners. Students of Sanbo Kyodan make up the largest group of all Zen teachers currently active in the United States, Germany, Switzerland, the Philippines, and Australia.

Sanbo Kyodan originated with Harada Da'un Sogaku Roshi (1871–1961), a Soto Zen teacher who also had credentials in Rinzai Zen. Most important for the development of Sanbo Kyodan was Harada Roshi's successor, Yasutani Haku'un Ryoko Roshi (1885–1973). Already a Soto monk, Yasutani Roshi met Harada in 1925. Over the years, especially in the decades following World War II, he became critical of the superficial emphases on practice he found in the Soto community and in 1954 left the Soto organization and founded Sanbo Kyodan, as an independent school. The name *Sanbo,* or "Three treasures," refers to the three things in which a Buddhist takes refuge—the Buddha, the Dharma, and the Sangha.

Yasutani Roshi attracted a number of Western students and beginning in 1962 made frequent trips to North America and Europe. In 1970 he retired from his administrative role as head of Sanbo Kyodan and passed the leadership to his student Yamada Koun Roshi (1907–89).

At least 40 Zen teachers have been authorized by the Sanbo Kyodan, the majority non-Japanese. Possibly the most famous are ROBERT BAKER AITKEN, who founded the Diamond Sangha in Hawaii, and Philip Kapleau, who founded the Zen Center of Rochester. Among the teachers were two Roman Catholic priests, Hugo Makibi Enomiya-LaSalle (1898–1991) and Willigis Jäger (1925–), who went on to become leading figures in the CHRISTIAN ZEN movement of the 1970s. Besides the several groups such as the Diamond Sangha, which carry the Sanbo Kyodan lineage while becoming independent international Zen organizations in their own right, there are some 20 centers around the world directly affiliated with the Sanbo Kyodan organization. Besides the centers in Japan there are centers in the United States, Canada, Switzerland, Germany, France, the Netherlands, Spain, the Philippines, and Australia. The school is currently led by Kubata Akira Ji'un-ken Roshi (1932–   ).

Further reading: Philip Kapleau, *The Three Pillars of Zen: Teaching, Practice, and Enlightenment* (Boston: Beacon Press, 1967); Sanbô Kôryûkai, ed., *In Memoriam: Kôun Yamada Roshi* (Tokyo: Kamakura, 1997); Robert H. Scharf, "Sanbokyodan: Zen and the Way of New Religions," *Japanese Journal of Religious Studies* 22, nos. 3–4 (1995): 417–458; Koun Yamada, *Gateless Gate* (Tucson: University of Arizona Press, 1990); Yasutani Haku'un Roshi, *Flowers Fall: A Commentary on Dogen's Genjokoan.* Translated by Paul Jaffe (Boston: Shambhala, 1996).

Sanghabhadra (fourth century C.E.)

Sanghabhadra was a contemporary and rival of the YOGACARA philosopher VASUBANDHU. Sanghabhadra's work *Treatise on Accordance with the Correct Doctrine* was a detailed explanation of SARVASTIVADA doctrine and a defense against Vasubandhu's point of view. He was a representative of the VAIBHASIKA school, a branch of Sarvastivada, one of the early 18 SCHOOLS OF BUDDHISM. He developed a unique theory of the existence of dharmas (elements of existence). Dharmas, he taught, exist concurrently in the past, present, and future, in other words, throughout all three periods.

Sanghamitta (280–220 B.C.E.) *daughter of Emperor Asoka*

Sanghamitta, the daughter of the emperor ASOKA, was, along with her brother, MAHINDA, responsible for the founding of Buddhism in Sri Lanka. As a young woman, she joined her brother in the religious life and became a Buddhist BHIKSUNI (nun). In 247 B.C.E., Mahinda gained the initial foothold for Buddhism in Sri Lanka in the court of King Devanampiyatissa (c. 250–210 B.C.E.).

According to the story, Mahinda received a request from Queen Anula, wife of a subking in Sri Lanka, to become a *bhiksuni*. Since he did not have the power to receive her into the religious life, he suggested that a request be made that his sister go to Sri Lanka. At the same time, Mahinda requested that a branch of the BODHI TREE also be sent to Sri Lanka.

According to the *MAHAVAMSA,* the ancient chronicle of Sri Lanka, in due time, Sanghamitta and several sister *bhiksunis* arrived at Jambukolapattana (today Point Pedro). Mahinda and an entourage from the capital met Sanghamitta and began a formal procession back to Anuradhapura, where the Bodhi tree was planted at a prepared spot.

A short time later, Sanghamitta ordained Anula and a group of 500 women, thus establishing Bhiksuni Sasana in Sri Lanka. The Sri Lankan sisters would later be the source of the Chinese Order of Nuns.

Sanghamitta remained in Sri Lanka for the rest of her life working with her brother to establish Buddhism among the population. She is honored on Sanghamitta Day, celebrated on the full moon in the month of December.

Further reading: Lorna Dewaraja, "Sanghamitta Their: A Liberated Woman." North American Buddhist Network. Available online. URL: http://www.buddhistinformation.com/sanghamitta_theri.htm. Accessed on November 3, 2003; Monica Lindberg Falk, "Thammacarini Witthaya: The First Buddhist School for Girls in Thailand," in Karma Lekshe Tsomo, ed., *Innovative Buddhist Women: Swimming against the Stream* (Richmond, U.K.: Curzon, 2000), 61–71; Walpola Rahula, *History of Buddhism in Ceylon: The Anuradhapura Period, 3rd Century B.C.–10th Century A.D.* (Colombo, Sri Lanka: M.D. Gunasena, 1966).

Sangha organization in Sri Lanka

Sangha is a Sanskrit term meaning "crowd." It later referred to a "virtuous assembly." In general a sangha is a group of followers around a teacher. In Buddhist usage the sangha is the Buddhist community of monks, nuns, and novices. It may also be taken to include devout lay followers, *upasaka.* The sangha is defined rigorously through the Vinaya, the body of texts that specify the rules for action of all members.

INSTITUTIONAL ORGANIZATION

In Sri Lanka there was early on a simple two-tier organization. Under the main temple, Mahathera, there were several *ganas,* or group of monks, in single congregations. Each *gana* was led by a *gana-detu,* or leader. In the 12th century this structure evolved into one in which a supreme leader (called *mahasami, mahimi,* or *sangharaja*) was given authority over the entire sangha in Sri Lanka. A council known as the Karaka Sabha (Executive Committee) gave guidance and represented the sangha. The council was made up of heads of monastic centers, especially those involved in learning. Under the *mahimi* were two *mahastha-viras* elected by the body of BHIKSUs. One of them would later be chosen to replace the *mahimi* when the office became vacant. Under the *mahasthaviras* were heads of *ayatanas* (major learning centers) and *pirivenas* (minor learning centers).

Sri Lanka is today divided into three main *nikayas,* or sects, the Siam, the largest; the Amarapura; and the Ramanna. Each temple (*vihara*) pays allegiance to one of the *nikayas.* Each temple has a chief monk (*viharadhipati*), *bhiksus,* and *samaneras* (novices).

Each *nikaya* has committees that report to the Karaka Sabha. These are called Palaka Maha Sangha Sabha (PMSS) and handle general as well as ecclesiastical affairs. The PMSS meets every six months. There are also a working committee (the Karaka Sangha Sabha) and a committee of officials (Niladhari Mandalaya) formed from the PMSS. Finally, atop the *nikaya* is the *maha nayaka.* His successor is chosen by the Karaka Sangha Sabha. In addition to this administrative structure is a juridical one that deals with succession disputes.

SOCIAL FUNCTION OF THE SANGHA

In Theravadin countries the sangha performs multiple social functions. Priests are called upon to perform significant rite of passage rituals. The priest is also a community wiseman and, often, the local doctor. The *vihara* may also own land and have tenants. Hermit, or Tapasa, monks are imbued with additional reverence and symbolize the ideals of Buddhism. Finally, the *vihara* and its *bhiksus* were traditionally the sole educational source in most village communities.

Further reading: Ruth-Inge Heinze, *The Role of the Sangha in Modern Thailand* (Taipei, Taiwan: Orient Cultural Service, 1977); Gunaratne Panabokke, *History of the Buddhist Sangha in India and Sri Lanka* (Dalugama, Kelaniya, Sri Lanka: Postgraduate Institute of Pali and Buddhist Studies, University of Kelaniya, 1993); Sangharakshita, *The Three Jewels: An Introduction to Buddhism* (London: Rider, 1967); Sunanda Putuwar *The Buddhist Sangha: Paradigm of the Ideal Human Society* (Lanham, Md.: University Press of America, 1991); Mohan Wijayaratna, *Buddhist Monastic Life: According to the Texts of the Theravada Tradition.* Translated by Claude Grangier and Steven Collins (Cambridge: Cambridge University Press, 1990).

sanja takusen (Oracles of the Three Shrines)

The Shinto gods who inhabit the shrines at Ise, Hachiman, and Kasuaga in Japan occasionally issued oracular pronouncements. These took the form of the *sanja takusen,* and for 600 years these pronouncements from the three shrines have been grouped together and written on hanging scrolls. The scrolls generally list the names of the three shrines; one, two, or three oracular texts (*takusen*); and one or more images. The image and text from the deity of Ise, Amaterasu, are usually placed in the center of the scroll, showing her higher status. The oracular texts deal with any subject but generally made moralistic or philosophical points. They were normally issued in response to specific requests for guidance.

The *sanja takusen* were most likely originally separate oracular utterances that were united into a single form. The earliest recorded *sanja takusen* dates from the Oei period (1394–1428), probably no later than 1409. It is significant in that the three deities associated with the three most powerful clans in medieval Japan were united in a single form in the *sanja takusen*. The appearance of this form was also related to the destruction of KAMAKURA in 1333 and the establishment of two competing emperors. The *sanja takusen* form reflects a desire for unity and an understanding in medieval exoteric Buddhism thought of underlying interdependence.

The *sanja takusen* form was influenced by the MEIJI RESTORATION and the efforts by the government to promote SHINTO as a state religion. The oracular texts became less moralistic and values based, and more interested in establishing the territory and commanding obedience. The style of writing then became "pure Shinto," with Buddhist elements purged. This style was nonexistent before 1868 and certainly reflects efforts to promote a pure Shinto. The *sanja takusen* from this period all reflect the government's efforts to reorganize Japanese society and especially to promote the role of the emperor. Under the new system all Japanese citizens were parishioners (*ujiko*) of the ISE SHRINE. The *sanja takusen* then became tools to promote the strong connection between emperor and Amaterasu, the divine ancestress.

Further reading: Brian Bocking, "Changing Images of Shinto: Sanja Takusen or the Three Oracles," in John Breen and Mark Teeuwen, eds., *Shinto in History: Ways of the Kami* (Richmond, U.K.: Curzon, 2000), 167–185; *The World of Shinto* (Tokyo: Bukkyo Dendo Kyokai, 1985).

Sanno Ichijitsu Shinto (Tendai Shinto)

Ichijitsu Shinto was the union of Shinto and Tendai Buddhism. This union flourished during the Tokugawa period (1603–1867) in Japan. The founding concept was that the Shinto *kami* (gods) were reflections of Buddhist deities. Ichijitsu in fact takes this idea from its predecessor, RYOBU SHINTO. But unlike Ryobu, which focused on the *kami* at ISE SHRINE, Ichijijitsu's development was stimulated largely by the location of Tendai's main temple. That temple was established on Mt. HIEI, near Kyoto. The local deity there was Sanno, "Mountain King." Sanno was easily identified with the Buddha Sakyamuni. Taking the idea of unity further, Sakyamuni was equated with Dainichi (Mahavairocana), who was equal to Amaterasu, who was therefore equal to Sanno. The concept of *ichijitsu,* "one truth," is a fundamental TENDAI (TIAN TAI) belief.

Further reading: Kazuo Kasahara, ed., *A History of Japanese Religion.* Translated by Paul McCarthy and Gaynor Sekimori (Tokyo: Dosei, 2001), 308–309.

Sanron school

The Sanron (Three Treatises) school was one of the original six schools of Buddhism established in the eighth century at NARA, Japan. The school originated in two texts written by NAGARJUNA (third century)—Treatise on the Middle Way and Treatise on the Twelve Gates—and one authored by his student Aryadeva, One-Hundred Verse Treatise.

The position of the three treatises was described as the Middle Way. The school did not generate ideas of its own so much as it used the refutation of existing concepts as a means to arrive at truth. It especially opposed all polarities and extreme views. In following this view, teachers had a problem. The refutation of error seems logically to imply the selection of a correct opposing view. The three treatises tried to avoid this seeming logical necessity, by making the refutation of error itself the explication of truth. The right view is gained only by the negation of all error.

Sanron texts were introduced into Japan from Korea during the reign of the regent SHOTOKU

(573–621), who studied them along with the Jojitsu texts. From that point, both the JOJITSU and Sanron (and KUSHA) texts tended to be studied together. Academies for all three schools were established at Nara. The Sanron school later absorbed the Jojitsu school, but none of the three schools survived more than a few centuries, and Japanese Buddhism moved on to other problems.

Further reading: K. Krishna Murthy, *Buddhism in Japan* (Delhi: Sundeep Prakashan, 1989); E. Dale Saunders, *Buddhism in Japan* (Philadelphia: University of Pennsylvania Press, 1964).

Sanskrit (Samskritam)

Sanskrit (*sam,* "complete" + *krita,* "done"), "that which is done completely, the perfected, the refined," is the ancient liturgical or ritual language of India. In its designation it is contrasted with *prakrit,* which indicates a "common" or vernacular language of ancient India. *Sanskrit* is actually the term for the language in modern Hindi; the proper "Sanskrit" form of the word is *Samskritam.*

Sanskrit is the cultural link language of India. It was used as the language for cultural activity in India for nearly 3,000 years. The body of extant writing in Sanskrit is staggeringly vast. Along with the Vedic MANTRA collections themselves are the Brahmanas and Aranyakas, which are attached to the Vedic collections. Similarly, the classical Upanishads are attached to the Vedas (but there are hundreds of texts called "Upanishad" that are not part of the older Vedic collections).

Sanskrit is written in a script called the Devanagari script made up of 48 to 51 letters, and different ways of presenting the alphabet are common. The script appears to have been devised during the Gupta era (fourth to sixth centuries C.E.)

Sanskrit represents the oldest extant Indo-European language. It is linguistically related, then, to such European languages as English, French, and German as well as to other languages such as Persian. The earliest evidence for Sanskrit is in the ancient Indian texts, the Vedas. The earliest of the four Vedas, the Rg Veda, dates from approximately 1500 B.C.E. The Sanskrit of the Vedas has noticeable differences from its classical form, which was set down linguistically by Panini in about 450 B.C.E.

After the grammar of Panini, there were virtually no changes made in the Sanskrit language through the many centuries up to the modern era. Sanskrit was a spoken language whose grammar was frozen in the fifth century B.C.E. Today Sanskrit is still spoken by pandits and people learned in Indian philosophy. There are several Sanskrit universities today in India, where all classes are conducted only in Sanskrit. The number of true Sanskrit speakers in India would number a few million in a population of a billion or more, a very small minority. Among these there would be no one who would speak Sanskrit only.

The ancient Vedas were received by seers, rishis, and recorded. They were considered to be divine revelation, in effect, and not composed by anyone. There are many theories regarding the Sanskrit language, and the many philosophical schools and sects in India have developed numerous viewpoints. Common is the understanding that the Vedas themselves are eternal and always existent. That means that Sanskrit is also considered to be eternal and always existent, not an arbitrary language created by humans, but the "language of the gods" (*devavani*).

When Jainism and Buddhism began to develop traditions counter to the Vedic ritual tradition, they both used languages other than Sanskrit, languages called Prakrits. These were the vernacular languages that had begun to develop. It must be understood that in those times (c. 800 B.C.E. to 0 C.E.), Sanskrit was still the spoken language of the educated classes and the language of high culture. By 0 C.E., the Buddhists and Jains also began to write their works in Sanskrit, an indication that the cultural force of developing Hinduism had overwhelmed these heterodox traditions.

Later than the Vedas are the Sanskrit epics, *Ramayana* and *Mahabharata*. The *Ramayana* is itself about 40,000 verses in length and the *Mahabharata* more than 100,000 verses. Included alongside the epics are the 18 *Puranas*, which tell the tales of the divinities. There are also 18 minor *Puranas* and hundreds of *Sthalapuranas*, or local works, which tell the tale of localized divinities.

Other genres were prolifically produced over the long history of the Sanskrit language. There are classical works that include hundreds of plays, longer poems, and other classical forms. There are works on aesthetics, erotics, medicine, philosophy, theology, and logic; there are devotional hymns, dictionaries, works on astronomy and astrology, and works on mathematics, ritual, law, architecture, TANTRISM, history, music, sculpture, and painting. Additionally, there is much panegyric literature and many, many inscriptions. Every one of the genres can be found in Jain Sanskrit literature also. The body of extant Sanskrit literature that is Hindu, Jain, or from other sects would total hundreds of thousands of texts, most of which have never been studied for centuries and are not edited, let alone translated.

Most Indian languages rely on Sanskrit-derived vocabulary. Even a Dravidian language such as Telegu has more than 50 percent of its vocabulary derived from Sanskrit.

At about the time of the arrival of the Muslims in India in the 13th century, Sanskrit learning began to decline. The vital and central role that Sanskrit had played in Indian culture for 3,000 years began to fade and the vernacular languages began to develop as alternatives in the cultural arena. This is not to say that Sanskrit died out, however. Many texts continued to be written in Sanskrit throughout the period of the Muslims in India (roughly 13th–18th centuries), and many current works are still being composed in Sanskrit. On both Indian television and India radio one can still hear Sanskrit newscasts and bulletins. There also are Sanskrit newspapers in certain areas.

See also SACRED LANGUAGES OF BUDDHISM.

Further reading: K. C. Aryan, *The Little Goddesses (Matrikas)* (New Delhi: Rekha, 1980); T. Burrow, *The Sanskrit Language* (London: Faber, 1973); John Grimes, *A Concise Dictionary of Indian Philosophy: Sanskrit Terms Defined in English* (Albany: State University of New York Press, 1989); Jan Gonda, ed., *A History of Sanskrit Literature.* 10 vols. (Wiesbaden: Otto Harrosowitz, 1975–1982); Arthur Berriedale Keith, *A History of Sanskrit Literature* (London: Oxford University Press, 1920); Diana Morrison, *A Glossary of Sanskrit from the Spiritual Tradition of India* (Petaluma: Nilgiri Press, 1977); Sheldon Pollock, ed., *Literary Cultures In History: Reconstructions from South Asia* (Berkeley: University of California Press, 2003); M. N. Srinivas, *The Cohesive Role of Sanskritization and Other Essays* (Delhi: Oxford University Press, 1989); Judith M. Tyberg. *The Language of the Gods: Sanskrit Keys to India's Wisdom* (Los Angeles: East-West Cultural Centre, 1970).

Santaraksita (725–788) *Indian Buddhist who disseminated Buddhism in Tibet*

Santaraksita was a major figure in the histories of Indian and Tibetan Buddhism. He was an important scholar of Indian Buddhist philosophy and played a pivotal role in the early transmission of Buddhism to Tibet. According to Tibetan sources, he was born into an aristocratic family in Bengal. Very little is know about his activities in India; his activities in Tibet are better known, because of the survival of Tibetan records. During the middle of the eighth century, the Himalayan region of Mangyul, then part of Tibet but now within the borders of Nepal, was governed by a Tibetan named Ba Salnang, who traveled to India and met Santaraksita there. At his instigation, King Trisongdetsen (742 C.E.–c. 797 C.E.) invited Santaraksita to Tibet. He traveled to Tibet twice, first in 763 C.E., and again shortly thereafter, and remained there for the rest of his life.

In Tibet, Santaraksita was responsible for the design of the first Buddhist monastery at Samye and the ordination of the first Tibetan monks. At Trisong Detsen's request, he designed a monastery to be built at Samye. His design was based upon the Odantapuri monastic complex in India. According to Tibetan accounts, the king encountered supernatural obstacles in his attempts to build the monastery at Samye. At Santaraksita's suggestion, he invited the great saint PADMASAMBHAVA to Tibet to serve as an exorcist. Together they completed the monastery in 779 C.E. Tibetans see this as a landmark moment in their history, and see Santaraksita and Padmasambhava as founding figures in the establishment of their tradition. He also ordained the first seven Tibetan monks, according to the monastic discipline tradition of the Mulasarvastivada (SARVASTIVADA), a tradition that had flourished in northwest India and is still followed by all of the Tibetan monastic orders.

Santaraksita was accompanied to Tibet by his disciple Kamalashila, who was an important scholar in his own right. According to the Tibetan tradition, Kamalashila defended the Indian "gradual" approach to Buddhist theory and practice in a great debate with the Chinese master Heshang ("monk") Moheyan, who advocated the Chinese CHAN "sudden" approach. This debate lasted for three years, from 792 to 794 C.E., and the king ultimately ruled in Kamalashila's favor.

Santaraksita was the founder of the Buddhist Yogacara-Madhyamaka philosophical tradition, so called because it advocated a synthesis of the positions of YOGACARA BUDDHISM and the MADHYAMIAKA. This approach was extremely influential, and it appears to have been the dominant position advanced at major Indian Buddhist institutions such as the NALANDA and Vikramashila monastic complex for several centuries. This synthesis seems to have been supplanted by the Prasangika-Madhyamiaka school by the 11th century, at least in Tibet. He authored a number of philosophical works, the most important his massive *Gathering the Elements of Reality (Tattvasamgraha)* and *Ornament of the Middle Way.*

Further reading: James Blumenthal, *The Ornament of the Middle Way: A Study of the Madhyamiaka Thought of Santaraksita* (Ithaca, N.Y.: Snow Lion, 2004); Matthew Kapstein and Gyurme Dorje., trans., *The Nyingma School of Tibetan Buddhism: Its Fundamentals and History* (Boston: Wisdom, 2002); David S. Ruegg, *Buddha-Nature, Mind and the Problem of Gradualism in a Comparative Perspective: On the Transmission and Reception of Buddhism in India and Tibet* (London: School of Oriental and African Studies, 1989).

Santi Asok

Santi Asok is a major contemporary Buddhist movement in Thailand. It grew up in the 1970s, a period of political tumult in Thai culture and politics. The founder, Bodhiraksa (1934–   ), believed the Thai sangha was too lax. Beginning in 1970, he attracted followers who were popularly known as the "Asoka Group," or *Santi Asok.* Santi Asok followers live a life of relative austerity, eating one meal per day. They eat only vegetarian food, an unusual practice in Thai Buddhism. There are also no Buddha statues in Santi Asok temples. They then established a center at Nakorn Pathom, near Bangkok, called "Asoka's Land." Under pressure to disband his center, Bodhiraksa resigned from the monkhood in 1975 and formally established Santi Asok.

Santi Asok has so far remained critical of mainstream Buddhism and Thai society in general. This stringent criticism has led to problems with authority. In 1989 Bodhiraksa and 79 followers were briefly arrested under charges of falsely claiming to be Buddhists. They were then banned from preaching. In 1995 several followers were also put on trial.

Santi Asok's troubled relationship with Thai authorities is to some extent related to politics. A follower, General Chamlong Srimuang, was elected governor of Bangkok in 1992 and his party, Phalang Dhamma (Power of Dhamma), is a force in the Thai parliament. Chamlong leads an austere lifestyle reminiscent of that of Santi Asok.

Further reading: John Powers, *A Concise Encyclopedia of Buddhism* (Oxford: One World, 2000); Sulak Sivaraksa, "Thai Spirituality and Modernization," in Takeuchi Yoshinori, ed. in association with Jan Van Bragt, James W. Heisig, Joseph S. O'Leary, and Paul L. Swanson, *Buddhist Spirituality: Indian, Southeast Asian, Tibetan, and Early Chinese* (New York: Crossroad, 1993), 112–134; Donald K. Swearer, *The Buddhist World of Southeast Asia* (Albany: State University of New York Press, 1995).

Santideva (c. 650 C.E.) *Indian interpreter of the bodhisattva path*

Santideva was a monk in the famous Buddhist monastery-university of NALANDA. He wrote two extant works, one of them the *Bodhicharyavatara* (Entering the path of enlightenment). This work traces the path of the six PARAMITAS (perfections), a path all BODHISATTVAS were expected to follow. He also explains two refined methods of meditation through which a bodhisattva can keep focus on helping others attain enlightenment.

Further reading: Reginald A. Ray, *Buddhist Saints in India: A Study in Buddhist Values and Orientations* (Oxford: Oxford University Press, 1994).

San Yuan Gong

San Yuan Gong is a long-established Daoist temple in Guangzhou, the largest city in China's south. San Yuan is purported to be the site where three Daoist adepts riding rams descended from the sky and founded the city. Three rams are the symbol of Guangzhou to this day. The temple today is well preserved but not an active center of worship.

Further reading: Taoist Information and Culture. "Grotto Heavens and Blissful Realms: Three Origins Temple (Sanyuangong)." Available online. URL: http://www.eng.taoism.org.hk/general-daoism/grotto-heavens&blissful-realms/pg1-5 -6–7.asp. Accessed on May 23, 2006.

Sariputra (c. 500 B.C.E.) *early disciple of the Buddha*

Sariputra, one of the Buddha's primary disciples, appears in many sutras, in which he is known for his wisdom. Sariputra was highly respected, second in the sangha only to the Buddha himself. Saruputra represents the force of monastic development. His impressive powers were developed through effort in accord with the rules of Buddhist monasticism. He was, in other words, a representative of settled spiritual development, the renouncer, as opposed to the ascetic, forest-oriented individual in early Buddhism.

Sariputra was the force behind the ABHIDHARMA SCHOOL. He was very analytical and arranged knowledge in easily taught groupings. As the modern scholar EDWARD CONZE notes, Sariputra's approach had "a certain soberness and dryness" that we feel even to this day. Other groups within the sangha preferred Maudgalyayana, who had psychic power, or ANANDA, the Buddha's personal attendant.

Sariputra was born in MAGADHA of a Brahman, upper-caste family. Sariputra was originally a follower of the ascetic Sanjayin. While traveling in the city of Rajagrha, Sariputra met a follower of the Buddha and converted to the Buddha's path, taking with him Maudgalyayana and the other followers of Sanjayin, who soon died.

Sariputra went on to become identified with scholarly learning and an understanding of doctrine. In such texts as the *Mahavastu* he is said to have a Brahman background and to have been highly literate before he met the Buddha. His abilities in memorization were prodigious. Sariputra was in later years focused on clarifying the correct understanding of doctrine and teachings. He fought heretical views and was able to expound on the meanings of the original teachings. In a word, he was an abhidharmic scholar not unlike the later figures VASUBHANDU and NAGARJUNA. In fact, he is said to have expounded on the Abhidharma along with the Buddha, in heaven.

Nevertheless, Sariputra continued to be seen as a paradigmatic ascetic in some later depictions in the Buddhist canon. After the development of MAHAYANA BUDDHISM literature Sariputra became a symbol for a certain kind of learning, a programmatic as opposed to a scholarly approach. In the PRAJNAPARAMITA, LOTUS SUTRA, and Avatamsaka Sutra Sariputra represents an inferior form of wisdom, one who is slow and not bright, unable to "understand" the essence of the Buddha's teachings. In other words, the Mahayana writers associated Sariputra with the HINAYANA form of Buddhism, a good but limited version in comparison with Mahayana Buddhism.

See also DISCIPLES OF THE BUDDHA.

Further reading: Edward Conze, *Buddhism: Its Essence and Development* (New York: Philosophical Library, 1951); Nyanaponika, *The Life of Sariputta* (Kandy: Wheel Series, 1966); Reginald Ray, *Buddhist Saints in India: A Study in Buddhist Values and Orientations* (Oxford: Oxford University Press, 1994).

sarira

Sarira are relics of the Buddha. The word *sarira* had the meaning of "body," in the singular, but in the plural form meant "relics." *Sarira* were an important subject of debate in early Buddhism and remain important objects of veneration today.

There is still debate on the Buddha's injunction to his disciple Ananda, in the Mahaparinibbana-sutta, not to perform *sarira-puja,* worship of his remains, after his death. One interpretation is that sangha members should not attend to such rituals, which could, however, be handled by lay followers. This interpretation implies that veneration of Buddha relics was not practiced by monks at all, at least not at first, and was primarily a lay phenomenon. However, other scholars have concluded the Buddha's statement referred only to participation in the funeral rites, not in relic veneration.

Regardless, by the second century B.C.E., during ASOKA's time, in rock monasteries of Sanci and Bharhut, the STUPA and veneration of the stupa occupied the center of monastic life. The worship halls by that time were built around the stupas.

See also RELICS OF THE BUDDHA.

Further reading: David Germano and Kenin Trainor, eds., *Embodying the Dharma: Buddhist Relic Veneration in Asia* (Albany: State University of New York Press, 2004); John S. Strong, *Relics of the Buddha* (Princeton, N.J.: Princeton University Press, 2004); Kevin Trainor, *Relics, Ritual, and Representation in Buddhism: Rematerializing the Sri Lankan Theravada Tradition* (Cambridge: Cambridge University Press, 1997).

Sarnath (Isipathana, Deer Park)

Sarnath, located around 10 miles from the holy city of Varanasi (Benares), is the place where the Buddha gave his first lectures after achieving enlightenment. It is therefore seen by Buddhists as the birthplace of Buddhism. Sarnath is not the place where he achieved enlightenment, however—that was at 135 miles away at BODHGAYA. Sarnath, also called Deer Park, was the site of the gathering of the first group of Buddhist monks and the formation of the initial Buddhist monastic community.

The Buddha is said to have taught two important lessons at the Deer Park, now recorded in the form of two early sutras: the Dhammacakkhapa-vathana Sutta and the Anattalakhana Sutta. ASOKA, the third-century B.C.E. emperor who converted to Buddhism, helped expand the monastic life at Sarnath. The community, which grew to include more than 1,000 monks, flourished through the ninth century but declined after the establishment of Muslim rule in the area. Eventually everything Buddhist would be destroyed. In the late 19th century, the British launched archaeological work in the area. They uncovered a number of the old Buddhist sites. Control of the Buddhist ruins has been placed in the hands of the MAHABODHI SOCIETY, which has expanded its initial concern with recovering Bodhgaya and again placing it in Buddhist hands.

The visitor to Sarnath today can see Asoka's pillar and several archaeological remains. The Dharmarajika Stupa was built by Asoka to hold some relics of Gautama Buddha. Only the base of the Nulghandhakuti Shrine, an elaborate building used by the Buddha for meditation, remains.

At the beginning of the 1930s, the Mahabodhi Society erected a modern temple, the Mulagandhakuti Vihara. It is decorated with scenes of the Buddha's life, but its main attraction is a silver casket found in the Punjab in 1913. On it is an inscription dated to 79 C.E. that claims the casket holds some relics of the Buddha. Given to the society in 1935, it was subsequently taken to Sarnath. The Deer Park is near the Mulagandhakuti temple. There are also many new Buddhist temples built nearby in the styles of various Buddhist cultures—Thailand, Tibet, Japan, Burma, China, and Korea.

Further reading: Buddhanet. "Sarnath: The Deer Park Where Buddha Preached His First Two Discourses." Available online. URL: http://www.buddhanet.net/e-learning/pilgrim/pg_25.html. Accessed on March 1, 2005; Trilok Chndra Majupuria, *Holy Places of Buddhism in Nepal and India: A Guide to Sacred Places in Buddha's Lands* (Columbia, Mo.: South Asia Books, 1987); Gunaratne Panabokke, *History of the Buddhist Sangha in India and Sri Lanka* (Dalugama, Kelaniya, Sri Lanka: Postgraduate Institute of Pali and Buddhist Studies, University of Kelaniya, 1993); Tarthang Tulku, *Holy Places of the Buddha.* Vol. 9, *Crystal Mirror* (Berkeley, Calif.: Dharma, 1994).

Sarvastivada (Sarvastivadin) school

Sarvastivada, the "All Things Exist" school, is one of the 18 SCHOOLS OF EARLY BUDDHISM. The Sarvastivadins propounded the doctrine of the existence of matter. This did not extend to the self however; the Sarvastivadins did not refute the ANATMAN concept whereby the Buddha taught that the ATMAN, or "self," had no substance. VASUBANDHU, one of the founders of YOGACARA BUDDHISM, wrote the great

Sarvastivadin-inspired work the ABHIDHARMA-KOSA before he renounced the Sarvastivadin premises.

Further reading: Sakurabe Hajime, "Abhidharma," in Takeuchi Yoshinori, ed. in association with Jan Van Bragt, James W. Heisig, Joseph S. O'Leary, and Paul L. Swanson, *Buddhist Spirituality: Indian, Southeast Asian, Tibetan, and Early Chinese* (New York: Crossroad, 1993), 67–78; Kogen Mizuno, *Essentials of Buddhism: Basic Terminology of Buddhist Philosophy and Practice.* Translated by Gaynor Sekimori (1972. Reprint, Tokyo: Kosei, 1996); Charles S. Prebish, *The A to Z of Buddhism* (Lanham, Md.: Scarecrow Press, 2001).

Sarvodya Shramadana

This Sri Lankan self-help movement, a prime example of ENGAGED BUDDHISM to Buddhists outside Sri Lanka, began in 1958 and is based on the use of Buddhist principles as a cure for the problems of modern urban life. Sarvodya conducts training programs in villages, covering infrastructure, education, women's issues, health, and welfare. Its work depends on volunteers. The founder, T. T. Ariyaratne, interprets his movement as an extension of Buddhism's teachings of liberation. Liberation here means individual liberation, freedom from one's defilements, as well as freedom from socioeconomic restrictions. Sarvodaya is an example of an active reinterpretation of Buddhist principles for the modern condition. While the movement does accept financial assistance from international sources, it has declined support from the Sri Lankan government.

Further reading: Richard F. Gombrich and Gananath Obeyesekere, *Buddhism Transformed: Religious Change in Sri Lanka* (Princeton, N.J.: Princeton University Press, 1988).

Sasaki, Ruth Fuller Everett (1893–1967)
pioneer American Buddhist leader

Ruth Fuller, one of the first Americans to study ZEN BUDDHISM in Japan, developed an interest in

Asian religion as a young woman. She married a Chicago attorney, Charles Everett (d. 1940), and the two spent time in the ashram on Long Island founded by Pierre Arnold Bernard (1875–1925), an early American teacher of Hinduism. In 1930 the two took a world tour, and while stopping over in Japan, met DAISETSU TEITARO SUZUKI. He gave her some initial instructions in Zen meditation. She returned to Japan several years later and Suzuki arranged for her to study at Nanzen-ji with the abbot Nanshinken Roshi.

In 1938, she settled in New York and discovered the existence of the Buddhist Society of America (later the First Zen Institute of America) and became a student of its founder, SHIGETSU SASAKI ROSHI (1882–1945). She was soon editor of the society's periodical, *Cat's Yawn*. Meanwhile her daughter met and married ALAN WILSON WATTS, who had recently migrated to the United States from England. After their marriage he pursued studies for the priesthood of the Episcopal Church.

In 1942, Shigetsu Sasaki was moved into an internment camp, as were most Japanese Americans. Everett arranged for his release and since she was now a widow, in 1944 she married him. He died the next year. To fulfill his wish that she finish the translation of the writings of RINZAI ZEN, she moved to Japan to further her own study and to learn Japanese and Chinese. She settled in at Daitoku-ji to sit with Zuigen Goto Roshi, the abbot. She eventually became Daitoku-ji's abbess. In 1965 she organized a Japanese branch of the First Zen Institute of America to help Americans to study Zen Buddhism in Japan. Among the many people whom she assisted in their travel to Japan was GARY SNYDER.

Further reading: Isshu Miura and Ruth Fuller Sasaki. *The Zen Koan: Its History and Use in Rinzai Zen* (New York: Harcourt, Brace & World, 1965); Sasaki, Ruth Fuller, trans., *Recorded Sayings of Ch'an Master Lin-chi* (Kyoto: Institute for Zen Studies, 1975); ——— et al., trans., *The Recorded Sayings of Layman P'ang* (New York

and Tokyo: Weatherhill, 1971); ———, Zen: A *Method for Religious Awakening* (Kyoto: First Zen Institute of America in Japan, 1959).

Sasaki Roshi, Kyozan Joshu
(1907–   ) *Japanese American Rinzai Zen master*
Joshu Roshi, founder of Rinzai-ji, an association of RINZAI ZEN centers in the United States, was born in Miyagi, Japan. He became a Buddhist novice at the age of 14 at a temple in Hokkaido under the oversight of Joten Soko Miura Roshi. He was ordained a priest at the age of 21, at which time he took the name Kyozan. At the age of 40, he received authority as a roshi. From 1953 to 1962, he served as abbot of Shoju-an, a temple in Iiyama, Nagano Prefecture. In 1962 Joshu Roshu arrived in America and the following year established the Rinzai Zen Dojo Association in Southern California. The name was later changed to Rinzai-ji, Inc. As it expanded, centers were founded in various locations in California North Carolina, New York, and New Mexico. The first Canadian center opened in 1979. For a period of nearly 10 years, he held regular sesshins for Trappist monks at St. Joseph's Abbey in Spencer, Massachusetts.

As of November 2005, Joshu Roshi, age 98, continued to teach. Meanwhile, his students now lead Zen centers in places as diverse as Redondo Beach, California; Vienna, Austria; Puerto Rico; Vancouver, British Columbia; Ithaca, New York; Miami; Mt. Cobb, California; and Princeton, New Jersey.

Further reading: Albuquerque Zen Center. "Joshu Sasaki Roshi in the United States." Available online. URL: www.azc.org/azc-about-roshi.thml, accessed June 2, 2005; Yoshin David Radin, *The Zen of Myoshin-ji Comes to the West: 25 Years of Joshu Roshi in America, 1962–1987* (Los Angeles: Rinzai-ji, 1987); ———, *Zen Master Joshu Sasaki: The Great Celebration* (Los Angeles: Rinzai-ji, 1992); Joshu Sasaki, *Buddha Is the Center of Gravity* (San Christobal, N. Mex.: Lama Foundation, 1974).

Sasaki Roshi, Shigetsu (1882–1945)
pioneering Japanese Zen monk in America

Shigetsu Sasaki Roshi, better known as Sokei-an, founded the Buddhist Society of America, one of the first Buddhist associations in the New York City metropolitan area. As a young man in Japan, Sasaki became a part of a lay ZEN BUDDHISM practitioner group. In 1906 he accompanied his teacher Sokatsu Shaku in a missionary effort to spread Zen in the West. The group found little initial response, and only Sasaki stayed in America. He made his way to New York City and worked as an artist through the years of World War I.

After the war, he returned to Japan to complete his training, which was finished in 1928. He subsequently settled permanently in the United States. He founded the First Zen Institute of America and found a small but growing number of students.

Sokei-an was briefly interned as a Japanese national in 1942. He subsequently married one of his students, RUTH FULLER EVERETT SASAKI, an American, part of an effort to get him released. He was able to return to New York in 1944 but eventually died of an illness he acquired while in the camp. His widow emerged as his successor and went on to become a notable Zen leader in her own right.

Further reading: Mary Farkas, "Footsteps in the Invisible World," *Wind Bell* 8, nos. 1–2 (Fall 1969): 15–19; Shigetsu Sasaki and Michael Hotz, *Holding the Lotus to the Rock: The Autobiography of Sokei-An, America's First Zen Master* (New York: Weatherhill, 1998).

sastra

Sastras are a category of Buddhist literature. Meaning literally "rule," a *sastra* is a commentary or essay on some aspect of Buddhist thought or practice. The *sastras* are contrasted to the SUTRAS, which are in all cases said to be the actual words of the Buddha. An example of a *sastra* is VASUBANDHU's *Abhidharmakos-sastra basyam*, his commentary (*basyam*) on the treasury (*kosa*) of the ABHIDHARMA. Although the concept is found in Theravada literature as well, the comparable term in PALI (*sattha*) is not often used.

Further reading: Damien Keown, *Oxford Dictionary of Buddhism* (Oxford: Oxford University Press, 2003, 2004); Kogen Mizuno, *Essentials of Buddhism: Basic Terminology of Buddhist Philosophy and Practice.* Translated by Gaynor Sekimori (1972. Reprint, Tokyo: Kosei, 1996); Charles S. Prebish, *The A to Z of Buddhism* (Lanham, Md.: Scarecrow Press, 2001).

satori   See ENLIGHTENMENT.

Sawaki Roshi, Kodo (1880–1965) Japanese
Soto Zen Master

Kodo Sawaki Roshi, one of the most outstanding SOTO ZEN masters in 20th-century Japan, was born in Tsu-shi, Mie Prefecture. Orphaned at an early age, he was adopted by Bunkicki Sawaki, a professional gambler. As a youth, he developed a desire to become a Zen monk, and in 1896 he moved to Eihei-ji. He was ordained the next year and took the name *Kodo* from his teacher, Kodo Sawada, the abbot of Soshin-ji.

In 1900, Sawaki was drafted into the army and in 1904–05 he fought in the Sino-Japanese War in China. He recovered from a near-fatal wound and after the war resumed his practice. In 1912 he became the instructor of monks at Yosen-ji in Mie Prefecture and held several similar positions at different locations over the next years. Then in 1923 he began to travel around Japan lecturing and leading meditation sessions for what he termed the "moving monastery." It is during his wandering years that he acquired a student, Taisen Deshimaru, who would remain with him for the rest of his life.

In 1935, Sawaki's accomplishments were recognized when he was appointed as a professor at Komazawa University. He would continue to teach for almost 30 years, while holding different positions at nearby Zen monasteries, initially as the overseer of practice at Soji-ji (1935–40).

In 1940, with World War II in full force, he became the head of another temple, Tengyo Zen-en. After the war, he again assumed a wandering life and became known for his activities teaching lay people and holding ZAZEN sessions in typical places such as jails. He continued this activity until 1963, when illness forced him to resign his professorship and to cease his travels. He died two years later. Shortly before his death, he ordained Taisen Deshimaru, a married man, as a monk and commissioned him to go to the West to spread Zen. Deshimaru subsequently established the Association Zen Internationale, one of the West's largest associations of Zen centers.

Further reading: Kosho Uchimaya, *The Zen Teaching of "Homeless" Kodo* (Tokyo: Sotoshu Shumuvcho, 1990).

sayadaw   *See* TITLES AND TERMS OF ADDRESS, BUDDHIST.

Scandinavia, Buddhism in

Though beginning the 21st century while experiencing growth, Buddhism remains a small religious community in Scandinavia (Denmark, Finland, Iceland, Norway, and Sweden), yet to claim even 1 percent of the population. That does not seem likely to change in the near future given its low-key proselytizing methods and the slowing of immigration from Asia.

The Scandinavian countries were, through the 19th century, home exclusively to the Christian faith. During the 16th century, the countries moved from Roman Catholicism in adopting Lutheranism as the state religion. In the 19th century, various alternative forms of Protestantism developed, but not until the early 20th century did forms of spirituality other than Christianity appear.

Asian religions in general and Buddhism in particular found individual advocates through the 20th century but only after World War II did worshipping communities begin to appear. In a few cases, individuals traveled to Asian countries, where they discovered Buddhist teachers, teachings, and practice. Then, in the 1960s, Asians began to move to Scandinavia, especially Denmark and Sweden, and the first Buddhist meditation halls and temples appeared. By the end of the century, a network of Buddhist groups had emerged across Scandinavia. One study estimated that the Buddhist community in Denmark had grown from approximately 2,000 adherents in 1980 to around 17,000 in 2004.

Important to the growth of Buddhism have been those Scandinavians who have traveled to other countries to gain leadership skills and credentials and returned home to head their own organizations. Of these, none are as important as Ole Nydahl and his wife, Hannah. In 1969 they traveled to India and became the first Western students accepted by the 16th Gyalwa *karmapa*. After three years of meditation and study, Nydahl was commissioned to return to the West and spread KAGYU KARMA Tibetan Buddhism. He returned to his native Denmark and as Lama Ole Nydahl has been most aggressive in founding centers and training teachers for what he terms DIAMOND WAY BUDDHISM. Centers associated with Lama Nydahl can now be found across Scandinavia.

As in North America, ZEN BUDDHISM has been the most attractive form of Buddhism in many Scandinavian nations. A number of Zen centers have emerged across Scandinavia, one group associated with the Association Zen Internationale (AZI) headquartered in Paris, France.

After Zen, Tibetan Buddhism has been most successful. A variety of Tibetan groups have opened centers representative of the four major schools of Tibetan Buddhism and a few of the lesser schools such as the Aro gTer (a subschool of the NYINGMA tradition). Several of the international associations of Tibetan centers are active, including the Foundation for the Preservation of the Mahayana Tradition, the Dzogchen Community, and the NEW KARMAPA TRADITION, and the DALAI LAMA has made periodic visits.

Immigrants from Taiwan, Sri Lanka, Vietnam, Japan, and Thailand have established temples in Scandinavia. The Vietnamese have possibly the largest network, with some 15 temples, primarily in Norway and Denmark. The Taiwan-based FOGUANGSHAN has opened a temple in Sweden and has affiliated centers in Norway and Denmark. SOKA GAKKAI INTERNATIONAL has centers across Scandinavia and is one of the few organizations with an affiliated group in the rather isolated Iceland. The socially active ORDER OF INTERBEING has also found support among native Scandinavians.

Further reading: Graham Coleman, ed., *A Handbook of Tibetan Culture: A Guide to Tibetan Centres and Resources throughout the World* (Boston: Shambhala, 1994); Peter Lorie and Julie Fookes, comp., *The Buddhist Guide* (London: Boxtree, 1996); ———, *The Buddhist Directory: The Total Resource Guide* (Rutland, Vt.: Charles E. Tuttle, 1997); Ole Nydahl, *Riding the Tiger: Twenty Years on the Road: Risks and Joys of Bringing Buddhism to the West* (Grass Valley, Calif.: Blue Dolphin Press, 1992).

schools of Chinese Buddhism

Chinese Buddhism is traditionally divided into 10 schools, all of which flourished during the Tang dynasty (618–907). The early ones were reinterpretations of existing teachings from India. However, over time the Chinese began to reinterpret Buddhist teachings in their own way, leading to new channels of thought. The four major schools of TIAN TAI, HUA YAN, PURE LAND, and CHAN are original Chinese contributions to Buddhist thought.

These schools of the Tang period were not always distinct and separate. It has been argued they were simply polemical vehicles used by different groups of monk-scholars to put forward their ideas. As such it is a mistake to assume that the division into schools is the major characteristic of Chinese Buddhist practice. Chinese Buddhism is found in the monasteries and temples, in popular literature, in ritual, and in the very phrases and idioms of the spoken language. These forms care little about schools and narrow distinctions. At the same time the major Chinese schools such as Tian Tai and Chan have left behind a strong image of proper Buddhist practice, a cultural memory of ideals, rituals, and ways of seeing the world, that survives wherever Buddhism is found in China.

THREE STAGES SCHOOL

This school was established by a Chinese monk, Xin Xing (540–594), to teach the idea of three stages. Such works as the LOTUS SUTRA and the Avatamsaka Sutra contain the theory of the three stages. This holds that the Buddha's teachings will go through three stages: one of the true DHARMA, when the teachings are followed closely; one of the counterfeit Dharma, when the true Dharma is hidden, and similar but false teachings prevail; and one of decay (in Japanese, MAPPO), when the Dharma will be ignored and disappear. The stages will last for between 500 and 1,000 years each, depending on which version is followed. The most popular version taught that the first, true stage would last 500 years, and the second, counterfeit one 1,000. Most Chinese of Xin Xing's period felt the third stage would begin in their time, in 550 C.E.

This sect was important as an example of Buddhist donation practice. A large storehouse, the Inexhaustible Treasury, was set up in the Huatu Temple at the Tang dynasty capital, Chang An. Donations poured in to support it. The treasury was finally appropriated in 713 C.E. by the emperor Xuan Zong, who also proscribed the sect. The Three Stages school did not survive the general persecution of 845.

DISCIPLINARY (LU) SCHOOL

This school was started in the Tang by Tao Xuan (596–667). The school's purpose was to remind followers that adherence to rules was as important as understanding of Buddhist concepts; it emphasized the 250 rules for monks and the 348 rules for nuns. These rules are found in the VINAYA, the section of the Buddhist canon dealing with monastic discipline.

KOSA SCHOOL

The Kosa (or Realist) school was stimulated by the translation of the ABHIDHARMA-KOSA, the work written by VASUBANDHU and translated into Chinese twice, once by PARAMARTHA in 563–567 and later by XUAN ZANG in 651–654. This school considered that DHARMAS (events) were facts, and that things had their own existence. Such dharmas include notions of time, such as the past, the present, and the future. Although things were impermanent, a kernel of their nature was transmitted into the future.

This school, with its SARVASTIVADA-leaning (so-called Hinayana) teachings, was by 795 absorbed into the Fa Xiang, or Idealist, school.

SAN LUN SCHOOL

San Lun means "Three Sastras." The SASTRAS, or commentaries, are three well-known works by NAGARJUNA and ARYADEVA: the *Madhyamika Sastra and Dvadasanikaya Sastra* by Nagarjuna, and, by Aryadeva, the *Sata Sastra*. These three *sastras* were translated by KUMARAJIVA (fifth century). These three texts form the core of MADHYAMIKA philosophy. Madhyamika taught followers to distinguish and find the middle ground between extremes. Although it did not last as an independent movement, Madhyamika has survived as a well-established branch of traditional MAHAYANA BUDDHISM. In the modern period the Chinese monk YIN SHUN (1906–2005) was known as an advocate of Madhyamika thought.

TIAN TAI

This syncretic school was established around the figure of ZHI YI (538–597) and held that the LOTUS SUTRA is the highest teaching of Buddhism. In Japan it was known as the TENDAI school.

HUA YAN

The Hua Yan masters promoted the Avatamsaka Sutra as the most profound of the Buddha's teachings. The last patriarch was Zongmi (780–841), who died just before the HUI CHANG PERSECUTION of 845, and the school did not generate additional masters later.

FA XIANG

Fa Xiang means "characteristics of the dharmas." It came into existence after the writings of VASUBANDHU and ASANGA (fl. fourth century C.E.) became popular, beginning with PARAMARTHA's translation of the Mahayanasamgraha in 563. This stimulated the Kosa (She Lun) school, which became absorbed into the Fa Xiang. The great Chinese translator Xuan Zang's return from India stimulated even more translation work.

The key philosophical emphasis of the Fa Xiang (also called the *Dharmalaksana*, or Mindonly, school) is an idealistic picture of the universe. The mind contains the ALAYA-VIJNANA, storehouse consciousness, which holds and mixes all ideas. The outside reality is simply a manifestation of the storehouse; in Vasubhandu's words, "All this world is ideation only."

This school was popular during Xuan Zang's time (602–664 C.E.), but with his death it declined. It was heavily criticized by the Hua Yan school as being too "Hinayana" and overly philosophical.

TANTRA

The Tantra school, which first developed in India in the seventh and eight centuries C.E., refers to the vast number of deities and sees them as creations of mind. The world is characterized in fact by SUNYATA, or emptiness. This interpretation married the Hindu Tantric elements with core Mahayana teachings on emptiness. The Tantric school put great emphasis on MANTRAS, MUDRAS (hand symbols), and MANDALAS, cosmograms showing the universe.

PURE LAND

The Pure Land school focuses on the Sukha-vativyuha, the Pure Land Sutra, which describes the Pure Land, the paradise in the west where the Buddha AMITABHA resides. Followers to this day are strongly attracted by the images of a peaceful afterlife accessible to all. Therefore, Pure Land remains a strong branch of contemporary Buddhist practice.

CHAN

The Chan school began with the entry into China of BODHIDHARMA, who in traditional accounts arrived there in 520 (or 526).

Chan was able to flourish in Tang dynasty China (618–906) because it fit the overall epoch. Artistic expression and experimentation reached a new peak during the Tang, and Chan fit well with that milieu. It also mixed well with DAOISM and did not focus excessively on philosophical speculations. Chan's rejection of the traditional scriptures and images of the Buddha was radical, but it fit the personality of the Chinese well.

Further reading: Buddhanet. "The Chinese Buddhist Schools." Available online. URL: http://www.buddhanet.net/e-learning/history/b3schchn.htm. Accessed on December 5, 2005.

Scripture of the Yellow Register   *See* THREE REGISTER RITUALS.

Seiran   *See* OUCHI SEIRAN KOJI.

self-immolation and disfigurement in Buddhism

Self-immolation is, simply, setting oneself on fire. It is not widespread or common in Buddhist practice. Nevertheless there are instances and references to this and other extreme ascetic practices in the Buddhist tradition. Other similar practices include self-disfigurement, especially intentionally cutting off one's own limb or body part.

It may seem paradoxical that such practices are found if not condoned in Buddhist history. Most people are aware that the Buddha himself expressly taught a Middle Way between extremes of indulgence and self-abnegation. He in particular noted that extreme ascetic practices such as limiting diet and physical postures do not lead one to a fundamental understanding of the nature of reality. How, then, did such practices develop in Buddhism after the Buddha's time?

Overcoming the natural urges of the physical body is part of the way of Buddhism. "Overcoming" is here perhaps too indicative of forced discipline; "not allowing desires to overshadow one's true nature" is more in line with the spirit of Buddhism. And to aid in this monitoring, the SANGHA, the community of monks and other cultivators, developed practices and regulations that all members were expected to follow. Chief among such regulations are rules on celibacy and eating habits. Naturally these have developed differently in various Buddhist contexts; for instance, not all Buddhist monastics are required to be vegetarian, and some can marry. However, it is widely recognized that the Buddhist practitioner must become aware of and regulate the urges of the body, as well as other desires that arise in life.

In China as well as India, the regulation of physical urges had been a focus of individual religious practice well before Buddhism. Inevitably, in every location Buddhist thought and practice mixed with existing ascetic practices. In China and other East Asian cultures, there was already a Daoist image of the cultivator separate from society, willing to sacrifice all links with fellow beings. The primary link was of course marriage and family. But membership in society also meant the caring for one's own body. Han Chinese to this day believe that one's physical body, including the nails and hair, is a precious inheritance from the ancestors and must be cared for in order to perpetuate the family line. Dismemberment in particular is seen as a disrespectful act, since it destroys the continuity of the body's various parts. Thus a person serious enough about religious cultivation to oppose these ingrained cultural habits was a devoted cultivator indeed.

Self-immolation and disfigurement are thus acts that symbolize religious devotion and sincerity. They carry such symbolic weight in those cultural contexts precisely because they run counter to cultural instincts. Such examples are present in Buddhist texts because they serve as symbols of sincere practice. They are, thus, usually literary tropes.

The 23rd chapter of the LOTUS SUTRA, one of the great texts of MAHAYANA BUDDHISM, states that such monks are worthy of emulation. The autobiography of HSING YUN (Xing Yun) (1927–), the contemporary Chinese monk-leader of the FOGUANGSHAN movement in Taiwan, gives an example of self-immolation from his youth. That monk was seen as a monk of high virtue. The CHAN literature is similarly full of examples of disfigurement.

In actual practice one finds little of this in contemporary Chinese Buddhism. One Western follower of HSUAN HUA (Xuan Hua) (1908–99), a 20th-century Chinese monk who migrated to America, actually did cut off a portion of his finger in order to show sincerity of belief. He was sent to intensive care and severely reprimanded by his master, who said such practices were meant for those extremely rare individuals of high cultivation. It is also possible that the idea of such practices attracts unbalanced individuals. At any rate, it is clear that this emphasis on extreme asceticism is not typical of Buddhist practice in general.

Self-immolation jumped onto center stage of the world's media during the Vietnam War (1950–75). In a series of widely publicized protests, several Buddhist monks led by THICH QUANG DUC (1897–63) lit themselves on fire. They were in this case going beyond symbolic statements of religious practice to political statements of protest. The act, by a highly respected Vietnamese monk, was taken very seriously indeed and broadcast around the world. At the time the Buddhist sangha in Vietnam was becoming increasingly marginalized by the intense political forces locked in the struggle for control of the society in southern Vietnam. It was, however, an essentially political act, not in any way required or condoned by Buddhist practice.

Further reading: Buddhist Information of North America. "Self Immolation." Available online. URL: http://www.buddhistinformation.com/self_immolation.htm. Accessed on November 7, 2005; Leon Hurvitz, trans., *Scripture of the Lotus Blossom of the Fine Dharma* (The Lotus Sutra) (New York: Columbia University Press, 1976); Thich Nhat Hanh, *Lotus in a Sea of Fire* (London: S.C.M. Press, 1967).

sensei   *See* TITLES AND TERMS OF ADDRESS, BUDDHIST.

Senzaki, Nyogen (1882–1958) *Japanese monk who worked in America*

A student of SOYEN SHAKU, Senzaki was born in Asian Russia (on the Kamchatka Peninsula) and taken to Japan as an infant after his mother's death. He had read the entire TRIPITAKA by the age of 19, and he was able to compose poetry in both Chinese and Japanese. He studied with Soyen Shaku and was asked by him to set up a kindergarten, in 1901. Senzaki lived in America for 17 years, from 1905, before he began to teach on Buddhism. At that point he held lectures in different places, a "floating *zendo*." He finally set up a permanent *zendo*, or "zen hall," in 1927 in Los Angeles, the Mentorgarten Mediation Hall (also called the Tosen-zenkutus, "Meditation Hall for the Eastern Dharma"). Interned in Wyoming under Executive Order 9066 as a Japanese, Senzaki continued to teach and lead ZAZEN groups.

Further reading: Rick Fields, *How the Swans Came to the Lake: A Narrative History of Buddhism in America* (Boston: Shambala, 1992); Nyogen Senzaki, *Like a Dream, like a Fantasy: The Zen Writings and Translations of Nyogen Senzaki*. Edited by Eido Shimano (Tokyo: Japan, 1978); ———, "Reflections on Zen Buddhism," *Pacific World* third series 6 (Fall 2005): 139–149; ———, and Ruth Strout McCandless, *Buddhism and Zen* (New York: Philosophical Library, 1953).

Setsubun (Bean Throwing Ceremony)

Setsubun is the traditional Japanese festival that celebrates the beginning of spring; it served as well to exorcise wandering spirits. There was an ancient belief that ghosts wandered the streets at night in the new season. The ceremony was originally performed on New Year's Eve by the imperial court. In the performance some actors took on the role of blue and red ghosts who were chased by the others. Beans were also thrown around the ground to ward off devils. The festival gradually spread into the general populace.

Today, on February 3 of the solar calendar, people throw roasted soybeans in and around their homes, intoning, "In with good luck, out with devil." This Setsubun-derived act is a ceremony to drive out demons. In shrines and temples well-known celebrities perform the same actions.

Another feature of Setsubun still practiced in many households is to put food out for the Mother Deity, HARITI. The traditional legend is that Hariti was a demon who ate the children of humans, until her own child was hidden by the Buddha. From that point she became a disciple of the Buddha.

Setsubun festivals are held at many SHINGON temples in Japan, such as Hoko-ji and Eifuku-ji in Nara.

Further reading: Hiroyuki Ozawa, *The Great Festivals of Japan*. Translated by John Bester. (Tokyo: Kodansha, 2000).

Seung Sahn Sunim   *See* KWAN UM SCHOOL.

sexuality, Buddhist approaches to

Buddhist practice is heavily monastic and therefore celibate. However, there exist a great multiplicity of approaches to sexuality in Buddhist literature and practice, and there are many teachings concerning what it means to be a sexual being.

Unlike Western monastic practice, which prohibits sex because it is seen as being immoral, Buddhist monastic practice prohibits it because it is a major distraction for anyone engaged on the Buddhist path. This view of sex is connected to the position that suffering is supported by cravings. These cravings ensnare one in the cycle of samsaric existence. Sex is an entanglement, and it produces additional entanglements in the form of family relations. Just as the Buddha felt the need to renounce these entanglements of family in order to cultivate, so too do Buddhist monks. Thus sexuality is not a moral issue; it is a practical one.

For laypeople, sexual conduct is not greatly discussed in the Buddhist literature. All devout lay Buddhists take the five vows (PANCA SILA), which include the injunction not to engage in inappropriate sexual behavior. But the norms for that behavior are left unexpectedly open. Thus modern Buddhists in some countries accept birth control, homosexuality, and even abortion. In contrast, life inside the Buddhist monastery is strictly regulated by the VINAYA rules of conduct. Sexual intercourse results in expulsion. Intercourse is carefully defined as any type of penetration of any orifice, including the anus and the mouth.

The rules for nuns are equally onerous. Nuns cannot touch another person's body between shoulders and knees and cannot meet alone with a man. And unlike monks, nuns are not allowed to meet with other women. They are also not allowed to sleep two in a single bed, unless one is sick.

Masturbation is an offense for both monks and nuns, although not as serious as intercourse.

The Vinaya rules for monks were, of course, written by men. That they spell out sexual rules in such detail may indicate the difficulties monks experienced in living up to the demands of celibacy. And since many of the cultures were patriarchal, much of the blame for their difficulties was placed on women. Women in Buddhist thinking were considered to be more subject to sexual desire than men and less able to control their desires, hence their more elaborate rules.

MAHAYANA BUDDHISM thought allowed that the act was less important than the intention behind it. Thus it was possible for an individual to engage in sex while not being influenced by it.

The BODHISATTVA precepts, which reflect this newer Mahayana way of thinking, now dominate monastic discipline in Japan. In Japan sexual misconduct no longer leads to expulsion, rather to the need for repentance. Male homosexuality also became more widespread in Japanese monasteries. Japan eventually eliminated the requirement for celibacy altogether. It is the only Buddhist culture to do so.

sexuality, Daoist approaches to

Daoism, with its core mission to investigate immortality, devoted much attention to the relations between the sexes. In contrast to Buddhism and other moralities of celibacy, Daoism has consistently taught that sex is a necessary part of life and, indeed, important as a cultivation practice. The sexual act itself seemed to recreate the creation of matter on a microscopic scale.

The unique approach of Daoist thinkers was to focus on retention of the male's vitality (*yuan jing*). One view of intercourse is that it nourishes the male. Some writers state it can feed the longevity of women also. The man's *jing* energy is limited and so should not be shed without control. In contrast, a woman's sexual energy, a form of QI, is inexhaustible. Therefore, a man should not ejaculate, while a woman may reach orgasm

often. A balanced view would be that both sexes benefit from the sexual act.

The urge to limit male ejaculation may also have been related to the keeping of many concubines, of course, a strictly social, patriarchal practice.

There are reports of communal rituals of ejaculation control in Daoism. The so-called *he qi* (union of energies) ritual of the second century C.E. was held after fasting, meditation, and prayer. Partners then disrobed and performed union. Not surprisingly, such communal rites, probably of ancient pedigree, were strongly criticized by Buddhists and Confucians.

Further reading: Bernard Faure, *The Red Thread: Buddhist Approaches to Sexuality* (Princeton, N.J.: Princeton University Press, 1998); Rita M. Gross, "Sexuality: Buddhist Perspectives," in William M. Johnston, ed., *Encyclopedia of Monasticism* (London: Fitzroy Dearborn, 2000), 1154–1156; Julian F. Pas, *Historical Dictionary of Taoism* (Lanham, Md.: Scarecrow Press, 1998); Douglas Wile, *Art of the Bedchamber: The Chinese Sexual Yoga Classics including Women's Solo Meditation Texts* (Albany: State University of New York Press, 1992).

Shaku, Soyen (1859–1919) *first Zen Buddhist priest in America*

Soyen Shaku, the first ZEN BUDDHISM teacher in the United States, was ordained as a monk at the age of 12. He studied under Imakita Kosen Roshi, who passed to him a desire for higher education. After receiving DHARMA transmission in 1884, Shaku went on to study at Keio University and then travel to Sri Lanka to study SANSKRIT and THERAVADA Buddhism.

Kosen died in 1892, and Shaku succeeded him as the head monk at the Engaku-ji temple in KAMAKURA. Shortly thereafter he accepted an invitation to speak at the World's Parliament of Religions held in Chicago in 1893. He delivered speeches on the law of cause and effect and on alternatives to war. At the parliament, he met PAUL CARUS, the owner of Open Court Press. The meeting generated an interest in Buddhism in Carus, who went on to publish a number of works on the subject and himself become an active practitioner.

In 1905, Shaku accepted an invitation from Alexander Russell to visit San Francisco. His most famous student, DAISETSU TEITARO SUZUKI, accompanied him and served as translator for his public lectures. In addition to Suzuki, two other students would become pioneers of the American Buddhist movement, NYOGEN SENZAKI and Sokatsu Shaku.

Further reading: Rick Fields, *How the Swans Came to the Lake: A Narrative History of Buddhism in America* (Boston: Shambala, 1992); Soyen Shaku, "The Law of Cause and Effect as Taught by the Buddha," in J. W. Hansen, ed., *The World's Parliament of Religions* (Chicago: Monarch Book Company, 1894); 388–390; ———, *Sermons of a Zen Buddhist Abbot* (Chicago: Open Court Publishing Company, 1906); ———, *Zen for Americans* (LaSalle, Ill.: Open Court, 1974).

Shambhala International

Shambhala International is an international Buddhist organization that originated in the teaching activities of CHOGYAM TRUNGPA Rinpoche (1939–87), a Tibetan lama from the KAGYU tradition who taught in Great Britain and North America from the 1960s until his death in 1987. Having already established several meditation centers in Great Britain and the United States, Trungpa in 1970 founded Vajradhatu with headquarters in Boulder, Colorado, as an umbrella organization for the loosely affiliated group of Buddhist institutions that had emerged around Trungpa among his students in the United States, Canada, and Europe. These local centers became known as dharmadhatus. Vajradhatu also included the Nalanda Foundation, which Trungpa founded as the organization to oversee his Nalanda Institute,

a secular educational institution for instruction in traditional subjects with a grounding in the Buddhist tradition. He also founded the system of Shambhala training, a secular path of spiritual training based on his popular book *Shambhala: The Sacred Path of the Warrior.*

In 1976, Chogyam Trungpa appointed Thomas Rich, an American also known as Osel Tendzin, as his regent. Osel Tendzin was responsible for day-to-day administration of this organization and assumed full leadership after the death of Chogyam Trungpa in 1987. Osel Tenzin's leadership did not last long, because of a severe health condition and a major lapse in ethical judgment. He contracted acquired immunodeficiency syndrome (AIDS) in 1988, and concealing this fact, infected at least one of his students with the disease before dying in 1990. When his condition was made public, this news led to a serious crisis throughout Vajradhatu.

After Osel Tendzin's death, Trungpa Rinpoche's eldest son, Sakyong Mipham Rinpoche (1962–   ), was in 1995 named the new leader of Vajradhatu. Meanwhile, in 1992, the leadership chose a new name for the movement and its various parts, Shambhala International. Today Vajradhatu primarily designates the way of Buddhist practice and study within the movement.

Shambhala International is headquartered in Nova Scotia, Canada; it is rooted in six residential contemplative communities in the United States, Canada, and France and the extensive network of dharmadhatus throughout North America and Europe.

Further reading: Chogyam Trungpa, *Born in Tibet* (Boulder, Colo.: Shambhala, 1976); ———, *Shambhala: Sacred Path of the Warrior* (Boulder, Colo.: Shambhala, 1985); Charles S. Prebish, *Luminous Passage: The Practice and Study of Buddhism in America* (Berkeley: University of California Press, 1999); Amy Lavine, "Tibetan Buddhism in America: The Development of American Vajrayana," in Charles S. Prebish and Kenneth K.

Tanaka, eds., *Faces of Buddhism in America* (Berkeley: University of California Press, 1998): 99–115.

Shangqing Daoism (Shang-ch'ing)

Shangqing (high clarity) DAOISM is a movement that was active between c. 370 C.E. and the Yuan (1270–1368) dynasty. Unlike some earlier Daoist movements associated with popular beliefs, Shangqing was Daoism as practiced by the upper classes. It was highly influential on Daoist ritual and is especially known for its focus on visualization techniques.

The classic work of Chinese alchemy, BAOPUZI NEIPIAN, was issued in 317 C.E. In another 50 years a new series of *Baopuzi*-inspired texts appeared, known collectively as *Shangqing* (high clarity). These form the core of the Shangqing branch of Daoism.

In the classic account by Dao Hongjing (456–536), most of the Shangqing scriptures came into existence when Lady Wei descended from heaven to give or recite the texts to Yang Xi (330–386). Lady Wei was in fact a historical person who died in 364, at the age of 83. According to GE HONG, author of the *Baopuzi*, Lady Wei had studied Daoism and become an immortal. Thus the Shangqing texts recorded by Yang Xi were revealed texts, in which the writer is somehow possessed by or privy to the words of a god.

Dao Hongjing collected many texts and recorded the early history of this process of text transmission and as a result is seen by some as the true founder of Shangqing. Dao was also the major practitioner of Shangqing Daoism in his time. And because Dao lived on Mt. Mao (Mao Shan), Shangqing became known as the Mao Shan lineage, although the association is not exclusive because other influences and schools were present on Mao Shan as well as Shangqing. Regardless, Shangqing existed as a separate school from the time of Dao Hongjing until the Yuan, when it effectively merged into the Zhengyi school of Daoism.

The merger with Zhengyi Daoism was not surprising, since most of the early members of Shangqing had a background in Zhengyi Daoism. Like Zhengyi Daoists, Shangqing leaders were members of the elite, ruling classes. Once a new ruling dynasty, the Eastern Jin, took power in 317, the elite members of the southern gentry class adopted Daoism and reinterpreted it in their own way. Thus Shangqing was an elite, southern Chinese reinterpretation of Daoism concepts.

The key work of Shangqing Daoism is the Perfect Scripture of Great Grotto (*Datong zhenjing,* also called Dragon Book of Three Heavens of Scripture of Thirty-nine Chapters). Thirty-nine was said to be important because it matched the number of Daoist gods (39) and the number of "seats" of the human body. The idea was to ask a god to descend to all of the body's "seats" and guard them. There are three key rituals described in the Perfect Scripture—the visualization of the five directions, the visualization of the sun and moon merging inside the body by swallowing 27 times, and a visualization of drawing in the energy from 24 stars, mixing this with saliva and breath, then swallowing 24 times. These early Shangqing rituals used key sounds—*chui, hu, xi, ah, xu,* and *si*—during meditation, sounds that are still used also in contemporary QIGONG.

In line with its essentially elitist background, Shangqing religious practice focused on inner contemplation, rather than communal rituals. Those contemplations made ample use of visualizations and invocations of the gods, allowing them entry into the individual's body. Such "entries" were of course on a subtle, nonvisible level. Practitioners also visualized themselves taking out-of-body trips to sacred sites and journeys to the limits of the five directions. Finally, Shangqing practitioners also used drugs, a reflection of experiments with alchemy.

Organizationally, Shangqing for many years had its own set of patriarchs, some of whom were powerful during the Tang (618–906) dynasty. With headquarters on Mao Shan, the patriarchs were at one point, 721 C.E., given supervision rights over all localized and mountain-related gods throughout the empire.

Further reading: Isabelle Robinet, "Shangqing—Highest Clarity," in Livia Kohn, ed., *Daoism Handbook* (Leiden: Brill, 2004), 196–224; Qing Xitai et al., *History of Chinese Daoism*. Vol. 1. Translated by David Yu (Lanham, Md.: University Press of America, 2000).

Sheng Yen (1931–) *founder of Dharma Drum Mountain Association (Taiwan)*

The Taiwanese Buddhist teacher Sheng Yen, the founder of the DHARMA DRUM MOUNTAIN ASSOCIATION, heads an international organization, one of the largest fellowships of Chan practitioners in the world, with more than 300,000 students. Sheng Yen was born near Shanghai. He entered a monastery in the CHAN BUDDHISM tradition at the age of 13 and began a decade of study and practice at various related facilities in and around Shanghai.

During the Chinese Civil War, he joined the Nationalist Army and was assigned to Taiwan. He continued in the army (while continuing to pursue his Buddhist studies) for a decade, during which he published his first book on Buddhism (1956). About the same time he left the army, he had several deep meditational experiences, as a result of which he was recognized as a DHARMA HEIR (successor) in both the LINJI CHAN (Lin Chi) and CAODONG (Tsao-tung) Chan BUDDHISM traditions. He became a full-time monk at the Buddhist Culture Center in Beitou, near Taipei. Sheng-yen engaged in a solitary retreat at the Chao Yuan Monastery (1961–68) and subsequently became a lecturer at Shan Dao Monastery in Taipei. His academic accomplishments were later recognized with a master's degree (1971) and a doctorate (1975) from Rissho University in Japan.

He followed his early status as a Dharma heir by receiving full transmission in the Caodong tradition (1975) and the Linji tradition (1978). He now began the organizational steps that led to the founding of Dharma Drum Mountain. In 1978 he became the president of the Chung-Hwa Buddhist Cultural Institute in Taipei. The next year he assumed duties as the abbot of Nung Ch'an Monastery in Taiwan, and in 1980 founded the Ch'an Meditation Center and the Institute of Chung-Hwa Buddhist Culture in New York. In 1985, with a growing following, he opened a graduate school, the CHUNG-HWA INSTITUTE OF BUDDHIST STUDIES, in Taipei.

In 1989 he founded the International Cultural and Educational Foundation of Dharma Drum Mountain. In 1996, this foundation was merged with the Institute of Chung-Hwa Buddhist Culture in New York to form the Dharma Drum Mountain Association. As these organizational changes were occurring through the 1980s and 1990s, Sheng Yen authored more than 90 books, many of which were translated into the languages of the Pacific region. He developed an active travel schedule, which sees him annually spending up to six months of the year in North America. He has also assumed a role as an environmental activist.

Further reading: Master Sheng-yen, *Faith in Mind: A Guide to Ch'an Practice* (Elmhurst, N.Y.: Dharma Drum, 1987); ———, *Getting the Buddha Mind: On the Practice of Ch'an Retreat* (Elmhurst, N.Y.: Ch'an Meditation Center, 1982); ———, with Dan Stevenson, *Hoofprint of the Ox: Principles of the Chan Buddhist Path as Taught by a Modern Chinese Master* (Oxford: Oxford University Press, 2001); ———, *Illuminating Silence: The Practice of Chinese Zen*. Edited by John Cook (London: Watkins, 2002).

Shen Hui (Heze Shenhui, Ho-tse Shen Hui) (684–758) *Chinese Chan Buddhism leader*

The Chinese Chan Buddhist Shen Hui (Heze Shenhui) was one of the most controversial and influential Buddhist teachers in the first half of the eighth century of China. This was the period during the transition of CHAN BUDDHISM from a relatively obscure branch of Chinese Buddhism, emphasizing seated meditation, to the most vigorous and stimulating sect of Buddhism in China.

Heze Shenhui was a student of HUI NENG (638–713), who is now known as the sixth patriarch of Chan. Heze Shenhui influenced the history of Chan Buddhism with three important contributions: (1) he added support to the myth that Chan existed in India and was taken to China by BODHIDHARMA; (2) he created the myth that Hui Neng was the one and only sixth patriarch in an unbroken line originating with the Buddha; (3) he seemingly also was an important instigator of the sectarian division of Chan into a Northern "gradual" tradition and a Southern "sudden" tradition.

Although a later biography states that Heze Shenhui met his teacher, Hui Neng, when Heze Shenhui was only 14 years old, it is likely that Heze Shenhui first encountered the sixth patriarch sometime later, between 701 and 709. Shenhui may have studied briefly with SHEN XIU of the Northern branch of Chan before study with Hui Neng in the south of China.

Seven years after the death of the sixth patriarch Hui Neng in 713, Heze Shenhui began teaching. Shenhui does not seem to have emphasized seated meditation or used shouting or striking in his teaching style; rather, he seems to have relied on talking, explaining, and eloquent and forceful sermons. Certainly the nonrational dialogs that appear in the KOANS barely 100 years after Heze Shenhui's death are nowhere in evidence in his recorded dialogs. Shenhui stressed the class of Buddhist wisdom texts called the PRAJNAPARAMITA literature, which included the DIAMOND SUTRA and the HEART SUTRA His central themes involve wu-nien (no-thought; freedom from conceptualization), the identity of wisdom and concentration, seeing and knowing one's BUDDHA NATURE, and the wisdom (PRAJNA) and emptiness (SUNYATA) teachings of the Diamond Sutra. In addition to study of doctrine he strongly recommended the recitation and study of SUTRAS to aid in the quest for awakening.

In those decades the most popular Chan Buddhist school in the capital city was the Northern school of SHEN XIU. In 732, Heze Shenhui began public criticisms of the Northern school's teachings and teachers: (1) that Heze Shenhui's own teacher, Hui Neng, was the one and only sixth patriarch of Chan in China, and thus the Northern Chan teachers were merely a sideline of the genuine transmission of Chan; and (2) that the understanding of the Northern Chan lineage was gradualist and incorrect.

Heze Shenhui's influence and popularity began to increase after 745, when he continued his dissection of the Northern line and instituted monthly meetings when he quoted prajnaparamita texts; criticized the teachings, techniques, and lineage of the north; and responded to questions from the audience. A follower of the rival Northern line of Chan sent a false report to the emperor claiming that Heze Shenhui was gathering followers for seditious purposes, and the 69-year-old Heze Shenhui was banished. However, in 755, two years later, General An Lu-shan began a rebellion and the emperor had to flee for his life. The government needed funds. Despite the fact that Heze Shenhui was now 73 years old, he was called upon to assist in the fund-raising and was so successful that he substantially increased the royal treasury. As a result, he was summoned to the imperial court and shown many royal favors. Until his death in 758 Heze Shenhui was the recipient of much royal patronage and his Southern school flourished.

Because of his forceful presentation, in the following decades Heze Shenhui's Southern school became the dominant sect of Chan. Thirty-eight years after Heze Shenhui's death, a meeting of Chan masters was called to determine which schools and which doctrines were orthodox. The Southern school was declared the orthodox school, Hui Neng was recognized as the sixth patriarch after Bodhidharma, and Heze Shenhui was decreed the seventh patriarch, successor to Hui Neng.

Shen Hui was instrumental in establishing the official list of Chan transmission. He used a list of Indian Buddhist teachers found in the introduction to the Dharmatr-dhyana Sutra (a manual of DHYANA meditation practice) to establish a fictitious connection between Chan in China and Indian Buddhism. Inspired by this list, Heze Shenhui created a line of patriarchal transmission for his own branch of Chan, to establish the legitimacy of what he called the "Southern school of Bodhidharma." In the minds of his audience Shenhui had established a connection between the Buddha in India and his own teacher, Hui Neng, by means of the story of Bodhidharma. Bodhidharma and Hui Neng were now regarded as inheritors in a line of a historical transmission of a doctrine that did not depend on written texts—Chan Buddhism. The Oxhead school of Chan also had a list of 29 patriarchs, and the two lists became combined into the official history of Chan.

See also CHAN BUDDHISM; SCHOOLS OF CHINESE BUDDHISM.

Further reading: J. C. Cleary, "Treatise on the True Principle," in Zen Dawn (Shambhala: 1986); Walter Liebenthal, trans., "Sermon of Shen-hui," Asia Major III, 1952; John McRae, "Shen-hui and the Teaching of Sudden Enlightenment," in Peter Gregory, ed., Sudden and Gradual (Honolulu: University of Hawaii Press, 1987); D. T. Suzuki, The Zen Doctrine of No-Mind (Weirs Beach, Maine: Weiser Books, 1991); Philip Yampolsky, The Platform Sutra of the Sixth Patriarch (New York: Columbia University Press, 1967); Robert B. Zeuschner, "A Sermon by the Zen Master Shen-hui," The Middle Way 49, no. 3 (November 1974): 45–47; ———, "The Hsien-tsung-chi: An Early Chan Text," Journal of Chinese Philosophy 3 (1976): 253–268.

Shen Xiu (Shen Hsiu) (600–706) leader of Northern school of Chan and one successor to the fifth patriarch of Chan Buddhism

Shen Xiu was a famous successor to the fifth patriarch of CHAN BUDDHISM, Hong Ren (601–674).

Shen Xiu is most known as a contemporary and "adversary" of the sixth patriarch, HUI NENG (638–713), and Hui Neng's advocate, SHEN HUI (670–762). While Hui Neng and his followers advocated a sudden theory of enlightenment, Shen Xiu promoted the idea of gradual "unfoldment" of enlightenment. In competitions for the attention of the master Hong Ren, Shen Xiu is depicted as being learned, with a solid foundation in the classics and vast understanding of the subtleties of Chinese literature. In a famous passage of the PLATFORM SUTRA, Shen Hui wrote the poem

This body is the Bodhi tree
The soul is like a mirror bright
Take heed to keep it always clean
And let not dust collect upon it.

Hui Neng then gave his additional stanza in response (see HUI NENG), which has ever since been seen as besting Shen Xiu's.

Shen Xiu did not become a follower of his master Hong Ren until he was more than 50 years old. After the death of Hong Ren, Shen Xiu became abbot of a monastery in Hubei, in central China. There he became famous and influential, and his followers were known as the Northern school of Chan. He was in one well-known incident called to meet EMPRESS WU CHAO (r. 684–705), who bowed before him as a mark of singular honor.

Further reading: D. T. Suzuki, Essays in Zen Buddhism (Second Series). Edited by Christmas Humphreys (London: Rider, 1970).

Shimaji Mokurai (1838–1911) modernist Japanese Jodo Shinshu priest

Shimaji Mokurai helped guide the JODO SHINSHU community during the difficult years of the MEIJI RESTORATION.

Shimaji became a Shin priest in the HONPA HONGWANJI. After the fall of the TOKUGAWA shogunate, the restoration of the emperor to power, and the disestablishment of Buddhism from its previously favored place vis-à-vis the government, Shimaji and a colleague, Akamatsu Renjo (1841–1919), led an effort to reorganize the entire sect. In 1872, as part of their reorganization, Shimaji and four colleagues traveled to Europe to study government-religion relationships and to examine the new critical approaches to the study of religion. Shimaji's observations of the North American and European religious scenes led to his most famous literary piece, the "Critique of the Three Standards," in which he criticized government policy toward religion (specifically a plan to revive and teach SHINTO throughout the country) and called for the separation of religion and government. The Shin Buddhists' refusal to support the government program led to its failure. In 1880, the government to a great extent ended its attempt to manage Japanese Buddhism; Shimaji interpreted the trend as indication that Japan had attained the separation he sought.

Motivated by the obvious favoring of Shinto by the government, Shimaji's efforts were always in support of Buddhism. Much of his thought was given to creating a picture of Buddhism as essential to the nation. Thus he cooperated with representatives from other Buddhist groups in publishing the *Essentials of the Buddhist Sects,* a statement detailing both the common ground and unique approaches of 12 major Japanese Buddhist groups. He wrote the lengthy introduction, in which he reviewed the whole of Buddhist history.

Further reading: James Edward Ketelaar, *Of Heretics and Martyrs in Meiji Japan: Buddhism and Its Persecution* (Princeton, N.J.: Princeton University Press, 1990); Brian Victoria, *Zen at War* (New York: Weatherhill, 1997).

Shingon

Shingon (literally, true word) Buddhism is a prominent Japanese Buddhist school that began with KUKAI (774–835) and his introduction of Chinese Vajrayana Buddhism to Japan. Kukai designated his religion "True Word" as a translation of the SANSKRIT term MANTRA. He referred to the secret mystical words spoken by VAIROCANA in the SUTRA. These words are chanted in Shingon rituals as part of their esoteric (secretly transmitted) practices. Kukai also taught that a believer could become a Buddha in this present lifetime by union with the vital life force of the universe. Today, the 12 million Shingon believers represent the largest community of VAJRAYANA BUDDHISM practitioners in the world.

Kukai found authority for Shingon teachings primarily in two sutras, the Mahavairocana Sutra and the Diamond Crown Sutra. As the major speaker in the Mahavairocana Sutra, the Buddha VAIROCANA is seen as the ultimate source of Shingon teachings. Originally transmitted by Vairocana to Vajrasattva, the esoteric (not openly transmitted) truth was passed through a line of eighth-century figures, including NAGARJUNA, VAJRABODHI, Pukong (or AMOGHAVAJRA, who translated the Diamond Crown Sutra), Subhakarasimha (who translated the Mahavairocana Sutra), and Hui Guo (with whom Kukai studied). These individuals are considered by Shingon, along with Kukai, to be the patriarchs of the tradition—in other words, the teachings are transmitted down through the ages by means of this line of teachers.

Kukai began his propagation of his brand of Vajrayana Buddhism in 806, upon his return to Japan from China. In 816 the emperor granted him land on Mt. KOYA, and in 823 he was granted land in Kyoto, which became the site of To-ji temple. Mt. Koya and To-ji became the main centers of the dissemination of Shingon through the country. Over the next centuries, a belief arose that Kukai had not died but had entered a deep trance from which he would awaken when the future MAITREYA, the future Buddha, would make his appearance.

Shingon spread through the ninth century but experienced two major schisms led by Yakusan and Shobo, two prominent priests who resided in Kyoto, at the end of the ninth century. Other schisms would occur over the years and there are now more than 50 Shingon sects in Japan, though the older group headquartered on Mt. Koya is still the largest. In the 20th century, Shingon Buddhism spread through the Japanese Buddhist diaspora in North America, South America, and Europe.

Further reading: Ryuichi Abe, *The Weaving of Mantra: Kukai and the Construction of Esoteric Buddhist Discourse* (New York: Columbia University Press, 1999); *Light of Buddha* (Los Angeles: Koyasan Buddhist Temple, 1968); Richard Karl Payne, *The Tantric Ritual of Japan Feeding the Gods: The Shingon Fire Ritual* (Delhi: International Academy of Indian Culture and Aditya Prakashan, 1991); Taiko Yamazaki, *Shingon Japanese Esoteric Buddhism* (Boston: Shambhala, 1988).

shinjin   See FAITH, PRACTICE, AND STUDY.

Shinkyo (1237–1319) *founder of Ji-shu Buddhism*

Shinkyo was a follower of IPPEN (1239–89), the wandering ecstatic who preached a somewhat mystical form of PURE LAND BUDDHISM. He believed that everyone who said the *NEMBUTSU*, the mantralike prayer calling upon the grace of AMITABHA, would be taken to the heavenly Pure Land. Ippen spent the last years of his life distributing medallions with the *nembutsu* stamped on them and teaching people an ecstatic dance that grew out of the joy of the realization of Pure Land truth. When Ippen died, he said that the teaching work was complete.

Shinkyo initially accepted Ippen at his word and claimed a mountain, there to await death while reciting the *nembutsu*. However, the local governor convinced Shinkyo that there was still work to be done, namely, sharing the word about the *nembutsu* with those who still were unaware of it. He finally agreed to assume leadership of Ippen's large following. He began to travel, distributed the medallions, and encouraged the ecstatic dance.

Unlike his master, however, Shinkyo began to build centers where believers could gather.

He also began to ordain priests (both male and female) to head the centers. By 1316, there were some 100 such centers scattered around the country. Thus in stages, the JI-SHU sect took shape. Shinkyo died in 1318. He was succeeded by Chitaku (1261–1320).

Further reading: Kazuo Kasahara, ed., *A History of Japanese Religion.* Translated by Paul McCarthy and Gaynor Sekimori (Tokyo: Kosei, 2001).

Shinnyo-en

Shinnyo-en is a new Buddhist religion founded soon after World War II by Shinjo Ito (1906–89) in Tachikawa, near Tokyo, Japan. Shinnyo-en offers training in *sesshin* (touch the essence) sittings, the central practice. This practice began when Shinjo, the founder, interpreted the divine instructions received by his wife, Tomoji, in trance. The group also focuses attention on the NIRVANA SUTRA as the highest expression of the Buddha's knowledge.

Ito had served as an engineer before becoming ordained as a SHINGON priest in 1941 at the Daigo-ji monastery in Kyoto. Ito's wife and cousin, Tomoji (Shojushinin) (1912–67), was also in a leadership position; Ito tended to specialize in divination while his wife was known for falling into trance and doing exorcism work. The two founded the Shingonshe Daigoha Tachikawa Fudoson Kyokai in 1938. After his formal ordination Ito began to teach his wife, Tomoji, and the two established a new organization, the Makoto Kyodan, in 1948. After a court case brought by a former follower, known as the Makoto Kyodan affair, the two registered their group as a denomination of Shingon, in 1952. The stated purpose in starting the new group was to allow all followers equal access to enlightenment.

Shinnyo-en's current leader is Shinso Ito, daughter of Shinjo Ito.

Further reading: Usui Atsuko, "Women's 'Experience' in New Religious Movements: The Case of Shinnyoen,"

Japanese Journal of Religious Studies 30, nos. 3–4 (2003): 217–241; Peter Clarke, *Bibliography of Japanese New Religious Movements* (Richmond, U.K.: Japan Library, 1999); *The Resonating Harmony of Buddha's Law* (Tokyo: Shinnoyen, 1994); Shinnyo-en. "Shinnyo-en." Available online. URL: http://www.shinnyo-en.org/shinnyoen/index.php. Accessed May 5, 2006.

Shinran (1173–1263) *founder of Jodo Shinshu Buddhism in Japan*

Shinran is the spiritual and institutional founder of the Japanese JODO SHINSHU tradition. Very little is known about his early history and the reasons why he chose the clerical life, but in 1181 he became a monk at the TENDAI monastic complex on Mt. HIEI in Kyoto. After 20 years Shinran left Mt. Hiei, disenchanted with the monastic politics and drawn to the teachings of HONEN (1133–1212). Shinran studied with Honen from 1201 to 1207. Shinran would later expand Honen's belief that anyone who recites the NEMBUTSU (a repeated chanting of the Buddha Amida's name, *Namu Amida Butsu*) and entrusts himself or herself to Amida Buddha's compassionate vow would attain birth in the PURE LAND, where the devotee would be able to fulfill the practices that led to Buddhahood.

In 1207 Honen and seven of his leading disciples, including Shinran, were banished from the capital for essentially political reasons. Shinran was exiled to Echigo (present-day Fukui and Toyama Prefectures) on the Japan Sea coast. The banishment also entailed a loss of their Tendai ordinations and a return to secular life.

Shinran took the name *Fuji'i Yoshizane* and married Eshinni, with whom he had six children. In 1214 Shinran moved his family to Hitachi (present-day Ibaraki Prefecture) in the Kanto region, where he actively began to build a large following, primarily farmers and tradepersons, and established meeting places called DOJOS. In 1234 Shinran entrusted management of the dojos and their respective congregations to his followers and departed for Kyoto with his family. In

1256 Eshinni returned to Echigo with three of their children to oversee property that she had inherited. Their youngest daughter, Kakushinni, remained in Kyoto to tend to her elderly father. Later she established the gravesite and chapel that would evolve into the Hongan-ji, the main temple of the Shin tradition.

Shinran spent the remainder of his life revising the *Kyogyo shinshu* (the full title is *A Collection of Passages Revealing the True Teaching, Practice and Realization of the Pure Land Way*) and composing other essays. Consisting almost wholly of passages drawn from the Chinese Buddhist canon and interspersed with short passages by Shinran, *Kyagyo shinshu* articulates the spiritual vision of the Larger Sukhavativyuha-sutra, the Amitayurdhyana-sutra, or the Meditation Sutra, and the Smaller Sukhavativyuha-sutra.

Together with the insights from these three SUTRAS, Shinran departed from the need for rigorous spiritual discipline to the centrality of *shinjin*, true or sincere faith, as seen in the writings of the seven patriarchs of Jodo Shinshu. In asserting that faith is central, Shinran assumed that the devotee possesses nothing true or absolute. Spiritual release occurs when the devotee perceives his or her inadequacies and surrenders to the absolute Other Power (*tariki*) of Amida Buddha. Amida Buddha's compassionate efficacy is the source of salvific power. Even *shinjin*, the prime condition for birth in the Pure Land, is a gift, and the sincere utterance of the *nembutsu* is an invocation of gratitude and joy for Amida's compassion. For Shinran, birth in the Pure Land is the most conducive way station for the ultimate realization of enlightenment (BODHI), or NIRVANA.

Further reading: James C. Dobbins, *Jodo Shinshu, Shin Buddhism in Medieval Japan* (Bloomington: Indiana University Press, 1989); Alicia Matsunaga and Matsunaga Daigan, Foundation of Japanese Buddhism. Vol. 2 (Los Angeles: Buddhist Books International, 1976); Ronald Y. Nakasone, *Ethics of Enlightenment, Essays and Sermons in Search of a Buddhist Ethic* (Fremont, Calif.:

Dharma Cloud, 1990); Yoshifumi Ueda and Dennis Hirota, *Shinran, an Introduction to His Thought* (Kyoto: Hongwanji International Center, 1989).

Shinshu Buddhism   *See* JODO SHINSHU.

Shinto (Way of the Gods)

Shinto is an indigenous Japanese belief system and set of institutionalized worship practices. Shinto is often described as the original religion of the Japanese people, comparable to BON RELIGION beliefs among Tibetan cultures and beliefs in indigenous spirits in Myanmar. However, as in most indigenous systems of belief its development and meaning are complex.

Shinto did develop as a system until far into Japanese recorded history, and then it appears to have attained its own identity as a result of Buddhism's presence as well as political developments. It was also not always seen as a "religion" in the same way Buddhism was perceived. To this day many people who respect the KAMI, or Shinto deities, do not necessarily see themselves as believers in a Shinto religion. At the same time, governments have often tried hard to develop a Shinto institution or symbol for their own purposes.

EARLY RELIGION IN JAPAN

Early religious beliefs are tied with burial practices. In fact, the religious beliefs of the inhabitants of the Japanese islands were varied and, in many parts, still not developed even when parts of Japan had an advanced civilization. Some of the earliest inhabitants of the Japanese islands left behind *dogu,* highly feminized ceramic figures that probably indicated fertility and ancient mother worship. The *dogu* were often broken then placed inside graves.

A larger variety of ceramic figures and objects were created in the Yayoi period (300 B.C.E.–300 C.E.). Some of these funerary objects were houses that resemble the architectural style of the ISE SHRINE, the most important of all Shinto shrines. Many *ujigami,* Shinto deities connected to clans (*uji*), date from the Yayoi period. Thus early burial practices and clan organizations clearly influenced Shinto.

RYOBU SHINTO

By the 600s the Yamato clan had exerted influence over most of central Japan, the Kanto plain. Buddhism appeared at this time and in 592 was accepted as the official religion. Buddhism spread widely in the Heian (794–1185 C.E.) and Kamakura (795–1333) periods. Buddhist temples were often built beside existing Shinto shrines. Buddhism was adaptable to its new environment. Eventually people began to equate the gods and saints of the new religion with existing *kami,* or deities. *Ryobu Shinto,* "Double" Shinto, combined Buddhist *bosatsu* (BODHISATTVAS) with Shinto *kami.*

The years from the Heian to the Tokugawa are generally considered the medieval period in Japanese history. Buddhism was dominant. In the Tokugawa (1600–1867) NEO-CONFUCIANISM was also popular. However, a scholarly movement to study ancient texts, the KOJIKI AND NIHONSHOKI, led to increasing interest in Shinto. This interest played a part in the regaining of the emperor's powers in the MEIJI RESTORATION of 1868. Shinto, as the imperial house's cult, was the official religion, "STATE SHINTO."

THE *KAMI* (DEITIES)

Kami are the primary objects of worship in Shinto. *Kami* is a category that includes a wide variety of beings and forces. Some are imported, for instance, from Buddhism. Others are mountain spirits. And still others are forces of nature or spirits of place. The kamikaze, the sacred wind—probably a typhoon—that saved Japan from Mongol invasion in the late 1200s, was a kind of *kami.*

Strictly speaking, *kami* are of three types: *ujigami* (clan ancestors), deified humans or nature spirits, and souls of dead leaders, especially emperors and war heroes. AMATERASU is the best known *uji-gami,* since she is the clan *kami* for the Yamato clan, the imperial household. But there are other clan shrines throughout Japan.

There are creative *kami (musubi),* which represent growth and reproduction. There are also mountain and river *kami.* Tenmangu, the god of learning, is an example of a deified human.

SHINTO AND THE CREATION MYTHS

The myths of creation are found in the *Kojiki* and the *Nihonshiki,* texts dating to the 700s C.E. There was an age of the gods in which gods were active before they departed to stay in heaven. The *kami* from these accounts are either *amatsukami* (heavenly *kami*) or *kunitsukami* (earthly *kami*). In the main creation myth Izanagi and his wife, Izanami, procreated and bore the sun goddess, Amaterasu. Amaterasu became the most important Shinto deity. She established the Yamato imperial line through her descendant Jimmu Tenno, Japan's first emperor, who is said to have reigned around 660 B.C.E.

Amaterasu's brother, SUSANO-O NO MIKOTO, went to earth and married. He built a palace at Izumo. He began a dynasty of deities who ruled the earth. The most powerful was Okuninushi, the Great Lord. In response to these developments, Amaterasu sent her grandson, Honinigi (also called Ninigi), to help reestablish her rule over the world.

Honinigi carried three talismans, or symbols of power: a mirror; a magic sword, called the Kusanagi; and a jewel, the Magatama, which gave him advantages. Honinigi eventually made piece with Okuninushi. He promised to allow Okuninushi recognition as protector of the imperial family, in return for his loyalty. Okuninushi is today worshipped in the Izumo taisha shrine.

Another myth from the *Kojiki* relates the domestication of agriculture. Susano-o, upon arriving at earth, visits Ogetsuhime. Ogetsuhime prepares a meal with material from her nose, mouth, and anus. Susano-o, thoroughly enraged, kills her. But her body then transforms into a place of growth: from her head emerge silkworms, rice seems to appear from her eyes, millet from the ears, beans from the nose, wheat from her genitals, and large beans from her anus. This ancient myth appears to reflect the close relationship between *kami* and the development of civilization itself.

Other *kami* stories reflect the natural environment. In the *Nihonshoki* one story follows Susano-o. Upon his arrival he notices that Japan will require wood for ships. He then pulls out the hairs from his beard and scatters them, and each hair becomes a *sugi* (cedar) tree. The hairs from his chest become cypress, those from his buttocks black pines, and those from his eyebrows camphor. After this Japan becomes a string of green islands. Japanese history is full of instances of concern for preserving trees and greenery.

SACRED TEXTS AND PRACTICES

Three essential texts that describe the birth and development of Japanese culture, the *Kojiki, Nihonjiki,* and *Engishiki* (Procedures of the Engi era, 927 C.E.), contain much of the mythology from which Shinto developed its own narratives. The *Engishiki* is a collection of codes, rites, and prayers that contain references to Shinto elements.

Doctrine and beliefs are not strongly emphasized in Shinto. Instead, followers are expected to perform rituals of purification on a regular basis, and when visiting shrines.

Further reading: W. G. Aston, trans., *Nihongi: Chronicles of Japan from the Earliest Times to A.D. 697* (Rutland, Vt.: Tuttle, 1972); Stacy Buko, "Shintoism." New Religious Movements. Available online. URL: http://religiousmovements.lib.virginia.edu/nrms/Shinto.html. Accessed on August 25, 2005; C. Scott Littleton, *Shinto: Origins, Rituals, Festivals, Spirits, Sacred Places* (New York: Oxford University Press, 2002); Sonoda Minoru, "Shinto and the Natural Environment," in John Breen and Mark Teeuwen, eds. *Shinto in History:*

Ways of the Kami (Richmond, U.K.: Curzon, 2000), 32–46; Sokyo One, in collaboration with William P. Woodard, *Shinto: The Kami Way* (Rutland, Vt.: Charles E. Tuttle, 1962).

Shinto New Religions

New religions began to appear in the Edo period in Japan (1600–1867 C.E.). These religious groups developed as a reaction to the forces of modernization, which began in the Edo period and extended into the later MEIJI RESTORATION (1868–1911) and contemporary Japan.

The newly established groups that formed in the late Edo, Meiji, and later periods fall into two categories. The first group is called Sect Shinto and is composed of 13 separate sects formed in the prewar years. The second group consists of Shinto-related new religions.

SECT SHINTO (KYOHA SHINTO)

In 1882 the government separated several Shinto groups from the officially sponsored STATE SHINTO. These groups were cut off completely from funding. By 1908, after some struggles, they had all been recognized as independent religions. The 13 sects today are the following:

Kurozumikyo
Shinto shuseiha
Izumo oyashirokyo
Fusokyo
Jikkokyo
Shinshukyo
Shinto taiseikyo
Ontoakekyo
Shinto taikyo
Misogikyo
Shinrikyo
Konkokyo
Tenrikyo

The list of 13 was in fact an administrative convenience. During the Meiji many newly established groups merged or combined temporarily in order to achieve government approval and function easily in society. And the official list masked important differences among the groups. Some, such as Izumo oyashirokyo, were classic Shinto. Others, such as Ontakekyo, focused on mountain worship. And three, Tenrikyo, Konkokyo, and Kurozumikyo, were distinct enough that they should be treated as new religions.

Why did these groups come into being in the early Meiji? Government policies were critical. The government announced that any organized Shinto group would be granted official recognition. Such an open-door policy naturally caused many groups to knock, each ready to proselytize. These groups were, as a result, only loosely related to the overall Shinto religious paradigm.

They were, however, more related to Shrine Shinto (Shinto based on shrine worship) than to one another. For instance, as in Shrine Shinto, the traditional network of shrines throughout Japan, they often focused on *kami*, rites, and the Shinto worldview. Additional influences in the growth of Sect Shinto were National Learning and the group of traveling *oshi* priests from the regions of Ise and Izumo. National Learning (Kokugaku) was an influential intellectual current that involved scholarly reappraisal of Japan's history and culture, with the goal to find the earliest, purist form of Japanese culture. It was, perhaps inevitably, also connected with rampant nationalism. The *oshi* were wandering priests from Ise who distributed talismans in the countryside.

The Sect Shinto groups were most popular in the Meiji and have declined since, at least in terms of number of adherents. After World War II many branches splintered off and formed into separate religious groups, further reducing the official rosters. Their declines paralleled the growth of Shinto New Religions.

SHINTO-DERIVED NEW RELIGIONS

These religious groups thrived because they proved adaptable to the new conditions in Japanese society. The vast social changes in the Taisho period (1912–26), and again in the Showa period (1926–89), especially after World War II, were challenges that the three Shinto-derived religions handled well.

TENRIKYO, or the religion of heavenly principle, is typical of the category of Shinto New Religions. First, the founder was a woman. Second, the group used the *tandoku fukyo,* or "independent proselytization," method. Any member could travel to a new area, care for people there, and teach the founder's message. The emphasis on healing the sick meant those who recovered often attributed their health to Tenrikyo's teachings. Organizationally, Tenrikyo groups were linked vertically with parent and child and grandchild churches. This was in contrast to the traditional Buddhist head temple–branch temple organization. And doctrinally Tenrikyo emphasized the responsibility of all to redeem the entire world. This meant in practice starting to spread salvation to those on the lowest rungs of society. Tenrikyo ultimately lived a strong ideal of equality and the pursuit of happiness in this world.

While Shinto groups thrive in contemporary Japan, it is the Shinto New Religions, especially Tenrikyo, Konkokyo, and Kurozumikyo, that have had the greatest success.

Further reading: Peter Clarke, *Bibliography of Japanese New Religious Movements* (Richmond, U.K.: Japan Library, 1999); Kazuo Kasahara, ed., *A History of Japanese Religion.* Translated by Paul McCarthy and Gaynor Sekimori (Tokyo: Dosei, 2001), 573–581. Sakamoto Koremaru, "The Structure of State Shinto: Its Creation, Development and Demise," in John Breen and Mark Teeuwen, eds., *Shinto in History* (Richmond, U.K.: Curzon Press, 2000), 329–330.

shobo (Chinese *zhengfa,* or *cheng-fa*)

Shobo is a Japanese term for the true Dharma, the correct doctrine. In the Buddhist context the true Dharma is, of course, the entirety of the Buddha's teachings.

When the Japanese ZEN BUDDHISM master DOGEN wrote his masterpiece *SHOBOGENZO* the term *shobo* had another sense, of things that are present prior to their being named or thought of. DHARMA (Japanese *-bo*) in this sense refers to something already present.

Shobo also refers to the first of the three periods of Buddhist history, as foretold in the LOTUS SUTRA. The *shobo* is that period in which the Dharma is healthy and revered; it will last 500 (in some versions, 1,000) years. It is followed by the *zobo,* the Middle (semblance) period, of 1,000 years; and, finally, by the MAPPO, Latter Period, of 10,000 years. Teachings revolving around the three periods are key in NICHIREN and other Lotus Sutra–based teachings.

See also SCHOOLS OF CHINESE BUDDHISM.

Further reading: Dogen, *Shobogenzo.* Translated by Thomas Cleary (Honolulu: University of Hawaii Press, 1986); Kosen Nishiyama, trans., *A Complete English Translation of Dogen Zenji's Shobogenzo (The Eye and Treasury of the True Law)* (Tokyo: Nakayama Shobo, 1975).

Shobogenzo

Shobogenzo (Treasury of knowledge regarding the true dharma), a major text in Japanese Buddhism, was written in the 13th century by DOGEN (1200–53), who introduced CAODONG CHAN BUDDHISM to Japan (where it is known as SOTO ZEN). The *Shobogenzo* is a collection of more than 300 KOANS, with commentaries. Less known is that Dogen wrote two books with very similar names, the *Kana Shobogenzo* and the *Mana Gozobenzo.*

In the Treasury of Knowledge (the *Kana Gozobenzo*), Dogen discussed the use of single-minded seated meditation (ZAZEN) as the primary practice, the daily life of practitioners, and the rules and teachings of the Soto school, among other topics.

The book became standard reading for Soto Zen monks.

It is also the case that in 1235 Dogen assembled a collection of some 300 koans from Song dynasty Zen texts. This work is entitled the *Mana Shobogenzo,* or *Sambyaku-soku shobogenzo* (The Shobogenzo of three hundred koans). This book was largely lost until 1934, when Professor Oya Tokujo discovered it and made it available to his scholarly colleagues. Only in the 1990s was it confirmed as a true work of Dogen.

Further reading: Dogen, *Flowers of Emptiness: Selections from Dogen's Shobogenzo.* Translated by Hee-Jin Kim (Lewiston, N.Y.: Edwin Mellen Press, 1985); ———, *Shobogenzo.* Translated by Thomas Cleary (Honolulu University of Hawaii Press, 1986); Steven Heine, *Dogen and the Koan Tradition: A Tale of Two Shobogenzo Texts* (Albany: State University of New York, 1994).

shogun/shogunate See TOKUGAWA SHOGUNATE.

Shotoku (574–622) *early patron of Japanese Buddhism*

Considered by many as the real founder of Buddhism in Japan, Crown Prince Shotoku Taishi actively supported the initial transmission of Buddhism from China and wrote some of the first Japanese Buddhist texts. He was born in Yamato, Japan, the son of Emperor Yomei (r. 586–587), who during his short reign had expressed interest in converting to Buddhism. Yomei was succeeded by Sujun (r. 587–592). Sujun's reign ended with his assassination and the installation of Shotoku's aunt as the empress Suiko (r. 592–628). In 593, Shotoku was named crown prince and regent, titles he retained until his death.

By the time she rose to the throne, the Empress Suiko was herself a Buddhist, but Shotoku became the active force in establishing Buddhism in Japan. Without giving up the throne, Suiko took vows as a Buddhist nun and gradually withdrew from her duties as a ruler. Thus without the title, Shotoku assumed more and more power. He was also a scholar who read the Chinese classics, and he wrote voluminously on a wide range of subjects.

Early in his public career, he sent envoys to China to begin a significant influx of Chinese learning and culture into the country. A secular ruler, he made his most notable accomplishment through writing a new constitution (604) based on Confucian ideals. The reorganized government was a major step in installing a government administration in which officials obtained their jobs by their accomplishments rather than family connections. Japan also adopted the Chinese calendar. While largely Confucian in orientation, the second article of the new constitution enjoins the Japanese ruler to value the Three Treasures of Buddhism—the Buddha, the Dharma, and the Sangha.

Shotoku primarily turned his scholarship to Buddhism and is known to have lectured on various Buddhist themes such as the LOTUS SUTRA, upon which he authored a commentary. He sponsored temples and saw to the creation of many images of the Buddha, the most impressive a 16-foot bronze Buddha. He supported Japanese monks-scholars on long-term visits to China. By the time of his death, there were a reported 46 temples, 816 priests, and 569 nuns serving a thriving Japanese Buddhist community.

Further reading: Joseph M. Kitigawa, *Religion in Japanese History* (New York: Columbia University Press, 1966); Kazaunori Mochizuki, *A Treatise on Prince Shotoku* (Tokyo: New Educational Research Institute, 1959); E. Dale Saunders, *Buddhism in Japan* (Philadelphia: University of Pennsylvania Press, 1964); George B. Sansom, *A History of Japan to 1334* (Stanford, Calif.: Stanford University Press, 1958).

shrines

The shrine developed as an extension of Buddhist practice centered on the *posadha*. The *posadha* was a form of sabbath. In ancient India, it was one night on which a community of ascetics (*sramanas*) assembled to discuss doctrine. It took place on the eighth, 14th, and 15th days of each lunar half-month—in other words, on the full moon and then weekly thereafter. The institution was first proposed by King Bimbisara and approved by the Buddha after his initial enlightenment. The Buddha also suggested that the monks recite their rules of training at this time.

The Buddha did visit shrines to meditate. He preferred to visit them at night because there would be few local people to disturb him. Most of these shrines were in forests and may have involved sacred trees seen as residences of spirits. There was no formal system of shrines proposed by the Buddha; however, some scholars believe he did try to hold *posadha* assemblies at fixed locations.

However, after the Buddha's PARINIRVANA another institution, that of the STUPA, or pagoda, was instituted to hold his ashes or relics. The practice of venerating the relics of the Buddha was specifically supported by the Mahaparinirvana Sutta, one of the oldest documents in the Pali Canon. In this text the Buddha gave instructions concerning his own burial: "As . . . they treat the body of a Wheel-Turning King, so should they treat the body of the TATHAGATA," spoke the Buddha to ANANDA. The Mahaparinirvana Sutta also notes that the Buddha says his remains can be placed in a stupa. Furthermore, the maintenance of this stupa should be the responsibility of the laity, not the wandering monks. Since the sutra was written later, well after the Buddha's death, it may have simply recorded an explanation for what was actual practice. This practice of building stupas to honor the Buddha may have sprung up spontaneously. Regardless of how it started, the stupa quickly became one of the most common Buddhist institutional and architectural forms.

See also ART, AESTHETICS, AND ARCHITECTURE; BUDDHIST MONASTERY; NIRVANA SUTRA; PRATIMOKSA/PATIMOKKHA.

Further reading: Johg C. Huntington, "Stupa," in William M. Johnston, ed., *Encyclopedia of Monasticism* (London: Fitzroy Dearborn, 2000), 1204–1212; Kevin Trainor, *Relics, Ritual, and Representation in Buddhism: Rematerializing the Sri Lankan Theravada Tradition* (Cambridge: Cambridge University Press, 1997); A. K. Warder, *Indian Buddhism* (Delhi: Motilal Banarsidass, 1970).

Shrine, Shinto   *See* SHINTO.

Shugendo

Shugendo is an ascetic faith built around the sacred mountains of Japan. The individualistic nature of Shugendo makes estimation of the number of practitioners and adherents difficult.

Shugendo traces its beginnings to En no Ozunu, a seventh-century figure, popularly called En the ascetic. A person around whom many legends have gathered, he appears to have been an unordained Buddhist practitioner of esotericism, beliefs and practices that are generally transmitted in secret, who was banished from society for trying to control others with his magical powers. He eventually went to dwell on Mt. Katsuragi.

En no Ozunu became the exemplar for a group of very loosely organized ascetics who roamed the mountains. Their various ascetic practices, including ordeals, diets, and strenuous spiritual exercises, were pursued as a means to acquire magical and supernatural powers. The unregulated environment in the mountains allowed them the freedom to engage unhindered in almost any outrageous behavior they chose.

As Shugendo evolved, practitioners generally selected elements from the various religious communities active in the country. It, of course, drew on variant traditions that showed great respect for mountains and the ascetic elements of the VINAYA, the Buddhist rules for monastic life. It drew magical elements from DAOISM and VAJRAYANA BUDDHISM—TENDAI and later SHINGON.

The foothills of the mountains became the site of meetings between the Shugendo practitioners and lay folk went to them for supernatural support. Over the centuries, the practitioners, the *yamabushi,* developed a complex relationship with Shingon, Japan's major community of esoteric Buddhists, and at times when Shingon was on the wane, the *yamabushi* became important in keeping esotericism alive and a vital element in Japanese religion.

Further reading: Erik Krautbauer, "About Shugendo." Available online at The Way of the Spiritual Warrior website. URL: http://shugendo.bravehost.com/about. htm. Accessed on December 2, 2005; Hitoshi Miyake, *Shugendo: Essays on the Structure of Japanese Folk Religion* (Ann Arbor: University of Michigan Press, 2001).

Shwedagon

The primary Buddhist site in Yangon (Rangoon), the capital of Myanmar, Shwedagon is unique because it houses a large quantity RELICS OF THE BUDDHA. There are, it is said, in addition to eight hairs from the head of Gautama Buddha, remains of three previous Buddhas—in other words, Buddhas from before the time of the historical Buddha.

The Shwedagon is imposing. It consists of an extremely large (99 meters high) STUPA, built in the 1770s, on a raised platform, surrounded by a series of smaller reliquaries, stupas, and halls. Around its base are four large devotional halls, called *tazaung,* in the center of each of the four sides surrounding the stupa. There are an additional 64 smaller shrines, called *zeidi-yan,* between each of the *tazaung.* These *zeidi-yan* were not added until the early 1900s. All of the stupa rests on a 6.5-meter-thick plinth, around which are placed an additional 64 stupas. At

the very top of the stupa's spire is the "diamond bud" (*sein-bu*), which holds an orb encrusted with 4,351 diamonds—including one 76-carat diamond.

The founding of Shwedagon harks back to the founding of Yangon itself. It was probably inhabited from the sixth century B.C.E.; since the area was then marshy, the Shwedagon hill may have been a relatively inhabitable location. At that time it may have been associated with a community of people from Orissa, in India. Legendary stories also relate that ASOKA, the great Indian king and champion of Buddhism, visited Shwedagon and repaired the shrine.

The earliest written evidence of Shwedagon is found in an inscription dating from the 15th century C.E., in both Mon and Burmese languages. The inscription records the hill and the visit of Burmese monks to Sri Lanka for ordination.

The pagoda today is the center of Buddhist life in Rangoon. It is managed by more than 100 staff people and a nine-member board, the Pagoda Trustees.

See also SHRINES; STUPA.

Further reading: Elizabeth Moor, "Shwedagon: Its History and Architecture," in Elizabeth Moor, Hansjorg Mayer, and U Win Pe, *Shwedagon: Golden Pagoda of Myanmar* (London: Thames and Hudson, 1999), 101–154.

Siddhartha *See* BUDDHA.

Sigalaka Sutta (Sigalovada Sutta)

The story within this early Buddha SUTRA is an early indication of Buddhist teachings on social relations. This section from the Pali canon (31st discourse of the Digha Nikaya) describes the Buddha's meeting a man, Sigala, and performing a ritual of worshipping the six directions—north, south, east, west, zenith, and nadir. The Buddha further interprets each direction as representing an important human relationship and explains the mutual obligations involved in each relationship. The east is for parents, so children are urged to honor and take care of parents, while parents are obliged to urge children to take the path of goodness. The southerly direction is associated with the relation between teachers and students, the west stands for the connection between husband with wife and children, the north is for one's ties to friends and relatives, the zenith symbolizes the relationship of *sramanas* (religious practitioners) with followers, and, finally, the nadir is associated with the way a master should treat servants and workers.

While the original ritual was a Brahmanic ceremony of worshipping the six directions, the Buddha's commentary in this sutra transforms it into a code of ethics, a basic guide for human relations.

See also ETHICS, TRADITIONAL BUDDHIST.

Further reading: Donald K. Swearer, *The Buddhist World of Southeast Asia* (Albany: State University of New York Press, 1995).

sila

Sila, or ethical conduct, includes right speech, right action, and right livelihood. In Buddhist thought right speech means one should not lie; slander; be harsh, rude, or impolite; or gossip. Right action means not taking life, stealing, dealing dishonestly, or having improper sexual actions. In essence, ethical conduct means one should act morally. In practice these precepts have been interpreted variously in different cultural contexts. The Buddha did not require his followers to be vegetarian, for instance, yet some of the Buddhist cultures, such as China's, have interpreted the injunction not to take life as requiring vegetarianism. In fact, all of these injunctions are subject to reinterpretation in different contexts. Right livelihood admonishes people to adopt a profession that will not cause harm to others. In

practice what is interpreted as right livelihood has varied over time.

See also ETHICS, TRADITIONAL BUDDHIST.

Further reading: Kogen Mizuno, *Essentials of Buddhism: Basic Terminology and Concepts of Buddhist Philosophy and Practice.* Translated by Gaynor Sekimori (1972. Reprint. Tokyo: Kosei, 1996); Charles S. Prebish, *The A to Z of Buddhism* (Lanham, Md.: Scarecrow Press, 2001).

Silk Road   *See* CENTRAL ASIA.

Silla

The Silla kingdom, which eventually unified the three Korean kingdoms into one, is significant as the period during which Buddhism spread from being a religion of the elites to a religion of all the people. In the early centuries of the Common Era, in part because of influence from China, the people of the Korean Peninsula began to unite into what would emerge as three kingdoms. On the southern half of the peninsula, two rival kingdoms came into existence, PAEKCHE and Silla. Silla, occupying the southeastern part of the peninsula, was resistant to the new faith. While Paekche adopted Buddhism toward the end of the fourth century, not until the early sixth century (527 C.E.) would Silla's ruler adopt it. However, once adopted, it received official support integrated into the country's rigidly pyramidal hierarchical social organization and used to sanction it.

The three kingdoms existed side by side for several centuries. However, in 660, Silla made common cause with the China Tang rulers and began a conquest of the peninsula. Paekche fell first and was incorporated into Silla. Eight years later, Silla and China defeated KOGURYO, and Silla was able to unite the whole of the Korean Peninsula into a single state.

In the early years of Unified Silla, WONHYO (617–686) and his younger colleague, UISANG

(625–702), would have their great impact with their basic idea of unifying the different schools of Buddhist thought and practice. They also worked to spread Buddhism, to that point largely limited to the elites of the society, as a popular movement among the masses. As Wonhyo was attempting to unify the older schools of Korean Buddhism, a new school, called Soen (or SON BUDDHISM), was imported from China, where it had been known as CHAN BUDDHISM, a meditation-based form of practice.

One of the Unified Silla rulers, King Kyongdok (r. 742–765), is remembered for his support of Buddhism and the many temples and other Buddhist facilities erected during his reign. Among the most notable was Sokkuram, a grotto shrine constructed in 751 and nestled in the mountains near the Silla capital at Kyongju.

At the end of the ninth century, the Silla dynasty collapsed and for a brief time the old three kingdoms reemerged. These were reunited in 918 by Taejo (r. 918–943), who seized control of the land and established the Goryeo dynasty. During the next century, Son Buddhism would blossom and become the favored Buddhism of Korea's rulers, who would favor it with many gifts and allow it privileges denied the other schools.

Further reading: Edward B. Adams, *Korea's Golden Age: Cultural Spirit of Silla in Kyongju* (Seoul: Seoul International Publishing House, 1991); Thera Nyanaponika, *Assimilation of Buddhism in Korea: Religious Maturity and Innovation in the Silla Dynasty* (Berkeley, Calif.: Asian Humanities Press, 1991); Narendra M. Pankaj, "The Buddhist Transformation of Silla Kingship: Buddha as a King and King as a Buddha," *Transactions of the Korea Branch of the Royal Asiatic Society* 70 (1995): 15–35.

Singapore, Buddhism in

Buddhism is today one of the major religions in Singapore, with the number of adherents estimated at between 25 and 50 percent of the total population.

Buddhism originally spread into Singapore from China and India. MAHAYANA BUDDHISM was primarily based in the Chinese community when the British purchased Singapore in the early 19th century, and British rule in Singapore stimulated the growth of the Chinese community substantially. Today almost half of Singaporeans can be said to follow the Chinese traditional religions—a mixture of folk religion, DAOISM, and Buddhism.

Buddhism exists on a spectrum from that practiced in the traditional Chinese temples that dot the island to the pristine practice found in the THERAVADA temples and in more recent ethnic forms of Buddhism imported from, for example, Tibet or Thailand.

Since Singapore's emergence as an independent country, the Buddhist community has reorganized both to meet the needs of a rapidly progressing urban society and to slow the inroads of an aggressive Christian community. The primary organizations for Buddhists (estimated at between 500,000 and 2 million) are the Singapore Buddhist Federation and Singapore Buddhist Mission, both of which carry on outreach efforts among the Chinese population and work to modernize Buddhist thought and practice. In the 1980s, they began targeting college and university students. This effort has led to the formation of several campus organizations such as the National University of Singapore Buddhist Society.

The federation works with the Singapore Buddhist Sangha Organization and the Singapore Regional Centre of the World Fellowship of Buddhists to join Mahayana and Theravada Buddhists in cooperative activities. Also serving the larger Buddhist community is the Buddhist Library in Singapore, which not only houses Buddhist books and other resource materials for use of the general public, but provides a venue for a variety of Buddhist programs—classes, lectures, and religious events.

While Mahayana is the dominant Buddhism in Singapore, Theravada has a significant following, especially among residents of Sri Lankan heritage. Theravada Buddhists find their focus in the Buddha Dhamma Mandala Society, which carries on a substantial publication program in both Chinese and English. The small Thai community has been organized by the DHAMMAKAYA Foundation founded in 1970 and based in Potumthani, Thailand. Societies have also been founded to serve the Korean, Burmese, and Tibetan communities. The primary Tibetan organization is affiliated with the KARMA KAGYU Tibetan tradition under the guidance of the 17th Gyalwa *karmapa*. There is also a CHAN BUDDHISM community operating primarily among ethnic Chinese.

More Westerners residing in Singapore have been attracted to Buddhism in the last generation. SOKA GAKKAI INTERNATIONAL leads the way along with Tibetan Buddhism in finding a home among European Singaporeans. Meanwhile, the five large Taiwan-based Buddhist groups—FOGUANGSHAN, THE BUDDHIST COMPASSION RELIEF TZU CHI ASSOCIATION, DHARMA DRUM MOUNTAIN ASSOCIATION, Amitabha Buddhist Societies, and the TRUE BUDDHA SCHOOL—have also found a home in Singapore.

Further reading: Ven. Shravasti Dhammika, *All about Buddhism: A Modern Introduction to an Ancient Spiritual Tradition* (Singapore: Buddha Dhamma Mandala Society, 1990); Narada Maha Thera, *The Buddha and His Teachings* (Singapore: Singapore Buddhist Meditation Centre, 1973); Cheu Hock Tong, ed., *Chinese Beliefs and Practices in Southeast Asia* (Selangor Daruk Ehsan, Malaysia: Pelunduk, 1993); Lio-Fan Yuan, *The Key to Creating One's Destiny.* Translated by Chiu-Nan Lai (Singapore: Lapis Lazuri Pte, n.d.).

Sivaraksa, Sulak (1933–) *Thai Buddhist social activist*

A prominent Thai exponent of ENGAGED BUDDHISM, Sivaraksa has been a strong, biting voice of a new spirit in Thai Buddhism. Sivaraksa attended school in England and received his law degree in 1961. He subsequently returned to his homeland to become a lecturer at several universities (1962) and launch his activist career by becoming the founding editor of the very influential *Social Science Review.*

Over the next years, Sivaraksa founded several nongovernmental movements in Thailand, including the Asian Cultural Forum on Development, the Coordinating Group for Religion and Society, and the Thai Inter-Religious Commission for Development. He also founded the International Network of Engaged Buddhists to focus on human rights and welfare issues on a regional basis. His actions are based on his own reinterpretation of Buddhist teachings in order to make them relevant to current issues. He criticizes commercial advertising, for example, as contrary to the fourth precept, the injunction against lying. He has also openly criticized Thai monasteries as being too affluent and comfortable.

His activism has generated problems for him. He was arrested briefly in 1984 and in 1991 went into exile overseas after an arrest warrant was issued.

Further reading: Donald S. Lopez, Jr., *Modern Buddhism: Readings for the Unenlightened* (London: Penguin, 2002); Sulak Sivaraksa, *Loyalty Demands Dissent: Autobiography of an Engaged Buddhist* (Berkeley, Calif.: Parallax Press 1998); Donald K. Swearer, *The Buddhist World of Southeast Asia* (Albany: State University of New York Press, 1995).

six realms of existence

Traditional Buddhist thought divides living beings into six categories, each of which resides in one "realm," or *dhatu.* These are the realms of gods (*devas*), demons (*asuras*), humans, animals, spirits or ghosts (*pretas*), and those in hell. An individual is born into a certain realm or path depending on past KARMA.

Humans in the realm of desire (*kama dhatu*), as well as animals, live on the surface of Mt MERU. The ghosts, demons, and those in hell live beneath the surface of the earth; gods live in the higher reaches of the mountain, in the realm of form (*rupa dhatu*) and, for some, in the realm of formlessness (*arupya dhatu*). Thus all beings live in one of the three realms, the *tri-dhatu*. And all living beings, including the more exalted gods living atop Mt. Sumeru, are subject to the law of karma and rebirth.

One psychological interpretation of this concept is that the six realms reflect internal states. We choose to live within a certain realm on the basis of our own volition and understanding. We may live as a PRETA, a "hungry ghost," constantly wanting more yet never achieving fulfillment, or we may live as a *deva*, a god, with ultimate awareness.

Further reading: Akira Sakakata, *Buddhist Cosmology: Philosophy and Origins* (Tokyo: Kosei, 1997 and 1999).

Skandhas

Literally meaning "bundles," the *Skandhas* are in English normally referred to as the "five aggregates." The Buddha spelled out a theory for five types of *Skandhas,* which in aggregate constitute the person: matter, feelings, perception, mind, and consciousness. The five *Skandhas* are also known as *nama-rupa* (name-form). The *Skandhas* form upon birth and the first thought and disperse upon death. This theory underlies the Buddha's criticism of the concept of *atman,* or self.

The individual human is simply a "bundle of perceptions" (*sankharapunja*), which is labeled with individual names for convenience only. A common metaphor used to explain the function of the *Skandhas* is the chariot, which is a label for what are after all a collection of components. Significantly, there is no inner essence or soul that can be identified with any one of the five *Skandhas.*

An ARHAT was defined as one who was able to see the nature of the self, thoroughly understanding the truth that the *Skandhas* are impermanent and have no self. The association of the *Skandhas* with a sense of self leads to wrong views and, ultimately, to the suffering of human existence.

See also ANATMAN; SVABHAVA.

Further reading: David J. Kalupahana, *Buddhist Philosophy: A Historical Analysis* (Honolulu: University Press of Hawaii, 1976); Kogen Mizuno, *Essentials of Buddhism: Basic Terminology of Buddhist Philosophy and Practice.* Translated by Gaynor Sekimori (1972, Reprint, Tokyo: Kosei, 1996).

smrti (mindfulness)

Smrti, or mindfulness, has a number of interpretations in Buddhist literature. Today perhaps the most important is mindfulness meditation.

Smrti literally means "being aware of all processes and phenomena, mental or physical." In the Buddhist ABHIDHARMA/ABHIDHAMMA literature, *smrti* is one of many mental functions. *Smrti* is a type of mental constituent (*samskara*). *Samskara* in turn is one of the five SKANDHAS, or aggregates, that collectively merge in the individual.

The SARVASTIVADA (SARVASTIVADIN) SCHOOL writers listed 10 types of functions, the *mahabhumika,* which included *smrti* as well as such states as desire (CANDA) and concentration (SAMADHI). According to Sarvastivadin writings *smrti* is also a key element in religious practice; it is one of the five roots of emancipation, an aspect of practice without which one cannot make progress on the Buddhist path.

Developing mindfulness is a key goal of THERAVADA as well as MAHAYANA BUDDHISM. The *smrti upasthana,* or "four awakenings," are meditations that help one develop mindfulness of body, feelings, mind, and mental objects. This practice is detailed in the Satipatthana-sutta in the PALI canon. This meditation is usually subsumed under the title of VIPASSANA meditation. In fact *vipassana,* or insight, refers to a cognitive apprehension of reality. Mindfulness is necessary for the development of such insight.

Further reading: John Daiushin Buksbazen, *Zen Meditation in Plain English* (Boston: Wisdom, 2002); The Dalai Lama, *How to Practice: The Way to a Meaningful Life.* Translated and edited by Jeffrey Hopkins (Waterville, Maine: Thorndike Press and Bath, U.K.: Chivers Press, 2002); Henepola Gunaratana, *Mindfulness in Plain English* (Taipei, Taiwan: The Corporate Body of the Buddha Educational Foundation, 1991); Santideva, *The Bodhicaryavatara.* Translated by Kate Crosby and Andrew Skilton (Oxford: Oxford University Press, 1995).

Snyder, Gary (1930–) *Zen poet and social activist*

Gary Snyder, an American poet who identified with the BEAT ZEN movement of the 1950s and then transcended it, was born in San Francisco but raised in Washington and Oregon. When he attended Reed College, he had developed an interest in Buddhism and Japan. After college (1951) he moved back to the San Francisco Bay Area to study Asian languages at the University of California in Berkeley (1953–56). In Berkeley he attended meetings of the Young Buddhist Association, which met near where he resided. He also associated with Beat writers such as Allen Ginsburg (1926–97) and Jack Kerouac.

He finally traveled to Japan in 1956 and remained there for eight years. He studied RINZAI ZEN and worked on translating texts. In 1962 he took a trip to India, where he met the DALAI LAMA. His first book of poems, *Riprap* (1959), was published while he was in Japan, though the poems reflected his experiences in the early 1950s. This book was a significant step in establishing him as a major American poet. The clarity of description attributed to his ZEN BUDDHISM meditation would appear in his later works such as *Cold Mountain Poems* (1965).

Upon his return to the United States in the mid-1960s he became a peace activist and then in 1969 purchased a farm in the foothills of the northern Sierra Nevada, from which he became one of the early voices of the deep ECOLOGY AND ENVIRONMENTALISM movement. At the farm he established a lay Zen center and ecology center. His social activism was expressed in his work to found the San Juan Ridge Tax Payers Association, the Ridge Study Group, and the Yuba Watershed Institute.

Meanwhile, Snyder continued to write and publish his poems, which earned him numerous awards and honors, including a Guggenheim Fellowship in 1968 and the Pulitzer Prize in 1975. In 1985 he became a professor in the English Department at the University of California at Davis. He is now a professor emeritus. In 1988 he received the Buddhism Transmission Award from the Bukkyo Dendo Kyokai, the first American so honored.

Further reading: Gary Snyder, *Riprap and Cold Mountain Poems* (San Francisco: Four Seasons, 1969); ———, *Passage through India* (San Francisco: Gray Fox, 1984); ———, *The Practice of the Wild* (San Francisco: North Point, 1990); ———, *No Nature* (New York: Pantheon, 1992); *The Gary Snyder Reader* (Washington, D.C.: Counterpoint, 1999).

Soen, Nakagawa (1907–1984) *Japanese Zen master who trained many Western Buddhists*

Nakagawa Soen Roshi was for many years the abbot of the Ryutaku-ji Monastery in Mishima, Japan, one of the leading RINZAI ZEN monastic centers in the country. Nakagawa Soen was unusual among Japanese teachers in the mid 20th-century in accepting Western students. Among the first of his American students was ROBERT BAKER AITKEN, who in 1959 was given permission to conduct a sitting group in his home in Honolulu, Hawaii, the seed of the Diamond Sangha, founded in part as a vehicle for bring Nakagawa to the United

States. Through both his acceptance of American students and his many trips to and talks in America, he helped shape the Zen environment of the later 20th century.

The extent of his influence is seen in the number of students who have assumed leadership positions. As early as 1955, he accepted Ruth Strout McCandless, the first Western woman to stay at a Zen monastery, as a student. Dan Welch practiced as a layman at Ryutaku-ji under Soen Nakagawa-roshi from 1962 to 1964. He later worked at the San Francisco Zen Center and is now the assistant abbot at the Crestone Mountain Zen Center. Eido Tai Shimano, a Japanese monk who in 1972 received Dharma transmission from Nakagawa, is now the leader of the Zen Studies Society (New York City) and its several affiliated centers including Dai Bosatsu Zendo Kongo-ji, in the Catskill Mountains of upstate New York. His assistant, John Mortensen, a Dane, began his study under Nakagawa at Ryutaku-ji in 1971.

Other 1970s students of Nakagawa's include Kyudo Nakagawa Roshi (Zen master), who in 1981 founded the Soho Zen Buddhist Society in New York City, and John Daido Loori, who in 1980 founded the Zen Arts Center in Mount Tremper, New York.

Further reading: Eido Shimano, ed., *Namu Dai Bosa: A Transmission of Zen Buddhism to America* (New York: Zen Studies Society, 1976); Kazuaki Tanahashi, *Endless Vow: The Zen Path of Soen Nakagawa* (Boston: Shambhala, 1996).

Soka Gakkai International

Soka Gakkai International (SGI) was formed in 1975 in recognition of the global development of Soka Kyoiku Gakkai (Society for the Education in the Creation of Value). As the 21st century began, SGI reported 12 million members scattered in 180 countries.

Formed in 1937 by TSUNESABURO MAKIGUCHI (1871–1944), it was originally established to reform education so to assist people to live lives that in turn created beauty, benefit, and goodness. An adherent of NICHIREN SHOSHU Buddhism, Makiguchi saw value creation in line with the teachings and practices articulated by NICHIREN (1222–82). Neither Makiguchi's Buddhist perspective nor Soka Gakkai's program fit well with the emphasis of the Japanese government in the 1930s—its focus on a nationalist mobilization that religious groups were expected to support fully. Eventually he and a number of Soka Gakkai's leaders were arrested as World War II heated up. Makiguchi died in prison, but his colleague JOSEI TODA (1900–58), who succeeded him as president, revived the organization after the war.

Under Toda, Soka Gakkai took its place as a lay arm of Nichiren Shoshu and focused upon the spreading of Nichiren's teachings and the conversion of the nation and the world. An early goal of winning 750,000 new adherents was met in the 1950s, before he turned over the leadership to DAISAKU IKEDA, who subsequently built it into an expansive international organization. In 1975, when Soka Gakkai International was formed, Ikeda was named its first president.

Soka Gakkai perpetuated the teachings of Nichiren concerning the primacy of the LOTUS SUTRA and the chanting of its title in Japanese, *Nam-myoho-renge-kyo,* before the GOHONZON, the object of worship, originally designed by Nichiren. Most SGI members have a replica of the Gohonzon on an altar in their home.

In the 1960s, Soka Gakkai became the most controversial of the many "new religions" that emerged in postwar Japan. The focus of controversy was their aggressive recruitment practice, *shakabuku,* which, it was charged, used intimidation and even physical force to persuade people to join. At the same time, Soka Gakkai had formed a political party, the Komeito, which, with the growth of the organization, began to have an impact on national elections in Japan. The controversy spilled over into the international scene, especially in North America and Europe, where in the 1970s a vigorous anticult movement, which included Soka Gakkai on its list of destructive cults, had developed. In spite of the controversy, Soka Gakkai grew and became the largest Buddhist organization in most of the countries it entered.

The controversy over Soka Gakkai intensified in the 1990s. In 1991, ongoing tension between the organization and the parent Nichiren Shoshu came to a head when the Nichiren Shoshu excommunicated Ikeda and the Soka Gakkai leadership and broke all attachments to it. This action created one immediate problem, as the priests of the Nichiren Shoshu had supplied the Gohonzon replicas that SGI members received.

However, the break with Nichiren Shoshu was mild in relation to the fallout experienced by the organization after the gassing of the Tokyo subway station in 1995 by the AUM SHINRIKYO. Aum Shinrikyo had no relation to SGI apart from envying the role it had assumed in Japan. However, after the gassing event, a wave of anticult sentiment swept Japan, and legislation was introduced to prevent similar occurrences. Much of that legislation was aimed at Soka Gakkai.

Then just as suddenly as the controversy peaked, it came to a sudden end in 1999. After the Japanese election, the ruling party fell short of a majority and needed the Komeito to continue in power. Suddenly, government pressure was taken off Soka Gakkai and criticism dropped dramatically, though the larger Buddhist community has not moved to embrace the organization. The change in Japan has been reflected around the world, as criticism suddenly dropped to minuscule levels.

Further reading: Karel Dobbelaere, *Soka Gakkai: From Lay Movement to Religion* (Salt Lake City, Utah: Sinature Books, 2001); Philip Hammond and David Machacek, *Soka Gakkai in America: Accommodation and Conversion* (Oxford: Oxford University Press, 1999); Kiyoaki Murata, *Japan's New Buddhism: An Objective Account of Soka Gakkai* (New York: Weatherhill, 1968); David Machecek and Bryan Wilson, eds., *Global Citizens: The Soka Gakkai Buddhist Movement in the World* (Oxford: Oxford University Press, 2000); Daniel Metraux, *The History and Theology of the Soka Gakkai* (Lewiston, N.Y.: Edwin Mellen Press, 1988); ———, *The Soka Gakkai Revolution* (Lanham, Md.: University Press of America, 1994).

Sokei-an   *See* SASAKI ROSHI, SHIGETSU.

Son Buddhism

Son Buddhism, the Korean form of CHAN BUDDHISM, which is centered upon the practice of meditation, traces its origin to Pomnang (seventh century), who studied in China with Tai Xin (Tai-hsin) (580–651), the fourth Chan patriarch. Pomnang's lineage died out and Chan had to be reintroduced to Korea, as it was on several occasions by students of the Chinese Chan master Mazu (709–788). The growth of Son Buddhism initially led to a perception that it was incompatible with the other forms of Buddhism that centered on the study of the SUTRAS. By the 10th century, Son was focused on nine prominent monasteries/temples and became generally referred to as the Nine Mountains tradition.

Son received new life with the career of CHINUL (1158–1210). Objecting to what he saw as the degenerating state of Son practice in his own day, he founded the Samadhi and Prajna (Enlightenment and Wisdom) Community. Meanwhile, in each case after his study of a particular sutra, he had three insightful experiences, the result of which was his conclusion that the practice of meditation and study of the sutras were not mutually exclusive activities. On the basis of his new perspective, the community began to grow and with growth, a new center on Songgwang Mountain was erected.

The three texts that had prompted Chinul's awakening insights—the PLATFORM SUTRA, THE Avatamsaka Sutra, and the *Record of Dahui Zongkao* (1089–1163), an innovative LINJI CHAN practitioner—became the basis of the CHOGYE Order he founded, still the main school of Korean Buddhism. On the basis of Chinul's insights, T'aego Pou (1301–82) was able to reconcile the remaining elements of Korean Buddhism, especially the more conservative Son practitioners of the Nine Mountains. Korean Buddhism has since the 14th century been characterized by the tendency to seek reconciliation between practice and study and the drive for unity.

Son Buddhism and the Chogye Order have been able to survive the ups and downs of Korea's checkered political situation (which in the 20th century included the Japanese occupation, World War II, and the Korean War) and has experienced a notable revival since the end of the Korean War. It has also been successfully exported to the West by individuals such as Seung Sahn Sunim, founder of the KWAN UM SCHOOL of Zen, and Samu Sunim, founder of the Buddhist Society for Compassionate Wisdom.

Further reading: Hee-Sung Keel, *Chinul: The Founder of the Korean Son Tradition* (Berkeley: Center for South and South East Asian Studies, University of California, Berkeley, Institute of Buddhist Studies, 1984); Korean Buddhist Research Institute, ed., *Son Thought in Korean Buddhism* (Seoul: Dongguk University Press, 1998); Mu Soeng, *Thousand Peaks: Korean Zen: Tradition and Teachers* (Cumberland, R.I.: Primary Point Press, 1991).

Soryu Kagahi (dates unknown) *first Japanese Buddhist missionary to the United States*

Soryu Kagahi was sent to Hawaii in 1898. He preceded the first missionaries to the American mainland, Shuye Sonoda and Kakuryo Nishimjima, by one year. Kagahi had been sent by the HONPA HONGWANJI headquarters in Kyoto in response to requests from the Japanese workers in Hawaii. Although he only stayed in Hawaii one year, he oversaw the building of the first Japanese temple in Hawaii, in Hilo.

See also UNITED STATES, BUDDHISM IN.

Further reading: Rick Fields, *How the Swans Came to the Lake: A Narrative History of Buddhism in America* (Boston: Shambhala, 1992).

Sosan Taesa (Ch'ongho Hyujeong) (1520–1604) *Korean Zen "warrior monk"*

Sosan Taesa was, along with CHINUL and WONHYO, one of the three most important figures in Korean Buddhism. He taught many important students and helped solidify Korean SON BUDDHISM practice. His *Songa kwigam* (A guide to Son practice) is studied to this day. Most modern Son lineages are traced back to him and his four disciples Yujeong, Eongi, T'ainung, and Ilseon. His words are often quoted to students, for instance, the following: "In studying Zen, one must have three things: a foundation of great faith, a zealous determination, and a great feeling of doubt. If one is lacking, it is like a tripod with a broken foot."

Along with his fellow monk Samyon Taesa (1543–1610), Sosan Taesa organized and led a guerrilla army to fight against the Japanese invasions under Hideyoshi between 1592 and 1598. He is thus held up as an example of active participation by Buddhist practitioners in war.

Further reading: Golden Wind Zen Group. "Ch'ongho Hyueiong Sosan Taesa 63rd Patriarch, Chogye Order (1520–1604)." Available online. URL: www.goldenwindzen.org/sosan.htm. Accessed on October 2, 2005; John Goulde, "Traditional Korean Views of War and Peace: A Historical Investigation." Sweet Briar College. Available online. URL: www.faculty.sbc.edu/goulde/peaceinkorea. Accessed on October 2, 2005; Sosan Taesa et al., *A Paragon of Zen House.* Translated by Ohyn Park (London: Peter Lang, 2000).

Sosurim (r. 371–384) *ruler who introduced Buddhism to Korea*

In 371 C.E. Sosurim, whose diplomatic ties with the Chinese emperor led to the establishment of Buddhism in Korea, became king of Goguryeo (KOGURYO) (from which the modern word *Korea* is derived), the northernmost of the three kingdoms then in existence on the Korean Peninsula. Inheriting a somewhat weakened and disorganized land, he immediately initiated a complete restructuring of its governing institutions. He introduced a new legal code and revised the centralized government bureaucracy. He then founded the T'aehak, the National Confucian Academy; Confucianism was the moral philosophy dominating governmental organization.

Sosurim also initiated diplomatic ties with the Chinese emperor Fujian (r. 357–384) and imported a number of elements of Chinese culture and technology. In 272, Fujian sent to Sosurim a Buddhist monk, SUNDO (or Shun Dao). Sundo was able to establish Buddhism in Sosurim's court, and Sosurim promoted the ideal of an unified land under this new system of belief and practice. The form of Buddhism Sundo advocated supported a strong centralized imperial governance of a unified land.

As the court accepted the new religion, Sosurim moved to make Buddhism the state religion of his kingdom and supported the building of the first Buddhist temple. He did not, however, move to spread Buddhism among the masses. The faith would, during the remaining years of his reign, be confined largely to the country's elite. It would be limited to those who participated in court life for a number of decades and only slowly move out among the masses. After his death in 384, Sosurim was succeeded by King Gogugyang (384–391).

Further reading: *Focus on Korea.* 3 vols. (Seoul: Seoul International Publishing House, 1988); James Huntley Grayson, *Korea: A Religious History* (Oxford: Oxford University Press, 1989); Duk-Whang Kim, *A History of Religions in Korea* (Seoul: Daeji Monoonwha-sa, 1988).

Soto Zen

Soto Zen is the Japanese form of the Chinese CAODONG (Ts'ao-tung) meditational school of Buddhism. Along with RINZAI ZEN, Soto is one of the two major Zen sects in Japan. In 1214 DOGEN (1200–53), a TENDAI monk, learned about Caodong in China. He studied ZAZEN (sitting meditation) for two years, then returned to Japan to teach. Dogen opted for a more gradual approach to enlightenment and did not use the KOANS so much a part of Rinzai practice. Dogen eventually settled in Echizen Province and there in 1245 built Eihei-ji (Enduring Peace Temple), which would become the center of the Soto movement in the country.

Dogen was succeeded by his disciple Ejo (1198–1280). As abbot at Eihei-ji, he would complete the compilation of Dogen's major work, the SHOBOGENZO. After Ejo's death, the Soto movement found itself in an era of rapid spread and of controversy over new tendencies. Several factions emerged, a conservative, monk-oriented one at Eihei-ji and a more popular lay-oriented branch that developed around Keizan Jokin (1268–1325), a rather charismatic leader based in Noto Province north of Echizen. In the 15th century, representatives of the Keizan school took over Eihei-ji and became the dominant force in the movement. Over the next century they united the various Soto factions and received imperial recognition as the rightful heirs of Dogen. Eihei-ji was given official imperial patronage. Over the next century, the TOKUGAWA SHOGUNATE also threw its support behind Eihei-ji and Keizan's temple, Soto-ji, and designated them the main temples of the movement and honored their abbots.

Unlike the Rinzai movement, which exists in a number of factions, the Soto movement has remained largely united, with more than 14,500 temples under its authorities at the beginning of the 21st century. It operates out of its two main temples, Eihei-ji and Soto-ji, which was moved to Yokohama in 1911.

In the 20th century, Soto Zen began to spread across the Pacific, first to Hawaii, then to the mainland United States. Although at first most U.S. Soto adherents were of Japanese descent, in the decades after World War II, the California temples would begin to attract non-Japanese who wished to learn Zen. In 1959, after the arrival of SHUNRYU SUZUKI (1904–71) to head the San Francisco temple, an English-speaking group began to emerge. There are now several influential Soto Zen groups in North America.

Further reading: Heinrich Dumoulin, Zen Buddhism: A History, 2 vols. 2d rev. ed. (New York: Macmillan, 1988); Juyi Kennett, The Wild White Goose. 2 vols. (Mt Shasta, Calif.: Shasta Abbey, 1970, 1978); E. Dale Saunders, Buddhism in Japan (Philadelphia: University of Pennsylvania Press, 1964); Shunryu Suzuki, Zen Mind, Beginner's Mind (New York: Weatherhill, 1970).

South America, Buddhism in

Buddhism in South America remains concentrated among residents of Japanese ancestry living in two countries, Brazil and Peru. And the vast number of Buddhists belong to groups with roots in Japanese Buddhism.

Buddhism was introduced to South America in 1899 when the ship Sakura Maru arrived at Callao, Peru, with 790 people from Japan. Additional ships would follow over the next decade; the first group arrived in 1908 at Santos, in São Paulo State, Brazil. Later immigrants spread out to Argentina and Bolivia.

The Japanese traveled to South America in search of jobs on plantations and assumed that as Japan's economy recovered and they accumulated money, they would return home. Not particularly religious as a group, they found that their religious sentiments began to emerge as their stays lengthened. The fact that initially Japanese authorities had prohibited Buddhist (and SHINTO) religious functionaries from joining the immigrants opened the community to religious proselytization. Many

turned to Christianity. Meanwhile, over the first generation, the community proved upwardly mobile and most escaped the plantation life to move into business and professional jobs. The majority dropped the Japanese language and any Japanese faith. Then, after Japan's defeat in World War II, they dropped any surviving plans to return to their homeland.

When Japanese religion did emerge among the immigrants, STATE SHINTO with its veneration of the emperor took the lead. Buddhism, however, had an early start, as several Buddhist priests evaded the law and traveled to South America. The first, a NICHIREN SHOSHU priest who accompanied the original group to Brazil in 1908, seems to have established the first Buddhist temple in Bauru, in São Paulo State. A short time later a SHINGON priest arrived. The first JODO SHINSHU priest did not arrive until 1925. He would erect the first Jodo temple in Cafelândia, also in São Paulo State.

Not until after World War II would Buddhism spread significantly among the Japanese in South America. By this time, the community had been virtually neglected for half a century, though the fall of State Shinto created a vacuum for a new wave of Buddhist teachers to fill. The HONPA HONGWANJI, HIGASHI HONGWANJI, JODO-SHU, Nichiren Sonshu, and Soto Zenshu all sent missionaries to Brazil in the years after the war. The first ZEN temple opened in 1955 in Mogi das Cruzes, outside São Paulo City, where the largest concentration of Japanese Brazilians had formed. That same year, the first Buddhist organization of non-Japanese origin, the Buddhist Society of Brazil (Sociedade Budista do Brasil), was founded by Murillo Nunes de Azevedo in Rio de Janeiro. Azevedo, a former Roman Catholic and philosophy professor, later translated DAISETSU TEITARO SUZUKI's Introduction to Zen Buddhism into Portuguese. In 1958, all of these Buddhist schools were united in the Federation of the Buddhist Sects of Brazil (Federação das Seitas Budistas do Brasil). Buddhism has continued to expand and now claims more than 20 percent of Japanese Brazilians as adherents.

In 1988, Tibetan Buddhism began to proselytize in Brazil with the Chagdud Gonpa Foundation taking the lead. The foundation's founder, Chagdud Rinpoche, moved from the United States to Brazil in the mid-1990s and has built two monasteries and opened a number of centers.

A similar course was followed by Japanese immigrants in Peru, where the second-largest community in South America developed. The relative success of the Japanese Peruvians was demonstrated in 1990 when Alberto Fujimori became the country's president (1990–2000), the first Japanese politician elected to lead a country other than Japan. The larger Japanese Buddhist groups have also found a home in the Japanese communities in Argentina, Bolivia, and Paraguay.

As in North America, the growth of Buddhism in South America was radically altered by the appearance of SOKA GAKKAI INTERNATIONAL, which has opened centers across South America and not limited itself to the Japanese communities. Today, it claims more than 250,000 adherents, making it the largest single Buddhist group on the continent.

While Buddhism has grown, several of the Japanese NEW RELIGIONS have also entered South America. Seicho-No-Ie, a group that was strongly affected by the American new thought movement, has had the most success. However, TENRIKYO, Sekai Kyusei Kyo, and Mahikari Bumei Kyodan now have a very visible presence, and several with primarily Buddhist roots, including RISSHO KOSEI-KAI and Buts-Ryu-Shu, have also established followings.

As of the year 2000, the Brazilian Buddhist community was estimated to be as many as half a million, with an additional 50,000 in Peru. Together, they constitute more than 90 percent of the Buddhist community in South and Central America, though there is some minimal Buddhist presence (at times a single center) in almost all of the Latin American countries.

Further reading: Peter B. Clarke, "Japanese 'Old,' 'New,' and 'New, New' Religious Movements in Brazil," in Peter B. Clarke and Jeffrey Somers, *Japanese New Religious Movements in the West* (Sandgate, U.K.: Japan Library, 1994); Cristina Moreira da Rocha, "Zen Buddhism in Brazil: Japanese or Brazilian?" Journal of Global Buddhism. Available online. URL: http://www.globalbuddhism.org/1/derocha001.html. Accessed on September 12, 2005; Usumu Shimazono, "The Expansion of Japan's New Religions into Foreign Cultures," *Japanese Journal of Religious Studies* 18, nos. 2–3 (1991): 105–132.

Soyen Shaku   *See* SHAKU, SOYEN.

sramana

The *sramana* is a renunciant who abandons conventional society. The term was used widely during the Buddha's time to refer to heterodox ascetics who did not accept the conventional teachings of Brahmanism. The Buddha himself was called the Mahasramana, the great *sramana,* and his followers were called *sramanas.* Many other groups also had communal lifestyles outside traditional society. In addition, some individual *sramanas* lived in seclusion, shunning society completely.

These two ends of the spectrum—ascetics, who have cut all ties with society, and renouncers, who still have ties with conventional society—form two trends that surface within the earliest Buddhist literature, the NIKAYAS. The ascetic tradition developed into the forest dwelling tradition. The renouncer tradition led to the SANGHA as later developed, the key aspect of Buddhist religious society.

Further reading: Seven Collins, *Selfless Persons: Imagery and Thought in Theravada Buddhism* (Cambridge: Cambridge University Press, 1990); Reginald Ray, *Buddhist Saints in India: A Study in Buddhist Values and Orientations* (Oxford: Oxford University Press, 1994).

sramanera/sramaneri

A *sramanera* is a novice monk, while a *sramaneri* is a novice nun. The *sramanera* completes a ceremony of initial ordination, the *pravrajya,* which includes having the head shaved, receiving the three robes and alms bowl of the monk, and reciting the *dasasila* (10-vows) as well as the statement of refuge.

The novice stage is a type of probation required prior to full ordination. In many countries such as Thailand and Myanmar young boys are required to become a *sramanera* for a certain time, sometimes as short as three months, sometimes a year or two, after which they return to lay life. In MAHAYANA BUDDHISM countries older novices are given the full precepts in the *upasampada* ceremony (*see* ORDINATION) only after they complete the *sramanera* stage.

Further reading: Charles S. Prebish, *The A to Z of Buddhism* (Lanham, Md.: Scarecrow Press, 2001).

sravaka/sravakayana

A *sravaka* (Pali, *savaka*) is, literally, a "hearer." The *sravaka* appears in MAHAYANA BUDDHISM texts as a term of veiled criticism for followers of "HINAYANA," or early Buddhist, groups. These early groups were said to have taught that enlightenment was possible only for those who heard the Buddha's teachings directly from the Buddha—in other words, his original group of followers. This was interpreted as a criticism because the idea of the *sravaka* indicated later believers in the Buddha's Dharma had no chance of gaining enlightenment.

Mahayana writers also developed the related term *Sravakayana*—"*sravaka* vehicle"—to refer to early Buddhist groups, in other words, "Hinayana."

The SRAVAKA was also compared to the PRATYEK-ABUDDHA and the BODHISATTVA when Mahayanaists discussed the model of the three vehicles. In this model the *sravaka* and the *pratyekabuddha* are the two vehicles of Hinayana practice, and the bod-

Novice monks (*sramanera*) seated for the noonday meal, Maha Ganayan monastery, Amarapura, near Mandalay, northern Myanmar (Burma)

hisattva is the practitioner of Mahayana ("greater vehicle") Buddhism.

Further reading: Kogen Mizuno, *Essentials of Buddhism: Basic Terminology of Buddhist Philosophy and Practice.* Translated by Gaynor Sekimori (1972. Reprint, Tokyo: Kosei, 1996); Charles S. Prebish, *The A to Z of Buddhism* (Lanham, Md.: Scarecrow Press, 2001).

Sri Lanka, Buddhism in

Sri Lanka has been part of Buddhist history from the earliest days and is today the culture with the longest continuing tradition of Buddhist practice. Accounts from the Buddhist canon tell the story of MAHINDA, the Buddhist monk and son of the great Mauryan emperor ASOKA. Asoka sent Mahinda to Sri Lanka around 240 B.C.E., a few hundred years after the death of the historical Buddha. Mahinda converted the local king, Devnampiya Tissa (r. 244–207 B.C.E.). The king in turn donated a tract of land for a temple, later known as the Mahavihara. A section of the BODHI TREE under which the Buddha was said to have attained enlightenment was planted at Mahavihara. Mahinda's sister,

SANGHAMITTA, accompanied her brother on his mission and established Sri Lanka's first order of Buddhist nuns.

Ethnically Sri Lanka is characterized by two great populations, Singhalese, currently 70 percent of the population, and Tamils, who today are either Hindu or Muslim. The interaction between these two groups began soon after the development of Buddhism there, with invasions of Tamil forces beginning in the last century before the Common Era.

The PALI canon, which is considered by THERAVADIN Buddhists to be the collection of all the Buddha's words, was written on palm leaf books during the reign of King Vattagamani (r. 29–17 B.C.E.). The king was concerned the teachings of the Buddha might be lost in his turbulent times. He also founded a monastery at Abhayagiri. The two monastic centers of Mahavihara and Abhayagiri have been rival centers of Sri Lankan Buddhism throughout Sri Lankan history.

MEDIEVAL PERIOD

One of the greatest Buddhist scholars of all time, BUDDHAGHOSA, lived in Sri Lanka in the 300–400s C.E. Although he was originally from India he moved to Sri Lanka to study and master the Pali language. He composed the well-known *Visuddhimagga* (Path of purification) as a meditation primer for novice monks. This work is still used today.

At about the same time King Mahasena (r. 334–362) built a monastery at Jetavana, which was originally intended for Mahayana monks. This illustrates the continuous cross-currents at play in these times: Tantric and Brahmanic (the Indian priestly class) influences continued to flow into Sri Lanka, though Theravada eventually became the dominant tradition.

Monastic practice in Sri Lanka did not continue smoothly of its own accord. In fact, on two occasions the Sri Lankan sangha requested help from overseas monasteries to reestablish Buddhist lineages. In the first instance, around 1000 C.E., help was requested from Burma, and in the second, during the long period of colonial occupation, help was asked from Thailand. The general weakness in Sri Lankan monastic institutions was related to both internal and external factors.

Internally, the support of the ruling authorities for the Theravadin sangha came and went. The long-reigning king Parakrama Bahu VI (1153–86), for instance, attempted to rebuild Buddhist institutions. He established monasteries and collected funds. However, this strong state-sangha relationship was weakened under the later Kotte kings, who favored the Brahmans. In contrast, the subsequent kingdom of Kandy under the ruler Senasammata Vikramabahu favored Buddhism once again.

During the 15th and 16th centuries two new central monastic institutions appeared, the Vanavasa and the Gamavasa. Both claimed to follow the ancient school of the Mahavihara and so were ideologically aligned with each other. The Vanavasi monks attempted to live lives completely cut off from outside society, while the Gamavasi had more contact with laity.

By the end of the 15th century these two institutions had declined in their own turn. The teacher-pupil relationship and various lineages took their place. Such teacher-pupil lineages often specialized. For instance, the Dharmakirti lineage of Palabatgala focused on literary activities. Caste and family background also influenced the composition of the lineages.

Buddhism developed specialized schools called *pirivenas* in the 15th century. The previous institution, *ayatanas,* then disappeared from the scene. *Pirivenas* trained all males in general as well as monks, and instruction was free.

Externally, Catholic missionaries arrived with the Portuguese in the 16th century. The ruler Dharmapala converted to Catholicism and as a result several monasteries were transferred to the Catholic Church. Later colonial regimes under the Dutch and British naturally favored their own brands of religious practices. Support for the traditional Buddhist educational system already in place, the *pirivenas,* decreased, and the monasteries were no longer able to provide broad-based free education.

Throughout this period regional connections were critical to the survival of Sri Lankan Buddhism. Neighboring Theravada cultures maintained close contact with the Kotte kingdom. Even at this relatively late stage in Buddhism's history in Sri Lanka most outside countries saw Sri Lankan Buddhism as a center of "pure" Theravada. Pilgrims arrived there and returned home with scriptures. This resulted in the development of the Sihala Shanga network throughout Southeast Asia, a tightly knit connection that circulated texts and cult veneration practices. For instance, tooth relics veneration—worshipping of the Buddha's tooth—emerged as a common practice. The maintenance and protection of the relic at Samantakuta in Sri Lanka were key political tasks of the ruling Polonnaru dynasty.

MODERN PERIOD

Colonial rule finally ended in 1948. Buddhism made a comeback with the awakening national consciousness that accompanied the departure of the British. As in other Southeast Asian countries Buddhism became identified as an intrinsic part of the national character. In Sri Lanka's case, however, this happened in tandem with a rise of intolerance toward non-Buddhist traditions, especially the beliefs of Hindu Tamils. Political leaders in the modern period have generally been pro-Singhalese and have not hesitated to use Buddhism as a symbol of insider status. S. W. R. D. Bandaranaike, elected in 1956, went so far as to identify Tamils publicly as responsible for the destruction of Sri Lanka's "golden age." Bandaranaike actively encouraged participation of the sangha and monks in politics. His "Buddhist socialism"

combined a belief in democracy with socialism and Buddhist compassion. (Ironically he was later assassinated by a Buddhist monk.)

The results of such extremist ideological views have been evident over the past 20 years, with a bloody civil war between Singhalese and Tamils. That this should happen in a culture so adamantly Buddhist is a sign that no religion, including Buddhism, is able to disengage itself from politics completely.

Further reading: H. B. M. Ilangasinha, *Buddhism in Medieval Sri Lanka* (Delhi: Sri Satguru, 1992); Damien Keown, ed., *Oxford Dictionary of Buddhism* (Oxford: Oxford University Press, 2003); John Powers, *A Concise Encyclopedia of Buddhism* (Oxford: One World, 2000); Donald K. Swearer, *The Buddhist World of Southeast Asia* (Albany: State University of New York Press, 1995).

State Shinto (Kokka Shinto)

State Shinto was the official religion in Japan from the MEIJI RESTORATION (1868) through the end of World War II in 1945. This form of Shinto harked back to the earliest version of state-supported Shinto, which had developed in the seventh century C.E. However, there were many modern innovations.

State Shinto developed during the Meiji period (1868–1912) as an official means to establish a Japanese cult that would support the revival of the emperor's social standing. In 1871 the government issued an edict, which directed that shrines were to be used for state ritual. Yet no official body was established to oversee Shinto. (The Jingikan, a traditional government office that had been reestablished in 1868, oversaw the *kami,* or gods, in general, but not Shinto specifically.) The government also did not want to allocate funds for the upkeep of most shrines—only the most famous ones such as Ise received support. The government's relation to Shinto was vague and conflicted until 1900, when the Jinjakyoku, or Shrine Bureau, was established.

As a unit of the Home Ministry, the establishment of the Jinjakyoku indicated the state would take a stronger role in regard to Shinto. Before its establishment yet another bureau, the Sajikyoku, the Bureau for Shrines and Temples, oversaw both Buddhist temples and Shinto shrines. But from 1900, Shinto was managed by its own bureau, and all other religions including Buddhism were overseen by the newly established Shukyokyoku, the Bureau for Religions. State Shinto could now become a separate reality.

In 1906, after the Russo-Japanese War of 1904–05, the government established a means to ensure Shinto shrines received constant funding. Funds were simply appropriated from all local government budgets. The national government went on to establish further rules for shrines, including such areas as etiquette and ritual (1907), finance (1908), and rites (1914). Garb and Ritual at the imperial ISE SHRINE were a special concern, and there were three separate laws promulgated to handle these areas.

During this period the government promoted the concept of the nonreligious function of Shinto shrines. It was seen as every citizen's civic duty to visit and pay obeisance to the *kami* and the emperor. This patriotic task was said to transcend religious beliefs, so believers in Christianity and Buddhism were expected to perform such rituals, as well as Shinto believers. It was common for school classes to visit Shinto shrines throughout the school year. Despite the official stance in favor of a "nonreligious" Shinto system, the provincial shrines continued such religious practices as selling charms and performing funerals.

The death of the Meiji emperor in 1912 and the building of a shrine to honor him (the Meiji Jingu, or shrine, was begun in 1915) made shrines important during the Taisho era (1912–26). Nevertheless, most shrines continued to be underfunded and neglected by the government. In fact, the government had an essentially "opportunistic" approach to Shinto shrines: promote their use inasmuch as they helped promote a uniquely Japanese ideology and the imperial family, but do not support their other religious functions. Reverence for the deities was seen as a simple matter of performing rites, not a deeply religious impulse.

At the same time Japanese society in the 1920s underwent significant changes and pressures. The Kanto earthquake of 1923, the advent of socialist thought, the post–World War I recession, and the weakness of the party system put the Diet (Japan's parliament) under intense pressure. The Diet increasingly saw the management of Shinto shrines and deities as a way to increase social solidarity. The government finally agreed to establish the Commission for Shrine Research in 1929, which would investigate legal status and economic resources, rank the shrines, and review their ritual practices. However, this bureau was still criticized for ignoring issues of true religiosity.

In 1940 the cabinet approved the establishment of yet another new bureau, the Jingiin, or Office of State for Deity Affairs. The charge was not simply to oversee state ritual, but to manage the entire shrine network. The Jingiin was responsible for the Ise shrines, all other shrines, all priests and shrine officials, and anything regarding "reverence" paid to deities. This marked the first time the government had actually become directly involved in spreading the ideology of State Shinto as an institution. Henceforth the Home Ministry was involved in maintaining as well as promoting State Shinto.

With Japan's defeat the Allied occupation forces introduced a new focus on the system of State Shinto. In one decree in 1945 the government was forbidden to support Shinto shrines. More shockingly, the emperor was said to be a mortal person, not a divine entity. With this the increasingly interwoven fate of modern Shinto and the Japanese state came to an end. Most of the shrines simply reorganized and today operate under the umbrella of Shrine Shinto.

Further reading: Kazuo Kasahara, ed., *A History of Japanese Religion.* Translated by Paul McCarthy and Gaynor Sekimori (Tokyo: Kosei, 2001), 529–544; Sakamoto Koremaru, "The Structure of State Shinto: Its Creation, Development and Demise," in John Breen and Mark Teeuwen, eds., *Shinto in History* (Richmond, U.K.: Curzon Press, 2000), 272–294.

Stein, Aurel (1862–1943) *Austrian-British explorer and geographer*

The explorer Aurel Stein discovered and obtained what may be the greatest single quantity of Chinese Buddhist art and literature in history. Stein was originally based in India and worked with the British government there as a surveyor and mapmaker. He began his first trip into Central Asia in May 1900. For some two years, he attempted to follow the route of the seventh-century Chinese monk/traveler XUAN ZANG and identify the Buddhist sites he described. His initial finds alerted the world to the possible treasures and set off a race by Western explorers.

In 1907, Stein set his sight on Lou Lan and Dunhuang (China), and at Dunhuang he made his greatest discovery, a great hoard of documents stored for centuries in the CAVES OF THE THOUSAND BUDDHAS. Stein bribed the leader of the monastic group in charge of the caves and took away thousands of manuscripts written in Chinese and other languages used in the region, including the world's oldest printed document, the DIAMOND SUTRA, dating from 863 C.E. Most of this collection is today in the British Museum.

Further reading: Jeannette Mirsky, *Sir Aurel Stein: Archaeological Explorer* (Chicago: University of Chicago Press, 1977); Annabel Walker, *Aurel Stein: Pioneer of the Silk Road* (London: John Murray, 1995).

Sthaviravada school

The Sthaviravada, or "Way of the Elders," was the first and most powerful of the original 18 SCHOOLS OF EARLY BUDDHISM. This school dominated the Second Council at Vesali, where they debated and expelled another group, the MAHASANGHIKA. The Sthaviravada were also the predecessors of the THERAVADA.

Further reading: Kogen Mizuno, *Essentials of Buddhism: Basic Terminology of Buddhist Philosophy and Practice.* Translated by Gaynor Sekimori (1972. Reprint, Tokyo: Kosei, 1996); Charles S. Prebish, *The A to Z of Buddhism* (Lanham, Md.: Scarecrow Press, 2001).

Stove God (*zao jun*)

The Stove God is a folk deity known to all Chinese people because of the role he plays in the New Year celebrations. The Stove God is tasked with watching over the family. Thus every household has a Stove God. He is represented, sometimes with his wife, on a piece of paper that is hung over the stove, in the kitchen. But because he "lives" with the family he knows all affairs and misdeeds. His wife, in fact, helps to write down everything said so he can report it. The Stove God is called to heaven by the Jade Emperor every New Year to report on the family's behavior, on the 23rd day of the 12th (lunar) month. Before this happens families typically hold a short ceremony to show respect for the Stove God and, more to the point, to offer him something in return for making a favorable report. The family often symbolically performs this transaction by smearing sugar or honey over the mouth of the Stove God image, hoping that his words will be "sweet." His image, typically on a piece of paper, is then burned, and a new image placed over the stove for the remainder of the year.

Worship of the Stove God is ancient, going back at least to the Zhou period in Chinese history (1111–249 B.C.E.). One version of the Stove God's origin relates that a Zhang Lang fell in love with another woman and spurned his wife. When his luck turned bad he became a wandering beggar, blind. Eventually he visited his wife's ancestral home. There she gave him sight again. But he was so ashamed of his actions he committed suicide by jumping into the stove.

Further reading: Cal Poly Pomona. "The Kitchen God." Available online. URL: www.scupomona.edu/~plin/ folkreligion/kitchengod.html. Accessed on December 5, 2005; Micha F. Lindemans, "Zao-jun." Encyclopedia Mythica. Available online. URL: http://www. pantheon.org/areas/mythology/asia/chinese/articles. html. Accessed on December 5, 2005.

Strauss, Charles T. (1852–1937) *first American convert to Buddhism*

Charles T. Strauss was a Swiss-American Jewish businessman (he sold lace curtains) who converted to Buddhism after a public lecture by ANGARIKA DHARMAPALA in 1893, after the World's Parliament of Religions meeting in Chicago. Soon afterward he became the first non-Asian North American to take refuge in the Buddha, or formally convert to Buddhism. He never sought ordination but became an active member of the MAHABODHI SOCIETY and assisted Dharmapala in building the organization. He wrote one book, *The Buddha and His Doctrine* (1923), in which he emphasized the nonmystical, ethical nature of Buddhism.

Further reading: Rick Fields, *How the Swans Came to the Lake: A Narrative History of Buddhism in America* (Boston: Shambala, 1992); C. T. Strauss, *The Buddha and His Doctrine* (Kolkata: R. N. Bhattacharya, 2003); Thomas A. Tweed, *The American Encounter with Buddhism, 1844–1912: Victorian Culture and the Limits of Dissent* (Bloomington: Indiana University Press, 1992).

stupa

In Buddhist culture, a stupa (in Tibetan, a *chorten*) is a shrine to the dead. Their origin can be traced to prehistoric times, when they were simple mounds where important people were buried. Toward the end of his life, Gautama BUDDHA requested that after his cremation the remains be placed in a stupa. He also suggested a different interpretation of the stupa. It should, he indicated, be thought of as a symbol of the enlightened mind, as opposed to merely being a place to house the deceased. When he passed away in 483 B.C.E. his lay devotees divided and erected stupas over his cremated remains to honor his memory. Fusing the earthly and transcendent, this ancient sepulchral monument became the signature icon of Buddhism.

THE STUPA AND THE CAITYA

Stupa and *caitya* are nearly equivalent terms, as is the case throughout most of Pali literature. Early (pre-400 C.E.) literature made a distinction, however. In the early literature a *caitya* was a site with a sacred grove, or a tree. These sites were often used for meditation by the Buddha, and they had names. They were thus also places where wandering monks could stay. They were also often associated with *yakkhas,* a type of semidivine being. The *caitya* space may also have been used for funeral rites—the word *caitya* derives from *cita,* a "funeral pyre."

In the MAHASANGHIKA school literature a stupa was a structure that contained the Buddha's remains, while a *caitya* was simply a memorial that did not contain remains.

FORMS OF THE STUPA

Most stupas contain the same basic structural elements, each of which symbolizes something about Buddhism. The stupa often incorporates a stone fence, called a *vedika.* This indicates the separation of the stupa from the world. The stupa is usually approached by four entrance gates, called *torana.* These open the stupa to the four quarters of the world and emphasize the universal spirit of the Buddha dharma.

Stupas vary in material, size, and shape, depending on the culture. In Sri Lanka the stupa is round and called a *dagoba.* In Tibet the *chorten,* or "Dharma receptable," performs the stupa's function. In Thailand the term is *chedi,* the Thai pronunciation of *caitya*. And in East Asian cultures they are typically eight-sided towers, called pagodas in English, which range from two to 13 stories. In Chinese these structures are called *ta*, in Japan *to*, both meaning "tower."

Architecturally, stupas were originally divided into three sections—terrace, dome, and superstructure.

The *terraces* or bases (*mehdi*) were probably originally used as altars for such offerings as flowers. In later periods retaining walls and processional paths were often added around the entire stupa.

The *hemispherical dome* is called the *anda*, or "egg." This rests on the terrace. There are traditionally six dome shapes used: bell, pot, bubble, "heap of paddy," lotus, and Amalaka. Relics are meant to be placed within the *anda*.

The *superstructures* have probably seen the most evolution as the stupa form was transferred to different cultural settings. In Sri Lanka there is a square, boxlike structure on the dome, the *tee*. In India it was originally called a *harmika*, "small pavilion." Railings were often set up around the *tees* as well as around the entire stupa base. Later, spires were added above the *tee*. And a *chattra*, or umbrella, was often placed atop the entire structure.

All stupas share the following symbolic characteristics. In addition to the terrace, dome, and superstructurer, there is a *yasti*, a central shaft. The *yasti* is nothing less than the axis of the world and allows the various heavens to be separated from the Earth. The base along with the *anda* are symbolic of Mt. Sumeru, the mythological center of the universe. And the *harmika* delineates the sacred space atop Mt. Sumeru, where the gods reside.

Taken as a whole, the classic stupa design shows the 37 stages, or wings, in ENLIGHTENMENT, called the *bodhipaksa*. These are most often symbolized by the different levels of the stupa, from the base through the top spire. In addition Theravada Buddhist cultures also added

elements symbolizing the 10 *jnanam*, or insights, of the ARHAT. These 10 layers are found above the *harmika*.

A third symbolic aspect found on many stupas are the 13 *bhumis*, an idea taken from the 10 *bhumis*, or stages, in the text the Dasabhumika. This book describes the 10 stages through which a BODHISATTVA must progress on the path of enlightenment. The final three *bhumis* are qualities of the Buddha's mind. These 13 stages are symbolized by 13 separate *chattras*, or umbrellas, found atop the *yasti*.

Finally, we should distinguish between the monastery and the stupa. These two architectural forms developed in tandem but performed separate functions. Every monastery normally contains at least one stupa. However, the stupa is fundamentally an object of lay worship. The presence of the monastery with the stupa symbolizes the symbiotic relationship between SANGHA and laity in Buddhism.

DEVELOPMENT OF THE STUPA

Architectural imagination manipulated the formal elements of the stupa to produce myriad

Central stupa and western entranceway to Schwedagon Temple, surrounded by smaller stupas, Yangon (Rangoon), Myanmar (Burma)

variations. The evolution of the stupa can be determined by examining the Great Stupa at Sanchi, the oldest existing example. Dating to the third century B.C.E. and enlarged in the second century B.C.E. to twice its original size, the Great Stupa has a 120-foot-diameter *anda*. The *anda* is slightly flattened at the top to accommodate the *harmika* that encloses the *yasti*, which supports three evenly spaced flattened *chattavali*.

At the base of the *anda* is the *pradakshina-patha*, a narrow pathway 16 feet above the ground along which devotees circumambulated, following the path of the sun; the *pradakshina-patha* is accessible by two flights of stairs, on the east and west meridians, respectively. A second similar pathway at the base is enclosed by the *vedika*, or stone

Rare cloisonné (metal with inlaid enamel) stupa dating from Qing dynasty (1648–1911), China; in the Freer Gallery, Smithsonian Museum, Washington, D.C.

fence, that demarcates the sacred from the secular world. Access to the sacred site is through four 34-foot monumental *torana*, or gateways, whose uprights and crossbars are elaborately carved. The gateways open to the four cardinal directions from which the spiritual energy from the *anda*, meaning "egg," flows throughout the world. When viewed from the top, the right-angled entries attached to the gateways suggest the SWASTIKA emblem. Probably derived from the design of farmers' gates used to keep out cattle, the swastika (*sathiya*) has no connection to the sinister connotations of modern times.

In contrast to the austerity at Sanchi, the Great Stupa at Amaravati in present-day Andhra Pradesh was covered with limestone sculptural reliefs that depict seminal events in the Buddha's life. Founded in the Asokan period (c. 268–321 B.C.E.) and completed in the second century C.E., bas-reliefs reveal the transformation from aniconic (negative image) to iconic representations of the Buddha.

Meanwhile, northern and western Indian architects raised the *medhi* (circular base), giving the stupa a more cylindrical shape; in the process the *anda* became proportionally smaller and elevated. Examples of these cylindrical stupas can be seen at communal places of worship (*chaitya*) at Karle and Ajanta. By the Gupta period (c. 319–550 C.E.), sculptors placed the image of the Buddha on the elongated cylindrical base. In other developments the architects also experimented with square bases, cornices, articulated by pilasters, niches, and arcades, developments that prefigure the East Asian pagoda.

The regions under the direct influence of India experimented with the different configurations of the stupa. The great stupa at Anuradhapura in Sri Lanka gives greater portion to the *anda* and *harmika* and enlarges the *chattavali*. By increasing and crowding the honorific parasols, the stupa is transformed into a slender needlelike spire. The hemispheric *anda* is placed on a low platform without the *torana* that set off the sacred site;

shrines are set directly into the *anda* at cardinal points of the compass. To the north, the Nepalese painters adorned the stupa at Kathmandu with half-closed eyes on each side of the prominent *harmika*. The *chorten* is the Tibetan version of the stupa, which has a functional interior chapel.

The Burmese, Thai, and Laotian stupas are topped with a distinctive elongated and tapering *chattavali* that rises from an inverted bell-shaped *anda*. Burmese architects dispensed with the *harmika*, creating seamless elongated spiral form. The 12th-century Ananda Stupa in Pagan and the gold covered stupa at Phra Si Ratana Chedi in Bangkok, Thailand, are outstanding examples. That Luang in Vientiane, Laos, has unique undulating and tapering *chattavali*. In Vietnam and Cambodia small votive stupas are found in temple structures.

At first glance the Far Eastern pagoda exhibits no similarity to its Indian progenitor. But the vertical rectilinear pagoda preserves all of the essential features found at the Great Stupa at Sanchi. The development of the pagoda can be traced in part to developments in Gandhara, present-day Pakistan, and Tajikistan, where architects experimented with a square and multisided and multilayered bases; the traditional multistoried Chinese watch tower with its overhanging tiled eaves is another source. The early Chinese pagoda is multisided, but it evolved into a four-sided structure. The *anda*, *harmika*, and *chattavali* form a finale placed on the top of the multistoried base.

The largest stupa in the world is BOROBODUR, an Indonesian temple complex near Yogyakarta, Java, which incorporates many small stupas surrounding a large main stupa at the temple's highest point. Stupas became especially identified with Tibet. In the last half of the 20th century, Tibetan refugees erected stupas around the world.

In the West, the construction of stupas has taken on new meaning, a sign that an emergent commitment to Buddhism has attained a new level of permanence. The first stupa for many Western believers may be the one erected to con- tain the relics of the founder of the community to which they belong.

See also ART, AESTHETICS, AND ARCHITECTURE; SHRINES.

Further reading: Joe Cummings with Bill Wassman, *Buddhist Stupas in Asia: The Shape of Perfection* (Oakland, Calif.: Lonely Planet, 2001); Sushila Pant, *Origin and Development of Stupa Architecture in India* (Columbia, Mo.: South Asia Books, 1977); Adrian Snodgrass, *Symbolism of the Stupa* (Delhi: Motilal Banarsidass, 1992).

Subhuti (c. 500 B.C.E.) *one of the 10 major disciples of the Buddha*

Subhuti is mentioned in many MAHAYANA BUDDHISM sutras, including the LOTUS SUTRA. But he is most well known for his role as the Buddha's discussant in the DIAMOND SUTRA. He was prophesied to become the Buddha of Wonderful Form.

Further reading: Edward J. Thomas, *The Life of Buddha as Legend and History* (Delhi: Munshiram Manoharlal, 1992).

successors to the Buddha   *See* TWENTY-EIGHT PATRIARCHS.

Suddodhana *Buddha's father and king of the Sakya nation*

Suddodhana acted to shield his son and heir from taking up the life of spiritual advancement that was foretold by a fortune teller. The king wanted his son to become a powerful monarch and arranged for Siddhartha to have every creature comfort and to be prevented from learning of suffering. Yet after being inadvertently exposed to the Four Omens (people with old age, sickness, death, and ascetic wandering), Siddhartha opposed his father's wishes anyway. The father was full of wrath, but helpless.

Further reading: Thera Piyadassi, *The Buddha: His Life and His Teachings*. The Wheel Publication No. 5, A/B (Kandy: Buddhist Publication Society, 1982). Available online. URL: http://www.buddhanet.net/pdf_file/life-buddha.pdf. Accessed on June 2, 2006.

Suika Shinto

Suika Shinto was a creative mix of SHINTO and Neo-Confucian thought. Suika Shinto focuses on study of the virtues of AMATERASU OMI-KAMI, the creator God. Worship of the emperor was also a form of worshipping Amaterasu. At the same time Suika teachings emphasized the divine nature of the emperor. Suika Shinto arose in the early TOKUGAWA SHOGUNATE period (1600–1867), when the government adopted NEO-CONFUCIANISM as the official ideology. The word *Suika* refers to two of the words (*sui* and *ka*, "blessings" and "protection") used in the title of one of the five books of Shinto, the Shinto Gobusho.

The movement was established by Yamazaki Anzai (1618–82), who believed one had to maintain a childlike innocence when discussing the divine. He tried in such ways to merge Neo-Confucianist ideas such as the FIVE ELEMENTS with Japanese ideas of the *kami*.

Further reading: Kazuo Kasahara, ed., *A History of Japanese Religion*. Translated by Paul McCarthy and Gaynor Sekimori (Tokyo: Kosei, 2001), 348–350.

sukhavati (heaven)

Sukhavati (realm of bliss) is the Pure Land in the west described in detail in PURE LAND BUDDHISM teachings. It is the western paradise, belief in which may have been common among many peoples in the regions of early Buddhist activity. Individuals reborn into *sukhavati* find themselves gaining consciousness in lotus flowers. They awaken to unimaginable bliss, surrounded by light beams emitted by AMITABHA. The surroundings are also filled with wonderful fragrances, flowers, trees with jewels, and rivers whose very sounds are music. And of course there are no negative entities such as evil or sadness. The individual remains in *sukhavati* until he (all individuals are reborn as men) is ready to enter NIRVANA.

The way to enter into *sukhavati* varied over time. In the beginning the key element stressed was faith in the teachings, but in East Asia the emphasis became faith as a devotional practice. In the early period, in India, it was assumed that meditation on AMITABHA Buddha would cause the development of "good roots," or wholesome faculties developed through individual efforts at cultivation, which would in turn lead to rebirth in *sukhavati*. But in China the translator Shan Dao taught that invoking the name of Amitabha was in itself sufficient to ensure rebirth in *sukhavati*. In other words, a transition developed as Pure Land teachings entered China and, later, Japan.

Further reading: Kogen Mizuno, *Essentials of Buddhism: Basic Terminology of Buddhist Philosophy and Practice*. Translated by Gaynor Sekimori (1972. Reprint, Tokyo: Kosei, 1996); Hajime Nakamura, *Indian Buddhism: A Survey with Bibliographical Notes* (1980. Reprint, Delhi: Motilal Banarsidass, 1996); "Sukhavati," in Charles S. Prebish, *The A to Z of Buddhism* (Lanham, Md.: Scarecrow Press, 2001), 241–242.

Sumedho, Ajahn (1934–) *monk who introduced the Thai Forest Meditation Tradition to the West*

The American-born Ajahn Sumedho, a follower of AJAHN CHAH, was largely responsible for taking the THAI FOREST MEDITATION TRADITION to the West. Ajahn Sumedho was born Robert Jackman in Seattle, Washington. He originally discovered Buddhism while in the United States Navy and stationed in Japan. He returned to the States, finished college, and then left for Thailand. There he received ordination as a BHIKSU (monk) at a monastery near the Laotian border. Then in 1967 he moved to Wat Pah Pong in northeast Thailand to study and practice with the Venerable Ajahn Chah (1918–81) and became his first Western student.

In 1975, with other Western students who had subsequently arrived at Wat Pah Pong, Sumedho started Wat Pa Nanachat (International Forest Monastery) at the nearby village of Bung Wai. It was to be a monastic training center led by Westerners for Westerners. It would become the parent of additional similar MONASTERIES in Thailand.

In 1976, Sumedho accompanied Ajahn Chah on a trip to England at the invitation of the English Sangha Trust. While there, he was requested to start a Thai Forest monastic community in Great Britain, and when Chah returned to Thailand, Sumedho remained behind. Two years later he and several fellow monks founded Wat Pah Cittavieka, better known as the Chithurst Forest Monastery, in Sussex, England. This institution would become the mother of like communities in France, Australia, New Zealand, Switzerland, Italy, Canada, and the United States.

Further reading: Ven. Ajahn Sumedho, *The Mind and the Way: Buddhist Reflections on Life* (Somerville, Mass.: Wisdom, 1996); ———, *The Path to the Deathless* (Hemel Hempstead, U.K.: Amaravati, 1985); ———, *Teachings of a Buddhist Monk* (Devon, U.K.: Buddhist Publication Group, 1990); ———, *The Way It Is* (Hemel Hempstead, U.K.: Amaravati, 1991).

Sumeru, Mt. (Mt. Meru)

In traditional Buddhist and Hindu thought Mt. Sumeru stands at the center of the world. It is said to rise 84,000 yojana (about 8,500 miles) high. The Hindu deity Indra resides on top, and the Four Heavenly Kings live on the sides. Sumeru is in turn surrounded by seven rings of mountains separated by seven perfumed seas. Around the final ring of mountains is a salt sea containing the four continents to the east, west, north, and south. Around the salt ocean is a ring of iron mountains that stand at the edge of the world. The doctrine of the BUDDHA is found only on the southern continent, Jambudvipa.

Mt. KAILAS, one of Asia's most sacred mountains, is located in a high and isolated enclave of west Tibet. To the Buddhist believers, it is the abode of Demchok, the wrathful manifestation of Buddha. For Hindus, Kailash is the dwelling of Shiva the destroyer, and according to SANSKRIT tradition of Vishnu Puran (The Hindu pilgrimage books, 200 B.C.E.), it is a representation of Mt. Sumeru, the cosmic mountain at the center of the universe.

Further reading: Charles Allen, *A Mountain in Tibet: The Search for Mount Kailas and the Sources of the Great Rivers of India* (London: Andre Deutsch, 1982).

Sundo (fourth century C.E.) *Chinese monk who introduced Buddhism to Korea*

Little is known of Sundo, the monk who in 372 occasioned the effective transmission of Buddhism into what is now Korea. A Chinese monk, Sundo was sent by the emperor Fujian (r. 357–384) to assist King SOSURIM of Yoguryo, the northernmost kingdom on the Korean Peninsula. Buddhism had spread to Korea earlier but had had little success. Sundo introduced a form of Buddhism that attracted Sosurim as it appeared to support the reforming and centralizing of the government that he had already initiated.

Sundo was able to attract many of the people at Sosurim's court to Buddhism and took the lead in the establishment of the first Buddhist temple in Korea. However, his aristocratic form of the faith had little appeal beyond the country's elite, and only in the next century would Buddhism spread as a popular faith.

Further reading: *Focus on Korea.* 3 vols. (Seoul: Seoul International Publishing House, 1988); James Huntley Grayson, *Korea: A Religious History* (Oxford: Oxford University Press, 1989); Duk-Whang Kim, *A History of Religions in Korea* (Seoul: Daeji Monoonwha-sa, 1988).

sunim See TITLES AND TERMS OF ADDRESS, BUDDHIST.

sunyata

Sunyata, generally translated as "emptiness," is the central concept of the MADHYAMIKA school of Buddhism, which in turn is based on the Indian philosopher NAGARUNA's teachings. MAHAYANA BUDDHISM taught that there is in addition to the emptiness of the self an additional emptiness of all DHARMAS. The noneternal existence of all dharmas was probably emphasized to counter the SARVASTI-VADA (SARVASTIVADIN) school focus on the eternal existence of dharmas.

Emptiness was a concept fully developed by the Mahayana thinkers. However, its source no doubt lies in the earlier teachings on non-self, or ANATMAN. Both these terms are in turn related to the ZEN BUDDHISM concept of WU (in Japanese, *mu*), or nonbeing.

Sunyata does not simply involve a denial of existence or nihilism. *Sunyata* means that the phenomena of existence, all dharmas, have no *intrinsic* identities. Every aspect of reality is, according to the principles of PRATITYA-SAMUTPADA, conditioned in some way. And *sunyata* is ultimately equal to another Buddhist concept, TATHATA, "suchness."

Further reading: Kogen Mizuno, *Essentials of Buddhism: Basic Terminology of Buddhist Philosophy and Practice.* Translated by Gaynor Sekimori (1972. Reprint, Tokyo: Kosei, 1996); "Sunyata," in Charles S. Prebish, *The A to Z of Buddhism* (Lanham, Md.: Scarecrow Press, 2001), 242.

Susano-o no Mikoto

One of the major Shinto deities (*KAMI*), Susano-o no Mikoto is variously described as the sea deity or storm deity, the ruler of the oceans, which completely surround the island nation of Japan. Susano-o emerges from the ancient SHINTO creation myths. For example, in the eighth-century text, the *KOJIKI,* the process of forming Japan and populating it with *kami* is described. That process hinges on a couple, Izanagi no Mikoto and Izanami no Mikoto. Their creative acts are interrupted by the death of Izanami, the female. The grieving Izanagi travels through the underworld in search of her, but his goal of resurrecting her fails. After he returns, he engages in a purification ritual in which he first cleans his eyes and nose. From his right eye arises Amaterasu no Mikoto, the sun goddess, and from his left eye Tsukiyomi no Mikoto. Susano-o no Mikoto, the third god to appear (from the nose cleaning), is assigned hegemony over the sea. (There are alternate versions of this story that offer different details of how Izanagi created the three deities.)

Susano-o is particularly related to two important Shinto shrines. First, Izumo Taisha is dedicated to Susano-o's son, Okuninushi-no-Mikoto. As the story goes, at one point Susano-o had a conflict with the sun deity, Amaterasu, who expelled him from the heavenly realm. He took up residence at Izumo, where he earned the gratitude of the humans by killing a giant serpent. He subsequently married a princess. Okuninushi was the product of their love and he became the *kami* overseeing the benefits of marriage. At this shrine, one also finds the road to the underworld, also under the domain of Susano-o, as the god of the dead. Second, Susano-o is honored at Itsuku-shima, a seaside shrine on Miyajima Island a short distance from Hiroshima. The main shrine at Ituku-shima is dedicated to Susano-o's three daughters, Ichikishima, Tagori, and Tagitsu, the beloved of sailors. Susano-o is also enshrined at the Kumano Shrine in Hongu, along with Amaterasu.

See also KAMI.

Further reading: Genchi Kato, *A Study of Shinto* (Richmond, U.K.: Curzon Press, 1971); ———, and Hikoshiro Hoshino, *Kogoshui: Gleanings from Ancient Stories* (Richmond, U.K.: Curzon Press, 1972); Sokyo Ono, *Shinto the Kami Way* (Rutland: Charles E. Tuttle, 1972);

Floyd Hiatt Ross, *Shinto the Way of Japan* (Westport, Conn.: Greenwood Press, 1983).

sutra (Pali, sutta)

Sutras are the texts that record the teachings of the Buddha between the time he gained ENLIGHTENMENT and his MAHAPARINIRVANA (death). Perhaps unfortunately, these teachings were not written down at the time they were delivered. According to the story, Buddha's primary disciple, ANANDA, during the meeting of the First Buddhist Council is said to have repeated the discourses for those followers of the Buddha so gathered. Subsequently, the teachings were committed to the memory of the 500 ARHATS (a number of respected practitioners) and for several centuries the teachings were passed from generation to generation orally. In the process of the growth of the Buddhist community, and in spite of the high accuracy of memory in nonliterary communities, some variations in the discourses did occur.

It was not until the first century B.C.E. that the sutras began to be written down. The language chosen for these early texts was PALI. The early texts of the Buddha's teachings were compiled into five collections (*agamas*), the Long Sutras (Digha-nikaya), the Medium-length Sutras (Majjhima-nikaya), Sutras on Related Topics (Samyutta-nikaya), Sutras of Numerical Doctrines (Anguttara-nikaya), and the Minor Sutras (Khuddaka-nikaya). These five *agamas* now constitute one of the three sections of the TRIPITAKA, the canon of Buddhist scripture recognized by THERAVADA Buddhism.

NEW SCHOOLS OF BUDDHISM

During the period in which the sutras were being written down, approximately 100 B.C.E. to 100 C.E., not only had the Indian Buddhists divided into a number of sects (some 18 were noted by observers), but a new form, MAHAYANA BUDDHISM, had begun to emerge. Proponents of Mahayana ideas began to produce new sutras, occasionally claiming that the texts were newly discovered lost texts that had been hidden since the Buddha's lifetime. The texts laid out the Mahayana teachings on such subjects as emptiness, the role of BODHISATTVAS, and the multiple bodies of the Buddha. Possibly the most noticeable characteristic of the new sutras was their being written in SANSKRIT rather than Pali. It was also the case that they were originally composed as a written document rather than an oral text later committed to writing. They tended to be longer and make use of more luxuriant language.

Among the earliest of the Mahayana sutras are the several Prajnaparamita (Perfection of wisdom) Sutras (c. 100 C.E.), the LOTUS SUTRA (c. 200 C.E.), and the NIRVANA SUTRA (c. 200–400 C.E.). NAGARJUNA, the great third-century Mahayana scholar, is known for compiling and writing a systematic presentation on the Wisdom sutra teachings, the Treatise on the Middle Way. The special devotion to AMITABHA (or Amida) Buddha also emerged in the second century C.E. and found literary expression in the Amida Sutra, the Buddha Infinite Life Sutra, and the Meditation on the Buddha Infinite Life Sutra.

In the fourth century C.E., a new set of sutras were written, most significantly, the Flower Ornament Sutra (AVATAMSAKA SUTRA), the Descent into Lanka Sutra (Lankavatara Sutra), and the Resolution of Enigmas Sutra (Sandhinirmocana Sutra). On the basis of these sutras, several teachers such as ASANGA and VASUBANDHU formed the YOGACARA (or Consciousness Only) school.

BUDDHISM AND SUTRAS IN CHINA

The centuries of the rise and development of Mahayana Buddhism were also the time of the transmission of Buddhism to China, generally dated from the reign of the Emperor Ming Ti (r. 58–75 C.E.). The move to China was characterized by two important factors, namely, the use of DAOISM to interpret Buddhism and the periodic and unsystematic injection of Buddhist sutras (both THERAVADA and Mahayana) into China. The first sutra translated into Chinese (some suggest it was originally written in Chinese) was the Sutra of Forty-two Sections, which presented an introduction to basic Buddhist doctrines.

The first documented translations of Indian texts into Chinese began in 148 C.E. at Luoyang, the capital of the Chinese Han dynasty, where AN SHIGAO established a center for translation that continued to produce Chinese copies of Sanskrit (that is, Mahayana) texts into the next century. In the third century, DHARMARAKSA (1) (230 C.E.) translated the Lotus Sutra and Large Perfection of Wisdom Sutra, both of which were to have a significant role in Chinese (and later Japanese) Buddhism. The work of translation, including the retranslation of the early poorly translated texts, was given a boost at the beginning of the fifth century by more capable scholars, such as KUMARAJIVA (344–413) and HUI YUAN (1) (344–416). Kumarajiva translated the Amida Sutra so central to Pure Land Buddhism, and most of the Wisdom Sutras including the DIAMOND SUTRA and the HEART SUTRA, and his version of the Lotus Sutra became an especially popular text chanted in Buddhist temples.

Eventually, the first four NIKAYAS (collections) of the Pali canon Sutras would be translated into Chinese, but the many Mahayana sutras would find the most response and Mahayana Buddhism would become dominant throughout China. The often chaotic and unsystematic manner in which texts were taken to China, translated, and then disseminated for study would have a marked effect on the development of uniquely Chinese schools of Buddhism. (And at the same time sutras were also finding their way to Tibet and being translated in a similar disjunct manner.)

In the period from the fifth to the ninth century, Chinese Buddhist scholars began the process of examining the various schools of Buddhist thought to be encountered in the sutras and as more and more texts appeared tried to develop comprehensive views of Buddhism. This problem led to several types of solution. ZHI YI (538–597), for example, the leading light of the TIAN TAI school, offered one explanation. He attempted to develop a typology of Buddhist sutras, which ranked them according to their ability to express truth most clearly. He concluded that the Lotus, Nirvana, and Flower Ornament Sutras were closest to stating the truth, which was itself beyond words, though the Lotus Sutra was slightly the superior of the three. CHAN BUDDHISM took a quite different approach, distancing itself from most Buddhist texts and centering its life on the practice of meditation. As the tradition developed, the discourse of its "sixth patriarch," HUI NENG (638–713), would be collected and published as the PLATFORM SUTRA of the sixth patriarch, though unlike other sutras, the Platform Sutra made no claim to be the words of the Buddha.

SUTRAS IN JAPAN

Over the next centuries, different sects of Chinese Buddhists would identify with and favor different sutras that provided the foundation for their particular approach to Buddhist belief and practice. Chinese teachers would also host individuals from Korea and Japan who wished to absorb the teachings of the sutras and would gather copies to take back to their homeland. At the same time, Chinese teachers would take sutras to Korea and Japan, where they would undergo another translation into the new language.

Of particular importance to the larger world of Buddhism, in the eighth century, six schools of Buddhism were set in place in the new imperial capital of NARA in Japan. Five of these six schools were, in fact, six centers for the study of the particular sutras and/or sastras (commentaries on the sutras). The sixth school concentrated on the VINAYA, another part of the Buddhist sacred literature, dealing with the discipline to be followed by monks and nuns. The KEGON school built its teachings, for example, on the Flower Ornament (AVATAMSAKA) Sutra. The HOSSO school based its teachings on six sutras, especially the Profound Secrets Sutra (Samdhinir-mochana-sutra) and the Flower Ornament Sutra, and 11 *sastra* texts.

As Japanese Buddhism developed, NICHIREN SHOSHU and those groups derived from it would become well known for their championing of the Lotus Sutra as the only Buddhist text of any great importance. Beginning with TENDAI Buddhism, in which the Lotus Sutra was well honored, Nichiren concluded that it was the best of the Buddhist sacred texts and then the exclusive text that embodied the truth of the Buddha within it.

THE SUTRAS IN THE WEST

One result of Western attempts to dominate traditionally Buddhist lands, both economically and politically, in the 19th century was the emergence of interest in Buddhism and Buddhist writings among Westerners. That interest led to both the translation of the sutras into Western languages and their publication and broad dissemination using modern printing advances. Through the 20th century, copies of the Buddhist sutras became available to almost anyone in his or her native language at little to no cost, a fact that is in itself having a long-term transforming effect on the Buddhist community.

Beginning with the emergence of Mahayana Buddhism, commentaries on the sutras, SAS-TRAS, began to appear and multiplied over the centuries.

Further reading: G. C. C. Chang, trans. and ed., *A Treasury of Mahayana Sutras: Selections from the Maharatnakuta Sutra* (University Park: Pennsylvania State University Press, 1983); Edward Conze, trans., *Buddhist Wisdom Books: The Diamond Sutra and the Heart Sutra.* 2d ed. (London: George Allen & Unwin, 1975); Dwight Goddard, ed., *A Buddhist Bible* (Thetford, Vt.: author, 1932); Kogen Mizuno, *Buddhist Sutras: Origin, Development, Transmission* (Tokyo: Kosei, 1982); Philip B. Yampolsky, ed., *Platform Sutra of the Sixth Patriarch* (New York: Columbia University Press, 1967); *Zen Bud-*

dhist English Sutras (Honolulu: Hawaii Soto Mission Association, 1948).

Suzuki, Daisetsu Teitaro (1870–1966)
Zen teacher influential in introducing Zen Buddhism to the West

Daisetsu Teitaro "D. T." Suzuki, a major force in bringing ZEN BUDDHISM to the West in the 20th century, was born in Kanazawa, a rural village in the north of Japan. Though his family was of modest means, they were of a dignified samurai lineage. As a young man, Suzuki stayed in his small town as a teacher for the local children. Then, after his mother's death, he moved to Tokyo, where he would have more opportunities for advancement.

He studied at Imperial University while studying Zen. He was a precocious student of MAHAYANA BUDDHISM and successfully integrated its variant teachings. His excellence in Zen coupled with his formal education propelled him onward. In 1897, he was chosen by SOYEN SHAKU (1859–1919), a pioneer in the introduction of Zen to Western countries, to go to America and serve as a consultant and translator for PAUL CARUS (1852–1919), owner of Open Court Press, who was publishing a number of Buddhist texts. Carus appointed him editor when he arrived in America in 1897.

Suzuki was responsible for the translations of books that reflected the heart of Buddhism and related Eastern volumes such as ASVAGHOSA's The Awakening of Faith in Mahayana and the DAODEJING (*Tao Te Ching*). When that mission had been accomplished, Soyen Shakyu asked him to accompany him on his promotional Western tour in 1905–06.

When young Suzuki returned to Japan from the speaking tour he settled in as a lay disciple. In 1911, he married Beatrice Erskine Lane (1878–1938) and they relocated to Tokyo so that he could accept a teaching position at Otani University, the foremost school of the HIGASHI HONGWANJI

Buddhists. He together with his wife started the publication of a seminal academic periodical, *The Eastern Buddhist*. He began to turn out a number of important texts in Buddhist studies including *Essays in Zen Buddhism, Zen and the Japanese Culture, On Indian Mahayana Buddhism*, concentrating on Jodo SHINSHU and ZEN BUDDHISM. This creative period was a watershed moment in his career.

Partially because of his prolific writing, in 1949, Suzuki was invited to teach as a visiting professor at the University of Hawaii. He was already 78 years old. The following year he journeyed to California and taught at the Claremont Graduate School. He then went to Columbia University for a period of six years. While living in New York and lecturing at Columbia he attracted the so-called Beatniks, whose acceptance and propagation of his writing propelled him forward as a public figure of popular culture. His presence in New York fueled the development of the Zen Studies Society.

He relocated to Cambridge, Massachusetts, in the mid-1950s and while lecturing at Harvard also helped inspire the founding of the Cambridge Buddhist Association. He finally returned home to Japan in 1958. He died in Kamakura, Japan, in 1966. He was nearly 96 years old when he died, a hero of Zen missionary activity.

Further reading: Maseo Abe, ed., *A Zen Life: D. T. Suzuki Remembered* (New York: Weatherhill, 1986); D. T. Suzuki, *An Introduction To Zen Buddhism* (1964. Reprint, New York: Grove Weidenfeld, 1991); ———, *Zen And Japanese Buddhism* (Rutland, Vt.: Charles E. Tuttle, 1958); ———, *Zen Buddhism: Selected Writings of D. T. Suzuki* (New York: Doubleday, 1956).

Suzuki, Shunryu (1904–1971) *Japanese American Zen leader*

Shunryu Suzuki, a teacher of SOTO ZEN in San Francisco, California, had as a young man followed in his father, Butsumon Sogaku Suzuki's, footsteps by becoming a ZEN BUDDHISM priest in

Japan. He deviated from the traditional path of discipleship, however, as he chose to study with a colleague of his father instead of his father. Suzuki later attended Komazawa Buddhist University. He continued in his practice of Zen while nurturing a desire to go to America. Instead he remained in Japan and became a priest of Zoun-ji temple and then later of Rinso-in.

Suzuki did not support World War II and spoke against it. After the armistice, he led in the creation of social services sponsored by Rinso-in Temple, including two kindergartens, one of which was taught by his second wife, Mitsu Matsuna.

Then, during the 1950s, Suzuki's interest in visiting the United States was revived by an invitation to become the interim director of Soko-ji, the Soto Zen temple in San Francisco. He moved to California in 1959. The temple at that time was home to a number of ethnic Japanese, though a few non-Japanese converts had also found their way to its doors.

Through the 1960s, Suzuki became increasingly popular as the "hippie" generation responded to the call from the East. It was the era of thinkers such as ALAN WILSON WATTS, who wished to build a bridge between cultures and religions. It was not long before Suzuki was teaching the path of SOTO and the practice of ZAZEN (sitting meditation) to cadres of young people. By the autumn of 1966 his work had grown enormously and was being transmitted by disciples all over America. The Zen Center of San Francisco, formed out of Soko-ji, became the hub of growth from which centers emerged in Berkeley, Mill Valley, and Los Altos, California. In 1967 Roshi Suzuki and his followers purchased a vacant hot springs site that became a rural retreat—the Zenshin-ji Monastery located at Tassajara Springs, California. Suzuki Roshi continued to teach *zazen* until his death in 1971. The leadership of the temple and retreat passed to his American disciple, Richard Baker Roshi, and continues today under a collective leadership.

Further reading: David Chadwick, *Crooked Cucumber: The Life and Zen Teaching of Shunryu Suzuki* (New York: Broadway Books, 1999); David Chadwick and Students of Shunryu Suzuki, *To Shine One Corner of the World: Moments with Shunryu Suzuki* (New York: Broadway Books, 2001); Rick Fields, *How the Swans Came to the Lake: A Narrative History of Buddhism in America.* Rev. ed. (Boston: Shambhala, 1986); Shunryu Suzuki Roshi, *Not Always So* (New York: HarperCollins, 2002); ———, *Zen Mind, Beginners Mind* (New York: Weatherhill, 1970).

Suzuki Shosan (1579–1655) *medieval samurai who became a well-known Zen monk*

Suzuki Shosan was born into a samurai family in Misawa (current Aichi Prefecture). He was a member of Tokugawa Ieyasu's army during Japan's civil war period and fought in the important Battle of Sekigahara. But at the age of 41 he became a devoted monk. He studied with several ZEN BUDDHISM masters and wrote a well-received manual of Zen in 1636, *Fumoto no Kusawake* (Parting the Grasses at the Foot of the Mountain). Suzuki emphasized the warrior metaphor and its application to Buddhism. The Zen monk needed the same kind of courage and ability to confront death as the warrior. He also saw the value of everyday acts such as farming. Enlightenment, however incomplete, can occur in the midst of everyday work, he taught.

Suzuki eventually returned to live in a small town near his hometown of Misawa, where he became known as a healer. He eventually began to teach from town to town about "True Buddhism," what he saw as the Buddha's teachings in practice. He spoke against becoming a priest or worshipping images of the Buddha. He eventually enlisted his brother, Shigenari's, help, and they worked to establish 32 temples throughout Japan.

Suzuki was also anti-Christian at a time when Christian missionaries were increasingly visible. His *Ha Kirishitan* (Christianity Refuted) was an anti-Christian text. Suzuki moved to Edo (present-day Tokyo) in 1648 and published the *Banmin Tokuyu* (The Meritorious Practice for All).

Further reading: Arthur Braverman, *Warrior Of Zen: The Diamond-Hard Wisdom of Suzuki Shosan* (Tokyo: Kodansha Globe, 1994); "The Diamond-Hard Wisdom of Suzuki Shosan." The DailyZen Journal. Available online at The DailyZen Journal: On The Way. URL: www.dailyzen.com/zen/zen_reading2.asp. Accessed on July 3, 2006; Anthony M. Wen, "The History and Life of Suzuki Shósan." California State University, Chico. Available online at Chico: California State University, Chico website. URL: http://www.csuchico.edu/~cheinz/syllabi/asst001/fall97/anth-wen.htm. Accessed on May 22, 2006.

svabhava ("own-being")

Svabhava is a Sanskrit term found in Hindu literature as well as early Buddhism. It can be translated as "innate nature" or "own-being." It indicates the principle of self-becoming, the essential character of any entity. It assumes that a phenomenon can exist without reference to a conditioning context; a thing simply "is." In other words, it has a permanent nature. Buddhism refutes this idea, holding that all phenomena are codependent with all other phenomena. NAGARJUNA, the great MAHAYANA BUDDHISM philosopher, concluded that nothing in the universe has *svabhava.* In fact, the universe is characterized by *sunyata,* emptiness. *Sunyata* assumes the opposite of *svabhava, asvabhava.*

Svabhava was a key issue of debate among the early schools of Buddhism, in India. They all generally held that every dharma, or constituent of reality, had its own nature.

Further reading: Etienne Lamotte, *History of Indian Buddhism from the Origins to the Shaku Era.* Translated by Sara Webb-Boin, (Nouvain-la-Neuve: Institute Orientaliste de l'Universite Catholique de Louvain, 1988); Religio. "Shunyata and Pratitya Samutpada in Mahayana." Available online. URL: www.humboldt.edu/~wh1/6.Buddhism.OV/6.Sunyata.html. Accessed on November 28, 2005.

swastika

Contemporary Western travelers to Asia are often surprised to find the swastika used as a decorative symbol on religious buildings and various religious objects. However, *swastika* is a Sanskrit word meaning "well-being." In ancient Hindu lore it was often associated with the serpent, a symbol of the creative life from the Supreme Spirit. The swastika symbolized the life force being set in motion to start up the various cyclic workings of nature. Its use by the Nazis and association with the Holocaust have identified the symbol with the worst kind of evil that humanity can perpetrate, hence the startled expressions that often follow initial encounters with the swastika in the non-Western world.

Buddhists borrowed the swastika from the Hindus and as Buddhism spread, especially northward into China (and from there to Japan and Korea), the swastika spread also. It is generally oriented horizontally but may appear with the arms pointing in either direction. It was quite often placed over the heart on statues of the Buddha and could be found stamped on the breasts of departed initiates. It was freely used to decorate temples and appeared on amulets. One popular representation of the Buddha was the Sri-Pada, or holy footprint (also a sacred mountain in Sri Lanka). Such images have a swastika on each of the toes.

In China, the swastika is placed on food packaging to identify vegetarian products. The symbol is sometimes sewn into the clothing of children as a protective amulet. In Korea, besides decorating the houses of fortune tellers and temples, swastikas also appear on maps, where they are used to mark the locations of temples (similarly, Western maps often use a box with a cross to identify the location of churches). The faithful also wear swastikas in necklaces in order to identify themselves as Buddhists. Early in the 20th century, the

Rubbing of a stone carving showing the Buddha's feet, with symbols showing different elements of his teachings; in the Da Yan pagoda, Xi'an, western China

Theosophical Society (based in South India) used a swastika as part of its symbol. At least one of the cofounders, HENRY STEEL OLCOTT, identified himself as a Buddhist.

Contemporary Buddhists have become aware of the Nazi swastika and the negative emotions that it arouses. Many have abandoned it, though no effort has been made to erase it from temples and other pre-Nazi structures. In recent decades, Asian artists, noting that the Nazi swastika was right facing, almost always draw any swastikas designed for a Buddhist context facing left.

Further reading: Donald A. MacKenzie, *The Migration of Symbols and their Relations to Beliefs and Customs* (New York: AMS Press, 1970); Barbara G. Walker, *The Woman's Dictionary of Symbols and Sacred Objects* (New York: Harper & Row, 1988); Thomas Wilson, *Swastika the Earliest Known Symbol and Its Migrations* (Washington, D.C.: Smithsonian Institution and Government Printing Office, 1896).

T

Tachikawa

Tachikawa was a Japanese Buddhist sect founded at the end of the 11th century by Nin-kan (1057–1123), a SHINGON priest. The group was distinctive in that, drawing on various Indian Tantric texts, Nin-kan advocated a form of TANTRA that included the practice of sexual intercourse. All of VAJRAYANA BUDDHISM has teachings that include a significant amount of sexual symbolism, but most who practice tantrism embody that symbolism in a spectrum of rituals that do not themselves include any sexual contact.

Early in the 12th century, the Japanese government outlawed the movement and its growth was quickly stunted. However, it appears to have survived as an underground movement into the 17th century. Rumors have persisted that some of the writings representative of the group have survived but are locked away and have not been made available to modern researchers.

Further reading: Rufus C. Camphausen, *Encyclopedia of Erotic Wisdom: A Reference Guide to the Symbolism, Techniques, Rituals, Sacred Texts, Psychology, Anatomy, and History of Sexuality* (Rochester, Vt.: Inner Traditions International, 1991).

T'aego Pou (1301–1382) *Korean Son (Zen) teacher*

T'aego Pou, to whom most practitioners of Korean SON BUDDHISM trace their lineage, was born in Kwangju, in southern Korea. He was ordained as a monk at the age of 13 and had his first awakening six years later. He was 37 when he attained his deeper ENLIGHTENMENT. Several years later he settled at Mt. Samgak (near present-day Seoul) at Chungheungsa temple. He built Sosolam Hermitage east of the temple and attracted many students. Here he completed his first major writing, the *Gailpyeon*. Over the course of his life, he authored many poems.

T'aego's life was divided by a visit to China for two years (1346–48) during which he met a number of CHAN BUDDHISM leaders, among them Shi Wu Jingkong (1270–1352), the patriarch in the LINJI CHAN school. Shi Wu certified T'aego's awakening and in 1348 sent him back to Korea to spread the Linji (in Korea, Imje) teachings. T'aego settled back at Sosolam, prepared to remain there the rest of his life. However, Korea had entered a tumultuous period. The Chinese Yuan dynasty (1271–1368) that ruled Korea at the time was in its last years, and in 1351, Kongmon (1351–74) asserted Korea's independence. In 1352 he invited T'aego to his court. T'aego assumed the role of teacher to the king and used his position to gain the king's backing for his goal of uniting the various Son groups into a single organization. Because of his study and authorization from China, his popularity was high. In 1356, the king appointed him the teacher of the nation and backed his unification plan.

T'aego worked for a decade on unifying the Korean Son centers and then retired from public life. When he died in 1382, he was honored with the title Son Master of Perfect Realization. His relics now lie in a granite STUPA on Mt. Samgak.

Further reading: J. C. Cleary, trans., *T'aego Pou: A Buddha from Korea* (Boston: Shambhala, 1992); Jaihiun J. Kim, trans., *Poems by Zen Masters* (Seoul: Hanshin, 1988); Mu Soeng, *Thousand Peaks: Korean Zen: Traditions and Teachers* (Cumberland, R.I.: Primary Point Press, 1991).

Tai Chi Chuan   *See* TAIJIQUAN.

Taijiquan (Tai Chi Chuan)

Taijiquan is a MARTIAL ARTS form developed in central China in the late 18th and mid-19th centuries. Although Taijiquan is only one of the many Chinese martial arts traditions, today it continues to be practiced by many and is the best known worldwide. As with most martial arts there is a strong element of inner cultivation in Taijiquan. Over the course of its development Taijiquan also became a magnet for popular religious and spiritual ideas.

Chinese martial arts schools can be generally classified as either outer styles (*waijia*) or inner styles (*neijia*). Shaolinquan, the boxing style said to have originated at the Shaolin Temple in Henan, central China, is an example of outer-directed style. And Aijiquan, Baguaquan (eight trigram boxing), and Xingyiquan are inner styles,

also known collectively as *wudang pai* (Wudang style), after the Wudang Mountains in Hubei, central China. In general the outer styles rely on force and technique, while the inner styles focus on inner phenomena such as *jin* (internal force) and *qi* (spiritual energy). All traditions are transmitted from individual teachers to students, usually forming a master-disciple lineage. And over time they add such elements as stories, theories, and written records.

THE THREE LINEAGES AND THE ORIGINS OF TAIJIQUAN

Stories of the origin of Taijiquan center on three families active in northern China in the late 18th and early 19th centuries, the heyday of the Qing dynasty (1644–1911). One family, the Chens, lived in the Chen family village (Chenjiagou) in Henan Province and had developed their own boxing style over generations. Much of their style is in fact related to a book written by a Ming dynasty (1368–1644) general and hero in the fight against coastal pirates, Qi Jiguang (1528–88). Qi wrote a military classic, the *Jixiao xinshu* (New book of effective techniques), in which he devoted one chapter to martial arts. This chapter, called the "Quanjing" (Classic of boxing), lists 16 styles and 32 boxing postures.

The Chen style had never been taught to people outside the Chen clan, however. Eventually a member of the Yang family from Yongnian County, Hebei Province, Yang Luchan (1799–1872), was allowed to become the first outsider taught the Chen boxing style. The Chen style of Taijiquan was finally described in writing in the book *Chen-shi taijiquan tujie* (Chen family Taijiquan illustrated), written by Chen Xin (1849–1929) and published in the 1930s.

After staying in Chenjiagou for 30 years Yang Luchan returned to his hometown of Yongnian and taught boxing. At this point it was called simply *ruanquan* (soft boxing) or *mianquan* (cotton boxing)—the name *Taijiquan* had not yet been developed. Yang taught the youngest member of the local gentry family in Yongnian, one Wu Yuxiang (1812–80). The Wu family was the local aristocracy. Through the Wu connections Yang was introduced to people in other cities. For instance, he taught members of the Manchu Imperial Guards stationed in Beijing. Yang eventually moved to Beijing and continued to teach, as did his children and grandchildren. They trained generations of *taiji* masters, some of whom lived into the 1990s. The Yang family also produced a large amount of literature concerning Taijiquan. This material was published in two books by Yang Chengfu (1883–1936), a grandson of Yang Luchan, in the 1930s.

Meanwhile, Yang Luchan's student Wu Yuxiang developed the boxing style in a different direction. Wu developed his own style called the Wu/Hao style, and passed it to his nephew, Li Yiyu (1832–92). Although this school did not spread widely, both Wu and his nephew Li wrote several important works on both the Wu and Yang styles of boxing.

In looking at the development of Taijiquan tradition so far, the pattern is of close personal connections between a handful of families in the same general area, and of later development, through teaching and publishing, in order to reach a wider audience. Already there is a complex net involving three family lineages, each promoting similar versions of a boxing style.

Sometime in the late 1880s the label *taiji* was used to describe the style of boxing. This title was probably used by the Wu/Li branch of Taijiquan. The use of *taiji,* "the supreme ultimate," a term used in the YIJING (*Book of Changes*), was a clear association with a key concept from DAOISM.

THE ASSOCIATION WITH ZHANG SANFENG

Because of their publishing efforts we have written accounts of these three families. However, over time additional legendary accounts were added to the Taijiquan tradition. This is a common phenomenon in Chinese culture: the involvement of legendary figures bestows a kind of popular legiti-macy to a practice, and more people become more disposed to take it up.

Beginning in the 1900s the Daoist Zhang Sanfeng was said to be the founder of Yang style boxing. Zhang was a late Song (960–1279) or early Ming (1368–1644) figure associated with the Wudang Mountains in northern Henan. The Wudang Mountains are near the Chen family village of Chenjiagou, and, as noted earlier, there is a strong connection between the Wudang Mountains and martial arts in general. Zhang's name had already been associated with inner style boxing as early as 1669. In a memorial he was said to have founded the Inner School of boxing during the Song dynasty after being visited by the God of War before a battle with bandits.

By the 1930s a new legend had been formulated about how Zhang Sanfeng developed Taijiquan. While chanting one day in his room he was said to have witnessed a battle between a snake and a bird. He was impressed with the way the snake evaded capture by constantly attacking and withdrawing. He then realized the principle of "soft overcoming hard," an expression frequently used in Taijiquan. And as in the development of Shaolinquan by BODHIDHARMA, the famous founder of CHAN (Zen) Buddhism, Zhang Sanfeng developed Taijiquan in order to help monks stimulate their *qi,* which had become stagnant.

The link between Taijiquan and Zhang Sanfeng is historically suspect. None of the Chen family writings or documents in Chenjiagou mention Zhang Sanfeng. However, the link is ideologically important, because it allows Taijiquan practitioners to claim that Taijiquan is Daoist. Zhang is therefore honored in many Taijiquan halls and schools.

MODERN TAIJIQUAN

Beginning in the Republican period of Chinese history (1911–49) the martial arts took on a more popular, public role than they had had in the past. We saw how various traditions had been essentially passed from master to disciple. They were of particular interest to soldiers as well as, to some extent, religious practitioners. By the Republican period access was broadened, allowing many people to learn these techniques. Martial arts associations such as the Beijing Physical Education Research Association were established. Teachers in the Yang tradition were active in this particular organization. And beginning in 1921 teachers began to publish popular guides to Taijiquan.

In the communist period, which began in 1949, Taijiquan was at first seen as one of the many feudal superstitions that should be eliminated to make way for the enlightened, socialist stage of Chinese history. Yet martial arts were popular and practiced throughout society. So instead of stamping out the practices altogether, the government decided to control and streamline practice. Taijiquan was made into a health exercise and a sport. Competitions were encouraged. Performances were staged for visitors. The health aspect, something that as we have seen has always been part of Taijiquan's attraction, became its sole purpose, to the detriment of its spiritual and martial sides. And as a result the Chen, Yang, and Wu lineages were phased out.

Lineages survived outside China, however, in places such as Taiwan and Hong Kong. And such masters as Zheng Manqing taught Taijiquan to a new generation of curious Westerners as well as Chinese. Today the state's control of Taijiquan is relatively lax, and individual masters are once again allowed to practice. However, any association with the QIGONG field in general is avoided; Taijiquan in China is perceived simply as a non-controversial, traditional series of exercises.

THE *TAIJIQUAN CLASSICS*

From the early 1900s a collection of written works involving Taijiquan was loosely called the *Taijiquan jing* (*Taijiquan classics*). These works include poems, essays, and instruction manuals. There are today two overlapping versions. The Wu/Li version, collected and published by followers of

Wu Yuxiang and Li Yiyu, mentioned earlier, is the older. This version dates as far back as 1881 and contains 12 works. Since the Wu/Li lineage had few students, none of the classics were printed; they were all circulated in hand-copied versions.

The Yang version of the classics overlaps with the Wu/Li version completely in three texts and partially in another four. It was first published by the Beijing Physical Education Research Institute in 1912. That printing contained six texts. A later printing by Chen Weiming in 1925 listed five texts in the Classics. This list is taken as definitive today. The following works are included:

1. *Taijiquan lun* (*The taijiquan treatise*), attributed to Zhang Sanfeng
2. *Taijiquan jing* (*The taijiquan classic*), attributed to Wang Zongyue
3. *Shisanshi ge* (*The thirteen postures song*)
4. *Shisan shi xinggong xinjue* (*Exposition of insights into the workings of the thirteen postures*)
5. *Dashou ge* (*Playing hands song*)

Since the Yang version of the texts occurred much later than the Wu/Li version and is simplified, many scholars think the Yang version derived from the Wu/Li version.

TAIJIQUAN THEORY AND PRACTICE

The *Taijiquan Classics* are filled with references to such Daoist concepts as *qi* (energy), yin-yang, and the five phases. However, Taijiquan practice tends to focus on these additional principles:

Softness (*rou*): overcome hardness with softness; remain stable while the opponent becomes decentered.

Relaxation (*song*): achieve a state of flexible relaxation in order to allow the *qi* to flow.

Emptiness/fullness: know weight distribution in the feet, and fullness in the hands and throughout the body.

Following/sticking/listening: stay with the
   opponent; do not attempt to set the agenda;
   "give up the self and listen to others."
Internal force (*jin*): like a bent sapling, *jin*
   allows you to remain rooted.
Rooting (*gen*): the feet are rooted from the soles.
Quietness (*jing*): be quiet like a mountain.
Qi (energy): attain a unified *qi,* flowing freely
   throughout the body.
Yao (waist): all movements originate here.

A visit to public parks in any Chinese city will
reveal many people practicing Taijiquan, as well
as other exercise techniques. The 13 postures are
taught step by step, so that a student will eventually be able to perform all the motions in a flowing
sequence. During practice the student focuses on
inner energy (*qi*) as well as posture and muscular
movement.

Such practices form a vital part of Chinese
popular culture. Taijiquan, although only several
hundred years old, reflects an innate desire for a
bodily practice that encapsulates ancient philosophical understandings.

Further reading: Barbara Davis, *The Taijiquan Classics:
An Annotated Translation: Including a Commentary by
Chen Weiming* (Berkeley, Calif.: North Atlantic Books,
2004); Jeaneane Fowler and Shifu Keith Ewers, *T'ai Chi
Ch'uan: Harmonizing Taoist Belief and Practice* (Brigh-
ton, U.K.: Sussex Academic Press, 2005); Jarek Szyman-
ski, "Brief Analysis of Chen Family Boxing Manuals."
ChinaFromInside.com. Available online. URL: www.
chinafrominside.com/ma.taiji/chenboxingmanuals.
html. Accessed on August 25, 2005; Wong shiu Hong,
*Investigations into the Authenticity of Chang San-Feng
Ch'uan-Chi: The Complete Works of Chang San-feng*
(Canberra: National Australian University Press, 1982);
———, *Mortal or Immortal: A Study of Chang San-feng
the Taoist* (Hong Kong: Calvarden, 1993).

Taiwan   *See* CHINA-TAIWAN, BUDDHISM IN;
CHINA-TAIWAN, DAOISM IN.

Tai Xu (T'ai Hsu) (1890–1947) *Chinese Buddhist reformer*
Tai Xu, a Chinese Buddhist reformer and founder
of the CHINESE BUDDHIST ASSOCIATION, was born Lu
Peilin in the city of Haining in Zhejiang Province,
China. At the age of 16 he entered the Linji Buddhist monastery and became a monk of the CHAN
BUDDHISM school. Well educated, Tai Xu launched
a variety of efforts to assist the Buddhist community in its dealing with modernity and the changes
that were coming upon his country through its
encounters with the West, including the rise of
Christianity.

As early as 1912, on the heels of the founding
of the secular Republic of China under Sun Yat
Sen, he formed the Fojiao Xiejin Hui (Association
for the Advancement of Buddhism) but was overwhelmed by opposition from his fellow monks. He
had more success in 1917 with the Enlightenment
Society he founded in Shanghai, which developed
a strong program of public education on Buddhism. Five years later he founded the Wuchang
Buddhist Institute, a Buddhist seminary.

In the years after World War I, Tai Xu had
developed a variety of international contacts,
which led him in 1923 to take the lead in founding a World Buddhist Federation. He also led the
Chinese delegation to the 1925 meeting of the
Conference of East Asian Buddhists in Tokyo.
In 1929 he assumed a role in the formation of
the first nationwide Buddhist organization, the
Chinese Buddhist Association, and served on its
standing committee. He used his position to help
build support for China after the 1937 invasion
by Japan. After the war he was honored by the
government for his activities, though the government otherwise ignored his efforts on behalf of the
Buddhist community.

Tai Xu died in 1947. His writings were later
gathered and published in a 333-volume collected version. While his ideas were popular with
many, the mainstream of the Buddhist community
was not in tune with his far-reaching vision of a
national and international Buddhist community.

He was appreciated more after the Chinese Revolution for his intellectual accomplishments and development of a contemporary language to communicate Buddhism. The Chinese Buddhist Association he helped found would rise and fall several times but now gives organizational oversight to the Buddhist temples in China.

Tai Xu has had a significant influence in Taiwan, where his perspective was spread by YIN SHUN (1906–2005) and became integral to the work of teachers such as CHENG YEN, a direct student of Yin Shun and founder of the BUDDHIST COMPASSION RELIEF TZU CHI ASSOCIATION, Taiwan's largest Buddhist group; Xingyun, founder of FOGUANGSHAN; and SHENG YEN, founder of the DHARMA DRUM MOUNTAIN ASSOCIATION.

Further reading: Chou Hsiang-kuang, *T'ai-hsü: His Life and Teachings* (Allahabad, India: Indo-Chinese Literature, 1957); Donald S. Lopez, Jr., *Modern Buddhism: Readings for the Unenlightened* (London: Penguin Books, 2002); Don A. Pittman, "The Modern Buddhist Reformer T'ai-hsu on Christianity," *Buddhist Christian Studies* 13 (1993): 71–83; T'ai Hsu, *Lectures in Buddhism* (Paris, 1928); Holmes Welch, *The Buddhist Revival in China* (Cambridge: Harvard University Press, 1968).

Takuan Soho (1573–1645) *Rinzai Zen leader*

Takuan Soho, who took the lead in a revival of RINZAI ZEN in the early 17th century, became a practitioner as a young man. His studies culminated in a period with Itto Shoteki (1539–1612), a leading Rinzai master and head of Yoshun-ji temple at Sakai (near present-day Osaka). Takuan emerged on the scene when the discipline at the main Rinzai centers was believed to have slipped, especially at the main Kyoto temples, Daitoku-ji and Myoshin-ji. Takuan went on to become the abbot of Daitoku-ji (1608), and along with his contemporary, Gudo Toshoku, he took the lead in reforming the training at the two temples.

Trouble developed in 1626 when the shogunate stepped into the affairs of Daitoku-ji and Myoshin-ji by laying down a new set of regulations that both were expected to follow. One regulation concerned the appointment of new chief abbots. Shortly thereafter, the emperor, who traditionally had a voice in the selection process, approved the appointment of a new abbot named Shoin, but the shogun opposed the new abbot. Takuan protested the shogun's intrusion, but as a result of the controversy, he was forced into exile and the emperor had to abdicate. With several other high-ranking Rinzai officials, Takuan moved to the north of Honshu, far away from Kyoto. He would later be pardoned and even welcomed by the new shogun, Tokugawa Iemitsu (1571–1646), who assumed power in 1632.

In his postexile years, Takuan also became the spiritual adviser of the famed swordsman Yagyu Murenori (1571–1646), the shogun's tutor in the use of the sword, and Tukuan's treatise on ZEN BUDDHISM and swordsmanship is the primary source of his contemporary fame. Tukuan wrote widely and remains a very influential voice within the Rinzai community.

Further reading: Nobuko Hirose, *Immovable Wisdom: The Art of Zen Strategy: The Teachings of Takuan Soho* (Shaftsbury, U.K.: Element Books, 1992); Takuan Soho, *The Unfettered Mind: Writings of the Zen Master to the Sword Master* (Tokyo: Kodansha International, 1988).

tanha

Tanha, or "craving," is one of the 12 links in the 12-fold chain of causation. An understanding of *tanha* is crucial in the practice of Buddhism, since craving creates new karma, which ties one to the world of SAMSARA, or suffering. One counters the strong, overpowering urges of craving through the development of *smrti* (mindfulness).

Further reading: Buddhanet. "The Buddhanet Basic Buddhism Guide: Dependent Arising." Available online. URL: http://www.buddhanet.net/e-learning/depend.htm. Accessed on May 22, 2006.

Tan Luan (476–542) *founder of the Pure Land school of Chinese Buddhism*

Tan Luan was a scholar-monk during the Northern and Southern dynasties (439–589 C.E.) period in Chinese history. He also studied DAOISM with an influential SHANGQING DAOISM master, Tao Hongjing, who focused on the quest for immortality. He later met BODHIRUCI (d. 527 C.E.), a famous translator originally from India. Bodhiruci was a proponent of PURE LAND BUDDHISM teachings, and he explained to Tan Luan that immortality could only be achieved through devotion to the Pure Land. Tan Luan thereafter left the Daoist teachings behind and focused on study of such Pure Land texts as the Meditation on the Buddha of Infinite Light Sutra. Tan Luan saw Pure Land practice as the easy way to achieve release from SAMSARA. He wrote several commentaries on Pure Land sutras. He is the first of the five Chinese Pure Land patriarchs.

Tantra

Tantra means, literally, "web" or "woof," and by extension Tantra refers to a system or collection of teachings. The teachings to which the term *Tantra* refers are the reality beyond the surface of experience, that continuum where SAMSARA merges with NIRVANA. A *tantra* is a shortened form of a mantra that would be extremely long if not reduced. It may be related to the root *tatri*, "to explain."

Tantra teachings began as a literary form in the early Gupta period in India. Religious activity during this period, the fourth and fifth centuries C.E., moved from oral to written religious texts. There was at that time a great effort to record legends, philosophical thoughts, and political treatises. Buddhist Tantras were one form of the many materials recorded during this period. These early texts included such revealed Tantra works as Guhyasamaja (Assembly of secrets), one of the root texts of VAJRAYANA BUDDHISM, which developed later.

Tantra was a revolution in religious practice, Hindu as well as Buddhist. The Tantrikas (practitioners of Tantra) did not engage in metaphysical speculation and instead focused on practice and exercises. The main thrust was devotional mysticism. At the same time Buddhism was waning in India, and Brahmanism had begun to redefine itself as "Hinduism." Tantra was one reason for these shifts.

Tantrika teachers held that there were four classes of literature, Venda, Smrti, Purana, and Agama, and that these were related to the historical period: *satya, treat, dvapara,* and *kali.* Therefore, the correct type of literature for the current age, that of *kali,* should be Agama or Tantra.

Tantra is often taken to mean the worship of female deities, and so need take no special forms of worship. However, Tantra does specify *how* worship is to proceed. Tantra, strictly speaking, means the worship of Sakti, or female energy, the cult of Sakti.

Besides Buddhist Tantras there are several Hindu cults: the Saivas, Vaisnavas, Sauras, Ganapatyas.

Further reading: Georg Feurerstein, *Tantra: The Path of Ecstasy* (Boston: Shambhala, 1998); Pranabananda Jash, "The Tantras: An Excursus into Origins," in N. N. Bhattacharyya and Amartya Ghosh, eds., *Tantric Buddhism: Centennial Tribute to Dr. Benoytosh Bhattacharyya* (New Delhi: Manohar, 1999), 137–145; John Powers, *Introduction to Tibetan Buddhism* (Ithaca, N.Y.: Snow Lion, 1995); Giuseppe Tucci, *The Religions of Tibet.* Translated by Geoffrey Samuel (London: Routledge & Kegan Paul, 1970); Alex Wayman, *The Buddhist Tantras: Light on Indo-Tibetan Esotericism* (Delhi: Motilal Banarsidass, 1973).

Tantric Buddhism (Tantrayana, Mantrayana, Vajrayana)

Tantric Buddhism, or Tantrayana, is the *yana,* or "vehicle," of the Tantra. It is often said to be the third vehicle, after HINAYANA and MAHAYANA, although this interpretation is not accepted by all Buddhists. Alternative terms are *Mantrayana* and *Vajrayana,* the "Indomitable Vehicle."

Tantric Buddhism developed in northeastern India in the region of Orissa and Bengal, from the 7th century C.E. It had a general emphasis on magical elements and worship of deities as a means to reach ENLIGHTENMENT. It had its major expansion in Tibet but also spread to China, Mongolia, and Japan, where it is known as SHINGON.

See also CHINA, BUDDHISM IN; CHINA-TIBET; CHINESE ESOTERIC BUDDHISM; MONGOLIA, BUDDHISM IN; SHINGON.

Further reading: BuddhaNet. "Tantrayana." Available online. URL: http://www.buddhanet.net/e-learning/dharmadata/fdd4.htm. Accessed on May 15, 2006.

tanuki

Often called a Japanese raccoon, the *tanuki* is actually a dog species native to Japan and parts of the Asia mainland. There are many legendary stories about magical *tanuki* in Japanese mythology. *Tanuki* tend to play tricks on hunters. They can cause illusions such as changing excrement into a meal. They love to drink Japanese rice wine and are often imagined carrying a bottle of sake. Sculpted depictions of *tanuki* usually include huge testicles, which are symbols of good luck. As has the *kitsune* (fox), the *tanuki* has magical powers. Both are said to be messengers of the god Shinto Inari.

Further reading: Juliet Piggot, *Japanese Mythology* (New York: Peter Bedrick Books, 1991); Norman A. Rubin, "Ghosts, Demons and Spirits in Japanese Lore." Asianart.com. Available online. URL: www.asianart.com/articles/rubin. Accessed on August 26, 2005; Mark Schumaker, "Tanuki, Odanuki, Mujina." Shinto and Buddhist Corner. Available online. URL: www.Onmarkproductions.com/html/tanuki.shtml. Accessed on August 26, 2005.

Taoism   *See* DAOISM.

tariki   *See* JIRIKI.

tathagata

Tathagata, "the thus-come one," is one of the 10 titles of the historical Buddha. "Thus-come," from the Sanskrit term *tatha-gata,* indicates that the individual appears in the same way as preceding Buddhas, from "thusness." The Buddha referred to himself as the Tathagata, indicating that as an enlightened being he considered himself to be different from other beings.

Tathagata is also a title used with other Buddhas and enlightened beings. For instance, Japanese SHINGON and TENDAI writings often refer to the Five Tathagatas: VAIROCANA, Amoghasiddhi, Ratnasambhava, Aksobhya, and AMITABHA. These five are pictured in the Kongokai (Diamond-world) and Taizokai (Womb-world) MANDALAS.

MAHAYANA BUDDHISM writers developed the Tathagata concept in several directions. In the Nirvana Sutra the Buddha states, "The Tathagata is the Dharma," thus equating himself with his teachings at the most abstract level. In YOGACARA BUDDHISM writings Tathagata refers to the Buddha in his NIRMANAKAYA nature. In this aspect of TRIKAYA (three-body) theory the *nirmanakaya,* or transformation, body is the form in which Buddha appears to other humans, the historical form in which he appeared (as Gautama).

See also TATHATA.

Further reading: Kogen Mizuno, *Essentials of Buddhism: Basic Terminology of Buddhist Philosophy and Practice.* Translated by Gaynor Sekimori (1972. Reprint, Tokyo: Kosei Publishing, 1996).

tathagata-garbha

TATHAGATA is the enlightened individual, the "thus come one." This is a term of respect for the Buddha himself. In the middle period of MAHAYANA BUDDHISM development in India, roughly 300–700 C.E., a related idea, the concept of the *tathagata-garbha* (embryo), was introduced. It reflected that all beings carry the potential to become enlightened.

The Tathagata-garbha Sutra and another nine works, including the NIRVANA SUTRA, spelled out the nature of the *tathagata-gharba*. These Mahayana sutras appeared after the PRAJNAPARAMITA group of Buddhist scriptures. The *prajnaparamita* (perfection of wisdom) writings performed the initial function of what we could call deconstructing the nature of the self. Based solidly on the Buddha's teachings of non-self, the *prajnaparamita* formulated the presence of emptiness (*sunyata*), a "general emptiness" throughout nature.

When the *tathagata-garbha* sutras appeared they reinterpreted the Buddha's teachings in light of something else, a pure mind, called a Buddha seed or embryo. This in a way allowed the ATMAN (self) concept, which had been all but banished in the face of the *prajnaparamita* criticisms, to be reinserted into Buddhism, in a highly refined way. The *tathagata-garbha* teachings held that the mind is originally pure but becomes defiled. The *tathagata-garbha* concept, as well as the idea of *sunyata* and the later YOGACARA concept of storehouse consciousness, would later form important parts of the Chinese concept of BUDDHA NATURE.

The *tathagata-garbha* concept was used later as the basis to explain codependent arising (PRATITYA SAMUTPADA) in the text The Awaking of Faith in the Mahayana. In this work the *tathagata-garbha* gives rise to all phenomena through the mechanism of *pratitya-samutpada.*

In the *tathagata-garbha* concept we see the importance of cultural differences between India, where the concept of Buddha nature was developed in detail, and China, which added its own interpretations. The Sanskrit term *garbha* (embryo) was translated in Chinese as *zang* (womb or "storehouse"), a difference that led to further development of the *foxing* (Buddha nature) concept in China.

Further reading: Shenpen Hookham, trans., *The Shrimaladevi Sutra* (Oxford: Longchen Foundation, 1998).

tathata

Tathata literally means "suchness." The *tathata* is the ground of ultimate reality, the absolute nature of phenomena. A Buddha, by definition, can effortlessly see the true nature of reality.

Further reading: Mizuno Kogen, *Basic Buddhist Concepts.* (Tokyo: Kosei, 1987).

tea ceremony

The tea ceremony, at once intricate and exact and promoting values of simplicity and attention to the present moment, attempted to raise everyday life to its artistic potential. It also became a supplement to ZAZEN, sitting meditation, in that attention to the successive acts of the ceremony focused participants' concentration on the present moment, which ZEN BUDDHISM teaches is the only reality in one's life.

Buddhism played an important role in the diffusion of tea into Japanese culture, beginning with its initial importation from China in the eighth century and the several new schools of Buddhism that settled in at NARA. The original form of the tea was termed "brick tea." The bricks were created by pounding tea leaves into a round ball. The ball could then be cut into pieces and placed in boiling water. The primary use of tea was medicinal (including its use as a substitute for alcohol, a prescription for excessive drinkers), as it did not taste very good. The drinking of tea was often ritualized and accompanied, for example, the recitation of Buddhist sutras.

EISAI (1141–1215), best known as the founder of Zen Buddhism, the Japanese form of Buddhism emphasizing meditation as the primary means of ENLIGHTENMENT, also introduced a new form of tea from China, powdered tea, an improvement on the foul-tasting brick tea. In his primary treatise *On Drinking Tea and Prolonging One's Life,* however, he initially attempted to promote the drinking of tea to the shogun by emphasizing its medicinal qualities. DOGEN (1200–53), the founder of SOTO ZEN, also had tea with him when he returned from China. He later developed an improved tea cup and made tea drinking part of the Soto Zen lifestyle.

Within the Zen community, tea drinking became a popular activity and was gradually incorporated into the Zen view of the world. It was during the time of Ikkyu Sojun (a RINZAI ZEN leader and abbot of the Daitoku-ji), who promoted the arts in all their aspects, that the full-blown tea ceremony developed. Among the many people hosted at Daitoku-ji was Murata Juko (1423–1501), known as a tea master, who developed the ceremony. He was succeeded by Takeno Joo (1502–55) and Sen no Riyku (1522–91), who created the "way of tea" (*chado*) as an integral part of Zen life. Daitoku-ji became the center from which the way of tea was disseminated through the Zen world and beyond.

As the ceremony developed, it was also moved into separate space, the tea hut. The hut, located in a garden, and its surrounding developed symbolic meanings such that moving into the tearoom was itself a foretaste of entering NIRVANA.

Tea ceremonies are still popular in Japan. They involve a host and one or more guests. The main guest works closely with the host to ensure all steps in the tea preparation sequence are performed smoothly and that nothing stands in the way of the guests' appreciation of the flavor, care, and visual pleasures of the carefully planned ritual.

Further reading: Heinrich Dumoulin, *Zen Buddhism: A History.* 2 vols. 2d ed. (New York: Macmillan, 1988); Kazuo Kasahara, ed., *A History of Japanese Religion.* Translated by Paul McCarthy and Gaynor Sekimori (Tokyo: Kosei, 2001); E. Dale Saunders, *Buddhism in Japan* (Philadelphia: University of Pennsylvania Press, 1964); Toichi Yoshioka, *Zen* (Kawamata, Japan: Hoikusha, 2002).

Temple of Heaven   *See* TIANTAN.

Tendai

Tendai is one of the oldest schools of Japanese Buddhism and remains a major group in contemporary Japanese religions. There are more than 2,500 Tendai temples in Japan today and hundreds of thousands of followers. Tendai, the Japanese version of the Chinese TIAN TAI BUDDHISM, was founded by SAICHO (767–822), who as a young priest in Japan encountered the works of ZHI YI (538–597), the founder of Tian Tai Buddhism. In 804, he went to China, where he studied for a year at Mount Tian T'ai and returned with a number of Tian Tai texts. The founding of the Tendai school he had established outside Kyoto on Mt. HIEI was signaled by the emperor's agreement to allow two priests trained by Saicho to be formally ordained each year.

Saicho, later known by the honorific title *Dengyo Daishi,* followed the Tian Tai perspective that attempted to classify the spectrum of Buddhist SUTRAS and approaches to Buddhism on a fourfold scale: the HINAYANA teachings, the teachings common to all MAHAYANA BUDDHISM, the teachings unique to Mahayana as opposed to Hinayana, and the perfect teachings, as contained in the LOTUS SUTRA. He angered the Buddhist officials at NARA by suggesting that they taught Hinayana Buddhism.

The Lotus Sutra was seen as above all other Buddhist texts. On the basis of his reading of the sutra, Saicho declared the potential Buddhahood of all beings, an idea that stood in stark contrast to the view of the most established Buddhist leadership of the time at Nara, who taught that some people were unable to arrive at enlightenment and only a few could reach complete Buddhahood. This disagreement became the basis of Saicho's appeal to the government to allow the independence of the Tendai community from the Nara officials.

The belief that all partook of BUDDHA NATURE also led Saicho to show great respect toward all the Buddhas and bodhisattvas, and as a result Tendai temples tended to include a number and variety of BODHISATTVA images. It also led to an essential teaching that all believers should have the bodhisattva ideal—seeking self-perfection and benefiting others—as the goal that guides their outward lives.

While Saicho had pursued some aspects of VAJRAYANA Buddhism, the distinctive outline of Tendai Esotericism would be developed by his disciples, primarily ENNIN (794–864) and ANNEN (c. 841–c. 901). Beginning in 838, Ennin spent nine years in China studying esoteric practices. Among the practices he encountered was meditation upon and invocation of the bodhisattva AMITABHA. The establishment of the veneration of Amitabha at Mt. Hiei would later nurture the emergence of PURE LAND BUDDHISM.

Ennin also studied the secret meditations and rituals related to the bodhisattva VAIROCANA as represented in two MANDALAS, the Diamond Realm mandala and the Womb Realm mandala. Ennin tended to see the esoteric teachings as superior to those of the Lotus Sutra, a perspective clearly stated by Annen. Mandalas pictorially present the spiritual world and proper actions related to them allow the believer to partake of that spiritual realm.

With the rise of Esotericism within Tendai, various subgroups developed among the leaders and various lineages of practice. In many cases, these lineages became the basis of separate Tendai sects, which today number more than 20 in Japan.

The year 966 was a landmark for the Tendai community as a great fire engulfed Engakyu-ji, the Tendai headquarters complex on Mt. Hiei. It fell to the then-abbot Ryogen (912–985) to raise the funds for the rebuilding, and he did. At the same time he gave a new emphasis to education and initiated an era of Tendai learning and expansion.

The largest segment of the Tendai community is that with headquarters at Mt. Hiei. It has associated temples across Japan divided into 25 districts. It sponsored Taisho University (operated in cooperation with the JODO SHU and SHINGON Buddhists). It has some 600,000 adherents in Japan, and a few centers outside the country.

Further reading: *Buddhist Denominations and Schools in Japan* (Tokyo: Bukkto Dendo Kyokai, 1984); Paul Groner, *Ryogen and Mount Hiei: Japanese Tendai in the Tenth Century* (Honolulu: University of Hawaii Press, 2002); Leo M. Pruden and Paul L. Swanson, trans., *The Essentials of the Vinaya Tradition: The Collected Teachings of the Tendai Lotus School* (Berkeley, Calif.: Numata Center for Buddhist Translation & Research, 1996); Michael R. Saso, *Tantric Art and Meditation: The Tendai Tradition* (Honolulu: Tendai Educational Foundation, 1990).

Tengu

Tengu are Japanese popular deities with both Shinto and Buddhist roots. *Tengu* literally means "Heavenly Dog." However, their features are similar to those of crows, not dogs. They are birdlike and have wings. They like to play tricks and are famed for making fun of monks and samurai alike. Tengu, as skilled warriors, are the patron deities of MARTIAL ARTS in Japan.

Tengu probably entered Japan along with Buddhism in the sixth and seventh centuries C.E. They combine features of the Chinese Tiangou mountain deity and the Hindu-Buddhist winged deity Garuda. Tengu were interpreted to be transformations of SHINTO gods of the mountains (*yama no kami*). There are generally two types of Tengu: those with birds' head and beak and those with human torso but bird's wings and a long nose (called Yamabushi Tengu). The long nose is also associated with the Shinto god Sarudahiko, who can look like a monkey. The long nose symbolizes the Tengu's dislike of arrogance; arrogant Buddhist priests were given long noses as Yamabushi Tengu or, after dying, sent to a special part of hell, the Tengudo, Realm of the Tengu.

Tengu is also said in some versions to be an emanation of SUSANO-O NO MIKOTO, the ancient Shinto deity.

Tengu masks are common in religious festivals and parades in Japan. Images of Tengu first appeared in KAMAKURA period (1192–1333) paintings. They are frequently found as characters in Noh and Kabuki plays.

Further reading: Mark Schumaker, "Tengu: The Slayer of Vanity." Shinto and Buddhist Corner. Available online. URL: www. Onmarkproductions.com/html/tengu.shtml. Accessed on August 26, 2005.

Tenmangu shrines

Tenmangu refers to the shrines built to honor the Shinto god of scholarship and learning, Tenman. Since success in school has much importance in Japan, the more than 12,000 Tenmangu shrines across Japan are well used.

This deity developed from a historical figure, Suguwara no Michizane (845–903 C.E.). Michizane served in the imperial court at Kyoto as a high-ranking government official, scholar, and trusted counselor to Emperor Uda. In spite of his position, he became the enemy of the powerful Fujiwara clan; controversy developed over a disagreement concerning Japan's relation with China, and the Fujiwaras conspired to rid the court of Michizane. Their slander of him eventually led to his exile to Daizaifu, near Fukuoka on the southern island of Kyushu, in 901. His life at Dazaifu, Kyushu, was one of relative hardship compared to his life in Kyoto, but he became known for the forbearance, the serenity of his person, and his scholarly studies. He died in 903.

According to the traditional story, the shrine in Dazaifu was a result of his ill-fated funeral. Only a few people attended, including his single follower, Yasuyuki Umasake. His coffin had been placed on a carriage pulled by a cow. As they progressed to the planned gravesite, the cow suddenly stopped and refused to go forward. As a result, the body was buried where the procession had halted. The Dazaifu Tenmangu Shrine was built over the burial site. It has subsequently become one the largest and most visited in the country. The shrine is known for the many plum trees on the grounds.

Meanwhile, after his death, over a period of several decades, severe earthquakes and notably strong thunderstorms hit Kyoto and the surrounding regions. Meanwhile, Michizane was undergoing a process of divinization, partially a result of what many considered a great wrong done to him. The disasters were seen as a result of Michizane's displeasure. Eventually, the imperial court moved to appease the deceased scholar. The emperor gave him the posthumous title *Karai Ten jin,* or God of Fire and Thunder. By the later Heian period (845–1185) Tenman was venerated as a Shinto KAMI (deity) of literature and calligraphy.

Michizane's gradual rise in status culminated in the erection of a shrine to his memory in Kyoto in the 940s, the Kitano Tenmangu shrine. It has subsequently grown into a large complex. The first visit by an emperor was in 1004, but it has since been a favorite spot for visits by emperors and high government officials. The shrine has additional fame that due to the presence of a cinnamon tree, the oldest tree in Kyoto. It is considered the head shrine of all the various Tenmangu shrines in Japan. Besides this temple and the Dazaifu Tenmangu, there is another major Tenmangu at Kobiragata, near Fukushima.

Further reading: Robert Borgen, *Sugawara no Michizane and the Early Heian Court* (Honolulu: University of Hawaii Press, 1986); Fuchu Internet. "Tenmangu." Available online. URL: www.fuchu.or.jp/~eguma/e%20tenmanguu.htm. Accessed on August 22, 2005; Kitano Tenman-gu. "Kitano Tenman-Gu" Available online. URL: www.kitanotenmangu.or.jp/eigo/. Accessed on August 22, 2005; John H. Martin and Phyllis G. Martin, *Kyoto: A Cultural Guide* (Rutland, Vt.: Charles E. Tuttle, 1998).

ten *paramitas*   *See* PARAMITA.

Tenrikyo

Tenrikyo is a major contemporary, independent Japanese religion. Tenriyko has more than 1 million members worldwide, mainly in Japan. Although it was influenced by SHINTO to some extent, it is very much a separate religious group, with its own ideas and history. Tenrikyo is the first of an important category of Japanese religion known as *shin shukyo*, or NEW RELIGIONS. The "New Religions" such as Tenrikyo have had a strong influence on religious studies worldwide.

Tenrikyo is, literally, the "religion of heavenly principle." Tenrikyo teaches the fundamental principle of heaven—healing.

Tenrikyo was founded by Nakayama Miki (1798–1887), a farmer's wife, in 1838. Her reason for founding Tenrikyo resulted from a healing experience. The healing deity Great General of Heaven (*Ten no daishogun*) announced Miki would be his carrier on earth. This experience of *kami* possession was not new in Shinto, but in the so-called Shinto New Religions, such as Tenrikyo, its orientation changed. Not only were the chosen people messengers for the *kami*, they were aware of their chosen status and worked to build the religion.

Miki was assisted in the work of early development by Iburi Izo, a carpenter whose wife had been healed by Miki. Izo became leader when Miki died in 1887. At this point he took on the additional role of *honseki*, or oracle. In this role he spoke for Miki's spirit. The words of Miki, uttered through Izo, were eventually collected and formed part of the Tenrikyo sacred writings, the Osashizu. Additional sacred writings are the Ofudesaki, a communication from God (referred to as Tenri O no Midoto) to Nakayama Miki, and the Mikagura-uta, a collection of poems.

Tenrikyo was oppressed by the government for many years and did not receive recognition as a religion until 1908. Nakayama Miki herself was imprisoned 17 times for various minor offenses. Nakayama remained critical of the government and the leaders. When Tenrikyo was finally recognized it was as one of the 13 sect Shinto groups. Its association with Shinto was formally terminated in 1970 when Tenrikyo withdrew from the Association of Shinto Sects.

Today Tenrikyo's main offices are in Tenri City, a town near Nara. Here is located the *jiba,* the piece of land from which the human race is said to have originated. In the Shinden, or principal place of worship, is the *kanrondai*, a sacred pillar that is a center of pilgrimage and healing. In addition at Tenri City can be found the Kyosoden, the sanctuary of the foundress, in which Miki's spirit is said to reside.

Tenrikyo ritual centers on the *kagura tsutome,* or the dance of creation. This is performed on the 26th of each month in the presence of the Shinbashira, a descendant of Nakayama Miki. The *kagura tsutome* is performed around the Kanrodai pillar in the Shinden. Tenrikyo offers new members several courses of study for initiation. The *besseki* are nine lectures required for initiation, and the *shuyoka* is a three-month-long intensive course. Once members have completed *shuyoka,* they are allowed to perform healing rituals using hand gestures. These gestures are the *teodori,* or hand dance.

Tenrikyo operates several community institutions, including a hospital and museum. Tenri University was founded in 1925. These are all located at Tenri City.

Further reading: Peter Clarke, *Bibliography of Japanese New Religious Movements* (Richmond, U.K.: Japan Library, 1999); Robert S. Elwood, Jr., *Tenrikyo: A Pilgrimage Faith* (Tenri City, Japan: Oyasato Research Institute, 1982); Henry Van Straelen, *The Religion of Divine Wisdom* (Kyoto: Veritas Shoin, 1957).

terma

A *terma* is a secret treasure, usually a text containing secret teachings that has been hidden to await discovery by a specially inspired person, a *terton,* at a later, more auspicious time. In Tibetan

Buddhism, a number of texts are believed to have been written in the eighth century by PADMASAMBHAVA and his disciple (and teacher in her own right) YESHE TSOGYAL (both eighth century C.E.). Toward the end of their lives, Buddhism underwent a period of suppression that threatened its very existence. Thus they took pains to hide some of their teachings.

In general *terma* are said to be texts that are either deemed to be too advanced for the faithful at the time they were written or texts that were threatened with being destroyed. In each case they were hidden to preserve them for future generations. Among the best known of *terma* texts is the Bar do thos grad, Tibetan teachings concerning the afterlife generally ascribed to Padmasambhava, but rediscovered by Karma Lingpa in the 14th century.

Obviously, the hiding of texts to prevent their destruction by enemies of the faith is practical during times when there is a real threat. It is also the case that most *terma* texts appear to be products of the time in which they were "rediscovered" and serve to give credentials to new and innovative teachings by ascribing them to a revered teacher of an earlier time. Using such means to introduce new writings is by no means unique to Buddhism; numerous examples could be cited from Christian and Western esoteric history.

Further reading: Padmasambhava, *Bardo Thödol: The Tibetan Book of the Dead.* Translated by Robert A. Thurman (New York: Bantam, 1993); Tulku Thondup, *Hidden Teachings of Tibet: An Explanation of the Terma Tradition of Tibetan Buddhism* (Somerville, Mass.: Wisdom, 1997).

Thai Forest Meditation Tradition

Today Thai Forest Meditation is an important strain of THERAVADA Buddhism, although it is not organized tightly enough to be called a "school." The movement emphasizes strict adherence to the VINAYA and meditation, and its teachers are popular in America and Europe, as well as Thailand, its place of origin. In the late-19th century, the Thai Buddhist establishment began to react to a variety of new currents in intellectual thought brought on by interaction with the West as well as internal challenges to the role of the SANGHA in Thai culture. Voices arose calling for both reform and development of the sangha and a return to traditionalist standards. In the midst of these tensions, there arose individual monks who were concerned about the laxity of many monasteries in regard to the discipline of the monk's life and a deemphasis on the teachings and practice, especially regarding meditation.

Thus it was that by the end of the century a few monks began to drop out of the mainstream of sangha life and move into isolated regions in the northeast region of the country to practice meditation (VIPASSANA) and study the Vinaya, the original rules for the Buddhist monastic life. In the first generation, the most outstanding teacher was Phra Mun Bhuridatta Thera (1870–1949), better known as AJAAN MUN. Ordained as a BHIKSU in 1893, he spent most of his life in the forests of northeast Thailand and began to attract other monks to him. Toward the end of his life, he received a young seeker who had found his way to Mun's isolated forest home. AJAHN CHAH (1918–81) would carry on the Forest Tradition, wandering through northern Thailand for seven years.

In 1954, Chah founded Wat Pah Pong, a monastery that would give an institutional base to the loosely organized movement from the years before World War II. As word of the *wat* spread, Chah attracted some of Mun's students and a host of new monks. Life was severe with long hours spent each day in meditation and strict adherence to the Vinaya expected of all residents. While never as popular as some of the concurrent movements spawned in the urban centers, the meditation movement led by Chah attracted a number of intellectuals and those drawn to the simple monastic environment he advocated. Over his life some 20 additional monasteries modeled on Wat Pah Pong were established.

Among the monasteries inspired by Wat Pah Pong was Wat Pah Nanachat (or International Forest Monastery), founded in 1975 by AJAHN SUMEDHO, an American, to provide a place to receive men from the West attracted to the movement. It would in turn become the launching pad for transplantation of the Forest Tradition to the West. Sumedho traveled to England in 1977 and remained to found Wat Pah Cittaviveka, the Chithurst Forest Monastery, the first of a network of Thai monasteries in Europe and North America.

The Thai Forest Meditation Tradition continues in Thailand through Chah's students and in the West through Sumedho and his students. Internationally, it has become a valued element in the spread of VIPASSANA meditation among an emerging lay Buddhist public.

Further reading: Ajahn Chah, *Seeing the Way: Buddhist Reflections on the Spiritual Life* (Hemel Hempstead, U.K.: Amaravati, 1989); Venerable Acariya Mun Bhuridatta, *The Biography of the Venerable Acariya Mun.* Than Acharn Maha Boowa Nanasampanno. Available online. URL: http://www.luangta.or.th/english/site/books.php. Accessed on September 22, 2005; Phra Rajavaramuni, *Thai Buddhism in the Buddhist World* (North Hollywood, Calif.: Wat Thai of Los Angeles, 1984).

Thailand, Buddhism in

The Tai people migrated into the area of modern Thailand and other parts of Southeast Asia around the eighth century C.E. There are in fact no written records from this migration, and this theory about their early development is based largely on linguistic reconstructions. These early migrants speaking a similar language are referred to as Tai to distinguish them from the later, modern Thai people and nation. They probably migrated south into Southeast Asia from China.

A state established by a related ethnic group and that spoke a form of Tai formed in Yunnan, southern China. By 752 this state was strong enough to defeat the forces of Tang dynasty China (689–907 C.E.). This kingdom, Nan Chao, served as a northern buffer to the Tai peoples as they moved south. During this period no other Tai states were significant; Southeast Asia was dominated by the Champa in Vietnam, the Khmer Empire centered on Angkor Wat, and, always in the background, the Chinese empire, then experiencing a period of significant success under the Tang rulers. The Khmers eventually dominated most of the region through Laos to the Malay Peninsula. The various Tai groups were, in effect, sandwiched between the inland Nan Chao and the expansive Khmer.

In the meantime a separate culture, the Dvaravati, had developed around 600 centered on the Gulf of Thailand. This early culture was Buddhist and spoke the Mon language. It left significant though few records in stone; there are ruins in sites in central Thailand. The Dvaravati civilization was soon superseded by the Khmer, but many elements of Dvaravati culture were retained as a kind of cultural memory by the subsequent Thai civilization. As Tai peoples continued to settle in the Dvaravati area, portions of the Mon peoples in turn migrated west and established states centered in Pagan and Thaton, Burma.

However, the various small Tai states in the period 1000–1200 existed essentially as peripheral client states of the powerful Khmer empire. These groups were situated on the fringe of the more powerful states in Angkor, Pagan, and Vietnam. All of these states became unified in their worldview of Buddhism.

In the 13th century two events changed this balance. First was the pressure of Tai peoples moving south; they had become the majority throughout the central Chao Phrya plains. The second development was the sudden appearance of Mongol armies who, having conquered China, invaded Nan Chao in 1253 and attacked Burma in 1283 and 1286.

THE FIRST THAI KINGDOMS

From this period, the mid-13th-century C.E., we have written records of Thai states. The first of these, Lan Na, was in northern Thailand around the new city of Chiang Mai.

New states also emerged to the south, in Nakhon Si Thammarat on the Malay Peninsula and Sukothai in the central Thai plains. Little is known about Nakhon Si Thammarat, except that it was a trading nation with extensive ties with Sri Lanka, including connections with the Theravadin monastery of Mahavihara there.

Sukhothai was originally a Khmer outpost established in the 1100s. It was taken over by Thai groups and, under Ramkhamhaeng (r. 1279–98), became a powerful local power, careful to maintain diplomatic ties with Lan Na and Nakhon Si Thammarat. The new state was solidly Buddhist and promoted monasteries. Ramkhamhaeng himself is said to have invented a new script in 1293 that is the foundation of today's Thai script.

Lan Na revived as a cultural center in the reign of Ku Na (1355–85). He established a new sect of forest monks and in 1369 invited a Sukhothai monk to establish the Singhalese Order. This monk, Sumana, became abbot of a new monastery in Chiang Mai in 1371. This Singhalese sect was a dominant cultural force in northern Thailand for several centuries.

In 1475–78 King Tilokaracha of Lan Na built the great *chedi* (STUPA) still visible in Chiang Mai, Maha Chedi Luang. A major Pali history, *Jinakalamali,* was written in Chiang Mai during the reign of Muang Kaeo (r. 1495–1526). This work chronicles the importance of Buddhism to the state; the king was said to have founded monasteries, copied the Buddhist texts, and cast new images of the Buddha, in works of great merit. Muang Kaeo also continued to support the scholarly sect of Singhalese Buddhism established by Sumana.

LUANG PRABANG

The people of the Laotian kingdom centered on the city of Luang Prabang were basically Tai and to this day speak a language, Laotian, very close to Thai. As with Sukhothai and many other kingdoms, Luang Prabang became powerful with the growth of Tai peoples and the weakening of the Khmer state in the 13th and 14th centuries. Luang Prabang state was said to have been founded by the legendary Cambodian prince Fa Ngum in 1353. Subsequent kings engaged in constant struggles with the Vietnamese and the northern Thai at Lan Na. One ruler, Visun (r. 1501–20), imported a Buddha image to Vientiane, the new capital, in 1512, a sign that an identity was growing among the previously homogeneous Tai groups. King Phothisarat (r. 1520–47) proscribed Brahmanic and animistic elements in religious or ceremonial practices current at the time; in contrast, to practice in Ayudhya or Lan Na, he favored a strict application of Buddhist ritual.

AYUDHYA

These minor states in the area of the Tai peoples were eventually superseded by a much more powerful Thai entity, Ayudhya, which held sway from 1351 to 1569 and dominated trade and populations in central Southeast Asia. Ayudhya absorbed the older Kingdom of Sukhothai in 1438. With the Khmer empire now a memory, Ayudhya's primary rival was Burma.

The Ayudhya kings attempted to expand their empires through trade and the use of awe-inspiring projects. King Ramathibodi II (r. 1491–1529) built the largest Buddha image known until recent times—a cast image 16 meters high covered with 173 kilograms of gold. Subsequent kings continued to make such gestures even as they increased trade with European powers and built up their own military powers. Ayudhya was then so powerful that it was requested to help the sangha in Ceylon (Sri Lanka) restore Singhalese Buddhism. Borommakot sent 18 monks to Kandy in Sri Lanka to establish the Siam order there in 1751. A second mission was sent in 1755.

Ayudhaya's period of greatness was not to last, however. The empire experienced increasing pressure, especially from France and, to the west, the ancient enemy Burma. The Burmese struck fatally in 1767, razing the capital and taking Lan Na, before they were forced out.

THE BANGKOK PERIOD
(1767–TODAY)

The eventual victor in the battle with Burma was Chaophrya Chakri ("Commander of Chaophrya") Thong Duang (1737–1809). He unified the Thai land again and reigned as Rama I (r. 1782–1809). He and his brother retook Vientiane in Laos and took two important Buddha images to their new Thai capital, the Emerald Buddha and the Phrabang. Rama I beat off a major Burmese invasion in 1785 and built his new capital at Bangkok.

Rama IV (r. 1851–68) was the popular and modernizing King Mongkut. He had become a monk one week before his elder brother, Rama III (r. 1824–51), became king. While still a monk he devoted himself to study of Pali and Buddhist writings. In 1826, he sat for the Pali examinations, the usual route for promotion in the monastic hierarchy. Mongkut was critical of the ordination rituals then prevalent in Thai Buddhism and in 1833 established a new sect, the DHAMMAYUTTIKA NIKAYA, or "Order Adhering to the Dhamma." He and his followers wore monks' robes with both shoulders covered, instead of one uncovered, and followed austere daily practices. The new group was officially recognized by the king and housed at Wat Bowonniwet, where Mongkut was abbot. To this day the Dhammayuttika and the MAHANIKAYA, the followers of mainstream Thai Buddhism, remain the two traditional orders in Thailand.

Mongkut's successor, Rama V (Chulalongkorn) (r. 1886–1910), encouraged further reform in all areas of life in Thailand, including Buddhist education. These reforms inevitably provoked reactionary responses in some areas. In the northeast and Laos a Holy Men's Rebellion in 1902 was led by people who claimed that the end of the world was near. They also claimed to have supernatural powers. They prophesied that *thao thammikarat*, the Lord of the Law, was about to arrive. These rebellions were put down, and modernization proceeded.

MODERN DEVELOPMENTS
AND POPULAR BUDDHISM

Thailand has experienced Westernization and rapid change beginning with the reign of Mongkut and extending to the present day. Of particular interest were Mongkut's reforms of Buddhism. The Thammayutika sect spread deep into the countryside under the leadership of Prince Wachirayanwarorot (1860–1921), who later became supreme patriarch of the Thai sangha.

The Thai monarchs maintained their close relations with Buddhism into the modern period. Thai Buddhism was reformed again during Chulalongkorn's (Rama V's) reign. Rama V announced the Buddhist Order Act, which stated that it is the government's duty to oversee the Buddhist sangha, in 1902. Commissioners were assigned to all regions, and Buddhist practice became standardized throughout the kingdom, from villages to the capital. This reform of religious organization was in turn found to be useful in the development of Thai nationalism.

Today Buddhism is a presence throughout Thai society. This is not to say there are not other religious traditions at work. The far south is predominantly Muslim and today is an area of unrest. There are pockets of animistic worship among tribal groups, mainly in the far north and east. And Christians, though never successful as missionaries, are found in the major cities. MAHAYANA BUDDHISM is a presence among ethnic Chinese, who blend in easily with local Buddhist beliefs. And there are areas of Hindu, New Age, and Daoist activity in the larger cities.

Thai Buddhism defies easy classification. Yes, it is solidly Theravadin, as Buddhism is in Burma, Laos, Kampuchea, and Sri Lanka. And yes, in each of these cultures Buddhism enjoys a status that we can call hegemonic—Buddhism is the dominant religious tradition practiced.

At the state level Buddhism is unquestionably the state religion, and the sangha is its institutional base. King Rama V organized the Thai sangha under supreme patriarch (sangha-raja). The identification of state, sangha, and education, which was first handled by the monasteries, has intensified throughout the modern period. A national ideology formed under the banner of "Nation, Religion, King." The sangha has as a matter of course cooperated with such major state programs as rural literacy campaigns. Under the Thammathut Program of the 1960s and 1970s, for instance, monks were sent to propagate the DHARMA among the hill tribes of the north in a fairly open effort to merge these ethnic groups into the larger mass of Thai society. Organizationally the sangha is hierarchical and state controlled to this day.

At the level of popular culture Buddhist influence is pervasive. Traditional moral stories of the Buddha's previous lives, the JATAKA TALES, are still popular. And monks officiate over a large slice of the ceremonies of everyday life, from kathina ceremonies (involving the ordination of new monks during the rainy season) to the consecration of new Buddha images and preaching ceremonies such as the Desana Mahajati. Monasteries are also the center of popular festivals such as New Year's (in April), Buddha's Day, and Loin Krathong, the Festival of the Floating Boats. Monks also naturally officiate over funerals; marriages, however, are handled by lay "spirit doctors."

One modern development has been the resurgence of forest dwelling Buddhism (ARANNAVASI), generally in the hilly north of Thailand. THAI FOREST MEDITATION TRADITION monks generally live in isolation or, more commonly, in small monastic communities. Because of their reputation for piety they often attract followers, including many Westerners. The tradition was first reinterpreted by Achan Sao, AJAAN MUN (1870–1949), and AJAAN CHAH, three masters in a lineage. Their examples in turn stimulated BUDDHADASA and the SANTI ASOK movement. Buddhadasa (1906–93) was a forest monk and prolific writer who established a hermitage, Suan Mokkh. He advocated a "spiritual politics" that emphasizes balance with nature.

The continuing popularity of the forest dwelling tradition can be seen as a reflection of Thailand's breakneck industrial development, a yearning for a simpler relationship with nature, and a focus on traditional values. In contrast to traditional Buddhism, the forest tradition offers a direct alternative, one that emphasizes the core practice of meditation.

Another important trend has been growing lay participation in Thai Buddhism. The DHAMMAKAYA movement, which attracts well-educated urban youth as well as politicians, was founded by Chaiyaboon Sitthiphon and Phadet Phongasawad in the early 1970s. Today it controls many of the Buddhist associations in Thai universities.

Another popular Buddhist thinker, SULAK SIVARAKSA (1933–), promotes the idea of a lay-based sangha.

A third example of a lay movement has been Santi Asok. While its founder, Bodhirak, was originally a Dhammayut monk, then a Mahanikaya monk, the movement has now severed all connections with the official Thai sangha. Members live simply, often eating one vegetarian meal a day, and are critical of the luxurious lifestyle of sangha monks. This movement has in turn become involved in national politics, with the establishment of the Phaland Dhamma Party, a major power in Parliament in the 1990s.

Further reading: Yoneo Ishii, *Sangha, State, and Society: Thai Buddhism in History* (Honolulu: University of Hawaii Press, 1986); Manich Jumsai, *Understanding Thai Buddhism* (Bangkok: Chalermnit Press, 1973); Phra Rajavaramuni, *Thai Buddhism in the Buddhist World*

(North Hollywood, Calif.: Wat Thai of Los Angeles, 1984); Donald K. Swearer, *The Buddhist World of Southeast Asia* (Albany: State University of New York Press, 1995); David K. Wyatt, *Thailand: A Short History* (New Haven, Conn.: Yale University Press, 1982, 1984).

tham khwan

A *khwan* ceremony is performed in Thailand at key periods of transition: during illness or mental stress, upon the newborn's first haircut, upon coming of age (when a boy's topknot was traditionally cut), upon ordination into the priesthood, during a wedding ceremony, and when one returns home after a long absence. It is not a strictly Buddhist ceremony but is often performed in the Buddhist wats of Thailand.

The first type of *khwan* ceremony is for newborns. The *khwan,* or individual soul, is bound to the body when a string is tied around the infant's wrist. At the same time all the hair on the infant's head is cut except one lock. This lock of hair then becomes the child's topknot, which is traditionally cut in another *tham khwan* ceremony when the child reaches puberty. The postnatal *tham khwan* ceremony derives from the traditional Indian rite of *sikhathapana mangalam,* which is recorded in the *Code of Manu,* an ancient Indian text, and is associated with nine other rites (together, the *dasakarman,* "the 10 rites").

A related *khwan* ceremony, the *phuk khwan* (tying of the essence of life), involves tying a string around the wrist of a university freshman. And a third ceremony, the *tham khwan nag* (making of a novice's essence of life), is done for young men undergoing initiation into the Buddhist monkhood. Young Thai Buddhist men traditionally enter the monkhood for some time ranging from several months to several years before proceeding to military service.

Tham khwan ceremonies may be performed by Buddhist monks, *mo khwan* (soul doctors), a relative, a senior village elder, or a *nai phram* (a Thai descended from Brahmanic priests). Tying

the wrist with a cotton bracelet is a practice common throughout Southeast Asia, among pregnant women, shamans, and even people who attend cremations. Tying grass or string around the wrist was also an ancient practice in India. The sacred cord (*yajnopavita*), a loose belt hung from the left shoulder to the waist, is mentioned in the *Code of Manu.*

In Thailand today the *saj sincana,* or bracelet of unspun cotton, is still worn by many. Buddhist monks give such bracelets as gifts to temple visitors. But the bracelet can be much larger; in theory a *saj sincana* can also be wrapped around a larger site such as a city or building to protect it.

See also SRAMANERA/SRAMANERI.

Thammakaya *See* DHAMMAKAYA.

Thammayuttica Nikaya *See* DHAMMAYUTTIKA NIKAYA.

thera *See* TITLES AND TERMS OF ADDRESS, BUDDHIST.

Theravada

Theravada, literally "Teaching of the Elders," is one of the original 18 schools of early Buddhism. Theravada is today the only one of the original schools to survive. It is today a major category of Buddhist practice and tradition, along with MAHAYANA BUDDHISM, VAJRAYANA BUDDHISM, and ZEN BUDDHISM.

The Theravada derived from the STHAVIRAVADA SCHOOL, which was introduced to Sri Lanka (then called Lanka) by missionaries inspired by King ASOKA, in 240 B.C. This school thrived and later spread to Burma, Thailand, Laos, Cambodia, and adjacent areas. According to tradition, the Theravadin canon, the TRIPITAKA, was written down in Pali after that the Third Council in the first century B.C.E.

See also COUNCILS OF BUDDHISM; 18 SCHOOLS OF EARLY BUDDHISM; SRI LANKA, BUDDHISM IN.

Further reading: Richard F. Gombrich, *Theravada Buddhism: A Social History from Ancient Benares to Modern Colombo* (London: Routledge and Kegan Paul, 1988); R. C. Lester, *Theravada Buddhism in Southeast Asia* (Ann Arbor: University of Michigan Press, 1973).

Thich Nhat Hanh (1926–   ) *major contemporary teacher of Buddhism*

Thich Nhat Hanh, an antiwar activist and Buddhist monk, was born in Vietnam and became a monk at the age of 16. He lived a quiet existence for the first decade of his monastic life. In the 1950s he left Vietnam for studies in America, but he returned to his homeland as the Vietnam War heated up; there he joined with others in the Buddhist priesthood to protest the destruction of life it was causing. In the early 1960s, he founded the School of Youth for Social Services, a lay relief organization that provided a spectrum of services to those affected by the war. At its height, the school mobilized some 10,000 student volunteers.

In 1966, he traveled to the United States, where he participated in a variety of antiwar activities that gave him a high profile, including a nomination for the Nobel Peace Prize. He was not allowed to return to Vietnam. He then applied for and was granted asylum in France. He currently resides in France at the meditation center he founded in 1982, Plum Village, designed as a nonsectarian Buddhist community that privileges ZEN BUDDHISM meditation.

Thich Nhat Hanh excels at reinterpreting basic Buddhist concepts with contemporary imagery. Thich Nhat Hahn developed the concept of ENGAGED BUDDHISM, by which he meant a socially aware and active Buddhism. While still in Vietnam, he had posed the question of whether he and his fellow monks should continue to practice in the monasteries or should go out into the world to assist people who were suffering. He answered that they should do both, but do so in the state of consciousness they attained in their meditation, that is, mindfulness.

Once aware that he was shut out of Vietnam, Hanh moved to found a set of structures that have served as vehicles for organizing support to his several causes. In 1969 he founded the Unified Buddhist Church in France. The church oversees the various centers of those who wish to be united with Hanh in his practice of Zen. Hanh, now in his 80s, lives in France in the community Plum Village, the main center of the Unified Buddhist Church.

In 1972, he founded the ORDER OF INTERBEING, an international organization that draws Buddhists together across sectarian boundaries to practice a form of engaged Buddhism. In 1983, followers of Hahn founded the Community of Mindful Living (CML), an organization to provide support for individuals and meditation groups (sanghas) who wish to practice in the Hanh tradition. It is now an official agency within the Unified Buddhist Church.

Through the last half of the 20th century, Hanh wrote more than 100 books, many translated into Western languages, expounding upon his position. Most are published by the church's publishing house, Parallax Press.

Further reading: Thich Nhat Hanh, *Be Free Where You Are* (Berkeley, Calif.: Parallax Press, 2002); ———, *Creating True Peace: Ending Violence in Yourself, Your Family, Your Community, and the World* (New York: Free Press 2003); ———, *Friends on the Path: Living Spiritual Communities.* Compiled by Jack Lawlor (Berkeley, Calif.: Parallax Press, 2002); ———, *Love in Action: Writings on Nonviolent Social Change* (Berkeley, Calif.: Parallax Press, 1993); Robert H. King, *Thomas Merton and Thich Nhat Hanh: Engaged Spirituality in an Age of Globalization* (New York: Continuum, 2001).

Thich Quang Duc (1897–1963) *Vietnamese monk*

Thich Quang Duc, who immolated himself on a major intersection of Saigon (now Ho Chi Minh City) on June 11, 1963, as the Vietnam War was heating up, had lived in a Vietnamese Buddhist monastic community from his seventh year. He was ordained as a BHIKSU when he was 20 years old. He spent most of his adult life rebuilding Buddhist temples. In the 1960s he became the director of rituals for the United Vietnamese Buddhist Congregation, the largest Buddhist organization in Vietnam. At the time he was affiliated with Linh-Mu Pagoda in Hue. The occasion for his action appears to have been the dispersing by government troops of a Buddhist gathering on May 8, 1963, in Hue, where Buddhists were demonstrating for the right to fly the BUDDHIST FLAG.

In the months prior to his action, Thich had joined other Buddhist leaders in a protest to the government of South Vietnam, then headed by Ngo Dinh Diem. They had requested that the government (1) lift its ban on flying the traditional Buddhist flag, (2) grant Buddhists the same rights enjoyed by Roman Catholics, (3) stop detaining Buddhists, (4) give Buddhist monks and nuns the right to practice and spread their religion, and (5) pay fair compensations to the families of victims of government abuse and punish those responsible for their deaths.

The action, which he and his supporters, such as his fellow monk THICH NHAT HANH, had seen as very different from suicide, occurred only after some months of consideration of the possible consequences, the issuing of explanatory letters to both the government and the Buddhist community, and several weeks of meditation. Thich Nhat Hanh saw the action (and several similar acts that followed) as courageous, full of hope, and aspiring toward a better future.

Thich Quang Duc's action has subsequently become the object of significant analysis from ethical, theological, and political perspectives, in light of the fall of the Diem government less than six months later. The withdrawal of American support for Diem occurred in the context of the growing civil rights movement in the United States. In the light of the actions of Thich Quang Duc and those who copied him, Buddhists were left with an ethical question over the rightness of such deaths. A major response was provided by Jan Yiin-Hua, who in 1965 sought justification for the immolations in the prior acts of elite devotees, inspired by their understanding of Buddhism, to demonstrate a significant act of selflessness.

On June 11, 2003, Vietnamese Buddhist and government officials gathered at the spot of Thich's immolation to commemorate his act.

Further reading: Russell T. McCutcheon, "The Self-Immolation of Thich Quang Duc." Buddhist Information of North America. Available online. URL: http://www.buddhistinformation.com/self_immolation. htm. Accessed on November 7, 2005.

Thittila, Sayadaw U (1896–1997) *learned Burmese Buddhist monk*

The Venerable Thittila was a major Burmese Buddhist leader who wrote *The Book of Analysis,* a major modern interpretation of ABHIDHARMA teachings (published in English in 1969). He was ordained as a BHIKSU (monk) at the age of 20, in the southern Burmese city of Moulmein. He attained the highest level of monastic scholarship when he passed the Panyattisasanahita examinations in 1923. He was said to have phenomenal powers of memorization. He was immediately made head of a monastery near the capital, Rangoon. He subsequently spent time in Ceylon (Sri Lanka) and India. He was elected president of the South India Buddhist Associations, a group founded in 1903.

Thittila went to England for further study in 1938. He spent the remainder of World War II there, living in quite difficult conditions and supporting himself through occasional lectures. His condition improved with the founding of the Sasana Kari Vihara in London, in 1949. In 1952, he finally returned to Burma, where he stayed another eight years giving academic lectures. He was then awarded the Agga Maha Pandita title, the highest government award for *bhiksus*. In later years he frequently toured the United States, Europe, Australia, and Japan. He finally returned to Burma in 1966. He was later made Ovadacariya, or spiritual adviser, to the central council of the Burmese sangha.

Thittila spent much of his energy teaching on the Abhidhamma Pitaka, that huge body of work in the Buddhist tradition that focuses on the explanation of Buddhist principles and philosophy. He made the first English translation of the Vibhanga, the second book of the Abhidharma.

Thittila lived a full, long life of teaching and learning; he was 100 when he died.

Further reading: Claudine W. Iggleden, "Sayadaw U Thittila." Nibbana.com: Presenting Theravada Buddhism in its Pristine Form. Available online. URL: http://www.triplegem.plus.com/biogrphy.htm#uthittila. Accessed on March 6, 2005; Sayadaw U Thittila, *The Book of Analysis* (Lancaster, U.K: Pali Text Society, 1969).

Thrangu Monastery

Thrangu is a major KAGYU monastery in Yushu, Chinghai, western China. Today it is managed by Lama Thutop, the most senior monk present, but the traditional head is the KENCHEN THRANGU, Khenpo Thrangu Rinpoche (1933–), now residing in Nepal.

Thrangu is said to have a history of 1,300 years. It was rebuilt and enlarged around 1400 C.E. by the seventh *karmapa*, Chodrak Gyamtso. He appointed Shwu Palgyi Sengey as the first Thrangu Rinpoche and abbot.

Thrangu Monastery is near the Princess Wen Cheng Temple. The temple was established in the seventh century C.E. when the princess married the Tibetan king Songtsen Gampo. It is now managed by the Thrangu Monastery.

At one time Thrangu Monastery was known as the "Monastery of the 10,000 Lamas." There were approximately 300 monks before the CULTURAL REVOLUTION period in China (1966–78). Today there are approximately 150 monks in residence. The monastery is today rebuilding, under the supervision of Lodro Nyima Rinpoche. An institute with 13 classrooms is under construction.

Another monastery also named Thrangu is currently under construction in Vancouver, Canada.

Further reading: Thrangu Dharma Society, PJ Malaysia. "Biography of Lama Thutop." Available online. URL: www.dharma-meida.org/tdspj/lama_tutop.html. Accessed on August 25, 2005; "Thrangu Monastery, Qinghai, China." Available online. URL: www.rinpoche.com/Yushu/page2.htm. Accessed on August 25, 2005.

three flaws

The three flaws was conceptual shorthand in early Buddhist discourse for three views that characterize all of reality. They are ANITYA, impermanence; ANATMAN, no-self; and DUKKHA, suffering. All existence is impermanent and nonlasting, beyond a brief period. Any belief we may hold in the permanence of any idea or thing is illusory. *Anatman* holds that impermanence applies to the self also. There is no substance in anything, beyond a brief joint arising of characteristics. Not only is there no individual self, there is no core self or underlying reality to any part of the universe or experience.

In *dukkha* suffering is explained as the result of attachment to false concepts. These false concepts include belief in permanence and belief in the self. *Dukkha* is therefore a part of the realm of SAMSARA, the world of recycled karmic conditions. The only release from this condition is to achieve NIRVANA, ultimate extinction.

Further reading: "The Noble 8-Fold Path: An Illustration of Right Belief and Right Aspiration (Prajna): The three Great Flaws of All Beings in Samsara." Available online. URL: www.humboldt.edu/~wh1/6. Buddhism.OV/6.ThreeFlaws.html. Posted January 20, 2000. Accessed on November 28, 2005.

three periods

This concept divides human history into three separate periods and associates each with a phase or style of Buddha Dharma, the teachings of Buddhism. The three periods are the former, middle, and later days. The period of the former days began after the PARINIRVANA (death) of the Buddha and extended for 500 (or in some versions 1,000) years. In this period the truth of the Buddha's teachings survived, and sincere practice allowed individuals to attain ENLIGHTENMENT. In the period of the middle days Buddhism was established and accepted in society, but the teachings become too formal and few people benefited. In the final period of the latter day (MAPPO) people lost their longing for ENLIGHTENMENT altogether, and at any rate Buddhism has degenerated and is ineffective in helping people to attain enlightenment. Each of the former day and middle day periods will last for 500 or 1,000 years, depending on the version of this teaching. The latter day period will extend for thousands of years. Since the Buddha taught more than 2,000 years ago, regardless of the calculation method, we clearly live today in the period of the latter day.

See also SCHOOLS OF CHINESE BUDDHISM; *SHOBO.*

three poisons

The three poisons are the major vices in Buddhist teachings—ignorance, hatred, and greed. They are often represented by three animals (a pig, a snake, and a cock, respectively). These three forces in life stand at the center of the Wheel of Life, endlessly powering the revolving cycle.

See also WHEEL OF LIFE.

Further reading: Kalachakranet. "A View on Buddhism: Working with Delusional Emotions." Available online. URL: http://buddhism.kalachakranet.org/delusion_introduction.html. Accessed on May 22, 2006.

three pure ones (*san qing*)

These three deities govern the three Daoist heavens. The first heaven is Yu Qing (Jade Purity), governed by Yuanshi Tianzun, the "Celestial Venerable of the Primordial Beginning." The second pure one is Shang Qing (Great Purity), governed by Lingbao Tianzun, the "Heavenly Venerable of the Numinous Treasure." This deity regulates time and guards mystical writings. The third of the three pure ones is Daode Tianzun, the "Heavenly Venerable of the DAO and *de.*" He rules over the third heaven of Tai Qing (Highest Purity). He is in fact Taishang Laozun, or Supreme Master Lao, another term for LAOZI. This figure interprets the teachings contained in the *ling bao* (numinous treasures).

In terms of the celestial hierarchy of religious Daoism, the three pure ones rank lower than Yu Huang, the Jade Emperor. Nevertheless, temples and altars set up to in their honor are common throughout Daoism.

three realms

The three realms (*triloka, tridhatu*) is shorthand for the Buddhism vision of the cosmos, including the world of the living. The three realms are the world of (sensual) desire, the world of form or matter, and the world of formlessness (or spirit). These in SANSKRIT are the *karmadhatu, rupadhatu,* and *arupadhatu,* and they parallel (but are not equivalent to) the ancient Indian Vedic idea of the *bhuvanatraya,* earth, atmosphere, and heaven.

The realm of desire includes nearly all of the SIX REALMS OF EXISTENCE—beings in hell; PRETAS, or hungry spirits; animals, *asuras* (demons), humans; and *devas,* or gods. The realm of desire is found on the four continents that surround Mt.

Sumeru, where humans and some deities live, and the space beneath, where beings in hell, *pretas*, animals, and *asuras* live.

The realm of form is located above that of desire, including sexual desire, although the beings in the realm of form retain the capacity to experience joy. The formless realm of *arupadhatu* contains only spirit.

One way of conceptualizing the three realms (following the contemporary writer Red Pine) is to consider them as the realms of the subjective, the objective, and the nonobjective. In theory an individual passes through each realm in succession in making progress on the path of cultivation.

Daoism also imitated the Buddhist concept of the three worlds in its cosmology. The *Duming miaojing* (Wondrous Scripture on the Salvation of Life), a text in Lingbao Daoism, for example, standardized a system of 36 heavens. Of these the lower 28 were divided into three groups: the realms of formlessness (four worlds), form (18), and desire (6).

Further reading: Red Pine, trans., *The Diamond Sutra: The Perfection of Wisdom* (Washington, D.C.: Counterpoint, 2001).

three register rituals

The three register rituals are Daoist rituals dating at least as far back as the Song dynasty (960–1279). They are the Golden Register Ritual, the Jade Register Ritual, and the Yellow Register Ritual. The Golden Register Ritual was concerned with imperial affairs. The purpose of the ritual was to ask for blessings and offer repentance of sins. It was used to remove the threat of disasters. This ritual is mentioned 17 times in the Daoist canon, each time focusing on the emperor and his affairs.

The Jade Register Ritual was mentioned eight times in various parts of the Daoist canon. Each time it referred to an action performed by kings,

the nobility, or ministers. Through this ritual the performer attempts to harmonize the extremes of yin and yang and bless the people. The Yellow Register Ritual acts to reduce disasters and give benefits to the living and the deceased. This ritual process is mentioned in many spots throughout the Daozang (Daoist canon). While Golden Register and Jade Register Rituals are extremely rare, Yellow Register Rituals continue to be performed today.

Further reading: Chen Yaoting, "rituals: The Three Registers Fasts." Luo tongbing, trans. Taoist Culture * Information Centre. Available online. URL: www.eng.taoism.org.hk/religious0-activities&rituals/rituals/pg4-6-1.asp. Accessed on January 7, 2005.

three rulers (*san guan*)

The three Daoist figures govern heaven, earth, and the waters, respectively. (They are named Tian Guan, Di Guan, and Shui Guan in Chinese.) As with all Daoist deities in the pantheon, each performs a fixed function. The ruler of heaven controls luck, the ruler of earth keeps track of transgressions, and the ruler of water overseas the obstacles met by people in life.

These three deities were worshipped in China at least from the late Han dynasty (207 B.C.E.–220 C.E.), often with temples devoted to their worship. The three are generally depicted as bureaucratic officials.

Further reading: Micha F. Lindemans, "Three Rulers." Encyclopedia Mythica. Available online. URL: http://www.pantheon.org/articles/s/san-guan.html. Accessed on May 22, 2006.

three stars (*san xing*)

These are the traditional Chinese folk deities of fortune, specifically Fu Xing (lucky star), Lu Xing (Star of Honor), and Shou Xing (Star of Longevity). They are typically pictured together, smiling, and add to the festive atmosphere during such holidays as Lunar New Year.

As with many Chinese deities, the three stars were historical individuals honored in their own period who were later deified. In many cases several folk traditions or individuals were combined into the contemporary figure. Fu Xing was a sixth-century government official. Another tradition identifies him as an eighth-century general who communicated with the Heavenly Weaver, a female deity. Lu Xing was a noble in the Han dynasty (207 B.C.E.–220 C.E.) or, alternatively, the god of literature, Wen Chang. And Shou Xing, also called the god of the south pole, was a child who could guarantee a long life span.

The three stars are also found on altars in many popular Chinese religions.

Further reading: Chen Yaoting, "Daoist Beliefs: Immortals and Immortalism: The Stars of Luck, Wealth and Longevity." Taoist Culture and Information. Available online. URL: http://www.eng.taoism.org.hk/daoist-beliefs/immortals&immortalism/pg2-4-6-2. Accessed on May 22, 2006.

three times

In Buddhist thought, the three times are, simply, the past, the present, and the future.

Further reading: Lewis R. Lancaster, "Discussion of Time in Mahayana Texts," Philosophy East and West 24, no. 2 (April 1974): 209–214. Excerpt available online at thezensite homepage. URL: http://www.thezensite. com/zen%20essays/DiscussionoftimeinMahayanatexts. htm. Accessed on May 22, 2006.

three treasures (triratna, "three jewels"; Chinese sanbao, Japanese sambo)

The three treasures are the three essential aspects of Buddhism—the BUDDHA the SANGHA, and the DHARMA. The terms stand for the founder of Buddhism, the community of believers, and the body of teachings passed down through time. The Buddha is not only the historical figure but also the ideal of the awakened person who leaves the cycle of suffering in life. The Dharma is the teachings of the Buddha, as well as all later teachings by the established traditions. And the Sangha is the community of believers. Today the Sangha is generally seen as including both lay followers of Buddhism as well as those who lead a monastic life.

A Buddhist is expected to honor and serve these three aspects. Buddhism is a multifaceted collection of systems of thought and practice, all of which would be unimaginable without the three treasures. The formulation of the three jewels was present from the earliest times.

In MAHAYANA BUDDHISM practice the three jewels concept was transformed into a complex model for understanding Buddhist practice. The three levels of the three treasures are unity, manifestation, and verification. Unity is represented by VAIROCANA Buddha; manifestation is Sakyamuni, the historical Buddha; and verification is found in the textual traditions and the totality of all contemporary Buddhist practitioners.

Further reading: Charles S. Prebish, Historical Dictionary of Buddhism (Metuchen, N.J.: Scarecrow Press, 1993) 263–264; Sangharakshita, The Three Jewels: An Introduction to Buddhism (London: Rider, 1967).

three worms (sancong)

In the Daoist concept also called the "three corpses" (sanshi), the three worms were spiritual entities said to inhabit every person's CINNABAR fields (dan tian). (These are the spiritual field centered in the head, the field around the heart, and the field around the navel.) The three worms take on mutable forms, sometimes appearing as humans, sometimes as demons. Their goal is to "devitalize" or shorten the life spans of people whose bodies they inhabit, usually by causing diseases. In other words, they represent forces that oppose Daoist efforts to attain immortality.

The Daoist cultivator, in attempting to attain immortality, tries to rid his or her body of the three worms. The most direct way to do this is to abstain from eating meat or grains.

The three worms are given suitably terrifying names: Old Blue, White Maiden, Bloody Corpse. They not only eat each person's vital energies, on *gengshen* (the 57th day of the traditional 60-day calendar cycle), they also spy and report to higher deities in heaven and hell about a person's actions.

The key characteristic of the three worms is that they are born through the consumption of grains. They actually preexist the individual, and as grains are absorbed in the body they gain more strength and are able to suck away the person's life force. The cultivator must therefore cease to eat any of the five cereals (rice, millet, wheat, oats, or beans).

The worms in the three areas show different symptoms: blindness and deafness, baldness, bad teeth, and bad breath in the top *dantian;* heart trouble, asthma, depression in the middle; and rheumatism, poor willpower, and confusion in the bottom *dantian.*

Abstaining from the five grains is insufficient, however. The true cultivator will also not consume wine or meat or any of the five strong flavors (including garlic and onions). Finally conquering the three worms requires a combination of breathing, cleansing, and dietary practices. Certain elixirs prepared in specified ways also help guard against the three worms.

Further reading: Julian F. Pas, *Historical Dictionary of Taoism* (Lanham, Md.: Scarecrow Press, 1998); Kristofer Schipper, *The Taoist Body* (Berkeley: University of California Press, 1993).

tian (t'ien, heaven)

Tian is the Chinese term for "heaven" or "sky." However, in ancient times it had extreme cosmological significance. In fact, it was such an over-arching concern of early Chinese authors that it is perhaps more accurate to translate *Tian* as "God" instead of "heaven," as is recommended by Russell Kirkland. Therefore, it is best simply to use the Chinese term *tian*. Early Chinese thinkers saw *tian* as a universal force behind the functioning of nature. These included Daoists, who accepted the idea of *tian* and did not simply replace it with the more mystical concept of DAO. The *Daodejing* discusses TIAN DAO (THE WAY OF HEAVEN). In fact, the two concepts of Dao and *tian* recur throughout the Chinese classics. *Tian* is often counterposed to *di*, earth, in a male/female opposition, and Dao as the primordial, original forces was thus associated with *tian*. The *Taiping jing* (Scripture of great peace), an early Daoist classic, completes the associations: *tian* is Dao, yang, the primordial. *Di* (earth) is mutable, yin, nurturing, *de* (literally, "power").

Further reading: Russell Kirkland, *Taoism: The Enduring Tradition* (New York: Routledge, 2004); Chi-tim Lai, "The Daoist Concept of Central Harmony in the Scripture of Great Peace: Human Responsibility for the Maladies of Nature," in N. J. Girardot, James Miller, and Liu Xiaogan, eds., *Daoism and Ecology: Ways within a Cosmic Landscape* (Cambridge: Harvard University Press, 2001), 95–111.

tian dao (t'ien tao, the Way of Heaven)

Tian dao is a Chinese term meaning "the Way [Dao] of heaven." The term is found in the earliest works of Chinese philosophy, including the classic Daoist text DAODEJING. *Tian dao* perhaps approximates the Christian sense of providence, God's agency. In Zhou period China (1122 B.C.E.–256 B.C.E.) Tian was the ultimate deity, the absolute. And on a practical level, ascertaining the will of the absolute became an important issue in establishing political authority.

Neo-Confucian writers such as Zhu Xi (1130–1200) simply equated *tian dao* with TIAN MING (MANDATE OF HEAVEN). This implied a moral order or "Way" but lessened the sense of a creator god implicit in the earlier uses of *tian dao.*

Further reading: Rodney L. Taylor, *The Way of Heaven: An Introduction to the Confucian Religious Life* (Leiden: E. J. Brill, 1986).

Tian Dao/Yiguandao

Tian dao is a philosophical concept. Today the term *Tian Dao* is also largely associated with a Chinese New Religion dating from the 1930s. In scholarly publication often referred to as *Yiguandao;* many affiliated groups now use the term *Tian Dao,* perhaps as a way to dissociate themselves from the older, original term. It is convenient to use *Yiguandao* for the earlier phase of the group, and *Tian Dao* in discussing its current manifestations. But regardless of the label chosen, the religious spirit of Tian Dao groups is clearly definable.

Yiguandao began as a minor cult probably based in a single temple, in the city of Jining, Shangdong, a populous province in eastern China. In 1933 the leadership of the small group passed to Zhang Tianran, the son-in-law of the previous leader. Zhang then set about building the movement he inherited to the point where it was present in nearly every corner of Chinese society. Although solid figures are difficult to come by, it can be argued that by the time of his death in 1947 Yiguandao had become the largest single religious grouping in China.

Zhang did this by several means. He first streamlined the official ritual and the regulations that all members were expected to follow. He no longer required sexual abstinence, for example. And he shortened the time required to perform

Worshippers in front of a Tiandao altar at a new temple near Xinzhu, central Taiwan

the ritual bows and prostrations so characteristic of Yiguandao temples. He also emphasized the benefits of Yiguandao proselytization: by introducing new converts, one would gain immeasurable merit that could be transferred to the benefit of one's own ancestors, most of whom were in hell with little hope of release. In effect Yiguandao conversion would benefit the inductee and their own ancestors, as well as the person who introduced him/her into Yiguandao.

Zhang expanded along the rail networks and urban trade routes of a newly modernizing China. Many of the first branch temples were in the port cities of Shanghai, Tianjin, and Guangzhou. While some of the branches were associated with MARTIAL ARTS studios, many later became associated with petty capitalism: store owners and clerks who made up the beginnings of a new middle class. Yiguandao, although associated strongly with capitalism and trading networks, yet retained the allure of traditional values of religiosity.

Most controversially, Yiguandao expanded significantly during the Sino-Japanese War (1936–45), especially in those areas under control of the Japanese puppet regimes established in Manchuria and Nanjing. After the Japanese defeat, charges began to fly that Yiguandao leaders cooperated with the Japanese. Zhang Tianran retired and died soon thereafter. The movement for years was suppressed by both Nationalist and Communist regimes, in China and Taiwan.

While it was effectively stamped out in mainland China after the victory of Communist forces there, it is remarkable that Tian Dao has been able to survive in Taiwan and other overseas centers of Chinese population.

Further reading: David D. Jordan and Daniel L. Overmyer, *The Flying Phoenix: Aspects of Chinese Sectarianism in Taiwan* (Princeton, N.J.: Princeton University Press, 1986); Hubert Seiwert, *Popular Religious Movements and Heterodox Sects in Chinese History* (Leiden: Brill, 2003).

Tian Ming (T'ien Ming, Mandate of Heaven)

A *ming* is a command, an order. The Mandate of Heaven is an ordering of events that is dictated by heaven, the highest authority in the (Confucian) universe; it is, in other words, a force against which humans cannot fight. The concept was found in classic descriptions of the universe, and especially in relation to governance; the Mandate is given to those deserving and lost to any ruler who lacks virtue. The *Shi Jing*, or Book of Songs, no. 267, mentions the connection between the virtue of King Wen and the fate of his descendants: as long as they continued to act with virtue, they, too, would enjoy the Mandate of Heaven. This concept, then, had obvious application to any group wishing to assert dominance—by claiming the Mandate one achieved legitimacy. There were frequent efforts to find portents such as shooting stars that indicated that the Mandate had shifted—in your direction.

Two extraordinary rites, Feng and Shan sacrifices on Mt. Tai in Shandong, confirmed the emperor's receipt of the Mandate of Heaven. During the Feng performance the emperor stated publicly to heaven the conditions of his rule, stressing his benign influence and many successes during his reign, and expressed thanks to heaven for assigning the Mandate to him. In the Shan performance, held on a smaller hill near Mt. Tai, called Sheshou, the emperor made sacrifices to the god of the earth and ancestral deities. These sacrifices were quite rare, however—they were performed only seven times in imperial China and were meant to be held only in times of abundant prosperity. We can assume, then, that the inevitable temptation to perform one to indicate receipt of the Tian Ming was resisted.

Further reading: Chen Jo-shui, "Empress Wu and Proto-Feminist Sentiments in T'ang China," in Frederick P. Brandauer and Chun-Chieh Huang, eds., *Imperial Rulership and Cultural Change in Traditional China* (Seattle: University of Washington Press, 1994), 77–116.

Tian Tai school (T'ien Tai)

Tian Tai developed as a distinct school or, perhaps more accurately, "flavor" of Chinese Buddhism, in the early Tang (618–907) Dynasty. This school created a wide-ranging and comprehensive philosophy from different elements of Buddhism. As such Tian Tai is a true native reaction to the many varieties of Buddhist doctrine available in China in that period.

Tian Tai takes its name from the Tian Tai mountains in eastern Zhejiang, China, a spot of rolling if not dramatic mountain ranges and many rivers. Tian Tai's founder, ZHI YI (538–597), built the Guoqing Temple there in 598 after dreaming of it and receiving the support of the Sui emperor, his sponsor. This temple continues to function to this day. In fact, the surrounding area is filled with spiritual significance; a mountain near the temple is one of the 10 Daoist caves, and Tian Tai is the location where the popular deity figure JI GONG (Duke Ji) was born.

Zhi Yi took the teachings of his predecessors, Hui Wen (fl. 550) and HUI SI (515–577), and created a systematic body of knowledge. Zhi Yi in fact wrote nearly nothing. His teachings were recorded by his disciple Guan Ding (561–632).

Zhi Yi's teachings focused on the LOTUS SUTRA, the central text of this school. The major works in Tian Tai teachings are the *Profound Meaning of the Lotus Sutra* (*Miaofa lianhua jing xuan'yi*), which surveys all the Buddha's teachings; the Textual Commentary on the Lotus Sutra (Miaofa lianhua jing wenzhu); and the Great Concentration and Insight (*MOHE ZHIGUAN*), a densely written manual of practice.

A key element of Zhi Yi's systematic approach was his idea of the five periods and the eight teachings (*wushi bajiao*), a way of classifying Buddhist texts and teachings. This system, a variety of the PANJIAO (discernment of teachings) system, was an attempt to combine all previous teachings into one vast school, to draw together all strands of Buddhism. While Tian Tai eventually merged into the general practice of Chinese Buddhism and did not survive as a distinct school, its ideas and in particular this synthetic impulse, still influences Chinese Buddhism today.

Further reading: Neal Donner and Daniel B. Stevenson, *The Great Calming and Contemplation: A Study and Annotated Translation of the First Chapter of Chih-I's Mo-Ho Chih-Kuan* (Honolulu: University of Hawaii Press, 1993); Paul L. Swanson, *Foundations of T'ien-T'ai Philosophy: The Flowering of the Two Truths Theory in Chinese Buddhism* (Berkeley, Calif.: Asia Humanities Press, 1989).

Tiantan (T'ien T'an)

Tiantan, the Temple of Heaven, the largest temple complex in China and a major artifact of the traditional Chinese worldview (pre-Buddhist). In imperial times Tiantan was the primary site for the annual ritual of thanksgiving performed by the emperor during the winter solstice.

The first major segment of the complex, erected to the southeast of central Beijing, was begun in 1410 by Emperor Yongle (r. 1403–24), whose building program also included the Forbidden City. For the first 100 years, Tiantan was termed the Temple of Heaven and Earth, but in 1530 a separate Temple of Earth was constructed on the northern edge of Beijing.

There are three main parts of the Tiantan complex, all laid out along a north-south axis. Entrance was at the Western Gate and the first stop for the emperor was at the Zhaigong, the Fasting Palace. Here the emperor would initiate the annual winter ceremony with three days of fasting during which he consumed no meat or wine, did not engage in sex, and handled no official matters related to criminal cases. He also engaged in ritual bathing.

The northern part of the complex is dominated by the Qiniandian, Great Enjoyment Hall; the Huangqiandian, or Heavenly Emperor Hall;

Qiniandian (Hall of Prayer for Good Harvests) at Tiantan (Temple of Heaven), Beijing, China

and the large circular Qigutan, or Altar of Prayer for a Rich Crop. Inside the Huangqiandian is an altar table at which the emperor burned incense.

The Danbi Bridge connects the northern part of Tiantan with the Imperial Vault of Heaven. Inside this circular building are the memorial tablets for the Heavenly Emperor and the ancestors of the royal family. On the winter solstice, the emperor began the day in this hall, where he read prayers and invited those memorialized to participate in the upcoming ceremonies.

From its construction in 1530, the main event of the year occurred on the Heaven-Worshipping Altar, a large circular structure at the southern end of the complex. This large outdoor structure was carefully constructed using multiples of 9 in its measurements and decorations, recognizing that the Heavenly Emperor was believed to reside in the ninth tier of heaven. On and around this altar the central elaborate ceremonies of the winter solstice occurred. The emperor reported to the Heavenly Emperor on the past year's abundance and interceded for the country as a whole with prayers for a new year of prosperity and peace.

Besides the several main buildings are a number of lesser structures, such as the side halls at the Qiniandian where the sun, moon, stars, wind, cloud, thunder, and rain were worshipped, or the Butcher Pavilion where the sacrificial animals for the ceremonies were actually killed. On the edge of the Danbi Bridge there is a platform where the emperor could change clothing.

The winter solstice was not the only ceremony to acknowledge heaven on behalf of the nation. For example, at the summer solstice the emperor went to the Heaven-Worshipping Altar to pray for rain.

Given the importance of the ceremonies that took place at Tiantan, it is not surprising that the key buildings are among the most important architectural treasures of the country, prized for both their beauty and their architectural innovation. The entire complex covers 675 acres.

Further reading: *Tiantan—Temple of Heaven* (Beijing: China Esperanto Press, 1998).

Tibetan Book of the Dead

This text, also known as the Bardo thosgrol chenmo, or Great liberation by hearing in the intermediate states, is a great work of NYINGMA literature. It was first partially translated into English by Lama Kazi Dawa Samdup and W. Y. Evans-Wentz in 1927, after which it became widely known in the West as the Tibetan Book of the Dead.

The Tibetan Book of the Dead was first written by the Tibetan saint PADMASAMBHAVA, who, with his consort Yeshe Tsogyal, concealed many texts (called TERMA) in Tibet and prophesied that Karma Lingpa would discover them. In the 11th century, Karma Lingpa's third-generation disciple Gyarawa Namka Chokyi Gyatso is responsible for disseminating these teachings throughout Tibet.

Much of the text is in verse and was intended to be sung. The teachings follow various stages in the path of VAJRAYANA BUDDHISM practice: from preparatory verses to such categories as liberation from negativity, acts of confession, liberation from fear, liberation from recollection, and rebirth. In particular, in the 49 days between death and rebirth, the Book of the Dead states there are six in-between (BARDO) states: birth *bardo*, dream *bardo*, meditation *bardo*, experience of death *bardo*, supreme reality *bardo*, and state of becoming *bardo*.

The symbolism of the Book of the Dead is based in large part on the Guhyagarbha Tantra, a revealed text dating from sixth-century India, said to be the words of the BODHISATTVA SAMANTABHADRA. The Guhyagarbha describes psychological states in terms of two MANDALAS, one for the 42 "peaceful" deities, and one for the 58 "wrathful" deities. All subsequent literature based on these two groups of 100 deities was known as Cycles of the Peaceful and Wrathful Deities (*zhi-khro*). The Tibetan Book of the Dead is one of those works of *zhi-khro* literature.

Further reading: Padmasambhava, *The Tibetan Book of the Dead: The Great Liberation by Hearing in the Intermediate States.* Composed by Padmasambhava, revealed by Terton Karma Lingpa and Gyurme Dorje and translated by Graham Coleman, with editing by Thupten Jinpa (London and New York: Penguin Books, 2005).

Tibetan Government-in-Exile

The Government-in-Exile is the provisional governmental organization established by the DALAI LAMA and his followers after his departure from Tibet to India in 1959.

See also CHINA-TIBET; DALAI LAMA XIV, TENZIN GYATSU; DHARMASALA.

Further reading: The Tibetan Government in Exile. "An Introduction Central Tibetan Administration." Available online. URL: http://www.tibet.net/tgie/eng/. Accessed on May 22, 2006.

T'ien-T'ai   *See* TIAN TAI.

Tilopa (988–1069) *early Indian Tantric Buddhist and teacher of Naropa*

The KARMA KAGYU school of Tibetan Buddhism traces its beginning through a lineage of teachers that reaches back to India and NAGARJUNA. Tilopa, a Brahmin from eastern India, studied with Nagarjuna. Later, for a time, Tilopa was the ruler of a small kingdom in India, though he later resigned his kingship, not wishing to exercise further political power. He dropped his royal attire for a monk's robes and settled in at Somapuri temple, a Tantric center in Bengal.

According to the legends that have grown around him, the life-changing event for Tilopa was a vision in which a DAKINI (a female teacher) offered him knowledge leading to ENLIGHTENMENT. Tilopa accepted the offer and was subsequently initiated into Chakrasamvara Tantra.

Tantric Buddhists believe that Chakrasamvara, a manifest form of Shakyamuni BUDDHA, has taught the highest yogic methods for enlightenment, the "spontaneous great bliss." The practice leads to the realization of the emptiness of all phenomena. Chakrasamvara Tantra can also include sexual union. Tilopa practiced Chakrasamvara tantra for some 12 years. Then, one day, his fellow monks found him with a female with whom he practiced union yoga, and they forced him to leave Somapuri.

Tilopa subsequently traveled widely through India and broadened his understanding of the spiritual life by his study with a variety of teachers. He also paid for his support by grinding sesame seeds for oil (the source of the name by which he would later be known—*til* means "oil" in SANSKRIT). During this time, his major teacher was the Buddha Vajradhara, like Chakrasamvara, a manifest form of Shakyamuni Buddha. From Vajradhara he learned of MAHAMUDRA, the great seal, the teaching about emptiness as the ultimate nature of reality—all phenomena are ultimately empty of any inherent existence.

In the last years of his life, Tilopa lived in a remote rural area. Among the students who sought him out was NAROPA, whom he chose to become the holder of his lineage. MARPA would also travel from Tibet to study with Tilopa on *mahamudra* meditation and later succeed Naropa as the third lineage holder.

Further reading: Marpa Chos-Kyi bLo-gros, *The Life of the Mahasiddha Tilopa*. Translated by Fabrizio Torricelli and Acharya Sangye T. Naga (Dharamsala, India: Paljor, 1995); Tai Situ Rinpoche, *Tilopa* (Eskdalemuir, Scotland: Kagyu Samye Ling, 1988); Thrangu Rinpoche Geshe Lharampa, *The Spiritual Biography of Marpa: The Translator* (Delhi: Sri Satguru, 2001).

titles and terms of address, Buddhist

In Buddhism there are, broadly speaking, two categories of titles: those relating to position within the SANGHA, the community of monks and nuns, and those titles of respect used in the local culture. While the Buddhist community of religious specialists has an amazing unity of functions and positions, each culture has a unique way of referring to such specialists as members of society overall.

LAYPEOPLE

From the earliest days lay people were referred to with special terms. They were generally called *upasaka* (female *upasika*), "devotees." Anyone who

had taken refuge and repeated the five precepts (*PANCA SILA*) was considered an *upasaka/upasika*.

MONASTIC TITLES

The first position, naturally, is monk—in SANSKRIT we use the term BHIKSU (BHIKSUNI for nuns). There are, of course, different grades of monks. The novice, who has taken the initial 10 precepts, is a SRAMANA/SRAMANERA. He/she is guided by a preceptor, the *upajjhaya*. Another traditional position in monasteries is the *acarya*, the instructor of doctrine.

Most revealing for understanding the meaning of ORDINATION as a monk is the monk's surname. Unlike in most Western religious traditions, the Buddhist monk changes his or her surname to that of the Buddha. In Chinese, for example, the monk henceforth uses the surname *Shi*, the Chinese version of the Buddha's clan name, *Sakya*. All monks thus share the same family surname and are therefore normally referred to by their personal names alone. Nevertheless, adoption of the new surname indicates that the person has left his or her previous family and joined the new one of the Buddha.

The highest position within a national sangha organization is called by different terms in different places. In Thailand the Sangharaja (king of the community) is appointed by the monarch, while in Sri Lanka the Maha Nayaka (great leaders) are elected by the entire sangha. In contemporary China the position of *fashi* (Dharma master) is an appointed one under the Bureau of Religious Affairs.

CHINESE TERMS OF RESPECT

At one point the titles used in Chinese temples reflected lineage or school affiliations. In the Song dynasty (960–1270) these various titles were broadly associated with CHAN, TIAN TAI, and VINAYA (*lu*) orientations. Senior monks were given specific titles in each tradition: *Chanshi* (meditation masters) were found in Chan, *fashi* (Dharma masters) in Tian Tai, and *Lushi* (Vinaya masters) in the Vinaya traditions, respectively. All these titles had been used in different contexts previous to the Song, however. For instance, ABHIDHARMA specialists had often been called *lushi*. *Chanshi* and *fashi* also appear as designations in early sources, such as the *Gaoseng Zhuan* by Hui Zhao (497–554). Thus all these terms were originally markers of respect and learning and were not affiliated with certain schools. Today any learned or respected monk may be called a *fashi* or the colloquial term *shifu* (master or teacher).

TIBETAN BUDDHIST TERMS

The Tibetan term *rinpoche*—literally "precious jewel"—refers to an individual who is a reincarnate lama. Such individuals normally are but may not necessarily be Buddhist monks (in Tibetan, *gelong*). In general the titles *geshe* and *khenpo* are less widely found than *rinpoche*; they are reserved for individuals of exceptional learning and spiritual accomplishment.

The word *lama* is equivalent to the Sanskrit/Indian title *guru*. Strictly speaking a lama has completed a three-year period of cultivation and need not necessarily be a monk who has taken the precepts. As is *guru*, the title *lama* is often used simply as a sign of respect.

Other titles sometimes found used in Tibetan traditions include *chogyal*, "Dharma king"; *chuje*, "Lord of Dharma"; *getsul*, a novice *sramanera*; *gyalwa*, "Conqueror"; *Lopon*, equivalent to the Sanskrit *acarya*, a meditation master; *ngakpa*, a MANTRA specialist in the NYINGMA school; *terton*, "discoverer of hidden texts"; and *TULKU*, an incarnate lama.

Several titles found in Tibetan Buddhism reflect academic degrees or honors. *Geshe*, originally a title used in the GELUG school, indicates academic achievement. *Lharampa* is the highest *geshe* degree attainable. *Khenpo* indicates a scholar in NYINGMA, SAKYA, or KAGYU schools.

THERAVADA TERMS

In Southeast Asian THERAVADA countries a common honorific title is *thera*, "elder," which simply

A novice lama assists a worshipper in lighting incense at the Yonghe Gong (temple) in Beijing, China

indicates one who has been a fully ordained monk for 10 years. After 20 years one is assigned the title *mahathera*, "great elder." The Thai term *ajahn* (also spelled *achaan*) indicates a Buddhist teacher. This word derives from the term *acarya*, a Sanskrit term originally meaning "great teacher" or "master." Although nuns are normally not called *thera* in Thailand, because the lineage of nuns no longer exists there, nuns may still be called *ajahn*.

The Burmese title of respect *sayadaw* means "exalted monk," or, strictly speaking, the chief monk of a monastery. In Sri Lanka *bhante* is simply a term for monk. In English such terms are usually translated as *Venerable*, also indicated by the *Ven.* title attached to names for formal usage. Other titles found in Theravadin cultures include *anagarika*, meaning "one without a home," a "wanderer" (and not necessarily a monk); *luang por,* in Thai and Laos, "Venerable grandfather monk;" *phra,* the Thai equivalent of *thera; phramaha,* a monk who has studied Pali; and *tan* (*than*), the Thai word for "Venerable."

JAPANESE AND KOREAN TITLES

In Japan many Zen BUDDHISM monks may be called *sensei,* "teacher," while more renowned or accomplished masters will be known as *roshi,* "elder master." Strictly speaking, a *sensei* has received a DHARMA transmission and so has higher status than a *hoshi,* a Dharma holder and apprentice instructor. Other titles also encountered in Japanese Buddhism include *daishi,* "great master" (assigned posthumously); *daiosho,* "great priest"; *hassu,* Dharma successor or "Dharma heir"; *jisha,* a roshi's attendant; *osho,* a priest; *sekko,* a Zen master; *shamon,* a novice (also a wanderer, monk, or priest); *shiso,* a teacher or tutor; *shoshi,* a "genuine master"; *taiko,* a priest who has undergone at least five years of training; and *unsu,* "cloud water," a novice.

In Korea priests and nuns are given the formal title of *sunim.*

Further reading: Robert E. Buswell, Jr., *The Zen Monastic Experience: Buddhist Practice in Contemporary Korea* (Princeton, N.J.: Princeton University Press, 1992); George Draffan, "Guidance on Finding a Buddhist Teacher or Organizations." Northwest Dharma Association. Available online. URL: www.nwdharma.org. Accessed on May 5, 2006; Mohan Wijayaratna, *Buddhist Monastic Life: According to the Texts of the Theravada Tradition.* Translated by Claude Grangier and Steven Collins (New York: Cambridge University Press, 1990).

Toda, Josei (1900–1958) *early leader of Soka Gakkai*

Josei Toda, who revived the Soka Gakkai movement (now SOKA GAKKAI INTERNATIONAL) in Japan in the years after World War II, was born in Ishikawa and grew up on Hokkaido, Japan's northern island. He became an elementary school teacher and at the age of 21 moved to Tokyo, where he obtained a job at Nishimachi Elementary School. As it happened, TSUNESABURO MAKIGUCHI, the future founder of Soka Gakkai, was the school's principal.

Toda resigned his teaching position after only a few years and worked as a private tutor and developed a publishing company. However, he stayed in contact with his former boss. Together they discovered the teachings of NICHIREN and affiliated with NICHIREN SHOSHU. When Soka Gakkai was founded, Toda was named its vice president. In July 1943, he was also arrested by the government. After Makiguchi's death in prison, Toda vowed to resume the work after World War II ended.

In 1946, in the new atmosphere of religious freedom imposed by the United States, Todo revived Soka Gakkai with the goal of converting the nation to the wisdom of Nichiren. He served as chairman of the board for the revived organization until 1949, when he was implicated in a major financial fraud. Ultimately all charges against him were dropped. Thus, when the new Soka Gakkai was formally initiated in 1951, he was named the president. The emphasis also shifted from the promotion of Mikiguchi's educational ideal to the spread of Nichiren's belief and the practice of chanting the LOTUS SUTRA MANTRA, *Namu Myoho-rengekyo,* before the GOHONZON (object of worship).

Among the early accomplishments of the movement under Toda were the initiation of two periodicals and the publication of a one-volume edition of the works of Nichiren and his disciple NIKKO, the founder of Nichiren Shoshu. Toda also wrote a commentary on Nichiren's writings and the Lotus Sutra, which he believed to be the quintessence of Buddhist teachings.

Toda led the organization to take its first movement into politics by successfully running candidates in the Tokyo local elections of 1955. The focus quickly turned to national politics—these members were elected to parliament in 1958.

In March 1958, the movement dedicated a great lecture hall at Taiseki-ji, Japan. Toda celebrated the event, at which it was announced that the goal he had set for the movement of winning 750,000 households to its cause had been met. The next month, he returned to Tokyo, where he unexpectedly became ill and died. His body was buried at Taiseki-ji and he was honored as the "chief of all the preachers of the Lotus Sutra."

Toda was succeeded two years later by DAISAKU IKEDA, the third president of Soka Gakkai.

Further reading: Noah S. Brannen, *Soka Gakkai: Japan's Militant Buddhists* (Richmond, Va.: John Knox Press, 1968); David Machachek and Bryan Wilson, eds., *Global Citizens: The Soka Gakkai Buddhist Movement in the World* (Oxford: Oxford University Press, 2000); Koichi Miyata, "The Lotus Sutra and Tsunesaburo Makiguchi and Josei Toda," *The Journal of Oriental Studies* 10 (2000): 56–71; Josei Toda, *Essays on Buddhism* (Tokyo: Seikyo Press, 1961).

Todai-ji

Todai-ji, the head temple of the KEGON school of Japanese Buddhism, was constructed in the new capital city of NARA in the middle of the eighth century. Kegon entered Japan from China in 736 and moved to construct a temple in Nara, which was named Konkomyo-ji. Buddhism was at this time intimately connected with the state and seen as a valuable force for its protection. The government sponsored the spread of Buddhism, especially among the country's elites. In 741, the government mandated the erection of two temples in each province of Japan.

In 743, the emperor ordered the building of a giant statue of VAIROCANA Buddha, the Buddha who shines like the sun, the principal Buddha of the Kegon school. The statue was cast in bronze and completed in 749, with the Konkomyo-ji temple taking responsibility for completing it. Meanwhile, in 747 Konkomyo-ji had been renamed Todai-ji. Also, in 749, gold was discovered in Japan, and it was used to cover the 53-foot-high statue. A great hall, the Dai-butsu-den, was then built around the statue to protect it. That hall was the largest wooden building in the world.

In 854 an ordination platform was erected at Todai-ji, and the Chinese monk Jian Jianzhen (also known in Japan as GANJIN), led a ceremony formally conferring the Buddhist precepts on the emperor Shommu, then living in a retired state. Todai-ji retained its important role in subsequent centuries in part because of its control over the ordination of Buddhist priests.

Todai-ji, including the Great Hall housing the Buddha, was burned during a civil war in 1180 and again in 1567. The giant statue survived the fires (as well as several earthquakes) but was damaged. The statue and the current building dating from the 18th century remain major pilgrimage sites in Nara. Though a third smaller than the eighth-century original, the present great hall is still the largest wooden structure in the world. The statue of Buddha was the largest bronze statue (49 feet in height) in the world for many years, slightly larger than the Amida Buddha at KAMAKURA, however, it was eclipsed in 1990 by the Giant Buddha in Hong Kong, which at 79.25 feet is almost twice as high.

Further reading: Kazuo Kasahara, ed., *A History of Japanese Religion*. Translated by Paul McCarthy and Gaynor Sekimori (Tokyo: Kosei, 2001); Takeshi Kobayashi, *Nara Buddhist Art, Todai-ji* (New York: Weatherhill, 1975); E. Dale Saunders, *Buddhism in Japan* (Philadelphia: University of Pennsylvania Press, 1964).

Tokugawa Shogunate

A shogun is, in Japan, a general or military ruler. In 1603, Tokugawa Ieyasu, a shogun of the Tokugawa family, established himself in power over Japan. He and his successors ruled from Tokyo, which at the time was called Edo, and the era of their rule (1603–1868) is often called the Edo period. The rule of the successive heads of the Tokugawa family would last until the middle of the 19th century.

By the time of the Tokugawa Shogunate a warrior class, the samurai, had emerged as the leading class in what had become a rigidly hierarchical society. The Shogunate privileged Buddhism in general and ZEN BUDDHISM in particular. Buddhism was acknowledged as the state religion, and significant sums of state money were given to build and maintain temples and monasteries. Buddhist priests were assigned an elevated place in the hierarchy (above peasants but below the samurai).

The Tokugawa government also moved to restructure the Buddhist community. During the last years of Tokugawa Ieyasu, sets of detailed regulations for each of the Buddhist sects were issued. Everyone was ordered to construct a Buddhist altar in the home, and, more significantly, to register as a "member" of their local temple. Forms of popular Buddhism, especially *kito* Buddhism, were discouraged. The reorganization effectively divided the country into a system of Buddhist "parishes" into which everyone fit. Buddhism was thoroughly integrated into the government administration.

Meanwhile, Zen Buddhism, both RINZAI ZEN and SOTO ZEN, had become the faith of samurai, the warrior class (who functioned as feudal lords). Their belief filtered down to special groups, such as the professional swordsmen. A new school, the OBAKU ZEN school, was introduced to Japan in 1654 by Yin Yuan, or as he came to be known in Japan, INGEN (1592–1673), a Zen practitioner from China. Obaku mixed Rinzai Zen with the veneration of AMITABHA. Receiving a grant from the shogunate, Yin Yuan built a monastery near Kyoto. Though it was never the largest Zen sect, Obaku Zen's arrival and spread assisted a revival of Zen in the late 17th century.

During the Tokugawa era, the imperial family continued to exist as the titular ruler of Japan. In the middle of the 19th century, the shogunate was shaken by the opening of Japan and the end of its heretofore isolationist foreign policy. This event created an opening for the overthrow of the Tokugawa Shogunate rule and the restoration of the emperor as the real ruler of Japan. The move from the Tokugawa era to the MEIJI RESTORATION era would also end Buddhism's privileged position in Japanese society.

Further reading: Helen J. Baroni, *Obaku Zen: The Emergence of the Third Sect of Zen in Tokugawa Japan* (Honolulu: University of Hawaii Press, 2000); Robert N. Bellah, *Tokugawa Religion: The Values of Pre-Industrial Japan* (New York: The Free Press, 1969); H. Byron Earhart, *Religion in the Japanese Experience: Sources and Interpretations* (Belmont, Calif.: Wadsworth, 1997); Kazuo Kasahara, ed., *A History of Japanese Religion.* Translated by Paul McCarthy and Gaynor Sekimori (Tokyo: Kosei, 2001).

tonsure

A tonsure is a rite of shaving the head in preparation for receiving monastic ORDINATION. In Buddhist practice all monks and nuns have their head shaved. This practice is symbolic of their leaving the family and society—in the Chinese term, *chu jia*, "leaving home."

The ceremony of shaving the head reflects a key event in the Buddha's own life. When he resolved to leave his family and his position as heir to his father's kingdom, he set out with his horse KANTAKA and groom Chandaka. He sent them back to the palace, and his next action was to cut off his hair with his sword. Several early Buddhist texts—the Lalitavistara and the Jatakattakatha, as well as the Mulasarvastivada Vinaya—relate what happens next. He throws the hairknot, called a *cuda*, into the air, where it is caught by the gods and held in Trayastrimasa Heaven. The gods there preserve the hairknot in a special *caitya* (STUPA), known as the Cudapratigrahana. In the JATAKA TALES it is Indra, king of the gods, who establishes the shrine, called the Culamani Shrine, in his own heaven, Trayastrimsa.

The *caitya* that contains the Buddha's top-knot is in heaven, not on earth. Such caitya were in general related to key events of his life, but were not sacred in the sense of belonging to an enlightened Buddha. They were not, therefore, relics with miraculous powers. Hence the relics are kept in heaven, not on earth, as a way to remind humans of the Buddha's passage toward enlightenment. Thus the tonsure is a preliminary step, symbolic of the will to cultivate the Buddha's DHARMA, not the actual achievement of enlightenment.

Further reading: John S. Strong, *Relics of the Buddha* (Princeton, N.J.: Princeton University Press, 2004).

torii

Standing at the entrance to SHINTO shrines (*jinga*), the *torii* (gate) is an archway that defines the sacred space into which the believer enters. Immediately beyond the *torii*, the believer finds a place for symbolic purification of the hands and mouth. Upon passing through the *torii*, a visitor also often claps his or her hands three times and bows three times, actions seen as a means to catch the attention of the KAMI (deity).

The *torii* is a freestanding structure, most often constructed of wood, minimally made with two vertical posts joined by two horizontal bars. From the basic structure a variety of innovations and decorations can be created, though most *torii* are painted orange (or more precisely, vermilion, a color available from ancient times made from cinnabar).

Among the more notable *torii* are the offshore *torii* that marks the entrance to the ITSUKU-SHIMA, on Miyajima Island, across the bay from Hiroshima, Japan, and the hundreds of *torii* that have been erected by successful businessmen at the Fushimi Inari shrine, a symbol of the positive

Torii at shrine to the Shinto deity Zeni-arai Benten, Kamakura, Japan

answers to their prayers for prosperity. The many *torii* at Fushimi Inari now cover paths several miles in length.

Further reading: H. Byron Earhart, *Japanese Religion: Unity and Diversity* (Belmont, Calif.: Wadsworth, 1982).

trikaya

The *trikaya*, or three body doctrine, is a major MAHAYANA BUDDHISM elaboration of the Buddha's nature. The Buddha was said to have had three manifestations at the same time. The NIRMANAKAYA, or transformation body, was his appearance; the DHAMMAKAYA, or DHARMA body, his eternal truth; and the *SAMBHOGAKAYA,* or bliss body, his celestial form.

triloka   *See* THREE REALMS.

Tripitaka

Literally meaning "three baskets," the *Tripitaka* is a name for the Buddhist canon. The Buddhist canon is traditionally divided into three types of texts, or *pitaka* ("baskets"). First are the Vinaya, which include the PATIMOKSA, or rules of behavior for monks and nuns. Second is the Sutra Pitaka, or discourses of the Buddha. And third are the Abhidarma Pitaka, commentaries on the Sutras and Buddhist concepts added over the years.

Marble slab incised with a portion of the Pali Tripitaka, part of a series of 729 that contains the entire Tripitaka, built between 1857 and 1900 and now housed at Kuthodaw Paya Temple, Mandalay, northern Myanmar (Burma)

The Pali Tipitaka (in Sanskrit, Tripitaka) is probably the oldest version of the Buddhist Tripitaka. The Pali Sutra Pitaka, discourses, are traditionally broken up into five bodies of work, or NIKAYA, and total some 5,398 separate suttas (SUTRAS) of various lengths. The Pali Abhidhamma Pitaka is composed of seven separate foundational texts: Dhammasangani (Enumeration of *dhammas*), Vibhanga (further analysis), Dhatukatha (discussion of elements), Puggalapannatti (description of individuals), Kathavatthu (discussion of the controversies among various BUDDHISM groups), Yamaka (Book of pairs), and Patthana (Book of relations).

The Mahayana canon is much vaster than the Pali Pitaka. It includes 3,053 separate texts, and in its standard Chinese version (the Taisho, 1922 version) takes up 85 volumes. Approximately 20–30 percent of the Pali Pitaka is present in the Taisho. However the Pali canon and its translations into Chinese or Tibetan are generally considered the core Tripitaka.

triratna   *See* THREE TREASURES.

True Buddha school

The True Buddha school emerged in the 1990s out of the life and experience of Master LU SHEN-YEN (1945–   ). Master Lu had a deep religious experience in 1971 that led him from his Christian upbringing into a period of seeking, study, and learning. During this period, which lasted for some 14 years, he studied with a succession of teachers of different religious traditions and several forms of Buddhism. Crucial, however, was his encounter with Tibetan Buddhism in 1976. He met Rangjung Rigpe Dorje (1924–81), the 16th *karmapa* of the KARMA KAGYU school. He was formally initiated into Tibetan Buddhism in 1981 by the KARMAPA. The next year, he moved to the United States.

On July 10, 1982, a Tibetan Buddhist deity appeared to Lu and assigned him a mission as the

Three major deities (Bodhisattva Kshitigarbha, left; Master Lu Sheng Yan, center; Guan Yin, right) worshipped in a True Buddhist school temple, in Taipei, Taiwan *(Institute for the Study of American Religion, Santa Barbara, California)*

one chosen to spread VAJRAYANA BUDDHISM teachings. The deity also bestowed upon him the title of "Holy Red Crown Venerable Vajra Master." Through this contact, Lu received the transmission of the Tibetan Buddhist teachings and his status as a master.

In 1983, Lu reorganized his by now quite substantial following from his year of teaching as the True Buddha school. Headquarters was established in a newly constructed temple in Redmond (suburban Seattle), Washington. With a Taiwanese following and an American headquarters he saw himself as positioned to build a large follow-

ing for Vajrayana Buddhism, especially among the many Chinese residing in Southeast Asia, North America, and Europe.

The teachings offered by the True Buddha school rest upon Master Lu's authority, which in turn rests upon his years of study with various Taiwanese, Taoist, and Buddhist teachers and his many spiritual contacts with a number of deity figures. This latter authority is emphasized to believers at the very beginning of their membership when they acknowledge the taking of refuge with a true teacher. They accept Master Lu as that true teacher (guru). Through his direct spiritual contacts with different BODHISATTVAS, Master Lu has claimed the status of *TULKU*, the emanation of a deity. His students acknowledge his enlightened state. This affirmation of Master Lu as a living Buddha places him at a level of other Tibetan teachers whose students claim to be tulkus.

For the student, the act of taking refuge may be made by visiting the temple in Redmond (not possible for most) or by joining in the twice-monthly remote initiation ceremonies performed by Master Lu. That process begins with the prospective student's rising early on one of the prescribed days (the first or 15th of any month on the lunar calendar) and at 7 A.M. (at their local time) repeating the basic refuge MANTRA three times, *Namo guru bei, namo Buddha ye, namo Dharma ye, namo Sangha ye.* On that same day, Master Lu will perform the empowering initiation ceremony wherever he happens to be. He will subsequently send a certificate acknowledging the student's membership and a note concerning

the practice the student is expected to begin. Students set up an altar in their home before which they daily chant and burn incense. They then begin practicing several of a number of spiritual exercises that include breath control, the use of mantras, and visualization techniques designed to improve the quality of their life and lead to enlightenment.

As of 2005, the students of the True Buddha school (TBS) had established more than 300 centers for TBS practice and worship. These temples operate independently of Master Lu and the school's international leadership but receive a charter and basic guidelines from the school. Participation in a center is not required, but most students find the local centers and the senior disciples in residence helpful to their progress.

Master Lu has appointed a number of teaching masters. It is from among the teaching masters that a central committee is selected to oversee the

True Buddha School lead temple, Seattle, Washington *(Institute for the Study of American Religion, Santa Barbara, California)*

school internationally. It oversees, for example, publishing and outreach programs. These have somewhat gone hand in hand, and while the school is still based primarily in the Chinese diaspora, a concerted effort has begun to translate Master Lu's writings into different local languages from Malay and Indonesian to English, French, Spanish, and Russian.

In 1992, he opened Rainbow Villa, in Washington's Cascade Mountains, as a facility for training senior leaders. In one early session at the Rainbow Villa, he delivered a set of lectures later collected into *A Complete and Detailed Exposition of the True Buddha Tantric Dharma,* the school's basic handbook.

Further reading: Lu Sheng-Yen, *Dharma Talks by a Living Buddha* (San Bruno, Calif.: Amitabha Enterprise, 1995); ———, *The Inner World of the Lake* (San Bruno, Calif.: Amitabha Enterprise, 1992); ———, *A Complete and Detailed Exposition of the True Buddha Tantric Dharma* (San Bruno, Calif.: Purple Lotus Society, 1995); Tam Wai Lun, "Integration of the Magical and Cultivational Discourses: A Study of a New Religious Movement Called the True Buddha School," *Monumenta Serica* 49 (2001): 141–169.

tsam dance

Festivals were a key way in which Buddhism spread from Tibet into Mongolia in the 16th and 17th centuries. Many of the Buddhist festivals involved ritual dances that exorcised evil. Called *tsam,* these were modeled on the Tibetan *cham* ceremonies and included both Buddhist and shamanic deity figures. The participants in the dance generally wore masks that today are highly prized for their artistic value.

Tsam performances were censored from the 1930s but have been revived from the 1990s. Today they can involve more than 100 dancers. The major *tsam* dance in the Mongolian capital of Ulaanbaatar is the ceremony for the 10 Dharma Protectors. It is held in early September at the Dashchoiling monastery. Deity figures include Erlik Khan, the god of death (in Sanskrit, YAMA), and Shridevi, the female protector of religion. Erlik Khan and his followers, in masks, dance around a MANDALA. A dough figure of a person is cut to pieces, signifying sacrifice.

A connected ceremony is the Sor Zalah, throwing the Sor, which takes place in the evening. Barley grains are thrown onto the ground and burned.

See also FESTIVALS, BUDDHIST; FESTIVALS, MONGOLIA.

Further reading: "Face Music—Projects—Tsam Dance Mongolia." Available online. URL: http://www.face-music.ch/tsam/tsamhistory_en.html. Accessed on July 10, 2006; "Festivals:" Available online. URL: http://www.asiasociety.org/arts/mongolia/festivals.html. Accessed on July 10, 2006; Walther Heissig, *The Religions of Mongolia.* Translated by G. Samuel (Berkeley: University of California Press, 1980); L. W. Moses and S. A. Halkovic Jr., *Introduction to Mongolian History and Culture* (Bloomington: Research Institute for Inner Asian Studies, Indiana University, 1985).

Ts'ao-tung   *See* CAODONG.

Tsong Khapa (Losang Drakpa) (1357–1419) *founder of the Gelug school of Tibetan Buddhism*

Tsong Khapa, known to his devotees as "Je Rinpoche" (Precious Master), was born in Amdo Province of eastern Tibet in 1357 and is regarded as an enlightened being. He is recognized by all schools and sects of Tibetan Buddhism as one of the foremost scholar-practitioners in their history. He was a reformer dedicated to the revitalization of the philosophical, ritual, and meditative practice of Buddhism.

According to his traditional spiritual biography, Tsong Khapa's life story begins long before his birth in 1357. As the story goes, in a previous birth, Tsong Khapa lived in the time of Sakyamuni Buddha. As a boy, he offered a crystal rosary to the Buddha, who gave him a conch shell in return and prophesied that in a future life he would be a great teacher born in Tibet named Losang Drakpa—this was the name given to Tsong Khapa when he took his novice monastic vows at seven years of age. Tsong Khapa's birth was heralded by the auspicious dreams of his mother and father and he is said to be the emanation of the BODHISATTVAS of Compassion and Wisdom—AVALOKITESVARA and MANJUSRI.

Tsong Khapa was nonsectarian in his outlook and studied under the best teachers of his day from several different lineages. He was ordained as a child by the fourth KARMAPA and his main teacher was the SAKYA master Rendawa. His own study and understanding led him to establish a new school of Buddhism in Tibet, the GELUG, which means "System of Virtue." The center of his reformed school was at Ganden monastery near Lhasa. Ganden is the Tibetan name for the heaven in which MAITREYA (the Buddha of the future) dwells, waiting for the right time to take birth.

Tsong Khapa became famous for his profound understanding of Buddhist teachings, his skill in debate, and his accomplishments in meditation practice. He completed many long retreats lasting for four and five years at a time. On one such retreat he is said to have prepared himself by doing three and a half million prostrations. The stone floor with grooves worn into it where he performed the prostrations is still there and serves to inspire his followers today. Among Tsong Khapa's most important works are the *Golden Rosary of the Good Explanations,* a commentary on the Perfection of Wisdom Sutras; *The Great Exposition of Secret Mantra* (*Ngakrim chenmo*); and the work which forms the foundation practice of the Gelugpa school, *The Great Exposition of the Stages of the Path* (*Lamrim chenmo*). As a devout monk and religious reformer, Tsong Khapa was concerned with the restoration of pure monas-

tic discipline and the reconciliation of TANTRA, which includes esoteric (transmitted secretly from teacher to student) sexual practices, with monastic vows.

The four great deeds attributed to Tsong Khapa are (1) the restoration of a Maitreya statue in Lhasa carried out at the end of a four-year retreat in which he and eight disciples received a vision of Maitreya; (2) an utterly clear and profound teaching on the rules of the monastic discipline; (3) the offering of a golden crown to the statue of Sakyamuni Buddha in Lhasa when he inaugurated the Monlam Great Prayer Festival that begins the Tibetan New Year; (4) the building of the great hall of Ganden monastery. Tsong Khapa died at the age of 62 at Ganden monastery. It is said that he died sitting in meditation and that his body appeared to his disciples as a body of rainbow light.

Further reading: John Powers, *Introduction to Tibetan Buddhism* (Ithaca, N.Y.: Snow Lion, 1995), 402–410; Robert A. F. Thurman, ed., *The Life and Teachings of Tsong Khapa* (Dharamsala, India: Library of Tibetan Works and Archives, 1982).

Tsukiyomi no Mikoto

One of the major SHINTO deities, Tsukiyomi no Mikoto, is the moon deity (KAMI), the ruler of the night. Tsukiyomi first appears in the ancient Shinto creation myths. According to the eighth-century text the *KOJIKI,* in the process of creating Japan to appear from the primordial ocean, the creative couple, Izanagi no Mikoto and Izanami no Mikoto, suffer a tragedy. Izanami, the female, dies, and Izanagi goes on a fruitless search for her in the underworld. After his return, he goes through a purification ritual in which he first cleans his eyes and nose. From his right eye emerges AMATERASU OMI-KAMI, the sun goddess, and from his left eye Tsukiyomi no Mikoto, while SUSANO-O NO MIKOTO, the sea god, emerges from nose cleaning. (There are alternate versions of this story that offer different details of the way Izanagi created the three deities).

According to another ancient Japanese scripture, Amaterasu and Tsukiyomi had a later falling out, a story that explains the separation between the Sun and the Moon in the heavens.

Veneration of Tsukiyomi is spread throughout Japan, though it takes second place to that offered Amaterasu. The most ubiquitous rites are the "watching of the moon" ceremonies. At the ISE SHRINE, the main Shinto shrine in central Japan, Amaterasu is venerated in the Inner Shrine and Tsukiyomi in the Outer Shrine. Tsukiyomi has his own shrines such as the Wakamiya Shrine in Kyoto and the Gassai-den shrine on Mt. Haguro in northern Japan.

Further reading: D. C. Holtom, *The National Faith of Japan* (New York: Paragon Book Reprint, 1965); *Kojiki.* Translated by Donald L. Philippi (Tokyo: University of Tokyo Press, 1968); *Nihongi: Chronicles of Japan from the Earliest Times to* A.D. 697. Translated by W. G. Aston (London: George Allen & Unwin, 1956); Sokyo Ono, *Shinto the Kami Way* (Rutland, Vt.: Charles E. Tuttle, 1972).

tulku

Most Tibetan and Mongolian Buddhist teachers (lamas) are also tulku; that is, they are considered to be existing as the emanation body of a deity or an enlightened being, a Buddha or a BODHISATTVA. In MAHAYANA BUDDHISM, the Buddha had three bodies—the higher DHARMAKAYA, the *bhoga-kaya* (enjoyment body), and the NIRMANAKAYA. The *nirmanakaya*, or transformation body, is understood to be the physical manifestation of his/her DHARMA qualities. A Buddha or bodhisattva has an excess of dharma qualities that may become visible as a physical body. Believers thus approach a lama as a semidivine being.

Once a Buddha or bodhisattva incarnates, reincarnation seems assured. Thus when a *tulku*/lama

passes from the physical, those around him or her begin to search for the next manifestation. Usually, a list of children born within a year or two of the deceased is assembled and these children are visited and tested. Tests include observation of the child's reaction to objects that belonged to the deceased lama. Those who knew the deceased will also look for any similarities.

Through the early 20th century, the search for new lamas/tulkus had been limited to Tibet and Mongolia, where until 1959 all *tulku* resided. That situation changed in the last half of the 20th century with the rise of communist China, the movement of so many Tibetans and their leaders into exile, and the development of a large body of Western Tibetan Buddhists. Then in 1976, O. K. Maclise was "recognized" as the reincarnation of Sangye Nyenpa Rinpoche, a KARMA KAGYU lama, considered to be an emanation of MANJUSRI. Since that time, a number of Western children have also been recognized as reincarnated lamas. Among the most interesting of the Western tulkus is Alyce Zeoli (1949–). A female, Zeoli was an adult when she was recognized as the reincarnation of JETSUNMA AHKON NORBU LHAMO.

The conflict between the Peoples' Republic of China and the TIBETAN GOVERNMENT-IN-EXILE has created a most significant competition over the authority to "recognize" a *tulku* formally in the case of the current PANCHEN LAMA. After the death of the 10th Panchen Lama in 1989, two searches began for his successor. One took place in Tibet with the cooperation of Chinese authorities. The second was carried out by Tibetans associated with the DALAI LAMA. Both announced their findings in 1995. These two candidates, both approaching adulthood, now look to the larger Tibetan community for support.

The leaders of the several Tibetan Buddhist schools and leading subschools are seen as tulku, but there are several hundred additional tulku, a number of whom have founded new Buddhist organizations in the West as branches of one of the larger schools. By far the most famous *tulku* is, of course, the Dalai Lama, who is considered the emanation of GUAN YIN.

Further reading: Graham Coleman, *A Handbook of Tibetan Culture* (Boston: Shambhala, 1994); *The Confirmation and Enthronement of the 11th Bainqen Erden* (Beijing: China Tibetology Publishing House, 1996); Isabel Hilton, *The Search for the Panchen Lama* (New York: W. W. Norton, 2001); Vicki Mackenzie, *Reborn in the West: The Reincarnation Masters* (London: Marlowe, 1995); Andrew Rawlinson, *The Book of Enlightened Masters: Western Teachers in Eastern Traditions* (La Salle, Ill.: Open Court, 1997).

tumo (tummo)

Tumo, literally "inner heat," is a meditation technique in Tibetan Buddhism in which the practitioner actually raises his or her body temperature. This result is achieved by a combination of breath control, visualization, MANTRAS, and a focus on parts of the body. In the 11th century, NAROPA borrowed techniques from Indian yogas and initially spelled out the *tumo* process.

ALEXANDRA DAVID-NÉEL first made practice of *tumo* known in the West in her book *Magic and Mystery in Tibet* (1931). Through the last half of the 20th century, several Western esoteric groups—part of a multifaceted tradition uniting spiritualism, occultism, and other mystical practices—incorporated *tumo* practice into their course of spiritual development. Most recently, several Tibetan teachers have offered training in the meditation practices associated with *tumo*.

Further reading: Alexandria David-Néel, *Magic and Mystery in Tibet* (London: John Lane, The Bodley Head, 1931); Reginald A. Ray, *Secret of the Vajra World: The Tantric Buddhism of Tibet* (Boston: Shambhala, 2001); Thubten Yeshe et al., *The Bliss of Inner Fire: Heart Practice of the Six Yogas of Naropa* (Somerville, Mass.: Wisdom, 1998).

twenty-eight patriarchs

The twenty-eight patriarchs is the standard list of CHAN BUDDHISM (ZEN BUDDHISM) masters, beginning with Mahakasyapa, the Buddha's great disciple and expert on doctrine, and extending through ANANDA, Sanakavasa, Upagupta, Dhrtaka, Mikkaka, Vasumitra, Buddhanandi, Buddhamitra, Parsva, Punyayasas, Asvaghosa, Kapimala, NAGARJUNA, Kanadeva, Rahulata, Sanghanandi, Gayasata, Kumarata, Jayata, VASUBANDHU, Manorhita, Haklena, Aryasimha, Basiasita, Punyamitra, Prajnatara, and BODHIDHARMA. The TIAN TAI SCHOOL traditionally counts 23 patriarchs, but all Chan schools count 28. This same list has been adopted by TIAN DAO/YIGUANDAO groups as part of their own patriarchal line of succession.

Further reading: Internet Sacred Text Archive. "List of Patriarchs." Available online. URL: http://www.sacred-texts.com/bud/taf/taf10.htm. Accessed on May 22, 2006; William Edward Soothill and Lewis Hodous, comps., *A Dictionary of Chinese Buddhist Terms: With Sanskrit and English Equivalents and a Sanskrit-Pali Index* (London: Kegan Paul, Trench, Trubner, 1937).

Tzu Chi   *See* BUDDHIST COMPASSION RELIEF TZU CHI ASSOCIATION.

U

U Ba Khin (1899–1971) *Burmese vipassana meditation master*

U Ba Khin, founder of the INTERNATIONAL MEDITATION CENTRE, was born in Rangoon, Burma (now Yangon, Myanmar). As a young man he obtained a job as a civil servant in the British colonial government. He first encountered meditation in 1937 and responded so powerfully to the experience that he immediate sought out Saya Thetgyi, a VIPASSANA teacher who had a center at Pyawbwegyi, outside Rangoon, and studied with him. In 1941 he met Webu Sayadaw, a monk proficient in meditation, who urged U Ba Khin to teach. He did not begin teaching, however, until some 10 years later. Meanwhile he worked at his government job even after Burma gained its independence. Only in the 1960s, four years before his death, did he retire and become a full-time meditation teacher.

Along the way, in 1950, he founded the Vipassana Association to facilitate his coworkers' learning to meditate, and two years later he opened the International Meditation Centre, where he received student from across the country and many foreign lands. He accepted many Western students as he was one of the very few *vipassana* teachers at the time who spoke English.

Among his most prominent students was SATYA NARAYAN GOENKA, an Indian who grew up in Burma. After studying with U Ba Khin Goenka established the VIPASSANA INTERNATIONAL ACADEMY in India and has developed an international following.

Further reading: *The Clock of Vipassana Has Struck: A Tribute to the Life and Legacy of Sayagyi U Ba Khin* (Igatpuri, India: Vipassana Research, 1999); U Ba Khin, *The Essentials of Buddha Dhamma in Meditative Practice, with an Essay on U Ba Khin by Eric Lerner* (Kandy, Sri Lanka: Buddhist Publication, 1981).

Uisang (625–702) *Korean Buddhist teacher*

Master Uisang Sunim, a major figure in the transmission to Korea of HWAOM BUDDHISM (the Korean form of Chinese HUA YAN Buddhism), is seen as the founder of Korean Buddhist philosophy. Uisang emerges on the historical stage as a companion of WONHYO (617–686 C.E.). In 650, the pair tried to travel from their native KOGURYO (the northern Korean kingdom) to China to study but were taken for spies and arrested at the border. Eleven years later, they made a second attempt, this time planning to sail from a port city in PAEKCHE (one of the southern Korean kingdoms). Delayed by a storm, they took refuge in what proved to be an old tomb, where Wonhyo had a vision that convinced him that the journey was a waste of his time.

Uisang traveled on to China, where he would spend 10 years, during which he studied with Zhi-yan (or Chih-yen, 602–668), the second patriarch of the Hua Yan school. Uisang returned home, according to one source, because he became privy to a Chinese plot to launch a surprise attack on his homeland, which had just gone through a lengthy period of warfare that united the peninsula into the kingdom of SILLA (668). After he returned to Korea in 671, Uisang spent the rest of his life establishing Hua Yan, or Hwaom Buddhism, across Korea.

The Hwaom school emphasized a doctrine of the interpenetrability of all of the phenomena of the universe, all of which arise from the original One Mind, or BUDDHA NATURE. One popular expression of this doctrine appeared in Uisang's book *Ocean Seal of Hwaeom Buddhism,* "In one is all, in all is one, one is identical to all, all is identical to one."

Uisang would gather many disciples and greatly influence his former companion Wonhyo, who used Hwaom perspectives to argue for the merger of the different Korean Buddhist schools. He also established the headquarters for Hwaom Buddhists at Pusok Temple, originally constructed in 676 C.E. under the patronage of Silla's King Munmu. Over three decades he would make Hwaon Buddhism the most important school of Buddhism until the 12th century.

Further reading: Sae Hyang Chung, "The Silla Priests Uisang and Wonhyo," *Korean Culture* 3, no. 4 (December 1982): 36–43; Peter H. Lee, "Fa-tsang and āisang." *Journal of the American Oriental Society* 82 (1962): 56–62.

Ullambana

Ullambana is a major festival celebrated in many countries in Asia, such as China, Japan, and Korea, through which Buddhists affirm their attachments to their ancestors. Held in August, it is variously known as the festival of All Souls and the festival of Hungry Ghosts. The observance of Ullambana is based in the Ullambana Sutra, a text of Chinese origin, which tells the story of the ARHAT MAUDGALYAYANA (in Chinese known as Mulian) and his mother. Having discovered that his deceased mother now exists in a realm of pain and suffering, marked by the inability to eat, he journeys to the netherworld to find a means of changing her condition. He finds her, but all his efforts to stop her suffering backfire. When he appeals to the Buddha, he is told that he alone cannot directly accomplish an end to her problem. The Buddha then tells Maudgalyayana to make offerings of various items to the monks and nuns, and then to join them in prayers for the liberation of his mother's soul from hell. The effect of his action will not just affect his mother, but also his other deceased relatives. Ullambana observes the day on which Maudgalyayana performed as the Buddha had suggested.

Ullambana merged with a preexisting general Chinese belief that in the seventh month of the Chinese calendar the souls of those trapped in the underworld, whose descendants have made no offerings for them, are free to wander the boundaries where the underworld and the visible world meet. These souls are described as PRETAS or, in everyday terms, "hungry ghosts" (and celebrated in Hong Kong movies as vampires) and may manifest a variety of mischief and evil.

Today, the festival occurs each August (the 15th day of the seventh lunar month). Participants offer prayers for the souls of their ancestors for the last seven generations, but especially deceased parents, and carry offerings to the local monasteries for the monks and nuns. The activities of the festival are believed to alleviate the suffering of ancestors and allow them to escape to the heavenly realm. To appease the hungry ghosts, people gather to offer them food, drink, and entertainment and use the occasion to imbibe them as well.

Further reading: Richard H. Robinson and Willard L. Johnson, *The Buddhist Religion: A Historical Introduction* (Belmont, Calif.: Wadsworth, 1997); Carol Stepanchuk and Charles Wong, *Mooncakes and Hungry Ghosts: Festivals of China* (South San Francisco, Calif.: China Books & Periodicals, 1992); Laurence G. Thompson, *Chinese Religion* (Belmont, Calif.: Wadsworth, 1996).

Unified Buddhist Church

The Unified Buddhist Church is the governing body for the variety of centers associated with THICH NHAT HANH, including Plum Village, France; the Maple Forest Monastery and Green Mountain Dharma Center (Vermont, United States); and the Community of Mindful Living, Parallax Press, and Deer Park Monastery (California, United States). It was established in Vietnam by Thich Nhat Hanh in the 1960s and was registered in the United States in 1997.

Further reading: "About the Community of Mindful Living." Community of Mindful Living. Available online. URL: http://www.iamhome.org/cml_about.html. Accessed on May 5, 2005.

United States, Buddhism in

Many contemporary observers argue that a new form of Buddhism is taking shape in the West, especially in the United States. This new Buddhism is eclectic, egalitarian, and practical. It allows equal treatment of men and women. Teachers borrow from many traditions that had largely been kept separate in Asian home countries. Rituals are simplified. And meditation is offered to all members, lay and SANGHA alike. American Buddhism can be generally described as consisting of three groups: old-line congregations, converts to Buddhism, and a group often called "ethnic Buddhists," those who are Buddhist because they are from an ethnic group which is normally Buddhist. We begin by describing these three aspects of Buddhism in the United States,

then discuss the history of Buddhism in the United States.

OLD LINE CONGREGATIONS

The prototypical group here is the BUDDHIST CHURCHES OF AMERICA, a Japanese JODO SHINSHU group established in San Francisco in 1900 as the Buddhist Mission of North America. At the same time YOUNG MEN'S BUDDHIST ASSOCIATIONS (BMNAs) were founded in many West Coast cities, as well as a Buddhist Women's Association (the Fujinakai). There were also Chinese temples in California, with informal temple associations, but these did not formally organize in the same way the Japanese ethnic groups, in Hawaii and along the West Coast, did.

The BMNA, which was formally renamed the Buddhist Churches of America (BCA) in 1944, was affected seriously by the internment of around 100,000 ethnic Japanese U.S. citizens during World War II. After this collective experience the members moved to become more mainstream and Americanized. Reforms gave second-generation (nisei) leaders more authority, and the bishop was elected from native-born candidates, not sent from Japan. Services, while obviously Buddhist, reflect some simplifications and, to some observers, "Protestantization" (simplification and deletion of ritual). Still primarily composed of descendants of ethnic Japanese, the BCA today has approximately 5,000–10,000 members.

CONVERTS

"Convert Buddhism" is the fastest growing and most visible side of Buddhism in America. The number of converts mushroomed from the 1960s, until today there are more than 1,000 meditation centers in use throughout the United States. Buddhist publishing targeting these new Buddhists is also a vast industry, with publishers such as SHAMBHALA INTERNATIONAL and magazines such as *Tricycle* readily available on bookshelves. The various convert Buddhist groups tend to cluster into communities associated with traditions—Tibetan

Buddhism, THERAVADA, ZEN BUDDHISM, JODO SHIN-SHU, and, increasingly, Chinese, Korean, and Vietnamese. Americans of all backgrounds have been attracted to each of these traditions. So each tradition has a unique institutional history within the American context.

Zen

Conditioned largely by the refined writings of DAISETSU TEITARO SUZUKI and the early missionary work of Zen masters such as SHIGETSU SASAKI ROSHI, NYOGEN SENZAKI KYOZAN, JOSHU SASAKI ROSHI, and SHUNRYU SUZUKI, the Japanese tradition of Zen took root early in the United States and has left a strong stamp on the general perception of Buddhism in American culture. Zen was influential to the BEAT ZEN poets of the 1950s. Both SOTO ZEN and RINZAI ZEN temples were established on both coasts. Today such centers as the San Francisco Zen Center and the White Plum Sangha continue Zen practice. But non-Japanese Zen groups have also been established and have thrived. These include Seung Sahn Sunim's KWAN UM SCHOOL and THICH NHAT HANH's centers.

Tibetan Buddhism

Tibetan Buddhism moved onto the worldwide stage after the Chinese invasion of Tibet in 1959, and the subsequent mass migration of Tibetan masters to India. The first Tibetan monastery in the United States was founded by Geshe Wangal in 1955. This was followed by strong growth in the 1970s when CHOGYAM TRUNGPA, Tarthang Tulku, and KALU RINPOCHE arrived and began to attract students. Chogyam Trungpa was especially successful and founded significant institutions of learning (NAROPA University) and publishing (Shambhala).

Just as Zen was closely associated with the Beat movement of the 1950s, so Tibetan Buddhism became associated with the counterculture movement of the 1960s and 1970s. Once this movement tapered off, a strong attraction remained for elements of Tibetan practice, study, and, uniquely, political activism. Tibetan Buddhism also became a major focus of academic work in American universities. Political support, under the banner of the Free Tibet movement, also became a significant aspect, with several high-profile Hollywood actors involved in supporting Tibetan political issues.

Vipassana Buddhism

VIPASSANA, insight meditation, is the typical meditation technique associated with THERAVADA practitioners in America. Many teachers were American-born individuals who picked up Theravada practice in Theravada countries during the 1960s and 1970s then returned to teach in America. These included Jack KORNFIELD, Sharon Salzberg, and Joseph Goldstein, cofounders of the Insight Meditation Society. Most of the *vipassana* teachers are lay practitioners and prolific writers. Many have also shown a keen interest in PSYCHOLOGY and the integration of Buddhist techniques as practical tools of psychology.

Nichiren

The major representative of this form of Japanese PURE LAND BUDDHISM is SOKA GAKKAI INTERNATIONAL, a worldwide movement very strong in the United States. Soka Gakkai, known in the United States as SGI-USA, is a form of NICHIREN SHOSHU, a *NEMBUTSU*-based religion that expanded quickly after World War II through its effective proselytization techniques. Many early American converts were Japanese women married to American servicemen, who on arriving in America maintained their involvement in Soka Gakkai.

ETHNIC BUDDHISMS

The label *ethnic Buddhisms* refers to the Buddhist practices of a wide variety of contemporary immigrant groups, from Vietnamese to Chinese to Thai to Mongolian, Korean, and Sri Lankan. These practices tend to be confined to the ethnic community, and the focus is generally not on reaching out to the larger community, although such contact certainly occurs. Ethnic-based groups, while low-profile and not always well organized, account for at least half of the 1- to 2-million Buddhist practitioners in America. They have blossomed largely as a result of the liberalized immigration policies of the 1960s. The Buddhist Churches of America can in this sense be seen as a forerunner of the way such groups may develop in the future. There will, for instance, be inevitable conflicts between the various generations in the ethnic community, with the second and third generations losing use of the mother tongue and depending on English. Some can be expected to develop strong institutional forms in America, and some will become ingrained fixtures in the everyday life of America.

HISTORICAL SURVEY OF BUDDHISM IN AMERICA

Buddhism first became a topic of interest to Americans through the Transcendentalists. This was a 19th-century intellectual movement centered in New England whose members sought new direction from the romantic philosophers and writers of Europe. The Transcendentalists included Ralph Waldo Emerson (1803–82) and Henry David Thoreau (1817–62), most prominently, but also such influential figures as Margaret Fuller (1810–50), a feminist, and Bronson Alcott (1799–1888), an educator. This group, in the pages of their magazine, the *Dial*, explored Hindu and, later, Buddhist writings that had only recently been translated through the efforts of such early Orientalists as William Jones (1746–94). The group published the LOTUS SUTRA in America for the first time in 1844. While their interests lay mainly with Hindu literature, they can be considered pre-Buddhist in their sympathies. Once more translations and writings on Buddhism began to appear in the later 1800s—such important works as Sir EDWIN ARNOLD's *The Light of Asia*, in 1878—they found a ready audience in readers familiar with the Transcendentalists.

By the late 1800s something quite different from the Transcendentalists was happening on the West Coast—mass migrations from Buddhist cultures. The discovery of gold, beginning in 1848 in California, generated strong demand for labor from China and, later, Japan. By 1860 10 percent of Californians were Chinese. And by 1900 there were more than 400 Chinese temples scattered throughout the West Coast, including some in Vancouver, Canada. Some of these temples were strictly Buddhist while others were dedicated to local deities.

A similar flood of immigrants, this time from Japan, transformed Hawaii in the late 1800s. Hawaii's King Kalakaua (1836–91)—Hawaii at the time was still an independent kingdom—actually visited Japan in 1881 to request more labor be sent from Japan. The first Buddhist priest from Japan, a representative of the HONPA HONGWANJI branch of JODO SHINSHU, visited Hawaii in 1889 to look after the welfare of Japanese workers and before returning oversaw the building of the first Buddhist temple, in Hilo. Japanese immigrants also began to move to the West Coast, generally to work in agriculture, although their numbers were much lower than those of the Chinese working in mining and the railroads.

Theosophy and Reinvented Traditions

The Theosophy movement, established in New York in 1875, gave America yet another angle on Buddhism. While the key early figure in the movement, Madame HELENA BLAVATSKY PETROVNA, was a spiritualist and a mystic and did not solely focus on Buddhism, Buddhism became a key symbol of alternative religiosity for the movement. It was Theosophy's cofounder, HENRY STEEL OLCOTT, who would fully explore this alternative spiritual tradition. He spent years in India and Sri Lanka and was crucial in the movement to restore Buddhism's place of privilege in Sri Lanka. Olcott became a committed Buddhist. And unlike Blavatsky, Olcott was seeking an alternative to materialism as a life philosophy. His *Buddhist Catechism* was an influential example of his efforts to introduce Buddhism to his home society.

The World's Parliament of Religions

By the end of the 19th century Buddhism had become more familiar to Americans, first as an object of curiosity, but second also as an alternative to modern society. There is a long tradition of critical social commentary in Western culture, including America's. Modern life was moving in a direction that troubled many, and Buddhism was seen by some as a viable alternative. LAFCADIO HEARN (1849–1904), an early representative of this trend, saw Buddhism as well as SHINTO and Japanese values as an alternative to "the ugliness of things new." Another American who had visited and studied Buddhism in Japan, William Bigelow (1850–1926), saw Buddhism as a repudiation of the Western idea of the self.

A turning point was reached at the World's Parliament of Religions, held at Chicago in 1893 as part of the Columbian Exhibition. The organizers sought to underline the unity of all religions and invited representatives of many major Asian traditions to which Americans had rarely been exposed. The result was a smorgasbord of alternative, nonmainstream faiths seated together—the Catholic cardinal with Swami Vivekananda (1863–1902) from India, and representatives from China and Japan. ANGARIKA DHARMAPALA reminded those present at the council of ASOKA held in India more than 2,000 years earlier, and the great "mild-garbed" missionary effort that had resulted from that council. Other Buddhists present included SOYEN SHAKU, a RINZAI ZEN master, as well as representatives from NICHIREN SHOSHU, SHINGON, TENDAI, and Jodo Shinshu traditions. Prince Chandradat from Thailand lectured on the DHARMA.

The parliament initially exposed many Americans who would go on to power the dissemination of Buddhist ideas for the next half-century to the new faith. One of the most prominent of these individuals was PAUL CARUS, who was then editing a series on Oriental classics. Soyen Shaku introduced him to Daisetsu Teitaro Suzuki, then a student, who would go on to publish highly popular writings on MAHAYANA BUDDHISM. and ZEN BUDDHISM. And the businessman CHARLES T. STRAUSS, made an unexpected profession of faith in Buddhism at the parliament, the first person to do so in America.

The Missionary Wave

The first missionary from Japanese Buddhism was SORYU KAGAHI, who arrived in Hawaii in 1898. On the U.S. mainland, Eryu Honda arrived in San Francisco in 1898 and quickly established the first Young Men's Buddhist Association (Bukkyo Seinenkai) there. This association requested that the Hongwanji head office in Kyoto send permanent priest-monks. This happened in 1899 when Shuei Sonada and Kakuryo Nishimjima arrived. They were in turn instrumental in establishing a small group of ethnic Japanese and non-Japanese, the Dharma Sangha of Buddha, one of the precursors of the Buddhist Churches of America. The most influential early missionary, however, was Soyen Shaku, who had attended the World's Parliament in 1893. He returned to America to stay for a few years in 1905. His follower Nyogen Senzaki would remain after Soyen Shaku's return to Japan and go on to found the mentorgarten, a ZAZEN group in Los Angeles.

Soyen Shaku's group was followed in 1906 by a group led by Sokatsu Shaku and Shigetsu Sasaki Roshi (better known as Sokei-an), a sculptor. Sokei-an would remain in America. He moved eventually to New York in 1916, where he founded, in 1931, the Buddhist Society of America (later the First Zen Institute).

Alan Watts and Beat Zen

A prolific writer on Zen and Eastern spirituality, ALAN WILSON WATTS (1915–73), was interested in Buddhism from an early age. However, after traveling to America from England in 1938 he also became interested in the possibilities of Christian mysticism, and he became a Christian (Episcopalian) cleric. Watt studied off and on with a string of teachers, including Sokei-an, founder of the First Zen Institute. However, he was never a monk and saw himself more as an individualist outside mainstream society, a member of the Beat generation who lived and breathed alienation.

For the Beat generation, Buddhism was less an expression of alienation than a way to explore the self more fully. The Beats were detached from but not wholly despairing of modern social life. BEAT ZEN was a concept that attempted to merge Beat culture with Zen practice. It never became a widespread movement, however, and was confined to the small number of artists curious about Buddhism.

Besides Watts, Buddhism and especially Zen attracted other well-known Beat figures, of course, including Jack Kerouac, Allen Ginsburg, and the poet GARY SNYDER. But from the point of view of organizational advancement of Buddhism the two most influential members of the Beat generation were Philip Kapleau, who had originally served in Tokyo after World War II, and ROBERT BAKER AITKEN. Aitken, who also studied literature at Berkeley and Hawaii, became a student of YASUTANI HAKUUN ROSHI in Japan. He eventually established the Diamond Sangha in Hawaii. Kapleau established the Zen Meditation Center in Rochester, New York.

The Sixties and Seventies: Competing Traditions Flood In

The missionary wave of the previous generation became a flood in the 1960s, as representatives from Japanese Zen continued to arrive along with teachers from other ethnic groups who had not been present previously. Two new Zen masters, SHUNRYU SUZUKI ROSHI and Yasutani Roshi, were the most influential of the new Zen masters. Suzuki arrived in San Francisco in 1959 and stayed at Soko-ji, a Soto Zen temple begun in 1934. He offered classes in strict *zazen* (sitting). The San Francisco Zen Center was an offshoot of Suzuki's teachings at Sokoji.

Yasutani Roshi arrived in 1962, by then 77. He began to hold *sesshin* meetings, intense Rinzai meditation sessions intended to force students to break through barriers to ENLIGHTENMENT, throughout the country.

Shunryu Suzuki's San Francisco Zen Center later developed the Tassajara Zen Mountain Center on the California coast. It was here that both Sensaki's and Suzuki Roshi's ashes were scattered after their deaths. Along with the San Francisco Zen Center, Tassajara and later the Green Gulch Zen Farm were showcases for American Zen.

Overall the 1960s saw a broad transformation of focus in Zen groups away from theory and toward practice. Zen practice groups were established in New York, Maine, Boston, Philadelphia, Washington, San Francisco, and Hawaii.

In addition to Zen activities, teachers from non-Japanese traditions began to arrive. Master HSUAN HUA, a strict CHAN BUDDHISM teacher originally from northern China, attracted a following in San Francisco.

Tibetan Buddhism began a gradual entry into America with the arrival of Geshe Wangyal, a monk from Lhasa who had lived in Russia. He taught a first generation of Tibetan scholar-specialists—including Robert Thurman and Jeffrey Hopkins. Thurman went on to become the first American-born Tibetan monk.

Tibetan teachers arrived in full force in the 1970s, with Tarthang Tulku, a NYINGMA monk, in Berkeley in 1969, and Chogyam Trungpa in Vermont and, eventually, Colorado in 1970. Chogyam Trungpa established VAJRADHATU (now SHAMBHALA INTERNATIONAL and headed by Trungpa's son, Jamgön Mipham Rinpoche), and Tarthang established the Nyingma Institute, in 1973.

Theravada also became established in America in the 1970s, especially through the work of Joseph Goldstein and JACK KORNFIELD, two former Peace Corps volunteers who had studied *vipassana* in, respectively, BODHGAYA (the site of the Buddha's ENLIGHTENMENT) and Thailand. They set up the Insight Meditation Center in Barre, Massachusetts, in 1976.

Korean and Vietnamese strands of Mahayana practice also arrived in the 1970s. The first Korean to enter was Soen-sa-nim, in 1972, who established SON BUDDHISM (Korean Zen) centers in Los Angeles, New York, Connecticut, Boston, and Berkeley. He was followed by Ku San Sunim, who taught at the Korean Buddhist Sambosa in Carmel, California.

The Vietnamese first arrived in the form of Dr. Thien-an, a scholar monk trained in Rinzai Zen. He founded a Vietnamese group, the International Buddhist Meditation Center, in Los Angeles.

Buddhism as a Contemporary Social Presence

By the late 1980s Buddhism had clearly established a multifaceted institutional presence throughout the United States. Groups ranged from small meditation circles to larger, congregation-sized churches meeting regularly. And as part of the American social scene Buddhist groups experienced the strains and issues current at the time. Most prominent were cases of sexual misconduct that surfaced in a variety of traditions. The San Francisco Zen Center was engulfed in controversy concerning the lifestyle of its leader, Zentatsu Baker Roshi. And the Vajradhatu, the organization founded by Chogyam Trungpa, was rocked by rumors that its leader, Osel Tendzin, had contracted acquired immunodeficiency syndrome (AIDS) and continued to have unprotected sex. In various ways the members of these groups were learning that no leadership was immune to issues in the society at large.

Another major theme in both American society and many Buddhist groups was the status of women. One survey has found that 57 percent of Buddhist members in the United States were women, with the highest number of women from *vipassana* groups. These American women began to question the lower status of women in many Buddhist traditions. Major female teachers, from Sharon Salzberg, a cofounder of the Insight Meditation Society in Barre, Massachusetts, to ANE PEMA CHODRON, have emerged. Some but not all of these leaders have adopted feminist positions. Retreats for women have been held. And many Buddhist groups have experimented with nonhierarchical forms of organization.

Modern American Buddhism has also given birth to unique mixtures. Special interest groups combine with Buddhism on the American scene, with unexpected results. Despite decades of dis-

cussion, modern America remains homophobic. It is not surprising, then, to see that gay Buddhists have organized. The Gay Buddhist Fellowship and the Dharma Sisters were formed in San Francisco in the 1990s. Some members felt that their original SANGHAS did not provide an environment in which they could openly express gay identity. In a Buddhist sense the setting up of such environments can be seen as an act of compassion toward others.

American Buddhism also has an activist bent, in line with the traditional involvement of religious groups in American society. Most American Buddhists desire social involvement from their spiritual community, including charitable activities. However, meditation is still seen as the core activity for American Buddhists, not community building or ritual. There thus exists some tension around this issue, and different groups have effected different creative outcomes. A final important development in the American context is ecumenical: the different groups, once established in America, have become fully aware of each other's presence as fellow Buddhists and now engage in dialog and explore mutual cooperation. Such contact may result in the strengthening of an overarching Buddhist identity. This trend gives some support to the thesis of the development of a uniquely American form of Buddhism. While this new form of Buddhism has yet to form fully, its arrival has been discussed, perhaps prematurely. There is no doubt that so far all forms of American Buddhism remain highly dependent on the support and the impetus given by overseas teachers, masters, and in some cases temples and institutions.

Further reading: James William Coleman, "The New Buddhism: Some Empirical Findings," in Duncan Ryuken Williams and Christopher S. Queen, *American Buddhism: Methods and Findings in Recent Scholarship* (Richmond, U.K.: Curzon, 1999), 91–99; Roger Coreless, "Coming Out in the Sangha: Queer Community in American Buddhism," in Charles S. Prebish and Kenneth

K. Tanaka, *The Faces of Buddhism in America* (Berkeley: University of California Press, 1998), 253–265; Rick Fields, *How the Swans Came to the Lake: A Narrative History of Buddhism in America*. 3d ed. (Boston: Shambhala, 1992); Joseph Goldstein, *One Dharma: The Emerging Western Buddhism* (New York: HarperCollins, 2003); Brian D. Hotchkiss, ed., Al Rapaport, comp., *Buddhism in America: Proceedings of the First Buddhism in America Congress* (Rutland, Vt.: Charles E. Tuttle, 1998); Jeffrey Paine, *Re-Enchantment: Tibetan Buddhism Comes to the West* (New York: W. W. Norton, 2004); Richard Hughes Seager, "American Buddhism in the Making," in Charles S. Prebish and Martin Baumann, eds., *Westward Dharma: Buddhism beyond Asia* (Berkeley, Calif.: University of California Press, 2002), 106–119; ———, *Buddhism in America* (New York: Columbia University Press, 1999); Joseph B. Tamney, *American Society in the Buddhist Mirror* (New York: Garland, 1992).

United States, Daoism in

DAOISM in the United States consists of a series of related practices and values that may have some connection to the Daoist tradition in China. However, the nature of that connection differs in important ways from American Daoists' own concepts about their movement.

There are anywhere from 10,000 to 30,000 thousand American Daoists in the United States and Canada. Typically, they are well educated, middle-class, and white. The majority of them first heard about Daoism in a college or high school class or were lent a book (usually the *Daodejing*) by a friend or family member. The *Daodejing* remains the single greatest influence on North Americans who self-identify as Daoists.

Thanks to the several major institutional forms of Daoism in North America, today American Daoism is defined less as an ancient, mystical philosophy than as an individual regimen of practice. American Daoist groups all teach practices through a combination of weekly classes and yearly or seasonal retreats or seminars. What all these practices have in common is that they can be performed individually, not collectively, as a modular part of a daily regimen. This may well be inevitable in the American context.

Daoism, more so even than most other Asian religions, was imported to the West as a series of ideas. In the late 19th century the new field of Sinology, which developed concurrently with the "science of religion," valued the classical traditions of China, found in ancient texts, while despising their modern manifestations.

Twentieth-century scholars, while bringing to light new information on Chinese religions, in particular Daoism, helped to construct a romantic picture of Daoism that might cure the illnesses of the modern West. Popular writers took this idea further, seeing Daoism as an age-old philosophy that could be conserved in the West and restored to its original purity.

PAUL CARUS and the future Zen BUDDHISM exponent DAISETSU TEITARO SUZUKI published the first American translation of the *Daodejing* in 1898. But it would not be the last; by 1950, there were 10 in print. And in the last 30 years new English translations appear in bookstores with great regularity. The values the *Daodejing* seems to advocate include many that coincide with counterculture spontaneity, naturalness, quietude, and concern for the environment.

The *Daodejing*'s fascination for Westerners, as well as its status as the second most translated text in the world (after the Bible), can be attributed to its brevity, its lack of proper names, and especially its multiplicity of possible meanings. These traits continue to make the *Daodejing* central to American Daoism.

Another subject of scholarly interest was investigation into longevity practices and Chinese alchemy. The ideas advanced by scholars about Daoist conceptions of health, longevity, immortality, and transcendence appealed to the West's growing need for body-centered spirituality. Popular scholarship argued that China had a "healthier" attitude toward sex while titillating readers with hints of an "exotic" sexuality. Thus, the language of transformation and cultivation found its way into the popular discourse.

By the early 1960s this discourse had found a home in the human potential movement, a generic name for a gamut of therapeutic techniques based on self-transformation, and indeed American Daoism, more than any other Asian tradition in the West, is historically and conceptually linked to that movement, often thought to have been born at the famed California retreat center Esalen. From the beginning *taijiquan*, a practice of physical cultivation that uses Daoist ideas, was taught at Esalen.

The 1970s saw the birth and growth of exclusively American Daoist organizations, led by Chinese masters. This development was due mainly to the 1965 changes in the immigration laws of the United States and Canada, which drew more Chinese to North America. Since the 1960s, the Chinese population of the United States has been doubling every decade and by 2000 was hovering around 2 million. This growth had several effects on the consumption of Chinese religion in the West. First, with so many Chinese living in North America, Chinese culture—from *martial arts* to eating with chopsticks—no longer seemed so exotic as it had in the 1940s through the early 1970s. Second, a handful of these immigrants were experienced in various Chinese religiophysical techniques and eager to teach these skills to willing Americans. At approximately the same time, young North Americans' search for spirituality outside traditional institutions (often called "the new religious consciousness") led them to embrace teachers and practices from Asia. Thus, the situation was ripe for the creation of American Daoist masters and organizations.

The first American Daoist organization officially recognized as a tax-exempt religious institution in the United States was the Taoist Sanctuary, founded in North Hollywood, California, in 1970. However, the founder of the sanctuary was not Chinese—though he often played Chinese characters on TV (most famously the Red Chinese agent

Wo Fat on *Hawaii 5-0*). Khigh Dhiegh (1910–91) was of Anglo-Egyptian descent and was born Kenneth Dickerson in New Jersey. Nonetheless, his sanctuary was the first comprehensive Daoist organization in America, teaching TAIJIQUAN, MARTIAL ARTS, the *DAODEJING*, and the YI JING, and conducting seasonal Daoist rituals (albeit invented by Dhiegh himself). Dhiegh recruited to the sanctuary teachers who were from China, including one who had been trained at a Daoist mountaintop monastery in Guangdong, China. The Taoist Sanctuary currently operates in San Diego, directed by Bill Helm, a former student of Dhiegh's.

In 1976, three students of the Taoist Sanctuary, studying Chinese medicine in Taiwan, met a Chinese doctor whom they invited to the United States. Hua-Ching Ni settled in Malibu, California, and opened a shrine called the Eternal Breath of Tao and began teaching classes privately in a venue he named the College of Tao. Over the years, Ni-sponsored organizations have multiplied. His private acupuncture clinic was known as the Union of Tao and Man. He also founded, in 1989, Yo San University of Traditional Chinese Medicine, an accredited degree-granting college. His sons, Maoshing and Daoshing, now head both the clinic and the university while Master Ni lives in semiseclusion.

A Thai-born Chinese named Mantak Chia moved to New York City in 1979 and opened the Taoist Esoteric Yoga Center, later renamed the HEALING TAO Center. Today, Chia attracts an international clientele to his Tao Garden in Thailand, while the Healing Tao USA is headed by Chia's former student, Michael Winn. Chia's classes and books are best described as a popularized, streamlined system of QIGONG based on Chinese internal alchemy (*neidan*).

Moy Lin-Shin founded the Taoist Tai Chi Society (TTCS) in 1970 in Toronto. This is perhaps the largest Daoist group in the Western Hemisphere, though largely unknown within the Daoist community in the United States, in part because it is based in Canada. The Taoist Tai Chi Society teaches "Taoist Tai Chi," a modified form of yang-style TAIJIQUAN, and has taught thousands of classes in more than 400 locations on four continents. It claims to have some 10,000 dues-paying members worldwide. The Taoist Tai Chi Society's religious arm is Fung Loy Kok Temple (FLK), dedicated in 1981. The original temple was located upstairs from the Taijiquan studio. Most Taoist Taijiquan studios around the world dedicate at least a corner of their space to a small shrine.

Each practice has been radically recontextualized in North America. The *Daodejing* and the Yi Jing entered the American scene through the field of Sinology, which never imagined these texts would be construed as modern practice. Once Taijiquan was in common circulation in the early 1970s and linked to the philosophy of the *Daodejing* and the Yi Jing, spiritual practice groups could offer courses in the study of these two texts as well as in Taijiquan, linking them by a common vocabulary (QI, YIN-YANG). This is exactly what the Taoist Sanctuary did in 1970, setting the stage for the current group of contemporary North American Daoist institutions.

See also JAPAN, DAOISM IN.

Further reading: J. J. Clarke, *The Tao of the West* (London: Routledge, 2000); Louis Komjathy, "Tracing the Contours of Daoism in North America," *Nova Religio* 8, no. 2 (November 2004): 5–27; Solala Towler, *A Gathering of Cranes Bringing the Tao to the West* (Eugene, Oreg.: Abode of the Eternal Tao, 1996).

Upali (c. 500 B.C.E.) *reciter of the first version of the Vinaya code governing Buddhist monks and nuns*
Upali was one of the Buddha's major followers. Originally a barber for the king in the city of Kapilavastu, he became a follower of the Buddha as soon as he heard the Buddha's teachings.

After the Buddha's PARINIRVANA Upali was present at the first of the COUNCILS OF BUDDHISM, held at RAJAGAHA. Upali recited the Vinaya, or code for BHIKSUS and BHIKSUNIS present there. He was thus considered to be an expert in the Vinaya, the code for monks and nuns.

Further reading: Soka Gakkai Dictionary of Buddhism. "Upali." Available online. URL: http://www.sgi-usa.org/buddhism/dictionary/define?tid=414. Accessed on May 21, 2006; Edward J. Thomas, *The Life of Buddha as Legend and History* (New Delhi: Munshiram Manoharlal, 1992).

upasampada *See* ORDINATION.

upaya
Upaya is "skill in means." The concept indicates that one should use variable means to communicate and act, in order to achieve goals efficiently. The BODHISATTVA, as well as any Buddha, acts in all things with an orientation toward the ENLIGHTENMENT of others. This orientation, the use of *upaya*, or skill in means, is defined by the Buddha, in the Upayakausalya-sutra, as "performing with an aspiration for omniscience." It also entails the idea of dedicating any merit earned to the fulfillment of the goal of universal enlightenment. This ideal of skillful means is still part of the bodhisattva's program of cultivation. *Upaya* is one of the 10 *paramitas* (perfections) to be practiced by bodhisattvas.

While the concept of skill in means did appear in the THERAVADA literature as well as early MAHAYANA BUDDHISM texts, the idea was most fully developed in such texts as the LOTUS SUTRA and the VIMALAKIRTI-NIRDESA SUTRA. In the Vimalakirti the hero, the bodhisattva Vimalakirti, often finds himself in situations in which as a monk he should not be found. Yet he is able to maintain such monkly vows as celibacy through the use of skillful means. In this general sense skill in means reflects the trait of not wavering from your dedication to the path, and keeping the absolute goal of enlightenment for all in mind. *Upaya-kausalya* also means, by extension, the use of practical techniques to attain an overarching goal. Thus the Buddha is said, in TIAN TAI and other PANJIAO (categorization) formulations, to have used skill in means by adjusting his message to match the abilities of his audience to comprehend. *Upaya* also explains why some SUTRAS were not revealed to earlier audiences but were hidden for centuries until the right time for their propagation.

Further reading: John W. Schroeder, *Skillful Means: The Heart of Buddhist Compassion* (Delhi: Motilal Banarsidass, 2004); Mark Tatz, trans., *The Skill in Means (Upayakausalya Sutra)* (Delhi: Motilal Banarsidass 1994); Tarthang Tulku, *Skillful Means* (Berkeley, Calif.: Dharma, 1978).

V

Vaibhasika

The Vaibhasikas were a branch of the SARVASTI-VADA (SARVASTIVADIN) SCHOOL, one of the major schools of early Buddhism in India. Both schools flourished in the northern Indian region, near Kashmir and Gandhar, from c. 250 B.C.E. The Sarvastivadins generally emphasized a text called the *Mahavibhasa,* or *Vibhasa,* which means simply "commentary." The Vibhasa is a vast commentary on the *Jnanaprasthanasutra,* the main treatise in the Sarvastivadin ABHIDHARMA/ABDHAMMA. The *Vibhasa* was compiled by Vasumitra (c. 45 B.C.E.). Those who continued this emphasis on the *Maha-vibhasa* were later known as Vaibhasikas in reference to this text.

Further reading: Charles S. Prebish, "Vaibhasika," in Charles S. Prebish, ed., *The A to Z of Buddhism* (Lanham, Md. Scarecrow Press, 2001), 263.

Vairocana

Vairocana—which means "illuminating all places"—was a solar deity who later developed into an extremely abstract Buddha, Mahavairo-cana, the Buddha that is beyond form or shape. Because this Buddha was associated with an extreme concept of the absolute, the image of Vairocana was popular in many places, especially those practicing VAJRAYANA BUDDHISM, or SHINGON Buddhism. The great Buddha at TODAI-JI in NARA, Japan, is a Vairocana image.

The figure of Vairocana is found in several places in Buddhist literature. In the LOTUS SUTRA, for instance, one passage states, "In every grain of dust of the Lotus Repository World can be seen the dharma essence." In the Sutra of Meditation on the Bodhisattva Universal Virtue Vairocana is equated with the universal aspects of Sakyamuni, the historical Buddha: Sakyamuni Buddha is called Vairocana Who Pervades All Places, and his dwelling place is called Eternally Tranquil Light, the place which is composed of permanency-PARAMITA, and stabilized by self-*paramita,* the place where purity-*paramita* extinguishes the aspect of existence, where bliss-*paramita* does not abide in the aspect of one's body and mind and where the aspects of all the laws cannot be seen as either existing or non-existing, the place of tranquil emancipation or PRAJNAPARAMITA. (trans. Kato, Tamua, and Miyasaka, 362–363)

In addition, the Brahmajala Sutra (Sutra of the Perfect Net), from the third century C.E., describes Vairocana seated on a 1,000-petaled lotus. Each petal of the lotus supports a separate world. Vairocana incarnates into one Sakyamuni Buddha for each world. And in each world there are 10 billion Mt. SUMERUS. The Sakyamuni Buddhas in turn transform into 10 billion Sakyamuni BODHISATTVAS, all of whom live within the Mt. Sumeru worlds. Thus from one Vairocana are generated 10 *trillion* Sakyamuni bodhisattvas.

This description of the Vairocana Buddha in his place in the universe had a powerful influence on iconographic depictions in many Buddhist cultures. The great Buddha of TODAI-JI in NARA, Japan, is based on the same description from the Brahmajala Sutra, as are other great Buddhas at Yun Gang, China, and the giant Buddha at Bamiyan, Afghanistan, destroyed in 2002. The popularity of such depictions developed in tandem with a form of Mahayana BUDDHISM called VAJRAYANA BUDDHISM, and is also reflected in Buddhist mandalas. The vast complex at BOROBUDUR, Indonesia, features 504 Buddhas arranged in a MANDALA pattern, with Vairocana in the center. Vairocana is thus coterminous with the universe itself, transcending all form and limitations.

See also ART, AESTHETICS, AND ARCHITECTURE.

Further reading: Bunno Kato, Yoshiro Tamura, and Kojiro Miyasaka, trans., *The Threefold Lotus Sutra* (New York: Weatherhill, 1975); Akira Sakakata, *Buddhist Cosmology: Philosophy and Origins* (Tokyo: Kosei, 1997, 1999).

vajra

The *vajra* (in Tibetan, *dorje*) is one of several instruments that derive from weapons of warfare, in this case the trident. In the hands of a teacher, it is seen as a weapon to use against the ego, the root of evil. They are weapons of transformation that destroy illusion. In their ritualistic form, they become scepters.

A Buddhist *vajra* has between one and nine prongs. It has a central shaft and a middle section made of two lotuses. From the lotuses the prongs emerge and then bend back into the shaft. Typically, six prongs emerge; when added to the central shaft, they form a seven-pronged instrument not unlike a pitchfork. *Vajras* are among the most ubiquitous objects used in VAJRAYANA BUDDHISM, or TANTRIC BUDDHISM and are frequently seen in the hands of lamas and priests.

As a thunderbolt, the *vajra* was the weapon most associated with the Vedic sky god Indra. It controlled the forces of nature and could be used against clouds to generate rains to break the droughts of summer. Indra slew the saintly sage Dadhichi and used his bones to fashion a weapon to slay the demons. Indra's weapon had open prongs. Gautama Buddha is said to have taken the weapon from Indra and forced the prongs into a closed position, thus creating the Buddhist scepter, a peaceful weapon. In Buddhist hands, the *vajra* retained its unbreakable and indestructible power.

The *vajra/dorje* is usually paired with the bell (SANSKRIT, *ghanta*). The *vajra* is held in the right hand as a male object and the bell in the left hand as a female object. Together they also represent the union of wisdom and method in the attainment of ENLIGHTENMENT. The *ghanta* has a round base and may be of different sizes, measured in finger-widths of height. There are two basic parts. The handle has a representation of a female deity wearing a crown, surmounted by a five-pointed *vajra*. The body of the bell represents wisdom comprehending emptiness. The clapper makes the sound of emptiness.

Further reading: Nitin Kumar, "Ritual Implements in Tibetan Buddhism: A Symbolic Appraisal." Exotic India. Available online. URL: http://www.exoticindiaart.com/article/ritual. Accessed on February 20, 2005; Reginald A. Ray, *Secret of the Vajra World: the Tantric Buddhism of Tibet* (Boston: Shambhala, 2001).

Vajrabodhi (671–741) *Indian monk who introduced Vajrayana teaching to China*

Vajrabodhi (known in China as Jingangzhi) was one of three VAJRAYANA BUDDHISM teachers who traveled to China in response to a request from the emperor Xuan Zong (r. 712–756). Vajrabodhi's efforts at integrating Indian and Chinese thought helped create the unique Chinese form of Vajrayana, sometimes known as Hanmi Buddhism.

Vajrabodhi was born into a prominent south Indian Hindu family but seems to have converted to Buddhism as a teenager. He studied at the Buddhist university at NALANDA. Both at the university and on travels to Sri Lanka, he was exposed to different varieties of Buddhist thought and practice. He seems to have been initiated into Vajrayana in Sri Lanka. He made his way to China around 720, accompanied by his young disciple, Amoghavajra (705–774). His colleague Subhakarasimha (637–735) had arrived several years earlier.

Subhakarasimha and Vajrabodhi both spent a considerable amount of their time in China translating various texts, none more important than the *Tattvasamgraha,* a project that Amoghavajra would continue and complete. This text would become essential to the Vajrayana school in both China and Japan. When Vajrabodhi died in 741, he was given the title *Guoshi* (teacher of the realm).

Further reading: Kenneth K. S. Ch'en, *Buddhism* (Woodbury, N.Y.: Barron's Educational Series, 1968); Arthur F. Wright, *Buddhism in Chinese History* (Stanford, Calif.: Stanford University Press, 1959); Zhou Yiliang, "Tantrism in China," *Harvard Journal of Asiatic Studies* 8 (March 1945): 241–332.

Vajradhatu

Vajradhatu is the original name for SHAMBHALA INTERNATIONAL, said to be one of the largest Buddhist groups in the United States, with an estimated 3,500 to 5,000 adherents. It was founded in Boulder, Colorado, in 1973, by CHOGYAM TRUNGPA Rinpoche (1939–87). In 1992 the movement's name was changed to Shambhala International, and Vajradhatu has continued as a division. Vajradhatu is also considered the way of Buddhist practice and study within the movement. The local branches are known as *dharmadhatus* and there are said to be 150 *dharmadhatus* worldwide.

Trungpa Rinpoche also founded the Naropa Institute, the first accredited Buddhist institute of university-level education in the United States, in 1974. Before his death he decided to transfer headquarters for his movement to Halifax, Nova Scotia, Canada, and asked his followers to join him. He was succeeded by Osel Tendzin (Thomas F. Rich, 1943–90); the organization is now headed by Sakyong Mipham Rinpoche (1962–), the eldest son of Trungpa Rinpoche.

Further reading: Chogyam Trungpa, *Born in Tibet* (Boulder, Colo.: Shambhala, 1976); ———, *Shambhala: Sacred Path of the Warrior* (Boulder, Colo.: Shambhala, 1988); Charles S. Prebish, *Luminous Passage: The Practice and Study of Buddhism in America* (Berkeley, Calif.: University of California Press, 1999); Amy Lavine, "Tibetan Buddhism in America: The Development of American Vajrayana," in Charles S. Prebish and Kenneth K. Tanaka, eds., *The Faces of Buddhism in America* (Berkeley: University of California Press, 1998): 99–115; Shambhala. "Shambhala." Available online. URL: http://www.shambhala.org/vdh/. Accessed on May 15, 2006; Loveena Rajanayakam, "Shambhala International." The Religious Movements Homepage Project @ The University of Virginia. Available online. URL: http://religiousmovements.lib.virginia.edu/nrms/shamb.html. Accessed on May 15, 2006; Dyan Zaslowsky, "Buddhists in U.S. Agonize on AIDS Issue," *New York Times,* 21 February, 1989. Available online at the New York Times website. URL: http://query.nytimes.com/gst/fullpage.html?res=950DE7D61F39F932A1. Accessed on May 15, 2006.

vajra-world (*kongo-kai, vajradhatu*) meditation

This Japanese VAJRAYANA BUDDHISM rite is usually performed after the LOTUS-WOMB MEDITATION. While the Lotus-womb meditation locks in the compassion of VAIROCANA Buddha, the purpose of the Vajra-world meditation is to unlock that spirit and spread its energy throughout the world. Together with the *Juhachi-do* (18 paths) ritual and the GOMA FIRE RITE, these four MANDALA-based rituals form the core of contemporary Japanese Vajrayana practice, in both the TENDAI and SHINGON schools. They are called mandala-based because the person performing the ritual is expected to imagine and internalize the images from a mandala. Novice monks in both traditions learn these rituals during the 60-day *shugyo* (cultivation) period, which precedes full ORDINATION as a monk.

Mandalas depicting the two rites (Vajra-world and Lotus-womb) can be found in many Shingon and Tendai temples in Japan, normally at right angles to the direction of the main altar. Collectively these two mandalas are called the Ryokai (two world) Mandala.

The Vajra-world meditation has nine steps and is usually performed by the practitioner alone, or before an altar.

On Mt. HIEI, the center of Japanese Tendai practice, the Lotus-womb meditations are normally performed for a year, then the *vajra*-world ceremonies are performed for another year, and the two liturgies are performed together for a third year.

Further reading: Michael Saso, *Homa Rites and Mandala Meditation in Tendai Buddhism* (Delhi: Pradeep Kumar Goel, 1991).

Vajrayana Buddhism

Vajrayana is the "diamond vehicle," that branch of Buddhist practice that developed first in India about 900 C.E. and the spread north, into Tibet, China and, eventually, Japan. Vajrayana takes MAHAYANA BUDDHISM, principles as its foundation and adds esoteric practices related to TANTRIC BUDDHISM literature. One characteristic of Vajrayana is an emphasis on the role of the master, or guru. The master uses a range of tools, including MANTRAS, MANDALAS, and MUDRAS, to help disciples gain

ENLIGHTENMENT. Rituals are relatively complex compared to THERAVADA and standard Mahayana practice; these rituals were then integrated into monastic life. The most highly respected figures in Vajrayana were Mahasiddhas, individuals who had supernatural powers, around whom a great oral literature developed.

In Tibetan Vajrayana is the "Vehicle of Indestructile Reality" (*rdo-rje'i theg-pa*), so named because this form of practice results in full manifestation of the Buddha body, speech, and mind, which are indestructible. An alternative name is the "Vehicle of Secret Mantras" (Guhyamantrayana), and Vajrayana is today normally taken to be equivalent to Tantric Buddhism and esoteric Buddhism.

Vassa rains retreat (Chinese, *jie xia*; Sanskrit, *visakha puja*)

The most important of SANGHA-specific commemorative dates is Vassa, which marks the beginning of the annual retreats commemorated by all monks. The monks typically spend the 15th day of the fourth lunar month in busy preparation. The abbot arrives to lecture all monks on proper procedures. A sign is hung inside the temple stating, "Annual retreat [Vassa]." All monks are carefully counted and registered.

On the 16th the monks enter the main hall of the temple and perform rituals to honor the Buddha, known in Theravadin countries as the Magha Puja (ritual of the month of Magha; see the discussion of Theravada countries). The lead monk leads the assembly to chant, "Sakyamuni Buddha, Summer Retreat." After this the lead monk leads the assembly to chant the Retreat Text three times. Then the assembly chant the Great Compassion Mantra three times, circumambulate the Buddha figures, and return to their positions to chant, "Sentient beings without end—I promise to save them, distress without end—I vow to end it, the Dharma Gate is unending—I vow to study, the Path of the Buddha is unsurpassed—I vow to complete it." At this point the monks stand and recite another promise three times. The assembly finally bow three times to Sakyamuni's image and retire to the Dharma Hall of the temple. This is the formal start of the three-month summer retreat. During this time the morning and evening rituals are performed as usual, but other time is spent in meditation. The temple also holds lectures and recitation sessions during the retreat.

Vassa began during the Buddha's time and matched the conditions in India. With the onset of the annual monsoon rains there was a profusion of new life—insects, plants, flowers—and limiting travel at this time was seen as a way to limit the chance of taking the lives of newly born beings inadvertently during walking. Of course the retreat served practical purposes as well: travel was difficult anyway during the heavy rains, which often resulted in flooding, and the retreat gave the monks an opportunity to focus on inner cultivation.

The Vassa also quickly became an occasion to reinforce community, a social event for the SANGHA. In the beginning some monks took the opportunity to sit in silence, without interacting. The Buddha noted this and thereafter forbade vows of silence.

The midpoint of the retreat was called midsummer. Those who withdrew from the retreat early were said to "break the summer." Overall, while there was some flexibility in fixing the start date of the retreat, it was strictly required to last a full 90 days.

The 15th of the seventh month marks the traditional end to the Vassa retreat. Monks normally recite sutras on the evening of the 14th. On the 15th they enter the hall and prepare cakes.

On the final day of Vassa, called Paravana day, the monks also hold a special ritual of confession and contrition. They review their faults and publicly call on others to review those faults of which they are unaware. This confessional practice also served as the origin of the ULLAMBANA festival.

Vasubandhu (late fourth-century C.E.) *Indian Buddhist philosopher and cofounder of the Yogacara school*

Little is known of the early life of Vasubandhu. He is believed to have been born in northern India to a Brahmin family. He initially became known as a proponent of the SARVASTIVADA (SARVASTIVADIN) SCHOOL of Buddhism, a branch of early Buddhism, which he had studied while at Ayodhya, an ancient Indian city located in today's province of Uttar Pradesh. During this period of his life, he wrote a commentary on the ABHIDHARMA-KOSA, the primary scripture of the Sarvastivadin. The work was later translated by PARAMARTHA (563–567) and XUAN ZANG and became the foundation of the Kosa, one of the SCHOOLS OF CHINESE BUDDHISM. He later repudiated the Sarvastivadin principles and adopted a MAHAYANA BUDDHISM perspective. In conjunction with his older brother, Asanga, he went on to found the YOGACARA BUDDHISM school.

Throughout his life he was known to have written numerous works, only a small percentage of which have survived. Among surviving books are his commentary on the LOTUS SUTRA and his exposition of the BUDDHA NATURE.

Further reading: Stefan Anackor, *Seven Works of Vasubandhu* (Delhi: Motilal Banarsidass, 1984); Thomas A. Kochumuttom, *A Buddhist Doctrine of Experience: A New Translation and Interpretation of the Works of Vasubandhu the Yog c rin* (Delhi: Motilal Banarsidass, 1982); Robert Kritzer, *Vasubandhu and the Yog c rabh mi: Yog c ra Elements in the Abhidharmako abh sya* (Tokyo: International Institute for Buddhist Studies, 2005).

vegetarianism

Vegetarianism is a dietary practice that excludes eating meat. There are several approaches to vegetarianism. Some vegetarians eat only vegetables, fruits, nuts, grains, and pulses. Others include dairy foods in their diet. Still others also include fish.

Many people are surprised to discover that not all Buddhist traditions call for vegetarianism. Perhaps there is an assumption that monks who lead a celibate life separate from everyday society will also have extreme ascetic dietary requirements. And some Buddhist cultures do require vegetarianism.

The major doctrinal objection to eating meat is that it is counter the First Precept, which prohibits killing. This precept includes one who causes another's life to cease. In the Buddha's EIGHTFOLD PATH he forbids laymen to take up such trades as weapons, meat, or poison dealing. However, support for and against meat eating can be found in the THERAVADA and MAHAYANA BUDDHISM scriptures.

PRO–MEAT EATING

There are references to meat in the Buddhist SUTRAS. The Buddha is quoted as saying, "I have allowed fish and meat that is pure in the three aspects, when it is not seen or heard or suspected to have been killed for one personally." Today in fact meat eating is widely allowed in Theravada Buddhist cultures. When monks make their morning rounds to beg, they are strictly not allowed to choose which foods to take and are instructed to take and eat *all* foods supplied by donations, including meat. Meat eating is also accepted in Tibetan Buddhism.

ANTI–MEAT EATING

At the same time, parts of the Mahayana are filled with injunctions, again said to have been uttered by the Buddha, not to eat meat. The Surangama Sutra, an important Mahayana text, states that the Buddha said, "If a man can (control) his body and mind and thereby refrains from eating animal flesh and wearing animal products, I say he will really be liberated." It goes on to say, The reason for practicing DHYANA and seeking to attain SAMADHI is to escape from the suffering of life, but in seeking to escape from the suffering ourselves why should we inflict it upon others? Unless you

can so control your minds that even the thought of brutal unkindness and killing is abhorrent, you will never be able to escape from the bondage of the world's life. . . . After my PARINIRVANA in the last *kalpa* (age) different kinds of ghosts will be encountered everywhere deceiving people and teaching them that they can eat meat and still attain enlightenment. . . . How can a BHIKSU, who hopes to become a deliverer of others, himself be living on the flesh of other sentient beings?

The Lankavatara Sutra says, simply, "The Blessed One said this to him: For innumerable reasons, Mahamati, the BODHISATTVA, whose nature is compassion, is not to eat any meat." Further, the text goes on to state, "It is not true, Mahamati, that meat is proper food and permissible for the SRAVAKA (a hearer, hence a pupil or beginner) when (the victim) was not killed by himself, when he did not order others to kill it. When it was not specially meant for him" (D. T. Suzuki translation).

Finally, the *Scripture of Brahma's Net* states very clearly that eating meat is a grave offense: "Disciples of the Buddha, should you willingly and knowingly eat flesh, you defile yourself by acting contrary to this less grave Precept. Pray, let us not eat any flesh or meat whatsoever coming from living beings" (translated from the Chinese by the Reverend Hubert Nearman with the Reverend Master Jiyu-Kennett and the Reverend Daizui MacPhillamy as consultants and editors).

Clearly, there is strong sutra-specific support in Mahayana texts for a meatless diet. And in fact, many, though not all, Mahayana cultures prohibit monks to eat meat.

In addition, it is quite likely that Buddhist ideas about preserving life found positive reception in certain of the East Asian cultures in which they developed, especially China. China had a pre-existing discourse on diet that proscribed, among other things, strong herbs or grains, although we do not know how widely such proscriptions were followed. And in general it is among the Chinese that vegetarianism remains strongest in Asia. In Japan and Korea there is some meat eating, although there are some monks in each country who adhere to a stricter interpretation of the sutra and VINAYA regulations. A similar process is at work in the West today, as Western ideas concerning vegetarianism intersect with Buddhist practices and teachings.

SUMMARY

Monks in the Buddha's time had to beg and so should be expected to eat broadly of what is given. However, today, when vegetarianism is a viable option in many modern societies, some argue the Buddha would not have held a lenient attitude toward meat eating. And then again, he may have recommended that followers not become overly concerned about this issue, which, after all, is not the key teaching in Buddhism.

Further reading: Richard M. Jaffe, "The Debate over Meat Eating in Japanese Buddhism," in William Bodiford, ed., *Going Forth: Visions of Buddhist Vinaya, Essays Presented in Honor of Professor Stanley Weinstein* (Honolulu: University of Hawaii Press, 2005), 255–275; Hsu Yun Buddhist Association. "Vegetarianism and Buddhism." Available online. URL: http://www.hsuyun.net/vegetarian.html. Accessed on January 26, 2006; Lambert Schmithausen, *The Problem of the Sentience of Plants in Earliest Buddhism* (Tokyo: The International Institute for Buddhist Studies, 2001).

Vessantara *legendary prince featured in the Jataka Tales, and the Buddha's incarnation before his rebirth as Siddhartha*

The story of Prince Vessantara is the final chapter of the 547 JATAKA TALES. As such it is given special status in Buddhist cultures, and Vessantara is the most popular figure from the Jatakas. He personifies the virtue of giving, DANA.

Vessantara was a prince of Sivi who offered a white elephant to the neighboring land of Kalinga to resolve a drought. This act of generosity made the people of Sivi angry, and Vessantara and fam-

ily were then expelled. Vessantara then gave away, in turn, his possessions, his chariot, his children, and, in a final act of giving, his wife. In fact he was being tested by the gods, and all was soon enough returned to him and he was made king of Sivi.

Vessantara's life is commemorated in THERAVADA cultures in the elaborate Desana Mahajati ceremony. This ceremony is normally held in early November, after the rainy season, over two or three days.

Further reading: John Powers, *A Concise Encyclopedia of Buddhism* (Oxford: One World, 2000); Donald K. Swearer, *The Buddhist World of Southeast Asia* (Albany: State University of New York Press, 1995).

Vetterling, Herman C.   *See* PHILANGI DASA.

Vietnam, Buddhism in

Buddhism was introduced into Vietnam through ocean trade routes as early as the second century B.C.E., and early in the Common Era a flourishing community of THERAVADA monks resided originally from Scythia and Sogdia, two Central Asian cultures, in Vietnam. Today Vietnam is dominated by a Theravada-influenced ZEN BUDDHISM unique to the country. While some surveys state that the country today is 80 percent atheist, other estimates estimate the total number of Vietnamese who are Buddhists or heavily influenced by Buddhist beliefs at 50 million, of a total population of 84 million.

The spread of Buddhism in Vietnam coincided with the occupation of the region by the pre-Buddhist Chinese. They introduced the art of writing and provided the context for the earliest Vietnamese Buddhist treatise, *Ly Hoac Luan* (Reason and doubt), by the scholar Mau Tu (c. 165 C.E.). As Buddhism spread into China, MAHAYANA BUDDHISM perspectives also were introduced.

CHAN BUDDHISM was transported to Vietnam almost as soon as it sprang up in China, around

520, and over the next centuries four different forms of Chan were established. Vinitaruci, a native of India who had studied with the third Chan patriarch, Seng Can (d. 606), traveled to Vietnam in 580 and founded there the Ty Ni Da Luu Chin Chan school. A second Chan sect was established in 820 with the arrival of a Chinese monk, Wuyan Tong (d. 826). A third Chan school, a syncretic mix of Chan and PURE LAND BUDDHISM practice, arrived with Caotang, a follower of Xuitou Congxian of the Yunmen lineage of Chinese Chan Buddhism. The final Chan school to arrive, the LINJI CHAN or, in Vietnamese, Lam Te, entered with the Vietnamese monk Nguyen Thieu (d. 1712). The Lam Te spread under the efforts of Master Lieu Quan, and the sect eventually became the dominant institutional presence in central Vietnamese Buddhism.

The Chinese were expelled from Vietnam toward the end of the 10th century C.E. and a new Vietnamese-led kingdom arose whose ruler was seen as semidivine. Over the next centuries, indigenous Buddhist leaders supported the monarchy. In turn, Buddhism was actively supported by the Ly (1010–1225) and Tran (1225–1400) dynasties. As in China, however, Buddhism was not always the most privileged religion; Buddhism grew in competition with DAOISM and CONFUCIANISM. Through the middle Tran dynasties (968–1314) Buddhism (especially Thien, the Vietnamese form of Chan), enjoyed "official" status, but Confucianism moved into the ascendant during the later Tran (1225–1400).

After Vietnam's colonization by France, Buddhism shared the stage with Catholicism and such indigenous religions as CAODAISM. The Roman Catholic church built the second largest church in Asia in Vietnam (second only to that in the Philippines). Yet Buddhism remained a vibrant part of Vietnamese society. Vietnam became the crucible from which ENGAGED BUDDHISM emerged, as a number of monks (THICH NHAT HANH, THICH QUANC DUC) became politically active during the Vietnam War of the 1960s and 1970s.

Temples have remained open under the Marxist-dominated government that gained power after the war, though interaction with the government had been tense at times. While Buddhism in Vietnam is influenced by Theravada Buddhism, continuing Mahayana dominance is seen in the images of Sakyamuni BUDDHA, AMITABHA, and MAITREYA that are found in most Buddhist temples.

The most important date on the Vietnamese Buddhist calendar is WESAK, the Buddha's birthday, celebrated April 8–15 on the lunar calendar. April 15–July 15 is the period of An Cu, during which all monks and nuns are confined to their temples. This period is concluded with the Vu Lan (ULLAMBANA, Yulan) festival on July 15. During this celebration ceremonies are held to offer spiritual merit accumulated during An Cu to parents, suffering beings, beings in hell, PRETA, and animals.

Further reading: Phra Rajavaramuni, *Thai Buddhism in the Buddhist World* (North Hollywood, Calif.: Wat Thai of Los Angeles, 1984); Thich Nhat Hanh, *Vietnam: Lotus in a Sea of Fire* (New York: Hill & Wang, 1867); Thich Thien-An, *Buddhism and Zen in Vietnam in Relation to the Development of Buddhism in Asia.* Edited, annotated, and developed by Carol Smith (Rutland, Vt.: Charles E. Tuttle, 1975); Thich Thien-Tam, *Buddhism of Wisdom and Faith: Pure Land Principles and Practice* (Sepulveda, Calif.: International Buddhist Monastic Institute, 1991).

vihara

As the Buddhist monastic community evolved, the original building in which the SANGHA resided was joined by other associated buildings. The term *vihara* designated the main hall in which rituals were performed and into which an image of the Buddha or another deity figure was placed and, by extension, the monastery itself. The term is most commonly (though by no means exclusively) used in southern and southeastern Asia, those countries dominated by THERAVADA Buddhism. As

Theravada spread to the West, in the absence of a strong Sangha, the *vihara* was most often the first building opened for an emerging worshipping community. It also refers to the monastery as a whole.

See also ART, AESTHETICS, AND ARCHITECTURE.

Further reading: Senake Bandaranayake, *Sinhalese Monastic Architecture: The Viharas of Anuradhapura* (Leiden: Brill, 1997); Kalalalle Sekhara, *Early Buddhist Sanghas and Viharas in Sri Lanka* (*Up to the 4th Century A.D.*) (Varanasi, India: Rishi, 1998).

vijnana (consciousness)

In Buddhist theory, there are six kinds of consciousness, each associated with a sense organ and the mind. *Vijnana* is the core of the sense of "self" that Buddhism denies. As such *vijnana* is one of the links in the 12-fold chain of causation in PRATITYA-SAMUTPADA theory. In this formulation, ignorance (of the true nature of reality) leads to karmic actions, speech, and thoughts, which in turn create *vijnana* (consciousness), which then allows the development of mental and bodily aggregates, and on through the eight remaining links.

The YOGACARA BUDDHISM school of Mahayana Buddhism theorized there are two additional types of consciousness in addition to the original six *vijnanas*. The additional types are *mana,* which is the discriminating consciousness, and ALAYA-VIJNANA, the storehouse consciousness.

Further reading: Buddhanet. "The Fundamentals of Buddhism: The Five Aggregates." Available online. URL: http://www.buddhanet.net/funbud14.htm. Accessed on May 20, 2006.

Vimalakirti-nirdesa Sutra

The Vimalakirti-nirdesa Sutra, the Discourse on Vimalakirti, is an extremely popular sutra in eastern Asian Buddhism. It presents the principles of MAHAYANA BUDDHISM teachings as opposed to those of Theravada Buddhism, explaining such Mahayana concepts as SUNYATA (emptiness).

The Vimalakirti-nirdesa Sutra describes discussions between Vimalakirti, a wealthy layman, and the BODHISATTVA MANJUSRI. Vimalakirti lies on his deathbed, and the Buddha, out of concern, sends Manjusri to inquire about Vimalakirti's health. Vimalakirti explains that his sickness is that of the bodhisattva who is sick until all sentient beings are enlightened. Vimalakirti uses dichotomies to describe extreme alternatives and finally reconcile them. Thus his words express the Middle Way, teachings that would be formulated clearly by the philosopher NAGARJUNA (c. 150–250 C.E.) in the MADHYAMIKA school. However, Vimalakirti actually advocates extreme practices if they are on the path of liberation, a foretaste of Tantric concepts that rose in India from the 700s.

The Vimalakirti Sutra was probably composed in the second century C.E. Vimalakirti was a lay practitioner who debated the proper role of a person wishing to seek enlightenment outside the SANGHA, or monastic community. He thus idealized this image of the enlightened householder. Although it no longer exists in the original version, there are seven versions in Chinese, two in Tibetan, and several in French and English.

This SUTRA is important for its concise explanations of key Mahayana concepts. It also illustrates how the nonordained person can practice the Buddha's DHARMA even while surrounded by the things of the world. Virmalakirti thus represents the ideal of the enlightened lay follower of the Buddha, a type of person who has been present in Buddhist literature from the beginning. In such practically oriented societies of East Asia as China, Korea, and Japan, Vimalakirti serves as a powerful cultural hero to this day.

Further reading: Charles Luk, trans., *The Vimalakirti Nirdesa Sutra* (Boston: Shambhala, 1972); Robert A. F. Thurma, trans., *The Holy Teaching of Vimalakirti: A Mahayana Scripture* (1976. Reprint, University Park: Pennsylvania State University Press, 1986).

Vinaya

The Vinaya, one of the three divisions of the Buddhist scriptures, is the "basket" (*pitaka*) that spells out the rules for monks and nuns. It is therefore also referred to as the Vinaya-pitaka. It gains its authority from the belief that the Vinaya presents in a systematic fashion the precepts voiced by Sakyamuni BUDDHA for the conduct of those who assumed monastic orders. According to tradition, these rules were compiled soon after the Buddha's MAHAPARANIVIRNA (death) and were then memorized. They were passed on orally until around 100 B.C.E., when they were written down.

Study of the Vinaya is important because it gives an insight into the way Buddhist practice developed over time. Although it may seem that much of the Vinaya is focused on codes and punishment for offenses, this simply reflects the actual occurrence of such issues, and the continuing influence of human nature on human institutions. Because of such transgressions and the efforts to deal with them we have a full picture of Buddhist values and monastic life.

THE VINAYA IN THERAVADA CULTURES

The oldest texts of the Vinaya that have survived are written in PALI. They contain all the regulations that give structure to the life of the THERAVADA BHIKSUs (monks) and BHIKSUNIs (nuns), as well as listing a number of procedures and conventions of etiquette that promote positive relationships within the monastic community, and between the monks and nuns and those lay people upon whom they rely for support. One part of the Vinaya, the Sutravibhanga, offers reflections on each rule and the rationale for its application. The existence of such material indicates that the rules were not just to be considered a matter of outward behavior but were part of the training of the mind.

As might be expected, over the first centuries of the Buddhist movement, as time passed and the movement spread around India and to Sri Lanka, variations in the oral Vinaya occurred, and these variations are manifested in the early Pali texts.

THOMAS WILLIAM RHYS DAVIDS, founder of the PALI TEXT SOCIETY, made the translation of the Vinaya one of the initial tasks of the society. The original edition appeared in multiple volumes published by Clarendon Press (and more recently reprinted in several editions).

THE VINAYA IN CHINA AND JAPAN

No complete Vinaya texts have survived in SANSKRIT, the language used by the early Mahayana groups, but Chinese translations of four of the early Buddhist schools have survived. These texts contain a variety of differences both with the Pali Vinaya and with each other. One of these texts, The Fourfold Rules of Discipline, emerged as the primary text for several Chinese groups, collectively known as the Precepts school, the most notable branch being the Nanshan school. The volume contains 348 precepts divided into seven categories, beginning with the eight major unpardonable rules whose violation would cause one to be expelled from the monastic order, to a variety of lesser offenses. The Nanshan school was founded in the seventh century by Dao Xuan (596–667) who resided on Zhongnan Shan, the mountain that gave the school its name. Dao Xuan later wrote a commentary on the *Fourfold Rules* that served as the primary text for Nanshan practitioners.

A student of the Nanshan school, Jianzhoujian (Chien-chen, also known as GANJIN) migrated to NARA, Japan, in 753, and established a new school modeled on the Nanshan, which in Japan became known as the RITSU SCHOOL. Amid the several schools headquartered at Nara, the Ritsu was the one that primarily focused on the rules for the monastic life. The Ritsu-shu survives as a small sect of Japanese Buddhism, still headquartered in Nara. In the 13th century, a group that combines SHINGON doctrines with observation of the Vinaya as found in the *Fourfold Rules of Discipline* was founded by Eizon (1201–90). It is headquartered at Saidai-ji temple in Nara.

ELEMENTS OF THE VINAYA

There are traditionally three sections to this material: the Sutravibhanga, Skandhaka, and Parivara ("Appendices" or "Accessories"). This forms the Vinaya material proper. There are two additional types of Vinaya-related material, the paracanonical and the commentarial. The "paracanonical" Vinaya consists of the PRATIMOKSA/PATIMOKKHA and the Karmavacana, two ancient works still in use in monasteries today.

Pratimoksa

The Pratimoksa is simply a collection of rules of conduct. These rules were designed to detail daily life in the monastery—such mundane areas as eating, cleaning, and assemblies. The Buddha ordered that the Pratimoksa be recited on every Posadha day, the celebrations that occurred twice each month during the full and new moon cycles. There were punishments spelled out for not following the rules—eight types for monks and seven for nuns.

Karmavacana

A *karmavacana* was a formula used to follow through on *sanghakarmas,* or acts reflecting the SANGHA's decision on general issues or disputes. *Sanghakarmas* required the presence of enough monks, consideration of all absentee ballots, proposal of a motion, and the final proclamation of the *karmavacana.*

Karmavacanas dealt with such important issues as admission, ordination, confession, preparation of medicines, discipline, dwellings, schisms, and relations between students and teachers. They provide a window on the democratic way the Buddhist Sangha operated.

Sutravibhanga

Vibhanga literally means "analysis." In the Vinaya the Sutravibhanga provides an analysis of the sections of the Pratimoksa. For each rule, the Sutravibhanga discusses stories illustrating the rule, the rule itself, a commentary, and stories concerning mitigating circumstances. There text also discusses additional offenses not included in the Pratimoksa: *duskrta* (light offenses), *sthulatyaya* (grave offenses), and *durbhasita* (offenses of improper speech).

Skandhaka

The Skandhaka involves acts and ceremonies important to the Sangha as a body. Just as the Sutravibhanga analyzes the Pratimoksa, the Skandhaka analyzes the Karmavacana. The Skandhaka is organized into 20 chapters, each focused on a single *vastu,* or subject area, such as admission to monkhood, confession, clothing, and food and medicine.

Noncanonical Commentaries

The Vinaya section of the TRIPITAKA was closed to amendments quite early in Buddhism's history. Because of that a massive commentarial literature grew as well, in many languages. The most famous Pali commentaries are those by BUDDHAGHOSA. His *Vamantapasadika* is a commentary on the entire Vinaya. His *Kankhavitarani* is a commentary on the Pali Patimokkha (Pratimoksa).

VERSIONS OF THE VINAYA

Theravada Sanghas, such as those in Sri Lanka, Burma, and Thailand, today follow the Pali version of the Vinaya. The Chinese and other East Asian Sanghas have five versions to choose from. And there is a Tibetan version.

The Chinese Buddhist monastic code is based overwhelmingly on one supplemental text, the Brahmajala Sutra (*fanwang jing*). This work was translated into Chinese by KUMARAJIVA in 406. It is in fact one chapter of a larger work, the Bodhisattvahrdayasutra, now lost. The Brahmajala Sutra blends Mahayana idealism with earlier monastic practice. Other texts, such as the various versions of the early Vinayas, are also influential in Chinese practice. Overall, it is clear that Chinese monastic practice is based solidly on codes of the earlier schools such as the STHAVIRAVADA SCHOOL.

Versions of Vinayas from the earliest schools of Buddhism have survived. The Vinaya of the MAHASANGHIKAS was translated into Chinese by BUDDHABHADRA and FA XIAN, who also translated the Mahasanghikan Pratimoksa. Another Pratimoksa version, that of the Mahisasaka school, was translated by Buddhajiva in 423–424. The corresponding Karmavacana was translated by Ai Tong between 705 and 706. Buddhajiva also translated the Vinaya. The Chinese Buddhist canon also contains translations of the Pratimoksa, Karmavacana, and Vinaya from the DHARMAGUPTAKA SCHOOL, SARVASTIVADA (SARVASTIVADIN) SCHOOL, and Mulasarvastivadin school. The Mulasarvastivadin version also exists in Tibetan, while many of the Sarvastivadin version's parts exist in SANSKRIT.

Further reading: William M. Bodiford, ed., *Going Forth: Visions of Buddhist Vinaya, Essays Presented in Honor of Professor Stanley Weinstein* (Honolulu: University of Hawaii Press, 2005); Jotiya Dhirasekhera, *Buddhist Monastic Discipline: A Study of Its Origins and Development in Relation to the Sutta and Vinaya Pitakas* (Colombo, Sri Lanka: M. D. Gunasena, 1982); Sukumar Dutt, *Early Buddhist Monachism*. Rev. ed. (Bombay: Asian Publishing House, 1960); E. Frauwallner, *The Earliest Vinaya and the Beginnings of Buddhist Literature* (Rome: Instituto Italiano per il Medio ed Estremo Oriente, 1956); Kogen Mizuno, *Essentials of Buddhism: Basic Terminology of Buddhist Philosophy and Practice*. Translated by Gaynor Sekimori (1972. Reprint, Tokyo: Kosei, 1996); Charles S. Prebish, *A Survey of Vinaya Literature* (Taipei: Jin Luen, 1974); T. W. Rhys-Davids, trans., *Vinaya Texts* (Reprint, London: RoutledgeCurzon, 2001); Mohan Wijayaratna, *Buddhist Monastic Life*. Translated by Claude Grangier and Steven Collins (Cambridge: Cambridge University Press, 1990).

vipassana

Literally meaning "insight" or "direct perception," *vipassana* refers to one of the two major forms of Buddhist-inspired meditation, or BHAVANA. The aim of *vipassana* is the development of insight into the nature of perceived reality through full awareness of the mind and body. It assumes the practitioner has learned the practice of SAMADHI, or calming meditation. In THERAVADA practice it is approached through regimented meditative practices. In MAHAYANA BUDDHISM it indicates analytical study of phenomena, which should give understanding of the nature of the world, its emptiness (SUNYATA).

Theravada teachers traditionally teach *vipassana* techniques during seven-week retreats, often at monasteries. These today are offered in shorter one- to two-week sessions. A large portion of the time is often spent in total silence, with the object of focusing attention on sensations, impressions, and the internal. Through painstaking self-observation of internal phenomena the practitioner becomes aware of the links between the outside world and mental phenomena.

Further reading: John E. Coleman, *The Quiet Mind* (*Vipassana Meditation and the Buddha's Teachings*) (Onalaska, Wash.: Pariyatti Press, 1971); Mitchell Ginsberg, *The Far Shore: Vipassana, the Practice of Insight* (New Delhi: Motilal Banarsidass, 2001); Joseph Goldstein and Jack Kornfield, *Seeking the Heart of Wisdom: The Path of Insight Meditation* (Boston: Shambhala, 1987); William Hart, *The Art of Living: Vipassana Meditation, As Taught by S. N. Goenka* (Igatpuri: Vipassana Research Institute, 1987); Piyadassi Thera, *Buddhist Meditation: The Way to Inner Calm and Clarity* (Kandy, Sri Lanka: Buddhist Publication Society, 1978); Haracarana Singha Sobati, *Vipassana, the Buddhist Way: Based on Pali Sources* (Delhi: Eastern Book Linkers, 1992).

Vipassana International Academy

The Vipassana International Academy in India is the central structure of the association of centers that teach VIPASSANA meditation in the tradition of SATYA NARAYAN GOENKA. Of Indian heritage, Goenka was nevertheless born (1924) and raised in Burma (Myanmar). As a young man he met the Burmese meditation master U BA KHIN (1899–1971), founder of the INTERNATIONAL MEDITATION CENTRE, with whom he studied for 14 years. Goenka then moved to India and in 1969 and began teaching *vipassana*.

Over several years he worked toward establishing a permanent center for teaching and in the mid-1970s land was purchased at Igatpuri, Maharashtra, not far from Mumbai. As the site was developed, he named it Dhamma Giri (or Mountain of Dhamma). The first classes were held at the Vapassana International Academy, the initial facility at Dharma Giri, in December 1976. By the end of the century, upward of 20,000 people a year were taking courses at the academy. In 1982 Goenka began to appoint assistant teachers to assist him in his work. In 1985, he founded the Vipassana Research Institute, also located at Dhamma Giri. The institute conducts research into *vipassana* meditation and translates Buddhist literature, especially works from PALI, and publishes a variety of books and other literature.

As people visited the academy, *vipassana* centers associated with it have emerged throughout southern and Southeast Asia and in the United States, Australia, New Zealand, France, the United Kingdom, Japan, Sri Lanka, Thailand, Burma, and Nepal. Currently, there are approximately 50 centers affiliated with the academy.

Further reading: S. N. Goenka, *The Discourse Summaries* (Igatpuri, India: Vipassana Research Publications, 2000); ———, *The Gracious Flow of Dharma* (Igatpuri, India: Vipassana Research Institute, 1994); ———, *Meditation Now: Inner Peace through Inner Wisdom* (Onalaska, Wash.: Pariyatti, 2002); William Hart, *The Art of Living: Vipassana Meditation as Taught by S. N. Goenka* (San Francisco: Harper & Row, 1993).

virya

Virya, "strength" or "zeal," describes the power and effort needed to transform impure events or tendencies into positive ones. Rather than physical strength, it refers to the strength of character required for sustained effort. *Virya* is key in any cultivation path such as Buddhism. *Virya* is one of the eight parts of the EIGHTFOLD PATH and one of the five (or 10) PARAMITAs, or perfections.

Further reading: Santideva, *The Bodhicaryavatara.* Translated by Kate Crosby and Andrew Skilton (Oxford: Oxford University Press, 1995).

W

Wang Bi (Wang Pi) (226–249 C.E.) *Chinese philosopher and commentator on the Daoist classics*

Wang made his contributions to Chinese thought primarily through his commentaries to the *Daodejing* and the *Yijing* (BOOK OF CHANGES), both of which remain authoritative to this day. In his commentary to the *Daodejing,* Wang views DAO as equivalent to the primordial source of all things. This source (*wu,* "nonbeing" or "nothing") is the ground from which Being (*you*) arises. Language, however, can only describe actual things, not their source. Hence, *wu* cannot be truly named but must remain "nameless," the "origin of the ten-thousand thing" (*Daodejing,* 1). As Wang comments, "The ultimate of the truly real cannot be named. 'Nameless' is indeed its name." This decidedly ontological interpretation of the *Daodejing* has had tremendous influence on Chinese philosophy, becoming the basic metaphysical scheme taken up by Chinese Buddhism and NEO-CONFUCIANISM. Wang also was one of the first thinkers to interpret the *Yijing* as a book of "wisdom" rather than just a divination manual, opening that work to much deeper philosophical exploration. In addition, he also left behind a partial commentary to the ANALECTS entitled Resolving Uncertainties in the Analects (*Lunyu shiyi*) that uncovered important philosophical depths to the work that had been previously overlooked.

Wang Bi holds a curious place in Chinese history. He is generally considered the first truly ontological thinker, that is, a person self-consciously focused on understanding issues of "being" and "nonbeing." He also had a reputation as something of an enfant terrible—a reputation fueled by his alleged egotism and undeniable brilliance. He is one of the main representatives of *xuanxue* ("mysterious/dark learning"), the more or less philosophical side of the post-Han intellectual movement known as "Neo-Daoism." Wang Bi traveled in the highest intellectual circles of his day, impressing his elders with his insights and understanding. He died of an unknown illness at the young age of 24.

There is little doubt that Wang Bi ranks among the most important of China's many philosophers. Wang Bi, as did other thinkers who were part of the *xuanxue* movement, sought the deeper meaning of Daoist texts such as the *Daodejing* and the *Yijing.* He also imprinted himself on Chinese history, leaving several anecdotes concerning his "Dao" much like those of other noted personalities (e.g. LAOZI, ZHUANGZI).

Further reading: Alan K. L. Chan, *Two Visions of the Way: A Study of the Wang Pi and the Ho-shang Commentaries on the Lao-Tzu* (Albany: State University of New York Press, 1991); W. Theodore De Bary and Irene Bloom, eds., *Sources of Chinese Tradition.* Vol. 1, *From Earliest Times to 1600,* 2d ed. (New York: Columbia University Press, 1999), 378–386; Ariane Rump and Wing-tsit Chan, trans., *Commentary on the Lao Tzu by Wang Pi.* Society for Asian and Comparative Philosophy, Monograph no. 6 (Honolulu: The University of Hawaii Press, 1979).

Wang Changyue (Wang Ch'ang-yüeh)
(d.1680) *Daoist monk and abbot of the Baiyun Monastery*

Wang Changyue was responsible for the renewal of QUANZHEN DAOISM, and especially the Longmen school, in the Qing dynasty (1644–1911). Wang decided to seek the DAO—in other words, embark on a spiritual journey—in the final days of the Ming (1368–1644) dynasty. According to legend Wang met the Quanzhen Dao ordination master Zhao Zhensong and was accepted by him as a disciple. However, Zhao refused to transmit the true teachings. They separately wandered an additional 10 more years. When they met again, in 1628, on Mt. Jiugong in Hubei, Zhiao relented and agreed to transmit the liturgy to Wang.

In 1655, after the military triumph of the Manchu forces over the Ming, Wang settled in Beijing. The fighting had emptied the BAIYUN GUAN, the major Quanzhen temple in Beijing, except for one caretaker. He invited Wang Changyue to live there. Wang then set about building an organization. Importantly, he established an ordination process for Quanzhen monks.

Wang was able to promote Longmen DAOISM because he imposed a strict discipline on followers that was in accord with the ruling Qing dynasty's wishes. The Qing's Manchu rulers in general looked on Daoism with suspicion, largely because they suspected it served as a conduit for people dissatisfied with the advent of their new dynasty. Wang lessened their concerns by imposing strict monastic guidelines. He also put a renewed emphasis on the Southern traditions of inner alchemy. Under Wang Changyue's leadership Longmen set up a presence in many traditional Daoist centers throughout China, including West Mountain (Xishan) in Nanchang, Jiangxi Province, and Mt. Wudang in Shanxi.

Further reading: Bartholomew P. M. Tsui, *Taoist Tradition and Change: The Story of the Complete Perfection Sect in Hong Kong* (Hong Kong: Christian Study Centre on Chinese Religion and Culture, 1991).

Wang Chongyang (Yangqun, Wang Zhe, Wang Ch'ung-yang) (1112–1170) *founder of Quanzhen Daoism*

Wang Chongyang is one of the great synthesizers in Chinese religious history. He mixed Daoist, Buddhist, and Neo-Confucianism concepts into a powerful school, QUANZHEN DAOISM. As were many Daoists, Wang was originally a member of the literati during the Jin dynasty (1115–1234). This was a period of sudden political dislocation, with the passing of the Song (960–1279) dynasty and the advent of a new dynasty ruled by foreigners. Wang had retired to a solitary life in the mountains, when he had several meetings with such immortals as LU DONGBIN. Impelled to start a tradition of teaching, he developed a syncretic mixture of practices and morality well suited to the times.

Wang's Quanzhen, or Complete Perfection, sect put greatest emphasis on self-cultivation and less emphasis on intricate visualization exercises, elaborate rituals, or talismanic magic. The particular goal was to refine the body's energies through the practices of inner alchemy (*neidan.*) Wang called his meditative practice *jing zuo,* "quiet sitting," a term probably borrowed from CHAN BUDDHISM. He also borrowed an emphasis on the Confucian virtue of filial piety and ascetic practices. In particular Wang taught abstention from sex, alcohol, and strong vegetables (called the *wu xin*). He and his disciples lived a rustic lifestyle.

When he died in 1127 there were around 15 followers. The subsequent growth in the Quenzhen sect of Daoism was managed by his successors.

Further reading: Bartholomew P. M. Tsui, *Taoist Tradition and Change: The Story of the Complete Perfection Sect in Hong Kong* (Hong Kong: Christian Study Centre on Chinese Religion and Culture, 1991).

Wang Yangming (Wang Shouren) (1472–1529) *action-oriented Chinese philosopher*

A well-known scholar, official, and historical figure in Chinese history, Wang Yangming was also a religious innovator. Under his leadership Neo-Confucianism was transformed into a large-scale religious movement, something that in its mass appeal appears quite modern to us. Although the philosophical system of Zhu Xi (1130–1200) became state orthodoxy, it was challenged in some quarters during the Ming dynasty (1368–1644). Throughout the Ming, Chinese society was becoming more complex; literacy was spreading, commercial activity was on the rise, and there was tremendous growth in international trade and craft specialization. The new problem that dominated intellectual circles was how one could be engaged in this complex world yet achieve the self-integration of a sage. The answer was supplied by an extraordinary teacher named Wang Shouren (later dubbed *Yangming*—"bright clarity"—by his disciples). Wang directly challenged Zhu's metaphysics and ideas on cultivation, sparking much debate among those who followed. His philosophical "protest" to the state institutionalization of Zhu's ideas left the way open for more individualistic, mystical approaches to life.

Wang himself led a very colorful life. After attaining his *jinshi* degree, the highest scholarly attainment, he held many official posts over his career, including that of general. It seems that he ran afoul of the throne, however, and was publicly flogged before being banished to the southwestern frontier. According to later accounts, it was while in exile that he had an intuitive awakening after failing to realize the principle of bamboo according to Zhu Xi's method of "investigating things." Wang recognized the intuitive moral knowledge residing within each person—an idea directly contrary to Zhu Xi's insistence that principle is realized through careful, rational investigation entailing years of study. For Wang principle exists in each person's mind. We need only clear away the obstructions (e.g., selfishness, material desires) to let this inborn knowledge rise to the surface.

Wang's teachings became the basis of a new school of Confucianism called the "New Learning of the Mind-Heart" (*xinfa*). His primary focus was on the original unity of the mind-heart with heaven, earth, and all things. Wang held that there exists a natural empathy within us, an "innate knowing" (LIANGZHI). There is no need to study principles as if they exist "outside" the mind. Instead, one should start from the basic, ontological unity and expand on it through moral self-cultivation. As Wang notes, "The original substance of the mind is nothing other than the heavenly principle . . . It is your True Self. This True Self is the master of your physical body. With it, one lives, without it, one dies." Here he is clearly using Daoist and Buddhist terms yet giving them a Confucian "spin."

Wang's philosophy has a strongly activist bent. Wang saw it as the basis for moral action and disliked the practice of "quiet sitting" (*jing zuo*), a form of meditation advocated by many teachings such as Neo-Confucianism and Quanzhen Daoism. Moral action is just the natural extension of one's innate knowing. For example, FILIAL PIETY (*xiao*) is part of human nature but one may only be said *truly to know* it by observing it in one's own life and actions. For Wang, moral principles are innate; sagehood is thus open to all. He even speaks in places of the "streets filled with sages." Sagely cultivation is not just the special province of the elite. We all can (and should) cultivate our moral nature in our daily affairs, not as an endeavor detached from real life. Wang's own writings show this practical focus and he had specific recommendations for local schooling, community organizations, and common defense.

Overall Wang Yangming was a very dynamic, charismatic personality. His was a truly popular movement open (at least in theory) to far greater social participation than Zhu Xi's school. Wang and his school exerted tremendous influence on Ming society, and his followers extended his views into new areas. Some even turned to DAOISM and BUDDHISM while others questioned the traditional hierarchy of Chinese society.

Further reading: W. Theodore de Bary and Irene Bloom, eds., *Sources of Chinese Tradition.* Vol. 1, *From Earliest Times to 1600,* 2d ed. (New York: Columbia University Press, 1999), 842–857; Wang Yang-ming, *Instructions for Practical Living, and Other Neo-Confucian Writings of Wang Yang-ming.* Translated by Wing-tsit Chan (New York: Columbia University Press, 1963).

war and violence

The injunction against killing is one of the first precepts, a vow taken by all monks as well as lay Buddhists. In the Brahma Net Sutra the individual is forbidden to participate in war or rebellion, or to possess weapons or even observe fighting. Yet Buddhism has in many times and situations been reinterpreted to allow killing. King Duttha-Gamani of Sri Lanka used a Buddha image to lead troops into battle. In China Fa Zang led 50,000 troops into battle in 515 C.E., saying each soldier who killed an enemy would become a BODHISAT-TVA. And monks from the Shaolin Temple helped the Tang dynasty founder gain power. In the Ming dynasty monks from another Shaolin temple, this one in Fujian, fought against Japanese pirates with their faces painted blue. Fighting monks were even more common in Japan and Korea.

What justifications from the Buddhist SUTRAS can be found for involvement in fighting? The French scholar Paul Demieville has pointed out that the MAHAYANA BUDDHISM version of the MAHAPARINIRVANA SUTRA tells how the Buddha, in a previous life, was forced to kill Brahmins in order to protect Buddhism and, ironically, to protect the Brahmins from the damnation that harming Buddhism would incur. Protecting the DHARMA at all costs was justified, even if it meant opposing the precepts. Here is very powerful justification for involvement in violence.

Another rationalization for violence is to save other lives. The great YOGACARA BUDDHISM scholar ASANGA noted in the Yogacarabhumi that a bodhisattva who killed in order to prevent further killing would gain merit if he had a mind of compassion (KARUNA) while performing the act. Again, there is a story from the Jnanottara-bodhisattva-pariprccha Sutra of the BUDDHA's killing a bandit in order to save the lives of 500 merchants.

A final argument, as listed by Demieville, was metaphysical. Since in orthodox Buddhist philosophy the individual had no actual "soul," there was no true loss when someone was killed. One passage in the Ratnakuta Sutra describes how the bodhisattva MANJUSRI pretends to stick a sword into the Buddha. The Buddha then approves, saying this shows that Manjusri understands there is no substance or reality to the Buddha; there is neither sin nor sinner.

These arguments help explain the support of some modern Buddhists and associations for warfare in certain cases.

Further reading: Holmes Welch, *Buddhism under Mao* (Cambridge, Mass.: Harvard University Press, 1972).

wat

The *wat,* the name used for a monastic complex, is the central institution in Thai and Laotian traditional culture and continues to serve as the symbolic center of most communities. As Buddhism spread into Thailand and the surrounding countries, the monastery became the place where social life and village activities were concentrated.

Here holy days and secular celebrations would occur and young boys would go through some of their manhood ceremonies.

Monasteries typically have a hall in which ceremonies are performed and living quarters for the monks. There may also be a STUPA for relics, a bell tower, a library, a preaching hall, and/or a crematorium. Many wats have a school for children and youth and increasingly in the modern world a room for literature distribution. The wat's community is headed by an abbot. In Thailand, there are two distinct types of wats, the royal wats supported by public funds, and the community wats supported by private funds. The many wats of the THAI FOREST MEDITATION TRADITION are community wats. Of Thailand's more than 28,000 wats, less than 2 percent are royal wats; however, among these are most of the large, more artistically notable, and famous ones.

On the average about a dozen men (monks and novices) reside at the monastery, along with some young boys who might live there while attending school. Almost all young males live for a short time at a *wat*, as a symbolic joining of the SANGHA is part of the recognition of their coming of age.

Further reading: Joe Cummings, *The Meditation Temples of Thailand: A Guide* (Bangkok: Wayfarer Books and Trasvin, 1990); Phra Rajavaramuni, *Thai Buddhism in the Buddhist World* (North Hollywood, Calif.: Wat Thai of Los Angeles, 1984).

Watts, Alan Wilson (1915–1973) *American writer on Buddhism and Zen*

Watts, a major spokesperson for ZEN BUDDHISM in the 1950s and 1960s, was born in England. As a young man he found his way to the Buddhist Society in England, where he was introduced to ZEN BUDDHISM by the society's president, CHRISTMAS HUMPHREYS, and the writings of DAISETSU TEITARO SUZUKI. He was but 19 years old when he wrote his first book, *The Spirit of Zen* (1935).

He moved to the United States in 1938 and shortly thereafter married Eleanor Everett, the daughter of Ruth Fuller Everett (who as RUTH FULLER EVERETT SASAKI would later have an outstanding career as a Buddhist leader). As World War II progressed, Watts entered Seabury-Western Theological Seminary and upon completion of his coursework in 1945 was ordained in the Episcopal Church.

In 1951 he moved to San Francisco as an instructor at the American Academy of Asian Studies. While there he encountered the founders of the "Beat" movement, many of whom, such as the poet GARY SNYDER, were identifying with BEAT ZEN Buddhism. He also became one of the pioneers of the psychedelic culture being advocated by Timothy Leary (1920–96) and Richard Alpert (1931–   ) (later known as Baba Ram Dass).

Watt's wide-ranging interest in Eastern religion, mood-altering drugs, and counterculture themes became the focus of a series of books beginning with *The Wisdom of Insecurity* (1951), which made him one of the most popular spokespersons in the cause of developing a new American spirituality apart from traditional Christianity. Always at the core of his writings, however, was his appropriation of Zen, most clearly presented in his *The Spirit of Zen* (1958) and *The Way of Zen* (1968). Shortly before his death he issued his autobiography, *In My Own Way* (1973).

Watts's work has been carried on by the Society for Comparative Psychology.

Further reading: David Stuart, *Alan Watts* (New York: Stein & Day, 1976); Alan Watts, *Cloud Hidden, Whereabouts Unknown* (New York: Pantheon, 1973); ———, *In My Own Way* (New York: Pantheon, 1972); ———, *The Spirit of Zen* (New York: Grove Press, 1958); ———, *This Is It* (New York: Random House, 1962); ———, *The Way of Zen* (New York: Pantheon Books, 1968).

Wesak (Vesak)

In early, if extracanonical, accounts of Sakyamuni BUDDHA, his birthday, the day of his ENLIGHTEN-

MENT, and his PARINIRVANA (death) are all said to have occurred on the same day, the night of the full moon of Vaisakha, the second month of the Hindu calendar (usually in May of the Western calendar). Traditionally, Wesak was primarily an event remembered by THERAVADA Buddhists and its celebration became the most important festival of their year. It was a time to remember the birth and death of Buddha, but eventually the celebration of his enlightenment moved to the fore. In the 20th century it became a favorite celebration within most Buddhist traditions, especially in the West.

The celebration of Wesak includes both a formal and an informal aspect. The formal part usually includes a procession by the monks, the presentation of an offering, and the chanting of SUTRAS. In more recent times, the ceremony often includes a talk on some aspect of the *dhamma* (DHARMA) and the bathing of a statue of the Buddha. In the evening of the full moon, a Vaisakha Puja (sacramental offering) celebrates the Buddha's birth.

The informal part of Wesak allows lay believers to take the lead and may include events over several days. Celebrations include liberal amounts of food and drink, artistic and cultural performances, and possibly academic discussions of Buddhist history and theology. This more informal part usually begins immediately after the more formal rituals.

As Buddhism has taken its place within the world's religious community and as many Buddhists have moved from predominantly Buddhist lands to settings around the world, Wesak has taken on new functions as a platform for interaction between Buddhists of different sects and ethnic groups and a showcase for dialogue between Buddhists and their non-Buddhist neighbors. These functions have become very important in the West, where Buddhists often exist as a beleaguered minority. In 1998, Wesak was accepted as the official Buddhist holiday by the United Nations.

In Korea, Wesak is known as the Festival of the Lanterns. Along with the normal rituals conducted at Buddhist temples, paper lanterns, decorated with Buddhist symbols and inscribed with wishes for a long life, are hung in the temple courtyards and are featured in parades through the street. The festival was designated as a Korean national holiday in 1975.

Through the 20th century, Western esoteric groups—part of a complex tradition including such practices as occultism, spiritualism, and Rosicrucianism—made an interesting appropriation of Wesak. The Theosophical teacher Alice A. Bailey (1880–1949) proposed that those associated with the Arcane School she founded celebrate three holidays she saw as particularly relevant to the quest for spiritual enlightenment—Easter (full moon in April), the Day of Goodwill (full moon in June), and Wesak (full moon in May). In the 1970s, Bailey's thought became an important aspect of the New Age movement, and the celebration of Wesak and a ceremonial occasion spread beyond the Arcane School and the several groups that had originated from it.

See also FESTIVALS, BUDDHIST.

Further reading: Aneri Ganeri, *Buddhist Festivals through The Year* (London: Watts Group, 2003); ———, *Wesak* (London: Heinemann Educational Books, 2002); Alice A. Bailey, "The Wesak Festival." Lucis Trust. Available online. URL: http://www.lucistrust.org/meetings/wesak2.shtml. Accessed on September 15, 2005; John Snelling, *Buddhist Festivals* (Vero Beach, Fla.: Rourke Enterprises, 1987); David Turpie, "Wesak and the Re-Creation of Buddhist Tradition." Montreal Religious Sites Project. Available online. URL: http://www.mrsp.mcgill.ca/reports/html/Wesak/#111. Accessed on September 15, 2005.

Wheel of Life

The Wheel of Life is a symbolic illustration of numerous aspects of the Buddhist worldview: reincarnation in the six realms; imprisonment in cyclic existence as a result of ignorance, attachment, and hatred; and responsibility for our own situation, among other things. Although there are many Buddhas and gods, no creator god who is responsible for existence is asserted. Instead, we are what our own minds have created. Ethical behavior does yield happiness, and wisdom will conquer ignorance. For humans, nirvana is always a possibility.

It is said that the Wheel of Life painting was designed by the BUDDHA Sakyamuni himself to display his essential teachings in a single illustration. Legend has it that a royal acquaintance of the Buddha, King Bimbisara of MAGADHA, once received a jeweled gift from another ruler, King Udayana. Not having a fabulous gift to present in return, Bimbisara asked the Buddha for advice. The Buddha described this didactic painting to Bimbisara's court painter. The following stanza is one of those that traditionally accompany it:

> Undertaking this and leaving that,
> Enter into the teaching of the Buddha.
> Like an elephant in a thatched house,
> Destroy the forces of the Lord of Death.

It is said that Bimbisara attained nirvana upon seeing it, and it is no wonder that the picture has remained popular even to the present day, gracing the entryways and courtyards of many Buddhist establishments. The Wheel of Life is especially popular in Tibet. Its many vivid details combine to present an eloquent and easily understandable view of our universe—the Desire Realm—according to the Buddha.

All the various versions of the painting vividly depict YAMA, the king of death and impermanence, clutching a round mirror in his teeth and claws. Reflected in the mirror are 24 aspects of the Desire Realm. Moving outward from the center, these are the three poisons, the two paths of virtue and nonvirtue, the six realms of rebirth in cyclic existence (along with the form and formless realms, not depicted here), and the 12 links of dependent origination. Above Death's left shoulder stands the Buddha, pointing across the painting to the moon, representing the passing beyond suffering of NIRVANA.

THE THREE POISONS

The Buddhist worldview presents a stark picture of individual responsibility. As the Wheel of Life painting points out, all of the many pleasant and unpleasant events that occur in our lives—including death and rebirth—are the results of our own actions, be they virtuous, nonvirtuous, or neutral. These actions are motivated by the THREE POISONS, of ignorance, desire, and hatred. These three are represented within the central section of the painting by a pig, a rooster, and a snake, respectively.

Looking more closely at these three symbolic animals, we see that they are linked, tails to mouths. This represents their psychological interdependence. The root of karmic actions, ignorance, arises as a precursor to desire and hatred.

THE PATHS OF VIRTUE AND NONVIRTUE

Even under the sway of ignorance, we are not solely nonvirtuous in our actions. Since beginningless time, we have inevitably committed physical, verbal, and mental nonvirtues. Nevertheless, there have also been times when we have acted virtuously, thinking of the well-being of others. These two paths of activity, the virtuous and the nonvirtuous, are represented surrounding the innermost circle of the three poisons. On the dark right side we see those who persist in nonvirtue being pulled down into suffering by demons. On the bright left side those who have forsworn nonvirtue are elevated into the happier realms through the excellent advice of spiritual friends. These fortunate beings have discovered the path to happiness by abandoning killing, stealing, sexual misconduct, lying, divisive talk, harsh speech, senseless chatter, covetousness, harmful intent, and wrong views.

THE SIX REALMS OF REBIRTH

According to the teachings of the Buddha, a person's body ends at death, but not the continuum of consciousness. Instead, impelled by actions motivated by ignorance (KARMA), a person

The Wheel of Life, showing the six births, clockwise from top: gods, jealous gods (firing arrows at the gods), animals, hell-beings, hungry ghosts, and humans. Thangka (mineral paints on cotton), kept in the Burat Historical Museum. From *Buddiiskaia zhivopis' Buriatii* (1995).

powerlessly takes another birth somewhere in one of the SIX REALMS OF EXISTENCE: the realms of gods, the jealous gods, humans, animals, hungry ghosts, or hell beings. Much of the Wheel of Life painting is concerned with depicting these realms. Notice that the figure of a Buddha is present in each of the realms, indicating that there is no place in the universe that is abandoned by these enlightened beings.

The realm of the gods is by far the most glorious. Because of their good karma, the gods live long, pleasure-filled lives. They live in fabulous mansions, their bodies shine from within, and they are adorned with garlands of flowers. Nevertheless, although they are gods, they too are mortal. In the days before they die, they see clearly that they have exhausted their good karma and are destined to be reborn in a lower realm. Their flower garlands wilt, their bodies begin to stink, and the suffering of their final days is terrible.

Next to the god realms are the abodes of the jealous gods. As can be seen in the illustration, in the jealous god realm there grows a tree. The fruit of this tree always falls into the god realms, depriving the jealous gods (asuras) of its beneficial effects. In their jealousy they wage war on the gods, but they are always defeated. They too fall into the lower realms after their death.

The human realm, in the upper left of the circular mirror, depicts our own world. Although we humans must endure the sufferings of birth, aging, sickness, and death, as well as not getting what we want and getting what we do not want, ours is the best realm for religious practice. Humans are smart, logical, and capable of understanding fully the teachings of the Buddha. It is often said that a human physical support is required for the attainment of nirvana.

The animal realm is the only other realm we humans can observe. There are animals on and under the land as well as in the sea. Animals are plagued by a lack of intelligence, by being food for other creatures, and by enslavement to humans,

among other problems. Their lives are generally short.

The PRETA, hungry ghosts, are shown below the human realm. Their lot is to be continually deprived of food and drink. They have large bellies but minuscule mouths. Even on the rare occasions when they find food, they cannot ingest it. Their throats are too small to pass nutriment, and morsels of food catch fire in their mouths. Their environment is barren, hot, and sandy.

Although the hungry ghosts endure terrible suffering, the suffering of the HELL realms is far worse. ASANGA's *Levels of Yogic Deeds* describes eight great hells and a number of neighboring hells. One hell is called the Howling Hell. There, beings who search for shelter are herded into an iron house, where they are incinerated by blazing fires. Death does not occur until the force of nonvirtue has been spent. Hence, it is possible to suffer in the hells for a billion years before release, and even then one might take rebirth in an adjoining hell, such as the Pit of Embers. Still, the sufferings of the hells are impermanent, just as are the causes of rebirth in them.

THE 12 LINKS OF CODEPENDENT ARISING

The outermost section of the Wheel of Life mirror consists of 12 cause-and-effect links called the links of codependent arising. These links describe the process of taking rebirth in cyclic existence. As do the links of a chain, one leads to the next, but should one link be broken the entire process ends.

The first link in the chain is ignorance, represented by a blind mind walking with a cane. Ignorance, as we have already seen, refers to misunderstanding how the self actually exists. Ignorance is the only link that can be broken, since there is an antidote to ignorance: the wisdom that realizes selflessness.

A moment of ignorance often leads to the next link, action. Actions that are undertaken under the sway of ignorance are virtuous, nonvirtuous, and neutral karmas. These stain the consciousness of the actor. These three links impel a new rebirth.

The fourth link, name and form, is represented by a person in a boat. The boat symbolizes the form aggregate while the person represents the mental aggregates. Within the process of rebirth, name and form are the beginning of a new life in a mother's womb. The next three links represent the developing child: the six sense fields lead to contact with the world, which in turn leads to feelings (represented vividly by a person with an arrow in his eye). Feelings can be pleasant, painful, or neutral.

When feelings are generated, one becomes attached to pleasant feelings and the wish to avoid unpleasant feelings. Attachment is the eighth link (a person drinking beer), which leads to an even stronger form of attachment called grasping (a monkey taking fruit). These two links are types of desire. Attachment and grasping empower a karmic potential to generate a new life in cyclic existence. This empowered karmic potency is called existence, the 10th link, which will produce another lifetime somewhere in the Desire Realm. The 11th link is birth, and the 12th link is aging and death.

NIRVANA

The first link, ignorance, can be broken through application of its antidote, the wisdom that realizes selflessness. When wisdom eradicates ignorance, actions motivated by ignorance cease. When ignorant actions cease, so too does the staining of consciousness. Without stains on the consciousness, there is no birth as name and form. When there is no name and form, the six sense fields do not develop. Without the six sense fields there are no contact, no feeling, no attachment, and no grasping. Therefore, there is no empowering of existence, and hence no birth. Without birth there is no aging and there is no death. In this way the cycle of rebirth is broken. Suffering is ended for the individual forever. Nirvana, the final liberation, is attained.

See also PRTATITYA-SAMUTPADA; SIX REALMS OF EXISTENCE; HELL.

Further reading: Tenzin Gyatso, the Fourteenth Dalai Lama, *Kindness, Clarity, and Insight* (Ithaca, N.Y.: Snow Lion, 1980); ———, *The Meaning of Life from a Buddhist Perspective* (Somerville, Mass.: Wisdom, 1992); Geshe Lobsang Tharchin, *King Udrayana and the Wheel of Life* (Howell, N.J.: Mahayana Sutra and Tantra Press, 1984).

White Horse Temple See BAIMASI.

Wilber, Ken (1949–) *American Buddhist and transpersonal psychologist*

Ken Wilbur, a popular American writer of books on spirituality, was born in Oklahoma City, Oklahoma, the son of an air force officer. While in school at Duke University he became interested in psychology. In graduate school he grabbed public attention with his first book, *The Spectrum of Consciousness,* an overview of the state of human consciousness that paid particular attention to the similarities and contrasts of Eastern and Western understandings. He pictured the human consciousness to waves of light that had stepped down to participate in time and space. From his interest in consciousness, he became a leading voice of the subdiscipline of transpersonal psychology and its quest for information about the higher states of conscious experience. Transpersonal psychology places particular emphasis on the study of spirituality and such related issues as self-actualization and peak experiences.

Wilbur continued his exploration of consciousness, adding insights form various social sciences and religions. He became a Buddhist during this time, moving from ZEN BUDDHISM to

Tibetan meditation practice. He has suggested that scholars who seek to study consciousness should previously have experienced some of the spiritual states of consciousness.

In the late 1980s he made public his very conscious experience of his relationship with his wife, Treya, who was dying of cancer. In order to identify with her, he shaved his head and went through a very public expression of compassion. Two years after her death he published an account of the time in his book *Grace and Grit* (1991).

Through the 1980s he had become increasingly identified with the popular New Age movement, a movement he found to be both soaked in an uncritical antiintellectualism and holding views that conflicted with his own Buddhism. He became vocally critical of the movement and has continued to criticize it in more recent books.

Further reading: Ken Wilber, *The Atman Project: A Transpersonal View of Human Development* (Wheaton, Ill.: Quest, 1980); ———, *The Essential Ken Wilber: An Introductory Reader* (Boston: Shambhala, 1998); ———, *No Boundary: Eastern and Western Approaches to Personal Growth* (1979. Reprint, Boston: Shambhala, 1981); ———, *The Spectrum of Consciousness* (Wheaton, Ill.: Quest, 1977).

women in Buddhism

Women became involved with Buddhism even before Siddhartha Gautama of the Sakya clan became an awakened one known as the BUDDHA (563–483 B.C.E.). As the story goes, his mother, MAHAMAYA, dreamed that a white elephant merged with her side. Subsequently, nine months later she delivered Siddhartha from under her arm near her heart. He took seven steps and declared that this was his last lifetime. Seven days later his mother died. Her sister, MAHAPRAJAPATI GOTAMI, married Siddhartha's father. After some years of questioning about why life was so hard Siddhartha left home on a pilgrimage when he was 29, leaving his wife and son behind.

It took six long and intensive years of study and meditation for him to realize ENLIGHTENMENT. He soon was able to develop a spiritual philosophy that would allow anyone to follow, the EIGHTFOLD PATH. Years later when he was near his hometown teaching about taking REFUGE in the Three Jewels of Buddhism:—the Buddha, the DHARMA (teachings), and SANGHA (order of monks)—a neighbor reported that Siddhartha was teaching in the town square. Quickly, his family ran to see him.

Buddha's stepmother, Mahaprajapati, heard his sermon about the Four Auspicious sights, the FOUR NOBLE TRUTHS, and the Eightfold Path. She decided to become a nun and attempted to gain Buddha's permission to start a women's order of the sangha. Neither the monks (BHIKSU) nor Buddha himself favored women's having a monastic type order. After repeated pleas, however, Buddha relented and allowed women to be ordained as nuns (BHIKSUNI), beginning with Mahaprajapati.

In instituting the order of nuns, Buddha asserted that women could attain *arhat* (enlightenment) but at the same time added eight restrictive rules that they had to follow. These rules were designed to maintain their subordinate relationship within the sangha and assure that no *bhiksuni* could ever have authority over any *bhiksu*. Other rules forbade the *bhiksu* to abuse his authority. In the context of the times, the rules elevated the status of women, especially in recognizing their spiritual equality.

HISTORICAL DEVELOPMENT

Over the next centuries, Buddhism would spread as believers carried it along the caravan and sea routes to other countries, but also as a missionary religion, planted by the self-conscious efforts of dedicated leaders. The jump from India to Sri Lanka, for example, occurred through the efforts of King ASOKA. His son, MAHINDA, introduced Buddhism to Sri Lanka. Since the rules of the priesthood forbade Mahinda to ordain women, he asked Asoka to send his sister, SANGHAMITTA, and a group of nuns to Sri Lanka. Sanghamitta arrived accompanied by the nuns and with a branch of the BODHI TREE. From Sri Lanka, the Theravada Bhiksuni Sangha (order of nuns) spread eastward into Burma (Myanmar). However, the order was largely destroyed at the time of the Mongol attack on the Burmese kingdom of Pagan in the 13th century. Partly as a result, there are currently a few Buddhist nuns in Southeast Asia, and those there are generally detached from the main sangha community.

There have been major obstacles for women to overcome to be admitted to holy orders. They have to seek ORDINATION where they can. Recently those in Sri Lanka after a long arduous struggle have been legitimized and are part of the organizational sangha (male monks). Since the third SAKYADHITA Conference in 1993, many nuns have been encouraged by laywomen to pursue their quest. In April 2000, 22 Sri Lankan nuns and three Indonesian nuns traveled to the FOGUANGSHAN monastery in Taiwan to be ordained.

The possibility of the religious life for Chinese women emerged as Buddhism was transmitted northward from India. Beginning in the fourth century Buddhism made tremendous progress throughout both northern and southern China. In 317 Zhu Qingjian (Chu Ching Chien) (292–361) became the first Chinese woman to take the initiation as novice. Twenty-four other Chinese women who also wanted to live collectively joined her, and they founded a convent in Chang An, the Chinese capital at the time. However, it would not be until the year 434 that the Bhiksuni Sangha from Sri Lanka founded a formal order in China. Thus the Indian Sangha lineage survived in China and this particular lineage has never ceased to be. Today it continues in Taiwan, Singapore, and Hong Kong.

The development of the sangha provided the first opportunity for Chinese women to leave roles as mother, daughter, and wife. It was also the case, unfortunately, that on those occasions that authorities discovered corruption among the secular political ranks, the women's order was often the first to suffer reprisals.

Buddhism in China took a great step forward during the reign of Empress WU CHAO (c. 625–705). Wu, a concubine of the emperor Tai Zong (r. 626–649), entered a Buddhist nunnery when he died. She later left the nunnery to become the wife of Tai Zong's son and, eventually, the empress of China herself. However, she remembered her former sister nuns and as empress became a patron to the women of several Buddhist sects and encouraged them to assume roles equal to those of males in various rituals. She also worked to elevate the role of women in general and commissioned the biographies of several outstanding women so their contributions would not be forgotten.

From China, the order of nuns was transmitted to Korea and Japan. Three Japanese women—Zenshin, Zenso, and Eizen—were sent to the Korean kingdom of PAEKCHE in 587 to study among the nuns there. Three years later they returned to Japan and instituted the process of ORDINATION for Japanese nuns. The women's orders have survived to the present, and especially in Korea women have assumed a more prominent role in leadership in the last generation.

VAJRAYANA BUDDHISM emerged among practitioners of MAHAYANA BUDDHISM in India in the fourth century C.E., probably in the northwest. This new perspective took some of its basic teachings from Tantric Hinduism. In these teachings sexual union serves as the model for overcoming duality in perceptions and achieving a realization of unity, described as an "adamantine union of light." Not all TANTRA teachings involves physical practices; the goal is to learn from within yourself—on a subtle level—how to mix male and female energy for enlightenment.

Princess Laksminkara was an early outstanding female figure in Tantrism, the avenue to enlightenment within Vajrayana Buddhism. The semimythical princess lived in what is now Pakistan. As the story goes, the princess was to marry a prince. Unfortunately, he hunted for sport, and her own belief in nonviolence caused her to leave him. Pretending lunacy, she lived for a period near a cremation ground. While there she experienced holy visions of Buddhas and BODHISATTVAS (the illumined souls who chose to reincarnate to help a suffering humanity). While there, the visionary Laksminkara attracted a substantial following of men and women from all castes. She taught them a form of sexual yoga as a way to bliss and enlightenment that transcended ordinary reality. Her students transmitted the extensive teachings all over the Indian subcontinent. She stressed that teachers remove the emotional blocks that prevented the student from obtaining NIRVANA.

As Buddhism was transmitted to Tibet, stories of figures such as Princess Laksminkara and a pantheon filled with female as well as male deities helped women to find a place in the tradition. Communities of nuns emerged throughout Tibet and most of the main male monastic groups had an affiliated order of nuns. Some nunneries were headed by women recognized as TULKUs (emanations of a bodhisattva). Women were not, however, ordained as *bhiksunis* and were in general seen as less possessed of ritual powers.

Buddhism in the Modern West

In moving into the modern West, Buddhism was forced to accommodate the changing attitudes toward women and their traditional assignments to second-class status. This changing context is no better symbolized that in the career of the Western Buddhist pioneer ALEXANDRA DAVID-NÉEL (1868–1969). David-Néel, an adventurer who pushed the envelope on women's status even for the late 19th century, spent years exploring India, Tibet, China, and Japan. A citizen of France, a former opera singer, and learned in a number of languages including Tibetan, she translated many Buddhist texts into French. Her labors to enter Tibet spanned years. Foreigners were forbidden to enter Lhasa and she wanted to meet the DALAI LAMA. Much of the early information about Tibetan Buddhism was gained through her works published in the late 1800s and early 1900s. She

lived to be 101—working on Buddhist translations until shortly before her death.

Another prominent early female Western Buddhist was MARY ELIZABETH FOSTER (d. 1930), a native of Hawaii. She had an accidental meeting with ANGARIKA DHARMAPALA from Sri Lanka when his ship docked in Honolulu in 1893. He was homeward bound after being a dignitary and guest speaker for Buddhism at the World's Parliament of Religions, in Chicago. Foster, already involved with Theosophy, managed to create a bridge encompassing the two belief systems. During the remaining years of her life she used her wealth to underwrite numerous Buddhist organizations throughout the islands.

As Buddhism was transmitted to the West in general and America in particular ZEN BUDDHISM had an early significant role. Many people in the United States primarily discovered Buddhism first through DAISETSU TEITARO SUZUKI and his teaching of Zen, in the 1940s and 1950s. Among the early female leaders within the American Zen community, RUTH FULLER EVERETT SASAKI (1893–1967) was given significant help by Suzuki, who arranged for her early study at a Zen monastery in Japan. She would later become the head of the First Zen Institute of America.

Elsie Mitchell was an early American woman who traveled to Japan for study. She authored one of the early Zen Buddhist books by a female, *Sun Buddhas, Moon Buddhas* (1973). She later became involved with running the Cambridge Buddhist Association and emerged as the keeper of the archives. She also became the mentor of Maurine Stuart, who had left one Zen group over gender submission issues. Now the president of the Cambridge Association, Stuart credits Mitchell as her role model.

The Order of Buddhist Contemplatives was founded by Jiyu-Kennett Roshi (1924–96). Initially, she studied Theravada Buddhism, but then in 1962 she moved to Malaysia seeking ORDINATION in the CHAN BUDDHISM tradition. Afterward, she traveled to Japan, where she became the personal disciple of the Very Reverend Chisan Koho Zenji, a SOTO ZEN master. In 1969, she returned to the United States and founded the Zen Mission Society in San Francisco. Operating amid a number of male *roshis* then in the West, Kennett Roshi attracted a number of students and in 1970 relocated to Mt. Shasta, where she founded a monastery and seminary. Those who completed their training, women and men, were ordained at Mt. Shasta, then founded monastic branches across North America and in England.

In spite of people like Sasaki and Kennett, women's entry into positions of power in the larger Zen community occurred slowly. They were given some assistance by a few American male leaders such as Philip Kapleau (1909–2004) and ROBERT BAKER AITKEN (1917–   ), who worked to transform antifemale attitudes in the many centers that grew out of their pioneering efforts. Anne Aitken and Robert Aitken, for example, cofounded the Diamond Zen Center in Hawaii, a center of the SANBO KYODAN (Order of the Three Treasures). In the 1970s, the Diamond Zen Center became one of the places where the roles of women in American Buddhism, especially in light of the transfer of traditional patriarchal patterns from Japan, were identified and discussed, and advocacy for their elimination occurred.

Meanwhile, some of the women associated with Kapleau's center in Rochester, New York, challenged a variety of the trappings of Zen practice and etiquette as inherently patriarchal. In 1981, unhappy with the state of change, Toni Packer and her allies withdrew from the Rochester Zen Center and started the Genesee Valley Zen Center. Her move raised a variety of issues about Zen practice related to women and the nature of authority. In the pilgrimage that later led from the Genesee Center to the Springwater Center that she now heads, Packer renounced her Zen credentials and adopted a new style of nonauthoritarian teachings.

A somewhat different trajectory was followed by Roshi Gessin Prabhasa Dharma (1931–99).

After a quarter-century of study and leadership, she resigned her post as head of an American RINZAI ZEN center. She formed a liaison with the Vietnamese leadership of the International Buddhist Meditation Center in Los Angeles. She ultimately received the Dharma Mind Seal Transmission from the Venerable Thich Man Giac of the United Buddhist Churches of America. She subsequently founded the International Zen Institute of America, which now has affiliated centers in the United States and several European countries.

The Zen Center of Los Angeles and its founding teacher, Taizan Maezumi Roshi (1931–95), also became a vehicle for the rise of women in American Zen. Prior to his death, Maezumi Roshi elevated several women to leadership positions and Charlotte Joko Beck was named as one of his DHARMA HEIRS, or designated successors. Today she leads the Ordinary Mind Zen School based in San Diego.

Along with Zen, in the 1960s and 1970s many Western Buddhists were attracted to Tibetan Buddhism. The largest of the Western Tibetan groups, Vajradhatu International, was founded by the KAGYU teacher CHOGYAM TRUNGPA Rinpoche (1939–87). Trungpa attracted many students with his unusual manner of teaching and his stress on the centrality of the teacher-and-student relationship. His goal was to strip away the ego of the student (in a manner similar to that advocated in Gestalt therapy). His teachings also advocated the trespassing of various sexual mores, which created a situation in which a number of his female disciples found themselves the victims of sexual abuse. As questions of male authority were raised in Zen in the 1980s, women from Tibetan traditions joined the conversations demanding changes.

In the summer of 1981, Naropa Institute in Boulder, Colorado, an educational institution founded by Trungpa, became the site of the first conference on women in Buddhism. Women representatives of the three major traditions of American Buddhism—Tibetan, Japanese Zen, and

Theravada—were invited to participate. The focus of the conferences were the numerous liaisons that had developed between male Buddhist leaders and their female students, and the unbalanced power relationship upon which such relationships were based. These conversations paralleled those that were also occurring in Protestant churches at the time.

The 1981–82 conferences were in part made possible by the women-only retreats that had emerged in the 1970s. Among the first to host such retreats was Ruth Denison, a Theravada meditation master and founder of Dhamma Dena, a retreat center near Joshua Tree, California. Considered somewhat unorthodox by some of her Theravada colleagues, she found support from the American-based VIPASSANA groups such as the Insight Mediation Society in Massachusetts. In London, the FRIENDS OF THE WESTERN BUDDHIST ORDER have also hosted female-only retreats for many years.

The challenges to the subordinate role for women that had developed out of the secular gender role assignments in the Asian countries where Buddhism was dominant would remake Western Buddhism. Women, always present, found themselves rising to leadership roles of every kind, and the changing patterns within groups founded in the West would rebound, however slowly, on the groups founded by various Asian diaspora groups. The environment created by the Western context has provided opportunities for talented women to assume a host of new roles. Among the many symbols of the new roles available to women was the recognition of Jetsunma Ahkon Norbu Lhamo (1949–   ) as a TULKU and her formal enthronement by her male colleagues as a lineage holder in the NYINGMA Tibetan tradition.

As indicative as any of the changing role of women in Buddhism has been the emergence of outstanding female Buddhist scholars, notable among them Rita Gross at the University of Wisconsin, Janet Gyatso at Amherst, and Karma Lek-she Tsomo at the University of San Diego. Lenore Friedman, the author of *Meetings with Remarkable Women: Buddhist Teachers in America,* set the standards for writing about Buddhist religious women. Such scholars have taken the lead in reexamining and recovering the achievements and accomplishments of Buddhist women through the centuries. Initially finding only minimal support in their own communities, they are doing what Christian women are doing: providing their own interpretations to the age-old challenges of cultures and societies that support male authority. One result has been that Western Buddhist women have projected multiple ways to express their need and desire for spirituality, while building lines of communication and action across the many Buddhist traditions.

See also CHENG YEN; *DAKINI;* NIGUMA; SAKYAD-HITA; YESHE TSOGYAL.

Further reading: Tessa Bartholomeusz, *Women under the Bo Tree: Buddhist Nuns in Sri Lanka* (New York: Cambridge University Press, 1994); Sandy Boucher, *Opening the Lotus: A Women's Guide to Buddhism* (Boston: Beacon Press, 1997); Marianne Dresser, ed., *Buddhist Women on the Edge: Contemporary Perspectives from the Western Frontier* (Berkeley, Calif.: North Atlantic Books, 1996); Lenore Friedman, *Meetings with Remarkable Women: Buddhist Teachers in America* (Boston: Shambhala, 1987); Rita Gross, *Buddhism after Patriarchy: A Feminist History, Analysis, and Reconstruction of Buddhism* (Albany, New York: State University of New York Press, 1993); Isaline B. Horner, *Women under Primitive Buddhism* (London: Routledge & Kegan Paul, 1930); Chatsumarn Kabilsingh, *Thai Women in Buddhism* (Berkeley, Calif.: Parallax Press, 1991); Diana Paul, *Women in Buddhism: Images of the Feminine in the Mahayana Tradition* (Berkeley: University of California Press, 1985); Ellen S. Sidor, ed., *A Gathering of Spirit: Women Teaching in American Buddhism* (Cumberland, R.I.: Primary Point Press, 1987); Karma Lekshe Tsomo, ed., *Buddhism through American Women's Eyes* (Ithaca, N.Y.: Snow Lion, 1995).

Won Buddhism

Won Buddhism is a relatively new form of Buddhism founded in Korea in the early 20th century. Its founder, Soe-tae San (1891–1943), attempted to strip Buddhism of its superstitious elements and reformulate it as a modern religion adaptable to present needs. Soe-tae San attempted to combine elements from both the Korean Son Buddhism (Zen Buddhism) tradition and the Pure Land Buddhism tradition. From the latter, the NEMBUTSU is chanted to the BODHISATTVA Amida, though the Won centers are devoid of any statues representing Amida or other Buddhas. Adherents also engage in periods of meditation at the temple; however, the goal of practice is what is termed "timeless and placeless" meditation, that is, living in such a way as to see the Buddha, ENLIGHTENMENT, in all things. A step along the way is to realize one's BUDDHA NATURE, one's original consciousness, which is equivalent to the consciousness of all enlightened ones.

Won Buddhism has only one prime symbol and object of meditation—a black circle painted on a white field, as a symbolic representation of the cosmic body of Buddha, the DHARMAKAYA. From his enlightened state, So-tae San wrote Chong-jon, the basic scriptural text used in the movement. At the same time respect is accorded the other SUTRAS common to Korean Buddhism.

The founder of Won Buddhism was born into a peasant family on May 5, 1891, in Chunnam Province, Korea. As a child he had begun his search for truth, much of which involved his observing and analyzing the phenomenal world. After some 20 years of striving, he was granted an awakening that followed his entering a state of NIRVANA. He concluded that the common human problem of the modern age was enslavement to materialism, which entrapped people in SAMSARA, the cycle of birth, death, and reincarnation. Won Buddhism attempts to facilitate people's escaping samsara.

The founder is now known by his Dharma name, *Soe-tae San,* and his Dharma title, *Tae-jongsa.* After receiving enlightenment in 1915, Soe-tae San Taejongsa drew around him nine original disciples who wished to study Buddhism and engage in its practice. In 1924, they founded the Association for the Study of the Buddha-Dharma, which remained a rather small association through the Japanese occupation of Korea that only ended with Japan's defeat in World War II. In the meantime, Soe-tae San died in 1943. However, as Won Buddhism, his teachings were propagated across Korea from 1946.

Soe-tae San had established the headquarters of his movement in Iksan City, where it remains. He was succeeded as head of the movement by Kyu Song (1900–62), one of his original disciples. He became known for the relief work he led and organized both after the Japanese occupation and after the Korean War. In 1962 he was succeeded by Taesan, Taego Kim (1916–   ), the third prime master. Social service has been a hallmark of Won Buddhism as its has emerged, and it has established a number of charitable/welfare facilities for the homeless, orphans, the disabled, the elderly, the ill, and people otherwise neglected and forgotten by society.

Won Buddhism sponsors Won Kwang University and the Won Buddhist Graduate School in Korea, and the Won Institute of Graduate Studies recently opened in suburban Philadelphia, Pennsylvania (the United States).

Further reading: Bongkil Chung, *The Scriptures of Won Buddhism: A Translation of the Wŏnbulgyo kyojŏn with Introduction* (Honolulu: University of Hawaii Press, 2003); ———, "Won Buddhism: The Historical Context of Sot'aesan's Reformation of Buddhism for the Modern World," in Steven Heine and Charles Prebish, eds., *Buddhism in the Modern World: Adaptation of an Ancient Tradition* (London: Oxford University Press, 2003), 143–168; Bokin Kim (Gim Bog'in), *Concerns and Issues in Won Buddhism* (Philadelphia: Won, 2000); Kwangsoo Park, *The Won Buddhism (Wŏnbulgyo) of Sot'aesan: A Twentieth-Century Reli-*

gious Movement in Korea (San Francisco: International Scholars, 1997).

Wonhyo (617–686) *Korean Buddhist pioneer*

Buddhist life in Korea began in the fifth century, but its effective establishment across the peninsula occurred in the seventh century under the leadership of Wonhyo. Wonhyo was born into a noble family and grew up near Sorabal, the capital of the SILLA Kingdom. His mature work was carried out in the years of the struggle to create a united Korea under the Silla ruler (completed in 668). He decided to become a Buddhist monk at the age of 15 and at the time of his ordination allowed his former home to be converted into a Buddhist temple. He would remain a monk for some three decades.

At one point, he decided it was necessary for him to go to China to study in some of the famous temples there. According to the story, when he was on his way to China with his younger colleague, UISANG (625–702), the pair was caught in a rainstorm. They took refuge in an underground shelter as darkness approached. During their stay in what turned out to be a mausoleum, Wonhyo arrived at a realization about the nature of the world as made of mind alone. When the mind is stilled, the differences in the world cease to matter. A tomb and a temple are all the same. With this realization, he no longer needed to go to China.

Abandoning his career as a monk in 661, he would spend the next decade contemplating his insight and writing a number of works expanding upon it. Then beginning in 676 he would devote a decade to popularizing Buddhism among the masses. His most famous book, the *Commentary on the Awakening of Faith in Mahayana*, explained his insight on the mind. Then, in his *Treatise on Ten Approaches to Reconciliation of the Doctrinal Controversy*, he turned to the problem of the divisions among a still minority faith on the Korean Peninsula. He argued that all religious positions have at least some validity and different perspectives find their reconciliation in the experience of the One Mind beyond all distinctions.

While articulating a mystical philosophy that could lead to inactivity, Wonhyo also refused to move in that direction. Rather, he called upon his contemporaries to give priority to their concern for all sentient being and orient themselves toward action. He suggested that human life was relatively short, the years should not be wasted, and efforts should be made to assist others in their appropriation of Buddhist truth.

Wonhyo continued to be active until his death at a cave temple near Kyongju, Korea, in 686. His own teachings prevented him from organizing a new school, and in the short term his contributions were less recognized than that of his own student Uisang. Some of his many writings were lost over the next centuries. However, as Korean Buddhists struggled with their own divisions and with the pressure of hostile rulers and foreign invaders, Wonhyo was rediscovered and his work recognized. At the end of the 11th century he was named the "National Preceptor of Harmonizing Controversies."

Further reading: Lewis R. Lancaster and C. S. Yu, eds., *Assimilation of Buddhism in Korea: Religious Minority and Innovation in the Silla Dynasty* (Berkeley, Calif.: Asian Humanities Press, 1991); Ian P. McGreal, ed., *Great Thinkers of the Eastern World* (New York: HarperCollins, 1995).

World Buddhist Sangha Council

The World Buddhist Sangha Council (WBSC) focuses on issues of widespread concern within the Buddhist community. Leadership education has been a particular concern, and it has tried to isolate various "extreme" elements on the fringe of the Buddhist community, which it considers outside the mainstream. The WBSC was founded in Colombo, Sri Lanka, in 1966 as an expression of the international Buddhist Sangha, in this case, the community of BHIKSUs (monks). Within the THERAVADA tradition, the monks constitute the Sammati-Sangha, or conventional SANGHA. They provide vital expression of Buddhist life, especially in Southeast Asia, where the council has its strongest support. By their leading of exemplary and noble lives, the monks lead, guide, and inspire the whole world of Buddhist believers.

While finding its origin in the Theravada world, the council quickly spread among MAHAYANA BUDDHISM monastic communities and currently is headquartered in Taiwan. The original secretary-general, the late Venerable Panditha Pimbure Sorata Thera, a Sri Lankan, championed the idea of uniting the Theravada and Mahayana Buddhist communities. At the organizational gathering, the WBSC adopted a statement, written by Walpola Ruhala, summarizing what it saw as the "Points Unifying Theravada and the Mahayana":

1. The Buddha is our only master.
2. We take refuge in the BUDDHA, the DHARMA, and the SANGHA.
3. We do not believe that this world is created and ruled by a god.
4. Following the example of the Buddha, who is the embodiment of the Great Compassion and Great Wisdom, we consider that the purpose of life is to develop compassion for all living beings without discrimination and to work for their good, happiness, and peace; and to develop wisdom leading to the realization of ultimate truth.
5. We accept the FOUR NOBLE TRUTHS, namely, DUKKHA [suffering], the arising of *dukkha,* the cessation of *dukkha,* and the path leading to the cessation of *dukkha;* and the universal law of cause and effect as taught in the PRATITYA-SAMUTPADA (codependent arising).
6. We understand, according to the teaching of the Buddha, that all conditioned things are impermanent and *dukkha,* and that

all conditioned and unconditioned things (DHARMA) are without self.
7. We accept the 37 qualities conducive to enlightenment as different aspects of the path taught by the Buddha leading to ENLIGHTENMENT.
8. There are three ways of attaining BODHI, or enlightenment, according to the ability and capacity of each individual: namely, as a disciple (SRAVAKA/SRAVAKAYA), as a PRATYEKABUDDHA, and as a *samyak-sam-Buddha* (perfectly and fully enlightened Buddha). We accept as the highest, noblest, and most heroic to follow the career of a BODHISATTVA and to become a *samyak-sam-Buddha* in order to save others.
9. We admit that in different countries there are differences with regard to the life of Buddhist monks, popular Buddhist beliefs and practices, rites and ceremonies, customs and habits. These external forms and expressions should not be confused with the essential teachings of the Buddha.

It is notable that there are no VAJRAYANA Buddhist groups associated with the council. Two Chinese monks, Wu Ming (of Taiwan) and Kok Kwong (of Hong Kong), have recently been named honorary president and vice president of the council.

The council periodically holds a variety of international gatherings. The Seventh General Conference of the WBSC was held in Taiwan in 2000 and the Third World General Conference of the World Buddhist Sangha Council Youth Committee met in Sydney, Australia, in 2004.

Further reading: Madhyamika Prasangika. "First International Congress of the World Buddhist Sangha Council, Sri Lanka, 1967." Available online. URL: http://www.angelfire.com/rings/prasangika/Congress_Buddhist.htm. Accessed on October 10, 2005; Ven. Prayudh Payutto, "Sangha: The Ideal World Community." Yahoo! Geocities. Available online. URL: http://www.geocities.

com/Athens/Academy/9280/sangha.htm. Accessed on October 10, 2005; Walpola Rahula, *The Heritage of the Bhiksu* (New York: Grove Press, 1974).

World Buddhist University

The World Buddhist University (WBU) was established in 1998 by the WORLD FELLOWSHIP OF BUDDHISTS' general conference held in New South Wales, Australia. The university is not a new school competing with already existing institutions so much as a specialized center to conduct advanced Buddhist studies, network with Buddhist scholars worldwide, and coordinate work with other Buddhist academic institutions, especially in matters of research, training, spiritual practice, cultural exchange, and education based on Buddhism. It carries out these aims through five institutes each with a focused objective. Thus the university serves as an international community of Buddhist scholars engaged in research and postgraduate training, with interests in spiritual practice and Buddhist studies at a high academic level. In cooperation with the University of the West in Los Angeles, California, the World Buddhist University offers two distance-learning degrees in Buddhist studies at the master's level. It also publishes a journal, *World Buddhism*.

Further reading: World Buddhist University. Available online. URL: http://www.wb-university.org/. Accessed on December 3, 2005.

World Fellowship of Buddhists

The World Fellowship of Buddhists (WFB), an international cooperative organization, has five primary objectives: the promotion of the observance and practice of Buddhism; unity of the Buddhist community; propagation of Buddhism; social, education, and humanitarian service; and work for world peace and harmony. To that end the organization establishes regional centers wherever there are a sufficient number of Buddhists, establishes Dhamma centers for disseminating Buddhist teaching and encouraging Buddhist observance, nurtures Buddhist educational institutions, nurtures Buddhist social service agencies, and coordinates Buddhist propagation centers worldwide.

The WFB was formed in 1950 in Colombo, Sri Lanka, by representatives from 27 countries, including priests, monks, and laity from across the spectrum of THERAVADA, MAHAYANA BUDDHISM, and VAJRAYANA BUDDHISM traditions. The formation of such an organization (which mirrored Christianity's World Council of Churches formed that same year) was proposed by the Sri Lankan scholar G. P. Malalasekera (1899–1973), who was also selected as its first president (1950–58).

The 1950 meeting made several important decisions, including the adoption of the eight-spoked Wheel of the Law and the BUDDHIST FLAG, which had been developed late in the 19th century in Sri Lanka, as international Buddhist symbols. It also called for the discarding of the term *HINAYANA* (lesser vehicle) as a designation of Theravada Buddhism.

The WFB received enthusiastic support among the majority of Buddhists in every country in which Buddhism was in the majority and was welcomed as a valued additional resource where its was a minority. Many Buddhist groups were honored by being named WFB regional centers.

The WFB meets twice a year. At its organization, it designated the country of its current president as the site of the international headquarters. For its first eight years, it was in Sri Lanka, then moved to Burma, and then to Thailand. In 1969 it was permanently established in Bangkok.

In May 1972, at the Tenth General Conference in Sri Lanka, the WFB established a youth division, the World Fellowship of Buddhist Youth (WFBY). The WFBY has established its central office in the same building where the WFB is located.

The WFB considers itself a completely apolitical organization and has welcomed Buddhist participation from countries across the political spectrum. It has attained nongovernmental organization status with the United Nations and consultative status with the United Nations Educational, Scientific, and Cultural Organization (UNESCO). In 2002 it reported some 140 regional centers in 37 countries. In 1998, the WFB founded the WORLD BUDDHIST UNIVERSITY located in Bangkok.

Further reading: *The World Fellowship of Buddhists Fortieth Anniversary (1950–1990)* (Bangkok: World Fellowship of Buddhists Headquarters, 1990).

wu (*mu*; nothingness) *See* SUNYATA.

wu (enlightenment) *See* ENLIGHTENMENT.

Wu Chao, Empress (Empress Wu)

(c. 625–705) (r. 690–705) *only female emperor of China*

Wu Chao, who rose from relative obscurity to become the ruler of the Chinese empire, was born into a wealthy noble family and received a good education. Her beauty and intelligence attracted the attention of the emperor Tai Zong (r. 626–649), and at the age of 13 she was invited to the court. She soon found her way to his bed. After Tai Zong's death, the relatively young Wu Chao was briefly a nun, then became the concubine of the new emperor, Gao Zong (r. 649–683). She also bore him sons, whereas his wife had failed to do so. Eventually, Gao Zong put aside his wife and married Wu.

Five years later Gao Zong suffered a stroke, and Empress Wu assumed his duties. When he finally died in 683, Wu was able to have her younger son named as emperor and she continued to run the country through him. In 690, the emperor resigned and Wu had herself declared the emperor of China. She would rule for 15 years.

Unable to find support from either Daoists or Confucianists as she rose to power, Empress Wu gave Buddhism the favored status in her land. She invited gifted scholars from India to travel to China and she built new Buddhist temples and sponsored the translation of important texts. Her greatest support went to the CHAN BUDDHISM and HUA YAN leadership. Buddhism expanded rapidly, though many who were attracted to it appeared to convert because of the mundane advantages (avoidance of taxes) it produced. She also supported female practitioners, and to encourage nuns in their practice allowed female clergy to assume roles in the rituals alongside the male priests. As she approached her 80th birthday, the aging empress was forced off the throne in favor of her third son. She died of natural causes a few months later.

Further reading: Cheng An Jiang, *Empress of China Wu Ze Tian* (Monterey, Calif.: Victory Press, 1998); Nancy Falk and Rita Gross, eds., *Unspoken Worlds: Women's Religious Lives in Non-Western Cultures* (New York: Harper & Row, 1980); R. W. L. Guisso, *Wu Tse-t'ien and the Politics of Legitimation in T'ang China* (Bellingham: Western Washington University, 1978).

wuwei (wu wei)

One of the key concepts in the *DAODEJING*, *wuwei* is normally translated as "nonaction." It is a means by which one obtains harmony with DAO. In fact, it is associated with much more than passivity; one scholar, James Miller, prefers the translation "action as nonaction" to "nonaction." Through *wu wei* the Dao is manifest in creation. *Wu wei* implies a state of harmony among heaven, earth, and humans, the triad that underlies harmony. *Wu wei*, then, is a technology: by tapping into the Dao, the adept is able to cultivate his or her own nature. There is no difference, then, between maintaining harmony in the self—the body—and the state—society. In no way does this imply a take-it-as-you-find-it attitude about life, as is often interpreted in popular Western writings. Instead *wu wei* implies a form of active cultivation by the individual.

Wuwei in fact underlies the idea of *ziran*, "natural," another key concept found in the *Daodejing*. Through practicing quiet and simplicity one attains *wu wei*, and thereby through complete convergence understands *ziran*. Wuwei is a kind of discernment that cuts through language and convention; it is nonideological.

See also DAOISM; WANG YANGMING; XUNZI.

Further reading: Alan Chan, "The Daode jing and Its tradition," in Livia Kohn, ed., *Daoism Handbook* (Leiden: Brill, 2004), 1–29; James Miller, *Daoism: A Short Introduction* (Oxford: Oneworld, 2003).

Wusheng Laomu

Wusheng Laomu, the Eternal Mother, is a major deity in popular Chinese religion. A composite figure whose roots stretch to XIWANG MU and GUAN YIN, the Eternal Mother does not belong to such major traditions of Chinese religiosity as BUDDHISM or DAOISM; nor is she based on a local veneration cult, such as MAZU. Instead she appears to be a manifestation of the feminine spirit within the patriarchal order that has dominated Chinese spiritual practice since imperial times.

Worship of the Eternal Mother became widespread in the Ming and Qing periods, to such an extent that we are justified in calling such worship a separate religious tradition, *Wusheng Laomuism*. The Eternal Mother was the centerpiece in many traditions of the time that were heterodox, not following traditionally approved forms. The sectarian groups who worshipped her nearly always included MAITREYA worship (called sometimes Maitreyanism) along with Wusheng Laomu veneration. Maitreya, the Buddha of the future, often depicted since the Song dynasty as the laughing Buddha, was imagined as the emissary or messenger of Wusheng Laomu. Maitreya would intervene in human affairs, while the Eternal Mother would watch in sorrow at the ignorance and tragedy of the human condition. She is to this day often depicted in a kind of splendid isolation, the figure to whom those in need can turn, but nevertheless separate from human existence.

Although feminine figures have been present in Chinese popular worship from the beginning, hard evidence of Wusheng Laomu cannot be located before the writings of Luo Qing (1443–1527), a seminal figure in sectarian, nonorthodox worship. Luo spelled out elements of the Eternal Mother myth. He associated AMITABHA Buddha with *wusheng fumu* (the eternal parents), a reference to PURE LAND BUDDHISM practice. He saw the spiritual journey as a quest to return to one's native place (*jiaxiang*). And he described the true self as *xusheng*, or "unbegotten." Later writers built on Luo's foundations and spelled out a complete Wusheng Laomu myth. The earliest text of the complete myth is a precious scroll dated 1523, in which the original creator, the *wuji* (unlimited ultimate), is referred to as the Eternal Mother. She is mother of all the gods. She orders Amitabha as well as Maitreya to descend to earth to assist the suffering humans. She sees they are ensconced in desires and have no awareness of their original natures, and her heart is filled with compassion for their plight. She longs for the return of all her children.

In some versions of the myth she is depicted as an elderly blind woman.

The myth assumed most complete form in the Longhua Baojing (Dragon-flower Precious Sutra) produced around 1650. Here the three-part division of history into calamities is clearly spelled out; the eternal mother has prepared for the return of her children, who are trapped in materiality.

Later sectarian groups such as TIAN DAO/ YIGUANDAO incorporated the myth of the Eternal Mother into their core doctrines.

The Eternal Mother teachings emphasized the immanence of heaven, for true believers. The elect would find a guaranteed place in heaven. Eternal Mother teachings also emphasized group ties over family and clan; one's true family, after all, was headed by Wusheng Laomu. Such teachings obviously went against the grain of established Confucian orthodoxy. The Eternal Mother was also a key figure for the independent, powerful woman, another teaching at odds with orthodoxy. Women were offered important positions of power within most of these sectarian groups of the Ming and Qing periods.

Further reading: Daniel Overmyer, *Precious Volumes: An Introduction to Chinese Sectarian Scriptures from the Sixteenth and Seventeenth Centuries* (Cambridge, Mass: Harvard University Press, 1999); Richard Shek and Tetsuro Noguchi, "Eternal Mother Religion: Its History and Ethics," in Kwang-Ching Liu and Richard Shek, *Heterodoxy in Late Imperial China* (Honolulu: University of Hawaii Press, 2004), 241–280; Hubert Seiwert, in Collaboration with Ma Xisha, *Popular Religious Movements and Heterodox Sects in Chinese History* (Leiden: Brill, 2003).

wushi bajiao (five periods and eight teachings)   *See* PANJIAO.

X

xin/xing (hsin/hsing, mind and human nature)

In Confucian thought, *xin* is the mind that is developed through cultivation. One understands one's own nature, *xing*, only through such cultivation of mind. The Confucian philosopher MENCIUS stated that people's original nature is good. Moral failings occur through a failure to develop one's *xin*. Thus original nature, while good, is blocked until the superior person makes it fully manifest. And through understanding of one's nature (*xing*) one is able to commune with heaven, to understand fully TIAN DAO (THE WAY OF HEAVEN). The ultimate goal is for the individual to be in complete accord with the will of heaven.

Further reading: Rodney L. Taylor, *The Confucian Way of Contemplation: Okada Takehiko and the Tradition of Quiet-Sitting* (Columbia: University of South Carolina Press, 1988); ———, *The Religious Dimensions of Confucianism* (Albany: State University of New York Press, 1990).

xing (hsing, human nature)   *See* XIN.

Xiwang Mu

Xiwang Mu, the "Royal Mother of the West," one of the most important female Daoist deities, is said to be the primary keeper of the secrets of immortality. Perhaps the foremost ruler of immortals, Xiwang Mu resides in a palace hidden in vast reaches of the Kunlun Mountains, located in the far western regions of China. As described in the early classic of imaginative DAOISM *Huainanzi* (c. 140 B.C.E.), this place is the very axis of the world. This mystic land cannot be reached by ordinary means as it is surrounded by a vast moat of "weak water" upon which even a feather cannot float. Within this paradise, Xiwang Mu dwells in her magnificent jade palace, which towers nine stories and is surrounded by a wall of pure gold measuring more than 1,000 miles in circumference.

In her secret garden Xiwang Mu cultivates the legendary magic peaches that bestow immortality on whoever partakes of them. These peaches form one at a time every 3,000 years and then take an additional 3,000 years to ripen. When it is ripe, Xiwang Mu invites all immortals to feast upon the fruit and so renew their immortal powers.

As one of the most formidable of Daoist deities, Xiwang Mu has enormous powers and numerous duties. She can, for instance, summon spiritual forces from throughout the universe and call upon all sages and worthies in the world. Above all, she is the keeper of the doorway to immortality. She also oversees all covenants and examines the quality of ordinary people's faith. In the heavenly realms she presides at all formal banquets and other observances and supervises the editing of various portions of the DAOZANG (Daoist sacred canon).

Over the course of history, the figure of Xiwang Mu has undergone numerous transformations. Most often she has been portrayed as a beautiful young woman wearing an elegant royal gown, often astride a resplendent peacock. This form, however, seems to have become popular only during the early years of the Common Era. In earlier texts such as the *Shanhai jing* (Classic of mountains and oceans) she is described as a monstrous being with a human face, the teeth of a tiger, and a leopard's tail. Early texts also call her the goddess of epidemics who ruled over the demons of plague. Historically, veneration of Xiwang Mu seems to have reached its height during the Han dynasty (206 B.C.E.–220 C.E.), and during this time murals depicting her were painted in numerous tombs. She also seems to have been the focus of various Daoist-inspired millenarian movements that arose near the dynasty's collapse. According to legend, she is alleged to have visited various worldly rulers, presenting them precious gifts of jade (or even her famous peaches).

Xiwang Mu sometimes appears to have a "dark" side—rather appropriate considering that she is the embodiment of "pure yin." Some traditions say that she achieved and maintains her immortal status by engaging in sexual intercourse with young men and robbing them of their vital energies (*jing,* "semen").

In some later apocalyptic texts of LINGBAO DAOISM, there are predictions that Xiwang Mu will appear at the end of the world to gather up the virtuous few (described as "seed people") and spirit them away to her "Land of Bliss" deep in the Kunlun Mountains. There they will be safe from the catastrophes that the world will endure.

Temples to Xiwang Mu can still be found in China, particularly in the western regions. Most Daoist communities honor her on the seventh day of the seventh lunar month with special feasts.

Overall she remains one of the most important figures in Chinese religious tradition and continues to play a significant role in Daoism.

See also WUSHENG LAOMU.

Further reading: Livia Kohn, *Daoism and Chinese Culture* (Cambridge, Mass.: Three Pines Press, 2001), 50, 56, 65, 206; ———, ed., *The Taoist Experience* (Albany: State University of New York Press, 1993), 56–62; Isabelle Robinet, *Taoism: Growth of a Religion.* Translated by Phyllis Brooks (Stanford, Calif.: Stanford University Press, 1997), 18, 94, 108, 139, 161; Eva Wong, *The Shambhala Guide to Taoism* (Boston: Shambhala, 1997), 150–151, 160–162, 164.

Xuan Zang (Xuanzang, Hsuan-tsang, Hsuan Tsang) (602–644/664) *Chinese traveler and translator*

Xuan Zang was one of the most important translators of texts from SANSKRIT into Chinese. His translations continue to be admired to this day as models of accuracy and balance. His translation of the Thirty Verses was so admired that it became the basis of a short-lived school of Chinese and Japanese Buddhism, the Faxiang (HOSSO).

Xuan Zang was a major player in the religious politics of the Tang period (618–906). He tried but failed to get the blessings of the emperor to set out on his 16-year voyage to India, intended to study and collect Buddhist materials, between 629 and 645. But upon his return to the capital he was hailed as a hero and honored by the emperor, who felt he could gain valuable information from Xuan Zang.

During his voyage Xuan Zang had visited the oasis states along the Gobi Desert and all the major sites of Buddhism in India. He lectured at the Buddhist University at NALANDA, under his master Silabhadra. He toured southern India and Sri Lanka and returned home laden with documents and texts, enough to keep an army busy translating.

After his return the emperor Taizong (549–649) supported Xuan Zang's translation efforts.

A 212-foot bronze image of the Buddhist pilgrim Xuan Zang (602–664), in Xian, western China

He was assigned assistants and copyists—some 23 monks—and based himself in the capital, Chang An. The next emperor, Gaozong (628–683), agreed to build a pagoda, named the Wild Goose Pagoda, to house the many SUTRA texts taken back by Xuan Zang. This pagoda stands to this day.

A major figure in Chinese Buddhism, Xuan Zang has over the years also become a key figure in the popular imagination. He is the model for Tang Sanzang ("Tripitika"), a key character in the *Journey to the West* (*Xiyouji*), a classic Chinese novel first published in 1592. In this story the author added significantly to Xuan Zang's biographical details and mixed them with those of his fellow travelers, including Monkey, who are charged with protecting Xuan Zang on his sacred mission to retrieve sutras. In large part because of the popularity of this tale, Xuan Zang is a fixture in the popular imagination throughout East Asia and is often depicted in movies and cartoons.

Further reading: D. Devahuti, ed., *The Unknown Hsuan Tsang* (Oxford: Oxford University Press, 2001); Geln Dudbridge, *The His-yu chi: A Study of Antecedents to the Sixteenth Century Chinese Novel* (Cambridge: Cambridge University Press, 1970); Sally Hovey Wriggins, *The Silk Road Journey with Xuanzang* (Boulder, Colo.: Westview, 2004); Anthony C. Yu, trans., *Journey to the West.* 4 vols. (Chicago: University of Chicago Press, 1977–1981).

Xunzi (Xun Kuang, Xun Qing, Hsün-tzu)
(310–220 B.C.E.) *rationalist philosopher in ancient China*

The Confucian philosopher Xunzi, or "Master Xun," is the first Chinese thinker to use extended arguments. Xunzi was connected to the school of legalism (*fajia*) and two of his disciples went on to become great legalist thinkers. Yet he himself remained a strict Confucian. He served as a regional administrator for many years, and his managerial experience shaped his work, which tends to be orderly, analytic, and practical. The book the *Xunzi* was in the main written by him (as opposed to his followers) and, unlike the *Analects* or the *Book of Mencius*, consists of philosophical discourses and arguments of the kind usually found in Western philosophical texts. Xunzi's style is generally no-nonsense and highly persuasive. His work remained very influential among Confucians until the Song dynasty (960–1279), when the more Mencian perspective came into favor.

Xunzi is particularly famous for his views of human nature (*xing*) and the role of ritual (LI). For Xunzi, human nature is "evil." By this he means that it is slothful, animalistic, and greedy. It must be curbed and reshaped by culture. This view diametrically opposes that of Mencius, who holds that human nature is originally "good." Xunzi's view, however, is not pessimistic. For him, culture is what makes us into good, refined human beings. However, culture is not natural but must be instilled through education; we become civilized and moral by learning. According to Xunzi, civilized education is a process of "conscious activity" (intellect, thinking) that the sage-kings of old used to establish civilized ways. In that sense we become full human beings only through the process of education. Moreover, we all can do this. We all can learn to be good; we all can become sages.

The key to such education, in Xunzi's eyes, are the *li* (rites, rituals). The *li* form a comprehensive blueprint for conduct as a human being in both public and private. The *li* establish the field upon which we can live. They set basic parameters, purify and refine our emotions, and direct us in interacting with others. Becoming fully schooled in *li* makes us gentlemen and gentlewomen.

Xunzi is a supreme rationalist. Our ability to think, to sort things out, and to classify them, makes us human and enables us to participate in society. Education in *li*, observance of the rites, reinforces this ability. To submit to such norms is eminently reasonable, for such submission allows us to live well and become who we can be. A life guided by *li* is not dry or harsh, even if learning them is difficult. Education in the *li* allows us to appreciate beauty, music, and art. But Xunzi stresses that this is all a human-centered project. Our concern is with the human world; heaven (*TIAN*) has little to do with this. Most certainly heaven is not moral; nor are natural events indications of "supernatural" forces. All can be explained in an obvious, natural fashion. There is, therefore, no need to look for omens or seek out the works of gods or spirits. Such rationalism, it must be said, never really caught on in China.

Xunzi is a great debater, and he argues at length against not only Mencius but other schools of thought in pre-Han China. He understands the "mind" (*XIN*) as being based on the power to organize and classify things accurately, that is, in conformity to objective reality. He is especially concerned with the "rectification of names," ensuring names and words are used properly. In Xunzi's perspective, language is integral to culture. Names and terms are essential human inventions for society to function harmoniously but they are based purely on convention and social agreement.

Xunzi is far more "philosophical" in the Western sense than any other early Chinese thinker. He has a sober view of human nature that bears some resemblance to the views of Augustine of Hippo (354–430) and John Calvin (1509–64).

Further reading: Julia Ching, *Chinese Religions* (Maryknoll, N.Y.: Orbis Books, 1993), 72–77; W. Theodore de Bary and Irene Bloom, eds., *Sources of Chinese Tradition.* Vol. 1, *From Earliest Times to 1600.* 2d ed. (New York: Columbia University Press, 1999), 159–183.

Y

Yama (Chinese, Yanluo; Japanese, Emma)

Yama is the Buddhist lord of the underworld. Yama was originally mentioned in the Indian Rg Veda as one of two twin brothers, Yama and Yami. The myth of Yama and Yami was of Indo-Iranian origin and corresponded to the story of Yima and Yimeh. According to the Rg Veda account Yama and Yami were the first humans. When Yama eventually died, he lived in a heavenly paradise, called *yamarajya*. It was the goal of all *rishis,* or holy people of merit in the period of the Rg Veda, to pass into Yama's paradise, a place without decay where all desires were met.

Over time Yama's heavenly paradise was shifted to the underworld and he became the overlord of hell. However, he is not without compassion. He acts as one of the 10 wardens in hell and as a judge. Unlike his other bureaucratically minded wardens, Yama is able to use compassion as a criterion in judging people's fates. In addition although Yama is depicted as having a fierce face, it is meant to scare people away from the practices that will lead them to hell, a compassionate act.

Further reading: Akira Sakakata, *Buddhist Cosmology: Philosophy and Origins* (Tokyo: Kosei, 1997 and 1999).

Yan Hui (Yan Yuan) (c. late sixth century–early fifth century B.C.E.) *ideal Confucian role model*

As far as we know, Yan Hui wrote nothing, had no disciples, and never served in any official position. Nevertheless, he exemplifies the spiritual dimensions of Confucian tradition and is regarded as a supreme model by later followers of CONFUCIANISM (*rujia*). He has become a symbol of the ideal Confucian person: eager to learn, insightful, morally scrupulous, and deeply respectful of his teacher and the traditions being imparted.

According to the *Shiji* (Records of the Grand Historian, compiled c. 100 B.C.E.), CONFUCIUS had some 3,000 pupils. Several of these are mentioned by name in the ANALECTS, but Yan Hui's name stands out from the rest. Indeed, there are more than a dozen passages in the *Analects* in which Yan Hui appears in some form. We know little about him, but from what we are able to glean, he was a remarkable man in terms of his intelligence, moral integrity, and loyalty. Clearly he was Confucius's favorite, and some passages (e.g., *Analects* 7.11) indicate that the master regarded him as an equal.

Unwavering in his integrity no matter his circumstances (cf. *Analects* 7.11), Yan Hui seems to display an almost mystical reconciliation with TIAN DAO (THE WAY OF HEAVEN). Confucius said of him that he never vented his anger on an innocent person nor made the same mistake twice (*Analects* 6.3). Yan, always modest, merely said that his goal was never to boast of his own virtue or impose burdens upon others (*Analects* 5.26). From the perspective of the *rujia,* Yan was the very embodiment of *cheng* ("sincerity," "authenticity"), the key virtue expounded upon in the *Zhongyong* ("Doctrine of the Mean"). His example, thus, serves as an important corrective to stereotypes of Confucianism as a primarily secular "philosophy" rather than a "religion." Interestingly, later Daoist and Buddhist thinkers also take Yan Hui as a model.

Further reading: D. C. Lau, trans., *The Analects* (New York: Viking Penguin, 1979), 201–203.

yantra

A yantra is a geometric design, used as a meditation diagram, whose various elements carry meanings that can be multiplied by juxtaposition. The yantra is said to be helpful to the individual's meditation practice. A yantra may be identified with a specific deity and serve as a contact point with the powers of that deity. Yantras are drawn and may then be memorized so that they can be recalled at any time. They first developed as tools used by Shaktaite Hindus (those who follow Tantric teachings), who passed the practice to adherents of VAJRAYANA BUDDHISM (primarily in Tibet).

Every yantra has a border that separates the design from the environment and functions much as a magical circle, to contain and focus cosmic energies. Each yantra is composed of combinations of geometric elements, each of which adds meaning to the design. Most often, in the center there is a dot (*bindu*) that serves as the center of concentration. The dot is often identified with the deity Shiva.

Triangles symbolize Shakti, the female deity, and her energy. The triangle (*trikona*) may point downward as a symbol of the female sexual organ (*yoni*) and hence of the source of creation. It may point upward as the symbol of the energy seen in the flame. Two triangles, one pointed upward and one downward, may be imposed on each other, thus forming a symbol (*shatkona*) very like what is known in the West as David's Star (Judaism) or Solomon's Seal (Western esotericism). In yantric theory this pattern represents the union of Shakta and Shiva in the act of creation, with obvious sexual connotations.

Circles (*chakras*), symbols of air, resemble the whirling energy of the *chakras,* the points of concentration of the subtle energy body that Tantric Hindus and Vajrayana Buddhists believe mirror the physical body. The square (*bhapura*) is a symbol of earth. The square most often appears as the border of the yantra. More complex yantras may also include a lotus (*padma*), a symbol of purity.

The most famous yantra is the Sri Yantra. It consists of nine intersecting triangles, six concentric circles, and several lotus petals, all within a complex border pattern that represents four doors to the outside world. It is seen as a model of the cosmos with a *bindu* on the center representing the absolute. The Sri Yantra is one connection between the yantra and the more complicated MANDALAS, which often use yantras as design elements.

Believers use yantras as part of their development of higher states of consciousness as well as objects of worship (since they often symbolized and carry the power of a deity). Yantras can be found decorating the temples of Hindus and Buddhists in the Tantric Vajrayana tradition.

Further reading: N. J. Bolton and D. N. MacLeod, "The Geometry of the Sri-Yantra," *Religion* 7, no. 1 (Spring 1977) 66–85; K. P. Kulaichev, "Sriyantra and Its Mathematical Properties," *Indian Journal of History of Science* 19, no. 3 (1984) 279–292; Ajit Mookerjee, *Tantra Art: Its Philosophy and Physics* (New York: Ravi Kumar, 1971); Philip Rawson, *The Art of Tantra* (Greenwich, Conn.: New York Graphic Society, 1973).

Yasodara *the Buddha's wife*

Yasodara was married to the young prince Sakya-muni. She bore him one son, RAHULA. She later became a follower of the Buddha herself. She stands in many Buddhist stories as a symbol of wifely devotion and love. Despite her love for him, the future Buddha chose to leave home, a key symbolic act of renunciation. In fact, in explaining the Buddha's decision to leave on that fateful night—on the very day his son was born—it is Yasodara's love and the impending duties of fatherhood that were seen by the young prince as the greatest obstacles to his leading a life of renunciation. Yasodara is thus a symbol of the enticements of human life, the realm of SAMSARA, as well as a paragon of devotion.

Further reading: "Yasodhara," in Charles S. Prebish, *The A to Z of Buddhism* (Lanham, Md.: The Scarecrow Press, 2001), 276.

Yasukuni Jinja

This controversial SHINTO shrine in Tokyo has become a symbol of Japan's nationalist past. Yasukuni Jinja was built in 1869, at the beginning of the MEIJI RESTORATION (1868–1912). The immediate reason for its establishment was to commemorate those who died in the Boshin civil war (1867–68), which preceded the Meiji. The emperor Meiji issued his proclamation in June 1869 to establish the shrine. *Yasu* means "peaceful," while *kuni* refers to "place" or "country." The name reflects the desire that the departed souls housed at Yasukuni will find peace. There were originally 3,500 souls, or KAMI, worshipped at Yasukuni. There are now, officially, 2,466,532 *kami* "enshrined" there and listed on the "Book of Souls." The annual spring festival held at Yasukuni commemorates the *mitama,* or souls of those *kami.*

For several reasons, the Yasukuni shrine is today a hot point in relations between Japan and its neighbors. First, the nearly 2.5 million souls enshrined at Yasukuni include many of Japan's military and government leaders from the Second World War, including 14 Class A war criminals. These 14 were not originally included in the shrine and were not added until 1978. They include Hideki Tojo, Japan's wartime prime minister. This act of including these figures in the shrine was controversial and fans the flames of anger in many other countries. The shrine's own Web site gives expression to strong feelings that those found guilty at the war tribunal, some 1,068 people, were unfairly branded as criminals and deserve to be honored at Yasukuni. It is just this point of view that angers many Chinese and Koreans. They see Yasukuni as a symbol of Japan's past aggression and a reminder of the potential for further right-wing adventurism.

The second immediate cause of controversy concerning Yasukuni is the former prime minister's practice of visiting the site to pay respects to the dead. While the emperor himself ceased such visits in 1979, when the 14 criminals were installed there, three separate prime ministers have visited since 1979. Junichiro Koizumi, who became prime minister in 2001, visited yearly after taking office. This action ensured that Yasukuni was never out of the news for long.

In fact Yasukuni has been at the center of debates over STATE SHINTO ever since the end of World War II. Sentiment against Japan's postwar pacifist constitution grew in the 1950s. Leaders of the Jinja Honcho, the Association of Shinto Shrines, wanted a revival of State Shinto. The ruling Liberal Democratic Party began to introduce a bill every year, the Yasukuni Shrine Bill, which was never able to pass. This bill would treat the Yasukuni Shrine as a nonreligious institution and allow tax support for it. The government later created a watered-down measure, the Memorial Respect Proposal, in order to allow state support for the Yasukuni Shrine.

The problem is the shrine's murky status as a religious institution. Yasukuni's political and religious roles are mixed. Unlike in most countries, there is no other civil memorial to those fallen in Japan's past wars. Most politicians insist that the dead should be commemorated at Yasukuni, which is legally speaking a self-funding religious shrine, not a state-supported site. Thus the controversy concerns a political act by politicians in a religious site. Politicians act in their personal capacity and are in a way protected ostensibly from saying their acts reflect government policy. Few observers accept this explanation, however.

Further reading: Kazuo Kasahara, ed., *A History of Japanese Religion*. Translated by Paul McCarthy and Gaynor Sekimori (Tokyo: Kosei, 2001), 543–544; Yasukuni Jinja. "Yasukuni Jinja." Available online. URL: www.yasukuni.or.jp/english/index.html. Accessed on August 1, 2005.

Yasutani Hakuun Roshi (1885–1973)
independent Japanese Zen teacher

The Japanese Zen Master Yasutani Hakuun Roshi, an important figure in the development of a Japanese Zen BUDDHISM organization, SANBO KYODAN, became one of the most famous figures in the transmission of Zen to the West. His influence rivaled that of DAISETSU TEITARO SUZUKI. His students founded two independent international associations of Zen centers, the Diamond Sangha (Aitken) and the Zen Center of Rochester (Kapleau), and others now form Sanbo Kyodan's own international association. Though the Sanbo Kyodan has a relatively marginal role in the Japanese Zen community, its students form the largest segment of the Western Zen community.

Yasutani was born into a poor family, a fact that led first to his adoption into another family and then his entrance into a RINZAI ZEN temple as a "monk" at the age of five. From the original temple he moved to several others during his early years. While at Teishin-ji, a SOTO ZEN temple, he studied with Yasutani Ryogi, from whom he took his religious name.

The years of his early adulthood were characterized by his movement among several temples and his encounters with a variety of Zen masters. Then at the age of 30, he left the rather confined world in which he had lived and became a school-

teacher. He married and fathered five children. He also pursued a quest to find one he could accept as a true master. He found that master in 1925 in the person of Harada Daiun Sogaku Roshi (1871–1961). Yasutani quit his teaching job and became a full-time Soto Zen priest at Hosshin-ji temple. In 1943 he received the seal of transmission from Harada Roshi. In 1954, he left the Soto Zen organization and founded the independent Sanbo Kyodan (Three Treasures Association) as a small independent Zen group. Yasutani maintained Harada's emphasis on synthesizing Soto and Rinzai Zen into a new teaching lineage.

Yasutani Roshi began to accept Americans and other Westerners as students, including Philip Kapleau and ROBERT BAKER AITKEN, both to have illustrious careers as founders of American Zen organizations. Then in 1962, the years after Harada's death, Yasutani made annual trips to the United States. He made stops in Hawaii and on both coasts. Through the 1960s, the publicity given his tours and his acceptance of many Westerners made Yasutani one of the best-known Zen figures in the West. Yasutani passed his lineage to Taizan Maezumi Roshi (1931–95), the founder of the Zen Center of Los Angeles.

Further reading: Robert Aitken, "Yasutani Hakuun Rôshi, 1885–1973," *Eastern Buddhist* 7, no. 1 (1974): 150–152; Philip Kapleau, *The Three Pillars of Zen: Teaching, Practice, and Enlightenment* (Boston: Beacon Press, 1967); Robert H. Scharf, *Sanbokyodan: Zen and the Way of New Religions, Japanese Journal of Religious Studies* 22, nos. 3–4 (1995): 417–458; Yasutani Haku'un Roshi, *Flowers Fall: A Commentary on Dogen's Genjokoan*. Translated by Paul Jaffe (Boston: Shambhala, 1996).

Yeshe Tsogyal (757–817) *female Tibetan Buddhist teacher*

Yeshe Tsogyal was one of the five prominent female students and consorts of PADMASAMBHAVA, who introduced Buddhism to Tibet. She was 16 when she met him in 772 and was initiated into esoteric VAJRAYANA BUDDHISM the next year. She worked with Padmasambhava to establish Buddhism in the face of the stronghold the indigenous BON RELIGION maintained on the Tibetan people of the eighth century. Over the years, she not only assisted Padmasambhava but began to emerge as a independent teacher and visionary in her own right. As her star rose, people began to think of her as a DAKINI, or semidivine being. She was the author of two important books, the biography of her teacher and her own autobiography, both of which have been translated into English.

In later centuries, two other prominent female teachers have been acknowledged as reincarnations of Tsogyal: Nachig Lapdron (1055–1145) and Yomo Memo (1248–83).

Further reading: Keith Dowman, *Sky Dancer: The Secret Life and Songs of Lady Yeshe Tsogyal* (London: Routledge & Kegan Paul, 1984); Erik Pema Kunsang, *Dakini Teachings: Padmasambhava's Oral Instructions to Lady Tsogyal* (Boston: Shambhala, 1990); Thinley Norbu, *Magic Dance: The Display of the Self-Nature of the Five Wisdom Dakinis,* 2d ed. (Boston: Shambhala, 1985); Yeshe Tsogyal, *The Lotus-Born: The Life Story of Padmasambhava.* Translated by Erik Pema Kunsang (Boston: Shambhala, 1993).

yi (rightness)

Yi is one of the most important yet inherently ambiguous concepts in Confucian tradition. The term is most often translated as "righteousness" or "propriety" but perhaps better rendered as "rightness," since an action can only be deemed "proper" or even "righteous" if, in fact, if it is "right," that is, suitable given the specific circumstances. As "rightness," *yi* has ethical, aesthetic, and intellectual connotations—very fitting considering how closely these concerns are intertwined in most of traditional Chinese thought. Various Chinese dictionaries relate *yi* to the term *wo* ("I," or more broadly, "personal self"), follow-

ing the lead of the Han Confucian thinker DONG ZHONGSHU (195–105 B.C.E.), who speaks of *yi* as related to "rightness" concerning the "self" (*wo*). Recent scholars such as Hall and Ames have said that *yi* might better be understood as a key component of the process of becoming fully human, a *junzi* (superior person).

From what we can see in the ANALECTS, *yi* was a crucial idea for CONFUCIUS. *Yi* seems to be the basic "rightness" marking the behavior of an ethical person in situations where there is no specifically recommended LI, or "ritual action." As such, *yi* is intimately related to REN in its more generalized sense, implying a skilled and graceful understanding of what is required. Thus, for instance, Confucius says that the *junzi* is concerned with *yi*, whereas the "petty person" focuses on profit (4 16). Elsewhere Confucius states that the *junzi* considers *yi* to be paramount in acting (17 23). Indeed, so basic is *yi* in ethical and spiritual cultivation that Confucius speaks of it as the "raw stuff" from which the *junzi* fashions his or her character (15 18).

MENCIUS, as is so often the case, expands upon and clarifies Confucius's views. Not surprisingly, Mencius locates the origins of *yi* within our heavenly endowed, innately good nature. Mencius argues that *yi* is internal, not external; it is one of the "four buds" of virtue that composes our original mind-heart. Specifically, Mencius holds that *yi* originates in the innate feeling of "shame and disgrace" that we all possess (2A 6). For Mencius, this inherent sense of shame is part of our prereflective way of being, not something that is instilled from without (6A 6).

Of the early Confucian thinkers, however, it is XUNZI who has the most intriguing view of *yi*. In his more or less "rationalistic" fashion, Xunzi speaks of *yi* as not just rooted in our innate ethical-spiritual nature but as a definitive characteristic of a human being, a trait that sets us apart from the birds and the beasts. In terms of what Xunzi says, then, *yi* is *not* simply "righteousness." Rather, it is more like the ethical self-awareness by which we take action that is "right" in whatever circumstances we find ourselves. It is in this more nuanced sense, then, that we can understand why *yi* sometimes has the sense of "meaning" or "significance"—it is the *ethical and spiritual meaning that human beings alone manifest in the world through deliberate, consciously chosen actions.*

The complex notion of *yi* reveals the distinctly humanistic, social, even existential, dimension of the Confucian tradition. The parallels on these points between Confucian tradition and the ethical and political philosophy of both Plato and Aristotle provide much food for thought. Only human beings can exemplify *yi*, and doing so requires living within a larger human community. It is for these reasons that the late Tang Confucian HAN YU (768–824) rightly criticizes LAOZI, the legendary author of the Daoist classic the *DAODEJING.* By speaking of DAO as the Way of Nature over and above human civilization, Laozi would necessarily overlook the *human* world; he is unconcerned with a human-centered approach to life. Confucians, by contrast, seek Dao within society; the Confucian Dao is realized through ethical, intellectual, and spiritual striving as part of a larger human community. Of the 10,000 things, only humans have a sense of *yi*; thus it is only those schools of Chinese thought focused on humanity that take *yi*—and other human concerns—seriously.

Further reading: Theodore W. De Bary and Irene Bloom, eds., *Sources of Chinese Tradition.* Vol. I, *From Earliest Times to 1600,* 2d ed. (New York: Columbia University Press, 1999), 49, 58, 63, 126–128, 149–150, 307–309, 569–570; David L. Hall and Roger T. Ames, *Thinking Through Confucius* (Albany: State University of New York Press, 1987), 89–110; Benjamin I. Schwartz, *The World of Thought in Ancient China* (Cambridge, Mass.: Harvard University Press, 1985), 79–80, 89.

Yijing   *See* BOOK OF CHANGES.

Yi Jing (I-ching) (635–713)   *Chinese traveler to India*

Yi Jing was one of the handful of significant travelers to India from China who have left detailed, extremely useful records of their travels. His accounts of BUDDHISM in northern India are the last textual source before the Muslim invasions in the period 1000–1200. Yi Jing described his visits to key Buddhist sites such as LUMBINI and NARANDA, the center of Buddhist learning. Many of the temples he described were becoming deteriorated, the numbers of devotees and monks dwindling. Local communities seemed to prefer the panoply of Hindu deities to the Buddha, who at any rate was easily incorporated into the vast Hindu pantheon. Yi Jing's account leads us to conclude that the decline of Buddhism in India was not solely caused by the Muslim incursions of the 13th century.

Yi Jing is also important for the records he left of the Srivijaya kingdom located in present-day Sumatra, Indonesia. He also carried 400 texts back to China from India and translated 60 SUTRAS himself.

Further reading: S. Dutt, *Buddhist Monks and Monasteries of India* (London: George Allen & Unwin, 1962); I-Tsing, *A Record of the Buddhist Religion: As Practiced in India and the Malay Archipelago* (A.D. 671–695). Translated by J. Takakusu (New Delhi: AES, 2005).

Yiguandao   *See* TIAN DAO.

Yin Shun (1906–2005)   *Taiwanese teacher of humanistic Buddhism*

Yin Shun, one of the most prominent contemporary figures in Taiwanese Buddhism, committed his life to spreading the message of humanized Buddhism, which built on the belief in the ultimate enlightenment of all. Yin Shun was born in Haining, Zhejiang Province, China. His father encouraged him to study medicine, but his initial studies awakened a number of religious issues and led to a lengthy spiritual quest. He was led to DAO-ISM, CONFUCIANISM, and Christianity, before stumbling upon BUDDHISM. The death of his mother (1928) and father (1929) occasioned a personal crisis and led him to become a monk. In 1930, he made his way to Fu Chun Monastery near Mt. PUTU (one of China's sacred mountains).

As a monk, he began to observe the decline and decadence of Buddhism as it was being practiced in China. He was also sensitive to the critique of Buddhism being offered by many intellectuals. He found his answers in his study of the Agama Sutra, the earliest teachings of the Buddha. He found the purpose of Buddhism to be to end the suffering in the world, to assist the liberation of people, and to elevate human beings. He concluded that the Buddha had found ENLIGHTENMENT in the real human world. From this insight, he began to assemble the basic ideas of what would be called humanized Buddhism. Individual Buddhists need to cultivate compassion by helping people become free of suffering and to expect no reward in return. These ideas were very close to those articulated several decades earlier by the eminent Chinese teacher T'AI HSU (Tai Xu) (1890–1947).

The troubles through which China passed, World War II and the Chinese revolution, led Yin Shun to relocate to Hong Kong in 1949 and then to Taiwan in 1952. In Taiwan, Yin Shun put his ideas into practice first by attacking the idea of women's inferiority. He inspired the head of a Buddhist convent, Shuan Shen, to open the Hsinchu Women's Buddhist Institute. Yin Shun then established a lecture hall, the first on Taiwan, the Hui Jih Lecture Hall, as a primary center for the dissemination of his perspective.

In 1963, CHENG YEN, a woman who wanted to become a nun, visited his hall. She asked to become his student. From their relationship, in 1966 Cheng Yen would found the Buddhist Compassion Relief Tzu Chi Association as an extension of humanized Buddhism. The work of Yin Shun and Cheng Yen ran parallel for a decade. Then in 1979, Yin Shun visited Hualien, where the Tzu Chi Association was headquartered and where Cheng Yen planned to build a hospital. He committed himself to the hospital and diverted the gift money he received to its construction.

Yin Shun authored several books through the years. One of these, *The Zen History of China* (1971), occasioned his receiving an honorary doctorate from Taisho University in Japan. He died in 2005. His ashes were placed at Fu Yan Monastery in Hsinchu, where he lived during most of his years in Taiwan.

See also CHINA-TAIWAN.

Further reading: Pan Shuen, "The Story of Dharma Master Yin Shun." Translated by Teresa Chang and Adrian Yiu. Tzu Chi Foreign Language Publications Department. Available online. URL: taipei.tzuchi.org.tw/tzquart/2002su/qs5.htm. Accessed on October 10, 2005; Yin Shun, *The Road from Man to Buddha* (Bronx, N.Y.: Buddhist Association of the United States, n.d.); ———, *The Way to Buddhahood: Instructions from a Modern Chinese Master* (Somerville, Mass.: Wisdom, 1998).

yin-yang

Yin/yang is a philosophic concept deeply embedded in Chinese thinking, especially DAOISM. The two terms signify the fundamental forces in nature, the yang and yin. Yin and yang are not comparable to dualistic ideas such as good/bad. In fact, each force cannot exist without the other; the one force by its existence creates a space for the other. Yin and yang interact throughout all matter and in their multiplicity create all phenomena. They are polar extremes around which all other forces and phenomena cluster.

Yang phenomena are male, light, brightness, sky, action, husband, ruler, father, rational, hot, the living.

Yin phenomena are female, darkness, shade, cloudiness, water, wife, subject, mother, mysterious, cold, the dead.

The concept of yin-yang first surfaced in the thought of Zhou Yan, a third-century B.C.E. philosopher associated with the school of naturalism, and the idea was eventually absorbed into other philosophical schools, including CONFUCIANISM. The concept meshed well with the Daoist creation narrative: "The Dao produced One; One produced Two; Two produced Three; Three produced All things" (*Daodejing*, Ch. 42; based on Legge).

Further reading: Christian Jochim, *Chinese Religions: A Cultural Perspective* (Englewood Cliffs, N.J.: Prentice Hall, 1986); James Legge, trans., *The Tao Teh King [Daodejing], or The Tao and Its Characteristics, by Lao-Tse [Lao Zi].* UCLA Center for East Asian Studies, East Asian Studies Documents. Available online. URL: http://www.isop. ucla.edu/eas/documents/DaoDeJingP2.htm. Accessed on June 5, 2006; Julian F. Pas, *Historical Dictionary of Taoism* (Lanham, Md.: Scarecrow Press, 1998).

Yogacara Buddhism

The Yogacara is one of the two major schools of Indian MAHAYANA BUDDHISM—that is, Buddhist thought that developed in distinction to such earlier schools as THERAVADA. Its fundamental doctrine is *cittamatra,* "mind only." Because of this, Yogacara is often known as the "mind only" school. In Yogacara thinking, the world experienced is simply an extension or by-product of mind.

The school's writers delineated a theory of consciousness that spelled out eight types of consciousness: in addition to the original six found in most early schools (those consciousnesses associated with the six senses, including "mind" as a sense organ), the Yogacara added two more consciousnesses. These were *manas* and ALAYA-VIJNANA, the storehouse consciousness. The school also built upon the MADHYAMIKA idea of two truths to include three "natures" that make up reality: the *parikalpita,* or imagined level; the *parantantra,* or relative reality; and the *parinispanna,* or ultimate reality.

While the other great Mahayana school, MADHYAMIKA, is associated with a thinker about whom little is known—NAGARJUNA—we know quite a bit about the founders of Yogacara. The school's founding is attributed to two brothers, ASANGA and VASUBANDHU, who lived in northwest India in the fourth century C.E. While the older brother, Asanga, had earlier become a monk and tried to interest his younger brother in the Mahayana, Vasubandhu was originally an advocate of the SARVASTIVADA (SARVASTIVADIN) SCHOOL. During this time he wrote the great ABHIDHARMA-KOSA, a commentary and compilation of basic Sarvastivadin doctrine. Soon after this, however, he joined his brother in advocating a form of Buddhism that emphasized the role of the mind in creating all the reality we experience.

The Yogacara was not simply a philosophical movement. Its thinkers spelled out a detailed path of cultivation, stated most clearly in Asanga's Yogacarabhuma-sastra. Other important Yogacara texts include the Mahasayanasamgraha, the Abhidharmasamuccaya by Asanga, and the Vimsatika and Trimsika by Vasubandhu. The school's name indicates an emphasis on the "practice" (*cara*) of "union" (yoga). Practice centered on the Yogacara school was most influential at such centers as Nalanda. Yogacara ideas were influential in East Asia and led directly to the establishment of the Faxiang and HOSSO schools in China and Japan, respectively.

See also 18 SCHOOLS OF EARLY BUDDHISM; SIX BUDDHIST SCHOOLS OF NARA; XUAN ZANG.

Further reading: "Yogacara," in Charles S. Prebish, *The A to Z of Buddhism* (Lanham, Md.: Scarecrow Press, 2001), 277.

Yonghegong (Yung-ho kung, Palace of Harmony and Peace)

The lamasery Yonghegong (the Palace of Harmony and Peace) in Beijing, first built in the late 1600s, is today the main center of Tibetan

Buddhism in China (outside Tibet), serving as both a ritual center for prominent celebratory events and a welcoming center for visiting dignitaries. On a day-to-day basis, it is one of Beijing's most popular tourist stops and the home to a large collection of Tibetan Buddhist artifacts and manuscripts.

The palace dates to 1694, when it was built as a palace for the then-prince and future ruler of China, Yong Zheng (r. 1722–35). However, by the middle of the 18th century, the Manchu Qing dynasty was at its height, and the emperor Qian Long (1711–99) wished to provide a place for visiting Tibetans (and Mongolians), whose territory had been incorporated into his kingdom. Thus in 1744 the palace was transformed into a Buddhist temple complex and a royal guesthouse in which to receive Mongolian and Tibetan officials.

The 66,000 square meters that the lamasery inhabits includes six main halls, seven courtyards, and a number of additional buildings. In each of the main halls are spectacular statues of major Buddhist figures such as Sakyamuni Buddha, the BODHISATTVAS GUAN YIN and MAITREYA, and TSONG KHAPA, the founder of the GELUG sect (the dominant school of Buddhism in Tibet and Mongolia). Notable among the statues is one of Sakyamuni

Wanfodian (Hall of 10,000 Buddhas), Yonghegong, Beijing

Buddha in the Hall of Infinite Happiness (Wan-fu-ge), made of a single piece of sandalwood and standing 18 meters high, the largest such Buddha in the world. Among the more unique items to be found at Yonghegong is the Mountain of Five Hundred Arhats, a carved wooden landscape housing hundreds of small statues of the enlightened ones.

Much of the history of Yonghegong has been written in the visits of its prominent guests. For example, the Ordination Altar Pavilion (Je-tai-lou) was erected in 1780 for the visit of the Sixth Bainqen Erdeni (or PANCHEN LAMA), when Qian Long accepted ordination from him. The pavilion has served as a site for many ordinations of Tibetan monks in the years since. An adjacent hall, the Panchen Pavilion, now houses a silver statue of the Bainqen Erdeni as part of the main collection of artifacts now on view for visitors.

In the decades after its building, Yonghegong served as a vehicle for the spread of the Gelug school. Not only did the emperor Qian Long identify with it, but he also saw it as an instrument for uniting the many different peoples in his empire. He subsequently sponsored the building of numerous Tibetan Buddhist temples, especially in those areas in which various minority groups resided. The erection of these temples then encouraged the relocation of many Mongolian and Buddhist priests.

During the CULTURAL REVOLUTION, Yonghegong suffered some damage, but as were other religious sites in the capital was protected by the government from the Red Guard. Most recently, in 1996 it hosted the young boy accepted within the People's Republic of China as the 11th Panchen Lama, Gyaincain Norbu, born in 1990.

Further reading: *The Confirmation and Enthronement of the 11th Bainqen Erden* (Beijing: China Tibetology Publishing House, 1996); *Yonghegong* (Beijing, 2001).

Yosai *See* EISAI.

Yoshida Shinto (Genpon Sogen Shinto)

Yoshida Shinto is also known as Genpon Sogen ("one-source") Shinto, and Yui-itsu ("unique") Shinto. This form of Shinto, which incorporated magical practices, was developed by the priest Yoshida Kanetomo. He established the school that dominated SHINTO thought until well into the Edo period (1600–1867), Yoshida Shinto.

Yoshida Kanetomo (1423–1511) was a priest at the Yoshida Shrine in Kyoto, which today sits near Kyoto University. Kanetomo was also a member of the powerful Yoshida clan, a family who in the 14th and 15th centuries became important interpreters of the ancient text the *Nihonshiki*. Yoshida Kanetomo was the culmination of his clan's great attainments in research and religious authority.

From the age of 39 Kanetomo began to promote a reinterpretation and scholarly investigation of the KAMI, the Shinto gods. He built the Taigenkyu, a hall for abstinence and purification, in the Yoshida Shrine. This was a replica of the Hall of the Eight Imperial Kami in the imperial palace. Kanetomo also lectured frequently on the *Nihonshiki*, especially the Age of the Kami section.

Kanetomo's concepts of Shinto contrasted with the popular RYOBU SHINTO, or Shrine Shinto, of his day. He saw Shinto as present everywhere, in the manifest and the hidden. Shinto was a divine principle. He insisted that Shinto was unique and different from CONFUCIANISM and BUDDHISM. Shinto, he argued, was in fact the true root of the ideas of Confucianism and Buddhism.

In terms of ritual Kanetomo borrowed much from SHINGON Buddhist practice, which emphasized esotericism (secret knowledge passed from master to pupil). Kanetomo made many of the Shinto rituals more complex than they had been previously.

One major factor in the growth of this form of Shinto was the practice of giving ranks to *kami*, or spirits of the dead. The bestowing of ranks, with official honors, had been an established practice for the living. Starting in the late 1400s Kanetomo applied for official rank for several local *kami.* Eventually the authority to grant rank was given to the Yoshida clan itself. This meant that Kanetomo's descendants held the same authority previously held by the imperial family. The document used to bestow rank and title on *kami* was a *Sogen Senji* (announcement of the original source). In this way the Yoshida clan itself began to dominate the governance of Shinto shrines.

Inevitably many Shinto priests went to the Yoshida to ask for recognition and certification with Yoshida Shinto. Some 121 priests and shrines were granted titles between 1482 and 1569. The Yoshida clan also gave out AMULETS for protection, and they were authorized to relax such regulations for Shinto clergy as those proscribing certain garments or prohibiting meat eating.

Yoshida Shinto grew in influence after Yoshida's death in 1511. His grandson and great-grandson were important leaders. The influence of Yoshida Shinto began to wane in the 19th century as newer strands of Shinto—Kokugaku (National Learning) and FUKKO SHINTO—became more popular. When the MEIJI RESTORATION government centralized shrine ranking functions in the government the power of the Yoshida system was spent.

Further reading: Kazuo Kasahara, ed., *A History of Japanese Religion.* Translated by Paul McCarthy and Gaynor Sekimori (Tokyo: Kosei, 2001), 310–313; Bernhard Scheid, "Reading the Yuiistu Shinto mybo yoshu: A Modern Exegesis of an Esoteric Shinto Text," in John Breen and Mark Teeuwen, eds., *Shinto in History: Ways of the Kami* (Richmond, U.K.: Curzon, 2000); St. Martin's College. "Yui-itsu Shinto." Available online. URL: ucsm.ac.uk/encyclopedia/Shinto/yui.html. Accessed on August 26, 2005.

Young Men's Buddhist Association

The Young Men's Buddhist Association (YMBA) provides Dhamma-based education and examinations for young people who want a traditional grounding in Dhamma (DHARMA) knowledge. The first association was founded in Colombo, Sri Lanka, around 1899 by D. D. Jayatilaka. Jayatilaka was a lay leader in the movement to strengthen BUDDHISM through an emphasis on Western-style education. The YMBA functions today in more than 3,000 centers throughout Sri Lanka. Parallel but separate YMBA organizations were later established in other countries, such as Burma (1906) and the United States (1974).

Further reading: John Powers, *A Concise Encyclopedia of Buddhism* (Oxford: One World, 2000); Donald K. Swearer, *The Buddhist World of Southeast Asia* (Albany: State University of New York Press, 1995).

Yuzu-Nembutsu

The YUZU-NEMBUTSU subgroup within the larger world of Japanese PURE LAND BUDDHISM emphasizes group chanting and obtaining of formal promises from people to continue daily chanting. Yuzu-Nembutsu is traced to RYONIN (1072–1132). An early student of TENDAI Buddhism, he adopted a common practice at their main center on Mt. HIEI of reciting the LOTUS SUTRA in the morning and the *NEMBUTSU,* or name of the Buddha, in the evening. He also absorbed a key Tendai belief of the connection of all things: each individual incorporates the whole and the whole is shown in each thing. From this insight, he developed the idea of interrelatedness and communication as applied especially to good deeds and chanting. When one does a good deed, he suggested, it communicates with other good deeds and even calls forth further good deeds. In like measure, when one chants the *nembutsu,* it communicates with the chanting of others, and the merit of the group's chanting reverberates on the individual who chants.

From his insights Ryonin made two proposals. First, he advocated chanting the *nembutsu* in group settings, in unison with all present, in the knowledge that such chanting permeates all beings. Second, on the basis of a dream in which a BODHISATTVA appeared to him, he began to call for pledges from people, both nobles and commoners, to recite the *nembutsu* daily and sign their name in a pledge book verifying their commitment.

During the last seven years of his life, Ryonin traveled the land promoting *Yuzu-Nembutsu* practice, accepting pledges from people, and organizing recitation groups. From this activity a new sect of Pure Land Buddhism emerged.

Although the Yuzu-Nimbutsu group was never large, its practice reverberated through the entire Pure Land community. It remains active in Japan, especially in Ise and Iga Provinces.

Further reading: *Buddhist Denominations and Schools in Japan* (Tokyo: Bukkyo Dendo Kyokai [Society for the Promotion of Buddhism], 1984); Kazuo Kasahara, ed., *A History of Japanese Religion.* Translated by Paul McCarthy and Gaynor Sekimori (Tokyo: Kosei, 2001).

Z

zazen

Zazen, sitting meditation, is a form of meditation distinctive to ZEN BUDDHISM practice. It consists of both proper posture and breathing and a state of mind. Clothing should be loose and nonbinding.

There are several options in positioning the body. Most commonly, the practitioner sits on the floor with the legs crossed. The rear end is raised slightly with a small pillow called a *zafu.* Practitioners may also sit in the yogic positions called the lotus or the half-lotus. For those who cannot sit cross-legged, sitting in a chair with the soles of the feet on the floor is permitted. The important aspect of the position of the body is the straightened back, which allows proper, natural breathing. Breathing is normally through the nose. The tongue rests against the upper palate.

Once the body is in place, the head and arms are positioned. The chin is lowered and the eyes focused on the ground in front of the body. The hands are placed in what is termed the cosmic MUDRA. The hands rest in front of the body, one hand holding the other, palms up. The ends of the thumbs lightly touch. Attention is placed in the *hara,* a place within the body slightly below the navel believed to be the body's physical and spiritual center.

Meditation, especially for the beginner, often begins with counting breaths, a technique to assist the mind in concentration, termed *joriki.* Thus the first goal of Zen meditation is unifying the mind and taking it to one point so that it no longer freely wanders.

The second goal of *zazen* is *kensho,* discovering one's BUDDHA NATURE, which occurs as a sudden realization that one is complete and perfect and has the power to realize full ENLIGHTENMENT. *Kensho* then leads to *mujodo no taigen,* the unfolding of one's Buddha nature in one's daily life and in one's beingness. Different Zen traditions place differing relative emphases on the three goals of *joriki, kensho,* and *mujodo no taigen.*

Further reading: Rindo Fujimoto, *The Way of Zazen* (Cambridge, Mass.: Cambridge Buddhist Association, 1966); Phillip Kapleau, *The Three Pillars of Zen* (Garden City, N.Y.: Doubleday, 1989); Katsuki Sekida, *Zen Training: Methods and Philosophy* (New York: Weatherhill, 1996); Shunryu Suzuki, *Zen Mind, Beginner's Mind* (New York: Weatherhill, 1970).

Zen Buddhism

Zen Buddhism is the meditational school of Buddhism as it has developed in Japan. It differs from other form of Buddhism in its emphasis on a particular form of meditation, the object of which is to practice present-mindedness and to reach a level of awareness or ENLIGHTENMENT. Through the practice of meditation one learns to know the truth about one's own nature.

In emphasizing meditation, Zen also tends to reduce the attention paid to Buddhist SUTRAS and other holy writings, the study of which is important in most other Buddhist traditions, and downplays the role of BODHISATTVAS, almost a distinguishing aspect of the larger MAHAYANA BUDDHISM tradition out of which Zen developed.

Zen entered Japan from China, where this school emphasizing meditation was known as CHAN BUDDHISM. Its development in Japan can be traced to DOSHO (629–700), a Japanese priest who had spent eight years studying under XUAN ZANG (602–664) and the Chan master Hui Man in China. Dosho is best known as the founder of the HOSSO (Dharma Marks) sect of Buddhism, but he also taught some of the Chan doctrine he had learned in China. A century later, SAICHO (767–822), the founder of TENDAI Buddhism, introduced a form of Zen into Tendai, and it has continued to be practiced to the present, though as one among many practices in Japanese religion. And while Zen Buddhism developed in Japan, Chan Buddhism underwent substantial changes in China.

Chan in China seems to have reached its height in the decades prior to the brief but devastating persecution of Buddhism in 845 under Emperor Wuzong (r. 841–846). This period saw the beginning of the use of the KOAN, the questions and stories presented to the individual practitioner that confound the intellect and lead it to make intuitive jumps toward realization of truth. It is in the generation after the persecution that the two main divisions of Zen, LINJI CHAN and CAODONG Chan, emerged, the latter rejecting the use of koans. Both schools developed out of the southern Chan movement that emphasized sudden as opposed to gradual enlightenment. Linji is most important to Japanese Zen, as it would be the first Zen school formally introduced to the island nation. Linji also separated into a number

of different schools, each with slightly different teachings and approaches to meditation and a distinctive lineage through which authority would be passed.

In the generations following the original transmission of Zen, teachers would go to China and receive credentials from the different Chinese schools of Linji and establish those schools as distinct RINZAI ZEN groups in Japan. Each Rinzai group would be built around a head temple/monastic complex, with a number of subtemples established around the country. Today in Japan there are no fewer than 18 separate Rinzai schools (denominations).

EISAI (1141–1215), raised a Shintoist and drawn to Tendai Buddhism as a young man, went to China in 1168 and there initially encountered Zen. He saw in the movement the answer for Japanese Buddhism. After his return to Japan in 1187, he finally received the seal of enlightenment in 1191 from the Huanglong Rinzai school. Meeting opposition from his former Tendai colleagues, he found favor with the shogun. In 1200, the shogun allowed him to establish Jufuku-ji in KAMAKURA; two years later he established Kinnin-ji. Both temples sought to reform Tendai along Zen lines.

A generation after Eisai, Enni Bennen (1202–80) traveled to China. Upon his return in 1241, he began to propagate the Yangqi school of Linji from his new temple, Tofuku-ji in Kyoto. A contemporary of Enni, Muhon Kakushin (1207–98) also traveled to China and upon his return in the 1260s founded Kokoku-ji, the lead temple of what became the Saiho school.

As Japanese practitioners traveled to China to learn, so a few Chinese adepts went to Japan to teach. Among them, Lanji Daoling (1213–78) would found Kencho-ji at Kamakura, the head temple of the Daikaku school of Rinzai. Another Chinese priest, Wuxue Zuyuan (also known as Mugaku Sogen) (1226–86), became the founding abbot of Engaku-ji, the famous monastic complex immediately north of Kamakura. Wuxue was a dominant influence in the city for the seven years he resided there, just enough time to establish the Bukko school of Linji.

As Rinzai Zen was growing through its various schools, Caodong Zen was introduced to Japan by DOGEN (1200–53). As did Eisai, Dogen started as a Tendai practitioner. His own religious questions led him away from Tendai to Einnin-ji, the Rinzai center founded by Eisai in Kyoto, and then on to China. At Mt. Tian Tai Tong he discovered Caodong Chan, and upon his return to Einnin-ji began to promote ZAZEN (sitting meditation) as the essential act of Zen practice. His new approach led to his dismissal from Einnin-ji and he eventually settled in the remote Echizen Province, where he founded EIHEI-JI, the center of what would become Soto Buddhism. For a variety of reasons, Soto avoided the many divisions into which Rinzai fell.

Rinzai and Soto remain the two primary schools of Zen, thought a third form was introduced by the Chinese priest Yin Yuan (or INGEN) (1592–1673) in the middle of the 17th century. OBAKU ZEN differed from the other schools in that, along with use of the koan, practitioners recited the NEMBUTSU, calling upon the name of AMITABHA (Amida) Buddha, considered the Buddha spirit in everyday life. Obaku was able to establish itself with the encouragement of the shoguns of the era.

Zen was especially strong in Japan through the years of rule by the shogunate, first in Kamakura and later in Tokyo. As did other forms of Buddhism, it suffered under the MEIJI RESTORATION. Zen Buddhism was introduced to North America in the person of SOYEN SHAKU (1859–1919), who spoke at the World's Parliament of Religions in 1893. Soyen had studied with Imakita Kosen (1816–92), who had been a student of Western culture; another of Imakita Kosen's students, Sokatsu Shaku (1869–1954), who arrived in 1906, became the second Zen teacher in the United States. Meanwhile, Senyei Kawahara had erected a Zen temple in Honolulu, Hawaii, where many Japanese lived.

Through the first half of the 20th century, additional Japanese Zen teachers would enter North America (as well as following the Japanese diaspora to South America). In the years after World War II, Americans would begin to travel to Japan to study, taking back both Soto and the various schools of Rinzai Zen. Zen would enjoy a certain popularity in the 1950s as the preferred religion of leaders in the BEAT ZEN movement— Jack Kerouac, Allen Ginsberg, and GARY SNYDER. After 1965, when anti–Asian immigration laws were rescinded, Zen would develop as a flourishing community.

Early in the 20th century, Zen found an initial advocate in England in the person of CHRISTMAS HUMPHREYS, the founder and longtime president of the BUDDHIST SOCIETY in London. For many years, the small Zen group with which he practiced in London was the only Zen center in the country.

A significant boost to Zen in both Europe and the United States was provided by DAISETSU TEITARO SUZUKI (1870–1966). As a young scholar, Suzuki traveled to the United States to work on translating various Buddhist texts. He spent the years between the world wars writing his major books on both Jodo Shin-shu and Zen Buddhism. Then, beginning in 1949, he taught for a decade in various American universities and became a popular speaker for emerging Zen groups. On a trip to England, he prompted the first growth spurt of the small Zen group headed by Humphreys.

As the 21st century begins, Zen has permeated the Western world and Zen groups can be found in most countries, with a full spectrum of groups operating in the United States, England, and Germany. The ASSOCIATION ZEN INTERNATIONALE, based in Paris, is the largest Zen organization in Europe.

Further reading: Helen Josephine Baroni, *The Illustrated Encyclopedia of Zen Buddhism* (New York: Rosen Publishing Group, 2002); Heinrich Dumoulin, *Zen Buddhism: A History.* 2 vols. 2d rev. ed. (New York: Macmillan, 1988); Kazuo Kasahara, ed., *A History of Japanese*

Religion. Translated by Paul McCarthy and Gaynor Sekimori (Tokyo: Kosei, 2001); Martin Roth and John Stevens, *Zen Guide* (New York: Weatherhill, 1985); E. Dale Saunders, *Buddhism in Japan* (Philadelphia: University of Pennsylvania Press, 1964); D. T. Suzuki, *Zen Buddhism* (Garden City, N.Y.: Doubleday, 1956); Kosho Yamamoto, *Buddhism in Europe* (Ube City, Japan: Karinbunko, 1967); Toichi Yoshioka, *Zen* (Kawamata, Japan: Hoikusha, 2002).

Zeng Yiguan (Tseng I-kuan) (c. 1000) *Quanzhen master who established Quanzhen Daoism in southern China's Guangdong Province*

An 11th-generation Quanzhen monk from Shandong in northern China, Zeng was asked by the provincial governor of Guangdong Province to perform a ritual to alleviate a severe drought. When rains followed the completed ritual, Zeng was considered a hero and enjoyed prestige for his spiritual efficacy. Zeng was easily able to extend his authority over the five Daoist temples (then called *an*) at Mt. LUOFU and to send his own disciples to establish new temples and posts in nearby urban centers of Guangzhou, Huizhou, and Panyu.

Further reading: Bartholomew P. M. Tsui, *Taoist Tradition and Change: The Story of the Complete Perfection Sect in Hong Kong* (Hong Kong: Christian Study Centre on Chinese Religion and Culture, 1991).

Zen Lotus Society   *See* BUDDHIST SOCIETY FOR COMPASSIONATE WISDOM.

Zhang Daoling (Chang Tao-ling) (second century C.E.) *founder of the Wudoumi sect of Daoism and first patriarch in the Zhengyi lineage of Daoism*

The beginning of DAOISM as an institutionalized religion is due to the efforts of one man in particular, Zhang Ling (later known as Zhang Daoling), a mysterious figure who was a hermit in the mountains in the far western regions of Sichuan. According to legend, LAOZI himself (under the title *Taishang Laojun,* "The Most High Lord Lao") appeared to Zhang in a vision in 142, complaining of people's failure to honor the true Way. Because of such degeneration, Lord Lao had withdrawn the Mandate of Heaven from the Han emperor and was bestowing it upon Zhang, along with the official title *tian shi* (heavenly master). He was also given a new covenant, which authorized him to subdue demons and spread the orthodox teachings. From this point onward, Zhang became the official heavenly master, serving as Laozi's spokesperson on Earth.

Zhang quickly founded a movement dubbed the DAO of the Five Pecks of Rice, after the tax of grain levied on its followers. In exchange for this levy, followers were given registers listing the names of various spirits and deities whom they could call upon for assistance. This essentially meant that the original sect was composed entirely of ordained priests. The most senior and accomplished followers received the longest registers listing the most powerful deities.

The Five Pecks of Rice sect opposed the traditional practice of offering bloody sacrifices to ancestors, substituting cooked vegetables instead. Healing was usually done via the confession of "sins" in which the sick wrote down their transgressions while the priests offered prayers. The writings were then left on mountaintops (as offerings to heaven), buried (as offerings to earth), or drowned (as offerings to rivers).

One of the notable features of Zhang's Five Pecks of Rice sect was its impressive organization. Zhang organized his many followers into various "parishes" headed by "libationers," male or female priests who conducted rituals, healed illness, drove out evil spirits, and taught others the religion's message. The title *heavenly master* denoted the chief of these priests and became the hereditary property of the Zhang lineage. The movement flourished under the direction of Zhang's eldest son and grandson, eventually establishing its own independent state in Sichuan. Although it eventually failed as a political movement, over the years the heavenly masters religious lineage has received official recognition by many imperial regimes, especially since the Song (960–1279) dynasty, and is still recognized as having unique authority.

Many practicing Daoist priests today trace their lineage back to Zhang Daoling. His movement is officially known as *Tianshi zhengyi Dao* (The Way of the orthodox unity of the heavenly master), and the heavenly master still is the recognized source of orthodox ordination. It has continued to be especially popular in southern China. After the Communist takeover in 1949, the headquarters was moved to Taiwan, where it continues as a lineage.

Further reading: Julia Ching, *Chinese Religions* (Maryknoll: Orbis Books, 1993), 103–104; James Miller, *Daoism: A Short Introduction* (Oxford: Oneworld, 2003), 8–9; Isabelle Robinet, *Taoism: Growth of a Religion.* Translated by Phyllis Brooks (Stanford, Calif.: Stanford University Press, 1997), 54–56; Laurence G. Thompson, *Chinese Religion: An Introduction.* 5th ed. (Belmont, Calif.: Wadsworth, 1996), 88–89.

Zhang Zai (Zhang Hengqu, Chang Tsai)

(1020–1077) *Chinese philosopher who clarified the concept of qi*

A native of Chang'an, the ancient capital of China, Zhang is the second leading figure in the "Succession of the Way" (*Daotong*) according to the Song philosopher Zhu Xi. In his youth he was deeply interested in military craft. Dissatisfied with traditional Confucian teachings, he explored DAOISM and BUDDHISM for a number of years before returning to the classics and was especially fond of the *Yijing* and *Zhongyong*. He obtained his *jinshi* degree in 1057 and held various offices. In 1077 he resigned his post as director of the Board of Imperial Sacrifices and died of illness on his way home.

As was ZHOU DUNYI, Zhang was deeply influenced by the teachings of the *Yijing, the Book of Changes.* According to Zhang, all things are united in their shared psychophysical substance, QI ("matter-energy"). They exist as productions of primal force emerging from the Supreme Ultimate in a constant process of change understood as a natural, orderly growth. *Qi* as a dynamic substance forms all creatures. Over the course of time, the particular formations of *qi* disintegrate, thus returning all things to their primal, undifferentiated state. The primary task of human beings is to understand and harmonize with the changes, not transcend them. Zhou's teachings are most fully articulated in *Zhengmeng* (Correcting youthful ignorance). However, his essay *Ximing* (western inscription, so named because it was inscribed on the west wall of his study) is his most celebrated work and remains one of the great works of Chinese literature. It is a concise, deeply moving statement of ontological and ethical unity and seems to be something of a Confucianized version of Buddhist Great Compassion (*mahakaruna*). The final lines, "In life I follow and serve Heaven and Earth. In death I will be at peace," are a profound statement of Confucian faith and ideals. Zhu Xi described it as "perfect," and the greatest statement since MENCIUS.

Further reading: Carson Chang, *The Development of Neo-Confucian Thought* (New York: Bookman Associates, 1957); Ira E. Kasoff, *The Thought of Chang Tsai (1020–1077)* (Cambridge: Cambridge University Press, 1984); Ian P. McGreal, ed., *Great Thinkers of the Eastern World* (New York: HarperCollins, 1995).

Zhan Ran (Chan Jan) (711–782) *sixth patriarch of the Tian Tai school of Chinese Buddhism*

Zhan Ran solidified the status of the TIAN TAI SCHOOL as a major strand of Chinese BUDDHISM. In his period, the late eighth century, Tian Tai competed with HUA YAN and CHAN BUDDHISM. All of these set themselves up as schools (*zong*) with a founder (*zu*) and an unbroken lineage of masters. And all argued for the superiority of their own teachings. Zhan Ran recognized the danger that Tian Tai would become marginalized by the competition. He dedicated his life to clarifying and spreading Tian Tai teachings.

He was born to a Confucian family in Chang Zhou, in today's Jiangsu Province, near present-day Shanghai. He was given a strict Confucian education. By his 20s he had become a monk and was attached to the master Xuan Lang (673–754), who lived on Mt. Zuoqi, near Wuzhou in modern Zhejiang Province. Xuan Lang taught Zhan Ran the Tian Tai meditative practice of *zhiguan*, "contemplation and insight." Zhan Ran stayed on Mt Zuoqi for 19 years, until he was finally ordained as a monk in 748, at the age of 38.

From this period Zhan Ran began a prolific writing career. His first major work was a commentary on ZHI YI's MOHE ZHIGUAN, the *Zhiguan fuxing quanhong jeu* (Extensive teachings in the form of a commentary as an aid to the practice of the great concentration and insight), completed between 755 and 765. This was the first commentary on Zhi Yi's great book, one of the three foundational works of Tian Tai Buddhism. Zhan Ran went on to write commentaries on all of Zhi Yi's major works. Thereafter Zhi Yi's works were generally read together with Zhan Ran's commentaries.

Zhan Ran spent most of his life after leaving Mt. Zuoqing at Fo Long, near Mt. Tian Tai, the home of Tian Tai Buddhism. He left for an extended trip in 769 and is said to have led 40 monks in a pilgrimage around 774 to Mt. Wutai, where he visited the Tantric master Han Guang (662–732). His last major work, the *Jingang Bei* (Diamond scalpel), was published near his death in 782. This work confirmed that BUDDHA NATURE is present in all things, including insentient objects, a theory that was later adopted by all East Asian Buddhists. In all Zhan Ran is credited with 33 works, 21 of which survive today. (But of those 11 are today considered suspect, not written by Zhan Ran.)

Zhan Ran's major contribution to Tian Tai theory was the theory of the five periods and eight teachings (*wushi bajiao*), a form of PAN-JIAO (teaching classifications) that was originally attributed to Zhi Yi. Zhan Ran used this framework to explain all Buddhist teachings. He can thus be seen as a major syncretic thinker, in addition to being a strong advocate for the Tian Tai school.

Further reading: Linda Penkower, "T'ian-t'ai during the T'ang dynasty: Chan-jan and the Signification of Buddhism" (Ph.D. diss., Columbia University, 1993).

Zheng Yen   *See* BUDDHIST COMPASSION RELIEF TZU CHI ASSOCIATION; CHENG YEN.

Zhi Li (Chih Li)   (960–1028)   *Tian Tai advocate*

Zhi Li was a Song dynasty (960–1279) TIAN TAI SCHOOL master and reformer who represents the later flowering of Tian Tai thought. He was also a vocal champion of his school and was especially critical of Dao Sui and Gan Shu's interpretation of such Tian Tai concepts as the nonduality of matter (*sixin buer*).

Zhi Li advocated a lineage transmission from the Tian Tai master ZHAN RAN through Xing Man to Guang Xiu, Wu Wai, Yuan Xiu, and Qing Song, followed by Xi Ji, Yi Tong, and, finally to Zhi Li himself in the Song dynasty. This lineage was at odds with the one championed on Mt. HIEI in Japan. The orthodox transmission was fixed by Zhi Pan, who reverted to using Dao Sui. The final line of figures included several previously unknown individuals who had resided on Mt. Tian Tai. The so-called *shan jia* tradition gave greater emphasis to those who championed values of mountain monasticism.

Further reading: Linda Penkower, "T'ian-t'ai during the T'ang Dynasty: Chan-jan and the Signification of Buddhism" (Ph.D. diss., Columbia University, 1993).

Zhi Yi (Chih Yi) (538–597) *founder of Tian Tai Buddhism*

Zhi Yi was the founder of a major branch of Chinese MAHAYANA BUDDHISM, the TIAN TAI SCHOOL, which places emphasis on the LOTUS SUTRA as the key SUTRA containing the essential knowledge of the Buddha's teachings. Zhi Yi also developed a categorization structure for Buddhist teachings, the PANJIAO. Contemporary practitioners in China, Japan, and Korea also remember him for his development of the *zhi guan* ("cessation of contemplation") meditative technique. Zhi Yi himself left no writings. His teachings were recorded by his major disciple, Guan Ding (561–632), in the work MOHE ZHIGUAN.

Zhi Yi was born near present-day Nanjing, in central China, to a wealthy family. His first master was Hui Si (515–576), who instructed him in the Lotus Sutra and the Prajnparamita Sutras. Zhi Yi spent many years in the area of present-day Nanjing, where he enjoyed strong support from the Yang imperial family of the short-lived Sui dynasty (589–618). When Zhi Yi recounted a dream vision in which he was instructed to establish a temple near Mt. Tian Tai, he was quickly given imperial funds. The temple, Guoqing Si, is still in use. Zhi Yi remained at Mt. Tian Tai until his death.

Further reading: "Chih-I," in Charles S. Prebish, *The A to Z of Buddhism* (Lanham, Md.: Scarecrow Press, 2001), 87.

Zhou Dunyi (Zhou Lianxi, Chou Lienhsi) (1017–1073) *early Neo-Confucian thinker*

Often regarded as the pioneering thinker of NEO-CONFUCIANISM, Zhou Dunyi has a high place in the history of Chinese thought. Although promoted by Zhu Xi as the first true Confucian sage since MENCIUS, he had only a tenuous connection to later Neo-Confucian thinkers.

During his lifetime Zhou had little influence on Song political and intellectual life. Born into a family of scholar-officials, Zhou himself only held minor posts and never obtained the *jinshi* degree, the highest rank in the Chinese imperial civil service system. For a short time, the brothers CHENG HAO and CHENG YI were his students. Zhou is especially remembered for his warm, humane temperament and mystical insight into the Way of Heaven. According to later thinkers, he was the very embodiment of *cheng* ("sincerity," "authenticity"). Zhou was a deep admirer of natural beauty and allegedly loved life so much that he would not cut the grass outside his window. His student Cheng Yi is said to have referred to him as "poor Chan fellow," indicating he may have been perceived as being overly partial to CHAN BUDDHISM.

Zhou's teachings are found in two key texts, the *Explanation of the diagram of the supreme ultimate* (Taijitu shuo) and *Penetrating the classic of changes* (Tongshu). With them he established the basic metaphysical scheme of Neo-Confucianism. Zhou's scheme is essentially a cosmological explanation of the world that also serves as a road map for spiritual cultivation. Beginning in ultimate nothingness (*wuji*), which also manifests as the Supreme Ultimate (*taiji*), there is mysterious movement of YIN and YANG (two basic cosmic modes). These together generate water, fire, wood, metal, and earth (*wuxing*, "five phases"), which, in turn, become "pure yang" (*qian*, "Heaven," in the *Yijing*) and "pure yin" (*kun*, "Earth," in the *Yijing*). These two complementary QI stimulate each other, transforming and generating the myriad things without end. Zhou then takes this basic Daoist scheme and gives it a decided Confucian twist by emphasizing that humanity receives the purest *qi*, which must be developed through exercising moral virtue.

In the *Tongshu* Zhou focuses on the sage as a model person. Following the *Zhongyong* (Doctrine of the mean), Zhou maintains that sagehood, the actualizing of one's cosmic-moral nature, occurs only through developing *cheng* (sincerity, authenticity).

Zhou has been regarded with suspicion by some more sectarian Confucians for his Daoist and Buddhist connections. Certainly *Explanation of the diagram* seems to have originated in Daoist circles and did make its way into the DAOZANG (Daoist Canon). In addition, he does seem to have been a great admirer of BUDDHISM. Nonetheless, his emphasis on social virtue and its development shows his deeply Confucian formation.

See also TIAN DAO (The Way of Heaven).

Further reading: Carson Chang, *The Development of Neo-Confucian Thought* (New York: Bookman Associates, 1957); Ian P. McGreal, ed., *Great Thinkers of the Eastern World* (New York: HarperCollins, 1995).

Zhuangzi (Chuang-tzu)

The *Zhuangzi* is a major literary text in Chinese literature; its influence as literature far exceeds that of other religious texts such as the *Laozi* or the *Analects*. This is due to the vast imagination and broad use of literary techniques found within. The *Zhuangzi* is part fable, part poetry, part prose. It has provided images and themes for nearly all later Chinese writers. The *Zhuangzi* also includes many religious themes of interest, including meditation practices, transcendence, and ruminations on death. Because of the vividness of its contents the *Zhuangzi* has had an important impact on the later development of SHANGQING DAOISM, Buddhism, and especially CHAN BUDDHISM.

The *Zhuangzi*, "Master Zhuang," is named for its author, Zhuang Zhou, a thinker said to have lived in the third century B.C.E. The existing version contains 33 chapters. It is apparent that more than one writer contributed to this work, over time. The original Zhuang would not have been expected to refer to himself as "Zhuangzi," for instance, but this happens in several places. However, it is safe to say that there was such a person as Master Zhuang, and that he was associated with a "school" active in the areas of Chu and Qi during the Warring States period.

In fact, textual analysis of the *Zhuangzi* has uncovered the influence of five separate "schools" or strands of thinking within the text: primitivists who followed LAOZI and other older masters but who were active around the Qin dynasty; hedonist followers from around 200 B.C.E.; a syncretist group active in 180–130 B.C.E.; direct followers of Zhuang Zhou; and anthologists who collected materials and added sections later.

The main spirit of the *Zhuangzi* is an emphasis on "naturalness," *ziran*. This term today means "nature," but in ancient times it may have indicated doing what is natural. One who practices the Way is at all times *ziran*. In order to attain this state a person should calm the mind by sitting. As does LAOZI, the *Zhuangzi* presents the DAO as the source of all in the universe. Because the sages of the past understood and embodied Dao, it makes sense for contemporary cultivators to do so also. In this way it was not necessary to mind moral codes or rules.

The *Zhuangzi* also presented a nuanced doctrine of relativity. The writers were adept at identifying the fallacies of rigid thinking. Because of the constant transformations of Dao, all phenomena are relative. This is, then, the *Zhuangzi*'s definition of freedom—becoming attuned to Dao.

The *Zhuangzi* also emphasized such innovative techniques as stilling the senses and circulating energy, called *xinzhai* (fasting the mind) and going into deep trance (*zuo wang*, "sitting in absorption"), both early forms of Chinese non-Buddhist meditation.

Further reading: Sam Hamill and J. P. Seaton, trans., *The Essential Chuang Tzu* (Boston: Shambhala, 1998); Victor Mair, "The *Zhuangzi* and Its Impact," in Livia Kohn, ed., *Daoism Handbook* (Leiden and Koln: Brill, 2000), 30–52.

Zong Mi (Guifeng Zongmi, Tsung-mi)
(780–841) *fifth patriarch in the Hua Yan school of Chinese Buddhism*

HUA YAN Buddhism flourished briefly in the Tang dynasty (618–907), and there were a mere five patriarchs in the tradition. The final patriarch,

Zong Mi, was in many ways the most brilliant. In addition to being a promoter of Hua Yan, he was also a patriarch of CHAN BUDDHISM. His major work, the *Inquiry into the Origin of Humanity* (*Yuanrenlun*), is a concise summation of the teachings of various schools in his time. This work used the concept of PANJIAO, classification of doctrines, to analyze each school, a common practice in Buddhist teachings during the Tang. Zong Mi's innovation was to include CONFUCIANISM and DAOISM in his discussions of doctrine.

Zong Mi received a traditional Confucian education. Before he could take the official civil service exams he met a Chan monk, Dao Yuan, and soon after became a monk himself. He received full ordination as a monk in 807. He was later attracted to the teachings of Cheng Guan (738–839), a Hua Yan master. Zong Mi emphasized study of the *Yuanjue jing* (Scripture of perfect enlightenment), and he focused his teaching energy on this text for the next 20 years.

Further reading: Peter N. Gregory, trans., *Inquiry into the Origin of Humanity: An Annotated Translation of Tsumg-mi's Yuan jen lun with a Modern Commentary* (Honolulu: University of Hawaii Press, 1995).

APPENDIX

Major Dynasties and Modern Periods in Chinese History

- Xia (Hsia) dynasty about 1994 B.C.E.–1766 B.C.E.
- Shang dynasty 1766 b.c.e.–1027 b.c.e.
- Zhou (Chou) dynasty 1122 b.c.e.–256 b.c.e. plus supplement
- Qin (Ch'in) dynasty 221 b.c.e.–206 b.c.e.
- Han dynasty 206 b.c.e.–220 c.e.
- Three Kingdoms—Period of Disunion 220 c.e.–280 c.e.
- Sui dynasty 589 c.e.–618 c.e.
- Tang (T'ang) dynasty 618 c.e.–907 c.e.
- Song (Sung) dynasty 969 c.e.–1279 c.e.
- Yuan (Mongol) dynasty 1279 c.e.–1368 c.e.
- Ming dynasty 1368 c.e.–1644 c.e.
- Manchu, or Qing (Ch'ing), dynasty 1644 c.e.–1912 c.e.
- Republic of China 1911–1949
- People's Republic of China 1949–

Japanese Historical Periods

- Jomon period 300 b.c.e.
- Yayoi period c. 300 b.c.e.–300 c.e.
- Kofun period 300–552 (538?)
- Asuka period 552–645
- Nara 645–794 710–784?
- Heian 794–1185
- Kamakura 1185–1333
- Muromachi 1336–1573
- Momoyama 1573–1603
- Edo 1603–1868
- Meiji 1868–1914
- Taisho 1914–1918
- Showa 1926–1989
- Heisei 1989–

The First Six Patriarchs of Chan/Zen

- Bodhidharma (–535)(28th Indian patriarch, first Chan patriarch)
- Hui Ke (487–593)
- Seng Can (–606)
- Dao Xin (580–651)
- Hong Ren (602–675)
- Hui Neng (638–713)

Major Mahayana Sutras

- Amitabha Sutra
- Avatamsaka Sutra

- Diamond Sutra (Vajracchedika-prajnaparamita Sutra)
- Heart Sutra (Pranjnaparamita-hrdaya Sutra)
- Lankavatara Sutra
- Lotus Sutra (Saddharma-pundarika Sutra)
- Mahavairocana Sutra
- Srimaladevi Sutra
- Sutra of Hui Neng
- Sutra of Ksitigarbha Bodhisattva
- The Brahma Net Sutra
- Mahaparinirvana Sutra
- Virmalakirti-nirdesa Sutra

The Books of the Pali Sutta-pittaka

- Digha Nikaya (The "Long" Discourses)
- Majjhima Nikaya (The "Middle-length" Discourses)
- Samyutta Nikaya (The "Grouped" Discourses)
- Anguttara Nikaya (The "Further-factored" Discourses)
- Khuddaka Nikaya (The "Division of Short Books"—18 books, in the Burmese tradition):

1. Khuddakapatha—The Short Passages
2. Dhammapada—The Path of Dhamma
3. Udana—Exclamations
4. Itivuttaka—The Thus-saids
5. Sutta Nipata—The Sutta Collection
6. Vimanavatthu—Stories of the Celestial Mansions
7. Petavatthu—Stories of the Hungry Ghosts
8. Theragatha—Verses of the Elder Monks
9. Therigatha—Verses of the Elder Nuns
10. Jataka—Birth Stories
11. Niddesa—Exposition
12. Patisambhidamagga—Path of Discrimination
13. Apadana—Stories
14. Buddhavamsa—History of the Buddhas
15. Cariyapitaka—Basket of Conduct
16. Nettippakarana (Burmese Tipitaka only)
17. Petakopadesa (Burmese Tipitaka only)
18. Milindapañha—Questions of Milinda (Burmese Tipitaka only)

A Bibliography of Buddhism and Related Eastern Asian Religions (Bon, Confucianism, Daoism, Shinto, and New Religions)

Buddhism

Adam, Enid, and Philip J. Hughes. *The Buddhists in Australia.* Canberra: Australian Government Publishing Service, 1992.

Adikaram, E. W. *Early History of Buddhism in Ceylon.* Migoda: D. S. Puswella, 1946.

An Outline of Buddhism. Honolulu: Hongwanji Buddhist Temple, 1929.

Anderson, Walt. *Open Secrets.* New York: Viking Press, 1979.

Anesaki, Masaharu. *Nichiren, The Buddhist Prophet.* Cambridge, Mass.: Harvard University Press, 1949. 160 pp.

Armstrong, Vessie Patricia. *Zen Buddhism: A Bibliography of Books and Articles in English 1892–1975.* Ann Arbor: University Microfilms International, 1976.

Baroni, Helen Josephine. *The Illustrated Encyclopedia of Zen Buddhism.* New York: Rosen Publishing Group, 2002.

Bartholemeusz, Tessa. *Women under the Bo Tree: Buddhist Nuns in Sri Lanka.* Cambridge: Cambridge University Press, 1994.

Baumann, Martin. *Deutsche Buddhisten: Geschichte und Gemeinschaften.* Marburg: Diagonal, 1995.

Becker, Ernest. *Zen: A Rational Critique.* New York: W. W. Norton, 1961.

Bellah, Robert N. *Tokugawa Religion: The Values of Pre-Industrial Japan.* New York: Free Press, 1969.

Bercholz, Samuel, and Sherab Chodzin Kohn. *Entering the Stream: An Introduction to The Buddha and His Teachings.* Foreword by Bernardo Bertolucci. Boston: Shambala, 1993.

Bibhuti Baruah. *Buddhist Sects and Sectarianism.* Delhi, Sarup, 2000.

Birnbaum, Edwin. *Sacred Mountains of the World.* San Francisco: Sierra Club, 1990.

Bischoff, Roger. *Buddhism in Myanmar: A Short History.* Kandy, Sri Lanka: Buddhist Publication Society, 1995.

Bissio, Roberto Remo et al. *Third World Guide 93/94.* Montevideo, Uruguay: Instituto del Tercer Mundo, 1992.

Blofeld, John. *The Tantric Mysticism of Tibet.* New York: Causeway Books, 1974.

Bloom, Alfred. *Shinran's Gospel of Pure Grace.* Tuscon: University of Arizona Press, 1965.

Bodiford, William M. *Soto Zen in Medieval Japan.* Honolulu: University of Hawaii Press, 1993.

Boucher, Sandy. *Opening the Lotus: A Women's Guide to Buddhism.* Boston: Beacon Press, 1997.

Brief Introduction to Korean Buddhism. Los Angeles: Korean Buddhist Sangha Association of Western Territory of the U.S.A., 1984.

Buddhaghosa. *The Path of Purification (Visuddhimagga).* Translated by Bhiksu Nyanomili. 2d ed. Colombo, Ceylon: A. Semage, 1964.

Buddhism in Japan. Philadelphia: University of Pennsylvania Press, 1964.

Buddhist Churches of America: Seventy-Five Year History, 1899–1974. 2 vols. Chicago: Nobart, 1974.

Buddhist Denominations and Schools in Japan. Tokyo: Bukkto Dendo Kyokai, 1984.

Burlingame, Eugene Watson. *Buddhist Legends.* Cambridge, Mass.: Harvard University Press, 1921.

Buswell, Robert E., Jr. *The Zen Monastic Experience.* Princeton, N.J.: Princeton University Press, 1992.

———, ed. *Encyclopedia of Buddhism.* 2 Vols. Detroit: Thomson/Gale, 2004.

Byron, Earhart H. *Religion in the Japanese Experience: Sources and Interpretations.* Belmont, Calif.: Wadsworth, 1997.

Cabrzón, José Innacio. *Buddhism, Sexuality and Gender.* Albany: State University Press of New York, 1992.

Chakravarti, Balaram. *A Cultural History of Bhutan.* Chittaranjan: Hilltop, 1979–1980.

Chegwan. *T'ien-T'ai Buddhism An Outline of the Fourfold Teachings.* Introduced and edited by David W. Chappell and compiled by Masao Ichishima. Tokyo: Daiichi-Shobo, 1983.

Ch'en, Kenneth. *Buddhism.* Woodbury, N.Y.: Barron's Educational Series, 1968.

———. *Buddhism in China: A Historical Survey.* Princeton, N.J.: Princeton University Press, 1964.

Chitkara, M. G. *Encyclopaedia of Buddhism: A World Faith: The Middle Path.* New Delhi: APH, 2001.

Chödrön, Prema. *No Time to Lose: A Timely Guide to the Way of the Bodhisattva.* Boston: Shambhala, 2005.

Chogay Trichen Rinpoche. *The History of the Sakya Tradition.* Translated by Jennifer Stott. Bristol: Ganesha Press, 1983.

Clasquin, Michel, and Jacobus S. Krüger. *Buddhism and Africa.* Pretoria: University of South Africa Press, 2000.

Cleary, Thomas. *The Original Face: An Anthology of Rinzai Zen.* New York: Grove Press, 1978.

———, trans. *Shobogenzo: Zen Essays by Dogen.* Honolulu: University of Hawaii Press, 1986.

Coleman, Graham, ed. *A Handbook of Tibetan Culture: A Guide to Tibetan Centres and Resources throughout the World.* Boston: Shambhala, 1994.

Coleman, James William. *The New Buddhism: The Western Transformation of an Ancient Tradition.* New York: Oxford University Press, 2001.

Conze, Edward. *Buddhism: Its Essence and Development.* New York: Philosophical Library, 1951.

Corless, Roger J. *The Vision of Buddhism.* New York: Paragon House, 1989.

Croucher, Paul. *Buddhism in Australia. 1848–1988.* Kensington, Australia: New South Wales University Press, 1989.

Dasgupta, Shashi Bhushan. *An Introduction to Tantric Buddhism.* Boulder, Colo.: Shambhala, 1974.

Davidson, Linda Kay, and David M. Gitlitz. *Pilgrimage from the Ganges to Graceland: An Encyclopedia.* Santa Barbara, Calif.: ABC-Clio, 2002.

Davidson, Ronald M. *Indian Esoteric Buddhism: A Social History of the Tantric Movement.* New York: Columbia University Press, 2002.

———. *Tibetan Renaissance: Tantric Buddhism in the Rebirth of Tibetan Culture.* New York: Columbia University Press, 2005.

Day, Terence P. *Great Tradition and Little Tradition in Theravada Buddhist Studies.* Lewiston, N.Y.: Edwin Mellen Press, 1988.

de Bary, William, ed. *Sources of Chinese Tradition.* 2d ed. 2 Vols. New York: Columbia University Press, 1999.

De Silva, Lynn. *Buddhism: Beliefs and Practices in Sri Lanka.* Colombo: Wesley Press, 1974.

Dewaraja, L. S. *The Position of Women in Buddhism.* The Wheel Publication No. 280. Kandy: Buddhist Publication Society, 1981.

Dumoulin, Heinrich, *Zen Buddhism: A History.* 2 vols. 2d rev. ed. New York: Macmillan, 1988.

Dutt, Nalinaksha. *Buddhist Sects in India.* Delhi: Motilal Banarsidass, 1978.

Dutt, Sukumar. *Buddhism in East Asia.* New Delhi: Indian Council for Cultural Relations, 1966.

———. *Buddhist Monks and Monasteries of India: Their History and Their Contribution to Indian Culture.* London: George Allen & Unwin, 1962.

Earhart, H. Byron. *Japanese Religion: Unity and Diversity.* 3d ed. Belmont, Calif.: Wadsworth, 1982.

————. *Religion in the Japanese Experience: Sources and Interpretations*. 2d ed. Belmont, Calif.: Wadsworth, 1997.

English Buddhist Dictionary Committee. *The Soka Gakkai Dictionary of Buddhism*. Tokyo: Soka Gakkai, 2002.

Farrer-Halls, Gill. *The Illustrated Encyclopedia of Buddhist Wisdom: A Complete Introduction to the Principles and Practices of Buddhism*. Wheaton, Ill.: Quest Books, 2000.

Faure, Bernard. *The Red Thread: Buddhist Approaches to Sexuality*. Princeton, N.J.: Princeton University Press, 1998.

Fields, Rick. *How the Swans Came to the Lake: A Narrative History of Buddhism in America*. Boston: Shambala, 1992.

Fischer-Schreiber, Ingrid, Franz-Karl Ehrhard, Kurt Friedrichs, and Michael S. Diener, eds. *The Encyclopedia of Eastern Philosophy and Religion: Buddhism, Hinduism, Taoism, Zen*. Boston: Shambhala, 1989.

Friedman, Lenore. *Meetings with Remarkable Women*. Boston: Shambhala, 1987. Rev. ed. New York: Random House, 2000.

Fujimoto, Rindo. *The Way of Zazen*. Cambridge, Mass.: Cambridge Buddhist Association, 1966.

Ganeri, Aneri. *Buddhist Festivals through the Year*. London: Watts Group, 2003.

Gardner, James L. *Zen Buddhism: A Classified Bibliography of Western-Language Publications through 1990*. Salt Lake City, Utah: Wings of Fire Press, 1991.

Gaulier, Simone, Robert Jera-Bezard, and Monique Maillard, *Buddhism in Afghanistan and Central Asia*. Leiden: Brill, 1976.

Gellner, David N. *Monk, Householder, and Tantric Priest: Newar Religion and Its Hierarchy of Ritual*. Cambridge: Cambridge University Press, 1992.

Gladstone, Cary. *Afghanistan: History, Issues, Bibliography*. Huntington, N.Y.: Novinka Books, 2001.

Goleman, Daniel, ed., *Healing Emotions: Conversations with the Dalai Lama on Mindfulness, Emotions, and Health*. Boston and London: Shamballa, 2003.

Gombrich, Richard F. *Theravāda Buddhism: A Social History from Ancient Benares to Modern Colombo*. London and New York: Routledge & Kegan Paul, 1988.

Gross, Rita. *Buddhism after Patriarchy: A Feminist History, Analysis, and Reconstruction of Buddhism*. Albany: State University of New York Press, 1993.

Gyatso, Geshe Kelsang. *Buddhism in the Tibetan Tradition: A Guide*. London: Tharpa, 1984.

Hanayama, Shinsho, ed. *Bibliography on Buddhism*. Tokyo: Hokuseido Press, 1961.

Hardacre, Helen. *Lay Buddhism in Contemporary Japan: Reiyukai Kyodan*. Princeton, N.J.: Princeton University Press, 1984.

Harvey, B. Peter. *An Introduction to Buddhism: Teachings, History, and Practices*. New York: Cambridge University Press, 1990.

Hasrat, Bikrama Jit. *History of Bhutan: Land of the Peaceful Dragon*. Thimphu, Bhutan: Education Department, 1980.

Heissig, W. *The Religions of Mongolia*. Translated by G. Samuel. Berkeley: University of California Press, 1980.

Hirakawa, Akira. *A History of Indian Buddhism: From Sakyamuni to Early Mahayana*. Translated and edited by Paul Groner. Honolulu: University of Hawaii Press, 1990.

Hoffman, Helmut. *The Religions of Tibet*. New York: Macmillan, 1961.

Horner, Isaline B. *Women under Primitive Buddhism*. London: Routledge & Kegan Paul, 1930.

Humphreys, Christmas. *A Popular Dictionary of Buddhism*. New York: Citadel Press, 1963.

————. *Sixty Years of Buddhism in England, 1907–1967*. London: Buddhist Society, 1968.

Hunter, Louise H. *Buddhism in Hawaii*. Honolulu: University of Hawaii Press, 1971.

Hurvitz, Leon, *Scripture of the Lotus Blossom of the Fine Dharma (The Lotus Sutra)*. New York: Columbia University Press, 1986.

Hyams, Joe. *Zen in the Martial Arts*. New York: Bantam, 1982.

International Buddhist Directory. London: Wisdom, 1985.

Introvigne, Massimo, PierLuigi Zoccatelli, Nelly Ippolito Macrina, and Verónica Roldán. *Enciclopedia delle*

Religioni in Italia. Leumann (Torino): Elledici, 2001.

Jacobson, Nolan Pliny. *Buddhism and the Contemporary World: Change and Self-Correction*. Carbondale: Southern Illinois: University Press, 1983.

Jayatilleke, K. N. *The Message of the Buddha*. New York: The Free Press, 1974.

Jera-Bezard, Robert, and Monique Maillard. *Buddhism in Afghanistan and Central Asia*. Leiden: Brill, 1976.

Jochim, Christian. *Chinese Religions: A Cultural Perspective*. Englewood Cliffs, N.J.: Prentice Hall, 1986.

Johnson, Sandy. *The Book of Tibetan Elders: The Life Stories and Wisdom of the Great Spiritual Masters of Tibet*. New York: Riverhead Books, 1996.

Jones, Charles B. "Buddhism in Taiwan: A Historical Survey." Ph.D. diss., University of Virginia, 1996.

Jumsai, M. L. Manich. *Understanding Thai Buddhism*. Bangkok: Chalermnit Press, 1973.

Kabilsingh, Chatsumarn Kabilsingh. *Thai Women in Buddhism*. Berkeley: Parallax Press, 1991.

Kalbacker, Catherine Elmes. *Zen in America*. Ph.D. diss., University of Michigan, 1972.

Kalupahana, David J. *Buddhist Philosophy*. Honolulu: University Press of Hawaii, 1976.

Kapleau, Phillip. *The Three Pillars of Zen*. Garden City, N.Y.: Doubleday, 1989.

Kasahara, Kazuo, ed. and Paul McCarthy and Gaynor Sekimori, trans. *A History of Japanese Religion*. Tokyo: Dosei, 2001.

Keisuke, Serizawa. *The Ten Disciples of Buddha*. Japan: Ohara Museum of Art, 1982.

Keown, Damien. *A Dictionary of Buddhism*. New York: Oxford University Press, 2003.

———. *The Nature of Buddhist Ethics*. New York: St. Martin's Press, 1992.

———, ed. *Oxford Dictionary of Buddhism*. Oxford: Oxford University Press, 2003.

Keshima, Tetsuden. *Buddhism in America*. Westport, Conn.: Greenwood Press, 1977.

Kim, Duk-Whang. *A History of Religions in Korea*. Seoul: Daeji Monoonwha-sa, 1988.

Kitigawa, Joseph M. *Religion in Japanese History*. New York: Columbia University Press, 1966.

Kodansha Encyclopaedia of Japan. Tokyo: Kodansha, 1983.

Kohn, Michael H., trans. *The Shambhala Dictionary of Buddhism and Zen*. Boston: Shambhala, 1991.

Korean Buddhism. Seoul, Korea: Korean Buddhist Chogye Order, 1996.

Korean Buddhist Research Institute, ed. *Buddhist Thought in Korea*. Seoul: Dongguk University Press, 1994.

———, ed. *Son Thought in Korean Buddhism*. Seoul: Dongguk University Press, 1998.

Kosho Yamamoto, *Buddhism in Europe*. Ube City, Japan: Karinbunko, 1967.

Kraft, Kenneth, ed. *Zen: Tradition and Transition*. New York: Grove Press, 1988.

Lamotte, Etienne. *History of India Buddhism*. Louvain: Peeters Press, 1988.

———. *History of Indian Buddhism from the Origins to the Shaku Era*. Translated by Sara Webb-Boin. Nouvain-la-Neuve: Institute Orientaliste de l'Universite Catholique de Louvain, 1988.

Lancaster, Lewis R., and C. S. Yu, eds. *Introduction of Buddhism to Korea: New Cultural Patterns*. Berkeley, Calif.: Asian Humanities Press, 1989.

Law, Bimala Churn. *Women in Buddhist Literature*. Varanasi: Indological Book House, 1981.

Layman, Emma McCoy. *Buddhism in America*. Chicago: Nelson-Hall, 1976.

Leyland, Winston, ed., *Queer Dharma: Voices of Gay Buddhism*. San Francisco: Gay Sunshine Press, 1989.

Liebert, Gosta. *Iconographic Dictionary of the Indian Religions: Hinduism, Buddhism, Jainism*. Leiden: Brill, 1976.

Ling, T. O. *A Dictionary of Buddhism: A Guide to Thought and Tradition*. New York: Charles Scribner's Sons, 1972.

Lopez, Donald S., Jr. *Buddhism in Practice*. Princeton, N.J.: Princeton University Press, 1995.

———. *Buddhist Scriptures*. London: Penguin, 2004.

———. *The Story of Buddhism A Concise Guide to its History and Teachings*. San Francisco: HarperSanFrancisco, 2001.

————, ed. *Curators of the Buddha: the Study of Buddhism Under Colonialism.* Chicago: University of Chicago Press, 1995.

————, ed. *Religions of China in Practice.* Princeton, N.J.: Princeton University Press, 1999.

Lorie, Peter, and Julie Fookes. *The Buddhist Directory: The Total Resource Guide.* Rutland, Vt.: Charles E. Tuttle, 1997.

Lorie, Peter, and Julie Fookes, comp. *The Buddhist Guide.* London: Boxtree, 1996.

MacInnis, Donald E. *Religion in China Today.* Maryknoll, N.Y.: Orbis Books, 1989.

Mann, Gurinder Singh et al. *Buddhists, Hindus and Sikhs in America.* New York: Oxford University Press, 2001.

March, Arthur C. *A Buddhist Bibliography.* London: Buddhist Lodge, 1935.

Matsunami, Kodo. *Introducing Buddhism.* Honolulu: Hawaii Jodo Mission, 1965.

Mayeda, Egaku, ed. *Contemporary Buddhism in Sinhalese Society.* Nagoya: Aichigakuin University, 1982.

McDougall, Colin. *Buddhism in Malaysia.* Singapore: Donald Moore, 1956.

McGreal, Ian P., ed. *Great Thinkers of the Eastern World.* New York: HarperCollins, 1995.

Melton, J. Gordon. *A Bibliography of Buddhism in America, 1880–1940.* Santa Barbara, Calif.: Institute for the Study of American Religion, 1985.

————. *Encyclopedia of American Religions.* 7th ed. Detroit: Thomson/Gale, 2003.

————. *Religious Leaders of America.* Detroit: Gale Research, 1991.

————, and Martin Baumann. *Religions of the World: A Comprehensive Encyclopedia of Beliefs and Practices.* 4 vols. Santa Barbara, Calif.: ABC-Clio, 2002.

Mizuno, Kogen. *Essentials of Buddhism: Basic Terminology and Concepts of Buddhist Philosophy and Practice.* Translated by Gaynor Sekimori, with a foreword by J. W. de Jong. 1972. Reprint, Tokyo: Kosei, 1996.

Mizuno Kogen, ed. *Buddhist Sutras: Origin, Development, Transmission.* Tokyo: Kosei, 1982.

Moor, Elizabeth, Hansjorg Mayer, and U Win Pe. *Shwedagon: Golden Pagoda of Myanmar.* London: Thames and Hudson, 1999.

Morreale, Don, ed. *The Complete Guide to Buddhist America.* Boston: Shambhala, 1973.

Moses, L. W. *The Political Role of Mongol Buddhism.* Bloomington: Research Institute for Inner Asian Studies, Indiana University, 1977.

Murthy, K. Krishna. *Buddhism in Japan.* Delhi: Sundeep Prakashan, 1989.

Murti, T. R. V. *The Central Philosophy of Buddhism: A Study of the Madhyamika System.* London: George Allen and Unwin, 1955.

Nakai, Gendo. *Shinran and His Religion of Pure Faith.* Kyoto: Shinshu Research Institute, 1937.

Nakamura, Hajime. *Indian Buddhism: A Survey with Bibliographical Notes.* Delhi: Motilal Banarsidass, 1980, 1987, 1989, 1996.

Narada Maha Thera. *The Buddha and His Teachings.* Singapore: Singapore Buddhist Meditation Centre, 1973.

Nath, Samir. *Encyclopaedic Dictionary of Buddhism.* 3 vols. New Delhi: Prabhat Kumar Sharma for Sarup & Sons, 1998.

Niharranjan, Ray. *Theravada Buddhism in Burma.* Calcutta: University of Calcutta, 1946.

Norman, Kenneth Roy. *Pali Literature: Including the Canonical Literature in Prakrit and Sanskrit of All the Hinayana Schools of Buddhism.* Wiesbaden: O. Harrassowitz, 1983.

Nyanaponika and Hellmuth Heckler. *Great Disciples of the Buddha.* Kandy, Sri Lanka: Buddhist Publication Society, 1997.

Nyanatiloka. *Buddhist Dictionary Manual of Buddhist Terms and Doctrines.* San Francisco: Chinese Materials Center, 1997.

Obermiller, E., trans. *The History of Buddhism in India and Tibet by Bu-ston.* Delhi: Sri Satguru, 1986.

Oliver, Ian P. *Buddhism in Britain.* London: Rider, 1979.

Omvedt, Gail. *Buddhism in India: Challenging Brahmanism and Caste.* New Delhi: Thousand Oaks and London: Sage, 2003.

Ortner, S. *High Religion: A Cultural and Political History of Sherpa Buddhism.* Princeton, N.J.: Princeton University Press, 1989.

Pachow, W. *Chinese Buddhism.* Washington, D.C.: University Press of America, 1980.

Paul, Diana. *Women in Buddhism: Images of the Feminine in the Mahayana Tradition*. Berkeley: University of California Press, 1985.

Peiris, William. *The Western Contribution to Buddhism*. Delhi: Motilal Bonarsidass, 1973.

Petzol, Bruno. *The Classification of Buddhism Bukkyou Kyohan Comprising the Classification of Buddhist Doctrines in India, China and Japan*. Wiesbaden: Arrassowtz Verlag, 1995.

Powers, John. *A Concise Encyclopedia of Buddhism*. Oxford: One World, 2000.

———. *Tibetan Buddhism*. Ithaca, N.Y.: Snow Lion, 1995.

———. *The Yogacara School of Buddhism: A Bibliography*. Lanham, Md.: Rowman & Littlefield, 1991.

Prebish, Charles S. *American Buddhism*. North Scituate, Mass.: Duxbury Press, 1979.

———. *Historical Dictionary of Buddhism*. Lanham, Md.: Rowman & Littlefield, 1993.

———. *Luminous Passage. The Practice and Study of Buddhism in America*. Berkeley: University of California Press, 1999.

———, ed. *Buddhism: A Modern Perspective*. University Park: Pennsylvania State University Press, 1975.

———, and Kenneth K. Tanaka, eds. *The Faces of Buddhism in America*. Berkeley: University of California Press, 1998.

Rahula, Walpola. *History of Buddhism in Ceylon: The Anur dhapura Period 3rd Century B.C.–10th Century A.D.* Colombo: M. D. Gunasena, 1956.

Rajavaramuni, Phra. *Thai Buddhism in the Buddhist World*. North Hollywood, Calif.: Wat Thai of Los Angeles, 1984.

Ramachandra Rao, S. K. *Encyclopedia of Indian Iconography, Hinduism, Buddhism and Jainism*. 3 vols. New Delhi: Sri Satguru, 2003.

Rawlinson. Andrew. *The Book of Enlightened Masters*. Chicago: Open Court, 1997.

Ray, Reginald A. *Buddhist Saints in India: A Study in Buddhist Values and Orientation*. New York and Oxford: Oxford University Press, 1994.

Reader, Ian. *Religion in Contemporary Japan*. Honolulu: University of Hawaii Press, 1991.

Reat, Noble Ross. *Buddhism: A History*. Fremont, Calif.: Jain, 1994.

Reynolds, Frank E. *Guide to the Buddhist Religion*. Boston: G. K. Hall, 1981.

Rice, Edward. *Eastern Definitions: A Short Encyclopedia of Religions of the Orient with Terms from Hinduism, Sufism, Buddhism, Islam, Zen, Tao, the Sikhs, Zoroastrianism and Other Eastern Religions*. Garden City, N.Y.: Doubleday, 1978.

Richard, Pierre, and Prancois Lagirarde. *The Buddhist Monastery: A Cross-Cultural Survey*. Paris: Ecole Prancaise D'Extreme-Orient, 2003.

Robinson, Richard H., and Willard L. Johnson. *The Buddhist Religion: A Historical Introduction* Belmont, Calif.: Wadsworth, 1997.

Sakakata, Akira. *Buddhist Cosmology: Philosophy and Origins*. Tokyo: Kosei, 1997 and 1999.

Sakar, Anil Kumar. *The Mysteries of Vajrayana Buddhism: From Atisha to Dalai Lama*. Colombia, Mo.: South Asia Books, 1993.

Samuel, Geoffrey. *Civilized Shamans: Buddhism in Tibetan Societies*. Washington, D.C.: Smithsonian, 1993.

Sangharakshita. *A Survey of Buddhism*. Boulder, Colo.: Shambhala and London: Windhorse, 1980.

Sangpo, Khetsun. *Biographical Dictionary of Tibet and Tibetan Buddhism*. Dharamsala: Library of Tibetan Works and Archives, 1973.

Satyaprakash. *Buddhism: A Select Bibliography*. New Delhi: Indian Documentation Service, 1976.

Saunders, E. Dale. *Buddhism in Japan*. Philadelphia: University of Pennsylvania Press, 1964.

Schumacher, Stephen, and Gert Woerner, eds., *The Rider Encyclopedia of Eastern Philosophy and Religion—Buddhism, Hinduism, Taoism, Zen*. London: Rider, 1986.

Schuman, Hans Wolfgang. *Buddhism*. Wheaton, Ill.: Theosophical Publishing House, 1973.

Seager, Richard Hughes. *Buddhism in America*. Columbia Contemporary American Religion Series. New York: Columbia University Press, 2000.

Sekida, Katsuki. *Zen Training: Methods and Philosophy*. New York: Weatherhill, 1996.

Seneviratne, H. L. *The Work of Kings: The New Buddhism in Sri Lanka.* Chicago: University of Chicago Press, 1999.

Shin-yong, Chun, ed. *Buddhist Culture in Korea.* Seoul, Korea: Si-sa-yong-o-sa, 1982.

Shojun, Bando et al., eds. *A Bibliography of Japanese Buddhism.* Tokyo: CIIB Press, 1958.

Singh, Nagendra, Jr., ed. *International Encyclopaedia of Buddhism.* New Delhi: Anmol, 1999.

Skilton, Andrew. *A Concise History of Buddhism.* Birmingham, U.K.: Windhorse, 1994.

Snellgrove, David, and Hugh Richardson, *A Cultural History of Tibet.* Boston: Shambhala, 1986.

Snelling, John. *Buddhist Festivals.* Vero Beach, Fla.: Rourke Enterprises, 1987.

———. *The Buddhist Handbook A Complete Guide to Buddhist Teaching and Practice.* London: Rider, 1987.

Sonoda, Koyu, and Yusen Kashiwahara, eds. *Shapers of Japanese Buddhism.* Rutland, Vt.: Charles E. Tuttle, 1994.

Sopa, Lhundup, and Jeffery Hopkins. *Practice and Theory of Tibetan Buddhism.* New York: Grove Press, 1976.

Spiro, Melford E. *Buddhism and Society: A Great Tradition and Its Burmese Vicissitudes.* Berkeley: University of California Press, 1982.

Spuler, Michelle. *Developments in Australian Buddhism: Facets of the Diamond.* London: Routledge Curzon, 2003.

Storlie, Erik Fraser. *Nothing on My Mind: An Intimate Account of American Zen.* Boston: Shambhala, 1996.

———. *The Experience of Buddhism: Sources and Interpretation.* Belmont, Calif.: Wadsworth, 1995.

———. *The Legend of King Asoka: A Study and Translation of the Asokavadana.* Princeton, N.J.: Princeton University Press, 1983.

Strong, John S., ed. *The Buddha: A Short Biography.* Oxford: Oneworld, 2001.

Suzuki, Beatrice Lane. *Mahayana Buddhism.* New York: Macmillan, 1969.

Suzuki, D. T. *An Introduction To Zen Buddhism.* 1964. Reprint, New York: Grove Weidenfeld, 1991.

———. *Zen Buddhism.* Garden City, N.Y.: Doubleday, 1956.

Swearer, Donald K. *The Buddhist World of Southeast Asia.* Albany: State University of New York Press, 1995.

Takeuchi Yoshinori, ed. *Buddhist Spirituality: Later China, Korea, Japan and the Modern World.* New York: Crossroad, 1999.

Tamney, Joseph B. *American Society in the Buddhist Mirror.* New York: Garland, 1992.

Thakur, Amarnath. *Buddha and Buddhist Synods in India and Abroad.* Delhi: Abhinav, 1996.

The Teaching of Buddha. Tokyo: Bukkyo Dendo Kyokai, 1966.

Thompson, Laurence G. *Chinese Religion: An Introduction.* 5th ed. Belmont, Calif.: Wadsworth, 1996.

Tong, Cheu Hock, ed. *Chinese Beliefs and Practices in Southeast Asia.* Selangor Daruk Ehsan, Malaysia: Pelunduk, 1993.

Tsomo, Karma Kedshe, ed. *Innovative Buddhist Women Swimming against the Stream.* Richmond, U.K.: Curzon, 2000.

Turnbull, Colin. *Tibet: Its History, Religion and People.* Reprint. London: Penguin Books, 1987.

Tweed, Thomas A. *The American Encounter with Buddhism, 1844–1912: Victorian Culture and the Limits of Dissent.* Chapel Hill: University of North Carolina Press, 2000.

Tworkov, Helen. *Zen in America: Five Teachers and the Search for an American Buddhism.* New York: Kodansha International, 1994.

Unno, Taisetsu. *River of Fire, River of Water: An Introduction to the Pure Land Tradition of Shin Buddhism.* New York: Doubleday, 1998.

Upasak, C. S. *History of Buddhism in Afghanistan.* Sarnath, Varanasi, India: Central Institute of Higher Tibetan Studies, 1990.

Warder, A. K. *Indian Buddhism.* Delhi, Patna, Varanasi: Motilal Banarsidass, 1970.

Weller, Paul, ed. *Religions in the UK: A Multi-Faith Directory.* Derby, U.K.: University of Derby/Inter Faith Network for the United Kingdom, 1993.

William, Edward Soothill, and Lewis Hodous, comp. *A Dictionary of Chinese Buddhist Terms. With Sanskrit and English Equivalents and a Sanskrit-Pali Index.* London: Kegan Paul, Tranch Trubner, 1937.

Williams, Duncan Ryuken, and Christopher S. Queen, eds. *American Buddhism: Methods and Findings in Recent Scholarship*. Richmond, U.K.: Curzon Press, 1999.

Williams, Paul. *Mahayana Buddhism: The Doctrinal Foundations*. London and New York: Routledge, 1989.

Wood, Jessica. "Buddhist Nuns in Sri Lanka." Bachelor's thesis, Lancaster University, 1977.

Wright, Arthur F. *Buddhism in Chinese History*. Stanford, Calif.: Stanford University Press, 1959.

Yamamoto, George Y. *The Origin of Buddhism in Hawaii*. Honolulu: YMB of Honolulu, 1955.

Yamamoto, Kosho. *Buddhism in Europe*. Ube City, Japan: Karinbunko, 1967.

Yanagawa, Keiichi, ed. *Japanese Religions in California*. Tokyo: University of Tokyo, 1983.

Yoo, Yushin. *Books on Buddhism*. Metuchen, N.J.: Scarecrow Press, 1976.

Yoshioka, Toichi. *Zen*. Kawamata, Japan: Hoikusha, 2002.

Yu, David C. *Guide to Chinese Religion*. With contributions by Laurence G. Thompson. Boston: G. K. Hall, 1985.

Yu, Lu K'uan (Charles Luk). *Practical Buddhism*. Wheaton, Ill.: Theosophical Publishing House, 1973.

BON

David L. Snellgrove, trans. *The Nine Ways of Bon*. Boulder, Colo.: Prajna Press, 1980.

Karmay, Samten G. *Treasury of Good Sayings: A Tibetan History of Bon*. Delhi: Motilal Banarsidass, 2001.

———, and Yasuhiko Nagano, eds. *New Horizons in Bon Studies*. New Delhi: M Saujanya, 2004.

Per Kvaerne. *The Bon Religion of Tibet: The Iconography of a Living Tradition*. Boston: Shambhala Press, 2001.

CONFUCIANISM

Berthrong, John H., and Evelyn Nagai. *Confucianism: A Short Introduction*. Oxford: Oneworld, 2000.

Chai, Ch'u, and Winberg. *Confucianism*. Woodbury, N.Y.: Barron's Educational Series, 1973.

Fingarette, Herbert. *Confucius: The Secular as Sacred*. New York: Harper Torchbooks, 1972.

Hall, David L., and Roger T. Ames. *Thinking Through Confucius*. Albany: State University of New York Press, 1987.

Oldstone-Moore, Jennifer. *Confucianism: Origins, Beliefs, Practices, Holy Texts, Sacred Places*. Oxford: Oxford University Press, 2002.

Yao, Xizhong. *Introduction to Confucianism*. Cambridge: Cambridge University Press, 2000.

Taylor, Rodney L. *The Way of Heaven: An Introduction to the Confucian Religious Life*. Boston: Shambhala, 1986.

DAOISM

Blofeld, John. *Taoism: The Road to Immortality*. Boulder, Colo.: Shambhala, 1978.

Boltz, Judith M. *A Survey of Taoist Literature: Tenth to Seventeenth Centuries*. China Research Monograph 32. Berkeley: University of California, 1987.

Chan, Wing-tsit, ed. and trans. *A Source Book in Chinese Philosophy*. Princeton, N.J.: Princeton University Press, 1963.

Cleary, Thomas S. *Vitality, Energy, Spirit: A Taoist Source Book*. Boston: Shambhala, 1991.

Ho, Kwok Man, and Joanne O'Brien, trans. and ed., with an introduction by Martin Palmer. *The Eight Immortals of Taoism*. New York: Penguin, 1990.

Kaltenmark, Max. *Lao Tzu and Taoism*. Translated from the French by Roger Greaves. Stanford, Calif.: Stanford University Press, 1969.

Kohn, Livia. *Daoism and Chinese Culture*. Cambridge, Mass.: Three Pines Press, 2001.

———, ed. *Daoism Handbook*. Leiden: E. Brill, 2000.

Pas, Julian F. *Historical Dictionary of Taoism*. Lanham, Md.: Scarecrow Press, 1998.

Pregadio, Fabrizio E. *Encyclopedia of Taoism*. London: Curzo Press, 2001.

Robinet, Isabelle. *Taoism: Growth of a Religion*. Translated by Phyllis Brooks. Stanford, Calif.: Stanford University Press, 1997.

Shahar, Meir. *Crazy Ji: Chinese Religion and Popular Literature*. Cambridge, Mass.: Harvard University Press, 1998.

Waley, Arthur. *The Way and Its Power.* New York: Grove Press, 1968.

Welch, Holmes. *Taoism: The Parting of the Way.* Boston: Beacon Press, 1965.

———. *Taoism: The Parting of the Way.* Boston: Beacon Press, 1966.

———, and Anna Seidel. *Facets of Taoism: Essays in Chinese Religion.* New Haven, Conn.: Yale University Press, 1979.

Wong, Eva Wong, *The Shambhala Guide to Taoism.* Boston: Shambhala, 1997.

———. *Tales of the Taoist Immortals.* Boston: Shambhala, 2001.

NEW RELIGIONS

Clarke, Peter B. *Bibliography of Japanese New Religious Movements.* Richmond, U.K.: Japan Library, 1999.

———. *Encyclopedia of New Religious Movements.* London: Routledge, 2006.

———. *New Religions in Global Perspective.* London: Routledge, 2005.

———, ed. *Japanese New Religions in Global Perspective.* Richmond, U.K.: Curzon Press, 2000.

———, and Jeffrey Somers, eds. *Japanese New Religions in the West.* Richmond, U.K.: Curzon Press, 1994.

Ellwood, Robert S., Jr. *The Eagle and the Rising Sun.* Philadelphia: Westminster Press, 1974.

Guthrie, Stewart. *A Japanese New Religion: Rissho Kosei-Kai in a Mountain Hamlet.* Ann Arbor: University of Michigan Press, 1988.

Inaba, Keishin. *Altruism in New Religious Movements: The Jesus Army and the Friends of the Western Buddhist Order in Britain.* Okayama, Japan: University Education Press, 2004.

Jordan, David K., and Daniel L. Overmyer. *The Flying Phoenix: Aspects of Chinese Sectarianism in Taiwan.* Princeton, N.J.: Princeton University Press, 1986.

Kisala, Robert J., and Mark R. Mullins. *Religion and Social Crisis in Japan: Understanding Japanese Society through the Aum Affair.* New York: Palgrave, 2001.

McFarland, H. Neil. *The Rush Hour of the Gods: A Study of New Religious Movements in Japan.* New York: Macmillan, 1967.

Offner, Clark B. *Modern Japanese Religions.* New York: Twayne, 1963.

Shimazono, Susumu. *From Salvation to Spirituality: Popular Religious Movements in Modern Japan.* Melbourne: Trans Pacific Press, 2004.

Wong, John, and William T. Liu. *The Mystery of China's Falun Gong: Its Rise and Its Sociological Implications.* Singapore: World Scientific, and Singapore University Press, 1999.

Thomsen, Harry. *The New Religions of Japan.* Rutland, Vt.: Charles E. Tuttle, 1963.

SHINTO

Akiyama. *Shinto and Its Architecture.* Tokyo: Tokyo News Service, 1955.

Aston, W. G. *Shinto: The Way of the Gods.* London: Longmans Green, 1905.

Ballou, Robert O. *Shinto: The Unconquered Enemy.* New York: Viking Press, 1945.

Bocking, Brian. *A Popular Dictionary of Shinto.* New York: McGraw-Hill, 1997.

Breen, John, and Mark Teeuwen, eds., *Shinto in History: Ways of the Kami.* Richmond: Curzon, 2000.

Hardacre, Helen. *Shinto and the State, 1868–1988.* Princeton, N.J.: Princeton University Press, 1991.

Huntly, Hope. *Kami-No-Michi: The Way of the Gods in Japan.* London: Rebman, 1910.

Littleton, Scott. *Shinto: Origins, Rituals, Festivals, Spirits, Sacred Places.* New York: Oxford University Press, 2002.

Mason, Joseph W. T. *The Meaning of Shinto: The Primæval Foundation of Creative Spirit in Modern Japan.* Port Washington, N.Y.: Kennikat Press, 1967.

Ono, Sokyo. *Shinto the Kami Way.* Rutland, Vt.: Charles E. Tuttle, 1972.

Picken Stuart D. B. *Historical Dictionary of Shinto.* Lanham, Md.: Scarecrow Press, 2001.

Picken, S. *Essentials of Shinto: An Analytical Guide to Principal Teachings* Westport, Conn.: Greenwood Press, 1994.

Reader, Ian, and George J. Tanabe, Jr., *Practically Religious: Worldly Benefits and the Common Religion of Japan.* Honolulu: University of Hawaii Press, 1998.

Ross, Floyd Hiatt. *Shinto, The Way of the Gods.* Boston: Beacon Press, 1965.

Sectarian Shinto (The Way of the Gods). Tokyo: The Japan Times & Mail, 1939.

INDEX